Contemporary Authors®

NEW REVISION SERIES

ISSN 0275-7176

Contemporary Authors®

A Bio-Bibliographical Guide to
Current Writers in Fiction, General Nonfiction,
Poetry, Journalism, Drama, Motion Pictures,
Television, and Other Fields

JEFF CHAPMAN
JOHN D. JORGENSON
Editors

NEW REVISION SERIES
volume 57

DETROIT • NEW YORK • TORONTO • LONDON

STAFF

Jeff Chapman and John D. Jorgenson, *Editors, New Revision Series*

Daniel Jones, *Pre-Manuscript Coordinator*
Thomas Wiloch, *Sketchwriting Coordinator* and *Online Research Specialist*

Pamela S. Dear, Jeff Hunter, Jerry Moore, Deborah A. Stanley, Polly A. Vedder, and Kathleen Wilson, *Contributing Editors*

Bruce Boston, Gary Corseri, Mary Gillis, Joan Goldsworthy, Anne Janette Johnson, Jane Kelly Kosek, Robert Miltner, Ronald Radtke, Trudy Ring, Bryan Ryan, Sue Salter, Pamela L. Shelton, Kenneth R. Shepherd, Arlene True, Denise Wiloch, Michaela Swart Wilson, and Tim Winter-Damon, *Sketchwriters*

Tracy Arnold-Chapman, Emily J. McMurray, Trudy Ring, and Pamela L. Shelton, *Copyeditors*

James P. Draper, *Managing Editor*

Laura C. Bissey, *Research Coordinator*

Victoria B. Cariappa, *Research Manager*

Barbara McNeil, *Research Specialist*

Julia C. Daniel, Tamara C. Nott, Tracie A. Richardson, Norma Sawaya, and Cheryl L. Warnock, *Research Associates*

™ This book is printed on acid-free paper that meets the minimum requirements of American National Standard for Information Sciences-Permanence Paper for Printed Library Materials, ANSI Z39.48-1984.

Library of Congress Catalog Card Number 81-640179

ISBN 0-7876-1198-0
ISSN 0275-7176

Printed in the United States of America.

Gale Research, an International Thomson Publishing Company.

10 9 8 7 6 5 4 3 2 1

Contents

Indexing note: All *Contemporary Authors New Revision Series* entries are indexed in the *Contemporary Authors* cumulative index, which is published separately and distributed with even-numbered *Contemporary Authors* original volumes and odd-numbered *Contemporary Authors New Revision Series* volumes.

As always, the most recent *Contemporary Authors* cumulative index continues to be the user's guide to the location of an individual author's listing.

Contemporary Authors *was named an* ***"Outstanding Reference Source"*** *by the American Library Association Reference and Adult Services Division after its 1962 inception.*
In 1985 it was listed by the same organization as one of the twenty-five most distinguished reference titles published in the past twenty-five years.

Preface

The *Contemporary Authors New Revision Series* (*CANR*) provides updated information on authors listed in earlier volumes of *Contemporary Authors* (*CA*). Although entries for individual authors from *any* volume of *CA* may be included in a volume of the *New Revision Series, CANR* updates only those sketches requiring significant change. However, in response to requests from librarians and library patrons for the most current information possible on high-profile writers of greater public and critical interest, *CANR* revises entries for these authors whenever new and noteworthy information becomes available.

Authors are included on the basis of specific criteria that indicate the need for a revision. These criteria include a combination of bibliographical additions, changes in addresses or career, major awards, and personal information such as name changes or death dates. All listings in this volume have been revised or augmented in various ways and contain up-to-the-minute publication information in the Writings section, most often verified by the author and/or by consulting a variety of online sources. Many sketches have been extensively rewritten, often including informative new sidelights. As always, a *CANR* listing entails no charge or obligation.

The key to locating an author's most recent entry is the *CA* cumulative index, which is published separately and distributed with even-numbered original volumes and odd-numbered revision volumes. It provides access to *all* entries in *CA* and *CANR*. Always consult the latest index to find an author's most recent entry.

For the convenience of users, the *CA* cumulative index also includes references to all entries in these Gale literary series: *Authors and Artists for Young Adults, Authors in the News, Bestsellers, Black Literature Criticism, Black Writers, Children's Literature Review, Concise Dictionary of American Literary Biography, Concise Dictionary of British Literary Biography, Contemporary Authors Autobiography Series, Contemporary Authors Bibliographical Series, Contemporary Literary Criticism, Dictionary of Literary Biography, Dictionary of Literary Biography Documentary Series, Dictionary of Literary Biography Yearbook, DISCovering Authors, DISCovering Authors: British, DISCovering Authors: Canadian, DISCovering Authors: Modules, Drama Criticism, Hispanic Literature Criticism, Hispanic Writers, Junior DISCovering Authors, Major Authors and Illustrators for Children and Young Adults, Major 20th-Century Writers, Native North American Literature, Poetry Criticism, Short Story Criticism, Something about the Author, Something about the Author Autobiography Series, Twentieth-Century Literary Criticism, World Literature Criticism,* and *Yesterday's Authors of Books for Children.*

A Sample Index Entry:

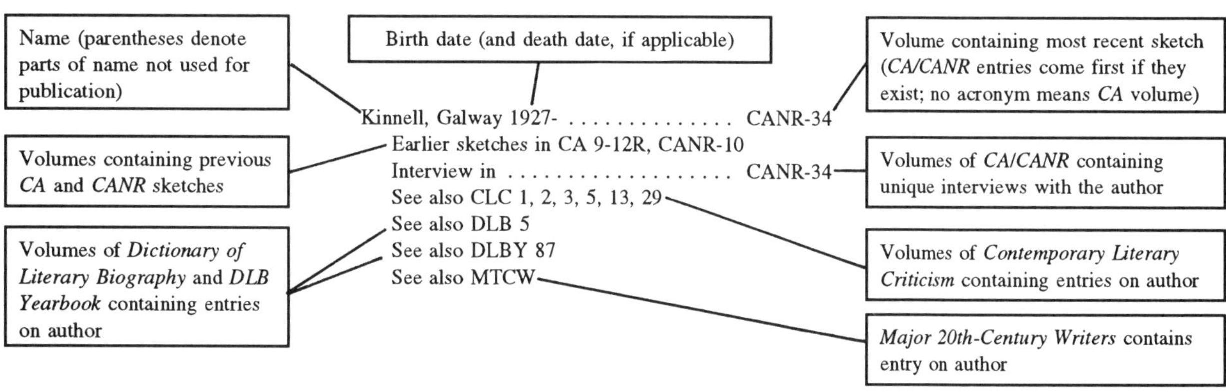

For the most recent *CA* information on Kinnell, users should refer to Volume 34 of the *New Revision Series,* as designated by "CANR-34"; if that volume is unavailable, refer to CANR-10. And if CANR-10 is unavailable, refer to CA 9-12R, published in 1974, for Kinnell's First Revision entry.

How Are Entries Compiled?

The editors make every effort to secure new information directly from the authors. Copies of all sketches in selected *CA* and *CANR* volumes previously published are routinely sent to listees at their last-known addresses, and returns from these authors are then assessed. For deceased writers, or those who fail to reply to requests for data, we consult other reliable biographical sources, such as those indexed in Gale's *Biography and Genealogy Master Index,* and bibliographical sources, such as *Magazine Index, Newspaper Abstracts, LC MARC,* and a variety of online databases. Further details come from published interviews, feature stories, book reviews, online literary magazines and journals, author web sites, and often the authors' publishers supply material.

** Indicates that a listing has been compiled from secondary sources but has not been personally verified for this edition by the author under review.*

What Kinds of Information Does an Entry Provide?

Sketches in *CANR* contain the following biographical and bibliographical information:

- **Entry heading:** the most complete form of author's name, plus any pseudonyms or name variations used for writing
- **Personal information:** author's date and place of birth, family data, ethnicity, educational background, political and religious affiliations, and hobbies and leisure interests
- **Addresses:** author's home, office, email, or agent's addresses, as available
- **Career summary:** name of employer, position, and dates held for each career post; resume of other vocational achievements; military service
- **Membership information:** professional, civic, and other association memberships and any official posts held
- **Awards and honors:** military and civic citations, major prizes and nominations, fellowships, grants, and honorary degrees
- **Writings:** a comprehensive, chronological list of titles, publishers, dates of original publication and revised editions, and production information for plays, television scripts, and screenplays
- **Adaptations:** a list of films, plays, and other media which have been adapted from the author's work
- **Work in progress:** current or planned projects, with dates of completion and/or publication, and expected publisher, when known
- **Sidelights:** a biographical portrait of the author's development; information about the critical reception of the author's works; revealing comments, often by the author, on personal interests, aspirations, motivations, and thoughts on writing
- **Biographical and critical sources:** a list of books and periodicals in which additional information on an author's life and/or writings appears

Related Titles in the *CA* Series

Contemporary Authors Autobiography Series complements *CA* original and revised volumes with specially commissioned autobiographical essays by important current authors, illustrated with personal photographs they provide. Common topics include their motivations for writing, the people and experiences that shaped their careers, the rewards they derive from their work, and their impressions of the current literary scene.

Contemporary Authors Bibliographical Series surveys writings by and about important American authors since World War II. Each volume concentrates on a specific genre and features approximately ten writers; entries list works written by and about the author and contain a bibliographical essay discussing the merits and deficiencies of major critical and scholarly studies in detail.

Available in Electronic Formats

CD-ROM. Full-text bio-bibliographic entries from the entire *CA* series, covering approximately 101,000 writers, are available on CD-ROM through lease and purchase plans. The disc combines entries from the *CA, CANR,* and *Contemporary Authors Permanent Series* (*CAP*) print series to provide the most recent author listing. It can be searched by name, title, subject/genre, and personal data, and by using boolean logic. The disc will be updated every six months. For more information, call 1-800-877-GALE.

Magnetic Tape. *CA* is available for licensing on magnetic tape in a fielded format. Either the complete database or a custom selection of entries may be ordered. The database is available for internal data processing and nonpublishing purposes only. For more information, call 1-800-877-GALE.

Online. The *Contemporary Authors* database is made available online to libraries and their patrons through online public access catalog (OPAC) vendors. Currently, *CA* is offered through Ameritech Library Services' Vista Online (formerly Dynix), and is expected to become available through CARL Systems. More OPAC vendor offerings will follow soon.

GaleNet. *CA* is available on a subscription basis through GaleNet, a new online information resource that features an easy-to-use end-user interface, the powerful search capabilities of the BRS/Search retrieval software, and ease of access through the World Wide Web. For more information, call Melissa Kolehmainen at 1-800-877-GALE, ext. 1598.

Suggestions Are Welcome

The editors welcome comments and suggestions from users on any aspects of the *CA* series. If readers would like to recommend authors whose entries should appear in future volumes of the series, they are cordially invited to write: The Editors, *Contemporary Authors,* 835 Penobscot Bldg., Detroit, MI 48226-4094; call toll-free at 1-800-347-GALE; fax to 1-313-961-6599; or e-mail at conauth@gale.com.

CA Numbering System and Volume Update Chart

Occasionally questions arise about the *CA* numbering system and which volumes, if any, can be discarded. Despite numbers like "29-32R," "97-100" and "150," the entire *CA* series consists of only 140 physical volumes with the publication of *CA New Revision Series* Volume 57. The following charts note changes in the numbering system and cover design, and indicate which volumes are essential for the most complete, up-to-date coverage.

CA First Revision

- 1-4R through 41-44R (11 books)
  Cover: Brown with black and gold trim.
  There will be no further First Revision volumes because revised entries are now being handled exclusively through the more efficient *New Revision Series* mentioned below.

CA Original Volumes

- 45-48 through 97-100 (14 books)
  Cover: Brown with black and gold trim.
- 101 through 156 (56 books)
  Cover: Blue and black with orange bands.
  The same as previous *CA* original volumes but with a new, simplified numbering system and new cover design.

CA Permanent Series

- *CAP*-1 and *CAP*-2 (2 books)
  Cover: Brown with red and gold trim.
  There will be no further *Permanent Series* volumes because revised entries are now being handled exclusively through the more efficient *New Revision Series* mentioned below.

CA New Revision Series

- *CANR*-1 through *CANR*-57 (57 books)
  Cover: Blue and black with green bands.
  Includes only sketches requiring extensive changes; **sketches are taken from any previously published *CA, CAP,* or *CANR* volume.**

If You Have:	You May Discard:
CA First Revision Volumes 1-4R through 41-44R **and** *CA Permanent Series* Volumes 1 and 2	*CA* Original Volumes 1, 2, 3, 4 and Volumes 5-6 through 41-44
CA Original Volumes 45-48 through 97-100 **and** 101 through 156	**NONE:** These volumes will not be superseded by corresponding revised volumes. Individual entries from these and all other volumes appearing in the left column of this chart may be revised and included in the various volumes of the *New Revision Series.*
CA New Revision Series Volumes *CANR*-1 through *CANR*-57	**NONE:** The *New Revision Series* does not replace any single volume of *CA.* Instead, volumes of *CANR* include entries from many previous *CA* series volumes. All *New Revision Series* volumes must be retained for full coverage.

A Sampling of Authors and Media People Featured in This Volume

Chaim Bermant

A novelist celebrated for his tales about Scotland's Jewish community, Bermant, asserts one critic, "writes about Jews with a curious blend of intimacy and objectivity, like an affectionate anthropologist." His works, often filled with wry humor and subtle wit, include *Jericho Sleep Alone, Roses Are Blooming in Picardy, Diary of an Old Man, The Patriarch: A Jewish Family Saga, Dancing Bear,* and *The Companion.*

Thomas Bernhard

An Austrian playwright, Bernhard was best known for his stylistic virtuosity and grim meditations on futility, death, hatred, and contempt. His works often presented German culture in a critical light; subsequently, he has gained a reputation as German literature's most melancholy and bitter writer. Despite such criticism, many critics praised Bernhard, calling him "one of the bravest and most unusual novelists of the post-war world." His titles include *Gargoyles, The Force of Habit, Before Retirement, Heroes' Square,* and *The Woodcutters.*

Barbara T. Christian

Respected for her critical insight into literature by and about African-American women, Christian is the author of the award-winning *Black Women Novelists: The Development of a Tradition, 1892-1976.* According to Christian, this study seeks "to trace the development of stereotypical images imposed on black women and assess how these images have affected the works of black women artists." Her other titles include *Black Feminist Criticism: Perspectives on Black Women Writers* and *From the Inside Out: Afro-American Women's Literary Tradition and the State.*

Douglas Coupland

Proclaimed by at least one reviewer as "the self-wrought oracle of our age" and "the Jack Kerouac of his generation," Canadian novelist Coupland achieved instant and widespread success with his debut hit, *Generation X: Tales for an Accelerated Culture.* Despite coining the term "Generation X" to refer to those Americans born in the 1960s to early-1970s, Coupland resists such proclamations labeling him as the generation's spokesperson. His other works include *Shampoo Planet, Life after God, Microserfs,* and *Polaroids from the Dead.*

Harry Crews

A novelist known for his grotesque characters in the gothic tradition of the American South, Crews' writing is often riddled with violence, obsession, and an extremely bleak outlook on human existence. Praised by one critic for displaying "a gift at once formidable and frightening," his titles include *Naked in Garden Hills, Karate Is a Thing of the Spirit, Car,* and *The Mulching of America.*

Stacey B. Day

Self-described as the "psychospiritual concept of the pastoral physician," Day combines his successful medical practice with a similarly significant literary career. In his scientific publications, he often stresses the importance of cultural anthropology, sociology, and psychology when treating the biological conditions of a patient. Once honored by former U.S. President Ronald Reagan as one who "builds on a community approach to medicine which is truly international in scope," Day's works include *Rosalita, Comprehensive Immunology,* and *Developing Health in the West African Bush.*

Bohumil Hrabal

Critically acclaimed as one of the Czech Republic's best fiction writers, Hrabal often places ordinary men and women in circumstances over which they have no control, weaving elements of surrealism within both his short stories and novellas. Best known for his Academy Award-winning screenplay adaptation of his own novel *Closely Watched Trains,* Hrabal's other works include *These Premises Are in the Joint Care of Citizens, Too Loud a Solitude, I Served the King of England,* and his biography, the two-volume *Kdo jsem,* which was published in 1989.

Irene Hunt

Hunt, described by one critic as "one of America's finest historical novelists," writes young adult fiction that explores places and time periods ranging from 1860s Illinois to the Depression-era Rocky Mountains. Often praised for creating realistic characters who learn to cope with their problems while maturing in the process, Hunt received a Newbery Medal in 1967 for her second book, *Up a Road Slowly.* Her other notable titles include *Across Five Aprils, No Promises in the Wind, Claws of a Young Century,* and *The Everlasting Hills.*

David Ignatow

A poet who, according to one reviewer, struggles "to create a living American poetry from the immediacies of existence in this country," Brooklyn native Ignatow is as relentless during self-evaluation as when diagnosing social ills. Robert Bly described him as both "a poet of the community, of people who work for a living" and as "a great poet of the collective." His collections include *Figures of the Human, The Animal in the Bush: Poems on Poetry, Leaving the Door Open,* and *Gleanings: Uncollected Poems, 1950s and 1960s.*

Kenneth Koch

Koch, winner of the 1995 Bollingen Prize, has published numerous collections of poetry, avant-garde plays, and short fiction while working as one of America's best-known creative writing teachers. He has been associated with the New York School of poetry for most of his career and employs surrealism, satire, irony, and an element of surprise throughout much of his work. Heralded by one critic for "reclaiming the humorous for serious writers of poetry," Koch's titles include *When the Sun Tries to Go On* and *On the Great Atlantic Rainway: Selected Poems, 1950-1988.*

Rita Kramer

In her controversial work *In Defense of the Family: Raising Children in America Today,* Kramer provides a theoretical basis for her assertions that a home environment with continuous parental involvement is crucial to a child's development. While many reviewers praised the study for challenging men and women to reclaim their parental responsibilities, others criticized it for being "a diatribe against feminism." Kramer's other works examining child development and education include *How to Raise a Human Being, Maria Montessori: A Biography, At a Tender Age: Violent Youth and Juvenile Justice,* and *Ed School Follies: The Miseducation of America's Teachers.*

Stanley Kunitz

Winner of a Pulitzer Prize and National Book Award for his poetry, Kunitz has exerted a subtle but steady influence on such major poets as W. H. Auden, and Robert Lowell. One reviewer commented, "the restraints of Kunitz's art combine with a fierce dedication to clarity and intellectual grace," while another said that his poetry has "the intellectual courage that insists on the truth, which is never simple." A longtime resident of New York City, Kunitz's works include, *Selected Poems, 1928-1958, The Testing-Tree: Poems,* and *Passing Through: Later Poems, New and Selected.*

Claude Levi-Strauss

Often ranked alongside Jean-Paul Sartre and Andre Malraux as one of France's great modern intellectuals, Levi-Strauss is, according to one critic, "the last uncontested giant of French letters." In addition to founding the movement known as structural anthropology, he is credited with influencing such fields as language theory, history, and psychology. *Tristes Tropiques,* his study of Brazilian Indians, has been called "one of the great books of our century." His other works include *The Savage Mind, Introduction to a Science of Mythology,* and *The Story of Lynx.*

Walter Mosley

In addition to being known as one of U.S. President Bill Clinton's favorite writers, hard-boiled detective novelist Mosley is credited with "taking familiar territory—the gritty urban landscape of post-World War II Los Angeles—and turning it inside out." Largely recognized for his "Easy" Rawlins series, Mosley has explained his aim in the series is less to create a memorable gumshoe than it is to explore the ethical dilemmas constantly faced by the character. His works include *Devil in a Blue Dress, A Red Death, Gone Fishin',* and *Always Outnumbered, Always Outgunned: The Socrates Fortlow Stories.*

Bapsy Sidhwa

Sidhwa, described by one critic as Pakistan's finest English-language novelist, writes stories that reflect her experience as a woman, a member of a religious minority in Pakistan, and as an immigrant to the United States. Although her works often attempt to explain what really happens to women in a tribal society, Sidhwa also manages to convey her compassion for the people who live by a strict social code of honor. Her titles include *The Crow Eaters, The Bride, Ice-Candy-Man, Cracking India* and *An American Brat.*

Frank Zappa

Described as bizarre, disgusting, avant-garde, grotesque, obscene, and Dadaistic, the lyrics of Zappa's songs, which largely critique contemporary cultural phenomena and middle-class values, were in many cases deemed unfit for public broadcasting. Despite such reaction, many considered Zappa a genius, with one critic calling him "one of the most important, and misunderstood, musical figures of the last half-century." His recordings included *Freak Out!, Hot Rats, 200 Motels, The Best Band You Never Heard in Your Life,* and the posthumously-released *Have I Offended Someone?*

Contemporary Authors®

NEW REVISION SERIES

***Indicates that a listing has been compiled from secondary sources believed to be reliable but has not been personally verified for this edition by the author sketched.**

ABSALOM, Roger Neil Lewis 1929-

PERSONAL: Born October 28, 1929, in Bebington, England. *Ethnicity:* "White." *Education:* Christ Church, Oxford, B.A. (with honors), 1952; Institute of Linguists, F.I.L., 1960.

ADDRESSES: *Office*—Cultural Research Institute, Sheffield Hallam University, 36 Collegiate Crescent, Sheffield S10 2BP, England. *E-mail*—100045.2243@compuserve.com.

CAREER: English teacher at British schools in Pescara and Milan, Italy, 1956-60; Cambridgeshire College of Arts and Technology, Cambridge, England, lecturer, 1960-66, senior lecturer, 1966-70, principal lecturer in Italian, 1970-73; Sheffield Hallam University, Sheffield, England, lecturer in Italian history and language and head of department of modern languages, 1973-86, reader in modern languages, 1986-89, honorary research fellow in Italian history, 1989—. Visiting scholar, Woodrow Wilson Institute, Washington, DC, 1982. Visiting lecturer and consultant.

MEMBER: Society for Italian Studies, Royal Institute of International Affairs, Association for the Study of Modern Italy, Society for the Study of Labour History.

AWARDS, HONORS: Corecipient of Premio Prato from City of Prato Council, 1980, for article (in Italian) on the role of the Allies in Florence, Italy, 1944-45; grants from British Academy, 1983, Gladys Krieble-Delmas Foundation, 1984, and Australian War Memorial, 1988.

WRITINGS:

"A" Level French, National Extension College (NEC), 1966.
Passages for Translation from Italian, Cambridge University Press (Cambridge, England), 1967.
"A" Level Italian, NEC, 1968.
Mussolini and the Rise of Italian Fascism, Methuen (London), 1969.
(Editor) *The May Events: France, 1968,* Longman (London), 1970, published as *France: The May Events, 1968,* 1971.
(Editor with Sandra Potesta) *Advanced Italian,* Cambridge University Press, 1970.
Comprehension of Spoken Italian, Cambridge University Press, 1978.
(With others) *French: Advanced Level* (six volumes), NEC, 1980.
Leo S. Olschki, editor, *Gli Alleati e la ricostruzione in Toscana (1944-1945): Documenti anglo-americani,* Volume 1, Accademia Toscana di Scienze e Lettere la Colombaria (Florence), 1988.
Olschki, editor, *A Strange Alliance: Aspects of Escape and Survival in Italy, 1943-45,* Accademia Toscana di Scienze e Lettere la Colombaria, 1991.
Italy since 1800: A Nation in the Balance?, Longman, 1995.

Also contributor to various publications, including *Italia e Gran Bretagna nella lotta di liberazione* (title means "Italy and Great Britain in the Fight for Freedom"), edited by Ian Greenlees, La Nuova Italia, 1977; *Socialism and Nationalism,* Volumes 1 and 3, edited by Eric Cahm and Vladimir Fisera, Spokesman Books, 1979; *La ricostruzione in*

Toscana dal CLN ai partiti (title means "Reconstruction in Tuscany from the National Liberation Committee to the Restoration of Party Rule"), Volume 1, edited by Ettore Rotelli, Il Mulino (Bologna), 1980; *Linea Gotica,* edited by G. Rochat and others, [Milan], 1986; *Moving in Measure,* Hull University Press (Hull, England), 1989; and *Prato storia di una citta. 4. Il modello pratese (1943-a oggi),* edited by G. Becattini, Le Monnier (Florence), 1997.

Also contributor to scholarly journals, including *The Historical Journal, Italian Studies, Oral History Journal,* and *Journal of Institutional Management in Higher Education.*

SIDELIGHTS: Roger Neil Lewis Absalom once told *CA:* "I have moved steadily from languages and linguistics to contemporary history over the last thirty years. I now regard myself as a (somewhat eccentric) historian of mentalities. The seed of this was sown during the four years I lived in Italy (from 1956 to 1960), when I became obsessed with trying to understand the historical roots of current Italian political behaviors and culture.

"These seemed (and still seem) to have little to do with the Risorgimento and 'The Making of Italy' as described in the textbooks. What fascinates the close observer in Italy is the unique blend—in its material and cultural life—of the archaic and the ultramodern. Italians, moreover, are Europe's greatest experts in the art of eluding the encroachments of the State: even Fascist dictatorship scarcely scratched the surface of this profoundly-rooted culture of individual survival and the preservation of identity.

"Exploring the remoter parts of the central Apennines in the 1950s (before they were touched by the 'economic miracle'), I came to realize the central role of the Italian hill-peasants and their values in maintaining the vitality of this culture. When they migrated en masse to the towns they took these values—this cultural armor—with them. They are, paradoxically, entrepreneurial and egalitarian at one and the same time: the two major parties in Italy have, in their own ways, learned to benefit politically from this contradiction and, consequently, are in no hurry to resolve it. Both, in practice, want to limit 'modernization' in order to continue their informal power-sharing. The Church has always known how to play this game; the Italian post-Communists have learned it better than any others. The matter is important because Italy's post-1945 developmental path may help us to understand the workings of 'cities of peasants' elsewhere in the world, and the kind of political arrangements that may prevent them from exploding."

* * *

ADLARD, (Peter) Mark 1932-

PERSONAL: Born June 19, 1932, in Seaton Carew, County Durham, England; son of A. M. (an auctioneer) and E. (Leech) Adlard; married Sheila Rosemary Skuse, October 19, 1968; children: Vanessa, Robert. *Education:* Trinity College, Cambridge, B.A., 1954; University of London, B.Sc.

ADDRESSES: Home—43 Enterpen, Hutton Rudby, Cleveland TS15 0EL, England. *Agent*—John Farquharson Ltd., 15 Red Lion Sq., London WC1R 4QW, England.

CAREER: Writer. Executive in the steel industry management in Middlesbrough, Yorkshire, Cardiff, and Kent, England, 1956-76; teacher of economics, 1985-92.

WRITINGS:

SCIENCE FICTION NOVELS; "TCITY TRILOGY"

Interface: Science Fiction, Sidgwick & Jackson (London), 1971, Ace (New York City), 1977.

Volteface: Science Fiction, Sidgwick & Jackson, 1972, Ace, 1978.

Multiface: Science Fiction, Sidgwick & Jackson, 1975, Ace, 1978.

OTHER

The Greenlander (novel), Summit (New York City), 1978.

SIDELIGHTS: Mark Adlard began writing science fiction not because he was a fan of the genre, but because he felt it would be an interesting way to explore the importance of work. He once told *CA,* "One of my main preoccupations is with the way economic activity can somehow give meaning or significance to individual lives, and why it often fails to do so." He decided to explore this subject by creating a fictional future world in which work had become a form of therapy, and economic activity had been largely made redundant. His imaginary civilization unfolds in his TCity trilogy, *Interface, Volteface,* and *Multiface.*

A *Times Literary Supplement* reviewer praised *Interface* as "a first novel by an English writer of considerable promise." In this book, Adlard presents a picture of a 22nd-century British society marked by hedonism and leisure—at least, for the upper classes. But the common people are discontent, and although the elite enjoy the great artistic works of the past, there is virtually no human creativity within the culture. The fate of this culture is further chronicled in *Volteface* and *Multiface.* T. A. Shippey commented in the *Times Literary Supplement: "Multiface* exemplifies one of the strengths of science fiction—its ability to consider events formed on a larger scale than human lives—as well as confirming its author's talent for transposing mirages of the past into the future."

Michael J. Tolley discussed the entire trilogy in the *St. James Guide to Science Fiction Writers.* In his opinion, the individual books are better than the trilogy as a whole. Still, he praises the complete work as "a highly interesting and readable work. The parts are considerable and the project ambitious." Tolley rated *Interface* as the least successful of the three, deeming it "overloaded with exposition at the expense of narrative and, although Adlard is clearly aware of the problem (throughout the series, a stock joke is the blunt interruption of robotic exposition), information whether cultural or technological appears to be simply dropped into the text and does not resonate within it."

Tolley characterizes *Interface* as being concerned with "weaknesses at the interface between an enclosed society of drugged citizens and their benevolent, superior managers, weaknesses on both sides which end in destruction for some but salvation for others." In the failed Utopia of *Interface,* work is reintroduced to Tcity by the executives, who deliberately create a 20th-century-like managerial structure merely to make work. Tolley explains: "This scheme enables Adlard to write splendid satire as he traces both the collective volte-face and some individual reversals of life in Tcity. The *Inferno* of work-free pleasure is exchanged for a dubious *Purgatorio.* . . .. If idle pleasure was hell, work purgatory, then *Multiface* seems to be asking what is the ideal mode of life. The answer is that it depends on the individual life."

Adlard moves from the future to the past with his fourth novel, although the underlying preoccupation with economic activity remains. *The Greenlander* tells about the end of the whaling era and one young man's journey into adulthood. A *Publishers Weekly* reviewer called it a "rawboned saga" and continued: "What Adlard works together here is not a conventional drama. Instead, the reader, like the toughened hero, returns from a voyage impressed with images of what whaling must have been like." Peter Kemp also reviewed the book positively, writing in *Listener* that "Mr. Adlard spins a robust yarn. . . . There is plenty of action: though the ships run aground, the story never does. If you do not mind scrambling over heaps of nautical vocabulary—futtock shrouds, tholes and grommets, clustered deadeyes, and topgallant braces—it is invigorating stuff."

BIOGRAPHICAL/CRITICAL SOURCES:

BOOKS

St. James Guide to Science Fiction Writers, St. James Press (Detroit), 1996.

PERIODICALS

Library Journal, November 1, 1978, p. 2259.
Listener, October 5, 1978, pp. 454-55.
Observer, October 1, 1978, p. 33.
Publishers Weekly, November 6, 1978, p. 66.
Times Literary Supplement, April 16, 1971, p. 455; December 5, 1975, p. 1438.

* * *

ALEXANDER, Sue 1933-

PERSONAL: Born August 20, 1933, in Tucson, AZ; daughter of Jack M. (an electronic component manufacturer) and Edith (Pollock) Ratner; married second husband, Joel Alexander (a car agency sales manager), November 29, 1959; children: (first marriage) Glenn David; (second marriage) Marc Jeffry, Stacey Joy. *Education:* Attended Drake University, Des Moines, IA, 1950-52, and Northwestern University, 1952-53. *Religion:* Jewish.

ADDRESSES: Home and office—6846 McLaren, Canoga Park, CA 91307; fax: 818-347-2617. *Agent*—Marilyn Marlow, Curtis Brown Ltd., Ten Astor Pl., New York, NY 10003.

CAREER: Writer, 1969—.

MEMBER: Society of Children's Book Writers and Illustrators (member of board of directors, 1972—), Southern California Council on Literature for Children and Young People.

AWARDS, HONORS: Children's Choice citation, International Reading Association-Children's Book Council, 1977, for *Witch, Goblin and Sometimes Ghost,* and 1982, for *Witch, Goblin and Ghost in the Haunted Woods;* Child Study Association children's book of the year, 1978, for *Marc the Magnificent;* Dorothy C. McKenzie Award, Southern California Council of Literature for Children and Young People, 1980, for distinguished contribution to the field of children's literature; Golden Kite honor plaque, Society of Children's Book Writers, 1980, Notable Children's Book in the Field of Social Studies citation, 1980, and High/Low Booklist citation, Young Adult Services Division/American Library Association, 1982, all for *Finding Your First Job;* teacher's choice citation, National Council of Teachers of English, 1983, American Library Association Booklist children's reviewer's choice, 1983, Notable Children's Book in the Field of Social Studies citation, 1983, Child Study Association children's book of the year, 1984, and distinguished work of fiction honor, Southern California Council of Literature for Children and Young People, 1984, all for *Nadia the Willful;* outstanding work of fiction honor, Southern California Council of Literature for Children and Young People, 1987, for *Lila on the Landing;* Alexander has had an award named in her honor by the Society of Children's Book Writers and Illustrators: the Sue Alexander Service and Encouragement (SASE) Award.

WRITINGS:

FOR CHILDREN

Small Plays for You and a Friend, illustrated by Olivia H. H. Cole, Scholastic (New York City), 1973.

Nadir of the Streets, Macmillan (New York City), 1975.

Peacocks Are Very Special, illustrated by Victoria Chess, Doubleday (New York City), 1976.

Witch, Goblin and Sometimes Ghost, illustrated by Jeanette Winter, Pantheon (New York City), 1976.

Small Plays for Special Days, illustrated by Tom Huffman, Clarion (New York City), 1977.

Marc the Magnificent, illustrated by Tomie dePaola, Pantheon, 1978.

More Witch, Goblin and Ghost Stories, illustrated by Winter, Pantheon, 1978.

Seymour the Prince, illustrated by Lillian Hoban, Pantheon, 1979.

Finding Your First Job (nonfiction), photographs by George Ancona, Dutton (New York City), 1980.

Whatever Happened to Uncle Albert? and Other Puzzling Plays, illustrated by Huffman, Clarion, 1980.

Witch, Goblin and Ghost in the Haunted Woods, illustrated by Winter, Pantheon, 1981.

Witch, Goblin and Ghost's Book of Things to Do, Pantheon, 1982.

Nadia the Willful, illustrated by Lloyd Bloom, Pantheon, 1983.

Dear Phoebe, illustrated by Eileen Christelow, Little, Brown (Boston), 1984.

World Famous Muriel, illustrated by Chris C. Demarest, Little, Brown, 1984.

Witch, Goblin and Ghost Are Back, illustrated by Winter, Pantheon, 1985.

World Famous Muriel and the Scary Dragon, illustrated by Demarest, Little, Brown, 1985.

Lila on the Landing, illustrated by Ellen Eagle, Clarion, 1987.

There's More . . . Much More, illustrated by Patience Brewster, Harcourt (New York City), 1987.

America's Own Holidays (nonfiction), illustrated by Leslie Morrill, F. Watts (New York City), 1988.

World Famous Muriel and the Magic Mystery, illustrated by Marla Frazee, Crowell (New York City), 1990.

Who Goes Out on Halloween?, illustrated by G. Brian Karas, Bantam, 1990.

Sara's City, illustrated by Ronald Himler, Clarion, 1995.

What's Wrong Now, Millicent? illustrated by David Scott Meier, Simon & Schuster (New York City), 1996.

OTHER

Contributor of short stories to *Children's Playmate, Weekly Reader*, and Walt Disney Studios. Contributor of book reviews to *Los Angeles Times*.

ADAPTATIONS: Witch, Goblin and Sometimes Ghost and *Witch, Goblin and Ghost Are Back* were adapted for audio cassette by Caedmon in 1987.

SIDELIGHTS: Sue Alexander is an award-winning writer of such children's picture books as *Witch, Goblin and Sometimes Ghost, Nadia the Willful*, and *Lila on the Landing*. Her work is characterized by a lively sense of humor, as well as sharp insight into the emotional ups and downs of childhood.

"Most of the stories I write are fantasy," Alexander once explained. "That is, they are about goblins and talking peacocks and ghosts instead of real people. But all the stories I write begin the same way: with how I *feel* about something." Alexander's *Witch, Goblin and Sometimes Ghost* first brought her a larger audience, as well as critical notice and awards. Goblin has difficulty flying his kite, until he figures out he needs wind. Thinking that growing older will make him smarter about such things, he is disappointed when his birthday comes around and he doesn't automatically become more intelligent. But Witch's gift of an encyclopedia that he can read and learn from makes him happy again. Set in the form of six read-aloud tales, the book "is useful as additional material for the beginning reader," notes a *Bulletin of the Center for Children's Books* contributor.

Goblin proved so popular with readers that he appears in several other books as well. *Witch, Goblin and Ghost in the Haunted Woods* was another award-winner in the series, returning to the mutually supportive spooky friends in five simple stories about swimming, gardening, and a snow storm. Each tale blends "mystery and the supernatural," according to Virginia Haviland in *Horn Book*. Zena Sutherland comments in *Bulletin of the Center for Children's Books* on the "reassuring texts" in these stories that deal with, among other things, a treasure hunt and storytelling.

"As more of my work was published," Alexander writes in her entry for *Something About the Author Autobiography Series* (*SAAS*), "I began to feel like a professional writer. More importantly, I came to realize that the more of me that went into my writing, the better my stories were. The warm and enthusiastic response of young readers to the first of my books about Goblin, *Witch, Goblin and Sometimes Ghost*, had given me the insight in a way that was unmistakable. Each of the stories in that book—and in the subsequent books about Goblin and his friends—has, at its core, feelings taken directly from my childhood."

One book taken directly from Alexander's childhood is *Lila on the Landing*, which evokes her own sense of humiliation and frustration as a child having to play all by herself on her apartment house landing. Lila succeeds in sharing her landing with Jon and Amy and even manages to win over the scornful Alan. But art does not always reproduce life; in Alexander's case it enhances it. Susan McCord, writing in *School Library Journal*, notes that Alexander "adeptly" deals with childhood loneliness and rejection, and that hers "is a meaningful story for an age for who it's often hard to find something good." A *Bulletin of the Center for Children's Books* contributor comments on Lila's patience and wit in solving her problems, suggesting to readers "the possibility of overcoming rejection," while *Kirkus Reviews* critic Anne Larsen calls the book "a winning tale of an old-fashioned, non-high-tech child."

In 1983 Alexander's agent was finally able to find a publisher for a book written eleven years earlier upon the death of Alexander's brother. Devastated by his death, Alexander turned to writing for comfort, dealing with her bereavement in a story. "As I began it, however," she explains in *SAAS*, "I recognized that I couldn't deal emotionally with the subject matter in a here-and-now setting. It would have to take place somewhere far away, preferably in another culture. No sooner had I made that decision than my fifth-grade fascination with Bedouins came to mind." What resulted was *Nadia the Willful*, the story of a young girl who disobeys her disconsolate father's command not to mention the death of his son and her beloved brother, Hamed. But Nadia must talk to someone:

she turns to her mother and then to shepherds who are fearful of the power of her father, yet still want to talk about Hamed and thereby keep his memory alive. Ultimately, even the father learns the simple lesson that no one is truly dead unless they are forgotten. A *Booklist* reviewer calls the story "moving" and "universal," and commented upon the desert setting, which is not typically seen in children's books. Maria Salvadore notes in *School Library Journal* that Alexander's language "is soft and fluid" and "affirms universal emotions."

Other favorite Alexander books include the "World-Famous Muriel" series, which is about a clever little tight-rope walker who loves to solve mysteries. The Muriel series once again mines many of the universal themes Alexander most enjoys—food, magic, mysteries, and friendship. Bessie Egan, reviewing the third book in the series, *World Famous Muriel and the Magic Mystery,* concludes in *School Library Journal* that it is "a picture book that will keep children interested and amused."

In addition to the books she has written, Alexander has also been active as a teacher of picture book writing at the University of California at Los Angeles and as a long-time board member with the Society of Children's Book Writers and Illustrators. "I love writing stories," she once explained. "It's my work and my joy. It satisfies my sense of fun and my need to share. I wouldn't trade what I do for any profession in the world. I write for young people because they have imaginations that soar, touched off by a word, a phrase, an image . . . a condition I share. To be able to provide the spark for this process gives me the greatest personal joy." Alexander recently told *CA:* "Hearing from children who have read my books tells me that they share the same feelings that I have and wonder about the same things that I do. That's what keeps me writing for them-and keeps me young inside."

BIOGRAPHICAL/CRITICAL SOURCES:

BOOKS

Roginski, James W., *Behind the Covers,* Volume 2: *Interviews with Authors and Illustrators of Books for Children and Young Adults,* Libraries Unlimited, 1989, pp. 1-15.

Something about the Author Autobiography Series, Volume 15, Gale (Detroit), 1993, pp. 51-66.

PERIODICALS

Booklist, September 15, 1976, p. 140; June 1, 1977, pp. 2, 1492; November 1, 1978, p. 473; December 15, 1979, p. 618; October 15, 1980, p. 322; January 15, 1981, p. 695; November 15, 1982, p. 450; April 1, 1983, p. 1022; August, 1983, p. 1460; September 15, 1984, p. 136; April 15, 1986, p. 1214; September 15, 1987, p. 139; November 15, 1987, p. 557; February 1, 1989, p. 935; March 15, 1990, p. 1440; October 1, 1995, p. 325.

Bulletin of the Center for Children's Books, April, 1977, p. 117; September, 1977, p. 1; January, 1980, p. 85; April, 1981, p. 145; October, 1981, p. 21; September, 1987, p. 1.

Horn Book, February, 1981, p. 62; June, 1981, p. 295.

Kirkus Reviews, October 15, 1976, p. 1135; October 1, 1987, p. 1457.

Publishers Weekly, August 20, 1979, p. 81; March 20, 1981, p. 62; August 20, 1982, p. 72; June 17, 1983, p. 74; February 24, 1984, p. 130; March 2, 1984, p. 93; July 6, 1984, p. 64; September, 25, 1987, p. 108; April 27, 1990, p. 63.

School Library Journal, January, 1975, p. 36; February, 1977, p. 53; September, 1977, p. 99; December, 1978, p. 65; December, 1980, p. 72; March, 1981, p. 153; May, 1981, p. 80; October, 1983, p. 145; August, 1984, p. 55; January, 1985, p. 62; April, 1986, p. 67; November, 1987, p. 102; December, 1987, p. 66; August, 1989, p. 158; July, 1990, p. 55; May, 1991, p. 74.

* * *

ALLINGTON, Richard L(loyd) 1947-

PERSONAL: Born May 13, 1947, in Grand Rapids, MI; son of George C. (a farmer) and Eldona (a copy editor; maiden name, Weller) Allington; married Susan Gordon, April 6, 1968 (divorced May 5, 1978); married Anne McGill (a legislative analyst), January 11, 1980; children: Heidi Jo, Tinker Marie, Margaret Anne, Richard Bo, Michael McGill. *Ethnicity:* "White." *Education:*

Western Michigan University, B.A., 1968, M.A., 1969; Michigan State University, Ph.D., 1973.

ADDRESSES: Home—246 Van Wie Point Rd., Glenmont, NY 12077; fax 518-442-4953. *Office*—Department of Reading, State University of New York at Albany, Albany, NY 12222. *E-mail*—dickasunya@aol.com.

CAREER: Elementary school teacher in Rockford, MI, and Kent City, MI, 1968-69; Belding Area Schools, Belding, MI, Title I director, 1969-71; Michigan State University, East Lansing, graduate assistant and lecturer, 1971-73; State University of New York at Albany, assistant professor, 1973-78, associate professor, 1978-83, professor, 1983—, chair of department of reading, 1982-88, 1994—. Visiting professor at the University of Minnesota, 1976, and Eastern Montana College, 1981. Consultant to National Assessment of Educational Progress, 1976-78, Institute for Research on Teaching, Michigan State University, 1977-80, New York State Insurance Department, 1982-83, U.S. Department of Education, 1987-89, and Center for the Study of Reading, 1988-89.

MEMBER: International Reading Association (chair of advisory group for analysis of reading programs data, 1976-77; chair of studies and research committee, 1987—; member, board of directors, 1995-98), American Educational Research Association (Division C assistant program chair, 1986-87), National Conference of Research in English (fellow), National Reading Conference (member of board of directors, 1988—), New York State Reading Association (director of preconference institute, 1982; chair of studies and research committee, 1985-88).

AWARDS, HONORS: Grants from State University of New York Research Foundation, 1976-79, National Institute of Education, 1977-78, National Institutes of Health, 1977-79, International Reading Association, 1983-84, Office of Educational Research and Improvement, 1985-86, 1993-97, and Office of Special Education Programs, 1987-88; Albert J. Harris Award from International Reading Association, 1990; Outstanding Reading Educator, New York State Reading Association, 1993; Literary Lectureship Award, Center for Literary and Disability Studies, University of North Carolina, 1996.

WRITINGS:

(With Gerald G. Duffy, George S. Sherman, Michael McElwee, and Laura R. Roehler) *How to Teach Reading Systematically,* Harper (New York City), 1973.

(With Michael Strange) *Learning through Reading: An Introduction for Content Area Teachers,* Heath (Lexington, MA), 1980.

(With Patricia Cunningham) *Classrooms that Work: They Can All Read and Write,* Longmans (New York City), 1994.

(With Sean Walmsley) *No Quick Fix: Rethinking Literary Instruction in America's Elementary Schools,* Teachers College (New York City), 1995.

(With Cunningham) *Schools that Work: Where All Children Read and Write,* Longmans, 1996.

INTERACTIONAL MATERIALS FOR CHILDREN

The Reading Fact (remedial reading program), Macdonald-Raintree, 1979.

Focus: Reading for Success (basal reading program), Scott, Foresman (Glenview, IL), 1984.

Scott, Foresman Reading: An American Tradition (basal reading program), Scott, Foresman, 1987.

Collections (a literary anthology), Scott, Foresman, 1989.

Celebrate Reading (a literary anthology) Scott, Foresman, 1993.

"BEGINNING TO LEARN ABOUT" SERIES; PUBLISHED BY MACDONALD-RAINTREE

Beginning to Learn about Colors, illustrations by Noel Spangler, 1979.

Beginning to Learn about Numbers, illustrated by Tom Garcia, 1979.

Beginning to Learn about Opposites, illustrated by Eulala Connor, 1979.

Beginning to Learn about Shapes, illustrated by Lois Ehlert, 1979.

(With Kathleen Cowles, pseudonym of Kathleen Krull) *Beginning to Learn about Feelings,* illustrated by Brian Cody, 1980.

(With Cowles) *Beginning to Learn about Hearing,* illustrated by Wayne Dober, 1980.

(With Cowles) *Beginning to Learn about Looking,* illustrated by Bill Bober, 1980.

(With Cowles) *Beginning to Learn about Smelling,* illustrated by Rick Thrun, 1980.

(With Cowles) *Beginning to Learn about Tasting,* illustrated by Spangler, 1980.
(With Cowles) *Beginning to Learn about Touching,* illustrated by Yoshi Miyake, 1980.
(With Kathleen Krull) *Beginning to Learn about Reading,* illustrated by Joel Naprstek, 1980.
(With Krull) *Beginning to Learn about Talking,* illustrated by Thrun, 1980.
(With Krull) *Beginning to Learn about Thinking,* illustrated by Garcia, 1980.
(With Krull) *Beginning to Learn about Writing,* illustrated by Miyake, 1980.
(With Krull) *Beginning to Learn about Autumn,* illustrated by Bruce Bond, 1981.
(With Krull) *Beginning to Learn about Spring,* illustrated by Dee Rahn, 1981.
(With Krull) *Beginning to Learn about Summer,* illustrated by Dennis Hockerman, 1981.
(With Krull) *Beginning to Learn about Winter,* illustrated by John Wallner, 1981.
(With Krull) *Beginning to Learn about Measuring,* illustrated by Spangler, 1983.
(With Krull) *Beginning to Learn about Science,* illustrated by James Teason, 1983.
(With Krull) *Beginning to Learn about Stories,* illustrated by Helen Cogancherry, 1983.
(With Krull) *Beginning to Learn about Time,* illustrated by Miyake, 1983.
(With Krull) *Beginning to Learn about Words,* illustrated by Ray Cruz, 1983.
Beginning to Learn about Letters, illustrated by Garcia, 1983.

OTHER

Contributor of over 100 articles and reviews to education and reading journals, including *Journal of Educational Psychology, Journal of Reading Behavior,* and *Reading Research Quarterly.*

Coeditor, *Journal of Reading Behavior,* 1978-83; member of editorial advisory boards of *Elementary School Journal* and *Remedial and Special Education.*

WORK IN PROGRESS: Children Who Find Learning to Read Difficult.

SIDELIGHTS: Richard L. Allington once told *CA:* "I grew up in Cedar Springs, Michigan, the eldest of six children. I was raised on a dairy farm and attended a one-room country school. I now work as a university professor and live in an old Victorian summer home on the Hudson River south of Albany, New York. I have five children, all of whom think it is nice to be able to go to the library and check out a book written by their father."

About his work in progress, *Children Who Find Learning to Read Difficult,* Allington later added: "[This book] discusses the problems that current practices, such as retention in grade, special education placement, ability grouping, tracking, and remedial services, present for children. It attempts to explain why these practices rarely work in the best interests of children and offers workable models for eliminating school failure generally and reading failure particularly."

* * *

AMBROSE, Stephen E(dward) 1936-

PERSONAL: Born January 10, 1936, in Decatur, IL; son of Stephen Hedges (a family physician) and Rosepha (Trippe) Ambrose; married Judith Dorlester, 1957 (deceased, 1966); married Moira Buckley, 1967; children: Stephanie (Tubbs), Barry Halleck, Andrew, Grace, Hugh. *Ethnicity:* "English." *Education:* University of Wisconsin, B.S., 1957, Ph.D., 1963; Louisiana State University, M.A.. *Politics:* Republican. *Religion:* Protestant. *Avocational interests:* Canoes, Woodworking, mountain hiking.

ADDRESSES: Home and Office—1606 Hauser, Helena, MT 59601.

CAREER: Louisiana State University in New Orleans (now University of New Orleans), assistant professor, 1960-64, professor, 1971-89, Alumni Distinguished Professor of History, 1982-95, Boyd Professor of History, 1989-95, and director of the Eisenhower Center, 1983; Johns Hopkins University, Baltimore, MD, associate professor, 1964-69; U.S. Naval War College, Newport, RI, Ernest J. King Professor of Maritime History, 1969-1970; Kansas State University, Manhattan, Dwight D. Eisenhower Professor of War and Peace, 1970-71. Visiting assistant professor, Louisiana State University, Baton Rouge, 1963-64; Mary Ball Washington Professor, University College, Dublin, Ireland, 1981-82; visiting professor, University of California, Berkeley, 1986; Howard Johnson Visiting Professor of Military

History, Army War College, 1989; senior fellow, Rutgers Center for Historic Analysis, 1993. *Military service:* ROTC.

MEMBER: American Committee on World War II (member, board of directors), American Historical Association, American Military Institute (member, board of directors; member, board of trustees, 1971-74), Conference on History of Second World War (member of American Committee), SANE (member, board of directors), Society for American Historians of Foreign Relations, Southern Historical Association, Lewis and Clark Heritage Trail Foundation (member, board of directors), Big Blue Athletic Association, Chi Psi.

AWARDS, HONORS: Eisenhower: Soldier, General of the Army, President-Elect, 1890-1952, won the Freedom Foundation's National Book Award.

WRITINGS:

Halleck: Lincoln's Chief of Staff, Louisiana State University Press (Baton Rouge), 1962.

Upton and the Army, Louisiana State University Press, 1964.

Duty, Honor, and Country: A History of West Point, Johns Hopkins Press (Baltimore, MD), 1966.

Eisenhower and Berlin, 1945: The Decision to Halt at the Elbe, Norton (New York City), 1967.

The Supreme Commander: The War Years of General Dwight D. Eisenhower, Doubleday (New York City), 1970.

Rise to Globalism: American Foreign Policy since 1938, Penguin (New York City), 1971, sixth edition, 1991.

General Ike: Abeline to Berlin (juvenile), Harper (New York City), 1973.

Crazy Horse and Custer: The Parallel Lives of Two American Warriors, illustrations by Kenneth Francis Dewey, Doubleday, 1975.

(With Richard H. Immerman) *Ike's Spies: Eisenhower and the Espionage Establishment,* Doubleday, 1981.

(With Immerman) *Milton S. Eisenhower: Educational Statesman,* Johns Hopkins University Press, 1983.

Eisenhower: Soldier, General of the Army, President-Elect, 1890-1952 (Book of the Month Club choice; also see below), Simon & Schuster (New York City), 1983.

Eisenhower: The President (also see below), Simon & Schuster, 1984.

Pegasus Bridge: 6 June, 1944, Allen & Unwin (London, England), 1984, Simon & Schuster, 1985.

Nixon: The Education of a Politician, 1913-1962, Simon & Schuster, 1987.

Nixon: The Triumph of a Politician, 1962-1972 (Book of the Month Club alternate), Simon & Schuster, 1989.

Eisenhower: Soldier and President (condensed version of *Eisenhower: Soldier and President,* Simon & Schuster, 1990.

Nixon: The Ruin and Recovery of a Politician, 1973-1990, Simon & Schuster, 1991.

Band of Brothers: E Company, 506th Regiment, 101st Airborne, from Normandy to Hitler's Eagle's Nest, Simon & Schuster, 1992.

D-Day June 6, 1944: The Climactic Battle of World War II, Simon & Schuster, 1994.

EDITOR

A Wisconsin Boy in Dixie, University of Wisconsin Press (Madison), 1961.

Institutions in Modern America: Innovation in Structure and Process, Johns Hopkins Press, 1967.

(Assistant editor) Alfred Chandler, editor, *The Papers of Dwight David Eisenhower: The War Years,* five volumes, Johns Hopkins Press, 1970.

(With James A. Barber, Jr.) *The Military and American Society,* Free Press (New York City), 1972.

Dwight D. Eisenhower, *The Wisdom of Dwight D. Eisenhower: Quotations from Ike's Speeches and Writings, 1939-1969,* Eisenhower Center, 1990.

(With Gunter Bischof) *Eisenhower and the German POWs: Facts against Falsehood,* Louisiana State University Press, 1992.

OTHER

Also author of a television documentary, *Eisenhower: Supreme Commander,* British Broadcasting Corporation, 1973. Author of biweekly column, *Baltimore Evening Sun,* 1968—. Author of introductions for Ronald Lewin, *Hitler's Mistakes,* Morrow, 1987, and *Handbook on German Military Forces,* Louisiana State University Press, 1990. Contributor to *The Harry S. Truman Encyclopedia,* edited by Richard S. Kirkendall, G. K.

Hall (Boston), 1989. Contributor of reviews and articles to numerous journals and newspapers, including *American Heritage, American History Illustrated, American Historical Review, Foreign Affairs, Harvard Magazine, Historic New Orleans Collection Quarterly, Journal of Contemporary History, Times Literary Supplement, New York Times Book Review, Prologue: Quarterly of the National Archives, Quarterly Journal of Military History,* and *U.S. News and World Report.* Contributing editor of *The Quarterly Journal of Military History.* Member of board of editors of *Military Affairs.*

Ambrose's *Duty, Honor, and Country: A History of West Point* has been translated into Spanish; *Eisenhower: The President, Eisenhower: Soldier, General of the Army, President-Elect, 1890-1952,* and *Pegasus Bridge: 6 June, 1944,* have been translated into French; *Crazy Horse and Custer: The Parallel Lives of Two American Warriors* has been translated into German and Italian; *The Supreme Commander: The War Years of General Dwight D. Eisenhower* has been translated into Norwegian, Spanish and Romanian; *Eisenhower: Soldier and President* has been translated into French, German and Russian; and *Rise to Globalism: American Foreign Policy since 1938,* has been translated into Arabic, Norwegian, Romanian, Spanish, and Turkish. An abridged edition of *Ike's Spies: Eisenhower and the Espionage Establishment* was translated into French and published under the title *"Les Services Secrets d'Eisenhower."*

WORK IN PROGRESS: The Crusade: The Campaign in Northern Europe.

SIDELIGHTS: Historian and biographer Stephen E. Ambrose has written about generals, presidents, major military battles, and foreign policy in his twenty-plus books, always demonstrating an uncommon ability to bring history and historical actors to vivid life. The University of New Orleans professor is best known for his multi-volume biographies of Presidents Dwight D. Eisenhower and Richard M. Nixon. Ambrose labored for nearly twenty years on the Eisenhower volumes and ten years on the Nixon volumes, both times with results that critics praised for meticulous research and balance.

Ambrose grew up in Whitewater, Wisconsin. A high-school football captain and prom king, he went to the University of Wisconsin in Madison, where he decided to major in history. After receiving his B.A. in 1957, Ambrose moved on to the Masters program at Louisiana State University, returning to the University of Wisconsin to receive his Ph.D. in history in 1963. During graduate school, Ambrose published a biography of General Henry Halleck, who had served as Chief of Staff to President Abraham Lincoln. A few years later, when Ambrose was working as an assistant professor at Louisiana State University, he received a phone call from an admirer of the book. The caller was former President Dwight D. Eisenhower.

"I was flabbergasted," Ambrose told *New York Times Book Review* contributor Herbert Mitgang. President Eisenhower told Ambrose that he liked the author's book, had thought about writing a work on Halleck himself, and wondered if the historian would come to his Gettysburg, Pennsylvania, home to talk; he also asked Ambrose if he would be interested in working on the Eisenhower papers. Ambrose recalled: "I told him, 'General, I'd prefer to write your biography.' He replied, 'I'd like to have you any way I can.'" So began Ambrose's long association with the life and reputation of President Eisenhower, an association that allowed him to produce a multi-volume set of edited papers, a biography of Milton Eisenhower (the President's brother), two books on Eisenhower's military career (*Eisenhower and Berlin, 1945: The Decision to Halt at the Elbe* and *The Supreme Commander: Eisenhower*), an analysis of Eisenhower's relationship with the espionage community, and the two-volume biography.

In the introduction to *Eisenhower: Soldier, General of the Army, President-Elect, 1890-1952,* Ambrose describes Eisenhower as "decisive, well disciplined, courageous, dedicated . . . intensely curious about people and places, often refreshingly naive, fun-loving—in short a wonderful man to know or be around." Despite his clear liking for the former President, most reviewers found that Ambrose developed an even-handed portrait of the man who is widely perceived to have been, in the words of *Time* reviewer Donald Morrison, both a "canny leader who brilliantly outmaneuvered subordinates and statesman," and a "mediocre President . . . slow of wit and out of touch with the currents of upheaval swirling beneath the calm surface of the 1950s." In reconciling these two views, Ambrose "has provided the most complete and objective work yet on the general who became President," wrote Drew Middleton in the *New York Times Book Review. New Yorker* contributor Naomi Bliven said that the biography "offers the beguiling mixture of nostalgia and illumination we find in old newsreels, along with an abundance of themes for reflection."

Reviewers praised Ambrose's reassessment of a president who had been reviled as a bumbling, inefficient leader, a President who, in the words of *Chicago Tribune Book World* reviewer Richard Rhodes, "golfed too much, knew little and did nothing." Ambrose acknowledges such public perception, wrote Henry Brandon in the *Washington Post Book World,* but his biography portrays Eisenhower as "a man in charge if not always in control, a born leader and a deft pilot who knows how to weather storms." In volume two, *Eisenhower: The President,* Ambrose highlights the fact that "Ike," as he was affectionately known, kept his country out of war for eight turbulent years, stood up to a burgeoning military-industrial complex, and managed to maintain domestic economic prosperity.

Though most reviewers praised Ambrose for his equanimity, some thought that he failed to advance a compelling interpretation of the voluminous data he compiled. *Los Angeles Times Book Review* contributor Kenneth Reich complained that the book was too restrained."It seems sad," he wrote, "when someone has obviously put in so much effort yet fails to go beyond evenhandedness. . . . [This] biography of Eisenhower emerges as a dull parade of data." Ivan R. Dee, writing in the *Chicago Tribune Book World,* said that the problem was that "a reader can arrive at opposite judgments about Eisenhower's performance based upon the evidence Ambrose presents," pointing to Eisenhower's handling of civil rights, the U-2 spying incident, and Middle Eastern politics as examples of failed leadership which Ambrose does not acknowledge.

After nearly twenty years of writing about one of the most loved American presidents, Ambrose turned his attention to a man he said had once been "the most hated and feared man in America," President Richard M. Nixon. A number of writers had penned psychological portraits of Nixon that attempted to account for his seeming cruelty, his terrific drive to succeed, and his failure to admit fault for the Watergate controversy and his subsequent resignation in the face of impeachment proceedings. But by 1987, no one had written a carefully-researched scholarly biography on the most controversial president of the twentieth century. With *Nixon: The Education of a Politician, 1913-1962,* the first of three-volumes, Ambrose wrote that kind of biography. *Washington Post Book World* reviewer Richard Harwood echoed the praise of many critics in noting Ambrose's ability to "examine with a surgeon's neutrality all the cliches and stereotypical assumptions about the character of this strange and fascinating man." Political analyst Sidney Blumenthal wrote in the *New Republic* that "Ambrose has written the standard, a middle point of reference, around which all Nixonia may be organized."

In three volumes, Ambrose follows Nixon from his humble beginnings in Yorba Linda, California, to his academic success at Duke University, to his bitter 1950 Senate campaign, to his troubled tenure as Eisenhower's vice-president, and finally to his rise to and fall from the presidency of the United States. Along the way, Ambrose debunks many of the myths about Nixon, picturing Nixon's childhood as happy, not sad, showing that Nixon's opponents initiated the mud-slinging for which he became known, and demonstrating that the political dirty work Nixon performed while vice-president to Eisenhower was done at the President's insistence. The final volume, *Nixon: Ruin and Recovery,* follows the resuscitation of the former President's reputation throughout the 1980s. *Spectator* reviewer Anthony Howard wrote that Ambrose "has crowned the edifice of his impressive trilogy with an admirably fair-minded last volume covering easily the most controversial aspect of what was already a singularly resilient political career." Throughout the three volumes, Ambrose does not excuse Nixon for the excesses that characterized his political career nor does he attempt to provide a explanation of what motivated Nixon to behave as he did; instead, he shows what happened and lets the reader decide.

Ambrose's reluctance to offer insights into Nixon's motivations frustrated some reviewers. *New York Times* reviewer Christopher Lehmann-Haupt complained that "there is something passive about the way Mr. Ambrose tells Mr. Nixon's story. He seems always confined by context, praising his subject for this, condemning him for that. He lacks the lift of a driving thesis." Ronald Steel, writing in the *New York Times Book Review,* echoed this appraisal, suggesting that Ambrose "is better at providing information than at delving into the dark recesses of character." And Gary Wills, whose own *Nixon Agonistes* attempted to probe the dark recesses of Nixon's character, thought that Ambrose's concern for the facts made him overlook an essential undercurrent in Nixon's life.

Edward Z. Friedenberg saw Ambrose's hesitancy to pass judgment on Nixon in a slightly different light. Writing in the Toronto *Globe and Mail,* he claimed that "Ambrose seems largely content to explain the hostility Nixon aroused in terms of his personality," but contended that "Nixon's enemies hated not merely the man but his (and his country's) policies." Thus Ambrose's equanimity led him to excuse the most sinister elements of Nixon's presidency: his policy toward Vietnam, and his willingness to do whatever it took to win. R. W. Apple, Jr. wrote in the *New York Times Book Review,* however, that "it is Mr. Ambrose's achievement to immerse himself in Mr. Nixon's life and keep his cool. . . . The result is a portrait that is all its subject is not: evenhanded and thoroughly reliable." Ambrose himself told *New York Times Book Review* contributor Alex Ward, "I make no claim to finding the key to the man—he's so complicated that it would take Shakespeare to do him justice."

Ambrose turned to less controversial material with his 1992 *Band of Brothers,* a history of the military exploits of Company E, 506th Parachute Infantry Regiment, 101st Airborne Division during their numerous engagements in World War II. Ambrose based his book on the stories he collected from the surviving members of the company as part of his work for the Eisenhower Center at the University of New Orleans. The soldiers told Ambrose of their predawn drop behind enemy lines on D-Day and of their eventual capture of German leader Adolf Hitler's beloved retreat, "Eagle Nest." The result, wrote *New York Times Book Review* contributor and combat veteran Harry G. Summers, Jr., is "a harrowing story," that captures "the true essence of a combat rifle company." *Times Literary Supplement* reviewer M. R. D. Foot wrote that the book "is full of insights into the nature of comradeship, as well as brutally frank description: noise, stench, discomfort, hunger and fear are all there, tied together in a masterly narrative flow."

BIOGRAPHICAL/CRITICAL SOURCES:

BOOKS

Ambrose, Stephen E., *Eisenhower: Soldier, General of the Army, President-Elect, 1890-1952,* Simon & Schuster, 1983.

PERIODICALS

Chicago Tribune, March 24, 1985.
Chicago Tribune Book World, October 16, 1983; October 7, 1984, pp. 1, 24; April 12, 1987.
Globe and Mail (Toronto), March 16, 1985; July 25, 1987; November 4, 1989.
London Review of Books, July 4, 1985, pp. 5-6.
Los Angeles Times, February 13, 1981.
Los Angeles Times Book Review, November 4, 1984; June 21, 1987, p. 12; October 15, 1989; November 24, 1991, pp. 4, 11.
Nation, February 28, 1972.
New Leader, March 5, 1990, pp. 16-17.
New Republic, July 6, 1987, pp. 30-34.
Newsweek, April 27, 1987.
New Yorker, July 1, 1985, pp. 95-97.
New York Review of Books, May 6, 1971.
New York Times, April 23, 1987; November 9, 1989.
New York Times Book Review, October 4, 1970, p. 5; September 19, 1983; December 9, 1984, pp. 1, 46-47; April 28, 1985; April 26, 1987; November 12, 1989, pp. 1, 65-66; November 24, 1991, pp. 3, 25; September 6, 1992, p. 11.
Spectator, July 4, 1987; February 1, 1992.
Time, October 3, 1983, pp. 79-80; May 4, 1987, p. 101; November 6, 1989, pp. 100-102.
Times Literary Supplement, June 1, 1967, p. 486; November 5, 1971, p. 1398; February 8, 1985, p. 135; December 25, 1987, p. 1424; August 21, 1992, p. 20.
Tribune Books (Chicago), July 19, 1992, p. 6.
Washington Post Book World, September 11, 1983, pp. 1, 4; September 30, 1984; May 3, 1987; November 12, 1989, pp. 1, 13; November 10, 1991, p. 5.

* * *

ANDERSON, (Helen) Jean 1931-

PERSONAL: Born October 12, 1931, in Raleigh, NC; daughter of Donald Benton (a university vice president) and Marian (Johnson) Anderson. *Ethnicity:* "WASP." *Education:* Attended Miami University, Oxford, Ohio, 1947-49; Cornell University, B.S., 1951; Columbia University, M.S., 1957. *Politics:* Independent. *Avocational interests:* Photography, painting, music, kitchen design, and fiction writing.

ADDRESSES: *Home*—1 Lexington Ave., New York, NY 10010. *Agent*—The Karpfinger Agency, Suite 2800, 500 Fifth Ave., New York, NY 10010.

CAREER: Iredell County, NC, assistant home demonstration agent, 1951-52; North Carolina Agricultural Extension Service, Raleigh, woman's editor, 1952-55; *Raleigh Times,* Raleigh, NC, food editor, 1955-56; *Ladies' Home Journal,* New York City, assistant editor, 1957-61, editorial associate, 1961-62, copy editor, 1962, managing editor, 1963-64; *Venture* (magazine), senior editor, 1964-68, contributing editor, 1968-71; freelance writer, 1968—. Contributing editor, *Family Circle,* 1975-85; columnist, *Newsday* (New York City), and Los Angeles Times Syndicate, 1990-92. Cookbook consultant, Reader's Digest General Books, 1984—.

MEMBER: American Home Economics Association, Home Economists in Business, Les Dames D'Escoffier (served as its first vice president, its membership chair, and on its board of directors), New York Women's Culinary Alliance, New York Travel Writers, New York Culinary Historians, James Beard Foundation, Gamma Phi Beta, Phi Kappa Phi, Omicron Nu.

AWARDS, HONORS: Pulitzer traveling scholarship, 1957; Southern Women's Achievement Award, 1962; George Hedman Memorial Award, 1971; R. T. French Tastemaker Award for best basic cookbook of the year and best overall cookbook of the year, 1975, for *The Doubleday Cookbook;* R. T. French Tastemaker Award for best specialty cookbook of the year, 1980, for *Half a Can of Tomato Paste and Other Culinary Dilemmas;* Seagram Award for best international cookbook of the year, International Association of Cooking Professionals, 1986, for *The Food of Portugal;* R. T. French Tastemaker Award for best foreign cookbook, 1986, for *The Food of Portugal;* two awards of merit from the Government of Portugal; named editor of the year by James Beard Foundation, 1992.

WRITINGS:

Henry the Navigator: Prince of Portugal, Westminster (Philadelphia, PA), 1969.

The Haunting of America: Ghost Stories from Our Past, Houghton (Boston, MA), 1973.

COOKBOOKS

(With Yeffe Kimball) *The Art of American Indian Cooking,* Doubleday (New York City), 1965.

Food Is More than Cooking: A Basic Guide for Young Cooks, Westminster, 1968.

(Editor) *The Family Circle Illustrated Library of Cooking: Your Ready Reference for a Lifetime of Good Eating,* twelve volumes, Rockville House, 1972.

The Family Circle Cookbook (Literary Guild main selection), Quadrangle, 1974.

(With Elaine Hanna) *The Doubleday Cookbook* (Literary Guild main selection), Doubleday, 1975, revised edition published as *The New Doubleday Cookbook,* 1985.

Recipes from America's Restored Villages, Doubleday, 1975.

The Green Thumb Preserving Guide: The Best and Safest Way to Can and Freeze, Dry and Store, Pickle, Preserve and Relish Home-Grown Vegetables and Fruits, Morrow (New York City), 1976.

The Grass Roots Cookbook, Quadrangle, 1977, reprinted, Doubleday, 1992.

(With Ruth Buchan) *Half a Can of Tomato Paste and Other Culinary Dilemmas,* Harper (New York City), 1980.

Jean Anderson's Processor Cooking, Morrow, 1980.

Jean Anderson Cooks, Morrow, 1982.

Unforbidden Sweets: More than 100 Classic Desserts You Can Now Enjoy without Counting Calories, Arbor House (New York City), 1982.

Jean Anderson's New Processor Cooking, Morrow, 1983.

Jean Anderson's New Green Thumb Preserving Guide, Morrow, 1985.

The Food of Portugal, Morrow, 1986, updated second edition, 1994.

(With Hanna) *Micro Ways: Every Cook's Complete Guide to Microwaving* (Literary Guild selection), Doubleday, 1990.

Sin-Free Desserts: 150 Low-Cholesterol Desserts You Can Enjoy with a Clear Conscience, Doubleday, 1991.

(With Hedy Wuerz) *The New German Cookbook* (Book-of-the-Month Club selection), Harper, 1993.
1,001 Secrets of Great Cooks: Tricks of the Trade from the Best in the Business, Morrow, 1995.
(With Barbara Deskins) *The Nutrition Bible,* Morrow, 1995.

Contributor of articles to periodicals, including *Family Circle, Bon Appetit, Gourmet, Food and Wine, Ladies Home Journal, Better Homes and Gardens, Connoisseur, New York Times Magazine,* and *Travel and Leisure.*

WORK IN PROGRESS: The Century Cookbook, a history of food and drink in the U.S. from 1900 to the present.

SIDELIGHTS: Jean Anderson's cookbooks have "sensible comments on just about everything gastronomic," reports *Time* reviewer Michael Demarest. For instance, *The Food of Portugal,* Anderson's examination of a relatively unknown cuisine, goes into some detail about Portuguese specialties and local ingredients. Minnie Bernardino, writing in the *Los Angeles Times,* explains that Anderson's "style of thoroughness in recipes from her past cookbooks is carried through in this new book."

Anderson told *CA:* "I love to cook, especially when I don't have to measure everything—imperative, of course, when testing recipes."

BIOGRAPHICAL/CRITICAL SOURCES:

PERIODICALS

Los Angeles Times, December 21, 1986.
Time, November 22, 1982.

* * *

APPLEBEE, Arthur N(oble) 1946-

PERSONAL: Born June 20, 1946, in Sherbrooke, Quebec, Canada; born a U.S. citizen; son of Roger K. (a university dean) and Margaret (Aitken) Applebee; married Marcia Lynn Hull (a teacher), June 15, 1968 (divorced); married Judith A. Langer (a university professor), May 23, 1982. *Education:* Yale University, B.A. (cum laude), 1968; Harvard University, M.A.T., 1970; University of London, Ph.D., 1973.

ADDRESSES: Home—Vly Creek Farm, 103 New Salem South Rd., Voorheesville, NY 12186. *Office*—School of Education, University of Albany, State University of New York, 1400 Washington Ave., Albany, NY 12222. *E-mail*—a.applebee@albany.edu.

CAREER: National Council of Teachers of English, Urbana, IL, parttime staff assistant, 1964-69; Massachusetts General Hospital, Child Development Laboratory, Boston, research assistant and psychologist, 1969-71; University of Lancaster, Lancaster, England, research associate at International Microteaching Unit, 1973-74; Tarleton High School, Tarleton, England, English and drama teacher, 1974-76; National Council of Teachers of English, staff associate, 1976-80, and associate director of ERIC Clearinghouse on Reading and Communication Skills, 1978-80; Stanford University, School of Education, Stanford, CA, associate professor, 1980-86, professor of education, 1987; State University of New York-Albany, professor, 1987—, director of Center for the Learning and Teaching of Literature, 1987-96, director of Center on English Learning and Achievement, 1996—. Visiting lecturer, University of California, Berkeley, summer, 1978.

MEMBER: International Reading Association, National Conference on Research in English (president, 1986), American Educational Research Association, National Council of Teachers of English, National Association of Teachers of English (England).

AWARDS, HONORS: Columbia University Teachers College Book Prize, 1967, for "outstanding constructive interest in educational issues"; Promising Researcher Award from National Council of Teachers of English, 1974; Outstanding Young Men of America Award, 1978; National Conference on Research in English fellow, 1984; Richard A. Meade Award for research in English education, 1989, for *How Writing Shapes Thinking: A Study of Teaching and Learning;* recipient of grants from U.S. Department of Education and National Council of Teachers of English.

WRITINGS:

Tradition and Reform in the Teaching of English: A History, National Council of Teachers of English (Urbana, IL), 1974.

The Child's Concept of Story: Ages Two to Seventeen, University of Chicago Press (Chicago), 1978.

A Survey of Teaching Conditions in English, 1977, National Council of Teachers of English, 1978.

Writing in the Secondary School: Current Practice in English and the Content Areas, National Council of Teachers of English, 1981.

(With others) *Reading, Thinking and Writing: Results from the 1979-80 National Assessment of Reading and Literature,* Education Commission of the States (Denver, CO), 1981.

Contexts for Learning to Write: Studies of Secondary School Instruction, Ablex Publishing (Norwood, NJ), 1984.

(Coauthor) *How Writing Shapes Thinking: A Study of Teaching and Learning,* National Council of Teachers of English, 1987.

Literature in the Secondary School: Studies of Curriculum and Instruction in the U.S., National Council of Teachers of English, 1993.

Curriculum as Conversation: Transforming Traditional Teaching and Learning, University of Chicago Press, 1996.

WITH J. LANGER AND I. MULLIS

The Reading Report Card: Progress toward Excellence in Our Schools; Trends in Reading over Four National Assessments, 1971-1984, National Assessment of Educational Progress, 1985.

Writing: Trends across the Decade, 1974-1984, National Assessment of Educational Progress, 1986.

The Writing Report Card; Writing Achievement in American Schools, National Assessment of Educational Progress, 1986.

Literature and U.S. History: The Instructional Experiences and Factual Knowledge of High School Juniors, National Assessment of Educational Progress, 1987.

Learning to Be Literate in America: Reading, Writing, and Reasoning, National Assessment of Educational Progress, 1987.

Spelling, Punctuation, and Grammar: The Conventions of Writing Used by 9-, 13-, and 17-Year-Olds, National Assessment of Educational Progress, 1987.

Who Reads Best? Factors Related to Reading Achievement, National Assessment of Educational Progress, 1988.

Understanding Direct Writing Assessment: Reflections on a South Carolina Writing Study, National Assessment of Educational Progress, 1989.

(And with L. Jenkins) *The Writing Report Card, 1984-88: Findings from the Nation's Report Card,* National Assessment of Educational Progress, 1990.

Crossroads in American Education: A Summary of Findings, National Assessment of Educational Progress, 1990.

The 1992 NAEP Writing Report Card, National Assessment of Educational Progress, 1994.

OTHER

Contributor to numerous publications, including *Language As a Way of Knowing,* Ontario Institute for Studies in Education, 1977; *Workload Starter Kit for Secondary English Teachers,* by Leon F. Williams, National Council of Teachers of English, 1980; *What Writers Know: The Language, Process, and Structure of Written Discourse,* edited by Martin Nystrand, Academic Press (New York City), 1982; *Encyclopedia of Educational Research,* Macmillan, 1982; *Researching Response to Literature and the Teaching of Literature,* edited by Charles R. Cooper, Ablex Publishing, 1985; and *The Word for Teaching is Learning,* by Martin Lightfoot and Nancy Martin, Heinemann (Exeter, NH), 1988.

Also contributor to *Informal Reasoning in Education, Vital Signs: Bringing Together Reading and Writing, Handbook of Curriculum Research, Literacy and Diversity, Encyclopedia of English Studies and the Language Arts,* and *Handbook of Research on Teaching the Language Arts.* Contributor to psychology and education journals in England and the United States. Editor, *Research in the Teaching of English,* 1984-91.

SIDELIGHTS: Arthur N. Applebee told *CA:* "Early involvement in various projects and activities of the National Council of Teachers of English led to a continuing concern with educational issues and a specific interest in language and language learning. This interest has had diverse manifestations, leading to studies in educational psychology, learning disabilities, educational history, curriculum evaluation, and the teaching of writing and literature. Various studies that I have directed have provided a not particularly encouraging portrait of students' experiences in American schools. My work has sought to understand why conditions are so bleak, and to propose some viable alternatives. Writing about learning is itself a learning process; it is never clear exactly what the recommendations will look like until we begin to write them up to share outside of our research group."

* * *

ARMS, Johnson
See HALLIWELL, David (William)

* * *

ARMSTRONG, Joe C. W.
See ARMSTRONG, Joseph Charles Woodland

* * *

ARMSTRONG, Joseph Charles Woodland 1934-
(Joe C. W. Armstrong)

PERSONAL: Born January 30, 1934, in Toronto, Ontario, Canada; son of James Shelley Phipps (a provincial agent general) and Helen Strawn (Woodland) Armstrong; married Barbara Anne Grace Johnson (a law clerk), July 18, 1970; children: Geoffrey, Jill, Katherine, Jamie. *Ethnicity:* "Canadian (6th generation)." *Education:* Bishop's University, B.A., 1957. *Politics:* "Philosophical conservative." *Religion:* Anglican. *Avocational interests:* Flying, travel (over 100 countries), photography.

ADDRESSES: Home and office—347 Keewatin Ave., Toronto, Ontario, Canada M4P 2A4. *E-mail*—joe.armstrong@sympatico.ca.

CAREER: Rolph-Clark-Stone Ltd., Toronto, Ontario, account executive and manager, 1958-63; Charterhouse Canada Ltd., London, England, and Toronto, nominee director and investment officer, 1963-67; Canadian Manoir Industries Ltd., Montreal, Quebec, executive vice-president, 1968-70; Northern Hardware Distributors Ltd., North Bay, Ontario, general manager, 1970-72; Federal Department of Regional Industrial Expansion, senior incentives officer, 1972-85; Expo '86, Vancouver, British Columbia, senior industrial development adviser for government of Canada, 1986; Canadian Council for Native Business, Toronto, director of economic development, 1987—; government of Canada, Toronto, senior industrial development officer, 1988-95. Professional photographer; television and radio broadcaster; creator of Canadian Broadcasting Corp. radio series "The Explorer." President of personal investment company, Port Franks Properties Ltd., 1971-86. Director of Ontario Heritage Foundation, 1987-90. Consultant for Bruce Beresford's film, *Black Robe,* 1991.

MEMBER: Canadian Institute of Surveyors (honorary member of board of directors, 1983—), Royal Canadian Geographic Society (fellow), Royal Geographic Society (fellow), Ontario Heritage Foundation (director, 1987—), Galiano Cultural and Historical Society (member of board of directors, 1986-87).

AWARDS, HONORS: First appointed honorary Membre Le Mouvement Francite (Quebec), 1990; Magna for Canada Scholarship Award, invitational category for "recognized Canadians", 1996.

WRITINGS:

UNDER NAME JOE C. W. ARMSTRONG

From Sea to Sea: Art and Discovery Maps of Canada, Lester & Orpen Dennys, 1982.

Champlain, Macmillan of Canada, 1987, French translation published as *Samuel de Champlain,* Les Edition de l'Homme, 1988.

Meech Plus: The Charlatan Accord, Committee of One, 1992.

Farewell the Peaceful Kingdom: The Seduction and Rape of Canada, 1963-1994, Stoddart Publishing Company, Ltd., 1995.

As Prime Minister I Would (satirical essay: "Days of Our Lives" [excerpts from the official Armstrong Memoirs]), Key Porter Books, 1996.

Contributor of articles and reviews to magazines, including *Canadian Collector,* and *Quill and Quire.*

WORK IN PROGRESS: An overview of current conservative thinking and conservative politics in Canada, expected publication in 1997.

SIDELIGHTS: Canadian entrepreneur, real estate investor, and government administrator Joe C. W. Armstrong's interest in history led him to publish two critically-successful volumes on the early exploration, cartography, and settlement of Canada. His first, an annotated selection of reproductions from his private Canadiana Collection of antique North American maps, is titled *From Sea to Sea: Art and Discovery Maps of Canada.* Containing thirty-eight maps, Armstrong's large-formatted book presents, as quoted by Lorna Inness in the *Novascotian,* "the process of discovery of the nation . . . after decades of pursuit and struggle," from the explorations of Henry Hudson in the east, to John Rapkin's 1851 trek across Ontario—then known as western Canada, to George Vancouver's voyages on the Canadian Pacific coast. The volume also includes anecdotes about Canadian explorers and descriptions of the methods used to create the maps, such as the woodcut printing technique used to produce the oldest map in the collection, drawn by Venetian mapmaker Giacomo Gastaldi in 1556.

Armstrong's second book, a biography of the seventeenth-century French explorer Samuel de Champlain, took him ten years to write. In researching original source materials such as the explorer's journals and maps and in traveling many of the same routes as Champlain had taken, Armstrong discovered that modern scholars had minimized Champlain's importance in Canadian history. Consequently, he portrayed Champlain as a courageous and heroic seaman and artist whose persistence through twenty-nine voyages across the Atlantic Ocean led to the colonization of Canada, most notably at Quebec, the oldest permanent settlement in North America. Describing Champlain's discovery and cartography of Niagra Falls, the Great Lakes, and much of the area that is now New York and Ontario, Armstrong makes a strong case for the position, in the words of John D. Harbron in the Toronto *Globe and Mail,* "that a Frenchman, not an Englishman, was [Canada's] true founder." Published in both English and French, *Champlain,* according to James Adams in the *Edmonton Journal,* "is a thoroughly readable book, chockful of wonderful stories, intriguing graphics and deft scholarship."

In reference to his first two books, Armstrong told *CA:* "Canada, for many decades now, has been and continues to be a nation rife with constitutional and cultural struggles. A major cause of these divisive forces is a stunning and dangerous lack of education regarding the nation's heritage and, in particular, the early cultural foundations. The teaching of Canadian history, for example, has been gradually provincialized, petrified, and relegated by academicians, politicians, and bureaucrats to the learning back-burner, often as a pathetic adjunct of the humanistic fields of political science, social studies, and social economics. The result of this modernistic indifference and neglect, this radical extrication of history from the more traditional lexicon of the liberal arts venue, has had a philosophically and intellectually devastating effect. Profoundly ignorant of their roots, Canadians are often politically victimized by anti-democratic forces. But also as a result of the impoverished educational foundation for the preservation of nationhood, in frustration and in search of a national vision of consequence, Canadians are often seen seemingly endlessly enduring monumental acts of self-flagellation. Indeed, this has become the predominant national pastime in recent years.

"In June of 1978 I chose my mission—to try something new. I decided to invest as a collector in what I have labeled the 'art and discovery' maps of Canada. The idea was to pioneer and build a small but very high-quality and well-focused cartographic display that could easily be made available, free of charge, to responsible public and private institutions for heritage events throughout Canada. The priority is, through these fascinating and often magnificent graphics (some even emblazoned in gold leaf), to create a new dimension of expression. By bringing greater public attention to the graphics of the nation's discovery foundation, as well as to the heroic accomplishments this artistry reflects, I hoped to effectively capture the interest of a busy younger generation ever in search of the entertainment quick-fix. I was lucky. After three years of intensive research and international purchasing activity, and with the assistance of W. Graham Arader III, a leading dealer in atlases and maps, the Canadiana Collection of rare maps was born. I soon found out, however, that even as a prominent and high-profiled collector sharing and publicizing the significance of the many captured cartographic treasures, the message, through the spoken and visual media alone, wore thin. Something was missing.

"*From Sea Unto Sea: Art and Discovery Maps of Canada* was the result. Following the 1983 publication of this best-selling anecdotal and full-color graphic atlas was the comprehensive 1988 biography *Champlain* and the updated edition in French, *Samuel de Champlain,* the latter distributed worldwide in November of that year. Although sized to a much smaller scale than the previous work, the Champlain biography contains some forty illustrations and maps, in effect the entire inventory of Champlain's graphics pertaining to North America. This is the first comprehensive biography of Champlain ever to be published in both English and French. In this work many of the longstanding Champlain controversies are put to rest with the tabling of considerable new evidence and research as to the Champlain exploits in Canada, New England, and New York."

BIOGRAPHICAL/CRITICAL SOURCES:

PERIODICALS

Alberta Report, August 14, 1995.
Canadian Geographic, December, 1981/January, 1982; December, 1982/January, 1983.
Canadian Heritage, August 20, 1980.
Edmonton Journal, January 9, 1988.
Globe and Mail (Toronto), January 16, 1988.
Kingston Whig-Standard, January 2, 1988.
Maclean's, November 6, 1978.
Novascotian, December 18, 1982.
Washington Times, July 10, 1996.

* * *

ASCHERSON, (Charles) Neal 1932-

PERSONAL: Born October 5, 1932, in Edinburgh, Scotland; son of Stephen Romer (a sailor) and Evelyn (Gilbertson) Ascherson; married Corinna Adam (a journalist), November 20, 1958 (divorced); married Isabel Hilton (a journalist), August, 1984; children: (first marriage) Marina, Isobel; (current marriage) Alexander, Iona. *Education:* King's College, Cambridge, degree (with distinction), 1955. *Politics:* Socialist.

ADDRESSES: Home—27 Corsica St., London N5, England.

CAREER: East African Institute of Social Research, Kampala, East Africa, researcher, 1955-56; journalist with *Guardian,* 1956-58, *Scotsman,* 1958-59, 1975-79; *Observer,* London, journalist, 1960-75, associate editor, 1985-89; *The Independent on Sunday,* London, assistant editor, 1989—. *Military service:* Royal Marines; served in Malaya.

MEMBER: Society of Antiquaries of Scotland (fellow).

AWARDS, HONORS: Granada Awards for Reporter of the Year, 1982, and Journalist of the Year, 1987; James Cameron Award, 1988; George Orwell Prize for Political Journalism, 1993; Golden Insignia of Polish Order of Merit, 1993; Satire Award for Literature (joint award), 1995.

WRITINGS:

The King Incorporated, Allen & Unwin (London), 1963, Doubleday (New York City), 1964.
(Editor and author of introduction) *"The Times" Reports the French Revolution: Extracts from "The Times," 1789-1794,* Times Books (London), 1975.
(Author of introduction) *The Book of Lech Walesa,* Simon & Schuster (New York City), 1982.
The Polish August: The Self-Limiting Revolution, Viking (New York City), 1982.
(Contributor) *The Fourth Reich: Klaus Barbie and the Neo-Fascist Connection,* Hodder & Stoughton (London), 1984, published in America as *The Nazi Legacy: Klaus Barbie and the International Fascist Connection,* Holt (New York City), 1985.
The Struggles for Poland, M. Joseph (London), 1987, Random House (New York City), 1988.
Games with Shadows, Radius (London), 1988.
Black Sea, Hill & Wang (New York City), 1995.

Also author of *New Europe!,* 1990. Contributor to the *New Statesman, New York Review of Books,* and other periodicals.

SIDELIGHTS: Neal Ascherson has served as a journalist, reporter, and columnist for several

British publications, most notably the *Observer.* His work as a foreign correspondent has taken him all over the world, but especially to Eastern Europe. Ascherson's writing is characterized by a deep grasp of history and an ability to apply its lessons to contemporary social and political situations. In the *Times Literary Supplement,* John Dunn wrote of the author: "A person's views are always a blend of sentiments and beliefs. On the page Ascherson is a marvellous companion. His sentiments are consistently engaging, his beliefs invariably intelligent, and the experience on which he draws, both vicariously and directly, is impressively wide and intense."

In the late 1970s and early 1980s Ascherson worked as a foreign correspondent in Poland. He was present on many of the occasions that marked the founding and rise to power of the Solidarity movement. His books on the movement and its leadership include *The Polish August: The Self-Limiting Revolution* and the introduction to *The Book of Lech Walesa.* Additionally he has published a wider-ranging history of Poland in conjunction with a British Broadcasting Corporation television series, *The Struggles for Poland.* These books draw not only upon Ascherson's own experiences as a reporter in that nation, but also upon his knowledge of several hundred years of Polish history. "Neal Ascherson has a matchless ability to evoke periods of intense experience with a few strokes of his pen," observed Timothy Garton Ash in the *Observer.* "*The Polish August* is repeatedly illuminated by such flashes of evocative brilliance." *New York Times Book Review* correspondent Richard M. Watt noted that Ascherson's work "contributes mightily to understanding . . . Poland," adding that *The Polish August* "is a major work by an author who is at once a political scientist, a historian and a very good writer, indeed."

Between 1985 and 1989 Ascherson wrote a political column for the *Observer.* Some of this column work is collected in *Games with Shadows,* published in 1988. In his review of the book for the *Observer,* Michael Frayn wrote: "Journalism is about the here and now; but Ascherson approaches these two familiar points from everywhere in space and time except here and now; and very strange he makes them look." The critic concluded that Ascherson "writes with a wonderful sinewy expressiveness, always colloquial but always elegant. . . . His idiosyncratic intelligence and shameless erudition give me hope each week; hope for newspapers, hope for all of us."

Another well-received Ascherson title is *Black Sea,* a wide-ranging meditation on the countries and states, past and present, that fringe the Black Sea. Traveling through Turkey, Georgia, Ukraine, Russia, and Abkhazia, Ascherson pondered the legacy the region has given the world in its perhaps unparalleled blending of divergent cultures. In a review of the work for *The Spectator,* Dominic Lieven contended that the author "understands both classical and modern history. He uses both to illuminate issues which haunt contemporary mankind. Because he combines interests and approaches which are not usually found in one head he can make connections which most authors would miss." Lieven concluded: "Ascherson's book has sweep and style. It makes one ponder the transience of civilisations, our own included. Above all, it simply encourages its readers to think. It is a glorious antidote to a contemporary university education in the social sciences." In the *New York Times,* Richard Bernstein called *Black Sea* "a fascinating hodgepodge with something to learn on almost every page. With ethnic conflicts much in the headlines, Mr. Ascherson's portrait of a place whose chief characteristic is the durability of its many ethnic identities comes at the right moment, providing perspective on a primordial element in human history."

BIOGRAPHICAL/CRITICAL SOURCES:

PERIODICALS

American Book Review, March 1985, p. 19.
London Review of Books, November 24, 1988, p. 7; May 9, 1996, p. 19.
New Statesman & Society, July 7, 1995, p. 40.
New York Review of Books, February 4, 1982, p. 3; September 29, 1983, pp. 18-27; April 18, 1996, pp. 50-54.
New York Times, December 6, 1995, p. C21.
New York Times Book Review, April 25, 1982, pp. 11, 19; November 26, 1995, p. 17.
Observer, December 6, 1981; August 16, 1987, p. 23; May 15, 1988, p. 23.
Spectator, February 6, 1982, pp. 20-21; June 20, 1987, pp. 23-24; July 15, 1995, pp. 29-30.
Times Literary Supplement, June 11, 1982, p. 640; July 1, 1988, p. 724; July 28, 1995, p. 4.

ASHABRANNER, Brent (Kenneth) 1921-

PERSONAL: Born November 3, 1921, in Shawnee, OK; son of Dudley (a pharmacist) and Rose Thelma (Cotton) Ashabranner; married Martha White, August 9, 1941; children: Melissa Lynn, Jennifer Ann. *Education:* Oklahoma State University, B.S., 1948, M.A., 1951; additional study at University of Michigan, 1955, and Boston University and Oxford University, 1959-60. *Avocational interests:* Bridge, golf, African art.

ADDRESSES: Home and office—15 Spring W., Williamsburg, VA 23188.

CAREER: Oklahoma State University, Stillwater, instructor in English, 1952-55; Ministry of Education, Technical Cooperation Administration, Addis Ababa, Ethiopia, educational materials adviser, 1955-57; International Cooperation Administration, Tripoli, Libya, chief of Education Materials Development Division, 1957-59; Agency for International Development, Lagos, Nigeria, education program officer, 1960-61; Peace Corps, Washington, DC, acting director of program in Nigeria, 1961-62, deputy director of program in India, 1962-64, director of program in India, 1964-66, director of Office of Training, 1966-67, deputy director of Peace Corps, 1967-69; Harvard University, Center for Studies in Education and Development, Cambridge, MA, research associate, 1969-70; Pathfinder Fund, Boston, MA, director of Near East-South Asia Population Program, 1970-71; director of project development, World Population International Assistance Division, Planned Parenthood, 1971-72; Ford Foundation, New York, NY, associate representative and population program officer, 1972-80, deputy representative to Philippines, 1972-75, deputy representative to Indonesia, 1975-80; fulltime writer, 1980—. *Military service:* U.S. Navy, 1942-45.

AWARDS, HONORS: National Civil Service League career service award, 1968; Notable Children's Trade Book in the Field of Social Studies, 1982, and Carter G. Woodson Book Award, National Council for the Social Studies, 1983, both for *Morning Star, Black Sun: The Northern Cheyenne Indians and America's Energy Crisis;* Notable Children's Trade Book in the Field of Social Studies, American Library Association (ALA) Notable Book, and Books for the Teen-Age, New York Public Library, all 1983, all for *The New Americans: Changing Patterns in U.S. Immigration;* Notable Children's Trade Book in the Field of Social Studies, 1984, ALA Best Book for Young Adults, 1984, and Carter G. Woodson Book Award, 1985, all for *To Live in Two Worlds: American Indian Youth Today;* Notable Children's Book in the Field of Social Studies, and ALA Notable Book, both 1984, both for *Gavriel and Jemal: Two Boys of Jerusalem;* ALA Notable Book, 1985, *Boston Horn-Globe* Honor Book, 1986, and Carter G. Woodson Book Award, 1986, all for *Dark Harvest: Migrant Farmworkers in America;* ALA Notable Book, *School Library Journal* Best Book of the Year, both 1986, both for *Children of the Maya: A Guatemalan Indian Odyssey;* Notable Children's Trade Book in the Field of Social Studies, *School Library Journal* Best Book of the Year, ALA Notable Book, and Christopher Award, all 1987, all for *Into a Strange Land: Unaccompanied Refugee Youth in America;* Notable Children's Trade Book in the Field of Social Studies, 1987, for *The Vanishing Border: A Photographic Journey along Our Frontier with Mexico; Washington Post*/Children's Book Guild of Washington, D.C. Award for nonfiction, 1990, for body of work; *Always to Remember: The Story of the Vietnam Veterans Memorial* was named by ALA as a notable book and best book for young adults; *People Who Make a Difference, Counting America: The Story of the United States Census, Born to the Land: An American Portrait,* and *The Times of My Life: A Memoir* were named Books for the Teen Age by the New York Public Library.

WRITINGS:

(Editor) *The Stakes Are High,* Bantam (New York City), 1954.

(With Judson Milburn and Cecil B. Williams) *A First Course in College English* (textbook), Houghton (Boston), 1962.

A Moment in History: The First Ten Years of the Peace Corps, Doubleday (New York City), 1971.

The Times of My Life: A Memoir, Dutton (New York City), 1990.

JUVENILE

(Editor, with Russell Davis) *The Lion's Whiskers: Tales of High Africa,* Little, Brown (Boston), 1959, revised as *The Lion's Whiskers and Other Ethiopian Tales,* illustrated by Helen Siegl, Linnet Books (North Haven, CA), 1997.

(With Davis) *Point Four Assignment: Stories from the Records of Those Who Work in Foreign Fields for the Mutual Security of Free Nations,* Little, Brown, 1959.

(With Davis) *Ten Thousand Desert Swords,* Little, Brown, 1960.

(With Davis) *The Choctaw Code,* McGraw (New York City), 1961, reprinted, Linnet Books (Hamden, CT), 1994.

(With Davis) *Chief Joseph: War Chief of the Nez Perce,* McGraw, 1962.

(With Davis) *Land in the Sun: The Story of West Africa,* Little, Brown, 1963.

(With Davis) *Strangers in Africa,* McGraw, 1963.

Morning Star, Black Sun: The Northern Cheyenne Indians and America's Energy Crisis (Junior Literary Guild selection), photographs by Paul Conklin, Dodd (New York City), 1982.

The New Americans: Changing Patterns in U.S. Immigration (Junior Literary Guild selection), photographs by Conklin, Dodd, 1983.

To Live in Two Worlds: American Indian Youth Today (Junior Literary Guild selection), photographs by Conklin, Dodd, 1984, reprinted, Putnam (New York City), 1989.

Gavriel and Jemal: Two Boys of Jerusalem (Junior Literary Guild selection), photographs by Conklin, Dodd, 1984.

Dark Harvest: Migrant Farmworkers in America, Dodd, 1985, reprinted, Linnett, 1993.

Children of the Maya: A Guatemalan Indian Odyssey, photographs by Paul Conklin, Dodd, 1986.

(With daughter, Melissa Ashabranner) *Into a Strange Land: Unaccompanied Refugee Youth in America* (Junior Literary Guild selection), Dodd, 1987.

The Vanishing Border: A Photographic Journey along Our Frontier with Mexico (Junior Literary Guild selection), photographs by Conklin, Dodd, 1987.

Always to Remember: The Story of the Vietnam Veterans Memorial (Junior Literary Guild selection), photographs by daughter, Jennifer Ashabranner, Dodd, 1988, reprinted, Putnam, 1990.

Born to the Land: An American Portrait (Junior Literary Guild selection), photographs by Conklin, Putnam, 1989.

(With daughter, Melissa Ashabranner) *Counting America: The Story of the United States Census* (Junior Literary Guild selection), Putnam, 1989.

I'm in the Zoo, Too!, illustrated by Janet Stevens, Dutton, 1989.

People Who Make a Difference, photographs by Conklin, Dutton, 1989.

Crazy about German Shepherds, photographs by Jennifer Ashabranner, Cobblehill Books (New York City), 1990.

A Grateful Nation: The Story of Arlington National Cemetery (Junior Literary Guild selection), photographs by Jennifer Ashabranner, Putnam, 1990.

An Ancient Heritage: The Arab-American Minority, photographs by Conklin, HarperCollins (New York City), 1991.

(Author of text) *Land of Yesterday, Land of Tomorrow: Discovering Chinese Central Asia,* photographs by Paul, David, and Peter Conklin, Cobblehill Books, 1992.

A Memorial for Mr. Lincoln (Junior Literary Guild selection), photographs by Jennifer Ashabranner, Putnam, 1992.

Still a Nation of Immigrants, photographs by Jennifer Ashabranner, Dutton, 1993.

A New Frontier: The Peace Corps in Eastern Europe (Junior Literary Guild selection), photographs by Conklin, Dutton, 1994.

(Author of Text) *Lithuania: The Nation That Would Be Free,* photographs by Stephen Chicoine, Dutton, 1995.

Our Beckoning Borders: Illegal Immigration to America, photographs by Conklin, Cobblehill Books, 1996.

A Strange and Distant Shore: Indians of the Great Plains in Exile, Dutton, 1996.

To Seek a Better World: The Haitian Minority in America, photographs by Conklin, Cobblehill Books, 1997.

OTHER

Contributor of articles and short stories to periodicals.

SIDELIGHTS: Brent Ashabranner's career has taken him across the globe and has provided him with opportunities to study cultures in other countries as well as America. As a result, many of his books for young adults address cross-cultural issues involving Africans, Arabs, Jews, Native Americans, immigrants, refugees, and migrant workers. Ashabranner has been praised for his sensitive portrayals of individuals in these groups and for his carefully researched history and sociology of the groups themselves. "Many of my books deal with serious social issues and problems," Ashabranner stated in thc *Something about the Author Autobiography Series.* "I think I can make these issues and problems interesting to readers of all ages by keeping the focus on the people who are caught up in them." He added: "No matter what social issues or problems my books may deal with, I have one overriding hope for each of them: that the people I write about will emerge as human beings whose lives are real and valuable and who have a right to strive for decent lives. If I can get that truth across, young readers will hear it and know what I am talking about."

Ashabranner was born and raised in Oklahoma, and at first he seemed destined to live his whole life there. He went to college in Oklahoma—helping to defray his tuition by selling fiction to pulp magazines—and after graduating began teaching English at Oklahoma State University. In 1955, however, he accepted a position with the U.S. Technical Cooperation Administration and journeyed to Ethiopia, Libya, and Nigeria to assist those countries's ministries of education. While in Nigeria he was invited to join the fledgling Peace Corps as an administrator.

Ashabranner was involved with the Peace Corps from its beginning, helping to shape and develop a number of its programs. From 1964 to 1966 he was director of the program in India, which at the time was the largest with over 750 volunteers. Before he left the Peace Corps in 1969, Ashabranner had become the deputy director of the entire agency. Years later he wrote a history of those years in *A Moment in History: The First Ten Years of the Peace Corps.*

Critics have observed that *A Moment in History* contains an honest portrayal of the corps during its first decade. Although he cites the Peace Corps's successes, Ashabranner also outlines examples of the agency's failures and explains the reasons behind them. *Library Journal* contributor R. F. Chapman noted that the book is "a frank account of the first decade of the Peace Corps," calling the author's approach "a human presentation." Similarly, a *New York Times Book Review* writer remarked that Ashabranner is "particularly good on the Peace Corps inception and the bureaucratic infighting that accompanied it."

Although Ashabranner left the Peace Corps in 1969, he continued working abroad for various charitable agencies until 1980, when he began writing full-time. The author's experiences with different cultures, both in America and abroad, led him to write about people who live outside mainstream culture. "The things I felt I was learning about understanding other cultures and about people of different cultures trying to understand each other seemed worth sharing with young readers," the author observed in *Authors and Artists for Young Adults.* "Since returning to the United States to live, I have concentrated on nonfiction and have written mostly about minorities, including Native Americans, and the growing ethnic groups in America. My years of living and working overseas have helped me to understand better their hopes, desires, frustrations, and fears."

Ashabranner gears most of his work toward young adults, frequently writing about children in crisis. For example, in *Children of the Maya: A Guatemalan Indian Odyssey,* the author recounts the everyday village life of young Indian children, often using the children's own memories. The result, commented Michael Dirda in the *Washington Post Book World,* is "as usual with Ashabranner. . . . His book—powerfully enhanced by [Paul] Conklin's black and white photographs—blends careful reporting with social conscience."

In recent years Ashabranner has been living in Williamsburg, Virginia. His grown daughters live in the Washington, D.C. area, and both have helped him with some of his books. His daughter Jennifer provided photographs for such well-received works as *Always to Remember: The Story of the Vietnam Veterans Memorial* and *A Memorial for Mr. Lincoln.* His other daughter Melissa has served as coauthor of *Counting America: The Story of the United States Census,* among others.

Ashabranner told *CA:* "Perhaps the hardest task of the nonfiction writer is to find the story and its proper form in the material. Speaking of the sculptor's task, Henry Moore wrote, 'You begin with a block and have to find the sculpture that's inside it. You have to overcome the resistance of the material by sheer determination and hard work.'

"Moore might have been talking about the nonfiction writer's task. You have collected a tremendous amount of material on your subject: stacks of interview and field notes, books, reports, newspaper and periodical clippings. They are stacked on your desk, on the shelves around you, on the floor. That is your block, and you must find the story that is somewhere inside. You have to keep searching no matter how long it takes.

"I collected material on refugees and interviewed refugees for two years before my daughter Melissa and I, in our book *Into a Strange Land: Unaccompanied Refugee Youth in America,* found the way to tell our story through the voices of refugee children who had been set adrift in the world alone, without parents, family, or loved ones. Here was the story inside this great mass of material, the story that would touch young readers and make them think deeply and feel deeply about the plight of refugees.

"A few years ago I talked with a class of sixth-graders. Afterward one of the students came up to tell me that he had just read my book about immigrants, *The New Americans: Changing Patterns in U.S. Immigration.* 'I liked the stories about people best,' he said, 'but all that other stuff was okay, too.'

"I confess to a certain awe at his nonchalance in lumping together 'all that other stuff,' which happened to be some immigration history, law, and politics; demographic projections; and speculations about America as a multicultural society. I had tried to integrate that information smoothly into the immigrant stories, and I hope I succeeded. But that young man put his finger squarely on the best way—the only way, really—to make the subjects I write about interesting to my young audience: stories about people. And of this I am sure: no matter what else they may be, every one of my books is a book about people worth knowing."

BIOGRAPHICAL/CRITICAL SOURCES:

BOOKS

Ashabranner, Brent, *A Moment in History: The First Ten Years of the Peace Corps,* Doubleday, 1971.

Ashabranner, *The Times of My Life: A Memoir,* Dutton, 1990.

Authors and Artists for Young Adults, Volume 6, Gale (Detroit, MI), 1992.

Children's Literature Review, Volume 28, Gale, 1992.

Something about the Author Autobiography Series, Volume 14, Gale, 1993.

PERIODICALS

Booklist, November 15, 1990, p. 64; September 1, 1993, p. 46; October 1, 1994, p. 315; June 1995, p. 1974.

Horn Book, November/December, 1988; January/February, 1995, p. 74; July/August, 1995, p. 477.

Junior Literary Guild, April-September, 1988.

Library Journal, August, 1971.

Los Angeles Times, October 17, 1987.

New York Times Book Review, August 5, 1962; April 4, 1971; December 30, 1990, p. 19.

School Library Journal, September, 1989, p. 220; April, 1991, p. 126; June, 1992, p. 127; November, 1994, p. 110.

Washington Post Book World, June 8, 1986.

* * *

ASHBROOK, James B(arbour) 1925-

PERSONAL: Born November 1, 1925, in Adrian, MI; son of Milan Forest (a minister) and Elizabeth (Barbour) Ashbrook; married Patricia Cober (a social worker), August 14, 1948; children: Peter, Susan, Martha, Karen. *Ethnicity:* "Caucasian." *Education:* Denison University, B.A. (with honors), 1947; Colgate Rochester Divinity School, B.D., 1950; Union Theological Seminary and William White Institute of Psychiatry, graduate fellow, 1954-55; Ohio State University, M.A., 1962, Ph.D., 1964. *Politics:* Democrat.

ADDRESSES: *Home*—1205 Wesley Ave., Evanston, IL 60202. *E-mail*—j-ashbrook@nwv.edu.

CAREER: Clergyman of American Baptist Church; pastor in Rochester, NY, 1950-54, and Granville, OH, 1955-60; Colgate Rochester Divinity School, Rochester, NY, associate professor, 1960-65, professor of pastoral theology, 1965-69, professor of psychology and theology, 1969-81; Northwestern University, Garrett-Evangelical Theological Seminary, Evanston, IL, professor of religion and personality and advisory member of graduate faculty, 1982-93, senior scholar of religion and personality, 1993-96, professor emeritus, 1996—. Teaching fellow, Graduate Theological Union, 1987-93; adjunct professor, Northern Baptist Theological Seminary, 1984-89. Visiting lecturer at Denison University, 1958-60, and Princeton Theological Seminary, 1970-71. Summer clinical pastoral training at Rochester State Hospital, 1949, Bellevue General Hospital, 1950, and Illinois State Training School for Boys, 1951. Consultant and supervisor, Counseling Center, University of Rochester, 1969-75, and Genesee Ecumenical Pastoral Counseling Center, 1975-81; consultant to Chief of U.S. Air Force Chaplains, 1969, to Rochester Board of Education, 1969-73, to Family Court of Monroe County (NY), 1972-74, and to St. Ann's Home for the Elderly, 1972-85.

MEMBER: American Association of Pastoral Counselors (diplomate; chair of centers and training committee, 1970-71), American Academy of Religion, Society for the Scientific Study of Religion, American Psychological Association, American Board of Professional Psychology (clinical), Phi Beta Kappa.

AWARDS, HONORS: Faculty fellowship, American Association of Theology Schools, 1963-64, 1971-72; postdoctoral fellowship, University of Rochester Center for Community Studies, 1971-73; alumni citation, Denison University, 1972; LL.D., Denison University, 1976; designated "a pioneer in pastoral psychotherapy," American Association of Pastoral Counselors/Institutes of Religion and Health, 1987; Distinguished Contribution Award from American Association of Pastoral Counselors, 1990; Academic fellow, Institute of Religion in an Age of Science, 1995.

WRITINGS:

Be/Come Community, Judson (Valley Forge, PA), 1971.

In Human Presence: Hope, Judson, 1971.

Humanitas: Human Becoming and Being Human, Abingdon (Nashville, TN), 1973.

The Old Me and a New i: An Exploration of Personal Identity, Judson, 1974.

Responding to Human Pain, Judson, 1975.

(With Paul W. Walaskay) *Christianity for Pious Skeptics,* Abingdon, 1977.

The Human Mind and the Mind of God: Theological Promise in Brain Research, University Press of America (Lanham, MD), 1984.

The Brain and Belief: Faith in Light of Brain Research, Wyndham Hall Press, 1988.

(Editor with John E. Hukle, Jr.) *At the Point of Need—Living Human Experience: Essays in Honor of Carroll A. Wise,* University Press of America, 1988.

Paul Tillich in Conversation, Wyndham Hall Press, 1988.

(Editor) *Faith and Ministry in Light of the Double Brain,* Wyndham Hall Press, 1989.

(Editor) *Brain, Culture, and the Human Spirit: Essays from an Emergent Evolution Perspective,* University Press of America, 1993.

Minding the Soul: Pastoral Counseling and Remembering, Fortress (Philadelphia), 1996.

(With Carol Rausch Albright) *The Humanizing Brain,* Pilgrim Press (Long Island City, NY), 1997.

Also contributor to publications, including *The Minister's Consultation Clinic,* edited by Simon Doniger, Channel Press, 1955; *Religion and Mental Health,* edited by Hans Hoffman, Harper (New York City), 1961; *Religion and Medicine,* edited by David Belgum, Iowa State University Press (Ames), 1967; and *Psychological Testing for Ministerial Selection,* edited by William Bier, Fordham University Press (Bronx, NY), 1970.

Member of editorial board, "Ministry Monograph" series, 1965-70. Contributor to psychology and religion journals. Associate editor, *Review of Religious Research,* 1982-89; member of editorial advisory board, *Journal of Pastoral Care,* 1965—; consulting editor, *Journal of Counseling Psychology,* 1968-74.

* * *

ASHE, Geoffrey (Thomas) 1923-

PERSONAL: Born March 29, 1923, in London, England; son of Arthur William (a travel agency general manager) and Thelma (Hoodless) Ashe; married Dorothy Irene Train (a teacher), May 3, 1946; children: Thomas, John, Michael, Sheila, Brendan. *Education:* University of British Columbia, B.A. (first class honors), 1943; Trinity College, Cambridge University, B.A. (first in English Tripos), 1948. *Religion:* Catholic.

ADDRESSES: *Home*—Chalice Orchard, Well House Lane, Glastonbury, Somerset BA6 8BJ England.

CAREER: Writer. Polish University College, London, lecturer in English, 1948-50; Newman Neame (publishers), London, industrial research assistant, 1949-51; Ford Motor Co. of Canada, Windsor, Ontario, administrative assistant, 1952-54; Post Office Department, Toronto, Ontario, technical officer, 1954-55; Polytechnic, London, lecturer in management studies, 1956-68. Visiting professor of English, University of Southern Mississippi, 1982, University of Alabama at Birmingham, 1984, Wilfred Laurier University, Canada, 1985, University of Minnesota, Duluth, 1986, Drew University, 1989, Portland State University, 1990-95 (summers), and University of Northern Iowa, 1995; Thomas Lamont Visiting Professor, Union College, Schenectady, NY, 1984; lecturer and contributor to television programs; guide to study-tours in Britain.

MEMBER: International Arthurian Society, Royal Society of Literature (fellow).

WRITINGS:

The Tale of the Tub: A Survey of the Art of Bathing through the Ages, Newman Neame, 1950.
King Arthur's Avalon: The Story of Glastonbury, Collins (London), 1957.
From Caesar to Arthur, Collins, 1960.
Land to the West: St. Brendan's Voyage to America, Collins, 1962.
The Land and the Book, Collins, 1965.
The Carmelite Order, Carmelite Press, 1965.
Gandhi: A Study in Revolution, Stein & Day (London), 1968.
(Editor and contributor) *The Quest for Arthur's Britain,* Pall Mall (London), 1968.
All About King Arthur (juvenile), W. H. Allen (London), 1969, published in the United States as *King Arthur in Fact and Legend,* T. Nelson (Nashville, TN), 1971.
Camelot and the Vision of Albion, Heinemann (Exeter, NH), 1971.
(With others) *The Quest for America,* Pall Mall, 1971.
The Art of Writing Made Simple, W. H. Allen, 1972.
The Finger and the Moon (novel), Heinemann, 1973.
Do What You Will: A History of Anti-morality, W. H. Allen, 1974.
The Virgin, Routledge & Kegan Paul (London), 1976.
The Ancient Wisdom, Macmillan (New York City), 1977.
Miracles, Routledge & Kegan Paul, 1978.
A Guidebook to Arthurian Britain, Longman (London), 1980.
Kings and Queens of Early Britain, Methuen (London), 1982.
Avalonian Quest, Methuen, 1982.
The Discovery of King Arthur, Doubleday (New York City), 1985.
The Landscape of King Arthur, Webb & Bower (New York City), 1987.
(With Norris J. Lacy) *The Arthurian Handbook,* Garland (New York City), 1988.
Mythology of the British Isles, Methuen, 1990.
King Arthur: The Dream of a Golden Age, Thames & Hudson (London), 1990.
Atlantis: Lost Lands, Ancient Wisdom, Thames & Hudson, 1992.
Dawn behind the Dawn, Henry Holt, 1992.

Author of play, "The Glass Island," 1964. Columnist in *Resurgence* magazine, 1973-78. Contributor to numerous periodicals, including *Speculum.* Associate editor of *The Arthurian Encyclopedia,* Garland Press, 1986, and *The New Arthurian Encyclopedia,* Garland Press, 1991.

SIDELIGHTS: The writings of Geoffrey Ashe represent an eclectic selection of religious, historical, and mythological topics. He has written extensively on the historical and literary aspects of Arthurian legend and has been involved with archaeological excavations in search of Camelot, but the scope of his works remains essentially diverse. "Geoffrey Ashe has written the best biography of Gandhi that I know," writes Henrietta Buckmaster in the *Christian Science Monitor. Gandhi: A Study in Revolution* is "a model of fairness, proportion and restraint," according to Martin E. Marty in the *New York Times Book Review.* "In a time when Gandhi usually receives ideological or tractarian treatment, it is refreshing to have a simple narrative, a straight biography of a very human being." Marty makes reference to one of the central difficulties confronting the Gandhi biographer: overcoming the cult of personality and mythology surrounding the religious and political leader to reveal the "very human" man beneath. Describing the success with which Ashe copes with this problem, Francis Watson says in *Spectator* that "Mr. Ashe has sunk his shafts in the immense material to convince us of what Einstein suggested wc might one day scarcely believe, 'that such a one as this ever in flesh and blood walked upon this earth.' While the tribute is quoted, its suggestion of the superhuman is satisfactorily avoided."

Another formidable task for the biographer of Gandhi is the task of making a balanced and coherent presentation of the different periods in the Indian leader's life, while sifting through an enormous mass of detail. Philip Altbach, reviewing *Gandhi* in *Commonweal,* believes that the focus of the book is uneven: "Like most of Gandhi's other biographers, [Ashe] spends too much time on the South African experience and does not go into enough detail about India." Marty, however, disagrees: "The plot line of Gandhi's life in Britain, South Africa, and India is necessarily complex, [but] the reader will not be lost in detail. [Ashe's] quotations from Gandhi are pithy and pointed; the anecdotes are spare but illuminating." In a *Punch* article on the book, Honoria J. Scannard asserts that Ashe's "greatest achievement is to present this eminently spiritual leader as a man who was also ruthlessly practical and passionately human."

Ashe has also written about the cult of the Virgin Mary, the search for Camelot, and other interrelated topics of religion, philosophy, and mythology. Writing in the *New Statesman,* Jonathan Raban calls *Camelot and the Vision of Albion* "an enterprising foray into [the] rich seam of indigenous English mythology." The volume proposes the idea that Arthurian legend, in all of its many manifestations, reflects an innate desire in mankind for a golden age as embodied in a paradisiacal setting such as Camelot. According to Raban, Ashe's "real interest lies in the notion of a submerged 'British spirit,' personified by an Arthur/Albion figure" traced through figures such as Shelley and Gandhi, and a hero of Arthurian dimensions who is yet to come.

Ashe's focus on the legendary king continues in a number of books published in the 1980s and 1990s. In *The Discovery of King Arthur,* Ashe proposes to locate the historical monarch. A likely candidate, he maintains, is a military leader famous for his exploits in the Gallic campaign of 469-470 A.D. During this time, "there was indeed military action among the pro-Roman Burgundians who were aided by their British cousins," James P. Carley comments in the *Globe and Mail.* "[Ashe] also notes that the subsequent retreat led them near the Burgundian town of Avalon," writes Carley, who calls Ashe's arguments "persuasive." Carley suggests that this discovery is not celebrated more because, in his words, "the real Arthur is the *legend,* not the *fact*—a conclusion Ashe himself would probably accept."

Ashe told *CA:* "*Gandhi* expressed lasting interests and aspirations of mine which admiration of Gandhi had partly inspired. But those [books] on the Arthurian Legend and other mythological topics are far better known, and more characteristic [of my work].

"The initial impulse came from discovering the history and legends of Glastonbury, a very ancient place where I now live. These involve Arthur but much more, and raise profound issues, especially about early religion in Britain. I have been much concerned in various ways with Glastonbury's modern revival as a cultural and spiritual centre.

"One major presence at Glastonbury is the mythos of Mary. Writing *The Virgin* required a preliminary study of pre-Christian Goddess-worship. An academic writer on the Mary cult, Michael P. Carroll, accepted the general thesis of Goddess influence and described *The Virgin* as 'the only work I know that tries to account for the historical origins of the Mary cult using a reasonably systematic methodology'. Taken up by Carolyn Shaefer, in Santa Cruz, my work played a part in bringing about a conference on 'The Great Goddess Re-Emerging' which was sponsored by the University of California Extension and launched an important trend in Women's Spirituality. I retained the interest and, at Portland State University, gave courses on Goddess mythology. *Dawn behind the Dawn,* a development of *The Ancient Wisdom,* is a contribution to prehistory in this field. There are connections with Hindu cults that attracted Gandhi: the link remains.

"Much of what I've done has been exploration of the past in the belief that it embodies clues, often obscure and overlooked, to a possible future. My work is functional, not purely antiquarian. Thus, it seems to me that the early Christianity of the Celtic people in Britain and Ireland can suggest neglected potentialities for Christianity today. I have become fascinated with certain medieval ideas—never condemned, but generally overlooked—about a future revolutionary change in the Church. With those in mind, and many other matters already examined, I am working on a study of Prophecy."

BIOGRAPHICAL/CRITICAL SOURCES:

PERIODICALS

Booklist, May 15, 1972.
Christian Science Monitor, July 18, 1968.
Commonweal, March 13, 1970.
Globe and Mail (Toronto), April 13, 1985.
New Statesman, January 15, 1971.
New York Review of Books, November 11, 1976.
New York Times Book Review, July 21, 1968; August 29, 1977.
Punch, May 8, 1968.
Spectator, March 22, 1968.
Times Literary Supplement, October 16, 1969.

* * *

ASHTON, Dore 1928-

PERSONAL: Born May 21, 1928, in Newark, NJ; daughter of Ralph Neil (a physician) and Sylvia Smith (Ashton) Shapiro; married Adja Yunkers (an artist), July 8, 1953 (died, 1983); married Matti Megged, March 5, 1985; children: (first marriage) Alexandra Louise, Marina Svietlana. *Ethnicity:* "Jewish." *Education:* University of Wisconsin, B.A., 1949; Harvard University, M.A., 1950. *Politics:* "Ranging from liberal to radical." *Avocational interests:* Preservation of world peace.

ADDRESSES: Home—217 East 11th St., New York, NY 10003. *Office*—Cooper Union, New York, NY 10003.

CAREER: Art Digest, New York City, associate editor, 1951-54; *New York Times,* New York City, associate art critic, 1955-60; Pratt Institute, Brooklyn, NY, lecturer, 1962-63; School of Visual Arts, New York City, lecturer in philosophy of art, head of department of humanities, 1965-68; Cooper Union, New York City, professor of art history, 1969—. Writer, teacher, and lecturer, 1960—; curator of exhibitions for the Museum of Modern Art, the American Federation of Artists, and individual museums in the United States and abroad. Instructor, City University of New York, 1973, Columbia University, 1975, and New School for Social Research, 1986—. Member of advisory boards, John Simon Guggenheim Foundation and Swann Foundation.

MEMBER: International Association of Art Critics, PEN, Phi Beta Kappa.

AWARDS, HONORS: Ford Foundation fellowship, 1960; F. J. Mather Award for art criticism, College Art Association, 1963; Graham Foundation Grant, 1963; Guggenheim fellowship, 1964; honorary doctorates from Moore College of Art, 1975, and Hamline University, 1982; National Endowment for the Humanities grant, 1980; Asian Cultural Council grant, 1989.

WRITINGS:

Abstract Art before Columbus, A. Emmerich, 1957.
Poets and the Past, A. Emmerich, 1959.
Philip Guston (monograph), Grove (New York City), 1960.
(Author of commentary) Robert Rauschenberg, *Rauschenberg's Dante,* Abrams (New York City), 1964.
Modern American Sculpture, Abrams, 1968.
A Reading of Modern Art, Harper (New York City), 1969.
Richard Lindner: A Full-Length Study, Abrams, 1970.
The Sculpture of Pol Bury, Maeght, 1970.
The Life and Times of the New York School, Adams & Dart, 1972, published as *The New York School: A Cultural Reckoning,* Viking (New York City), 1973.
Drawings by New York Artists (exhibition catalogue), Utah Museum of Fine Arts (Salt Lake City, UT), 1972.
(With others) *New York: Cultural Capital of the World, 1940-1965,* edited by Leonard Wallock, photographs by Mario Carrieri, Holt (New York City), 1972, reprinted, Rizzoli International (New York City), 1988.
A Joseph Cornell Album, Viking, 1974.
Yes, but . . .: A Critical Study of Philip Guston, Viking, 1976.
(With Suzanne Delehanty) *Eight Abstract Painters,* University of Pennsylvania, Institute of Contemporary Art (Philadelphia, PA), 1978.
(With Peter Howard Selz) *Zwei Jahrzehnte amerikanischer Malerei, 1920-1940* (Duesseldorf, Germany), 1979.

A Fable of Modern Art, Thames & Hudson (London, England), 1980.
(With Denise Brown Hare) *Rosa Bonheur: A Life and a Legend,* Viking, 1981.
American Art since 1945, Oxford University Press (New York City), 1982.
(With Jack Flam) *Robert Motherwell,* Abrams, 1982.
(With Joan M. Marter) *Jose de Rivera Constructions,* Abner Schram, 1983.
About Rothko, Oxford University Press, 1983.
Jacobo Borges (Caracas, Venezuela), 1983.
Deborah Remington: A 20-Year Survey, Newport Harbor Art Museum, 1983.
Multiplicity in Clay, Metal, Fiber: Skidmore College Craft Invitational, The College (Saratoga Springs, NY), 1984.
Jean Cocteau and the French Scene, edited by Arthur Peters, Abbeville Press (New York City), 1984.
Out of the Whirlwind: Three Decades of Arts Commentary, edited by Donald Kuspit, UMI Research Press, 1987.
Fragonard in the Universe of Painting, Smithsonian Institution Press (Washington, DC), 1988.
Terence LaNoue, Hudson Hills (New York City), 1992.
Gunther Gerszo, Latin American Masters, 1995.
The Delicate Thread: Hiroshi Teshigahara, Kodansha, 1996.

EDITOR

(Coeditor) *Redon, Moreau, Bresdin,* Museum of Modern Art, 1961.
The Unknown Shore, Atlantic/Little, Brown, 1962.
Pablo Picasso, *Picasso on Art: A Selection of Views,* Viking, 1972.
20th-Century Artists on Art, Pantheon (New York City), 1985.
Antonio Sant'Elia, A. Mondadori (Milan, Italy), 1986.

OTHER

Contributor to the "Vision and Value" series, edited by Gyorgy Kepes, Braziller, 1966, and to *On Art,* edited by Rudolf Baranik. Contributor of articles to over seventy journals, including *Aujourd'hui, Cimaise* and *XXieme Siecle.* New York contributing editor for *Cimaise* and *XXieme Siecle,* 1955-70, *Studio International,* 1961-74, *Opus International,* 1968-74, and *Art International,* 1987—; associate editor and columnist, *Arts,* 1974—.

SIDELIGHTS: Art critic and educator Dore Ashton specializes in the study of 20th-century art. She is well known for her books concerning the New York School of art and such New York artists as Mark Rothko and Joseph Cornell.

Ashton told *CA:* "What I seek in all arts is to be moved. As I have to translate my responses to myself, I write."

BIOGRAPHICAL/CRITICAL SOURCES:

PERIODICALS

Los Angeles Times Book Review, June 22, 1980; April 26, 1981; January 29, 1984.
New York Review of Books, August 21, 1969; June 14, 1973.
New York Times, April 24, 1980; November 7, 1983.
New York Times Book Review, December 6, 1970; December 2, 1973; December 29, 1974; July 4, 1976; May 24, 1981; January 1, 1984.
Spectator, May 29, 1982; September 8, 1984.
Times Literary Supplement, February 11, 1965; November 9, 1973; December 5, 1980; October 16, 1981; March 19, 1982.
Village Voice, May 29, 1984; March 15, 1988.
Washington Post Book World, July 6, 1980; April 12, 1981; February 19, 1984.

* * *

ASPRIN, Robert L(ynn) 1946-

PERSONAL: Born June 28, 1946, in St. John's, MI; son of Daniel D. (a machinist) and Lorraine (an elementary school teacher; maiden name, Coon) Asprin; married Anne Brett (a bookkeeper), December 28, 1968; married Lynn Abbey; children: (first marriage) Annette Maria, Daniel Mather. *Education:* Attended University of Michigan, 1964-65.

ADDRESSES: Office—c/o Ace Books, 200 Madison Ave., New York, NY 10016.

CAREER: University Microfilm, Ann Arbor, MI, accounts payable clerk, 1966-69, accounts receivable correspondent, 1969-70, payroll-labor analyst, 1970-74; junior cost accountant, 1974-76, cost accountant, 1976-78; freelance writer, 1978—. *Military service:* U.S. Army, 1965-66.

MEMBER: Science Fiction Writers of America.

AWARDS, HONORS: Hugo Award nomination, World Science Fiction Convention, 1976, for *The Capture; Locus* Award for editing, 1982.

WRITINGS:

SCIENCE FICTION NOVELS

The Cold Cash War, St. Martin's (New York City), 1977.
The Bug Wars, St. Martin's, 1979.
The Star Stalkers, Playboy Press, 1979.
(With George Takei) *Mirror Friend, Mirror Foe,* Playboy Press, 1979.
Tambu, Ace Books (New York City), 1979.
Tambu Anthology (short fiction), Ace Books, 1980.
(With Lynn Abbey) *Act of God,* Ace Books, 1980.
(With Bill Fawcett) *Cold Cash Warrior,* Ace Books, 1989.
Phule's Company, Ace Books, 1990.
Phule's Paradise, Ace Books, 1992.
(With Abbey) *Catwoman: Tiger Hunt,* Warner (New York City), 1992.
(With Linda Evans) *Time Scout,* Baen (New York City), 1995.
Wagers of Sin, Baen, 1996.

FANTASY NOVELS

Another Fine Myth, Donning (Norfolk, VA), 1978, revised edition, illustrated by Phil Foglio, 1985.
Myth Conceptions, illustrated by Polly and Kelly Freas, Donning, 1980.
The Demon Blade, St. Martin's, 1980.
Myth Directions, illustrated by Foglio, Donning, 1982.
Hit or Myth, illustrated by Foglio, Donning, 1983.
Myth Adventures (includes *Another Fine Myth, Myth Directions,* and *Hit or Myth*), Doubleday (Garden City, NY), 1984.
Myth-ing Persons, illustrated by Foglio, Donning, 1984.
Little Myth Marker, illustrated by Foglio, Donning, 1985.
(With Kay Reynolds) *M.Y.T.H. Inc. Link,* illustrated by Foglio, Donning, 1986.
Myth Alliances (includes *Myth-ing Persons, Little Myth Marker,* and *M.Y.T.H. Inc. Link*), Doubleday, 1987.
Myth-Nomers and Im-Pervections, illustrated by Foglio, Donning, 1987.
M.Y.T.H. Inc. in Action, illustrated by Foglio, Donning, 1990.
Sweet Myth-tery of Life, illustrated by Foglio, Donning, 1994.

GRAPHIC NOVELS

(With Foglio) *Myth Adventures One* (previously published in magazine form), art by Foglio, Starblaze Graphics (Norfolk, VA), 1985.
(With Foglio) *Myth Adventures Two* (previously published in magazine form), art by Foglio, Starblaze Graphics, 1985.
(With Abbey) *Thieves' World Graphics,* art by Tim Sales, six volumes, Starblaze Graphics, 1985-87.
(With Mel White) *Duncan and Mallory,* Starblaze Graphics, 1986.
(With White) *Duncan and Mallory: The Bar-None Ranch,* Starblaze Graphics, 1987.
(With White) *Duncan and Mallory: The Raiders,* Starblaze Graphics, 1988.

EDITOR

Thieves' World, Ace Books, 1979.
Tales from the Vulgar Unicorn, Ace Books, 1980.
Shadows of Sanctuary, Ace Books, 1981.
Sanctuary (includes *Thieves' World, Tales from the Vulgar Unicorn,* and *Shadows of Sanctuary*), Doubleday, 1982.
Storm Season, Ace Books, 1982.
(With Abbey) *The Face of Chaos,* Ace Books, 1983.
(With Abbey) *Wings of Omen,* Ace Books, 1984.
(With Abbey) *Birds of Prey,* Ace Books, 1984.
(With Abbey) *Cross-Currents* (includes *Storm Season, The Face of Chaos,* and *Wings of Omen*), Doubleday, 1984.
(With Abbey) *The Dead of Winter,* Ace Books, 1985.
(With Abbey) *Soul of the City,* Ace Books, 1986.
(With Abbey) *Blood Ties,* Ace Books, 1986.
(With Abbey) *The Shattered Sphere* (includes *The Dead of Winter, Soul of the City,* and *Blood Ties*), Doubleday, 1986.

(With Abbey and Richard Pini) *The Blood of Ten Chiefs,* Tor (New York City), 1986.
(With Abbey) *Aftermath,* Ace Books, 1987.
(With Abbey) *Uneasy Alliances,* Ace Books, 1988.
(With Abbey and Pini) *Wolfsong: The Blood of Ten Chiefs,* Tor, 1988.
(With Abbey) *Stealers' Sky,* Ace Books, 1989.
(With Abbey) *The Price of Victory* (includes *Aftermath, Uneasy Alliances,* and *Stealers' Sky*), Doubleday, 1990.

OTHER

The Capture (script), Boojums Press, 1975.

ADAPTATIONS: Several of Asprin's novels have been recorded on cassette tape.

SIDELIGHTS: Robert L. Asprin is known in the science fiction and fantasy genres for his humorous novels which parody genre conventions and for his coeditorship, with wife Lynn Abbey, of the "Thieves' World" anthologies. Writing in the *St. James Guide to Fantasy Writers,* Stan Nicholls explains that "Asprin can take some credit for helping to move humorous fantasy away from the short form in which it was more usually found and making it acceptable at novel length. Sales as large as his suggest a readership extending far beyond fantasy enthusiasts, so it would be fair to assume he has contributed to the process of bringing the [fantasy] sub-genre to general attention." Comparing his work to that of author L. Sprague de Camp, Richard A. Lupoff comments in the *St. James Guide to Science Fiction Writers* on the "typical Asprin characteristics of rapid pace, slapstick action, and broad humor."

The Cold Cash War was Asprin's first published novel. Drawing from his personal experience as a financial analyst, Asprin wove a futuristic tale about mega-corporations that wage bloodless "warfare" on each other using war-game simulations. Ignoring the efforts of actual governments to stop them, these moneyed superpowers eventually lose control of the game when real weapons enter the picture and the hits become lethal. Calling it a "very good treatment of a SF concept popular in the 50s," a *Publishers Weekly* reviewer praises *The Cold Cash War*'s "satire, action, and character."

Asprin's second novel, the fantasy *Another Fine Myth,* was inspired by such heroic characters as Kane and Conan the Barbarian. Basing his two main characters—an apprentice wizard named Skeeve (who also serves as narrator) and his shifty-eyed cohort, Aahz—on the relationship between Bob Hope and Bing Crosby in their classic screwball "Road" films of the 1940s, Asprin developed a winning duo whose antics have fuelled an entire series of humorous "Myth" books. Dragons, demons, and an amazing assortment of fantastic ne'er-do-wells keep Asprin's fumbling heroes on their toes throughout the series. The lighthearted tone and steady barrage of puns, jokes, and bumbling antics have made the series a popular and entertaining read. "Asprin isn't trying to be profound," Tom Easton notes in a review in *Analog Science Fiction/Science Fact.* "He's having fun."

In his continuing effort to keep the job of writing fun, Asprin has strived to keep his subject matter from becoming stale. As he once noted, "my first three books are intentionally dissimilar. *The Cold Cash War* is speculative near-future fiction involving corporate takeover of world government. *Another Fine Myth* is a sword-and-sorcery farce full of dragons, stranded demons, and very bad puns. *The Bug Wars* does not have a human in the entire book. It was written 'first-person alien, reptile to be specific' and has been one of my greatest writing challenges to date."

In 1990 Asprin added a new hero to his catalogue of space adventurers with *Phule's Company.* Willard Phule is a captain in the Space Legion, but his devil-may-care attitude soon finds him exiled to a remote command, where he is put in charge of a rag-tag band of fellow miscreants. Undaunted, the savvy Phule eventually shapes his troops into a highly effective—and profitable—military outfit. "This lighthearted tale is part science fiction, part spoof, part heart-warmer," notes a *Publishers Weekly* critic.

Another novel leaning more towards science fiction than fantasy is Asprin's *Time Scout,* which he cowrote with Linda Evans. Taking place in the near future, the novel features a world where time travel has become a common vacation pastime. Kit Carson, a retired "time scout"—one of the daring explorers who enter new passages through time in advance of the commonfolk—must train his headstrong granddaughter to survive as the first female time scout. Calling the novel "engaging, fast moving, historically literate," and reflective of

Asprin's broad knowledge of the martial arts, *Booklist* reviewer Roland Green dubs *Time Scout* "first-class action sf."

In addition to novel-writing, Asprin has also collaborated with Lynn Abbey to edit the popular "Thieves' World" series. Called "the toughest, seamiest backwater in the realm of fantasy" by *Voice of Youth Advocates* reviewer Carolyn Caywood, the "Thieves' World" anthologies bring together a collection of original short fiction written by a host of predominately women writers, including Abbey, Janet Morris, and C. J. Cherryh. Each book in the series centers around the ongoing struggle between the evil Queen Roxanne and her nemesis, a blood-sucking enchantress named Ischade. The continuing battle between these two powerful witches continues through such collections as *Soul of the City* and *Blood Ties,* each of which takes place in a mythic city called Sanctuary.

Asprin has characterized the overall message behind his writing as "the case for Everyman. Like all science fiction writers, I promote space travel and development. I feel, however, that we will never see it until the average guy on the street can see a place for himself in space. We will have to have the support of the common man, not just the scientists and test pilots. . . . We are going to need grease monkeys as well as computer programmers. Few people see themselves as Superman, and as long as science fiction writers portray space travelers in that light, the taxpayers and voters could not care less about getting off the planet."

BIOGRAPHICAL/CRITICAL SOURCES:

BOOKS

St. James Guide to Fantasy Writers, St. James Press (Detroit), 1996.

St. James Guide to Science Fiction Writers, St. James Press, 1995.

PERIODICALS

Analog Science Fiction-Science Fact, October, 1984, p. 147; September, 1987, p. 163; February, 1991, p. 181.

Booklist, December 1, 1977, p. 598; January 15, 1984, p. 715; April 1, 1986, p. 1120; March 15, 1987, p. 1097; June 15, 1990, p. 1960; January 15, 1992, pp. 915, 921; January 15, 1995, p. 689; December 15, 1995, p. 689.

Library Journal, November 1, 1977, p. 2279; January 15, 1980, p. 228.

Publishers Weekly, July 11, 1977, p. 75; June 8, 1990, p. 50; January 20, 1992, p. 60.

School Library Journal, March, 1980, p. 146.

Voice of Youth Advocates, April, 1981, p. 52; June, 1986, p. 84; February, 1987, p. 290; December, 1987, p. 241.

B

BAIRD, Joseph Armstrong (Jr.) 1922-

PERSONAL: Born November 22, 1922, in Pittsburgh, PA; son of Joseph A. (a physician) and Lulu Charlotte (Fuller) Baird. *Education:* Oberlin College, B.A. (magna cum laude), 1944; Harvard University, M.A., 1947, Ph.D., 1951.

CAREER: University of Toronto, Toronto, Ontario, 1949-53, began as lecturer, became instructor in art history; University of California, Davis, 1953-85, began as instructor, became professor of art history. Visiting professor, University of Southern California, 1952, 1970, University of Mexico, Mexico City, 1957, University of Oregon, 1963. Curator and consultant, California Historical Society, 1961-62, 1967-70; cataloger of Robert B. Honeyman, Jr. Collection in Bancroft Library, University of California, Berkeley, 1964-65. Owner of North Point Gallery, San Francisco, CA, 1972-85. Lecturer in United States and Mexico at cultural institutions, including Toronto Art Gallery, Royal Ontario Museum of Art, National Gallery (Washington), and Crocker Art Museum (San Francisco).

MEMBER: Society of Architectural Historians, American Society for Hispanic Art Historical Studies, Phi Beta Kappa.

AWARDS, HONORS: Award of Merit, California Historical Society, 1961.

WRITINGS:

The Churches of Mexico, 1530-1810, University of California Press (Berkeley), 1962.

Time's Wondrous Changes: San Francisco Architecture, 1776-1915, California Historical Society (San Diego, CA), 1962.

California's Pictorial Letter Sheets, 1849-1869, David Magee (San Francisco, CA), 1967.

(Editor) *Pre-Impressionism, 1860-1869: A Formative Decade in French Art and Culture,* University of California at Davis, 1969.

Historic Lithographs of San Francisco, Burger & Evans, 1972.

The West Remembered, California Historical Society, 1973.

Theodore Wores, the Japanese Years, Oakland Museum (Oakland, CA), 1976.

(Editor) *Theodore Wores and the Beginnings of Internationalism in Northern California Painting, 1874-1915,* University of California at Davis, 1978.

(Author of commentary) *Wine and the Artist,* Dover (New York City), 1979.

(Editor) *From Exposition to Exposition: Progressive and Conservative Northern California Painting, 1915-1939,* Crocker Art Museum (Sacramento, CA), 1981.

(Author of architectural commentary) *Sacred Places of San Francisco,* Presidio Press (Novato, CA), 1985.

(Author of architectural commentary) *Los Retablos del siglo XVIII, en el sur de Espana, Portugal y Mexico,* Universidad Nacional Autonoma de Mexico, 1987.

(Author of architectural commentary) *Rincon Hill and South Park: San Francisco's Early Fashionable Neighborhoods,* Windgate Press, 1988.

(Author of architectural commentary) *If Pictures Could Talk: Stories about California Paintings in Our Collection,* WIM (Oakland, CA), 1989.

Also contributor of articles and reviews to professional journals.*

* * *

BALLIETT, Whitney 1926-

PERSONAL: Born April 17, 1926, in New York, NY; son of Fargo and Dorothy (Lyon) Balliett; married Elizabeth Hurley King, July 21, 1951; married Nancy Kraemer, June 4, 1965; children: (first marriage) Julia Lyon, Elizabeth Erving, Will King; (second marriage) Whitney Lyon, Jr., James Fargo. *Ethnicity:* "White." *Education:* Cornell University, B.A., 1951. *Politics:* Democrat.

ADDRESSES: Office—New Yorker, 20 West 43rd St., New York, NY 10036. *Agent*—Harold Ober Associates, Inc., 40 East 49th St., New York, NY 10017.

CAREER: New Yorker, New York, NY, collator, proofreader, then reporter, 1951-57, staff writer, 1957—. Originator of Columbia Broadcasting System television show "Sound of Jazz," 1957; writer and broadcaster of two segments of National Educational Television series "Trio," 1962. *Military service:* U.S. Army Air Corps, 1946-47; became sergeant.

MEMBER: Delta Phi.

AWARDS, HONORS: Academy Award in Literature, American Academy of Arts and Letters, 1996.

WRITINGS:

The Sound of Surprise: Forty-six Pieces on Jazz, Dutton (New York City), 1959.

Dinosaurs in the Morning: Forty-one Pieces on Jazz, Lippincott (Philadelphia, PA), 1962.

Such Sweet Thunder: Forty-nine Pieces on Jazz, Bobbs-Merrill (New York City), 1966.

Super-Drummer: A Profile of Buddy Rich, Bobbs-Merrill, 1968.

Ecstasy at the Onion: Thirty-one Pieces on Jazz, Bobbs-Merrill, 1971.

Alec Wilder and His Friends, Houghton (Burlington, MA), 1974.

New York Notes: A Journal of Jazz, 1972-74, Houghton, 1975.

Improvising: Sixteen Jazz Musicians and Their Art, Oxford University Press (New York City), 1977.

Night Creature: A Journal of Jazz, 1974-1980, Oxford University Press, 1981.

Jelly Roll, Jabbo, and Fats: Nineteen Portraits in Jazz, Oxford University Press, 1983.

American Musicians: Fifty-six Portraits in Jazz, Oxford University Press, 1986.

American Singers: Twenty-seven Portraits in Song, Oxford University Press, 1988.

Barney, Bradley, and Max: Fifteen Portraits in Jazz, Oxford University Press, 1989.

Goodbyes and Other Messages, Oxford University Press, 1991.

American Musicians II: Seventy-two Portraits in Jazz, Oxford University Press, 1996.

Contributor of articles and reviews to *Atlantic, New Republic, Reporter,* and *Saturday Review;* contributor of poetry to *Atlantic, New Yorker* and *Saturday Review.*

SIDELIGHTS: "Whitney Balliett has covered jazz for the *New Yorker* since 1957; he has done so with taste, knowledge, consistency and splendid skill as a writer," claims Don Gold in the *New York Times Book Review.* Gold goes on to comment that "it is not easy to communicate what jazz sounds like to people who weren't there. Balliett masters it better than anyone else writing about jazz today." Considered informed about his subject and gifted in his presentation by most reviewers, Balliett writes both substantive studies of jazz artists and short, impressionistic articles likened to diary entries by several critics. According to Joseph McLellan in the *Washington Post,* "Balliett's job is to be entertaining as well as illuminative and not to take too long about it. . . . [He] does it superbly. . . . [His] musicology is largely impressionistic, descriptive, and focused on such points as the textures and rhythms of the sound, looseness or tightness of structures, and above all on what the music is saying." Echoing American critics' praise for Balliett's treatment of an American genre, Bill Luckin concludes in the *Times Literary Supplement* that "Balliett is among the most stylish and perceptive of living jazz writers."

American Musicians: Fifty-six Portraits in Jazz is a compilation of biographical profiles that Balliett had written for the *New Yorker* from the early 1960s to 1985. In the *New York Times Book Review,* John Litweiler remarks that "of Mr. Balliett's 11 previous books—mostly shorter collections—'American Musicians' makes at least three entire volumes plus hunks of several others obsolete. His biographical articles are his best, so this is his most valuable book." According to Litweiler, Balliett had interviewed all but fifteen of his subjects and "the quality of his portraits depends on his subjects and his patience. He says he generally chose his subjects because they were 'irresistible.'" In his *Washington Post Book World* assessment, David Nicholson likewise comments about the book's interview format: "When the musicians were alive to be interviewed, Balliett—for the most part—allowed them to speak for themselves. Thus we get a sense of each person, as well as insights into the personal connections between musicians and the evolving of musical eras and styles. . . . There are also telling (and sometimes amusing) details of the rigors of musicians' lives." With respect to overall style, Nicholson maintains that Balliett "writes with grace, style and insight. While reading, one wishes for a complete record collection so that one could listen to samples of each musician's work: Balliett is unmatched at describing how a particular musician sounds."

The chief flaw that critics detect in this work is Balliett's omission of many of the more contemporary artists in the field of jazz; "He leaves unexplored so many mansions in the house of jazz," states Nicholson. "Apart from anecdotes included in other essays, Dizzy Gillespie and Charlie Parker, the co-founders of be-bop, go unacknowledged, as do Miles Davis and, more important, John Coltrane, for many *the* greatest jazz musician of all time." Francis Davis for the *Times Literary Supplement* detects this same flaw when he notes that Balliett presents studies of only two contemporary jazz artists under fifty years of age, which he feels is"in no way indicative of current directions within the genre." Nevertheless, David concludes that "the musicians on whom Balliett lavishes his attentions emerge as unique, and that, one suspects, is what has drawn him to them, regardless of their musical style. One is drawn to Whitney Balliett for much the same reason. Say what one will about his profiles, there is no mistaking them for the work of anyone else."

BIOGRAPHICAL/CRITICAL SOURCES:

PERIODICALS

American Scholar, spring, 1982.
Los Angeles Times, June 12, 1981.
Los Angeles Times Book Review, April 24, 1983.
New Republic, May 5, 1979.
New York Review of Books, February 12, 1987.
New York Times Book Review, September 12, 1976; April 1, 1979; July 19, 1981; December 21, 1986.
Time, March 19, 1979.
Times Literary Supplement, February 24, 1978; May 4, 1984; April 1, 1988.
Washington Post, June 4, 1981; July 19, 1983.
Washington Post Book World, December 21, 1986.

* * *

BALTAZZI, Evan S(erge) 1921-

PERSONAL: Born April 11, 1921, in Izmir, Turkey; came to the United States in 1959; naturalized citizen, 1964; son of Phocion (a civil engineer) and Agnes (an author; maiden name Varda) Baltazzi; married Nellie Biorlaro (a parliamentarian and civic activist), July 17, 1945; children: Vittoria, James, Maria. *Education:* Studied industrial chemistry at the University of Athens, Greece; Sorbonne, Paris, D.Sc., 1949; Oxford University, England, D.Phil. *Avocational interests:* The American Self-Protection (A.S.P.) system, the combative arts, volunteering in national parks, fencing, history, dogs.

ADDRESSES: Home and office—825 Greengate Oval, Greenwood Village, Sagamore Hills, OH 44967-2311.

CAREER: International Red Cross Committee, Thessaloniki (Salonika), Greece, chemist, 1941-45; chemist at the Institute Pasteur, Paris, the Dyson Perrins Laboratory, Oxford, and Nalco Chemical Company, Chicago, IL; IIT Research Institute, manager; the Bruning Company (later part of the Addressograph-Multigraph Corporation), director of exploratory research and the organic chemistry laboratory. Formed engineering consulting firm in 1978 and served as a consultant to American, European, and Japanese companies until 1988. Organized and chaired national and international symposia and conferences on chemistry. Served on the U.S. Olympic and A.A.U. Committees for Judo, 1964-72, and on the U.S. Currency Committee of the National Academy of Sciences, National Research Council, Washington, DC, 1984-86. Served as an official at the Panamerican Games, Winnipeg, and chaired the National YMCA Judo Committee, both 1967. Chaired the Health and Physical Education Research Methods conferences, Chicago, IL, 1969-70. *Military service:* Served in the Greek Army during World War II.

MEMBER: American Chemical Society (senior member), American Institute of Chemists (vice president of the Chicago chapter), Society of Photographic Scientists and Engineers, Chicago Research Directors Society.

AWARDS, HONORS: New Citizen of the Year Award, Citizenship Council of Metropolitan Chicago, 1964; Distinguished Service Award (Sciences), Immigrants' Service League, 1965; Best Program of the Year Award for developing the A.S.P. program, Metropolitan Chicago YMCA, 1967; fellow of the Royal Chemical Society, the American Institute of Chemists, and the French Chemical Society; fellowship to the Canadian National Research Center in Ottawa, Ontario, Canada.

WRITINGS:

American Self-Protection: ASP, System of Mind-Body Self-Protection for Self-Defense, for Fitness, for Sport, Evanel (Northfield, OH), 1972.

Kickboxing: A Safe Sport, a Deadly Defense, Tuttle (Rutland, VT), 1976.

Stickfighting: A Practical Guide for Self-Protection, Tuttle, 1983.

Plato and Socrates' Trial, Evanel, 1991.

Self-Protection, the A.S.P. System: A Complete System of Holistic Body-Mind Self-Protection, for Mental and Physical Fitness, for Self-Defense and Prevention, for Sport, Evanel, 1992.

Dog Gone West: A Western for Dog Lovers (children's book), illustrated by Gregory Kyziridis, Evanel, 1994.

Contributor to scientific publications. Former editor, *Journal of Photographic Science and Engineering.*

WORK IN PROGRESS: Africa My Love, an autobiography based on Baltazzi's experiences as a young man in French Equatorial Africa before World War II.

SIDELIGHTS: Evan S. Baltazzi once commented: "From my early teens to the present, I have been active in various combative arts and sports." As a student at the Sorbonne, he was a member of the Faculty of Sciences Fencing Team, and he is currently recognized as a fencing master. During his years at Oxford, Baltazzi was captain of the varsity Judo team, which remained unbeaten during his stay; he has achieved high black belt rankings in both Judo and Akido. In the early 1970s, Baltazzi decided to devote himself to developing the American Self-Protection (A.S.P.) method and system. Baltazzi notes: "Several physical educators here and abroad, including the Administrators of the President's Council on Physical Fitness under Presidents Johnson and Bush, have recognized the outstanding qualities of A.S.P. A.S.P. is superior to all combative systems from the standpoint of yield for expended effort, degree of retention of the techniques learned over long periods, didactic value, and holistic approach. It is at least as effective as any other art."

* * *

BANISTER, Judith 1943-

PERSONAL: Born September 10, 1943, in Washington, DC; daughter of William Price (a court reporter) and Helen Barbara (a speech therapist; maiden name, Myers) Banister; married Kim Woodard (a China business manager for John Deere Company), December 17, 1966; children: Adrian Banard, Dawn Banard. *Ethnicity:* "Caucasian." *Education:* Attended University of Glasgow, 1963-64; Swarthmore College, B.A., 1965; graduate study at Middlebury College, 1966, University of Denver, 1966-67, and Princeton University, 1976-77; Stanford University, Ph.D., 1978.

ADDRESSES: Office—International Programs Center, U.S. Bureau of the Census, 312 Washington Plaza II, Washington, DC 20233-8860. *E-mail*—judith_banister@ccmail.census.gov; fax: 301-457-3034.

CAREER: East-West Population Institute, Honolulu, HI, research fellow in demography, 1978-80; U.S. Bureau of the Census, Washington, DC, statistician and demographer, 1980-82, chief of China Branch, 1982-92, chief of Center for International Research, 1992-94, chief of International Programs Center, 1994—. Adjunct professor at George Washington University, 1981-91; East-West Population Institute, coordinator of China Population Analysis Conference and Workshop, 1980, coordinator of Workshop on China's 1982 Population Census, 1984; organizer and chair of workshops for Population Association of America annual meetings, 1990, 1992-96; U.S. representative to United Nations Population Commission meetings, 1994-96; guest on television programs.

MEMBER: International Union for the Scientific Study of Population, Population Association of America (chair, Committee on China Study and Exchange, 1994—).

AWARDS, HONORS: Fellow of East-West Population Institute, 1977-80.

WRITINGS:

(With Shyam Thapa) *The Population Dynamics of Nepal,* East-West Center (Honolulu, HI), 1981.

The Population of Vietnam, U.S. Government Printing Office (Washington, DC), 1985.

China: Recent Trends in Health and Mortality, U.S. Bureau of the Census, 1986.

China's Changing Population, Stanford University Press (Stanford, CA), 1987.

Contributor to various publications, including *The Economic Basis of Pacific Security,* edited by John E. Starron, Jr. and Patricia J. Hymson, National Defense University, 1982; *China: The Eighties Era,* edited by Norton Ginsburg and Bernard A. Lalor, Westview (Boulder, CO), 1984; *Political Developments and Human Rights in the People's Republic of China,* edited by U.S. House of Representatives, Committee on Foreign Affairs, U.S. Government Printing Office, 1986; *China's Economy Looks Toward the Year 2000,* Volume I: *The Four Modernizations,* edited by U.S. Congress, Joint Economic Committee, U.S. Government Printing Office, 1986; *A Census of One Billion People,* edited by Li Chengrui and others, Population Census Office (Beijing, China), 1986; *Changing Family Structure and Population Aging in China,* edited by Zeng Yi and others, Beijing University Press (Beijing, China), 1990; *China's Dilemmas in the 1990s: The Problems of Reforms, Modernization, and Interdependence,* U.S. Government Printing Office, 1991; *The Uneven Landscape: Geographical Studies in Post-Reform China,* edited by Gregory Veeck, Geoscience Publications (Baton Rouge, LA), 1991; *The Population of Modern China,* edited by Dudley L. Poston and David Yaukey, Plenum (New York City), 1992; *Genocide and Democracy in Cambodia: The Khmer Rouge, the U.N., and the International Community,* edited by Ben Kiernan, Southeast Asia Studies, Yale University Press (New Haven, CT), 1993; *The Chinese and Their Future: Beijing, Taipei, and Hong Kong,* edited by Zhiling Lin and Thomas W. Robinson, American Enterprise Institute Press (Washington, DC), 1994; and *China's Economic Future: Challenges to U.S. Policy,* U.S. Government Printing Office, 1996.

Also contributor to numerous professional journals.

WORK IN PROGRESS: Research and population projections on China's provinces, mortality and fertility trends in China, and the current and future migration out of China's rural areas.

SIDELIGHTS: Judith Banister once told *CA:* "In 1966, after graduating from college, my fiance and I decided to emphasize international affairs in our subsequent educations. When searching for a region of the world in which to specialize, we asked ourselves, 'What is a country or region that is poorly understood, yet vital for Americans to comprehend?' An obvious answer was China, with over a fifth of the world's people, an enigmatic country then enduring its disastrous Cultural Revolution. We decided to focus on China, began Chinese language study, and launched our present careers.

"From 1969 to 1971 we lived in Taiwan and Hong Kong, then had the unexpected opportunity to travel to the People's Republic of China just after the famous precedent-setting visit of the U.S. ping-pong team. Our delegation consisted of American graduate students focusing on China studies. On the trip, Premier Zhou Enlai spent four hours discussing with us why China's leaders had decided to invite President Nixon to visit.

"In the 1970s I got a Ph.D. in demography and wrote my dissertation on China's population, based on the very spotty information being released at the time. My book *China's Changing Population* evolved gradually as China's government gathered more population statistics and began to release such information to the world for the first time."

Banister later told *CA:* "Throughout my writing career, I have emphasized demographic research on countries whose population trends were unknown, hidden, or highly controversial at the time. In my work as sole author or co-author, I have revealed, evaluated, and documented the population situation and changes in selected countries, as well as the social, economic, political, and environmental trends associated with each country's demographic evolution or crises. I am best known as one of the few leading experts on the continuing population transformations in the People's Republic of China, as well as North Korea, Vietnam, Cambodia, and Nepal."

* * *

BARROL, Grady
See BOGRAD, Larry

* * *

BARRY, Sheila Anne

PERSONAL: Born in New York, NY; daughter of Mark Henry (a lawyer) and Bertha (a lawyer; maiden name, Robinson) Shulman; married Paul Weissman, 1960 (divorced, 1974); married Julian Barry (divorced); children: (first marriage) Mark John, Lael Tiu Kimble. *Education:* Columbia University, B.F.A.; also attended Cornell University. *Avocational interests:* Neurolinguistic programming, hypnosis.

ADDRESSES: *Office*—Sterling Publishing Co., Inc., 387 Park Ave. S., New York, NY 10016.

CAREER: Taplinger Publishing Co., New York City, senior editor, 1962-69; Sterling Publishing, New York City, acquisitions director, 1971—.

WRITINGS:

FOR CHILDREN

The Super-Colossal Book of Puzzles, Tricks & Games, illustrated by Doug Anderson, Sterling (New York City), 1978.
Our New Home, Sterling, 1981.
Tricks and Stunts to Fool Your Friends, illustrated by Anderson, Sterling, 1984.
Test Your Wits!, illustrated by Anderson, Sterling, 1986.
The World's Best Party Games, illustrated by Anderson, Sterling, 1987.
The World's Best Travel Games, illustrated by Anderson, Sterling, 1987.
The World's Most Spine-Chilling "True" Ghost Stories, illustrated by Jim Sharpe, Sterling, 1992.
The World's Best Card Games for One, illustrated by Myron Miller, Sterling, 1992.
(Editor) *Kids' Funniest Jokes,* illustrated by Jeff Sinclair, Sterling, 1993.

OTHER

(Compiler) Lady Wilde, *Irish Cures, Mystic Charms, and Superstitions,* illustrated by Marlene Ekman, Sterling, 1991, revised edition published as *Ancient Legends of Ireland,* 1996.

BIOGRAPHICAL/CRITICAL SOURCES:

PERIODICALS

Booklist, October 15, 1978, p. 370; November 1, 1979, p. 458; January 1, 1985, p. 637; February 15, 1986, p. 875; August, 1987, p. 1740; January 15, 1988, p. 860.
Children's Book Review Service, February, 1979, p. 66.
Horn Book Guide, spring, 1993, p. 86.
Kliatt, fall, 1984, p. 72.
School Library Journal, February, 1979, p. 51.

* * *

BARTON, Byron 1930-

PERSONAL: Surname originally Vartanian; name legally changed in 1953; born September 8, 1930, in Pawtucket, RI; son of Toros and Elizabeth (Krekorian) Vartanian; married Harriett Wyatt, December, 1967 (divorced, April, 1973). *Education:* Attended Los Angeles City College, 1948-50, and Chouinard Art Institute, 1953-56.

ADDRESSES: Home—2 Washington Square Village, New York, NY 10012.

CAREER: Freelance writer, illustrator, and designer. Studio 7 Los Angeles, Los Angeles, CA, illustrator, 1956-57; Equitable Life Assurance Co., New York City, designer, 1957-60; Columbia Broadcasting System, Inc., New York City, designer, 1960-66. *Military service:* U.S. Army, 1950-52.

AWARDS, HONORS: Spring Book Festival Middle Honor, *New York Herald Tribune,* 1969, for *A Girl Called Al; New York Times* Choice of Best Illustrated Children's Books of the Year, 1972, for *Where's Al?,* and 1988, for *I Want to Be an Astronaut;* Children's Book Showcase Title, Children's Book Council, 1972, for *The Paper Airplane Book,* and 1973, for *Where's Al?; Airport* was selected a *New York Times* Notable Book, 1982; Please Touch Award, Please Touch Museum for Children, 1990, for *Dinosaurs, Dinosaurs.*

WRITINGS:

FOR CHILDREN; SELF-ILLUSTRATED

Elephant, Seabury (New York City), 1971.
Where's Al?, Seabury, 1972.
Applebet Story, Viking (New York City), 1973.
Buzz Buzz Buzz, Macmillan (New York City), 1973.
Harry Is a Scaredy-Cat, Macmillan, 1974.
Jack and Fred, Macmillan, 1974.
Hester, Greenwillow (New York City), 1975.
Wheels, Crowell (New York City), 1979.
Building a House, Greenwillow, 1981.
Airport, Crowell, 1982.
Airplanes, Crowell, 1986.
Boats, Crowell, 1986.
Trains, Crowell, 1986.
Trucks, Crowell, 1986.
Machines at Work, Crowell, 1987.
I Want to Be an Astronaut, Crowell, 1988.
Dinosaurs, Dinosaurs, Crowell, 1989.
Bones, Bones, Dinosaur Bones, Crowell, 1990.
(Reteller) *The Three Bears,* HarperCollins (New York City), 1991.
Building a House: Big Book, Hampton-Brown, 1992.
Building a House: Small Book, Hampton-Brown, 1992.
(Reteller) *The Little Red Hen,* HarperCollins, 1993.
Dinosaurs, Dinosaurs Board Book, HarperCollins, 1994.
(Reteller) *Little Red Hen Big Book,* HarperCollins, 1994.
(Reteller) *Three Bears Big Book,* HarperCollins, 1994.
Planes, HarperCollins, 1994.
The Wee Little Woman, HarperCollins, 1995.
Big Machines, HarperCollins, 1996.
Dinosaurs, HarperCollins, 1996.
Tools, HarperCollins, 1996.
Zoo Animals, HarperCollins, 1996.

ILLUSTRATOR

Constance C. Greene, *A Girl Called Al,* Viking, 1969.
Alan Venable, *The Checker Players,* Lippincott (New York City), 1973.
Seymour Simon, *The Paper Airplane Book,* Viking, 1973.
Franklyn Branley, *How Little and How Much: A Book about Scales,* Crowell, 1976.
David A. Adler, *Roman Numerals,* HarperCollins, 1977.
Jack Prelutsky, *The Snopp on the Sidewalk and Other Poems,* Greenwillow, 1977.
Russell Hoban, *Arthur's New Power,* HarperCollins, 1978.
Marjorie Weinman Sharmat, *Gila Monsters Meet You at the Airport,* Simon & Schuster (New York City), 1980.
Mirra Ginsburg, *Good Morning, Chick,* Greenwillow, 1980.
Robert Kalan, *Jump, Frog, Jump!,* Greenwillow, 1981.
Charlotte Pomerantz, *Where's the Bear?,* Greenwillow, 1984.
Diane Siebert, *Truck Song,* Crowell, 1984.
Greene, *Al's Blind Date,* Puffin Books (New York City), 1991.
Greene, *Ask Anybody,* Puffin Books, 1991.
Pomerantz, *The Tamarindo Puppy,* Greenwillow, 1993.

SIDELIGHTS: Through the use of simple text and bright, bold illustrations with thick black outlines, children's author and illustrator Byron Barton makes such activities as building a house, going on a space mission, and reassembling dinosaur bones accessible to young readers. With just a few rhythmic words running along the bottom of his illustrations, Barton tells his stories with pictures that give readers all the necessary details about his subject. Barton is "a master of simplicity," declares a reviewer in *Publishers Weekly*. Cathryn A. Camper, writing in *Five Owls*, praises Barton's colorful, well-defined drawings which make "his books fun even for children too young to read."

Action plays a big part in most of Barton's stories, especially those that teach children about a certain activity, such as the construction of a house. *Building a House* starts with a plot of land being surveyed, moves on to laying the foundation, describes the electrical wiring and plumbing process, shows the walls being painted, and concludes with a family moving into the finished product. "In *Building a House* I wanted to show, with simple words and pictures, the different workers coming one after the other to do their part: digging the hole, making the floor, putting up the walls, putting in the plumbing," explains Barton in *Junior Literary Guild*. "Then, when all the work is done, the family comes to live inside the house."

With *Airport* Barton similarly shows his young audience the activities in an airport that surround the preparations for a flight before it takes off. Mary M. Burns showers praise on Barton in her *Horn Book* review for capturing all the "excitement and bustle of a major airport" while keeping the flow of events in a clear, well-focused order. A contributor to *Publishers Weekly* points out that the picture book is filled with Barton's hallmark "flashy primary colors and inspired characterizations" and goes on to say that *Airport* "is a wonder."

Airplanes are described again as part of Barton's series focusing on different forms of transportation. The books in this series, including *Trucks, Boats, Airplanes,* and *Trains,* feature illustrations of different vehicles that fall into these categories, as well as some of the activities surrounding them, such as a boat docking and a train stopping to pick up passengers. Linda Wicher, writing in *School Library Journal,* relates that all the books in the series feature "brightly colored illustrations" which present many "accurate details that preschoolers find so fascinating." A critic in *Publishers Weekly* applauds Barton's understandable concepts and illustrations, noting that "a little says a great deal here."

The details of a trip to outer space are the focus of Barton's *I Want to Be an Astronaut.* A crew of six children who want to be astronauts now, as opposed to waiting until they grow up, make up the crew of the space shuttle. Along with enjoying the new sensations of weightlessness and ready-to-eat space food, the young crew also fixes a satellite and builds a space factory before journeying back to earth. In *I Want to Be an Astronaut,* "Barton has provided an especially evocative early career book," according to Zena Sutherland in *Bulletin of the Center for Children's Books. Horn Book* contributor Nancy Vasilakis praises Barton's illustrations, stating that "astronauts, spaceships, and the earth itself unite in dramatic visual harmonies." Writing in the *New York Times Book Review,* Roger Sutton describes Barton's vision of space as "downright giddy," going on to conclude: "*I Want to Be an Astronaut* has a sense of adventure that enlarges its context beyond space to the realm of imaginative journey."

Another profession is explored in *Bones, Bones, Dinosaur Bones.* In the beginning of the book, six young paleontologists methodically dig up dinosaur bones, carefully package their findings, and then travel with them to the natural history museum. The process of cleaning each bone and then assembling them into a recognizable dinosaur skeleton is detailed at the museum. And once the project is complete, the young workers leave in search of more bones, starting the cycle over again. *Horn Book* contributor Ellen Fader applauds Barton's "accuracy, simplicity, appropriateness, appeal for intended audience, and timeliness" in describing paleontological work. In *Five Owls* Camper calls *Bones, Bones, Dinosaur Bones* "a gentle rainbow procession of discovery, mixing a little magic into this search for bones."

In a departure from his more realistic stories, Barton tells the tale of a tiny woman in *The Wee Little Woman.* The daily activities of the wee little woman are the focus of this book. She starts her day by milking her wee little cow, placing the milk on her wee little table. Things go awry, though, when her wee little cat drinks the milk and runs away for a wee little time after being scolded. By the time the cat returns home, all is forgiven and a new bowl of milk is waiting for the petite feline. "This reassuring story is told in simple words with lots of repetition," observes Leone McDermott in *Booklist*. And Marcia Hupp, writing in *School Library Journal*, notices that the illustrations in *The Wee Little Woman* "have a satisfying heft well suited to this most satisfying little tale."

BIOGRAPHICAL/CRITICAL SOURCES:

PERIODICALS

Booklist, July, 1995, p. 1882.
Bulletin of the Center for Children's Books, October, 1975, p. 21; September, 1979, p. 2; May, 1982, p. 162; October, 1988, p. 26; September, 1989, p. 3; January, 1992, p. 117.
Five Owls, November/December, 1990, p. 28.
Horn Book, June, 1974, p. 271; June, 1979, pp. 290-91; August, 1981, p. 412; April, 1982, pp. 152-53; January/February, 1988, pp. 49-50; July/August, 1988, p. 476; May/June, 1989; November/December, 1990, pp. 724-25.
Junior Literary Guild, March, 1981.
Kirkus Reviews, July 15, 1973, p. 750; March 1, 1982, p. 269; June 15, 1986, p. 935; June 15, 1988, p. 896; July 15, 1991, p. 937.
New York Times Book Review, May 5, 1974, p. 46; October 26, 1975, p. 17; April 29, 1979, p. 45; November 13, 1988, p. 46.
Publishers Weekly, October 4, 1971, p. 60; September 18, 1972, p. 73; February 25, 1974, p. 114; January 29, 1982, p. 67; May 30, 1986, p. 61; August 10, 1990, p. 443; November 1, 1991, p. 79; May 3, 1993, pp. 304-305; May 8, 1995, p. 294.
School Library Journal, April, 1979, p. 39; April, 1981, p. 108; September, 1986, p. 116; May, 1988, p. 76; July, 1993, p. 80; August, 1995, p. 114.

* * *

BATTIN, B(rinton) W(arner) 1941-
(S. W. Bradford, Alexander Brinton, Warner Lee, Casey McAllister)

PERSONAL: Born November 15, 1941, in Ridgewood, NJ; son of Harold Taylor (an engineer) and Dorothy (Warner) Battin; married Leslie Sue Curb, August 27, 1966 (divorced, 1974); married Sandra McCraw (a journalist), February 14, 1976. *Ethnicity:* "Caucasian." *Education:* University of New Mexico, B.A., 1969. *Religion:* None.

ADDRESSES: Home and office—711 North Mesa Rd., Belen, NM 87002; *E-mail*—bbattin@ix.netcom.com; fax: 505-864-2558. *Agent*—Dominick Abel Literary Agency, Inc., 146 West 82nd St., New York, NY 10024.

CAREER: KOAT-TV, Albuquerque, NM, reporter, 1969, 1971-75; KTBS-TV, Shreveport, LA, assistant news director, 1975-76; KEVN-TV, Rapid City, SD, news director, 1976; KDAL-TV, Duluth, MN, news director, 1976-77; freelance writer, 1977—. *Military service:* U.S. Coast Guard, 1959-63.

AWARDS, HONORS: Awards from Albuquerque Press Club, 1973, for documentary "When the Dream Becomes a Nightmare" and feature story about an outlaw motorcycle gang, and 1974, for news story on housing contractor fraud.

WRITINGS:

NOVELS

Angel of the Night, Fawcett (New York City), 1983.
The Boogeyman, Fawcett, 1984.
Mary, Mary, Pocket Books (New York City), 1984.
Satan's Servant, Paper Jacks, 1984.
Programmed for Terror, Fawcett, 1985.
The Attraction, Fawcett, 1986.
The Creep, Fawcett, 1986.
Smithereens, Fawcett, 1987.
Demented, Fawcett, 1988.
(Under pseudonym Warner Lee) *Into the Pit*, Pocket Books, 1988.
(Under pseudonym Warner Lee) *It's Loose*, Pocket Books, 1990.
(Under pseudonym S. W. Bradford) *Tender Prey*, Jove (New York City), 1990.
(Under pseudonym S. W. Bradford) *Fair Game*, Jove, 1992.
(Under pseudonym Warner Lee) *Night Sounds*, Pocket Books, 1992.
(Under pseudonym Alexander Brinton) *Serial Blood*, Zebra (New York City), 1992.
(Under pseudonym Casey McAllister) *Catch Me If You Can*, Avon (New York City), 1993.

Work also included in anthologies, including (as B. W. Battin) *Cat Crimes,* Donald Fine, 1992, and (as Warner Lee) *Dracula: Prince of Darkness,* DAW, 1992.

SIDELIGHTS: B. W. Battin once told *CA:* "I gave up on television a few years ago, unable to contend with the backstabbing and the general rat race. My wife handed me a copy of a horror novel and, after reading it, I thought, 'I can do this!' Since my wife was working and I wouldn't starve, I started writing. After I'd sold five novels, we decided to leave Minnesota, where we'd lived for eight years, and return to New Mexico to be near our families.

"I enjoy writing, the manipulation of words as well as trying to make my characters come to life. I take special care with the women I write about in my suspense stories. I like then to be self-sufficient, level-headed, and not the sort who go to pieces when terrible things begin to happen in their lives. They're not screamers like so many women in the movies. My women characters don't want for some man to come and rescue them; they take care of themselves—in ingenious ways, I hope. But if they happen to fall in love along the way, well, more power to them."

Battin later told *CA:* "Recently I have been ghost writing. Because my contracts contain a secrecy clause, I can not reveal anything about them, except to say I have done more work than shows here.

"I write for two reasons. First, it gives me the freedom to be self-employed—to be my own boss, on my own schedule. Second, I love wordcraft: creating with language, choosing and arranging words, selecting from among the myriad of possible sentence structures, manipulating syntax and style and flow.

"Over the years, I've been influenced by all sorts of writers, authors from various genres who write in a multitude of styles. They include Robert Ludlum, Stephen King, Dean R. Koontz, Mary Higgins Clark, Jack Higgins, Elmore Leonard, and Carl Hiaasen. Though each is different, I've gained something from reading all of them—from the thrill of Hiassen's humor and exuberance to Dean Koontz's dazzling imagination.

"When I begin to write, I consider how many pages I have to produce and how much time I have to complete them. This enables me to determine how many pages I need to do per day. I finish that number of pages no matter what. If I get done early, I have some extra free time. On the other hand, if I run into difficulties, I may have to work all day and into the evening.

"Why do I write the things I do? The answer is quite simple, really. I've always loved horror and suspense and science fiction—whether in the form of books, movies, or television. For some reason, I have never been able to write science fiction, but I found I could write in the other genres—and perhaps most important of all, that I could actually sell what I wrote."

* * *

BENEDICT, Morgan (a joint pseudonym)
See MORGAN, Fidelis

* * *

BERMANT, Chaim (Icyk) 1929-

PERSONAL: Born February 26, 1929, in Breslev, Poland; son of Azriel (a rabbi) and Feiga Tzirl (Daets) Bermant; married Judith Weil, December 17, 1962; children: Alisa, Eve, Azriel, Daniel. *Ethnicity:* "Jewish." *Education:* Attended Rabbinical College, Glasgow, Scotland, 1948-50; University of Glasgow, M.A., 1955, M.Litt., 1960; London School of Economics and Political Science, M.Sc., 1957. *Politics:* Liberal conservative. *Religion:* Jewish.

ADDRESSES: *Home*—18 Hill Rise, London NW11 6NA, England. *Agent*—Aitken & Stone, 29 Fernshaw Rd., London SW10 0TG, England.

CAREER: Teacher in London, 1955-56; economist in London, 1956-58; television writer in Glasgow, Scotland, 1958-59, and in London, 1959-61; *London Jewish Chronicle,* London, features editor, 1961-66; freelance writer, 1966—.

WRITINGS:

FICTION

Jericho Sleep Alone, Holt (New York City), 1963.
Berl Make Tea, Holt, 1964.
Ben Preserve Us, Holt, 1964.
Diary of an Old Man, Holt, 1966.
Swinging in the Rain, Hodder & Stoughton (London), 1967.
Here Endeth the Lesson, Eyre & Spottiswoode (London), 1969.
Now Dowager, Eyre & Spottiswoode, 1971.
Roses Are Blooming in Picardy, Eyre & Spottiswoode, 1972.
The Last Supper, St. Martin's (New York City), 1973.
The Second Mrs. Whitberg, Allen & Unwin (London), 1976, St. Martin's, 1977.
The Squire of Bor Shachor, Allen & Unwin, 1977.
Now Newman Was Old, Allen & Unwin, 1978, St. Martin's, 1979.
Belshazzar: A Cat's Story for Humans (juvenile), Allen & Unwin, 1979.
The Patriarch: A Jewish Family Saga, St. Martin's, 1981.
On the Other Hand, Robson Books, 1982.
House of Women, St. Martin's, 1983.
Dancing Bear, Weidenfeld & Nicolson (London), 1984, St. Martin's, 1985.
Titch, St. Martin's, 1987.
The Companion, Robson Books, 1987, St. Martin's, 1988.

OTHER

Israel, Walker & Co. (New York City), 1967.
(Editor with Murray Mindlin) *Explorations: An Annual on Jewish Themes,* Barrie & Rockliff (London), 1967.
Troubled Eden: The Anatomy of Anglo-Jewry, Basic Books (New York City), 1969.
The Cousinhood: The Anglo-Jewish Gentry, Macmillan (New York City), 1971.
The Walled Garden: The Saga of Jewish Family Life and Tradition, Macmillan, 1975.
Point of Arrival: A Study of London's East End, Macmillan, 1975.
Coming Home, Allen & Unwin, 1976.
The Jews, New York Times Co. (New York City), 1977.
(With others) *My LSE,* edited and introduced by Joan Abse, Robson Books, 1977.
(With M. Weitzman) *Ebla: An Archeological Enigma,* New York Times Co., 1979.
What's the Joke?: A Study of Jewish Humour through the Ages, Weidenfeld & Nicolson, 1986.
Lord Jakobovits: The Authorized Biography of the Chief Rabbi, Weidenfeld & Nicolson, 1990.
Murmurings of a Licensed Heretic, Peter Halban, 1990.

SIDELIGHTS: "If you haven't run into Chaim Bermant before, you are in for a treat," asserts Martin Levin of the *New York Times Book Review.* "His field of specialization concerns middle-class Orthodox Jews, habitat Glasgow. But you don't have to be Jewish to enjoy his wry humor," explains the critic, for the author "excels at creating a social climate rich in ethnic commonalities and personal differences. Both are instantly recognizable." For example, Bermant's first novel *Jericho Sleep Alone* presents "a fresh landscape in which some familiar figures are animated with a wit often subtle and oblique," notes Levin. Jericho Broch is a young Jewish Scotsman who cannot overcome his own indecisiveness and lack of specific ambition, and subsequently drifts through school and relationships. "The story, though, is not a great deal," comments *New Statesman* contributor Stephen Hugh-Jones; "what is, is the sense of place, of age, the particularities of word and feeling." The critic adds that *Jericho Sleep Alone* "is told with (and in no way diminished by) a very lively and unsubtly funny wit."

Bermant moves his subject from the uncertain tumult of youth to the staunch passivity of the elderly in *The Diary of an Old Man;* nevertheless, notes Robert Taubman in the *New Statesman,* the narrative "has the same colloquial style, scepticism and liveliness as the 60-years-younger lot—and less sentimentality." Covering a month in diarist Cyril's life, the novel relates his reaction to the deaths of his last two friends—"and it's a relief to read a novel so much about death that doesn't do it for black jokes," remarks Taubman. Nicholas Samstag presents a similar assessment, stating in the *Saturday Review:* "That [the passing of time until death] is [the elderly's] chief preoccupation is made clear, without sentimentality but with great skill and a wry precision." "The special quality of Chaim Bermant's most unusual novel can only be conveyed in the expressions [of the characters]," states Aileen Pippett in the *New York Times Book Review.* The critic elaborates, remarking that Bermant "reproduces [the characters] with exactitude, never striking a false note, giving unforgettable glimpses into the tragicomic life of lonely old age in Britain's welfare state today. Each character is firmly realized."

A *Times Literary Supplement* reviewer believes that it is Cyril's character in particular which enhances the work: "[This] is a book which clearly might have been depressing, or trivial, or sentimental. . . . But Mr. Bermant manages to avoid the dangers, mainly because he achieves an extraordinary completeness of identification with his diarist." Cyril, continues the critic, makes *The Diary of an Old Man* "into something which is often richly funny, occasionally touching, and always true to the facts." As Samstag similarly comments, the novel is "a little masterpiece . . . because Mr. Bermant has written here a superb fantasy disguised as a realistic novel. Into his dreary tapestry he has managed to work threads of gold, crimson, and lettuce green, expressing gallantry, gusto, gaiety, and a human goodness that I wish I believed in." Concludes the critic: "For a little while, experiencing that suspension of disbelief which only the most artful of fantasists can create, I was convinced."

These accurate portrayals have led some critics to observe an anthropological tendency in Bermant's work. In *The Patriarch: A Jewish Family Saga,* for example, Bermant "writes about Jews with a curious blend of intimacy and objectivity, like an affectionate anthropologist," asserts Annie Gottlieb in the *New York Times Book Review;* "he captures the specialness without the shame." And *Spectator* contributor Nick Totton observes that in *The Second Mrs. Whitberg,* "like any self-respecting anthropologist, Mr. Bermant's formal role is not to judge but to describe. However, as with the most interesting anthropology," the critic adds, "scientific objectivity is tempered with enough pure affection to leave the reader gently wondering if civilisation is worth so much after all." Totton concludes: "Information, wit, invention, style, conviction—what more can one ask from an anthropological whodunnit?"

Although he has had success in "providing an entirely new perspective on that tough old recidivist, the Jewish Family Novel," as the *Los Angeles Times*'s Elaine Kendall describes it, Bermant departs from type in his novel *The Companion.* Relating the relationship of stingy widow Martha Crystal and her "lady's companion," Phyllis, through a series of difficulties, *The Companion* is a "funny, original and surprisingly poignant novel," maintains Kendall. The critic adds that while the relatively simple characters "may seem unprepossessing ingredients for a comic novel, Bermant does wonders with them." Told through the voice of fifty-five-year-old Phyllis, the novel's "successes are the moments at which humor and pathos, riding in tandem, emerge from behind the calculated sparsity of Phyllis's account," comments Penelope Lively in the *New York Times Book Review.* While Lively finds Phyllis's first-person chronicle inconsistent at times, *Washington Post Book World* contributor Linda Barrett Osborne believes that Bermant's narrative "is perfectly, irreverently sustained: a devastating series of one-liners highlighting the symbiotic relationship of his eccentric protagonists." "By taking a fundamentally bleak and static situation, inventing two remarkably complementary characters supported by assorted figures of fun," concludes Kendall, in *The Companion* "Bermant has created and ironic and altogether memorable novel, as delicately calibrated as a jeweler's scale."

Bermant once told *CA:* "I suppose I was driven to write by a sort of hedonism, for it gave me a pleasure offered by no other occupation and, unlike other activities which I need not name, it still does. Yet, I did not think it could offer a livelihood, and I dabbled at many things before taking my life in my hands in 1966 and throwing up a secure and fairly lucrative post to devote myself to full time writing and, somehow, I have survived. I used to be in television and journalism before taking up full-time authorship, and I still turn to both between books because they get me out of the house and keep me in touch with people and events, and because I value them—journalism especially—as a discipline. Writing books can be a form of self-indulgence because one has almost all the time and space in the world, whereas journalism with its deadlines and space limitations concentrates the mind wonderfully.

"As I have a fairly large family and live in a fairly spacious house, I am compelled to approach my work in a thoroughly professional manner and am at my typewriter daily from 9:30 to 1:30, whether I have anything to write or not (for I don't know whether I have until I start). In the afternoon I answer letters, fend off creditors, etc., and return to my desk again after dinner. On most working days I do not rise from my labors 'til about 10 P.M. I sometimes shudder at the torrents of words I produce—on average about five thousand a day. I begin my working day by re-reading my previous day's output, and if it yields a thousand usable words I feel I have done well."

BIOGRAPHICAL/CRITICAL SOURCES:

BOOKS

Contemporary Literary Criticism, Volume 40, Gale, 1986.

PERIODICALS

Los Angeles Times, February 21, 1985; December 22, 1987; October 28, 1988.
New Statesman, April 3, 1964; March 12, 1965; October 1, 1965; June 24, 1966.
New Yorker, February 18, 1974; January 25, 1988.
New York Times Book Review, June 12, 1966; May 21, 1967; January 13, 1974; October 3, 1976; August 2, 1981; January 31, 1988; October 23, 1988.
Observer, October 28, 1990.
Saturday Review, May 13, 1967.
Spectator, April 7, 1973; August 28, 1976.
Times Literary Supplement, April 9, 1964; March 11, 1965; September 23, 1965; June 23, 1966; March 31, 1972; April 20, 1973.
Washington Post Book World, September 4, 1988.

* * *

BERNHARD, Thomas 1931-1989

PERSONAL: Born February 9 or 10 (one source says September 11), 1931, in Heerland, Holland; Austrian citizen; died of heart failure and lung problems, February 12, 1989, in Gmunden, Austria; son of Alois Zuckerstatter (a carpenter) and Hertha Bernhard; grandson of Johannes Freumbichler (a carpenter). *Education:* Mozarteum (Salzburg, Austria), received degree, 1957.

CAREER: Novelist, dramatist, poet, and journalist. Also worked as a court reporter, critic, and librarian.

AWARDS, HONORS: Julius Campe Prize, 1964; Bremen Prize, 1965; Austrian State Prize for Literature, 1967; Anton Wildgans Prize, 1968; George Buechner Prize from German Academy of Language and Literature, 1970; Grillparzer Prize, 1971; Theodor Csokor Prize of Austrian PEN Club, 1972; Hannover Dramatists Prize and Seguier Prize, 1974; Literature Prize from Austrian Chamber of Commerce, 1976; Premio Prato, 1982; Premio Modello, 1983; Prix Medicis, 1988.

WRITINGS:

IN ENGLISH TRANSLATION

Vestoerung (novel; title means "Perturbation"), Insel (Frankfurt-am-Main), 1967, translation by Richard Wilson and Clara Wilson published as *Gargoyles,* Knopf (New York City), 1970, University of Chicago Press (Chicago, IL), 1986.

Das Kalkwerk (novel), Suhrkamp (Frankfurt-am-Main), 1970, translation by Sophie Wilkins published as *The Lime Works,* Random House (New York City), 1973, University of Chicago Press, 1986.

Die Macht der Gewohnheit: Komoedie (play; also see below; first produced in Salzburg, 1974), Suhrkamp, 1974, translation by Neville Plaice and Stephen Plaice published as *The Force of Habit: A Comedy* (produced in London, 1976), Heinemann Educational (Exeter, NH), 1976, text edition published as *Die Salzburger Stucke* (title means "National Theatre Plays: The Force of Habit, a Comedy").

Der Praesident, Suhrkamp, 1975, translation by Gitta Honegger published in *The President and Eve of Retirement: Two Plays,* Performing Arts Journal, 1982.

Korrektur (novel), Suhrkamp, 1975, translation by Wilkins published as *Correction,* Knopf, 1979.

Ja, Suhrkamp, 1978, translation by Ewald Osers published as *Yes,* University of Chicago Press, 1992.

Vor dem Ruhestand (play; title means "Before Retirement"; first produced in Bochom, 1980; English version produced as "Eve of Retirement" in Minneapolis, 1982), Suhrkamp, 1979, translation by Honegger published in *The President and Eve of Retirement: Two Plays,* Performing Arts Journal, 1982.

Der Schein truegt, Suhrkamp, 1983, translation by Honegger published as *Appearances Are Deceiving,* in *Theater,* Volume 15, 1983, pp. 13-51.

Beton, Suhrkamp, 1983, translation by David McLintock published as *Concrete,* Knopf, 1984.

Gathering Evidence: A Memoir (contains five volumes first published in German by Residenz (Salzburg), 1983: *An Indication of the Cause* [originally published as *Die Ursache: Eine Andeutung* (also see below), 1975]; *The Cellar: An Escape* [originally published as *Der Keller: Eine Entziehung* (also see below), 1976]; *Breath: A Decision* [originally published as *Der Atem: Eine Entscheidung* (also see below) 1978]; *In the Cold* [originally published as *Die Kaelte: Eine Isolation* (also see below) 1981]; and *A Child* [originally published as *Ein Kind* (also see below), 1982]), translation by McLintock, Knopf, 1986, reprinted, 1995.

Die Untergeher, Suhrkamp, 1983, translation by Jack Dawson published as *The Loser,* Knopf, 1991.

Wittgenstein's Neffe: Eine Freundschaft (autobiographical; title means "Wittgenstein's Nephew: A Friendship"), 1983, translation by McLintock published as *Wittgenstein's Nephew: A Novel,* Knopf, 1989.

Holzfaellen, Suhrkamp, 1984, translation by McLintock published as *The Woodcutters,* Knopf, 1988.

Ausloeschung, Suhrkamp, 1986, translation by McLintock published as *Extinction,* Knopf, 1995.

In der Hohe, translation by Russell Stockman published as *On the Mountain: Rescue Attempt, Nonsense,* Marlboro Press (Marlboro, VT), 1991.

Alte Meister, translation by Ewald Osers published as *Old Masters: A Comedy,* University of Chicago Press, 1992.

IN GERMAN

Auf der Erde und in der Hoelle (poetry; title means "On Earth and in Hell"), Mueller (Salzburg), 1957.

In hora mortis (poetry; title means "In the Hour of Death"), Mueller, 1958.

Unter dem Eisen des Mondes (poetry; title means "Under the Iron of the Moon"), Kipenheuer & Witsch, 1958.

Die Rosen der Einoede: fuenf Saetze fuer Ballet, Stimmen und Orchester, S. Fischer, 1959.

Frost (novel), Insel, 1963.

Amras (prose), Suhrkamp, 1967.

Prosa, Suhrkamp, 1967.

Ungenach (prose; title means "Trouble"), Suhrkamp, 1968.

An der Baumgrenze (novel; title means "At the Timberline"), illustrations by Anton Lehmden, Residenz, 1969.

Ereignisse (title means "Events"), Literarisches Colloquium, 1969.

Watten: ein Nachlass (prose; title means "Mudflats"), Suhrkamp, 1969.

Ein Fest fuer Boris (play; title means "A Party for Boris"; produced in Hamburg, Germany, 1970), Suhrkamp, 1970.

"Der Berg," published in *Literatur und Kritik,* Number 5, June, 1970.

Gehen, Suhrkamp, 1970.

Midland in Stilfs: Drei Erzaelungen, Suhrkamp, 1970.

Der Italiener (screenplay; title means "The Italian"), Residenz, 1971.

Der Ignorant und der Wahnsinnige (play; first produced in Salzburg, Austria, at Salzburg Festival, 1972; title means "The Ignoramus and the Madman"), Suhrkamp, 1972.

Der Kulterer (screenplay), Residenz, 1974.

Die Jagdgesellschaft (play; title means "The Hunting Party"; first produced in Vienna, 1974), Suhrkamp, 1974.

Die Salzburger Stuecke (also includes *Die Macht der Gewohnheit*), Suhrkamp, 1975.

Die Ursache: Eine Andeutung (autobiographical stories; title means "An Indication of the Cause"; also see below), Residenz, 1975.

Der Beruehmten (play; title means "The Famous"; first produced at the Burgtheater in Vienna, Austria, 1988), Suhrkamp, 1976.

Der Keller: Eine Entziehung (autobiographical; sequel to *Die Ursache;* title means "The Cellar: An Escape"), Residenz, 1976.

Der Wetterfleck, illustrations by Otto F. Best, Reclam, 1976.

Heldenplatz (play; title means "Heroes' Square"), first produced in Vienna, 1976.

Minetti: ein Portrait des Kuenstlers als alter Mann (a play; first produced in Stuttgart, 1976), photographs by Digne Meller Marcovicz, Suhrkamp, 1977.

Der Atem: Eine Entscheidung (autobiographical; sequel to *Der Keller;* title means "Breath: A Decision"), Residenz, 1978.

Immanuel Kant (comedy; first produced in Stuttgart, 1978), Suhrkamp, 1978.
Die Erzaelungen, edited by Ulrich Greiner, Suhrkamp, 1979.
Der Weltverbesserer (play; title means "Worldimprover"; first produced in Bochum, 1980), Suhrkamp, 1979.
Die Billigesser, Suhrkamp, 1980.
Der Stimmenimitator (title means "The Voice-Mime"), Suhrkamp, 1980.
Am Ziel (play), Suhrkamp, 1981.
Ave Vergil (poems), Suhrkamp, 1981.
Die Kaelte: Eine Isolation (autobiographical; sequel to *Der Atem;* title means "In the Cold"), Residenz, 1981.
Ein Kind (autobiographical; sequel to *Die Kaelte;* title means "A Child"), Residenz, 1982.
Ueber allen Gipfeln ist Ruh: Ein deutscher Dichtertag um 1980 (play), Suhrkamp, 1981.
Die Stuecke, 1969-1981, Suhrkamp, 1983.
Der Theatermacher, Suhrkamp, 1984.
Ritter, Dene, Voss, Suhrkamp, 1984.
Ausloschung: Ein Zerfall, Suhrkamp, 1986.
Einfach Kompliziert, Suhrkamp, 1986.
Elisabeth II, Suhrkamp, 1987.
Der deutsche Mittagstisch, Suhrkamp, 1988.
Andrae Meuller im Gespreach mit Thomas Bernhard, Bibliothek der Provinz, 1992.

Also author of *Die heiligen drei Koenige von St. Vitus* (title means "The Three Wise Men of St. Vitus"), 1955, *Der Schweinehueter* (title means "The Swineherd"), 1956, and *Die Jause* (title means "The Afternoon Snack"), 1965.

SIDELIGHTS: Austrian playwright Thomas Bernhard's pessimistic view of human nature was ever-present in his controversial plays and novels. Because his works often presented the faults of his culture in a critical light, he gained a reputation as German literature's most melancholy and bitter writer. Like the works of Mark Twain, Bernhard's later plays were indictments of a culture in decline. His 1984 novel *Holzfaellen* (*The Woodcutters*) was seized by the police because they thought it drew an unflattering portrait of a famous Viennese personage. His play *Heldenplatz* (*Heroes' Square*), forthright in its charges that anti-Semitism is widespread in Austria, angered his audiences and the Austrian government, who began to discuss whether or not such work should be censored. Considered by some to be unimportant due to the views he expressed, he was esteemed by others as "one of the greatest writers of the century," noted a writer for the London *Times.*

The perceived greatness in Bernhard's works has rested in their stylistic virtuosity as well as their grim meditations on futility, death, madness, hatred, contempt, and disease. "Bernhard's writing is like printed music not only in the regularity of its lines but also in being the notation of an essentially aural phenomenon, a voice," observed *Times Literary Supplement* reviewer Paul Griffiths. "His are, with a vengeance, talking books. They are monologues, but they are also . . . polyphonies." These monologues, whether in play or fictive form, attack modern Austria and its pretenses with a vengeance hardly matched anywhere in literature. According to Ursula Hegi in the *New York Times Book Review,* Bernhard "nurtured a love-hate connection to his native land and took pleasure in shocking and antagonizing its citizens with his work. His practice of blurring the lines between fiction and fact even resulted in lawsuits for libel." This penchant for misanthropy and denunciation—both in and out of print—has done little to erode the author's popularity in Europe and America. The recipient of numerous literature prizes during his lifetime, he has left a legacy as "one of the bravest and most unusual . . . novelists of the post-war world," to quote Benjamin Weissman in the *Los Angeles Times Book Review.*

Bernhard's novel *Vestoerung,* translated as *Gargoyles,* revealed his belief in the hopelessness of the human condition. In the story, "the patients are the gargoyles of the title and their peculiar arrangements could be well skipped were it not for the brilliance, erudition, and suggestiveness with which Bernhard writes about them," commented a critic in *Antioch Review.* The book was not widely read in the United States, but was very popular in Europe.

Grotesque figures that depict Bernhard's view of human nature appeared often in his other works, as well. The works unanimously stress that man is motivated primarily by madness and disease, noted Martin Esslin in *Modern Drama.* "Life itself is a disease only curable by death. Cripples and madmen merely exhibit, more plainly and therefore perhaps more frankly, what all men suffer from beneath the surface. And even 'genius is a disease,' as the doctor asserts in *The Ignoramus and the Madman,*" Esslin maintained. In *German*

Life and Letters, D. A. Craig observed that "the introspective sickness" of many of Bernhard's characters indirectly represent the troubles besetting the Austrian people in the wake of two world wars.

Many of Bernhard's characters are diseased or disabled. The ringmaster of the circus in *Die Macht der Gewohnheit* (*The Force of Habit*) has a wooden leg; the narrator of *Korrektur* (*Correction*), an idealistic scientist, has a psychotic hatred, and commits suicide. In *Ein Fest fuer Boris* (*A Party for Boris*), thirteen legless guests attend a party hosted by a wealthy woman who also has no legs. The woman, misnamed the "Gute" or "Good," is married to Boris, also legless, who dies while pounding on a drum; because the guests are absorbed in sharing their morbid experiences and dreams with one another, they don't notice the death until the end of the party.

Death and disease almost always inform Bernhard's major works because the author himself struggled with ill health throughout his life. After an impoverished and troubled childhood, recorded in his memoir *Gathering Evidence,* Bernhard contracted first pneumonia and then tuberculosis as a young man. At one point he was so ill that he was consigned to a terminal ward in a public health facility. In and out of sanatoriums during a long convalescence, he was forced to give up any hopes of the singing career he had imagined. Instead he became interested in reading and writing. During his years of illness Bernhard composed his first poems, plays, and short fiction. *Partisan Review* contributor Betty Falkenberg generalized: "All Bernhard's books, all his plays, are really about one thing: death. Death in death, death in life, the futility of all human contact or attempts at understanding, the senselessness of all existence and the cruelty of creating new life, the stupidity of all human beings, the futility of all systems, political or religious, both encompassing as they do the same corruption and stupidity to be found everywhere else." This focus on death paradoxically led his more sensitive characters to an appreciation of the value of commitment; explained Falkenberg, "If there is one thing that can bind people together . . . it can only be the awareness of the total hopelessness of all human endeavor in the light of the fact of death."

Similarly, *Dictionary of Literary Biography* contributor Steve Dowden noted: "For Bernhard, death defines the human condition; a joke played by nature, death is both comic and tragic, a brute fact against which all else is measured. Bernhard's subsequent dramatic work hardly deviates from the underlying theme of *Ein Fest fuer Boris,* that human beings are wretched creatures and death is a certainty."

Though Bernhard's works often reveal common themes, they do so by means of a variety of unusual techniques. For example, the novel *Das Kalkwerk* (*The Lime Works*) is narrated by a life insurance salesman who weaves the story from rumors about a frustrated Austrian writer who has blasted his crippled wife in the head with a shot from her own rifle. "The book is a jungle of meaning, the opposite of simplistic allegory, and a major achievement because of this. . . . *The Lime Works* invites comparison with the run-on novels of Beckett," a *New Republic* reviewer wrote. Ronald De Feo concluded in *National Review* that in this book Bernhard had again demonstrated that he was "one of the most substantive and intense" among German writers.

Bernhard's facility with a variety of techniques brought him the ongoing appreciation of writers and critics. Between 1960 and 1980, he won a number of literary prizes, including the Austrian State Prize for Literature in 1967. American critics valued the masterful style in which he couched his social criticism and bleak world view. Of *The Woodcutters,* a novel in which the narrator deflates the pretentiousness of local artists, *New York Times Book Review* contributor Mark Anderson commented, "What raises this denunciation of Austria's cultural parochialism above the level of mere satire is Mr. Bernhard's supremely ironic tone of voice and musical sensibility. The narrator's own credibility is constantly undermined by the anxious excessiveness of his attacks, which one gradually comes to see as being aimed as much at himself and his own fear of death as at the guests."

In *The Woodcutters,* a dinner party for artists and intellectuals is the springboard from which the narrator—a vituperative artist largely isolated from the others—berates them in a manner that begins to sound unsound. Part of the attraction for readers is the question of the narrator's reliability as he recounts observations based on thirty years' experience with the aristocrats of culture. In this novel, said *Chicago Tribune* writer Joseph Coates,

Bernhard "comes close to the novelist's ideal of making every gesture meaningful, bathing it in a garish light from the past whose quality of illumination we can never entirely trust." Richard Eder in the *Los Angeles Times* praised the novel's finish, in which the narrator demonstrates that he practices the same kind of pretention that so offends him in the others. Though the reviewer would have liked to see the revelation come sooner, "it is an abrupt reversal, and startlingly effective," he remarked.

Critics also admired Bernhard's mature prose for achieving its effects in the same way that music does. Coates explained that all Bernhard's work shows his training in music. "His books embody such musical values as counterpoint, fugue, leitmotif and harmony, and in at least two of them a play-within-the-novel obliquely reflects on the action." For these reasons and more, *The Woodcutters,* said Martin Seymour-Smith in a *Washington Post Book World* review, is a representative work that can well serve as an "introduction to Bernhard's work as a whole. Apart from perfectly illustrating his shrewdness, disgruntlement and acute awareness, *Woodcutters* is very funny." The novel's success firmly established Bernhard's reputation as a world class novelist to the extent that in the year before his death, some critics regarded the playwright as a candidate for the Nobel Prize.

Bernhard's depiction of the least admirable facets of human nature endeared him to some readers and enraged others. Some critics pointed out that one need not share Bernhard's views to appreciate his mastery of dramatic and novelistic techniques. Speaking of the later plays which had sharpened into "savage aggression against the public itself," Esslin remarked that what makes the playwright's misanthropic works notable is "the artistry with which these impulses are hammered into shape. Bernhard's theatre is essentially a *mannerist* theatre. If his characters are puppets, all the greater the skill with which they perform their intricate dance; if his subject-matter is venom and derision, all the more admirable the perfection of the language in which the venom is spat out, the intricacy of the pattern it creates."

Not everyone has shared the view that Bernhard's virtuosity of language reveals an unerring genius at work. *New Republic* reviewer Robert Boyers commented: "Taken as a whole, Bernhard's work seems repetitious, suffocating, impoverished." The critic added: "Repetition, compulsion, and emotional impoverishment need not be fatal characteristics for an ambitious novelist who knows how to make them his subject. . . . The great problem with Bernhard is that he seems, in the end, to be entirely the helpless servant of his obsessions. He is not writing about pathology, or Austria, or the vicissitudes of consciousness. He is not writing about subjects at all. He is exhibiting symptoms." Weissman likewise maintained that Bernhard "tells a skewed version of his personal history over and over again, mixing autobiographical details with a fanatical subjectivity that's obsessed with exaggeration." In an essay on the author's plays, Dowden too concluded: "The intention that drives Bernhard's theater is not revolution or social reform or even constructive criticism; it is personal outrage at the course of modern Austrian history. Bernhard, the misanthrope, was an uncompromising moralist."

This "uncompromising moralism" remained a staple of Bernhard's work until his death in 1989. His last two published novels, translated into English as *The Loser* and *Extinction,* both offer obsessive and contemptuous narrators confronted by the sudden death of a friend, in the case of *The Loser,* and family, in *Extinction.* Dowden explained that *Extinction* is "Bernhard's longest prose work and his final major piece of fiction," adding that the work "is a great synthesis of his interests and concerns: music, Nazism, family, Catholicism, selfishness, death, and Austria's squandered history."

Even in death Bernhard reflected his lifelong disdain for Austria. After succumbing to a heart attack while living alone in a rural farmhouse, he was buried in a small private ceremony before the press was informed of his death. His will specified that none of his novels or plays were to be published or performed in Austria—and none of his papers or unfinished works released—for the duration of his copyright, 70 years. Immediately the existing Austrian editions of his work disappeared from shops, bought frantically by those who never expected to see his work in print again. The publishing ban has not led to out-of-print situations, however, since Bernhard works are still being translated from the German and are being reprinted in other countries. Dowden, for one, has found this unusual posthumous legacy quite in conformity with Bernhard's singular life and work.

"A loner both in art and in life," summarized the critic, "[Bernhard] cultivated the image of an intellectual curmudgeon."

BIOGRAPHICAL/CRITICAL SOURCES:

BOOKS

Arnold, Heinz Ludwig, editor, *Bernhard,* Boorberg, 1974.
Bernhard, Thomas, *Der Ignorant und der Wahnsinnige,* Suhrkamp, 1972.
Bernhard, *Die Ursache: Eine Andeutung,* Residenz, 1975.
Bernhard, *Der Keller: Eine Entziehung,* Residenz, 1976.
Bernhard, *Der Atem: Eine Entscheidung,* Residenz, 1978.
Bernhard, *Die Kaelte: Eine Isolation,* Residenz, 1981.
Bernhard, *Ein Kind,* Residenz, 1982.
Bernhard, *Wittgenstein's Neffe: Eine Freundschaft,* Suhrkamp, 1983.
Bernhard, *Gathering Evidence: A Memoir,* translation by David McLintock, Knopf, 1986.
Birkerts, Sven, *An Artificial Wilderness: Essays on 20th-Century Literature,* Morrow (New York City), 1987, pp. 77-84.
Botond, Anneliese, editor, *Ueber Bernhard,* Suhrkamp, 1970.
Bullivant, Keith, editor, *The Modern German Novel,* Berg (Leamington Spa, England), 1987.
Calandra, Denis, *New German Dramatists,* Macmillan (New York City), 1983.
Contemporary Literary Criticism, Gale (Detroit, MI), Volume 3, 1975; Volume 32, 1985; Volume 61, 1990.
Demetz, Peter, *After the Fires: Recent Writings in the Germanies, Switzerland, and Austria,* Harcourt (San Diego, CA), 1986, pp. 199-212.
Dictionary of Literary Biography, Gale, Volume 85: *Austrian Fiction Writers after 1914,* 1989; Volume 124: *Twentieth-Century German Dramatists, 1919-1992,* 1992.
Dittmar, Jens, *Bernhard Wergeschichte,* Suhrkamp, 1981.
Dowden, Stephen D., *Understanding Thomas Bernhard,* University of South Carolina Press (Columbia), 1991.
Fleischmann, Krista, *Thomas Bernhard—Eine Erinnerung: Interviews zur Person,* Osterreichische Staatsdruckerei, 1992.
Markolin, Caroline, *Thomas Bernhard and His Grandfather Johannes Freumbichler: Our Grandfathers Are Our Teachers,* Ariadne Press (Riverside, CA), 1993.
Mittermayer, Manfred, *Thomas Bernhard,* J. B. Metzler (Stuttgart), 1995.
Sorg, Bernard, *Bernhard,* Beck, 1977.
Waitzbauer, Harald, *Thomas Bernhard in Salzburg: Alltagsgeschichte einer Provinzstadt, 1943-1955,* Bohlau, 1995.

PERIODICALS

American Book Review, February-March, 1996, p. 25.
Antioch Review, fall, 1970.
Booklist, February 15, 1971; July 15, 1975.
Book World, January 3, 1971.
Chicago Tribune, February 24, 1989.
German Life and Letters, July, 1972.
Globe and Mail (Toronto), August 18, 1984.
Los Angeles Times, January 20, 1988.
Los Angeles Times Book Review, October 8, 1995, p. 3.
Modern Austrian Literature, number 1, 1978, pp. 21-48; number 11, 1978; number 12, 1979.
Modern Drama, January, 1981; March, 1987, pp. 104-14.
National Review, February 1, 1974.
New Republic, December 1973; April 27, 1992, pp. 41-44.
New Yorker, February 4, 1985, pp. 97-101; July 21, 1986, pp. 90-93.
New York Review of Books, March 28, 1985, pp. 31-32.
New York Times Book Review, July 1, 1984; February 16, 1986, p. 12; February 19, 1989; September 8, 1991, p. 15; September 10, 1995, p. 42.
Partisan Review, Volume 47, number 2, 1980.
Saturday Review, October 31, 1970.
Theater, winter, 1983, pp. 58-62.
Times Literary Supplement, February 12, 1971; September 29, 1972; February 13, 1976; June 11, 1976; May 1, 1992, p. 21.
Tribune Books (Chicago), January 31, 1988.
Village Voice, March 18, 1986, pp. 45-46; September 30, 1986, p. 56.
Washington Post Book World, April 17, 1988; February 19, 1989; March 5, 1989; October 8, 1995, pp. 1, 14.
World Literature Today, summer, 1977; winter, 1978.

OBITUARIES:

PERIODICALS

Chicago Tribune, February 17, 1989.
Los Angeles Times, February 17, 1989.
New York Times, February 17, 1989.
New York Times Book Review, February 14, 1988.
Times (London), February 17, 1989.
Washington Post, February 21, 1989.*

* * *

BOGRAD, Larry 1953-
(Grady Barrol)

PERSONAL: Born May 5, 1953, in Denver, CO; son of Nathan (a physician) and Ruth (a gerontologist; maiden name, Parker) Bograd; married Coleen Hubbard (a playwright), 1988; children: Allie, Natalie, Willa. *Education:* University of Colorado, B.A., 1975; University of Washington, Seattle, M.A., 1977. *Politics:* "Off-center and increasingly depressing." *Avocational interests:* Athletics, movies, photography, reading, computers, gardening, camping, and theater.

ADDRESSES: Home—P.O. Box 200651, Denver, CO 80220. *Agent*—Christine Tomasino, RLR Associates, 7 West 51st St., New York, NY 10019.

CAREER: Writer, 1975—; Harvey House Publishers, New York City, managing editor, 1977-79; teacher of English at colleges in Denver, CO, and in Ohio, 1986-96; writer and consultant, 1996—.

AWARDS, HONORS: Irma Simonton Black Award, Bank Street College, 1979, for *Felix in the Attic;* selected among 100 most important authors for young adults, National Council of Teachers of English, 1990.

WRITINGS:

FOR CHILDREN

(Under pseudonym Grady Barrol) *Little Book of Anagrams,* illustrated by Liz Victor, Harvey House (New York City), 1978.
Felix in the Attic, illustrated by Dirk Zimmer, Harvey House, 1978.
Egon, illustrated by Zimmer, Macmillan (New York City), 1980.
Lost in the Store, illustrated by Victoria Chess, Macmillan, 1981.
Poor Gertie, illustrated by Zimmer, Delacorte (New York City), 1986.
Bernie Entertaining, illustrated by Richard Lauter, Delacorte, 1987.
The Fourth-Grade Dinosaur Club, illustrated by Lauter, Delacorte, 1989.

YOUNG ADULT NOVELS

The Kolokol Papers, Farrar, Straus (New York City), 1981.
Bad Apple, Farrar, Straus, 1982.
Los Alamos Light, Farrar, Straus, 1983.
The Better Angel, Lippincott (New York City), 1985.
Travelers, Lippincott, 1986.

PLAYS

Shelter Me (one-act play), produced in Denver, CO, at The Changing Scene, 1987.
Lab Rats, produced in Denver at Writers Lab, 1988.
Horn of Plenty, produced in Denver at Writers Lab, 1989.
Western Slope, produced in Denver at Writers Lab, 1990.
Ludlow, produced in Denver at Writers Lab, 1991.
The Half-Life of Karen Silkwood, produced in Detroit at Attic Theater, 1993.

OTHER

Also author of screenplays, including *Travelers* (adaptation of novel), 1991; *Dinosaur Wars* (original screenplay), 1992; *The Dinosaur Club* (adaptation of *The Fourth-Grade Dinosaur Club*), 1994; *Western Slope* (adaptation of play), 1994; and *Josie's Railroad* (original screenplay), 1995. Author of children's stage musical, *Poor Gertie* (adapted from novel), 1993. Also author of a television pilot screenplay, "Ghost Town," 1994, and video "Keepers of the Dream," history of the OCAW (Oil, Chemical, and Atomic Workers union), 1991. Contributor of short stories to anthologies, including *Short Circuits,* edited by Don Gallo, Delacorte, 1992, and *Within Reach,* edited by Gallo, HarperCollins, 1993. Contributor to periodicals, including *ALAN Review, Westword,* and *Working Mother.*

WORK IN PROGRESS: Adult fiction; children's fiction; screenplays.

SIDELIGHTS: Larry Bograd is a playwright and author of young adult novels and juvenile picture books. His collaboration with Dirk Zimmer, *Felix in the Attic,* is perhaps his best known children's book. He wrote in an essay for *Something about the Author Autobiography Series* (*SAAS*), "I went further than thousands of other writers attempting to get published. . . . I'm glad that writing and I found each other. I like the life."

Bograd wrote *Felix in the Attic* while working with the children's publisher Harvey House. "When the publisher needed a manuscript for illustrator Dirk Zimmer, I offered to write one for $250," Bograd recalls. That manuscript would be published as *Felix in the Attic* in 1978. The story of a small boy who actually enjoys serving "time" in the attic, *Felix* went on to win the Irma Simonton Black Award for best children's book the next year. "An article about me was published in the *New York Times,*" Bograd notes, describing his first writing success. "I was taken out to lunch by several curious and powerful editors. I was asked to meet with a producer at [Children's Television Workshop], which produces *Sesame Street.* I hardly cared when I lost my job. I was a hero prince to my relatives. Not bad for a kid from Colorado who never cared much for writing when he was young."

Felix in the Attic would be followed by another Zimmer-Bograd collaboration, 1980's *Egon.* In this allegory of learning to make one's own way in the world, a young, bushy-tailed fox named Egon leaves his familiar den to discover what lies beyond. He learns from each of the creatures he meets and, in return for that knowledge, shares his artistic talents by drawing a picture of his new acquaintances. Bograd's *Lost in the Store,* a picture book illustrated by Victoria Chess, was next published in 1981. The story of Molly and Bruno and their adventures while separated from their parents in a large department store, *Lost in the Store* would mark its author's third well-received effort in the picture-book market.

"While I enjoyed this early success," Bograd noted in (*SAAS*), "I wrote dozens of other picture book stories which never were published. My job came to an end in 1979. I stayed in New York for another seven years, taking odd jobs so I could focus on my writing. . . . Still wanting to write serious novels, I wrote a book for teenagers about a boy whose parents are human rights activists in the Soviet Union." *The Kolokol Papers* is narrated by young Lev Kolokol, a Russian teen who has grown up as a social outsider. Taking place during the Cold War, Lev's father is a political dissident whose remarks against the communist party ultimately find him standing trial. The elder Kolokol's refusal to conform to the standard party line inspires his son to also act on his personal beliefs rather than go with the popular majority. "Bograd's simple, eloquent prose strengthens the effects of his powerful novel," noted a reviewer in *Publishers Weekly;* the novel was recommended by other critics for use as a supplemental text to history classes on the Cold War.

"I suppose if I'd continued to produce easy-to-admire books, my career might have unfolded more smoothly," Bograd reflected in *SAAS.* "Instead, I refused to restrict myself. I never liked to be too predictable. Yet it was more than simply refusing to write 'safe' books that caused me to write my next novel, *Bad Apple;* it was the acknowledgment of people's sometimes accidental and sometimes purposeful cruelty and its effects on children." In fact, child abuse, criminal behavior, violence, and alcohol abuse figure prominently in the life of the novel's disturbed young protagonist, fifteen-year-old Nicky, who inflicts some cruelty of his own by robbing and beating an elderly couple. Calling the work a "masterful blend of storytelling and emotional insight," *Voice of Youth Advocates* reviewer Frank Perry praised *Bad Apple* as "richly flavored and delicately seasoned with sprigs of caustic humor."

Bograd's favorite novel, *Travelers,* depicts the life of another troubled adolescent male. In this 1986 tale, seventeen-year-old Jack is still haunted by the loss of his father, who was killed in Vietnam when Jack was four. A high-spirited trip to California courtesy of a party-loving friend enables the teen to follow the threads of his father's life through talking to Air-Force buddies. In the process of coming to terms with his father's death, Jack also learns to appreciate what he does have in what *School Library Journal* reviewer Elizabeth Reardon called "an entertaining and moving story—one filled with beautifully written descriptions of the land and of the people Jack meets." In addition to writing several realistic novels for young-adult readers, Bograd made a foray into historical fiction with 1984's *Los Alamos Light.* Taking place in Los Alamos, New Mexico, while the first atomic bomb was being developed there, the book helps readers gain an understanding of the arguments for and against the development and use of this terrifying new weapon. The story is told through the eyes of Maggie, who accompanies her scientist father to Los Alamos where he is to assist Robert Oppenheimer in the Manhattan Project. "The historical, geographical and cultural details of *Los Alamos Midnight* are authentic and illuminating," commented Marguerite M. Lambert in *School Library Journal,* praising Bograd's well-researched efforts. The author himself enjoyed the work involved in accurately recreating a historical epoch. "When I have something to learn in order to make a manuscript more believable," he explained in *SAAS,* "I take time for research. I like libraries—a trait I've had since earliest memory. I like to learn, and I find, for certain things, I'm my own best teacher. As a writer, it's a tickle that, at times, someone actually pays me to learn."

Poor Gertie, which was published in 1986, is a novel for elementary school readers. Featuring an artistic girl from a struggling, single-parent family, the story focuses on Gertie's ability to use her imagination to make the best of a bad situation. "Both the first-person narrative and the dialogue are natural," wrote reviewer Betsy Hearne in the *Bulletin of the Center for Children's Books,* "and the plot, despite some occasionally exaggerated scenes, carries the episodic chapters to a convincingly happy conclusion." The following year's *Bernie Entertaining* depicts a young boy's attempts to survive entering adolescence and being the class nerd to boot. While some critics found the book's plot trite, Robert Strang praised it in *Bulletin of the Center for Children's Books,* writing that *Bernie Entertaining* "is a fun read that may provide some insight into the kid who likes science, hates sports, and 'was among the first in his class to get glasses.'"

After the publication of *The Fourth-Grade Dinosaur Club* in 1989, Bograd became involved in theater and wrote and produced several plays, often with his wife, fellow playwright Coleen Hubbard. Together, the couple started their own theater, Writers Lab, which remained open from 1987 until 1995, when Coleen got a job in Cleveland with the Cleveland Play House. The Hubbard-Bograds moved back to Denver a year later.

BIOGRAPHICAL/CRITICAL SOURCES:

BOOKS

Something about the Author Autobiography Series, Volume 21, Gale (Detroit), 1996.

PERIODICALS

Booklist, October 15, 1983, p. 337.

Bulletin of the Center for Children's Books, July/August, 1980, p. 207; January, 1982, pp. 81-82; May, 1982, p. 164; April, 1983, p. 143; January, 1986, pp. 82-83; March, 1986; June, 1986; May, 1987, p. 162.

Kirkus Reviews, November 15, 1981, p. 1.

New York Times, May 29, 1979.

Publishers Weekly, June 13, 1980, p. 73; November 20, 1981, p. 55; June 27, 1986, p. 95.

School Library Journal, January, 1979, p. 39; March, 1979, p. 120; March, 1982, p. 155; December, 1982, p. 70; November, 1983, p. 87; August, 1986, p. 98.

Voice of Youth Advocates, June, 1983, p. 96; April, 1984, p. 28; April, 1987, p. 28.

* * *

BOULTON, Jane 1921-

PERSONAL: Born September 25, 1921, in Indianapolis, IN; daughter of John W. and Martha (Morris) Balch; married Peter Boulton (divorced, 1980); married DeWitt Whittlesey, February 6, 1942 (deceased, 1992); children: Ann, Michael Dorn, Celeinne Ysunza. *Education:* Rollins College, B.A. *Politics:* Democrat.

ADDRESSES: Home—649 University Ave., H 441, Palo Alto, CA 94301-2032. *Agent*—Laurie Harper, Sebastian Agency, 333 Kearny St., No. 708, San Francisco, CA 94108.

CAREER: Poet and children's author.

WRITINGS:

Opal, Macmillan (New York City), 1976.
Opal: The Journal of an Understanding Heart, Tigoa (Palo Alto, CA), 1984.
Only Opal: The Diary of a Young Girl, illustrated by Barbara Cooney, Philomel (New York City), 1994.

WORK IN PROGRESS: A novel, *Journey within a Journey.*

SIDELIGHTS: Jane Boulton is the author of three books drawn from the journals kept by Opal Whitely, a young pioneer girl in late eighteenth-century Oregon. Orphaned at five, Opal spent her remaining childhood with a foster family, following the logging family as they worked at nineteen different lumber camps. Calling her foster mother "the mama where I live," Whitely escapes the harsh treatment of her adoptive family by keeping a diary of her "fifth and sixth year." In *Opal,* Boulton collected Opal's diary entries into a single work. She used selections from the diary and arranged them like a poem for the picture book *Only Opal: The Diary of a Young Girl.*

A critic writing in *Kirkus Reviews* calls *Only Opal* "a touching, fascinating portrait," while in *Horn Book,* Mary M. Burns applauds the book's "ingenious quality which speaks directly to the emotions." *School Library Journal* contributor Martha Rosen notes that some of Whitely's wording is "awkward," but she insists "readers will respond positively to this glimpse of history." However, Ann Banks questions the authenticity of the poetical text in the *New York Times Book Review.* While calling *Only Opal* "intense, poetic, and quaintly ungrammatical in places," Banks tells of skeptics who believe Whitely wrote the diary as an adult and how one of Whitely's own relatives claims that Whitely's so-called foster family was indeed her own birth family. Although she makes no judgement in terms of whether the diary is original, Banks does offer an opinion of the work, wondering how anyone "could judge such a bleak story appropriate for a picture book."

BIOGRAPHICAL/CRITICAL SOURCES:

PERIODICALS

Booklist, March 15, 1994, p. 1348.
Bulletin of the Center for Children's Books, June, 1994, p. 338.
Children's Book Review Service, March, 1994, p. 90.
Children's Book Watch, May, 1994, p. 4.
Horn Book, May/June, 1994, p. 338.
Horn Book Guide, fall, 1994, p. 387.
Kirkus Reviews, February 15, 1994, p. 235.
New York Times Book Review, May 22, 1994, p. 20.
Quill & Quire, May, 1994, p. 38; February, 1995, p. 35.
Reading Time, October, 1994, p. 167.
School Library Journal, May, 1994, p. 106.

* * *

BRADFORD, S. W.
See BATTIN, B(rinton) W(arner)

* * *

BRENDON, Piers (George Rundle) 1940-

PERSONAL: Born December 21, 1940, in Cornwall, England; son of George (a writer) and Frances (a journalist; maiden name, Cook) Brendon; married Vyvyen Davis (a teacher), 1968; children: George, Oliver. *Ethnicity:* "Caucasian." *Education:* Magdalene College, Cambridge, M.A., 1965, Ph.D., 1970. *Politics:* Labour.

ADDRESSES: Home—4B Millington Rd., Cambridge, England. *Agent*—Curtis Brown Ltd., 162-168 Regent St., London W1R 5TA, England.

CAREER: Cambridgeshire College of Arts and Technology, Cambridge, England, lecturer in history, 1966-79, head of department, 1977-79; writer, 1979—. Occasional lecturer and broadcaster. Keeper of the Archives Center and fellow, Churchill College, Cambridge, 1995—.

WRITINGS:

(Editor with William Shaw) *Reading They've Liked,* Macmillan (London), 1967.
(Editor with Shaw) *Reading Matters,* Macmillan, 1969.

(Editor with Shaw) *By What Authority?*, Macmillan, 1972.

Hurrell Froude and the Oxford Movement, Merrimack Books Service (Topsfield, MA), 1974.

Hawker of Morwenstow: Portrait of a Victorian Eccentric, J. Cape (London), 1975.

Eminent Edwardians, Secker & Warburg (London), 1979, Houghton (Boston), 1980.

(With Rex Bloomstein) *Auschwitz and the Allies* (documentary), British Broadcasting Corp. (BBC-TV), 1981.

The Life and Death of the Press Barons, Secker & Warburg, 1982, Atheneum (New York City), 1983.

Winston Churchill: A Biography, Harper (New York City), 1984, published in England as *Winston Churchill: A Brief Life,* Secker & Warburg, 1984.

(With Bloomstein) *Human Rights* (documentary), Thames TV, 1984.

Ike: His Life and Times, Harper, 1986 (published in England as *Ike: The Life and Times of Dwight D. Eisenhower,* Secker & Warburg, 1986).

Our Own Dear Queen, Secker & Warburg, 1986, David & Charles (North Pomfret, VT), 1987.

Thomas Cook: 150 Years of Popular Tourism, Secker & Warburg, 1991.

(With Phillip Whitehead) *The Windsors: A Dynasty Revealed,* Hodder & Stoughton (London), 1995.

The Motoring Century: The Story of the Royal Automobile Club, Bloomsbury, 1997.

Coauthor of other television documentary scripts. Script consultant, *The Windsors* (four-part documentary), and *The Churchills* (three-part documentary). Contributor of reviews to numerous periodicals and newspapers, including the London *Times, New York Times, Observer, Mail on Sunday,* and *Columbia Journalism Review.*

WORK IN PROGRESS: Research on a history of the 1930s.

SIDELIGHTS: With *The Life and Death of the Press Barons,* "Piers Brendon has revived, with elegance and distinction, the discipline of digestible history which gave writers like Barbara Tuchman their early success: a 'tissue of innumerable biographies,' only lightly drawn together with generalizations, strongly spiced by anecdote, and written in a style that combines bravura with allusiveness," states Roy Foster in the *Times Literary Supplement.* "This is a more substantial achievement than it may sound; the subjects for such an approach need to be carefully selected, the terrain well mapped, and the material produced with a sustained flourish," the critic continues. "His new book succeeds on these levels." *The Life and Death of the Press Barons* is a "witty study of the press lords of England and America," summarizes *Washington Post Book World* contributor Bernard A. Weisberger, containing "some 250 of the funniest and shrewdest pages of business and cultural history that you are likely to find between covers in any given year." Tracing the careers and idiosyncracies of executives such as Joseph Pulitzer, Horace Greeley, William Randolph Hearst, and James Gordon Bennett, the author "offers routine cautions on the growth of conglomerates and other sober matters," observes *New York Times* reviewer Walter Goodman, "but the main pleasures of his book lie in the portraits of the men who made the papers." Although these anecdotes constitute a major portion of the book, "the range of sources behind *The Life and Death of the Press Barons* is eclectic and interesting, and some of the best material . . . comes from unpublished sources," Foster concludes. "What emerges is on one level a gallery of eccentrics, and on another a series of studies in the tactics of power."

Brendon narrows his focus to a single individual in *Winston Churchill: A Biography.* Because many in-depth studies of the former British Prime Minister have been written, "Brendon has wisely settled for a 'brief life,' which is in effect a brilliant sketch for a portrait," remarks *Times Literary Supplement* contributor C. M. Woodhouse. Despite its brevity, "*Winston Churchill* is nonetheless a brilliant *tour de force,*" asserts Joe Mysak in the *National Review,* "even if it is not quite Winston Churchill. Recounting ninety years at breakneck speed, especially ninety years as densely packed as Churchill's, inevitably produces distortion." The critic explains that while the author "is not seduced by the minutiae of experience, and he is not tedious," nevertheless "he is better at telling what his subject did than what he was like."

London *Times* contributor Woodrow Wyatt, however, claims that "small blemishes apart, a reader who does not want to know too much about Churchill can safely begin here." By using a variety of anecdotes, "Brendon builds a convincing picture of the great man," Woodhouse notes. "His judgment is good and his style succinct. His view of Churchill is entirely without hagiography. . . [exposing] the warts and all." "Most important of all," concludes Mysak, "Mr. Brendon demonstrates that Churchill was one of those relics, those dinosaurs, who fought all his life for duty, honor, and country." That the author "does so within the boundaries he has set for himself, in a Churchillian 'reconnaissance in force,' proves a stylish mastery that the flaws of this book cannot vitiate."

The author's aim in *Ike: His Life and Times,* "as with his previously acclaimed study of Winston Churchill, was to write a succinct and readable biography and this he has achieved admirably," Edward Hamilton observes in the *Spectator.* Brendon's study of former U.S. president Dwight D. Eisenhower "is fluently written, witty and never loses sight of the subject," the critic adds. "If sometimes the judgments are too sweeping, the tone too flippant in the desire for the memorable phrase, all can be forgiven. This is a tour-de-force and should confirm Brendon as one of the best writers of history at work today." *New York Times Book Review* contributor Townsend Hoopes similarly calls *Ike* a "witty [and] perceptive" analysis that is "new and arresting in . . . the author's moral penetration and his concentration on gathering evidence to show Eisenhower's chronic vacillation and remarkably opaque moral standards." While the critic also faults Brendon for the occasional oversimplification, "nevertheless, this is a telling analysis that is bound to have an impact on the current debate over Eisenhower's proper place in history."

"Rich with insight and good humor, taking Eisenhower from boyhood through his two presidential terms," as Guy Halverson describes it in the *Christian Science Monitor,* Brendon's biography "is especially useful . . . [in] demythologiz[ing] the Eisenhower-as-instant-hero viewpoint that has arisen in recent years." Fred Greenstein explains in a *Washington Post Book World* article that "there are two quite separable kinds of Eisenhower revisionism" that have improved the former president's rating over previous assessments. "Brendon has read [this] new scholarship on Eisenhower and delved into the archives," the critic elaborates. "He is familiar with the seeming contradictions" of Eisenhower's presidential career, and his challenges to the new theories "lead him to raise important questions." Greenstein adds that "although Brendon is unable to do full justice to his subject or his own commendable aims, he provides an original account of an historical actor about whom much more remains to be said." "As the author convincingly demonstrates," writes Hamilton, "Eisenhower was a highly complex man whom it was all too easy to take at his own apparent estimation. . . . Brendon calls him 'one of the most enigmatic characters ever to occupy the White House' and admits there will never be a last word on him," the critic concludes. "Meanwhile however, Piers Brendon's book will do just fine."

Brendon once told *CA:* "Were I to fill in this section properly, it would consist of a paean of nihilistic hatred and Swiftian vituperation directed at almost every aspect of public life I can think of, from Mrs. Thatcher to dumping nuclear waste in the seas, from racialism to killing whales, from sports and sportspersons to the drivel excreted by the media. In short, the only optimistic features on my horizon are private ones—family, friends, and work."

BIOGRAPHICAL/CRITICAL SOURCES:

PERIODICALS

Christian Science Monitor, June 24, 1983; October 3, 1986.
National Review, November 2, 1984.
New York Times, April 7, 1983.
New York Times Book Review, April 20, 1980; November 30, 1986.
Observer, January 13, 1991.
Spectator, January 10, 1987.
Times (London), April 5, 1984; November 13, 1986.
Times Literary Supplement, February 18, 1983; April 13, 1984; January 25, 1991.
Washington Post Book World, April 24, 1983; September 7, 1986.

* * *

BRENNER, Barbara (Johnes) 1925-

PERSONAL: Born June 26, 1925, in Brooklyn, NY; daughter of Robert Lawrence (a real estate broker) and Marguerite (Furboter) Johnes; married Fred Brenner (an illustrator), March 16, 1947; children: Mark, Carl. *Ethnicity:* "Russian, German, half-Jewish." *Education:* Attended Seton Hall College (now University), 1942-43, Rutgers University, 1944-46, New York University, 1953-54, and New School for Social Research, 1960-62. *Politics:* Independent. *Avocational interests:* Gardening, swimming, travel, birdwatching.

ADDRESSES: Home—Box 1826, Hemlock Farms, Hawley, PA 18428.

CAREER: Prudential Insurance Co., copywriter, 1942-46; freelance artist's agent, 1946-52; freelance writer, 1957—. Senior editor, Bank Street College of Education, publications division, 1980-90.

MEMBER: Authors Guild, Authors League of America, PEN, Royal Society for the Arts, National Audubon Society.

AWARDS, HONORS: New York Herald Tribune Children's Spring Book Festival honor book award, 1961, for *Barto Takes the Subway; Washington Post Book World* Spring Book Festival honor book award, 1970, and American Library Association notable book citation, both for *A Snake-Lover's Diary;* National Science Teachers Association and Children's Book Council award, 1974, for *Lizard Tails and Cactus Spines,* 1977, for *On the Frontier with Mr. Audubon,* 1979, for *Beware! These Animals Are Poison,* and 1980, for *Have You Heard of a Kangeroo Bird?: Fascinating Facts about Unusual Birds;* American Library Association notable book citation, 1978, for *Wagon Wheels;* Best of the Best Award from *School Library Journal,* 1982, for *On the Frontier with Mr. Audubon.*

WRITINGS:

JUVENILE

Somebody's Slippers, Somebody's Shoes, W. R. Scott, 1957.

Barto Takes the Subway, Knopf (New York City), 1961.

A Bird in the Family (Junior Literary Guild selection), W. R. Scott, 1962.

Amy's Doll, Knopf, 1963.

The Five Pennies, Knopf, 1963.

Our Class Presents Ostrich Feathers: A Play in Two Acts (first produced Off-Broadway, 1965), illustrated by Vera B. Williams, Parents' Magazine Press, 1978.

Beef Stew, Knopf, 1965, reprinted, Random House (New York City), 1990.

The Flying Patchwork Quilt, illustrated by husband Fred Brenner, Knopf, 1965.

Mr. Tall and Mr. Small, W. R. Scott, 1966, reprinted, Holt (New York City), 1994.

Nicky's Sister, Knopf, 1966.

Summer of the Houseboat, Knopf, 1968.

Faces, illustrated with photographs by George Ancona, Dutton (New York City), 1970.

A Snake-Lover's Diary, W. R. Scott, 1970.

A Year in the Life of Rosie Bernard, Harper (New York City), 1971, revised edition, Avon (New York City), 1983.

Is It Bigger Than a Sparrow?: A Box for Young Bird Watchers, Knopf, 1972.

Walt Disney's "Three Little Pigs," Random House, 1972.

Bodies, illustrated with photographs by Ancona, Dutton, 1973.

If You Were an Ant, Harper, 1973.

Walt Disney's "The Penguin That Hated the Cold," Random House, 1973.

Hemi: A Mule, Harper, 1973.

Baltimore Orioles, illustrated by J. Winslow Higginbottom, Harper, 1974.

Cunningham's Rooster, illustrated by Anne Rockwell, Parents Magazine Press (New York City), 1975.

Lizard Tails and Cactus Spines, illustrated with photographs by Merrit S. Keasey III, Harper, 1975.

Little One Inch, illustrated by F. Brenner, Coward, 1977.

On the Frontier with Mr. Audubon, Coward, 1977, reprinted, Boyds Mills, 1998.

We're Off to See the Lizard, illustrated by Shelley Dietreichs, Raintree (Milwaukee, WI), 1977.

Wagon Wheels, illustrated by Don Bolognese, Harper, 1978.

Beware! These Animals Are Poison, illustrated by Jim Spanfeller, Coward, 1979.

(With May Garelick) *The Tremendous Tree Book,* Four Winds Press (New York City), 1979, reprinted, Boyds Mills, 1992.

Have You Ever Heard of a Kangeroo Bird?: Fascinating Facts about Unusual Birds, illustrated by Irene Brady, Coward, 1980.

The Prince and the Pink Blanket, illustrated by Nola Langner, Four Winds Press, 1980.

A Killing Season, Four Winds Press, 1981.
Mystery of the Plumed Serpent, Knopf, 1981.
Mystery of the Disappearing Dogs, Knopf, 1982.
A Dog I Know, Harper, 1983.
The Gorilla Signs Love, Lothrop (New York City), 1984.
The Snow Parade, Crown (New York City), 1984.
Saving the President, Messner (New York City), 1987.
The Falcon Sting, Bradbury (Scarsdale, NY), 1988.
(With Garelick) *Two Orphan Cubs,* Walker (New York City), 1989.
(With William H. Hooks) *Lion and Lamb,* Bantam (New York City), 1989.
Annie's Pet, Bantam, 1989.
The Color Wizard, Bantam, 1989.
(With Hooks) *Lion and Lamb Step Out,* Bantam, 1990.
Moon Boy, Bantam, 1990.
The Magic Box, Bantam, 1990.
Good News, Bantam, 1991.
If You Were There in 1492, Atheneum (New York City), 1991.
(With Hooks) *Ups and Downs with Lion and Lamb,* Bantam, 1991.
Beavers Beware, Bantam, 1991.
Too Many Mice, Bantam, 1992.
Group Soup, Viking (New York City), 1992.
(With Bernice Chardiet) *Where's That Reptile?,* Scholastic (New York City), 1993.
(With Chardiet) *Where's That Insect?,* Scholastic, 1993.
Dinosaurium, Bantam, 1993.
Planetarium, Bantam, 1993.
If You Were There in 1776, Atheneum, 1994.
(With Chardiet) *Where's That Fish?,* Scholastic, 1994.
(Editor) *The Earth Is Painted Green* (poetry anthology), Scholastic, 1994.
The UN Fiftieth Anniversary Book, Atheneum, 1995.
(With Chardiet) *Where's That Cat?,* Scholastic, 1995.
(With Julia Takaya) *Chibi,* Clarion (Boston), 1996.
The Plant That Kept on Growing, Bantam, 1996.
Thinking about Ants, Mondo, 1997.
Lucky Dog, Scholastic, 1997.

OTHER

Careers and Opportunities in Fashion (young adult), Dutton, 1964.
(Editor) Edward Turner and Clive Turner, *Frogs and Toads,* Raintree, 1976.
(Editor) Ralph Whitlock, *Spiders,* Raintree, 1976.
Love and Discipline (adult), Ballantine (New York City), 1983.
Bank Street's Family Guide to Home Computers (adult), Ballantine, 1984.
(With Joanne Oppenheim and Betty Boeghold) *Raising a Confident Child: The Bank Street Year-by-Year Guide,* (adult), Pantheon (New York City), 1984.
(With Oppenheim and Boeghold) *Choosing Books for Kids* (adult), Ballantine, 1986.

Contributor of articles to periodicals. Editor of "Talkabout Program" for Adult Resource Books.

SIDELIGHTS: Barbara Brenner is a respected, award-winning author specializing in works of both juvenile fiction and nonfiction that deal with animals, nature, and ecology. Reviewers praise Brenner for writing interesting and appealing books that are at the same time informative and educational. One example of Brenner's talent is her book on the life of the great ornithologist, John James Audubon. In a review of *On the Frontier with Mr. Audubon,* Paul Showers writes in the *New York Times Book Review* that "Brenner again demonstrates her gift for invention and respect for facts. This is a combination of fiction and fact that works so well it might almost be the thing it imitates." Showers goes on to explain that this book is "written in the polite but colloquial language of the frontier sketching in Audubon's biographical background and recording events of the journey as they might have been observed by a serious, very perceptive 13-year-old."

Barbara Brenner discussed with *CA* some of her thoughts on being a writer: "All the circumstances of my life conspired to make me a writer—just lucky, I guess. I grew up in Brooklyn, which supplied the color, and my mother had died when I was a year old, which supplied the sensitivity. We were poor, which gave me the social outlook and my father was ambitious for me, which developed the intellectual curiosity. Not to carry this any further, here I am, loving what I do and still surrounded by extraordinary stimuli. My husband is an artist, and we work together on books whenever we can. Our sons are both grown; one is a biologist, to whom I owe my interest in reptiles, and the other one is a musician, with whom I share an interest in music which has crept into at least one of my books. The wild animals here in rural Pennsylvania are rich sources of inspiration for my work, and the many historical sites around here have whetted my appetite for writing about American history."

BIOGRAPHICAL/CRITICAL SOURCES:

BOOKS

Something about the Author Autobiography Series, Volume 14, Gale (Detroit), 1992.

PERIODICALS

New York Times Book Review, March 27, 1977.

* * *

BRINTON, Alexander
See BATTIN, B(rinton) W(arner)

* * *

BRISTOW, Allen P. 1929-

PERSONAL: Born July 11, 1929, in Kearney, NE; son of George P. and Mary (Nye) Bristow; married Patricia Ann DeWeber; children: Bradley, Scott, Teresa. *Ethnicity:* "White Anglo Saxon." *Education:* Los Angeles Valley College, A.A., 1952; Los Angeles State College of Applied Arts and Sciences (now California State University, Los Angeles), B.S., 1952; University of Southern California, M.S., 1957. *Avocational interests:* Shooting sports, antique arms collecting, military and western history.

ADDRESSES: Home—P.O. Box 1109, Atascadero, CA 93423.

CAREER: San Fernando Police Department, San Fernando, CA, police officer, 1952-53; Los Angeles County Sheriff's Department, Los Angeles, CA, 1953-59, began as deputy, became sergeant; California State University, Los Angeles, 1959—, began as assistant professor, professor of police science, 1967-83. Parttime or visiting professor at University of Hawaii, University of Southern California, Los Angeles Harbor College, and Orange Coast College. Developer and director of police training institutes, 1960—; consultant to President's Commission on Law Enforcement and Administration of Justice, 1966. *Military service:* U.S. Army, Corps of Military Police, 1950-51; retired as Lieutenant Colonel, California State Military Department, 1996.

MEMBER: Academy of Criminal Justice Sciences (founding member), International Association of Polygraph Examiners (vice president, 1962), Southern California Police Training Officers Association (founding member), California State Peace Officers Association (honorary life member).

WRITINGS:

Police Decision Making, Donner Foundation, University of Southern California, 1957.
Field Interrogation, C. C. Thomas (Springfield, IL), 1958, second edition, 1964.
Analysis of Chart and Graph Tests, Davis Publishing (San Francisco, CA), 1959.
(With E. Carol Gabard) *Decision Making in Police Administration,* C. C. Thomas, 1961.
(With G. Douglas Gourley) *Patrol Administration,* C. C. Thomas, 1961.
Police Film Guide, Police Research Associates, 1962, second edition, 1968.
(Editor) *Readings in Police Supervision,* Los Angeles State College Foundation, 1963.
(With John B. Williams) *Criminal Procedure and the Administration of Justice,* Police Research Associates, 1964, second edition, Glencoe (New York City), 1966.
Effective Police Manpower Utilization, C. C. Thomas, 1969.
(With Willis Roberts) *Introduction to Modern Police Firearms,* Glencoe, 1969.
Police Supervision, C. C. Thomas, 1971.
Police Disaster Operations, C. C. Thomas, 1972.
Search for an Effective Police Handgun, C. C. Thomas, 1973.
You and the Law Enforcement Code of Ethics, Davis Publishing, 1976.
Police Unusual Occurrence Management, Trident Publishers, 1979.
Rural Law Enforcement, Allyn & Bacon (Boston), 1982.
203rd Infantry Battalion: A Military History, privately published, 1991.
History of the California State Guard in San Luis Obispo County, 1942-1945, privately published, 1992.

Contributor of articles to law enforcement and western history publications. Member of board of editors, *Police,* 1961-72.

WORK IN PROGRESS: Ride the Man Down: A Collection of Notable Western Manhunts; The Presley Chronicles (fiction).

SIDELIGHTS: Allen P. Bristow and G. Douglas Gourley's *Patrol Administration* has been published in Spanish and Vietnamese.

* * *

BRITTAIN, Bill
See BRITTAIN, William (E.)

* * *

BRITTAIN, William (E.) 1930-
(Bill Brittain; James Knox, a pseudonym)

PERSONAL: Born December 16, 1930, in Rochester, NY; son of Knox (a medical doctor) and Dorothy (a nurse; maiden name, Sunderlin) Brittain; married Virginia Ann Connorton (a teacher), February 6, 1954; children: James, Susan. *Education:* Attended Colgate University, 1948-50; State Teachers College at Brockport (now New York State University at Brockport), B.S., 1952; Hofstra University, M.S., 1958.

ADDRESSES: Home—17 Wisteria Dr., Asheville, NC 28804.

CAREER: Writer. English teacher in LeRoy, NY, 1952-54; elementary teacher in Lawrence, NY, 1954-60; Lawrence Junior High School, Lawrence, remedial reading teacher, 1960-86.

MEMBER: Mystery Writers of America, Society of Children's Book Writers.

AWARDS, HONORS: Children's Choice citation, International Reading Association/Children's Book Council, 1980, and Charlie May Simon award, 1982, for *All the Money in the World;* Notable Children's Book citation, American Library Association, 1981, for *Devil's Donkey;* Newbery Award honor book citation, 1984, for *The Wish Giver: Three Tales of Coven Tree.*

WRITINGS:

Survival Outdoors, Monarch, 1977.

UNDER NAME BILL BRITTAIN

All the Money in the World, illustrations by Charles Robinson, Harper (New York City), 1979.
Devil's Donkey, illustrations by Andrew Glass, Harper, 1981.
The Wish Giver: Three Tales of Coven Tree, illustrations by Glass, Harper, 1983.
Who Knew There'd Be Ghosts?, Harper, 1985.
Dr. Dredd's Wagon of Wonders, Harper, 1987.
The Fantastic Freshman, Harper, 1988.
My Buddy, the King, Harper, 1989.
Professor Popkin's Prodigious Polish, illustrated by Glass, Harper, 1990.
Wings, Harper, 1991.
The Ghost from beneath the Sea, illustrated by Michele Chessare, Harper, 1992.
Shape Changer, Harper, 1994.
The Wizards and the Monster, illustrated by James Warhola, Harper, 1994.
The Mystery of the Several Sevens, illustrated by Warhola, Harper, 1994.

OTHER

Contributor of stories to *Ellery Queen's Mystery Magazine* and *Alfred Hitchcock's Mystery Magazine,* sometimes under pseudonym James Knox.

WORK IN PROGRESS: Controller, for Harper.

SIDELIGHTS: William Brittain told *CA:* "Retirement, after thirty-six years of teaching, has provided a lot more time for my writing. I still, however, regard this writing as a hobby which I enjoy very much. Any 'teaching' in my stories is purely in the eye of the beholder. I'm quite content to produce a tale that's interesting and exciting, both to me and to the boys and girls who read my books. I'm extremely grateful to all the established authors who were so helpful when, as a teacher, I was doing my best to make it as a part-time writer. Chief among those offering assistance was Frederic Dannay, editor of *Ellery Queen's Mystery Magazine,* whose help and encouragement were invaluable. I'm also blessed with a wife who has the patience of Job, coupled with razor-sharp critical faculties. Without her, it's doubtful that any of my books would have been completed."

* * *

BROGAN, Jacque Vaught
See BROGAN, Jacqueline Vaught

* * *

BROGAN, Jacqueline Vaught 1952-
(Jacque Vaught Brogan)

PERSONAL: Born July 23, 1952, in Odessa, TX; daughter of N. R. (a professor) and M. I. (a professor; maiden name, Alcorn) Vaught; married T. V. F. Brogan (a professor), June 28, 1981; children: Jessica Leigh, Evan Lloyd. *Education:* Southern Methodist University, B.A. (magna cum laude), 1974, M.A., 1975; attended Tufts University, 1976; University of Texas at Austin, Ph.D., 1982.

ADDRESSES: *Office*—Department of English, University of Notre Dame, Notre Dame, IN 46556.

CAREER: Midland College, Midland, TX, and Odessa College, Odessa, TX, instructor in world literature, 1977; University of Texas at Austin, assistant instructor in English, 1977-82; University of Hawaii at Manoa, Honolulu, assistant professor of English, 1983-86; University of Notre Dame, Notre Dame, IN, assistant professor, 1986-89, associate professor, 1989-93, professor of English, 1993—. Visiting professor, Lancaster University (England), 1994.

MEMBER: International Association of Philosophy and Literature, American Literature Associate, Elizabeth Bishop Society, Hemingway Society, Modern Language Association of America, Wallace Stevens Society, Phi Beta Kappa, Phi Kappa Phi.

WRITINGS:

Stevens and Simile: A Theory of Language, Princeton University Press (Princeton, NJ), 1986.

Part of the Climate: An Anthology of American Cubist Poetry, University of California Press (Santa Cruz), 1991.

(Editor) *Women Poets of the Americas,* University of Notre Dame Press (Notre Dame, IN), 1996.

Contributor of articles, poems (under name Jacque Vaught Brogan), and reviews to magazines, including *American Literature, American Poetry, Bamboo Ridge, Diacritics, Formalist, Hemingway Review, HOW(ever), Kalliope, Man and World, Trinity Review, Wallace Stevens Journal, Women's Studies;* guest editor of *Wallace Stevens Journal* (special issue on Stevens and structures of sound), Volume 15, Number 2, 1991, and (special issue on Stevens and Bishop), Volume 19, Number 2, 1995.

WORK IN PROGRESS: *War, Words, and Women: The Critical Stages of Wallace Stevens' Poetry* and *Notes from the Body* (collection of poetry).

SIDELIGHTS: Jacqueline Vaught Brogan once told *CA:* "Despite the rather abstract nature of my book on Stevens, what prompted my work on Stevens and simile was actually quite *personal:* the question of what I was doing to myself and how I was naming myself and the world in writing my own poetry. I was especially perplexed by what seemed to be the power of language to make personal problems disappear and, conversely, the power of language to make things appear by naming them. I began to take classes in the philosophy of language as a sidelight to my work as an English graduate student.

"My poetry is probably most colored by growing up in the west Texas desert—a place full, as it were, of vast empty spaces, a constant wind, and mental freedom. Living for three years in Hawaii, a place as different from west Texas culturally as geographically, changed my writing completely. My most recent work is much less private or confessional than my earlier work. It has become increasingly experimental (including 'experiment' with traditional forms) and increasingly political."

* * *

BROUGHTON, James (Richard) 1913-

PERSONAL: Born November 10, 1913, in Modesto, CA; son of Irwin (a banker) and Olga

(Jungbluth) Broughton; married Suzanna Hart (an artist), December 6, 1962 (divorced, 1978); children: Serena, Orion. *Education:* Stanford University, B.A., 1936; advanced study, New School for Social Research, 1943-45.

ADDRESSES: *Office*—P.O. Box 1330, Port Townsend, WA 98368.

CAREER: Poet, playwright, filmmaker. Was involved with Art in Cinema experimental film group at the San Francisco Museum in late 1940s, and with San Francisco Renaissance poetry movement in late 1950s and early 1960s; resident playwright with Playhouse Repertory Theatre in San Francisco, 1958-64; lecturer in creative arts, San Francisco State University, 1964-76, and instructor in film, San Francisco Art Institute, 1968-82. Has given public readings of his poetry. Member of board of directors, Farallone Films, 1948—, and Anthology Film Archives, 1969—.

AWARDS, HONORS: Alden Award, 1945, for play *Summer Fury;* James D. Phelan Award in Literature, 1948, for play *The Playground,* and 1987, for creative cinema; Avon Foundation grant-in-aid, 1968; Eugene O'Neill Theatre Foundation playwright fellow, 1969; Guggenheim fellowships, 1970-71 and 1973-74; National Endowment for the Arts grant, 1976 and 1982; Citation of Honor, City of San Francisco, 1983, for contributions to the arts; Doctor of Fine Arts degree, San Francisco Art Institute, 1984; Edinburgh Film Festival Award of Merit, 1953; Cannes Film Festival Prix du fantaisie poetique, 1954, for *The Pleasure Garden;* Oberhausen Film Festival Hauptpreis der Kurzfilmtage, 1968, for *The Bed;* Bellevue Film Festival grand prize, 1970, for *The Golden Positions;* Twelfth Independent Film Award from *Film Culture* magazine, 1975, for "outstanding work of thirty years" as "grand classic master of independent cinema"; Maya Deren award, American Film Institute, 1989, for lifetime achievement; Lifetime Achievement in Poetry Award from National Poetry Association, 1992.

WRITINGS:

POETRY

Songs for Certain Children, Adrian Wilson, 1947.
The Playground (also see below), Centaur Press, 1949.
The Ballad of Mad Jenny, Centaur Press, 1949.
Musical Chairs: A Songbook for Anxious Children, Centaur Press, 1950.
An Almanac for Amorists, Collection Merlin (Paris), 1954, Grove Press (New York City), 1954.
True and False Unicorn, Grove Press, 1957.
The Water Circle: A Poem of Celebration, Pterodactyl Press, 1965.
Tidings, Pterodactyl Press, 1966.
Look In, Look Out, Toad Press, 1968.
High Kukus (also see below), Jargon Society (East Haven, CT), 1968.
A Long Undressing: Collected Poems, 1949-1969, Jargon Society, 1971.
Going through Customs, Arion Press (San Francisco, CA), 1976.
Erogeny (also see below), ManRoot Press, 1976.
Odes for Odd Occasions, ManRoot Press, 1977.
Song of the Godbody (also see below), ManRoot Press, 1979.
Hymns to Hermes, ManRoot Press, 1979.
Shaman Psalm (also see below), Syzygy Press (Mill Valley, CA), 1981.
Graffiti for the Johns of Heaven, Syzygy Press, 1982.
Ecstasies, Syzygy Press, 1983.
Atteindre l'inevitable, Nadir Press (France), 1985.
A to Z, Syzygy Press, 1986.
Vrai et Fausse Licorne, Editions Aeolian (France), 1987.
Hooplas, Pennywhistle Press, 1988.
75 Life Lines, Jargon Society, 1988.
The Last Sermon of Gnarley Never, Syzygy Press, 1989.
Special Deliveries, Broken Moon (Tacoma, WA), 1990.
Little Sermons of the Big Joy, Insight to Riot Press, 1994.
Little Prayers to Big Joy's Mother, Syzygy Press, 1995.
Collected Poems, Black Sparrow (Santa Barbara, CA), 1997.

PLAYS

A Love for Lionel, first produced in New York, NY at Actors Stage, 1944.
Summer Fury (one-act; first produced in Palo Alto, CA, at Stanford University, 1945), published in *Best One Act Plays of 1945,* edited by Margaret Mayorga, Dodd (New York City), 1946, reprinted as *Best Short Plays,* 1957.

The Playground (first produced in Oakland, CA, at Mills College, 1948), Centaur Press, 1949, reprinted, Baker's Plays, 1965.

Burning Questions (four-act), first produced in San Francisco, CA, at Playhouse Repertory Theatre, 1958.

The Last Word (one-act; first produced in San Francisco at Playhouse Repertory Theatre, 1958; also see below), Baker, 1958.

Where Helen Lies (first produced in New York at American Theatre Wing, 1959), University of Colorado Press, 1961.

The Rites of Women (two-act), first produced in San Francisco at Playhouse Repertory Theatre, 1959.

How Pleasant It Is to Have Money, first produced in San Francisco at Playhouse Repertory Theatre, 1964.

Bedlam; or, America the Beautiful Mother (one-act), first produced at San Francisco State College, 1967; produced in Waterford, CT, by Eugene O'Neill Theatre Foundation, 1969.

Also author of *Eggs of the Ostrich,* adapted from the French of Andre Roussin, 1956.

FILMS

(With Sydney Peterson) *The Potted Psalm,* Farallone Films, 1946.

Mother's Day, Farallone Films, 1950.

Adventures of Jimmy, Farallone Films, 1951.

Four in the Afternoon, Farallone Films, 1951.

Loony Tom and Happy Lover, Farallone Films, 1951.

The Pleasure Garden, Flights of Fancy Committee for Farallone Films, 1953.

The Bed, Farallone Films, 1968.

Nuptiae, Farallone FIlms, 1969.

The Golden Positions, Farallone Films, 1970.

This Is It, Farallone Films, 1971.

Dreamwood, Farallone Films, 1972.

High Kukus (with poems from *High Kukus*) Farallone Films, 1973.

Testament, Farallone Films, 1974.

The Water Circle, Farallone Films, 1975.

Erogeny, Farallone Films, 1976.

(With Joel Singer) *Together,* Farallone Films, 1976.

(With Singer) *Windowmobile,* Farallone Films, 1977.

(With Singer) *Song of the Godbody* (with poems from *Song of the Godbody*), Farallone Films, 1978.

Hermes Bird, Farallone Films, 1979.

(With Singer) *The Gardener of Eden,* Farallone Films, 1981.

(With Singer) *Shaman Psalm* (with poems from *Shaman Psalm*), Farallone Films, 1982.

(With Singer) *Devotion,* Farallone Films, 1983.

(With Singer) *Scattered Remains,* Farallone Films, 1988.

OTHER

The Right Playmate, Farrar, Straus (New York City), 1952, revised edition, Pterodactyl Press, 1964.

San Francisco Poets (sound recording), Evergreen Records, 1958.

The Bard & the Harper (sound recording), MEA Records, 1965.

Something Just for You, Pisani Press, 1966.

The Androgyne Journal (autobiographical), Scrimshaw Press, 1977, revised edition, Broken Moon, 1991.

Seeing the Light, City Lights Books (San Francisco, CA), 1977.

(Editor) *Whitman's Wild Children* (anthology), Lapis Press, 1988.

(Editor) *Gay and Lesbian Poetry in Our Time* (anthology), St. Martin's Press (New York City), 1988.

The Broughton Songs (compact disc), Syzygy Records, 1995.

Films and poems also recorded on video and audio cassettes. Contributor to more than a dozen anthologies, including *Sparks of Fire,* edited by James Bogan, 1982, and *Practicing Angels,* 1986. Contributor of articles to *Theatre Arts, Sight and Sound* (London), *Film Culture, Film Quarterly,* and *Filmagazine;* frequent contributor to *Canyon Cinemanews.* Broughton's manuscripts, papers and memorabilia are housed in the special collections section of the Kent State University Library, Kent, Ohio.

ADAPTATIONS: An opera based on the play *The Last Word* was composed by Craig Carnahan of Minneapolis, MN.

SIDELIGHTS: Since 1948 James Broughton has made his international reputation as a poet, playwright, and "'guru' of the independent film subculture in the United States," notes Janis Crystal Lipzin in the *Antioch Review. Dictionary of Literary Biography* contributor Idris McElveen relates that Broughton describes himself as "a visionary and a parodist" who is "happy among the Transcendentalists." His poetry expresses Zen philosophy and celebrates the ecstasies of life, particularly eroticism. In both poetry and film, he uses the possibilities of the art forms to their full extent, often extending the recognized boundaries of technique. In both genres, "he insists . . . that both the original impulse and the product of his work be natural, spontaneous leaps of his own imagination, without artifice, without novelty for the sake of novelty, and without masks," reports McElveen. Nudity—emotional and physical—characterizes his works. Thus he fulfills his role as a poet, which to him means "being obstreperous, outlandish and obscene. [The poet's] business is to ignite a revolution of insight in the soul," he says in *Seeing the Light.*

The Modesto-born, third-generation Californian says in "Testament" that he received a vision of his destiny early in life: "When I was three years old I was wakened in the night by a glittering stranger, who told me I was a poet and never to fear being alone or being laughed at. That was my first meeting with my angel, who is the most interesting poet I have ever met." Sent to military school at age ten, Broughton developed a love for language and soon began to write imitations of the poems in the *Oxford Book of English Verse.* After earning a B.A. from Stanford in 1936, Broughton joined the merchant marines and visited the Near East. He then returned to New York and two years of study at the New School for Social Research, then home to San Francisco, where he learned poetry reading from Robert Duncan and Madeline Gleason. His initiation to filmmaking came in 1946 when Sydney Peterson suggested they abandon the play they were writing together to make a film instead. The result was *The Potted Psalm,* "a rather crazy thing" exploring camera techniques on location in an abandoned graveyard, Broughton explained in *Film Culture.* The film, which he later referred to as "an energetic surrealist lark," was completed in time to be part of the Art in Cinema movement in San Francisco, which helped its makers to become known as pioneers in the art world.

The originality of his works, in which he expresses an essentially comic and erotic vision of life, verifies Broughton's often-stated independence from social and aesthetic norms. His first independent offering, *Mother's Day,* "was not meant to please anyone but myself," he says in *Seeing the Light.* "It was done out of absolute necessity, to discover what my inner haunting looked like. I accepted it as my first and last chance, a one and only shot: I risked everything. All work should be approached that way. Still today every film I make is my 'last.'" To critics who see in *Mother's Day* the influence of earlier avant garde films, Broughton says, "That sort of thing is only a critic's means of putting one in one's place (or someplace where he can file you away) so that originality can be discounted." Because "it linked a specifically American way of seeing to the French avant-garde tradition," Broughton reports in *Film Culture, Mother's Day* has been the subject of detailed study in France and has had an important shaping influence on the American avant garde.

Broughton's next major work was *The Pleasure Garden,* made in London at the request of the director of the British Film Institute. "That film was a bit ahead of its time, being maybe the first Love-In in a public park," Broughton told *Film Culture.* He added that at first it was most popular among Europeans, who viewed it as "a satire on the English." It won the Edinburgh Festival award in 1953 and the Cannes Festival award the following year. The making of the film plunged him deeply into debt, and when he returned to San Francisco he rejoined the flourishing poetry scene, not intending to make another film. Eventually, however, he was to produce another prizewinner, *The Bed,* a tribute to the piece of furniture so closely linked to birth, death, and all the major events of human life. He explains in *Seeing the Light,* "I had not made a film for 13 years and I was prodded into making 'just one more' by Jaques Ledoux of the Belgian Film Archive for his international experimental powwow of 1968. All I did was express how life felt to me in my 50s. . . . I wanted to show as directly as possible my vision of the flowing river of existence and I thought of it as a private communication to an old friend in Brussels. The public success of the film astounded me." His enthusiasm for making films thus renewed, he continued making films, including *The Golden Positions,* which won the Bellevue Film Festival grand prize in 1970.

Broughton has shared his enthusiasm with students at the San Francisco Playhouse, San Francisco State College Poetry Center, San Francisco State University, and the San Francisco Art Institute.

He has also worked at film institutes in Denmark and England. His lifetime achievement was recognized in 1975, when he received the 12th annual Independent Film Award from *Film Culture* magazine for thirty years of "outstanding work" as "the grand classic master of independent cinema." About success, he advises in a *Film Culture* essay, "One asks merely for a little magic. If the magician's act turns out to be Great Art, that part of it will not be his concern."

Broughton told *CA:* "In whatever I do—writing, filming, lecturing—I am first and always a poet, trying to live poetically. Because that is the only way I can feel well. And a poet is in the service of something greater than his published works or his public reputation. Poetry is an act of love, it asks no rewards. Therefore all my work is celebrational and passionate, my hobby is the care and feeding of ecstasy, and my goal in life is to attain my own inevitability.

"I write and have always written because I am a born poet. I am not in good health if my heart is not singing. I never took any writing course in my life. I was always intoxicated by the riches of the English language. Inspiration is a grace from above, a gift from one's angels."

BIOGRAPHICAL/CRITICAL SOURCES:

BOOKS

Broughton, James, *A Long Undressing: Collected Poems, 1949-1969,* Jargon Society, 1971.
Broughton, *Seeing the Light,* City Lights Books, 1977.
Broughton, *The Androgyne Journal* (autobiographical), Scrimshaw Press, 1977, revised edition, Broken Moon, 1991.
Contemporary Authors Autobiography Series, Volume 12, Gale (Detroit), 1992.
Curtis, David, *Experimental Cinema,* Universe Books (New York City), 1971.
Dictionary of Literary Biography, Volume 5: *American Poets since World War II,* Gale, 1980.
Sitney, P. Adams, *Visionary Film,* Oxford University Press (Oxford, England), 1974.

PERIODICALS

Antioch Review, summer, 1978.
Cahiers du Cinema (Paris), number 10, 1952.
Canyon Cinemanews, September/October, 1974; January/February, 1975; July/August, 1975; November/December, 1975; September/October, 1976; November/December, 1976.
Cinema News, November/December, 1977; September/October, 1978; number 3, 1980; number 6, 1980-81.
Credences, March, 1978.
Ekran, Volume 8, number 5/6, 1983.
Evergreen Review, Volume 1, number 2, 1957.
Film Comment, summer, 1964.
Film Culture, summer, 1963; Number 61, 1975-76.
Film Quarterly, spring, 1960; summer, 1968; Volume 29, number 4, 1976; summer, 1978.
Film & Filmmakers, November, 1954.
Lamp, Volume 74, 1984.
Los Angeles Free Press, March 15, 1968.
Millennium, winter, 1977/78.
New Leader, December 13, 1971.
Poetry, March, 1951; December, 1967.
Saturday Review, October 13, 1951.
Sight and Sound (London), January/March, 1952; January/March, 1954.
Small Press Review, August, 1980.
Spiral, October, 1986.
Take One (Montreal), July, 1972.
Theatre Arts, August, 1946.
University Film Studies, Volume 8, number 1, 1977.
Village Voice, July 9, 1979.

OTHER

Testament (film autobiography), Farallone Films, 1974.

* * *

BYARS, Betsy (Cromer) 1928-

PERSONAL: Born August 7, 1928, in Charlotte, NC; daughter of George Guy and Nan (Rugheimer) Cromer; married Edward Ford Byars (a professor of engineering and writer), June 24, 1950; children: Laurie, Betsy Ann, Nan, Guy. *Education:* Attended Furman University, 1946-48; Queens College, B.A., 1950. *Avocational interests:* Flying (licensed pilot).

ADDRESSES: Home—126 Riverpoint, Clemson, SC 29631.

CAREER: Writer.

AWARDS, HONORS: America's Book of the Year selection, Child Study Association, 1968, for *The Midnight Fox,* 1969, for *Trouble River,* 1970, for *The Summer of the Swans,* 1972, for *The House of Wings,* 1973, for *The Winged Colt of Casa Mia* and *The 18th Emergency,* 1974, for *After the Goat Man,* 1975, for *The Lace Snail,* 1976, for *The TV Kid,* and 1980, for *The Night Swimmers;* Notable Book Award, American Library Association, 1969, for *Trouble River,* 1970, for *The Summer of the Swans,* 1972, for *The House of Wings,* 1977, for *The Pinballs,* and 1996, for *My Brother Ant;* Lewis Carroll Shelf Award, 1970, for *The Midnight Fox;* John Newbery Medal, American Library Association, 1971, for *The Summer of the Swans;* Best Books for Spring selection, *School Library Journal,* 1971, for *Go and Hush the Baby;* Booklist, *Library Journal,* 1972, and National Book Award finalist, 1973, both for *House of Wings; New York Times* Outstanding Book of the Year, 1973, for *The Winged Colt of Casa Mia* and *The 18th Emergency,* 1979, for *Good-bye Chicken Little,* and 1982, for *The Two-Thousand Pound Goldfish;* Dorothy Canfield Fisher Memorial Book Award, Vermont Congress of Parents and Teachers, 1975, for *The 18th Emergency.*

Woodward Park School Annual Book Award, 1977; Children's Book Award, Child Study Children's Book Committee at Bank Street College of Education, 1977; Hans Christian Andersen Honor List for Promoting Concern for the Disadvantaged and Handicapped, 1979; Georgia Children's Book Award, 1979; Charlie May Simon Book Award, Arkansas Elementary School Council, 1980 and 1987; Surrey School Book of the Year Award, School Librarians of Surrey, British Colombia, 1980; Mark Twain Award, Missouri Library Association, 1980, William Allen White Children's Book Award, Emporia State University, 1980, Young Readers Medal, California Reading Association, 1980, Nene Award runner up, 1981 and 1983, and Golden Archer Award, Department of Library Science, University of Wisconsin—Oshkosh, 1982, all for *The Pinballs;* Best Book of the Year, *School Library Journal,* 1980, and American Book Award for Children's Fiction, 1981, both for *The Night Swimmers;* Children's Choice, International Reading Association, 1982, Tennessee Children's Choice Book Award, Tennessee Library Association, 1983, and Sequoyah Children's Book Award, 1984, all for *The Cybil War;* Parent's Choice Award for Literature, Parent's Choice Foundation, 1982, Best Children's Books, *School Library Journal,* 1982, CRABbery Award, Oxon Hill Branch of Prince George's County Library, 1983, Mark Twain Award, 1985, all for *The Animal, the Vegetable, and John D. Jones;* Notable Book of the Year award, *New York Times,* 1982, for *The Two-Thousand Pound Goldfish;* Regina Medal, Catholic Library Association, 1987; Charlie May Simon Award, 1987, for *The Computer Nut;* South Carolina Children's Book Award, William Allen White Award, and Maryland Children's Book Award, all 1988, all for *Cracker Jackson;* Edgar Alan Poe Award, Mystery Writers of America, 1992, for *Wanted . . . Mud Blossom.*

WRITINGS:

FOR CHILDREN

Clementine (illustrated by Charles Wilton), Houghton (New York City), 1962.

The Dancing Camel (illustrated by Harold Berson), Viking (New York City), 1965.

Rama, the Gypsy Cat (illustrated by Peggy Bacon), Viking, 1966.

The Groober (self-illustrated), Harper (New York City), 1967.

The Midnight Fox (illustrated by Ann Grifalconi), Viking, 1968.

Trouble River (illustrated by Rocco Negri), Viking, 1969.

The Summer of the Swans (illustrated by Ted CoConis), Viking, 1970.

Go and Hush the Baby (illustrated by Emily A. McCully), Viking, 1971.

The House of Wings (illustrated by Daniel Schwartz), Viking, 1972.

The 18th Emergency (illustrated by Robert Grossman), Viking, 1973.

The Winged Colt of Casa Mia (illustrated by Richard Cuffari), Viking, 1973.

After the Goat Man (illustrated by Ronald Himler), Viking, 1974.

The Lace Snail (self-illustrated), Viking, 1975.

The TV Kid (illustrated by Cuffari), Viking, 1976.

The Pinballs, Harper, 1977.

The Cartoonist (illustrated by Cuffari), Viking, 1978.

Good-bye Chicken Little, Harper, 1979.

The Night Swimmers (illustrated by Troy Howell), Delacorte (New York City), 1980, reprinted, Cornerstone Books (Santa Barbara, CA), 1990.
The Cybil War (illustrated by Gail Owens), Viking, 1981.
The Animal, the Vegetable, and John D. Jones (illustrated by Ruth Sanderson), Delacorte, 1982.
The Two-Thousand Pound Goldfish, Harper, 1982.
The Glory Girl, Viking, 1983.
The Computer Nut (illustrated with computer graphics by son Guy Byars), Viking, 1984.
Cracker Jackson, Viking, 1985.
The Not-Just-Anybody Family (illustrated by Jacqueline Rogers), Delacorte, 1986.
The Golly Sisters Go West (illustrated by Sue Truesdale), Harper, 1986.
The Blossoms Meet the Vulture Lady (illustrated by Rogers), Delacorte, 1986.
The Blossoms and the Green Phantom (illustrated by Rogers), Delacorte, 1987.
A Blossom Promise (illustrated by Rogers), Delacorte, 1987.
Beans on the Roof (illustrated by Melodye Rosales), Delacorte, 1988.
The Burning Question of Bingo Brown (illustrated by Cathy Bobak), Viking, 1988.
Bingo Brown and the Language of Love (illustrated by Bobak), Viking, 1988.
Hooray for the Golly Sisters (illustrated by Truesdale), Harper, 1990.
Bingo Brown, Gypsy Lover, Viking, 1990.
The Seven Treasure Hunts, Harper, 1991.
Wanted . . . Mud Blossom, Delacorte, 1991.
Bingo Brown's Guide to Romance, Viking, 1992.
Coast to Coast, Delacorte, 1992.
McMummy, Viking, 1993.
The Golly Sisters Ride Again (illustrated by Truesdale), HarperCollins (New York City), 1994.
The Dark Stairs: A Herculeah Jones Mystery, Viking, 1994.
(Compiler) *Growing Up Stories,* Kingfisher (New York City), 1995.
Tarot Says Beware, Viking, 1995.
My Brother, Ant (illustrated by Marc Simont), Viking, 1996.
The Joy Boys (illustrated by Frank Remkiewicz), Yearling First Choice Chapter Book (New York City), 1996.
Tornado (illustrated by Doron Ben-Ami), HarperCollins, 1996.
Dead Letter, Viking, 1996.
Ant Plays Bear (illustrated by Simont), Viking, 1997.
Death's Door, Viking, 1997.

OTHER

(Author of afterword) Margaret Sidney, *The Five Little Peppers and How They Grew,* Dell (New York City), 1985.
(Author of preface) Margaret M. Kimmel, *For Reading Out Loud,* Dell, 1987.
The Moon and I (autobiography), J. Messner (New York City), 1991, reprinted, Beech Tree Books (New York City), 1996.

Contributor of articles to numerous magazines, including *Saturday Evening Post, TV Guide,* and *Look.*

Byars's works have been translated into nine languages.

ADAPTATIONS: The following books have been adapted for ABC-TV and broadcast as episodes of the *ABC Afterschool Special: The 18th Emergency,* broadcast as "Psst! Hammerman's After You," 1973, *The Summer of the Swans,* broadcast as "Sara's Summer of the Swans," 1974, *The Pinballs,* 1977, and *The Night Swimmers,* broadcast as "Daddy, I'm Their Mamma Now," 1981; *Trouble River,* 1975, and *The Winged Colt of Casa Mia* (adapted as "The Winged Colt"), 1976, were broadcast as *Saturday Morning Specials,* ABC-TV; *The Lace Snail* was adapted as a filmstrip and cassette by Viking; *The Midnight Fox, The Summer of the Swans, Go and Hush the Baby,* and *The TV Kid* were adapted as record/audio cassette recordings by Miller-Brody.

SIDELIGHTS: Over the course of her long and productive career, Betsy Byars has received extensive critical praise for her insightful portrayals of adolescents suffering from feelings of isolation and loneliness. "In a succession of psychologically-sound stories," wrote a *New York Times Book Review* critic, "she has developed her theme: that the extreme inward pain of adolescence lessens as a person reaches outward." Byars has produced books for children of several different ages, including chapter books for beginning readers and novels aimed at an early adolescent audience. Though her works are intended for children, Byars does not shy away from controversial subjects. Mental retardation, teenage sexuality, and physical abuse are among the volatile topics considered in Byars's work, and her skillful handling of the material has helped convince critics that such issues can be effectively portrayed in juvenile literature.

Raised in North Carolina, Byars entered college as a math major but soon found English more to her liking. After marrying and starting a family, she turned to writing. She got her start by penning magazine articles, but eventually devoted her talents to children's literature. Her first published book, *Clementine,* appeared in 1962, but the negative reviews it received caused Byars to turn away from the personal material she had included in the book. "I went back to writing books that anyone could have written," Byars related in an interview for *Children's Literature in Education,* "like *Rama the Gypsy Cat*—very impersonal." Though she continued to publish regularly throughout the 1960s, it was not until she wrote *The Midnight Fox* that Byars again returned to events from her own life as a source of her fiction.

The Summer of the Swans, Byars's next effort, was drawn from the author's work with mentally retarded children. *The Summer of the Swans* tells the story of Sara, an awkward adolescent who struggles both with doubts about herself, and with the mixed feelings she has for her mentally-impaired brother, Charlie. When Charlie wanders away from the house and becomes lost in a forest, Sara understands how valuable her brother is to her. In the end, Sara locates Charlie, and in the process, gains a new and positive sense of herself.

In a *Horn Book* review of *Summer of the Swans,* Ethel L. Haines stated: "Seldom are the pain of adolescence and the tragedy of mental retardation presented as sensitively and unpretentiously as in the story of Sara and Charlie." A *Top of the News* reviewer also lauded the book: "Betsy Byars, a sensitive writer with an ear and heart attuned to the subtleties of growing up, has created a story of extraordinary understanding and warmth." Barbara H. Baskin and Karen H. Harris, writing in *Notes from a Different Drummer: A Guide to Juvenile Fiction Portraying the Handicapped,* attributed the book's strengths, in part, to the way in which Byars handled the sentimental aspects of the story. "The descriptions of behavior are both tender and accurate," the authors wrote. "[Byars] can describe scenes revealing limitations in ways that reflect reality and avoid maudlin pity."

Byars's ability to avoid an overly sentimental treatment of her subjects has been praised frequently by reviewers of her work. Another factor contributing to the author's critical success is her appealing use of comedy. In *Children and Books,* Zena Sutherland, Dianne L. Monson, and May Hill Arbuthnot wrote that Byars's writing exhibits a "quiet, understated sense of humor that children quickly recognize and enjoy." *Times Literary Supplement* reviewer Diane Moss seconded this opinion, pointing out Byars's use of funny situations to soften her books' serious messages. "There are many ways in which the author can distance the agonies children endure," Moss wrote. "Humor is Betsy Byars's chosen path."

An example of this process comes from a more recent Byars work, *Cracker Jackson.* In the course of the book, eleven year old Jackson discovers that his former baby sitter, Alma, is being physically abused by her husband. When the abuse spreads to Alma's baby, Jackson and a friend take action. Their attempt to drive Alma to a shelter for battered women is related as a humorous adventure, and the comedy of Jackson's day-to-day mischief is also woven throughout the story.

A *Horn Book* reviewer noted that this combination "would be an audacious undertaking in the hands of a less-skilled storyteller," but found Byars's effort to be an "expert blend of humor and compassion." Patricia Craig, writing in the *Times Literary Supplement,* found the book's subject "grim indeed; yet the atmosphere in which the events of the story are located is full of bounce." In addition to Byars's use of humor, Craig also credited the author's skill at "keeping the reprehensible actions of one of her characters very much in the background." *New York Times Book Review* contributor Mary Louise Cuneo also cited Byars's ability to "write low-key humor deftly," but registered a minor complaint about the characterization of Goat, Jackson's friend. "Goat regularly acts so much like a standard free spirit," Cuneo wrote, "that a reader could tire or disbelieve him."

Such criticism of Byars's characterization is rare. Her books have often been hailed for containing vivid characters that appeal to young readers. Critic Jane Langton of the *New York Times Book Review* wrote that "there is something uncanny about the way that Betsy Byars transcends the book in your hand and gives you living, feeling people instead." Jean Fritz, also writing in the *New York Times Book Review,* noted that Byars "has always had the capacity to create unique and believable characters." This ability is ably demonstrated in her series of novels featuring the Blossom family. Junior Blossom has a knack for unsuccessful inventions such as his subterranean hamster resort. Junior's sister, Maggie, wants to be a trick horseback rider like her mother and deceased father, and Vicki, the mother, occasionally leaves her children to rejoin the professional rodeo circuit. The family's acquaintances are also unusual, including Ralphie, a boy with an artificial leg, and Mad Mary, who lives in a cave and makes her dinner from the dead animals that she finds on the road.

In her review of *A Blossom Promise, Los Angeles Times Book Review* contributor Kristiana Gregory wrote that Byars's "perception of kids' feelings is keen." She also praised the author for creating a "cast so memorably quirky that you hate to say good-bye." Elizabeth-Ann Sachs's review of *Wanted . . . Mud Blossom* in the *New York Times Book Review* sounded a cautionary note regarding the bizarre characters. "The adults are atypical," Sachs wrote, "more flawed than it is comfortable to think about—indeed somewhat alarming in their eccentricity." Despite this reservation, Sachs found that "Ms. Byars's dialogue rings true. She captures the whining and the teasing and the playfulness of children."

The Blossom series also demonstrates Byars's attempt to create a detailed view of her protagonists by devoting several books to their adventures. She has applied this approach to other characters as well, including Bingo Brown. In the first installment of this series, *The Burning Questions of Bingo Brown,* the title character grapples with uncertainty by writing down his questions about various adolescent concerns. Many of Bingo's questions deal with the three girls he has fallen in love with simultaneously. There are also questions regarding Bingo's English teacher, Mr. Markham, who has begun to give the class strange lectures on suicide and the woman that he loves. When Mr. Markham is involved in a motorcycle crash, Bingo wonders if the teacher was attempting to take his own life.

Ellen Fader, reviewing the book in *School Library Journal,* called *The Burning Questions of Bingo Brown* a "humorous and poignant novel," but also warned readers about the book's consideration of suicide. "Byars's light handling of a serious subject may disturb some adults," the critic wrote. Despite this reservation, Fader ultimately judged the book a success: "Accurate characterization developed through believable dialogue and fresh language, give this tremendous child appeal and read-aloud potential." A *Publishers Weekly* reviewer also praised the book. "Byars relays Bingo's questions and his answers in a way that is so believable," the critic wrote, "that readers may wonder if there isn't a Bingo Brown in their classrooms."

Over the course of her career Betsy Byars has gained a great respect for her young readers. "Boys and girls are very sharp today," Byars told Rachel Fordyce in an interview for *Twentieth-Century Children's Writers.* "When I visit classrooms and talk with students I am always impressed to find how many of them are writing stories and how knowledgeable they are about writing." Her personal contact with children has also affected the way she shapes her stories. "Living with my own teenagers has taught me that not only must I not write down to my readers," Byars said, "I must write up to them."

BIOGRAPHICAL/CRITICAL SOURCES:

BOOKS

Baskin, Barbara H., and Karen H. Harris, *Notes from a Different Drummer: A Guide to Juvenile Fiction Portraying the Handicapped,* Bowker (New York City), 1977.

Children's Literature Review, Volume I, Gale (Detroit, MI), 1976.

Contemporary Literary Criticism, Volume 32, Gale, 1985.

Fordyce, Rachel, "Betsy Byars," *Twentieth-Century Children's Writers,* edited by D. L. Kirkpatrick, St. Martin's (New York City), 1978.

Rees, David, *Painted Desert, Green Shade: Essays on Contemporary Writers of Fiction for Children and Young Adults,* Horn Book (Boston, MA), 1984.

Something about the Author Autobiography Series, Volume One, Gale, 1986.

Sutherland, Zena, Dianne L. Monson, and May Hill Arbuthnot, editors, *Children and Books,* sixth edition, Scott Foresman (New York City), 1981.

Usrey, Malcolm, *Betsy Byars,* Twayne (New York City), 1995.

PERIODICALS

Book Week, October 10, 1965.

Bulletin of the Center for Children's Books, November, 1972; September, 1973; March, 1974; March, 1975; September, 1976; April, 1977.

Children's Book Review, September, 1973; April, 1979.

Children's Literature in Education, winter, 1982.

Christian Science Monitor, November 4, 1965; May 7, 1970; October 3, 1973; November 7, 1973; June 10, 1975; May 3, 1978.

Commonweal, November 22, 1968.

Horn Book, February, 1971; May/June, 1985.

Language Arts, October, 1978; September, 1980; October, 1982.

Los Angeles Times Book Review, January 31, 1988, p. 7.

New York Review of Books, December 14, 1972.

New York Times, December 4, 1979; December 5, 1980; November 30, 1982.

New York Times Book Review, June 14, 1969; February 28, 1971; April 23, 1972; June 4, 1972; November 5, 1972; May 6, 1973; June 10, 1973; August 19, 1973; November 4, 1973; October 13, 1974; November 3, 1974; December 15, 1974; May 2, 1976; October 7, 1979; November 25, 1979; May 4, 1980; July 19, 1981; May 30, 1982; November 28, 1982; January 2, 1983; November 27, 1983; August 4, 1985; August 4, 1980, p. 21; December 15, 1991, p. 29.

Observer, September 25, 1977.

Psychology Today, January 10, 1974.

Publishers Weekly, September 16, 1971; April 17, 1978; April 8, 1988, p. 95.

Saturday Review, September 18, 1965; November 9, 1968; March 20, 1971; May 20, 1972; November 29, 1975.

School Library Journal, May, 1988, pp. 95-96; April, 1992, p. 112.

Times Literary Supplement, July 2, 1970; July 20, 1970; April 6, 1973; March 29, 1974; April 4, 1975; September 19, 1975; July 16, 1976; October 21, 1977; July 7, 1978; December 14, 1979; July 18, 1980; July 24, 1981; July 23, 1982; November 25, 1983; February 1, 1985; October 11, 1985, p. 1154.

Top of the News, April, 1971.

Washington Post Book World, May 7, 1972; April 10, 1977; May 13, 1979; April 11, 1980; May 10, 1981; July 12, 1981; October 11, 1981; April 11, 1982; October 10, 1982; October 9, 1983; January 13, 1985.

Young Reader's Review, January, 1967.*

C

CAIRNCROSS, Alec
See CAIRNCROSS, Alexander Kirkland

* * *

CAIRNCROSS, Alexander Kirkland 1911-
(Alec Cairncross)

PERSONAL: Born February 11, 1911, in Lesmahagow, Scotland; son of Alexander Kirkland and Elizabeth Andrew (Wishart) Cairncross; married Mary Frances Glynn, May 29, 1943; children: Frances Anne, Philip Wishart Glynn, Alexander Messent, David John, Elizabeth Mary. *Education:* University of Glasgow, M.A., 1933; Trinity College, Cambridge, Ph.D., 1936. *Avocational interests:* Color photography, travel.

ADDRESSES: Home—14 Staverton Rd., Oxford OX2 6XJ, England.

CAREER: University of Glasgow, Glasgow, Scotland, lecturer in political economy, 1935-39; West of Scotland Agricultural College, Glasgow, lecturer in agricultural economics, 1935-39; War Cabinet Office, London, staff member of Economic Section, 1939-41; administrative assistant, Board of Trade, 1941; Ministry of Aircraft Production, London, staff member of directorate of programs and planning, 1941-45; head of economic advisory panel, British Element, Control Commission for Germany, Berlin, 1945-46; *Economist,* London, staff member, 1946; economic advisor to Board of Trade, 1946-49; Organisation for European Economic Co-operation, Paris, director of Economic Division, 1949-50; University of Glasgow, professor of applied economics and director of department of social and economic research, 1951-61; first director of Economic Development Institute, Washington, DC, 1955-56; British Treasury, London, Economic Advisor to Her Majesty's Government, 1961-64, head of Economic Service, 1964-69; Oxford University, Oxford, England, Master of St. Peter's College, 1969-78. Member of Court of Governors of London School of Economics and Political Science, University of London; chancellor of University of Glasgow, 1972-96; fellow of St. Antony's College, Oxford University, 1978-89. Director of Ailsa and Alva Investments Trusts, 1959-61; trustee of Urwick Orr & Partners, 1970-81; Girls Public Day School Trust, president, 1972-92, vice president, 1992—; advisory committee chair to Houblon-Norman Trustees, 1982-86.

MEMBER: Royal Economic Society (president, 1968-70; vice president, 1970—), National Institute of Social and Economic Research, British Association for the Advancement of Science (section F president, 1969; president, 1970-71), British Academy (fellow), American Academy of Arts and Sciences (foreign honorary member), Scottish Economic Society (president, 1969-73; vice president, 1973—).

AWARDS, HONORS: Named to Order of St. Michael and St. George, 1950, named knight commander, 1966; honorary LL.D., Mount Allison University, 1962, University of Glasgow, 1966, and University of Exeter, 1969; D.Litt., University of Reading, 1968, and Heriot Watt University, 1969; D.Sc., University of Wales, 1971, and Queen's University,

Belfast, 1972; D.Univ., Stirling University, 1973; honorary fellow of St. Peter's College, Oxford University, St. Anthony's College, Oxford University, and of London School of Economics.

WRITINGS:

UNDER NAME ALEC CAIRNCROSS

Introduction to Economics, Butterworth (Sevenoaks, England), 1944, sixth edition, 1982.

Home and Foreign Investment, 1870-1913: Studies in Capital Accumulation, Cambridge University Press (Cambridge, England), 1953, Kelley, 1974.

(Editor) *The Scottish Economy: A Statistical Account of Scottish Life by Members of the Staff of Glasgow University,* Cambridge University Press, 1954.

Some Problems of Economic Planning, Foreign Trade Research Institute (Belgrade), 1957.

The International Bank for Reconstruction and Development, Princeton University International Finance Section (Princeton, NJ), 1959.

Monetary Policy in a Mixed Economy, Almqvist & Wiksell (Stockholm), 1960.

Economic Development and the Atlantic Provinces, Atlantic Provinces Research Board, 1961.

Factors in Economic Development, Allen & Unwin (London), 1962, Beekman, 1972.

The Short Term and the Long in Economic Planning, Economic Development Institute (Washington, DC), 1966.

(Editor) *The Managed Economy,* British Association for the Advancement of Science (London), 1969, Barnes & Noble (New York City), 1970.

(Editor) E. Devons, *Papers on Planning and Economic Management,* Manchester University Press (Manchester, England), 1970.

(Editor) *Britain's Economic Prospects Reconsidered,* Allen & Unwin, 1971, State University of New York Press (Albany), 1972.

Essays in Economic Management, Allen & Unwin, 1971, State University of New York Press, 1972.

(Contributor) G. D. N. Worswick, editor, *Uses of Economics,* Barnes & Noble, 1972.

Learning to Learn, University of Glasgow Press (Glasgow), 1972.

Control of Long-Term International Capital Movements: A Staff Paper, Brookings Institution (Washington, DC), 1973.

Control over International Capital Movements, University of Reading (Reading), 1973.

(Editor with others and contributor) *Economic Policy for the European Community,* Macmillan (London), 1974, Holmes & Meier (Hoddesdon, England), 1975.

Inflation, Growth, and International Finance, Allen & Unwin, 1975.

(Editor with Mohinder Puri) *H. W. Singer: The Strategy of International Development,* Macmillan, 1975.

(Editor with Puri) *Employment, Income Distribution, and Development Strategy: Essays in Honor of H. W. Singer,* Macmillan, 1976.

(Editor) R. W. B. Clarke, *Public Expenditure, Management, and Control,* Macmillan, 1978.

Science Studies, Nuffield Foundation, 1980.

Snatches (poetry), Colin Smythe Ltd., 1980.

(Contributor) Frances Anne Cairncross, editor, *Changing Perceptions of Economic Policy,* Methuen, 1981.

(Contributor) *The Economic History of Britain since 1700,* Cambridge University Press, 1981.

(Editor) Clarke, *Anglo-American Collaboration in War and Peace,* Oxford University Press (Oxford), 1982.

(With Barry Eichengreen) *Sterling in Decline: The Devaluations of 1931, 1949, and 1967,* Blackwell, 1983.

Years of Recovery: British Economic Policy, 1945-51, Methuen, 1985.

The Price of War: British Policy on German Reparations, 1941-49, Blackwell, 1986.

Economics and Economic Policy, Blackwell, 1987.

A Country to Play With: Level of Industry Negotiations in Berlin, 1945-46, Colin Smythe Ltd., 1987.

(With Nita Watts) *The Economic Section, 1939-1961: A Study in Economic Advising,* Routledge (London), 1989.

(Editor) Robert Hall, *The Robert Hall Diaries,* Unwin Hyman, Volume One, *1947-53,* 1989, Volume Two, *1954-61,* 1991.

Planning in Wartime: Aircraft Production in Britain, Germany, and the USA, St. Martin's (New York City), 1991.

The British Economy since 1945: Economic Policy and Performance, 1945-1990, Blackwell, 1992, revised edition published as *The British Economy since 1945: Economic Policy and Performance, 1945-1995,* Blackwell, 1995.

(With Kathleen Burk) *Goodbye, Great Britain: The 1976 IMF Crisis,* Yale University Press (New Haven, CT), 1992.
(Editor with F. Cairncross) *The Legacy of the Golden Age: The 1960s and Their Economic Consequences,* Routledge, 1992.
Austin Robinson: The Life of an Economic Adviser, St. Martin's, 1993.
Economic Ideas and Government Policy: Contributions to Contemporary Economic History, Routledge, 1996.
Managing the British Economy in the 1960s, Macmillan, 1996.
The Wilson Years: A Treasury Diary 1964-69, The Historian's Press, 1997.

Also coauthor of Radcliffe report, *The Working of the Monetary System,* 1959, and report on the Channel Link, 1982. General editor of "Social and Economic Studies" series, Department of Social and Economic Research, University of Glasgow, 1953-61. Coauthor of script for phonotape, "The British Economy," Holt Information Systems, 1972. Editor, *Scottish Journal of Political Economy,* 1954-61.

BIOGRAPHICAL/CRITICAL SOURCES:

PERIODICALS

London Review of Books, September 19, 1985, p. 6; December 21, 1989, p. 15.
Spectator, May 11, 1985, p. 23.
Times Literary Supplement, February 24, 1984, p. 188; June 21, 1985, p. 683; November 28, 1986, p. 1337; January 30, 1987, p. 105; November 3, 1989, p. 1206; March 4, 1994, p. 1190.

* * *

CALLAHAN, John
See GALLUN, Raymond Z.

* * *

CALLEO, David P(atrick) 1934-

PERSONAL: Born July 19, 1934, in Binghamton, NY; son of Patrick and Gertrude (Crowe) Calleo; married Avis Thayer Bohlen. *Education:* Yale University, B.A. (magna cum laude), 1955, M.A., 1957, Ph.D., 1959.

ADDRESSES: *Home*—626 A St. N.E., Washington, DC 20002. *Office*—School of Advanced International Studies, Department of European Studies, 1740 Massachusetts Ave. N.W., Washington, DC 20036-1984. *E-mail*—dcalleo@sais-jhu.edu; fax: 202-663-5784.

CAREER: Brown University, Providence, RI, instructor in political science, 1959-60; Yale University, New Haven, CT, 1961-67, began as instructor, became assistant professor of political science; U.S. Department of State, consultant to undersecretary for political affairs, 1967-68; Johns Hopkins University, School of Advanced International Studies, Washington, DC, professor and director of European Studies Program, 1968—, Dean Acheson chair, 1988—, Washington Center of Foreign Policy Research, research associate, 1968-79, director, 1974-75. Research fellow, Nuffield College, Oxford University, 1966-67; senior Fulbright lecturer in Germany, 1975; associate fellow, John Edwards College, Yale University. Project director, Twentieth Century Fund, 1981-85. Trustee, Jonathan Edwards Trust, Yale University. Vice president and member of board of trustees, Lehrman Institute. President and trustee, Washington Foundation for European Studies. *Military service:* U.S. Army Reserve, 1956-65; became captain.

MEMBER: International Institute for Strategic Studies, Council on Foreign Relations, American Political Science Association, Century Association, Metropolitan Club of Washington, D.C., Brook's (London).

AWARDS, HONORS: Gladys M. Kammerer Award for best book analyzing American national policy, American Political Science Association, 1973, for *America and the World Political Economy;* fellowships from Rockefeller Foundation, Guggenheim Foundation, and Social Science Research Council; Fulbright fellowship, 1982; NATO fellowship, 1983.

WRITINGS:

Europe's Future: The Grand Alternatives, Horizon, 1965.

Coleridge and the Idea of the Modern State, Yale University Press (New Haven, CT), 1966.

Europe's Future, Hodder & Stoughton (London), 1967.

Britain's Future, Horizon, 1968.

The Atlantic Fantasy, Johns Hopkins University Press (Baltimore, MD), 1970.

(With Benjamin M. Rowland) *America and the World Political Economy,* Indiana University Press (Bloomington), 1974.

(Editor with Cleveland, Kindleberger, and Lehrman, and contributor) *Money and the Coming World Order,* New York University Press (New York City), 1976.

The German Problem Reconsidered: Germany in the World Order, 1870 to the Present, Cambridge University Press (New York City), 1978.

The Imperious Economy, Harvard University Press (Cambridge, MA), 1982.

Beyond American Hegemony: The Future of the Western Alliance, Basic Books (New York City), 1987.

(Editor with Claudia Morgenstern) *Recasting Europe's Economies: National Strategies in the 1980s,* University Press of America (Lanham, MD), 1990.

NATO: Reconstruction or Dissolution?, SAIS Foreign Policy Institute (Washington, DC), 1992.

The Bankrupting of America: How the Federal Budget Is Impoverishing the Nation, Morrow (New York City), 1992.

(Editor with Philip Gordon) *From the Atlantic to the Urals: National Perspectives on the New Europe,* Seven Locks (Cabin John, MD), 1992.

Europe and World Order after the Cold War, Old Dominion University (Norfolk, VA), 1996.

Contributor to numerous publications, including *Retreat from Empire?: The First Nixon Administration,* edited by Robert Osgood, Johns Hopkins University Press, 1973; *The United States and Western Europe: The Political, Economic, and Strategic Perspectives,* edited by Wolfram F. Hanrieder, Winthrop, 1974; *Balance of Power or Hegemony: The Interwar Monetary System,* edited by Benjamin M. Rowland, New York University Press, 1976; *The Euro-American System: Economic and Political Relations between North America and Western Europe,* edited by Ernst-Otto Czempiel and Dankwart A. Rustow, Westview (Boulder, CO), 1976; *Atlantis Lost: U.S.-European Relations after the Cold War,* edited by James Chace and Earl Ravenal, New York University Press, 1976; *The End of the Keynesian Era: Essays on the Disintegration of the Keynesian Political Economy,* edited by Robert S. Skidelsky, Holmes & Meier (New York City), 1977; *West German Foreign Policy: 1949- 1979,* edited by Hanrieder, Westview, 1979; *SDI AND U.S. Foreign Policy,* Westview, 1987; *Economic and Strategic Issues in U.S. Foreign Policy,* edited by Carl-Ludwig Holtfrerich, Walter de Gruyter (Hawthorne, NY), 1989; *The External Relations of the European Community, in Particular EC-US Relations,* edited by Juergen Schwarze, Nomos Verlagsgesellschaft, 1989; *NATO at 40: Confronting a Changing World,* edited by Ted Galen Carpenter, Cato Institute (Washington, DC), 1990; *Europe and America Beyond 2000,* edited by Gregory F. Treverton, Council on Foreign Relations (Washington, DC), 1990; *The Rise and Decline of the Nation State,* edited by Michael Maurr, Blackwell (London), 1990; *The Future of American Foreign Policy,* edited by Charles W. Kegley Jr. and Eugene R. Wittkopf, St. Martin's (New York City), 1992; *The Rise and Decline of the Nation State,* edited by Michael Mann, Blackwell, 1992; *France-Germany 1983-1993: The Struggle to Cooperate,* edited by Patrick McCarthy, St. Martin's, 1993; and *Nationalism and Nationalities in the New Europe,* edited by Charles Kupchan, Council on Foreign Relations, 1995.

Also contributor to various periodicals, including *Social Research, World Policy Journal, Journal of International Affairs, Ethics and International Affairs, Political Science Quarterly, Foreign Affairs,* and *Foreign Policy.*

SIDELIGHTS: David P. Calleo's *The Imperious Economy* "presents a major challenge to conventional economic thinking about the causes of virulent inflation," states Grant D. Aldonas in the *Los Angeles Times Book Review.* In *The Imperious Economy,* Calleo charges that the devaluation of the American dollar during the past two decades is a result not of deficit spending during the Vietnam War, as is commonly assumed, but rather of older problems that stem from the United States' historic inability to reconcile domestic and foreign objectives. Calleo "unfolds a subtle analysis of how inflation became embedded in the national fabric," Daniel Yergin writes in *Washington Post Book World.* The importance of *The Imperious Economy,* comments Aldonas, is that it "challenges assumptions and forces us to confront the complex interdependence of decisions at home with stature abroad."

Calleo argues in *The Imperious Economy* that the United States' chronic monetary inflation began during the Kennedy era when the government pushed for full employment as a panacea for domestic social unrest while at the same time spending large amounts of capital to maintain its global economic hegemony and military superiority. In order to achieve both full employment and world dominance, Calleo maintains, the United States began a policy of deficit spending in both good times and bad, thus increasing the flow of American currency without any corresponding real growth.

Richard J. Barnett comments in the *New York Times Book Review* that *The Imperious Economy* "is really an essay on the paradoxes of American Power." Calleo's argument is that in its pursuit of greater economic and military power, the United States contradicts its goal of restoring post-World War II Europe and Japan to economic stability and independence and deriving a more equitable world economic balance. "Calleo has long been a student of U.S.-European relations," writes Aldonas. "He is at his best bringing out essential elements of our alliance and explaining why our security and economic interests sometimes differ. . . . This book is a must for those who hope to join the international economic debate."

BIOGRAPHICAL/CRITICAL SOURCES:

PERIODICALS

Los Angeles Times Book Review, July 4, 1982.
New York Times Book Review, July 18, 1982.
Washington Post Book World, November 5, 1978; August 29, 1982.
Times Literary Supplement, December 2, 1988.

* * *

CALTER, Paul (Arthur) 1934-

PERSONAL: Born June 18, 1934, in New York, NY; son of Arthur and Frances Calter; married Margaret Carey, May 13, 1959; children: Amy, Michael. *Ethnicity:* "Caucasian." *Education:* Cooper Union, B.S., 1962; Columbia University, M.S., 1966; Norwich University, M.F.A., 1993. *Avocational interests:* Painting, sculpture, mountaineering.

ADDRESSES: *Home*—33 South Pleasant St., Randolph, VT 05060. *Office*—Department of Mathematics, Vermont Technical College, Randolph, VT 05061. *E-mail*—pcalter@sover.net.

CAREER: Columbia University, New York City, senior research assistant at Heat and Mass Flow Analyzer Laboratory, 1952-57, 1959-60; Kollsman Instrument Corp., Elmhurst, NY, development engineer, 1960-65; Intertype Co., Brooklyn, NY, senior project engineer, 1965-68; Vermont Technical College, Randolph, began as assistant professor, became professor of mathematics, 1968-89, Director of Summer Mathematics Institutes, 1989-94. Visiting professor of mathematics, Dartmouth College, 1995—. *Military service:* U.S. Army, 1957-59; served in Medical Corps.

MEMBER: International Sculpture Society, Volunteers for International Technical Assistance, Leonardo, the International Society for the Arts, Sciences, and Technology, American Society of Mechanical Engineers, Mathematical Association of America, National Council of Teachers of Mathematics, American Mathematical Association of Two-Year Colleges, Authors Guild, College Art Association, New England Mathematics Association of Two Year Colleges.

AWARDS, HONORS: Ralph Horton Memorial Award in science, 1952; Faculty Fellow Award, Vermont State Colleges, 1987; Honorary Alumnus, Vermont State Colleges, 1991.

WRITINGS:

Problem Solving with Computers, McGraw (New York City), 1973.
Graphical and Numerical Solution of Differential Equations, Educational Development Center, 1977.
Magic Squares (mystery novel), Thomas Nelson (Nashville, TN), 1977.
Schaum's Outline of Technical Mathematics, McGraw, 1978.
Fundamentos di Matematica, McGraw, 1980.
Technical Mathematics, Prentice-Hall (Englewood Cliffs, NJ), 1983, third edition, 1995.

Practical Math Handbook for the Building Trades, Prentice-Hall, 1983.
Technical Mathematics with Calculus, Prentice-Hall, 1984, third edition, 1995.
Math for Electricity and Electronics, McGraw, 1984.
Math for Computer Technology, Prentice-Hall, 1986.
Technical Calculus, Prentice-Hall, 1988.
(Contributor) *Applications in Geometry,* Mathematical Association of America (Washington, DC), 1996.
Introductory Algebra and Trigonometry, with Applications, Prentice-Hall, 1997.

Also author of a learning module, "Graphical and Mechanical Solution of Differential Equations," Educational Development Center, 1977. Contributor to *Review of Scientific Instruments* and *Journal of Engineering Graphics.*

WORK IN PROGRESS: Technical Calculus, second edition, for Prentice-Hall; *Geometry in Art and Architecture.*

SIDELIGHTS: Paul Calter's personal home page on the World Wide Web is located at http://www.sover.net/~pcalter.

* * *

CAMERON, Ann 1943-

PERSONAL: Born October 21, 1943, in Rice Lake, WI; daughter of William Angus (a lawyer) and Lolita (a teacher; maiden name, Lofgren) Cameron; married Bill Cherry (a congressional committee staff director), 1990; children: Angela, Cristi (stepdaughters). *Education:* Radcliffe College, B.A. (with honors), 1965; University of Iowa, M.F.A., 1972. *Politics:* Democrat.

ADDRESSES: Home—Calle Principal, Panajachel, Solola, Guatemala. *Agent*—Ellen Levine Literary Agency, 15 East 26th St., Suite 1801, New York, NY 10010.

CAREER: Writer, editor, and teacher. Supervisor of the Panajachel, Guatemala municipal library; director of Amigos de la Biblioteca (a fundraising organization that supports the Panajachel municipal library).

MEMBER: Authors Guild, Authors League of America.

AWARDS, HONORS: MacDowell Colony fellow, 1968; guest at Yaddo Colony, 1968; grant from National Endowment for the Humanities, 1974; Irma Simonton Black Award, 1981, for *The Stories Julian Tells;* Parents' Choice Award, 1986, and Selectors' Choice, *Wilson Library Bulletin,* 1988, for *More Stories Julian Tells;* Children's Book Award, Child Study Children's Book Committee at Bank Street College, 1988, and Addams Award, 1989, both for *The Most Beautiful Place in the World;* Blue Ribbon book, *Bulletin of the Center for Children's Books,* 1995, for *The Stories Huey Tells.*

WRITINGS:

The Seed, Pantheon (New York City), 1975.
Harry, the Monster, Pantheon, 1980.
The Stories Julian Tells, illustrated by Ann Strugnell, Pantheon, 1981.
More Stories Julian Tells, illustrated by Strugnell, Knopf (New York City), 1986.
Julian's Glorious Summer, illustrated by Dora Leder, Random House (New York City), 1987.
Julian, Secret Agent, illustrated by Diane Allison, Random House, 1988.
The Most Beautiful Place in the World, illustrated by Thomas B. Allen, Knopf, 1988.
Julian, Dream Doctor, illustrated by Strugnell, Random House, 1990.
The Stories Huey Tells, Knopf, 1995.
(Adapter) *The Kidnapped Prince: The Life of Olaudah Equiano,* introduction by Henry L. Gates, Knopf, 1995.
More Stories Huey Tells, Farrar, Straus (New York City), 1997.

Also author of introduction, *The Angel Book,* Balance House, 1978. Contributor of stories to *Iowa Review* and *Northwest Review;* contributor of an essay to *Booktalk,* published by the National Council of Teachers of English.

WORK IN PROGRESS: Looking for Amanda, a novel about an eleven year old.

SIDELIGHTS: Ann Cameron once explained: "I try to write about characters who have inner abundance—sympathy, imagination, inventiveness, hope, intelligence—and who make happy lives despite modest outer resources." Cameron is best known for the series of books she introduced with *The Stories Julian Tells*. These stories feature Julian, a young black boy whom Julie Corsaro described in *Booklist* as "energetic, engaging, and intelligent"; his brother Huey; his best friend, Gloria; and his wise and loving parents. When Julian's creativity and enthusiasm lead him into trouble, his parents help him toward self-discovery, moral growth, and pride in his achievements.

Cameron once told *CA* that *The Stories Julian Tells* "was inspired by some stories a friend of mine, Julian DeWette, told me about his childhood." DeWette, a South African, and his brother had once eaten a pudding his father had made as a special present for their mother. Cameron's version ends with the two boys hiding under their bed from their angry father. The story reminded Cameron that much of childhood is spent trying to fathom the rules of adults and living up to one's own developing sense of morality.

Cameron stated that she has never believed in the traditional advice to writers: "write what you know." "We all know a great deal," according to the author, "which neither interests nor inspires us. Write what you care about," she advises, "and the force of your caring will lead you to questioning, imagining, learning—the opening of the heart and mind that lead to the best writing."

Because she had friends of diverse cultures and races as a child, Cameron once remarked, "I grew up with an almost instinctive conviction that people quite different from me would like me. . . . It has brought me wonderful and enduring friendships and a tremendous enrichment of my understanding of life." She recently added, "I see my character Julian as an Everychild, a child whose hopes and mishaps children everywhere can understand. Letters from young readers of many races and cultures saying his adventures remind them of themselves support me in viewing Julian this way. As an author I am more interested in what we have in common as human beings than in the things that divide us. I'm interested in how we conquer our hatreds and our fears, our lack of love, and our lack of hope."

Cameron grew up in rural Wisconsin in the late 1940s and 1950s, spending lots of time alone, riding her pony, Paint; fishing; looking for Indian arrowheads; and, as she recalled, dreaming "a lot about what the land was like before the arrival of Europeans. Motivating these dreams was an equal mix of my love of nature, interest in Native Americans, and dislike of school. I knew Native Americans had not had to spend nine months a year in school, and that in itself made me wish I could have been one of them."

Cameron's parents were traditional, uninfluenced by the child-rearing theories of Dr. Spock, and given to repeating, "Children should be seen and not heard." They had great curiosity about other cultures, great respect for learning, and faith that education and hard work were the keys to a good life. "I respected their values," Cameron has said, "but I resented their idea that children should be second-class citizens within the family." In *School Library Journal* the author described her family environment as often being an "icicle kingdom of silence," and she grew up determined to "say, for a lifetime and in the strongest form that [she] could devise, the things most important" to her.

Although she disliked grade school, Cameron read constantly. She once related: "I loved books about characters who struggled to make a happy life for themselves, and who succeeded. I knew from my own childhood that often I wasn't happy, that often even adults did not lead happy lives. The books I loved best taught me to hope, and helped me to believe life could be, if not all good, at least mostly good and even wonderful. Books—especially fiction and autobiography—gave me energy. They were a kind of magic—nothing but paper and ink and a little glue, and then you opened their covers and found they held life inside them. That's why from a very early age (about third grade) I wanted to be a writer—the person who captures the positive energy of life, wraps it in paper, and gives it, all shimmering and forever bright, to others."

Cameron earned a bachelor's degree with honors at Radcliffe College. There she heard Martin Luther King speak and participated in Civil Rights demonstrations. In her senior year, she studied poetry with the poet Robert Lowell, who encouraged her to write, calling one of her poems "magical." Lowell advised her to go to New York to work in publishing after college, as the best way to develop her writing. So in 1965 she moved to New York, getting a job as editorial assistant in the trade department of Harcourt Brace Jovanovich.

Cameron explained: "It was a thrill to work in publishing, to get a thank you letter for some reviews of Virginia Woolf's essays from her husband, Leonard Woolf; to read the correspondence in which Alfred Harcourt had rejected Faulkner's *The Sound and the Fury;* to see and meet many famous editors and authors—Lewis Mumford, Paula Fox, Anais Nin, Irving Howe; and to learn to edit books. However, after two and a half years in publishing, I thought it was time to take the leap into writing. I began an adult novel and on the basis of my incomplete manuscript received a fellowship for a master's degree in creative writing at the University of Iowa, plus invitations to the artists' colonies MacDowell and Yaddo for the summer of 1968. With fellowship and recognition heaped on me, I told my friend Paula Fox I felt like I was walking on God's hand. Paula responded, 'It's a very narrow hand.' She couldn't have been more right.

"At Iowa I became overwhelmed by all I hadn't read, all I didn't know. My adult novel ground to a halt; I couldn't figure out how to organize my experience. What did I really have to say that other writers hadn't already said much better?

"In the midst of my discouragement, I remembered that children's books were short. 'At least I might be able to get through one,' I thought. My second attempt at a children's book—about a seed in the ground who hears a storm above her head and becomes afraid to grow—was published in 1975."

Cameron received her M.F.A. at the University of Iowa in 1972. She lived in Berkeley, California for a year, and then returned to New York, working freelance as a manuscript reader for literary agents. She edited an archaeologists's thesis and worked as camp cook in the rain forest on a Mayan dig in Belize, Central America. She also evaluated the potential movie prospects of books for a Hollywood film company, and worked for the Doubleday Book Clubs. Her hardest but briefest job in these years, she has said, was babysitting twenty-three cats, two of whom had eye infections, needed daily eye drops, and hid in kitchen cabinets because they didn't feel well.

With *The Stories Julian Tells,* published in 1981, Cameron's work began to receive wide recognition. According to Liz Waterland in *Books for Keeps,* the "Julian stories have been deservedly popular ever since they first appeared." Along with the pudding story, *The Stories Julian Tells* includes tales about making a first friend; cats that do gardening work; and Julian's attempt to grow tall by eating a fig tree's leaves, nearly killing the tree. *More Stories Julian Tells* provides five additional stories which, as David Gale wrote in *School Library Journal,* "reflect incidents true to children." In this work, Julian learns the destructive effects of name-calling; discovers that his best friend, Gloria, really can move the sun; and sends a message in a bottle that unfortunately gets stuck very close to home.

Three of the Julian books present longer stories with chapters for young readers. *Julian's Glorious Summer* begins when his friend Gloria offers to help him learn to ride the new bike she received for her birthday. Julian can't tell her that he is afraid of falling, so he gives a false excuse for not riding. He pretends that his father is putting him to work, nights and days. When Julian persuades his father to give him work so that Gloria will believe his excuse, Dad responds with more work than Julian would prefer. Julian finally confides to his mother that he is afraid of falling off a bicycle. His parents then give him a bike for all the work he has done, and he learns to ride and enjoy it. A *Booklist* critic appreciated Cameron's "well-paced plot" and "fine characterizations of Julian's struggles."

Julian, Secret Agent finds Julian, Gloria, and Huey pretending to be "crimebusters." They decide to track down the criminals on the most-wanted posters they see at the post office, but their visits to the supermarket and hospital give them opportunities to rescue a dog from a hot car and a child from a fountain instead. When the secret agents visit a cafe, they are certain the cook is a wanted bank robber. It takes the police chief himself to convince the children that the "bank robber" is really his son! A critic for *Junior Bookshelf* praised Cameron's "enviable knack of weaving intriguing stories out of small incidents."

Julian is busy sleuthing again in *Julian, Dream Doctor.* This time, however, Julian is trying to figure out what his father wants for his birthday. Julian and Huey first try to use the brainwave machine they've made, and when that fails, they prompt their sleeping father to tell them his "biggest dream," which turns out to be "two snakes. Big ones." When the boys present Dad with the gift they worked so hard to find, Dad is horrified and must confess that snakes are his biggest nightmare. A critic for *Junior Bookshelf* asserted that "Julian's parents are a bit too good to be true." In her *Booklist* review, Corsaro appreciated Cameron's ability to develop "well-realized characters and situations."

In 1983 Cameron traveled to Guatemala to visit a New York filmmaker from Guatemala, Pablo Zavala, who was a close friend. Cameron explained: "I had always wanted to immerse myself in another culture. We have such brief, narrow lives and learn so little of all the ways to experience being human. Each culture sees the world and the meaning of life with slightly different eyes. I wanted to grow, to see things more than one way, to find more than one way of seeing myself.

"I went to Guatemala for a short vacation, but with the hope that I might stay. In the highland town of Panajachel, which is on the shore of an enormous lake overshadowed by majestic volcanoes, I found a new home. I was in the garden of a Panajachel restaurant, when I looked down into my coffee cup and saw it full of the golden reflections of flowers, and knew this was the place I wanted to stay."

The Most Beautiful Place in the World is set in a Guatemalan town much like Panajachel, where Cameron now lives. As she wrote in *School Library Journal,* the character of the narrator of this book, a seven-year-old boy named Juan, is based on a boy Cameron knows. In *The Most Beautiful Place in the World,* Juan's father has abandoned the family, and when his mother finds a new husband, she is forced to leave Juan with his grandmother. Grandmother's house is already full of children; Juan must help support the family by working as a shoe-shine boy. Juan works hard, but he cannot help wishing that he could go to school like the children he sees in the morning. He begins to teach himself to read by studying the street signs near the tourist office. After Juan relates his dream of going to school to his grandmother, she grants his wish, and Juan optimistically enters the first grade. As Ethel R. Twichell observed in *Horn Book,* this story provides an "unsentimental picture of Juan's hard life" as well as "a modest hope for his brighter future." Phillis Wilson concluded in *Booklist* that Juan tells his "bittersweet story with warmth and dignity."

In *The Kidnapped Prince: The Life of Olaudah Equiano,* a shortened, retold version of Olaudah Equiano's 1789 autobiography, Cameron gives children insight into the life of another child suffering hardship. Equiano was brutally kidnapped from Benin, Africa, and separated from his family when he was just eleven years old. He was subjected to forced labor in England, the United States, and a plantation in the West Indies, until, having learned to read and write, he managed to buy his way to freedom. According to Hazel Rochman in *Booklist,* Cameron's version remains "true to the spirit of the original."

"I am sure that my writing has been influenced by a long time spent in a poor country, where only the very rich live in the equivalent of the U.S. 'consumer culture,'" the author said. After dividing her time between Guatemala and New York for six years, Cameron met Bill Cherry, the staff director of a congressional sub-committee on agriculture, in 1989. They were married in 1990, and since then have lived full time in Guatemala.

"In 1993," Cameron stated, "the mayor and city council of Panajachel named me unpaid supervisor of the town's public library. I was very honored by this trust from my adoptive community. In Guatemala, illiteracy is about eighty percent. The whole country has only a handful of very ill-equipped libraries. In public schools, children study without books, because parents have no money to buy them. Nationally, only thirty-eight percent of children attend school. Most of those who attend do not get beyond sixth grade.

"With the help of U.S. donations, we are building the Panajachel library into a first-class library for students. We've added over three thousand volumes in Spanish for children—plus new lights, windows, fans, and tables. The library is filled with children every day that it is open. Many older students come from other towns to use the library as well, and we are building a collection of university-level books for them."

Cameron once described what it was like to be a writer: "Now that I've grown up, and become a writer, people say to me, 'I have a story for you'; or 'You could make a story out of that.' They seem to think that writers are like piggy banks, empty inside, and just waiting for some nice person to come along and put in a coin! But stories are not like that. My story will never be exactly like yours. I could never tell yours for you. Your story, if it's really the way you want to tell it, can never be wrong the way an arithmetic answer is wrong; and even if your mother, your father, your teacher or your best friend doesn't understand it, it's still right for you. Right answers in arithmetic are the same for everybody; but stories are individual, special, and all different—brand new thought-flowers blooming in the garden of your head."

The author added, "We are all born with the capacity to discover and use our own inner abundance, but if we are put down, discriminated against, or abused, we lose access to our inner selves. We don't become who we are meant to be, and unfortunately, we pass our frustration and disappointments on to the next generation.

"This was epitomized for me on a school visit to a fourth grade class in Wisconsin. I told the students they could be authors, too, when they grew up. To my horror, the teacher immediately disagreed: 'No, nobody in *this* class could be an author!,' she said. (Before I left the class, one boy in it had developed a scene for me that I later used in *Julian, Dream Doctor.*)

"I try to write about characters who haven't lost touch with their own inner abundance. I hope my characters can connect or re-connect children to the richness inside themselves."

BIOGRAPHICAL/CRITICAL SOURCES:

BOOKS

Something about the Author Autobiography Series, Volume 20, Gale (Detroit), 1995.

PERIODICALS

Booklist, December 15, 1987, pp. 702-703; January 1, 1989, p. 784; May 15, 1990, p. 1797; January 1, 1995, p. 816.

Books for Keeps, July, 1990, p. 9.

Bulletin of the Center for Children's Books, June, 1980; January, 1982.

Horn Book, January, 1989, p. 66.

Junior Bookshelf, April, 1990, pp. 80-81; June, 1990, p. 133; October, 1992, p. 196.

Junior Literary Guild, March, 1981.

School Library Journal, April, 1986, p. 84; June, 1989, pp. 50-51.

CANNON, Garland (Hampton) 1924-

PERSONAL: Born December 5, 1924, in Fort Worth, TX; son of Garland Hampton and Myrtle (Goss) Cannon; married Patricia Richardson, February 14, 1947; children: Margaret, India, Jennifer, William. *Ethnicity:* "Caucasian." *Education:* University of Texas, B.A., 1947, Ph.D., 1954; Stanford University, M.A., 1952. *Religion:* Episcopalian. *Avocational interests:* Stamp collecting, travel.

ADDRESSES: Home—805 Hawthorn, College Station, TX 77840. *Office*—Department of English, Texas A & M University, College Station, TX 77843.

CAREER: University of Hawaii, Honolulu, instructor, 1949-52; University of Texas at Austin, instructor, 1952-54; University of Michigan, Ann Arbor, instructor, 1954-55; University of California, Berkeley, assistant professor of speech, 1955-56; American University Language Center, Bangkok, Thailand, academic director, 1956-57; University of Florida, Gainesville, assistant professor, 1957-58; Columbia University, Teachers College, New York City, and Kabul, Afghanistan, assistant professor, 1959-62, director of English Language Program in Afghanistan, 1960-62; Northeastern Illinois State College (now Northeastern Illinois University), Chicago, associate professor, 1962-63; Queens College of the City University of New York, Flushing, NY, associate professor of English, 1963-66; Texas A & M University, College Station, associate professor, 1966-68, professor of English, 1968—; founder and director of linguistics program, 1970-94.

Visiting professor at University of Puerto Rico, Rio Piedras, 1958-59, University of Michigan, 1970-71, Kuwait University, 1979-81, and Institut Teknologi Mara, Kuala Lumpur, Malaysia, 1987-88; visiting summer professor at Massachusetts Institute of Technology, 1969, Oxford University, 1974, and Cambridge University, 1980. Has conducted field work in many countries, including Afghanistan, India, Kuwait, Malaysia, Pakistan, and the former Soviet Union. Public lecturer at British Library (London), Cambridge University, Oxford University, Columbia University, Cornell University, Oxford University, Princeton University, University of California (Berkeley and Los Angeles), and other institutions worldwide. Consultant. Has been interviewed on All-India Radio,

BBC World Service, Radio Japan, and Voice of America, and in various international print media. *Military service:* U.S. Marine Corps, 1943-46.

MEMBER: American Dialect Society (member of executive council, 1989-92), Dictionary Society of North America, Linguistic Society of America, Modern Language Association of America (member of delegate assembly, 1985-88), South Asian Literary Association (president, 1979-85).

AWARDS, HONORS: American Philosophical Society grants to England, 1964, 1966, 1974; *Sunday London Telegraph* Book of the Year Award, 1971, for *The Letters of Sir William Jones;* faculty distinguished achievement award in research, Texas A & M University, 1972; visiting fellow, Oxford University, 1974; Hospitality Grant, Indian Council for Cultural Relations, 1984; grants from Indian government, 1984, and from American Council of Learned Societies and Linguistic Society of America, 1984.

WRITINGS:

Sir William Jones, Orientalist: A Bibliography, University of Hawaii Press (Honolulu), 1952.
Oriental Jones: A Biography, Asia Publishing House, 1964.
A History of the English Language, Harcourt (New York City), 1972.
Teacher's Manual to a History of the English Language, Harcourt, 1972.
An Integrated Transformational Grammar of the English Language, Rodopi, 1978.
Sir William Jones: A Bibliography of Primary and Secondary Sources, Library and Information Sources in Linguistics, Volume 7, John Benjamins (Amsterdam, Netherlands), 1979.
Historical Change and English Word Formation: Recent Vocabulary, Peter Lang (New York City), 1987.
The Life and Mind of Oriental Jones, Cambridge University Press (Cambridge, England), 1990.
Arabic Loanwords in English: An Historical Dictionary, Otto Harrassowitz Verlag (Weisbaden, Germany), 1994.
(With Alan Pfeffer) *German Loanwords in English: An Historical Dictionary,* Cambridge University Press, 1994.
Japanese Loanwords in English: An Historical Dictionary, Otto Harrassowitz Verlag, 1996.

EDITOR

The Letters of Sir William Jones, two volumes, Clarendon Press (Oxford, England), 1970.
(With Helmut Esau and others, and contributor) *Language and Communication,* Hornbeam Press (Columbia, SC), 1980.
The Collected Works of Sir William Jones, 13 volumes (facsimile of the 1807 London edition), Curzon Press (London), 1993.
(With Kevin Brine) *Objects of Enquiry: The Life, Contributions, and Influences of Sir William Jones,* New York University Press, 1995.

OTHER

Contributor to *Biographical Dictionary of the Phonetic Sciences,* 1977, *Comparative Criticism: A Year Book,* 1981, *Oxford Companion to the English Language, Oxford International Encyclopedia of Linguistics,* and *Dictionary of Literary Biography.*

Contributor to approximately fifty linguistics and Asian studies journals, literary, and other journals, including *American Anthropologist, American Speech, Asian Affairs, College English, Language, Semiotica,* and *World.*

* * *

CARLSON, Nancy L(ee) 1953-

PERSONAL: Born October 10, 1953, in Minneapolis, MN; daughter of Walter J. (a contractor) and Louise (a homemaker; maiden name, Carlson) Carlson; married John Barry McCool (a graphic designer), June 30, 1979; children: Kelly Louise, John Patrick, Michael Barry. *Education:* Attended University of Minnesota, 1972-73, and Santa Fe Workshop of Contemporary Art, 1975; Minneapolis College of Art and Design, B.F.A., 1976. *Avocational interests:* "Physical fitness, running, biking, watching my children do sports."

ADDRESSES: Home—5900 Mount Normandale Dr., Bloomington, MN 55438.

CAREER: Artist and illustrator, 1975—. Visiting artist at schools, including Bemidji State University, 1983, Minnetonka Schools, MN, 1985, and Minneapolis School of Art and Design, 1986.

Lecturer and public speaker. Card Buyer for Center Book Shop, Walter Art Center, 1977-80; arts and craft specialist for city of South St. Paul, MN, 1978; illustrator of greeting cards for Recycled Paper Products, 1982. Creator of CD-ROM products. Illustrator of calendars, mugs, T-shirts, posters, hats, and gift wrap. *Exhibitions:* "Commencement Exhibition," Minneapolis College of Art and Design, 1976; "New Works by Three Artists," Honeywell Plaza, Minneapolis, MN, 1980; "Drawings: Scandinavian Reflections," Dolly Fiterman Gallery, 1980; "Minnesota Women," WARM Gallery, Minneapolis, 1981, 1982; Minnesota State Fair Art Exhibition, 1981; "American Art: The Challenge of the Land," Pillsbury World Headquarters, 1981; "Illustrator's Art," Inland Gallery, Minneapolis, 1982; "Young Minnesota Artists," University Gallery, University of Minnesota, 1982; "Hausman Years: 1975-1982," Minneapolis College of Art and Design, 1982; "Original Art," Master Eagle Gallery, New York City, 1983, 1985; "Alumni Show," Minneapolis College of Art and Design, 1986; "The Art of Author Illustrator Nancy Carlson," American Swedish Institute, Minneapolis, 1989; "Metaphorical Fish," University Art Museum, 1990; "Children's Book Illustration," Minneapolis College of Art and Design, 1993; "Children's Book Illustration," Plymouth Church, Minneapolis, 1994; "Whimsical World of Josie Winship and Nancy Carlson," Bloomington Art Center, Bloomington, MN, 1996.

AWARDS, HONORS: Drawing awards from Northshore Arts Festival, 1975, Minnesota State Fair Art Exhibition, 1981, Young Minnesota Artists, University of Minnesota, 1982, Women in International Design, 1983, and Minneapolis Graphic Design Association, 1985; Parents' Choice Award, Parents' Choice Foundation, 1985, for *Louanne the Pig in the Talent Show;* Children's Choice Award, 1996, for *Sit Still.*

WRITINGS:

SELF-ILLUSTRATED

Harriet's Recital, Carolrhoda (Minneapolis), 1982.
Harriet and Walt, Carolrhoda, 1982.
Harriet and the Roller Coaster, Carolrhoda, 1982.
Harriet and the Garden, Carolrhoda, 1982.
Harriet's Halloween Candy, Carolrhoda, 1982.
Loudmouth George and the Cornet, Carolrhoda, 1983.
Loudmouth George and the New Neighbors, Carolrhoda, 1983.
Loudmouth George and the Fishing Trip, Carolrhoda, 1983.
Loudmouth George and the Sixth-Grade Bully, Carolrhoda, 1983.
Loudmouth George and the Big Race, Carolrhoda, 1983.
Bunnies and Their Hobbies, Carolrhoda, 1984.
Louanne Pig in Making the Team, Carolrhoda, 1985.
Louanne Pig in the Mysterious Valentine, Carolrhoda, 1985.
Louanne Pig in the Perfect Family, Carolrhoda, 1985.
Louanne Pig in the Talent Show, Carolrhoda, 1985.
Louanne Pig in Witch Lady, Carolrhoda, 1985.
Bunnies and Their Sports, Viking (New York City), 1987.
Arnie and the Stolen Markers, Viking, 1987.
Arnie Goes to Camp, Viking, 1988.
I Like Me, Viking, 1988.
Poor Carl, Viking, 1988.
Arnie and the New Kid, Viking, 1990.
Take Time to Relax, Viking, 1991.
What If It Never Stops Raining?, Viking, 1992.
A Visit to Grandma's, Viking, 1993.
Life is Fun!, Viking, 1993.
How to Lose All Your Friends, Viking, 1994.
Arnie and the Skateboard Gang, Viking, 1995.
Sit Still, Viking, 1996.

ILLUSTRATOR

Joyce Kessel, *Halloween,* Carolrhoda, 1980.
Geoffrey Scott, *Egyptian Boats,* Carolrhoda, 1981.
(With Trina Schart Hyman, Hilary Knight, and Peter E. Hanson) Pamela Espeland and Marilyn Waniek, *The Cat Walked through the Casserole and Other Poems for Children,* Carolrhoda, 1984.
Susan Pearson, *The Baby and the Bear,* Viking, 1987.
Pearson, *When the Baby Went to Bed,* Viking, 1987.
Rufus Klein, *Watch Out for These Weirdos,* Viking, 1990.
Pearson, *Lenore's Big Break,* Viking, 1992.
Jacqueline K. Ogburg, *The Masked Maverick,* Lothrop (New York City), 1994.
Rick Walton, *When a Bug Craws in Your Mouth and Other Poems to Drive You Crazy,* Lothrop, 1995.

OTHER

Also author of stage adaptations of *Louanne Pig in the Talent Show* and *Loudmouth George and the 6th Grade Bully,* both produced in Hopkins, MN.

ADAPTATIONS: A number of Carlson's books have been adapted for cassette tape, including *Harriet and Walt,* Live Oak Media, 1984; *Harriet's Recital* (with filmstrip), Random House, 1984, Live Oak Media, 1985; *Harriet and the Roller Coaster,* Live Oak Media, 1985; *Harriet and the Garden,* Live Oak Media, 1985; *Harriet's Halloween Candy,* Live Oak Media, 1985; *Loudmouth George and the Cornet,* Live Oak Media, 1986; *Loudmouth George and the Fishing Trip,* Live Oak Media, 1986; *Loudmouth George and the Sixth-Grade Bully,* Live Oak Media, 1986; *Loudmouth George and the Big Race,* Live Oak Media, 1986; *Loudmouth George and the New Neighbors,* Live Oak Media, 1987; *Louanne Pig in the Talent Show,* Live Oak Media, 1987; *Louanne Pig in Witch Lady,* Live Oak Media, 1987; *Louanne Pig in the Perfect Family,* Live Oak Media, 1987; *Louanne Pig in Making the Team,* Live Oak Media, 1987; and *I Like Me* ("Read Along" cassette series), Weston Woods, 1988, (with filmstrip), Weston Woods, 1988.

WORK IN PROGRESS: A CD-ROM; *ABC, I Like Me Book.*

SIDELIGHTS: From the age of five, author and illustrator Nancy Carlson knew that she wanted to be an artist when she grew up; she began illustrating children's books soon after graduating from college. Quickly realizing she would rather illustrate books that she had written herself, Carlson began combining her own pictures with stories and produced her first book, *Harriet's Recital,* in 1982. She wrote four more books about Harriet before creating a series of books about Loudmouth George and another about Louanne Pig.

Another series by Carlson features the antics of Louanne and George's friend, Arnie the Cat. A cat who loves mice, Arnie first appeared in Carlson's books about Harriet before he received a book of his own, *Arnie and the Stolen Markers,* in 1987. One day Arnie sees a set of markers for sale at Harvey's Candy and Toy Shop and decides that he must have them. However, since he has wasted all his allowance on candy and his spendthrift friend Louanne refuses to lend him any money, Arnie slips the markers under his shirt and out of the store. Once he returns home, Arnie's mother discovers his thievery and returns him to the store, where the owner makes Arnie work for the stolen marker set. "Brightly spirited characters" help Carlson convey the message to children that stealing is wrong without the author "didactically haranguing the impropriety of stealing" according to Cathy Woodward in *School Library Journal.*

In *Arnie and the New Kid,* Carlson's 1990 picture book, a boy named Philip, who is in a wheelchair, enters Arnie's school. Arnie leads the other children in teasing Philip about his physical disability, but when Arnie injures his leg and finds out how difficult maneuvering on crutches is, he begins to sympathize with Philip. Philip and Arnie begin a friendship that continues long after Arnie's cast is removed. Writing in *School Library Journal,* Ellen Fader praised the happy ending, as well as Carlson's "lighthearted treatment of a common situation." *Bulletin of the Center for Children's Books* critic Deborah Stevenson applauded Carlson's illustrations, saying the characters complimented the text by "convey[ing] emotions that the text left unspoken."

While producing the Arnie series, Carlson also worked on other books to help youngsters calm their childhood fears and develop a healthy outlook on life. *Take Time to Relax,* the author's 1991 book, features a family of busy beavers who fill their every waking hour with activities from ballet classes and soccer games to tennis lessons and volleyball matches. When a terrible snowstorm prevents the beaver family from leaving their home, the ambitious family discovers that spending time alone with each other is more important than any other activity. A critic in *Publishers Weekly* liked the "hyperbole and humor" Carlson included in her text and noted that *Take Time to Relax* reinforces "an important message to today's over-programmed families."

Carlson followed *Take Time to Relax* with *What If It Never Stops Raining?,* another book that concentrates on children coping with their anxieties. Young Tim constantly worries about everything, even about a neverending rain flooding his house. However, with his mother's support, Tim learns how to distinguish between worrying about real dangers, like falling off of the playground equipment, and needless anxiety about unfamiliar situations, like his new school bus driver getting lost.

While admitting the ending is "a bit too tidy," a reviewer in *Publishers Weekly* said Carlson "proficiently handled" the delicate subject of how to quiet a child's irrational fears.

Carlson once explained: "I'm an artist who enjoys making up stories for children. When I'm not writing for kids, I'm drawing pictures for shows and galleries."

BIOGRAPHICAL/CRITICAL SOURCES:

PERIODICALS

Booklist, May 15, 1990, p. 1797; October 15, 1992, p. 438; January 1, 1993, p. 810; February 1, 1994, p. 1010; September, 1, 1994, p. 49; June 1, 1995, p. 1782.

Bulletin of the Center for Children's Books, February, 1989, p. 143; May, 1990, pp. 209-10.

Five Owls, September, 1988, p. 8; May, 1990, p. 93; May, 1993, pp. 104, 122. *Junior Bookshelf,* April, 1993, p. 57.

Horn Book Guide, spring, 1993, p. 23; spring, 1994, p. 28; spring, 1995, p. 28.

Kirkus Reviews, March 15, 1989, p. 460; May 15, 1990, p. 726; August 15, 1991, p. 1086; August 15, 1994, p. 1122.

Magpies, March, 1992, p. 27.

Publishers Weekly, October 9, 1987, p. 84; April 29, 1988, p. 74; September 9, 1988, p. 130; December 9, 1988, p. 61; December, 7, 1990, p. 81; August 30, 1991, p. 81; November 9, 1992, p. 82; March 1, 1993, p. 58; July 26, 1993, p. 70.

School Library Journal, February, 1988, p. 58; September, 1988, p. 154; June, 1990, p. 97; August, 1991, p. 143; November, 1991, p. 90; February, 1993, p. 70; November, 1993, p. 76; August, 1995, p. 121.

Times Educational Supplement, February 19, 1993, p. R2.

* * *

CARLSON, Natalie Savage 1906-

PERSONAL: Born October 3, 1906, in Kernstown, VA; daughter of Joseph Hamilton (in business) and Natalie Marie (Vallar) Savage; married Daniel Carlson (a naval officer), December 7, 1929; children: Stephanie Natalie Carlson Sullivan, Julie Anne Carlson McAlpine. *Education:* High school graduate. *Politics:* Republican. *Religion:* Roman Catholic. *Avocational interests:* Cooking, crossword puzzles, creating hand puppets of her storybook characters.

ADDRESSES: Home—3220 Highway 19, North Lot 17, Clearwater, FL 34615.

CAREER: Long Beach Morning Sun, Long Beach, CA, reporter, 1926-29; writer of children's books.

MEMBER: Society of Children's Book Writers.

AWARDS, HONORS: New York Herald Tribune Children's Spring Book Festival Awards, 1952, for *The Talking Cat and Other Stories of French Canada,* 1954, for *Alphonse, That Bearded One,* 1955, for *Wings against the Wind;* Honor Book Awards, 1955, for *Wings against the Wind,* and 1957, for *Hortense: The Cow for a Queen;* Boys Clubs of America Junior Book Awards, 1955, for *Alphonse, That Bearded One,* and 1956, for *Wings against the Wind;* Newbery Medal runner-up, 1959, for *The Family under the Bridge;* Wel-Met Children's Book Award, Child Study Association of America, 1966, for *The Empty Schoolhouse;* nominated U.S. candidate for International Hans Christian Andersen Award, 1966.

WRITINGS:

JUVENILE

The Talking Cat and Other Stories of French Canada, illustrated by Roger Duvoisin, Harper (New York City), 1952.

Alphonse, That Bearded One, illustrated by Nicolas Mordvinoff, Harcourt (New York City), 1954.

Wings against the Wind, illustrated by Mircea Vasiliu, Harper, 1955.

Sashes Red and Blue, illustrated by Rita Fava, Harper, 1956.

Hortense: The Cow for a Queen, illustrated by Mordvinoff, Harcourt, 1957.

The Happy Orpheline, illustrated by Garth Williams, Harper, 1957, illustrated by Pearl Falconer, Blackie & Son (London), 1960.

The Family under the Bridge, illustrated by Williams, Harper, 1958, published in England as *Under the Bridge,* Blackie & Son, 1969.

A Brother for the Orphelines, illustrated by Williams, Harper, 1959, illustrated by Falconer, Blackie & Son, 1961.

Evangeline: Pigeon of Paris, illustrated by Mordvinoff, Harcourt, 1960, published in England as *Pigeon of Paris,* illustrated by Quentin Blake, Blackie & Son, 1972.

The Tomahawk Family, illustrated by Stephen Cook, Harper, 1960.

The Song of the Lop-Eared Mule, illustrated by Janina Domanska, Harper, 1961.

Carnival in Paris, illustrated by Fermin Rocker, Harper, 1962, illustrated by Geraldine Spence, Blackie & Son, 1964.

A Pet for the Orphelines, illustrated by Rocker, Harper, 1962, illustrated by Falconer, Blackie & Son, 1963.

Jean-Claude's Island, illustrated by Nancy Ekholm Burkert, Harper, 1963.

School Bell in the Valley, illustrated by Gilbert Riswold, Harcourt, 1963.

The Letter on the Tree, illustrated by John Kaufmann, Harper, 1964.

The Orphelines in the Enchanted Castle, illustrated by Adriana Saviozzi, Harper, 1964, illustrated by Falconer, Blackie & Son, 1965.

The Empty Schoolhouse, illustrated by Kaufmann, Harper, 1965.

Sailor's Choice, illustrated by George Loh, Harper, 1966.

Chalou, illustrated by Loh, Harper, 1967, illustrated by Jillian Willett, Blackie & Son, 1968.

Luigi of the Streets, illustrated by Emily McCully, Harper, 1967, published in England as *The Family on the Waterfront,* illustrated by Victor Ambrus, Blackie & Son, 1969.

Ann Aurelia and Dorothy, illustrated by Dale Payson, Harper, 1968.

Befana's Gift, illustrated by Robert Quackenbush, Harper, 1969, published in England as *A Grandson for the Asking,* Blackie & Son, 1969.

Marchers for the Dream, illustrated by Alvin Smith, Harper, 1969, illustrated by Bernard Blatch, Blackie & Son, 1971.

The Half-Sisters, illustrated by Thomas di Grazia, Harper, 1970, illustrated by Faith Jaques, Blackie & Son, 1972.

Luvvy and the Girls, illustrated by di Grazia, Harper, 1971.

Marie Louise and Christophe, illustrated by Jose Areugo and Ariane Dewey, Scribner (New York City), 1974.

Marie Louise's Heydey, illustrated by Areugo and Dewey, Scribner, 1975.

Runaway Marie Louise, illustrated by Areugo and Dewey, Scribner, 1977.

Jaky or Dodo?, illustrated by Gail Owens, Scribner, 1978.

Time for the White Egret, illustrated by Charles Robinson, Scribner, 1978.

The Night the Scarecrow Walked, illustrated by Robinson, Scribner, 1979.

A Grandmother for the Orphelines, illustrated by David White, Harper, 1980.

King of the Cats and Other Tales, illustrated by David Frampton, Doubleday (Garden City, NY), 1980.

Marie Louise and Christophe at the Carnival, illustrated by Aruego and Dewey, Scribner, 1981.

Spooky Night, illustrated by Andrew Glass, Lothrop (New York City), 1982.

The Surprise in the Mountains, illustrated by Elise Primavera, Harper, 1983.

The Ghost in the Lagoon, illustrated by Glass, Lothrop, 1984.

Spooky and the Ghost Cat, illustrated by Glass, Lothrop, 1985.

Spooky and the Wizard's Bats, illustrated by Glass, Lothrop, 1986.

Spooky and the Bad Luck Raven, illustrated by Glass, Lothrop, 1988.

Spooky and the Witch's Goat, illustrated by Glass, Lothrop, 1989.

SIDELIGHTS: Natalie Savage Carlson is the author of more than forty novels and picture books for children. A former newspaper reporter, Carlson became inspired to write for the young while reading to her family. She received critical attention as a children's author after her first published book, *The Talking Cat and Other Stories of French Canada,* won the *New York Herald Tribune* Children's Spring Book Festival Award in 1952. As she continued her work, she developed a reputation for her keen ability to capture the unique settings, lifestyles, and traditions of the various lands and people of which she wrote. She has also been lauded for the realism in her books—an achievement, some critics claim, that springs from the fact that she often writes of situations that happened in her own life.

Born in Kernstown, Virginia, in 1906, Carlson was the daughter of American distiller Joseph Hamilton Savage and his French-Canadian wife

Natalie Marie (nee Vallar). Carlson later incorporated some of her family memories and childhood experiences into her fiction. Her novel *The Half-Sisters,* for example, contains a recollection of Shady Grove, the family farm in Maryland. The author's French-Canadian roots were also an important influence during her childhood. Her mother, Natalie Marie, told the family stories she had heard from her uncle Michel Meloche. Carlson was curious and enchanted by the folk tales and later based *The Talking Cat and Other Stories of French Canada* on such accounts. Her vast assortment of relatives, family, and friends would also filter into her writings as characters in her novels and picture books. Her sister Evangeline, for example, takes on the persona of Marylou in *Luvvy and the Girls,* while Carlson herself is depicted as Luvvy.

During the mid-1920's, the Savage family experienced hardship when Joseph lost his business due to some financial miscalculations. Carlson obtained a job as a reporter for the *Long Beach Morning Sun,* thereby meeting her financial needs and realizing her dream of writing professionally. She charted her ascension through the ranks at the *Sun* in *Something about the Author Autobiography Series (SAAS):* "I began as society reporter and worked up to drama critic and feature writer. My rise was fast because my city editor was in love with me. But I was in love with the police reporter who only was in love with himself."

Carlson, nevertheless, met and wed Daniel Carlson in the late 1920s. Her husband's career with the U.S. Navy required frequent relocations for the couple. As a result, the author can boast that she has lived or visited every state in America but Alaska and has resided in Paris, France. During the 1930s she gave birth to two daughters, Stephanie and Julie. As she read stories to them, she decided to focus her energies on writing children's literature. In the subsequent years, Carlson wrote *Alphonse, That Bearded One* and *Wings against the Wind,* both of which were honored at the *New York Herald Tribune* Children's Spring Book Festival.

A popular children's novel upon its release in 1955, *Wings against the Wind* describes the adventures of an abandoned baby sea gull named Fripoun and his honorary papa Jacot, a Breton fisherman. A story of trust, honor, and friendship, the book recounts the unusual relationship that develops between the so-called parent and child and the despair the duo faces when the sea gull is wrongfully accused of theft. Critics generally praised Carlson's story, pointing out her ability to narrate so vividly. Several reviewers cited the following passage for its effective presentation of the loneliness Fripoun feels when he is banished from the fishing boat and sent to live on a chicken farm: "Bewildered and still far from being a happy chicken, Fripoun sat down on his webbed feet and refused to budge again. He sat like a gray rock. Only his eyelids moved in blinks . . . . Never had he been so lonely since he was the yolk in an egg."

Wings against the Wind was also commended by reviewers for its humor and authentic flavor—an ambience Carlson evoked through references to Breton culture and traditions, such as "The Blessing of the Sea" festival. The tale "is told with wit, speed and a fine knowledge of place and character," wrote Marjorie Fischer in the *New York Times.* The critic's sentiments were echoed in the *Chicago Tribune* by Polly Goodwin, who asserted that *Wings against the Wind* should be "read aloud, so that young and old may fully savor its Gallic drolleries and amusing situations."

When her husband was assigned to the European Command Headquarters in Paris, France, Carldon ventured there for a three-year stay. In time, she incorporated her experiences in France in books such as her acclaimed "Orpheline" series. Carlson became acquainted with "orphelines," French for "orphans," through her work with an officers' wives group. In *SAAS* she explained: "I joined those helping the poor of the Paris area, not because I was so charitable but because I wanted to see the nitty-gritty side of French life. I might use it as background for some future books—which I did . . . . The most enjoyable work was doing things for the orphans . . . . These adorable children were the inspiration for my book, *The Happy Orpheline,* which was set in an orphanage unlike theirs or any in this country." Brigitte is the happy orpheline of the title, and she and the 19 other wards of the French government enjoy their life together so much that Brigitte commits a crime to make sure that she will never be adopted.

Carlson also wove her experiences with Paris's poor into other works like her 1958 novel, *The Family under the Bridge.* A Newbery Medal runner-up, the volume is considered by some critics to be among Carlson's finest. Centering around a tramp named Armand who lives on the streets of Paris, the story chronicles the hobo's transformation from a transient with little tolerance for children or work into a respectable citizen and honorary grandfather. A reviewer for the *Chicago Tribune* observed that, "The Paris the tourist seldom sees, the Paris of the poor and the homeless, is the setting of a story as wonderfully warm, as unabashedly sentimental as ever tugged at a reader's heart."

Like some critics of *Wings against the Wind,* various reviewers of *The Family under the Bridge* were enthusiastic about the author's ability to capture the cultural essence of the story's setting. As evidence, commentators offered Carlson's description of a party given by Notre Dame Cathedral's parishioners for the poor of Paris. In part it reads: "A large tent had been raised on the quay—a tent that would have delighted the gypsies. Young boys and girls of the parish were carrying out pans of steaming food from the tent. The warm smell of sauerkraut was overpowering . . . . Charcoal heaters had been set around to warm the air, and many of the ragged guests were huddled over them. Others sat on the curb greedily eating out of tin bowls." Carlson achieved a similar feat in *Luigi of the Streets* by describing the rough-and-tumble world of an exotic Marseilles slum. Praised Ellen Goodman in the *New York Times Book Review,* "In *Luigi of the Streets,* Natalie Savage Carlson again exercises her gift for fusing foreign locales and universal values into a strong, realistic story."

After three years in Paris, the Carlsons returned to Rhode Island, and eventually retired to Florida. Meanwhile, the author completed books with social themes like *The Empty Schoolhouse,* a tale of courage about the racial desegregation of a schoolhouse in Louisiana. Jean Fritz, writing in the *New York Times Book Review,* praised Carlson for keeping a sometimes violent and racially incendiary tale focussed on what matters most to children: the friendship of two ten-year old girls, one of whom is black and one, white. "It takes skill and restraint," observed Fritz, "to keep a story simple and the relationships warm against such a background; Mrs. Carlson succeeds admirably." At the same time, Carlson turned to writing picture books like *Marie Louise and Christophe,* a tale about the ambivalent friendship between a mongoose and a snake. Carlson told *CA:* "I have turned to writing picture book stories because they offer a fresh approach and a challenge whereas I feel 'written out' for older children." In the 1980s she and illustrator Andrew Glass began a series of books that follow the antics and adventures of a black cat named Spooky, which was once owned by a nasty witch. Maria B. Salvadore, writing in the *School Library Journal,* described *Spooky and the Ghost Cat* as "a satisfying, not-too-spooky story which should be an ideal Halloween read aloud both in homes and at story times." Reviewers have also applauded the collection for its incorporation of rhythmic language. For example, in the third book, *Spooky and the Wizard's Bats,* Carlson uses narration such as, "He had to race quickety-paw into the house to get away," and "He went creepy-crawl, creepy-crawl through the cave."

Of her distinguished writing career, Carlson told *SAAS* readers: "Most of my books have gone out of print but I have the satisfaction of knowing they are still in libraries for children to read. And I keep writing more . . . . I am old now but have so many memories to relive." Her significant contribution to children's literature has been noted by various reviewers who assert that Carlson's witty stories are as enjoyable to the adult as they are to the child. As Helen Adams Masten noted in *Saturday Review,* Carlson's books contain "a fresh quality and original humor . . . which make them delightful."

BIOGRAPHICAL/CRITICAL SOURCES:

BOOKS

Contemporary Authors, New Revision Series, Volume 3, Gale, 1981.

Something about the Author, Gale, Volume 2, 1971.

Something about the Author Autobiography Series, Gale, Volume 4, 1987.

PERIODICALS

Atlantic Monthly, December, 1965.

Booklist, March 1, 1988.

Book World, November 5, 1967; May 5, 1968; May 17, 1970.

Bulletin of the Center for Children's Books, March, 1980; October, 1982; November, 1983; April, 1985; February, 1986; November, 1986.

Chicago Tribune, June 5, 1955; November 17, 1957; November 2, 1958.
Chicago Tribune Book World, November 8, 1980; December 7, 1980; May 3, 1981; October 10, 1982.
Children's Book World, November 5, 1967.
Christian Science Monitor, November 6, 1958.
Commonweal, February 21, 1969; November 1, 1969; November 20, 1970; February 26, 1971; May 21, 1971.
Horn Book, June, 1955; August, 1955; December, 1958; February, 1981; October, 1982; March/April, 1986.
Kirkus Reviews, September 1, 1977; December 15, 1980.
New York Herald Tribune Book Review, May 15, 1955; November 17, 1957; November 2, 1958.
New York Times, May 15, 1955; November 30, 1958.
New York Times Book Review, September 12, 1965; February 12, 1967; May 7, 1967; November 5, 1967; May 5, 1968; May 4, 1969; September 27, 1970; May 5, 1974; November 16, 1975; November 13, 1977; February 25, 1979.
Publishers Weekly, October 3, 1966; April 29, 1968; March 18, 1974; October 17, 1980; August 22, 1986.
Saturday Review, September 17, 1955; December 21, 1957; December 20, 1958; May 13, 1967; July 25, 1970.
School Library Journal, January, 1983; February, 1984; March, 1984; February, 1985; October, 1985; December, 1986; May, 1988; September, 1988; June, 1989.
Society of Children's Writers Bulletin, August, 1986.
Times Literary Supplement, November 30, 1967; May 19, 1969; August 3, 1969; August 14, 1970; July 2, 1971; July 14, 1972; September 19, 1980.
Washington Post Book World, April 8, 1979.
Young Readers' Review, November, 1966; June, 1968; May, 1969.*

* * *

CARLSTROM, Nancy White 1948-

PERSONAL: Born August 4, 1948, in Washington, PA; daughter of William J. (a steel mill worker) and Eva (Lawrence) White; married David R. Carlstrom, September 7, 1974; children: Jesse David, Joshua White. *Education:* Wheaton College, Wheaton, IL, B.A., 1970; also attended Harvard Extension and Radcliffe College, 1974-76. *Religion:* Christian. *Avocational interests:* Reading, tennis, cross-country skiing, and birding.

ADDRESSES: *Agent*—Marilyn Marlow, Curtis Brown Ltd. 10 Astor Pl., New York, NY 10003.

CAREER: Writer, 1983—. A. Leo Weil Elementary School, Pittsburgh, PA, teacher, 1970-72; Plum Cove Elementary School, Gloucester, MA, teacher, 1972-74; Secret Garden Children's Bookshop, Seattle, WA, owner and manager, 1977-83. Worked with children in West Africa and the West Indies; worked at school for children with Down's Syndrome in Merida, Yucatan, Mexico.

MEMBER: Society of Children's Book Writers and Illustrators, National Council of Teachers of English, Authors Guild, Authors League of America.

AWARDS, HONORS: Editor's Choice, *Booklist,* 1986, and Children's Choice, International Reading Association/Children's Book Council (IRA/CBC), 1987, both for *Jesse Bear, What Will You Wear?;* American Booksellers Pick of the List, and Notable Book, National Council of Teachers of English (NCTE), both 1987, both for *Wild Wild Sunflower Child Anna;* Best Book of 1990, *Parents' Magazine,* for *Where Does the Night Hide?;* Children's Choice, IRA/CBC, and Parents' Choice, *Booklist,* both 1991, both for *Blow Me a Kiss, Miss Lilly;* Notable Book, NCTE, 1991, for *Goodbye Geese.*

WRITINGS:

Jesse Bear, What Will You Wear?, illustrated by Bruce Degen, Macmillan (New York City), 1986.
The Moon Came, Too, illustrated by Stella Ormai, Macmillan, 1987.
Wild Wild Sunflower Child Anna, illustrated by Jerry Pinkney, Macmillan, 1987.
Better Not Get Wet, Jesse Bear, illustrated by Bruce Degen, Macmillan, 1988.
Where Does the Night Hide?, illustrated by Thomas B. Allen and Laura Allen, Macmillan, 1988.

Blow Me a Kiss, Miss Lilly, illustrated by Amy Schwartz, Harper (New York City), 1989.

Graham Cracker Animals 1-2-3, illustrated by John Sandford, Macmillan, 1989.

Heather Hiding, illustrated by Dennis Nolan, Macmillan, 1990.

It's about Time, Jesse Bear, and Other Rhymes, illustrated by Bruce Degen, Macmillan, 1990.

I'm Not Moving, Mama!, illustrated by Thor Wickstrom, Macmillan, 1990.

Grandpappy, illustrated by Laurel Molk, Little, Brown (Boston), 1990.

No Nap for Benjamin Badger, illustrated by Dennis Nolan, Macmillan, 1990.

Light: Stories of a Small Kindness, illustrated by Lisa Desimini, Little, Brown, 1990.

Moose in the Garden, illustrated by Lisa Desimini, Harper, 1990.

Goodbye Geese, illustrated by Ed Young, Philomel (New York City), 1991.

Who Gets the Sun Out of Bed?, illustrated by David McPhail, Little, Brown, 1992.

Northern Lullaby, illustrated by Diane and Leo Dillon, Philomel, 1992.

Kiss Your Sister, Rose Marie!, illustrated by Thor Wickstrom, Macmillan, 1992.

How Do You Say It Today, Jesse Bear?, illustrated by Bruce Degen, Macmillan, 1992.

Baby-O, illustrated by Sucie Stevenson, Little, Brown, 1992.

The Snow Speaks, illustrated by Jane Dyer, Little, Brown, 1992.

What Does the Rain Play?, illustrated by Henri Sorensen, Macmillan, 1993.

Swim the Silver Sea, Joshie Otter, illustrated by Ken Kuori, Philomel, 1993.

Rise and Shine, illustrated by Dominic Catalano, HarperCollins, 1993.

How Does the Wind Walk?, illustrated by Deborah K. Ray, Macmillan, 1993.

Fish and Flamingo, illustrated by Lisa Desimini, Little, Brown, 1993.

Wishing at Dawn in Summer, illustrated by Diane Wolfolk Allison, Little, Brown, 1993.

Does God Know How to Tie Shoes?, illustrated by Lori McElrath-Eslick, Eerdmans (Grand Rapids, MI), 1993.

What Would You Do If You Lived at the Zoo?, illustrated by Lizi Boyd, Little, Brown, 1994.

Jesse Bear's Yum-Yum Crumble, Aladdin Books (New York City), 1994.

Jesse Bear's Wiggle-Jiggle Jump-Up, Aladdin Books, 1994.

Jesse Bear's Tum Tum Tickle, Aladdin Books, 1994.

Jesse Bear's Tra-La Tub, Aladdin Books, 1994.

Happy Birthday, Jesse Bear!, illustrated by Bruce Degen, Macmillan, 1994.

Barney Is Best, illustrated by James G. Hale, HarperCollins, 1994.

Who Said Boo?: Halloween Poems for the Very Young, illustrated by R. W. Alley, Simon & Schuster (New York City), 1995.

I Am Christmas, illustrated by Lori McElrath-Eslick, Eerdmans, 1995.

Let's Count It Out, Jesse Bear, illustrated by Bruce Degen, Simon & Schuster, 1996.

Ten Christmas Sheep, illustrated by Cynthia Fisher, Eerdmans, 1996.

Raven and River, illustrated by Jon Van Zyle, Little, Brown, 1997.

Midnight Dance of the Snowshoe Hare, illustrated by Ken Kuori, Philomel, 1997.

Glory, illustrated by Lori McElrath-Eslick, Eerdmans, in press.

WORK IN PROGRESS: A historical novel for young adults, *The Shape of Waiting.*

SIDELIGHTS: Author of the popular "Jesse Bear" series, Nancy White Carlstrom decided to become a writer of children's books at an early age; she worked in the children's department of her local library during her high school years, and "that's where my dream of writing children's books was born," she once told *SATA.* Known for her tight lines of verse filled with vivid description and evocation of the everyday, Carlstrom presents hopeful and humorous picture and board books for very young readers, books with simple vocabulary and subjects ranging from counting and colors to more sophisticated topics like inter-generational and multicultural relationships.

Carlstrom's themes reflect her own life and interests. The popular "Jesse Bear" books grew out of a poem written for her first son, Jesse. In these and other works, the author's concerns with society and nature are a reflection of her own upbringing and world view. Growing up without television, Carlstrom learned early on to create her own fantasies and to entertain herself. She loved books and writing from an early age, and as she reported in an interview with Jeffrey S. and Vicky L. Copeland in *Speaking of Poets,* "I primarily grew up on the Bible. Even as a young child I enjoyed the language of the Psalms." Another favorite of

Carlstrom's was *Little Women.* After earning a B.A. in education from Wheaton College, Carlstrom taught primary school in Pittsburgh while working summers with children in the West Indies and in West Africa. She also studied art and children's literature, then moved with her husband to the Yucatan where she worked at a school for children with Down's Syndrome. Upon their return to the United States, the couple moved to Seattle, where Carlstrom became proprietor of The Secret Garden, a children's bookstore. "As owner and manager of the bookshop I was constantly surrounded by children's books," Carlstrom once recalled, "and spent a good portion of my time promoting quality children's literature through book fairs, presentations at churches and parent groups, and in our shop newsletter. In 1981 the urge to write resurfaced and I participated in a two-week workshop led by children's book author Jane Yolen." During that workshop Carlstrom wrote the poem that forms the text of *Wild Wild Sunflower Child Anna,* although several years passed before this text found a publisher. In the meantime, Carlstrom wrote *Jesse Bear, What Will You Wear?* "My husband and I often called our son Jesse Bear," Carlstrom explained, "and the book . . . began as a little song I sang while dressing him. I finished the picture book text for Jesse's first birthday." The book progresses through the day as little Jesse dresses and then messes and must dress again. Liza Bliss, writing in *School Library Journal,* noted in particular that "the rhymes, besides having a charming lilt to them, are clean and catchy and beg to be recited." A *Bulletin of the Center for Children's Books* reviewer drew attention to Carlstrom's lyrics, as well, and determined that, "without crossing the line into sentimentality, this offers a happy, humorous soundfest that will associate reading aloud with a sense of play." Lines like Jesse's reply to his mother—"I'll wear the sun / On my legs that run / Sun on the run in the morning"—tempt one "to sing Carlstrom's words aloud," commented a *Kirkus Reviews* critic, who added: "[Carlstrom] has a rich imagination which, hopefully, will create many more books for children."

Carlstrom has, in fact, created many more books for children, a large number of which are further adventures of Jesse Bear, with illustrations by Bruce Degen. *Better Not Get Wet, Jesse Bear* is a "winsome picture book," according to a *Publishers Weekly* reviewer, with "lilting, strongly rhymed text"; Ellen Fader of *Horn Book* commented that "the book never loses its claim to the sensibility of young children, who will be won over by Jesse Bear's delight in water play and his final triumphant splash." Clocks and the times of the day are at the heart of Carlstrom's third "Jesse Bear" title, *It's about Time Jesse Bear, and Other Rhymes,* a book that "children are sure to enjoy," according to Patricia Pearl in *School Library Journal. How Do You Say It Today, Jesse Bear?* celebrates the holidays of the year, from Independence Day to Halloween and Christmas. Ilene Cooper of *Booklist* commented on this work: "A good way to learn about the months and holidays, or read it just for fun." The sixth in the series, a Main Selection of the Children's Book-of-the-Month Club, *Let's Count It Out, Jesse Bear,* finds the playful bear "in a high-impact counting game," according to a *Publishers Weekly* reviewer. The rhyme for number two in this counting book is indicative of the humor and joy of the whole: "Jumping high, / Landing loud. / New shoes dancing, / New shoes proud." At seven titles and counting, the "Jesse Bear" series has prompted spin-off board books and toys as well as a loyal following among readers.

Carlstrom has also written many books outside of the "Jesse Bear" series. The first text she wrote, *Wild Wild Sunflower Child Anna,* about a child's exploration and discovery of the natural world around her, found a publisher in 1987 and is, according to Carlstrom, "still my favorite book of all I have written." Denise M. Wilms of *Booklist* maintained that "audiences young and old will find [Anna's] pleasure in the day most contagious." Ellen Fader, writing in *Horn Book,* concluded that "an exceptional treat awaits the parent and child who lose themselves in this book." Carlstrom further celebrated the lives of preschoolers in books such as *Heather Hiding,* the tale of a hide-and-seek game, *Graham Cracker Animals 1-2-3,* and *Blow Me a Kiss, Miss Lilly,* which deals with the death of a loved one. *Light: Stories of a Small Kindness* draws somewhat on Carlstrom's time spent in Mexico, in that the gathered tales all have Hispanic settings and all deal with a small kindness. "Tender, thought-provoking, moving are just a few of the words to describe these seven short stories," commented Ilene Cooper in a *Booklist* review.

Much the same format is employed in *Baby-O,* in which the rhythms of the West Indies are celebrated in a rhyming cumulative story of a family on its way to market to sell their produce. "Sing it, chant it, clap it, or stamp it," Jane Marino declared in a *School Library Journal* review. "Just don't miss it." Carlstrom has dealt with topics as various as the relationship between a young boy and his grandfather in *Grandpappy,* unlikely friendships in *Fish and Flamingo,* a child's fears of a trip to the hospital in *Barney Is Best,* and even "new baby syndrome" in *Kiss Your Sister, Rose Marie!* Also, harking back to her own childhood enjoyment of the Bible and religion, she wrote a book to encourage a child's questions about God—*Does God Known How to Tie Shoes?*—as well as Christmas books such as *I Am Christmas* and *Ten Christmas Sheep.*

Carlstrom practices the craft of writing with care and intelligence. "A picture book, like a poem, is what I call a bare bones kind of writing," Carlstrom once explained. "Usually I start with many more words than I need or want. I keep cutting away until I am down to the bare bones of what I want to say. It is then up to the illustrator to create pictures that will enlarge and enhance the text. . . . Often a title of a story will come first. I write it down and tend to think about it for a long time before actually sitting down to work on it. Sometimes I just get a few pieces of the story and they have to simmer on the back burner, like a good pot of soup. When the time is right, the writing of the story comes easily." Carlstrom also explained, in *Books That Invite Talk, Wonder, and Play,* that she often sings her words to get the correct rhythm. "Language is a musical experience for me. Rhythm, rhyme and cadence all become an important part of the process. I love the way a young child, just learning the language, rolls a word around on her tongue and, if she likes the sound of it, may chant it over and over."

Moving to Alaska in 1987 provided the author with new settings and themes for her writing—"freely wandering moose, northern lights, and extreme seasonal changes to name a few," she said. Books such as *Moose in the Garden, The Snow Speaks, Northern Lullaby,* and *Goodbye Geese* have all been inspired by the wilderness and wildlife of the far north. "A first-rate choice for toddlers" is how *School Library Journal* contributor Ellen Fader described *Moose in the Garden,* which tells of a moose invading a garden and—to the delight of the young boy of the family—eating all the vegetables the boy does not like. The northern winter is lovingly examined in *Goodbye Geese* through the question and answer exchange between a father and his curious child: "Papa, is winter coming? / Yes, and when the winter comes, she'll touch every living thing." *Booklist* reviewer Carolyn Phelan found *Goodbye Geese* to be "an effective mood book for story hour . . . a vivid introduction to personification." In *Northern Lullaby,* Carlstrom also personifies the natural elements such as the moon and stars, along with wild creatures to conjure up a vision of the vastness of the far north. "The end effect," commented *Bulletin of the Center for Children's Books* reviewer Betsy Hearne, "is both simple and sophisticated." A *Kirkus Reviews* critic noted the book's "gently cadenced verse," and a *Publishers Weekly* reviewer concluded that *Northern Lullaby* was a "stunning, seamlessly executed work." Wintertime in Alaska also inspired Carlstrom's *The Snow Speaks,* in which two children experience the first snowfall of the season. *Booklist* reviewer Carolyn Phelan noted that Carlstrom used "lyrical language to turn down-to-earth experiences into something more," and Jane Marino in *School Library Journal* thought that it was "a book to be enjoyed all winter, long after the decorations have been packed away."

Natural phenomena form the core of many of Carlstrom's books, as she has been a nature lover since her own childhood. In books such as *Where Does the Night Hide?, Who Gets the Sun Out of Bed?, What Does the Rain Play?,* and *How Does the Wind Walk?,* Carlstrom uses question and answer rhymes and riddles to look at nature. With *Who Gets the Sun Out of Bed?,* the author reverses the goodnight story, relating instead a tale about waking up. *School Library Journal* contributor Ruth K. MacDonald found this work to be "an altogether successful story about the coming of the day," noting that "the persistent gentle patterns of questions and answers leads up to a climax that is warm but not boisterous—a fitting, final ending to a story that, despite its message, functions as an appropriate bedtime tale." The sounds of rain take center stage in *What Does the Rain Play?,* as the little boy in the tale loves all the various noises rain makes, even at night. Emily Melton in *Booklist* noted that "the gently calming writing and softly lulling rhythms of the rain sounds make this book a perfect bedtime choice." In *How Does the Wind Walk?,* a little boy looks at the different moods of the wind in different seasons in a question-and-answer format. *Kirkus Reviews* noted that Carlstrom's text employed "lots of alliteration and some subtle internal rhymes" to produce "wonderfully evocative effects."

All of Carlstrom's books share the common denominator of humor and hope. "No matter how bad things get, in this world or in my life," Carlstrom commented in her *Speaking of Poets* interview, "I do believe in joy and hope because I believe there's someone greater than myself in charge. It is my own religious faith that affects both the way I live my life and the way I write." The mystery of creation and of art are at the center of Carlstrom's inspiration, as she explained in the same interview: "I can't always explain exactly why my poems come out the way they do, but there is a joy that I have that I do want to express. And for me, writing is my way of celebrating."

BIOGRAPHICAL/CRITICAL SOURCES:

BOOKS

Copeland, Jeffrey S. and Vicky L. Copeland, editors, *Speaking of Poets*, Volume 2, National Council of Teachers of English, 1994, pp. 194-202.

McClure, Amy A. and Janice V. Kristo, editors, *Books That Invite Talk, Wonder, and Play*, National Council of Teachers of English, 1996, pp. 236-238.

PERIODICALS

Booklist, October 1, 1987, p. 257; December 1, 1989, pp. 740-741; March 15, 1990, p. 1443; December 15, 1990, pp. 855, 860; November 1, 1991, p. 530; November 15, 1991, p. 628; September 15, 1992, p. 154; March 15, 1993, p. 1358; April 1, 1993, p. 1436; December 1, 1993, p. 692; November 1, 1994, p. 505; September 1, 1995, p. 54.

Bulletin of the Center for Children's Books, May, 1986, p. 162; May, 1990, p. 210; October, 1992, p. 40; October, 1996, p. 51.

Horn Book, November-December, 1987, pp. 721-722; May-June, 1988, pp. 338-339; May-June, 1990, p. 319.

Kirkus Reviews, February 15, 1986, p. 300; October 15, 1992, p. 1307; April 1, 1993, p. 453; April 15, 1993, p. 525; September 1, 1993, p. 1141; October 15, 1994, p. 1406; October, 1995, p. 1424.

New York Times Book Review, July 20, 1986, p. 24; December 20, 1992, p. 19; April 18, 1993, p. 25; September 19, 1993, p. 36.

Publishers Weekly, February 27, 1987, p. 162; March 11, 1988, p. 102; October 19, 1992, p. 75; March 22, 1993, p. 78; April 12, 1993, p. 62; May 17, 1993, p. 77; July 5, 1993, p. 72; April 25, 1994, p. 76; October 3, 1994, p. 67; June 17, 1996, p. 63.

Quill & Quire, October, 1992, p. 39.

School Library Journal, April, 1986, pp. 68-69; June-July, 1987, p. 78; February, 1988, p. 58; May, 1988, p. 81; December, 1989, p. 77; April, 1990, p. 87; June, 1990, p. 97; July, 1990, p. 56; October, 1990, p. 86; December, 1990, p. 100; December, 1991, p. 80; April, 1992, p. 89; September, 1992, p. 199; October, 1992, p. 38; May, 1993, p. 82; March, 1994, p. 190; July, 1994, p. 74; December, 1994, p. 72; September, 1995, p. 192.

Times Literary Supplement, April 3, 1987, p. 356.*

* * *

CARR, Pat 1932-
(Pat M. Esslinger)

PERSONAL: Born March 13, 1932, in Grass Creek, WY; daughter of Stanley (an oil camp supervisor) and Bea (Parker) Moore; married Jack H. Esslinger, June 4, 1955 (divorced July, 1970); married Duane Carr (a professor and writer), March 26, 1971; children: Stephanie, Shelley, Sean, Jennifer. *Education:* Rice University, B.A., 1954, M.A., 1955; Tulane University, Ph.D., 1960.

ADDRESSES: Home—10695 Venice Rd., Elkins, AR 72727.

CAREER: Texas Southern University, Houston, instructor in English, 1956-58; Dillard University, New Orleans, LA, assistant professor of English, 1960-61; Louisiana State University in New Orleans (now University of New Orleans), assistant professor of English, 1961-62, 1965-69; University of Texas at El Paso, assistant professor, 1969-72, associate professor, 1972-78, professor of English, 1978-79; University of New Orleans, assistant professor of English, 1987-88; Western

Kentucky University, Bowling Green, assistant professor, 1988-90, associate professor, 1990-93, professor of English, 1993-96.

MEMBER: International Women's Writing Guild, Poets and Writers, Texas Institute of Letters, Phi Beta Kappa, Phi Kappa Phi.

AWARDS, HONORS: Short fiction award, *South and West,* 1969; Mark IV Award, Library of Congress, 1970, for *Beneath the Hill of the Three Crosses;* National Endowment for the Humanities grant, 1973; short fiction award, Iowa School of Letters, 1977, for *The Women in the Mirror;* short story award, Texas Institute of Letters, 1978, for "Indian Burial"; Arkansas Endowment for the Humanities grant, 1985; Green Mountain Fiction Award, 1987; First Stage Drama Award, 1990; Al Smith fiction fellowship, 1995.

WRITINGS:

(Under name Pat M. Esslinger) *Beneath the Hill of the Three Crosses* (stories), South & West, 1970.
The Grass Creek Chronicle (novel), Endeavors in Humanity, 1976, reprint, 1996.
Bernard Shaw, Ungar (New York City), 1976.
The Women in the Mirror, University of Iowa Press (Iowa City), 1977.
Mimbres Mythology, Texas Western Press (El Paso), 1979, reprint, 1997.
In Fine Spirits (U.S. Civil War letters), Washington County Historical Society, 1986.
Night of the Luminarias (stories), Slough (Austin, TX), 1986.
Sonahchi (myth-tales), Cinco Puntos Press, 1988, reprint, 1993.
Our Brothers' War (U.S. Civil War stories), Sulgrave Press, 1993.
Bluebirds (novella), in *Careless Weeds,* Southern Methodist University Press (Dallas, TX), 1993.

Also contributor to *Best American Short Stories, Encyclopedia of World Literature* and the *Guide to American Women Writers.* Contributor of articles and stories (before 1971, under name Pat M. Esslinger) to periodicals, including *Southern Review, Yale Review, Arizona Quarterly, Modern Fiction Studies, Kansas Quarterly, Seattle Review,* and *Western Humanities Review.*

WORK IN PROGRESS: A Perfectly Splendid Time, a novel set in Civil War Arkansas; a collection of modern stories set in the American South; a contemporary novel of manners.

SIDELIGHTS: Pat Carr told *CA:* "Every place I've lived—the Wyoming of my childhood and the South of my adult years—has marked my work. I've also been exceedingly fortunate in that my generation has been able to experience a wide range of conflicts and emotions from the most silent to the most articulate and has possibly come to Matthew Arnold's conclusion that 'Ah, love, let us be true to one another.' All of my own themes, at least, lead there."

* * *

CEBULASH, Mel 1937-
(Ben Farrell, Glen Harlan, Jared Jansen, Jeanette Mara)

PERSONAL: Surname is pronounced "*seb*-yu-lash"; born August 24, 1937, in Jersey City, NJ; son of Jack (a mail carrier) and Jeanette (Duthie) Cebulash; married Deanna Penn, August 19, 1962 (divorced); married Dolly Hasinbiller, June 19, 1977; children: (first marriage) Glen Harlan, Benjamin Farrell, Jeanette Mara; (second marriage) Patchin Hasinbiller. *Education:* Jersey City State College, B.A., 1962, M.A., 1964; University of South Carolina, graduate study, 1964-65. *Religion:* Jewish. *Avocational interests:* Literature and popular music of the 1930s, the works of James T. Farrell ("a friend and inspiration"), handicapping horses and prize fights.

ADDRESSES: Home—11820 North 112th St., Scottsdale, AZ 85259. *Office*—11811 North Tatum Blvd., Suite 1081, Phoenix, AZ 85028.

CAREER: Junior high school teacher of reading, Teaneck, NJ, 1962-64; Fairleigh Dickinson University, Rutherford, NJ, instructor in reading clinic, 1965-67; Scholastic Magazines, Inc., New York City, editor for language arts, 1966-76; Bowmar/Noble Publishing Co., Los Angeles, CA, editor in chief, 1976-80; Cebulash Associates, Phoenix, AZ (formerly Pasadena, CA), publisher, 1980-83, 1986—; Fearon Educational (imprint of Simon & Schuster), publisher, 1983-86. *Military service:* U.S. Army, 1955-58.

MEMBER: Authors Guild, Authors League of America, Mystery Writers of America (regional vice president, Southern California chapter, 1981-82).

AWARDS, HONORS: Author Award, New Jersey Association of Teachers of English, 1969, for *Through Basic Training with Walter Young;* New Jersey Institute of Technology award, 1972, for *The Ball That Wouldn't Bounce, Benny's Nose,* and *Dic-tion-ar-y Skilz,* 1983, for *Ruth Marini—Dodger Ace* and *Ruth Marini of the Dodgers;* Children's Choice Award, International Reading Association (IRA), 1975, for *Football Players Do Amazing Things,* and 1976, for *Basketball Players Do Amazing Things;* Children's Book of the Year, Child Study Association, Bank Street College, 1977, for *Basketball Players Do Amazing Things;* IRA Young Adult Choice Award, 1987, for *Ruth Marini—World Series Star;* Public Library Association (PLA) Certificate of Merit, 1994, for "Great Sports of the 20th Century" series and "Sully Gomez Mystery" series.

WRITINGS:

FICTION

The Ball That Wouldn't Bounce, illustrated by Tom Eaton, Scholastic (New York City), 1972.

Benny's Nose, illustrated by Ib Ohlsson, Scholastic, 1972.

(Under pseudonym Ben Farrell) *Nancy and Jeff,* Scholastic, 1972.

(Under pseudonym Jared Jansen) *Penny the Poodle,* Scholastic, 1972.

(Under pseudonym Glen Harlan) *Petey the Pup,* Scholastic, 1972.

The See-Saw, Scholastic, 1972.

The Grossest Book of World Records, Pocket Books (New York City), 1977.

The Grossest Book of World Records II, Pocket Books, 1978.

Blackouts, Scholastic, 1979.

The Champion's Jacket, Creative Education (Mankato, MN), 1979.

Ruth Marini of the Dodgers, Lerner Publications (Minneapolis), 1983.

Ruth Marini—Dodger Ace, Lerner Publications, 1983.

The Face That Stopped Time, Pitman Learning (Belmont, CA), 1984.

Ruth Marini—World Series Star, Lerner Publications, 1985.

Hot Like the Sun: A Terry Tyndale Mystery, Lerner Publications, 1986.

Campground Caper, Fawcett (New York City), 1990.

Carly and Company, Fawcett, 1990.

Part-Time Shadow, Fawcett, 1990.

(Under pseudonym Ben Farrell) *Dad Saves the Day,* Silver Burdett/Ginn (Morristown, NJ), 1991.

(Under pseudonym Jared Jansen) *Showtime,* Silver Burdett/Ginn, 1991.

Batboy, illustrated by Duane Krych, Child's World (Elgin, IL), 1993.

Catnapper, illustrated by Krych, Child's World, 1993.

Flipper's Boy, illustrated by Krych, Child's World, 1993.

Muscle Bound, illustrated by Krych, Child's World, 1993.

Rattler, illustrated by Krych, Child's World, 1993.

Snooperman, illustrated by Krych, Child's World, 1993.

Willie's Wonderful Pet, Scholastic, 1993.

Scared Silly, Trumpet Book Club, 1995.

(Under pseudonym Ben Farrell) *My Family Band,* Harcourt (San Diego), 1996.

(Under pseudonym Glen Harlan) *Play Ball!,* Harcourt, 1996.

(Under pseudonym Ben Farrell) *Let's Visit the Moon,* Harcourt, 1996.

(Under pseudonym Ben Farrell) *One More Time,* Harcourt, 1996.

(Under pseudonym Ben Farrell) *What a Shower!,* Harcourt, 1996.

NONFICTION

Through Basic Training with Walter Young, Scholastic, 1968.

Man in a Green Beret and Other Medal of Honor Winners, Scholastic, 1969.

Baseball Players Do Amazing Things, Random House (New York City), 1973.

Dic-tion-ar-y Skilz, Scholastic, 1974.

Football Players Do Amazing Things, Random House, 1975.

Basketball Players Do Amazing Things, Random House, 1976.

Math Zingo, Bowmar/Noble (New York City), 1978.

Reading Zingo, Bowmar/Noble, 1978.

Big League Baseball Reading Kit, Bowmar/Noble, 1979.

Crosswinds Reading Program, Bowmar/Noble, 1979.

Spanish Math Zingo, Bowmar/Noble, 1979.

The 1,000 Point Pro Sports Quiz Book: Football, Random House, 1979.

The 1,000 Point Pro Sports Quiz Book: Basketball, Random House, 1979.

The 1,000 Point Pro Sports Quiz Book: Baseball, Random House, 1980.

A Horse to Remember, Bowmar/Noble, 1980.

I'm an Expert: Motivating Independent Study Projects for Grades 4-6, Scott, Foresman (Glenview, IL), 1982.

"SPRING STREET BOYS" SERIES; PUBLISHED BY SCHOLASTIC

The Spring Street Boys Team Up, 1982.

The Spring Street Boys Settle a Score, 1982.

The Spring Street Boys Hit the Road, 1982.

The Spring Street Boys Go for Broke, 1982.

"CARLY AND COMPANY" SERIES; PUBLISHED BY FAWCETT

Carly and Company, 1990.

Campground Caper, 1990.

Part-time Shadow, 1990.

"GREAT SPORTS OF THE 20TH CENTURY" SERIES; PUBLISHED BY NEW READERS PRESS

Bases Loaded: Great Baseball of the 20th Century, 1993.

Fast Break: Great Basketball of the 20th Century, 1993.

Lights Out: Great Fights of the 20th Century, 1993.

Third and Goal: Great Football of the 20th Century, 1993.

"SULLY GOMEZ MYSTERY" SERIES; PUBLISHED BY NEW READERS PRESS

Dirty Money, 1993.

Knockout Punch, 1993.

Set to Explode, 1993.

A Sucker for Redheads, 1993.

SCREENPLAY NOVELIZATIONS

Monkeys, Go Home, Scholastic, 1967.

The Love Bug, Scholastic, 1969.

The Boatniks, Scholastic, 1970.

Herbie Rides Again, Scholastic, 1974.

The Strongest Man in the World, Scholastic, 1975.

Ghostdad, Berkley (New York City), 1990.

OTHER

Editor, "ACTION Reading Kit" series, Scholastic, 1970. Contributor, sometimes under pseudonyms Ben Farrell and Jeanette Mara, of short stories to university literary journals. Contributing editor, *Scholastic Scope.*

WORK IN PROGRESS: California Listing, an adult mystery about the high-stakes textbook adoption business; *Freak Times,* a humorous juvenile title.

SIDELIGHTS: Educator Mel Cebulash has written over sixty books for children, young adults, and adults. Most of his books deal with high-interest subjects—such as sports, mysteries, and movies—and are intended to encourage reluctant young people to read. During what he has described as an ordinary childhood in Union City, New Jersey, Cebulash developed a lifelong appreciation for the way that reading can open young minds. "My mother's deep respect for books led me to a library at a very early age, and reading allowed me to entertain all sorts of dreams and to become all sorts of people," he once explained. "I still believe that reading is the most important subject taught in school."

After teaching junior high school for a few years, Cebulash "left teaching and moved into writing and editing as a full-time activity," he recalled. "My parents and friends looked upon the move as the foolish pursuit of a far-fetched dream. Fortunately, years of reading had led me to believe in the possibility of dreams." He worked for several educational publishers, developing high-interest materials and programs for at-risk students, before starting his own company, Cebulash Associates, in 1980.

One of Cebulash's well-received series of books for reluctant readers includes the titles *Baseball Players Do Amazing Things,* published in 1973, and *Football Players Do Amazing Things,* published in 1975. The first book features thirteen short chapters, each describing an interesting story or event from baseball history. For example, one chapter recalls the time that the great power hitter Babe Ruth pointed to the spot in the grandstand where he predicted he would hit his next home run, and another discusses the career of Eddie Gaedel, who at three feet, seven inches was the shortest man ever to play professional baseball. Similarly, *Football Players Do Amazing Things* contains eleven chapters about famous football players and their feats. It tells the story of a 1948 game between the Chicago Cardinals and the Philadelphia Eagles that took place in a blinding blizzard, and describes the time that Viking player Jim Marshall ran sixty yards to score a touchdown in the opposition's end zone. Each book is illustrated with numerous black-and-white photographs. A reviewer for *Booklist* praised Cebulash's "smooth, down-to-earth style" and noted that the books "will impress and amuse readers."

In 1982 Cebulash published a series of four fictional works about the Spring Street Boys, a group of high school students who live in the same neighborhood and share many sports-related adventures. In *The Spring Street Boys Settle a Score,* the boys set out to avenge Tiny, a younger kid who was injured by a car when he ran into the street to retrieve his ball. Just before the accident, two mean older boys had been teasing Tiny and had thrown his ball into the street. The Spring Street Boys find out who the two boys are and get even with them, even though they end up losing an important game in the process. In a review for *The High-Low Report,* Thetis Powers Reeves commented that Cebulash's "kids are real and likeable and his complex plots fast paced and fun. The Spring Street Boys are well worth knowing."

In *Ruth Marini of the Dodgers,* published in 1983, as well as two sequels, Cebulash tells the fictional story of the first woman to break the gender barrier and play major league baseball. Ruth is a star pitcher on her high school baseball team, but she believes that her career is over after graduation. She initially takes an office job, but then she is thrilled to be invited to attend training camp for the Los Angeles Dodgers. As a rookie assigned to the Dodgers' minor league system, Ruth must face the sexist attitudes of some of her fellow players and fans as well as the hardships of playing frequently and living on the road. She also struggles to find a place in her life for a romantic relationship.

In the first sequel, *Ruth Marini—Dodger Ace,* Ruth makes it to the big leagues but is injured during the season. She also meets her father, who had left her family many years earlier. The final book in the series, *Ruth Marini—World Series Star,* follows Ruth as she recovers from her injury in time to help her team defeat the New York Yankees for the world championship. A reviewer for *School Library Journal* called Ruth "a winning character and a convincing one," while a writer for *Bulletin of the Center for Children's Books* added that the series has "plenty of action, an appealing idea, and baseball sequences that are well written."

In a writing career spanning thirty years, Cebulash has motivated many at-risk students to read with his entertaining, high-interest books. In addition to his sports-related stories, he has written book-length adaptations of several popular movies—such as *The Love Bug, The Strongest Man in the World,* and *Ghostdad*—as well as books of study projects and quizzes for students. "I've been pleased by the sales of my books, but my real joy in writing has come from the letters I've received from young people," Cebulash explained. "When I think I'm all alone with a computer, I remind myself of the many friends I've made through writing."

BIOGRAPHICAL/CRITICAL SOURCES:

PERIODICALS

Booklist, November 15, 1975; August, 1983, p. 1483; January 15, 1990, p. 990.

Bulletin of the Center for Children's Books, November, 1973; May, 1983; July-August, 1983; September, 1985; July-August, 1986.

Childhood Education, November-December, 1983, p. 136.

High-Low Report, February, 1982.

Kirkus Reviews, October 1, 1975.

Library Journal, October 15, 1973.

Publishers Weekly, March 4, 1983, p. 99.

Reading Teacher, May, 1983, p. 950.

School Library Journal, May, 1983, p. 95; August, 1983; January, 1994, p. 112.

* * *

CHABON, Michael 1963-

PERSONAL: Surname is pronounced "*shay*-bahn"; born in 1963, in Washington, DC; son of a Robert (a physician, lawyer and hospital manager) and Sharon (a lawyer) Chabon; married Lollie Groth (a poet; divorced, 1991); married Ayelet Waldman (a lawyer), 1993; children (second marriage): Sophie. *Education:* University of Pittsburgh, B.A., 1984; received M.F.A. from University of California, Irvine.

ADDRESSES: Agent—Mary Evans, Inc., 242 East 5th Street, New York, NY 10003.

CAREER: Writer and screenwriter.

AWARDS, HONORS: Publishers Weekly best books of 1995, and *New York Times* Notable Book of 1995, both for *Wonder Boys.*

WRITINGS:

The Mysteries of Pittsburgh (novel), Morrow (New York City), 1988.
A Model World, and Other Stories (includes "The Lost World," "The Little Knife," "More Than Human," and "Blumenthal on the Air"), Morrow, 1991.
Wonder Boys (novel), Villard Books (New York City), 1995.

Also author of screenplays, including *Gentleman Host,* and *The Martian Agent.* Author of introduction to Ben Katchor, *Julius Knipl, Real-Estate Photographer,* Little, Brown (Boston), 1996. Contributor to periodicals, including *Gentlemen's Quarterly, Mademoiselle, New Yorker, New York Times Magazine, Esquire, Playboy, Forward, Civilization,* and *Vogue.*

ADAPTATIONS: Film rights to *Wonder Boys* have been optioned by Scott Rudin.

*WORK IN PROGRESS:*A novel, tentatively titled *The Golden Age.*

SIDELIGHTS: Upon the publication of the coming-of-age novel *The Mysteries of Pittsburgh* in 1988, Michael Chabon earned recognition as a promising young fiction writer. The story centers on Art Bechstein, who has recently graduated from college and is about to experience what he perceives as the last summer of his youth. Shortly into that summer, Art befriends a witty homosexual, Arthur, and two appealing women. He becomes the lover of one of the women, Phlox. The other woman is the lover of Arthur's best friend, the opportunist Cleveland. When Cleveland learns that Art's father is a racketeer, he pressures Art into making introductions. Art cooperates, but it costs him his father's remaining respect. Frustrated by that paternal disdain, Art falls into an emotionally confusing, but nonetheless fulfilling, affair with Arthur. Cleveland, who has profited from the patronage of Art's father, then reappears with stolen goods. He is fleeing both the law and the mob—that is, Art's father. Violence ensues, and Art and Arthur are compelled to run for their lives.

The Mysteries of Pittsburgh won Chabon recognition as a gifted new storyteller. "Here," proclaimed Alice McDermott in the *New York Times Book Review,* "is a first novel by a talented young writer." Chabon, McDermott declared, "skillfully sets down the elements of his plot [and] diligently sets them spinning." She added that "his control over his story, the wonderful use he makes of each description, of Pittsburgh itself, are often astonishing." Another enthusiast, Brett Lott, wrote in the *Los Angeles Times Book Review* that *The Mysteries of Pittsburgh* constituted a "remarkable" achievement, and he lauded the novel for its "heart, [its] compassion for characters simply trying to wade through a world too filled with itself to let real love surface, breathe, and take us in." And *New Statesman* reviewer M. George Stevenson, who was not alone in likening Chabon to author F. Scott Fitzgerald, noted: "Making a reader experience again a sense of endless possibility is one of the most satisfying and quintessentially American things an American bildungsroman can do. Chabon's *The Mysteries of Pittsburgh* adds to the canon one of the rare novels actually able to do it."

Chabon followed *The Mysteries of Pittsburgh* with *A Model World, and Other Stories,* which includes tales he had already published in *New Yorker.* Many of the stories here involve unrequited love, and five of the tales—collectively termed "The Lost World"—chart the angst of adolescent Nathan Shapiro as he grows from age ten to sixteen. Among these chronicles is "The Little Knife," where he agonizes over both his parents' antagonistic relationship and the Washington Senators' imminent demise from major-league baseball. In "More Than Human," a tale focusing on Shapiro, he must come to terms with his shattered family after his father leaves home. Another story in *A Model World,* "Blumenthal on the Air," centers on an American narrator who marries an Iranian woman simply to provide her with United States citizenship. He then finds himself falling in love with her.

In her *New York Times Book Review* appraisal of *A Model World,* Elizabeth Benedict complained that Chabon sometimes uses his polished style as a means of remaining emotionally aloof from his material. "All too often he keeps his distance," she alleged. But she added that even in tales where Chabon remains reserved, he nonetheless manages to produce "fluent, astonishingly vivid prose." Benedict was particularly impressed with "The Lost World" group, which she lauded for its "breathtaking" descriptive passages. Other tales in the volume, Benedict noted, recalled *The Mysteries of Pittsburgh.* Such stories, she affirmed, "have a kaleidoscopic beauty."

Chabon experienced considerable difficulty in trying to follow up the success of *The Mysteries of Pittsburgh* and *A Model World.* While living on a large advance from his publisher, he wrote 1,500 pages of what he intended to be his second novel, *Fountain City.* It was, Chabon told *Los Angeles Times* contributor Erik Himmelsbach, "sort of a map of my brain," and in it, he attempted to express his love for Paris, architecture, baseball, Florida, and more. After four and a half years and four drafts, however, Chabon admitted to himself that he was never going to be able to craft *Fountain City* into a readable book. He explained to Himmelsbach, "Because I had taken that [advance] money, I felt like I couldn't dump the project, even when it was fairly clear to me that it wasn't working."

The *Fountain City* experience was demoralizing, but Chabon eventually turned it to his advantage. In early 1993, he began work on *Wonder Boys,* and in less than a year he had finished his second novel. *Wonder Boys* is a fast-paced, comic romp that chronicles one long, disastrous weekend in the life of Grady Tripp, a once-lauded writer now burdened with a 2,000-page manuscript he cannot finish. Joseph P. Kahn of the *Boston Globe* called Tripp "an instant classic . . . part Ginger Man, part Garp and altogether brilliantly original." The plot includes "an itchy editor, a pregnant mistress, a befuddled protege, a pilfered tuba, [and] a dead dog," noted Kahn. Chabon confided to Lisa See in *Publishers Weekly* that until his wife read the manuscript of *Wonder Boys* and he heard her laughing as she turned the pages, he had no idea that he was writing a comic novel. "To me, Grady has a wry tone, but I felt sad writing about him. In a lot of ways, he is a projection of my worst fears of what I was going to become if I kept working on *Fountain City.*" He continued: "To me, the book is about the disappointment of getting older and growing up and not measuring up to what you thought, and the world and the people in it not being what you expected. It's about disillusionment and acceptance."

Wonder Boys was hailed as a worthy successor to *The Mysteries of Pittsburgh* and *A Model World* by many critics. "Despite (or maybe because of) his failings, Grady Tripp is an appealing hero," affirmed Robert Ward in the *New York Times Book Review.* "We feel for him as he struggles with his behemoth of a novel, as he broods about love and literature. . . . He's very much a lovable mess." Ward found that "stylistically, Mr. Chabon is, as always, a pleasure to read. 'Wonder Boys' is filled with memorable lines and wonderful images. . . . Chabon is that rare thing, an intelligent lyrical writer. Because his comedy always reins in his romantic impulses, his work seems to reflect a nature that is at once passionate and satirical. The result is a tone of graceful melancholy punctuated by a gentle and humane good humor."

Some reviewers were less enthusiastic, however. *Time*'s John Skow remarked that *Wonder Boys* is "a series of funny scenes about not writing a novel that somehow don't hang together as a novel." Yet others, such as Roz Kaveney, differed sharply in their assessment of Chabon's achievement. Kaveney wrote in a *New Statesman & Society* review that *Wonder Boys* "is a virtuoso performance with a sequence of comprehensively visualised backdrops and enough well-rounded walk-ons to people a novel twice its length. . . . This is a great book about personal disaster."

Although he has often been grouped with other writers of his generation such as Bret Easton Ellis and Jay McInerney, many critics feel Chabon's work bears no resemblance to their enervated narratives of disaffected youth. "Unlike other authors of his age, Chabon embraced, rather than scorned, the power of words and language; his writing was lively, funny, involving, beautiful, the kind of stuff from which great literature is made," declared Himmelsbach. He quoted Chabon as saying: "I just want to write things that last. . . . My first intention has not been to reflect the time in which they were written. I'm not trying to get the '90s or the '80s or whatever down on paper in America at all. I'm just trying to write the best English I can write."

BIOGRAPHICAL/CRITICAL SOURCES:

BOOKS

Contemporary Literary Criticism, Volume 55, Gale (Detroit), 1989.

PERIODICALS

Atlanta Journal-Constitution, April 2, 1995, p. M12.
Boston Globe, May 14, 1995, p. 50; May 22, 1995, p. 30.
Chicago Tribune, April 2, 1995, Section 14, p. 5.
Entertainment Weekly, April 14, 1995, p. 61.
Gentlemen's Quarterly, March, 1995, p. 118.
Interview, March, 1988, p. 48.
Los Angeles Times, June 28, 1988; April 27, 1995, p. E1.
Los Angeles Times Book Review, April 17, 1988, pp. 1, 11; March 26, 1995, p. 3.
New Republic, June 26, 1995, p. 40.
New Statesman, May 13, 1988, pp. 34-35.
New Statesman & Society, June 9, 1995, p. 38.
Newsweek, April 10, 1995, pp. 76-77.
New York, April 3, 1988, p. 7; May 2, 1988, p. 30; April 1, 1991, p. 63.
New York Times, March 17, 1995, p. C28.
New York Times Book Review, April 3, 1988, p. 7; May 26, 1991, p. 7; April 9, 1995, p. 7.
People Weekly, May 1, 1995, p. 32; June 26, 1995, pp. 63-64.
Publishers Weekly, April 10, 1995, pp. 44-45; November 6, 1995, p. 58.
Time, May 16, 1988, p. 95; April 8, 1991, p. 77; April 10, 1995, p. 87.
Times Literary Supplement, June 17, 1988, p. 680.
Village Voice, April 19, 1988, p. 60.
Washington Post, June 9, 1995, p. B1.
Washington Post Book World, April 24, 1988, p. 5; April 26, 1991, p. 20; March 19, 1995, p. 3.

* * *

CHARLES, Henry
See HARRIS, Marion Rose (Young)

CHERRY, Gordon E(manuel) 1931-

PERSONAL: Born February 6, 1931, in Barnsley, Yorkshire, England; son of Emanuel (a former tenant farmer and bank clerk) and Nora (a homemaker) Cherry; married Margaret Mary London Cox (a homemaker), June 8, 1957; children: Shona Margaret, Shelagh Louise, Iain Gordon. *Education:* Queen Mary College, London, B.A. (with honors), 1953.

ADDRESSES: *Home*—Quaker Ridge, 66 Meriden Rd., Hampton in Arden, West Midlands B92 0BT, England. *Office*—Department of Geography, University of Birmingham, Birmingham B15 2TT, England.

CAREER: City planner in Durham, Hull, Doncaster, and Sheffield, 1956-63; City Planning Department, Newcastle upon Tyne, England, research officer, 1963-68; University of Birmingham, Birmingham, England, deputy director of Centre for Urban and Regional Studies, 1968-76, professor of urban and regional planning, 1976—, dean of faculty of commerce and social science, 1981-85, head of department of geography, 1986—. Member of Bournville Village Trust, 1979—, and chair, 1991—; director of groundwork, Birmingham, and Family Care Trust, Solihull; occasional chair of E.I.P. panels for D.O.E. *Military service:* British Army, Royal Army Education Corps, 1954-56.

MEMBER: Planning History Group (chair), Royal Institution of Chartered Surveyors (fellow), Royal Town Planning Institute (fellow and president, 1978-79).

AWARDS, HONORS: D.Sc. from Heriot-Watt University, 1984; outstanding service award from R.T.P.I., 1995.

WRITINGS:

Town Planning in Its Social Context, Leonard Hill Books (London), 1970, revised edition, 1973.
(With T. L. Burton) *Social Research Techniques for Planners,* Allen & Unwin (London), 1971.
Urban Change and Planning, G. T. Foulis (Sparkford, Yeovil, Somerset, England), 1972.
The Evolution of British Town Planning, Leonard Hill Books, 1974.

Environmental Planning, Volume II: *National Parks and Recreation in the Countryside,* H.M.S.O., 1976.

Urban and Regional Planning: Promise and Potential in the West Midlands: An Inaugural Lecture Delivered in the University of Birmingham on 4th November 1976, Centre for Urban and Regional Studies, University of Birmingham (Birmingham, England), 1976.

The Politics of Town Planning, Longman (London and New York City), 1982.

(With Leith Penny) *Holford: A Study in Architecture, Planning, and Civic Design,* Mansell (London and New York City), 1986.

Cities and Plans: The Shaping of Urban Britain in the Nineteenth and Twentieth Centuries, Edward Arnold (London), 1988.

Birmingham: A Study in Geography, History and Planning, John Wiley (New York City), 1994.

Town Planning in Britain since 1900: The Rise and Fall of the Planning Ideal, Blackwell Publishers (Cambridge, MA), 1996.

EDITOR

Urban Planning Problems, Leonard Hill Books, 1974.

Rural Planning Problems, Leonard Hill Books, 1976.

Shaping an Urban World, Mansell, 1980.

Pioneers in British Planning, Architectural Press (London), 1981.

OTHER

Coeditor of "Studies in History, Planning, and the Environment," Mansell, 1980—. Also coeditor of *Planning Perspectives: An International Journal of History, Planning, and the Environment,* 1986—.

WORK IN PROGRESS: Research on the history of town planning.

SIDELIGHTS: Gordon E. Cherry told *CA:* "I was trained as a geographer and made an easy transition into town planning (British style). I practiced as a town planner in local government. Since then I have taught the subject and analyzed it politically and historically. I am a curious observer of world cities: what they look like, how they function, how they change, how people live in them, and what life chances these people have."

CHRISTELOW, Eileen 1943-

PERSONAL: Born April 22, 1943, in Washington, DC; daughter of Allan (an historian and business executive) and Dorothy (an economist; maiden name, Beal) Christelow; married Albert B. Ahrenholz (a potter), December, 1965; children: Heather. *Education:* University of Pennsylvania, B.A. (architecture), 1965; graduate study, University of California, Berkeley.

ADDRESSES: *Agent*—Dilys Evans, 40 Park Ave., New York, NY 10016.

CAREER: Freelance photographer in Philadelphia, PA, 1965-71, and graphic designer and illustrator in Berkeley, CA, 1973-81; author and illustrator of books for children, 1982—.

MEMBER: Society of Children's Book Writers and Illustrators.

AWARDS, HONORS: Little Archer Award (Wisconsin), 1982, for *Henry and the Red Stripes;* Junior Literary Guild selections for *Henry and the Red Stripes, Mr. Murphy's Marvelous Invention,* and *Henry and the Dragon;* Washington Irving fiction award, 1984, Land of Enchantment award, 1986, and Maud Hart Lovelace award, 1986, all for *Zucchini; School Library Journal* Best Books list, 1995, for *What Do Authors Do?*

WRITINGS:

SELF-ILLUSTRATED BOOKS FOR CHILDREN

Henry and the Red Stripes, Clarion (Boston), 1982.

Mr. Murphy's Marvelous Invention, Clarion, 1983.

Henry and the Dragon, Clarion, 1984.

Jerome the Babysitter, Houghton (Boston), 1987.

Olive and the Magic Hat, Houghton, 1987.

Jerome and the Witchcraft Kids, Clarion, 1988.

The Robbery at the Diamond Dog Diner, Houghton, 1988.

(Reteller) *Five Little Monkeys Jumping on the Bed,* Clarion, 1989.

Glenda Feathers Casts a Spell, Clarion, 1990.

Five Little Monkeys Sitting in a Tree, Clarion, 1991.

Don't Wake Up Mama: Another Five Little Monkey's Story, Clarion, 1992.

Gertrude, the Bulldog Detective, Clarion, 1992.
The Five-Dog Night, Clarion, 1993.
The Great Pig Escape, Clarion, 1994.
What Do Authors Do?, Clarion, 1995.
Five Little Monkeys with Nothing to Do, Houghton, 1996.

ILLUSTRATOR

(With others) Diane Downie, *Math for Girls and Other Problem Solvers,* University of California Press (Berkeley), 1981.
Barbara Dana, *Zucchini,* Harper (New York City), 1982.
Thomas Rockwell, *Oatmeal Is Not for Moustaches,* Holt (New York City), 1984.
Sue Alexander, *Dear Phoebe,* Little, Brown (Boston), 1984.
Barbara Steiner, *Oliver Dibbs and the Dinosaur Cause,* Simon & Schuster (New York City), 1986.
Jim Aylesworth, *Two Terrible Frights,* Simon & Schuster, 1987.
Joy Elizabeth Handcock, *The Loudest Little Lion,* A. Whitman (Niles, IL), 1988.
Steiner, *Oliver Dibbs to the Rescue!* Avon (New York City), 1988.
Myra Cohn Livingston, selector, *Dilly Dilly Piccalilli: Poems for the Very Young,* McElderry Books, 1989.
Mary Elise Monsell, *The Mysterious Cases of Mr. Pin,* Atheneum (New York City), 1989.
Aylesworth, *The Completed Hickory Dickory Dock,* Atheneum, 1990.
Monsell, *Mr. Pin: The Chocolate Files,* Atheneum, 1990.
Peggy Christian, *The Old Coot,* Atheneum, 1991.
Steiner, *Dolby and the Woof-Off,* Morrow (New York City), 1991.
Jan Wahl, *Mrs. Owl and Mr. Pig,* Lodestar (New York City), 1991.
Monsell, *Mr. Pin: The Spy Who Came North from the Pole,* Atheneum, 1993.
Jennifer Brutschy, *Celeste and Crabapple Sam,* Lodestar, 1994.
Maryann Macdonald, *Secondhand Star,* Hyperion (New York City), 1994.
Monsell, *Mr. Pin: A Fish Named Yum,* Atheneum, 1994.
Macdonald, *No Room for Francie,* Hyperion, 1995.

Christelow's photographs have appeared in *Progressive Architecture, Colloquy, Ford Foundation, Home, Media and Method, New York Times Book Review, Pennsylvania Gazette, Youth, Teacher,* and in various textbooks. Creator of posters for the Children's Book Council.

SIDELIGHTS: Eileen Christelow is an award-winning author/illustrator who produces humorous, bright, and energetic picture books. Whether she is illustrating her own stories or those of other authors, her animal characters—from cats and dogs to alligators and penguins—are charming and expressive. Christelow once explained that her career as a picture-book creator developed from her interests in architecture and photography.

"I majored in architecture at the University of Pennsylvania in Philadelphia," she explained. "While I was there, I discovered the darkroom in the graphics department. I spent more time there than I should have, taking photographs. After graduation, I earned my living as a freelance photographer, photographing buildings rather than designing them. I also photographed in the Philadelphia public school classrooms, skid row, and Chinatown. I took several trips with my cameras across the United States and one trip to Mexico. My photos appeared in various magazines and textbooks."

After a visit to Cornwall, England, and the birth of a daughter, Christelow and her family moved to Berkeley, California. There, she "found that I was tired of constantly looking at the world through a camera lens, so I began to learn about type, graphic design, and illustration. I eventually started freelancing as a designer producing ads, brochures, catalogues, and books.

"When my daughter was fourteen months old, I decided that I wanted to write and illustrate picture books for young children. For several years my daughter and I researched the problem together, taking weekly trips to the library and reading at naptime and bedtime. I found the picture book format a fascinating and frustrating challenge. I learned about pacing and I learned to keep my text spare. I also found that the years I'd spent as a photographer, trying to capture one photo that would tell an entire story, were invaluable to the process of creating stories with pens and pencils." One of the results of her efforts was a large collection of children's books, which helped her daughter to read and write. "And I wrote and illustrated several books—one of which is *Henry and the Red Stripes*.

"The idea for *Henry and the Red Stripes* first came to me when I was half asleep in a hot, steamy bath. It had been percolating in the back of my mind for months as I researched and illustrated a poster picturing twenty-six insects, reptiles, birds, and mammals camouflaged in a forest setting. That poster, combined with observing my daughter and her friends decorating themselves with paints and magic markers, led to the creation of Henry Rabbit."

Henry and the Dragon, the second "Henry" book, portrays the rabbit after a bedtime story. He thinks there must be a dragon about, and builds a trap to catch it. As Christelow said in a *Junior Literary Guild* article, *Henry and the Dragon* "was inspired by memories" of her young daughter asking if any bears walked around the family house at night.

Jerome the Babysitter introduces a young alligator boy just as he begins his first job babysitting. His twelve charges trick and mistreat him, and even trap him on the roof, but in the end Jerome proves he is a clever as well as competent caretaker. According to Lisa Redd in *School Library Journal,* the alligator characters are "delightful," and rendered with "expressive faces." In the words of a *Publishers Weekly* critic, the book presents a "side-splitting story" and "luridly colored cartoons."

The Robbery at the Diamond Dog Diner features a little hen who can't keep her mouth shut. When she hides her dog friend's diamonds in her hollowed-out eggs, diamond thieves think she's a diamond-egg-laying hen, and kidnap her. *The Five-Dog Night,* which a *Kirkus Reviews* critic calls a "good-natured, entertaining yarn," surprises readers by demonstrating that a five-dog night is one so cold that five dogs in the bed make the best blanket. A young dog, intent on becoming a detective, spies on her neighbors in *Gertrude, the Bulldog Detective;* although the neighbors provide her with some fake clues in an effort to discourage her, Gertrude manages to catch some real thieves.

In *The Great Pig Escape* a pair of vegetable farmers decide to raise pigs. When it is time for the farmers to sell the pigs at the market, the pigs escape both the market and certain death by stealing clothes, disguising themselves as people, and blending in with the crowd. After safely reaching Florida, the pigs return the clothes, along with a postcard for their owners with the comment, "Oink!" *School Library Journal* contributor Cynthia K. Richey described the text as "lively" and "funny," and notes that the book's pen and ink and watercolor illustrations are "filled with humor." And a *Publishers Weekly* critic describes the book as a "strategic endorsement of vegetarianism."

Fans of Christelow's, as well as aspiring authors, may appreciate her book *What Do Author's Do?* By following the efforts of two writers who have witnessed the same event, Christelow demonstrates how writers begin their books and prepare them for publication. According to *Horn Book* contributor Elizabeth S. Watson, "If ever there was a book to encourage youngsters to try their hand at writing, this is one."

BIOGRAPHICAL/CRITICAL SOURCES:

PERIODICALS

Booklist, March 15, 1992, p. 1397.
Bulletin of the Center for Children's Books, July-August, 1985.
Horn Book, September-October, 1989, pp. 633-634; November/December, 1995, p. 754.
Junior Literary Guild, March, 1984.
Kirkus Reviews, July 1, 1993, p. 857.
Publishers Weekly, February 22, 1985, p. 158; June 28, 1993, p. 77; June 27, 1994, p. 78.
School Library Journal, March, 1986, p. 145; February, 1987, p. 66; June, 1992, p. 90; November, 1994, p. 73.

* * *

CHRISTIAN, Barbara T. 1943-

PERSONAL: Born December 12, 1943, in St. Thomas, U.S. Virgin Islands; divorced; one daughter. *Education:* Marquette University, A.B. (cum laude), 1963; Columbia University, M.A., 1964, Ph.D. (with honors), 1970.

ADDRESSES: Home—2920 Benvenue, Berkeley, CA 94705. *Office*—Department of Afro-American

Studies, University of California at Berkeley, 3335 Dwinelle, Berkeley, CA 94720.

CAREER: College of the Virgin Islands, instructor in English, 1963; Hunter College, New York City, instructor in English, 1963-64; City College of the City University of New York, New York City, lecturer, 1965-70, assistant professor of English, 1971-72; University of California, Berkeley, lecturer, 1971-72, assistant professor, 1972-78, associate professor and chairperson of Afro-American studies, 1978-86, professor of African-American studies and president of Women's Studies Board, 1986—. Consultant to Far West Laboratories.

MEMBER: Modern Language Association of America, National Women's Studies Association, National Council for Black Studies, Women's Studies Board (Berkeley).

AWARDS, HONORS: Afro-American Society Hall of Fame award, 1980; American Women's Educators Association award, 1982; Before Columbus American Book Award, 1983, for *Black Women Novelists: The Development of a Tradition, 1892-1976;* University of California, Berkeley, Feminist Institute grant, 1987; Louise Patterson African-American Studies Award, 1992, 1995; City of Berkeley Icon award for community service, 1994; Modern Language Association *MELUS* award for contribution to ethnic studies and African-American scholarship, 1994; Gwendolyn Brooks Center award, 1995.

WRITINGS:

(Contributor) Addison Gayle, editor, *Black Expression,* Weybright & Talley, 1969.

Black Women Novelists: The Development of a Tradition, 1892-1976, Greenwood Press (Westport, CT), 1980.

Black Feminist Criticism: Perspectives on Black Women Writers, Pergamon (New York City), 1985.

From the Inside Out: Afro-American Women's Literary Tradition and the State, University of Minnesota Center for Humanistic Studies (Minneapolis), 1987.

(Editor and author of introduction) Alice Walker, *Everyday Use,* Rutgers University Press, (New Brunswick, NJ), 1994.

(Editor, with Elizabeth Abel and Helene Moglen) *Female Subjects in Black and White: Race, Psychoanalysis, Feminism,* University of California Press (Berkeley), 1997.

OTHER

Also author of teaching guide for *Black Foremothers, Three Lives* by Dorothy Sterling, Feminist Press (Old Westbury, NY), 1980, revised edition, 1988. Contributor to anthologies, including *Female Immigrants to the U.S.: A Caribbean, Latin American, and African Experience,* edited by Bryce La Porte, Smithsonian Institute (Washington, DC), 1982; *Black Women Writers, 1950-1980,* edited by Mari Evans, Doubleday (Garden City, NY), 1984; and *Reading Black, Reading Feminist,* edited by Henry Louis Gates, Meridian (New York City), 1990. Coeditor, *Feminist Studies,* 1984-92; *Black American Literature Forum,* 1985-90; *Sage,* 1987-89; and *Contentions,* beginning 1990. Contributor of essays and reviews to numerous journals, including *Black Scholar* and *Journal of Ethnic Studies.*

SIDELIGHTS: Barbara Christian is noted for her insight into literature by and about African-American women and is the author of numerous essays on African-American and women's studies. Two of her best known books are *Black Women Novelists: The Development of a Tradition, 1872-1976* and *Black Feminist Criticism: Perspectives on Black Women Writers. Black Feminist Criticism* is a collection of 17 essays in which Christian first explains why she and other black women write and then demonstrates the writing process itself. Nancy Raye Tarcher observes in *Feminist Writers:* "Within these essays, written between 1975 and 1984, Christian examines, from a black feminist perspective, such issues as the importance of motherhood and the mother-child relationship within both the works of both African-American and Native-African writers; 19th-century black women novelists' efforts to transcend the prevailing racial and sexual stereotypes of their age; and the attempts by such writers as Paule Marshall to destroy the image of the domineering black matriarch—the 'superwoman,' if you will, in modern African-American literature." The book has won widespread praise for its thoughtful, well-written analysis.

In her introduction to *Black Women Novelists,* Christian describes the book as "an attempt to describe [the tradition of those few Black women able to get their works into print], to articulate its existence, to examine its origins, and to trace the development of stereotypical images imposed on black women and assess how these images have affected the works of black women artists." In Part One, Christian traces the evolution of the images of black women in black fiction, beginning in 1892 and continuing to 1976. In Part Two, she takes an in-depth look at the work of three contemporary novelists: Paule Marshall, Toni Morrison, and Alice Walker. "Christian's book . . . breaks new ground," declares Keith Byerman in *Modern Fiction Studies.* Janet Boyarin Blundell concurs in *Library Journal,* calling the book an "exciting survey. . . . The lucidity of the treatment, the broadness of scope, and the sheer heart that Christian has put in along with the scholarly trappings will make this compelling for both academics and lay readers." And a *Choice* reviewer was similarly enthusiastic, calling *Black Women Novelists* an "original and thoughtful study" that is "well-written" and "intellectually stimulating." The reviewer concludes: "It is an important contribution to Afro-American literary history, a ground-breaking work."

BIOGRAPHICAL/CRITICAL SOURCES:

BOOKS

Feminist Writers, St. James Press (Detroit), 1996.

PERIODICALS

Choice, April, 1981, p. 1095.
Feminist Studies, 11(1), spring 1985.
Library Journal, August, 1980, p. 1634.
Modern Fiction Studies, summer, 1982, p. 303.

* * *

CLIFFORD, David
See ROSENBERG, Ethel (Clifford)

* * *

CLIFFORD, Eth
See ROSENBERG, Ethel (Clifford)

COATES, David 1946-

PERSONAL: Born December 24, 1946, in Bury, England; son of Robert (a police officer) and Edna (a homemaker; maiden name, Todd) Coates; married Eileen Coates; children: Emma, Ben, Anna, Thomas, Edward, Jonathan. *Education:* University of York, B.A. (with first class honors), 1967; Oxford University, D.Phil., 1970. *Politics:* Socialist. *Religion:* None.

ADDRESSES: Home—33 Leeds Rd., Harrogate, North Yorkshire, HG2 8AY, England. *Office*—Department of Government, University of Manchester, Manchester M13 9PL, England.

CAREER: University of York, Heslington, England, lecturer in politics, 1970-77, chair of Graduate School, 1976-77; University of Leeds, Leeds, England, lecturer, 1977-83, senior lecturer in politics, 1983—, head of department, 1984-87, reader in contemporary political economy, 1992-93, professor, 1993-95; University of Manchester, Manchester, England, professor of government and codirector of the International Centre for Labour Studies, 1995—.

WRITINGS:

Teacher Unions and Interest Group Politics, Cambridge University Press (Cambridge, England), 1972.
(With George Bain and Valerie Ellis) *Social Stratification and Trade Unionism,* Heinemann (London), 1973.
The Labour Party and the Struggle for Socialism, Cambridge University Press, 1975.
Labour in Power? A Study of the Labour Government, 1974-1979, Longman (London), 1980.
The Context of British Politics, Hutchinson (London), 1984.
(With Hans Breitenbach and Tom Burden) *Features of a Viable Socialism,* Harvester Wheatsheaf (New York City), 1990.
Running the Country, Hodder & Stoughton in association with the Open University (Sevenoaks, Kent, England), 1991, second edition, 1995.
The Question of UK Doctrine, Harvester (Brighton, England), 1994.

EDITOR

A Socialist Primer, Volume I (with Gordon Johnson): *Socialist Arguments,* Martin Robertson, 1983, Volume II (with Johnson): *Socialist Strategies,* Martin Robertson, 1983, Volume III (with Johnson and Ray Bush): *A Socialist Anatomy of Britain,* Polity Press, 1984, Volume IV (with Johnson and Bush): *Two World Orders: Socialist Perspectives,* Polity Press (Oxford, England), 1987.
(With John Hillard) *The Economic Decline of Modern Britain: The Debate between Left and Right,* Wheatsheaf, 1987.
(With Hillard) *The Economic Revival of Modern Britain: The Debate Between Left and Right,* Edward Elgar Publications (Aldershot, Hants, England), 1987.
(With Hillard) *UK Economic Decline: Key Texts,* Prentice Hall/Harvester Wheatsheaf, 1995.
Economic and Industrial Performance in Europe: A Report Prepared for the Centre for Industrial Policy and Performance, University of Leeds (Aldershot, Hants, England), 1995.
Industrial Policy in Britain, St. Martin's (New York City), 1996.

OTHER

Contributor to *Dictionary of Marxist Thought* and the annual, *World View.* Also contributor to political science journals.

BIOGRAPHICAL/CRITICAL SOURCES:

PERIODICALS

Times Literary Supplement, November 19, 1987; January 8-14, 1988.

* * *

COMAROFF, John L(ionel) 1945-

PERSONAL: Born January 1, 1945, in Cape Town, South Africa; immigrated to United States, 1978, naturalized citizen, 1986; son of Lionel (a shopkeeper) and Jane (a homemaker; maiden name, Miller) Comaroff; married Jean Rakoff (a professor of anthropology), January 15, 1967; children: Joshua, Jane. *Education:* University of Cape Town, B.A., 1966; London School of Economics and Political Science, London, Ph.D., 1973. *Religion:* Jewish.

ADDRESSES: Home—5327 South University Ave., Chicago, IL 60615. *Office*—Department of Anthropology, University of Chicago, Chicago, IL 60637.

CAREER: University of Wales, University College of Swansea, lecturer in anthropology, 1971-72; Victoria University of Manchester, Manchester, England, lecturer in anthropology, 1972-78; University of Chicago, Chicago, assistant professor, 1978-81, associate professor, 1981-87, professor of anthropology and sociology, 1987-96, Harold H. Swift Distinguished Professor of Anthropology, 1996—, chair of anthropology department, 1991-94. Member of anti-apartheid organizations.

MEMBER: African Studies Association (England), African Studies Association (United States), American Anthropological Association (fellow), American Ethnological Society, Association of Political and Legal Anthropology (president, 1995-97), Association of Social Anthropologists (England; fellow), Royal Anthropological Institute (fellow).

WRITINGS:

(With Simon Roberts) *Rules and Processes: The Cultural Logic of Dispute in an African Context,* University of Chicago Press (Chicago, IL), 1981.
(With wife, Jean Comaroff) *From Revelation to Revolution: Christianity, Colonialism, and Black Consciousness in South Africa,* University of Chicago Press, Volume 1, 1991, Volume 2, 1996.
(With J. Comaroff) *Ethnography and the Historical Imagination,* University of Chicago Press, 1992.

EDITOR

The Diary of Solomon T. Plaatje: An African at Mafeking, Macmillan (New York City), 1973.
The Meaning of Marriage Payments, Academic Press (San Diego, CA), 1980.
(With Eileen Jensen Krige) *Essays on African Marriage in South Africa,* Juta, 1981.
(With J. Comaroff) *Modernity and Its Malcontents,* University of Chicago Press, 1993.

OTHER

Contributor to African studies and anthropology journals. Also member of editorial boards of *Africa, American Ethnologist,* and *Annual Reviews of Anthropology.*

WORK IN PROGRESS: Third volume of *From Revelation to Revolution,* with expected publication in 1997; a book of essays on the "new" South Africa.

SIDELIGHTS: John L. Comaroff told *CA:* "My theoretical concerns are to explore and develop the relationship between history and anthropology, to develop the methodology of a generic historical anthropology, and to investigate the nature of colonialism and post coloniality. I am also currently interested in the impact of globalism and the assertion of ethnic identities."

BIOGRAPHICAL/CRITICAL SOURCES:

PERIODICALS

Times Literary Supplement, May 7, 1982.

* * *

COOK, Thomas H. 1947-

PERSONAL: Born September 19, 1947, in Ft. Payne, AL; son of Virgil Richard (in management) and Myrick (a secretary; maiden name, Harper) Cook; married Susan Terner (a writer for radio), March 17, 1978; children: Justine Ariel. *Education:* Georgia State College, B.A., 1969; Hunter College, City University of New York, M.A., 1972; Columbia University, M.Phil., 1976.

ADDRESSES: Home—New York, NY. *Agent*—Tim Seldes, Russell & Volkening, 50 West 29th St., New York, NY 10017.

CAREER: U.S. Industrial Chemicals, New York City, advertising executive, 1970-72; Association for Help of Retarded Adults, New York City, clerk and typist, 1973-75; Dekalb Community College, Clarkston, GA, teacher of English and history, 1978-81; contributing editor and book review editor of *Atlanta* magazine, 1978-82; full-time writer, 1981—.

MEMBER: Authors Guild.

AWARDS, HONORS: Edgar Allan Poe Award nominations from Mystery Writers of America, 1981, for *Blood Innocents,* 1988, for *Sacrificial Ground,* 1992 for *Blood Echoes: The True Story of an Infamous Mass Murder and Its Aftermath,* and 1996 for *The Chatham School Affair;* Hammett Prize, International Association of Crime Writers, 1995, for *Breakheart Hill.*

WRITINGS:

NOVELS

Blood Innocents, Playboy Press (Chicago, IL), 1980.
The Orchids, Houghton (Boston, MA), 1982.
Tabernacle, Houghton, 1983.
Elena, Houghton, 1986.
Sacrificial Ground, Putnam (New York City), 1988.
Flesh and Blood, Putnam, 1989.
Streets of Fire, Putnam, 1989.
The City When It Rains, Putnam, 1991.
Evidence of Blood, Putnam, 1991.
Night Secrets, Thorndike Press (Thorndike, ME), 1991.
Mortal Memory, Putnam, 1993.
Breakheart Hill, Bantam Books (New York City), 1995.
The Chatham School Affair, Bantam Books, 1996.

OTHER

Blood Echoes: The True Story of an Infamous Mass Murder and Its Aftermath, Dutton (New York City), 1992.

Also author of *Early Graves: The Shocking True-Crime Story of the Youngest Woman Ever Sentenced to Death Row,* 1990.

SIDELIGHTS: Thomas H. Cook has written many works, including both literary novels and true crime novels. In both areas, the author is known for his meticulous attention to character development and setting. Cook's murder mysteries of the 1990s are often set in the rural southern United States. Many were well received, with critics highlighting the author's successful evocation of small-town life in the rural South and the often painful process of recollection. While Cook is occasionally faulted for overworking his simple stories, he is also viewed as one of the mystery genre's most accomplished storytellers.

Cook's first publication, *Blood Innocents,* was written while the author was in graduate school. A police procedural set in New York City, the novel is "essentially . . . about the capacity of a man to hold to his goodness while pursuing a rather squalid labor-police work," Cook once told *CA*. "My scheme, if I may call it that, is to write solid and artistically sound police procedurals like *Blood Innocents* and *Tabernacle* in order to buy the time needed to write such literary efforts as *The Orchids* and *Elena,*" Cook continued. *The Orchids,* a literary novel which followed *Blood Innocents,* was warmly received by critics such as S. L. Stebel, who, in a *Los Angeles Herald Examiner* review, found Cook's language "imbued with the kind of image and metaphor present in our very best poetry." And in *Literary Boston* Lee Grove deemed *The Orchids* "a Holocaust novel that will blow you away. . . . Cook wants you to be both comfortable and uncomfortable—and he succeeds, perfectly. You'll feel as cozy as a razor blade in a Halloween apple. You'll see just how easy it is for a brilliant, powerful, sensitive intellect to go bad, to weld itself to corruption. This novel, however, will never go bad and is anything but corrupt."

"In my literary novels I would like to help bring back what I think of as the 'meditative novel,'" Cook told *CA,* "that is, the work with a quiet, reasoned, and highly reflective voice. I prefer novels that depart somewhat from strictly linear forms of action and narrative as well as works that have taken on greater themes, rather than yet more books about middle-class or academic angst or restrictively autobiographical works, those that never venture beyond the usually rather limited experience of the novelist. In *The Orchids,* for example, I tried to render the density and precision of the German language into English, and to create a narrative voice that could convey the horrors of Langhof's experience without resorting to sensationalism of any kind. In *Elena* the narrative voice is that of a brother talking of his sister's life, a method by which not only a woman's life can be portrayed, but that of a man as well, so that the two genuinely merge into a single narrative tone."

Critics have spoken of Cook's detective novels of the 1990s, including *Breakheart Hill, Evidence of Blood,* and *Blood Echoes: the True Story of an Infamous Mass Murder and Its Aftermath,* in terms similar to those the author uses himself for his more literary efforts. In particular, the avoidance of linear structures and the inclusion of "greater themes" have brought critical acclaim for the mystery writer.

In *Evidence of Blood,* Cook's protagonist, Jackson Kinley, returns to his hometown in rural Georgia for the funeral of his oldest friend, and stays on to solve the thirty-year-old murder case his friend had been working on at the time of his death. The victim, a teenage girl, was never found, but a man was quickly arrested, tried, convicted, and electrocuted. Decades later the condemned man's daughter convinces first Kinley's friend and then Kinley himself to try to find the real murderer. "Mr. Cook knows this terrain, both in locale and in disquiet," remarked Steven Slosberg in the *New York Times Book Review.* Although Jon L. Breen, writing in the *Armchair Detective,* had a few "procedural quibbles" regarding Cook's rendering of transcripts from other cases Kinley looks into, Slosberg concluded: "*Evidence of Blood* is a highly satisfying story, strong in color and atmosphere, intelligent and exacting."

Like *Evidence of Blood,* Cook's novel *Mortal Memory* focuses on the long-term effects of a violent crime. In this work, a boy visiting friends for the afternoon returns home to find that his mother and siblings have been gruesomely killed, and his father, the presumed murderer, has run away. Years later, the young man's powerful emotions are brought to the surface again when a woman researching a book on fathers who kill their families contacts him. The *Atlanta Constitution*'s William A. Henry praised the book for its surprising plot twists and satisfying conclusion, but singled out for special praise the author's mode of storytelling, which relies on "repetition and insight" as the protagonist revisits his memory of the time of the murders from different perspectives, "almost as though he were on a Freudian analyst's couch." The result "gradually elevates a sordid personal history to mythic proportions—a 'Medea' for the middle class," Henry concluded.

Like *Evidence of Blood,* the murder at the center of *Breakheart Hill*—that of a high school girl—continues to affect her survivors decades after the crime. In this case, Ben Wade, the town doctor who was once secretly in love with classmate and victim Kelli Troy, continues to carry the guilt of Kelli's death with him twenty-five years later. Although the reviewer for the *Washington Post Book World* faulted Cook's execution of the scenario, and *New York Times Book Review*'s Marilyn Stasio found the author's "painstaking variations on his theme and the delicacy of his writing" somewhat wearying, the reviewer for *Publishers Weekly* felt that Cook's "expert storytelling" redeems his simple story. *Breakheart Hill* is "a haunting evocation that gains power and resonance with each twist of its spiral-like narration," the *Publishers Weekly* reviewer concluded.

Cook is a writer of mystery novels that evoke the feel of small-town life. Their skillful rendering of character and theme offer a glimpse into the more intelligent side of genre writing, according to the author's critics. The plots of three of Cook's mysteries published in the 1990s hinge on memory as well as murder, and some reviewers highlighted the author's expert rendering of the process of recollecting painful memories as an essential element of his success. While Cook himself has characterized these police procedurals as mere money-makers which enable him to write more literary fare, his attention to details of character and setting, as well as his skills as a storyteller, have earned him a respected place among successful mystery writers.

BIOGRAPHICAL/CRITICAL SOURCES:

PERIODICALS

Armchair Detective, summer, 1989, p. 238; summer, 1991, p. 293; spring, 1992, p. 247; fall, 1992, p. 505; winter, 1992, p. 36; spring, 1993, p. 12; fall, 1993, p. 115; spring, 1995, p. 204.

Atlanta Journal, October 17, 1982.

Atlanta Journal-Constitution, January 6, 1991, p. N10; March 3, 1991, p. N11; November 4, 1991, p. N10; March 22, 1992, p. N12; May 8, 1994, p. N11.

Booklist, January 1, 1986, p. 658; March 1, 1988, p. 1097; January 1, 1989, p. 753; June 1, 1989, p. 1673; April 15, 1990, p. 1585; November 1, 1990, p. 485; December 15, 1990, p. 804; September 15, 1991, pp. 123, 131; February 15, 1992, p. 1070; July, 1995, p. 1858.

Book Watch, May, 1992, p. 1.

Boston Globe, December 29, 1991, p. A15.

Chicago Tribune, April 18, 1993, sec. 14, p. 6.

Christian Science Monitor, August 4, 1989, p. 13.

Jerusalem Post, March 11, 1983.

Kirkus Reviews, November 1, 1985, p. 1147; March 1, 1988, p. 325; November 15, 1988, p. 1639; July 1, 1989, p. 953; May 1, 1990, p. 610; October 1, 1990, p. 1365; December 1, 1990, p. 1640; August 15, 1991, p. 1028; January 1, 1992, p. 28; February 15, 1993, p. 185.

Library Journal, January, 1986, p. 100; March 1, 1988, p. 79; January, 1989, p. 104; August, 1989, p. 162; October 1, 1990, p. 102; January, 1991, p. 147; February 1, 1992, p. 111; July, 1995, p. 118.

Literary Boston, December, 1982.

Los Angeles Herald Examiner, February 13, 1983.

Los Angeles Times, November 17, 1991, p. 12.

Los Angeles Times Book Review, March 13, 1988, p. 13; January 1, 1989, p. 9; September 10, 1989, p. 10; January 13, 1991, p. 8; November 17, 1991, p. 12; April 11, 1993, p. 8.

Minneapolis Star and Tribune, September 19, 1982.

New York Times Book Review, October 31, 1982; January 5, 1986, p. 23; February 19, 1989, p. 23; September 24, 1989, p. 29; June 24, 1990, p. 22; January 20, 1991, p. 27; June 9, 1991, p. 22; October 20, 1991, p. 47; January 26, 1992, p. 24; August 6, 1995, p. 23.

Observer (London), January 17, 1993, p. 49.

People, August 20, 1990, p. 29.

Publishers Weekly, November 1, 1985, p. 56; January 15, 1988, p. 82; October 21, 1988, p. 51; July 7, 1989, p. 50; May 4, 1990, p. 51; December 14, 1990, p. 52; August 9, 1991, p. 42; January 27, 1992, p. 81; May 18, 1992, p. 66; November 16, 1992, p. 60; February 15, 1993, p. 197; February 22, 1993, p. 90; May 1, 1995, p. 44.

Punch, December 9, 1988, p. 72.

School Library Journal, August, 1993, p. 205; February, 1996, p. 131.

Southern Living, April, 1992, p. 112.

Tribune Books (Chicago), April 18, 1993, p. 6.

Washington Post, March 7, 1992, p. B3; August 27, 1995, p. 4.

Washington Post Book World, November 6, 1983; February 2, 1986, p. 8; March 22, 1992, p. 12; August 27, 1995, p. 4.

West Coast Review of Books, April, 1989, p. 29.

Wilson Library Bulletin, December, 1980, p. 295.*

COUPLAND, Douglas 1961-

PERSONAL: Born December 30, 1961, on a Canadian military base in Baden-Soellingen, Germany; son of Douglas Charles Thomas (a doctor) and C. Janet (Campbell) Coupland. *Education:* Attended Emily Carr College of Art and Design, Vancouver, Canada, 1984; completed a two-year course in Japanese business science, Hawaii, 1986.

ADDRESSES: *Home*—Vancouver, British Columbia, Canada.

CAREER: Writer, sculptor, and editor. Host of *The Search for Generation X* (documentary), PBS, 1991.

WRITINGS:

Generation X: Tales for an Accelerated Culture (novel), St. Martin's (New York City), 1991.

Shampoo Planet (novel), Pocket Books (New York City), 1992.

Life after God (short fiction), Pocket Books, 1994.

Microserfs (novel), ReganBooks (New York City), 1995.

Polaroids from the Dead (essays and short fiction), ReganBooks, 1996.

Contributor of articles to periodicals, including *New Republic, New York Times, Wired,* and *Saturday Night.*

SIDELIGHTS: Douglas Coupland has become known as the voice of a generation, "the self-wrought oracle of our age," according to John Fraser in *Saturday Night,* who also called him "the Jack Kerouac of his generation." Coupland earned his reputation with his first novel, *Generation X: Tales for an Accelerated Culture,* which originated the term "Generation X" to refer to those Americans born in the 1960s to early-1970s, defining their aggregate interests, concerns, and problems. About Coupland's status as mouthpiece for Generation X-ers, Fraser added that the author achieved it "with a distinctive style and up-market hustle that still leaves me breathless. Not once, so far as I can tell, did he do a sleazy thing to get where he is. He trudged all the way on his talent alone."

Generation X chronicles the story of three "twenty-something" friends living in Palm Springs, California, and mired in "McJobs"—a term coined by Coupland to indicate jobs with low pay, low dignity, and little future. The book, which London *Times* contributor Michael Wright described as "part novel, part manifesto," launched its twenty-nine-year-old author straight to the top of the bestseller lists. Coupland is claimed by some to have written the defining document of his generation, "the new *Catcher in the Rye,*" a book about young people "with too many TVs and too few job opportunities," commented a *Newsweek* reviewer. In the novel, Andy, Claire, and Dag represent Generation X members and the stories they tell each other in their Palm Springs refuge predict a drab future of "lessness" and an accompanying tedium as the X-ers' fate in life. (One of many neologisms, along with the cartoons and slogans that appear in the book, "lessness" implies the acceptance of lower expectations than those of preceding generations.) "The trio's modern fables of love and death and spacemen and nuclear war, sparkle like lumps of quartz amid the granite of their desert life," commented Wright, "each tale offering a small epiphany or moment of spangled optimism amid the prevailing gloom."

Laurel Boone, writing in *Books in Canada,* found fault with Coupland's story and its annotations. "The cartoons, definitions, slogans, and other ephemera running beside the text in a separate column make shallow comments on the slightly less shallow story," she maintained. John Williams conceded in *New Statesman and Society* that Coupland's novel is "self-conscious as hell," but he still found *Generation X* "charming" and "a surprisingly endearing read." Describing the book as "funny, colourful and accessible," Wright stated that Coupland's first novel possesses "dizzying sparkle and originality," further lauding it as "a blazing debut."

In *Shampoo Planet,* published a year after *Generation X,* Coupland turns his attention to "the Global Teens," the generation following the X-ers who were raised in the age of information and video stimulation. Tyler Johnson, the youthful narrator and younger brother of *Generation X*'s narrator, has what Sophronia Scott Gregory described in *Time* as "a Smithsonian-class collection of shampoos" (thus the book's title) plus a sister named Daisy—a waif-like, pseudo-hippie sporting blond dreadlocks—and a twice-divorced mother, Jasmine, a true flower child who seems to Tyler more in need of parenting than is he. "Although the author is almost twice as old as the main characters in *Shampoo Planet,*" observed Victor Dwyer in *Maclean's,* "he creates in the book a fictional teenage world that is both convincing and highly entertaining."

Comparisons to Coupland's first novel were to be expected. Some, like Brian Fawcett's in *Books in Canada,* noted a certain heaviness in both books. "Like its predecessor," wrote Fawcett, "*Shampoo Planet* is relentlessly witty and sometimes insistently light-headed without ever quite becoming light-hearted." "Old people will always win," figures *Shampoo*'s narrator; he finds himself in a world experiencing "severe shopping withdrawal and severe goal withdrawal." Still, Tyler remains hopeful about his future. Coupland himself drew attention to this hopefulness as a difference between his two books. He was quoted in *Maclean's* as saying, "I'm not Pollyannaish, but I'm optimistic about the future. I think *Shampoo Planet* has an optimism about it that *Generation X* does not." Dwyer recognized the same distinction: "It is as though the decade that separates him from his latest crop of characters has provided Coupland with a sense of perspective, and levity, that was sometimes lacking in the often bleak, self-absorbed *Generation X.*"

Time contributor Gregory complained that Coupland's narrative in *Shampoo Planet* lacks motivation, but she praised the author's quirky descriptive passages, noting that "the book thrives with the energetically bizarre." Gregory further observed, "Fascinating characters abound, but unfortunately they have little to do." Michael Redhill offered a different characterization of the novel in his Toronto *Globe and Mail* review. "Coupland's challenge here was to write about the fascination with surfaces without being superficial himself," he commented. "*Generation X* was a novel filled with an empathetic rage and sadness. In *Shampoo Planet,* Coupland's tears run to jeers." Other critics hailed the book's fresh viewpoint and inventiveness. A *Publishers Weekly* reviewer called the novel "funny, sympathetic, and offhandedly brilliant." Dwyer assessed Coupland as "a maturing author artfully evoking the hopes and dreams of a generation that has good reason to have little of either."

Describing Coupland's 1994 collection of short fiction and essays, *Life after God,* Joe Chidley asserted in *Maclean's* that the book "strips away the paraphernalia of an age-group to investigate the origins of its angst. Unfortunately, he also strips away much of its anger and wit. What remains is the ennui." Terry Horton drew a similar conclusion in a *Quill and Quire* review. "Coupland has a knack for beautiful imagery . . . and each chapter's first page is topped with a lighthearted cartoon," wrote the reviewer. "But, in the end, neither beautiful imagery nor cartoons can sweep away the hopelessness that darkens these tales." Chidley further observed that, "cumulatively, eight stories about the passing of things end up sounding like an extended whine."

Brenda Peterson, reviewing *Life after God* in the *New York Times Book Review,* found that Coupland's effort missed the mark. "Though each of these very short tales has its own narrator, the voice never really varies: it drones where it might delve, it skims where it might seduce, it hoards where it might offer sustenance." Peterson concluded, "Mr. Coupland's vision is as perishable and trendy as the brand names that pass here for characters and story lines." *New Criterion* contributor Jeffrey Bloom explained the collection's shortcomings in the following manner: "Coupland has the eye and the ear of a good reporter, but lacks the vision of a good novelist. He sees the telling detail and hears the revealing bit of dialogue, but he never goes behind or beyond them. The result, *Life after God,* is rather thin gruel. But as such, it is an excellent guide to the thin spiritual life of the first generation raised without religion."

Coupland's 1995 novel, *Microserfs,* again explores the lives of the generation of young men and women in their twenties. However, the characters at the center of this novel are not mourning the hopelessness of their McWorld; they are young computer programmers hyperactively engaged in realizing the hopes of Bill Gates and his MicrosoftWorld. *New Statesman and Society* reviewer Peter Jukes suggested that Coupland has created "perhaps the first great work of *cyberrealism.* Where others are obsessed by pixels and bits, Coupland's subject is the 'biomass' squeezed between the silicon, the 'carbon-based forms' that still sweat, flake away, love, grieve and fail." He added, "*Microserfs* is a tough and raucous celebration of our ability to reinvent and remember ourselves. And it paints a vivid picture of the new geek priesthood, sitting like monks in their VDU-lit cells, embellishing the margins with hieroglyphs, keeping our culture alive."

Microserfs' "main characters are all highly observant, introspective, and almost painfully ironic," noted Dan Bortolotti in *Books in Canada.* "They are, in fact, like most of Coupland's characters: coldly viewing themselves in terms of consumer culture." Daniel, the narrator, and his friends share a house where they pass the few moments they are not working at Microsoft. They eat poorly, sleep rarely, and exercise only their brains. They think and speak in terms of popular culture, defining themselves by their ideal *Jeopardy* categories. "*Microserfs* is entertaining," Nadia Halim commented in *Canadian Forum.* "Coupland's skill at manipulating his pop-culture-reference-laden vocabulary remains as strong as ever. He is capable of producing passages that are funny, provocative and sublime all in the same breath." Even so, Halim found that "Coupland's weaknesses . . . are also on display here. The book's plot is banal: after a few predictable crises, everyone falls in love and lives happily ever after. The characters all talk the same way."

Such reservations notwithstanding, reviewers like *New York* magazine's John Homans pointed out that Coupland is "a journalist . . . and *Microserfs* is a giant, frightening collage, a novel of half-baked ideas about change and technology and obsolescence." Rick Perlstein touched on this quality of the novel and its author's role as a chronicler of social change. He wrote in the *Nation,* "Coupland here is mining urgent territory—a new social realism for the dawn of Postindustry and its unholy trinity of data, downsizing and Darwinism. He's investigating a curious sociological quirk of our age: What happens when the very cultural imagination of a society, nay, the very cultural imagination of a planet, is chartered by an elite of preternaturally gifted computer geeks who play with Nerf toys?"

Coupland has been lauded by some as an accurate and keen observer, the voice of his generation, and a seer; by others, he has been faulted as a gloomsayer who only scratches surfaces. Yet, according to Jay McInerney in the *New York Times Book Review,* "Douglas Coupland continues to register the buzz of his generation with a fidelity that should shame most professional *Zeitgeist* chasers."

Coupland's official homepage on the World Wide Web is located at http://www.coupland.com.

BIOGRAPHICAL/CRITICAL SOURCES:

BOOKS

Contemporary Literary Criticism, Volume 85, Gale (Detroit), 1995.

PERIODICALS

Books in Canada, September, 1991, pp. 50-51; April, 1992, p. 13; October, 1992; September 1995, p. 30.

Byte, October, 1995, p. 49.

Canadian Forum, January, 1993, p. 41; June, 1994, p. 44; December, 1995, p. 50.

Christian Century, October 5, 1994, p. 905.

Esquire, March, 1994, pp. 170-71.

Fortune, September 18, 1995, p. 235.

Globe and Mail (Toronto), September 5, 1992, p. C8.

Maclean's, August 24, 1992, p. 60; April 25, 1994, p. 62; June 26, 1995, p. 54.

Nation, June 26, 1995, p. 934.

New Criterion, April, 1994, pp. 79-80.

New Statesman and Society, May 29, 1992, p. 40; July 29, 1994, p. 39; November 10, 1995, p. 37.

Newsweek, January 27, 1992, p. 58; June 19, 1995, p. 12.

New York, June 5, 1995, p. 50.

New York Times Book Review, May 8, 1994, p. 13; May 8, 1994, p. 13; June 11, 1995, p. 54.

Observer, August 7, 1994, p. 22.

Paragraph, fall, 1994, pp. 32-33.

People Weekly, October 14, 1991, pp. 105-06; April 25, 1994, pp. 31-32; July 10, 1995, p. 30.

Progressive, January, 1994, p. 42.

Publishers Weekly, February 1, 1991, p. 77; June 15, 1992, p. 82; December 20, 1993, p. 48; May 13, 1996, p. 66.

Quill and Quire, February, 1994, p. 24; June, 1994, p. 38; May, 1995, p. 7; July, 1995, p. 51; May, 1996, p. 1.

Saturday Night, March, 1994, pp. 8-9.

Time, October 19, 1992, p. 78.

Times (London), June 4, 1992, p. 6.

Times Literary Supplement, February 19, 1993, p. 23; August 5, 1994, p. 18; November 10, 1995, p. 22.
USA Today, March 7, 1994, p. D1.
Vanity Fair, March, 1994, pp. 92, 94.
Voice Literary Supplement, November, 1992, p. 25.*

* * *

COVER, Arthur Byron 1950-
(Thomas Shadwell, a joint pseudonym)

PERSONAL: Born January 14, 1950, in Grundy, VA; son of William Arthur (a physician) and Margaret (a politician; maiden name, Peery) Cover. *Education:* Virginia Polytechnic Institute and State University, M.A., 1971.

ADDRESSES: *Agent*—Jane Rotrosen Agency, 318 East 51st St., New York, NY 10022.

CAREER: Writer. Interviewer for *Vertex,* Los Angeles, 1974-75. Member of extension faculty at University of California, Los Angeles.

MEMBER: Science Fiction Writers of America.

WRITINGS:

SCIENCE FICTION NOVELS, EXCEPT AS INDICATED

Autumn Angels, Pyramid Publications (New York City), 1975.
The Platypus of Doom and Other Nihilists (short stories), Warner (New York City), 1976.
The Sound of Winter, Pyramid Publications, 1976.
An East Wind Coming, Berkeley Publishing (New York City), 1979.
Flash Gordon (novelization of the motion picture), Jove (New York City), 1980.
The Rings of Saturn, Bantam (New York City), 1985.
American Revolutionary, illustrated by Walter Martishius, Bantam, 1985.
Blade of the Guillotine, illustrated by Scott Hampton, Bantam, 1986.
Isaac Asmiov's Robot City: Prodigy, Ace (New York City), 1988.
Planetfall: In Search of Floyd, Avon (New York City), 1988.
Stationfall, Avon, 1989.
(With Tim Sullivan and John Gregory Betancourt as Thomas Shadwell) *Robert Silverberg's Time Tours: The Dinosaur Trackers,* HarperPaperbacks (New York City), 1991.

Work represented in anthologies, including *Alien Condition,* edited by Steve Goldin, 1973, and *The Last Dangerous Visions,* edited by Harlan Ellison.

SIDELIGHTS: In much of Arthur Byron Cover's science fiction, plot often takes a back seat to unusual writing techniques and intellectual flights of fancy. Discussing Cover in the *St. James Guide to Science Fiction Writers,* Robert Reginald compares the author's work to a comic-strip version of the world of medieval artist Hieronymus Bosch: "Grotesqueries there are aplenty, unexplained and inexplicable, wandering the bizarre landscape of a caricature Earth, interacting with each other in curious and unique ways, seeking neither resolution nor evolution nor solution, but just existing as they are. Forget about plots, forget about the conventionalities of science fiction or fantasy, or of fiction in general: you won't find them here. What you *will* find are . . . pieces and snatches of characters, conversations, situations, perambulations, rearranged in new and interesting ways."

Cover's unique style surfaced in his first novel, *Autumn Angels.* The story takes place on a "strange, far-future or other-dimensional Earth dominated by godlike beings scrapping over philosophical nullities while trying to establish his or her own position," according to Reginald. Each of these beings has taken on the persona of some fictional character of the past, identifying themselves with labels like "the demon," "the lawyer," "the fat man," and "the other fat man." The only two characters really given names are Dwit and Xit, the aliens who, long ago, transformed humankind into its current "godlike" state as a joke. The narrative "meanders back and forth across a landscape of broken conversations and philosophical musings," according to Reginald. "Each of these beings is searching for a unique identity in a world where individuations have failed; each seeks something to give it purpose: a name, a self, a reason."

These beings were featured again in *An East Wind Coming,* which Reginald considers Cover's "major work." This novel further explores the theme of identity. In it, characters based on Sherlock Holmes and Dr. Watson must challenge a new

Jack the Ripper, who uses an antimatter knife to disembowel female godlike beings. At the book's climax, the ripper destroys himself, and the threat to the godlike beings is ended. "The right of the individual to be individual has thus been affirmed," comments Reginald.

BIOGRAPHICAL/CRITICAL SOURCES:

BOOKS

St. James Guide to Science Fiction Writers, St. James Press (Detroit), 1996.

PERIODICALS

Science Fiction Chronicle, January, 1988, p. 53; February, 1989, p. 37-38.

VOYA, August, 1988, p. 138.*

* * *

COWLEY, (Cassia) Joy 1936-

PERSONAL: Born August 7, 1936; daughter of Peter (a builder) and Cassia (Gedge) Summers; married Malcolm Mason (an accountant and writer), 1970 (died 1985); married Terry Coles, 1989; children: (from a previous marriage) Sharon, Edward, Judith, James. *Education:* Attended Girls' High School, Palmerston North, Wellington, New Zealand. *Politics:* None. *Religion:* Catholic. *Avocational interests:* Spinning, fishing, and "other soothing pastimes."

ADDRESSES: Home—Te Mangawa, Fish Bay, Kenepuru, R.D.2, Picton, New Zealand.

CAREER: Writer, 1967—. Pharmacists' apprentice in New Zealand, 1953-56.

AWARDS, HONORS: New Zealand Buckland Literary Award, 1970, for *Man of Straw;* New Zealand Literary Achievement Award, 1980; New Zealand AIM Children's Book Awards, 1982, for *The Silent One,* 1992, for *Bow Down Shadrach,* and 1996, for *The Cheese Trap;* Children's Book of the Year awards, 1983, for *The Silent One,* and 1993, for *Bow down Shadrach;* Russell Clark Award, 1985, for *The Duck in the Gun;* New Zealand Commemoration Medal, 1990; Order of the British Empire, 1992, for services to children's literature; Margaret Mahy Lecture Award, 1993; Women's Suffrage Centennial Medal, 1993; Honorary Doctorate of Literature, Massey University, 1994.

WRITINGS:

CHILDREN'S BOOKS

The Duck in the Gun, illustrated by Edward Sorel, Doubleday, 1969, illustrated by Robyn Belton, Shortland (Auckland), 1984.

The Silent One, illustrated by Hermann Greissle, Knopf, 1981, illustrated by Sherryl Jordan, Whitcoulls, 1981.

The Terrible Taniwha of Timberditch, Oxford University Press (Auckland), 1982.

Old Tuatara, illustrated by Clare Bowes, Department of Education School Publications Branch (Wellington), 1983, published as *Old Lizard,* Nelson (London), 1985.

(With Mona Williams) *Two of a Kind* (stories), illustrated by Jane Amos, Blackberry Press (Upper Hutt, New Zealand), 1984.

The Fierce Little Woman and the Wicked Pirate, illustrated by Jo Davies, Shortland, 1984.

Salmagundi, illustrated by Philip Webb, Oxford University Press, 1985.

Brith the Terrible, Shortland, 1986.

Captain Felonius, illustrated by Elizabeth Fuller, Shortland, 1986.

The Lucky Feather, illustrated by Philip Webb, Shortland, 1986.

My Tiger (stories), illustrated by Jan van der Voo, Shortland, 1986.

The King's Pudding, illustrated by Martin Bailey, Shortland, 1986.

Mrs. Grindy's Shoes, illustrated by Val Biro, Shortland, 1986.

Turnips for Dinner, illustrated by van der Voo, Shortland, 1986.

The Train Ride Story, illustrated by Biro, Shortland, 1987.

Giant on the Bus, illustrated by Ian McNee, Shortland, 1987.

Seventy Kilometers from Ice Cream, photographs by Winto Cleal, Department of Education School Publications Branch, 1987.

Pawprints in the Butter, Mallinson Rendel (Wellington, New Zealand), 1991.

Bow down Shadrach, illustrated by Robyn Belton, Hodder & Stoughton (Auckland), 1991, Wright Group (Seattle, WA), 1996.

Happy Birthday, Mrs. Felonius, Omnibus (Australia), 1992.
The Day of the Rain, Mallinson Rendel, 1993.
The Screaming Mean Machine, Scholastic, 1993.
Gladly Here I Come, Penguin (Harmondsworth), 1994, Wright Group, 1996.
Beyond the Rivers, Scholastic New Zealand, 1994.
Song of the River, Wright Group, 1994.
Write On, Scholastic New Zealand, 1994.
Guide for Young Authors, Wright Group, 1994.
The Day of the Snow, illustrated by Bob Kerr, Mallinson Rendel, 1994.
Tulevai, Scholastic New Zealand, 1995.
The Happy Hens Series, Scholastic New Zealand, 1995.
The Day of the Wind, Mallinson Rendel, 1995.
Sea Daughter, Scholastic New Zealand, 1995.
The Mouse Bride, paintings by David Christiana, Scholastic, 1995.
The Cheese Trap, Scholastic New Zealand, 1995.
Nicketty-Nacketty-Noo-Noo-Noo, Scholastic New Zealand, 1995.
Joy Cowley Answers Kids' Questions, Scholastic New Zealand, 1995.
Brave Mama Puss ("Puss Quartet") Reed (Auckland), 1995.
Papa Puss to the Rescue ("Puss Quartet") Reed, 1995.
Mabel and the Marvelous Meow ("Puss Quartet"), Reed, 1995.
Oscar in Danger ("Puss Quartet"), Reed, 1995.
Gracias the Thanksgiving Turkey, illustrated by Joe Cepeda, Scholastic, 1996.
Snake and Lizard, Wright Group, 1996.

JUVENILE READERS

Author of readers *Fish in the Trough, A New Friend, Johnny's Guitar, The Fire-Fighters, The Meeting House,* and *Wendy Makes a Poi,* all illustrated by Nancy Parker, Kea Press (Wellington), 1968, published as *The Tui and Sis Books,* Price Milburn (Wellington), 1977.

Author, with June Melser, of "Story Chest Read-Together" series: *Mrs. Wishy-Washy, Smarty Pants, The Big Toe, Boo-Hoo, Grandpa Grandpa, Hairy Bear, The Hungry Giant, In a Dark Dark Wood, Lazy Mary, Obadiah!, One Cold Wet Night, Poor Old Polly, Sing a Song, Three Little Ducks, Woosh!, Yes Ma'am, The Red Rose, To Town, Dan the Flying Man, The Farm Concert, The Jigaree, Meanies, The Monster's Party,* and *Who Will Be My Mother?,* Shortland, 1980-83.

Author, with June Melser, of "Story Chest Books" series: *The Birthday Cake, The Dragon, A Terrible Fright, A Barrel of Gold, Clever Mr. Brown, Hungry Monster, Jack-in-the-Box, The Kick-a-Lot Shoes, The Pirates, Wet Grass, Where Is My Spider?, Yum and Yuk, Captain Bumble, Countdown, A Day in Town, The Big Tease, Cat on the Roof, The Ghost and the Sausage, Grandma's Stick, Hatupatu and the Birdwoman, Little Brother's Haircut, The Sunflower That Went FLOP, Tell-Tale,* and *Sun Smile,* Shortland, 1981-82.

Author, with June Melser, of "Story Chest Ready-Set-Go" series: *The Bee, The Chocolate Cake, Come with Me, Copy-Cat, Flying, I Want an Ice Cream, Little Pig, Lost, My Home, Plop!, Round and Round, Splosh, To New York, Who Lives Here?, Where Are They Going?, Who's Going to Lick the Bowl?, Horace, The Night Train, The Pumpkin, Rum-Tum Tumm, Sleeping Out, Too Big for Me, What a Mess!,* and *Look for Me,* Shortland, 1981-82.

Author, with June Melser and Margaret Mahy, of *Cooking Pot, Fast and Funny, Roly Poly, Sing to the Moon,* and *Tiddalik,* Shortland, 1982.

Author of "Story Box Books" series: *The Pie Thief, The Tale of the Cook, The Trader from Currumbin, The War of the Winds,* and *Poor Old Robot,* Shortland, 1982-85.

Author of "Story Chest Ready-to-Read" series: *Number One, The Biggest Cake in the World, Fasi Sings, Fasi's Fish, Greedy Cat, Our Teacher Miss Pool, Rain Rain, Words, I'm the King of the Mountain, Rosie at the Zoo, The Wild Wet Wellington Wind, Did You Say Five?, The Smile,* and *Where Is Miss Pool?,* Department of Education School Publications Branch, 1982-87.

Author, with June Melser, of "Story Chest Get Ready Books": *The Bicycle, The Big Hill, Feet, The Ghost, Go Go Go, Houses, If You Meet a Dragon, In the Mirror, A Monster Sandwich, Mouse, Night-Time, On a Chair, Painting, The Party, The Storm,* and *The Tree-House,* Arnold Wheaton (Leeds, England), 1983.

Author of "Sunshine Books" series: *Yuk Soup, Baby Gets Dressed, Big and Little, Buzzing Flies, Dinner! Down to Town, A Hug Is Warm, Huggles' Breakfast, Huggles Can Juggle, Huggles Goes*

Away, I Am a Bookworm, I Can Fly, I Can Jump, I Love My Family, Ice Cream, Little Brother, The Long Long Tail, Major Jump, My Home, My Puppy, Our Granny, Our Street, The Race, Scat! Said the Cat, Shark in a Sack, Shoo! Snap!, Uncle Buncle's House, Up in a Tree, What Is a Huggles? When Itchy Witchy Sneezes, Along Comes Jake, Bread, Come for a Swim, The Cooking Pot, Dad's Headache, Don't You Laugh at Me! The Giant's Boy, Good for You, Goodbye Lucy, I'm Bigger Than You!, Let's Have a Swim!, Little Car, The Monkey Bridge, Mr. Grump, Mr. Whisper, My Boat, My Sloppy Tiger, Noise, Nowhere and Nothing, Old Grizzly, One Thousand Currant Buns, The Poor Sore Paw, Ratty-Tatty, Red Socks and Yellow Socks, The Seed, Spider Spider, The Terrible Tiger, The Tiny Woman's Coat, Wake Up, Mum!, What Would You Like?, Where Are You Going Aja Rose?, and *The Wind Blows Strong,* Heinemann (London), 1986-87.

Author of "Windmill" series: *Growing, The Little Red Hen, My Little Brother, Splish Splash!, Where Can We Put an Elephant?, Where's the Egg Cup, Lucy's Sore Knee,* and *My Wonderful Chair,* Heinemann, 1986-88.

Author of "Jellybeans" series: *Don't Wake the Baby, The Kangaroo from Wooloomooloo, Lavender the Library Cat, Let's Get a Pet, The Little Brown House, The Magician's Lunch, Morning Dance, The Most Scary Ghost, Mouse Monster, The Plants of My Aunt, Ten Loopy Caterpillars, The Terrible Armadillo, The Train That Ran Away, The Yukadoos, Monster, The Amazing Popple Seed, The Bull and the Matador, Cow Up a Tree, The Difficult Day, The Gumby Shop, A Handy Dragon, The Horrible Thing with Hairy Feet, Mr. Beep, Boggity-Bog, Do-Whacky-Do, The Shoe Grabber, A Silly Old Story, A Walk with Grandpa, The Wonder-Whizz,* and *The Wild Woolly Child,* Allan, 1988-89.

ADULT FICTION

Nest in a Falling Tree, Doubleday, 1967.
Man of Straw, Doubleday, 1970.
Of Men and Angels, Doubleday, 1973.
The Mandrake Root, Doubleday, 1976.
The Growing Season, Doubleday, 1979.
Heart Attack and Other Stories, Hodder & Stoughton, 1985.

OTHER

Whole Learning: Whole Child, Wright Group, 1994.

Contributor, *New Zealand Short Stories,* Volume 3, Oxford University Press, 1975. Stories have appeared in New Zealand literary periodicals and school readers; writer of radio scripts for New Zealand Broadcasting Corporation. Several of Cowley's books have been translated into Spanish.

ADAPTATIONS: Carry Me Back, a film produced by Kiwi Film Production/New Zealand Film Commission, and shown at the 1982 Cannes film festival, was based on a story by Cowley. *Nest in a Falling Tree* was adapted by Roald Dahl as the film *The Night Digger,* starring Patricia Neal. *The Silent One* has been adapted for film and aired on The Disney Channel.

WORK IN PROGRESS: Starbright and the Dream Eater, a children's book.

SIDELIGHTS: Joy Cowley, a prolific, award-winning writer of children's picture books and readers, first earned her reputation with *The Silent One.* This story, set in the South Pacific, tells how a deaf, mute boy named Jonasi is dreaded and ostracized by superstitious islanders because of his silence and his friendship with a rare albino turtle. Jonasi and the turtle are perceived as demons, and blamed for both a hurricane and a fatal shark attack. When Jonasi gets his chance to leave the island for a new life and an education at a school for the deaf, the life of his turtle is threatened. Jonasi jumps into the ocean to save it, and disappears forever.

The Silent One was favorably received by many critics, and it earned Cowley her first AIM Children's Book Award. Virginia Haviland, writing in *Horn Book,* found the prose in *The Silent One* to be "brilliantly evocative of the physical background as well as of the emotional atmosphere." The book "has a haunting quality," asserted a critic for *Bulletin of the Center for Children's Books.* And *Times Educational Supplement* critic Fred Urquhart declared that *The Silent One* "will not be forgotten easily."

More recently, Cowley has gained critical recognition for her picture book *The Mouse Bride,* illustrated by David Christiana. In this work, based on a traditional folktale spanning many cultures, a small mouse laments her weakness and desires to marry the strongest husband in the world, thereby seemingly ensuring strong children. Her search takes her to the sun, the cloud, the wind, and finally back again to the house before her quest is resolved.

Cowley, who has also penned books on the education of children and on children's writing, once explained how she approaches her work for children. "Writing for young people requires a memory; more than that—before starting a book it's necessary to peel away years of adult experience like the layers of an onion, and expose a self that's of an age corresponding with character and reader. Only by being once more ten or fourteen or whatever age I'm writing for, can I evaluate the work. I can 'live' with my characters and understand them as equals."

BIOGRAPHICAL/CRITICAL SOURCES:

PERIODICALS

Best Sellers, August 15, 1967.
Bulletin of the Center for Children's Books, June, 1981, p. 189.
Horn Book, June, 1981, pp. 301-302.
Kirkus Reviews, March 15, 1978, p. 321.
Library Journal, February 1, 1975, p. 310.
Magpies, March, 1996.
New York Times Book Review, August 13, 1967, p. 5; December 24, 1972, p. 14.
Observer Review, October 22, 1967.
Publishers Weekly, January 20, 1975, p. 65; April 3, 1978, p. 69; September 30, 1996, p. 86.
Reading Time, May, 1996, p. 23.
Times Educational Supplement, August 20, 1982.

* * *

CREWS, Harry (Eugene) 1935-

PERSONAL: Born June 6, 1935, in Alma, GA; son of Rey (a farmer) and Myrtice (Haselden) Crews; married Sally Thornton Ellis, January 24, 1960 (divorced); children: Patrick Scott (deceased), Byron Jason. *Education:* University of Florida, B.A., 1960, M.S.Ed., 1962.

CAREER: Writer. Broward Junior College, Ft. Lauderdale, FL, teacher of English, 1962-68; University of Florida, Gainesville, associate professor, 1968-74, professor of English, 1974-88. *Military service:* U.S. Marine Corps, 1953-56; became sergeant.

AWARDS, HONORS: Award from American Academy of Arts and Sciences, 1972.

WRITINGS:

NOVELS

The Gospel Singer, Morrow (New York City), 1968.
Naked in Garden Hills, Morrow, 1969.
This Thing Don't Lead to Heaven, Morrow, 1970.
Karate Is a Thing of the Spirit, Morrow, 1971.
Car, Morrow, 1972.
The Hawk Is Dying, Knopf (New York City), 1973.
The Gypsy's Curse, Knopf, 1974.
A Feast of Snakes, Atheneum (New York City), 1976.
All We Need of Hell, Harper (New York City), 1987.
The Knockout Artist, Harper, 1988.
Body, Poseidon Press (New York City), 1990.
Scar Lover, Poseidon Press, 1992.
The Mulching of America, Simon & Schuster (New York City), 1995.

SHORT STORIES

The Enthusiast, Palaemon Press, 1981.
Two, Lord John (Northridge, CA), 1984.

Contributor of stories to *Florida Quarterly* and *Craft and Vision.*

OTHER

A Childhood: The Biography of a Place (autobiography), Harper, 1978.
Blood and Grits (nonfiction), Harper, 1979.
Florida Frenzy (essays and stories), University Presses of Florida (Gainesville), 1982.
Blood Issue (play), produced in Louisville, KY, 1989.
Madonna at Ringside, Lord John, 1991.
Classic Crews: A Harry Crews Reader, Poseidon Press, 1993.

Author of column "Grits" for *Esquire.* Contributor to *Sewanee Review, Georgia Review,* and *Playboy.*

SIDELIGHTS: Reading novelist Harry Crews, Allen Shepherd maintains in the *Dictionary of Literary Biography,* "is not something one wants to do too much of at a single sitting; the intensity of his vision is unsettling." This vision is both comic and tragic, nostalgic and grotesque, and is focused on the American South, where Crews was raised and still lives. His characters, often physically deformed or strangely obsessed, are grotesques in the southern gothic tradition, and his stories are violent and extreme. Michael Mewshaw, writing in the *Nation,* explains that Crews "has taken a cast of the misfit and malformed—freaks, side-show performers, psychopaths, cripples, midgets and catatonics—and yoked it to plots which are even more improbable than his characters." Frank W. Shelton of the *Southern Literary Journal* defines the world of Crews's fiction as "mysterious, violent and dangerous" and calls his vision "a lonely and extremely sad one." But Mewshaw does not find Crews's vision essentially sad. He finds that Crews is "beset by existential nausea but, like any normal American, is not blind to the humor of it all. Bleak, mordant, appalling, Harry Crews can also be hilarious." Vivian Mercier of the *World* echoes this idea, remarking that "reading Crews is a bit like undergoing major surgery with laughing gas."

Crews first began to create stories as a boy in rural Georgia during the Depression. Living in an area where, he claims in *A Childhood: The Biography of a Place,* "there wasn't enough cash money . . . to close up a dead man's eyes," Crews and his friends found a wonderland in the Sears, Roebuck mail order catalog. The boys called the catalog their dream book because the models seemed unnaturally perfect to them, and the merchandise was far beyond their reach. While poring over the catalog pictures, Crews entertained his friends by spinning stories about the models and products. "I had decided that all the people in the catalog were related," he explains in *A Childhood,* "not necessarily blood kin but knew one another. . . . And it was out of this knowledge that I first began to make up stories."

After serving four years in the U.S. Marines, which he joined at the age of seventeen, Crews went to the University of Florida, where he was inspired by writer in residence Andrew Lyle to begin writing seriously. Crews studied Graham Greene's novel *The End of the Affair* while learning to write. He tells Steve Oney in the *New York Times Book Review* that he picked the book apart to see "how in the hell you do it." Crews reduced the novel to numbers: how many characters, how many scenes, how many rooms, and so on. Then he wrote a novel following that formula exactly. "It was the bad novel I knew it would be," Crews remembers. "But by doing it I learned more about writing fiction and writing a novel . . . than I had from any class."

Crews writes of his native Georgia in *The Gospel Singer,* his first published novel. A popular traveling evangelist, the Gospel Singer appears in his hometown of Enigma during a concert tour. His local sweetheart has recently been murdered and, it is suspected, raped by a black man. The Singer is trailed into town by the Freak Fair, a sideshow of human oddities—including the show's owner, a man with an oversized foot—working the crowds attracted by the Singer's revival meetings. When the accused murderer is threatened with lynching, the Gospel Singer tries to save him by revealing that the murdered woman was not in fact a violated virgin but "the biggest whore who ever walked in Enigma," as Shepherd writes. In the resulting chaos the townspeople lynch both men.

Response to *The Gospel Singer* was generally favorable. Though Walter Sullivan of *Sewanee Review* finds the book has "all the hallmarks of a first novel: it is energetic but uneven, competent but clumsy, not finally satisfactory but memorable nonetheless," he believes that "Crews has a good eye, an excellent ear for voices, and a fine dramatic sense." Martin Levin of the *New York Times Book Review* thinks *The Gospel Singer* "has a nice wild flavor and a dash of Grand Guignol strong enough to meet the severe standards of Southern decadence." And Guy Davenport of *National Review* calls the novel "a frenetic sideshow of Georgia poor white trash and their *Hochkultur.*"

Crews followed *The Gospel Singer* with *Naked in Garden Hills,* a book Jean Stafford of the *New York Times Book Review* believes "lives up to and beyond the shining promise of . . . 'The Gospel Singer.' It is southern Gothic at its best, a Hieronymus Bosch landscape in Dixie inhabited by monstrous, darling pets." The novel revolves around the almost helpless Mayhugh Aaron, known as the Fat Man because of his six-hundred-pound frame, and his valet John Henry Williams, a tiny black man who takes care of him. Fat Man owns most of Garden Hills, a town where the local phosphate mine is the only source of employment. When the mine is exhausted and closed, the town faces financial collapse. To avoid ruin, Dolly Ferguson opens a nightclub with go-go dancers and a sideshow to attract the tourist trade. She wants Fat Man as her star sideshow exhibit, but he refuses. As his employees, including Williams the valet, are one by one hired away by Dolly, and as his financial situation deteriorates, the Fat Man is reduced to a humiliated and helpless figure. He is finally forced to join the sideshow. "Bleeding, beaten by the mob of tourists, naked, and drooling, he crawls to his waiting cage and is lifted high in the light," Shepherd recounts.

Writing in the *New York Times Book Review,* Jonathan Yardley finds *Naked in Garden Hills* "a convincing grotesque of a rotting American landscape and its decadent inhabitants." Shelton believes the novel "treats religion in an almost allegorical way." He cites the novel's title as a reference to the Garden of Eden, sees Jack O'Boylan, the out-of-state mine owner, as a God figure, and pictures Dolly Ferguson as a kind of savior meant to restore the town. But the novel's ending, in which "everyone is consumed by Dolly's voracious appetite for success," shows that "man's desire to find meaning in his life leads to degradation, exploitation and the denial of love," Shelton writes.

A religious dimension can also be found in *Karate Is a Thing of the Spirit.* In this novel Crews writes of an outlaw karate class that meets on a Florida beach and is barred from tournament competition because of its deadly reputation. John Kaimon wanders into this circle and becomes a member, undergoing the rigorous training under the hot sun. The star member of the class, brown belt Gaye Nell Odell, becomes pregnant, possibly by Kaimon, and at novel's end the couple drive out of town together. Shelton finds both Kaimon and Odell searching for something—something they both find in the discipline of karate. The training, Shelton argues, "is an almost religious ritual through which people attempt to link and fulfill body and spirit." John Deck of the *New York Times Book Review* observes that, after a slow start, "the novel takes off, in the manner of a fire storm, rushing at amazing speed, eating up the oxygen, scorching everything it touches."

In *Car* Crews examines another physical discipline, this one far less common than karate. Herman Mack, whose family is in the automobile junkyard business, decides it is his destiny to eat an automobile, four ounces at a time each day. His daily ingestion of the cut-up auto is broadcast on national television as a sports event. At first pleased with his instant notoriety, Herman falls in love with a prostitute and ends by abandoning his spectacle before it is finished. Yardley calls the ending "mere sentimentality" and a "flabby resolution," but also believes the novel "a marvelous idea" and "exceedingly funny, indeed painfully so." The reviewer for the *Times Literary Supplement* finds the novel "a satire on two alleged vices of the American people: an extravagant fondness for motor-cars, and a taste for ghoulish spectacle." Christopher Lehmann-Haupt of the *New York Times* also sees larger implications in the story, concluding that *Car* "may very well be the best metaphor yet made up about America's passionate love affair with the automobile."

Another obsession dominates Crews's novel *The Hawk Is Dying.* George Gattling becomes obsessed with training a wild hawk, an obsession that estranges him from his family and friends. But his efforts eventually reach fruition when "the hawk has finally been 'manned,' and flies free to kill and return again to Gattling's hand," resulting in "one moment of absolute value—and hence absolute beauty," as the critic for the *Times Literary Supplement* explains. The story is told in "comic-horrific scenes," the critic remarks. Mercier also finds this odd mix in the novel, writing that "beauty and pity and terror coexist with satire and grotesque humor." Similarly, Phoebe Adams of *Atlantic* calls *The Hawk Is Dying* "a bizarre mixture of tragedy and farce." But she goes on to say that, though "the events of this novel are hardly realistic, . . . the book becomes immensely convincing because the underlying pattern of desperation over wasted time and neglected abilities is real and recognizable."

Crews examines a town's obsession with rattlesnakes in *A Feast of Snakes.* He fictionalizes a unique yearly custom in Mystic, Georgia, where the townspeople hold a Rattlesnake Roundup at which they crown a rattlesnake queen, hold a snake fight, and even dine on rattlesnake. The novel follows local resident Joe Lon Mackey, who is unhappily married, illiterate, and bitter abut his life. Crews shows the pressures which drive Mackey to go on a murderous rampage at the snake roundup.

The gruesome events leading up to this final outburst of violence are seen by many critics to be expertly handled by Crews. "Crews," Paul D. Zimmerman writes in *Newsweek,* "has an ugly knack for making the most sordid sequences amusing, for evoking an absolutely venomous atmosphere, unredeemed by charity or hope. Few writers could pull off the sort of finale that has mad-eyed red-necks rushing in sudden bursts across a snake-scattered, bonfire-bright field, their loins enflamed by the local beauty contestants, their blood racing with whisky, their hearts ready for violence. Crews does." The critic for the *New Yorker* judges Crews to be "a writer of extraordinary power. Joe Lon is a monster, but we are forced to accept him as human, and even as sympathetic. Mr. Crews' story makes us gag, but he holds us, in awe and admiration, to the sickening end."

Crews's nonfiction book *A Childhood* gives some insight into the sources of his fiction. In this book Crews recounts the first six years of his life. It was a period, he claims, when "what has been most significant in my life had all taken place." Crews's father died when he was two years old. His mother remarried his uncle, a man she later left because of his violent rages. Crews had a bout with polio, which paralyzed his legs for a time and forced him to hobble on the floor. A fall into a tub of scalding water, used for removing the skin off slaughtered hogs, removed the first layer of skin on most of Crews's body. "The skin on the top of the wrist and the back of my hand, along with the fingernails," he remembers in the book, "all just turned loose and slid on down to the ground." Crews recalls the poverty of this period for the *New York Times Book Review:* "None of the kids I played with ate very well—bless their hearts. We kind of came up on a steady diet of biscuits made with lard and water, no milk. Hardly ate any meat whatsoever. We ate clay to make up for mineral deficiency. I know it sounds kind of pitiful. I didn't think it was pitiful then, don't now. It's just the way it was." Roy Blount, Jr., comments in the *Chicago Tribune Book World,* "If any writer as accomplished as Crews has ever come through so much and from so far behind I would like for somebody to write in and tell me."

The book's subtitle, *The Biography of a Place,* refers to Georgia's rural Bacon County, where Crews's family lived as tenant farmers. Despite the hardships of his childhood, Crews presents the people of his home county in a warm, honest, and unapologetic manner. He tells of the faith healers who tried to cure his polio; of the old black nurse who threatened him with her hexing powers; and of the family friend who robbed their smokehouse on the night Crews's father died. As Crews recounts, "It was a world in which survival depended on raw courage, a courage born out of desperation and sustained by a lack of alternatives." Robert Sherrill of the *New York Times Book Review* admits: "It's easy to despise poor folks. *A Childhood* makes it more difficult. It raises almost to a level of heroism these people who seem of a different century."

Critical reaction to *A Childhood* was generally positive, with several critics citing Crews's restraint in recounting his life. Mewshaw, for example, finds that throughout the book Crews "maintains a precarious balance between sentiment and sensation, memory and madness, and manages to convince the reader of two mutually exclusive imperatives which have shaped his life—the desire to escape Bacon County and the constant ineluctable need to go back, if only in memory." The *New Yorker* critic writes that Crews remembers his childhood with "a sense of grateful escape and shattering loss which have the confusing certainty of truth." Allen Lacy of *Chronicle Review* calls *A Childhood* "a book of great emotional power, fashioned out of often savage stuff by a superb craftsman who possesses both a comic eye and a tragic sense of life."

Discussing *A Childhood* with Scott Hiaasen, a writer for the London *Observer,* Crews remarked that he had hoped to exorcise some of the pain of his childhood through composing the memoir. He found instead that it only made his memories more vivid. "I thought if I forced myself to relive the experience I could purge myself of it. . . . So much for good ideas. It almost killed me living it again." Already a heavy drinker, Crews plunged even deeper into alcoholism after writing the autobiography. He gave up writing novels and went on what Hiaasen called a "rampage around America," relying on short magazine features as his livelihood. "The world pissed me off so bad that if I didn't have a drink to tilt, I couldn't take it," Crews recalled to Hiaasen. The nonfiction book *Blood and Grits* and an essay and story collection titled *Florida Frenzy* emerged from this eleven-year period.

In 1987, Crews checked himself into a rehabilitation clinic. He described his month in group therapy to Hiaasen as "endless humiliation," and noted that "you spend a small fortune. But, finally, you're free of it." The author also resumed writing longer works of fiction in late 1980s, producing the novels *All We Need of Hell* and *The Knockout Artist.* Like his books from previous decades, the works have been acclaimed for their gritty Southern flavor and offbeat characters. *All We Need of Hell* concerns Duffy Deeter, a driven attorney who constantly seeks to prove his manliness. When his wife throws him out of the house, Duffy commences a spree of exercise and drinking, a session that ends when a former enemy teaches Duffy the virtues of love, friendship, and forgiveness.

"If *All We Need of Hell* ran according to Harry Crews's earlier fictional form," remarks Christopher Lehmann-Haupt in the *New York Times,* "Duffy's misadventures would lead him to some bizarre or even ghoulish fate." Noting, though, that "something new has been added" to Crews's fiction, the reviewer laments that "there is something decidedly forced and even sentimental about [the story's positive] turn of events. . . . We come away from the novel regarding it as a distinctly lesser effort." Beaufort Cranford writing in the *Detroit News* was similarly disappointed, commenting that "we readers of Crews suddenly find ourselves on alarmingly cheerful ground. . . . [The ending to] *All We Need of Hell* is a . . . shock, much like a sudden infusion of sugar." Despite complaints that Crews has softened his fiction, Lehmann-Haupt concludes that "we can't help forgiving him for it. There's still such a vividness to his characters. There's still such ease to his prose. . . . [And] he still has the power to make us smile and even laugh out loud."

Crews followed *All We Need of Hell* with *The Knockout Artist* in 1988. The story focuses on Eugene Biggs, a promising young boxer whose career ends after he develops a glass jaw and is rendered incapable of further fighting. To survive, Eugene earns money by staging shows wherein he knocks himself out. Humiliated by his own exploits and burdened by an assortment of unusual friends, Eugene finally decides to break the destructive pattern of his life and becomes a boxing trainer.

Like in *All We Need of Hell, The Knockout Artist*'s ending disappointed some reviewers. Lehmann-Haupt, for example, writes: "When Eugene Biggs makes up his mind to stop knocking himself out and to walk away from all the losers who are dragging him down, it has the effect of turning his hell into a comic book, where the colors are brighter than the world's and the people are less than real." Don Robertson in the *Washington Post Book World,* though, disagrees, declaring that "at the book's conclusion, . . . Eugene Biggs has been, in effect, a Hemingway hero, and he's responded heroically with that quality Hemingway so famously called grace under pressure." Summing up his opinion of *The Knockout Artist* while making reference to Crews's previous fiction, Robertson concludes: "It's masterful, and it's moving, and it's quite funny at times, . . . and here's hoping Harry Crews prevails and flourishes and gives us more karate and snakes and grits and blood and hell and all the rest of that stuff. Hooray for him, and hooray for this mean little masterpiece he's wound up and so skillfully thrown in the world's astonished collective face."

Crews's next novel, *Body,* centers around a backwoods Georgia girl, Dorothy Turnipseed, who takes to working out in a gym and eventually goes on to compete, under the name Shereel Dupont, in the Ms. Cosmos competition. "In the world of the Ms. Cosmos competition, sex is for losing weight, food is for fuel, other people for rivalry, love for exploitation, family for leaving," novelist Fay Weldon notes in her *New York Times Book Review* assessment of *Body*. Nevertheless, Dorothy/Shereel's family accompanies her all the way to the contest, where they are conspicuous among the bodybuilders because of their immense bulk. Merle Rubin is unforgiving in her criticism of the book in the *Wall Street Journal,* labeling it a "violent comic-strip of a novel" that "mixes clenched, muscle-bound humor with lashings of fairly standard-style pornography." He further charges that it "derives its comic moments from caricatures of blacks, whites, Southerners, Jews, gays and Vietnam veterans" and concludes that "any satiric edge has been blunted by a kind of syrupy affection the author hopes we will share for his thick-witted characters, whose simple-mindedness is meant to render their coarseness endearing."

Weldon, however, is extremely enthusiastic about *Body,* describing it as "electric" and as "a hard, fast and brilliant book." She has special praise for Crews's ability to create convincing women: "Not for a moment, such is this male writer's skill, the throttled-back energy of his writing, do I doubt Mr. Crews's right to be as intimate as he is with his female characters. . . . Shereel's struggle between love and honor provides the book's tender, perfect fleshing out; the will-she-win, won't-she-win tension, mounting page by page, gives muscle, nerve and fervor to the whole." She adds, however, that "it's Harry Crews's ability to describe physical existence, bodily sensation, that most impresses."

Scar Lover, Crews's next novel, featured a typical cast of outcasts and misfits, including a pair of scarred Rastafarian lovers and a woman who sings lullabies to her husband's skull. The protagonist is Peter Butcher, a man tormented by guilt because of an accident in which he left his younger brother permanently brain-damaged. Filled with self-loathing and reviled by the rest of his family, Peter eventually drifts into true love, fighting it all the way. "It may surprise the followers of Harry Crews to hear that his twelfth novel is a love story that is both life-affirming and tender," advises Robert Phillips in the *Hudson Review.* It is "a comic morality play which is less fierce and more tender than any of his previous works." In the reviewer's estimation, however, the positive messages in *Scar Lover* in no way blunt the power of the author's work. *Chicago Tribune* writer Gary Dretzka concurs that *Scar Lover* "is successful in promoting the healing powers of love and forgiveness," and he notes that "Crews' familiar tenderness toward his outcast characters is here in spades, driven by typically muscular writing and energetic pacing."

A darker tone permeated Crews's next effort, *The Mulching of America,* a book described by a *Washington Post Book World* reviewer as "a satire of corporate America and the credo of success at any cost." The reviewer goes on to say that "Crews's wicked satire sends up corporate culture's celebration of conformity and boundless personal sacrifice." The central characters are Hickum Looney, a door-to-door salesman for a soap company; Gaye Nell Odell, a homeless prostitute (seen previously in *Karate Is a Thing of the Spirit*); and the Boss—the harelipped, hard-driving chief of the Soap for Life Company. Valerie Sayers, a contributor to the *New York Times Book Review,* finds the characters predictable enough "for reader discomfort to set in." Still, she adds that especially in the case of Hickum and Gaye Nell, "that their love story is sweetly compelling is the measure of Mr. Crews's ability to have his cartoon characters remind us, vaguely and laughably, of our own most compelling fears and humiliations." She further credits the author with creating a successful portrayal of "Americans terrified of taking a step or making a moral choice," and concludes that "Harry Crews is a storyteller who bears down on American enterprise with fierce eyes and a cackle. By the end of the story, he's not laughing and we are all ready to look away."

Assessing Crews's career, Clarence Petersen in the *Chicago Tribune Book World* sees autobiography as a primary component in all of his fiction. Petersen writes that Crews's "writing is informed by an unimaginably brutal and grotesque childhood and by a deep love of language, literature, nature, blood sports and his own kind of people—namely rural, Southern, hard-drinking, honest-measure hell-raisers." Shaun O'Connell also believes that Crews draws heavily upon his own life experiences for his fiction, maintaining in an article for the *New Boston Review* that his books "simultaneously incorporate and transcend his personal history. . . . Crews has concocted elaborate metaphors, images more sustainingly inventive than most metafictionists, tropes which subsume his past, conceits which widen our sense of the possible as they make the magical and the freakish more plausible."

Crews's own explanation of how he writes stresses the spontaneous nature of his work and places little emphasis on his subject matter. Speaking to Al Burt of the *Miami Herald,* Crews reveals how he begins a novel: "I start with a place and somebody and then I just try to know the story. . . . I don't give a rat's ass where the novel's going." When writing *Naked in Garden Hills,* for example, he began with the first line in the book and the idea for the Fat Man character and began to write. Crews claims that the story itself is not important. "The important thing is the writer whose perceptions all of this is being filtered through. The writer's vision of the world," he tells Burt. "It doesn't matter what he writes about."

Some observers judge Crews's stories to be excessive. "His harshest critics claim that Crews always pushes things too far—to the point where his characters turn into caricatures and his plots become cartoons," Mewshaw explains. One such critic is Sarah Blackburn of the *New York Times Book Review,* who describes *The Hawk Is Dying* as "a festival of mangled animals, tortured sexuality and innocence betrayed." James Atlas in *Time* calls Crews "a Southern gothic novelist who often makes William Faulkner look pastoral by comparison." Crews's novel *A Feast of Snakes* was even banned in South Africa.

Admirers of Crews, however, cite his ability to transform unusual or extreme subjects into credible, moving stories. Doris Grumbach, writing in *Saturday Review,* admits that Crews's novels possess a "bizarre, mad, violent, and tragic quality," but believes that Crews "has a sympathy for maimed and deformed characters, a love of strange situations, and the talent to make it all, somehow, entirely believable." Shepherd, speaking of *Car, The Hawk Is Dying,* and *A Feast of Snakes* in an article for *Critique: Studies in Modern Fiction,* argues that Crews displays "in these strangely powerful, outlandish, excessive, grotesquely alive novels a gift at once formidable and frightening."

BIOGRAPHICAL/CRITICAL SOURCES:

BOOKS

Authors in the News, Volume 1, Gale (Detroit), 1976.

Contemporary Literary Criticism, Gale, Volume 6, 1976, Volume 23, 1983, Volume 49, 1988.

Crews, Harry, *A Childhood: The Biography of a Place,* Harper, 1978.

Dictionary of Literary Biography, Gale, Volume 6: *American Novelists since World War II, Second Series,* 1980; Volume 143: *American Novelists Since World War II, Third Series,* 1994.

Jeffrey, David K., editor, *A Grit's Triumph: Essays on the Works of Harry Crews,* Associated Faculty Press (Port Washington, NY), 1983.

PERIODICALS

America, December 23, 1978.

Arkansas Review, spring, 1995, pp. 1, 82-94.

Atlanta Journal-Constitution, January 18, 1987, p. J8; June 26, 1988, p. J8; April 9, 1989, pp. N1, N2; September 2, 1990, p. N14; January 26, 1992, p. N8; March 8, 1992, p. N1; November 28, 1993, p. K8.

Atlantic, April, 1973.

Booklist, February 15, 1992, p. 1086; October 1, 1993, p. 244.

Boston Globe, January 13, 1987, p. 59; May 3, 1988, p. 73; October 1, 1990, p. 32; February 21, 1992, p. 40; November 23, 1995, p. A26.

Chicago Tribune, February 1, 1987, section 14, p. 3; April 10, 1988, section 14, p. 6; August 27, 1990, section 5, p. 3; February 23, 1992, p. 6.

Chicago Tribune Book World, October 29, 1978; March 11, 1979; July 18, 1982; July 31, 1983; February 23, 1992, section 14, p. 6.

Chronicle Review, April 16, 1979.

Contemporary Review, April, 1977.

Critique: Studies in Modern Fiction, September, 1978; fall, 1986, pp. 45-53.

Detroit News, February 1, 1987, p. H2.

Entertainment Weekly, February 28, 1992, p. 50; March 27, 1992, p. 69; November 17, 1995, p. 75.

Georgia Review, fall, 1987, pp. 627-631; fall, 1994, pp. 3, 537-553.

Harper's, August, 1986, p. 35.

Hudson Review, autumn, 1993, pp. 492-493.

Journal of American Culture, fall, 1988, pp. 2, 47-54.

Library Journal, August, 1990, p. 139; February 1, 1992, p. 121; November 15, 1995, p. 98.

Los Angeles Times, May 3, 1987, p. B8; May 22, 1988, p. B6; January 31, 1992, p. E2.

Los Angeles Times Book Review, May 3, 1987; May 22, 1988, p. 6; September 23, 1990, p. 3; October 21, 1990, p. 3; January 14, 1996, p. 2.

Maclean's, March 26, 1979.

Miami Herald, June 30, 1974.

Mississippi Quarterly: The Journal of Southern Culture, winter, 1987-88, pp. 1, 69-88.

Nation, February 3, 1979.

National Review, April 21, 1970.

New Boston Review, February-March, 1979.

New Republic, March 31, 1973; May 8, 1989, p. 28.

Newsweek, August 2, 1976.

New Yorker, July 15, 1974; July 26, 1976; November 6, 1978.

New York Times, March 2, 1972; March 21, 1973; April 30, 1974; July 12, 1976; December 11, 1978; February 6, 1979; January 12, 1987, p. C19; February 1, 1987, section 7, p. 9; February 19, 1987; April 18, 1988, p. C21; May 1, 1988, section 7, p. 21; April 5, 1989, p. C19; November 20, 1995, p. C16.

New York Times Book Review, February 18, 1968; April 13, 1969; April 26, 1970; April 25, 1971; February 27, 1972; March 25, 1973; March 10, 1974; June 2, 1974; June 23, 1974; September 12, 1976; December 24, 1978; March 25, 1979; February 1, 1987, pp. 9, 11; May 1, 1988, p. 21; September 9, 1990, p. 14; March 15, 1992, p. 13; November 5, 1995, p. 18.

Observer (London), October 30, 1994, p. 4.

People, June 8, 1987, p. 75; October 1, 1990, p. 41.

Playboy, August, 1990, p. 64.

Prairie Schooner, spring, 1974.

Publishers Weekly, April 15, 1988; June 29, 1990, p. 86; December 13, 1991, p. 44; September 11, 1995.

Saturday Review, November 11, 1978.

Sewanee Review, winter, 1969.

Shenandoah, summer, 1974.

Southern Literary Journal, spring, 1980; spring, 1984, pp. 132-35; spring, 1992, pp. 2, 3-10.

Spectator, January 22, 1977.

Studies in the Literary Imagination, fall, 1994, pp. 2, 75-86.

Texas Review, spring-summer, 1988, pp. 1-2, 96-109.

Time, September 13, 1976; October 23, 1978; March 5, 1979; April 17, 1989, p. 70; March 2, 1992, p. 66.

Times Literary Supplement, February 2, 1973; January 11, 1974; January 24, 1975; January 21, 1977; December 7, 1979; December 30, 1994, p. 19.

Variety, April 19, 1989, p. 215.

Village Voice, October 30, 1978.

Virginia Quarterly Review, autumn, 1980.

Wall Street Journal, August 31, 1990, p. A9.

Washington Post, March 29, 1979.

Washington Post Book World, April 15, 1973; July 24, 1983; May 1, 1988; August 19, 1990, p. 3; February 16, 1992, p. 4; October 17, 1993, p. 3; February 4, 1996, p. 8.

World, April 24, 1973.

Writers Digest, June, 1982, p. 30.*

D

DANGERFIELD, Harlan
See PADGETT, Ron

* * *

DANIELOU, Alain 1907-1994

PERSONAL: Born October 4, 1907, in Paris, France; died January 27, 1994; son of Charles (a writer and politician) and Madeleine (an educator and founder of a religious order; maiden name, Clamorgan) Danielou. *Ethnicity:* "French." *Education:* Educated in France, India, and the United States; attended St. John's College, Annapolis, MD. *Religion:* Hindu. *Avocational interests:* Painting, playing Western and Indian music.

CAREER: Hindu University, Benares, India, research professor of Sanskrit literature on music, 1949-54; Adyar Library, Madras, India, director, beginning in 1954; International Institute for Comparative Music Studies, founder of institutes in Berlin, Germany, 1963, and Venice, Italy, 1970, director, 1963-79, appointed honorary president, 1980, and vice president of board of directors, 1982. Served as director of Rabindranath Tagore's school of music in Shantiniketan, India; also worked as a singer, dancer, and painter.

AWARDS, HONORS: Legion d'honneur, chevalier, 1967, officier, 1993; named Chevalier des Arts et Lettres, 1970, and Commandeur des Arts et Lettres, 1985; Prix Broquette-Gonin, Academie Francaise, 1971, for *Histoire de l'Inde;* officier, L'Ordre National du Merite, 1974; Prix Unesco, 1981; Medaille Kathmandu de l'Unesco, 1987; named Personnalite de l'Annee en France, 1987, and Personnalite de l'Annee a titre international, 1989; Prix Cervo (Italy), 1991.

WRITINGS:

Introduction to the Study of Musical Scales, India Society (London, England), 1943, South Asia Books (Columbia, MO), 1979.

Yoga: Methode de reintegration, originally published before 1950, reprinted, L'Arche (Paris), 1951, new edition, 1973, translation by the author published as *Yoga: The Method of Reintegration,* Johnson (London), 1949, University Books, 1973, new edition published as *Yoga: Mastering the Secrets of Matter and the Universe,* Inner Traditions International (Rochester, NY), 1991.

Visages de l'Inde Medievale, photographs by Raymond Burnier, Hermann (Paris), 1950, new edition, 1985.

Northern Indian Music, two volumes, Barrie & Rockliff (London), 1951-55, published as *The Ragas of Northern Indian Music,* 1968.

La Musique du Laos et du Cambodge, Institute Francais d'Indologie (Pondichery, India), 1957.

Tableau Comparatif des Intervalles Musicaux, Institute Francais d'Indologie, 1958.

Le Gitalamkara: L'ouvrage original de Bharata dur la Musique, Institut Francais d'Indologie, 1959.

Textes des Puranas sur la Theorie Musicale, Institut Francais d'Indologie, 1959, reprinted, 1987.

Le Polytheisme Hindou, Buchet-Chastel (Paris), 1960, third edition, 1982, new edition published as *Mythes et Dieux de l'Inde: Le Polytheisme Hindou,* Editions du Rocher (Paris), 1992, translation published as *Hindu Polytheism,* Princeton University Press (Princeton, NJ), 1964, published as *The Gods of India: Hindu Polytheism,* Inner Traditions International, 1985, and as *The Myths and Gods of India,* 1991.

(Translator from Tamil with R. S. Desikan) Prince Ilango Adigal, *Shilippadikaram: Le Roman de l'Anneau,* Gallimard (Paris), 1961, translation published as *Shilippadikaram: The Ankle Bracelet,* New Directions (New York City), 1965.

(Translator and composer of piano accompaniment) *Trois Chansons de Rabindranath Tagore,* Editions Ricordi France, 1961, translation published as *The Songs of Rabindranath Tagore: Original Bengali Texts and Melodies,* 1997.

Le Betail des Dieux (novel; title means "The Cattle of the Gods"), Buchet-Chastel, 1962, published in *Le Betail des Dieux et Autres Contes Gangetiques,* 1983, new edition, Editions du Rocher, 1994, translation by Kenneth F. Hurry published as *The Livestock of the Gods: Tales from the Ganges,* 1997.

L'Erotisme Divinise, photographs by Burnier, Buchet-Chastel, 1962, reprinted as *La Sculpture erotique hindoue* (title means "Erotic Hindu Sculpture"), 1973.

Les Quatre Sens de la vie: La Structure sociale de l'Inde traditionnelle (title means "The Four Aims of Life: Social Structures of Traditional India"), Librairie Academique Perrin (Paris), 1963, revised edition, Buchet-Chastel, 1976, new edition, Editions du Rocher, 1992, translation published as *Four Aims of Life,* Inner Traditions International, 1988, and as *Virtue, Success, Pleasure, and Liberation: Traditional India's Social Structures,* 1993.

Inde du nord: Les Traditions Musicales (title means "Musical Traditions of Northern India"), Buchet-Chastel, 1966, published as *La musique de l'Inde du nord,* 1985.

Semantique musicale: essai de psychophysiologie auditive (title means "Musical Semantics"), Hermann, 1967, new edition with preface by Fritz Winckel and introduction by Francoise Escal, 1978, translation published as *Musical Semantics,* Inner Traditions International, 1991.

Histoire de l'Inde (title means "History of India"), Fayard (Paris), 1971, revised edition, 1983.

(With Jacques Brunet) *La Situation de la musique et des musiciens dans les pays d'orient,* Leo S. Olschki Editore (Florence, Italy), 1971, translation by John Evarts published as *The Situation of Music and Musicians in the Countries of the Orient,* 1971.

Les Fous de Dieux: Contes Gangetiques (title means "God's Madmen"), Buchet-Chastel, 1975, published in *Le Betail des Dieux et Autres Contes Gangetiques,* 1983, new edition, Editions du Rocher, 1994, selections (translated by David Rattray) published as *Fools of God,* Hanuman Books (New York City), 1988.

Le Citta dell'Amore: Appendice sull'Amore Indiano, Franco Maria Ricci Editore (Parma, Italy), 1976, English translation, 1989.

(Translator and adaptor) *Trois pieces du theatre de Harsha* (title means "The Plays of Harsha"), Buchet-Chastel, 1977.

Le Temple hindou (title means "The Hindu Temple"), Buchet-Chastel, 1977.

Shiva et Dionysos: La Religion de la Nature et de l'Eros (also known as *Shiva et Dionysos: Mythes et rites d'une religion pre-aryenne*), Fayard, 1979, translation by Hurry published as *Shiva and Dionysus: The Religion of Nature and Eros,* East-West Publications (London), 1982, reprinted as *Shiva and Dionysus: The Omnipresent Gods of Transcendence and Ecstasy,* Inner Traditions International, 1984, and as *Gods of Love and Ecstasy: The Tradition of Shiva and Dionysus,* 1992.

Le chemin du labyrinthe: souvenirs d'Orient et d'Occident (autobiography), Laffont (Paris), 1982, new edition, Editions du Rocher, 1993, translation by Marie-Claire Cournand published as *The Way to the Labyrinth: Memories of East and West,* New Directions, 1987.

(Translator) *Le Shiva Svarodaya: Ancien traite de presages et premonitions d'apres le Souffle Vital,* Arche Milano (Milan, Italy), 1982.

La Fantaisie des Dieux et L'aventure Humaine: Nature et Destin du Monde dans la Tradition Shivaite, Editions du Rocher, 1985, reprinted as *Destin du Monde d'apres la tradition shivaite,* Livre de Poche, 1992, translation by Barbara Bailey, Michael Baker, and Deborah Lawlor published as *While the Gods Play: Shaiva Oracles and Predictions on the Cycles of History and the Destiny of Mankind,* Inner Traditions International, 1987.

Dhrupad Poemes: Themes d'improvisation des principaux Raga de la Musique de l'Inde du Nord, Editions Nulle Part, Cahiers des Brisants, 1986.

(Translator from Tamil with T. V. Gopala Iyer) Merchant Prince Shattan, *Manimekhalai ou le scandale de la Vertue,* Flammarion (Paris), 1987, translation (with Hurry) published as *Manimekhalai: The Dancer with the Magic Bowl,* New Directions, 1987.

Le Tour du Monde (collection of articles), Flammarion, 1987.

Les Contes du Labyrinthe, Editions du Rocher, 1990, translation by Hurry published as *Tales from the Labyrinth,* 1997.

Hierarchy and Social Order: Traditional India's Social Structures, Inner Traditions International, 1991.

(Translator) Vatsyayana, *Le Kama Sutra,* Editions du Rocher, 1992, English translation by the author (with Hurry) published as *The Complete Kama Sutra,* Inner Traditions International, 1994.

(Translator) Swami Karpatri, *Le Mystere du Culte du Lingua: Metaphysique de l'Inde,* Editions du Relie (Robion, France), 1993, translation published as *Indian Metaphysics: Basic Writings of Swami Karpatri,* 1997.

Le Phallus, Editions Pardes, 1993, translation published as *The Phallus: Sacred Symbol of Male Creative Power,* Inner Traditions International, 1996.

Music and the Power of Sound: The Influence of Tuning and Interval on Consciousness, Inner Traditions International, 1995.

Ricordo di Alain Danielou, Leo S. Olschki Editore, 1997.

Author of *La Musique dans la societe et la vie de l'Inde.* Works currently in press include *Vivre en Inde;* and *Les Cahiers du Mleccha,* Volume 1: *Shivaisme, Tantrisme, et Tradition primordiale,* Volume 2: *Castes, Egalitarisme, Genocodes Culturels,* Volume 3: *Le Message de l'Hindouisme,* Volume 4: *Origines et Pouvoirs de la Musique.* Contributor to books, including (author of introduction) *Le Congres du monde et les Secrets des Tantras,* by Jorge Luis Borges, Franco Maria Ricci Editore, 1979, published as *The Congress of the World,* introduction translated by John Shepley, translation by Alberto Manguel, 1981; and (author of introduction) *L'Epopee fantastique des dieux hindous dans le theatre d'ombre javanais,* Editions Trismegiste, 1982. Work represented in anthologies, including *The Game of Dice,* edited by James Turner, Pan Books (London), 1965. Founder and editor of Unesco collection of Oriental and traditional music recordings, beginning in 1981.

SIDELIGHTS: Alain Danielou, whom *Interview* contributor Andrew Harvey once called "the foremost living interpreter of Hinduism," spent his adolescence in Paris during the 1920s, where he befriended Jean Cocteau and Igor Stravinsky. The father of the king of Afghanistan (another boyhood friend) invited Danielou to visit the East. During this time he travelled to India, where he spent fifteen years; three of his books, *Shivan and Dionysus, The Four Aims of Life,* and *While the Gods Play* originated from his experiences there. The books, wrote Harvey, are "remarkable for their clarity, scholarship, and uninhibited celebration of erotic and mystical ecstasy."

Danielou once told *CA* that his "main interest is explaining Hindu traditional civilization, religion and culture to the outside world." He continued: "Hinduism especially in its oldest, Shivaite form, never destroyed its past. It is the sum of human experience from the earliest times. Non-dogmatic, it allows every one to find his own way. Ultimate reality being beyond man's understanding, the most contradictory theories or beliefs may be equally inadequate approaches to reality. Ecological (as we would say today), it sees man as part of a whole where trees, animals, men and spirits should live in harmony and mutual respect, and it asks everyone to cooperate and not endanger the artwork of the creator. It therefore opposes the destruction of nature, of species, the bastardization of races, the tendency of each one to do what he was not born for. It leaves every one free to find his own way of realization, human and spiritual, be it ascetic or erotic or both. It does not separate intellect and body, mind and matter, but sees the universe as a living continuum. I believe any sensible man is unknowingly a Hindu and that the only hope for man lies in the abolition of the erratic, dogmatic, unphilosophical creeds people today call religions."

Danielou told Harvey that he wanted to stress "the fundamental unity of human endeavors to understand the nature of the world and to re-create a love and admiration for what I would call 'the divinity of presence.'" He continued, "All the effort of Indian wisdom has been toward understanding things. The problem of the West is that it wants to change the world without understanding it."

Danielou's site on the World Wide Web is located at http://www.imaginet.fr/~jcloarec/danielou.

BIOGRAPHICAL/CRITICAL SOURCES:

PERIODICALS

Interview, January, 1989.*
[Date of death provided by Jacques Cloarec]

* * *

DASH, Joan 1925-

PERSONAL: Born July 18, 1925, in Brooklyn, NY; daughter of Samuel (a lawyer) and Louise (a lawyer; maiden name, Sachs) Zeiger; married Jay Gregory Dash (a professor of physics), June 23, 1945; children: Michael, Elizabeth, Anthony. *Education:* Barnard College, B.A. (with honors), 1946. *Religion:* Jewish.

ADDRESSES: *Home*—4542 52nd St. N.E., Seattle, WA 98105. *Agent*—Charlotte Gordon, 235 East 22nd St., New York, NY 10010.

CAREER: Writer.

MEMBER: Hadassah, Seattle Free-Lancers, Phi Beta Kappa.

WRITINGS:

A Life of One's Own: Three Gifted Women and the Men They Married, Harper (New York City), 1973, published as *A Life of One's Own: Margaret Sanger, Edna St. Vincent Millay, Maria Goeppert-Mayer,* Paragon House, 1988.
Summoned to Jerusalem: The Life of Henrietta Szold, Harper, 1979.
The Triumph of Discovery: Women Scientists Who Won the Nobel Prize (juvenile), Julian Messner (New York City), 1991.
We Shall Not Be Moved: The Women's Factory Strike of 1909 (juvenile), Scholastic (New York City), 1996.

Contributor of stories and articles to journals.

BIOGRAPHICAL/CRITICAL SOURCES:

PERIODICALS

Los Angeles Times, February 29, 1980.
New York Times, September 22, 1979.
New York Times Book Review, October 14, 1979; August 25, 1996.

* * *

DAVIDSON, (Marie) Diane 1924-

PERSONAL: Born March 6, 1924, in Los Angeles, CA; daughter of Charles C. (in the U.S. Cavalry) and Stella Ruth (a writer and art critic; maiden name, Bateman) Winnia; married William E. Davidson (a U.S. artillery captain), February 27, 1948 (divorced); children: David William, Ronald M. *Education:* University of California, Berkeley, A.B., 1943, teaching credential, 1944; Sacramento State University, M.A., 1959. *Politics:* Democrat. *Religion:* Episcopalian. *Avocational interests:* Gardening, photography, writing.

ADDRESSES: *Agent*—Swan Books, P.O. Box 2498, Fair Oaks, CA 95628.

CAREER: Actress in U.S.O. Camp Shows' Far East circuit, 1946-47; Kurokamiyama School, Nara, Japan, teacher and principal, 1947-49; El Camino High School, Sacramento, CA, teacher, 1954-84; Swan Books, Fair Oaks, CA, writer and publisher, 1979—.

MEMBER: National Education Association, Authors Guild, Authors League of America, PEN, Actor's Equity, National Association of Teachers of English, California Association of Teachers of English, California Writers Club, Phi Beta Kappa, Pi Lambda Theta.

WRITINGS:

Feversham (novel), Crown (New York City), 1969.
Shakespeare on Stage (eight volumes), Swan Books (Fair Oaks, CA), 1979-85.
Shakespeare for Young People (nine volumes), Swan Books, 1986-94.

History of Trinity Episcopal Church, Folsom, 1856-1994, Trinity (Folsom, CA), 1996.

WORK IN PROGRESS: Additional volumes in *Shakespeare for Young People,* including *Twelfth Night for Young People;* a novel entitled *A Very Likely Story.*

SIDELIGHTS: "My major works are the two series *Shakespeare on Stage* and *Shakespeare for Young People,* a total of seventeen books so far," Diane Davidson once explained. "They are easy-to-read editions of Shakespeare's plays without changing the words. The two series arose quite naturally from elements in my life: a background that includes a Phi Beta Kappa key in dramatic literature, professional acting, and an M.A. in playwriting, plus a career of teaching high school for thirty-five years.

"After years of teaching Shakespeare, I still marvelled that some intelligent college-prep students found the plays difficult. Why? Over and over, I would interrupt and explain the line till I felt like a robot. So I began to experiment by putting the plays on mimeograph with the explanations added in parentheses. The students approved. Then I typed new editions on dittos with the dialogue in modern running style, as an actor never uses an artificial end-of-line pause every ten syllables. Also, like a theater director, I cut the slow parts. Better and better. I added descriptions of fights and flirtations, modern style, so the students could visualize the plays easier. They asked for more explanations, and I rewrote endlessly. Finally I abolished my pet peeve—footnotes, with the attendant eye-jumps that cause a reader to lose his place and interrupt his concentration. Instead, I inserted headnotes in italics, giving explanations *before* a hard part. Much better! The last script in xerox was quite readable, and it moved so swiftly that the reader felt the full momentum of the play. The whole process had taken only eight years.

"What had happened was that I put Shakespeare's plays into modern playwriting format. To test my point that format caused the difficulty, I taped a sequence of *Magnum, P.I.* and typed it in sixteenth-century format with ten syllables per line, no stage direction, and no explanations. The seniors could not read even *Magnum, P.I.* in this style. Format was the key to intelligibility!

"After fifty-six rejections by professional publishers, I took out a second mortgage on my old house and became my own publisher of Swan Books. The eight original high school plays became the *Shakespeare on Stage* series. Then teachers at conventions asked me to do shorter editions for middle school. Thus emerged the forty-minute adaptations known as *Shakespeare for Young People,* nine playlets that proved even more popular than the high school series. My latest is *Twelfth Night for Young People.* All are endorsed by educators at the University of California, Berkeley, Folger Shakespeare Library, and the Ashland Shakespeare Festival.

"So far as I know, no one else has stumbled on this simple method for presenting the world's best writer so that he can be enjoyed in print."

BIOGRAPHICAL/CRITICAL SOURCES:

PERIODICALS

Kliatt, spring, 1980, p. 22.

* * *

DAY, Stacey B(iswas) 1927-

PERSONAL: Born December 31, 1927, in London, England; came to U.S. in 1955; became naturalized U.S. citizen in 1977; son of Satis Biswas (a barrister) and Emma Lenora (Camp) Day; married Noor Kassam Kanji (a microbiologist), March 17, 1952 (divorced, 1969); married Nasreen Y. Fazalbhoy (a psychologist), June 7, 1970 (divorced, 1973); married Ivana Podvalova (a research pharmacologist), October 18, 1973; children: (first marriage) Kahlil Amyn, Selim. *Education:* Royal College of Surgeons, Dublin, Ireland, M.D., 1955; McGill University, Montreal, Quebec, Ph.D., 1964; University of Cincinnati, D.Sc., 1971. *Politics:* "Moderate Republican."

ADDRESSES: *Home*—6 Lomond Ave., Chestnut Ridge, NY 10977. *Office*—Department of Medicine, New York Medical College, Valhalla, NY 10595. *Agent*—Robert Faher, c/o Cultural and

Educational Productions, 310 Craig St. E., Montreal, Quebec, Canada.

CAREER: University of Minnesota Hospitals, Minneapolis, surgeon, 1956-60; St. George's Hospital, London, honorary clinical assistant in surgery, 1960-61; McGill University, surgeon in Experimental Division, 1961-65; Hoffman La Roche (pharmaceutical manufacturer), Nutley, NJ, medical director for New England, 1966-68; Shriners Hospital Burns Institute, University of Cincinnati, Cincinnati, OH, associate director of basic medical research, 1969-70; University of Minnesota, Minneapolis, associate professor in pathology department, assistant professor of research surgery in the medical school, and conservator at the Bell Museum of Pathobiology, 1971-73; Cornell University, Graduate School of Medical Sciences, New York City, professor of biology and member and director of biomedical communication and medical education at Sloan-Kettering Institute for Cancer Research, 1974-80; New York Medical College, Valhalla, NY, clinical professor of medicine in division of behavioral medicine, 1980-92; University of Arizona, Tucson, adjunct professor of family and community medicine, 1985-88; World Health Organization Collaborating Center for Community Based and Multiprofessional Education for Health Personnel, Meharry Medical College, Nashville, TN, International Health Center founding director and visiting professor, 1985-89, emeritus director, 1990—.

Canadian Heart Association, research associate, 1964-66, senior research associate, 1966-67; New Jersey College of Medicine, assistant professor, 1968-69; Hoechst Pharmaceutical Co., Cincinnati, OH, Department of Medical Research, clinical investigator, 1966-68; Arris and Gale Lecturer, Royal College of Surgeons, England, 1971; SAMA Foundation, Calabar, Nigeria, lecturer, and consulting advisor and director for Health Services Management Board, 1982-84; Calabar University, Nigeria, College of Medical Sciences, founding professor of biopsychosocial medicine, and professor and chair of department of community medicine, 1982-84, and distinguished visiting professor of international health, 1989—; Oita Medical University, Japan, permanent visiting professor of medical education, 1992—.

Visiting professor to numerous institutions including Royal College of Surgeons, Dublin, Ireland, 1972, Oncologic Research Institute, 1976, University of California, Irvine, 1981, University of Mauritius, 1991, and Bratislava University, 1991. Exchange scientist to the Soviet Union for the National Cancer Institute, 1976. Cultural and Educational Productions Publishing, Montreal, Quebec, president and chair, 1966-86; Mario Negri Foundation, New York City, director and vice president for research and American scientific affairs, 1974-80; Lambo Foundation, member of board of directors and honorary chair, 1985; Project to Develop Oban Research Institute, Cross River State, Nigeria, founding director, 1988; Cross River State, Nigeria, founder of four Self-Health Primary Care Centers; National Association for Equal Opportunity in Higher Education/Agency for International Development, liaison officer US-AID, 1985-90; India League, Dublin, Ireland, former president; All India Radio, New Delhi and Calcutta, broadcaster and contributor; African Health Consulting Services, Nigeria, board member, 1986—.

Organizer and director of interdisciplinary conference education radio programs in Minnesota and Nigeria. Consultant to various organizations, including Cincinnati Zoological Society, 1969-71, Pan American Health Organization, Brazil, 1974, Sage Memorial Hospital, Navajo Nation Reservation, Ganado, AZ, 1984, U.S. Agency for International Development/African Regional Organization (US-AID/AFRO), 1985-88, World Health Organization, 1985-90, African Research Foundation, Lagos, 1986—, Institute for Creative Health, Chile, and consulting editor, Van Nostrand, Reinhold Co., Charles Scribner's Sons, and Plenum Publishing; editor-in-chief of *Health Communications and Biopsychosocial Health. Military service:* British Army, 1946-49; served in Royal Army Educational Corps.

MEMBER: World Academy of Arts and Sciences (fellow), International Communication Association, Institute International de Medicine Biologique, International Foundation for Biosocial Development and Human Health (founder; president, 1977-86), International Society for Burn Injuries (Edinburgh), World Priorities Population Committee, Canadian Authors Association, American Academy of Political and Social Science, American Institute of Stress (founding member, consultant, and member of board of directors, 1979-82), American Anthropological Association, American Association for the Advancement of Science, American Burns Association, American

Cybernetics Society, American Medical Association, American Rural Health Association (founding member; director and vice president of international affairs, 1977-81), Society of Pharmacological and Environmental Pathologists, Sloan-Kettering Institute for Cancer Research, Society for Anthropology of Visual Communication, Society for Medicine and Anthropology, Council of Biology Editors, Association of Surgeons of Great Britain and Ireland, Japanese Foundation of Biopsychosocial Health (international honorary fellow and most distinguished member), Zoological Society of London (fellow), Royal Microscopical Society (fellow, 1955—), Royal Society of Health (fellow), Medical Geographers of the USSR Geographic Society (honorary member), Harvey Society, New York Academy of Sciences, New York Historical Society, Bombay Society of Natural History, University of Minnesota Alumni Club (charter member), Sigma Xi.

AWARDS, HONORS: First prize and silver medal in biology, Royal College of Surgeons in Ireland, 1950, and silver medal for best scientific paper of academic year, Biology Society, 1953 and 1954, and Triennial Reuben Harvey Memorial Prize and Medal, 1957; second prize in clinical surgery, St. Laurence's Richmond Hospital, Dublin, 1955; Moynihan Prize and Medal, Association of Surgeons of Great Britain and Ireland, 1960; Ciba fellow in Canada, 1963; Arris and Gale award, Royal College of Surgeons, 1972; Gold Key, University of Minnesota Medical School, Bell Museum of Pathobiology, 1973; *Behavioral Medicine* selection for one of the best books of the year, 1979, for *Cancer, Stress, and Death;* distinguished scholar award, International Communication Association, Division of Health Communications, 1980. SAMA Foundation Award, Nigeria, 1982; initiation into the Mgbe (Ekpe) Society, and conferment of the chieftaincy title, Ntufam Ajan of Oban (title means "King of Medicines"), by the people of Oban, Cross River State, Nigeria, 1983; commendation from H. R. H. the Obong of Calabar, Edidem Bassey Eyo Ephraim Adam III, King of Calabar, 1983, in honor of World Health Day; decoration with chieftaincy costumes and conferment of chieftaincy title, Obong Nsong Idem Ibibio, by the people of Ikot Imo, Cross River State, Nigeria, 1983; WHO medal, 1987; awarded the Key to the City of Nashville, TN, 1987; presidential commendation, 1987, for the establishment of the World Health Organization Center in Nashville; proclaimed "ambassador for the State of Tennessee" by Governor Ned McWherter, 1987; outstanding citizen citation, the Assembly State of New York, 1987; citation in the U.S. Congressional Record, 1987; Maestro Honorario, Universidad Autonoma Agraria Antonio Narro, 1987; Fulbright professor, Prague, 1989-90; Pametni medal, Postgraduate Medical College, Prague, 1991; gold medal, University of Bratislava, 1991; Hagakure Research Society, Japan, named first foreign honorary member, 1991, distinguished citation, 1992; national service medal, Royal British Legion, 1993. Fellowships from Minnesota Heart Association, 1958-59, American Heart Association, 1959-60, American Cancer Society, 1961-62, Canadian Defense Board, 1962-63, Canadian Heart Association, 1964-66, and other organizations.

WRITINGS:

TECHNICAL

The Idle Thoughts of a Surgical Fellow: Being an Account of Experimental Surgical Studies, 1956-1966, foreword by Robert A. Good, Cultural and Educational Productions, 1968.

(Consultant and contributor) *Dictionary of Scientific Biography,* Scribner (New York City), 1968.

(With Bruce G. MacMillan and William A. Altemier) *Curling's Ulcer: An Experiment of Nature,* foreword by Owen H. Wangensteen, C. C. Thomas (Springfield, IL), 1971.

(Author of introduction) Joseph Black, *De Humore Acido a Cibis Orto et Magnesia Albo,* translation by Thomas Hanson, Bell Museum of Pathobiology, 1973.

Tuluak and Amaulik: Dialogues on Death and Mourning with the Inuit Eskimo of Point Barrow and Wainwright, Alaska, Bell Museum of Pathobiology, 1973.

Report of a Visit to the Soviet Union in January, 1976, as an Exchange Scientist for Three Weeks under the Aegis of the U.S.-U.S.S.R. Agreement for Health Cooperation, Biomedical Communications, Oncology, Education, and Cancer Research Imperatives in the Soviet Union, Day, 1976.

(With Good) *Comprehensive Immunology,* nine volumes, Plenum (New York City), 1976-80.

(With R. V. Cuddihy and H. H. Fudenberg) *The American Biomedical Network: Health Care Systems in America, Present and Future,* Scripta Medica, 1977.

Health Communications, International Foundation for Biosocial Development and Human Health (New York City), 1979.

Biologos and Biopsychosocial Synthesis: The SAMA Foundation Lectures, Calabar, West Africa, 1982, International Foundation for Biosocial Development and Human Health, 1985.

(With Jean Tache and Hans Selye) *Cancer, Stress, and Death,* Plenum, 1979, second edition, 1986.

(With Emmanuel Aban Oddaye and Habteab Zerit) *Primary Health Care Guide Lines: A Training Manual; Field Training Programs and Education for Health,* introduction by H. L. Mays, International Center for Health Sciences at Meharry Medical College, second edition, 1986.

(With K. Inokuchi and M. Kobayashi) *The Medical Student and the Mission of Medicine in the Twenty First Century,* University of Oita Press, 1994.

Developing Health in the West African Bush, two volumes, International Foundation for Biosocial Development and Human Health, 1996.

Also author with L. H. Schloen, *The Sloan-Kettering Institute of Cancer Research Annual Report,* 1973.

EDITOR; TECHNICAL

Death and Attitudes toward Death, Bell Museum of Pathobiology, 1972.

(With Robert A. Good) *Membranes, Viruses, and Immune Mechanisms in Experimental and Clinical Diseases,* Academic Press (San Diego, CA), 1972.

(With Good) *The Bulletin of the Bell Museum of Pathobiology,* Volumes 1-4, University of Minnesota Medical School, 1972-75.

Proceedings: Ethics in Medicine in a Changing Society, Bell Museum of Pathobiology, 1973.

(And contributor with Good and Ellis S. Benson) *Miscellaneous Papers of the Bell Museum of Pathobiology,* University of Minnesota Medical School, 1973.

(With Good and J. Yunis) *Molecular Pathology,* C. C. Thomas, 1975.

Trauma: Clinical and Biological Aspects, Plenum, 1975.

Communication of Scientific Information, S. Karger (New York City), 1975.

(With E. Teischoltz) *Computer Graphics: Application of Computer Graphics in Medicine and Health Care Science,* S. Karger, 1975.

(With W. P. Myers, W. P. Laird, P. Stanley, S. Garattini, and M. C. Lewis) *Cancer Invasion and Metastases: Biologic Mechanisms and Therapy,* Raven Press (New York City), 1977.

The Image of Science and Society, Biosciences Communications, volume 3, number 1, 1977.

Some Systems of Biological Communication, Biosciences Communication, 1977.

What Is a Scientist?: Memorial Issue for Professor Oscar Bodansky, Biosciences Communications, volume 4, number 5, 1978.

Companion to the Life Sciences, Volume I, Van Nostrand (New York City), 1979.

(With Fernando Lolas and Marc Kusinitz) *Biopsychosocial Health,* International Foundation for Biosocial Development and Human Health, 1980.

(With Everett Sugarbarker, Bruce A. Warren, and Paul J. Rosch) *Readings in Oncology,* International Foundation for Biosocial Development and Human Health, 1980.

Integrated Medicine: Volume II of the Companion to the Life Sciences, Van Nostrand, 1981.

(With Jan F. Brandejs) *Computers for Medical Office and Patient Management,* Van Nostrand, 1982.

(And author of introduction) *Life Stress: Volume III of the Companion to the Life Sciences,* Van Nostrand, 1982.

(With Thomas A. Lambo) *Issues in Contemporary International Health,* Plenum, 1990.

(With D. Salat and others) *Health and Quality of Life in Changing Europe in the Year 2000,* University of Martin Press (Slovakia), 1992.

NONFICTION

(Author of Introduction) Vera Stacey Wainwright, *Poems and Masks,* 1969, and *A Leaf of the Chaatim,* 1970.

Edward Stevens—Gastric Physiologist: Physician and American Statesman, Cultural and Educational Productions, 1969.

Ten Poems and a Letter from America for Mr. Sinha (cultural anthropology essay), Cultural and Educational Productions, 1970.

(Illustrator) George Dahl, *Of Physicians and Fairies,* Cultural and Educational Productions, 1973.

(With Satis Biswas Day) *A Hindu Interpretation of the Hand and Its Portents as Practiced by Palmists of India,* Bell Museum of Pathobiology, 1973.

East of the Navel and Afterbirth: Reflections and Song Poetry from Rapa Nui—Mysterious Easter Island, Cultural and Educational Productions, 1975.

As They See You: Letters from His Students, Colleagues, and Friends to Stacey B. Day, ICHS, 1988.

(Author of introduction) K. Inokuchi, *Three Essays on Humanism and Survival in the Twenty-First Century,* University of Kyushu Press, 1991.

(Editor with H. Koga) *Hagakure-Spirit of Bushido,* University of Kyushu Press, 1993.

(With K. Inokuchi) *Wisdom of Hagakure: Way of the Samurai of Saga Domain,* University of Kyushu Press, 1994.

Letters of Owen Wangensteen to a Surgical Fellow—With a Memoir, International Foundation for Biosocial Development and Human Health, 1996.

LITERARY

Collected Lines (verse), Cultural and Educational Productions, 1966.

By the Waters of Babylon (four-act play), Cultural and Educational Productions, 1966.

East and West: A Play in Three Acts, Cultural and Educational Productions, 1967.

American Lines (verse), Cultural and Educational Productions, 1967.

The Music Box (three-act play), Cultural and Educational Productions, 1967.

Poems and Etudes (verse), Cultural and Educational Productions, 1968.

Rosalita (novella), Cultural and Educational Productions, 1968.

Three One-Act Plays for Reading: Presenting Portland en Passant, The Cricket Cage, and Little Boy on a Red Horse, Cultural and Educational Productions, 1968.

Bellechasse (novella), Cultural and Educational Productions, 1970.

(Contributor) *The Broken Glass Factory* (poetry anthology), edited by Louis Safer, University of Minnesota, 1974.

Author of monographs for the International Foundation for Biosocial Development and Human Health, including *The Biopsychosocial Imperative: Understanding the Biologos and General Systems Theory Approach to Bio-Communications as the Psychospiritual Anatomy of Good Health,* 1981, *Creative Health and Health Enhancement: Individual Initiative and Responsibility for Self Health and Wellness,* 1982, and *The Way of a Physician: The Biologos, Biopsychosocial Way; Survival and the Parasympathetic towards an Ethic and a Way of Life,* 1982; *Three Folk Songs Set to Music* (guitar and harmonica music), 1967. Editor, narrator and author of script for the documentary films *AKAMPA,* 1983, and *Oban under the Mountain,* which aired in 1983 on Nigerian Television Authority (NTA-TV), Calabar, Nigeria. Contributing editor, *Postgraduate Medicine,* 1971; editor, member of editorial board, *University of Minnesota Medical Bulletin,* 1972-74; founder, editor-in-chief, contributor, and member of editorial board, *Health Communications and Informatics* (Basel, Switzerland; formerly, *Biosciences Communications*), 1974-80; consulting editor, *Life Sciences,* 1976—; editor, *Foundation One,* and *Monographs in Biopsychosocial Health,* 1980-84; member of editorial board, *Psyche et Cancer* (Switzerland), 1980—; editor, Contemporary International Health, 1986; member of editorial board for *Psychooncology, Kosmos, Annual Reviews on Stress, Lambo Foundation Newsletter,* and *Current Selected Research in Human Stress.* Contributor to journals, including *Surgery, Gynecology and Obstetrics,* and *Journal of the History of Medicine.*

SIDELIGHTS: Stacey B. Day is a poet-playwright-surgeon-philosopher who "feels that man should not follow a career or profession to the point of boredom," according to a writer for the *Montreal Weekly Post.* Medical writer and journalist Walter S. Alvarez considers him "one of the most remarkable physicians of today . . . [with] a great flair for doing splendid literary research." Initially calling himself a "perspective humanitarian," Day has come to view himself in terms of what he calls the "psychospiritual concept of the pastoral physician." Day told *CA* that over the last twenty years he has had an increasing intellectual curiosity for people, places, and events, which he visualizes "within a biopsychosocial space-time continuum." He further remarked that he is especially interested in the region between Europe and Asia, feudal economies coping with advanced technological societies, and the social, moral, and health problems of indigent inhabitants. The upsurge of political and social unrest in the Near East during the 1970s and 1980s has increased Day's concern for this area of the world even more.

Born in England of an English mother and Indian father, Day has traveled widely in Europe, Africa, Asia, the Americas, and Japan. Although his education originally trained him for a career in India, Day decided after his military service to learn about Russia and its economic history, studying at the University of Birmingham under the tutelage of the late Russian expatriate and economic historian, Alexander M. Baykov.

The writer's novella, *Rosalita,* is described as "a post-Ulysses Joycean psychoanalytic treatment of the generation gap and contemporary . . . living" in the United States during the 1960s. In comparing the lifestyle of the West to that of the East, Day observes that the "West is an external society, while the East is internal, more spiritual." Day continues, "I have tried to assimilate things of goodness from many cultures and to bring about synthesis of these expressions in my own life and writings."

Day's medical writings include studies on heart and circulatory disease and on the extinct Irish elk; and his research has led him to pioneer the studies of community-based education, health communications and informatics, and biopsychosocial health. As a poet and philosopher he has studied the American counterculture, appeared on radio and television programs (including *60 Minutes*), and given poetry readings in Africa, England, Canada, India, and the United States. In addition to appearances in these countries, he has lectured, led workshops, and been a guest speaker in Germany, Italy, Japan, Czechoslovakia, Ireland, and the former Soviet Union, where he appeared at the 13th International Congress of the History of Science in Moscow in 1971. His work in the United States includes the development of the World Health Organization at the Meharry Medical College in Tennessee. President Ronald Reagan awarded Day a commendation for this achievement, which begins: "The vision of Dr. Stacey Day, and his fine team at the Center, builds on a community approach to medicine which is truly international in scope."

The goodness that Day sees in all cultures is, for him, made manifest in everyday people. One of the physician's main concerns involves the way in which scientists often forget humanity in their pursuit of knowledge, or worse, fame. About his observations of those who tutored him and their struggles to win the Nobel Prize, Day told *CA:* "It was always the research, never the patient." He believes that "salvation, greatness, and importance exude from elegant self-deception, the crown of the 'successful' life." In a *Hindustan Times* article, he told writer Nandini Chandra: "We doctors and scientists are autocratic and live in ivory towers. We don't spread our knowledge." In order to raze these towers "we need a new system with scientists trained as communicators," he explained. According to Day, not only do doctors need to communicate better with others, they also need to focus more on sociology, cultural anthropology, and psychology, instead of only on the biology of change. "After all," he concludes, "we are dealing with people, not only with rats and guinea pigs."

BIOGRAPHICAL/CRITICAL SOURCES:

PERIODICALS

Ananda Bazar Patrika (Calcutta), March, 1968.
Cincinnati Enquirer, November 26, 1967.
East African Standard (Nairobi), February, 1968.
Gastroenterology, Number 6, 1969.
Hindustan Times, December 26, 1976.
Los Angeles Times, September 19, 1967.
Meharry Reporter, November 12, 1985.
Nashville Banner, October 26, 1987; November 27, 1987.
Nigerian Chronicle, June 1, 1983; June 3, 1983.
Tennessean, January 8, 1987.
Weekly Post (Montreal), September 7, 1967.

* * *

DEBUS, Allen G(eorge) 1926-

PERSONAL: Born August 16, 1926, in Chicago, IL; son of George Walter William (a manufacturer) and Edna Pauline (Schwenneke) Debus; married Brunilda Lopez-Rodriguez, August 25, 1951; children: Allen Anthony George, Richard William, Karl Edward. *Ethnicity:* "Caucasian." *Education:* Northwestern University, B.S., 1947; Indiana University, A.M., 1949, additional study, 1950-51; University College, London, graduate study, 1959-60; Harvard University, Ph.D., 1961.

ADDRESSES: Home—Deerfield, IL. *Office*—Social Sciences 209, University of Chicago, 1126 East 59th St., Chicago, IL 60637. *E-mail*—adebus@midway.uchicago.edu; fax: 773-834-1299.

CAREER: Abbott Laboratories, North Chicago, IL, research and development chemist, 1951-56; University of Chicago, Chicago, assistant professor, 1961-65, associate professor, 1965-68, professor of the history of science, 1968-78, Morris Fishbein Professor of the History of Science and Medicine, 1978-96, Morris Fishbein Professor Emeritus, 1996—, director of Morris Fishbein Center for the Study of the History of Science and Medicine, 1971-77. Visiting distinguished professor, Arizona Center for Medieval and Renaissance Studies, 1984. Member of Institute for Advanced Study, Princeton, 1972-73. Member of international advisory, Institute for the History of Science and Ideas, Tel-Aviv University, and Center for the History of Science and Philosophy, Hebrew University of Jerusalem. Holder of chemical patents.

MEMBER: Internationale Paracelsus Gesellschaft, Academie Internationale d'Histoire des Sciences, Societe Internationale d'Histoire de la Medicine, History of Science Society (member of council, 1962-65, 1987-89; program chair, 1972), American Institute of the History of Pharmacy, American Chemical Society (associate; member of executive committee, History of Chemistry Division, 1969-72), American Association for the Advancement of Science (fellow; chair of electorate nominating committee, 1974), American Association for the History of Medicine, British Society for the History of Science, Society for the Study of Alchemy and Early Chemistry (member of council, 1967—), Midwest Junto for the History of Science (president, 1983-84), Society of Medical History of Chicago (member of council, 1969-77; secretary-treasurer, 1971- 72; vice president, 1972-74; president, 1974-76).

AWARDS, HONORS: Research grants from American Philosophical Society, 1961-62, National Science Foundation, 1961-63, 1971-74, National Institutes of Health, 1962-70, and American Council of Learned Societies, 1966, 1974-75, 1977-78; Social Science Research Council and Fulbright fellow in England, 1959-60; Guggenheim fellow, 1966-67; overseas fellow, Churchill College, Cambridge University, 1966-67, 1969; National Endowment for the Humanities fellow at Newberry Library, 1975-76, fellow at Folger Shakespeare Library, 1987; Edward Kremers Award, American Institute of the History of Pharmacy, 1978; Pfizer Book Award, History of Science Society, 1978, for *The Chemical Philosophy;* fellow, Institute for Research in the Humanities, University of Wisconsin—Madison, 1981-82; honorary D.Sc., Catholic University of Louvain, 1985; Dexter Award, Division of the History of Chemistry, American Chemical Society, 1987; elected foreign associate member of Classe de Ciencias, Academia das Ciencias de Lisboa, 1987; Sarton Medal, History of Science Society, 1994.

WRITINGS:

The English Paracelsians, Oldbourne, 1965, F. Watts (New York City), 1966.

(With Robert P. Multhauf) *Alchemy and Chemistry in the Seventeenth Century,* William Andrews Clark Memorial Library, 1966.

(Author of introduction) Elias Ashmole, *Theatrum Chemicum Britannicum,* Johnson Reprint (New York City), 1967.

The Chemical Dream of the Renaissance (lecture at Churchill College, Cambridge University), Heffer, 1968, Bobbs-Merrill (New York City), 1972.

(Editor) *World Who's Who in Science from Antiquity to the Present,* Marquis (Chicago), 1968.

Science and Education in the Seventeenth Century: The Webster-Ward Debate, American Elsevier (New York City), 1970.

(Editor and contributor) *Science, Medicine and Society in the Renaissance: Essays in Honor of Walter Pagel,* two volumes, Neale Watson, 1972.

(With Brian A. L. Rust) *The Complete Entertainment Discography, 1898-1942,* Arlington House (New York City), 1973, revised edition, Da Capo Press (New York City), 1989.

(Editor and contributor) *Medicine in Seventeenth-Century England,* University of California Press (Berkeley), 1974.

(Author of introduction) John Dee, *The Mathematicall Praeface to the Elements of Geometrie of Euclid of Megara,* Science History Publications, 1975.

The Chemical Philosophy: Paracelsian Science and Medicine in the Sixteenth and Seventeenth Centuries, two volumes, Science History Publications, 1977.

Man and Nature in the Renaissance, Cambridge University Press (New York City), 1978.
Robert Fludd and His Philosophical Key, Science History Publications, 1979.
Science and History: A Chemist's Appraisal, University of Coimbra, 1984.
Chemistry, Alchemy and the New Philosophy, 1550-1700, Variorum, 1987.
(Editor with Ingrid Merkel, and contributor) *Hermeticism and the Renaissance: Intellectual History and the Occult in Early Modern Europe,* Folger Books (Cranburynswick, NY), 1988.
The French Paracelsians: The Chemical Challenge to Medical and Scientific Tradition in Early Modern France, Cambridge University Press, 1991.
Paracelso e la Tradizione Paracelsiana, La Citta del Sole (Naples), 1996.

Editor, "History of Science and Medicine" series, University of Chicago Press. Annotator of three-record set, *Music of Victor Herbert,* Smithsonian Institution, 1979. Contributor of about 200 articles to professional journals.

Man and Nature in the Renaissance has been translated into Italian, Spanish, Japanese, Greek, and Chinese, and has gone through fifteen printings in English.

WORK IN PROGRESS: Chemistry and Medical Debate, 1650-1750.

* * *

de GROAT, Diane 1947-

PERSONAL: Born May 24, 1947, in Newton, NJ; married Daniel Markham, 1975; children: Amanda Lee. *Education:* Attended Phoenix School of Design, New York, NY, 1964; Pratt Institute, B.F.A., 1969.

ADDRESSES: Agent—Crown Publishers, One Park Ave., New York, NY 10016.

CAREER: Illustrator and author of books for children, 1971—. Holt, Rinehart & Winston (book publishers), Basic Reading Program, New York City, 1969-72, began as book designer, became art director. *Exhibitions:* Work has appeared in shows, including Society of Illustrators Annual National Exhibition, New York, NY, 1973, 1975; Art Directors Club, New York, 1974; and American Institute of Graphic Arts Annual Book Show, New York, 1978.

WRITINGS:

SELF-ILLUSTRATED

Alligator's Toothache, Crown (New York City), 1977.
Annie Pitts, Artichoke, Simon & Schuster (New York City), 1992.
Annie Pitts, Swamp Monster, Simon & Schuster, 1993.
Roses Are Pink, Your Feet Really Stink, Morrow (New York City), 1995.

ILLUSTRATOR

Eleanor L. Clymer, *Luke Was There,* Holt (New York City), 1973.
Elinor Parker, *Four Seasons, Five Senses,* Scribner (New York City), 1974.
Marcia Newfield, *A Book for Jodan,* Atheneum (New York City), 1975.
Lucy Bate, *Little Rabbit's Loose Tooth,* Crown, 1975.
Mamie Hegwood, *My Friend Fish,* Holt, 1975.
Anne Snyder, *Nobody's Family,* Holt, 1975.
Miriam B. Young, *Truth and Consequences,* Four Winds Press (New York City), 1975.
Sylvia Sunderlin, *Antrim's Orange,* Scribner, 1976.
Maria Polushkin, *Bubba and Babba: Based on a Russian Folktale,* Crown, 1976.
Harriett M. Luger, *Chasing Trouble,* Viking (New York City), 1976.
Kathryn F. Ernst, *Mr. Tamarin's Trees,* Crown, 1976.
Eve Bunting, *One More Flight,* Warne (New York City), 1976.
K. F. Ernst, *Owl's New Cards,* Crown, 1977.
Ann Tompert, *Badger on His Own,* Crown, 1978.
Tobi Tobias, *How Your Mother and Father Met, and What Happened After,* McGraw (New York City), 1978.
Lois Lowry, *Anastasia Krupnik,* Houghton (Boston), 1979.
Seymour Simon, *Animal Fact/Animal Fable,* Crown, 1979.
Elizabeth T. Billington, *Part-Time Boy,* Warne, 1980.

Valerie Flournoy, *The Twins Strike Back,* Dial (New York City), 1980.
Lois Lowry, *Anastasia Again!,* Houghton, 1981.
Christine McDonnell, *Don't Be Mad, Ivy,* Dial, 1981.
Barbara Dillon, *Who Needs a Bear?,* Morrow, 1981.
Lynn Luderer, *The Toad Intruder,* Houghton, 1982.
Christine McDonnell, *Toad Food and Measle Soup,* Dial, 1982.
Johanna Hurwitz, *Tough Luck Karen,* Morrow, 1982.
Susan Shreve, *Bad Dreams of a Good Girl,* Knopf (New York City), 1982.
Lois Lowry, *Anastasia at Your Service,* Houghton, 1982.
Johanna Hurwitz, *DeDe Takes Charge!,* Morrow, 1984.
Susan Shreve, *The Flunking of Joshua T. Bates,* Knopf, 1984.
Bonnie Pryor, *Amanda and April,* Morrow, 1986.
Johanna Hurwitz, *Hurricane Elaine,* Morrow, 1986.
Niki Yektai, *Bears in Pairs,* Simon & Schuster, 1987.
Barbara Cohen, *The Christmas Revolution,* Lothrop (New York City), 1987.
Robin A. Thrush, *The Gray Whales Are Missing,* Harcourt (San Diego), 1987.
Christine McDonnell, *Just for the Summer,* Viking, 1987.
Barbara Isenberg, *Albert the Running Bear Gets the Jitters,* Houghton, 1988.
Lois Lowry, *All about Sam,* Houghton, 1988.
Barbara Cohen, *The Orphan Game,* Lothrop, 1988.
Kate McMullan, *Great Advice from Lila Fenwick,* Puffin (New York City), 1989.
Johanna Hurwitz, *Aldo Peanut Butter,* Morrow, 1990.
Joanne Rocklin, *Jace the Ace,* Simon & Schuster, 1990.
Bonnie Pryor, *Merry Christmas, Amanda and April,* Morrow, 1990.
Barbara Cohen, *The Long Way Home,* Lothrop, 1990.
Kate McMullan, *The Great Eggspectations of Lila Fenwick,* Farrar, Straus (New York City), 1991.
Jamie Gilson, *Itchy Richard,* Houghton, 1991.
Eve Bunting, *A Turkey for Thanksgiving,* Houghton, 1991.
Lois Lowry, *Attaboy, Sam!,* Houghton, 1992.
Lisa G. Evans, *An Elephant Never Forgets Its Snorkel: How Animals Survive without Tools and Gadgets,* Crown, 1992.
Jean Van Leeuwen, *The Great Summer Camp Catastrophe,* Dial, 1992.
Kevin Roth, *Lullabies for Little Dreamers,* Random House, 1992.
Carol P. Saul, *Peter's Song,* Simon & Schuster, 1992.
Eve Bunting, *Our Teacher's Having a Baby,* Clarion (New York City), 1992.
Susan Shreve, *Wait for Me,* Morrow, 1992.
Eve Merriam, *Where Is Everybody?: An Animal Alphabet,* Simon & Schuster, 1992.
Susan Shreve, *Amy Dunn Quits School,* Morrow, 1993.
Ruth Westheimer, *Dr. Ruth Talks to Kids: Where You Came From, How Your Body Changes, and What Sex Is All About,* Simon & Schuster, 1993.
Teddy Slater, *The Wrong-Way Rabbit,* Scholastic (New York City), 1993.
A. C. LeMieux, *Fruit Flies, Fish, and Fortune Cookies,* Morrow, 1994.
Jamie Gilson, *It Goes Eeeeeeeeeeee,* Houghton, 1994.
Stephanie Calmenson, *Kinderkittens: Show and Tell,* Scholastic, 1994.
P. J. Petersen, *Some Days, Other Days,* Scribner, 1994.
Eve Bunting, *Sunshine Home,* Houghton, 1994.
Jamie Gilson, *You Don't Know Beans about Bats,* Houghton, 1994.
John Dennis Fitzgerald, *The Great Brain Is Back,* Dial, 1995.

SIDELIGHTS: Besides writing her own picture books, Diane de Groat has illustrated over sixty books by some of the most prominent authors in children's literature. She has also exhibited her artwork. De Groat explains in *Illustrators of Children's Books:* "My picture books enable me to explore the world of fantasy, while the novels I've illustrated are very realistic in style. My work in fine art is an infusion of these two styles."

De Groat was inspired to write her first book, *Alligator's Toothache,* by a dream she had about her editor, who was then undergoing extensive dental work. In this wordless story, Alligator gets a terrible toothache after eating too much cake at his birthday party. He tries to ease the pain by tying a giant bandage around his snout, but it does not work. His friends decide to call the dentist, Dr. Possum, but Alligator is afraid of him and hides when he arrives at the house. Finally, Alligator's friends trick him into getting his tooth pulled, and then he feels better and they go on with the party. A contributor in *Kirkus Reviews* remarked that "the animals' clearly communicative expressions and gestures tell the story without words," while a reviewer in *Publishers Weekly* called the book "an uncommon treat for older children as well as for beginners."

In 1992, de Groat published the first of her two amusing stories about third-grader Annie Pitts, who wants nothing in the world more than to be a famous actress. She thinks that her big break to stardom is waiting around every corner, which leads her into many funny situations. In *Annie Pitts, Artichoke,* Annie accompanies her class on a field trip to the supermarket. While there, she hopes that the store manager will notice her and ask her to appear in his next commercial. When Annie winds up hitting her classmate Matthew in the head with a dead fish, however, the class is asked to leave the store. As punishment, the teacher makes Annie play the undesirable role of an artichoke in the school play. In a *Booklist* review, Ellen Mandel called *Annie Pitts, Artichoke* "amusing and highly palatable reading fare, with sprightly, realistically drawn illustrations that enhance the book's energy and fun."

In 1993's *Annie Pitts, Swamp Monster,* Annie jumps at the chance to star in a low-budget horror movie being produced by a high-school student as a class project. She takes her role as the swamp monster very seriously, hoping it could be the opportunity she has been waiting for to get into show business. The filming turns into one hilarious disaster after another, however, and Annie is embarrassed when the video is shown to her grade-school class. Lucinda Snyder Whitehurst, writing in *School Library Journal,* called the book "breezy and lighthearted" and noted that "the slapstick humor will have young readers giggling." *Booklist* reviewer Chris Sherman added that "the black-and-white illustrations are delightful" and claimed that the book was "sure to win new fans for author-illustrator de Groat."

Among the many books that de Groat has illustrated for other authors is Eve Bunting's 1994 book *Sunshine Home.* The story centers around seven-year-old Timmy, whose grandmother has been placed in a nursing home after injuring herself in a fall. On his first visit to Sunshine Home, Timmy is nervous about what he will find there. Although he does not like the "barf green" walls or the way the place smells, Timmy is relieved that his grandmother seems the same and their visit goes well. After his family leaves, however, Timmy's mother begins to cry. Discovering that he has forgotten to give his grandmother a copy of his school picture, Timmy runs back into the nursing home and finds his grandmother crying too. When he brings his parents back inside to talk to his grandmother again, everyone in the family is able to confront their true feelings about the situation. In *Booklist,* Ellen Mandel wrote that "in her realistic watercolors, de Groat defines the images of Bunting's tender, true-to-life story." Jody McCoy added in *School Library Journal* that de Groat's illustrations "are appropriately heavy on institutional green and poignantly support the text."

BIOGRAPHICAL/CRITICAL SOURCES:

BOOKS

Kingman, Lee, and others, compilers, *Illustrators of Children's Books, 1967-1976,* Horn Book, 1978.

PERIODICALS

Booklist, October 15, 1992, p. 428; March 15, 1994, p. 1371; June 1, 1994, p. 1815.

Bulletin of the Center for Children's Books, May, 1977, p. 140.

Horn Book, July/August, 1989, p. 476.

Kirkus Reviews, January 1, 1977, p. 1; September 15, 1992, p. 1185; June 15, 1994, p. 843.

Publishers Weekly, January 24, 1977, p. 333; May 19, 1989, p. 81; February 5, 1996, p. 89.

School Library Journal, July, 1989, p. 73; September, 1992, p. 202; April, 1994, p. 100; July, 1994, p. 102.

* * *

DENKER, Henry 1912-

PERSONAL: Born November 25, 1912, in New York, NY; son of Max (a fur manufacturer) and

Jennie (Geller) Denker; married Edith Rose Heckman, December 5, 1942. *Ethnicity:* "Jewish." *Education:* New York Law School, LL.B., 1934. *Politics:* Liberal Democrat. *Religion:* Jewish. *Avocational interests:* Travel and tennis.

ADDRESSES: Home—241 Central Park West, New York, NY 10024. *Agent*—Mitch Douglas, International Creative Management, 40 West 57th St., New York, NY 10019.

CAREER: Admitted to the Bar of New York State, 1935; practiced law in New York City, 1935-58; Research Institute of America, New York City, executive, 1938-40; Standard Statistics, New York City, tax consultant, 1940-42; novelist and writer for radio, television, stage and screen, 1947-97. Drama instructor, American Theatre Wing, 1961-63, College of the Desert, 1970.

MEMBER: Dramatists Guild (member of council, 1967-70), Authors Guild, Authors League of America (member of council), Academy of Television Arts and Sciences (member of council, 1967-70 and 1994-96), Writers Guild East.

AWARDS, HONORS: Peabody Award, Christopher Award, *Variety* Showmanship Award, and Brotherhood Award of National Conference of Christians and Jews, all for radio series *The Greatest Story Ever Told;* Ohio State Award.

WRITINGS:

I'll Be Right Home, Ma, Crowell (New York City), 1949.
My Son, the Lawyer, Crowell, 1950.
Salome, Princess of Galilee, Crowell, 1952.
That First Easter, illustrations by Ezra Jack Keats, Crowell, 1959.
The Director, R. W. Baron, 1970.
The Kingmaker, McKay (New York City), 1972.
A Place for the Mighty: A Novel about the Superlawyers, McKay, 1973.
The Physicians: A Novel of Malpractice, Simon & Schuster (New York City), 1974.
The Experiment, Simon & Schuster, 1975.
The Starmaker, Simon & Schuster, 1977.
The Scofield Diagnosis, Simon & Schuster, 1977.
The Actress, Simon & Schuster, 1978.
Error of Judgment, Simon & Schuster, 1979.
Horowitz and Mrs. Washington (also see below), Putnam (New York City), 1979.
The Warfield Syndrome, Putnam, 1980.
Outrage (also see below), Morrow (New York City), 1982.
The Healers, Morrow, 1983.
Kincaid, Morrow, 1984.
Robert, My Son, Morrow, 1985.
Judge Spencer Dissents, Morrow, 1986.
The Choice, Morrow, 1987.
The Retreat, Morrow, 1988.
A Gift of Life, Morrow, 1989.
Payment in Full, Morrow, 1990.
Doctor on Trial, Morrow, 1991.
Mrs. Washington and Horowitz Too, Morrow, 1992.
Labyrinth, Morrow, 1993.
This Child Is Mine, Morrow, 1994.
To Mary, with Love, Morrow, 1995.
A Place for Kathy, Morrow, 1997.

PLAYS

(With Ralph Berkey) *Time Limit* (first produced on Broadway at Booth Theatre, January 24, 1956; also see below), Samuel French (New York City), 1956, typescript entitled *Valour Will Weep,* [New York], 1956.
Olive Oglivie, first produced on West End at Aldwych Theatre, March 12, 1957.
A Far Country (three acts; first produced on Broadway at Music Box Theatre, April 4, 1961), Random House (New York City), 1961.
Venus at Large, first produced on Broadway at Morosco Theatre, April 12, 1962.
A Case of Libel (three act; based on *My Life in Court* by Louis Nizer; first produced on Broadway at Longacre Theatre, October 10, 1963), Random House, 1964.
A Sound of Distant Thunder, first produced in Paramus, NJ, at Paramus Playhouse, 1967.
What Did We Do Wrong? (two-act comedy; first produced on Broadway at Helen Hayes Theatre, October 22, 1967), French, 1967.
The Headhunters, first produced in New Hope, PA, at Bucks County Playhouse, September, 1971.
The Second Time Around (three-act comedy; first produced on Broadway at Morosco Theatre, 1976), French, 1977.
Horowitz and Mrs. Washington (two-act comedy based on his novel; produced on Broadway at Golden Theatre, 1980), French, 1980.
Outrage (based on his novel), produced in Washington, DC, at The Kennedy Center, 1983.

Also author of plays *Judge Spencer Dissents* and *Tea with Madame Bernhardt.*

SCREENPLAYS

Time Limit! (based on his play), United Artists, 1957.

The Hook (based on a novel by Vahe Katcha), Metro-Goldwyn-Mayer, 1962.

Twilight of Honor (based on a novel by Al Dewlen), Metro-Goldwyn-Mayer, 1963.

TELEVISION AND RADIO SCRIPTS

Laughter for the Leader (radio play), broadcast on *Columbia Workshop,* Columbia Broadcasting System (CBS), 1940.

Me? I Drive a Hack (radio play), broadcast on *Columbia Workshop,* CBS, 1941.

Radio Reader's Digest, CBS, 1943-46.

(And producer/director) *The Greatest Story Ever Told* (radio plays), American Broadcasting Co. (ABC), 1947-57.

The Wound Within (three-act television play broadcast on *U.S. Steel Hour,* CBS, September 10, 1958), Batten, Barton, Durstine & Osborn, Inc., 1958.

Give Us Barabbas (television play broadcast on *Hallmark Hall of Fame,* National Broadcasting Corp. [NBC], March, 1961), Compass Productions, 1961.

A Case of Libel (television play based on his play), ABC, February, 1969.

The Choice (television play), broadcast on *Prudential Onstage,* NBC, March, 1969.

The Man Who Wanted to Live Forever, broadcast on *Movie of the Week,* ABC, December, 1969.

First Easter, broadcast on *Hallmark Hall of Fame,* NBC, March, 1970.

The Heart Farm, broadcast on *Movie of the Week,* ABC, March, 1971.

The Court Martial of Lieutenant Calley (television play), ABC, 1975.

A Time for Miracles (television play), ABC, 1980.

WORK IN PROGRESS: HeadMistress, a screenplay; and *Follow My Lead,* a television play.

SIDELIGHTS: Novelist and playwright Henry Denker once told *CA* that he "found two areas of early education of enormous value in later writing. Early religious education with a view toward becoming a rabbi turned out to be of enormous importance in working on *The Greatest Story Ever Told* and the other religious books and TV specials I have done. Also legal training and experience turned out to be of great help in doing *A Case of Libel, Twilight of Honor,* and *The Adversaries.* In each instance, the work concerned a trial and much highly technical legal knowledge was required. For the rest, reading of periodicals provides a varied source of ideas. And research on a topic once selected seems to provide information for yet other subjects."

Denker has addressed the issues of race relations in *Horowitz and Mrs. Washington,* and the criminal justice system in *Outrage.* Both stories began as novels, then were adapted for the stage. In *Horowitz and Mrs. Washington,* Horowitz, an elderly Jewish man who has been mugged and suffered a stroke, forms an uneasy alliance with his black nurse, Mrs. Washington. As the author explains in a *Los Angeles Times* article, the idea for the play came from his years observing in New York's Central Park "the same sight: an elderly Jewish man either with a walker or in a chair and a black woman taking care of him. Having witnessed that scene for so many years, I thought,'There must be a story beyond that hour that they spend in the park.' So this is about the relationship of two people, totally mismatched." Denker drew on his years as a practicing lawyer for *Outrage,* the story of a man's quest for justice. After his daughter has been raped and killed and the convicted criminal released on a technicality, the protagonist, Dennis Riordan, tracks down and kills the rapist/murderer. After Riordan turns himself in to the police, he finds himself at the center of a heated trial of his own. Though not based on a real case, the legal proceedings involved in *Outrage* are accurate, according to the author in a *Washington Post* interview with Megan Rosenfeld. "I've been concerned about what I call an unfair administration of justice for several years," Denker told Rosenfeld. "It's great for legal scholars to sit around and debate the issues, but I'm worried about the people. Something has to be done before it's too late for the courts to reform themselves." Denker added that "writing is a hobby as well as a profession and one is never at ease when not engaged in writing on some work. As a result the tendency is to work seven days a week when engaged in a long project such as a novel or a play. Days of the week lose their relevance and it is actually a struggle to interrupt the work for any save the gravest of reasons."

BIOGRAPHICAL/CRITICAL SOURCES:

PERIODICALS

Los Angeles Times, March 6, 1988.
Washington Post, December 12, 1982.

* * *

DENZIN, Norman K(ent) 1941-

PERSONAL: Born March 24, 1941, in Iowa City, IA; son of Kenneth F. (a naval captain) and Betty (Townsley) Denzin; married Katherine Ryan; children: Johanna, Rachel, Nathan Stevens. *Education:* University of Iowa, A.B., 1963, Ph.D., 1966.

ADDRESSES: Home—107 South Prospect St., Champaign, IL 61820. *Office*—Department of Sociology, University of Illinois, Urbana, IL 61801.

CAREER: University of Illinois at Urbana-Champaign, assistant professor of sociology, 1966-69; University of California, Berkeley, assistant professor of sociology, 1969-71; University of Illinois at Urbana-Champaign, associate professor, 1971-73, professor of sociology, 1973-80, College of Communications, research communications scholar, distinguished professor of sociology, criticism and interpretive theory professor, 1981—. Referee on grant applications, National Foundation on the Arts and Humanities, 1970—.

MEMBER: International Sociological Association (secretary-treasurer of social psychology section, 1978-80), American Anthropological Association, American Psychological Association, American Association for Public Opinion Research, Society for the Study of Symbolic Interaction (vice president, 1975-76; president, 1993-95), Society for the Sociological Study of Social Problems, Society for the Psychological Study of Social Issues, Society for the Study of Applied Anthropology, Pacific Sociological Society, Midwest Sociological Society (president, 1988-89).

WRITINGS:

(Editor and contributor with Stephen P. Spitzer) *The Mental Patient: Studies in the Sociology of Deviance,* McGraw (New York City), 1968.

The Research Act: A Theoretical Introduction to Sociological Methods, Aldine (Hawthorne, NY), 1970, third edition, Prentice-Hall (Englewood Cliffs, NJ), 1989.

(Editor and contributor) *Sociological Methods: A Sourcebook,* Aldine, 1970, second edition, McGraw, 1977.

(Editor and contributor) *The Values of Social Science,* Aldine, 1970, second edition, Dutton (New York City), 1973.

(With others) *Social Relationships,* Aldine, 1970.

(Editor) *Children and Their Caretakers,* Dutton, 1973.

(With Lindesmith and Strauss) *Readings in Social Psychology,* second edition (Denzin was not associated with previous edition), Holt (New York City), 1975, eighth edition, Sage Publications (Beverly Hills, CA), 1997.

Childhood Socialization, Jossey-Bass (San Francisco), 1977.

(Editor) *Studies in Symbolic Interaction: A Research Annual,* eleven volumes, JAI Press (Greenwich, CT), 1978-89.

On Understanding Emotion, Jossey-Bass, 1984.

The Alcoholic Self, Sage Publications, 1987.

The Recovering Alcoholic, Sage Publications, 1987.

Treating Alcoholism, Sage Publications, 1987.

(With Alfred R. Lindesmith and A. R. Strauss) *Social Psychology,* sixth edition (Denzin was not associated with previous editions), Prentice-Hall, 1988.

Interpretive Interactionism, Sage Publications, 1989.

Doing Biography, Sage Publications, 1989.

Hollywood Shot By Shot, Aldine, 1991.

Images of Postmodern Society, Sage Publications, 1991.

Symbolic Interactionism and Cultural Studies, Blackwell (Oxford, England), 1992.

The Alcoholic Society: Addiction and Recovery of the Self, Transaction (New Brunswick, NJ), 1993.

(Coeditor with Yvonna S. Lincoln) *Handbook of Qualitative Research,* Sage Publications, 1994.

The Cinematic Society: The Voyeur's Gaze, Sage Publications, 1995.

Hollywood and the Cinema of Racial Violence, Sage Publications, 1997.

Interpretive Ethnography: Ethnographic Practices for the 21st Century, Sage Publications, 1997.

Also author of *Performance Narratives,* 1997. Contributor to numerous periodicals, including

Social Forces, Journal of Health and Social Behavior, Mental Hygiene, Sociological Quarterly, Social Problems, American Sociological Review, American Sociologist, American Journal of Sociology, Word, Quest, and *Slavic Review. Trans-action,* special issue editor, June-July, 1971; *Sociological Quarterly,* associate editor, 1972-82, editor, 1992—; *Urban Life,* associate editor, 1972—; *Contemporary Sociology,* associate editor, 1978-81; *Qualitative Inquiry,* coeditor, 1994—; *Cultural Studies: A Research Annual,* editor, 1995—; *American Journal of Sociology,* editorial referee.

SIDELIGHTS: Norman K. Denzin told *CA:* "[My] basic position is that human conduct can only be understood by grasping the historical and cultural perspectives, languages and points of view of those we study. Instrumental works have been by G. H. Mead, C. H. Cooley, H. Blumer, C. Peirce, W. James, J. Dewey, A. Smith, E. Husserl, M. Scheler, S. Freud, Karl Marx, Martin Heidegger, and Jean-Paul Sartre. [The] basic question guiding my work is 'How is meaning constructed and lived in the lives of ordinary people and how may we, as interpretive scholars, ground our understandings in the spoken prose of the people we study?'"

* * *

Des BARRES, Pamela (Ann) 1948-

PERSONAL: Also known as "Miss Pamela"; surname is pronounced "day-*bar*"; born September 9, 1948, in Los Angeles, CA; daughter of Oren Coy and Margaret Ruth (Hayes) Miller; married Michael Des Barres (a musician and actor), October, 1977 (separated); children: Nicholas Dean. *Education:* Attended University of California. *Politics:* Liberal Democrat. *Religion:* "All."

ADDRESSES: *Agent*—William Morris Agency, 1350 Avenue of the Americas, New York, NY 10019.

CAREER: Writer. Member of the GTOs (Girls Together Outrageously), a rock group inspired by Frank Zappa, 1969-71; governess for Zappa's children, Dweezil and Moon Unit; rock reporter for the Playboy Channel, 1988—, and for the Lifetime Channel, 1989—. Public speaker.

WRITINGS:

I'm with the Band: Confessions of a Groupie (memoirs), Morrow (New York City), 1987.

Take Another Little Piece of My Heart: A Groupie Grows Up (memoirs), Morrow, 1992.

(With Dick St. John and Sandy St. John) *The Rock and Roll Cookbook: Favorite Recipes from the Chart Toppers, Hitmakers and Legends of Rock and Roll,* General Pub. Group (Santa Monica, CA), 1993.

Rock Bottom: Dark Moments in Music Babylon, St. Martin's (New York City), 1996.

Contributor to numerous periodicals, including *Details, New York Times Book Review, Rolling Stone, Movieline,* and *Interview.*

SIDELIGHTS: Pamela Des Barres created a minor furor in 1987 when her controversial, tell-all autobiography *I'm with the Band: Confessions of a Groupie* appeared on bookstands. In it, the first-time author detailed her life in the fast lane of rock and roll during the 1960s and 1970s. Des Barres was a friend of legendary cult musician Frank Zappa and his family and a member of an all-female rock group produced by Zappa in the late 1960s called the GTOs—Girls Together Outrageously. The ubiquitous Miss Pamela, as she was known in the scene in those days, hung out in London, New York City, and Los Angeles with a plethora of dynamic rock musicians and kept a journal of it all. In her memoir, Des Barres described friendships and liaisons with Mick Jagger of the Rolling Stones, drummer Keith Moon of The Who, and Led Zeppelin's Jimmy Page. To some, Des Barres's book seemed to glorify promiscuity and substance abuse, and she was often criticized for speaking so openly about sex. Yet on the other hand, Des Barres's story is a tale that speaks volumes about the often misunderstood role of women in rock. The music scene is notorious for the legions of females who line up backstage hoping to catch a glimpse, or better yet the eye, of their favorite artist. Although swooning and adoring fans offering themselves up sexually have been around since the days of early eighteenth-century Romantic poets, the modern versions of these women are often vilified and unfairly lumped together with their more serious peers—the women who actually do win the hearts and minds of enigmatic musicians. Men who achieve success in the music business are often driven by a host of demons, but common to most is a well-concealed inner drive a CEO would envy combined with some rather unsavory personality traits that may include extreme self-centeredness and a penchant for substance abuse. They seek women whose traits often complement their shortcomings—partners who aren't prone to the chemical pitfalls of the music business, even-tempered companions who serve as an ameliorative buffer from the more sordid side of the exploitive music industry. As a matter of course, women who wind up married to such men are often themselves enigmatic figures who are addicted in their own right to the world of rock and roll, an addiction Des Barres unabashedly chronicled in her first book.

In *I'm with the Band,* Des Barres recounts her childhood and teenage years in the prototypical suburban Los Angeles community of Reseda and how the exciting new rock music of the early 1960s influenced her growing awareness of the opposite sex. After graduating from high school, Des Barres became a full-time devotee of the Southern California music scene. She reminisces about her contacts with influential musicians of the era and her relationships with an array of talented artists, such as Jimi Hendrix's bandmate Noel Redding. Des Barres also tells of the antics of her close band of daring female friends that included Cynthia Plaster Caster, a woman who made plaster casts of rock star's private members. But she also writes of the warm friendship she shared with the Zappa family, and the impression they made on her as a relatively normal, well-adjusted nuclear family whose breadwinner happened to be an experimental musician. As the 1960s progressed into the next decade, Des Barres herself also metamorphosed into one of the most well-known and respected women on the sidelines of the music world. She became involved with guitarist Jimmy Page of Led Zeppelin, a band whose excesses were well-documented by the media—throwing furniture out of hotel rooms, incorporating references to black magic in their music, and partaking of the women who relentlessly followed the group. Des Barres's involvement with Page was fraught with melodrama and heartache; he eventually left her, and Des Barres's chronicle of the break-up and its emotional effect on her is one of the most moving sections of *I'm with the Band.*

But Des Barres, ever the eternal optimist as the pages of her life attest, bounced back and a short while later met the man of her dreams. Michael Des Barres was not only an up-and-coming musician in the glitter rock scene of the early 1970s, he was also devastatingly handsome and a titled English aristocrat to boot. The two fell madly in love and *I'm with the Band* concludes with the heady triumph of the author's ultimate success in both love and life. The book's publication in 1987 catapulted Des Barres to the television talk-show circuit as she recounted for eager audiences the wild ride she took through the heyday of rock and roll. While she often fielded insensitive and downright rude questions from interviewers about her autobiography and her personal life, most reviews were favorable. "Miss Pamela represented something honorable and loving about Southern California and the 60's, about hippies and innocent hedonism," John Rockwell of the *New York Times* wrote about Des Barres's explicit account of life in the fast lane, "and even about the sexual honesty of modern women, that modern-day moralists ignore at their own peril." Kurt Loder, reviewing *I'm with the Band* for *Rolling Stone,* deemed it a "highly personalized, page-turning cultural history" and term it "terrifically entertaining stuff, not the least because it has about it the viscous, sticky texture of truth." Loder further noted that Des Barres's "total love of the music is endearing, and her concept of sex as simple, loving fun is, in this grimly posttumescent era, bracingly subversive."

The success of *I'm with the Band* fostered a new career for Des Barres and newfound celebrity status. She began writing articles for magazines like *Details* and *Interview* and contemplated penning a sequel. Yet personal conflicts put that project on hold until 1992, when *Take Another Little Piece of My Heart: A Groupie Grows Up* was published. In it, Des Barres candidly recounts the downside of her life as a rock wife and the struggles she faced over the years. The volume opens happily with marriage to Michael and the birth of their son, but Des Barres describes the dismal days and nights she spent waiting for her husband to return home from his drug and alcohol binges. Her unflinching support of him, what she terms "co-co-dependence," could not rescue her husband from his road to self-destruction after his career faltered. She also recounts the shaky financial footing on which their family life stood for many years, and her jobs that ranged from acting in commercials to selling cosmetics. Yet as the book progresses their son—an exceptionally bright and sensitive boy—begins to take center stage in Des Barres's life.

Despite his intelligence, or perhaps because of it, their son grew into a troubled child plagued by inner demons that made him hard to manage.

Eventually Michael Des Barres joined Alcoholics Anonymous and found a new career as an actor, but the couple grew apart and separated. Des Barres found the right professional help for her son and drew upon the strength to enter this new phase of her life from a rich circle of friends. Her journey to self-fulfillment is an integral element of *Take Another Little Piece of My Heart,* but, like its predecessor, is also filled with the celebrities and anecdotes of life in the fast lane. The Zappa family remains close to Des Barres, and she recounts her friendship and social activities with both former lover Don Johnson and his subsequent wives, Melanie Griffith and Patti D'Arbanville. Her coming-of-age memoir also offers a glimpse of late 1980's Hollywood, which was becoming older, cleaner, chaster. Des Barres renewed her passion for music with her new love, a musician seventeen years her junior, and eventually put her talents to use as manager of his band. Elyse Gardner, critiquing Des Barres's second autobiographical book for *Rolling Stone* and comparing it with her first, contended "the most compelling personality in this book is the author herself; its most compelling feature is her efforts to define herself less by age or physical attributes than by her accomplishments." Ann Powers of the *New York Times,* discussing both tomes, argued that despite the changing face of rock and roll and women's role in it, "there's still much to learn from Ms. Des Barres and her kind, about the rock world's hidden history and its groundings in desire."

Des Barres told *CA:* "I hope to unite people with each other and their own souls through my work. Perhaps make them laugh and see another view."

BIOGRAPHICAL/CRITICAL SOURCES:

PERIODICALS

Boston Phoenix, June 26, 1987.
Chicago Tribune, November 16, 1992, sec. 5, p. 3.
New York Times, August 16, 1987, p. 24; December 20, 1992, p. 30.
Publishers Weekly, May 22, 1987, p. 61; September 28, 1992, p. 60.
Rolling Stone, July 16, 1987, p. 22; October 20, 1988; March 18, 1993, p. 31.
Voice Literary Supplement, July, 1987.*

* * *

DIAMOND, Sander A. 1942-

PERSONAL: Born November 25, 1942, in New York, NY; son of William (a window designer) and Bess (Weltman) Diamond; married Susan Lee Dorfman (a nurse practitioner), March 20, 1966; children: Meredith Carolyn, Matthew Eric. *Ethnicity:* "American." *Education:* State University of New York College at New Paltz, B.A. (with highest honors), 1964; State University of New York at Binghamton, M.A., 1966, Ph.D., 1971. *Religion:* Jewish. *Avocational interests:* Travel, stamp collecting, cycling, sailing.

ADDRESSES: Home—619 Prospect Street, Keuka Park, NY 14478; fax 315-536-4689. *Office*—Department of History, Keuka College, Keuka Park, NY 14478-0176.

CAREER: State University of New York at Binghamton, instructor in history, 1968; Keuka College, Keuka Park, NY, instructor, 1968-71, assistant professor, 1971-73, became associate professor of history, currently professor of history, chair of department, 1973-80, chair of division of humanities, 1980-85. Visiting professor of German history at Hobart and William Smith Colleges, 1976, 1977. Director of American-U.S.S.R. Seminar, 1977—.

MEMBER: Conference Group on German and Central European History, European Historians of New York State.

AWARDS, HONORS: National Endowment for the Humanities fellow, 1979.

WRITINGS:

The Nazi Movement in the United States: 1924-1941, Cornell University Press (Ithaca, NY), 1974.
Herr Hitler: Amerikas Diplomaten, Washington, und der Untergang Weimars, Droste Verlag (Duesseldorf, Germany), 1985.

(Contributor) Hans Trefousse, editor, *Germany and America: Essays on Problems of International Relations,* Brooklyn College Press (Brooklyn), 1980.
(With Jeff Rovin) *Starik,* Dutton (New York City), 1988.
(With Rovin) *The Red Arrow,* Dutton, 1991.
The German Table: The Education of a Nation, Harper (New York City), 1996.

Author of *The Silent Artillery of Time: Essays on the End of the Epoch of the World Wars, 1914-1989,* 1996. Also contributor to various journals, including *Journal of American History, American Jewish Historical Quarterly, Vierteljahrshefte fuer zeitgeschichte,* and *Yivo Annual of Jewish Social Sciences.*

* * *

DICK, Kay 1915-
(Edward Lane)

PERSONAL: Born July 29, 1915, in London, England; daughter of Kate Frances Dick. *Education:* Educated in Geneva, Switzerland, and at Lycee Francais de Londres, London, England. *Politics:* Independent. *Religion:* None. *Avocational interests:* Friends, gardening, and walking the dog.

ADDRESSES: Home—Flat 5, 9 Arundel Terrace, Brighton BN2 1GA, Sussex, England. *Agent*—Rogers, Coleridge & White, 20 Powis Mews, London W11 1SN, London, England.

CAREER: Freelance writer, biographer and novelist. Worked variously in editorial, publicity, and production jobs and as a publisher's reader and broadcaster.

AWARDS, HONORS: South-East Arts Literature Prize, 1977, for *They: A Sequence of Unease;* Art Council awards; Queen Civil List Pension.

WRITINGS:

FICTION

By the Lake, Heinemann (London), 1949.
Young Man, Heinemann, 1951.
An Affair of Love, Heinemann, 1953.
Solitaire, Heinemann, 1958.
Sunday, Hutchinson, 1962.
They: A Sequence of Unease, Allen Lane, 1977.
The Shelf, Hamish Hamilton (London), 1984.

NONFICTION

Pierrot: An Investigation into the Commedia dell arte, Hutchinson, 1960.
Ivy and Stevie: Ivy Compton-Burnett and Stevie Smith, Conversations and Reflections, Duckworth (London), 1971, Schocken (New York City), 1983.
Friends and Friendship: Conversations and Reflections, Sidgwick & Jackson (London), 1974.

Contributor to numerous literary journals.

EDITOR

(And compiler) *The Mandrake Root: An Anthology of Fantastic Tales,* Jarrolds (London), 1946.
At the Close of Eve: An Anthology of New Curious Stories, Jarrolds, 1947.
The Uncertain Element: An Anthology of Fantastic Conceptions (three volumes), Jarrolds, 1950.
(And author of introduction) *Bizarre and Arabesque: A New Anthology of Tales, Poems and Prose* (anthology from Edgar Allan Poe), Panther (London), 1967.
Writers at Work: The Paris Review Interviews, Penguin (Harmondsworth, England), 1972.

Also editor of *London's Hour: As Seen through the Eyes of Fire-Fighters,* 1942, and *Late Joys at the Players Theatre,* 1943. As Edward Lane, edited thirteen issues of magazine, *The Windmill.*

SIDELIGHTS: In a review of *The Shelf, Times Literary Supplement* critic Anne Duchene comments that Kay Dick "is a very honourable novelist. Her readers must often regret the kind of determined monochrome in which she tends to present herself, and wish that she might come out in fuller colour, but she has always set her face against such lures, and gone on working steadfastly at her elected seam." Dick "was lucky enough" to know writers "Ivy Compton-Burnett and Stevie Smith, and to know them well enough to penetrate any social veneer," indicates Gillian Freeman in *Spectator.* "Both agreed to tape-record long and intimate conversations with her, and parts of these conversations are the basis of her book," *Ivy and Stevie: Ivy Compton-Burnett and*

Stevie Smith, Conversations and Reflections. "She follows them with personal recollections so telling, touching and revealing that this short book is a masterpiece of evocation," Freeman writes. According to Marghanita Laski in *Listener,* "the friendship is what gives these conversations quality above most tape-speaking, and renders them evidentially valuable. . . . With Stevie at least (and it seems so with Ivy) life and work were one. She was as she wrote, all of a piece, creator and creature, and to all her friends, to anyone she met and liked, she gave the fullness of both. So everything she said to Kay Dick is, recognisably, cut from the whole cloth."

BIOGRAPHICAL/CRITICAL SOURCES:

BOOKS

Friends and Friendship: Conversations and Reflections, Sidgwick & Jackson, 1974.

PERIODICALS

Listener, October 21, 1971; December 15, 1977.
New York Times Book Review, September 7, 1980.
Observer (London), October 17, 1971; April 21, 1974; November 6, 1977.
Spectator, October 9, 1971; April 20, 1974; October 29, 1977; April 7, 1984.
Times (London), February 23, 1984.
Times Literary Supplement, October 22, 1971; February 24, 1984.*

* * *

DiGIACOMO, James J(oseph) 1924-

PERSONAL: Born November 22, 1924, in Brooklyn, NY; son of Philip (a construction foreman) and Catherine Margaret (in insurance sales; maiden name, Gargiula) DiGiacomo. *Education:* Woodstock College, Woodstock, MD, Ph.L., 1950, M.A., 1952, S.T.L., 1957; International School of Religious Formation, Brussels, Belgium, Diplome de Lumen Vitae, 1965.

ADDRESSES: *Home*—106 West 56th St., New York, NY 10019-3803. *Office*—Regis High School, 55 East 84th St., New York, NY 10028.

CAREER: Entered Society of Jesus (Jesuits), 1943, ordained Roman Catholic priest, 1956; teacher in Roman Catholic high schools in Washington, DC, 1950-53, and in New York City, 1958—. Fordham University, assistant adjunct professor, 1965-93, member of board of trustees, 1981-87. Member of summer faculties at University of Notre Dame, Boston College, Loyola University, University of Detroit, University of San Francisco, Loyola-Marymount University, and University of St. Thomas, Houston. Lecturer in Australia, New Zealand, Germany, and Micronesia. Member of Jesuit Spirituality Seminar, 1991-94.

MEMBER: Religious Education Association, Jesuit Secondary Education Association (member of commission on religious education, 1970-88).

WRITINGS:

Conscience and Concern (series), Holt (New York City), 1969-73.
Violence, Holt, 1969.
Race, Holt, 1969.
Church Involvement, Holt, 1969.
Faith, Holt, 1969.
Sexuality, Holt, 1969.
See You in Church, Holt, 1970.
Meaning, Holt, 1970.
(With Edward Wakin) *We Were Never Their Age,* Holt, 1971.
Would You Believe. . . ?, Holt, 1971.
Jesus Who?, Winston Press (Minneapolis, MN), 1973.
(With John Walsh) *The Longest Step: Searching for God,* Winston Press, 1977.
(With Walsh) *Meet the Lord: Encounters with Jesus,* Winston Press, 1977.
(With Walsh) *Going Together: The Church of Christ,* Winston Press, 1978.
(With Thomas Shannon) *An Introduction to Bioethics,* Paulist Press (Ramsey, NJ), 1979.
When Your Teenager Stops Going to Church, Abbey Press, 1980.
(With Wakin) *Understanding Teenagers,* Argus Communications (Allen, TX), 1983.
(With Walsh) *So You Want to Do Ministry,* Sheed & Ward (London), 1986.
Teaching Religion in a Catholic Secondary School, NCEA, 1989.
Do the Right Thing, Sheed & Ward, 1990.
(With Walsh) *Christian Discovery: The Road to Justice,* Orbis, 1992.

Morality and Youth: Fostering Christian Identity, Sheed & Ward, 1993.

Featured in numerous tape and video recordings. Contributor to periodicals, including *Youth Update, Modern Liturgy, America, Marriage and Family Living, U.S. Catholic, Academy of Political Science, New Catholic World,* and *Family Digest.*

SIDELIGHTS: James J. DiGiacomo wrote *CA:* "My main audiences are those concerned with the religious and moral development of adolescents—youth ministers, parents, teachers, and young people themselves. For over forty years I have been in day-to-day contact with teenagers. Keeping up with the changing scene is a challenge. I started teaching high schoolers when Truman was president. I worked with youngsters in the quiet fifties, the explosive sixties, the laid-back seventies, and the mellow eighties.

"In some ways kids are always the same, but they are also different in significant, often dramatic ways. They are always trying to find themselves in the search for identity that is youth's main task. But the search takes different forms in different eras, as they grow up in times of comparative stability or upheaval. Their attitudes toward authority may be predominantly submissive or rebellious; they may identify with adult values or reject them; they may reject religious institutions and concerns or be open to the mystery at the heart of human life. To keep up with them, to help them, and to provide guidance and encouragement for the adults who love them has become my life's work.

"In young people today, a remarkable receptivity to religion and religious experience is combined with apathy and even alienation from institutional religion. Their yearning for ideals is mocked by a pervasive relativism that leaves them morally adrift, vulnerable to the ideological quick-fix offered by fundamentalist groups. Most will probably settle for consumerism in the plastic paradise, but many yearn for something more to do with their lives than devote them to earning and owning and conspicuously consuming.

"Authentic Christianity holds out the highest ideals, the fulfillment of their noblest aspirations, but the churches are uncertain trumpets that play weak tunes or false notes. In my writings, as in my teaching, I try not to lay out the paths they should take, but to challenge them with the Christian vision of a meaningful life and invite them to make that vision their own. As a Roman Catholic priest, I speak from within a church that is often perceived as repressive and authoritarian, the enemy of freedom and self-determination. I believe that at our best we are better than that, and I invite the young to help us realize our best collective self—a people faithful to a rich tradition, attentive to authority properly exercised, respectful of the rights of individual conscience, and obedient to the larger truth that makes claims on us all.

"It is not just the young who need to hear such a call. Their parents, ministers, and teachers need help to live up to the sublime vocation of guides on the way to the kingdom of God. I try to explain young people to them to help them hear, under their growing children's noise and even more threatening silence, the cry for a fuller life. I believe that God holds out such a life in the person of Jesus Christ, and whether I write of God or church or youth or freedom or sex or faith or war or peace or many other concerns, my aim is to nelp both young and old hear and respond to that call."

* * *

DRIVER, C(harles) J(onathan) 1939-

PERSONAL: Born August 19, 1939, in Cape Town, South Africa; son of Kingsley Ernest (an Anglican priest) and Phyllis (a university warden; maiden name, Gould) Driver; married Ann Elizabeth Hoogewerf (an occupational therapist), June 8, 1967; children: Dominic, Thackwray, Tamlyn. *Ethnicity:* "South African." *Education:* University of Cape Town, B.A., 1960, B.A. (honors), 1961, B.Ed., 1962; Trinity College, Oxford, M.Phil., 1967. *Politics:* Liberal Conservative. *Religion:* Anglican. *Avocational interests:* Long-distance running, rugby, reading, writing.

ADDRESSES: *Office*—Wellington College, Crowthorne, Berkshire RG11 7PU, England; fax (0) 1344 772261. *Agent*—John Johnson, 45-47 Clerkenwell Green, London EC1R 0HT, England.

CAREER: President, National Union of South African Students, 1963-64; left South Africa in 1964 after being detained in solitary confinement under 90 Day Detention Law; Sevenoaks School, Sevenoaks, Kent, England, teacher of English, 1964-73, housemaster of International Sixth Form Centre, 1968-73; Matthew Humberstone Comprehensive School, Cleethorpes, Humberside, England, director of sixth form studies, 1973-78; Island School, Hong Kong, principal, 1978-83; Berkhamsted School, Berkhamsted, Hertfordshire, England, headmaster, 1983-89; Wellington College, Crowthorne, Berkshire, England, Master, 1989—. Research fellow, University of York, 1976; Commonwealth Linking Trust fellow, North India, 1987. Member of governing bodies, Benenden School, Eagle House School; trustee, Lomans Trust.

MEMBER: Arts Council of Great Britain (member of literature panel, 1975-77), Royal Society of Arts (fellow), Headmasters' Conference.

WRITINGS:

Elegy for a Revolutionary (novel), Faber (London), 1969, Morrow (New York City), 1970.
Send War in Our Time, O Lord (novel), Faber, 1970.
Death of Fathers (novel), Faber, 1972.
A Messiah of the Last Days (novel), Faber, 1974.
(Editor with H. B. Joicey) *Landscape and Light: Photographs and Poems of Lincolnshire and Humberside,* Lincolnshire and Humberside Arts (Newport, England), 1978.
I Live Here Now (poetry), Lincolnshire and Humberside Arts, 1979.
(With Jack Cope) *Jack Cope/C. J. Driver* (poetry), Philip, 1979.
Patrick Duncan, South African and Pan-African (biography), Heinemann (London), 1980.
In the Water-Margins (poetry), Snailpress (Cape Town, South Africa), 1994.

Also author of poetry volume, *Hong Kong Portraits,* 1986. Contributor to various anthologies, including *Penguin Book of South African Verse,* Penguin (New York City), 1969; *Seven South African Poets,* Heinemann, 1969; and *Penguin Modern Stories,* Number 8, Penguin, 1971. Also contributor to *Contrast, New Review,* and *Times Literary Supplement.* Editor, *Conference and Common Room,* 1993-97.

WORK IN PROGRESS: REQUIEM, poems.

SIDELIGHTS: "A recurring theme in C. J. Driver's novels has been that of people obliged, in certain crucial circumstances, to take cognisance of grave issues almost against their will," a *Times Literary Supplement* contributor describes, explaining that "the nice, the sensitive, the unexceptional and the untypical suddenly find themselves having to answer large questions about society." *Elegy for a Revolutionary,* for example, relates the dilemma of six young, white South Africans who are arrested for planning sabotage as a form of protest against apartheid. While the novel's topic is political, it is the author's portrayal of his characters which stands out, as another *Times Literary Supplement* reviewer comments: "It is a tribute to [Driver's] skill that both the people and the setting in [this novel] emerge with immense vividness, that the clash of motives and temperaments among his six anti-apartheid saboteurs seems fresh, real, subtle and touching." A third *Times Literary Supplement* writer concludes that *Elegy for a Revolutionary* is "a first novel of remarkable power and promise: an understated yet immensely telling study of political activists restricted by their own conflicts."

Driver's later novels also present individuals in conflict with both their consciences and society; *Send War in Our Time, O Lord* explores a South African widow's examination of her own attitudes and ethics with "a beautifully simple and lucid prose [which] conceals a considerable unobtrusive sophistication in . . . plot and character," a *Times Literary Supplement* critic observes. In *A Messiah of the Last Days,* Driver "has transferred all the skill he showed in describing the South African political situation to his intelligent—and uncomfortable—analysis of English life today," notes a *Times Literary Supplement* commentator. The novel follows the enchantment of a middle-aged lawyer with a group of young, idealistic anarchists; "the most ambitious of the four novels, *A Messiah of the Last Days* contrasts a number of different life styles, and presents a complex image of contemporary Britain," states Ursula Edmands in *Contemporary Novelists,* concluding that the novel exemplifies what she calls "Driver's most persistent theme: the need society has for a 'leader' with a compelling vision, and its equal need to destroy him."

Driver's 1994 publication *In the Water-Margins,* is a volume of poetry that focuses on the author's twenty-year exile from South Africa and his visits to his homeland. Stephen Watson, in a review for *Southern African Review of Books,* describes this volume as "a haunted book, dealing with one of the greatest of all hauntings: the encounter with the shades of an earlier self." The same reviewer states that "this collection contains [Driver's] finest poetry to date. Which is to say, some of the best English-language poetry thus far produced by a South African or ex-South African."

BIOGRAPHICAL/CRITICAL SOURCES:

BOOKS

Contemporary Novelists, St. James Press/St. Martin's, 1986.

PERIODICALS

New Statesman, September 5, 1969; September 18, 1970; February 25, 1972.

Southern African Review of Books, November/December, 1994.

Times Literary Supplement, September 18, 1969; September 2, 1970; October 2, 1970; March 10, 1972; October 4, 1974; October 16, 1980.

* * *

DUNNAHOO, Terry Janson 1927-
(Margaret Terry)

PERSONAL: Born December 8, 1927, in Fall River, MA; daughter of Joseph Alfred (a mill worker) and Emma (a mill worker; maiden name, Dolbec) Janson; married Thomas William Dunnahoo (a cinematographer), September 18, 1954; children: Kim, Sean, Kelly. *Ethnicity:* "Caucasian." *Education:* Attended parochial schools in Massachusetts. *Politics:* "I vote for the man—or the woman." *Religion:* Roman Catholic.

ADDRESSES: *Home*—4061 Tropico Way, Los Angeles, CA 90065.

CAREER: Writer. Has worked as a teacher of creative writing in the gifted program, Los Angeles Public Schools, and as an instructor in creative writing and a mentor on the Teacher Advisory Board, UCLA Extension. Lecturer to private groups, writer's conferences, and seminars, colleges, and schools. Consultant to Disney Educational Media Company, Asselin Television Productions, and California Arts Commission.

MEMBER: International PEN (president, Los Angeles Center, 1975-77; member of board of directors), Authors Guild, Authors League of America, Society of Children's Book Writers, California Writer's Club (member of board of directors), Southern California Council on Literature for Children and Young People (member of board of directors), Friends of Children and Libraries (member of board of directors), Women in Film.

AWARDS, HONORS: Southern California Council on Literature for Children and Young People's nonfiction award, 1975, for *Before the Supreme Court: The Story of Belva Ann Lockwood;* Teacher of the Year, UCLA Extension, 1985; Dorothy C. McKenzie Award, 1988, for distinguished contribution to the field of children's literature.

WRITINGS:

Emily Dunning, Reilly & Lee, 1970.

Nellie Bly: A Portrait, Reilly & Lee, 1970.

Annie Sullivan: A Portrait, Reilly & Lee, 1970.

Before the Supreme Court: The Story of Belva Ann Lockwood, Houghton (Boston), 1974.

Who Cares about Espie Sanchez?, Dutton (New York City), 1976.

This Is Espie Sanchez, Dutton, 1976.

Who Needs Espie Sanchez?, Dutton, 1977.

(Under pseudonym Margaret Terry) *The Last of April,* Bouregy (New York City), 1981.

(Under pseudonym Margaret Terry) *Bridge to Tomorrow,* Bouregy, 1983.

Break Dancing, F. Watts (New York City), 1985.

How to Write Children's Books, Janson, 1985.

Alaska, F. Watts, 1987.

U.S. Territories, F. Watts, 1988.

How to Win a School Election, F. Watts, 1989.

The Lost Parrots of America, Crestwood (Mankato, MN), 1989.

The Truth about Pearl Harbor, F. Watts, 1991.

How to Survive High School, F. Watts, 1993.

Football Hall of Fame, Crestwood, 1994.

Basketball Hall of Fame, Crestwood, 1994.

Baseball Hall of Fame, Crestwood, 1994.

Boston's Freedom Trail, Dillon (Minneapolis, MN), 1994.

Plimoth Plantation, Dillon, 1995.

Sacramento, California, Dillon, 1997.

Contributor to *Los Angeles Herald-Examiner*. Editor, *West Coast Review of Books*.

SIDELIGHTS: Terry Janson Dunnahoo once told *CA:* "When I speak to groups of hopeful writers, whether they are children or adults, I'm asked what my favorite book was when I was a child. I tell them I didn't have a favorite book. My family was so poor we had no books and there was no library where I could get any. The only books I knew or heard about while I was in elementary school were my French and religious books. Then, when I got to high school, I had to work three jobs at the same time to stay in school and had no time to read. One of the jobs was in a sweat shop sewing parts of dresses. I was paid for each seam I sewed and if I didn't work at top speed I couldn't earn enough money to stay in school. Actually, if I didn't work at top speed I would have been fired, and then I definitely couldn't have stayed in school. Still, I felt slaving in a sweat shop was one step above slaving in a mill, which is where my parents worked. I was the first person in my family to graduate from high school. After that I worked my way through business school and, eventually, worked for an attorney in Fall River and as a civilian for the U.S. Navy on Guam. When I reached the point where I had no more classes and only one job to take up my time, I started reading several books a month. I still don't have a favorite book. I read anything that interests me.

"The other question I often get from children and adults is what and who influenced me to write. No particular incident influenced me. No teacher encouraged me. But when my daughter was thirteen, although she read fiction, she seldom read nonfiction. So I decided to write a biography she would read. That biography was *Nellie Bly*. The book sold to the first editor I sent it to and I was a writer. And, for a while, I couldn't imagine doing anything else. However, now I've branched out in different areas related to writing. I speak at writers' conferences throughout the United States, I teach creative writing, I review books, I do manuscript analysis, and I've become active in writer's organizations.

"Each gives me a feeling of helping others. But none gives me more satisfaction than meeting my audience during lecture tours, especially the young people who take Espie Sanchez, one of my fictional characters, so seriously that they believe she's a real person. One of those people was able to escape from the gang she belonged to, graduate from high school and get a job. My books have influenced other readers in different ways. One became a doctor because she read my book *Emily Dunning*. But the former gang member, who now lives a happy and productive life because of my books about Espie Sanchez, is the perfect example of how strongly writers can change people's lives."

E

EICHENBERG, Fritz 1901-1990

PERSONAL: Born October 24, 1901, in Cologne, Germany; immigrated to United States, 1933, naturalized citizen, 1940; died of complications of Parkinson's disease, November 30, 1990, in Peace Dale, RI; son of Seigfried and Ida (Marcus) Eichenberg; married Mary Altmann, 1926 (died, 1937); married Margaret Ladenberg, 1941 (divorced, 1965); married Antonie Ida Schulze-Forster (a graphic designer), January 7, 1975; children: (first marriage) Suzanne Eichenberg Jensen; (second marriage) Timothy. *Education:* Attended School of Applied Arts, Cologne, 1916-20; State Academy of Graphic Arts, Leipzig, M.F.A., 1923. *Politics:* Pacifist. *Religion:* Society of Friends (Quakers).

CAREER: Graphic artist and illustrator of classics and other books. Started as newspaper artist in Germany, 1923, and worked as an artist traveling correspondent for Ullstein Publications, Berlin, before settling in the United States; New School for Social Research, New York City, member of art faculty, 1935-45; Pratt Institute, Brooklyn, NY, professor of art, 1947-72, chair of department of graphic arts, 1956-63, founder-director of Graphic Arts Center, 1956-72; University of Rhode Island, Kingston, professor of art, 1966-71, chair of department, 1966-69; Albertus Magnus College, New Haven, CT, professor of art, 1972-73; Arbuthnot lecturer, 1984. Member of Pennell Committee, Library of Congress, 1959-65, and Yale University Library, 1979. *Exhibitions:* Work has been exhibited in one-man shows at New School for Social Research, 1939, 1949; Associated American Artists Gallery, 1967, 1977; Pratt Manhattan Center Gallery, 1972; and Klingspor Museum (Offenbach, Germany), 1974. Work has also been shown in Xylon international exhibitions in Switzerland, Yugoslavia, and other countries, in U.S. Information Agency traveling exhibits, and in Society of American Graphics Artists shows. An exhibition of six decades of Eichenberg's prints was circulated by the International Exhibition Foundation in 1979-81. A traveling exhibit of his art toured Europe, Asia, and Australia, 1988-90. Work represented in collections of National Gallery of Art, Hermitage Museum (Leningrad), Metropolitan Museum of Art, Philadelphia Museum of Art, and other museums.

MEMBER: National Academy of Design, Royal Society of Arts (London; fellow), Society of American Graphic Artists, Xylon International, Bund Deutscher Buchkuenstler.

AWARDS, HONORS: American Institute of Graphic Arts Fifty Books of the Year citation, 1937, for *Puss in Boots; New York Herald Tribune*'s Spring Book Festival middle honor award, 1942, for *Mischief in Fez;* Newbery Honor Book citation, 1943, for *"Have You Seen Tom Thumb?";* Joseph Pennell Medal, Pennsylvania Academy of Fine Arts, 1944, for a wood engraving; first prize, National Academy of Design, 1946, for a print; Caldecott Honor Book citation, American Library Association (ALA), 1953, for *Ape in a Cape: An Alphabet of Odd Animals;* Silver Medal, Limited Editions Club, 1954; Notable Book citation, ALA, 1955, for *Dancing in the Moon: Counting Rhymes;* Lewis Carroll Shelf Awards, 1962, for *Padre Porko: The Gentlemanly Pig,* and 1968, for *No Room: An Old Story Retold;* grant from John D.

Rockefeller III Fund, 1968; S. F. B. Morse Medal, National Academy of Design, 1973, for a wood engraving; Outstanding Educator of America Award, 1973; National Book Award nomination, 1979, for *Endangered Species, and Other Fables with a Twist;* Rhode Island Governor's Award for the Arts, 1981, for contributions to the world of art; *New York Times* Best Illustrated Children's Book citation, and Notable Book citation, ALA, both 1982, both for *Rainbows Are Made: Poems by Carl Sandburg;* D.F.A., Southeastern Massachusetts University, 1972, University of Rhode Island, 1974, California College of Arts and Crafts, 1976, Marymount College, 1984, and Stonehill College, 1985.

WRITINGS:

(Translator with William Hubben) Helmut A. P. Grieshaber, *H. A. P. Grieshaber,* Arts, 1965.

(Author of text) Naoko Matsubara, *Nantucket Woodcuts,* Barre (New York City), 1967.

(Editor) *Artist's Proof: A Collector's Edition of the First Eight Issues of the Distinguished Journal of Print and Printmaking,* New York Graphic Society (Boston), 1971.

The Print: Art, Masterpiece, History, Technics, Abrahams, 1975.

Endangered Species, and Other Fables with a Twist, Stemmer House (Owings Mills, MD), 1979.

Six Decades of Prints by Fritz Eichenberg, with introduction by Gene Baro, International Exhibitions Foundation (Washington, DC), 1979.

Artist on the Witness Stand, Pendle Hill (Wallingford, PA), 1984.

Fritz Eichenberg: Werkkatalog der illustriertern Beucher, 1922-1987, Edition C. Visel (Memmingen, Germany), 1987.

Robert Ellsberg, editor, *Works of Mercy,* Orbis Books (Maryknoll, NY), 1992.

SELF-ILLUSTRATED

Ape in a Cape: An Alphabet of Odd Animals (juvenile), Harcourt (New York City), 1952.

Art and Faith (booklet), Pendle Hill, 1952.

Dancing in the Moon: Counting Rhymes (juvenile), Harcourt, 1955, reprinted, Harcourt, 1975.

(Translator) Desiderius Erasmus, *In Praise of Folly,* Aquarius, 1972.

The Wood and the Graver: The Works of Fritz Eichenberg, C. N. Potter (New York City), 1977.

Yours in Peace: Prints with a Message, Fellowship of Reconciliation, 1977.

The Artist and the Book, Yale University Library (New Haven, CT), 1979.

(Reteller) *Poor Troll: The Story of Ruebezahl and the Princess,* Stemmer House, 1983.

Dance of Death Portfolio, Abbeville Press (New York City), 1983.

(Reteller) *Bell, Book and Candle,* American Library Association (Chicago), 1984.

ILLUSTRATOR

Puss in Boots, Holiday House (New York City), 1936.

Joel Chandler Harris, *Uncle Remus Stories,* limited edition, Peter Pauper (New York City), 1937.

Moritz A. Jagendorf, *Tyll Ulenspiegel's Merry Pranks,* Vanguard, 1938.

Therese Lenotre, *Mystery of Dog Flip,* translation from the French by Simone Chamoud, Stokes, 1939.

Robert Davis, *Padre: The Gentlemanly Pig,* Holiday House, 1939, enlarged edition, 1948.

Rosalys Hall, *Animals to Africa,* Holiday House, 1939.

Stewart Schackne, *Rowena, the Skating Cow,* Scribner (New York City), 1940.

Eula Griffin Duncan, *Big Road Walker,* Stokes, 1940.

Babette Deutsch, *Heroes of the Kalevala: Finland's Saga,* Messner (New York City), 1940.

Jonathan Swift, *Gulliver's Travels,* Heritage Press (Baltimore, MD), 1940, junior text edition, 1947, new edition, 1961.

Richard A. W. Hughes, *Don't Blame Me* (short stories), Harper (New York City), 1940.

William Shakespeare, *Tragedy of Richard the Third,* Limited Editions Club, 1940.

Henry Beston, *The Tree that Ran Away,* Macmillan (New York City), 1941.

Marjorie Fischer, *All on a Summer's Day,* Random House (New York City), 1941.

Irmengarde Eberle, *Phoebe-Bell,* Greystone Press, 1941.

Ivan S. Turgenev, *Fathers and Sons,* translation from the Russian by Constance Garnett, Heritage Press, 1941.

Mabel Leigh Hunt, *"Have You Seen Tom Thumb?,"* Stokes, 1942.

Charlotte Bronte, *Jane Eyre* [and] Emily Bronte, *Wuthering Heights* (companion volumes), Random House, 1943.

Henrik Ibsen, *Story of Peer Gynt,* retold by E. V. Sandys, Crowell (New York City), 1943.

Eberle, *Wide Fields: The Story of Henry Fabre,* Crowell, 1943.

Eleanor Hoffmann, *Mischief in Fez,* Holiday House, 1943.

Leo N. Tolstoi, *Anna Karenina,* translation by Garnett, two volumes, Doubleday (New York City), 1944.

Edgar Allen Poe, *Tales,* Random House, 1944.

Mark Keats, *Sancho and His Stubborn Mule,* W. R. Scott, 1944.

Rose Dobbs, *No Room: An Old Story Retold,* Coward, 1944.

Feodor M. Dostoevski, *Crime and Punishment,* translation by Garnett, Heritage Press, 1944.

Stephen Vincent Benet, *The Devil and Daniel Webster,* Kingsport, 1945.

Dostoevski, *The Grand Inquisitor,* Haddam House, 1945.

Glanville W. Smith, *Adventures of Sir Ignatius Tippitolio,* Harper, 1945.

Anna Sewell, *Black Beauty,* Grosset, 1945, reprint, 1995.

Terence H. White, *Mistress Masham's Repose,* Putnam (New York City), 1946.

E. Bronte, *Wuthering Heights,* Random House, 1946.

Maurice Doblier, *The Magic Shop,* Random House, 1946.

Felix Salten, compiler, *Favorite Animal Stories,* Messner, 1948.

Dostoevski, *Brothers Karamazov,* translation by Garnett revised with introduction by Avram Yarmolinsky, Limited Editions Club, 1949.

Ruth Stiles Gannett, *Wonderful House-Boat-Train,* Random House, 1949.

Rudyard Kipling, *The Jungle Book,* Grosset, 1950, reprint, 1995.

Mark van Doren, *The Witch of Ramoth,* Maple Press, 1950.

Wilkie Collins, *Short Stories,* Rodale Books, 1950.

(With Vassily Verestchagin) Tolstoi, *War and Peace,* translation by Louise and Aylmer Maude, two volumes in one, Heritage Press, 1951.

Margaret Cousins, *Ben Franklin of Old Philadelphia,* Random House, 1952.

Dorothy Day, *Long Loneliness* (autobiography), Harper, 1952.

Nathaniel Hawthorne, *Tale of King Midas and the Golden Touch,* Limited Editions Club, 1952.

Johann Wolfgang von Goethe, *Story of Reynard the Fox,* translation by Thomas J. Arnold from original German poem, Heritage Press, 1954.

Dostoevski, *The Idiot,* translation by Garnett revised with introduction by Yarmolinsky, Heritage Press, 1956.

Elizabeth J. Coatsworth, *The Peaceable Kingdom and Other Poems,* Pantheon (New York City), 1958.

Edna Johnson and others, compilers, *Anthology of Children's Literature,* third edition (Eichenberg did not illustrate earlier editions), Houghton (Boston), 1959, fourth edition, 1970.

Dostoevski, *The Possessed,* translation by Garnett, Heritage Press, 1960.

Tolstoi, *Resurrection,* translation by Leo Wiener revised and edited by F. D. Reeve, Heritage Press, 1963.

Jean Charlot, *Pasada's Dance of Death,* Graphic Arts Center, Pratt Institute (Brooklyn, NY), 1965.

Etienne Decroux, *Mime: The Art of Etienne Decroux,* Pratt Adlib Press, 1965.

Dylan Thomas, *A Child's Christmas in Wales,* limited edition, New Directions (New York City), 1969, redesigned edition, 1995.

Tolstoi, *Childhood, Boyhood, Youth,* translation by Wiener, Press of A. Colish, 1972.

John M. Langstaff, *The Two Magicians,* Atheneum (New York City), 1973.

Dostoevski, *A Raw Youth,* Limited Editions Club, 1974.

Philip S. Bernstein, *What the Jews Believe,* Greenwood, 1978.

Avon Neal, *Pigs and Eagles,* Thistle Hall Press, 1979.

Poe, *Eleanora,* Penmaen Press (Great Barrington, MA), 1979.

C. S. Lewis, *Till We Have Faces: A Myth Retold,* Harcourt, 1980.

J. C. Grimmelshausen, *The Adventurous Simplicissimus,* translation by John P. Spiegelman, Limited Editions Club, 1981.

Allen Hoffmann, *Kagan's Superfecta and Other Stories,* Abbeville Press, 1981.

Lee B. Hopkins, editor, *Rainbows Are Made: Poems by Carl Sandburg,* Harcourt, 1982.

Dostoevski, *The House of the Dead,* translation by Garnett, Limited Editions Club, 1982.

Thomas, *Rebecca's Daughters,* New Directions, 1983.

Georges Bernanos, *Diary of a Country Priest,* Limited Editions Club, 1986.

Hutterian Bretheren, editor, *The Gospel in Dostoevski: Selections from His Works,* Plough Publishing (Rifton, NY), 1988.

OTHER

Contributor to books, including *Education in Graphic Arts,* Boston Public Library, 1969; also contributor to *American Artist* and other journals. Founder and chief editor, *Artist's Proof: An Annual of Prints and Printmaking,* Pratt Institute, 1960-72.

Some of his books have been presented in British and Japanese editions. His works are collected in the Kerlan Collection of the University of Minnesota.

SIDELIGHTS: Children's book author and illustrator Fritz Eichenberg's career was varied. In addition to his work with children's books, he has also illustrated a number of adult classics and taught and lectured at a number of colleges. He explained in *Contemporary American Illustrators of Children's Books,* though, that doing children's books was always a gratifying and fulfilling experience. "I have always found the illustrating of children's books a refreshing relief, and profoundly satisfying because of the warm response of young readers, parents, and librarians. You are doubly blessed if you can illustrate your own stories. . . . I believe you produce your best work if it's addressed to your children—your own or others you love. They are your most honest and incorruptible critics."

Eichenberg was born in Cologne, Germany, in 1901. His strongest childhood memory is that of the day, when he was four years old, that his father took him window-shopping through the streets of Cologne for a pet mouse. It was the last time he saw his father walk. Soon after the trip, he became confined to bed with Parkinson's disease, dying ten years later. After his father's death, Eichenberg's mother began managing the small family business, drawing strength from the classical music she loved. These years left Eichenberg with few pleasant memories, mainly because of the difficult school years he endured. Discipline at the Gymnasium was brutal and he believes the frequent beatings explain the kind of person he later became: one who communicated to others primarily through his art.

His best teacher during that time taught literature, never used physical discipline, and expressed a sincere interest in Eichenberg's writing. The teacher's direction encouraged the young man to look forward to a career as a writer. He wrote in *The Wood and the Graver,* "I took refuge in literature because I had the urge to know what life—apart from my horrible environment—was all about. In a militaristic atmosphere you either succumb to it or become a rebel. I became a rebel."

He survived the bombing of Cologne during World War I by sleeping in the cellar, where the other people of his neighborhood also sought protection. He recalled in the same book, "During this time I wrote a school essay on *The Dance of Death* (which I would later illustrate). Why that particular subject caught my attention, I owe to the times—it was the war years, bombs were falling, trains arrived with prisoners of war. We all thought a lot about death in those days. My grandfather, who owned an internationally-famous matzoh bakery, was given the 'privilege' of picking prisoners of war to work for him for no pay. I remember, in particular, a German-speaking Russian Jewish soldier who befriended me one summer. I was a tiny shrimp of a lad, and we struck up a wonderful relationship. I remember his uniform of a great blouse and a hat with an emblem on it. I saw in him, not a prisoner of war, not a soldier, but a *human being*. This experience and the deep feelings it aroused in me were probably the beginnings of my pacifism." When the war ended in 1918, Eichenberg said, "Everything was in smithereens. Soldiers came back wearing the red arm bands of the Socialists. And so the new era began. And I would eventually play a political part in it, lampooning Hitler in my newspaper cartoons."

Hatred of the Jews was not commonly expressed in the years before Hitler came to power, Eichenberg remembered. Because his parents did not attend the local synagogue and did not emphasize his religious education, Eichenberg grew up thinking of himself as a German citizen who also happened to be a Jew. At about this time, he attended evening classes in drawing at the School of Applied Arts. He liked to sketch animals at the zoo during his spare time, and began to think of a career in art. As an apprentice in lithography, a method of printing by spreading ink on slabs of stone, he spent many hours in a print shop rubbing ink. His first artistic assignments included drawings for wine labels etched into stone and poster designs for Tietz, Cologne's large department store.

When eighteen, Eichenberg took a job in the store's art department. With a regular income, he started buying books and spent hours browsing in bookstores. "The most important find," he wrote in his autobiography, "was Frans Masereel's *Book of Hours*. A Belgian pacifist in exile in France, he was the first artist to create a book from a collection of woodcuts without words. He was obsessed with the challenge of expressing his ideas without the benefit of text. For him, illustration had to stand on its own merit. His *Ein Bilderoman,* comprised of sixty woodcuts, also deeply influenced me. I still see Masereel as one of my guiding lights."

Eichenberg became a staff artist at the store and decided to become a master graphic artist. The store's director agreed to send him to the State Academy of Graphic Arts in Leipzig for two years of study. His teacher, Hugo Steiner-Prag, allowed him to direct his own studies. While there, he illustrated *Gulliver's Travels* by Jonathan Swift, *Crime and Punishment* by Feodor Dostoevski, and one of his own creations, *Till Eulenspiegel's Merry Pranks*. Their publication confirmed his choice of vocation as an illustrator.

In 1926 he married Mary Altmann, and the couple returned to her home in Berlin. Ullstein Publications, a large and diverse publishing house, employed him as a staff artist and traveling correspondent. He wrote, "I wrote articles and illustrated them, made posters and cartoons for Ullstein and other German publishers. These were exhilarating years when theatre, films, dance and literature were flourishing, until suddenly a man named Hitler, whom I had lampooned in my cartoons, became Reichs Chancellor." Enthused about the changes promised by the revolution and the rise of the Weimar Republic, Eichenberg was disappointed to see Hitler take control. "That experience put an end to my affection for anything I would call 'German,'" he wrote.

By 1932 Eichenberg saw the necessity of leaving Germany, a goal he could achieve using his status as a correspondent. He also brought his wife and daughter to New York City. Like many other European craftspeople, Eichenberg found work with the Federal Artists project's Works Progress Administration. The program offered a living wage, quality materials to work with, comfortable deadlines, and complete artistic freedom. Together with income earned as a teacher at the New School for Social Research, he was able to support the family. By 1938, the household included his mother, sisters, and other relatives who had escaped the German pogroms in which many Jews lost their lives.

In 1936, he illustrated the children's book *Puss in Boots*. The American Institute of Graphic Arts named it one of fifty best books of that year. He was also commissioned to illustrate *Crime and Punishment,* welcoming the chance to add more mature artwork to the classic he had illustrated as a student. The new drawings expressed insights gained from his knowledge of the genocide in his homeland and his life as an exile.

In 1937 his young wife died of cancer. Three years later, Eichenberg joined the Quaker faith, and remarried the following year. In 1947, he became chair of the Department of Graphic Arts at Pratt Institute. The next year he also illustrated *The Brothers Karamazov,* a project funded by George Macy. His expert work led to a commission to illustrate a special edition of *The Grand Inquisitor*. The artist's deep appreciation of Dostoevski's theme of redemption by grace allowed him to do his best work on these projects. They have been appreciated by important people of many different political groups from the Pope to the Soviet Premier.

In 1956, Eichenberg returned to Germany to see what had changed since Hitler's demise. It pleased him greatly to see that the Gymnasium where he had been brutalized as a child had been completely destroyed. That year he founded the Graphic Arts Center in New York City.

Art was always Eichenberg's major link to the rest of the world. Even with his own children, who watched him draw and carve for hours, he allowed his pictures to serve as the foundation for communication. He believed that art has to be an obsession to be taken seriously. He once commented, "Art is a vocation—you can't recommend it to someone and it can't really be taught. You have to jump into the pool and sink or swim. Don't imitate anyone. You must be able to engage your own resources." He added, "It should be quite obvious when one reads the life of a Beethoven or Michelangelo or Goya that you don't make art because you want to make money; you do it because you *have* to. Even if no one else cares—*you* care."

BIOGRAPHICAL/CRITICAL SOURCES:

BOOKS

Catalogue Raisonne, 1988.
Contemporary American Illustrators of Children's Books, Rutgers, 1974.
Eichenberg, *The Wood and the Graver,* C. N. Potter, 1977.
Johnson, Edna, and others, editors, *Anthology of Children's Literature,* 4th edition, Houghton, 1970.
Kingman, Lee, and others, compilers, *Illustrators of Children's Books: 1957-1966,* Horn Book, 1968.
Kingman and others, compilers, *Illustrators of Children's Books: 1967-1976,* Horn Book, 1978.
Mahony, Bertha A., and others, editors, *Illustrators of Children's Books: 1744-1945,* Horn Book, 1947.
Miller, B. M., and others, compilers, *Illustrators of Children's Books: 1946-1956,* Horn Book, 1958.
Simon, Howard, *Five Hundred Years of Art Illustration,* Garden City Publishers, 1942.
Ward, Martha E., and Dorothy A. Marquardt, *Illustrators of Books for Young People,* Scarecrow, 1975.
Williamson, Richard, *Book Illustrators,* Kingsport Press, 1952.

PERIODICALS

American Artist, December, 1944; May, 1956; May, 1964; October, 1975.
Biography News, November, 1975.
Christian Century, November, 1983.
Commonweal, September, 1983.
Friends Journal, October, 1982.
Graphis, Volume 13, number 43, 1952; May, 1980.
Horn Book, February, 1960; December, 1980.
Idea (Tokyo), January, 1974.
Library of Congress Quarterly, April, 1965.
Print, May, 1976; September, 1976.
Publishers Weekly, February 4, 1957; May 7, 1979.
Rhode Islander, August 12, 1973.

OBITUARIES:

PERIODICALS

New York Times, December 4, 1990.*

* * *

ELLER, Scott
See HOLINGER, William (Jacques)

* * *

ELSTAR, Dow
See GALLUN, Raymond Z.

* * *

ELTING, John R(obert) 1911-

PERSONAL: Born February 15, 1911, in Spokane, WA; son of Robert C. (a business manager) and Myrtle (Welborn) Elting; married Ann M. Clancy, November 6, 1935. *Ethnicity:* "White (Scots-Dutch)." *Education:* Stanford University, B.S., 1932; Colorado State College of Education, M.A., 1948. *Religion:* Deist. *Avocational interests:* Travel (Scotland, Western Europe).

ADDRESSES: Home and office—28 Stillman, Cornwall-on-Hudson, NY 12520.

CAREER: Billings High School, Billings, MT, teacher of general science and biology, 1936-40 and 1947-48. Served in U.S. Army, 1933-36 and 1940-48, career officer, 1950-68, serving as a teacher at Armed Forces Information School, 1948-51, and at United States Military Academy, 1951-54 and 1957-65; retired as colonel, 1968. Military historian and consultant, 1968—.

MEMBER: Company of Military Historians (member of board of governors).

AWARDS, HONORS: Military—Legion of Merit, Bronze Star, Purple Heart, Army Commendation Ribbon with two Oak Leaf clusters.

WRITINGS:

(Associate editor) *West Point Atlas of American Wars,* Praeger (New York City), 1959.

(With Vincent Joseph Esposito) *A Military History and Atlas of the Napoleonic Wars,* Praeger, 1964.

(Editor) *Military Uniforms in America,* Presidio Press (Novato, CA), Volume 1: *The Era of the American Revolution, 1755-1795,* 1974, Volume 2: *Years of Growth, 1796-1851,* 1977, Volume 3 (with Michael J. McAfee): *Long Endure: The Civil War Period, 1852-1867,* 1982, Volume 4 (with McAfee): *The Modern Era,* 1988.

The Battle of Bunker's Hill, Philip Freneau (Monmouth Beach, NJ), 1975.

The Battles of Saratoga, Philip Freneau, 1977.

Battles for Scandinavia, Time-Life (Alexandria, VA), 1981.

American Army Life, Scribner (New York City), 1982.

(With Dan J. Cragg and Ernest L. Deal) *A Dictionary of Soldier Talk,* Scribner, 1984.

The Superstrategists: Great Captains, Theorists, and Fighting Men Who Have Shaped the History of Warfare, Scribner, 1985.

(Contributor) Donald D. Horward, editor, *Napoleonic Military History: A Bibliography,* Garland Publishing (New York City), 1986.

(Contributor) David D. Chandler, editor, *Napoleon's Marshals,* Macmillan (New York City), 1987.

Swords around a Throne: Napoleon's Grande Armee, Free Press (New York City), 1988.

Amateurs, to Arms! A Military History of the War of 1812, Algonquin Press (Chapel Hill, NC), 1991.

Napoleonic Uniforms, two volumes, Macmillan, 1993.

(Translator and editor) Elzear Blaze, *Military Life under Napoleon,* Emperor's Press, 1995.

Consultant to Time-Life Books on "World War II," "The Civil War," and "The Third Reich" series. Contributor to *Encyclopedia Americana* and *Random House Dictionary;* contributor to magazines, including *Military Collector* and *Historian.*

SIDELIGHTS: In *Swords around a Throne: Napoleon's Grande Armee,* which *Washington Post Book World* contributor Douglas Porch calls a "thorough and immensely entertaining book," Napoleonic historian John R. Elting "explains how Napoleon managed to meld 1.35 million French conscripts, . . . numerous French volunteers and legions of foreigners into a force that, between 1800 and 1815, deprived European diplomacy of much of its creativity." In detailing the numerous operations of Napoleon's forces, "almost no aspect of the life of the Grande Armee escapes Elting's attentions," the critic remarks; William Jackson explains in the London *Times* that in this "exceptional" book "Elting creates a fascinating picture of the people, their motives and their methods. . . . He exposes to our gaze all the inner workings of that incredibly complex human organism." As Porch concludes: "What is certain is that, as a social history of the men who made the Napoleonic era such a dynamic one, *Swords around a Throne* is unlikely to be surpassed."

Elting once told *CA:* "Military history and military intelligence are similar, and fascinating, disciplines. The military historian collects bits of information, sometimes conflicting, and must sift through them and put together a picture of events that makes sense. It's worse than any jigsaw puzzle, because many of those bits will prove false and must be discarded. After you at last get the job done, there may be additional frustrations—higher headquarters may ignore or flinch from acting on your intelligence estimate or the publisher may refuse your book.

"Sifting through military reports and serving, however briefly, in Bill Mauldin's fraternity of 'them as gets shot at' can give you a cynical outlook on our military past. My writing of *The Battle of Bunker's Hill* and *The Battles of Saratoga* was much inspired by a vast mistrust of the accepted versions of both and wonder as to what actually happened. As usual, once I had dug down, the facts were much more interesting than the fables. I've written some books—*Battles for Scandinavia, American Army Life, The Superstrategists*—because a publisher wanted them, and I concluded that I had a few useful ideas on the subjects.

"The longer I work at military history, the more impressed I am with how much I still have to learn. To merely scratch the surface, a military historian needs to know the weapons of the period he proposes to cover—their range, rate of fire, accuracy, reliability; he needs to know the means of transportation available for supply and the roads, rivers, seas, and canals by which supplies can be moved; and he needs to know the clothing and equipment of the individual soldier, the means of transmitting orders and information, the medical problems, weather, and terrain."

BIOGRAPHICAL/CRITICAL SOURCES:

PERIODICALS

Times (London), May 27, 1989.
Washington Post Book World, November 13, 1988.

* * *

EPSTEIN, June

PERSONAL: Born in Perth, Australia; daughter of Simon (in business) and Annie (Walters) Epstein; married Julius Guest (a lecturer in mathematics), March 7, 1949; children: Katharine-Anne, John Carey, Philip Ross (deceased). *Education:* Trinity College of Music, London, Licentiate; Royal Academy of Music, Licentiate; Royal Schools of Music, Licentiate.

ADDRESSES: *Home*—Victoria, Australia.

CAREER: Australian Broadcasting Commission, Melbourne, Australia, broadcaster and scriptwriter, 1933—; director of music at Melbourne Church of England Girls' Grammar School, 1946-49; Melbourne College of Advanced Education, Institute of Early Childhood Development, Kew, Australia, senior lecturer, 1972-78; University of Melbourne, School of Education, currently affiliated with Institute of Early Childhood Studies.

MEMBER: Australian Society of Authors, Fellowship of Australian Writers, Society of Women Writers, Kew Cottages' Parents' Association (foundation president, 1957).

AWARDS, HONORS: Overseas scholar at Trinity College of Music, London, 1936-39; silver medal from Worshipful Company of Musicians, 1938; Literature Board of the Australia Council grant, 1973 and 1982; Best Children's Book Award, Royal Zoological Society of New South Wales, 1981, for *The Friends of Burramys;* Rigby Literary Award, 1982, for *Scarecrow and Company;* Order of Australia Medal for services to the arts and to people with disabilities.

WRITINGS:

The Nine Muses, Robertson & Mullens, 1951.
Mermaid on Wheels: The Story of Margaret Lester, Ure Smith, 1967, Taplinger (New York City), 1968.
Image of the King: A Parent's Story of Mentally Handicapped Children, Ure Smith, 1970.
Enjoying Music with Young Children, Allans, 1972, second edition, 1984.
A Paltry Affair, first produced in Victoria, Australia, November, 1976.
Mr. Nightingale, Allans, 1978.
Boy on Sticks, National Press, 1979.
No Music by Request: A Portrait of the Gorman Family, Collins, 1980.
A Golden String: The Story of Dorothy J. Ross, Greenhouse, 1981.
The Friends of Burramys, Oxford University Press (Oxford), 1981.
A Swag of Songs (with cassette), Oxford University Press, 1984.
Scarecrow and Company, Rigby, 1984.
The Icecream Kids, Jacaranda-Wiley, 1984.
The Emperor's Tally, Jacaranda-Wiley, 1984.
Concert Pitch: The Story of the National Music Camp Association and the Australian Youth Orchestra, Hyland House, 1984.
A Second Swag of Songs (with cassette), Oxford University Press, 1986.
Woman with Two Hats, Hyland House, 1988.
Turn a Deaf Ear: The Story of the Bionic Ear, Hyland House, 1989.
Rosalie McCutcheon: A Memoir, Rosalie McCutcheon Memorial, 1993.

"BIG DIPPER" SERIES; WITH CASSETTES

Big Dipper, Oxford University Press, 1981.
Big Dipper Rides Again, Oxford University Press, 1982.
Big Dipper Returns, Oxford University Press, 1985.
Big Dipper Songs, Oxford University Press, 1985.

OTHER

Also author of educational recordings for children and composer of music. Music critic, *Australian Journal of Music Education.*

SIDELIGHTS: June Epstein once told *CA:* "I've always combined the two professional careers of music and writing. In music I began in childhood as a concert pianist, studied on an overseas scholarship, returned to tour Australia as a concert pianist for the Australian Broadcasting Commission, and later became involved in music education.

"In writing I have been influenced by my great interest and involvement with handicapped people and have written three full-length biographies of people with different handicaps, as well as a number of other books concerning disabilities. I also write many books for children of different ages."

* * *

ESMEIN, Jean 1923-

PERSONAL: Born December 1, 1923, in Poitiers, France; son of Paul (a law professor and author) and Marcelle (Roux) Esmein; married Suzanne Esteve (a museum librarian), August 4, 1945; children: Pierre, Bernard. *Ethnicity:* "French by origin." *Education:* Ecole Nationale des Langues Orientales Vivantes, diploma, 1956; Ecole Pratique des Hautes Etudes, titulaire, 1958; Tokyo University, graduate study, 1971, D.Litt., 1983.

ADDRESSES: Home—25 Rue Gay Lussac, Paris, France 75005. *Office*—Maitre de Recherche, Groupe D'Etude de Civilisation Japonaise, Instituts D'Asie du College de France, 52 Rue du Cardinal Lemoine, Paris, France 75005. *E-mail*—irene.schaeffer@u-paris10.fr; fax: 33-134710680.

CAREER: Marine Nationale (French Navy), career officer, 1942-58, became commander; Compagnie des Machines Bull (computers), Paris, manager of scientific computing center, 1959-65; French Embassy, Peking, China, press attache, 1965-68; Credit Lyonnais (bank), Tokyo, Japan, representative for the Far East, beginning 1969; INSEAD (European Business Administration Institute), Euro-Asia Centre, Fontainebleau, France, secretary general, 1979-82; Credit Lyonnais, Bombay, India, general representative for South Asia, 1982-84; CESTA, Paris, associate professor, 1985-88; University of Technology of Compiegne, Compiegne, France, associate professor, 1989-91; CEREM, CNRS-Universite Paris X, Nanterre, director of research, 1992—.

MEMBER: Association for Computing Machinery, Computers Art Society, Strategic Management Society, Academie de Marine, Association du Pacte d'Amitie Kyoto-Paris (assistant secretary general, 1958—).

AWARDS, HONORS: Prix Jean Mermoz, 1979, for body of literary work. Military: Croix du Combattant, Croix de Guerre, Officier de la Legion d'Honneur.

WRITINGS:

La Revolution culturelle chinoise, Le Seuil, 1970, translation by W. J. F. Jenner published as *The Chinese Cultural Revolution,* Doubleday (New York City), 1973.
(Contributor) *Melanges offerts a M. Charles Haguenauer,* Asiatheque, 1980.
1/2+, un demi plus, Fondation pour les Etudes de Defense Nationale, 1983.
L'Evolution des Systemes Japonais, Documentation Francaise, 1986.
Les Bases de la Puissance du Japon, College de France, Documentation Francaise, 1988.
(Contributor) *Histoire du Japon,* Horvath, 1990.
Pouvoir Politique au Japon, POF, 1994.

Contributor to *Larousse Encyclopedique* and *Universalia.*

WORK IN PROGRESS: Translating Ooka Shohei's *Leyte Senki* ("Chroniques de la bataille de Leyte"); translating Sakurai Tokutaro's *Nihon no Shamanizumu* ("Le chamanisme Japonais").

SIDELIGHTS: Jean Esmein told *CA:* "Through the books I write, I wish to release the history of what could have happened together with what did really happen. Raymond Aron influenced my work, and now the most striking model for me is Umberto Eco."

BIOGRAPHICAL/CRITICAL SOURCES:

PERIODICALS

Times Literary Supplement, May 28, 1970; May 21, 1976.

* * *

ESSLINGER, Pat M.
See CARR, Pat

* * *

EVANS, David Allan 1940-

PERSONAL: Born April 11, 1940, in Sioux City, IA; son of Arthur Clarence (an editor) and Ruth (Lyle) Evans; married Janice Kay (a secretary), July 4, 1958; children: Shelly, David Jr., Karlin. *Ethnicity:* "Caucasian." *Education:* Attended Augustana College, Sioux Falls, SD, 1958-60; Morningside College, B.A., 1962; University of Iowa, M.A., 1964; University of Arkansas, M.F.A., 1971. *Politics:* Democrat.

ADDRESSES: Home—1432 2nd St., Brookings, SD 57006. *Office*— English Department, Box 504 Scobey Hall, South Dakota State University, Brookings, SD 57007. *E-mail*—evans@brookings.net.

CAREER: Marshalltown Community College, Marshalltown, IA, instructor in English, 1964-65; Adams State College, Alamosa, CO, assistant professor of English, 1966-68; South Dakota State University, Brookings, assistant professor, 1968-75, associate professor, 1975-78, professor of English, 1978—. Artist in the Schools residencies, South Dakota Arts Council, 1973—, and Iowa Arts Council, 1975; writer and scholar in residence, Wayne State College, Wayne, NE, 1980.

MEMBER: Poetry Society of America, Association of Writers Programs, Sports Literature Association.

AWARDS, HONORS: Borestone Poetry Award, 1969; Breadloaf scholar, 1973; National Endowment for the Arts grant, 1974; writing grant, South Dakota Arts Council, 1982 and 1989; South Dakota Centennial Poet, 1989; Butler Award, South Dakota State University, 1989, for excellence through innovative and creative activity; Bush Artist fellowship, 1990; Fulbright scholar in People's Republic of China, 1992-93; Pushcart Prize nomination, 1995.

WRITINGS:

(Editor with Tom Kakonis) *From Language to Idea,* Holt (New York City), 1971.

(Editor with Kakonis) *Statement and Craft,* Prentice-Hall (Englewood Cliffs, NJ), 1972.

Among Athletes (poems), Folder Editions (New York City), 1972.

(Editor) *New Voices in American Poetry,* Winthrop, 1973.

Train Windows (poems), Ohio University Press (Athens), 1976.

(Contributor) *A Book of Readings,* Best Cellar Press (Rochester, NY), 1979.

(Coeditor) *The Poetry of Sport/The Sport of Poetry,* South Dakota State University Foundation (Brookings), 1979.

(General editor and contributor) *What the Tallgrass Says* (prose), Center for Western Studies (Sioux Falls, SD), 1982.

Real and False Alarms (poems), BkMk Press (Kansas City, MO), 1985.

Remembering the Soos (prose), Plains Press (Marshall, MN), 1986.

Hanging Out with the Crows (poems), BkMk Press, 1991.

(With wife, Jan Evans) *Double Happiness: Two Lives in China* (prose), University of South Dakota Press (Vermillion), 1995.

Contributor of poetry to numerous anthologies. Contributor of poems to periodicals, including *Esquire, Prairie Schooner, Poetry Northwest, Poetry Now, Bloomsbury Review, Saturday Review, New York Times, Shenandoah, Kansas Quarterly,* and *North American Review.*

WORK IN PROGRESS: Body Songs (poems), *Short Cut and Other Stories* (short stories), *Letters from My Father* (essays).

SIDELIGHTS: David Allan Evans told *CA:* "In the last half decade I've been writing more prose than poetry. I write almost every day. I still find a lot of my ideas and images in sports, if only for the reason that I have always been physically active.

"Since my high school years when my father talked about Darwin and Huxley, and especially since college, where I majored in biology for a time, I've been very intrigued by natural selection. I want to write about what one well-known recent biologist called the 'greatest intellectual advance of the twentieth century'—namely, the new findings about human nature. A writer can't overlook the important ideas in science in his or her own time. Furthermore, writers and artists are students of human nature. They have an insatiable curiosity about why we are here, who we are, where we are going. I plan to write about the Darwinian paradigm: in poems, stories, and essays, and hope to eventually publish a book on the subject."

F

FARRELL, Ben
See CEBULASH, Mel

* * *

FELDMAN, Ruth 1911-

PERSONAL: Born May 21, 1911, in East Liverpool, OH; daughter of Mendel (in business) and May (a musician; maiden name, Rosenthal) Wasby; married Moses D. Feldman (a lawyer), May 3, 1934 (died March 4, 1963). *Education:* Attended Western Reserve University (now Case Western Reserve University), 1927-29; Wellesley College, B.A., 1931.

ADDRESSES: Home and office—221 Mount Auburn St. Apt. 307, Cambridge, MA 02138-4847.

CAREER: Painter; work exhibited in shows. Poet, translator and editor. Has lectured at numerous universities and institutions in the United States and Italy, including Harvard University, Cornell University, Brandeis University, Boston University, Princeton University, University of Pennsylvania, Catholic University, Tufts University, Middlebury College, University of Bologna, University of Urbino, La Sapienza (Rome), and University of Venice.

MEMBER: American Literary Translators Association, Poetry Society of America.

AWARDS, HONORS: Devil's Advocate award, Poetry Society of America, 1971, for "Delos"; John Florio Award, Translators Association (England), 1976, for translating *Shema: Collected Poems of Primo Levi;* Members' Prize, New England Poetry Club, 1977; Sotheby's International Poetry Competition Prize, 1982, for "Eden"; International Translator's Prize, Circe Sabaudia (Italy), 1984; literary translators fellowship, National Endowment for the Arts, 1988.

WRITINGS:

POETRY

The Ambition of Ghosts, Green River Press (University Center, MI), 1979.
Poesie di Ruth Feldman, La Giuntina, 1981.
To Whom It May Concern, William Bauhan (Dublin, NH), 1986.
Perdere la strada nel tempo, Edizioni del Leone (Venice), 1990.
Birthmark, Cross-cultural Communications (Merrick, NY), 1993.

EDITOR AND TRANSLATOR; WITH BRIAN SWANN

Lucio Piccolo, *Collected Poems of Lucio Piccolo,* Princeton University Press (Princeton, NJ), 1972.
Andrea Zanzotto, *Selected Poetry of Andrea Zanzotto,* Princeton University Press, 1975.
Primo Levi, *Shema: Collected Poems of Primo Levi,* Menard Press, 1976.
Italian Poetry Today, New Rivers Press (St. Paul, MN), 1979.
Rocco Scotellaro, *The Dawn Is Always New: Selected Poetry of Rocco Scotellaro,* Princeton University Press, 1980.
Vittorio Bodini, *The Hands of the South: Selected Poetry of Vittorio Bodini,* Charioteer Press (Washington, DC), 1981.

Bartolo Cattafi, *The Dry Air of the Fire: Selected Poetry of Bartolo Cattafi,* Ardis (Ann Arbor, MI), 1982.

Primo Levi, *The Collected Poems of Primo Levi,* Faber & Faber (Winchester, MA), 1988.

TRANSLATOR

Primo Levi, *Moments of Reprieve,* Summit Books (New York City), 1986.

Margherita Guidacci, *Liber Fulguralis: Poems of Margherita Guidacci,* University of Messina Press, 1986.

Guidacci, *A Book of Sibyls,* Rowan Tree (Boston), 1989.

Guidacci, *Landscape with Ruins: Selected Poetry of Margherita Guidacci,* Wayne State University Press (Detroit), 1992.

(With John Welle) Andrea Zanzotto, *Peasants Wake and Other Poems,* University of Illinois Press (Champaign), 1997.

Contributor to various anthologies, including *Penguin Book of Women Poets,* Penguin (New York City), 1978; *A Book of Women Poets,* Schocken (New York City), 1980; *Anthology of Magazine Verse,* Monitor (Beverly Hills, CA), 1981; *Literary Olympians II,* Crosscurrents, 1987; *Editor's Choice II,* Spirit That Moves Us (Iowa City, IA), 1987; *Women at War,* Simon & Schuster (New York City), 1988; *The Age of Koestler,* Practices of the Wind, 1994; and *The Vintage Book of World Poetry,* Random House (New York City), 1996.

Also contributor to *Affinities I,* Latitudes Press; *Border Crossings,* Latitudes Press; and the *New York Times Book of Verse.* Contributor of poems and translations to numerous magazines and newspapers, including *Nation, Southern Review, AGNI, Sewanee Review, Nimrod, Yankee, Malahat Review, Yale Review, New York Times,* and *Prairie Schooner.* Coeditor, *Modern Poetry in Translation,* 1975.

SIDELIGHTS: Ruth Feldman once told *CA:* "I have loved Italy since my first trip there in 1936. I have worked with and visited many of Italy's leading poets. I find translating a constant and fascinating challenge. It is too often poorly done. My original motivation remains the same: to make things I like and admire accessible to people who do not know Italian, while preserving the language's spirit and style. I started writing my own poetry ten months after my husband died."

Many of Feldman's poems have been translated into Italian and published in Italian magazines. Her poems have also been translated into French, Spanish, and Bengali.

* * *

FENNER, Carol (Elizabeth) 1929-

PERSONAL: Born September 30, 1929, in Almond, NY; daughter of Andrew J. and Esther (Rowe) Fenner; married Jiles B. Williams (a retired U.S. Air Force major), July 3, 1965. *Avocational interests:* Horses, tennis, swimming, cooking, gardening.

ADDRESSES: Home—190 Rebecca Rd., Battle Creek, MI 49015-4137.

CAREER: Writer, illustrator, publicist, lecturer, and instructor. Member of Michigan Council for the Arts Literature Panel, 1976-79.

MEMBER: Authors Guild, Authors League of America, Society of Children's Book Writers and Illustrators.

AWARDS, HONORS: American Library Association (ALA) Notable Book citation, 1963, for *Tigers in the Cellar;* Coretta Scott King Freedom Award Runner-up, 1970, for *The Skates of Uncle Richard;* Christopher Medal, Library of Congress Book of the Year, Outstanding Science Trade Book for Children citation, and ALA Notable Book citation, all 1973, all for *Gorilla, Gorilla;* Michigan Council for the Arts Literature Grant, 1982; *Randall's Wall* was named to Readers' Choice Master Lists in eight states, 1991-92, and received a Maryland Children's Choice Book Award, Maryland International Reading Association Council; Newbery Honor Book, American Library Association, 1996, for *Yolonda's Genius.*

WRITINGS:

Gorilla, Gorilla, illustrated by Symeon Shimin, Random House (New York City), 1973.

The Skates of Uncle Richard, illustrated by Ati Forberg, Random House, 1978.

Saving Amelia Earhart, Wayne State University Press (Detroit), 1982.

A Summer of Horses, Knopf (New York City), 1989.
Randall's Wall, McElderry Books (New York City), 1991.
Yolonda's Genius, McElderry Books, 1995.

SELF-ILLUSTRATED

Tigers in the Cellar, Harcourt (San Diego), 1963.
Christmas Tree on the Mountain, Harcourt, 1966.
Lagalag, the Wanderer, Harcourt, 1968.

OTHER

Contributor of stories to magazines, including *Cricket* and *Kalamazoo Collective.*

ADAPTATIONS: The Skates of Uncle Richard was released on videocassette, Children's Television International, 1979.

WORK IN PROGRESS: At the Sugar Island Cafe, an adult novel; an untitled work about a homeless boy who lives in an abandoned hall of justice; an untitled story about Fenner's mother's childhood.

SIDELIGHTS: "It was spring when I wrote my first poem—about dandelions," children's book author and illustrator Carol Fenner once said. "I sat in a field of grass and sun and dandelions and felt a sudden richness, such a fullness, that I needed to say something. *Name* something. *A dandelion so fair/Had the prettiest hair.* The words were there in my head. I said them over and over to myself. I was about five or less and couldn't write yet. I ran to my mother with the poem dancing in my head. *One day I again was there/The dandelion grew old/And had white hair.* After that, my mother wrote down all my gems until I learned to write them down myself. My mother says I would come in from playing and tell her, 'I feel a poem coming on.'"

Born in the fall of 1929 in Almond, New York, Fenner spent parts of her childhood in Brooklyn and rural Connecticut. The oldest of five children, she considers herself and her siblings lucky to have had their "magic" aunt, Phyllis Fenner, a librarian, anthologist, reviewer, and writer about books for young people. "Whenever we could capture her, Phyllis told us unforgettable fairy tales drenched with her own excitement and pleasure," Fenner recalled. "I can still hear her voice dropping to a low chant when the Wee Red Man '*blew* the bellows and *blew* the bellows and *blew* the bellows. . . .'" Phyllis Fenner also provided her nieces and nephews with every wonderful children's book in print. "Phyl was for me, when I was a child," remarked Fenner, "and up until she died in her eighties, a treat the way ice cream is. She has been a delightful and unpretentious influence."

Fenner attributes her love of "cadence and word shape, the way words color each other," to her Aunt Phyl and to her mother, Esther, who read poetry aloud at bedtime in a voice that "purred with wonder." Fenner says she "loves to read aloud," even "to herself if no one is about, to hear the shape of the words." As a child, she read to her sister Faith and her best friend, Grace Marie, the three of them lying across the beds in the room the sisters shared. She read aloud poetry and stories that intrigued her, as well as her own writings. At the age of eleven, plays became the focus of Fenner's writing, and once complete these plays would be performed in the basement. "We performed my *A Modern Version of Romeo & Juliet—A Comedy* and an enthralling drama I entitled *The Mystery of the Arabian Dagger* (I thought of the title first, a practice I now warn against as the play had no dagger and no mystery and only as an afterthought did I write in Arabians)," Fenner explained. Novels were the next genre Fenner tackled as she moved into her teenage years. She remarked, "As a teenager, I began a novel about Joan of Arc because, at my hormonal dawn, I couldn't understand why Joan didn't fall in love with at least one of her soldiers. Although the world has not missed this uncompleted work, age and experience have not invalidated my original puzzlement. What *were* Joan's hormones doing?"

In addition to her writing, Fenner developed an interest in drawing while growing up, utilizing both her talents in her first three children's books. "I don't remember when I began to draw," she commented. "It seems as if I have always done it. I have no formal training in either writing or drawing but I'm an inveterate reader and I have an artist's eye, under-developed though it may be. I love words more than light and line; I love the shapes they make on the page, the way they rub against each other making different sounds. I love reading out loud to myself, to others. I enjoy writing more than drawing because spending words comes from delight and pleasure and need, whereas drawing is something I *can* do but am not compelled to."

Among these first picture books are *Tigers in the Cellar,* a story of a young girl who hears tigers in the cellar when she is in bed, and *Christmas Tree on the Mountain,* which follows three siblings as they search for and bring home the perfect Christmas tree for their family. A *Horn Book* reviewer describes *Tigers in the Cellar* as "a poetic, completely harmonious and beautiful picture book." And Ethel L. Heins, also writing in *Horn Book,* similarly points out that *Christmas Tree on the Mountain* is "a tender, childlike story written and illustrated with artless charm."

"Although my first two published stories, both picture books which I illustrated, were the capturing and holding of memories, most of my writing is still an exploration into that which perplexes, disturbs, or excites me," Fenner related. And so the inspiration for *Gorilla, Gorilla* was an actual gorilla Fenner encountered at Ueno Park Zoo in Tokyo. Based on this experience and additional research, Fenner created the story of a young gorilla who lives in the wild until he is captured and taken to a zoo. In his new surroundings, the gorilla is lifeless, until a young female is placed in the next cage; he then performs the same ritual of chest thumping and hooting he witnessed while still in the jungle. *Gorilla, Gorilla* is "an effectively personalized animal biography," writes Joyce Alpern in *Kirkus Reviews,* adding that the story is "a sound and vividly empathic account." A *Publishers Weekly* contributor states, "The illustrations are spellbinding and so is the story."

The hopes and dreams of a young girl are the focus of Fenner's 1978 story *The Skates of Uncle Richard.* Secretly dreaming of becoming a champion figure skater, Marsha wants nothing more than a gleaming new pair of ice skates for Christmas. Instead, though, she receives her Uncle Richard's old, ugly hockey skates that her mother has been saving for her. At first disappointed and a poor skater, Marsha begins to improve and reach for her dream again with the help of her Uncle Richard and his skates. *The Skates of Uncle Richard* is "an unpretentious story . . . told and pictured with sensitivity and care," relates Heins in her *Horn Book* review. A *Bulletin of the Center for Children's Books* contributor further asserts: "Fenner has an easy, natural writing style that has convincing dialogue and a smooth narrative flow."

Also written with a sympathetic slant, *Randall's Wall,* like *Gorilla, Gorilla,* began because of one of Fenner's real-life experiences. Fenner told *CA:* "*Randall's Wall* practically wrote itself, stimulated by an encounter with the dirtiest boy I have ever seen and whom I couldn't get out of my mind." Randall is just as dirty as his inspiration, but he is also withdrawn and friendless because of his home life (he lives with an abusive father and detached mother in a house with no running water). To escape his problems, Randall constructs "the wall," which is a barrier between himself and the outside world until a fellow classmate breaks it. Jean is also somewhat of an outcast, and the first thing she does is take Randall home and give him a bath. As their ensuing friendship develops Randall's wall falls down and his significant artistic talents are discovered at the same time.

"Fenner presents a disturbing yet believable story of a down-and-out family who has fallen through the cracks of the system," observes Laura Culberg in *School Library Journal.* Nancy Vasilakis, writing in *Horn Book,* also finds *Randall's Wall* to be a believable tale, stating that Randall's "story is achingly sad, but understated nonetheless. The characterizations are excellent, and the language is metaphoric and compelling." *Voice of Youth Advocates* reviewer Margaret Galloway similarly asserts that "Fenner's characters are drawn from real life and her story line is humorous and fast paced," and Culberg concludes that *Randall's Wall* is "a well-written, compassionate story."

Yolonda is close in age to Randall but experiences much different problems in Fenner's 1995 Newbery Honor Book *Yolonda's Genius.* Having just moved from Chicago to a Michigan suburb, Yolonda finds herself isolated because of her obesity and intellectual level. Eventually making a new friend who thinks she is a genius, Yolonda looks the word up in the dictionary and comes to the conclusion that her younger, slower brother Andrew is actually the genius. Trying to convince everyone else of his musical talents (he plays the harmonica), Yolonda gets Andrew backstage during a blues festival and he ends up on stage where his talents are finally revealed.

Fenner's "descriptions of Andrew's thoughts, his relationship with music, and perceptions of the world around him are thought-provoking and lyrical," relates Carol Jones Collins in her *School Library Journal* review of *Yolonda's Genius.* Lauren Peterson asserts in *Booklist* that "dynamic characters and fresh dialogue combine with a compelling story line to draw reader's into Yolonda's world." Vasilakis states in her *Horn Book* review that *Yolonda's Genius* "is suffused with humor and spirit and proves, as Yolonda comes to realize, that genius comes in many surprising forms."

Fenner told *CA,* "My husband . . . is responsible for my 'discovery' of Yolonda; it is his passion for live music which initiates visits to Chicago, Indianapolis, Toronto—whatever city is hosting jazz or blues festivals. His wanderlust also took us to Japan in the late sixties." Of her current work, she said, "Presently, I am setting aside work on an adult novel because of the fructifying stirrings of another book for young readers about a boy who lives in an abandoned hall of justice in the downtown of a small city. Who knows where it will lead? I am eager to take this journey, too."

BIOGRAPHICAL/CRITICAL SOURCES:

PERIODICALS

Booklist, August, 1989, p. 1974; April 1, 1991, p. 1567; June 1, 1995, pp. 1769-1770.

Bulletin of the Center for Children's Books, March, 1979.

Horn Book, April, 1963; December, 1966; April, 1979, p. 191; July/August, 1991, pp. 455-456; September/October, 1995, p. 598.

Kirkus Reviews, February 15, 1973, p. 190; June 15, 1989, p. 915.

Publishers Weekly, February 5, 1973, p. 89; June 19, 1995, p. 61.

School Library Journal, August, 1989, p. 139; April, 1991, p. 118; July, 1995, pp. 76, 78.

Voice of Youth Advocates, April, 1991, pp. 29-30.

* * *

FERGUSON, Helen
See KAVAN, Anna

* * *

FERRY, Charles 1927-

PERSONAL: Born October 8, 1927, in Chicago, IL; son of Ignatius Loyola (a postal clerk) and Madelyn Anne (Bartholemew) Ferry; married Ruth Louise Merz (an executive travel coordinator), September 26, 1958; children: Ronald Edmund Richardson (stepson). *Education:* Attended University of Illinois, 1952. *Politics:* Republican. *Religion:* Episcopalian. *Avocational interests:* "I cook, bake bread, and tutor persons of all ages in writing."

ADDRESSES: Home—Rochester Hills, MI. *Office*—Daisy Hill Press, P.O. Box 1681, Rochester, MI 48308.

CAREER: Radio and newspaper journalist, 1949-71; writer, 1971—. *Military service:* U.S. Navy, 1944-49.

AWARDS, HONORS: Best Children's Book, Friends of American Writers, Best Books of the Year selection, *School Library Journal,* and Best Books for Young Adults, American Library Association (ALA), all 1983, all for *Raspberry One;* Best Book for Young Adults, ALA, 1993, Books for the Teen Age, New York Public Library, 1994, and Best Book for High School Seniors, National Council of Teachers of English, 1995, all for *Binge.*

WRITINGS:

Up in Sister Bay, Houghton (Boston), 1975.

O Zebron Falls!, Houghton, 1977.

Raspberry One, Houghton, 1983.

One More Time!, Houghton, 1985.

Binge, Daisy Hill Press (Rochester, MI), 1992.

A Fresh Start, Proctor Publications (Ann Arbor, MI), 1996.

Love, Proctor Publications, in press.

ADAPTATIONS: Binge was optioned for film by Walt Disney Educational Productions.

SIDELIGHTS: A career as a children's book writer came relatively late in life for Charles Ferry. After working as a journalist and in related fields for several years, Ferry began writing his first book for young readers after he had reached his forties. Prompted by recollections of his own wide-ranging life experiences—from happy childhood vacations in the northern United States to tragic adult years during which his life was controlled by a growing dependence on alcohol—Ferry published the first of several novels that would vividly recreate young peoples' movement toward adulthood. While his early novels take place during the years surrounding World War II, his later fiction deals with contemporary—and controversial—topics, including alcoholism. "I have no interest in writing for adults," Ferry once told *CA*. "In general, I think the best writing is being done in the children's field. Authors have the freedom to give of themselves and to dream a little."

"I began writing vignettes about my boyhood summers in northern Wisconsin," Ferry once explained to *CA,* describing how he "eased into the role of author." He eventually collected these vignettes into the manuscript of his first novel, *Up in Sister Bay,* which was published in 1975. Set in northern Wisconsin in the year 1939, the story revolves around the challenges facing four teens during wartime. "In *Up in Sister Bay,* Hitler's armies invade Poland," the author noted, "triggering the war and changing the lives of simple people."

Up in Sister Bay would be the first of Ferry's books to illuminate the events of everyday life during the World War II era. 1977's *O Zebron Falls!* portrays a young woman approaching high school graduation, whose efforts to find a direction in her life are complicated by an unresolved conflict with her father and the onset of the Second World War. Sixteen-year-old Lukie Bishop tries to get the most from her last year in school, knowing her future as a woman in a small Midwestern town is limited. At a glance, Lukie's life seems idyllic—she's elected Class Sweetheart, serves as homecoming chairman, and enjoys the company of Billy Butts, football hero and school valedictorian. However, readers soon understand Lukie's sorrows. Her relationship with Billy, an African American, can never become serious because of the townspeople's prejudices; her uncle dies in a munitions factory while contributing to the war effort; and her elders suggest she should limit her goals to teaching or nursing, respectable professions for women. Critics praised Ferry for writing about times long past without sugar-coating or ignoring the difficulties young adults experienced. Marianne M. Rafalko, writing in *Best Sellers,* commended Ferry for his perceptive portrayal of a teenage girl of the 1940s, saying "today's young reader may readily identify with her problems and fears: growing up, falling in love, maturing sexually, relating to one's parents, and deciding one's future." In a *Horn Book* review, Ann A. Flowers applauded *O Zebron Falls!,* asserting that it "contains the sweetness of a simpler time but emphasizes that every era has its unsolvable problems."

Ferry's award-winning *Raspberry One,* published in 1983, also focuses on the tensions young Americans felt during the Second World War. The young protagonist, Nick Enright, attempts to deal with the brutalizing effects of combat while serving aboard a U.S. Navy torpedo bomber destined to fight in the bloody battle for control of the island of Iwo Jima. " *O Zebron Falls!* deals with life on the wartime home front, while *Raspberry One,* a hard look at the horrors of war, ends with V-J Day and victory," explained Ferry. "Prior to that war, in 1936, President Franklin Delano Roosevelt had told his countrymen, 'To some generations, much is given. Of some generations, much is expected. This generation of Americans has a rendezvous with destiny.' That generation had an awesome rendezvous, with history's greatest war," Ferry maintained, "and it acquitted itself admirably." Because he had never actually experienced a combat situation, Ferry put an enormous amount of effort into researching the historic backdrop of *Raspberry One.* He once said in a *Horn Book* article, "For two years . . . I relived the war, in all of its theaters. God, what a horror! . . . *Raspberry One* is my little prayer that it will never happen again." Ferry expects that his first four titles will soon be reissued, in a boxed set, as "The Rendezvous Quartet."

Calling the characters in *Raspberry One* "well-realized," Micki S. Nevett in *Voice of Youth Advocates* remarked on Ferry's ability to dramatize war without glorifying it and suggested the novel will give new readers an idea of "what a generation of young people in the 1940s experienced." In *School Library Journal,* reviewer David A. Lindsey appreciated Ferry's war narrative as a refreshing change of pace and described *Raspberry One* as being "long on action and strong in characterization."

Another of Ferry's historical novels, 1985's *One More Time!,* takes place during the same period, depicting the impact of the Japanese attack on Pearl Harbor on an older group of Americans: the members of a popular Big Band dance orchestra. Ferry details the life of a musician and American culture in general during the Big Band era. Writing in *Booklist,* Stephanie Zvirin complimented Ferry on "capturing the nostalgia and the trepidation of the American people" during the 1940s as they prepared for the "unknown." While admitting *One More Time!* may appeal to a smaller audience because of its subject, *School Library Journal* contributor Lindsey praised the novel's "well-crafted narrative," adding that Ferry presents solidly constructed characters and provides readers "a detailed knowledge of the milieu in which [these characters] live."

"In the writing of my first four titles, I was keenly aware that I was probably creating the most important body of work on life in America during World War II ever written for young people," Ferry once disclosed to *CA.* "I knew that because I was drawing heavily from personal experience and was confident of the integrity of my work." While providing his readers with a vivid recreation of life in the United States during wartime, Ferry also accomplished something of a personal nature while writing those first four novels. "I had an ambivalent relationship with my father," he explained to *CA.* "As a result, when I started my creative writing, I couldn't handle a father as a fictional character, even though my own father had passed away fifteen years earlier.

"And so in *Up in Sister Bay,* I wrote the father out of the story. He is away in Chicago looking for work. We learn about him indirectly through his son, Robbie, who remembers unkind things about him: his meanness, his drinking, things that applied to my own father. Yet it is clear that Robbie loves his father and looks up to him—again reflecting my own situation.

"In my second book, I could handle a father, but he is a gruff man who embarrasses his daughter in front of her friends, which my father often did. Then, in my third book, *Raspberry One,* the character George Enright is a marvelous father. The self-therapy had worked; I had come to terms with my own father. In researching that book, I learned about the horrors he had experienced in World War I. I came to understand him and to realize that I loved him dearly—and still do."

At this point in his career as an author, all of Ferry's books had focused on the lives of young people during the period of his own adolescence. A change in direction came in the 1990s with the publication of *Binge.* Considering it "the most personally important book" he would ever write, Ferry bravely confronted the reality of the addiction that had diminished his own life, career, and relationships with family and friends for more than two decades. "For much of my life I was plagued by the ravages of alcohol," he told *CA.* "I could fill a large volume, recounting the horrors it caused in my life. [In the early 1970s], I finally whipped the problem. Still, hardly a night goes by that some bad memory of that period doesn't return to haunt me." In his essay for *Something about the Author Autobiography Series,* Ferry shares how alcohol consumed his life for over twenty-five years, leading him to commit crimes and even spend time in prison. "Why was I sent to prison in the first place? Forgery, and uttering, and publishing—three-and-a-half to fourteen years. The sentence . . . may seem rather harsh, but it wasn't. [It] was merely the tip of the iceberg. [It] was the disgraceful culmination of my six-month, nine-state drinking binge. During that time I was a mini crime wave. Two stolen cars, one abandoned, one totaled. Five break-ins, most of them senseless. Bad checks, whenever I got my hands on a blank one. Larceny, whenever there was an opportunity. Anything to keep alcohol flowing through my bloodstream."

Ferry wanted to write these experiences out of his system; he did, publishing *Binge* in 1992. The story of Weldon Yeager, an eighteen-year-old petty criminal with a serious drinking problem, *Binge* follows its dissolute protagonist on a colossal binge that has tragic consequences. Waking up in a hospital ward under police guard—and not remembering how he got there—Weldon must eventually accept responsibility for actions that resulted in not only the loss of his own right foot, but in the deaths of two people struck and killed by the car he was driving. "If the book spares one young person the ravages of alcohol, I will consider it the greatest achievement of my life," Ferry declared. "You see, when I set out to write a young adult novel about how alcohol destroys young lives, my primary target was not young people who already have a drinking problem (although some would surely be influenced by such a book) but those who *don't,*" the author said in his *SAAS* essay. "Hopefully the images in *Binge* would remain fixed in the minds of some of them and spare them the horrors of alcoholism in future years. I would achieve that effect, I decided, with a short novel that could be read in one sitting and have a stunning impact on the reader."

Since its publication, critical reception has marked *Binge* a success: Mary K. Chelton in a review for *Voice of Youth Advocates* called the novel "an incredibly powerful, mesmerizing, tragic, read-in-one-sitting little book with an authenticity and understanding rare in adolescent literature." In the same publication, critic Carol Otis Hurst termed the work "a brutal book with a strong moral impact. It walks a thin line between being a tract on the evils of alcohol and a novelette and, thanks to the skills of Mr. Ferry, it succeeds."

Binge proved to be pivotal, both in the field of publishing as a whole—it was the first self-published book in the history of the American Library Association to receive an ALA Best Book citation—as well as in its author's personal life. "I had gone public with my troubled background: my twenty-five-year battle against alcohol, which had been a torment in my life: lost jobs, wrecked cars, dirty jail cells, prison. *Binge,* which tells a powerful story about how alcohol destroys young lives, was written as my personal redemption. When sixty-one mainstream publishers rejected it, I published the book myself . . . [and] when the American Library Association chose it as a Best Book for Young Adults, almost overnight I became something of a legend."

Ferry has continued writing in the candid, forthright vein characteristic of *Binge;* he released *A Fresh Start* in 1996. "*A Fresh Start* points the way to recovery from alcoholism [using] my Eight Steps to Sobriety and a Better You," the author explained. "This time, I ignored establishment publishers and went directly to small presses." The novel recounts the efforts of four high school seniors in fighting the demons of alcohol and regaining sobriety through an eight-step program that Ferry devised during his own recovery from alcoholism. After failing courses during their final year in school, these four students struggle to earn their diploma, all the while reflecting on how alcohol abuse has affected their relationships with friends, family, and classmates. In *Voice of Youth Advocates,* C. A. Nichols emphasized that *A Fresh Start*'s message would be lost if it were viewed as "a novel or short story." Instead the reviewer insisted the work be used "to empower teens (or adults) to examine and take control of their own lives."

A more recent novel, *Love,* departs from the topic of alcohol to focus on two terminally ill children—Robbie and Sue Ellen, both age eleven—and the strong bond of love that develops between them in a hospital cancer ward. "I think . . . *Love* is my best work to date," the author explained to *CA,* although he believes that, like *Binge, Love* will be regarded as controversial for dealing with issues that are not typical of children's literature.

Despite the controversy surrounding his most recent novels, Ferry remains dedicated to his work. "To one degree or another, all good fiction involves truth," he once told *CA*. "As William Faulkner put it, 'Truth is what a person holds to his or her heart.' What do my books offer that young people can hold to their hearts? It's not for me to say, really. My strong suit appears to be evoking mood and atmosphere. I tell stories of young people coming of age. . . . My books come from deep inside of me, and they are slow to develop." After more than two decades as a published author, Ferry continues to live modestly, researching, lecturing, and writing from his home in Rochester Hills, a suburb of Detroit, Michigan. There, he explains, "our gregarious Belgian sheepdog, Emily Anne, rules the household. My wife, Ruth, who is a partner in my work, and I have touched a lot of young lives throughout America. We feel privileged."

BIOGRAPHICAL/CRITICAL SOURCES:

PERIODICALS

Best Sellers, December, 1977, p. 293.

Booklist, May 15, 1983, p. 1196; May 15, 1985, p. 1325; March 15, 1993, p. 1342.

Children's Literature in Education, spring, 1985, pp. 15-20.

Horn Book, December, 1975, p. 601; October, 1977, p. 539; June, 1983, p. 310; December, 1983, p. 651; September-October, 1985, p. 563.

Kirkus Reviews, August 15, 1975, p. 924.

New York Times Book Review, November 2, 1975, p. 10; March 5, 1978, p. 26.

Publishers Weekly, March 29, 1985, p. 73.

School Library Journal, December, 1975, p. 59; October, 1977, p. 123; September, 1983, pp. 132-133; August, 1985, p. 74; May, 1996, p. 132.

Voice of Youth Advocates, April, 1984, p. 30; August, 1985, p. 183; June, 1993, p. 8; October, 1993, pp. 206-208; August, 1994; December, 1994, p. 272; October, 1996, p. 208.

* * *

FICKERT, Kurt J(on) 1920-

PERSONAL: Born December 19, 1920, in Pausa, Germany; son of Kurt Alfred (a mechanic) and Martha (Saerchinger) Fickert; married Lynn B. Janda, August 6, 1946; children: Linda (Mrs. Matthew Mosbacher), Jon, Chris. *Education:* Hofstra College (now University), A.B., 1941; New York University, M.A., 1947, Ph.D., 1952. *Politics:* Independent. *Religion:* Lutheran.

ADDRESSES: Home—33 South Kensington Pl., Springfield, OH 45504. *Office*—Department of Languages, Wittenberg University, Springfield, OH 45501.

CAREER: Hofstra College (now University), Hempstead, NY, instructor, 1947-52, assistant professor of German, 1952-53; Florida State University, Tallahassee, instructor in German, 1953-54; Fort Hays Kansas State College, Hays, assistant professor, 1956-60, associate professor, 1960-67, professor of German, 1967-86, professor emeritus, 1966—, adjunct professor, 1966-68, chair of department of languages, 1969-75. *Military service:* U.S. Army Air Forces, 1942-45; served in Pacific theater.

MEMBER: American Association of Teachers of German, German Studies Association, Ohio Poetry Day Association (president, 1971-75), Phi Eta Sigma, Phi Beta Kappa.

AWARDS, HONORS: Fulbright grant for teachers of German, Germany, 1957; Stephen Vincent Benet Narrative Poem Award, *Poet Lore,* 1968, for "Struggle with Loneliness;" citation for meritorious achievement, Society for German-American Studies, 1973; New England Prize, *Lyric,* 1976; second prize, Poets and Patrons, 1978; first prize, Yukuhara Haiku Society of Japan, 1978; first prize, Ohio Poetry Society, 1979; second prize, World Order of Narrative Poets, 1980, 1984; National Endowment for the Humanities grant, 1982; Panola Prize, *Lyric,* 1983; Poetry Prize, *Writer's Digest,* 1985; Broadside Series Winner, *The Red Pagoda,* 1987; first prize, Orbis Rhyme Revival Award; third prize, Erasmus Darwin Award, World Order of Narrative Poets, 1988.

WRITINGS:

To Heaven and Back: The New Morality in the Plays of Friedrich Duerrenmatt, University Press of Kentucky (Lexington), 1972.
Herman Hesse's Quest, York, 1978.
Kafka's Doubles, Peter Lang (New York City), 1979.
Signs and Portents: Myth in the Work of Wolfgang Borchert, York, 1980.
Franz Kafka: Life, Work, and Criticism, York, 1984.
Neither Left nor Right: The Politics of Individualism in Uwe Johnson's Work, Peter Lang, 1987.
End of a Mission: Kafka's Search for Truth in His Last Stories, Camden House (Columbia, SC), 1993.
Dialogue with the Reader: The Narrative Stance in Uwe Johnson's Fiction, Camden House, 1996.

CONTRIBUTOR

Anthology of German Poetry, Anchor Books (New York City), 1960.
(Author of introduction) Otto Dix, *Der Krieg,* Garland Publishing (New York City), 1972.
(Author of introduction) Ferdinand Avenarius, *Das Bild als Narr,* Garland Publishing, 1972.
Living in the Present, Acheron Press (Friendsville, MD), 1982.
Nachrichten aus den Staaten: Deutsche Literatur in den USA, Olms, 1983.
Manfred Jurgensen, *Johnson: Ansichten, Einsichten, Aussichten,* Francke, 1989.
Internationales Uwe-Johnson-Forum IV, Peter Lang, 1996.
Kafka's Legacy in Austrian Literature, Camden House, 1997.

Contributor of articles to *German Quarterly, Monatshefte, Germanic Notes, Germanic Review, Seminar, Colloquia Germanica, Contemporary Literature, Explicator,* and *Modern Drama,* of stories to *Beacon Review* and *Home Planet News,* and of poems to *Lyrica Germanica, German-American Studies, Poet Lore, Bitterroot, Poetry Venture, Speak Out, Lunatic Fringe, Change, Southern Humanities Review, Lyric, Blue Unicorn Thirteen, Home Planet News, New York Quarterly, Poetry Digest,* and *Z-Miscellaneous.* Also contributor of a translation of a story from German in *Dimension,* and of Emily Dickinson poems into German in the *Higginson Journal of Poetry.*

WORK IN PROGRESS: Fantastic Truth: Truth in Fiction.

SIDELIGHTS: Kurt J. Fickert wrote to *CA,* "The eye sees upside down, / but the mind knows the sky from the ground. / Clothed in a body of some mass / spun on a globe like a glass / tumbling through infinity, / the mind invented gravity. / In a world of barren sound / intelligence sought and found / words—a symbolic code / and gave us a name and abode. / To solve its own mystery, / the mind engages in poetry."

* * *

FONTENOT, Mary Alice 1910-

PERSONAL: Surname is pronounced *fon*-te-no; born April 16, 1910, in Eunice, LA; daughter of Elias Valrie and Kate (King) Barras; married Sidney J. Fontenot, September 6, 1925 (died, 1963); married Vincent L. Riehl, Sr., November 14, 1966; children: (first marriage) Edith Ziegler, R. D. (deceased), Julie Landry. *Education:* Attended school in Eunice, LA. *Religion:* Roman Catholic.

ADDRESSES: Home—1107 East 7th St., No. 4, Crowley, LA 70526. *Office*—Crowley Post-Signal, 602 North Parkerson Ave., Crowley, LA 70526-4354.

CAREER: New Era, Eunice, LA, reporter, columnist, and women's news writer, 1946-50; *Eunice News,* Eunice, editor, 1950-53; *Daily World,* Opelousas, LA, columnist, 1953-71, area editor, 1962-69; *Daily Advertiser,* Lafayette, LA, women's news reporter, 1958-60; *Rayne Tribune,* Rayne, LA, editor, 1960-62; *Crowley Post-Signal,* Crowley, LA, columnist and feature writer, 1977—.

MEMBER: League of American Pen Women, Louisiana Press Women.

AWARDS, HONORS: First Prize from National Press Women, 1966; Louisiana Literary Award, Louisiana Library Association, 1976, for *Acadia Parish, LA.*, Volume 1: *A History to 1900;* Children's Choice Award, 1984, for *Clovis Crawfish and the Orphan Zo-Zo.*

WRITINGS:

FOR CHILDREN

The Ghost of Bayou Tigre, Claitor's (Baton Rouge), 1964.
The Star Seed: A Story of the First Christmas, illustrated by Nannette Cregan, Pelican (Gretna, LA), 1983.
Mardi Gras in the Country, illustrated by Patrick Soper, Pelican, 1995.
Tah-Tye, the Last 'Possum in the Pouch, illustrated by Scott R. Blazek, Blue Heron Press (Thibodaux, LA), 1996.

"CLOVIS CRAWFISH" SERIES

Clovis Crawfish and His Friends, Claitor's, 1962, revised edition, illustrated by Keith Graves, Pelican, 1985.
Clovis Crawfish and the Big Betail, Claitor's, 1963, reprinted, Pelican, 1988.
Clovis Crawfish and the Singing Cigales, Claitor's, 1964, reprinted, illustrated by Eric Vincent, Pelican, 1981.
Clovis Crawfish and Petit Papillon, Claitor's, 1966, reprinted, illustrated by Keith Graves, Pelican, 1985.
Clovis Crawfish and the Spinning Spider, Claitor's, 1968, reprinted, illustrated by Christine Kidder, Pelican, 1987.
Clovis Crawfish and the Curious Craupaud, Claitor's, 1970, reprinted, illustrated by Christine Kidder, Pelican, 1986.
Clovis Crawfish and Michelle Mantis, Claitor's, 1976, reprinted, illustrated by Scott R. Blazek, Pelican, 1989.
Clovis Crawfish and Etienne Escargot, illustrated by Eric Vincent, Acadiana Press (Lafayette, LA), 1979, reprinted, illustrated by Scott R. Blazek, Pelican, 1992.
Clovis Crawfish and the Orphan Zo-Zo, illustrated by Eric Vincent, Pelican, 1983.
Clovis Crawfish and Simeon Suce-Fleur, illustrated by Scott K. Blazek, Pelican, 1990.
Clovis Crawfish and Bertile's Bon Voyage, illustrated by Scott K. Blazek, Pelican, 1991.
Clovis Crawfish and Batiste Baete Puante, illustrated by Scott K. Blazek, Pelican, 1993.
Clovis Crawfish and Bidon Box Turtle, illustrated by Scott K. Blazek, Pelican, 1996.
Clovis Crawfish and Paillasse Poule d'Eau, Pelican, 1997.

Several of Fontenot's "Clovis Crawfish" books have been translated into French by her daughter, Julie Landry.

FOR ADULTS

(Editor) *Quelque Chose Douce* (cookbook), Claitor's, 1964.
(Editor) *Quelque Chose Piquante* (cookbook), Claitor's, 1966.
(With husband, Vincent L. Riehl, Sr.) *The Cat and St. Landry* (biography), Claitor's, 1972.
(Editor with Mercedes Vidrine) *Beaucoup Bon* (cookbook), Claitor's, 1973.
(With Fran Dardeau and Cacky Riehl) *Cajun Accent* (cookbook), Cajun Classics Press, 1979.
Acadia Parish, LA, Volume 1 (with Paul B. Freedland): *A History to 1900,* 1976, Volume 2: *A History to 1920,* Claitor's, 1979.
(With daughter, Julie Landry) *The Louisiana Experience: An Introduction to the Culture of the Bayou State,* Claitor's, 1983.
(With daughter, Edith Ziegler) *The Tensas Story,* Claitor's, 1987.

WORK IN PROGRESS: Clovis Crawfish and Fedora Field Mouse; Clovis Crawfish and Raoul Raccoon.

SIDELIGHTS: A newspaper journalist and former kindergarten teacher, Louisiana-born writer Mary Alice Fontenot once told *CA* how she began writing children's books: "Three hours a day with thirty five-year-olds for two years is what led me into writing for children. This kindergarten teaching experience coincided with the start of the movement in south Louisiana to preserve the Acadian heritage and to restore the state to its former bilingual status. This revival of the French-Acadian culture strongly influenced my newspaper writings as well as the books I have written for children and adults."

One of Fontenot's most beloved creatures is the small Cajun-speaking crustacean named Clovis Crawfish.

The central character of thirteen children's books, Clovis and his bayou friends teach children the value of cooperation and the importance of preserving the wetlands environment of southern Louisiana. Fontenot weaves Cajun words and songs into her text, giving children a taste of the Acadian culture. In a review of *Clovis Crawfish and the Singing Cigales,* a critic writing in *Publishers Weekly* applauds the tale about Clovis saving a young cicada from M'sieu Blue Jay, saying, "The story has suspense, lessons in nature lore, in French and plenty of fun."

BIOGRAPHICAL/CRITICAL SOURCES:

PERIODICALS

Children's Book Watch, December, 1993, p. 2.

Horn Book, July, 1990, p. 58; spring, 1992, p. 32; spring, 1993, p. 28; spring, 1994, p. 33; fall, 1995, p. 291.

Publishers Weekly, January 1, 1982, p. 51.

Reading Time, December, 1982, p. 265.

School Library Journal, August, 1982, p. 96; December, 1983, p. 54.

* * *

FOWLER, William Morgan, Jr. 1944-

PERSONAL: Born July 25, 1944, in Clearwater, FL; son of William Morgan (a U.S. post office employee) and Eleanor (Brennan) Fowler; married Marilyn Louise Noble (an elementary school teacher), August 11, 1968; children: Alison Louise, Nathaniel Morgan. *Education:* Northeastern University, B.A. (magna cum laude), 1967; University of Notre Dame, M.A., 1969, Ph.D., 1971. *Politics:* Democrat. *Religion:* Roman Catholic.

ADDRESSES: Home—323 Franklin St., Reading, MA 01867. *Office*—Department of History, Northeastern University, Boston, MA 02115.

CAREER: Northeastern University, Boston, assistant professor, 1971-77, associate professor, 1977-80, professor of history, 1980—, acting associate dean of college of arts and sciences, 1977, vice provost, 1989-91, department chair, 1993—. Lecturer at universities and museums. Consultant to historical societies and other organizations. *Military service:* U.S. Army Reserve, 1970-84; became captain.

MEMBER: North American Society of Oceanic Historians, Organization of American Historians, U.S. Naval Institute, Naval Historical Foundation, Pilgrim Society (fellow), Paul Revere Memorial Association, New England Historic and Genealogical Society, Colonial Society of Massachusetts, Massachusetts Historical Society, Old South Association, Reading Antiquarian Society, Boston Marine Society (honorary member), USS *Constitution* Museum.

AWARDS, HONORS: National Endowment for the Humanities fellow, 1975; American Philosophical Society grant, 1976; Phi Alpha Theta Prize, *Choice* magazine best history book list, and Winship Award nomination, *Globe* Book Fair, all 1976, all for *Rebels under Sail: The American Navy during the Revolution;* named one of Boston's ten best teachers, *Real Paper,* 1977; Samuel Eliot Morison Distinguished Service Award, USS *Constitution* Museum, 1985; Northeastern University Outstanding Alumnus Award, 1994.

WRITINGS:

William Ellery: A Rhode Island Politico and Lord of Admiralty, Scarecrow (Metuchen, NJ), 1973.

Rebels under Sail: The American Navy during the Revolution, Scribner (New York City), 1976.

(Editor with Wallace Coyle) *The American Revolution: Changing Perspectives,* Northeastern University Press (Boston), 1979.

The Baron of Beacon Hill: A Biography of John Hancock, Houghton (Boston), 1980.

Jack Tars and Commodores: The American Navy, 1783-1815, Houghton, 1984.

(Contributor) James C. Bradford, editor, *Command under Sail: Makers of Naval Tradition,* Naval Institute Press (Annapolis, MD), 1985.

Under Two Flags: The American Navy in the Civil War, Norton (New York City), 1990.

Silas Talbot: An American Hero, Mystic, 1995.

Samuel Adams: Puritan Radical, Longman (New York City), 1997.

Contributor to *World Book Encyclopedia* and *Dictionary of American Military Biography;* contributor to professional journals, including *American Neptune, Rhode Island History, New York Historical Society Quarterly,* and *Harvard Magazine.* Managing editor, *New England Quarterly,* 1981—.

SIDELIGHTS: A professor of history at Northeastern University, William Morgan Fowler, Jr. has written several books about the early United States, including three works that trace the history of the U.S. Navy. "But it seems unfair to call this author a professor, or his book a lesson," novelist Tom Clancy states in his *Washington Post* review of *Jack Tars and Commodores: The American Navy, 1783-1815*. "Fowler does not write like many academics. His book is a lively mixture of hard facts and fluent prose, and he has the wit to alternate between the military and political arenas at a pace sufficiently brisk to maintain the reader's interest." In his account of the founding of the new nation's navy, Fowler "deals with the politics, sometimes schematically," notes *Los Angeles Times* correspondent Richard Eder; "but his real pleasure, and ours, is his account of shipbuilding, battles and the quirks and quarrels of the early captains and commodores. His writing tends to yo-ho-ho," the critic continues; nevertheless, "if [Fowler] is a mite touched by hemp and pitch it is an attractive excess, giving the book descriptive and narrative vigor." Clancy similarly observes that "the general reader could hardly ask for more, and this entertaining and informative volume could well have lasted longer. Fowler is easily a good enough writer to retain interest longer than a mere 264 pages." He concludes that *Jack Tars and Commodores* "is an uncommonly concise portrait of another age both different from and similar to our own."

BIOGRAPHICAL/CRITICAL SOURCES:

PERIODICALS

Christian Science Monitor, January 7, 1977.
Los Angeles Times, June 11, 1984.
Newsweek, January 14, 1980.
Washington Post, August 1, 1984.
Washington Post Book World, October 14, 1990.

* * *

FOX, Levi 1914-

PERSONAL: Born August 28, 1914, in Leicestershire, England; son of John William and Julia (Stinson) Fox; married Jane Richards; children: Roger James, Elizabeth Jane, Patricia Mary. *Ethnicity:* "British." *Education:* Oriel College, Oxford, B.A. (with first-class honors), 1936, M.A., 1938; University of Manchester, M.A., 1938.

ADDRESSES: Home—Silver Birches, 27 Welcombe Rd., Stratford-upon-Avon, Warwickshire, England. *Office*—Shakespeare Centre, Stratford-upon-Avon, Warwickshire, England.

CAREER: Shakespeare Centre, Stratford-upon-Avon, England, director of Shakespeare Birthplace Trust, 1945-89. *Military service:* British Army, 1940-43.

MEMBER: International Shakespeare Association (deputy chair), Royal Society of Literature (fellow), Royal Historical Society (fellow), Society of Antiquaries of London (fellow).

AWARDS, HONORS: Honorary doctorate, George Washington University, 1964; New York University medal, 1964; named officer of the Order of the British Empire, 1964; named deputy lieutenant of County of Warwick, 1967; D. Litt., Birmingham University, 1986; elected life trustee of Shakespeare's birthplace, 1989; director emeritus of the Shakespeare Birthplace Trust, 1989.

WRITINGS:

Leicester Abbey, City of Leicester Publicity Department, 1938.
The Administration of the Honor of Leicester in the Fourteenth Century, E. Backus, 1940.
The History of Coventry's Textile Industry, privately printed, 1944.
Leicester Castle (pamphlet), Leicester Publicity and Development Department, 1944.
Coventry's Heritage: An Introduction to the History of the City, Coventry Evening Telegraph, 1947, second edition, 1957.
(With Percy Russell) *Leicester Forest,* E. Backus, 1948.
Shakespeare's Town, Stratford-upon-Avon: A Pictorial Record with Historical Introduction and Descriptions, H. & J. Busst, 1949.
Stratford-upon-Avon, Garland Publishing (New York City), 1949.
(Author of introduction and notes) Gerald Gardiner, *Oxford: A Book of Drawings,* Garland Publishing, 1951.
Stratford-upon-Avon: An Appreciation, Jarrolds (London), 1952.
The Borough Town of Stratford-upon-Avon, privately printed, 1953.
(Editor) *English Historical Scholarship in the Sixteenth and Seventeenth Centuries,* Oxford University Press (Oxford, England), 1956.

Stratford-upon-Avon: Official Guide, privately printed, 1958.

William Shakespeare: A Concise Life (pamphlet), Jarrolds, 1959.

Shakespeare's Town and Country, Cotman House (London), 1959.

Shakespeare's Stratford-upon-Avon: A Souvenir in Colour with Historical Descriptions, J. Salmon, 1962.

Shakespeare's Birthplace: A History and Description, Jarrolds, 1963.

(Editor) William Shakespeare, *Sonnets,* Cotman House, 1963.

Stratford-upon-Avon in Colour: A New Pictorial Guide, Jarrolds, 1963.

The Shakespearian Properties, Jarrolds, 1964, new edition, 1981.

The Shakespeare Anniversary Book, Jarrolds, 1964.

(Editor) *Correspondence of the Reverend Joseph Greene: Parson, Schoolmaster, and Antiquary, 1712-1790,* H.M.S.O. (London), 1965.

Celebrating Shakespeare: A Pictorial Record of the Celebrations Held at Stratford-upon-Avon during 1964 to Mark the Four-Hundredth Anniversary of the Birth of William Shakespeare, privately printed, 1965.

New Place: Shakespeare's Home (pamphlet), Jarrolds, 1966.

(Editor) *A Shakespeare Treasury,* Cotman House, 1966.

A Country Grammar School: A History of Ashby-de-la-Zouch Grammar School through Four Centuries, 1567 to 1967, Oxford University Press, 1967.

(Editor) *The Stratford Shakespeare Anthology,* Cotman House, 1968.

The Shakespeare Book, Jarrolds, 1969, new edition, 1972.

Shakespeare's England, Putnam (New York City), 1972.

In Honour of Shakespeare: The History and Collections of the Shakespeare Birthplace Trust, Jarrolds, 1972.

A Splendid Occasion: The Stratford Jubilee of 1769 (pamphlet), V. Ridler, 1973.

Stratford Past and Present: A Pictorial Record of the Ancient Town of Stratford, Oxford Illustrated Press (Oxford, England), 1975.

Stratford-upon-Avon and the Shakespeare Country, Jarrolds, 1975.

Shakespeare's Flowers, Jarrolds, 1978.

Shakespeare's Birds, Jarrolds, 1978.

The Shakespeare Centre, Stratford-upon-Avon, Jarrolds, 1982.

The Early History of King Edward VI School, Stratford-upon-Avon, Dugdale Society (Warwickshire, England), 1984.

Stratford-upon-Avon, Shakespeare's Town, Jarrolds, 1986.

Historic Stratford-upon-Avon, Jarrolds, 1986.

Mary Arden's House and the Shakespeare Countryside Museum, Jarrolds, 1989.

Also author of *Minutes and Accounts of the Corporation of Stratford-upon-Avon, Volume V., 1592-1598,* 1992; and *The Shakespeare Birthplace Trust: A Personal Memoir,* 1997.

General editor of the publications of the Dugdale Society of Warwickshire. Contributor to Shakespeare studies and history journals.

WORK IN PROGRESS: Research on historical records of Stratford-upon-Avon and Warwickshire.

* * *

FRANCOEUR, Robert T(homas) 1931-

PERSONAL: Born October 18, 1931, in Detroit, MI; son of George Antoine (a steel consultant) and Julia Ann (Russell) Francoeur: married Anna Kotlarchyk (an accountant), September 24, 1966; children: Nicole Lynn, Danielle Ann. *Ethnicity:* "French-Canadian." *Education:* Sacred Heart College, B.A., 1953; St Vincent College, M.A., 1958; University of Detroit, M.S., 1961; University of Delaware, Ph.D., 1966; also attended Fordham University and Johns Hopkins University. *Politics:* Democrat. *Religion:* Roman Catholic.

ADDRESSES: Home—2 Circle Dr., Rockaway, NJ 07866. *Office*—Department of Biology, Fairleigh Dickinson University, Madison, NJ 07940. *E-mail*—rtfrancocu@aol.com; fax: 201-443-8766.

CAREER: Former Catholic priest; Fairleigh Dickinson University, Department of Biological and Allied Health Sciences, Madison, NJ, instructor, 1965-66, assistant professor, 1966-70, associate professor, 1970-75, professor of human embryology, sexuality, and biomedical ethics, 1975—, former chair of biological sciences. Visiting professor at twenty-two universities and medical schools; frequent lecturer at colleges, universities, and professional conferences; has appeared on national and local television and radio programs. Has completed documentary programs for Public Broadcasting Authority of New Jersey and Canadian Broadcasting Corp. (CBC). Participant in study of ethical, legal, and social implications of advances in biomedical and behavioral research and technology mandated by the U.S. Congress. Consultant to the United Nations, the American Medical Association, and the New York Bar.

MEMBER: World Future Society, Society for the Scientific Study of Sex (fellow, 1987; president, eastern region, 1988-90), American Association of Sex Educators, Counselors, and Therapists, American College of Sexologists (charter member).

AWARDS, HONORS: Annual award of the Educational Foundation for Human Sexuality, 1978.

WRITINGS:

Evolving World, Converging Man, Holt (New York City), 1970.

Utopian Motherhood: New Trends in Human Reproduction, Doubleday (New York City), 1970, revised edition, A. S. Barnes (San Diego, CA), 1972.

(Author of introduction) Beatrice Bruteau, *Worthy is the World: The Hindu Philosophy of Sri Aurobindo,* Fairleigh Dickinson University Press (Madison, NJ), 1971.

Eve's New Rib: Twenty Faces of Sex, Marriage and Family, Harcourt (San Diego, CA), 1972.

(With wife, Anna K. Francoeur) *Hot and Cool Sex: Cultures in Conflict,* Harcourt, 1974.

(Editor with A. K. Francoeur) *The Future of Sexual Relations,* Prentice-Hall (Englewood Cliffs, NJ), 1974.

Becoming a Sexual Person, Wiley (New York City), 1982, abridged edition published as *Becoming a Sexual Person: A Brief Edition,* 1984, second edition of original, Macmillan (New York City), 1990.

Biomedical Ethics: A Guide to Decisions, Wiley, 1983.

(Editor) *Taking Sides: Clashing Views on Controversial Issues in Human Sexuality,* Dushkin Publishing Group (Guilford, CT), 1987, sixth edition, 1998.

(Editor-in-chief) Norman A. Scherzer and Timothy Perper, coauthors, *A Descriptive Dictionary and Atlas of Sexuality,* Greenwood Press (Westport, CT), 1990.

(With James Vaughn Kohl) *The Scent of Eros: Mysteries of Odor in Human Sexuality,* Continuum (New York City), 1995.

(Editor-in-chief) *The Complete Dictionary of Sexology,* Continuum, new expanded edition, 1995.

(General editor) *The International Encyclopedia of Sexuality,* Volumes 1-3, Continuum, 1997.

(With Albert Freedman) *A Woman's Guide to Male Potency,* Future Medicine Publishing, 1998.

Contributor to various books, including *To Create a Different Future: Religious Hope and Technological Planning,* edited by Kenneth Vaux, Friendship (New York City), 1972; *Teilhard de Chardin: In Quest of the Perfection of Man,* edited by Seymour Farber and Joseph Alioto, Fairleigh Dickinson University Press, 1972; *Contemporary Families and Alternative Lifestyles, A Handbook of Research and Theory,* edited by Eleanor Macklin and Roger Rubin, Sage Publications (Beverly Hills, CA), 1983; *Marriage and the Family in the Year 2020,* edited by Lester Kirkendall and Arthur Gravatt, Prometheus, 1984; *The Vatican and Homosexuality,* edited by Crossroads (Los Angeles), 1988; *Sexology,* edited by W. Eicher and G. Kockott, Springer-Verlag (New York City), 1988; *Sexual Rehabilitation of the Spinal-Cord-Injured Patient,* edited by Jose Leyson, Humana Press (Clifton, NJ), 1989; *Abortion Rights and Fetal "Personhood,"* edited by Ed Doerr and James W. Prescott Centerline Press (Downey, CA), 1989; *The Gospel Imperative in the Midst of AIDS: Towards a Prophetic Theology,* edited by Robert H. Iles, Morehouse Publishing Co., 1990; *Handbook of Sexology, Volume 7: Childhood and Adolescent Sexology,* edited by Michael Perry, Elsevier Scientific Publishers (New York City), 1990; *American Families and the Future: Analyses of Possible Destinies,* edited by Barbara H. Settles, Roma S. Hanks, and Marvin B. Sussman, Haworth Press (New York City), 1993; *Human Sexuality: An Encyclopedia,* edited by Vern L. Bullough and Bonnie Bullough, Garland Publishing, 1994; and *Encyclopedia of the Future,* edited by George Thomas Kurian and Graham T. T. Molitor, Simon & Schuster, 1996.

Also contributor of articles to scientific and popular magazines, including *Forum, Journal of Sex Research, Medical Aspects of Human Sexuality, Journal of Allied Health, Journal of Bioethics,* and *The Truth Seeker.* Contributing editor, *Forum.*

WORK IN PROGRESS: Rejoining Sex and the Spirit: Personal Adventures in Redefining Marriage and Intimacy.

SIDELIGHTS: Robert T. Francoeur once told *CA* that his readers have always found it hard to label him or fit him into a comfortable pigeonhole. "I started off in college majoring in philosophy and English," he continued, "and graduated tied for last place in my class because I refused to fit into 'the mold.' Then I shifted gears, pursued Master's degrees in theology and biology. After working for three years as a Catholic priest, my interest in evolution, Teilhard de Chardin, and theology led me into a doctorate in experimental embryology and teaching in a large private secular university. In the past twenty years, I've worn many hats as a 'bioanthropologist,' a theologian, a sexologist, a medical ethicist, a specialist in alternative lifestyles, textbook writer, and expert on the social implications of reproductive technologies. My problem is I'm always looking for the whole picture. Using artificial insemination or embryo transplants to save endangered animal species is interesting in itself, but I'm also interested in the transfer of such technologies to humans and their impact on our values and lifestyles. The challenge of the whole picture leads me into many unusual situations but I really enjoy working and learning with people with different perspectives and professional interests."

BIOGRAPHICAL/CRITICAL SOURCES:

PERIODICALS

Baltimore Sun, February 7, 1971.
Medical World News, November 27, 1970.
Newsweek, November 23, 1970.

* * *

FRY, C(harles) George 1936-

PERSONAL: Born August 15, 1936, in Piqua, OH; son of Sylvan Jack and Lena Freda Marie (Ehle) Fry; children: Patricia Ann. *Ethnicity:* "Anglo-German." *Education:* Capital University, B.A. (with honors), 1958; Ohio State University, M.A., 1961, Ph.D., 1965; Evangelical Lutheran Theological Seminary, B.D. (with honors), 1962, M.Div., 1977; Winebrenner Theological Seminary, D.Min., 1978. *Politics:* Democrat. *Avocational interests:* Hiking, painting, science fiction.

ADDRESSES: *Home*—158 West Union St., Circleville, OH. *Office*—Lutheran College of Health Professions, 3024 Fairfield Ave., Fort Wayne, IN 46807-1697; fax: 219-458-3077.

CAREER: Clergyman of Lutheran Church, student pastorates, 1958-60; vicar in Columbus, OH, 1961-62; Wittenberg University, Springfield, OH, instructor in history, 1962-63; pastor in Columbus, 1963-66; Capital University, Columbus, instructor, 1963-65, assistant professor, 1966-71, associate professor of religion and history, 1971-75; Concordia Theological Seminary, Fort Wayne, IN, associate professor of historical theology and director of missions education, 1975-84; St. Francis College, Fort Wayne, protestant chaplain, 1982-92; Lutheran College of Health Professions, Fort Wayne, professor of philosophy and theology, 1992—. Interim minister, Arbor Grove Congregational Church, Jackson, MI, 1980, First Congregational Church, Detroit, MI, 1984-85, First Presbyterian Church, Huntington, IN, 1988-89, St. Luke's Lutheran Church, Fort Wayne, 1989-90, Mt. Pleasant and St. Mark Lutheran Churches, Albion, IN, 1990-91, Mt. Zion Lutheran Church, Fort Wayne, 1991-93, Community Church, New Carlisle, IN, 1993-94, First Lutheran Church, Styker, OH, 1994-95, and Zion Lutheran Church, Jefferson, OH, 1994—. Visiting professor, Damavand College, 1973-74, Reformed Bible College, 1975-80, Concordia Lutheran Seminary, 1978, 1982, Indiana University, 1982—, Purdue University, 1982—, Graduate School of Christian Ministries, Huntington College, 1986—, and Graduate School of Missions, Wheaton College, 1987, 1988.

Visiting lecturer, Wittenberg University, 1971, Northern England Institute for Christian Education, University of Durham, 1984, and Winebrenner Seminary, Findlay, OH, 1992; visiting theologian at churches in Columbus, 1971-72, National Presbyterian Church of Mexico, 1977, 1979, Conference of the Lutheran churches in Venezuela, 1981, the Lutheran church in Nigeria, 1983, and Queenstown Lutheran Church, Singapore, 1991. Instructor, John F. Kennedy Special Warfare Center, Fort Bragg, NC, 1983; Joseph J. Malone post-doctoral fellow, Egypt, 1986; visiting scholar, Al-Ain University, United Arab Emirates, 1987. Member of North American executive committee, Fellowship of Faith for the Muslims, 1970-80; member of North American Conference on Muslim Evangelization, 1977-78; member of Lutheran-Baptist dialogue team, Lutheran Council/United States of America, 1978-81. Member of board, Damavand College, 1976-94, Samuel Zwemer Institute, 1977-82, Fort Wayne International Affairs, 1982-92, Lutheran

Liturgical Renewal, 1983-90, 1994—, Greater Fort Wayne Campus Ministry, 1983-92, and Indiana Churches United for Ministry in Higher Education, 1984-92. Minister-in-residence, Deaconers Community Lutheran Church, Gladwyne, PA, 1993. Vice president, International Lutheran Fellowship, 1995—; editorial board member, *Bride of Christ,* 1995—. Consecrated bishop, Southern Region International Lutheran Fellowship, 1995.

MEMBER: Conference on Faith and History, Middle East Institute, American Association of University Professors, National Association of College and University Chaplains, American Association for Counseling and Development, Association for Religious and Values Issues in Counseling, Fellowship of St. Augustine (fellow), General Society of the War of 1812 (compatriot), Ohio Historical Society, Ohio Academy of History, Phi Alpha Theta, Kappa Alpha Pi.

AWARDS, HONORS: Research grant for study in Turkey, Regional Council for International Education, 1969; Praestantia Award, Capital University, 1970; Malone post-doctoral fellow, 1986-87; honorary member, House of Bishops, Southern Episcopal Church, 1995.

WRITINGS:

The Church and Israel, Hathaway, 1971.
A Book about the Bible, Hathaway, 1971.
The Supper Guest, Ohio State University Printing (Columbus), 1971.
Yesterday, Today and Forever, Hathaway, 1972.
Theological Reflections, Hathaway, 1972.
Under God's Guidance, Hathaway, 1972.
(With James R. King) *The Middle East: Crossroads of Civilization,* C. E. Merrill (Columbus, OH), 1973.
The Christian Ministry to Muslims Today, Fellowship of Faith for Muslims (Toronto), 1977.
A Guide to the Study of the World of Islam, Fellowship of Faith for Muslims, 1977.
(With King) *Islam: A Survey of the Muslim Faith,* Baker Book (Grand Rapids, MI), 1980, second edition, 1982.
(With Duane W. H. Arnold) *The Way, the Truth, and the Life: An Introduction to Lutheran Christianity,* Baker Book, 1982.
(With King) *Great Asian Religions,* Baker Book, 1984.
(With Arnold) *Francis: A Call to Conversion,* Zondervan (Grand Rapids, MI), 1988.
The Middle East: A History, St. Francis College, 1988.
(With Jon Paul Fry) *Congregationalists and Evolution: Asa Gray and Louis Agassiz,* University Press of America (Lanham, MD), 1989.
(With Fry) *Pioneering a Theology of Evolution: Washington Gladden and Pierre Teilhard de Chardin,* University Press of America, 1989.
(With Raymond J. Graves) *America and the Soviet Union, 1948-1988,* Westwood Community Press, 1989.
(With Graves) *America and the Third World,* Westwood Community Press, 1989.
(With Fry) *Avicenna's Philosophy of Education: An Introduction,* Three Continents (Washington, DC), 1990.
(With Fry) *Pioneers of Science Fiction: Jules Verne and H. G. Wells,* Westwood Community Press, 1991.
Introduction to Protestant Theology, St. Francis College, 1992.

PUBLISHED BY CONCORDIA THEOLOGICAL SEMINARY PRESS

Ten Contemporary Theologians, 1976.
Islam: An Evangelical Perspective, 1976.
(With Harold H. Zietlow) *Christian Missions: History,* 1976.
(With Zietlow) *Christian Missions: Strategy,* 1976.
(Editor) *European Theology, 1648-1914,* 1976.
The Christian Ministry to Muslims Today, 1976.
(Editor) *Protestant Theology, 1914-1975,* 1977.
(With John M. Drickamer) *A History of Lutheranism in America, 1619-1930,* 1979.
(With Drickamer) *The Age of Lutheran Orthodoxy, 1530-1648,* 1979.
(With Arnold) *A Lutheran Reader,* 1982.
Raymond Lull: Apostle to the Muslims, 1983.
Iran and Japan: Two Models of Modernization, 1983, second edition, Westwood Community Press, 1989.

EDITOR

(With Donald E. Bensch, and contributor) *The Middle East in Transition,* Capital University Press, 1970.
(With James L. Burke, and contributor) *The Past in Perspective,* MSS Educational Publishing, 1971.
(With Burke, and contributor) *The Emergence of the Modern World, 1300-1815,* MSS Educational Publishing, 1971.

(With Burke, and contributor) *The Search for a New Europe, 1919-1971,* MSS Educational Publishing, 1971.

Maritime History in the Western World, 1300-1815, Hathaway, 1972.

(With King) *An Anthology of Middle Eastern Literature from the Twentieth Century,* Wittenberg University, 1974.

Catholicism: A Bibliography, St. Francis College, 1985.

OTHER

Also contributor to *The New Schaff-Herzog Encyclopedia of Religious Knowledge,* Baker Book, *Dictionary of Christianity in America,* Inter-Varsity Press (Downers Grove, IL), *Great Lives from History,* Salem Press (Englewood Cliffs, NJ), *Evangelical Dictionary of Theology,* Baker Book, *Handbook of Evangelical Theology,* Baker Book, *Nobel Prize Winners,* Salem Press, *Magill's Medical Guide,* Science and Practice, *Ready Reference: Social Sciences,* Salem Press, *Ready Reference: American Indians,* Salem Press, *Ready Reference: Ethics,* Salem, and *Encyclopedia of World Authors,* Salem Press.

WORK IN PROGRESS: Washington Gladden as a Preacher; Life's Little Lessons; A Song in His Heart; Twelve Nativity Tales.

SIDELIGHTS: C. George Fry told *CA:* "Writing is my life and my life is a series of paradoxes.

"I am of both the Midwest and the Mideast. Born a sixth generation Ohioan, I remain very much a child of the American heartland. When I turned thirty-three, I discovered a second home. Time in Turkey, Iran, Egypt, the Persian Gulf and the Arabian Peninsula gave me a love of the Muslim world. That is why I write of both Western and Islamic civilization.

"I am both Lutheran and ecumenical. A 'cradle Lutheran,' raised within that tradition, I have served widely, from student minister to bishop. By the time I turned forty I realized that 'nothing Christian was alien to me' and I was invited to work in Roman Catholic, Congregational, Episcopal, Presbyterian, and Community Church settings. That is why I write of both Lutheran leaders, as Matthias Loy, and Catholic saints—as Francis of Assisi and Teilhard de Chardin—let alone Congregationalist sages as Washington Gladden and Louis Agassiz.

"I am both teacher and minister. I fell in love with education while attending a little red brick one room school house in Darke County, Ohio, in the forties. That was my portal to platform experiences in public and private college in the U.S. and overseas. Then, ten years later, I acquired a second love, ministry, preaching in a white frame open-country church in Pickaway County, Ohio. From there I went to serve from the country to the inner city, from the village to the heart of the city, a pastor among German refugees in Columbus, or Chinese in Singapore, or African-Americans in Detroit, or preaching in English to Persian Presbyterians in Tehran. That is why I write for both the platform and the pulpit, ranging from formal philosophy to down home homilies.

"Life is so much more than can be imagined or understood, but writing is an attempt to come to grips with its richness and diversity. I take as guidance what Sir Philip Sidney wrote, 'Biting my truant pen, beating myself for spite: Fool! said my Muse to me, look in thy heart and write.'"

* * *

FULTON, Alice 1952-

PERSONAL: Born January 25, 1952, in Troy, NY; daughter of John R. (in business) and Mary (a nurse; maiden name, Callahan) Fulton; married Hank De Leo (an artist), June, 1980. *Education:* State University of New York Empire State College, B.A., 1979; Cornell University, M.F.A., 1982.

ADDRESSES: Home—2370 Le Forge Road, R.R. 13, Ypsilanti, MI 48198-9638. *Office*—Department of English, Angell Hall, University of Michigan, Ann Arbor, MI 48109-1003.

CAREER: University of Michigan, Ann Arbor, assistant professor, 1983-86, William Wilhartz professor of English, 1986-89, professor of English, 1992—; Michigan Society of Fellows, fellow, 1983-86, senior fellow, 1996—. Visiting professor of creative writing, Vermont College, 1987; visiting professor of English, University of California, Los Angeles, 1991, Ohio

State University, 1995, University of North Caroline, 1997.

AWARDS, HONORS: MacDowell Colony fellow, 1978-79; Millay Colony fellow, 1980; Emily Dickinson Award from the Poetry Society of America, 1980; Academy of American Poets prize, 1982; award from Associated Writing Programs, 1982, for *Dance Script With Electric Ballerina;* Consuelo Ford Award from Poetry Society of America, 1984; Rainer Maria Rilke Award, 1984; Yaddo Colony fellow, 1987; Guggenheim fellowship, 1986-87; Bess Hokin prize from *Poetry,* 1989; Ingram Merrill Foundation award, 1990; MacArthur Foundation fellow, 1991; Elizabeth Matchett Stover Award from *Southwest Review,* 1993; Litt.D. from State University of New York, 1994.

WRITINGS:

Anchors of Light (poems; limited edition chapbook), Swamp Press (Oneonta, NY), 1979.

Dance Script with Electric Ballerina (poems), University of Pennsylvania Press (Philadelphia), 1983.

(With Katharyn M. Aal, Karen Marie Christa Minns, and Sy Smith) *The Wings, The Vines: Poems,* McBooks Press, 1983.

Palladium (poems), University of Illinois Press (Urbana), 1986.

Powers of Congress (poems), Godine (Boston), 1990.

Sensual Math (poems), Norton (New York City), 1995.

Work has also appeared in *The Best American Poetry* for 1989, 1991, 1992, and 1994, and *The Best American Short Stories, 1993.* Contributor to magazines, including *New Republic, New Yorker, Poetry, Georgia Review, Emily Dickinson Journal, Parnassus, Triquarterly,* and the *Washington Post.*

SIDELIGHTS: Alice Fulton's first book, *Dance Script with Electric Ballerina,* "made readers sit up and take notice," according to J. D. McClatchy in *Poetry,* and it was noticed equally by critics for its use of common speech and its incorporation of both high and low culture. According to Stephen C. Behrendt in *Prairie Schooner,* Fulton "established herself as an energetic, inventive risk taker." In the introduction to the book, Pulitzer prize-winning poet W. D. Snodgrass, as quoted by McClatchy, calls her "the lady of Logopoeia" and celebrated her "razzy exuberance and 'brass-assed language,'" characterizing her as "a poet of style, like [John] Berryman, rather than a poet of subject, like [Robert] Frost."

In discussing Fulton's second book, *Palladium,* McClatchy praises the performance and spoken-word quality of her poems, which are "hopped up, with a hard metallic tone and a cranky line." Fulton writes about subjects ranging from jaded waitresses to the nature of faith. As Calvin Bedient writes in *Sewanee Review,* "Fulton invites you to have a good time along with her." Yet she can also write of her family with love and respect, and does so in a six-poem series in *Palladium* in which McClatchy notes she "quiets down." The book remains, though, according to Behrendt, one in which Fulton takes risks that succeed and present her readers with a "brilliant verbal and psychological palette."

Powers of Congress, likewise, was warmly received by critics. Behrendt notes how Fulton "brings together the ordinary and the extraordinary" so "the juxtapositioning of effects is more assured now, the voices in the poems more craggy and eerily distinctive," than in her earlier works. One example Behrendt cites is the poem "Point of Purchase," which includes underlines, highlights, annotations, as used textbooks often carry, effectively "[reinstating] poetry as a *social activity,* a transactional dialogue among a community of writers and readers." Other poems, like "Fractal Lanes," also invite the reader to participate, notes Louise Horton in *Southern Humanities Review.* Eavan Boland, writing in *Partisan Review,* calls Fulton "an ambitious, powerful poet" who details "experiences of stress and force in the ironies of daily life." Like her contemporary, Albert Goldbarth, notes David Baker in *Poetry,* Fulton "is embarked on a project to redefine or recreate poetry according to the multiforms of experience and intellect, rather than to shape experience by modelling it on a received poetic vision." *Powers of Congress,* writes Baker, "is a rigorous, generous book, by one of the finest young poets in the country."

The very title of *Sensual Math,* according to Amy Gerstler in the *Los Angeles Times Book Review,* plays off "the tension between the two words," indicating the "tug of war going on . . . between the worlds of thinking and feeling." Gerstler notes that the four sections of the book offer "Darwinian musings, whiffs of Emily Dickinson and cameos by Elvis Presley," with the final section devoted to eleven poems that rework the Apollo and Daphne myth. As William Logan points out in the *New York Times Book Review,* "Apollo is a

Vegas lounge lizard with a taste for camo outfits and Daphne a compound of [Marianne] Moore, Emily Dickinson, Amelia Earhart and Annie Oakley." For this work, Fulton offers an invented punctuation, a double equal sign ("=="), which *Publishers Weekly* points out is "described variously as 'dash to the max' and 'sutures that dissolve into the self.'" Still, Logan admits, Fulton is "a nervy, skittish bandbox of a poet, thrilled by image." Though, as Gerstler points out, "in these poems '90s-minded concerns are tartly and smartly articulated." Fulton's voice and imagery suggest, in the words of a *Publishers Weekly* reviewer, that Alice Fulton "may be Dickinson's post-modern heir."

BIOGRAPHICAL/CRITICAL SOURCES:

BOOKS

Contemporary Poets, 5th edition, St. James Press (Detroit), 1991.

Keller, Lynn, and Miller, Cristanne, *Feminist Measures: Soundings in Poetry and Theory,* University of Michigan Press (Ann Arbor), 1994, pp. 317-43.

PERIODICALS

American Poetry Review, January 1988, p. 17.

Blue Penny Quarterly (online journal), summer, 1996.

Book Report, March, 1991, p. 22.

Booklist, October 15, 1986, p. 321.

Boston Book Review, August, 1995, p. 37.

Boston Herald, March 8, 1987, p. S17.

Boston Review, February, 1984, p. 31; December, 1986, p. 29.

Choice, June, 1984, p. 1465; December, 1986.

Emily Dickinson International Society Bulletin, volume 8, no. 2, 1996, pp. 10-11.

Epoch, Volume 36, number 3, 1986-87.

Georgia Review, winter, 1987, p. 800.

Harvard Book Review, July-August, 1991, p. 20.

Hudson Review, summer, 1987, p. 349.

Hungry Mind Review, winter, 1991, p. 49.

Iowa Review, volume 22, no. 2, 1992, pp. 190-92.

Library Journal, December 15, 1982, p. 2335; September 1, 1986, p. 204; February 1, 1991, p. 80; April 1, 1995, p. 98.

Los Angeles Times Book Review, July 23, 1995, p. 15.

Michigan Quarterly Review, summer, 1992, p. 425.

New York Times Book Review, December 10, 1995.

New Yorker, October 23, 1995, p. 95.

Newsday, December 18, 1983, pp. 17-8.

Partisan Review, February, 1993, p. 316.

Ploughshares, volume 17, no. 1, 1991, p. 230.

Poetry, November, 1984, p. 102; October, 1986, p. 43; June, 1991, p. 172.

Prairie Schooner, summer, 1985, p. 115; spring, 1993, p. 157.

Publishers Weekly, October 21, 1983, p. 55; July 4, 1986, p. 65; October 5, 1990, p. 94; February 27, 1995, p. 97.

Sewanee Review, winter, 1988, p. 137.

Southern Humanities Review, spring, 1982, p. 185.

Stand, spring, 1992, p. 107.

Virginia Quarterly Review, winter, 1987, p. 25.

Women's Review of Books, June, 1991, p. 24; July, 1995.

Writer's Digest, September, 1991, p. 36.

Yale Review, Volume 77, number 1, 1987.*

G

GALLAHUE, David L(ee) 1943-

PERSONAL: Born February 15, 1943, in Niagara Falls, NY; son of Douglas (a printer) and Loretta (a file clerk) Gallahue; married Elnora Bredenberg; children: David Lee, Jr., Jennifer. *Education:* Indiana University, B.S., 1964; Purdue University, M.S., 1967; Temple University, Ed.D., 1970. *Religion:* Christian. *Avocational interests:* Skiing, weight training, mountain climbing, farm work.

ADDRESSES: *Home*—Blackberry Ridge Farm, 8010 North St. Rd. 37, Bloomington, IN 47404. *Office*—School of Health, Physical Education, and Recreation, Indiana University, Bloomington, IN 47405. *E-mail*—gallahue@indiana.edu.

CAREER: Indiana University at Bloomington, assistant professor, 1970-74, associate professor, 1974-83, professor of kinesiology, 1983—, assistant dean for research and development, 1977-87, associate dean for academic affairs and research, 1996—. Visiting professor at universities in America and abroad, including State University of New York at Buffalo, 1975, 1977, University of Kuwait, 1979, University of Alaska at Fairbanks and Anchorage, 1989, university of Santa Maria, Brazil, 1991-92, Valparaiso University, Chile, 1993-94, and Macquarie University, Australia, 1995. Guest lecturer at universities, including Purdue University, Temple University, University of British Columbia, and Leeds University. Pubic lecturer and director of workshops on a national and international level. Chair, Council on Physical Education for Children, 1987; chair, Motor Development Academy, National Association for Sport and Physical Education, 1988; president, National Association for Sport and Physical Education, 1990. Consultant, National Institute for Fitness and Sport, 1991—, USA Gymnastic Federation, 1994—, Children's Television Workshop, 1995—, and USA Skiing Federation, 1996—.

MEMBER: International Playground Association, International Council for Health, Physical Education, Recreation, Sport, and Dance, American Camping Association, American Alliance for Health, Physical Education, Recreation, and Dance (life member), American Association for Leisure and Recreation, Indiana Association for Health, Physical Education, Recreation, and Dance, Phi Delta Kappa, Phi Epsilon Kappa (life member).

AWARDS, HONORS: Leadership-Recognition Award, Indiana Alliance for Health, Physical Education, Recreation and Dance, 1979; State of Indiana Recognition award, Governor's Task Force for the Year of the Child, 1980; Midwest Alliance Scholar Award, Midwest/American Alliance for Health, Physical Education, Recreation and Dance, 1987; distinguished service awards from National Association for Sport and Physical Education, 1993, and Council on Physical Education for Children, 1994; Healthy American Fitness Leadership Award, 1994; honor award, Indiana Alliance for Health, Physical Education, Recreation and Dance, 1995; Temple University Alumni Fellow Award, 1996; distinguished scholar at University of Delaware, 1987, Ball State University, 1988, Anderson University, 1988, Long Beach State University, 1989, University of Wisconsin, LaCrosse, 1990, and Murray State University, 1991.

WRITINGS:

(With Peter H. Werner and George C. Luedke) *A Conceptual Approach to Moving and Learning,* Wiley (New York City), 1971, 2nd edition, 1975.

(With Maryhelen Vannier and Mildred Foster) *Physical Education for Elementary School Children,* Saunders (Philadelphia, PA), 5th edition, 1973, 6th edition (with Vannier), 1978.

Individualized Movement Experiences for Young Children, Phi Delta Kappa (Bloomington, IN), 1974.

(With W. Meadors) *Let's Move: A Physical Education Program for Elementary Classroom Teachers,* Kendall/Hunt (Dubuque, IA), 1974, 2nd edition, 1979.

Individualized Movement Experiences for Young Children, Phi Delta Kappa, 1974.

Yes I Can!: Movement and the Developing Self (film strip), Phi Delta Kappa, 1975.

Developmental Play Equipment for Home and School, illustrations and instructional development by Rogers Glenn, Wiley, 1975.

Motor Development and Movement Experiences for Young Children, Wiley, 1976.

(With Bruce A. McClenaghan) *Fundamental Movement: A Developmental and Remedial Approach,* Saunders, 1978.

(With McClenaghan) *Fundamental Movement: An Observational Assessment Instrument,* Saunders, 1978.

(With M. Botha) *The Progressive Development of Fundamental Movement Abilities* (film strip), Indiana University, 1982.

Understanding Motor Development: Infants, Children, Adolescents, Adults, Brown & Benchmark (Dubuque, IA), 1982, 3rd edition, 1995.

Developmental Movement Experiences for Children, Wiley, 1982.

Developmental Physical Education for Today's Children, Brown & Benchmark, 1987, 3rd edition, 1996.

Contributor to books, including *Your Growing Child,* Time-Life Books (New York City), 1987; *Developing Your Child's Potential,* Time-Life Books, 1987; *Handbook of Research on the Education of Young Children,* edited by B. Spodek, Macmillan (New York City), 1993; *Reaching Potentials: Transforming Early Childhood Curriculum and Assessment,* edited by S. Bredenkamp and T. Rosegrant, National Association for the Education of Young Children (Washington, DC), 1995; and *Adapted Physical Education and Sport,* edited by J. P. Winnick, Human Kinetics (Champaign, IL), 1995.

Series editor, *United States Olympic Committee Sports Education Series,* published by Cooper Publishing Group (Indianapolis, IN). Contributor to numerous journals, including *Research Quarterly for Exercise and Sport, Physical Educator, Studies in Educational Evaluation,* and *Perceptual and Motor Skills.* Editor-in-chief of *The Physical Educator,* 1973-83.

WORK IN PROGRESS: Developmentally Appropriate Movement Activities for Young Children; Movement Literacy and the Young Child.

SIDELIGHTS: David L. Gallahue once told *CA:* "Writing must be a labor of love. The financial rewards are too uncertain and often too meager in the textbook market for it to be anything else. For the most part, writing is hard work. It is time-consuming, demanding of one's complete attention and long-range commitment. It is, however, a tremendous thrill to see a completed manuscript in print and to be able to express your views to people all over the world."

* * *

GALLUN, Raymond Z(inke) 1911-1994
(John Callahan, Dow Elstar, E. V. Raymond)

PERSONAL: Surname is pronounced Gall-*oon;* born March 22, 1911, in Beaver Dam, WS; died April 2, 1994, in Forest Hills, NY; son of Adolph (a farmer) and Martha (Zinke) Gallun; married Frieda Ernestine Talmey (a high-school foreign language teacher), December 26, 1959 (died May 19, 1974); married Bertha Erickson Backman, February 24, 1978. *Education:* Attended University of Wisconsin, Madison, 1929-30, Alliance Francaise, Paris, France, 1938-39, and San Marcos University, Lima, Peru, 1960. *Politics:* "No party affiliation." *Religion:* Agnostic.

CAREER: Science-fiction writer. Prior to 1942, worked as a laborer in a cannery, a shoe factory, and a hemp mill. Construction worker for U.S. Army Corps of Engineers, 1942-43; marine blacksmith at Pearl Harbor Navy Yard, 1944; technical writer on sonar equipment for EDO Corp., College Point, NY, 1964-75.

AWARDS, HONORS: First Fandom Hall of Fame Award, 1979; Lifetime Achievement Award (renamed The Raymond Z. Gallun Award for outstanding achievement in science fiction, and presented annually), I-Con IV.

WRITINGS:

SCIENCE FICTION

(Under pseudonym William Callahan) *The Machine That Thought,* Columbia (New York City), 1942.

People Minus X, Simon & Schuster (New York City), 1957.

The Planet Strappers, Pyramid Press (Benwood, WV), 1961.

The Eden Cycle, Ballantine (New York City), 1974.

The Best of Raymond Z. Gallun, edited by J.J. Pierce, Ballantine, 1977.

Bioblast!, Berkley (New York City), 1985.

NONFICTION

Skyclimber: The Literary Adventures and Autobiography of Raymond Z. Gallun, with Jeffrey M. Elliot, Tower Books (New York City), 1981, reprinted as *Starclimber,* Borgo Press (San Bernardino, CA), 1991.

CONTRIBUTOR TO ANTHOLOGIES

The Best of Science Fiction, edited by Groff Conklin, Crown (New York City), 1946.

Adventures in Time and Space, edited by J. Healy and J. Francis McComas, Random House (New York City), 1946, published as *Famous Science-Fiction Stories,* Modern Library (New York City), 1957.

Imagination Unlimited, edited by Everett F. Bleiler and T. E. Dikty, Farrar, Straus & Young (New York City), 1951.

Possible Worlds of Science Fiction, edited by Conklin, Vanguard Press (New York City), 1951.

Space Service, edited by Andre Norton, World Publishing, 1953.

Space Pioneers, edited by Norton, World Publishing, 1954.

Thinking Machines, edited by Conklin, Vanguard Press, 1954.

Escales dans l'infini, edited by Georges Gallet, Hachette (Paris, France), 1954.

Coming of the Robots, edited by Sam Moscowitz, Collier (New York City), 1963.

Five Unearthly Visions, edited by Conklin, Gold Medal Books (New York City), 1965.

Tomorrow's Worlds, edited by Robert Silverberg, Meredith Press, 1969.

The Astounding-Analog Reader, edited by Harry Harrison and Brian W. Aldiss, Doubleday (New York City), 1972.

Jupiter, edited by Carol Pohl and Frederik Pohl, Ballantine, 1973.

The Great Illusion, Tyne & Wear (Wallsend, England), 1973.

Before the Golden Age, edited by Isaac Asimov, Doubleday, 1974.

History of the Science-Fiction Magazine, edited by Michael Ashley, Pitman Press, 1974.

The Best of Planet Stories, edited by Leigh Brackett, Ballantine, 1975.

Earth Is the Strangest Planet, edited by Robert Silverberg, Thomas Nelson (Nashville, TN), 1977.

Science Fiction of the Forties, edited by Frederik Pohl, Avon (New York City), 1978.

Analog Readers' Choice, edited by Stanley Schmidt, Dial Press (New York City), 1981.

OTHER

Also author of unpublished novels *Gemi the Finder, Ormund House* (autobiographical fiction), *The Magnificent Mutation,* and *Legend Seed.* Contributor of several hundred stories, sometimes under pseudonyms John Callahan, Dow Elstar, and E. V. Raymond, to science fiction magazines and other popular periodicals, including *Astounding Stories, Collier's* and *Family Circle.*

SIDELIGHTS: Raymond Z. Gallun began writing science fiction in the 1930s and found a ready market for his work in the pulp magazines of the time. Over the course of the next twenty years he published hundreds of science fiction stories, many of them appearing in *Astounding Stories* magazine. Widely anthologized, these short stories have found a new audience among readers interested in the earlier stages of modern science fiction writing. Gallun also published novels and a memoir detailing his long and eventful life.

Born in a small Wisconsin town in 1911, Gallun developed an interest in science by reading college-level textbooks left in the attic of his home by a former owner. He discovered the pulp magazines as a teenager and began submitting stories to them while still in high school. By the mid-1930s his work was appearing regularly in *Astounding Stories*. The money he received for his submissions, bolstered by earnings from jobs in a shoe factory and a cannery, allowed him to travel to Europe in 1938. He spent a year in Paris teaching English to German refugees, then returned to America at the outbreak of World War II.

Gallun's career after that consisted of a series of day jobs, science fiction writing by night, and frequent travels. He eventually ceased writing fiction altogether and accepted a technical writer's post with a corporation. *Analog* book reviewer Tom Easton noted that Gallun "vanished so thoroughly that when he returned to SF in the seventies, his past contributions were long forgotten."

Forgotten they might have been at that time, but revived interest in pulp magazine fiction has brought renewed interest in Gallun's work—and has provided an audience for his more recent novels and memoirs. Of the Gallun autobiography *Starclimber,* Easton wrote: "The book's tale is smooth and lucid, with Gallun's voice coming through as if he were talking to you and you alone of his successes, frustrations, and intriguing interludes."

In a letter to *CA* written before he died, Gallun commented upon the current science-fiction scene: "Almost by definition, science fiction should be forward-looking, backward-looking, inward-looking, every-which-way-looking—innovative of possibly useful ideas as it used to be, not so often tedious and repetitious. Sorcerers and swordplay, pseudo-medieval settings and improbable, super-muscular heroes and anti-heroes, tired socio-political themes rehashed on planets of distant stars, still far out of the reach of our present reality. These things have their place, of course. Yet in such over-muchness? Is the readership truly scared into that degree of escape from what is actual? Or away from solid technology, which is still the best available approach to problem-solving?

"We are at the edge of a historic fledging from the Earth into the wider frontier of the universe. The first real steps are possible now—while we also listen for intelligent signals from the stars. So why isn't more attention paid to what is on our true horizon? Manned and womaned exploration of Mars and the first habitations there. Probes into local gas giants (Jupiter, Saturn, etc.) or down into their moons. Mysterious Io and its active sulphur-volcanoes; the dense, cryogenic nitrogen atmosphere of Titan. Probes onto Venus and the asteroids. Maybe the possible refurbishing of our own moon. . . . And as for the other—non-spatial—fields: How about, for instance, probing into ourselves? Isn't it obvious that our bodies know more than our conscious minds, controlling and monitoring, as they do, thousands of intricate processes, including the very existence of our conscious minds, which are like mere bubbles floating on top of all of that physical bio-complexity? Yes, we get a free ride through life atop a wonderful bio-machine about which our understanding remains very limited. As a very small example of the superiority of bodily knowledge, bodies (animal before human) recognized the existence of and successfully fought disease germs a billion years before Pasteur. But what if, by some minor mutation in the nervous system of some person, the barrier between body know-how and conscious mind were broken down, so that all that knowledge became available by means of an introspective sense?

"In other areas of science-fiction writing—instead of so much patterning from the historically dismal, louse-ridden, bigotry-pervaded Middle Ages, why not, for variation at least, draw from the cultures of Ancient Rome, Mesopotamia, Egypt, or from some possible first civilization of the latest ice age, in the then half-dry Mediterranean basin? Ready-made there would even be the menace of a great flood when the polar glaciers dwindled and much of their water went back into the oceans. "You see, I—along with other forward-and outward-looking writers and readers—have had my differences with what publishers have been putting out lately. Of course the publishers should know better than I what kind of yarns have had the best sales figures in the last couple of years. To a certain extent publishers lead and guide their readership and, in return, are influenced by reader feedback—some of which undoubtedly calls for yet more of the same. But where is the end of this except in dull monotony, which must adversely affect sales more and more, as more and more readers feel cheated when flowery blurbs and publicity fall flat while the books are being read?

"I don't think the fault is with the writers, who are pretty flexible people generally, nor do I think it is with the editors, who must conform to commands from higher up. I hope the time will soon return when book manuscripts will again be selected on the basis of their individual merit, instead of being picked, packaged, and marketed by name-trademark and category, as if they were detergents, pet-food, or sugary breakfast cereals."

BIOGRAPHICAL/CRITICAL SOURCES:

BOOKS

Ashley, Michael, *The History of the Science Fiction Magazine, Part I: 1926-1935,* Pitman Press, 1974.

Elliot, Jeffrey M., *The Work of Raymond Z. Gallun: An Annotated Bibliography and Guide,* R. Reginald (San Bernardino, CA), 1993.

PERIODICALS

Analog Science Fiction & Fact, March, 1992, pp. 164-65.

Foundation: The Review of Science Fiction, Number 22, 1981.

Science-Fiction Studies, November, 1991, pp. 456-57.

OBITUARIES:

PERIODICALS

Locus, May, 1994, p. 62.*

* * *

GEISERT, Arthur 1941-

PERSONAL: Born September 20, 1941, in Dallas, TX; son of Leonard (an engineer) and Doris (a homemaker; maiden name, Boland) Geisert; married Bonnie Meier (a teacher), June 1, 1963; children: Noah. *Education:* Concordia College, Seward, NE, B.S., 1963; University of California, Davis, M.A., 1965; additional study at Chouinard Art Institute, Otis Art Institute, and Art Institute of Chicago.

ADDRESSES: Home—P.O. Box 3, Galena, IL 61036.

CAREER: Printmaker and artist. Art teacher at Concordia College, River Forest, IL, Concordia College, Seward, NE, and Clark College, Dubuque, IA, 1965—. Lecturer at many colleges, universities, and institutions, including University of Wisconsin, Madison; University of Minnesota, Minneapolis; and the Smithsonian. *Exhibitions:* Has exhibited artwork at galleries and exhibitions, including the Society of American Graphic Artists, New York City, 1986, 1991, and 1993; and the Society of Illustrators Museum of American Illustration, New York City, 1991, 1992, and 1996.

MEMBER: National Artist's Equity Association, Los Angeles Printmaking Society, Boston Printmakers.

AWARDS, HONORS: Illinois Arts Council fellow, 1986; Ten Best Illustrated Children's Books selection, *New York Times,* 1986, for *Pigs from A to Z,* 1996, for *Roman Numerals I to MM; Reading Rainbow* Review Book selection and Reading Magic Award, *Parenting,* both 1991, both for *Oink;* Honor Book, *Parents Choice,* Ten Recommended Picture Books selection, *Time,* and Honor Book, *Boston Globe-Horn Book,* all 1995, all for *Haystack.*

WRITINGS:

SELF-ILLUSTRATED

Pa's Balloon and Other Pig Tales, Houghton (Boston), 1984.

Pigs from A to Z, Houghton, 1986.

The Ark, Houghton, 1988.

Oink, Houghton, 1991.

Pigs from 1 to 10, Houghton, 1992.

Oink Oink, Houghton, 1993.

After the Flood, Houghton, 1994.

(With wife, Bonnie Geisert) *Haystack,* Houghton, 1995.

Roman Numerals I to MM = Numerabilia Romana Uno Ad Duo Mila: liber de difficullimo, Houghton, 1996.

The Etcher's Studio, Houghton, 1997.

ILLUSTRATOR

F. N. Monjo, *Prisoners of the Scrambling Dragon,* Holt (New York City), 1980.

Barbara Bader, *Aesop and Company: With Scenes from His Legendary Life,* Houghton, 1991.

OTHER

The Orange Scarf, illustrated by Thomas Di Grazia, Simon & Schuster (New York City), 1970.

Contributor to numerous books, including *Paradis Perdu,* Atelier Contraste Fribourg, 1991; *Children's Book Illustration and Design,* edited by Julie Cummins, P.B.C. International, 1992; *World Book Encyclopedia,* 1993; and *The Very Best of Children's Book Illustration,* compiled by the Society of Illustrators, North Light Books, 1993. Geisert's books have been published in Japan, France, Spain, and Germany.

WORK IN PROGRESS: Prairie Town, for Houghton.

SIDELIGHTS: Arthur Geisert combines etching with wry humor to produce award-winning children's books. "My main interest is illustration," Geisert once commented. "I'm trying to combine a classic etching style inspired by Piranesi, Rembrandt, and Callot with humor and narrative."

Trained as a teacher, Geisert soon discovered that his real passion lay in the studio, not in the classroom. Taking up residence in rural Galena, Illinois, Geisert and his wife and child lived for many years a "dirt poor" existence, as he wrote in *Something about the Author Autobiography Series* (*SAAS*). While his wife taught at a local school, Geisert worked selling etchings and building two homes for the family. As he explained in *SAAS,* his early etching subjects focused on "Noah's Ark, with a lot of detailed cutaway pieces, pigs, views of Galena, and humorous prints." Beginning with a small business loan of $800, Geisert was able to develop a lucrative business in prints. For many years he also submitted proposals to publishers for children's books. Over the years he managed to collect a drawer full of rejections for his troubles.

In the end, publishers came to him, however. An editor at Houghton Mifflin, after seeing his etchings in an exhibition, took a look at his portfolio and the happy result was Geisert's picture book, *Pa's Balloon and Other Pig Tales.* "It was illustrated with etchings," Geisert explained in *SAAS,* "a rarely used technique in children's books, and the color was done with manual color separations." Relatively long for a picture book, *Pa's Balloon and Other Pig Tales* "has the look of a short novel," according to Karen Stang Hanley writing in *Booklist.* It contains three stories about a pig family: a disastrous picnic; a balloon race; and a journey to the North Pole. All are "narrated with childlike economy by a plucky piglet," Hanley noted. Writing in *Horn Book,* Karen Jameyson commented that while the stories themselves were slight, the illustrations "distinguish the book," utilizing "an array of perspectives to record the activity." A *Publishers Weekly* reviewer concluded that "Geisert's first book is sure to leave children wanting more from him."

Children did not have to wait long. Geisert's second title was a puzzle alphabet book, *Pigs from A to Z,* illustrated as all his books are, with original etchings. Minimal text accompanies full-page etchings in which various letters are hidden. A story line about the building of a tree house recalls Geisert's own boyhood carpentry efforts as well as his adult construction of houses. Denise M. Wilms in *Booklist* noted that the book was an "intriguing venture for curious, ambitious browsers," and *Horn Book*'s Jameyson concluded that "the graphically pleasing and very clever book may fascinate even those well beyond the picture-book age." *Pigs from A to Z* was selected by the *New York Times* as one of ten Best Illustrated Picture Books of 1986.

Animals figure in most of Geisert's graphic productions, and with *The Ark,* there is a definite plethora of all sorts of beasts in a retelling of the story from Genesis. "A dignified, somber retelling of the flood story," Ellen D. Warwick dubbed the book in a *School Library Journal* review. "I drew on material from many of my earlier etchings that deal with a Noah's Ark theme," Geisert wrote in *SAAS.* "I was especially interested in the interior views of the ark. I liked combining the rigid discipline of perspective with the organic chaos of the animals, birds, sacks of feed, etc." *Horn Book* reviewer Elizabeth S. Watson noted that "children will love finding the beasts who have wandered from their proper spaces. Parents and religious educators will welcome Geisert's handsome rendition of the story." Geisert, educated as an undergraduate at a Lutheran teacher's college, returned to this biblical theme with *After the Flood,* a story of what happens after the waters recede and the animals leave the Ark. "A glowing, impelling, visually stimulating panorama of hope and affirmation of life," is how Mary M. Burns described the book in *Horn Book.* Classical mythology forms the basis of another book, *Aesop and Company,* written by Barbara Bader, for which Geisert provided illustrations.

But Geisert never strays far from his beloved pigs. Four further titles have employed playful porkers: *Oink* and its sequel, *Oink Oink,* and two counting books, *Pigs from 1 to 10* and *Roman Numerals I to MM.* "*Oink* . . . was a silly one-word (oink, oink, oink, etc.) book," Geisert reported in *SAAS.* "Earlier versions done on a single etching-plate date back fifteen years. *Oink* was the culmination of an idea that I had worked at, on and off, for years. I used our neighbor's pigs for models. It was a popular little book which received several awards and was translated into Spanish, German, and Japanese." As the sound that a pig makes is rendered the same in those languages as in English, it was not much of a translation effort. *Publishers Weekly* noted that the book's "droll illustrations exude an understated hilarity," and *Kirkus Reviews* dubbed its wordless sequel, *Oink Oink,* "a joyful adventure." *Pigs from 1 to 10* is a sequel to Geisert's earlier *Pigs from A to Z,* and a suspension bridge that Geisert had been building on his property played an integral part in this counting puzzle book. Numbers from 0 to 9 are hidden in each double-page, black-and-white etching. These etchings in turn tell the story of a pig family searching for a lost land. Each of the illustrations shows the piglets building elaborate machinery that will allow them to explore from mountain top to mountain top. "Few will be able to resist the game," concluded Nancy Vasilakis in *Horn Book.*

Geisert also illuminated the world of Roman numerals in *Roman Numerals I to MM.* "You have to count pigs to find the value of the Roman numeral," explained Geisert in *SAAS.* "The total number of pigs in the book is MMMMDCCCLXIV or 4,864." Jennifer Fleming, writing in *School Library Journal,* commented that "there is plenty of visual detail for early-elementary children to pore over," and *Booklist*'s Carolyn Phelan concluded that "Geisert's etchings, tinted with washes, make lively and beautifully detailed illustrations for this unusual book."

Teaming up with his wife, Geisert created a "quiet tribute to a bygone era," according to *Publishers Weekly,* with the picture book *Haystack.* The narrative explains the cycle of hay, from growth to cutting and stacking. Eventually the hay is used for feed and to provide warmth, while the animals give back to the cycle with their manure which fertilizes the next crop of hay. Leone McDermott in *Booklist* concluded that "readers will gain not only knowledge about haystacks, but also a sense of the atmosphere of farm life," while *School Library Journal* contributor Lee Bock noted that "the prose is brisk and straightforward and the text is superbly illustrated." *Haystack* went on to win several awards, including Honor Book listings from *Parents Choice* and *Boston Globe-Horn Book.*

In another non-pig book, 1997's *The Etcher's Studio,* Geisert's etching technique wins pride of place. "It shows how an etching is made and the studio equipment used in the etching process," Geisert wrote in *SAAS.* "For me there is no more beautiful way of putting line on paper than by etching." With his blend of humor and classical method, Geisert has made believers of the publishing industry as well as the book-buying public.

BIOGRAPHICAL/CRITICAL SOURCES:

BOOKS

Silvey, Anita, ed., *Children's Books and Their Creators,* Houghton Mifflin, 1995.

Something about the Author Autobiography Series, Volume 23, Gale, 1997, pp. 95-109.

PERIODICALS

Booklist, August, 1984, p. 1625; November 15, 1986, p. 509; September 15, 1995, p. 161; May 1, 1996, p. 1509.

Bulletin of the Center for Children's Books, October, 1984, p. 25; February, 1987, p. 106; September, 1988, p. 7; February, 1993, p. 176; February, 1994, p. 185; October, 1995, p. 54.

Horn Book, August, 1984, p. 457; January-February, 1986, p. 43; January-February, 1989, pp. 52-53; September-October, 1992, p. 575; July-August, 1994, pp. 440-441.

Kirkus Reviews, May 1, 1984, p. J30; August 15, 1985, p. 1290; July 1, 1988, p. 972; August 1, 1992, p. 989; February 1, 1993, p. 146; February 1, 1994, p. 142; July 15, 1995, p. 1023; January 15, 1996, p. 133; February 15, 1997, p. 299.

New York Times Book Review, July 29, 1984, p. 146; November 9, 1986, p. 39; November 27, 1988, p. 36; July 14, 1991, p. 25; January 31, 1993, p. 22; March 27, 1994, p. 21; January 28, 1996, p. 27; November 10, 1996.

Publishers Weekly, June 22, 1984, p. 100; March 29, 1991, p. 92; August 28, 1995, p. 112.

School Library Journal, October, 1988, p. 120; September, 1995, p. 193; September, 1996.

* * *

GERRARD, Roy 1935-

PERSONAL: Born January 25, 1935, in Atherton, Lancashire, England; son of Arthur (a miner) and Elsie (Hackett) Gerrard; married Jean Thatcher (a teacher), March 29, 1958; children: Sally Gerrard Turpie, Paul. *Education:* Attended Salford School of Art, 1950-54. *Politics:* "Nonexistent." *Religion:* "Barely visible." *Avocational interests:* "My spare time is spent recuperating."

ADDRESSES: *Home*—10 Maynestone Rd., Chinley, Stockport, Cheshire SK12 6AQ, England.

CAREER: Egerton Park County Secondary School, Denton, England, art teacher and department head, 1956-66; Hyde Grammar School, Hyde, England, art teacher and department head, 1966-80; painter, 1980—; author and illustrator of children's books, 1980—. *Exhibitions:* Annual one-man shows at SEEN Gallery, London, 1975-85. Illustrations have been exhibited at National Theatre, London, and in New York galleries.

AWARDS, HONORS: Mother Goose Award runner-up, *Books for Your Children* Bookshop, 1982, for *Matilda Jane;* "Fiera di Bologna" Children's Graphic Art Prize, Bologna Children's Book Fair, Parents' Choice Award for Illustration in Children's Books, Parents' Choice Foundation, and Best Illustrated Children's Books of the Year, *New York Times,* all 1983, all for *The Favershams;* Best Illustrated Children's Books of the Year, *New York Times,* 1984, for *Sir Cedric,* and 1988, for *Sir Francis Drake: His Daring Deeds;* Parents' Choice Award for Picture Book, 1989, for *Rosie and the Rustlers.*

WRITINGS:

SELF-ILLUSTRATED CHILDREN'S BOOKS

The Favershams, Gollancz, 1982, Farrar, Straus (New York City), 1983.

Sir Cedric, Farrar, Straus, 1984.

Sir Cedric Rides Again, Farrar, Straus, 1986.

Sir Francis Drake: His Daring Deeds, Farrar, Straus, 1988.

Rosie and the Rustlers, Farrar, Straus, 1989.

Mik's Mammoth, Farrar, Straus, 1990.

A Pocketful of Posies, Farrar, Straus, 1991.

Jocasta Carr, Movie Star, Farrar, Straus, 1992.

Croconile, Farrar, Straus, 1994.

Wagons West!, Farrar, Straus, 1996.

ILLUSTRATOR

Jean Gerrard, *Matilda Jane,* Gollancz (London), 1981, Farrar, Straus, 1983.

WORK IN PROGRESS: A children's book set in ancient Rome.

SIDELIGHTS: English author-illustrator Roy Gerrard is the creator of a number of award-winning picture books in verse that feature historical settings. His thumb-shaped humans play out their adventures and misadventures amid a rich and varied backdrop of period detail, as Gerrard gently satirizes medieval life, the Victorian and Edwardian ages, and the American West. Gerrard's verse texts provide a light accompaniment to his highly decorative and slyly humorous illustrations. "My paintings express a sense of whimsy which owes much to Lewis Carroll and Edward Lear," Gerrard once told *CA.* "I think this helped when I started to write children's books. I'm not really an author—I am more an amateur dabbler in light verse."

Gerrard's books have found a following on both sides of the Atlantic and with parents as well as children. Indeed, some critics have noted that

Gerrard's satire and wit is directed more at adults than at young readers. Reviewing his first solo effort, *The Favershams,* in the *New York Times Book Review,* Janice Prindle commented that "an appreciation of the real humor here demands a grown-up sense of history and an ability to understand the irony that the point of the Favershams' story is its very pointlessness." But if children do not always understand the historical context of the story, they can surely empathize with Gerrard's curiously foreshortened characters and appreciate his playful ballads, such as this one that begins his 1989 romp set in the American West, *Rosie and the Rustlers:* "Where the mountains meet the prairie, where the men are wild and hairy / There's a little ranch where Rosie Jones is boss. / It's a place that's neat and cozy, and the boys employed by Rosie / Work extremely hard, to stop her getting cross."

The Wild West is a long way from the English Midlands, where Gerrard was born in 1935. "As a boy I was brought up 12 miles outside Manchester," Gerrard told Jean Russell in an interview for *Books for Your Children,* "and as a child always thought of it as a magical city, the streetlife, the trams, horses, and cobblestone." After studying at the Salford School of Art, Gerrard taught art at secondary and grammar schools for twenty-five years. At the same time he was a Sunday painter, working in oils, but at one point he decided to quit painting and destroyed all his works. "Then in 1972," he further related to Russell, "I was immobilized for several weeks after a climbing accident and started tinkering around with small watercolours." After three years of such tinkering, Gerrard had hit on his idiosyncratic style that he described for Russell as "small, highly-detailed watercolours, remorselessly whimsical and often [featuring] Victorian/Edwardian subjects."

There followed several one-man shows in London, and in 1980 Gerrard quit teaching to devote full time to painting. It was at one of his shows that someone suggested that his paintings would also make good book illustrations. Subsequently, he teamed up with his wife to create his first illustrated book, *Matilda Jane,* with text by his wife. Light verse tells the story—set in Edwardian England—of little Matilda, who takes a seaside vacation with her parents and nanny and sees and experiences extraordinary things. Critics were quick to respond to Gerrard's quirky illustrations. Margery Fisher, in *Growing Point,* called *Matilda Jane* a "delectable book," and drew special attention to the "meticulous details of the Edwardian scenes on the railway and at the seaside, with their picture-postcard colours." Writing in *School Library Journal,* Ruth K. MacDonald also commented favorably on Gerrard's watercolor illustrations for *Matilda Jane.* "The abundant detail of gingerbread trim on houses, wallpaper patterns and bathing costumes are whimsically pleasing," noted MacDonald.

With his next title, Gerrard also wrote the text, as he has done for each of his subsequent works. "*The Favershams* is a story in verse of a Victorian gentleman, soldier, and scholar," Gerrard told *CA.* "Based on my childhood memories of my great-uncle Sam, who served in the British Army during Victoria's reign, it's an affectionately satirical look at nineteenth-century values and behavior." The verse story follows the life of one Charles Augustus Faversham from his birth, through school, the Army, love and marriage, a honeymoon, service in India, hunting big game, family life, and into retirement during which he becomes an author. All of this is told in low-key, humorous iambic tetrameter, as in this verse introducing the protagonist: "One day in eighteen fifty-one / These parents posed beside their son, / The son (that's him inside the pram) / Was Charles Augustus Faversham." Above this verse is a signature Gerrard watercolor with the proud parents in their garden and the family mansion behind with its acres of roof and solarium addition. The round-faced baby sits in his pram, his head covered by a wide straw hat. A table is laid for tea; a cat peaks out from behind the table cloth. The rest of the story is told in similar verses with full-page illustrations, one even of the newly married Charles and his wife nude bathing.

"This is good fun, gentle satire, a relevant comment on a period of history, all in one happy book," commented Marcus Crouch in the *Junior Bookshelf.* Elaine Moss, in her *Picture Books for Young People 9-13,* called *The Favershams* "a loving satire on the life of the ruling class in Victorian England." Commenting especially on the illustrations, Ann A. Flowers in *Horn Book* described the details of fabrics, wallpaper, and other elements as "brilliantly rendered," while noting that the "dark, muted reds and browns are certainly Victorian in feeling." A reviewer for *Publishers Weekly* called Gerrard's watercolors for *The Favershams* "tender, affectionately satiric slants on the proper Victorian and astonishingly beautiful," and noted that the "story equals the paintings as humorous art." Donnarae MacCann and Olga Richard, writing in the *Wilson Library Bulletin,* praised the technique which allowed Gerrard to infuse his illustrations with such a wealth of detail while suffering from neither "confusion or claustrophobic excess." MacCann and Richard added that there is "a haunting charm about [Gerrard's] static, posed figures, who look frozen in time while they are still living out an entire life span against changing backdrops." *The Favershams* won several international awards, including the "Fiera de Bologna" from the Bologna Children's Book Fair, and established Gerrard's reputation as an innovative and highly original illustrator and writer.

Gerrard furthered this reputation with his next effort, *Sir Cedric,* "a verse story of a medieval knight who is a do-gooder but also an all-round nice guy," as the author described the book to *CA.* The story, Gerrard explained, "owes much to the derring-do books I used to read as a boy, such as Kipling, Conan Doyle, Sir Walter Scott, and the Arthurian legends. It's written in the style of the Victorian music-hall monologue—deliberately lugubrious. The setting of *Sir Cedric* is based on Beeston Castle, a thirteenth-century ruin set on a 300 foot rocky knoll which rises steeply and dramatically from a typical Cheshire landscape—sleepy village and rich agricultural land." This parody of a medieval knight's tale is a mock-biography of Sir Cedric, who rescues Princess Matilda from her evil jailor, Black Ned, and then marries her. Humor comes, as Fisher noted in *Growing Point,* from "Cedric's small size . . . and the satirical suggestions in such details as the cucumber sandwiches eaten on the journey." Roy Foster, writing in the *Times Literary Supplement,* commented that *Sir Cedric* "is crammed not only with jingling quatrains recounting stirring deeds, but also with pictures of breathtaking intricacy and verve." Foster concluded that the illustrations might make *Sir Cedric* "a classic," but that the text also deserved praise as "tough-minded, funny and convincing," as in this description of Princess Matilda and her jailor: "Matilda, though fat, was a princess, you see, / and could have any man that she chose, / But Black Ned was badtempered, dirty and mean, / and had hairs growing out of his nose." Laurance Wieder, in the *New York Times Book Review,* found similarities to Pieter Breughel, Albrecht Duerer, William Blake, and William Morris in Gerrard's illustrations, and noted that such "lavish illustrations incorporate his verses in their design, and neither is complete without the other." Zena Sutherland in the *Bulletin of the Center for Children's Books* also commented favorably on Gerrard's illustrations for *Sir Cedric,* calling them "deft in technique and composition, humorous in effect, and often beautifully detailed and ornamented."

Sir Cedric Rides Again revisits the diminutive medieval knight who in this adventure finds that his daughter Edwina needs rescuing from Arab bandits. Her suitor, Hubert the Hopeless, turns into an instant hero when called upon, and all turns out well in this book which, according to Carolyn Phelan in *Booklist,* "pleases the ear, the eye, and the funny bone." A commentator in *Kirkus Reviews* also noted that *Sir Cedric Rides Again* was "a book to pore over, read aloud, and share with delight," while Zena Sutherland in *Bulletin of the Center for Children's Books* concluded that "this is lively, witty narrative poetry, and the paintings are of comparably high quality." Lachlan Mackinnon, however, writing in the *Times Literary Supplement,* called attention to "sexual and racial undertones [that] unsettle because they distract from the story and invite speculation and inquiry more mature than the likely readership." A reviewer for *Publishers Weekly* efficiently summed up the criticisms for and against *Sir Cedric Rides Again* by concluding that "those who side with Sir Cedric will hail his latest adventure; others may find his views too absolute."

Such absolute views seemingly inform Gerrard's next title, as well. *Sir Francis Drake: His Daring Deeds* tells the story of a man who was the first Englishman to circumnavigate the globe and who helped to destroy the Spanish Armada, but who was also a privateer for Queen Elizabeth I and not necessarily renowned for his tender mercies. Gerrard, however, manages to tell the main points of Drake's life in his usual tongue-in-cheek verse accompanied with his foreshortened people set against lushly detailed backgrounds. Kay E. Vandergrift, writing in *School Library Journal,* concludes that this is "a book that children will love to discover and explore," with its "majestic and detailed illustrations" and playful language, such as this from the final battle scene with the Armada: "The discombobulated foe / decided it was time to go." Ellen Mandel of *Booklist* declared that "rarely is history recalled with such verve or inspired liberty." Other critics, however, wondered at the subtext. John Cech in the *New York Times Book Review* noted that Gerrard's choice of scenes from Drake's ambiguous career put the privateer in the best possible light. "Alas, once one starts trying to make literal sense of the fragments Mr. Gerrard has chosen from Drake's life, the text quickly loses its credibility. Finally, as an American reader, one wonders if this is trying to pass for a fragment of unreconstructed history in Thatcher England." Cech also drew attention to Gerrard's strange little characters, "all head and torso on legs without thighs," and their odd juxtaposition with backgrounds which have normal proportions. Cech commented that this mannerism might work in other stories, but "here it limits rather than enriches the story, trivializing the very events Mr. Gerrard wishes to celebrate." Other commentators disagreed with such an appraisal, like Marcus Crouch in the *Junior Bookshelf* who warned that "we mustn't take [Gerrard's] account of the 'daring deeds' too literally: there is more artistic truth than sound fact in them." A *Publishers Weekly* reviewer also noted that "the irony of his plundering Spanish 'chaps' and other calculated word choices will not be lost on adults reading the story aloud. . . . This is diverting and sophisticated fare." *Sir Francis Drake: His Daring Adventures* was chosen as one of the ten best illustrated children's books of 1988 by the *New York Times.*

In a departure from English history, Gerrard's next book, *Rosie and the Rustlers,* told the story of Rosie Jones and her band of hard-working cowboys in oversized ten-gallon hats and their battle with the rustlers led by Greasy Ben. Employing his usual blend of one or two quatrains per page along with detailed watercolors, Gerrard managed to reach "children with little details that will make them giggle and even explode into laughter," concluded Kay E. Vandergrift in *School Library Journal.* Gerrard had a new venue for his painting, creating something of a parody of a movie Western chase scene allowing for panoramic double-page spreads of mountains and canyons. Betsy Hearne, reviewing *Rosie and the Rustlers* for the *Bulletin of the Center for Children's Books,* asserted that "the patterned landscapes and detailed portraits make this one of Gerrard's best." Nancy Vasilakis, writing in *Horn Book,* commented that Gerrard's "solid, chunky" figures worked especially well in a Western setting, and concluded that this was a book that would "be enjoyed at story hours as much for its visual fun as for its word play."

More recent additions to Gerrard's playful menagerie have included *Mik's Mammoths,* in which a caveman proves that wit and intelligence can win out over brawn; *Jocasta Carr, Movie Star,* which combines images of Shirley Temple and Amelia Earhart with the young star Jocasta setting off in her plane to find her stolen dog; *Croconile,* set in ancient Egypt; and *Wagons West!,* a return to a frontier setting in the story of a wagon train's journey west. A reviewer for *Publishers Weekly* called *Mik's Mammoths* a "refreshingly original glimpse of prehistoric life," while Carolyn Phelan in *Booklist* concluded that "touches of droll humor in both artwork and verse will endear it to readers young and old." Reviewing *Jocasta Carr, Movie Star* for *Magpies,* Moira Robinson described the book as a "tongue in cheek send-up" of early Hollywood movies with "dastardly villains" and "plucky heroines," and Eve Larkin in *School Library Journal* called it "a smashing adventuring," praising its illustrations as both fun and informative. A commentator for *Publishers Weekly* also noted Gerrard's illustrations in *Jocasta Carr,* asserting: "An abundance of fetching Art Deco motifs, from the array of geometric borders surrounding text and illustrations to furnishing and architectural details, give the book a bold, graphic look suggestive of its pre-World War II era." *Croconile* follows the adventures of a brother and sister and their pet crocodile in ancient Egypt, and the illustrations include ten hieroglyphic messages for which a key has been provided on the jacket flap. Phelan noted in *Booklist* that *Croconile* would be "an entertaining addition to any elementary unit on ancient Egypt," and a *Publishers Weekly* reviewer dubbed Gerrard's book "an innovative amalgam of ancient history lesson, introduction to hieroglyphics and fanciful story."

Wagons West! details the 1850s journey of a wagon train from Independence, Missouri, to Oregon's Willamette Valley. Buckskin Dan leads this band of intrepid travelers until they reach "Oregon at last, with all hazards safely past." Such hazards include cattle bandits, rough terrain, and river crossings. "The rich, dramatic scenes are rendered in earth-tone watercolors," noted Wendy Lukehart in *School Library Journal.* Kay Weisman, writing in *Booklist,* pointed out that "primary classes studying the westward movement and young history buffs will find this a pleasing introduction to life on the Oregon Trail." A *Publishers Weekly* reviewer assessed *Wagons West!* in a manner that has become fairly common in analyses of Gerrard's works. While noting that the author's verse "rolls easily off the tongue," the reviewer concluded that the artwork provides the real flavor of the volume. "The stylized characters indicate not so much an artistic idiosyncracy as a fully realized imaginative vision just waiting to be shared with the reader."

BIOGRAPHICAL/CRITICAL SOURCES:

BOOKS

Children's Book Illustration and Design, edited by Julie Cummins, PBC International, 1992.
Children's Literature Review, Volume 23, Gale, 1991, pp. 118-23.
Picture Books for Young People 9-13, Thimble Press, 1985, p. 43.

PERIODICALS

Booklist, January 1, 1987, p. 70; August 8, 1988, p. 1924; December 1, 1990, p. 745; October 15, 1994, p. 435; March 15, 1996, p. 1268.
Books for Your Children, summer, 1981, p. 4; autumn, 1986, p. 9; spring, 1989, p. 7; autumn, 1992, p. 51; summer, 1995, p. 23.
Bulletin of the Center for Children's Books, January, 1985, p. 83; December, 1986, p. 66; July, 1988, p. 228; November, 1989, p. 55; November, 1990, p. 59; January, 1995, p. 164.
Growing Point, September, 1981, p. 3950; November, 1984, p. 4347.
Horn Book, October, 1983, p. 562; January, 1989, p. 53; March-April, 1990, pp. 188-89.
Junior Bookshelf, December, 1982, p. 220; June, 1988, p. 130.
Kirkus Reviews, October 15, 1986, p. 1576.
Magpies, July, 1993, p. 31; March, 1995, p. 27.
New York Times Book Review, June 19, 1983, p. 26; November 4, 1984, p. 23; April 10, 1988, p. 38; August 13, 1995, p. 23.
Publishers Weekly, April 15, 1983, p. 50; November 28, 1986, p. 71; April 29, 1988, p. 74; October 12, 1990, p. 63; October 26, 1992, p. 71; September 5, 1994, p. 109; March 18, 1996, p. 69.
School Library Journal, April, 1982, p. 58; August 8, 1988, p. 81; February, 1990, p. 74; November, 1992, p. 70; March, 1996, p. 173.
Times Literary Supplement, October 5, 1984, p. 1139; December 26, 1986, p. 1458; April 1, 1988, p. 371.
Wilson Library Bulletin, November, 1983, p. 210.

* * *

GERSHATOR, Phillis 1942-

PERSONAL: Born July 8, 1942, in New York, NY; daughter of Morton Dimondstein (an artist) and Miriam Honixfeld Green (an artist); married David Gershator (an author) October 19, 1962; children: Yonah, Daniel. *Education:* Attended University of California, Berkeley, 1959-63; Douglass College, B.A., 1966; Pratt Institute, M.L.S., 1975. *Avocational interests:* Reading, gardening, cooking.

ADDRESSES: *Home*—P.O. Box 303353, St. Thomas, Virgin Islands 00803-3353.

CAREER: St. Thomas Public Library, St. Thomas, Virgin Islands, librarian, 1974-75, 1988-89; Enid M. Baa and Leonard Dober Elementary School libraries, Brooklyn, NY, children's librarian, 1977-84; Department of Education, St. Thomas, children's librarian, 1984-86. Has also worked as a secretary and in library promotion for various New York City publishers. Reading Is Fundamental volunteer in St. Thomas, 1984—.

MEMBER: Society of Children's Book Writers and Illustrators, Virgin Islands Library Association, Friends of the St. Thomas Library (secretary, 1985-95).

AWARDS, HONORS: Cooperative Children's Book Center of the University of Wisconsin choice book, Children's Book of the Year, Bank Street's Child Study Children's Book Committee, American Children's and Young Adult literature Award commended title, Consortium of Latin American Studies Programs, and Blue Ribbon Book, *Bulletin of the Center for Children's Books,* all 1994, all for *Tukama Tootles the Flute: A Tale from the Antilles;* Children's Book of the Year, Bank Street's Child Study Children's Book Committee, 1994, for *The Iroko-man: A Yoruba Folktale;* Junior Library Guild selection, National Council of Teachers of English Notable Trade Book in the Language Arts, 1995, and Best Black History for

Young People, *Booklist,* 1995, all for *Rata-pata-scata-fata: A Caribbean Story.*

WRITINGS:

FOR CHILDREN

Honi and His Magic Circle, illustrated by Shay Rieger, Jewish Publications Society of America (Philadelphia), 1979, revised edition published as *Honi's Circle of Trees,* illustrated by Mim Green, 1994.

Rata-pata-scata-fata: A Caribbean Story, illustrated by Holly Meade, Little, Brown (Boston), 1993.

(Reteller) *Tukama Tootles the Flute: A Tale from the Antilles,* illustrated by Synthia St. James, Orchard Books (New York City), 1994.

(Reteller) *The Iroko-man: A Yoruba Folktale,* illustrated by Holly Kim, Orchard Books, 1994.

Sambalena Show-off, illustrated by Leonard Jenkins, Macmillan (New York City), 1995.

(With husband, David Gershator) *Bread Is for Eating,* illustrated by Emma Shaw-Smith, Holt (New York City), 1995.

Sweet, Sweet Fig Banana, illustrated by Fritz Millevoix, Albert Whitman (Morton Grove, IL), 1996.

Zzzng! Zzzng! Zzzng!: A Yoruba Tale, Orchard Books, 1996.

Sugar Cakes Cyril, Mondo (Greenvale, NY), 1997.

Palampam Day, Marshall Cavendish (Freeport, NY), 1997.

OTHER

A Bibliographic Guide to the Literature of Contemporary American Poetry, 1970-1975, Scarecrow Press (Metuchen, NJ), 1976.

Contributor of poems and book reviews to periodicals.

SIDELIGHTS: Phillis Gershator is the author of award-winning picture books based on the black folklore of such places as the Caribbean and Africa. Her stories have been either original works, like *Rata-pata-scata-fata: A Caribbean Story,* or retellings, such as *Tukama Tootles the Flute: A Tale from the Antilles.*

Gershator's career as an author began with an early love of books. "[My] family was in the book business in New York," she explained in a *Junior Library Guild* article, and she often received books as gifts. She read so much that her mother often had to force her to go outside to play and get some exercise. As a graduate student, Gershator majored in library science. Her first job as a librarian was on the island of St. Thomas, where her family had moved from New York City in 1969. The Caribbean eventually became the setting for *Rata-pata-scata-fata* and *Tukama Tootles the Flute.*

After working for several years at libraries and publishing companies in New York City, Gershator returned to St. Thomas in 1988. Gleaning much satisfaction through her library work and as a Reading Is Fundamental (RIF) volunteer, Gershator wanted to contribute even more to children by writing her own stories. Career and family kept her from spending much time on her writing, though she published her first book, *Honi and His Magic Circle,* in 1979 and has been composing poems and short stories since the early 1970s. It was not until the mid-1990s that her career would really take off, however. In 1993 and 1994 she published three very successful books: *Rata-pata-scata-fata, Tukama Tootles the Flute,* and *The Iroko-Man: A Yoruba Tale,* all of which have won awards.

Rata-pata-scata-fata is about a young St. Thomas boy named Junjun who tries to avoid household chores by chanting "Caribbean gobbledygook" in the hope that his tasks will be completed by magic. Although luck, not magic, smiles on him to grant him all his wishes, Junjun attributes everything to his gobbledygook. A *Kirkus Reviews* critic called the tale "an engagingly cadenced story that will be just right for sharing aloud." "Gershator has a light and lively sense of language," declared *Bulletin of the Center for Children's Books* contributor Betsy Hearne, "along with a storytelling rhythm that shows experience with keeping young listeners involved."

In a similar vein to *Rata-pata-scata-fata, Tukama Tootles the Flute* is about another St. Thomas boy who is unreliable in his chores. In this yarn, young Tukama loves to play his flute so much that he does not help his grandmother like he should, although she warns him that his disobedient ways might one day cause him to wind up in the stomach of the local two-headed giant. Tukama's grandmother's words prove unsurprisingly prophetic when the boy is captured by the giant, but he manages to escape by playing his flute for the giant's wife. The frightening experience teaches Tukama a lesson, and thereafter he restricts his playing until after his chores are done. Pointing out the similarities between this story and "Jack and the Beanstalk," *School Library Journal* reviewer Lyn Miller-Lachman commented that *Tukama Tootles the Flute* "offers an opportunity to observe similarities and differences in folklore around the world." A *Publishers Weekly* critic favorably remarked that the "text pulses with the rhythms of island dialect and is laced with the casual asides of an oral storyteller."

Like the Caribbean children in these stories, Gershator considers herself to be very lucky. "Wishes do, once in a while, [come true]," she said in *Junior Library Guild,* "so I don't consider *Rata-pata-scata-fata* a fairy tale, and oddly enough, that little boy seems very familiar."

BIOGRAPHICAL/CRITICAL SOURCES:

PERIODICALS

Booklist, April 15, 1994, p. 1541; May 1, 1994, p. 1603; May 15, 1994, p. 1676; February 15, 1995, p. 1094.
Bulletin of the Center for Children's Books, April, 1994, p. 257.
Horn Book Guide, fall, 1994, p. 340.
Junior Library Guild, April-September, 1994, p. 14.
Kirkus Reviews, February 1, 1994, p. 142; May 1, 1994, p. 629.
Publishers Weekly, January 10, 1994, p. 60; April 4, 1994, p. 79.
School Librarian, November, 1994, p. 145.
School Library Journal, April, 1994, p. 118; July, 1995, p. 27; September, 1995, p. 194.

* * *

GETHERS, Peter 1953-

PERSONAL: Born April 10, 1953, in New York, NY; son of Steven and Judith Gethers. *Education:* Attended University of California, Berkeley, 1970-72, University of London, 1972-73, and University of California, Los Angeles, 1973-74.

ADDRESSES: Home—74 5th Ave. #6A, New York, NY 10011. *Office*—Random House, Inc., 201 East 50th St., New York, NY 10022. *E-mail*—gushen@aol.com. *Agent*—Esther Newberg, International Creative Management, 40 West 57th St., New York, NY 10019.

CAREER: Bantam Books, Inc., New York City, executive editor, 1975-80; Random House, Inc., New York City, editor, 1980-83; Villard Books, New York City, vice president and editorial director, 1983-91; Random House, Inc., vice president and editor-at-large, 1991—.

MEMBER: National Academy of Television Arts and Sciences, Writers Guild of America (East), Authors League of America.

WRITINGS:

The Dandy (novel), Dutton (New York City), 1978.
(Coauthor) *Rotisserie League Baseball* (nonfiction annual), Bantam (New York City), 1985, 1987, 1989, 1990.
Getting Blue (novel), Delacorte (New York City), 1987.
The Cat Who Went to Paris (nonfiction), Crown/Ballantine (New York City), 1991.
A Cat Abroad (nonfiction), Crown/Ballantine, 1993.
Historical Cats (humor), Fawcett (New York City), 1996.

Author of several television scripts for the series *Kate and Allie.* Writer-producer for television series *Working It Out;* cocreator/executive producer of television series *Land's End.* Contributor to *Esquire, New York Times,* and *New York Daily News Sunday Magazine.*

WORK IN PROGRESS: Flame, a novel; *Say When It Hurts,* a screenplay.

SIDELIGHTS: The Dandy, Peter Gethers's first novel, describes a "monster of the '70s," according to Joseph McLellan in a *Washington Post* review. The protagonist of the novel is a 30-year-old man named Eugene Toddmann who deals with life by detaching himself from it emotionally. Thus, the only reaction he allows himself whenever tragedy strikes is curiosity. He becomes asocial, an attitude that leads him to kill the closest thing he has to a best friend in a duel over a woman he does not even care about. "Clearly, we are dealing here with a monster," writes McLellan, "a walking abstraction, but I suspect it is a monster that looms as a sort of ideal for more than one young man of our era." "It is no small undertaking to center a book on a nearly abstract character and yet hold the reader's interest for over 200 pages," McLellan later notes, "but Gethers has done it with a virtuoso flourish."

In another *Washington Post* article, Tom Miller praises the characters and writing in Gethers's *Getting Blue,* a novel about one athlete's rise to the top of professional baseball. "Often Gethers's personality sketches jump off the page and demand rereading in admiration of their precision," Miller attests. The reviewer also admires the author's accurate depiction of the earlier years of baseball: "His observations about black-white relations in 1950s minor-league baseball are sensitively—and, I suspect, accurately—portrayed." But despite the book's strengths, Miller concludes that "the three or four story lines don't end concurrently, and we're left with a book whose parts are far greater than their sum."

BIOGRAPHICAL/CRITICAL SOURCES:

PERIODICALS

New York Times Book Review, September 29, 1991.

Washington Post, August 24, 1978; April 7, 1987.

* * *

GILLESPIE, John T(homas) 1928-

PERSONAL: Born September 25, 1928, in Fort William, Ontario, Canada; immigrated to the United States, 1955, naturalized citizen, 1963; son of William and Jean (Barr) Gillespie. *Ethnicity:* "White." *Education:* University of British Columbia, B.A., 1948; Columbia University, M.A., 1957; New York University, Ph.D., 1970.

ADDRESSES: Home and office—360 East 72nd St., New York, NY 10021.

CAREER: Elementary schoolteacher in British Columbia, 1950-55; school librarian in Hicksville, NY, 1956-57, and Roslyn, NY, 1957-63; Long Island University, C. W. Post Center, Greenvale, NY, associate professor, 1963-71, professor of library science, 1971-86, dean of Palmer Graduate Library School, 1971-76, 1980-82, vice president for academic affairs, 1982-85. Long Island University, adjunct assistant professor, 1960-63. Hunter College of the City University of New York, circulation librarian, 1959-61.

MEMBER: American Library Association, Association of American Library Schools, Association for Educational Communication and Technology, National Education Association, New York Library Association (member of board of directors; president, 1962), New York Library Club, Nassau-Suffolk School Library Association (president, 1960), Phi Delta Kappa, Kappa Delta Pi.

WRITINGS:

(With Diana L. Lembo) *Junior Plots,* Bowker (New Providence, NJ), 1966.

The Secondary School Library as an Instructional Materials Center, New York State Department of Education, 1969.

(With Lembo and Ralph J. Folcarelli) *Library Learning Laboratory,* Fordham Publishing, 1969.

(With Lembo) *Introducing Books,* Bowker, 1970.

(With Diana L. Spirt) *The Young Phenomenon: Paperbacks in Our Schools,* American Library Association (Chicago), 1971.

Paperback Books for Young People, American Library Association, 1971, second edition, 1977.

(With Spirt) *Creating a School Media Program,* Bowker, 1973.

More Junior Plots, Bowker, 1977.

A Model School District Media Program, American Library Association, 1977.

(With Christine Gilbert) *Best Books for Children,* Bowker, 1978, fifth edition, 1994.

Home and School Reading and Study Guides, New Book of Knowledge, 1980.

(With Spirt) *Administering the School Library Media Center,* Bowker, 1983, third edition, 1992.

The Elementary School Paperback Collection, American Library Association, 1984.

The Junior High School Paperback Collection, American Library Association, 1984.

The Senior High School Paperback Collection, American Library Association, 1986.

Juniorplots 3, Bowker, 1987.

Seniorplots, Bowker, 1989.
Best Books for Junior High School Readers, Bowker, 1992.
Best Books for Senior High School Readers, Bowker, 1992.
Juniorplots 4, Bowker, 1993.
Middleplots, Bowker, 1994.
Guides to Library Collection Development, Libraries Unlimited (Englewood, CO), 1994.
The Newbery Companion, Libraries Unlimited, 1996.
Characters in Young Adult Literature, Gale (Detroit), 1997.
Guides to Library Collection Development for Children and Young Adults, Libraries Unlimited, 1997.

SIDELIGHTS: John T. Gillespie once told *CA:* "The basic principles of learning have remained the same throughout the years: children learn as individuals, children learn at various rates, children learn according to different styles and patterns, and education is a continuous process. In an attempt to translate these principles into practice, educators have realized that a unified media program involving all forms and types of educational materials and equipment is a necessity. There has been increased support of the library media center concept from many agencies, organizations, and professional personnel because those who are involved in education now realize that a sound media program is a prerequisite for high quality education."

* * *

GILLILAND, (Cleburne) Hap 1918-

PERSONAL: Born August 26, 1918, in Willard, CO; son of Samuel Smith (a teacher) and Esther J. (an artist; maiden name, Sandstedt) Gilliland; married Erma L. Roderick (a secretary), April 21, 1946; children: Lori Sargent, Diane Bakun, Dwight. *Education:* Western State College (Colorado), A.A., 1948, B.A., 1949, M.A., 1950; University of Northern Colorado, Ed.D., 1958; attended University of Colorado, Philippine Teachers College, and Eastern Montana College. *Religion:* Protestant.

ADDRESSES: Home—2032 Woody Dr., Billings, MT 59102.

CAREER: Public school teacher in Richland, WA, 1950-53; Humboldt State University, Arcata, CA, supervising teacher, 1953-60; Montana State University—Billings, professor, 1960-80; Lake and Peniasual Schools, Alaska, bilingual and multicultural specialist, 1980-84. Council for Indian Education (a publisher of educational and children's books), president and editor, 1970—. Has directed various educational programs serving Indian reservations and chaired numerous committees dealing with Indian and general education. Has conducted teacher training workshops. Has been a visiting lecturer and speaker at numerous institutions. *Military service:* U.S. Air Force, 1942-46.

MEMBER: International Reading Association (Montana state president, 1963-75), Montana Writers Coalition, Billings Arts Association (vice-president, 1963-64, 1988-90; president, 1990-92), Billings Friendship Force (vice-president, 1988-90, 1994-95), Kiwanis.

AWARDS, HONORS: Merit Award for Research and Creative Endeavor, Committee on Evaluation of Faculty, Eastern Montana College, 1977; Bronze Plaque in recognition of outstanding contributions to child's rights and education, Billings Committee for International Year of the Child, 1978; Outstanding Alumnus Award, Western State College of Colorado, 1979. Professor Emeritus, Montana State University—Billings.

WRITINGS:

FOR CHILDREN

No One Like a Brother, Council for Indian Education, 1970.
Broken Ice, Council for Indian Education, 1972.
Coyote's Pow-wow, Council for Indian Education, 1972.
The Flood, Montana Reading Publications, 1972.
Bill Red Coyote Is a Nut, Council for Indian Education, 1981.
(With Betty Greison and Sam Bloom) *Black Hawk and Jim Thorp: Super Heroes,* Council for Indian Education, 1983.
Drums of the Head Hunters (novel), Winston-Derek (Nashville), 1987.
O'Kohome: The Coyote Dog, illustrated by Tanya Hardgrove, 1989.

Mystery Tracks in the Snow: A Guide to Animal Tracks, Naturegraph (Happy Camp, CA), 1990.
(With others) *When We Went to the Mountains,* Council for Indian Education, 1991.
Flint's Rock (novel), illustrated by Pauline Livers-Lambert, Robert Rinehart (Niwot, CO), 1994.

Also author of *We Live on an Indian Reservation, How the Dogs Saved the Cheyennes, The Dark Side of the Moon,* and *Jumper;* author, with Royce Holland, Virginia Kroll, and Sylvia Mularchyk, of *Search for Identity* (stories).

TEXTBOOKS

Materials for Remedial Reading, Montana Reading Publications, 1965, revised, 1966, 1967, 1972, 1976.
Establishment and Operation of a Remedial Reading Program, Alpine, 1967.
Analysis Skills, Alpine, 1968.
A Practical Guide to Remedial Reading, C. E. Merrill (Columbus, OH), 1974.
Corrective and Remedial Reading, Alpine, 1973.

OTHER

Chant of the Red Man, Council for Indian Education, 1976.
(With others) *Teaching the Native American,* Kendall/Hunt (Dubuque, IA), 1988.
(With Bill Walters) *Challenging Education: A Positive Approach to Teaching Maori Students in New Zealand Schools,* Kupenga O Te Matouranga (New Zealand), 1994.
Voices of Native America, Kendall/Hunt, 1997.

Also author of *The Road to Happiness* (poetry), Council Publications. Author of three standardized tests. Contributor to *Reading Teacher, Reading Horizons,* and *Journal of the Reading Association of Ireland.* Editor of "Indian Culture Series" for Montana Reading Publications, beginning 1970. Editor of *Montana Journal of Reading,* 1962-68; member of editorial board of *Journal of Reading,* 1972-74, *ERIC Research Materials,* beginning 1973, *Reading Teacher,* beginning 1974, and *Reading Horizons,* beginning 1974.

WORK IN PROGRESS: Enhancing Your Wilderness Experience; Cooperative Learning for Hispanic and Native American Students.

SIDELIGHTS: Hap Gilliland told *CA:* "My two main interests for the last thirty years have been writing children's books and studying world cultures. Believing that the way to learn about and understand a culture is to live in it, I have lived in the homes of indigenous peoples on all five continents and the Pacific islands.

"I grew up on a horse ranch in Southeast Colorado. I still love to do ranch work and ride horseback. I also hike and climb, and spend one to two weeks each summer backpacking in the Montana wilderness areas."

* * *

GILSON, Jamie 1933-

PERSONAL: Born July 4, 1933, in Beardstown, IL; daughter of James Noyce (a flour miller) and Sallie (a teacher; maiden name, Wilkinson) Chisam; married Jerome Gilson (a lawyer), June 19, 1955; children: Tom, Matthew, Anne. *Education:* Attended University of Missouri, 1951-52; Northwestern University, B.S., 1955.

ADDRESSES: Home—Wilmette, IL.

CAREER: Thacker Junior High School, Des Plaines, IL, speech and English teacher, 1955-56; writer and producer for radio and television division of public school system in Chicago, IL, 1956-59; WFMT-Radio, Chicago, continuity director, 1959-63; Encyclopaedia Britannica, Chicago, writer in film division, 1963-65. Lecturer and writing workshop teacher, Wilmette Public Schools, 1974-90.

MEMBER: Society of Children's Book Writers and Illustrators, Children's Reading Round Table, Society of Midland Authors, PEN American Center, Authors Guild, Authors League of America.

AWARDS, HONORS: Merit Award, Friends of American Writers, 1979, for *Harvey, the Beer Can King;* Carl Sandburg Award, Friends of the Chicago Public Library, 1981, and Charlie May Simon Award, Arkansas Elementary School Council, 1983, both for *Do Bananas Chew Gum?;* Dallas Market Center Gift Editorial Award, 1983, for column "The Goods"; Sequoyah Award and Pacific Northwest Young Readers Choice Award, both 1985, Land of Enchantment Award, 1986, Buckeye Award and Sunshine Award, both 1987, all for *Thirteen Ways to Sink a Sub;* Children's Reading Round Table Award, 1992; *Do Bananas Chew Gum?* and *Can't Catch Me, I'm the Gingerbread Man* were Junior Literary Guild selections.

WRITINGS:

FOR CHILDREN

Harvey, the Beer Can King, illustrated by John Wallner, Lothrop (New York City), 1978.
Dial Leroi Rupert, DJ, illustrated by John Wallner, Lothrop, 1979.
Do Bananas Chew Gum?, Lothrop, 1980.
Can't Catch Me, I'm the Gingerbread Man, Lothrop, 1981.
Thirteen Ways to Sink a Sub, illustrated by Linda Strauss Edwards, Lothrop, 1982.
4-B Goes Wild, illustrated by Linda Straus Edwards, Lothrop, 1983.
Hello, My Name Is Scrambled Eggs, illustrated by John Wallner, Lothrop, 1985.
Hobie Hanson, You're Weird, illustrated by Elise Primavera, Lothrop, 1987.
Double Dog Dare, illustrated by Elise Primavera, Lothrop, 1988.
Hobie Hanson: Greatest Hero of the Mall, illustrated by Anita Riggio, Lothrop, 1989.
Itchy Richard, illustrated by Diane de Groat, Clarion (New York City), 1991.
Sticks and Stones and Skeleton Bones, illustrated by Dee DeRosa, Lothrop, 1991.
You Cheat!, illustrated by Maxine Chambliss, Bradbury Press (New York City), 1992.
Soccer Circus, illustrated by Dee DeRosa, Lothrop, 1993.
It Goes Eeeeeeeeeeeee!, illustrated by Diane de Groat, Clarion, 1994.
Wagon Train 911, Lothrop, 1996.

OTHER

Author of *Chicago Magazine* column "The Goods," 1977-87. Contributor of articles to *WFMT Guide* and *Perspective* magazine.

SIDELIGHTS: Jamie Gilson's humorous books for middle-grade readers, all written in first-person from the perspective of an adolescent, demonstrate her keen understanding of the priorities and concerns of younger teens. "Before writing books for children, all of my professional writing had been for the voice—radio, TV, films—so that my books, too, are *told,* as a child would tell them," Gilson once related to *CA*. "To keep that voice genuine, I work with children a good deal, speaking to them about my writing, teaching writing to sixth graders, sitting in with classes, going with a fifth grade class on a nature study overnight. . . . My research is a joy."

One of the early books to grow out of Gilson's experience with children is *Do Bananas Chew Gum?,* published in 1980. Gilson got the idea for the story from an assignment she had as a reporter for *Chicago Magazine,* covering an archaeological dig in southern Illinois. "I discovered the real excitement that comes from finding broken arrowheads and shards of once-used clay pots," she recalled for *CA*. "Sam Mott in *Bananas* shares that enthusiasm." Sam is a sixth-grader who has become the subject of his classmates' unkind jokes because he reads at a second-grade level. His reading difficulties make him feel stupid, so he tries to hide them from his family and friends. As the story progresses Sam receives encouragement and motivation to overcome his problem from a young archaeologist who shares her love of history with him, as well as from the kind woman for whom he baby-sits and from one of his classmates. He agrees to a series of tests and learns that he is not stupid after all—he has a learning disability. By working with an understanding teacher, Sam is not only able to read better, but also improves his confidence and outlook on life. "Told with humor and subtle compassion, this is a story that leaves you feeling good," reviewer Jane VanWiemokly commented in *Voice of Youth Advocates*. "I hope that children will not only find *Bananas* fun to read, but also revealing of the difficulties that a learning-disabled child faces," Gilson told *CA*.

Gilson introduced one of her most popular characters, Hobie Hanson, in *Thirteen Ways to Sink a Sub,* published in 1982. In this story, Hobie and his fourth-grade classmates are surprised to find a substitute teacher, Miss Svetlana Ivanovich, taking over their lessons for the day. The boys and the girls quickly face off to see which team can be the first to "sink the sub," or upset her to the point of tears. Some of their antics include switching names, pretending not to speak English, and faking the loss of a contact lens. Miss Ivanovich remains pleasant and good-natured throughout the contest, which eventually makes the class like her too much to continue trying to "sink" her. Barbara

Elleman of *Booklist* praised Gilson's book for its "crisp, inventive plot that is top drawer in the contemporary fiction genre for this age group."

Gilson rejoined Hobie and his friends in 1987's *Hobie Hanson, You're Weird.* When Hobie's best friend, Nick Rossi, goes away to computer camp for the summer, Hobie is left on his own. At first he is annoyed when his classroom rival, Molly Bosco, begins following him around, but before long they find out how much they have in common and share some entertaining adventures. Writing in *School Library Journal,* Julie Cummins noted that "with dialogue right on target for the age, Gilson writes with humor and appeal for kids." A *Booklist* reviewer praised Gilson's "bulls-eye wit and ease with the written word" and claimed that "kids will be attracted to this like steel to a magnet."

Hobie has a harrowing adventure in *Hobie Hanson: Greatest Hero of the Mall,* published in 1989. In this story, heavy rains cause the nearby Hawk River to overflow its banks and flood much of Hobie's hometown. He tries to be a hero, but instead Molly Bosco floats by on an inflatable giraffe and rescues him and the little boy he is baby-sitting. Since the elementary school was damaged in the flood, Hobie and his friends learn that school will be held temporarily in an empty department store at the local mall. In this unusual educational setting, the class finds a variety of new ways to make hilarious mischief. Hobie finally does become a hero by finding some diamond earrings that were lost in the flood and returning them to their owner, and he is only slightly less pleased with himself when he learns that the diamonds are fake. Denise Wilms, writing in *Booklist,* stated that the story "has action, humor, and a protagonist familiar enough to be the boy next door," and predicted that "Hobie's fans will be quick to line up for this one."

Gilson explores the relationship between two young brothers in 1992's *You Cheat!* Active, six-year-old Nathan longs to show up his video-game loving older brother, Hank. When he can't beat Hank at cards, Nathan challenges his brother to go fishing with him and see who can land the biggest fish. Since Hank thinks worms are gross and fishing is boring, Nathan convinces him to accept the challenge by promising to kiss every fish Hank catches on the mouth. Deciding that the prospect of Nathan kissing a fish is too good an opportunity to pass up, Hank agrees to the contest and makes Nathan deliver on his promise. In a review for *School Library Journal,* Maggie McEwen called *You Cheat!* "an excellent beginning chapter book" and noted that the "simple adventure will appeal to early readers."

Some of Gilson's remaining books for young readers deal with subjects like head lice (*Itchy Richard*), bats (*It Goes Eeeeeeeeeeeee!*), and ways to settle disputes peacefully (*Sticks and Stones and Skeleton Bones*). Hobie Hanson and friends are again featured at their temporary school in the mall in *Sticks and Stones and Skeleton Bones.* In this tale, Hobie and classmates Nick Rossi and Molly Bosco become embroiled in an accelerating cycle of practical jokes, misunderstandings, and retaliation, until all three end up in the school's new conflict management program, where they—and readers—learn that there are two sides to every story. Reviewing *Sticks and Stones and Skeleton Bones* for *Booklist,* Deborah Abbott maintained that Gilson "paints her characters with a refined brush, showing in an uncanny fashion the intricacies and nuances of the world of fifth-graders." *Itchy Richard* addresses a problem common to many grade schoolers: head lice. Someone in Mrs. Zookey's second-grade class has them, and rumors begin to fly among the children when the head nurse comes in to check each of their scalps. As the students exchange exaggerated ideas about these bugs and what they do, central protagonist Richard begins to feel kind of itchy himself. Mrs. Zookey settles everyone down with a simple explanation of head lice and how they are treated. "Loaded with kid-appealing humor and personalities straight out of a grade-school classroom," asserted Stephanie Zvirin for *Booklist,* "Gilson's sensitive story takes a fairly common elementary school problem and makes it seem, if no less 'yucky,' at least less scary." A reviewer for *Publishers Weekly* added that in *Itchy Richard* "Gilson displays the same snappy dialogue and brisk humor that have made her Hobie Hanson novels so popular with youngsters."

Richard and his friends from Mrs. Zookey's class return in *It Goes Eeeeeeeeeeeee!,* a story supplying a palatable dose of information about bats to again clear up the young students' misconceptions and fears. In her review of this tale in *Booklist,* Stephanie Zvirin noted that Gilson "feeds the facts smoothly and memorably into the fictional format." Other commentators cited Gilson's trademark warmth, humor, and first-person narration, while appreciatively underscoring her remarkable understanding of the world of grade school students.

BIOGRAPHICAL/CRITICAL SOURCES:

BOOKS

Sixth Book of Junior Authors and Illustrators, edited by Sally Holmes Holtze, H. W. Wilson (Bronx, NY), 1989.

PERIODICALS

Booklist, October 1, 1982, p. 244; September 1, 1983, p. 85; June 15, 1987, p. 1601; September 1, 1988, p. 76; September 1, 1989, p. 71; March 1, 1991, p. 1392; September 15, 1991, p. 150; August, 1992, p. 2011; April 1, 1993, p. 1431; April 1, 1994, p. 1446.

Bulletin of the Center for Children's Books, November, 1978, p. 43; March, 1981, p. 133; June, 1981, p. 171; December, 1982, p. 67; October, 1983, p. 27.

Kirkus Reviews, May 1, 1978, p. 497; December 15, 1980, p. 1570; July 15, 1981, p. 872; September 1, 1983, p. 161; March 1, 1985, p. 11; October 15, 1991, p. 1353; August 15, 1992, p. 1061; May 1, 1994, p. 629.

Publishers Weekly, June 24, 1988, p. 114; July 28, 1989, p. 222; January 18, 1991, p. 58; September 20, 1991, p. 134; March 8, 1993, pp. 79-80.

School Library Journal, September, 1981, p. 124; January, 1983, p. 75; August, 1985, p. 64; June, 1987, p. 95; September, 1988, p. 183; October, 1989, p. 118; March, 1991, p. 193; December, 1991, p. 90; September, 1992, p. 203; June, 1993, p. 106; June, 1994, p. 100.

Voice of Youth Advocates, April, 1981, p. 34.

* * *

GLASS, Andrew 1949-

PERSONAL: Born in 1949. *Education:* Attended Temple University and School of Visual Arts, New York, NY.

ADDRESSES: Home—New York, NY. *Office*—Doubleday & Co., Inc., 1540 Broadway, New York, NY, 10036-4094.

CAREER: Author and illustrator.

AWARDS, HONORS: Newbery honor book, American Library Association (ALA), 1983, for *Graven Images: Three Stories,* written by Paul Fleischman and illustrated by Andrew Glass, and 1984, for *The Wish Giver: Three Tales of Coven Tree,* written by William Brittain and illustrated by Glass.

WRITINGS:

FOR CHILDREN; SELF-ILLUSTRATED

Jackson Makes His Move, Warne (New York City), 1982.

My Brother Tries to Make Me Laugh, Lothrop (New York City), 1984.

Chickpea and the Talking Cow, Lothrop, 1987.

Charles T. McBiddle, Doubleday (New York City), 1993.

Folks Call Me Appleseed John, Doubleday, 1995.

The Sweetwater Run: The Story of Buffalo Bill Cody and the Pony Express, Doubleday, 1996.

A Right Fine Life: Kit Carson on the Santa Fe Trail, Holiday House, 1997.

ILLUSTRATOR

George E. Stanley, *Crime Lab,* Avon (New York City), 1980.

Nancy Etchemendy, *The Watchers of Space,* Avon, 1980.

Bill Brittain, *Devil's Donkey,* Harper (New York City), 1981.

Catherine E. Sadler, adapter, *The Adventures of Sherlock Holmes* (4 volumes), Avon, 1981.

Elizabeth Charlton, *Terrible Tyrannosaurus,* Elsevier/Nelson (New York City), 1981.

Theodore Taylor, *The Battle of Midway Island,* Avon, 1981.

Taylor, *H.M.S. Hood vs. Bismarck: The Battleship Battle,* Avon, 1982.

Robert Newton Peck, *Banjo,* Knopf (New York City), 1982.

Natalie Savage Carlson, *Spooky Night,* Lothrop, 1982.

Paul Fleischman, *Graven Images: Three Stories,* Harper, 1982.

Marilyn Singer, *The Fido Frame-Up,* Warne, 1983.

Taylor, *Battle in the English Channel,* Avon, 1983.

Joan Lowery Nixon, *The Gift,* Macmillan, 1983.

Brittain, *The Wish Giver: Three Tales of Coven Tree,* Harper, 1983.
Carlson, *The Ghost in the Lagoon,* Lothrop, 1984.
Singer, *A Nose for Trouble,* Holt (New York CIty), 1985.
Carlson, *Spooky and the Ghost Cat,* Lothrop, 1985.
Carlson, *Spooky and the Wizard's Bats,* Lothrop, 1986.
Singer, *Where There's a Will, There's a Wag,* Holt, 1986.
Brittain, *Dr. Dredd's Wagon of Wonders,* Harper, 1987.
Beverly Major, *Playing Sardines,* Scholastic (New York CIty), 1988.
Carlson, *Spooky and the Bad Luck Raven,* Lothrop, 1988.
Susan Beth Pfeffer, *Rewind to Yesterday,* Delacorte (New York City), 1988.
Pfeffer, *Future Forward,* Delacorte, 1989.
Carlson, *Spooky and the Witch's Goat,* Lothrop, 1989.
Robert D. San Souci, *Larger than Life: John Henry and Other Tall Tales,* Doubleday, 1991.
Brittain, *Professor Popkin's Prodigious Polish,* HarperCollins, 1991.
David Gifaldi, *Gregory, Maw, and the Mean One,* Clarion (New York City), 1992.
Tom Birdseye, reteller, *Soap Soap Don't Forget the Soap: An Appalachian Folktale,* Holiday House (New York City), 1993.
Karen Hesse, *Lavender,* Holt, 1993.
Susan Whitcher, *Real Mummies Don't Bleed: Friendly Tales for October Nights,* Farrar, Straus (New York CIty), 1993.
Susan Mathias Smith, *The Booford Summer,* Clarion, 1994.
T. Birdseye and Debbie Holsclaw Birdseye, adapters, *She'll Be Comin' Round the Mountain,* Holiday House, 1994.
Al Carusone, *Don't Open the Door after the Sun Goes Down: Tales of the Real and Unreal,* Clarion, 1994.
Tololwa M. Mollel, reteller, *Ananse's Feast: An Ashanti Tale,* Clarion, 1996.
Whitcher, *The Key to the Cupboard,* Farrar, Straus, 1996.
Emily Herman, *Liza and the Fossil,* Hyperion (New York CIty), 1996.
Bethany Roberts, *Monster Manners: A Guide to Monster Etiquette,* Clarion, 1996.
Alan Schroeder, *The Tale of Willie Monroe,* Clarion, 1997.

Also illustrator of *The Glass Ring,* Mary Kennedy, Dandelion Press.

SIDELIGHTS: A talented artist, Andrew Glass illustrates his own stories as well as those of other authors. In fact, art is so much a part of his life that the first book he authored and illustrated, *Jackson Makes His Move,* features a raccoon artist, rendered by Glass in pencil and watercolor. When Jackson realizes that he is no longer inspired by the country around him, and when he tires of his realistic paintings, he heads for the busy, chaotic city. There, instead of painting what he sees, he paints what he feels. The resulting works are large and abstract. According to Kenneth Marantz of *School Library Journal,* Jackson "helps readers come to grips with some of the rationale of such movements as Abstract Expressionism."

My Brother Tries to Make Me Laugh provides an example of the author-illustrator's whimsical talent. In crayon-colored illustrations, Glass portrays a brother and sister traveling to planet Earth on their spaceship. Odeon, a bright purple alien with a snout and stalk-eyes, attempts to get his sister to laugh to break up the monotony of a long journey. "How could this miss?" asked a critic from the *Bulletin of the Center for Children's Books.*

Another of Glass's works recalls the classic children's story, "Tom Thumb." In *Chickpea and the Talking Cow,* a tiny boy named Chickpea is swallowed up by his father's cow. Despite his misfortune, the boy is determined to make his father rich by speaking from within the cow and tricking the Emperor into thinking that the cow can talk. According to Patricia Dooley in *School Library Journal,* "everyone should enjoy" the book's line and wash illustrations, which are "warm, fuzzy, and light-struck."

Glass adopts a cartoon style, with natural colors and bright blues, to create the illustrations for his retelling, *Folks Call Me Appleseed John.* Narrated by John Chapman (also known as Johnny Appleseed), the book tells of winter travels and adventures. A *Publishers Weekly* critic remarked that the text has a "rough-hewn tone," and that the "homespun, almost unfinished appearance" of the illustrations "express a variety of moods."

Glass has illustrated the stories of other authors, including stories in the "Spooky" series by Natalie Savage Carlson. Ann F. Flowers in *Horn Book* comments on the variety of techniques that Glass incorporates into his illustrations, dubbing the art in *Spooky and the Ghost Cat* "vibrant" and "textured," while describing the illustrations for *Spooky Night* as "crosshatched" and "shadowy." In a review of *Spooky and the Wizard's Bats,* a critic in *Kirkus Reviews* concluded that Glass captured the "essence of . . . Halloween without being trite." Susan H. Patron in *School Library Journal* found the illustrations for the same book to be "dramatic and colorful."

BIOGRAPHICAL/CRITICAL SOURCES:

PERIODICALS

Bulletin of the Center for Children's Books, October, 1984, p. 25.
Horn Book, October, 1982, pp. 508-509; March/April, 1986, p. 190.
Kirkus Reviews, September 15, 1986, p. 1443; February 1, 1993, p. 146.
New York Times Book Review, June 5, 1983, p. 34.
Publishers Weekly, July 10, 1995, p. 58.
School Library Journal, May, 1982, pp. 52-53; December, 1986, p. 81; October, 1987, pp. 111-12; August, 1995, p. 134.

* * *

GLENDOWER, Rose
See HARRIS, Marion Rose (Young)

* * *

GOLDIN, Barbara Diamond 1946-

PERSONAL: Born October 4, 1946, in New York, NY; daughter of Morton (an accountant) and Anna (a medical secretary) Diamond; married Alan Goldin (a soil scientist), March 31, 1968 (divorced 1990); children: Josee Sarah, Jeremy Casey. *Education:* University of Chicago, B.A., 1968; Boston University, teaching certificate in primary and special education, 1970; attended Western Washington University, 1980. *Religion:* Jewish.

ADDRESSES: Office—P.O. Box 981, Northampton, MA 01061. *Agent*—Virginia Knowlton, Curtis Brown Ltd., 10 Astor Pl., New York, NY 10003.

CAREER: Special education teacher at public schools in Gloucester and Ipswich, MA, 1970-72; preschool teacher in Missoula, MT, and Yellow Springs, OH, 1972-75; Children's Bookshop, Missoula, co-owner and operator, 1975-76; Goldendale Public Library, Goldendale, WA, library assistant in children's section, 1976-78; preschool teacher in Bellingham, WA, 1980-82; Congregation B'nai Israel Preschool, Northampton, MA, head teacher, 1986-89; Heritage Academy, Longmeadow, MA, middle school English teacher, 1990—; freelance writer.

MEMBER: Society of Children's Book Writers and Illustrators.

AWARDS, HONORS: National Jewish Book Award, 1989, for *Just Enough Is Plenty: A Hanukkah Tale;* Association of Jewish Libraries Award, 1992, for *Cakes and Miracles: A Purim Tale;* American Library Association Notable Book, 1995, for *The Passover Journey: A Seder Companion.*

WRITINGS:

JUVENILE

Just Enough Is Plenty: A Hanukkah Tale, illustrated by Seymour Chwast, Viking (New York City), 1988.
The World's Birthday: A Story about Rosh Hashanah, illustrated by Jeanette Winter, Harcourt (San Diego), 1990.
The Family Book of Midrash: Fifty-two Stories from the Sages, J. Aronson (Northvale, NJ), 1990.
Cakes and Miracles: A Purim Tale, illustrated by Erika Weihs, Viking, 1991.
Fire!: The Beginnings of the Labor Movement, illustrated by James Watling, Viking, 1992.
The Magician's Visit: A Passover Tale, illustrated by Robert Andrew Parker, Viking, 1993.
The Passover Journey: A Seder Companion, illustrated by Neil Waldman, Viking, 1994.

Red Means Good Fortune: A Story of San Francisco's Chinatown, illustrated by Wenhai Ma, Viking, 1994.

Night Lights: A Sukkot Story, illustrated by Louise August, Harcourt, 1995.

Bat Mitzvah: A Jewish Girl's Coming of Age, illustrated by Erika Weihs, Viking, 1995.

Creating Angels: Stories of Tzedakah, J. Aronson, 1996.

Coyote and the Fire Stick: A Pacific Northwest Indian Tale, illustrated by Will Hillenbrand, Harcourt, 1996.

While the Candles Burn: Eight Stories for Hanukkah, illustrated by Elaine Greenstein, Viking, 1996.

The Girl Who Lived with the Bears, illustrated by Andrew Plewes, Gulliver Books (San Diego), 1997.

Elijah Tales, Harcourt, 1998.

Also author of adaptation of Tchaikovsky's ballet *The Sleeping Beauty* for boxed editions of compact discs, BMG Music, 1993. Contributor of story to *The Haunted House,* edited by Jane Yolen and Martin H. Greenberg, HarperCollins, 1995; contributor to children's magazines and newspapers, including *Highlights, Cricket, Shofar, Seattle's Child, Child Life,* and *Jack and Jill.*

WORK IN PROGRESS: Kids Talk about Religion, for Viking; *What Is Hidden Is Revealed: Tales of Revelation,* for Aronson.

SIDELIGHTS: Barbara Diamond Goldin is an author of children's picture books, novels for older children, story collections, and nonfiction. Her popular picture books deal mainly with holidays and the retelling of folktales, and they often emphasize her Jewish heritage. Her first picture book, *Just Enough Is Plenty: A Hanukkah Tale,* set the tone for much of her subsequent work: well researched stories often set in the "old country" of Eastern Europe, in the shtetls where three of Goldin's grandparents came from. Growing up in New York and Pennsylvania, Goldin was partially cut off from these beloved grandparents because of a language barrier. Yiddish was still their first language, and thus young Goldin was not able to share in their rich heritage. It was only with the research for her first children's book that she began to understand their histories.

This first book was a long time coming, however. Teaching, motherhood, and stints as a bookshop owner and librarian all came first. Then, in 1981, Goldin took a writing workshop with Jane Yolen and spent the next years placing articles and stories in magazines, but also in gathering rejection slips from book publishers. Increasingly, she became fascinated with the Eastern European origins of her relations and researched memoirs as well as the writings of Shalom Aleichem and Isaac Bashevis Singer. Black and white photographs of pre-Holocaust Eastern Europe also aided in this reconstruction, and such researches ultimately coalesced into the story of a poor shtetl family who take in a peddler at Hanukkah to share their holiday meal. The peddler repays their kindness by leaving behind a bag of gifts, just as the prophet Elijah does in the traditional stories. The book, *Just Enough Is Plenty,* is a "satisfying tale of traditional values," according to Hanna B. Zeiger in *Horn Book,* and a *Publishers Weekly* reviewer noted that "Goldin's tale and Chwast's vibrant, primitive paintings are masterfully combined." *Junior Bookshelf* critic Marcus Crouch offered a favorable estimation of "this admirable picture-book," commenting that "the simple story is told briefly but with due regard to the importance of its message." *Just Enough Is Plenty* went on to win the National Jewish Book Award.

Goldin continued with holiday themes in her later picture books. *The World's Birthday: A Story about Rosh Hashanah* explores the Jewish New Year, through the story of young Daniel who decides to throw a birthday party for the world and buys a birthday cake for the occasion. Zeiger, writing in *Horn Book,* noted that the blend of text and illustrations created a "tale that captures the spirit of the holiday." *Cakes and Miracles: A Purim Tale* returns to an Eastern European shtetl to tell a story of Purim, a celebration of spring. The young blind boy Hershel finds a place for himself in the life of his village when he helps his mother bake cakes for the holiday, shaping the dough with a special sensitivity he has as a result of his lack of sight. A *Booklist* reviewer stated that *Cakes and Miracles* is "a heartwarming story that is really about using one's special gifts," and Zeiger, in *Horn Book,* concluded that it is a "loving story." Betsy Hearne of the *Bulletin of the Center for Children's Books* called the work a "blessedly unsentimental picture of a blind boy" and also noted that an afterword to the book summarized the origins and customs of Purim.

The important Jewish holiday of Passover is depicted in two books by Goldin. *The Magician's*

Visit: A Passover Tale is a picture book in which the prophet Elijah himself comes to provide a feast for a poor couple, while *The Passover Journey: A Seder Companion,* a nonfiction work, looks at the history and customs of this holiday and the ceremonial evening meal, or Seder. Goldin explained that she worked on *The Passover Journey* on and off for four years in an attempt to organize her material and get it exactly right. Betsy Hearne of the *Bulletin of the Center for Children's Books* offered a favorable estimation of Goldin's efforts, stating: "More thorough than many children's books on *Pesach,* this takes great care to explore Jewish tradition and to encourage individual response to it." In a starred review, *Booklist*'s Stephanie Zvirin commended the intricate blending of text and illustration in the work, calling *The Passover Journey* "a beautiful wedding of the work of two talented individuals. . . . A book for family sharing as well as a rich source of information." Goldin has also compiled a collection of tales and retellings to be read aloud, one each night, for the Hanukkah season. *While the Candles Burn: Eight Stories for Hanukkah* is, according to Janice M. Del Negro of the *Bulletin of the Center for Children's Books,* "a solid addition to collections looking for something a little more unusual than typical holiday fare."

A departure from such picture books with strictly Jewish themes are two short novels for older readers focusing on historical issues such as the labor movement and immigration. *Fire!: The Beginnings of the Labor Movement* is a view of the 1911 Triangle Shirtwaist factory fire through the eyes of eleven-year-old Rosie who wants to quit school and go to work in the garment factory like her older sister. When a fire destroys the building and kills 146 workers, Rosie, the daughter of Russian immigrants, wakes up to her need for an education and for the labor movement to win strength. "Rosie and her friends will appeal to readers looking for a good story as well as to those needing information on the era," commented *School Library Journal* contributor Joyce Adams Burner. Goldin explores the lives of Chinese Americans in *Red Means Good Fortune: A Story of San Francisco's Chinatown,* set in 1869. Jin Mun, a twelve-year-old boy, helps out in his father's laundry, but when he discovers a young Chinese girl sold into slavery, he sets a new mission for himself: to free the girl. Carla Kozak, writing in *School Library Journal,* noted that the book was "well-researched and clearly written," while Carolyn Phelan of *Booklist* commented that the "characters and story are involving." Phelan, however, also felt that the book was "too short and the ending will leave the readers wondering what happened next."

Goldin has continued her eclectic mix of story material with a retelling of a Native American tale in *Coyote and the Fire Stick: A Pacific Northwest Indian Tale,* as well as further explication of Jewish tradition and customs in *Bat Mitzvah: A Jewish Girl's Coming of Age.* The former, a retelling of a pourquoi tale explaining the origin of fire, is raised "above the common" variety of such retellings, according to Patricia Lothrop Green in *School Library Journal,* by Goldin's characterization of Coyote and the illustrations of Will Hillenbrand. *Horn Book* reviewer Ann A. Flowers concurs, describing *Coyote and the Fire Stick* as "a well-told story with inventive oil and oil pastel illustrations." With the nonfiction *Bat Mitzvah,* Goldin explains the relatively recent ceremony of the celebration of a girl's coming of age at twelve or thirteen. Ellen Mandel of *Booklist* called the work "relevant, informative, and highly readable," and *School Library Journal* contributor Marsha W. Posner concluded that *Bat Mitzvah* would be "an insightful addition to all collections."

Goldin, whose favorite place to work is at a local college library, enjoys the process of research and writing. "I still love to write and research and discover new worlds on paper," she once said. "Writing is still an exciting process for me. I'm never certain when I sit down to write what the next few hours bring."

BIOGRAPHICAL/CRITICAL SOURCES:

PERIODICALS

Booklist, January 15, 1991, p. 1062; December, 15, 1993, p. 754; March 1, 1994, p. 1260; September 1, 1995, p. 56.

Bulletin of the Center for Children's Books, February, 1991, p. 141; April, 1992, p. 206; March, 1993, p. 233; April, 1994, pp. 257-258; November, 1996, pp. 96-97.

Horn Book, November-December, 1988, p. 763; November-December, 1990, pp. 718-719; July-August, 1991, p. 447; November-December, 1996, p. 748.

Junior Bookshelf, April, 1989, p. 60.

Kirkus Reviews, September 15, 1988, p. 1403; July 15, 1990, p. 1011; December 1, 1990, p. 1671; May 15, 1992, p. 677; January 1, 1993, p. 67; January 1, 1994, p. 67.
Publishers Weekly, September 30, 1988, p. 66; August 31, 1990, p. 64; December 7, 1990, p. 90; January 4, 1993, p. 72; January 24, 1994, p. 57; February 14, 1994, p. 65; November 13, 1995, p. 65.
School Library Journal, July, 1992, p. 73; May, 1994, p. 114; November, 1995; October, 1996, p. 114.
Springfield Republican, September 1, 1996, p. D5.

* * *

GOODRUM, Charles A(lvin) 1923-

PERSONAL: Born July 21, 1923, in Pittsburg, KS; son of Bernie Loy (a city director) and Mae (Beaver) Goodrum; married Donna Belle Mueller, September 2, 1950; children: Christopher Kent, Julia Belle, Geoffrey Paul. *Education:* University of Wichita (now Wichita State University), B.A., 1964; attended Princeton University, 1943-44; Columbia University, M.A., 1949.

ADDRESSES: Home—2808 Pierpont St., Alexandria, VA 22302.

CAREER: University of Wichita (now Wichita State University), Wichita, KS, librarian in charge of circulation, 1947-48; Library of Congress, Washington, DC, Legislative Reference Service, reference librarian, 1949-50, political science bibliographer, 1950-53, librarian, 1953-62, coordinator of research, 1963-70; Congressional Research Service, assistant director, 1970-76; Office of the Librarian of Congress, director of Office of Planning and Development, 1976-78. Writer and consultant, 1978—. *Military service:* U.S. Army, 1943-46.

WRITINGS:

NONFICTION

The Library of Congress, Praeger (New York City), 1974, 2nd revised edition, with Helen W. Darymple, Westview (Boulder, CO), 1982.
Treasures of the Library of Congress, Abrams (New York City), 1980, revised and expanded edition, 1991.
(With Darymple) *Guide to the Library of Congress,* Library of Congress (Washington, DC), 1983.
(With Darymple) *American Advertising: The First 200 Years,* Abrams, 1990.

MYSTERY NOVELS

Dewey Decimated, Crown (New York City), 1977.
Carnage of the Realm, Crown, 1979, published in England as *Dead for a Penny,* Gollancz, 1979.
The Best Cellar, St. Martin's (New York City), 1987.
A Slip of the Tong, St. Martin's, 1992.

OTHER

I'll Trade You an Elk (humorous memoir), Funk (New York City), 1967.

Contributor to books, including *The Craft of the Essay,* edited by Halsey P. Taylor, Harcourt, 1976; *Murderess Ink,* edited by Dilys Winn, Workman Publishing, 1979; and *Respectfully Quoted: A Dictionary of Quotations Requested from the Congressional Research Service,* Library of Congress, 1989. Contributor to *ALA World Encyclopedia of Library and Information Services,* American Library Association, 1980. Contributor to *Atlantic, New Yorker,* and library journals.

ADAPTATIONS: I'll Trade You an Elk was produced by Walt Disney Studios as a made-for-television movie.

SIDELIGHTS: Charles A. Goodrum told *CA:* "I try to keep a little variety going by doing a nonfiction, reasonably serious research book, immediately followed by a light, hopefully humorous mystery novel—and then starting the cycle over again. Regrettably, the money is in the non-fiction, while the fun is in the detective stories." Goodrum's mystery novels have all been detective stories set in a famous library of rare books. One of Goodrum's nonfiction books, *Treasures of the Library of Congress,* is described by *New York Times Book Review* critic Frances Taliaferro as "a large handsome volume whose text suggests the remarkable range of the Library's 76 million items; abundant photographs document the richness of books and objects that are the best of their kind." *Washington Post Book World* reviewer Herman W. Liebert reports that, here, Goodrum "writes with humor, a sure feel for the little-known and the unexpected, and a sense of the ticking of history's clock. No one who cares about our present as the child of its past and the parent of its future can read his book without being freshly instructed and deeply moved."

BIOGRAPHICAL/CRITICAL SOURCES:

PERIODICALS

New York Times Book Review, February 8, 1981.
Washington Post Book World, November 16, 1980.

* * *

GOSLING, Paula 1939-
(Ainslie Skinner)

PERSONAL: Born October 12, 1939, in Detroit, MI; daughter of Paul (a design engineer and inventor) and Sylvie (Van Slembrouck) Osius; married Christopher Gosling, July, 1968 (divorced, 1978); married John A. Hare (a management accountant), September 17, 1981; children: (first marriage) Abigail Judith, Emily Elizabeth. *Education:* Wayne State University, B.A., 1962.

ADDRESSES: *Home*—22 Shelley Rd., Beechen Cliff, Bath, Avon BA2 4RJ, England. *E-mail*—pgolsling@netcomuk.co.uk. *Agent*—Greene & Heaton Ltd., 37 Goldhawk Road, London W12 8QQ, England.

CAREER: Campbell-Ewald Co. (advertising agency), Detroit, MI, copywriter trainee, 1962-64; C. Mitchell & Co., London, England, copywriter, 1964-67, copy consultant, 1969-70; copywriter at advertising agencies in London, 1967-69; ATA Advertising, Bristol, England, copy consultant, 1976-79; full-time writer, 1979—.

MEMBER: Crime Writers' Association (chair, 1988-89), Mensa.

AWARDS, HONORS: John Creasey Memorial Award, 1978, for *A Running Duck;* Gold Dagger Award, 1986, for *Monkey Puzzle;* Arts Achievement Award, Wayne State University, 1993.

WRITINGS:

CRIME NOVELS

A Running Duck, Macmillan (London), 1978, published as *Fair Game,* Coward, 1979.
Zero Trap, Macmillan, 1979, Coward, 1980.
Loser's Blues, Macmillan, 1980, published as *Solo Blues,* Coward, 1981.
(Under pseudonym Ainslie Skinner) *Mind's Eye,* Secker & Warburg (England), 1980, published as *The Harrowing,* Rawson, Wade (New York City), 1981.
The Woman in Red, Macmillan, 1983, Doubleday (New York City), 1984.
Monkey Puzzle, Macmillan, 1985, Doubleday, 1986.
The Wychford Murders, Macmillan, 1986, Doubleday, 1987.
Hoodwink, Macmillan, 1987, Doubleday, 1987.
Backlash, Macmillan, 1988, Doubleday, 1989.
Death Penalties, Scribner (New York City), 1991, Mysterious Press (New York City), 1992.
The Body in Blackwater Bay, Scribner, 1992, Mysterious Press, 1993.
A Few Dying Words, Little, Brown (Boston, MA), 1993, Mysterious Press, 1994.
The Dead of Winter, Little Brown, 1995, Mysterious Press, 1996.

OTHER

Also author of magazine serials including "The Man in the Bicycle Shop," published in *Woman,* 1981.

ADAPTATIONS: *A Running Duck* was filmed twice by Warner Bros., in 1986 as *Cobra,* starring Sylvester Stallone, and in 1995 as *Fair Game,* starring Cindy Crawford.

WORK IN PROGRESS: "I never discuss my work in progress. I can only say that I am deep in research for my next thriller."

SIDELIGHTS: Paula Gosling wrote to *CA:* "Many people consider crime fiction to be a confining form, but I find in it a great challenge—and that is, to stick to the rule of playing fair with the reader, while bending and even breaking some of the other rules of form and content. Crime fiction allows me to show characters under the most intense pressure. Murder is the ultimate crime, and the ripples and vibrations it produces enable me not only to demonstrate each character's public personality, but also to gradually reveal the secret persona that hides behind it. It is that secret persona which drives someone to kill. Murder is an act of ego, and the killer's most primal motivation is simply this: 'you must die so I can live.' Crime writers today are encouraged to explore and experiment because their readers are knowledgeable and demanding—they want not only a challenging puzzle, but also a good, strong, well-written novel containing imaginative description, lively dialogue, and powerful characterization. That's why, in comparison to writing crime fiction, writing 'straight' novels seems like child's play to us—and these days often reads like it!"

* * *

GOTTLIEB, Alan M(erril) 1947-

PERSONAL: Born May 2, 1947, in Los Angeles, CA; son of Seymour and Sherry (Schutz) Gottlieb; married Julie Hoy Versnel, 1979; children: Amy, Sarah, Merril, Andrew. *Education:* Attended Georgetown University, 1970; University of Tennessee, B.S., 1971.

ADDRESSES: Home—12500 Northeast 10th Pl., Bellevue, WA 98005.

CAREER: Merril Associates, Bellevue, WA, president, 1974—. President of KSBN Radio, Spokane, WA, and KBNP Radio, Portland, OR; chair of Citizens Committee for the Right to Keep and Bear Arms. *Military service:* Army National Guard, 1968-74.

AWARDS, HONORS: Freedom Award from Young Americans for Freedom, 1974, for work protecting individual rights; Roy Rogers Award, 1987, from the National Antique Arms Association for Protecting Gun Rights.

WRITINGS:

The Gun Owner's Political Action Manual, Green Hill (Ottawa, IL), 1976.

The Rights of Gun Owners, Caroline House (Aurora, IL), 1981.

The Gun Grabbers, Merril Press (Bellevue, WA), 1986.

Guns for Women, Merril Press, 1987.

Gun Rights Fact Book, Merril Press, 1988.

(Editor) *The Wise Use Agenda: The Citizen's Policy Guide to Environmental Resource Issues,* Free Enterprise Press (Bellevue, WA), 1989.

The Rights of Gun Owners, Merril Press, 1991.

Trashing the Economy: How Runaway Environmentalism Is Wrecking America, Free Enterprise Press, 1993, 2nd edition, 1994.

In the Shadow of the Rockies: An Outsider's Look Inside a New Major League Baseball Team, Roberts Rinehart (Niwot, CO), 1994.

(With Ron Arnold) *Politically Correct Environment,* cartoons by Chuck Asay, Merril Press, 1996.

Politically Correct Guns, Merril Press, 1996.

Also author of *Things You Can Do to Defend Your Gun Rights,* 1994; and *More Things You Can Do To Defend Your Gun Rights,* 1995.

* * *

GOURSE, Leslie 1939-

PERSONAL: Born January 1, 1939, in Providence, RI; daughter of Harry Andrew (a clothing store owner) and H. Zelda (a homemaker; maiden name, Fisher) Gourse. *Education:* Columbia University, B.S. in creative writing, 1960.

ADDRESSES: Home and office—55 Bethune St., Apt. 222G, New York, NY 10014.

CAREER: Writer. CBS Network Radio News Morning Report, writer, 1966-68; *New York Times* national desk, stringer on regular general assignment in social trends, 1970-74.

MEMBER: Writers Room, Writers Union, PEN American Center.

AWARDS, HONORS: Deems Taylor Award, American Society of Composers, Authors and Publishers (ASCAP), 1991, for a series of seven articles about women jazz musicians in *Jazz Times;* scholarship to Breadloaf Writers Conference at Middlebury College; Columbia-Doubleday Opton Award and Book of the Month Club recommendation, both for *With Gall and Honey;* Ralph J. Gleason Award nominations, Broadcast Music, Incorporated (BMI), New York University and

Rolling Stone, for *Sassy: The Life of Sarah Vaughan* and *Unforgettable: The Life and Mystique of Nat King Cole.*

WRITINGS:

Student Guide to New York, Hippocrene (New York City), 1984.

Louis' Children: American Jazz Singers, Morrow (New York City), 1984.

Every Day: The Story of Joe Williams, Da Capo Press (New York City), 1985.

The Best Guided Walking Tours to New York City, Globe Pequot (Chester, CT), 1989.

Unforgettable: The Life and Mystique of Nat King Cole, St. Martin's (New York CIty), 1991.

Sassy: The Life of Sarah Vaughan, Scribner (New York City), 1993.

Dizzy Gillespie and the Birth of Bebop, Atheneum (New York City), 1994.

The Congress, Franklin Watts (New York City), 1994.

Aretha Franklin: Lady Soul, Franklin Watts, 1995.

Billie Holiday: The Tragedy and Triumph of Lady Day, Franklin Watts, 1995.

Madame Jazz: Contemporary Women Instrumentalists, Oxford University Press (New York City), 1995.

Mahalia Jackson: Queen of Gospel Song, Franklin Watts, 1996.

Pocahontas, Aladdin (New York City), 1996.

(Editor) *The Billie Holiday Companion: Seven Decades of Commentary,* Schirmer (New York City), 1997.

Swingers and Crooners: The Art of Jazz Singing, Franklin Watts, 1997.

Striders to Beboppers and Beyond: The Art of Jazz Piano, Franklin Watts, 1997.

Blowing on the Changes: The Art of the Jazz Horn Players, Franklin Watts, 1997.

Straight, No Chaser: The Life and Genius of Thelonious Monk, Schirmer, 1997.

Also author of *With Gall and Honey,* Doubleday, and of several other books about New York and of liner notes for albums and CDs. Contributor of articles to magazines and newspapers, including *New York Times, New York Post, Village Voice, Washington Post, Chicago Tribune, Harper's Bazaar, Cosmopolitan, Jazz Times, Jazz Iz, Keyboard, CD Review, Pulse,* and *Downbeat.* Correspondent for Paris magazine, *Jazz Hot,* 1995.

WORK IN PROGRESS: An anthology of writings about Ella Fitzgerald.

SIDELIGHTS: Leslie Gourse told *CA:* "I have always wanted to write, ever since I was a little girl, when I first saw a beautiful first edition of *Grimm's Fairy Tales.* The illustrations were so magnificent, and of course I loved the stories, and I decided that if 'they' made books that beautiful, I wanted to be a writer. My father collected books, and so I had many inspirations in that library.

"I began by writing poetry, and as I matured, I turned to fiction, then nonfiction, becoming interested in what was going on in the world at large. I wanted to express my observations. I particularly liked writing about people, social trends, and the arts. My work about jazz was well accepted by magazines, and that welcome led me to spend more time writing about jazz. I began to seek out book contracts. Pretty soon most of my time was devoted to writing about jazz. I have done it for all kinds of publications—music magazines, general interest publications, liner notes for albums, books for adults. And I thought it would be a wonderful idea to do books on jazz for kids, and now I am doing quite a few biographies and jazz histories by instrument."

Among Gourse's works are biographies of such jazz greats as Nat King Cole and Sarah Vaughan. In *Unforgettable: The Life and Mystique of Nat King Cole* Gourse starts with Cole's beginnings as a ground-breaking jazz pianist, describing his decision to instead pursue a more lucrative singing career which brought him fame and popularity. "This is a well-researched and readable biography," declares Tim LaBorie in *Library Journal.* Anne Larsen, writing in *Kirkus Reviews,* asserts, "The early jazz pages are magnetic, and Cole practically sits in the reader's lap throughout." *Sassy: The Life of Sarah Vaughan* similarly covers the choir-singing beginnings of Vaughan as well as her varied musical career in which she worked with such greats as Charlie Parker and Dizzy Gillespie. Gourse "evokes the voluptuous tone of Vaughan's signature songs," observes Leo Sacks in the *New York Times Book Review,* concluding that "*Sassy* is a deeply felt portrait."

A wide range of contemporary women jazz musicians is covered in Gourse's 1995 survey of the profession—*Madame Jazz: Contemporary Women*

Instrumentalists. First explaining the prejudice that women jazz instrumentalists have faced in the past, Gourse goes on to describe the slow change in attitude that enables today's musicians to be a force. In addition to this historical background, Gourse profiles a number of well-known women jazz musicians as well as several newcomers. Donna Seaman relates in *Booklist* that Gourse "brings lots of energy and knowledge" to *Madame Jazz,* adding that she "focuses most of her attention on the women themselves, describing their drive, confidence, and talent."

"I try to explain who jazz musicians are and what they do, whether I am writing for adults or children," Gourse relates to *CA,* adding: "I want people to be interested in jazz musicians as creative people and real people who have achieved a high degree of artistry in a very demanding field. And I want people to appreciate the history of the music within the context of American history."

Among the more recent of Gourse's biographical titles is her well-received *Mahalia Jackson: Queen of Gospel Song.* In this work, which *School Library Journal* contributor Tim Wadham describes as a "touching, even moving, biography," Gourse examines Jackson's life from her early childhood in New Orleans through her involvement in the civil rights movement and eventual rise to fame as a gospel singer. Wadham praises the detail that informs Gourse's biography, and concludes: "Gourse tells the story with the passion that was Mahalia Jackson herself."

BIOGRAPHICAL/CRITICAL SOURCES:

PERIODICALS

Booklist, June 15, 1991, p. 1922; January 1, 1995, pp. 791, 811.

Kirkus Reviews, May 1, 1991, p. 581; November 1, 1992, p. 1351; October 15, 1994, p. 1384.

Library Journal, July, 1991, p. 98.

New York Times Book Review, January 24, 1993, p. 16.

School Library Journal, August, 1996, p. 170.

* * *

GRAHAM, Arthur Kennon

See **HARRISON, David L(ee)**

GRAHAM, Kennon

See **HARRISON, David L(ee)**

* * *

GRAYSON, Richard (A.) 1951-

PERSONAL: Born June 4, 1951, in Brooklyn, NY; son of Daniel (in business) and Marilyn (a retailer; maiden name, Sarrett) Grayson. *Ethnicity:* "White/Jewish." *Education:* Brooklyn College of the City University of New York, B.A., 1973, M.F.A., 1976; Richmond College of the City University of New York, M.A., 1975; University of Florida, J.D., 1984.

ADDRESSES: Home—2001 Southwest 98th Terr., Fort Lauderdale, FL 33324. *Office*—Center for Governmental Responsibility, College of Law, University of Florida, Gainesville, FL 32611-7629. *E-mail*—rgrayson@delphi.com; fax 954-370-9460.

CAREER: Fiction Collective, Brooklyn, NY, editorial assistant, 1975-77; Long Island University, Brooklyn, lecturer in English, 1975-78; City University of New York, lecturer in English at Kingsborough Community College, Brooklyn, 1978-81, Brooklyn College, Brooklyn, 1979-81, John Jay College of Criminal Justice, 1984-86, and Bernard M. Baruch College, 1986-87; Broward Community College, Fort Lauderdale, FL, instructor in English, 1981-83; Florida International University, Miami, instructor in computer education, 1986-90; Nova Southeastern University, Fort Lauderdale, instructor in business, 1992—. University of Florida, staff attorney in social policy at Center for Governmental Responsibility, 1994—; Human Rights Council of North Central Florida, member of board of directors, 1995—; Lambda Legal Defense and Education Fund, member. Compu Learn Systems, director of training, 1986-90; Broward Community College, instructor, 1987-91. Rockland Center for the Arts, writer in residence, 1988-89; New Jersey Online, columnist, 1995—.

MEMBER: International PEN, Association of Computer Educators, Authors Guild, Authors League of America, Associated Writing Programs, Mensa, Brooklyn College Alumni Association (board of directors, 1973-81), Phi Beta Kappa, Coif.

AWARDS, HONORS: Scholar of National Arts Club at Bread Loaf Writer's Conference, 1977; scholar at Santa Cruz Writing Conference, 1978; fellowships from Virginia Center for the Creative Arts, 1979 and 1981, MacDowell Colony, 1980 and 1987, Florida Arts Council, 1982 and 1988, and Millay Colony for the Arts, 1984; fellow in residence, Center for Mark Twain Studies, Elmira College, 1990.

WRITINGS:

Disjointed Fictions, X Archives, 1978.
With Hitler in New York and Other Stories, Taplinger (New York City), 1979.
Lincoln's Doctor's Dog and Other Stories, White Ewe (Havre de Grace, MD), 1982.
Eating at Arby's: The South Florida Stories (pamphlet), Grinning Idiot Press, 1982.
I Brake for Delmore Schwartz, Zephyr Press, 1983.
The Greatest Short Story That Absolutely Ever Was, Lowlands (New Orleans, LA), 1989.
Narcissism and Me, Mule & Mule, 1990.
I Survived Caracas Traffic: Stories from the Me Decades, Avisson, 1996.

Contributor of short stories to more than a 165 periodicals, including *Epoch, Texas Quarterly, Confrontation, Shenandoah, Carleton Miscellany,* and *Transatlantic Review;* contributor of nonfiction to magazines and newspapers, including *People, Miami Herald, Orlando Sentinel,* and *Tampa Tribune.* Humor columnist, *Hollywood Sun-Tattler,* 1986-87.

WORK IN PROGRESS: A collection of related short stories.

SIDELIGHTS: Unconventional, imaginative, and possessed by an offbeat sense of humor, Richard Grayson is the author of several collections of short stories that examine life from a perspective many critics find refreshingly different. Originally published in a variety of small magazines, his stories "are full of insanity, nutty therapists, cancerous relatives, broken homes, fiction workshops, youthful theatricals at Catskill bungalow colonies and the morbid wizardry of telephone-answering machines," notes Ivan Gold in the *New York Times Book Review.* Some also feature such unlikely "characters" as the voice of the cold that "assassinated" President William Henry Harrison in 1841 and Sparky, Abraham Lincoln's doctor's puppy, who grows up to become a successful politician and lecturer (the latter story was inspired by an article Grayson once read that stated most recent best-sellers have dealt with presidents, diseases, or animals—hence, "Lincoln's Doctor's Dog"). As Mark Bernheim observes in *Israel Today,* "Grayson is able to create a full range of masks from behind which the artist peers out to make his criticisms of artificial modern life."

Commenting in *Best Sellers,* Nicholas J. Loprete, Jr., also asserts that Grayson's stories "display a versatility which commands attention. [The author] can parody human excess and human frailty, parent-child relationships, and recreate a 1960's scene with poignancy. He is serious and comic, charming, given to outrageous puns, and a sharp-eyed observer of and participant in Life's absurdities."

In short, declares Lynne Gagnon in the *Ventura County News,* "Richard Grayson gets the prize for making us laugh about the ridiculous insaneness surrounding our lives. But the award is two-fold; he also forces us to examine people and what they do to us. And more importantly what we do to them."

Richard Grayson once told *CA:* "Writing has been the primary way I've defined myself; at first it was therapy, but now, I hope, it has become something more. I see the writer's first job as giving the lowdown on himself, and through himself, on humanity. As I reluctantly leave the longest adolescence in history, I find myself happily becoming less self-conscious, more patient. I would like to avoid becoming pompous, but I'm afraid statements like these are among the mine fields on the road to absurd self-importance. I have a lot to learn about writing (and other things)."

BIOGRAPHICAL/CRITICAL SOURCES:

BOOKS

Contemporary Literary Criticism, Volume 38, Gale (Detroit), 1986.

PERIODICALS

Aspect, number 72/73, 1979.
Athens Daily News, July 18, 1983.
Best Sellers, May, 1982.
Des Moines Register, October 21, 1983.

Israel Today, May 8, 1983.
Kings Courier, August, 1978.
Los Angeles Times, July 17, 1979.
Miami News, April 13, 1984.
New York Times Book Review, August 14, 1983.
Orlando Sentinel, April 18, 1982; January 14, 1984.
Ventura County News, February 4, 1980.

* * *

GROSS, Joel 1951-

PERSONAL: Born March 22, 1951, in New York, NY; son of David Charles (an editor) and Esther (Pearl) Gross; married Linda Sanders, May, 1983. *Education:* Queens College of the City University of New York, B.A. (with honors), 1971; Columbia University, M.A. (with honors), 1973. *Politics:* Liberal Democrat. *Religion:* Jewish.

ADDRESSES: *Home*—165 East 66th St., New York, NY 10021. *E-mail*—joelgross@aol.com.

CAREER: Writer.

WRITINGS:

PLAYS

Clean Sweep, first produced off-Broadway at Perry Street Theater, New York City, February, 1984.
Haven, first produced off-Broadway at South Street Theater, 1985.
Mesmer, first produced at Williamstown Theater Festival, 1988.

NOVELS

Bubble's Shadow, Crown (New York City), 1970.
The Young Man Who Wrote Soap Operas, Scribner (New York City), 1975.
1407 Broadway, Seaview, 1978.
The Books of Rachel, Seaview, 1979.
Maura's Dream, Seaview, 1981.
Home of the Brave, Seaview, 1982.
This Year in Jerusalem, Putnam (New York City), 1983.
The Lives of Rachel, New American Library (New York City), 1984.
Spirit in the Flesh, New American Library, 1986.
Sarah, Morrow (New York City), 1987.

OTHER

Author of the television movie *Blind Man's Bluff,* 1991, and the screenplay *No Escape,* 1994.

SIDELIGHTS: Joel Gross began writing when he was nineteen. More than 3 million copies of his bestselling paperback novels are in print.

H-I

HALL, N(orman) John 1933-

PERSONAL: Born January 1, 1933, in Orange, NJ; son of Norman C. and Lucille (Hertlein) Hall; married Marianne E. Gsell, October 13, 1968; children: Jonathan. *Education:* Seton Hall University, A.B., 1955, M.A., 1967; New York University, Ph.D., 1970.

ADDRESSES: Home—44 West 10th St., New York, NY 10011. *Office*— Department of English, Bronx Community College of the City University of New York, Bronx, NY 10453. *E-mail*—nhall@email.-gc.cuny.edu.

CAREER: New York University, New York City, parttime lecturer in English, 1967-70; Bronx Community College of the City University of New York, Bronx, NY, assistant professor, 1970-75, associate professor, 1975-78, professor of English, 1978—. New School for Social Research, lecturer, 1970-74; Graduate School and University Center of the City University of New York, professor, 1980—; City University of New York, distinguished professor, 1983—.

MEMBER: Modern Language Association of America.

AWARDS, HONORS: Research awards from American Council of Learned Societies, 1973, and City University of New York; fellowships from National Endowment for the Humanities, 1974, Guggenheim Foundation, 1977 and 1984, and American Council of Learned Societies, 1980.

WRITINGS:

(Editor) Anthony Trollope, *The New Zealander,* Clarendon Press (Oxford, England), 1972.

Salmagundi: Byron, Allegra, and the Trollope Family, Beta Phi Mu, 1975.

Trollope and His Illustrators, Macmillan (London), 1980.

(Editor) *The Trollope Critics,* Macmillan, 1981.

(General editor) *Selected Works of Anthony Trollope,* 62 volumes, Arno Press, 1981.

(Editor) *The Letters of Anthony Trollope,* Volume 1: *1835-1870,* Volume 2: *1871-1882,* Stanford University Press (Stanford, CA), 1983.

(Editor) Max Beerbohm, *The Illustrated Zuleika Dobson,* Yale University Press (New Haven, CT), 1985.

(Editor) Beerbohm, *Rossetti and His Circle,* new and enlarged edition, Yale University Press, 1987.

Trollope: A Biography, Clarendon Press, 1991.

(Editor) Beerbohm, *A Christmas Garland,* new illustrated edition, Yale University Press, 1993.

Contributor to literature journals.

WORK IN PROGRESS: Max Beerbohm: Caricatures, for Yale University Press.

* * *

HALLIWELL, David (William) 1936- (Johnson Arms)

PERSONAL: Born July 31, 1936, in Brighouse, Yorkshire, England; son of Herbert (a managing director of a textile firm) and Ethel (Spencer) Halliwell. *Ethnicity:* "White, English." *Education:* Attended Huddersfield College of Art, 1953-59; Royal Academy of Dramatic Art, diploma, 1961. *Politics:* "I believe in democracy at all levels, from the ward to the world, and the delegation of power both upwards and downwards."

ADDRESSES: *Home*—8 Crawborough Villas, Charlbury, Oxford OX7 3TS, England.

CAREER: Actor in Nottingham, England, 1962, Stoke-on-Trent, England, 1962-63, and London, 1963-67; Quipu Productions, London, cofounder and director, 1966-76; director of plays in London at New Arts Theatre, 1966-67, Little Theatre, 1971-73, Bankside Globe Theatre, 1974, and New End Theatre, 1975; director for productions of other managements, in Edinburgh, Scotland, at Traverse Theatre, 1971, in London for National Theatre at Young Vic Theatre, 1975, Royal Court Theatre, 1976-77, and Kingston Overground Theatre, 1978, and in Sheffield, England, at Sheffield Crucible, 1978; director at Old Red Lion, London, 1982. University of Reading, visiting fellow, 1970; resident dramatist at Royal Court Theatre, 1976-77, and Hampstead Theatre, 1978-79. Thames Television, interviewer for *Question '68*, 1968. Charlbury Town Council, member, 1992—, vice chairperson, 1996-97; Chalbury Chamber of Commerce, member; Gifford Trust, member, 1992—, vice chairperson, 1996-97.

MEMBER: International Synaesthesia Association, Royal Society of Literature (fellow), Equity, Writers Guild of Great Britain (chairperson of radio committee, 1983-84, and theatre committee, 1984-86, 1995-96; member of executive council, 1983-86, 1995-96), Theatre Writers Union (member of negotiating team, 1976-82), Actors' Centre, Dramatists Club, Alibi Club.

AWARDS, HONORS: Named most promising playwright by *Evening Standard,* 1966, for *Little Malcolm and His Struggle against the Eunuchs;* John Whiting Award, 1978, for *Prejudice;* Hawthornden fellow, 1995.

WRITINGS:

PLAYS

Hail Scrawdyke (produced in New York City, 1966), Grove (New York City), 1966 (published in England as *Little Malcolm and His Struggle against the Eunuchs* [first produced in London at Unity Theatre, March 30, 1965], Faber, 1966).

K. D. Dufford Hears K. D. Dufford Ask K. D. Dufford How K. D. Dufford'll Make K. D. Dufford (first produced in London at Lambda Theatre, 1969; later retitled "K. D. Dufford"), Faber, 1970.

A Discussion, Faber, 1971.

Muck from Three Angles, Faber, 1971.

A Who's Who of Flapland and Other Plays, Faber, 1971.

An Amour, (first produced in London at Little Theatre, January, 1972), published in *Fun Art Bus Book,* Methuen, 1971.

Meriel the Ghost Girl (first produced as a television play, 1976; produced at Old Red Lion, 1982), published in *The Mind Beyond* (anthology), Penguin, 1976.

The House, Methuen, 1979.

Bonds, published in part in *Norwegian Journal of Group Analysis,* 1995.

UNPUBLISHED PLAYS

(With David Calderisi) *The Experiment,* first produced in London at New Arts Theatre, January 16, 1967.

The Girl Who Didn't Like Answers, first produced in London at Mercury Theatre, June 29, 1971.

A Last Belch for the Great Auk, first produced at Mercury Theatre, 1971.

Bleats from a Brighouse Pleasureground, first produced at Little Theatre, 1972.

Janitress Thrilled by Prehensile Penis, first produced at Little Theatre, 1972.

An Altercation, first produced in London at Covent Garden Street Festival, 1973.

The Freckled Bum (first play of quartet), first produced in London at Bankside Globe Theatre, 1974.

Minyip (second play of quartet), first produced at Bankside Globe Theatre, 1974.

Progs (third play of quartet), first produced at British Drama League, 1975.

A Process of Elimination (final play of quartet), first produced at Howff, 1975.

Prejudice (later retitled *Creatures of Another Kind*), first produced in Sheffield at Sheffield Crucible, 1978.

A Rite Kwik Metal Tata, first produced at Sheffield Crucible, 1979.

Was It Her?, first produced at Old Red Lion, 1982.

A Tomato Who Grew into a Mushroom, first produced by Oxfordshire Touring Theatre Co., 1987.

Brothers in Arms (working title), rehearsed reading presented in Oxford, England, by Oxford Stage Company, at Rose Theatre, 1996.

Also author of unpublished plays, *Wychways along the Evenlode,* 1986, and *The Cutteslowe Walls,* 1987.

OTHER

Also author, under pseudonym Johnson Arms, of *They Travelled by Tube* (biographies of notable people who moved by means of London's Underground subway system), Butterworth. Author of television plays, including *A Plastic Mac in Winter,* 1963, *Cock, Hen and Courting Pit,* 1966, *Triptych of Bathroom Users,* 1972, *Blur and Blank via Checkheaton,* 1972, *Triple Exposure,* 1972, *Steps Back,* 1972, *Daft Mam Blues,* 1976, *Pigmented Patter,* 1976, *Treewomen of Jagden Crag,* 1976, *Speculating about Orwell,* 1983, and *There's a Car Park in Witherton;* also author of radio plays, including *Spongehenge,* 1982, *Grandad's House,* 1984, *Shares of the Pudding,* 1985, *Do It Yourself,* 1986, *Bedsprings,* 1988, *Parts,* 1988, *Crossed Lines,* 1992, *There's a Car Park in Witherton,* 1992, and *Bird,* 1995, all for British Broadcasting Corp. (BBC).

ADAPTATIONS: The film *Little Malcolm,* released in 1973, was based on Halliwell's play of the same title, which was published in the United States as *Hail Scrawdyke.*

WORK IN PROGRESS: The Other Half of My Heartbeat; or, My Worthy Constituent, for BBC-Radio; adapting the radio play *Bird* into a screenplay; adapting the radio play *Parts* and the television play *Bonds* for the stage.

SIDELIGHTS: David Halliwell told *CA:* "A very basic motivating factor in my career has been a compulsion to surpass other people in some way (accompanied by a compulsion to be inferior to them). When I was an art student, I realised I had no chance of surpassing other students as a graphic artist, and so I turned to the theater, writing and acting in revue sketches. I work out the overall framework of a play in my head before I write a single word. This often takes longer than the writing. Then I write numerous drafts, each one a development on its predecessor, until I have a producible text. I revise this text during rehearsal.

"I like to direct my own plays in the theater, and I believe that the writing and directing of a play are both parts of the same task, given that the playwright is an experienced director. The opinion that a playwright is incapable of . . . directing his or her own work is a prejudice, an artificial separation not found in any other medium. In addition to directing my own plays, I have directed plays by Pinter, Shaw, Tony Connor, and Brian Friel, amongst others. I perform in my own plays and those of other playwrights.

"My advice to aspiring dramatists is: listen to people talking wherever you are. My own main interest as a playwright is the psychology underlying behavior. For the whole of my writing career I have been seeking the means to understand psychodynamics and express them in dramatic form. In 1988, I managed to first realize this endeavor in a radio play called *Parts,* and then in 1989 and 1990 in a television play called *Bonds.* Although these are relatively minor works, I intend to continue the approach in major works in all media, but particularly in the theater."

Halliwell adds, "I have been influenced by many people—by other writers, including Sean O'Casey, D. H. Lawrence, George Orwell, James Joyce, Norman Mailer, Samuel Beckett, Harold Pinter, and Sigmund Freud—but more by artists in other disciplines, including Charles Chaplin, George Burns, Bix Beiderbeck, Tommy Ladnier, Charles Parker, Tal Farlow, and Charles Mingus. Nowadays I am inspired by the lives and works of Henry Roth and James Ellroy."

BIOGRAPHICAL/CRITICAL SOURCES:

PERIODICALS

City Limits, November, 1981.
Event, November, 1981.
New Statesman, September 26, 1969.
Plays and Players, October, 1970.
Time Out, November, 1981.
Witney Gazette, January, 1987.

HALPERIN, John (William) 1941-

PERSONAL: Born September 15, 1941, in Chicago, IL; son of S. William (a historian) and Elaine (a translator; maiden name, Philipsborn) Halperin. *Education:* Bowdoin College, A.B., 1963; University of New Hampshire, M.A., 1966; Johns Hopkins University, M.A., 1968, Ph.D., 1969.

ADDRESSES: *Office*—Department of English, Vanderbilt University, Nashville, TN 37235.

CAREER: *Wall Street Journal,* New York, NY, reporter, 1963; Associated Press, Albany, NY, editor, 1963-64; State University of New York at Stony Brook, assistant professor of English, director of summer school, and assistant to academic vice president, 1969-72; University of Southern California, Los Angeles, associate professor, 1972-77, professor of English, 1977-83, director of graduate studies, 1973-75; Vanderbilt University, Nashville, Tennessee, Centennial Professor of English, beginning 1983. Honorary fellow, Wolfson College, Oxford University, 1976; visiting professor, University of Sheffield, England, 1979-80. *Military service:* U.S. Army Reserve, 1963-69; became staff sergeant.

MEMBER: International PEN, Modern Language Association of America, American Philosophical Society (fellow), Royal Society of Literature (fellow).

AWARDS, HONORS: Rockefeller Foundation fellow, 1976; Guggenheim Foundation fellow, 1978-79, 1985-86; American Council of Learned Societies fellow, 1981; distinguished Bowdoin educator, 1990.

WRITINGS:

The Language of Meditation, Stockwell (Ilfracombe, UK), 1973.
Egoism and Self-Discovery in the Victorian Novel, B. Franklin (New York City), 1974.
(With Janet Kunert) *Plots and Characters in the Fiction of Jane Austen, the Brontes, and George Eliot,* Archon Books (Handin, CT), 1976.
Trollope and Politics: A Study of the Pallisers and Others, Barnes & Noble (New York City), 1977.
Gissing: A Life in Books, Oxford University Press (Oxford, England), 1982.
C. P. Snow: An Oral Biography, Harvester (Brighton, Sussex, UK), 1983.
The Life of Jane Austen, Johns Hopkins University Press (Baltimore, MD), 1984, reprinted 1996.
Jane Austen's Lovers and Other Studies in Fiction and History from Austen to le Carre, St. Martin's (New York City), 1988.
Novelists in Their Youth, St. Martin's, 1990.
Eminent Georgians: The Lives of King George V, Elizabeth Bowen, St. John Philby, and Nancy Astor, St. Martin's, 1995.

EDITOR

Henry James, *The Golden Bowl,* Popular Library, 1973.
The Theory of the Novel: New Essays, Oxford University Press, 1974.
Jane Austen: Bicentenary Essays, Cambridge University Press (Cambridge, England), 1975.
George Gissing, *Denzil Quarrier,* Harvester (Hassocks, UK), 1979.
Anthony Trollope, *Lord Palmerston,* Arno, 1981.
Trollope, *Sir Harry Hotspur of Humblethwaite,* Arno, 1981.
Trollope Centenary Essays, Macmillan (London), 1982.
George Meredith, *The Ordeal of Richard Feverel,* Oxford University Press, 1984.
Trollope, *Dr. Wortle's School,* Oxford University Press, 1984.
Gissing, *The Emancipated,* Hogarth (London), 1985.
Gissing, *Will Warburton,* Hogarth, 1985.
Trollope, *The Belton Estate,* Oxford University Press, 1986.
Trollope, *The American Senator,* Oxford University Press, 1986.
Gissing, *In the Year of Jubilee,* Hogarth, 1987.
Gissing, *New Grub Street,* Ryburn Library Centennial Edition, 1991.
Trollope, *The Vice of Bulhampton,* Folio Society, 1997.

OTHER

Contributor of articles to academic journals, editor of *Proust,* a special issue of *Style,* 1988.

SIDELIGHTS: The literary scholarship of John Halperin focuses on a select few writers of the eighteenth and nineteenth centuries, notably Jane Austen, Anthony Trollope, and George Gissing. In his 1990 work *Novelists in Their Youth,* Halperin states: "Give me the first twenty or thirty years of an author's life, and I think I can explain, through examination of them and of various influences (historical, psychological, geographical, familial, social and whatever) exerted upon them, some of the reasons why the texts produced during the author's maturity came into being."

Such a challenge presented itself in Halperin's best-known book, *The Life of Jane Austen.* Published in 1984 and reissued in 1996, this book capitalized on Austen's continuing popularity (though it could hardly predict the mid-1990s surge of interest as evidenced by several feature-film and television adaptations of Austen's novels). This "detailed and exhaustive analysis," as Anne-Marie Foley describes it in the *Dictionary of Literary Biography,* attempts to "fill in many of the gaps left by other Austen biographies."

In Halperin's view, the continuing myths surrounding Austen's life—that of a "pleasant and practically angelic" writer, as Foley puts it—were perpetrated by the novelist's own relatives, particularly her sister Cassandra, who destroyed many of the letters Jane had written after the novelist's death at the age of 41. Austen's lifelong search for love and marriage, her wickedly satiric novels (including *Pride and Prejudice, Sense and Sensibility, Emma* and *Northanger Abbey*), and her early demise have so endeared her to generations of critics and readers that her most ardent fans could belong to the cult of what has become known as "Janeites."

"Laudably, [Halperin] is no Janeite," notes a *London Review of Books* critic. "He never speaks of his subject as 'Miss Austen,' that facetious, would be 'period' locution . . .[Austen herself] took care to avoid and avert." In the view of John Bayley, in a *New York Review of Books* article, Halperin's "great merit as a biographer is that he is the most unlikely spouse imaginable for Jane Austen. . . . [He] teases his Jane as he admires her, and by being so completely from another world does indeed make us see her in a different way. He takes her right out of the incestuous love or hate embrace in which Janeites and anti-Janeites have concealed her so long. That is quite an achievement."

"My interest here," writes Halperin in *The Life of Jane Austen,* "as elsewhere, is in the relation between the life of the artist and the work produced rather than in either by itself." The biography delves deeply into the "interrelatedness of life and art," according to Foley. By dissecting Austen's fictional characters, Foley continues, Halperin seeks a better understanding of the novelist's life and concerns. In doing so he "draws more extensively on Austen's letters than any previous biographer, uncovering evidence of personal events, and of her likes and dislikes, from seemingly trivial correspondence."

Not every reader of *The Life of Jane Austen* received the work as enthusiastically. Judith Martin, for one, takes Halperin to task for drawing certain conclusions. Austen's "use of marriage as a plot device is seen as the preoccupation of an embittered spinster, as if satisfactorily matched writers never ended their stories with a wedding," Martin writes in the *Washington Post Book World.* "Discussions of money and marriage are analyzed with an apparent innocence of the fact that what a couple was going to live on was once considered as important a condition to marriage as, say, sexual compatibility would be today." And to *Listener* critic Hugh Brogan, Halperin "has no *joie de vivre* and no understanding of English humour, which rather disqualifies him for treating this particular subject." Brogan goes on to characterize Halperin's modern-day reading of Austen as an attempt "to make her seem a modern writer, a fretful neurotic like the Martini-swilling chain-smokers of New York." To Marilyn Butler, in a *New York Times Book Review* article, Halperin "shows a sounder intuition when he depicts Austen as a tough professional, not the loyal, supportive younger daughter or maiden aunt that the family liked to imagine. The mystery is that he should regard this as somehow scandalous." "Ultimately," comments Hermione Lee in the *Times Literary Supplement,* Halperin's "'spinster novelist' is as sentimental, vulgar and naive a construct as the adorable Jane whose characters seemed part of the English landscape."

But to Bayley, the biographer's "admirable sense of the minutiae of the Austen menage, the alarms and tranquilities, the things to eat and to drink, . . . lead him also to some unexpected and penetrating critical judgements." Halperin, Bayley concludes, suggests "with considerable vividness what it must have felt to live like Jane Austen, and even to die like her at forty-one of adrenal tuberculosis."

BIOGRAPHICAL/CRITICAL SOURCES:

BOOKS

Dictionary of Literary Biography, Volume 111: *American Literary Biographers,* second series, Gale (Detroit), 1991.
Halperin, John, *Novelists in Their Youth,* St. Martin's 1990.
Halperin, *The Life of Jane Austen,* Johns Hopkins University Press, 1984.

PERIODICALS

Economist, April 14, 1990, p. 99.
Listener, August 7, 1986.
London Review of Books, February 7, 1985, p. 5.
New York Review of Books, May 9, 1985, p. 3.
New York Times Book Review, February 24, 1985, p. 25; December 3, 1995.
Spectator, January 19, 1985, p. 23.
Times Literary Supplement, August 2, 1985, p. 859; March 23, 1990, p. 308.
Washington Post Book World, January 13, 1985 p. 5.*

* * *

HARE, R(ichard) M(ervyn) 1919-

PERSONAL: Born March 21, 1919, in Backwell, near Bristol, England; son of Charles Francis Aubone (a paint manufacturer) and Louise Kathleen (Simonds) Hare; married Catherine Verney, December 7, 1947; children: John Edmund, Bridget Rachel, Amy Louise, Ellin Catherine. *Education:* Balliol College, Oxford, B.A., M.A., 1947. *Religion:* Church of England. *Avocational interests:* Music, gardening.

ADDRESSES: Home—Bywater, The Street, Ewelme, Wallingford, Oxfordshire OX10 6HQ, England.

CAREER: Oxford University, Oxford, England, fellow and tutor in philosophy at Balliol College, 1947-66, university lecturer in philosophy, 1951-66, Wilde Lecturer in Natural and Comparative Religion, 1963-66, White's Professor of Moral Philosophy and fellow of Corpus Christi College, 1966-83; University of Florida, Gainesville, graduate research professor of philosophy, 1983—. Visiting fellow at Princeton University, 1957, Australian National University, 1966, and Center for Advanced Study in Behavioral Sciences, Stanford University, 1980; visiting professor at University of Michigan, 1968, and University of Delaware, 1974; Axel Haegerstroem Lecturer in Uppsala, Sweden, 1991. Church of England, Board for Social Responsibility, member of committees on medical practices, 1962-79; National Road Safety Advisory Council, member, 1966-69. *Military service:* British Army, Royal Artillery, 1939-45; became lieutenant; served with Indian Mountain Artillery; prisoner of war in Singapore and Siam (now Thailand), 1942-45.

MEMBER: British Academy (fellow), Aristotelian Society (president, 1972-73), American Academy of Arts and Sciences (honorary foreign member).

AWARDS, HONORS: Honorary fellow, Balliol College, Oxford, 1974, and Corpus Christi College, Oxford, 1983; Tanner Award, 1979; honorary Ph.D. from University of Lund, 1991.

WRITINGS:

Oxford's Traffic: A Practical Remedy, privately printed, 1948.
The Language of Morals, Oxford University Press (Oxford, England), 1952.
Freedom and Reason, Oxford University Press, 1963.
Practical Inferences, Macmillan (London), 1971.
Essays on Philosophical Method, Macmillan, 1971.
Essays on the Moral Concepts, Macmillan, 1972.
Applications of Moral Philosophy, Macmillan, 1972.
Moral Thinking, Oxford University Press, 1981.
Plato, Oxford University Press, 1982.
Hare and Critics: Essays on Moral Thinking, edited by Douglas Seanor and N. Fotion, Oxford University Press, 1988.
Essays in Ethical Theory, Oxford University Press, 1989.
Essays on Political Morality, Oxford University Press, 1989.
Essays on Religion and Education, Oxford University Press, 1992.
Essays on Bioethics, Oxford University Press, 1993.

Sorting Out Ethics, Oxford University Press, 1997.

Contributor to volumes of essays, including *The Tanner Lectures on Human Values,* edited by Sterling M. McMurrin, Volume 1: *1980,* University of Utah Press (Salt Lake City), 1980. Contributor to professional journals.

BIOGRAPHICAL/CRITICAL SOURCES:

PERIODICALS

Times (London), January 7, 1982.
Times Literary Supplement, January 19, 1973; July 2, 1982; March 11, 1983.

* * *

HARLAN, Glen
See CEBULASH, Mel

* * *

HARRIS, David (Victor) 1946-

PERSONAL: Born February 28, 1946, in Fresno, CA; son of Clifton G. (an attorney) and Elaine (an attorney; maiden name, Jensen) Harris; married Joan Baez (a folk singer), March 26, 1968 (divorced March 26, 1973); married Lacey Fosburgh (a writer), May, 1977; children: (first marriage) Gabriel. *Education:* Attended Stanford University, 1963-67. *Politics:* Democrat. *Religion:* None.

ADDRESSES: Home—880 Berkeley Ave., Menlo Park, CA 94025. *Agent*—Helen Brann Inc., 94 Curtis Rd., Bridgewater, CT 06752.

CAREER: Civil rights worker in Quitman County, MS, 1964; organizer for United Farmworkers Union, 1965; anti-war organizer, 1966-73; *Rolling Stone,* San Francisco, contributing editor, 1973—. Democratic candidate for congress from 12th California district, 1976. Member of California Democratic State Central Committee and California Tax Reform Association.

MEMBER: Palo Alto Cooperative, Briarpath Auto Cooperative.

AWARDS, HONORS: Stanford Poetry Prize; Communication Arts Award of Excellence for editorial design.

WRITINGS:

Goliath, R. W. Baron, 1969.
(With wife, Joan Baez) *Coming Out,* Simon & Schuster (New York City), 1971.
I Shoulda Been Home Yesterday, Delacorte (New York City), 1976.
The Geologic Story of the National Parks and Monuments (for children), graphics by Gregory C. Nelson, Colorado State University Foundation Press, 1978, 4th edition (with Eugene P. Kiver), 1980.
Rights in Residence, Cooperative Press, 1979.
The Last Scam: A Novel, Delacorte, 1981.
Dreams Die Hard: Three Men's Journey through the Sixties, St. Martin's (New York City), 1982, revised edition, Mercury House (San Francisco), 1993.
The League: The Rise and Decline of the NFL, Bantam (New York City), 1986.
The Last Stand: The War between Wall Street and Main Street over California's Ancient Redwoods, Times Books (New York City), 1995.
Our War: What We Did in Vietnam and What It Did to Us, Times Books, 1996.

Contributor of articles and poetry to numerous periodicals, including the *New York Times.*

SIDELIGHTS: David Harris has chronicled the social, political, and cultural currents of mid- to late-twentieth-century America through autobiographical accounts of his involvement in Vietnam War-era protests and his more recent experiences as a journalist. He often finds the character of these currents in the lives of the people—including himself—caught up in them. While a student at Stanford University, where he served as student-body president, Harris joined in the protests for civil rights and against the Vietnam War, eventually marrying fellow-protestor and folk singer Joan Baez. For his resistance to the draft, he was sent to prison for twenty months, an experience that he recalls in his 1976 book, *I Shoulda Been Home Yesterday.* A reviewer for *Publishers Weekly* comments that the book is "not only an indictment of the mindless, brutalized system that erodes the prisoner's soul, but a shocking testament of the indiscriminate punishment meted political prisoners, even in the United States." Malcolm Braly writes of Harris' work in the *New York Times Book Review:* "As an activist, a social critic, and a candidate for political office we might have expected more from him. But having said this, it must also be said that Harris can write with power and economy; his incidents emerge as small gems, and many will read this book with pleasure. Beneath all the tough talk one senses a nice man who has bitten off more than he really wants to chew, whose optimism and world view has been damaged by his walk through the dark side of our Republic."

Dreams Die Hard: Three Men's Journey through the Sixties is Harris's second memoir of his protest years. This book tells the story of Harris, his friend and fellow-civil rights activist Dennis Sweeney, and their former mentor, Allard K. Lowenstein—a "liberal gadfly and later a Democratic Representative from New York," as Michiko Kakutani observes in the *New York Times. Dreams Die Hard* is Harris's record of these three and their political and personal relationships during the turbulent 1960s. Harris looks back on these lives and events through the intervening years and with the knowledge that in March of 1980 Sweeney murdered Lowenstein. "Things are not as simple as they once seemed," notes Kakutani, "and Mr. Harris looks back on his former friends and his younger self with both irony and a measure of nostalgia for what is now irretrievably past."

Harris describes Lowenstein as a man who could inspire younger people to follow his crusades, only to betray them through choosing the expedient or through unsolicited physical advances. Sweeney emerges as a man who never recaptured the passion of the movement and who eventually fell victim to mental illness and paranoia. Harris's revelations about Lowenstein have raised some controversy, as they concern a man remembered primarily as a successful reform leader, congressman, and member of the United Nations delegation for the Carter administration. But, as Jonathan Yardley explains in the *Washington Post Book World,* "Such are the sobriety and evenhandedness of Harris' analysis that he makes this speculation entirely plausible, and presents a persuasive case that Lowenstein's relationship with his 'proteges' must be considered within a sexual as well as moral and political context." He adds, "This is not gratuitous keyhole-peeping, as Lowenstein's more blinkered followers are sure to charge, but a brave, sensitive effort to understand a complex, troubled man."

Harris's ability to capture the characters and events of this period as well as his writing are the focus of many of the reviews of *Dreams Die Hard.* Joe Klein admits in the *New York Times Book Review,* Harris "is no doubt correct in sensing that there was symbolic resonance in the assassination of Allard Lowenstein, but this remains a cold, unsatisfying book." He explains, "The characters—compelling as Mr. Harris says they are—are cardboard statues seen through a scrim." For Yardley, however, "Though his prose becomes a trifle muddy from time to time, and though his efforts to weave into one seamless narrative the separate stories of three men are not entirely successful, Harris has written a work of unusual maturity and honesty. He is always fair, never judgmental." And according to Kakutani, "Although the book is marred by awkward and portentous passages . . . Mr. Harris has managed, through intelligent reporting and recollection, to create a portrait of a decade as it was mirrored in the lives of three men." It is, in Yardley's words, "a rarity: something of value and durability wrenched out of the empty dislocations of the '60s."

In *The League: The Rise and Decline of the NFL,* Harris writes about professional football without writing about the players or the fans. Instead, as Leigh Steinberg comments in the *Los Angeles Times Book Review,* Harris chooses to "focus on the politics of the inner circle of professional football leadership in the most complete volume yet written describing the past decade of the National Football League." Harris returns to the 1958 NFL Championship, in which the Baltimore Colts beat the New York Giants in overtime, and marks this as the point that would set football on a course to become number one in the hearts of sports fans. From there he follows the business of football through years of unity and prosperity under Commissioner Pete Rozelle to efforts by Raiders' owner Al Davis and others to call their own shots. According to Steinberg, "When Harris shifts focus to the owners themselves, his keen descriptive eye for color and detail brings *The League* to life. The author highlights a fascinating collection of personalities and life styles that often seem lifted from the television shows 'Dallas' or 'Dynasty.'"

Jonathan Yardley of *Washington Post Book World,* calls *The League* well-researched, but concludes that "although Harris has done his homework with great care, he has unearthed surprisingly little that will come as news to anyone who has paid attention to the NFL's affairs in recent years." Ron Rosenbaum offers a different view in the *New York Times Book Review.* He commends Harris's effort and states, "The secret of his success is his diligence as an investigative reporter. He's dug up a gold mine of fresh material on the N.F.L. owners from the dozens of lawsuits they've left in their wake." He concedes that Harris does not write as if he is a fan of the game, but believes that this is "the source of both the greatest strengths and the occasional weakness of his book. He brings considerable nonfan detachment to his dissection of the character and style of the N.F.L. owners, and no picture of the league will be complete without taking into account the muck he rakes. And yet, in another sense, his rogues' gallery of owner portraits only re-emphasizes, by contrast, the grace and courage of those figures who loom larger in their absence from his account—the players on the field." For a *West Coast Review of Books* reviewer, "Overall, the book is absorbing as Harris gives us more than we really had a right to expect to know. A monumental effort has been rewarded by a monumental book."

In his 1995 book, *Last Stand: The War between Wall Street and Main Street over California's Ancient Redwoods,* Harris "details the clash of three distinct cultures: greedy Wall Street financiers; idealistic environmentalists; and those attempting to earn their living from the forest," according to a reviewer in *Publishers Weekly.* Here Harris explores what happens to the people of a small, northern California lumber town when the local employer, committed to making money without exploiting its natural and human resources, becomes the target of a hostile, corporate takeover. Financier Charles Hurwitz, with help from Wall Street legends Michael Milken and Ivan Boesky, first secured control of the company and then set out to make money regardless of local concerns.

"Through the personal experiences of ordinary people affected by the takeover, Mr. Harris describes the painful transition of a town and its company from enlightened to unenlightened capitalism," notes Mark Dowie in the *New York Times Book Review.* "Mr. Harris quite reliably weaves a good parable," believes Dowie. "But unlike his earlier nonfiction books . . . this one . . . is long on narrative and short on analysis." Even so, concludes the reviewer, "'The Last Stand' remains an essential read for anyone curious about the innards of a hostile takeover, the *Realpolitik* of resource economics or the psychodynamics of radical environmentalism."

BIOGRAPHICAL/CRITICAL SOURCES:

PERIODICALS

Business Week, February 26, 1996, p. 16.
Chicago Tribune Book World, June 27, 1982, p. 1.
Economist, March 16, 1996, p. 10.
Los Angeles Times Book Review, June 20, 1982; November 9, 1986.
New York Times, November 16, 1981; June 29, 1982.
New York Times Book Review, August 22, 1976, pp. 3, 10; December 20, 1981, pp. 10, 19; June 13, 1982, p. 38; October 26, 1986, p. 9; January 28, 1996, p. 12.
People, January 30, 1978, p. 66.
Publishers Weekly, June 14, 1976, p. 109; October 9, 1981, pp. 66-68; September 5, 1986, p. 97; November 13, 1995, p. 53.
Washington Post Book World, June 27, 1982, pp. 5, 13; October 5, 1986, p. 3.
West Coast Review of Books, number 4, 1986, p. 40.*

* * *

HARRIS, Marion Rose (Young) 1925-
(Rose Young; pseudonyms: Henry Charles, Rose Glendower)

PERSONAL: Born July 12, 1925, in Cardiff, South Wales; daughter of Robert Henry and Marion (Phillips) Young; married Kenneth Mackenzie Harris (the director of a furnishing company), August 18, 1943; children: Roger Mackenzie, Pamela Daphne, Keith Mackenzie. *Education:* Attended Gillingham School and Cardiff Technical College.

ADDRESSES: Home and office—Walpole Cottage, Long Dr., Burnham, Buckinghamshire SL1 8AJ, England.

CAREER: Writer. Private secretary to managing director of builder's merchant, 1942-46; freelance journalist, 1946—; editor of Regional Feature Service, 1964-71; W. Foulsham & Co. Ltd., Slough, Buckinghamshire, England, editorial controller, 1974-83. Child care consultant for *Here's Health;* London correspondent for *Irish Leather and Footwear Journal* and *Futura* (fashion trade magazine). Furnishing consultant to builders, architects, and magazines, designing interiors for show houses at Ideal Homes Exhibition, Olympia, London, England, 1963-64, and for building estates in England.

MEMBER: Romantic Novelists Association, Society of Authors, Welsh Academy.

WRITINGS:

Fresh Fruit Dishes, Jenkins, 1963, reprinted, 1977.
Making a House a Home, Pan Books (England), 1963.
The Awful Slimmer's Book, Wolfe, 1967.
Teach Your Mum Flower Arranging, Wolfe, 1968.
(Under pseudonym Henry Charles) *Twenty-Five Easy to Grow Vegetables: In Any Size Plot,* Foulsham (England), 1975.
(Under name Rose Young) *When the Clouds Clear,* International Publishing Co. (New York City), 1975.
Captain of Her Heart, R. Hale (England), 1976.
(Under name Rose Young) *Love Can Conquer,* International Publishing Co., 1976.
(Under name Rose Young) *Secret of Abbey Place,* International Publishing Co., 1977.
Just a Handsome Stranger, Hamlyn, 1983.
The Queen's Windsor (nonfiction), Kensal Press, 1985.
Soldiers' Wives, Severn House Publishers, 1986.
Officers' Ladies, Severn House Publishers, 1987.
The Heart of the Dragon, Sphere Books, Book 1: *Nesta,* 1988, Book 2: *Amelda,* 1989.
(Under pseudonym Rose Glendower) *Sighing for the Moon,* 1991.
(Under name Rose Young) *To Love and Love Again,* D. C. Thomson, 1994.

Also scriptwriter for British Broadcasting Corp. schools broadcast *Do Manners Matter,* and for *Home This Afternoon* series. Contributor to *Dairy Book of Home Management,* Milk Marketing Board, 1969. Contributor of short stories and articles to periodicals, including *Top Secretary, Homefinder, Cupid Chronicle, Home Overseas, Moneymaker, Here's Health,* and *Writer's Review.*

SIDELIGHTS: Marion Rose Harris told *CA:* "Fiction can be therapeutic. Transporting readers from their mundane daily round into a fantasy world can prove more beneficial than valium or any other sedative. Fiction often helps the reader to sort out problems or avoid some of life's pitfalls, so it could even be claimed that it has some educational value."

Harris adds that since 1986, she "has been publishing family sagas which have strong, factual backgrounds and are listed as 'general fiction.'"

* * *

HARRISON, David L(ee) 1937-
(Arthur Kennon Graham, Kennon Graham)

PERSONAL: Born March 13, 1937, in Springfield, MO; son of John Alexander (a businessman) and Laura Neva (a homemaker; maiden name, Justice) Harrison; married Sandra Sue Kennon (a high school counselor), May 23, 1959; children: Robin Lynn Harrison Williams, Jeffrey Scott. *Education:* Drury College, A.B., 1959; Emory University, M.S., 1960; Evansville University, graduate studies, 1960-63.

ADDRESSES: Home—2634 Skyline Dr., Springfield, MO 65804. *Office*—928 South Glenstone, Springfield, MO 65802. *E-mail*—dharriso@mail.-orion.org.

CAREER: Mead Johnson Co., Evansville, IN, pharmacologist, 1960-63; Hallmark Cards, Kansas City, MO, editorial manager, 1963-73; Glenstone Block Co. (manufacturer and supply house of building materials), Springfield, MO, president and owner, 1973—. President and member of Springfield Board of Education, 1983-88; member of board, Springfield Public Schools Foundation, 1988-96; member of board of trustees, Ozarks Technical Community College, 1992-94; member of advisory board, *Springfield Parent* magazine, 1994—. Has been a professional musician, music teacher, and principal trombonist in the Springfield Symphony. Active in various activities supporting literacy, 1982—; presenter and speaker at workshops and conferences.

MEMBER: Society of Children's Book Writers and Illustrators, Missouri Writers Guild.

AWARDS, HONORS: Christopher Award, Christopher Foundation, 1973, for *The Book of Giant Stories;* award for Outstanding Contributions to Children's Literature, Central State University, 1978; Distinguished Alumni Award, Drury College, 1981; Kentucky Blue Grass Award nominee, Kentucky State Reading Association, 1993, for *Somebody Catch My Homework;* Celebrate Literacy Award, Missouri State Reading Association, 1994; Friend of Education Award, Missouri State Teachers Association, 1994; Children's Choice Award, International Reading Association and Children's Book Council (IRA/CBC), 1994, for *Somebody Catch My Homework,* and 1995, for *When Cows Come Home;* inclusion on Recommended Reading List, Kansas State Reading Association, 1995, and Master List of the Virginia Young Readers Program, Virginia State Reading Association, 1996-97, both for *When Cows Come Home.*

WRITINGS:

The Boy with a Drum, Golden Press (Racine, WI), 1969.
Little Turtle's Big Adventure, Random House (New York City), 1969.
The Little Boy in the Forest, Whitman Publishing, 1969.
About Me, Childcraft Education Corp., 1969.
The World of American Caves, Reilly & Lee, 1970.
The Case of Og the Missing Frog, Rand McNally (Chicago), 1972.
(With Mary Loberg) *The Backyard Zoo,* Hallmark Books (Shelby, OH), 1972.
(With Loberg) *The Kingdom of the Sea,* Hallmark Books, 1972.
(With Loberg) *The World of Horses,* Hallmark Books, 1972.
(With Loberg) *The Terrible Lizards,* Hallmark Books, 1972.
The Book of Giant Stories, illustrated by Philippe Fix, McGraw, 1972.
The Little Boy and the Giant, Golden Press, 1973.
Let's Go Trucks!, Golden Press, 1973.
Children Everywhere, Rand McNally, 1973.
Piggy Wiglet and the Great Adventure, Golden Press, 1973.
The Huffin Puff Express, Whitman Publishing, 1974.
The Busy Body Book, Whitman Publishing, 1975.
Monster! Monster!, Golden Press, 1975.
The Pink Panther in Z-Land, Whitman Publishing, 1976.
The Circus Is in Town, Golden Press, 1978.
Detective Bob and the Great Ape Escape, illustrated by Ned Delaney, Parents Magazine Press (New York City), 1980.
My Funny Bunny Phone Book, illustrated by Lyn McClure Butrick, Golden Press, 1980.
What Do You Know!: Mind-Boggling Questions, Astonishing Answers, illustrated by Rod Ruth, Rand McNally, 1981.
The Snoring Monster, illustrated by Richard Walz, Golden Press, 1985.
Busy Machines, illustrated by Walz, Golden Press, 1985.
Wake Up, Sun!, illustrated by Hans Wilhelm, Random House, 1986.
Little Boy Soup, Ladybird Books (England), 1989.
Somebody Catch My Homework: Poems, illustrated by Betsy Lewin, Boyds Mills Press, 1993.
When Cows Come Home, illustrated by Chris L. Demarest, Boyds Mills Press, 1994.
The Boy Who Counted Stars: Poems, illustrated by Betsy Lewin, Boyds Mills Press, 1994.
A Thousand Cousins: Poems of Family Life, illustrated by Betsy Lewin, Boyds Mills Press, 1996.
The Animals' Song, Boyds Mills Press, 1997.

UNDER PSEUDONYM KENNON GRAHAM

Smokey Bear Saves the Forest, Whitman Publishing, 1971.
Lassie and the Big Clean-Up Day, Golden Press, 1971.
Eloise and the Old Blue Truck, Whitman Publishing, 1971.
Lassie and the Secret Friend, Golden Press, 1972.
My Little Book of Cars and Trucks, Whitman Publishing, 1973.
Woodsy Owl and the Trail Bikers, Golden Press, 1974.
Land of the Lost: Surprise Guests, Golden Press, 1975.
The Pink Panther in the Haunted House, Golden Press, 1975.
The Pink Panther Rides Again, Whitman Publishing, 1976.
My Little Book about Flying, Whitman Publishing, 1978.
Bugs Bunny in Escape from Noddington Castle, illustrated by Darrell Baker, Golden Press, 1979.

EDITOR; PUBLISHED BY HALLMARK BOOKS

Peter Pan, 1964.
Cinderella, 1964.
Pinocchio, 1964.
The Adventures of Doctor Dolittle, 1965.
A Christmas Carol, 1965.
The Three Pigs, 1966.
Goldilocks and the Three Bears, 1966.

OTHER

Contributor of stories and poems to anthologies. Contributor of short stories, under pseudonyms Arthur Kennon Graham and Kennon Graham, to *The Witch Book,* edited by Dorothy F. Haas, Rand McNally, 1976. Contributor to periodicals, including *Highlights for Children, Family Circle, Journal of Reading, Creative Classroom, Hello Reader!, Senior Living,* and *Springfield News-Leader.* Some of Harrison's work has been presented on cassettes, on television, and on radio throughout the world; *Somebody Catch My Homework* was produced on CD-ROM, Discis, 1994. Harrison's work has been translated into more than twelve languages.

WORK IN PROGRESS: My Desk Is Haunted, "a collection of humorous school poems;" *The Purchase of Small Secrets,* "a collection of free verse comprising memories from teenage years;" *Farmer's Garden,* a picture book; *Don't Tell Said the Bell,* a picture book; a book for classroom teachers about writing poetry, with Bernice E. Cullinan.

SIDELIGHTS: Although the author of over fifty books for young people, David L. Harrison has not limited himself to the field of children's literature. He once told *CA:* "By the time I was twenty-one I had worked in a pet shop, done yard work, taught music, dug ditches, unloaded boxcars, played in dance bands, poured concrete, worked in the entomology department at a university, mined uranium, and explored caves. I had also begun to write seriously, but it took nearly six more years before my first story was accepted for publication." Using these wide and varied experiences as inspiration, Harrison has produced award winning children's stories, poetry, and retellings of classic tales.

Harrison's 1972 work, *The Book of Giant Stories,* blends limericks and stories together to create a world where giants live among men. In this make-believe book, one young boy escapes from the hands of giants by telling them a secret; another clever lad calms a temperamental giant by teaching him to whistle; and a third boy helps a sorry giant who has been cursed by a wicked witch. A reviewer in *Publishers Weekly* described Harrison's book as "farfetched and funny," while Evelyn Stewart noted in *Library Journal* that the "believable fantasy is perfect for reading aloud" to younger readers. *Wake Up, Sun!,* an easy-to-read book published in 1986, chronicles the humorous attempts of barnyard animals to awaken the sun when they arise one morning before daybreak.

Somebody Catch My Homework features a variety of poems addressing the trials and tribulations children often have about school. Missing homework excuses, asking permission for restroom privileges, and complaints about playground bullies are set to verse with a sense of humor that is accessible to children. According to *School Library Journal* contributor Lee Bock, *Somebody Catch My Homework* is "reminiscent of the styles of Prelutsky and Silverstein." Writing in *Booklist,* Hazel Rochman applauded the book's "immediacy and slapstick." A critic in *Kirkus Reviews* remarked that the book is "all recognizable, neatly scanned, and genuinely funny," further labeling the book "a winner—to read aloud, pass around, and chortle over again."

In his 1994 picture book, *When Cows Come Home,* Harrison reveals what really happens on the farm when the farmer's back is turned. As soon as the farmer tends to other business, all of his cows explode in silly and whimsical stunts, including square dancing, riding bicycles, and playing tag. A *Kirkus Reviews* critic complimented Harrison's "skillful versifying," while in *School Library Journal,* Mary Lou Budd admired "the motion in the rhythmic and evocative text." A *Publishers Weekly* reviewer described *When Cows Come Home* as "a bright, appealing volume with a mischievous nature."

Harrison's collection *A Thousand Cousins: Poems of Family Life* looks lightheartedly at numerous family situations which often confuse and confound children. The poet explores the relationships between siblings and extended family members and makes light of situations common to many children, such as fathers snoring loudly and mothers incessantly reminding their kids to keep clean. A critic in *Kirkus Reviews* observed that most of the poems "have punchy endings; each revolves around some gimmick." *School Library Journal* contributor Marjorie Lewis asserted that these poems will "elicit giggles from young readers and listeners."

About his work as a children's writer and poet, David L. Harrison told *CA:* "I've always maintained two careers. First I worked in a pharmacology lab by day and wrote at night. Then came editing greeting cards by day and writing by night, followed by managing a business by day and writing at night. That used to seem normal to me. Now I'm not as sure. Years ago I'd come home from my day job and work on some manuscript until late at night. Late comes earlier than it once did.

"Something else that's changed is the way folks react if you tell them you write for young people. They used to say something like, 'Oh?' beneath arched eyebrows, signifying that it was a darned pity you couldn't make it as a real writer. Worse yet, sometimes there wasn't even the spark of a question mark. 'Oh,' they'd say simply, a touch of sadness pursing their lips, their attention turning to the broccoli dip.

"Thanks to our nation's well-founded concerns about educating and developing our newest generations, writing for young people is now recognized as a worthy goal. Writers have always known that they must grow with their work. What could be a better strategy for success than to choose an audience that also must keep growing?"

BIOGRAPHICAL/CRITICAL SOURCES:

PERIODICALS

Booklist, December 1, 1986, p. 583; January 15, 1993, p. 914; May 1, 1994, p. 1608.

Kirkus Reviews, December 15, 1992, p. 1573; January 1, 1994, p. 68; December 15, 1995, p. 1770.

Library Journal, January 15, 1973, p. 253.

Publishers Weekly, December 11, 1972, p. 36; November 29, 1993, p. 64.

Reading Teacher, October, 1994.

St. Louis Post-Dispatch, June 5, 1994.

School Library Journal, December, 1986, pp. 122-123; January, 1993, p. 92; February, 1994, p. 86; November, 1994, p. 98; March, 1996, p. 209.

* * *

HARTLEY, Robert F(rank) 1927-

PERSONAL: Born December 15, 1927, in Beaver Falls, PA; son of Frank H. (a merchant) and Eleanor (Theis) Hartley; married Dorothy Mayou, June 30, 1962; children: Constance, Matthew. *Education:* Drake University, B.B.A., 1949; University of Minnesota, M.B.A., 1962, Ph.D., 1967.

ADDRESSES: *Home*—17405 South Woodland Rd., Shaker Heights, OH 44120. *Office*—Department of Marketing, Cleveland State University, Cleveland, OH 44115.

CAREER: Management employee for national department store chains, 1949-59; Dayton Corp., Minneapolis, MN, in merchandise management, 1959-63; University of Minnesota, Minneapolis, instructor in marketing, 1963-65; George Washington University, Washington, DC, assistant professor, 1965-69, associate professor of marketing, 1969-72; Cleveland State University, Cleveland, OH, professor of marketing, 1972—.

MEMBER: American Marketing Association.

WRITINGS:

Marketing Management and Social Change, International Textbook Co., 1972.

Retailing: Challenge and Opportunity, Houghton (Boston, MA), 1975, 3rd edition, 1984.

Marketing for Responsive Management, Dun Donnelly, 1976.

Marketing Mistakes, Grid Publishing, 1976, 6th edition, Wiley (New York City), 1995.

Sales Management, Houghton, 1979, 2nd edition, C. E. Merrill (Columbus, OH), 1989.

(Coauthor) *Essentials of Marketing Research,* PennWell (Tulsa, OK), 1983.

Management Mistakes & Successes, Grid Publishing (Columbus, OH), 1983, 5th edition, Wiley, 1997.

Marketing Fundamentals, Harper (New York City), 1983.

Marketing Successes, Historical to Present Day: What We Can Learn, Wiley, 1985, 2nd edition, 1990.

Bullseyes and Blunders, Wiley, 1987.

Pricing for Export, International Trade Centre, 1987.

Export Channel Management, International Trade Centre, 1987.

Business Ethics: Violations of the Public Trust, Wiley, 1993.

Also author of the novels *A Shuttered Life,* 1995; and *The Quest,* 1996. Contributor to business and marketing journals.

Some of Hartley's books have been translated into various languages, including Croation, Finnish, Hebrew, Japanese, and Spanish.

SIDELIGHTS: Robert F. Hartley told *CA:* "I have attempted in my academic and trade writings to blend the practical with the conceptual. An underlying theme in these books has been the desirability of business to be responsive to the needs and dictums of society, rather than strictly corporate short-term self-interest. We need to inspire as well as instruct.

"In recent years I have become intrigued with the challenge of fiction, and have at present written two novels, one having a contemporary theme and the other historical. It is my hope to write novels of courage and perseverance, ones that may somehow move the reader."

* * *

HARVEY, Nigel 1916-
(Hugh Willoughby)

PERSONAL: Born August 8, 1916, in Oxford, England; son of Godfrey Eric (a civil servant in India) and Stella Hope (Garratt) Harvey; married Barbara Anne Skemp; children: Charles Frazer, Geoffrey Rowland. *Ethnicity:* "English." *Education:* Exeter College, Oxford, B.A., 1938, M.A., 1950; also attended Purdue University, 1955.

ADDRESSES: Home—41 Corringham Rd., Golders Green, London NW11 7BS, England.

CAREER: Farm worker in Oxfordshire and land agent trainee in Suffolk, 1941-44; Ministry of Agriculture, Fisheries, and Food, London, member of staff, 1944-58; Agricultural Research Council, London, member of staff, 1958-76; fulltime writer, 1976—. Agricultural history adviser to Old Fort William project in Ontario for National Heritage Ltd., 1974. Honorary librarian of Royal Agricultural Society of England, 1979-94. Historic farm building adviser to Ministry of Agriculture, Fisheries, and Food, 1984. Historic Farm Buildings Group, chair, 1985, honorary president, 1991.

MEMBER: Royal Institution of Chartered Surveyors (associate), Royal Agricultural Society of England (honorary member).

AWARDS, HONORS: Kellogg fellowship to Purdue University, 1955.

WRITINGS:

The Story of Farm Buildings, National Federation of Young Farmers Clubs, 1953.

The Farming Kingdom, Turnstile, 1955.

Ditches, Dykes, and Deep Drainage, National Federation of Young Farmers Clubs, 1956.

(Under pseudonym Hugh Willoughby) *Amid the Alien Corn,* Bobbs-Merrill (New York City), 1958.

Farm Work Study, Farmer & Stockbreeder, 1958.

A History of Farm Buildings in England and Wales, David & Charles (London), 1970, second edition, 1984.

Old Farm Buildings, Shire Publications, 1975, fourth edition, 1997.

Fields, Hedges, and Ditches, Shire Publications, 1976, second edition, 1987.

Farms and Farming, Shire Publications, 1977.

Discovering Farm Livestock, Shire Publications, 1979.

(With Graham Cherry) *Effective Writing in Advisory Work,* Ministry of Agriculture, Fisheries, and Food, 1980.

The Industrial Archaeology of Farming in England and Wales, Batsford (London), 1980.

Trees, Woods, and Forests, Shire Publications, 1981.

(Editor) *Agricultural Research Centres: A World Directory of Organisations and Programmes,* Longmans (London), 1983.

Historic Farm Building Study: Sources of Information, Ministry of Agriculture, Fisheries, and Food, 1985.

Contributor to agriculture journals and to *New Statesman* and *Country Life.*

SIDELIGHTS: Nigel Harvey described himself to *CA* as "a general-purpose agricultural and rural writer, historical, professional, and for the general reader." His official work "was concerned with producing advisory leaflets and bulletins for farmers and a continuous supply of up-to-date technical information for extension workers." His freelance books are "mainly historical, some for readers already concerned with agricultural history, others, in short, simplified form, the equivalent of illustrated historical guidebooks for those visiting the countryside and interested in the origins and development of the farmlands they see." *Amid the Alien Corn* is a collection of Harvey's letters from Purdue University to his family at home in England. He told *CA:* "My letters were never intended for publication, of course. When I got home, I had copies run-off, omitting personal matters, to give to friends and one of them took it to Bobbs-Merrill who offered to publish it." A reviewer for the *Christian Science Monitor* wrote: "Since [Harvey] combines intellect with wit, his views make fast and easy reading, having for Americans all the fascination inherent in a chance to look over someone's shoulder and read private correspondence about ourselves."

According to Philip Riden writing in the *Times Literary Supplement,* Harvey's *Industrial Archaeology of Farming in England and Wales* describes "each stage in the farming process from 'The Winning of the Waste' through field, drainage, fertilizers, crops, stock, implements and machinery to the substantial section on farm buildings. . . . Harvey's style is plain and easy to follow; this is a book on technology which the non-technical can understand without difficulty."

BIOGRAPHICAL/CRITICAL SOURCES:

PERIODICALS

Architectural Review, March, 1985.
British Farmer, February 23, 1971.
Christian Science Monitor, December 6, 1958.
Times (London), October 2, 1980.
Times Literary Supplement, November 21, 1980.

HARWICK, B. L.
See KELLER, Beverly L(ou)

* * *

HASSLER, Donald M. (II) 1937-

PERSONAL: Born January 3, 1937, in Akron, OH; son of Donald M. (in business) and Fran (Parsons) Hassler; married Diana Cain, October 8, 1960 (died September 19, 1976); married Sue Smith, September 13, 1977; children: (first marriage) Donald M. III, David. *Ethnicity:* "German-British." *Education:* Williams College, B.A., 1959; Columbia University, M.A., 1960, Ph.D., 1967. *Religion:* Lutheran.

ADDRESSES: Home—1226 Woodhill, Kent, OH 44240. *Office*—Department of English, Kent State University, Kent, OH 44240. *E-mail*—dhassler-@kentum.kent.edu; fax: 330-672-3152.

CAREER: University of Montreal, Montreal, Quebec, instructor in English, 1961-65; Kent State University, Kent, OH, assistant professor, 1967-71, associate professor, 1971-77, professor of English, 1977—, director of experimental college, 1973-83, chair of undergraduate studies and director of writing certificate program in English, 1987-91, chair of graduate studies, 1991-94, secretary of faculty senate, 1996—.

MEMBER: Modern Language Association of America, American Society for Eighteenth-Century Studies, Keats-Shelley Association, American Association of University Professors, Science Fiction Research Association, Ohio Poets Association, Phi Beta Kappa.

AWARDS, HONORS: Woodrow Wilson fellow, 1959; J. Lloyd Eaton Award for best book of science fiction criticism, 1993, for *Isaac Asimov.*

WRITINGS:

The Comedian as the Letter D: Erasmus Darwin's Comic Materialism, Nijhoff, 1973.
On Weighing a Pound of Flesh (poetry), Defiance College Publications, 1973.
Erasmus Darwin, Twayne (Boston), 1974.

(Contributor) Theodore Besterman, editor, *Studies on Voltaire and the Eighteenth Century,* Voltaire Foundation, 1976.

(Contributor) Joseph Olander and Martin Greenberg, editors, *Isaac Asimov,* Taplinger (New York City), 1977.

Comic Tones in Science Fiction, Greenwood Press (Westport, CT), 1982.

Hal Clement, Starmont House (Mercer Island, WA), 1982.

Patterns of the Fantastic, Starmont House, Volume 1, 1983, Volume 2, 1984.

(Coeditor) *Death and the Serpent,* Greenwood Press, 1985.

Isaac Asimov, Starmont House, 1991.

(Coeditor) *The Letters of Arthur Machen and Montgomery Evans,* Kent State University Press (Kent, OH), 1994.

(Coeditor) *Political Science Fiction,* University of South Carolina Press, 1997.

Work appears in annual anthologies of Ohio Poets Association, 1969—. Contributor to *Hiram Poetry Review, Canadian Poetry, Fiddlehead, Descant, Canadian Forum,* and other periodicals. *Extrapolation* (science fiction journal), coeditor, 1987-89, editor, 1990—.

WORK IN PROGRESS: A collection of poems; a collection of essays on the relation of modern science fiction to the eighteenth century.

* * *

HAWKINS, Hugh (Dodge) 1929-

PERSONAL: Born September 3, 1929, in Topeka, KS; son of James Adam and Rena (Eddy) Hawkins. *Education:* DePauw University, A.B., 1950; Johns Hopkins University, Ph.D., 1954.

ADDRESSES: *Home*—Route 7, Amherst, MA 01002. *Office*—Department of American Studies, Amherst College, Amherst, MA 01002. *E-mail*—hhawkins@amherst.edu; fax 413-542-5838.

CAREER: University of North Carolina at Chapel Hill, instructor, 1956-57; Amherst College, Amherst, MA, instructor, 1957-59, assistant professor, 1959-64, associate professor, 1964-69, professor of history, 1969-75, Anson D. Morse Professor of History and American Studies, 1975—. Fulbright lecturer in Germany, 1973-74, 1993-94; University of California, Berkeley, visiting associate at Center for Studies in Higher Education, 1978-79, 1982-83.

MEMBER: American Historical Association, Organization of American Historians, American Association of University Professors, History of Education Society, Peace History Society.

AWARDS, HONORS: Moses Coit Tyler Award, American Historical Association, 1959, for *Pioneer: A History of the Johns Hopkins University, 1874-1889;* Guggenheim fellow, 1961-62; M.A., Amherst College, 1969; fellow, National Endowment for the Humanities, 1982-83.

WRITINGS:

Pioneer: A History of the Johns Hopkins University, 1874-1889, Cornell University Press (Ithaca, NY), 1960.

(Editor and author of introduction) *Booker T. Washington and His Critics: The Problem of Negro Leadership,* Heath (Lexington, MA), 1962, second edition published as *Booker T. Washington and His Critics: Black Leadership in Crisis,* 1974.

The Abolitionists: Immediatism and the Question of Means, Heath, 1964, second edition published as *The Abolitionists: Means, Ends, and Motivations,* 1972, third edition (with Lawrence B. Goodheart), 1994.

(Editor and author of introduction) *The Emerging University and Industrial America,* Heath, 1970, enlarged edition, R. E. Krieger, 1985.

Between Harvard and America: The Educational Leadership of Charles W. Eliot, Oxford University Press, 1972.

Banding Together: The Rise of National Associations in American Higher Education, 1887-1950, Johns Hopkins University Press (Baltimore, MD), 1992.

The Independent Intellectual as Academic Gadfly: One Variety of Antiacademicism, State University of New York Press (Albany), 1995.

* * *

HAYES, Geoffrey 1947-

PERSONAL: Born December 3, 1947, in Pasadena, CA; son of Philip Dutton (a waiter) and Juliette (a secretary; maiden name, Dante) Hayes. *Education:* Attended John O'Connell Institute, San Francisco Academy of Art, New York School of Visual Arts, and Hunter College.

ADDRESSES: Home—338 Bocana St., San Francisco, CA 94110. *Agent*—Edite Kroll, 12 Grayhurst Park, Portland, ME 04102.

CAREER: Marling, Marx & Seidman (advertising agency), New York City, worked in art department, 1972-73; Kajima International, New York City, interior designer, 1973-75; Harper & Row Publishers, Inc., New York City, artist and designer, 1975-1984; writer and illustrator, 1984—; Vanguard Public Foundation, San Francisco, grants associate, 1994—.

AWARDS, HONORS: When the Wind Blew (written by Margaret Wise Brown) was chosen by the *New York Times* as one of the ten best illustrated books of 1977.

WRITINGS:

FOR CHILDREN; SELF-ILLUSTRATED

Bear by Himself, Harper (New York City), 1976.
The Alligator and His Uncle Tooth: A Novel of the Sea, Harper, 1977.
Patrick Comes to Puttyville and Other Stories, Harper, 1978.
The Secret Inside, Harper, 1980.
Elroy and the Witch's Child, Harper, 1982.
Patrick and Ted, Four Winds Press (New York City), 1984.
Patrick Buys a Coat, Knopf (New York City), 1985.
Patrick Eats His Dinner, Knopf, 1985.
Patrick Takes a Bath, Knopf, 1985.
Patrick Goes to Bed, Knopf, 1985.
The Mystery of the Pirate Ghost: An Otto and Uncle Tooth Adventure, Random House (New York City), 1985.
Christmas in Puttyville, Random House, 1985.
Patrick and His Grandpa, Random House, 1986.
The Lantern Keeper's Bedtime Book, Random House, 1986.
Patrick and Ted at the Beach, Random House, 1987.
Patrick and Ted Ride the Train, Random House, 1988.
The Secret of Foghorn Island, Random House, 1988.
The Treasure of the Lost Lagoon, Random House, 1991.
The Curse of the Cobweb Queen, Random House, 1994.
The Night of the Circus Monsters, Random House, 1996.
Swamp of the Hideous Zombies, Random House, 1996.
House of the Horrible Ghosts, Random House, 1997.

ILLUSTRATOR

Margaret Wise Brown, *When the Wind Blew,* Harper, 1977.
Joan Lowery Nixon, *Muffie Mouse and the Busy Birthday,* Seabury (New York City), 1978.
Fran Manushkin, *Moon Dragon,* Macmillan (New York City), 1980.
Fran Manushkin, *Hocus & Pocus at the Circus,* Harper, 1981.

WORK IN PROGRESS: Valley of the Vicious Ducks, for Random House.

SIDELIGHTS: Author and illustrator Geoffrey Hayes has written several books for beginning readers that feature animal duos such as the young bears Patrick and Ted and amateur alligator sleuths Otto and the crusty Uncle Tooth. Through his whimsical watercolor illustrations of these and a menagerie of other animal characters, Hayes both entertains and educates young readers with books geared both to reluctant readers and those seeking more sophisticated material.

Readers are first introduced to Patrick in *Patrick Comes to Puttyville and Other Stories.* In this collection, the young bear moves with his family to a new house in a small town, where Patrick makes new friends—including Ted—and has several real-life adventures with which young children can identify. In *Patrick and Ted Ride the Train,* the two take a day trip on the Skitter & Scoo Railway to visit an elderly relative; fortunately armed with squirt guns, they make short work of a gang of annoying weasels.

The Alligator and His Uncle Tooth: A Novel of the Sea introduces readers to an entirely different community of animal characters, from young Corduroy Alligator and Captain Poopdeck, to the roving adventurer Uncle Tooth and the woebegone Ducky Doodle. Uncle Tooth is joined by young

Otto in mystery stories that include *The Treasure of the Lost Lagoon, Swamp of the Hideous Zombies,* and *The Curse of the Cobweb Queen.* Whether encountering treasure ships, mermaids, suspicious fortune tellers, a gang of dastardly rats, or a sinister, pearl-snatching witch, the long-jawed duo manage to save the day in the town of Boogle Bay. And in *Elroy and the Witch's Child* an orphaned kitten seeking his fortune encounters a witch and a little girl, with whom he travels after some misunderstandings and confused introductions. "Hayes's new romp, cause for rejoicing, sparkles with his recital of nonsense and the gaudy hues in the cartoons," noted a *Publishers Weekly* reviewer.

"Writing and drawing have always come naturally to me," Hayes once told *CA.* "My brother and I, being only two years apart, channeled our creative energies into stories and books which we gave to one another. All the writing I do now is an extension and development of those early works. Many authors relive their past in their fiction, but while some (such as Proust) do so in autobiographical novels, I find fantasy not only the best form for expressing my feelings, but as viable as any literary genre."

In addition to writing and illustrating books for young people, Hayes designs and builds custom, hand-painted furniture and is a member of a San Francisco dance troupe that performs locally. He is also involved in working for Vanguard Public Foundation, a non-profit organization that funds grassroots organizations in northern California. As the author/illustrator noted, "I find dealing with a diverse group of people to be a nice compliment to the rather solitary act of writing."

BIOGRAPHICAL/CRITICAL SOURCES:

PERIODICALS

Booklist, September 1, 1976, p. 38; May 15, 1977, p. 1420; November 15, 1978, p. 546; January 15, 1981, p. 1352; February 15, 1982, p. 762; June 15, 1984, p. 1483; June 15, 1985, p. 1457; October 1, 1988, p. 330; February 1, 1989, p. 935.

Bulletin of the Center for Children's Books, September, 1977; October, 1977, p. 33; March, 1979, p. 117.

Horn Book, August, 1977, p. 441.

Junior Bookshelf, April, 1978, p. 88.

Kirkus Reviews, June 15, 1976, p. 680; April 1, 1977, p. 350; December 15, 1978, p. 1357; May 15, 1980, p. 642; July 15, 1982, p. 795.

New York Times Book Review, November 14, 1976, p. 26; May 1, 1977, p. 47.

Publishers Weekly, May 2, 1980, p. 76; September 10, 1982, p. 76; January 21, 1983, p. 85; March 16, 1984, p. 87; April 25, 1986, p. 78; December, 1986, p. 55; June 12, 1987, p. 83; December 22, 1989, p. 57.

School Library Journal, October, 1976, p. 98; September, 1977, p. 109; October, 1978, p. 145; May, 1980, p. 58; September, 1982, p. 108; October, 1984, p. 147; November, 1985, p. 72; December, 1986, p. 80; December, 1988, p. 87; April, 1992, p. 92.

* * *

HEALD, Tim(othy Villiers) 1944-
(David Lancaster)

PERSONAL: Born January 28, 1944, in Dorchester, Dorset, England; son of Villiers Archer John (a businessman) and Jean (Vaughan) Heald; married Alison Martina Leslie, March 30, 1968; children: Emma, Alexander, Lucy, Tristram. *Education:* Balliol College, Oxford, B.A. (with honors), 1965, M.A., 1984. *Politics:* Liberal.

ADDRESSES: Home and office—66 The Esplanade, Fowey, Cornwall PL23 1JA, England. *Agent*—Richard Scott Simon, 43 Doughty St., London WC1N 2LF, England.

CAREER: Sunday Times, London, England, assistant diary columnist, 1965-67; *Town* magazine, London, features editor, 1967; *Daily Express,* London, feature writer, 1967-72; freelance journalist and writer, 1972-77; *Weekend* magazine, Toronto, Ontario, associate editor, 1977-78; freelance journalist and writer, 1978—. Visiting fellow, University of Tasmania.

MEMBER: PEN (coordinator of Writers in Prison Committee, 1986-89; executive council of English society), Society of Authors (council of management, 1988—), Crime Writers Association (chair, 1987-88), Annandale Society (former president), Marylebone Cricket Club, Lankelly-Fowey Rugby Football Club (vice president), Royal Tennis Court.

WRITINGS:

MYSTERY NOVELS

Unbecoming Habits, Stein & Day (New York City), 1973.
Blue Blood Will Out, Stein & Day, 1974.
Deadline, Stein & Day, 1975.
Let Sleeping Dogs Die, Stein & Day, 1976.
Just Desserts, Scribner (New York City), 1979.
Murder at Moose Jaw, Doubleday (New York City), 1981.
A Small Masterpiece, Doubleday, 1982, published in England as *Masterstroke,* Hutchinson, 1982.
Red Herrings, Doubleday, 1985.
Brought to Book, Doubleday, 1988.
Business Unusual, Macmillan (London), 1989.

OTHER

It's a Dog's Life, Elm Tree Books, 1971.
The Making of "Space 1999," Ballantine (New York City), 1976.
John Steed: An Authorized Biography, Weidenfeld & Nicolson (London), 1977.
(With Mayo Mohs) *H.R.H.: The Man Who Will Be King,* Arbor House (New York City), 1979, published with new prologue, Berkley Publishing (New York City), 1981.
Caroline R (novel), Arbor House, 1980, published in England under pseudonym David Lancaster, Hutchinson, 1981.
Networks: Who We Know and How We Use Them, Hodder & Stoughton (London), 1983, published as *Old Boy Networks,* Ticknor & Fields (New York City), 1984.
Class Distinctions (novel), Hutchinson, 1984.
The Character of Cricket, Pavilion Books (London), 1986.
(Editor) *The Newest London Spy,* Muller, 1988.
(Editor) *The Rigby File,* Hodder & Stoughton, 1989.
By Appointment: 150 Years of the Royal Warrant, Queen Anne Press, 1989.
(Editor) *A Classic English Crime,* Mysterious Press (New York City), 1991.
Philip: A Portrait of the Duke of Edinburgh, Morrow (New York City), 1991, published in England as *The Duke: A Portrait of Prince Philip,* Hodder & Stoughton, 1991.
Honourable Estates: The English and Their Country Houses, illustrated by Paul Cox, Pavilion Books, 1992.
Beating Retreat: Hong Kong under the Last Governor, Sinclair Stevenson, 1997.

Also author of *Denis: The Authorised Biography of the Incomparable Compton,* Pavilion Books; *A Life of Love: Barbara Cartland,* Sinclair Stevenson; and *Brian Johnston: The Authorised Biography,* Methuen. Contributor of articles and reviews to numerous periodicals, including the *Daily Telegraph,* and to British Broadcasting Corp. Regular reviewer, London *Times,* 1973—; regular fiction reviewer, *Daily Telegraph,* 1974-77.

ADAPTATIONS: Some of Heald's mysteries have been adapted for television by Thames Television.

WORK IN PROGRESS: A novel.

SIDELIGHTS: Although Tim Heald has written several nonfiction works and mainstream novels and has had a notable career as a journalist, he is best known for his series of mystery novels featuring bumbling Board of Trade investigator Simon Bognor. As Carol Cleveland describes him in *Twentieth-Century Crime and Mystery Writers,* Heald's sleuth "is cousin to other fallible, physically unimpressive heroes of the 1970's." "Bognor," she explains, "'mindful as ever of the idiocy of his job,' is introduced unwillingly into various modern institutions chosen for their qualities of flamboyance, or anachronism, or both. He then passes through adventures that range from the pathetic to the ludicrous and back again." In the typical Bognor mystery, "Simon pokes around and stumbles on a solution, which, as his boss Parkinson would observe, is not too satisfactory but will have to do," *Washington Post Book World* reviewer Jean M. White notes. "But then you don't read Heald for deft solutions or action but for stylish wit and satire."

In addition, Heald has a flair for "creat[ing] vignettes that stick in the mind," *New York Times Book Review*'s Newgate Callendar comments, supplemented by what White calls "a delightful cast of characters." In the novel *Brought to Book,* for example, Bognor attends a publishing conference where a publisher/pornographer is found crushed to death by his own bookshelves. "In the world of opportunistic writers and megalomaniac takeovers it is only mildly surprising to find Russian submarines lurking [and] a psychopathic SAS poet" among other oddities, comments Harriet Waugh in the *Spectator.* In between these strange occurrences, Bognor "flits enthusiastically among more jokes, literary puns, *bon mots,* and jokes-within-jokes than" any of his literary predecessors, Marcel Berlins states in the London *Times.* The result, both critics agree, is "great fun."

Heald told *CA:* "I've always had a facility for words. I won essay prizes at school and started magazines and I've never considered anything else, except briefly, and absurdly, the British Foreign Office. The most important circumstance has always been luck—mostly good. I started at school, edited my first magazine at about age ten. I'd like to make a reasonable living out of writing and I'd like as many people as possible to read what I write and I'd like them to be entertained by it. I don't believe I have any amazingly important message to convey but at the same time I don't want my readers to treat my books as a sort of literary musack. I want them to be alert throughout!

"I'm influenced by everything I read but it would take a book to explain precisely how and why. I review thrillers for the London *Times* at the moment so my view of other writers is somewhat jaundiced (I am not able to be as selective as I would like). A very few impress me a lot, but much more strike me as being of marginal worth. There are almost certainly too many books being published but unfortunately if the total were to be cut back, the wrong books would suffer. I do think the majority of commercially successful books are appalling. . . . I'm afraid I have a low opinion of public taste (the mass market) and an even lower one of the literary sensibilities of the average publisher!

"I'm now living in a part of the world with all sorts of literary connections. The immediate locality was once the home of Sir Arthur-Quiller-Couch, a tremendous figure in his day (novelist, essayist, critic, short-story writer and editor of the first ever Oxford book of English verse) and of Daphne du Maurier. So I hope perhaps something will rub off!

"I don't know that I will ever write another 'Simon Bognor' crime novel much as I enjoyed them. I felt that the publishers and to a certain extent readers were beginning to take them for granted. The last was quite unlike most of its predecessors and yet comparatively few people seemed to notice—and in commercial terms nothing much was happening. My nonfiction books are much more lucrative so in a way poor old Bognor has become something of an indulgence. At the popular end of the market there is a dire philistinism and at the 'literary' end there is an equally depressing portentousness. There seems to be very little room for stuff which is deft, sharp and above all funny."

BIOGRAPHICAL/CRITICAL SOURCES:

BOOKS

Twentieth-Century Crime and Mystery Writers, St. James Press (Detroit), 1985.

PERIODICALS

New York Times Book Review, November 25, 1973; October 20, 1974.
Spectator, September 24, 1988.
Times (London), February 18, 1988.
Washington Post Book World, September 15, 1974.

* * *

HEIMBERG, Marilyn Markham
See ROSS, Marilyn (Ann) Heimberg

* * *

HELLER, Francis H(oward) 1917-

PERSONAL: Born August 24, 1917, in Vienna, Austria; came to the United States, 1938; naturalized U.S. citizen, 1943; son of Charles A. and Lily (Grunwald) Heller; married Donna De Munn, September 3, 1949 (died, 1990); children: Denis Wayne. *Ethnicity:* "Caucasian." *Education:* Attended University of Vienna, 1935-37; University of Virginia, J.D., M.A., both 1941, Ph.D., 1948.

ADDRESSES: *Home*—3419 Seminole Dr., Lawrence, KS 66047. *Office*—School of Law, University of Kansas, Green Hall, Lawrence, KS 66045; fax: 913-864-5054.

CAREER: College of William and Mary, Williamsburg, VA, assistant professor of government,

1947; University of Kansas, Lawrence, assistant professor, 1948-51, associate professor, 1951-56, professor of political science, 1956-72, Roy A. Roberts Distinguished Professor of Law and Political Science, 1972-88, associate dean of faculties, 1966-67, dean of faculties, 1967-70, vice chancellor for academic affairs, 1970-72. Visiting professor, Institute for Advanced Studies, Vienna, 1965, University of Vienna Law School, 1985, and Trinity University (San Antonio, TX), 1992. Member, Kansas Governor's Commission on Constitutional Revision, 1957-61, and Lawrence City Planning Commission, 1957-63; Harry S Truman Library Institute, member of board of directors, 1958-96, vice president, 1962-96; Benedictine College, member of board of directors, 1971-79, chair, 1973-79. *Military service:* U.S. Army, 1942-47, 1951-52; became captain; awarded Silver Star and Bronze Star with oak leaf cluster. U.S. Army Reserve, 1956-65; retired as major.

MEMBER: American Political Science Association (executive council, 1958-60), American Association of University Professors, American Society for Legal History, Midwest Conference of Political Scientists, Phi Beta Kappa, Pi Sigma Alpha (executive council, 1958-60), Order of Coif.

AWARDS, HONORS: Higher Education Service Award, University of Kansas, 1973; Career Teaching award, University of Kansas Chancellor's Club, 1986; D.H.L., Benedictine College, 1988.

WRITINGS:

Virginia's State Government during the Second World War: Its Constitutional, Legislative, and Administrative Adaptations, Virginia State Library (Richmond), 1949.

The Sixth Amendment to the Constitution of the United States: A Study in Constitutional Development, University of Kansas Press, 1951, reprinted, Greenwood Press (Westport, CT), 1969.

Introduction to American Constitutional Law, Harper (New York City), 1952.

Our Stake in the Federal System, University of Kansas Governmental Research Center, 1954.

The Presidency, Random House (New York City), 1960.

Uniform State Laws in Kansas, University of Kansas Governmental Research Center, 1962.

(Editor) *The Korean War: A 25-Year Perspective,* Regents Press of Kansas, 1977.

(Compiler and editor) *Materials for the Study of the History, Method, and Process of the Law,* [Lawrence, KS], annual editions, 1978-82.

(Editor) *The Truman White House: The Administration of the Presidency, 1945-1953,* Regents Press of Kansas, 1980.

(Editor) *Economics and the Truman Administration,* Regents Press of Kansas, 1981.

USA: Verfassung und Politik, Boehlau Verlag (Vienna), 1987.

The Kansas State Constitution: A Reference Guide, Greenwood Press, 1992.

(Editor with John R. Gillingham) *NATO: The Founding of the Atlantic Alliance and the Integration of Europe,* St. Martin's (New York City), 1992.

(Compiler and editor) *American Legal History,* [Lawrence, KS], annual editions, 1993-97.

(Editor with Gillingham) *The United States and the Integration of Europe: Legacies of the Postwar Era,* St. Martin's, 1996.

Contributor to *Encyclopaedia Britannica,* political science reviews, and law journals.

* * *

HENNEMAN, John Bell, Jr. 1935-

PERSONAL: Born November 1, 1935, in New York, NY; son of John Bell (a banker) and Esther Gracie (Ogden) Henneman; married Margery Meigs Clifford, September 17, 1960; children: John, Charles, Margery Lawrence. *Ethnicity:* "English and German ancestry." *Education:* Princeton University, A.B., 1957; Harvard University, A.M., 1961, Ph.D. (history), 1966; University of Iowa, M.A. (library science), 1982. *Politics:* Republican. *Religion:* Episcopalian.

ADDRESSES: *Home*—78 Shady Brook Lane, Princeton, NJ 08540. *Office*—Princeton University Library, Princeton, NJ 08544. *E-mail*—henneman@princton.edu; fax: 609-258-4105.

CAREER: McMaster University, Hamilton, Ontario, lecturer, 1965-66, assistant professor of history, 1966-69; University of Iowa, Iowa City, associate professor, 1969-73, professor of history, 1973-83, chair of department, 1980-83; Princeton University, Princeton, NJ, history bibliographer,

1983—. *Military service:* U.S. Navy, 1957-60; became lieutenant.

MEMBER: International Commission for the History of Representative and Parliamentary Institutions, American Historical Association, American Library Association, Mediaeval Academy of America, Society for French Historical Studies, Phi Beta Kappa.

AWARDS, HONORS: Woodrow Wilson fellowship, 1960-61; Guggenheim fellowship, 1976.

WRITINGS:

Royal Taxation in Fourteenth Century France: The Development of War Financing, 1322-1356, Princeton University Press (Princeton, NJ), 1971.
(Editor) *The Medieval French Monarchy,* Dryden Press (Hinsdale, IL), 1973.
Royal Taxation in Fourteenth Century France: The Captivity and Ransom of John II, 1356-1370, American Philosophical Society (Philadelphia), 1976.
Olivier de Clisson and Political Society in France under Charles V and Charles VI, University of Pennsylvania Press (Philadelphia, PA), 1996.

Contributor to *Dictionary of the Middle Ages;* contributor and associate editor, *Medieval France: An Encyclopedia,* Garland Publishing (New York City). Contributor to *Speculum, Traditio, American Historical Review, Studia Gratiana,* and *Mediaeval Studies.*

SIDELIGHTS: John Bell Henneman, Jr. told *CA:* "In pursuing an academic career, I followed in the footsteps of my grandfather, John Bell Henneman (literature) and my uncle, Richard Hubard Henneman (psychology), but chose the field of medieval history. After devoting the years 1963-73 to studying and writing about French royal taxation, I began a second major project that entailed a study of the French military aristocracy in the later fourteenth century. In 1978, however, I halted this work because of other professional commitments including a change of career from professor to librarian.

"Only in 1986 did I return to my research, which now concentrated on the most important leader of the French military aristocracy, Olivier de Clisson. A man of great wealth and shrewd in military matters, Clisson was also litigious, brutal, quarrelsome, and relentless in bearing grudges—a most unattractive person and yet one whose political life made a fascinating and dramatic tale. Still convinced that the political behavior of elites has greater importance for their societies than recent academic historians have been prepared to concede, I attempted to make Clisson's story interesting to a general audience as well as informative to academic specialists."

* * *

HENSLEY, Joe L. 1926-

PERSONAL: Born March 19, 1926, in Bloomington, IN; son of Ralph Ramon and Frances Mae (Wilson) Hensley; married Charlotte R. Bettinger, June 18, 1950; children: Michael Joseph. *Ethnicity:* "Mostly English." *Education:* Indiana University, A.B., 1950, LL.B., 1955. *Politics:* Democrat. *Religion:* Presbyterian.

ADDRESSES: Home—2315 Blackmore, Madison, IN 47250. *Office*—Fifth Judicial Circuit Courthouse, Madison, IN 47250.

CAREER: Admitted to State Bar of Indiana, 1955; Metford & Hensley, Attorneys at Law, Madison, IN, associate, 1955-71; Ford, Hensley & Todd, Attorneys at Law, Madison, partner, 1971-73; Hensley, Todd & Castor, Madison, partner, 1973-75; Eightieth Judicial Circuit, Indiana, judge pro-tempore, 1975-76; Fifth Judicial Circuit, Indiana, judge, 1977-88; Hensley, Walro, Collins & Hensley, Madison, partner, 1988—. Member of Indiana General Assembly, 1961-62; prosecuting attorney of Fifth Judicial Indiana Circuit, 1963-66. *Military service:* U.S. Navy, hospital corpsman, 1944-46, journalist in Korea, 1951-52.

MEMBER: Mystery Writers of America, Science Fiction Writers of America, Indiana State Bar Association, Jefferson County Bar Association.

WRITINGS:

The Color of Hate, Ace Books (New York City), 1961.

Deliver Us to Evil, Doubleday (New York City), 1971.
Legislative Body, Doubleday, 1972.
The Poison Summer, Doubleday, 1974.
Song of Corpus Juris, Doubleday, 1974.
Rivertown Risk, Doubleday, 1977.
A Killing in Gold, Doubleday, 1978.
Minor Murders, Doubleday, 1980.
Outcasts, Doubleday, 1981.
Final Doors (short stories), 1981.
Robak's Cross, Doubleday, 1985.
Robak's Fire, Doubleday, 1986.
Color Him Guilty, Walker, 1987.
Robak's Firm (short stories), Doubleday, 1987.
Fort's Law, Doubleday, 1988.
Robak's Run, Doubleday, 1990.
Grim City, St. Martin's (New York City), 1994.
Robak's Witch, St. Martin's, 1997.

Contributor of more than sixty science fiction and suspense stories to magazines.

SIDELIGHTS: Joe L. Hensley, a judge and former attorney in Indiana, is creator of a series of suspense novels featuring Don Robak. With a background similar to the author's, lawyer Robak defends the innocent and tries to identify the guilty in Indiana. Hensley "always uses his knowledge [of the state and its judicial system] . . . to enhance his well-woven novels of chicanery and murder," states Alice Cromie in the *Chicago Tribune Book World.*

Hensley told *CA:* "I'm a former judge who retired from the bench unbeaten and unbowed. Time is still difficult, but these days I try to find more of it for writing. My books and stories are part of my legal life. Although they usually take the suspense form, my books are about people who must live in this complicated and devious world all of us try our best to exist within. I find that I can't easily stop writing. So I get up earlier, work harder, and hope to get more done. It isn't fun anymore, but it's something I do. I'm glad I do it and I doubt that anything could make me stop."

In 1997 Hensley added: "I have semi-retired as a lawyer, but I still write. Two new books are going now, numbers 20 and 21. Mostly I write about lawyers, but not always. I *always* write about people. It's still interesting."

BIOGRAPHICAL/CRITICAL SOURCES:

PERIODICALS

Chicago Tribune Book World, June 21, 1981.
New York Times Book Review, March 1, 1981; November 30, 1986.
Washington Post Book World, February 15, 1981; January 17, 1988.

* * *

HERMAND, Jost 1930-

PERSONAL: Born April 11, 1930, in Kassel, Germany; son of Heinz and Annelies (Hucke) Hermand; married Elisabeth Jagenburg, 1956. *Education:* University of Marburg, D.Phil., 1955.

ADDRESSES: Home—845 Terry Pl., Madison, WI 53711. *Office*—Department of German, University of Wisconsin, Madison, WI 53706.

CAREER: Freelance writer, 1955-58; University of Wisconsin—Madison, assistant professor, 1958-61, associate professor, 1961-63, professor of German, 1963-67, Vilas Research Professor of German, 1967—. Visiting professor at U.S. and European universities, including Harvard University, Free University of Berlin, University of Freiburg, and University of Texas.

AWARDS, HONORS: American Council of Learned Societies fellowship, 1963.

WRITINGS:

(With Richard Hamann) *Deutsche Kunst und Kultur,* five volumes, Akademie, 1959-75.
Von Mainz nach Weimar, Metzler, 1969.
Pop International, Athenaeum (Frankfurt), 1971.
Unbequeme Literatur, Stiehm, 1971.
Der Schein des schoenen Lebens, Athenaeum, 1972.
Streitobjekt Heine, Fischer Athenaeum, 1975.
Der fruehe Heine, Winkler, 1976.
(With Evelyn T. Beck) *Interpretive Synthesis,* Ungar (New York City), 1976.
Stile, Ismen, Etiketten, Athenaeum, 1978.
(With Frank Trommler) *Die Kultur der Weimarer Republik,* Nymphenburger, 1978.

Sieben Arten an Deutschland zu Leiden, Athenaeum, 1979.
Orte: Irgendwo, Athenaeum, 1981.
Konkretes Hoeren: Zum Inhalt der Instrumentalmusik, Argument, 1981.
Die Kultur der Bundesrepublik, Nymphenburger, Volume 1, 1985, Volume 2, 1988.
(With James Steakley) *Writings of German Composers,* Continuum (New York City), 1985.
Adolph Menzel, Rowohlt, 1986.
Arnold Zweig, Rowohlt, 1990.
Gruene Utopien in Deutschland, Fischer, 1991.
Old Dreams of a New Reich: Volkish Utopias and National Socialism, Indiana University Press (Bloomington), 1992.
Als Pimpf in Polen, Fischer, 1993.
Geschichte der Germanistik, Rowohlt, 1994.
Avantgarde und Regression, Edition Leipzig, 1995.
Judentum und deutsche Kultur, Boehlau, 1996.
Angewandte Literatur, Edition Sigma, 1996.

BIOGRAPHICAL/CRITICAL SOURCES:

BOOKS

Klaus L. Berghahn and others, editors, *Responsibility and Commitment: Ethische postulate der Kulturvermittlung. Festschrift fuer Jost Hermand,* Peter Lang (New York City), 1996.

* * *

HESTON, Charlton 1924-

PERSONAL: Born October 4, 1924, in Evanston, IL; son of Russell Whitford (a mill operator) and Lilla (Charlton) Carter; married Lydia Marie Clarke (an actress), March 17, 1944; children: Fraser Clarke, Holly Ann. *Education:* Attended Northwestern University, 1941-43.

ADDRESSES: *Home*—Beverly Hills, CA. *Office*—c/o Jack Gilardi, International Creative Management, 8942 Wilshire Blvd., Beverly Hills, CA 90211.

CAREER: Actor; has appeared in stage plays, including *State of the Union, The Glass Menagerie, Kiss and Tell, Antony and Cleopatra, Design for a Stained Glass Window, Leaf and Bough, The Tumbler, A Man for All Seasons, The Crucible, Macbeth, Long Day's Journey Into Night,* and *Crucifer of Blood;* in motion pictures, including *Dark City,* 1950, *The Greatest Show on Earth,* 1952, *Ruby Gentry,* 1953, *The Naked Jungle,* 1954, *The Ten Commandments,* 1956, *Touch of Evil,* 1957, *The Big Country,* 1958, *Ben-Hur,* 1959, *The Wreck of the Mary Deare,* 1959, *El Cid,* 1961, *Fifty-five Days at Peking,* 1963, *The Greatest Story Ever Told,* 1965, *Major Dundee,* 1965, *Planet of the Apes,* 1968, *Julius Caesar,* 1970, *The Omega Man,* 1971, *Antony and Cleopatra,* 1972, *Soylent Green,* 1973, *Airport 1975,* 1974, *Earthquake,* 1974, *The Last Hard Men,* 1976, *The Mountain Men,* 1980, *Mother Lode,* 1982, *Tombstone,* 1993, *True Lies,* 1994, *Alaska,* 1996, and *Hamlet,* 1996; and in television programs, including *Chiefs* (mini-series), 1983, *The Nairobi Affair,* 1984, *The Colbys* (series), 1985-87, *A Man For All Seasons,* 1988, *Original Sin,* 1989, *Treasure Island,* 1990, *The Little Kidnappers,* 1990, *Crash Landing: The Rescue of Flight 232,* 1992, *Charl-ton Heston Presents the Bible,* 1993, *The Avenging Angel,* 1995, *Wuthering Heights, Macbeth, Taming of the Shrew, Of Human Bondage, Studio One,* and *Jane Eyre.* Director of the play, *The Caine Mutiny Court-Martial;* director of films, including *Antony and Cleopatra,* 1973, and *Mother Lode,* 1982; also director of television movie, *A Man For All Seasons,* 1988. Member of the President's Council on Youth Opportunities, the National Council on the Arts (president, 1966-72), and the President's Task Force on the Arts and Humanities (co-chair, 1981). Visited troops in Vietnam; also toured under the State Department's Cultural Presentation Program. *Military service:* U.S. Army Air Forces during World War II; became staff sergeant.

MEMBER: American Film Institute (chair, 1973), National Arthritis and Rheumatism Foundation (film chair, 1955-56), Screen Actors Guild (president, 1966-71), Center Theatre Group (Los Angeles; former chair).

AWARDS, HONORS: Academy Award for best actor from the Academy of Motion Picture Arts and Sciences, 1959, for *Ben Hur;* Belgian Uilenspiegel, 1960, 1962, and 1969; German Bambi award, 1961; Jean Hersholt Award from the Academy of Motion Picture Arts and Sciences, 1978, for humanitarianism; award from Hollywood Women's Press Club, 1993.

WRITINGS:

Antony and Cleopatra (screenplay; based on the play by William Shakespeare), Folio, 1973.

The Actor's Life: Journals, 1956-1976, edited by Hollis Alpert, Dutton (New York City), 1978.

Beijing Diary, introduction, photographs, and captions by wife, Lydia Clarke Heston, Simon & Schuster (New York City), 1990.

In the Arena: An Autobiography, Simon & Schuster, 1995.

RECORDINGS; NARRATOR

Melville, Herman, *Moby Dick* (audio), Caedmon (New York City), 1975.

Hemingway, Ernest, *The Old Man and the Sea* (audio), Caedmon, 1976.

Andrew Wyeth—The Helga Pictures (video), directed by Dennis Powers, Videodisc Publishing, 1987.

Hemingway, *The Snows of Kilimanjaro* (audio), Caedmon, 1989.

Narrator of "The Giants of Philosophy" series of recordings from Knowledge Products (Nashville, TN), 1990; also narrator of *Charlton Heston's Voyage through the Bible* (CD-ROM), Campion, Volume 1: *The Old Testament: From Genesis to Moses,* 1995, Volume 2: *The New Testament: Life and Passion of Jesus the Nazarene,* 1996. Narrator of numerous other audio and video projects.

SIDELIGHTS: Charlton Heston, who recalls, "I can't remember a time when I didn't want to be an actor," made his movie debut at age sixteen in an amateur version of *Peer Gynt.* It was later, when playing Antony in David Bradley's 16mm *Julius Caesar,* that Heston's talents were recognized by producer Hall Wallis, who cast him as the lead in *Dark City.* With his next film, Cecil B. de Mille's *The Greatest Show on Earth,* Heston's career as an actor was firmly established: the film won the Academy Award for best picture of 1952, and Heston has been steadily employed ever since, starring in many motion pictures and performing on Broadway and in television productions.

According to Heston, "Producers seem to feel I have a medieval face." Therefore, some of his most memorable roles have been in historical epics, including Moses in *The Ten Commandments,* John the Baptist in *The Greatest Story Ever Told,* and the lead in *Ben-Hur,* for which he won the 1959 Oscar for best actor. Still, the bulk of Heston's film roles have been in contemporary dramas, adventures, and comedies. "By now, I've gradually worked my way into the 20th century," the actor explains.

Despite his hectic filming schedule, Heston finds time to act on stage and has performed with some regularity at Los Angeles's Ahmanson Theatre in productions that include *Macbeth, Long Day's Journey Into Night, A Man for All Seasons,* and *Crucifer of Blood.* Heston has also tried his hand at directing, his initial effort being a film version of Shakespeare's *Antony and Cleopatra,* in which he appeared as Antony, and later *Mother Lode,* in which he also starred.

Throughout his career, Heston has kept a journal in which he has recorded his impressions of his trade. His notes were published as *The Actor's Life: Journals, 1956-1976,* and the result is, according to Heston in an interview with Eric Pace of the *New York Times,* "a highly subjective, very personal record of my life." Stressing that "there's very little in the way of scandalous revelation" in his book, Heston relates: "It was undertaken as a work tool. . . . You can use something like this journal to teach yourself." In a *Washington Post* review of *The Actor's Life,* Charles Freund writes that in Heston's journal "a picture of the working actor emerges that is interesting in the light of the grand charioteering, swashbuckling characterizations that make up Heston's screen image." Noting Heston's devotion to his family and community, Freund claims: "Heston the man is less out of epic saga than he is out of Sinclair Lewis—complete with a lively abhorrence of eccentricity and a native midwestern sense of boosterism and civic responsibility." And in the *New York Times Book Review,* Seymour Peck deems *The Actor's Life* "an honorable publishing enterprise, undertaken seriously and deserving of the reader's trust."

Heston revisits the story of his life in both *Beijing Diary,* a collection of his thoughts while directing a production of Herman Wouk's stage play *The Caine Mutiny Court-Martial* in Communist China with a Chinese cast shortly before the Tiananmen Square incident, and *In the Arena: An Autobiography.* Based on the actor's private diaries, *In the Arena* covers the full range of Heston's experience: from his political views to his opinions of friends, co-workers, and colleagues. Beginning with his birth in Evanston, Illinois, continuing with his parents' divorce and his northern Michigan childhood, and concluding with his many stage, television and screen roles, Heston's autobiography, explains David Thomson in the *New Republic,* "lets us feel the cramped kid and the gruff man he became, as well as the unironic grandeur that grew up—in robes, armor and history's key light—to be nothing less than 'Charlton Heston,' a name forever echoed by the salute of trumpets." "Indeed," the reviewer continues, "he has become a world and an industry unto himself."

Critics praise *In the Arena* for its professional prose style and its vivid and generous description of life in the motion picture business. "There are two singularities resident in Charlton Heston's personal story of his cinema/stage life," writes Motion Picture Association of America chair and CEO Jack Valenti in the Chicago *Tribune Books.* "One, an authentic, accessible insight into the real world of moviemaking guaranteed to entice anyone who cares about films. Two, a rare instance of a superfamous star/artist actually writing his own material, no 'as told to' collaborators or ghost writers on the scene. The result: Sprightly prose, full of juice and elegance." Other critics echo Valenti's assessment of Heston's writing. "The voice is unmistakably Heston's own—clear, supremely confident, eloquent, candid, but also funny and sometimes even risque," states *Los Angeles Times Book Review* contributor Charles Champlin, "which is somehow startling given the majestic men he has so often played, from Moses forward." "The absence of ghost-buffed polish," declares Terry Teachout in the *American Spectator,* "is one of the nicest things about *In the Arena,* which sounds as if its author simply sat down at the typewriter one day and started reminiscing. Where he learned to write I don't know, but he learned it well." "His autobiography is orderly and detailed," concludes novelist and screenwriter George MacDonald Fraser in the *National Review,* "and as good a description of the strange business of making films as I have read. He writes without mock modesty and with a kindly if candid eye for his co-workers, most of whom he treats with a generosity rare in film memoirs."

Many reviewers comment on Heston's graciousness toward his associates. "I was pretty hard on Ava Gardner, who I worked with in 1963 on *55 Days at Peking,*" Heston tells *Los Angeles Times* contributor Kristine McKenna, "but you don't need to resort to attack language to suggest that someone was less than professional." He also tells McKenna that Sam Peckinpah "was his own worst enemy" and "seemed to have a suicidal death wish," and that Orson Welles "was a brilliant man, yet he seemed compulsively driven to alienate the money people." "Jason Robards," explains Champlin, ". . . catches some of the blame for the failure of *Antony and Cleopatra.* 'I have never seen a good actor so bad in a good part as Jason was as Brutus . . . terrible is the only word.'" On the other hand, Valenti notes that Heston credits writer Christopher Fry with rescuing the dialogue for *Ben Hur.* "Such, asserts Heston, is the difference between the merely good and the very best," Valenti asserts. "And that is why Willy Wyler, that smallish, taciturn artist, is Heston's hero director, though he also venerates George Stevens, Sr. in his pantheon of Gods of the Screen."

Heston's outspoken political views also receive commentary from reviewers. "Heston began his political life as a Roosevelt supporter," Thomson states. "He is proud of his early stand on civil rights. He reckoned Martin Luther King was 'put on earth, I do believe, to be a twentieth-century Moses for his people.'" Heston is best known, however, as a supporter of conservative views, and "the closing pages of *In the Arena,*" declares Champlin, "are a fervent statement of his credo and his angers." Despite his conservative reputation, in January of 1995 Heston spoke before the Republican-controlled Congress in support of Federal funding for the National Endowment for the Arts and the National Endowment for the Humanities. "Heston simply holds by values which were taken for granted fifty years ago, which means that today he is politically incorrect," writes Fraser. "Quite aside from his merits as a performer, he has projected an image, on screen and off, that is worthy. . . . It is no small thing to pass half a century of superstar exposure and come out with your dignity intact."

BIOGRAPHICAL/CRITICAL SOURCES:

BOOKS

Crowther, Bruce, *Charlton Heston: The Epic Presence,* Columbus Books (London), 1986.

Druxman, Michael B., *Charlton Heston,* Pyramid (New York City), 1976.

Heston, Charlton, *The Actor's Life: Journals, 1956-1976,* edited by Hollis Alpert, Dutton, 1978.
Munn, Michael, *Charlton Heston,* St. Martin's Press (New York City), 1986.
Reinhardt, Hans, and Andrea Rennschmidt, *Charlton Heston: Seine filmischen Werke,* Weber Verlag (Landshut, Germany), 1993.
Rovin, Jeff, *Films of Charlton Heston,* Citadel (Secaucus, NJ), 1977.
Shipman, David, *Great Movie Stars,* A & W Visual Library, 1976.
Williams, John, *The Films of Charlton Heston,* BCW (Bembridge), 1977.

PERIODICALS

American Spectator, January, 1996, pp. 68-69.
Booklist, October 1, 1990, p. 242.
Entertainment Weekly, September 8, 1995, p. 77.
Los Angeles Times, January 28, 1995, p. F1; September 16, 1995, p. F1.
Los Angeles Times Book Review, October 15, 1995, pp. 8, 13.
Maclean's Magazine, December 18, 1978; January 1, 1979.
National Review, October 9, 1995, pp. 58-60.
New Republic, October 30, 1995, pp. 43-45.
New Statesman, April 13, 1979.
New York, September 10, 1990, p. 116.
New York Times Book Review, December 17, 1978; October 15, 1995, p. 11.
Saturday Evening Post, July 3, 1965; January, 1976.
Time, August 12, 1966; August 23, 1976.
Tribune Books (Chicago), October 1, 1995, p. 23.
TV Guide, November 12, 1983.
Vanity Fair, September, 1994, p. 135.
Washington Post, November 16, 1978.
Washington Post Book World, October 15, 1995, p. 8.*

* * *

HIMLER, Ronald (Norbert) 1937-

PERSONAL: Born November 16, 1937, in Cleveland, OH; son of Norbert and Grace (Manning) Himler; married Ann Danowitz, June 18, 1972 (divorced); children: Daniel, Anna, Peer. *Education:* Cleveland Institute of Art, diploma, 1960; graduate study in painting at Cranbrook Academy of Art, Bloomfield Hills, MI, 1960-61, and New York University and Hunter College, New York City, 1968-70.

ADDRESSES: Home—11301 East Placita Cibuta, Tucson, AZ 85749.

CAREER: General Motors Technical Center, Warren, MI, technical sculptor (styling), 1961-63; artist and illustrator, 1963—. Toy designer and sculptor for Transogram Co., New York City, 1968, and Remco Industries, Newark, NJ, 1969. Co-founder and headmaster, Blue Rock School, NC, 1982-84. *Exhibitions:* Wolfe Galleries, Tucson, AZ, 1990.

AWARDS, HONORS: Award for Graphic Excellence, American Institute of Graphic Arts, and citation of merit, Society of Illustrators, both 1972, both for *Baby;* Printing Industries of America citation, 1972, for *Rocket in My Pocket;* Children's Book Showcase selection, Children's Book Council, 1975, for *Indian Harvests;* New Jersey Institute of Technology award (with Ann Himler), 1976, for *Little Owl, Keeper of the Trees;* Best of Bias-free Illustration citation, American Institute of Graphic Arts, 1976, for *Make a Circle, Keep Us In;* Children's Choice selection, International Reading Association/Children's Book Council (IRA/CBC), 1979, for *Bus Ride;* Best Children's Books, *School Library Journal,* 1979, for *Curly and the Wild Boar,* 1990, for *The Wall,* and 1991, for *Fly Away Home;* Children's Books of the Year selection, Child Study Children's Book Committee at Bank Street College (CSCBC), 1982, for *Moon Song* and *Jem's Island,* and 1992, for *Fly Away Home; Best Town in the World* was exhibited at the Brataslava Biennale of Illustration, 1985; Best Books of 1985, New York Public Library, and Notable book selection, American Library Association, 1986, both for *Dakota Dugout;* Pick of the Lists, American Booksellers, 1987, for *Nettie's Trip South,* 1990, for *The Wall,* 1991, for *I'm Going to Pet a Worm Today,* and 1992, for *Fly Away Home* and *Katie's Trunk;* Notable Children's Book, American Library Association and Association for Library Services to Children (ALSC), 1990, and Journal of Youth Services in Libraries, 1991, both for *The Wall;* Children's Books—100 titles for reading and sharing, New York Public Library, 1990, for *The Wall,* and 1992, for *The Lily Cupboard;* Notable Children's Books, American Library Association, 1991, and Editor's Choice, *Booklist,* 1991, both for *Fly Away Home;* Silver Medal, Society of Illustrators, 1992, for best western painting in book cover art.

WRITINGS:

FOR CHILDREN; SELF-ILLUSTRATED

(Compiler) *Glad Day, and Other Classical Poems for Children,* Putnam (New York City), 1972.
(With former wife, Ann Himler) *Little Owl, Keeper of the Trees,* Harper (New York City), 1974.
The Girl on the Yellow Giraffe, Harper, 1976.
Wake Up, Jeremiah, Harper, 1979.

ILLUSTRATOR

Robert Burgess, *Exploring a Coral Reef,* Macmillan (New York City), 1972.
Carl A. Withers, compiler, *Rocket in My Pocket* (poetry anthology), revised edition, Western Publishing (New York City), 1972.
Fran Manushkin, *Baby,* Harper, 1972.
Elizabeth Winthrop, *Bunk Beds,* Harper, 1972.
Millicent Brower, *I Am Going Nowhere,* Putnam, 1972.
Charlotte Zolotow, *Janey,* Harper, 1973.
Marjorie Weinman Sharmat, *Morris Brookside, a Dog,* Holiday House (New York City), 1973.
Tom Glazer, *Eye Winker, Tom Tinker, Chin Chopper,* Doubleday (New York City), 1973.
Fran Manushkin, *Bubblebath,* Harper, 1974.
William C. Grimm, *Indian Harvests,* McGraw-Hill (New York City), 1974.
Robert Burch, *Hut School and the Wartime Homefront Heroes,* Viking (New York City), 1974.
Marjorie Weinman Sharmat, *Morris Brookside Is Missing,* Holiday House, 1974.
Betsy Byars, *After the Goat Man,* Viking, 1974.
Polly Curran, *A Patch of Peas,* Golden Press (New York City), 1975.
Arnold Adoff, *Make a Circle, Keep Us In,* Delacorte (New York City), 1975.
Achim Broger, *Bruno,* Morrow (New York City), 1975.
Marty Kelly, *The House on Deer-Track Trail,* Harper, 1976.
Crescent Dragonwagon, *Windrose,* Harper, 1976.
Betty Boegehold, *Alone in the Cabin,* Harcourt (San Diego), 1976.
Yoshiko Uchida, *Another Goodbye,* Allyn & Bacon (Newton, MA), 1976.
Richard Kennedy, *The Blue Stone,* Holiday House, 1976.
Jeanette Caines, *Daddy,* Harper, 1977.
Johanna Johnston, *Harriet and the Runaway Book: The Story of Harriet Beecher Stowe and Uncle Tom's Cabin,* Harper, 1977.
Eleanor Coerr, *Sadako and the Thousand Paper Cranes,* Putnam, 1977.
Arnold Adoff, *Tornado,* Delacorte, 1977.
Louise Dickerson, *Good Wife, Good Wife,* McGraw-Hill, 1977.
Arnold Adoff, *Under the Early Morning Trees,* Dutton, 1978.
Clyde Bulla and Michael Syson, *Conquista,* Crowell (New York City), 1978.
Nancy Jewell, *Bus Ride,* Harper, 1978.
Fred Gipson, *Little Arliss,* Harper, 1978.
Fred Gipson, *Curly and the Wild Boar,* Harper, 1979.
Richard Kennedy, *Inside My Feet: The Story of a Giant,* Harper, 1979.
Carla Stevens, *Trouble for Lucy,* Houghton (Boston), 1979.
Arnold Adoff, *I Am the Running Girl,* Harper, 1979.
Douglas Davis, *The Lion's Tail,* Atheneum (New York City), 1980.
Elizabeth Parsons, *The Upside-Down Cat,* Atheneum, 1981.
Linda Peavy, *Allison's Grandfather,* Scribner (New York CIty), 1981.
Byrd Baylor, *Moon Song,* Scribner, 1982.
Katherine Lasky, *Jem's Island,* Scribner, 1982.
Byrd Baylor, *Best Town in the World,* Scribner, 1983.
Thor Heyerdahl, *Kon Tiki: A True Adventure of Survival at Sea,* Random House (New York City), 1984.
Anne Turner, *Dakota Dugout,* Macmillan, 1985.
Ellen Howard, *Edith Herself,* Atheneum, 1987.
Ann Turner, *Nettie's Trip South,* Macmillan, 1987.
Susan Pearson, *Happy Birthday, Grampie,* Dial (New York City), 1987.
Emily Cheney Neville, *The Bridge,* Harper, 1988.
Alice Fleming, *The King of Prussia and a Peanut Butter Sandwich,* Scribner, 1988.
Susan Nunes, *Coyote Dreams,* Atheneum, 1988.
Ann Herbert Scott, *Someday Rider,* Clarion (New York City), 1989.
(With John Gurney) Della Rowland, *A World of Cats,* Contemporary Books (Chicago), 1989.
Crescent Dragonwagon, *Winter Holding Spring,* Macmillan, 1990.
Eve Bunting, *The Wall,* Clarion, 1990.
Dorothy and Thomas Hoobler, *George Washington and Presidents' Day,* Silver Press (Englewood Cliffs, NJ), 1990.

Merry Banks, *Animals of the Night,* Scribner, 1990.

Liza Ketchum Murrow, *Dancing on the Table,* Holiday House, 1990.

Patricia Hubbell, *A Grass Green Gallop,* Atheneum, 1990.

Eve Bunting, *Fly Away Home,* Clarion, 1991.

Constance Levy, *I'm Going to Pet a Worm Today, and Other Poems,* McElderry Books (New York City), 1991.

Virginia T. Gross, *The Day It Rained Forever: A Story of the Johnstown Flood,* Viking, 1991.

Kathleen V. Kudlinski, *Pearl Harbor Is Burning,* Viking, 1991.

Shulamith Levey Oppenheim, *The Lily Cupboard,* HarperCollins, 1992.

Byrd Baylor, *One Small Blue Bead,* Scribner, 1992.

Ann Turner, *Katie's Trunk,* Macmillan, 1992.

Kate Aver, *Joey's Way,* McElderry Books, 1992.

Ann Herbert Scott, *A Brand Is Forever,* Clarion, 1993.

Eve Bunting, *Someday a Tree,* Clarion, 1993.

Virginia Driving Hawk Sneve, *The Sioux,* Holiday House, 1993.

Virginia Driving Hawk Sneve, *The Navajos,* Holiday House, 1993.

Virginia Driving Hawk Sneve, *The Seminoles,* Holiday House, 1994.

Virginia Driving Hawk Sneve, *The Nez Perce,* Holiday House, 1994.

Kathleen V. Kudlinski, *Lone Star,* Viking, 1994.

Kathleen V. Kudlinski, *Earthquake,* Viking, 1994.

Eve Bunting, *A Day's Work,* Clarion, 1994.

Nancy Luenn, *SQUISH! A Wetland Walk,* Atheneum, 1994.

Wendy Kesselman, *Sand in My Shoes,* Hyperion (New York City), 1995.

Virginia Driving Hawk Sneve, *The Hopis,* Holiday House, 1995.

Virginia Driving Hawk Sneve, *The Iroquois,* Holiday House, 1995.

D. Anne Love, *Bess's Log Cabin Quilt,* Holiday House, 1995.

D. Anne Love, *Dakota Spring,* Holiday House, 1995.

Sue Alexander, *Sara's City,* Clarion, 1995.

Virginia Driving Hawk Sneve, *The Cherokees,* Holiday House, 1996.

Virginia Driving Hawk Sneve, *The Cheyennes,* Holiday House, 1996.

Eve Bunting, *Train to Somewhere,* Clarion, 1996.

Barbara A. Steiner, *Desert Trip,* Sierra Club Books (San Francisco), 1996.

Ellen Howard, *The Log Cabin Quilt,* Holiday House, 1996.

Linda Oatman High, *A Christmas Star,* Holiday House, 1997.

Virginia Driving Hawk Sneve, *The Apaches,* Holiday House, 1997.

Several of Himler's books have been translated into other languages, including Dutch and Japanese.

SIDELIGHTS: Artist and illustrator Ronald Himler is known for his work in a variety of artistic media. Watercolor, oils, gouache, and pencil have all been used by Himler to present his imaginative interpretation of popular children's books to young readers. Trained in both painting and illustration, Himler offers characteristically gentle and sensitive depictions of stories and poems that help open the eyes of preschoolers and primary graders to the world that surrounds them.

Raised in Cleveland, Ohio, Himler spent many childhood hours immersed in drawing, especially during the weekly trips he took to his grandmother's home. After graduating from high school, he studied painting at the Cleveland Institute of Art, and went on to attend graduate school at the Cranbrook Academy of Art in Bloomfield Hills, Michigan. After holding various positions as a commercial artist, Himler decided to travel throughout Europe and Scandinavia, doing independent research in such major museums as the Louvre in Paris, the Uffizi Galleries in Florence, and Amsterdam's Rijksmuseum. His tours through some of the world's finest collections of fine art broadened the scope of Himler's own painting, while the contacts he made with people of so many different cultures increased his sensitivity to the diversity of the world's peoples.

Upon returning to the United States, Himler was determined to pursue a career as an illustrator of children's books. His first project was a verse anthology called *Glad Day, and Other Classical Poems for Children,* which was published in 1972. The *Glad Day* illustrations were quickly followed by others, including drawings to accompany a work of nonfiction entitled *Exploring a Coral Reef.* Requests for illustrations for other books continued to come his way, and Himler found himself working with texts written by a wide variety of popular children's writers, including Betsy

Byars, Tom Glazer, Marjorie Weinman Sharmat, and Charlotte Zolotow.

In 1974, Himler and his wife Ann collaborated on the children's book *Little Owl, Keeper of the Trees,* with Himler providing the illustrations. Three tales that center on a young owl living high up in a sycamore tree, *Little Owl* weaves magic into the world of forest-dwelling animals through the character of Jonas, a small, friendly monster who possesses special powers. Himler went on to write two other books, including his 1976 publication *The Girl on the Yellow Giraffe,* which features his pencil-sketch illustrations. Calling the book "an affectionate celebration of a child's imaginative powers," *Booklist* reviewer Denise M. Wilms praised the author/illustrator's picture book as an effective portrayal of a child's imaginary world. Himler wrote *The Girl on the Yellow Giraffe* for his daughter, Anna; four years later, he produced *Wake Up, Jeremiah* for his son, Peer. Accompanied by a minimum of text, Himler's impressionist-style, full-color illustrations depict a young boy's excitement at witnessing the start of a new day. Getting up extra early to watch the sunrise from the top of a hill near his home, Jeremiah then rushes home to share this fresh new day with his drowsy parents. "The evolution of dawn—from early murk to resplendent full light—in Mr. Himler's illustrations represent his best, most colorful performance to date," asserted *New York Times Book Review* contributor George A. Woods.

In the works he has illustrated since *Wake Up, Jeremiah,* Himler has focused on complex emotional issues. In Eve Bunting's *Fly Away Home,* for example, the homeless lifestyle of a young boy and his out-of-work dad is treated by Himler with muted shades of brown and blue watercolor, and the artist places father and son at the edge of his pictures as a way of reflecting their existence on the fringes of airport life. "Himler matches Bunting's understated text with gentle sensibility," noted a *Kirkus Reviews* commentator. Zena Sutherland of the *Bulletin of the Center for Children's Books* similarly noted that "Himler's quiet paintings echo the economy and the touching quality of the story," and *Horn Book* reviewer Ann A. Flowers commented: "The yearning sadness of the story, ameliorated only by the obvious and touching affection between father and son, is reflected in the subtle, expressive watercolors, dominated by shades of blue." In 1996 *Fly Away Home* was adapted as a major motion picture.

Other collaborations with Bunting have included the 1990 work *The Wall,* which sensitively presents a boy's impressions of a visit to Washington, D.C.'s Vietnam Memorial, and, in 1993, *Someday a Tree,* a gentle ecology message for primary graders centering on the fate of one sick tree. In a review of Bunting's highly regarded *The Wall,* Denise Wilms of *Booklist* maintained that "Himler's intense, quiet watercolors capture the dignity of the setting as Bunting's story reaches right to the heart of deep emotions." In a *Booklist* review of *Someday a Tree,* Hazel Rochman commented favorably on yet another effective Bunting/Himler collaboration, noting that "Himler's watercolors express the quiet harmony of the green shady scene where you can dream and hear leaves whisper and see 'clouds change like smoke.'"

While Himler has enjoyed writing and illustrating books for young readers, painting has remained his first love. In 1982, while traveling through the U.S. Southwest, the artist was permitted to attend several ceremonial dances performed by Native Americans. The powerful psychological effect of witnessing these traditional dances opened Himler's eyes to a people and a time with which he felt an inexplicable empathy. As a result, he sensed a growing need to understand and give expression to what he perceived as two very different cultures and histories: Plains Indian traditions and the history of the white man who had invaded and altered those traditions. Himler has since worked to capture the essence of Native American ceremony in oil paintings. Many of these works have won him critical acclaim; Himler's Indian paintings have been featured in both *Art of the West* magazine and the PBS television program *Arizona Illustrated.*

Acknowledged for his beautifully executed children's book illustrations on a variety of topics, Himler's area of greatest interest is the life and history of the American west. He has executed illustrations for "The First Americans," a series of books written by Virginia Driving Hawk Sneve that focus on Native American tribal culture. Series titles include *The Nez Perce, The Sioux,* and *The Seminoles,* of which *School Library Journal* contributor M. Colleen McDougall noted: "Himler's illustrations are the book's high point. . . . [His] figures and landscapes are both aesthetically pleasing and pertinent to the discussion." A *Publishers Weekly* commentator praised "Himler's striking oil paintings" in a review of Sneve's *The Sioux* and *The Navajos,* while *School Library Journal* contributor Jacqueline Elsner, reviewing *The Cherokees,* asserted: "Himler's familiar watercolors, rich, warm, and serene, grace the text." And the ranch stories of Ann Herbert Scott—*Someday Rider* in 1989 and *A Brand Is Forever* in 1993—have also benefited from Himler's artistic vision; each reflects the artist's sensitivity to western surroundings. Of *A Brand Is Forever,* Marianne Partridge noted in the *New York Times Book Review* that Himler's illustrations "capture the essentially unchanging nature of ranching while giving [the book] a thoroughly modern flavor." And Himler's illustrations for Byrd Baylor's stories of the U.S. southwest have also been hailed by reviewers: a *Publishers Weekly* critic refers to his illustrations for Baylor's *Moon Song* as "harmonious, lovely drawings, dominated by the touching presence of the lonely coyote." With scores of children's books to his credit, and hundreds of book cover illustrations, Himler continues to inspire young people through his artistic talents.

BIOGRAPHICAL/CRITICAL SOURCES:

PERIODICALS

Art of the West, January/February, 1989.

Booklist, October 1, 1976, p. 252; September 15, 1979, p. 120; April 1, 1990, p. 1544; March 1, 1993, p. 1234; December 15, 1993, p. 759; November 1, 1994, p. 505.

Bulletin of the Center for Children's Books, May, 1975, p. 148; February, 1980, p. 111; May, 1991, p. 212; October, 1994, pp. 38-39.

Horn Book, July-August, 1990, pp. 442-443; July-August, 1991, p. 445; March-April, 1992, p. 193; May-June, 1996, p. 353.

Kirkus Reviews, October 15, 1974, p. 1103; February 1, 1991, p. 172; February 15, 1993, p. 223; September 15, 1994, p. 1266.

New York Times Book Review, June 25, 1972; November 12, 1972; October 28, 1979, p. 18; February 19, 1989; May 30, 1993, p. 19.

Publishers Weekly, September 30, 1974, p. 60; June, 1982; January 1, 1992, p. 55; November 8, 1993, p. 80; August 8, 1994, pp. 434-435; February 5, 1996, p. 89.

Quill & Quire, June, 1993, p. 40.

School Library Journal, June, 1991, p. 74; April, 1994, p. 146; January, 1995, p. 82; March, 1996, p. 166; April, 1996, p. 130.

* * *

HINDE, Robert A(ubrey) 1923-

PERSONAL: Born October 26, 1923, in Norwich, England; son of Earnest Bertram (a physician) and Isabella (a nurse; maiden name, Taylor) Hinde; married Hester Coutts (divorced, 1971); married Joan Gladys Stevenson; children: two sons, four daughters. *Ethnicity:* "Caucasian." *Education:* University of London, B.Sc., 1948; St. John's College, Cambridge, B.A., 1948, M.A., 1950, Sc.D., 1958; Balliol College, Oxford, D.Phil., 1950.

ADDRESSES: Home—Park Lane, Madingley, Cambridgeshire, England; fax 01223 337720.

CAREER: Cambridge University, Cambridge, England, curator at Ornithological Field Station, 1950-65, research fellow at St. John's College, 1951-54, steward, 1956-58, tutor, 1958-63, fellow, 1958—, Royal Society Research Professor, 1963—. Honorary director of Medical Research Council Unit on Development and Integration of Behaviour, 1970—. *Military service:* Royal Air Force, Coastal Command, 1941-45.

MEMBER: British Psychological Society (honorary fellow), Royal Society (fellow), American Academy of Arts and Sciences (honorary foreign member), American Ornithologists Union (honorary foreign member), National Academy of Sciences (honorary foreign associate member).

AWARDS, HONORS: Commander, Order of the British Empire, 1988.

WRITINGS:

Animal Behaviour: A Synthesis of Ethology and Comparative Psychology, McGraw (New York City), 1966, 2nd edition, 1970.

Social Behaviour and Its Development in Subhuman Primates, University of Oregon Press (Eugene, OR), 1972.

Biological Bases of Human Social Behaviour, McGraw, 1974.

Towards Understanding Relationships, Academic Press (New York City), 1979.
Ethology: Its Nature and Relations with Other Sciences, Oxford University Press (New York City), 1982.
Individuals, Relationships and Culture, Cambridge University Press (New York City), 1987.
Relationships: A Dialectical Perspective, Psychology Press, 1997.

EDITOR

Advances in the Study of Behaviour, Academic Press, Volume 1 (with D. S. Lehrman and E. Shaw), 1965, Volume 2 (with Lehrman and Shaw), 1969, Volume 3 (with Lehrman and Shaw), 1970, Volume 4 (with Lehrman and Shaw), 1974, Volume 5 (with Lehrman,, Shaw, and J. S. Rosenblatt), 1974, Volume 6 (with Shaw, Rosenblatt, and C. Beer), 1976, Volume 7 (with Shaw, Rosenblatt, and Beer), 1976, Volume 8 (with Rosenblatt, Beer, and M. C. Busnel), 1978, Volume 9 (with Rosenblatt, Beer, and Busnel), 1979, Volume 10 (with Rosenblatt, Beer, and Busnel), 1979, Volume 11 (with Rosenblatt, Beer, and Busnel), 1980.
Bird Vocalizations, Cambridge University Press, 1969.
(With Gabriel Horn) *Short-Term Changes in Neural Activity and Behaviour,* Cambridge University Press, 1970.
Non-Verbal Communication, Cambridge University Press, 1972.
(With wife, J. S. Hinde) *Constraints on Learning,* Academic Press, 1973.
(With P. P. G. Bateson) *Growing Points in Ethology,* Cambridge University Press, 1976.
Primate Social Relationships, Blackwell Scientific Publications (Boston, MA), 1983.
(With G. Prins and others) *Defended to Death,* Penguin (New York City), 1983.
(With A-N. Perret-Clermont and J. S. Hinde) *Social Relationships and Cognitive Development,* Clarendon Press, 1985.
(With J. S. Hinde) *Relationships with Families,* Clarendon Press (England), 1988.
(With D. A. Parry) *Education for Peace,* Russell Press, 1989.
(With J. Groebel) *Aggression and War,* Cambridge University Press, 1989.
(With Groebel) *Cooperation and Prosocial Behavior,* Cambridge University Press, 1991.
The Institution of War, Macmillan (New York City), 1991.
(With H. Watson) *War: A Necessary Evil?,* Taurus, 1994.

OTHER

Contributor to scientific journals.

SIDELIGHTS: Robert A. Hinde told *CA:* "Having worked for some years on the effects of separation between mother and infant, using rhesus monkeys as experimental subjects, I have now focused on the nature of inter-individual relationships. My earlier research concerns the family and school relationships of pre-school age children and their role in the development of personality. I am now primarily interested in integrating research on adult relationships and in finding bridgeheads between biology and psychology.

"I am also involved in ex-Serviceman's Campaign for Nuclear Disarmament . . . and some of the edited volumes bear on that issue."

BIOGRAPHICAL/CRITICAL SOURCES:

PERIODICALS

Times Literary Supplement, June 24, 1983; May 6, 1988.

* * *

HOAGLAND, Edward 1932-

PERSONAL: Born December 21, 1932, in New York, NY; son of Warren Eugene (an attorney) and Helen (Morley) Hoagland; married Amy J. Ferrara, 1960 (divorced); married Marion Magid, March 28, 1968; children: Molly. *Education:* Harvard University, A.B., 1954.

ADDRESSES: Home—P.O. Box 51, Barton, VT 05822.

CAREER: Novelist and essayist, 1954—. Instructor at New School for Social Research, 1963-64, Rutgers University, 1966, City University of New York, 1967-68, University of Iowa, 1978 and 1982, Columbia University, 1980-81, Bennington College, 1987-97, Brown University, 1988, and

Beloit College, 1995. *Military service:* U.S. Army, 1955-57.

MEMBER: American Academy of Arts and Letters.

AWARDS, HONORS: Houghton Mifflin literary fellowship, 1954, for *Cat Man;* Longview Foundation Award, 1961; American Academy of Arts and Letters travelling fellowship and Guggenheim fellowship, both 1964; O. Henry Award, 1971; New York State Council on the Arts award and Brandeis University Creative Arts Awards Commission citation in literature, both 1972; National Book Award nomination, 1974, for *Walking the Dead Diamond River;* Guggenheim fellowship, 1975; National Book Critics Circle Award nomination in nonfiction, 1979, for *African Calliope: A Journey to the Sudan;* Harold D. Vursell Award from American Academy of Arts and Letters, 1981; American Book Award nomination, 1982, for paperback edition of *African Calliope;* Lannan Foundation Award, 1993.

WRITINGS:

NOVELS

Cat Man, Houghton (Boston), 1956.
The Circle Home, Crowell (New York City), 1960.
The Peacock's Tail, McGraw (New York City), 1965.
Seven Rivers West, Summit Books, 1986.

NONFICTION

Notes from the Century Before: A Journal from British Columbia, Random House (New York City), 1969, reprinted, Sierra Club Books (San Francisco, CA), 1995.
The Courage of Turtles: Fifteen Essays by Edward Hoagland, Random House, 1971.
Walking the Dead Diamond River, Random House, 1973.
The Moose on the Wall: Field Notes from the Vermont Wilderness, Barrie & Jenkins (England), 1974.
Red Wolves and Black Bears, Random House, 1976.
African Calliope: A Journey to the Sudan, Random House, 1979.
The Edward Hoagland Reader, edited by Geoffrey Wolff, Random House, 1979.
The Tugman's Passage, Random House, 1982.
(Editor) *The Penguin Nature Library,* 29 volumes, Penguin Books, 1985-97.
City Tales, Capra (Santa Barbara, CA), 1986.
Heart's Desire: The Best of Edward Hoagland, Summit Books, 1988.
Balancing Acts, Simon & Schuster (New York City), 1992.

OTHER

The Final Fate of the Alligators (stories), Capra, 1992.

Contributor to numerous periodicals, including *Esquire,* the *New Yorker, New American Review, Transatlantic Review, Sports Illustrated,* and the *New York Times.*

SIDELIGHTS: Edward Hoagland's award-winning essays explore the world of nature, the homely affairs of the human heart, and the dynamics of changing civilizations. Hoagland delights in presenting not only the sights of things but his insights into them as well, "trapping feeling and experience into an unexpected truth," to quote *New York Times Book Review* contributor Dan Wakefield. The author, a native of metropolitan New York, is best known for his closely observed pieces on wild animals and natural phenomena; *Washington Post Book World* correspondent Edwin M. Yoder, Jr. notes that Hoagland "is one of New York City's important links with the wilderness." Yoder continues: "In the editorial columns of the *New York Times* the reader unnerved by nerve gas or frayed by the cost of living index may suddenly come upon [a Hoagland] editorial that begins, 'There's nothing like a canoe'. . . . And since the call of the wild is rarely heard in the 21 Club, or even on 43rd Street, Hoagland's nature prose is the next best thing. And it is a good thing indeed." In the *New York Review of Books,* R. W. Flint calls Hoagland's work "a gem of atmospheric figure painting and imaginative anthropology: thousands of anecdotes and small observations resolving themselves into a gallery of shaped figures."

The son of an oil corporation attorney, Hoagland grew up in Connecticut and Manhattan. A severe stammer restricted his social contacts, and he found himself most at home on long, solitary strolls or in the company of animals. Hoagland is quoted in the *Dictionary of Literary Biography* on the results of his affliction: "Words are spoken at considerable cost to me, so a great value is placed on each one," he declares. "That has had some effect on me as a writer. As a child, since I couldn't talk to people, I became close to animals. I became an observer, and in all my books, even the novels, witnessing things is what counts." In his youth, Hoagland was able to enhance his conventional education by indulging in unconventional pursuits—he worked for a time as a Ringling Brothers and Barnum and Bailey circus hand, tramped across the country hobo-style, and worked in an army morgue. His first novel, *Cat Man,* was accepted by Houghton Mifflin shortly before he graduated from Harvard University.

Hoagland published three novels between 1956 and 1965. In the *Village Voice,* Ross Wetzsteon characterizes these works as "marvelously rendered settings (the circus, a boxing gym, a welfare hotel) in futile search of narrative." The critic adds: "Even more problematic, all three novels dealt with confrontations between unequals in narrowly confined settings, and while this allowed the novels to explore the nature of power in human relationships, their inability to achieve any kind of narrative or emotional resolution meant that their attempts at compassion too often had overtones of something close to sadism." *Dictionary of Literary Biography* contributor James A. Hart finds much to admire in Hoagland's early fiction. "We appreciate the individuality of the chapters, the varied nature of the prose (Hoagland has a good ear for dialogue), and the sympathetic recreation of life among the misfits and the oddballs," writes Hart. "The primitivism of his fiction may exclude a Jamesian exploration of a character's psychology, but it leads nevertheless to deeply moving and disturbing scenes. . . . Throughout the fiction, . . . one senses in Hoagland an educated sensitivity, a sturdy intelligence, and a tenacious individualism."

A regular contributor to magazines, Hoagland began to concentrate almost exclusively on nonfiction in the late 1960s. Since then, his interests have led him far and wide, from the waters surrounding Manhattan to the desert wastes of the Sudan. As James Kaufman notes in the *Los Angeles Times,* Hoagland has subsequently become "one of our best and most esteemed nature writers." A love of wild animals invests Hoagland's essays with both enthusiasm and elegy—he fears for the future of many species but avoids dogmatic assertions on the subject. "Hoagland is surely one of our most truthful writers about nature, one of the few who can be counted on to avoid the distracting theatricality of preaching or blaming or apocalypse-mongering," claims Thomas R. Edwards in the *New York Times Book Review.* "And his truthfulness doesn't rule out the pleasures of a brilliant image . . . or of passages of sustained inventive brio." *Newsweek* correspondent Peter S. Prescott writes: "Hoagland lives, diving from the city to Vermont to look for mountains, to Minnesota to stalk black bears, to Texas to see if the red wolf has a chance to survive. He seeks out the wildlife biologists and follows them through the woods. When he comes to write about what he has learned he writes complex essays in which a lot of good hard information is refracted through a distinctive, likable sensibility. . . . More than most writers, he seems to use everything that has ever happened to him, everything he has ever heard."

Subjects from nature often highlight Hoagland's essay collections, but a Hoagland book may also address an array of urban and personal topics. In the *New York Times Book Review,* Diane Johnson observes: "The best moments of [Hoagland's work] concern not actions or escapades but general matters of enduring interest—the death of a father, childbirth, the relation of man and animals, qualities of the human heart. These are subjects about which wisdom is of better use than wit, and rarer—wisdom and a lively sense of the role of the imagination in getting through life." Critic Alfred Kazin also contends in a *New York Times Book Review* piece that Hoagland is "one of the best 'personal essayists' in the business, a virtuoso of the reader-capsizing sentence, a splendid observer of city street, circus lot, go-go girls, freight trains, juries in the jury room plus, and especially, any and every surviving patch of North American wild he can get to moon around in."

Stylistically, writes Wetzsteon, Hoagland is "gifted at rescuing moribund adjectives and nursing them back to health, at combining the arcane with the colloquial, at guiding us through bewildering but suddenly gratifying digressions (like detours that turn out to save hours), and especially at jolting one's mind with abrupt, revelatory transitions. . . . He also rescues, combines, guides, and jolts, dealing with places and subjects we know little and care less about, . . . revealing that the universe can be glimpsed in a turtle or a tugboat as well as in a grain of sand." In the *National*

Review, poet Donald Hall suggests that Hoagland's writing "combines world and self, or creates a self that we watch with delight as it observes and renders the world. He mostly describes or recounts matters external to himself—a tugboat, a lion tamer, a settlement on the Blue Nile—but which he observes very much in his own person. . . . Always Hoagland is *there;* we feel him, we listen to him examine himself, remember, and even think. One has the impression not of egotism but of restless self-examination—skeptical, alert, and intelligent."

Many critics have responded warmly to Hoagland's work. Edwards claims that the author's essays offer "the welcome companionship of an unusual personality, a man determined to know the worst of us so that he can find something helpful to say, a lover of animals who will not have them sentimentalized simply because they are endangered . . . an intelligence that's quiet, speculative, sensible." In the *Village Voice,* L. S. Klepp writes: "These essays, conveying an individuality both stubborn and serene, remind us that resolute curiosity is an offspring of vitality. What comes through above all is Hoagland's love of life and of beings, human and otherwise, intensely alive." Diane Johnson similarly states that throughout his essays, fiction, and travel books, "it is against the deadness of life that Edward Hoagland writes, or at least that is the effect of his writing. Beneath the wise and faintly elegiac tone of regret for this deadness there always lies a confidence about life that is reassuring." *Washington Post Book World* contributor L. J. Davis concludes that Hoagland's pieces "are richly particular and often luminously beautiful, conveying a love of vanishing things and doomed places that is poignant, intensely personal, and moodily level-headed. . . . One may quarrel with him, on occasion one may be embarrassed for him, but there is a quiet magnificence in the way he doggedly keeps plugging away despite the risks and the pain and the cost, persistently refusing to shun the unpleasantness of truth. In that task, he is among the best we have."

Hoagland told the *Washington Post Book World:* "I write to live. Alfred Kazin once wrote that he suspected I'd die if I didn't write. And he may have been correct. I might die from hurrying, worrying, and scurrying, if I didn't have something so worth hurrying about. I love life and believe in its goodness and rightness, but I seem not to be terribly well fitted for it—that is, not without writing. Writing is my rod and staff. It saves me, exults me."

BIOGRAPHICAL/CRITICAL SOURCES:

BOOKS

Contemporary Literary Criticism, Volume 28, Gale (Detroit), 1984.

Dictionary of Literary Biography, Volume 6: *American Novelists since World War II, Second Series,* Gale, 1980.

Johnson, Diane, *Terrorists and Novelists,* Knopf (New York City), 1982.

Wolff, Geoffrey, editor, *The Edward Hoagland Reader,* Random House, 1979.

PERIODICALS

Book World, September 7, 1969; January 17, 1971.

Chicago Tribune, November 12, 1979; September 12, 1988.

Chicago Tribune Book World, September 23, 1979; April 4, 1982; December 12, 1993.

Commentary, September, 1969.

Detroit News, March 28, 1982; June 5, 1983.

Los Angeles Times, June 3, 1982.

Los Angeles Times Book Review, April 25, 1982; April 30, 1995.

National Review, May 30, 1980.

New Republic, December 29, 1979.

Newsweek, August 9, 1965; June 2, 1969; January 18, 1971; May 10, 1976; March 29, 1982.

New York Review of Books, September 11, 1969.

New York Times, January 15, 1971; September 11, 1979; March 17, 1982.

New York Times Book Review, January 15, 1956; June 8, 1969; February 7, 1971; March 25, 1973; June 13, 1976; September 16, 1979; March 21, 1982; September 21, 1986; November 21, 1993.

Saturday Review, May 29, 1976; September 15, 1979; March, 1982.

Sewanee Review, summer, 1980.

Time, May 3, 1976; September 10, 1979.

Village Voice, October 23, 1969; October 15, 1979.

Washington Post, January 14, 1971.

Washington Post Book World, May 16, 1976; September 23, 1979; February 28, 1982; October 12, 1986; November 28, 1993.

HOGE, Dean R(ichard) 1937-

PERSONAL: Surname rhymes with "stogie"; born May 27, 1937, in Ohio; son of Arthur F. (a lumber dealer) and Meta (Meckstroth) Hoge; married Josephine Jacobson, June 27, 1965; children: Christopher, Elizabeth. *Education:* Ohio State University, B.S. (summa cum laude), 1960; graduate study at University of Bonn, 1960-61; Harvard University, B.D. (cum laude), 1964, M.A., 1966, Ph.D., 1970. *Religion:* Presbyterian.

ADDRESSES: Home—7314 Holly Ave., Takoma Park, MD 20912. *Office*—Department of Sociology, Catholic University of America, Washington, DC 20064.

CAREER: Princeton Theological Seminary, Princeton, NJ, assistant professor of sociology, 1969-74; Catholic University of America, Washington, DC, associate professor, 1974-82, professor of sociology, 1982—.

MEMBER: International Society for the Sociology of Religion, American Sociological Association, Society for the Scientific Study of Religion, Religious Research Association (president, 1979-80), Association for the Sociology of Religion.

AWARDS, HONORS: Catholic Book Award for best professional book, Catholic Press Association, 1987, for *The Future of Catholic Leadership: Responses to the Priest Shortage;* Distinguished Book Award, Society for the Scientific Study of Religion, 1994, for *Vanishing Boundaries: The Religion of Protestant Baby Boomers.*

WRITINGS:

Commitment on Campus: Changes in Religion and Values over Five Decades, Westminster (Philadelphia, PA), 1974.

Division in the Protestant House: The Basic Reasons behind Intra-Church Conflicts, Westminster, 1976.

(With Hart M. Nelsen and Raymond H. Potvin) *Religion and American Youth, with Emphasis on Catholic Adolescents and Young Adults,* U.S. Catholic Conference (Washington, DC), 1976.

(Editor with David A. Roozen, and contributor) *Understanding Church Growth and Decline, 1950-1978,* Pilgrim Press (New York City), 1979.

(With others) *Converts, Dropouts, Returnees: A Study of Religious Change among Catholics,* Pilgrim Press, 1981.

(With Kathleen M. Ferry and Potvin) *Research on Men's Vocations to the Priesthood and the Religious Life,* U.S. Catholic Conference, 1984.

The Future of Catholic Leadership: Responses to the Priest Shortage, Sheed & Ward (Kansas City, MO), 1987.

(With others) *Seminary Life and Visions of the Priesthood: A National Survey of Seminarians,* National Catholic Educational Association (Washington, DC), 1987.

(With Jackson W. Carroll and Francis K. Scheets) *Patterns of Parish Leadership: Cost and Effectiveness in Four Denominations,* Sheed & Ward, 1988.

(With Benton Johnson and Donald A. Luides) *Vanishing Boundaries: The Religion of Protestant Baby Boomers,* Westminster, 1994.

(With others) *Money Matters: Personal Giving in American Churches,* Westminster, 1996.

Contributor to religion and sociology journals.

* * *

HOLINGER, William (Jacques) 1944-
(Scott Eller)

PERSONAL: Born June 12, 1944, in Chicago, IL; son of Paul H. (a physician) and Julia C. (Drake) Holinger; married Dorothy Helen Powe (a classical psychologist), August 18, 1978; stepchildren: Gordon Ondis, Jr., Aleta T. Ondis. *Education:* Wesleyan University, A.B., 1966; Brown University, A.M., 1977.

ADDRESSES: Home—20 Chapel St., Brookline, MA 02146. *Agent*—McIntosh & Otis, Inc., 310 Madison Ave., New York, NY 10017.

CAREER: University of Michigan, Ann Arbor, faculty member, 1978-90; Harvard University, Cambridge, MA, faculty member, 1990—. *Military service:* U.S. Army, 1966-69.

MEMBER: Authors Guild, Authors League of America.

AWARDS, HONORS: Associated Writing Programs award in the novel, 1984, for *The Fence-walker;* Eyster Award for fiction, 1984, for short story, "Younker's Jump"; creative artist grant from Michigan Council for the Arts, 1984.

WRITINGS:

YOUNG ADULT NOVELS; WITH JIM SHEPARD, UNDER JOINT PSEUDONYM SCOTT ELLER

Short Season, Scholastic (New York City), 1985.
21st Century Fox, Scholastic, 1989.

"THE JOHNSON BOYS" SERIES FOR YOUNG ADULTS; WITH JIM SHEPARD, UNDER JOINT PSEUDONYM SCOTT ELLER

The Football Wars, Scholastic, 1992.
First Base, First Place, Scholastic, 1993.
That Soccer Season, Scholastic, 1993.
Jump Shot, Scholastic, 1994.

OTHER

The Fence-walker (adult novel), State University of New York Press (Albany), 1985.

Contributor of short stories to *Delta Review, Texas Review,* and *Iowa Review.*

SIDELIGHTS: After English professor and author William Holinger published his first novel, *The Fence-walker,* which is based on his experiences as a soldier in Korea during the late 1960s, he teamed up with Jim Shepard to write stories for children under the name Scott Eller. All of the Scott Eller books involve sports in one way or another. The stories often blend game action with the personal struggles of their young protagonists. *Short Season,* for example, mixes play-by-play baseball action with twelve-year-old Brad Harris's problems with his developing sense of identity and his close relationship with his brother, Dean. Susan McCord, writing in *School Library Journal,* felt that the blend was a successful one. "Eller has woven a story of substance about growing up," she remarked. *21st Century Fox* continues the story of Brad and Dean, this time as players with the Adrian High School football team. When a teenage movie star named Christiana "Fox" Renard arrives in town to make a horror film, Brad is star-struck and begins to date her, while Dean is eager to get a part in the movie.

About his writing experiences, Holinger once commented in *The Writer:* "When writing fiction, try above all to tell a good story. Give your narrative a structure. If your material is based on experience, so much the better: The fiction will contain a loud ring of truth, and the passion you bring to it will infuse your work with energy and make it that much more powerful."

BIOGRAPHICAL/CRITICAL SOURCES:

PERIODICALS

Booklist, August, 1985, p. 1663.
Choice, February, 1986, p. 868.
Kliatt, November, 1992, p. 6.
Library Journal, July, 1985, p. 93.
New York Times Book Review, October 20, 1985.
Publishers Weekly, May 17, 1985, p. 98.
School Library Journal, October, 1985, p. 171; March, 1989, p. 198.
Sewanee Review, fall, 1986.
Voice of Youth Advocates, June, 1989, p. 100; October, 1990, p. 257.
Writer, May, 1986, pp. 7-9, 46.

* * *

HOMANS, Peter 1930-

PERSONAL: Born June 24, 1930, in New York, NY; married Celia Ann Edwards (secretary of the board of trustees, University of Chicago); children: Jennifer, Patricia, Elizabeth. *Education:* Princeton University, A.B., 1952; Johns Hopkins Medical School, 1953-54; Washington School of Psychiatry, 1955-56; Protestant Episcopal Theological Seminary, B.D., 1957; University of Chicago, M.A., 1962, Ph.D., 1964.

ADDRESSES: *Office*—1025 East 58th St., University of Chicago, Chicago, IL 60637.

CAREER: Institute for Juvenile Research, Chicago, IL, psychologist, 1961-62; University of Toronto, Trinity College, Toronto, Ontario, instructor in department of religion, 1962-64; Hartford Seminary Foundation, Hartford, CT, assistant professor of theology and psychology, 1964-65; University of Chicago, Divinity School, Chicago, associate professor, 1965-78, professor of religion and psychological studies, 1978—, and professor of social sciences. Member of the University of Chicago's Committee on Human Development and Committee on the History of Culture.

MEMBER: American Psychological Association, American Historical Association.

WRITINGS:

(Editor) LeRoy Aden and others, *The Dialogue between Theology and Psychology,* University of Chicago Press (Chicago), 1968.

Theology after Freud: An Interpretive Inquiry, Bobbs-Merrill (New York City), 1970.

(Editor and author of introduction) *Childhood and Selfhood: Essays on Tradition, Religion, and Modernity in the Psychology of Erik H. Erikson,* Bucknell University Press (Lewisburg, PA), 1978.

Jung in Context: Modernity and the Making of a Psychology, University of Chicago Press, 1979, 2nd edition, 1995.

The Ability to Mourn: Disillusionment and the Social Origins of Psychoanalysis, University of Chicago Press, 1989.

Jung in Context has been translated into Italian and Japanese.

WORK IN PROGRESS: A book comparing individual-psychological with social and historical understandings of loss, mourning, and memory.

SIDELIGHTS: Peter Homans told *CA:* "All the books I have written seek to understand a single, grandiose problem: the displacement or erosion of traditional religious authority and practice and its replacement by modern forms of thought and action which repudiate tradition and the past. Intellectuals of many different stripes will recognize this as the problem of modernization or secularization. Put simply, the religious past constitutes 'the way we were,' whereas the psychological present defines 'what we have become.'

"To explore this problem, I have concentrated principally on the rise of modern psychology, especially the depth psychologies (Freud, Jung, Erikson and others) because psychology is repeatedly cited as one of the most powerful expressions of modern, secular life. So, I ask, How did this change occur? Why? Where? and so forth.

"My answer: these psychologies have their origins (as do many other forms of modernization or secularization) in powerful experiences of disillusionment and disenchantment with the symbols, values and morals of the ancient past which the first moderns inherited but could no longer accept. These first 'moderns' were exceptionally sensitive and creative—and anguished—men and women. I think that their lives and works constitute sites where the transition from the traditional to the modern is best represented and studied.

"*Theology after Freud: An Interpretive Inquiry* described or framed the shift from a religious to a psychological view of the world at the cognitive level of systematic thought. It centered upon the then-prominent existentialist theologies of the self (e.g., Paul Tillich and Reinhold Niebuhr) because they defended the traditional religious point of view against the (then new) depth psychologies. It demonstrated that the depth psychologies not only clashed with, but also deconstructed the theological point of view and its unexamined psychological assumptions.

"*Jung in Context: Modernity and the Making of a Psychology* analyzed this shift at the personal, experiential and far more self-conscious level. It portrayed Carl G. Jung as an anguished but creative mind struggling inwardly with the loss of his inherited Christian faith, and evolving a new form of thinking—of consciousness, really—which reconciled the remaining scraps of religious faith with elements of Freud's new psychodynamic (and non-religious) system.

"*The Ability to Mourn: Disillusionment and the Social Origins of Psychoanalysis* developed this approach into a general theory. It studied the lives, works and socio-historical contexts of Freud, Jung, Otto Rank, and Ernest Jones, as well as those of Max Weber. It showed how all these men underwent a common experience, which it theorized as symbolic loss and collective mourning for a lost past. The experience began with disillusionment and loss of a sense of attachment to, and support from, ancient and cherished cultural ideals and symbols; followed by self-discovery and a redefinition of one's sense of self; leading to the creation of a new system of meaning.

"The path which led me to this area of study—a set of psychological and philosophical conflicts—was one which many in today's market-driven and fashion-conscious academies would, if wise, avoid. It was my good fortune to be able to work through a complex vocational conflict in a period of national prosperity (late 1950s-early 1960s), which made possible low tuitions, a high tolerance for interdisciplinarity, plentiful teaching jobs and, most of all, the luxury of time.

"In late adolescence I was torn intellectually between science and the humanities, and vocationally between becoming a physician or a minister. Over a period of six years I studied medicine, theology, psychiatry and psychology—each at a different graduate school—and underwent a period of personal psychotherapy. Gradually, I was able to place my intellectual conflicts in historical relation to each other: religion was the ancient context out of which modern science and psychology grew, and rigorous advanced study gave me an appreciation for teaching as a kind of work which combined rigorous thinking with a praxis of care and concern. As a result, exploring these relations became an overriding—and then lifelong—interest.

"Most important of all, this subject matter has of itself conferred an unexpected but very strong sense of self-confirmation. For, I have learned again and again that the men and women whose lives and works I admire and study also suffered from a cognitive conflict between the humanities and the sciences, and a conflict between the practice of medicine and the practice of a form of care and concern which, while it resembled the historical work of the minister, did not, alas, at that time exist, but had to be created."

Commenting on his current research, Homans stated: "Recently, I have been struck by the way scholars in fields other than psychology are appropriating the concept of mourning for their work. Literary critics think of it as a source for, and sometimes as a hindrance to, their subjects' creativity; architects write about monuments and the memorialization of loss; most of all, historians find the question of collective mourning and collective memory closely related.

"I think that the modern, psychodynamic understanding of mourning has much to contribute to the way historians understand the past and, in particular, to the problem created in part by cultural pluralism, the disintegration of collective memory. Therefore, I am currently working on a book which will, I hope, link up individual-psychological understandings of loss, mourning and memory with social and historical ones—which will, in effect, create a psychology of collective memory."

* * *

HOPKINS, Jasper (Stephen, Jr.) 1936-

PERSONAL: Born November 8, 1936, in Atlanta, GA; son of Jasper Stephen, Sr. (a barber) and Willie Ruth (Sorrow) Hopkins; married Gabriele Voight, December 13, 1967. *Education:* Wheaton College, Wheaton, IL, A.B., 1958; Harvard University, A.M., 1959, Ph.D., 1963.

ADDRESSES: *Office*—Department of Philosophy, University of Minnesota—Twin Cities, Minneapolis, MN 55455. *E-mail*—hopki001@maroon.tc.-umn.edu.

CAREER: Case Western Reserve University, Cleveland, OH, assistant professor, 1963-68; University of Massachusetts—Boston, associate professor, 1969-70; University of Minnesota—Twin Cities, Minneapolis, associate professor, 1970-74, professor of philosophy, 1974—. University of Arkansas, visiting associate professor, spring, 1969; visiting professor at University of Graz, 1981-82, and University of Munich, winter, 1986-87. University of Padua, visiting researcher at Instituto di Storia della Filosofia, spring, 1987; Pontificia Universita Gregoriana, Rome, visiting researcher, 1992-93.

AWARDS, HONORS: National Endowment for the Humanities, fellow in Munich, Germany, 1967-68, translation fellow, 1979; fellow in Paris, American Council of Learned Societies, 1973-74; Guggenheim fellow in Paris, 1980-81; National Humanities Center fellowship, 1983-84.

WRITINGS:

(Editor, translator, and author of introduction, with Herbert Richardson) St. Anselm of Canterbury, *Truth, Freedom, and Evil: Three Philosophical Dialogues,* Harper (New York City), 1967.

(Translator and author of introduction, with Richardson) St. Anselm of Canterbury, *Trin-*

ity, Incarnation, and Redemption: Theological Treatises, Harper, 1970.

A Companion to the Study of St. Anselm, University of Minnesota Press (Minneapolis), 1972.

(Editor and translator, with Richardson) *Anselm of Canterbury,* Edwin Mellen (Lewiston, NY), Volume 1: *Monologion; Proslogion; Debate with Gaunilo; A Meditation on Human Redemption,* 1974, Volume 2: *Philosophical Fragments; De Grammatico; On Truth; Freedom of Choice; The Fall of the Devil; The Harmony of the Foreknowledge, the Predestination, and the Grace of God with Free Choice,* 1976, Volume 3: *Two Letters Concerning Roscelin; The Incarnation of the Word; Why God Became a Man; The Virgin Conception and Original Sin; The Procession of the Holy Spirit; Three Letters on the Sacraments,* 1976, Volume 4 (sole author): *Hermeneutical and Textual Problems in the Complete Treatises of St. Anselm,* 1976.

A Concise Introduction to the Philosophy of Nicholas of Cusa, University of Minnesota Press, 1978, third edition, Banning Press (Minneapolis), 1986.

Nicholas of Cusa on God as Not-Other: A Translation and an Appraisal of De Li Non Aliud, University of Minnesota Press, 1979, third edition, Banning Press, 1987.

Nicholas of Cusa on Learned Ignorance: A Translation and an Appraisal of De Docta Ignorantia, Banning Press, 1981, second edition, 1985.

Nicholas of Cusa's Debate with John Wenck: A Translation and an Appraisal of De Ignota Litteratura and Apologia Doctae Ignorantiae, Banning Press, 1981, third edition, 1988.

Nicholas of Cusa's Metaphysic of Contraction, Banning Press, 1983.

Nicolas of Cusa's Dialectical Mysticism: Text, Translation, and Interpretive Study of De Visione Dei, Banning Press, 1985, second edition, 1988.

A New, Interpretive Translation of St. Anselm's Monologion and Proslogion, Banning Press, 1986.

Nicholas of Cusa's De Pace Fidei and Cribratio Alkorani: Translation and Analysis, Banning Press, 1990, second edition, 1994.

A Miscellany on Nicholas of Cusa, Banning Press, 1994.

Philosophical Criticism: Essays and Reviews, Banning Press, 1994.

Nicholas of Cusa on Wisdom and Knowledge, Banning Press, 1996.

Glaube und Vernunft im Denken des Nikolaus von Kues, Paulinus Verlag (Trier, Germany), 1996.

Nicholas of Cusa: Metaphysical Speculations, Banning Press, 1997.

* * *

HRABAL, Bohumil 1914-

PERSONAL: Born March 28, 1914, in Brno, Czechoslovakia. *Education:* Attended Charles University (Prague).

ADDRESSES: Home—Na Hrazi 24, Prague 8-Liben, Czech Republic.

CAREER: Employed as lawyer's clerk, railway worker, insurance agent, salesman, foundry worker, paper salvage worker, stage hand, and stage extra, 1939-62; writer, 1962—.

AWARDS, HONORS: Klement Gottwald State Prize, 1968; Academy Award for best foreign language film (with Jiri Menzel), Academy of Motion Picture Arts and Sciences, 1967, for *Closely Watched Trains.*

WRITINGS:

NOVELLAS

Tanecni hodiny pro starsi a pokrocile, Ceskoslovensky Spisovatel, 1964, translated by Michael Henry Heim as *Dancing Lessons for the Advanced in Age,* Harcourt (New York City), 1995.

Ostre sledovane vlaky, Ceskoslovensky Spisovatel, 1965, translated by Edith Pargeter as *Closely Watched Trains,* Grove (New York City), 1968, published as *A Close Watch on the Trains,* Cape (London), 1968.

Postriziny, Ceskoslovensky Spisovatel, 1976.

Morytaty a legendy (title means "These Premises Are in the Joint Care of Citizens"), Ceskoslovensky Spisovatel, 1978.

Krasosmutneni, 1979.

Kazdy den zazrak, 1979.

Priliz hlukna samota, 1980, translated by M. H. Heim as *Too Loud a Solitude,* Harcourt, 1990.

Kluby poezi, 1981.

Obsluhoval jsem anglickaho krale, 1982, translated by Paul Wilson as *I Served the King of England,* Harcourt (San Diego), 1989.

SHORT STORIES

Perlicka na dne (title means "Pearl at the Bottom"; includes "Baron Prasil" and "Krtiny 1947"), Ceskoslovensky Spisovatel, 1964.

Pabitete (title means "Palaverers"), Mlada Fronta, 1964, also published in *Automat svet,* 1966.

Inzerat na dum, ve kterem uz nechci bydlet (title means "An Advertisement for a House in Which I Don't Want to Live Anymore"), Mlada Fronta, 1965.

Automat svet (contains "Romance," "Palaverers," "Angel Eyes," "A Dull Afternoon," "Evening Course," "The Funeral," "The Notary," "At the Sign of the Greentree," "Diamond Eyes," "A Prague Nativity," "Little Eman," "The Death of Mr. Baltisberger," "The World Cafeteria," and "Want to See Golden Prague?"), Mlada Fronta, 1966, translated by M. H. Heim as *The Death of Mr. Baltisberger,* Doubleday (Garden City, NY), 1975.

Slavnosti snezenek, 1978.

Mistecko [and] *Kde se zastavil cas,* Aeskoslovenskio Spisovatel, 1982, translated by James Naughton as *The Little Town Where Time Stood Still* [and] *Cutting It Short,* Pantheon (New York City), 1993.

Contributor to anthologies, including *Czech and Slovak Short Stories,* edited by Jeanne Nemcova, Oxford University Press, 1968.

SCREENPLAYS

(With Ivan Passer) *Fadni odpoledne* (adapted from his short story, "A Dull Afternoon"), Barrandov Film Studio, 1965, released in the United States as *A Boring Afternoon,* 1968.

(With Jiri Menzel) *Ostre sledovane vlaky* (screenplay; adapted from his novella of the same title), translated by Joseph Holzbecher as *Closely Watched Trains,* Simon & Schuster (New York City), 1971, published as *Closely Observed Trains,* Lorrimer (London), 1971.

Postriziny (adapted from his novella of the same title), 1980.

OTHER

(Editor) *Vybor z ceske prczy* (anthology), Mlada Fronta, 1967.

Toto mesto je ve spoleane peci obyvatel; montaz (nonfiction), photographs by Miroslav Peterka, Ceskoslovensky Spisovatel, 1967.

Slavnosti snezenek, Ceskoslovensky Spisovatel, 1978.

Kdo jsem (autobiography), two volumes, Praoski imaginace, 1989.

Also contributor of poetry to periodicals.

ADAPTATIONS: Closely Watched Trains was produced by Barrandov Film Studio, 1967, released in the United States as *Closely Watched Trains,* Sigma III, 1968, and in Great Britain as *Closely Observed Trains,* 1968.

SIDELIGHTS: Critically acclaimed as one of the Czech Republic's most famous writers, Bohumil Hrabal posits ordinary men and women within circumstances over which they have no control, weaving the elements of surrealism within both his short stories and novellas. One of Hrabal's most well-known works is 1965's *Ostre sledovane vlaky,* translated in 1968 as the novel *Closely Watched Trains.* In addition to several screenplays and poems, Hrabal's works include the novels *I Served the King of England* and *Too Loud a Solitude.* His biography, the two-volume *Kdo jsem,* was published in 1989.

After training for a career in law as a young man, Hrabal found himself unable to practice his profession due to the political changes in post World-War II Czechoslovakia. Instead, he was forced to work at a variety of odd jobs after communism was imposed upon the Czech people in 1949. Although he had begun writing poetry as a student during the 1930s, Hrabal would be forty-eight years old before beginning his career as a writer.

Although written in a colloquial, rambling style, Hrabal's stories confront the vagaries of human existence; his characters reveal warmly human qualities that contrast with the cold indifference of the world in which they live. What is more, as critic Kvetoslav Chvatik observes in *Orientace,* "Hrabal's people . . . are able to see new, hitherto unsuspected, aspects of reality, allowing them to marvel at the inexhaustible miracles of a world that has been thrown off its bearings." In the author's own introduction to his first collection of short stories, 1963's *Perlicka na dne* ("Pearl at the Bottom"), "he attests that he has glimpsed at the bottom of these figures a pearl, that is, something pure and rare that gives us pleasure," according to Milan Jungmann in *Oblehani Troje*.

While international audiences praised Hrabal's works, Czech authorities found his characters too "unconstructive," in the words of Jungmann. In the wake of the invasion of Czechoslovakia by the Soviet Union and the Warsaw Pact allies in 1968, all of Hrabal's existing books were destroyed and his subsequent writings suppressed. Hrabal was not "rehabilitated" by the communist government until 1976. Consequently, for about eight years Czechs had no access to Hrabal's works except in underground editions.

Meanwhile, Hrabal had became known in the United States when the 1967 Academy Award for best foreign language film was conferred upon the motion picture adaptation of his novella, *Closely Watched Trains*. The book, set in Nazi-occupied Czechoslovakia, tells the story of a young railroad employee who becomes anxious to prove his manhood, especially when inexperience and youthful nervousness cause him to fail during a romantic encounter with a pretty young woman. Though praised for its wit and humor, the book also contains an underlying sense of violence and impending tragedy that finally erupts when the young man is killed during an attempt to blow up a German ammunition train. A *Times Literary Supplement* reviewer explained, "The blend of stoic and epicurean remains consistent to the conclusion of this witty, comprehensive tale, seeing the necessary murders of warfare through the eyes of Falstaff and Hotspur at once."

The internationally successful film adaptation of the novella, coauthored by Hrabal and director Jiri Menzel, has been praised by several critics. *New York Times* reviewer Bosley Crowther notes that the "charm" of *Closely Watched Trains* "is in the quietness and slyness of [its] earthy comedy, the wonderful finesse of understatements, the wise and humorous understanding of primal sex," while *Punch*'s Richard Mallett applauds its humor, stating that the film's "wittily written" screenplay "is as gay as a character comedy and very much funnier than most." Equally impressed by the work of Hrabal and Menzel, *Movies into Film* author John Simon maintains that "the best thing about *Closely Watched Trains* is that it impresses one as unique, indebted only to its individual genius." In addition to writing several other screenplays, Hrabal would also collaborate with director Ivan Passer on the film adaptation of his short story, "A Boring Afternoon." Set in a tavern where some older patrons reveal their resentment of the indifference of the young, the picture was released in the United States in 1968.

Among other of Hrabal's works to become available to English-speaking readers, his *The Death of Mr. Baltisberger* is a collection of fourteen short stories based upon tales told in the beer halls of Prague. "In these stories," writes Igor Hajek in the *Times Literary Supplement*, "Hrabal is as strong, sparkling and invigorating as Pilsner Urquell." Commenting on the author's method, *New York Times Book Review* critic Thomas Lask observes that Hrabal writes "with a splendid ear for the trivia, the ephemera that make up so much of our discourse." "The key to Hrabal," he adds, "is that though the details are always realistic, the uses he puts them to are not." According to Hajek, "Hrabal has his own particular way of looking at or reading the world, of exposing aspects of character or reality one hadn't thought of. It is a quasi-surrealist method, in which everything depends on an extraordinary angle of perception." Though admitting that weaknesses occasionally appear in Hrabal's work, Hajek insisted that, in 1975's *The Death of Mr. Baltisberger*, they "are avoided with bravura."

In 1976, after assuring the Czech government of his loyalty, Hrabal was granted permission to publish *Postriziny* ("The Haircutting"), a semi-fictional short story collection based upon the lives of his ancestors. The first work by Hrabal available in his native country in over a decade, the first printing of twenty thousand copies sold out in less than two hours.

The Czech publication of *I Served the King of England* followed in 1982, with its English translation following in 1989. The novel, which takes place prior to World War II, revolves around Dite, a self-serving hotel waiter whose career brings him into contact with a wealth of personalities and experiences, all of which carry him to a greater understanding of humankind and, ultimately, of self. Calling it "[Hrabal's] most ambitious work so far" in an essay published in *Czech Literature since 1956,* George Gilbian has high praise for the novel: "Acting on impulse, making a sweeping gesture, particularly when moved spontaneously by love, sex, beauty, these points are admiringly and vividly presented by Hrabal over and over and they impress the reader. . . . *I Served the King of England* is a book in which the absurd becomes the marvelous. . . . Hrabal, in his robust stories, is celebrating the discovery of true humaneness, of the marvellousness in people, of how the incredible became fact."

Hrabal's *The Little Town Where Time Stood Still* became available to English-speaking readers in 1994. Narrated by a young boy, the novel depicts family life during the communist takeover of Czechoslovakia. Despite the author's rich use of imagery, intuition, and emotion in painting his verbal landscapes, "We are never glutted by the excess of [his] language, and we never lose sight of the story's shape beneath its rhapsodic shapelessness," notes Nicci Gerrard in a review for the *Observer.* "Hrabal combines good humour and hilarity with tenderness and a tragic sense of his country's history. He writes like a poet and a politician, possessing the gallant hopefulness of one who has lived through too much despair."

After the collapse of communism in the Soviet Union and Eastern Europe, much literature from this part of the world now serves as a useful means of understanding the political and cultural milieu that remained hidden behind the Iron Curtain for so many years. As Howard Norman notes in the *Los Angeles Times Book Review,* Hrabal's works is perhaps best representative of this era of modern history: "Simply put, first-hand experience informs Hrabal's work with wonderful detail, deceptive folksiness, irascibility and charm. One of the grand patriarchs of the unprecedented cacophony of Czech film, writing and painting in the late 1960s . . . . Bohumil Hrabal has invented some of the most memorable characters in world literature."

BIOGRAPHICAL/CRITICAL SOURCES:

BOOKS

Contemporary Literary Criticism, Volume 13, Gale (Detroit), 1980.

Hajek, Jiri, *Lidska situace,* Ceskoslovensky Spisovatel, 1966.

Harkins, William E., and Paul I. Trensky, *Czech Literature since 1956: A Symposium,* Bohemica, 1980.

Jungmann, Milan, *Oblehani Troje,* Ceskoslovensky Spisovatel, 1969.

Simon, John, *Movies into Film: Film Criticism, 1967-1970,* Dial (New York City), 1971.

Souckova, Milada, *A Literary Satellite,* University of Chicago Press (Chicago), 1970.

PERIODICALS

Atlantic Monthly, February, 1975.

Listener, July 11, 1968, p. 55.

London Review of Books, May 18, 1990.

Los Angeles Times, October 22, 1995, pp. 2, 12.

Nation, November 1, 1993, p. 878.

New York Times Book Review, October 5, 1975, p. 46.

Observer, December 21, 1969; May 23, 1993, p. 71.

Orientace, Number 6, 1966.

Punch, May 15, 1968.

Times Literary Supplement, July 25, 1968; May 20, 1977, p. 632; December 3, 1993, p. 12.

Tribune Books (Chicago), October 17, 1993, p. 6.

Virginia Quarterly Review, autumn, 1975, p. 144.

Washington Post Book World, January 2, 1994, p. 9.*

* * *

HUNT, Irene 1907-

PERSONAL: Born May 18, 1907, in Pontiac, IL; daughter of Franklin Pierce and Sarah (Land) Hunt. *Education:* University of Illinois, A.B., 1939; University of Minnesota, M.A., 1946; graduate study, University of Colorado, Boulder.

ADDRESSES: *Home*—2307 Brookshire, West Champaign, IL 61821.

CAREER: Oak Park Public Schools, Oak Park, IL, teacher of French and English, 1930-45; University of South Dakota, Vermillion, instructor in psychology, 1946-50; Cicero Public Schools, Cicero, IL, teacher, 1950-65, consultant and director of language arts, 1965-69; writer, 1964—.

AWARDS, HONORS: Charles W. Follett Award, 1964, American Notable Book Award, 1965,

Newbery Honor Book citation, 1965, Dorothy Canfield Fisher Award, 1965, Clara Ingram Judson Memorial Award, 1965, Lewis Carroll Shelf Award, 1966, and American Library Association Notable Book citation, all for *Across Five Aprils;* Newbery Medal, 1967, and International Board on Books for Young People Honor List citation, 1970, both for *Up a Road Slowly;* Friends of Literature Award and Charles W. Follett Award, both 1971, both for *No Promises in the Wind;* Omar's Book Award, for *The Lottery Rose;* Certificate in Recognition of Contribution to Children's Literature, Twelfth Annual Children's Literature Festival, Central Missouri State University, 1980; Parents' Choice Award, 1985, for *The Everlasting Hills*.

WRITINGS:

Across Five Aprils, Follett (Chicago), 1964.
Up a Road Slowly, Follett, 1966.
Trail of Apple Blossoms, illustrated by Don Bolognese, Follett, 1968.
No Promises in the Wind, Follett, 1970.
The Lottery Rose, Scribner (New York City), 1976.
William, Scribner, 1978.
Claws of a Young Century, Scribner, 1980.
The Everlasting Hills, Scribner, 1985.

Also contributor to *Horn Book,* and to *The Writer's Handbook,* edited by A. S. Burack, 1973. Several of Hunt's manuscripts are housed in the Kerlan Collection of the University of Minnesota at Minneapolis.

ADAPTATIONS: No Promises in the Wind has been optioned for a motion picture.

SIDELIGHTS: "With her first book, *Across Five Aprils,*" writes Clyde Robert Bulla in *Twentieth-Century Children's Writers,* "Irene Hunt established herself as one of America's finest historical novelists." In her works Hunt explores places and time periods ranging from 1860s Illinois to the Depression-era Rocky Mountains. Despite what Zena Sutherland of the *Bulletin of the Center for Children's Books* calls her "historically authenticated" details, however, Hunt's strength lies in creating realistic characters learning to cope with their problems and maturing in the process. "Brilliant characterization, a telling sense of story, an uncanny ability to balance fact and fiction, and compassionate, graceful writing mark Hunt's small but distinguished body of work," maintains commentator Sheryl Lee Saunders in *Children's Books and Their Creators*. Hunt's devotion to quality literature for children brought her a Newbery honor citation in 1965 for *Across Five Aprils,* and her second book, *Up a Road Slowly,* won the Medal itself in 1967. "She has proven that she can write good books for children that please adults as well," notes Philip A. Sadler in the *Dictionary of Literary Biography,* "and she has established an international audience."

Hunt was born in Pontiac, Illinois—a small town about halfway between Springfield and Chicago—in 1907. When she was still quite young, however, her parents, Franklin and Sarah Hunt, moved to Newton, in the southeastern corner of the state. The family was living there in 1914 when her father died. Hunt and her mother relocated to her grandparents' farm nearby. She formed a close relationship with her grandfather, who had grown up during the Civil War and had a plentiful stock of stories about his childhood experiences. Hunt later drew on her grandfather's memories as the inspiration for *Across Five Aprils*. She based *Up a Road Slowly* on her own experiences.

Hunt began her career as a schoolteacher. For fifteen years, from 1930 until 1945, she worked as a teacher of French and English in the school system of Oak Park, Illinois, a suburb of Chicago. She earned her bachelor's degree from the University of Illinois at Urbana in 1939, and went on to obtain a master's degree from the University of Minnesota at Minneapolis in 1946. Hunt taught psychology at the University of South Dakota in Vermillion for the next four years before returning to Illinois. From 1950 until her retirement in 1969 she taught in the school system in Cicero, Illinois, another Chicago suburb. In her position as director of language arts Hunt found that good historical fiction for younger readers, which she felt was an effective teaching tool, was in short supply. *Across Five Aprils,* Sadler reveals, was "written to fit the needs of her students."

Across Five Aprils differs from other stories about the Civil War, such as Stephen Crane's *The Red Badge of Courage,* because the action of the war takes place, for the most part, elsewhere. The focus of the story is nine-year-old Jethro Creighton and how he grows and matures while the war rages on. "Jethro experiences the war through his relationships with his parents," writes Sadler, "his sisters, Jenny and Mary; his brothers, John and Bill; and his schoolmaster, Shadrach Yale." He has to learn to accept the fact that his brothers enlist to fight for different sides, John for the Union and Bill for the Confederacy. "The family respects their rights to act on their beliefs," Sadler states, "but because Bill's sympathies are with the Confederacy, the family is labeled 'Copperheads' and slated for retribution." "Once the pampered baby of the family," Patricia L. Bradley reveals in *Twentieth-Century Young Adult Writers,* "Jethro advances to adult status amid the disintegration of the family unit in which he had once felt security." In addition, he has to take up most of the responsibilities for the farm when his father suffers a heart attack. "At the end of the war," Sadler concludes, "Jethro, who has come to a knowledgeable understanding of it through letters and conversations, is taken east to school by Shadrach and Jenny, who are now married."

Hunt depicts the destruction and remaking of the Creighton family as a model of the destruction of the United States during the Civil War and the Reconstruction period. One major character, Jethro's cousin Ed, deserts from the Union Army and writes in desperation to President Lincoln for a pardon. Lincoln responds by offering to forgive all the deserters in Ed's party. "Hunt's research of historical details is impeccable," declares Bradley, "and her use of her grandfather's memories of his childhood during the war gives the reader a sense of great intimacy with the lives of the characters." Hunt has, according to a reviewer for *Booklist,* "in an uncommonly fine narrative, created living characters and vividly reconstructed a crucial period of history." "It is withal an intriguing and beautifully written book," states *New York Times Book Review* contributor John K. Bettersworth—"a prize to those who take the time to read it, whatever their ages."

Up a Road Slowly, Hunt's second book, chronicles ten years in the life of Julie Trelling. Julie's mother dies when she is only seven years old. Her father and her beloved older sister, unable to care for her, send Julie to live with her Aunt Cordelia, a country schoolteacher. "Willful and adventurous," Bradley declares, "Julie clashes frequently with her aunt, a strict and duty-bound woman who nonetheless exerts a loving and powerful influence over Julie." Despite her early problems, Julie matures into a gracious young lady. "Miss Hunt," claims Constantine Georgiou in *Children and Their Literature,* "relates with warmth and sympathetic insight the story of a young girl's growth to maturity."

Critics praised Hunt's depiction of her characters and her grasp of language and difficult themes in *Up a Road Slowly.* "Treating the story with a detached realism tempered with love," Sadler asserts, "Hunt introduces themes of jealousy, first love, parent-child and sibling relationships, foster-family relationships, and snobbishness and handles them in fresh new ways." Ruth Hill Viguers, writing in *Horn Book,* suggests that, while the characters in *Up a Road Slowly* "are no more unusual and varied than are most people's families and friends," Hunt "sees them so much more clearly . . . and gives them such vivid life that the reader is quickly and intensely interested in them." "She breaks new ground," concludes Sadler, "shattering old taboos in children's literature, to produce a book devoid of the artificiality and superficiality of many of the teenage novels of the time." "The author is adept at distinguishing the genuine from the spurious," writes a reviewer for *Virginia Kirkus' Service.* "Julie *is* a genuine character, and girls who go up the road with her will share in her growing up."

Like *Across Five Aprils, Up a Road Slowly* draws on Hunt's family history. It reflects her own experience growing up in relative isolation with only one parent after the death of the other. "Just as Hunt had been lonely, bewildered, and frightened upon the loss of her father," Sadler states, "another little girl . . . might, in her loneliness, wander into the woods quoting verses from Edna St. Vincent Millay or Shakespeare." Hunt, asserts *New York Times Book Review* contributor Dorothy M. Broderick, "brings off a difficult tour de force and turns personal reminiscence into art." Hunt herself acknowledged this debt in her Newbery acceptance speech, published in *Horn Book.* "Often children are troubled and in a state of guilt," Hunt wrote. "One can say to them, 'You are not unique. There is in all of us only a thin veneer of civilization that separates us from the primitive.'"

Trail of Apple Blossoms, Hunt's third book, drew for its inspiration on the American folk hero John Chapman, better known as Johnny Appleseed. The book "is not a biography, but a historical novel," Bulla reveals, "picturing Johnny Appleseed as he may have been—a heroic man with a reverence for life whose beneficent influence touched pioneer America." *Trail of Apple Blossoms* focuses not on Chapman's traditional planting and sowing of apple seeds, but on his reputation as a man of peace and a lover of life. The narrator of the story is Hoke Bryant, who is traveling with his parents and his two-year-old sister Rachel from their old home in Boston to a new place in the Ohio Valley. During the trip, Rachel becomes ill and refuses to eat. The Bryants encounter Chapman, who uses his skills to coax Rachel into eating. He becomes a close friend of the Bryant family and his gentle philosophy inspires the adult Hoke to take up a career as a minister. "Irene Hunt," declares Dorothy M. Broderick in the *New York Times Book Review,* "has written one of the best accounts of the gentle man who would harm neither man nor beast." *School Library Journal* contributor Helen Armstrong claims that in *Trail of Apple Blossoms* Hunt "has endowed her subject with a spiritual quality which shines through the story."

In *No Promises in the Wind,* Hunt moves on to the twentieth century and the era of the Great Depression. The Grodowski brothers, Josh and his little brother Joey, flee their home and their negligent father. In the company of Howie, a friend, the two hop a freight train for the west. However, Howie slips beneath the wheels of a freight car and is killed. Josh and Joey travel on, finding both trials and comfort in their travels. "They are befriended by a kindly truck driver who treats them as his own sons," Sadler writes. "When Josh recovers from a serious illness, the boys leave their benefactor and continue on their wanderings. Joining a carnival group, they again find others who will share with them their meager substance as well as their love. . . . Even the hungry hoboes offer assistance to the boys." Eventually the boys return home and are reconciled with their repentant father. "With all the problems that exist today," Ruth Hill Viguers writes in *Horn Book,* "such an honest picture of one of our country's most tragic periods may give readers a wider perspective. It is a deeply moving story."

"The writer who takes on a subject like child abuse," writes author Betsy Byars in the *New York Times Book Review,* "faces a problem—whether to show the deed in all its headline horror or to soften it for young readers." *The Lottery Rose* is Hunt's story of Georgie Burgess, neglected by his alcoholic mother and abused by her boyfriend. "In a lottery held by the new owners of a local grocery story, Georgie wins a rose bush," Byars notes. "Beautiful flowers . . . are the only meaningful things in his life, and he lavishes his concern on finding a place to plant his rose bush." After a particularly brutal beating Georgie is placed in a Catholic boarding school, where he encounters Mollie Harper, who is in mourning for her husband and son. "In the passage of time," Sadler explains, "Georgie emerges from his withdrawn state." He makes friends with Mrs. Harper's surviving son Robin and, when Robin is lost in an accident, gains her acceptance. "Though the book may not be as strong a novel as her earlier ones," Sadler concludes, "Hunt does provide a touching treatment of a theme out of the ordinary at the time of the book's creation—the abuse of a small child—in a manner suitable for young readers."

William looks at interracial relationships on an intergenerational level. A young, pregnant white teenager named Sarah moves in next door to William's family. William's Mama, the head of the household, helps nurse Sarah through a hurricane strike and the birth of her child. When Mama dies of cancer, states Nancy P. Bailey in *School Library Journal,* "Sarah takes over as head of the family, refusing to let William and his sisters be placed in a foster home." "William recognizes that the situation and the home he has grown up in will never be the same again," Sadler concludes, "but he realizes that he must assume responsibility for the family." "The love and concern for human beings other than oneself are basic elements underlying the development of strong family relationships," explains *Horn Book* reviewer Mary M. Burns. "Through the skill with which the author delineates the characters, their ultimate triumph over multiple adversities is made believable, and each one emerges as a distinct personality."

Hunt looks at feminist issues in *Claws of a Young Century,* the story of a young suffragette working for women's rights in the early years of the century. "On New Year's Eve, 1899, seventeen-year-old Ellen Archer has hopes of bringing change and progress into her life and into the lives of other women," writes *Horn Book* contributor Ann A. Flowers. She leaves her unenlightened father to live with her college-educated brother Alex, falls in love with his journalist friend Philip Wrenn, and becomes pregnant. Ellen and Philip marry, but separate and divorce so that Philip can work overseas as a foreign correspondent and Ellen can continue her campaign for women's rights. "Ellen goes to jail for her beliefs," explains Cyrisse Jaffee in *School Library Journal,* "and the brutal treatment she receives there proves fatal." "When Philip returns after sixteen years abroad to find Ellen dying," Sadler concludes, "they realize their love and that pride has kept them apart. He promises to continue her work for the ratification of the suffrage amendment."

The Everlasting Hills, published in 1985, is set in the Rocky Mountains during the 1930s. The protagonist is Jeremy Tydings, who has a learning disability. Alienated from his unfeeling father, Jeremy finds solace in his relationship with his sister Bethany. When he realizes that Bethany is sacrificing her own life in order to care for him, he runs away. Jeremy finds shelter with an old hermit named Ishmael. "In the time he spends with Ishmael, Jeremy matures and grows in self-esteem," writes Barbara Chatton in *School Library Journal.* "After Ishmael dies, Jeremy returns to the cabin and embarks upon a project the two had dreamed of together and a difficult reconciliation with his father." "Their relationship . . . [is] delicately portrayed," Bulla states, "and reveal[s] some of Hunt's finest qualities."

Critics continue to celebrate Hunt's literary accomplishments. Bradley states that Hunt "demonstrates her virtuosity as a storyteller by never duplicating her use of characters, setting, and plot within the genre of historical fiction. In addition, all of Hunt's novels consistently demonstrate other important elements such as poetic yet simple language and a delicate appreciation of the natural world." "Irene Hunt has a strong faith in the enduring qualities of courage, love, and mercy," Sadler concludes. "It is to reiterate this faith that she writes her books."

BIOGRAPHICAL/CRITICAL SOURCES:

BOOKS

Children's Literature Review, Volume 1, Gale, 1976.

Dictionary of Literary Biography, Volume 52: American Writers for Children since 1960: Fiction, Gale (Detroit), 1986, pp. 202-208.

Georgiou, Constantine, *Children and Their Literature,* Prentice-Hall, 1969, p. 379.

Hopkins, Lee Bennett, *More Books by More People,* Citation Press, 1974.

Larrick, Nancy, *A Parent's Guide to Children's Reading,* 3rd edition, Doubleday, 1969.

Silvey, Anita, editor, *Children's Books and Their Creators,* Houghton (Boston), 1995, p. 331.

Twentieth-Century Children's Writers, 3rd edition, St. James Press (Detroit), 1989, pp. 481-482.

Twentieth-Century Young Adult Writers, St. James Press, 1994, pp. 312-314.

PERIODICALS

Booklist, August, 1985, p. 1665.

Booklist and Subscription Books Bulletin, July 1, 1964, p. 1002.

Bulletin of the Center for Children's Books, July-August, 1964, p. 171.

Commonweal, May 24, 1968.

Horn Book, February, 1967, p. 73; August, 1967, pp. 424-429; June, 1970; October, 1977, pp. 540-541; October, 1980, pp. 525-526.

Kirkus Reviews, November 15, 1966, p. 1188.

New Yorker, December 14, 1968.

New York Times Book Review, May 10, 1964, pp. 8, 10; November 6, 1966, pp. 8, 12; March 19, 1967; April 14, 1968; April 5, 1970; May 16, 1976, pp. 16, 18.

Publishers Weekly, March 13, 1967; March 22, 1976, p. 46.

School Library Journal, May, 1968, p. 79; April, 1976, p. 74; April, 1977, p. 77; August, 1980, p. 77; September, 1985, p. 134; August, 1993, pp. 50-51; September, 1994, p. 140.

Writer, March, 1970.

Young Readers' Review, June, 1968.

* * *

IGNATOW, David 1914-

PERSONAL: Surname is accented on second syllable; born February 7, 1914, in Brooklyn, NY; son of Max (in business) and Henrietta (Wilkenfeld) Ignatow; married Rose Graubert (an artist and writer), August 11, 1939; children: David, Jr., Yaedi (daughter). *Ethnicity:* "Jewish." *Education:* High school graduate.

ADDRESSES: Home—P.O. Box 1458, East Hampton, NY 11937.

CAREER: Freelance writer and editor. Worked in family-owned butcher shop and a bindery in Brooklyn, NY, which he later owned and managed. Works Progress Administration, journalist with Writers Project, beginning 1932; New School for Social Research, New York City, instructor, 1962-64; University of Kentucky, Lexington, lecturer, 1964-65; University of Kansas, Lawrence, lecturer, 1966-67; Vassar College, Poughkeepsie, NY, instructor, 1967-68; Columbia University, New York City, adjunct professor, 1968-76, senior lecturer, 1977—; York College of the City University of New York, New York City, poet in residence and associate professor, 1968-84, professor emeritus, 1984—.

MEMBER: PEN, Poetry Society of America (member of executive board, 1979; president, 1980-84).

AWARDS, HONORS: Awards in literature, National Institute and American Academy, 1964, "for a lifetime of creative effort"; Guggenheim fellow, 1965, 1973; Poetry Society of America, Shelley Memorial Prize, 1966, Robert Frost Medal, 1992; grants from Rockefeller Foundation, 1968, and National Endowment for the Arts, 1970; Bollingen Prize, 1977; Wallace Stevens Fellow, Yale University, 1977; poet in residence award, Walt Whitman Birthplace Association, 1986-87; Long Island University, D.Litt., 1987, John Steinbeck Award, 1995.

WRITINGS:

Poems, Decker Press, 1948.
The Gentle Weight Lifter, Morris Gallery, 1955.
(Editor) *Political Poetry,* Chelsea, 1960.
Say Pardon, Wesleyan University Press (Hanover, NH), 1961.
(Editor) *Walt Whitman: A Centennial Celebration,* Beloit College (Beloit, WI), 1963.
(Editor) *William Carlos Williams: A Memorial Chapbook,* Beloit College, 1963.
Figures of the Human, Wesleyan University Press, 1964.
Rescue the Dead, Wesleyan University Press, 1968.
Earth Hard: Selected Poems, Rapp & Whiting, 1968.
Poems, 1939-1969, Wesleyan University Press, 1970.
The Notebooks of David Ignatow, edited by Ralph Mills, Jr., Swallow Press (Athens, OH), 1973, Sheep Meadow (Bronx, NY), 1981.
Facing the Tree: New Poems, Little, Brown (Boston), 1975.
Selected Poems, edited by Robert Bly, Wesleyan University Press, 1975.
The Animal in the Bush: Poems on Poetry, edited by Patrick Carey, Slow Loris Press, 1977.
Tread the Dark, Little, Brown, 1978.
Sunlight: A Sequence for My Daughter, BOA Limited Editions (Brockport, NY), 1979.
Conversations, Survivors' Manual Books, 1980.
Open between Us, edited by Ralph J. Mills, Jr., University of Michigan Press (Ann Arbor), 1980.
Whisper to the Earth, Little, Brown, 1981.
Leaving the Door Open, Sheep Meadow, 1984.
New and Collected Poems, 1970-1985, Wesleyan University Press, 1987.
The One in the Many: A Poet's Memoirs, Wesleyan University Press, 1988.
Shadowing the Ground, Wesleyan University Press, 1991.
Despite the Plainness of the Day, Mill Hunk Books (Pittsburgh, PA), 1991.
I Have a Name, Wesleyan University Press, 1996.
The End Came: Selected Short Stories, Cathedral Publishers, 1996.
Gleanings: Uncollected Poems, 1950s and 1960s, BOA Limited Editions, 1997.

Works represented in *Naked Poetry, A Big Jewish Book, News of the Universe,* and many other anthologies. Contributor of poems to periodicals, including *Quarterly Review of Literature, Sixties, Poetry, Kayak, Commentary, New Yorker,* and *Saturday Review. Beloit Poetry Journal,* editor, 1949-59, guest editor, 1963; poetry editor, *Nation,* 1962-63; coeditor, *Chelsea,* 1967-76; associate editor, *American Poetry Review,* 1972-74.

WORK IN PROGRESS: A new poetry collection.

SIDELIGHTS: David Ignatow once told *CA:* "My avocation is to stay alive; my vocation is to write about it; my motivation embraces both intentions, and my viewpoint is gained from a study and activity in both ambitions. The book important to my career is the next one or two or three on the fire." Fidelity to the details and issues of daily life in Ignatow's poetry has won for him a widespread reputation for being "the most autobiographical of writers," suggests *Dictionary of Lit-*

erary Biography contributor Christopher Brown. Ignatow added, "The modern poet most influential in my work was William Carlos Williams. Earlier influences were the Bible, Walt Whitman, Baudelaire, Rimbaud, Hart Crane." In Williams, as in the works of Peruvian surrealist Cesar Vallejo, Ignatow most appreciates "the language of hard living; the universal language," which is perceived "in the lines of the poets where you can feel the mind running like an electrical current through the muscles," he told *Paris Review* contributor Gerard Malanga. Ralph J. Mills observes in *Cry of the Human: Essays on Contemporary American Poetry* that Ignatow "has placed himself in the tradition of those genuine poets who have, in independent ways, struggled to create a living American poetry from the immediacies of existence in this country, from the tragedies and potentialities of its legacy, and from the abundant music and vitality of its language." The respected poet has edited several volumes of poetry and well-known poetry journals, including the *American Poetry Review*. He also addresses the topic of poetic theory in poems that discuss direct statement and clarity, the two objectives Ignatow keeps in mind when crafting a poem. Suggests Mills, "Authenticity speaks to us from every line of Ignatow's poetry, reaching into our lives with the force and deliberation of the seemingly unassuming art which he has subtly and skillfully shaped."

Critics trace several stages of development in the body of Ignatow's works. One line of development in the books is a gradual change in Ignatow's poetic technique. "His typical poem is a short lyric expressing what to all appearances are his genuine thoughts and feelings, yet he is expert at adopting personae, particularly those of insane businessmen and killers, to convey more effectively his vision of modern American life," notes Brown. As current events become increasingly macabre, Ignatow more frequently expresses his response to them in the form of the prose poem, which allows for the depiction of nightmarish sequences from a civilization reeling out of control. For example, in "A Political Cartoon," the President and cabinet members recklessly toss a gun around a conference room until two of them have been shot to death; backing a dump truck into the room, the poet arrives to bury them all under a load of grain.

Ignatow's poems—the lyrics and prose poems alike—are characterized by direct statement rendered with the minimum of poetic devices, achieving their effects through the poet's superb handling of the line, suggests Marvin Bell in the *American Poetry Review*. Coming from "a consciously skeletal aesthetic," says Bell, Ignatow's art is one "of apparent artlessness in the extreme." William Spanos, speaking to Ignatow in a *Boundary 2* interview, explains how the poet's spare, "flat" style of expression achieves maximum impact: unlike much modern poetry, which provides a release or escape from the tension or terror of life in the twentieth century, Ignatow's "poetry—and this is a stylistic as well as thematic matter—disintegrates the reader's expectation of release to demand a confrontation of the horror." The directness in the poems, Ignatow told Spanos, derives "from life itself and so they must always take into account the rawness with which life comes to me, its direct impact on my senses and the stance it alerts in me to keep myself from becoming overwhelmed by this direct impact." In the confessional volume *Leaving the Door Open,* a reflection on his performance as a husband and father, Ignatow is as relentless during self-evaluation as when diagnosing social ills. *Hudson Review* contributor James Finn Cotter admires both the "honesty . . . and the effort required to make such a confession."

Though events come to him without structure, in order to survive them, the poet "must try to structure [the poem] without losing the unstructured, random, elemental quality of things as they happen," Ignatow said in the *Boundary 2* interview. "I structure them through my person which is obliged to remain intact or consistent. . . . There is then a tension between myself and the world outside and it is on this tension that I build my poems. . . . The world has an identity of its own with which I cannot associate myself altogether, especially at crucial points. . . . Clarity as I seek it in my poems is to distinguish my person from the rest of everything else. Clarity together with directness make my style."

Elaborating on his aesthetic, Ignatow told Spanos, "I use my materials without receiving from them any vote of confidence at all, nor do I have any confidence or trust in the materials, full of hidden and not so hidden traps. I may only trust myself and so I go carefully among my objects and events, picking and choosing from among them, letting myself be led only where I will go and so my line is spare, selective, concise, in search of form to hold all this disparate material together always about to fly apart." He compares his writing process to taking a walk through his native Brooklyn: "I have to watch my step around an open manhole, a drunk sprawled on the sidewalk, dog shit, a nodding drug addict. I have to glance behind me from time to time to be sure I'm not being followed. My poetry has this touch of paranoia, this tight alertness to dangers, this militant preparedness for the worst, and above all, the sense of absurdity that arises as we seek for a meaning in this kind of life." He does not provide a meaningful resolution in the poems, "nothing conclusive or definitive," however, because life itself provides no solutions, he said in the Spanos interview. As he explained to Malanga, the lyric form also seemed to require more closure than the prose poem; therefore, for Ignatow, breaking out of the strictures of composition by line was an important step toward fuller and more accurate expression.

In another line of development, Ignatow's themes follow a progression from reflections on individual causes of social ills to problems of wider scope, Brown observes. "Generally, the early work tends to concentrate upon the evils of business and money-grubbing, while the later presents a more surreal vision of social violence and insanity," summarizes Brown. Money, and how we acquire it, is the major topic of the early books and *The Notebooks of David Ignatow,* and, according to Ignatow, "is the central issue of our time."

Poems declaiming the evils of money stem from the poet's personal history. As Ignatow reveals in *Open between Us,* his early years were dominated by his parents' anxieties about the family business. At first fascinated by the intensity of their conversations, Ignatow began to recognize that he did not value material success as much as the kind of personal freedom exemplified by the poet Walt Whitman. Therefore, instead of joining the family business after graduating from high school, he left home to find employment that would allow him the peace and leisure to write poetry.

However, his idealism drew him repeatedly into conflict with his bosses. Moving from job to job, he found that the pressure to provide for himself displaced the time and energy he needed to continue writing. He entered the family business feeling resigned and guilty about imposing on the freedom of his workers in order to make a profit. They told him, however, that they voluntarily submitted to the unpleasant demands of industry in order to maintain a standard of living they equated with happiness. Seeing no alternative to making this kind of trade-off himself, Ignatow concluded, "And so there was poetry to be written, about this paradox of the perpetual search for personal happiness and freedom in things other than oneself." His struggles to earn a living without compromising his personal values is often expressed in the early volumes *Poems, The Gentle Weight Lifter,* and *Say Pardon.*

Other poems in the early volumes speak out against social problems such as urban crime, war, and economic collapse. "In the 1930s he wrote poems about the depression, in the 1940s about World War II, in the 1960s about Vietnam," notes Brown. In *Figures of the Human,* the poet "directs his creative rage toward the . . . subject of violence and social dissolution in the America of the Vietnam era," Brown relates. *Rescue the Dead* ironically holds out no hope of rescue for the poet who identifies himself in one poem as a man forced by a nation of killers to kill his neighbor. "We are more used to poets open to the personal unconscious," comments Robert Bly in the afterword to Ignatow's *Selected Poems.* "If the 'dark side' [of human energy] is thought of as part of the personal unconscious, we notice that David Ignatow sees his dark side clearly only after he has seen it reflected in the angers and frustrations of the collective, when he sees it embodied in a stabber moving through a subway car. He is a poet of the community, of people who work for a living, as Whitman was too, but he is also a great poet of the collective."

In subsequent books, Ignatow's focus on his social environment broadens to include his relationship with nature. More philosophical and imaginative than his other poetry, the poems in *Facing the Tree: New Poems* and *Whisper to the Earth* ask of nature the same questions Ignatow raises elsewhere, L. M. Rosenberg comments in Chicago's *Tribune Books.* In meditations on stones, plants, and weather, Ignatow asks how humans can live, and affirms consciousness of his membership in an ecology that unifies all forms of life, Rosenberg observes. Brown, like other critics, suggests that the poet thus reconciles himself to the inevitability of his death. Responding to these poems reprinted in *New and Collected Poems, 1970-1985, New York Times Book Review* contributor Peter Stitt remarks that they provide "a positive response to the threat of isolation, death, political cruelty, godlessness and meaninglessness. The answer is love. . . . Faced with the fact of a strictly physical universe, Mr. Ignatow chooses to love that universe for all he, and it, are worth."

Ignatow commented on another significant difference between his earlier and later work; regarding "my early concentration in my poetry on injustice and cruelty," he told *CA,* "these poems were written with the assumption that somewhere, somehow there was a social system, idealized in faith by me, that practised justice and decency consistently and with pleasure. I was wrong. At seventy-five years of age, I no longer have such hopes and expectations, though my heart still leaps at any and all pieces and fragments of good news. Nevertheless, I have fallen back upon my study of the individual, taking myself primarily as an example and revealing to myself my shortcomings, my failures. Like Whitman, I think of myself as representative, and so what I write about myself and quite often about others, is intended as, by extension, a comment on most of us. We live in one world."

"If I were to make of this litany a steady diet," he continued, "I don't think I could easily absorb it, and so you will find humor in the later books, humor dealing with precisely those problems to which in my earlier books I gave my passionate concern. In other words, with humor I seem to be more at ease with the moral burdens I have taken on myself and I actually enjoy writing about them now with a sense of detachment, which humor affords." Ignatow elaborates on these changes in *The One in the Many: A Poet's Memoirs.*

Critical responses to Ignatow's work were more antagonistic than he expected, at first, but have gradually become more favorable. "After I had written the kind of poetry *I thought* deserved the respect and attention of people whose opinions *I* respected, I discovered to my dismay that I was writing a kind of poetry which really did not relate to the taste or interests of my generation in any way," he told Malanga. Ignatow's poetic stance—one of direct confrontation with life—opposes the widespread attitude, coming down to us from romanticism, that in poetry, "language takes precedence over content," he explained. From Williams, Ignatow had learned to guard against "a romantic view of life. Against elevated language. Against trying to make a leap into something which didn't exist." In contrast, the prevailing trend fosters a"withdrawal from life" by concerning itself with imaginative poetic devices; a substantial number of influential poets and critics "think through language you learn of life. I say you learn of life through sensibility which then has to be translated into language," he continued. Being thus at odds with critical opinion, Ignatow has produced an important body of work largely without the support of his own generation of writers and without critical acclaim. Later generations have been more appreciative, honoring him with the Shelley Memorial prize, the Wallace Stevens fellowship at Yale University, and the Bollingen prize.

Summing up Ignatow's lifetime accomplishment, which was recognized in 1964 by an award from the National Institute of Arts and Letters, Brown concludes, "Transmuting autobiography into art, he has examined the self's relationship with the environment over a long, productive career. He offers both the edifying spectacle of a man who has paid for his accommodation with life and a body of poetry combining deep-felt emotion, intellectual penetration, and a considerable technical facility."

Ignatow more recently told *CA:* "As I grow old, I find myself more bold in writing about death. My more recent poems treat the subject from almost every angle: without anger, with study and contemplation. Writing about death and dying calms what underlying fears impel me to bring the coming event out into the open. I think of this writing as a kind of triumph over time that remains to me. I look out upon trees and recognize my relationship to them, as organic quantities, in which I feel a satisfying companionship. Earth itself is for a time being, the universe no less. In short, I am a participant in a wordly epic, if significance can be found in living and dying, together with everything and everyone else. I bow to my higher self."

BIOGRAPHICAL/CRITICAL SOURCES:

BOOKS

Contemporary Authors Autobiography Series, Volume 3, Gale (Detroit), 1986.

Contemporary Literary Criticism, Gale, Volume 4, 1975, Volume 7, 1977, Volume 14, 1980, Volume 40, 1986.

Dickey, James, *From Babel to Byzantium,* Farrar, Straus (New York City), 1968.
Dickey, *The Suspect in Poetry,* Sixties Press, 1968.
Dictionary of Literary Biography, Volume 5: *American Poets since World War II,* Gale, 1980.
Ignatow, David, *The Notebooks of David Ignatow,* edited by Ralph J. Mills, Swallow Press, 1974.
Ignatow, *Selected Poems,* edited by Robert Bly, Wesleyan University Press, 1975.
Ignatow, *Open between Us,* edited by Ralph J. Mills, University of Michigan Press, 1980.
Ignatow, *The One in the Many: A Poet's Memoirs,* Wesleyan University Press, 1988.
Jackson, Richard, *Acts of Mind,* University of Alabama Press (Tuscaloosa), 1983.
Mazzaro, J., *Postmodern American Poetry,* University of Illinois Press (Champaign), 1980.
Mills, Ralph, J., Jr., *Cry of the Human: Essays on Contemporary American Poetry,* University of Illinois Press, 1975.
Smith, Robert A., *A Checklist of Writings,* University of Connecticut Library, 1966.

PERIODICALS

American Book Review, December/January, 1978-79; September/October, 1981; December, 1994.
American Poetry Review, March/April, 1974; January/February, 1976; March/April, 1976.
Boundary 2, spring, 1974 (interview); fall, 1975.
Contemporary Literature, summer, 1987 (interview).
Georgia Review, summer, 1979.
Hudson Review, autumn, 1984; autumn, 1985; spring, 1987.
Lamp in the Spine, spring, 1973.
New York Times Book Review, November 21, 1948; July 30, 1978; February 14, 1982; November 11, 1987.
Ontario Review, spring/summer, 1975.
Paris Review, fall, 1979 (interview).
Parnassus, fall/winter, 1975.
Poetry, April, 1976; June, 1980.
Salmagundi, spring/summer, 1973.
Sewanee Review, spring, 1976.
Some, winter, 1973 (interview).
Tennessee Poetry Journal, winter, 1970 (interview).
Times Literary Supplement, November 6, 1987.
Tribune Books, April 12, 1987.
University Review, spring, 1968.
World Literature Today, summer, 1979.
Yale Review, autumn, 1955; summer, 1961.

* * *

IRVINE, R. R.
See IRVINE, Robert (Ralstone)

* * *

IRVINE, Robert (Ralstone) 1936-
(R. R. Irvine)

PERSONAL: Born March 16, 1936, in Salt Lake City, UT; son of Garner Davis (a businessman) and Stacie (Ellsworth) Irvine; married Angela Prata (an engineer), January 31, 1959. *Education:* Attended University of Utah, 1954-55; University of California, A.B., 1959.

ADDRESSES: *Home*—5461 La Forest Dr., La Canada, CA 91011. *Agent*—Dominick Abel, 146 West 82nd St., New York, NY 10024.

CAREER: Writer. *Daily Signal,* Huntington Park, CA, reporter, 1962-63; *Citizens News,* Hollywood, CA, reporter and Los Angeles City Hall bureau chief, 1963-64; KTLA-TV, Los Angeles, CA, worked as newswriter, producer, assistant assignments editor, and secretary, 1964-65; KNX-Radio, Los Angeles, writer, producer, and news director, 1966-68; KABC-TV, Los Angeles, news director, 1968-71; KCBS-TV, Los Angeles, writer, 1980-82. Teacher at University of Southern California, 1977. *Military service:* U.S. Army, 1959-61; became first lieutenant.

MEMBER: Mystery Writers of America (director of Southern California chapter).

AWARDS, HONORS: Emmy Awards, Academy of Television Arts and Sciences, 1969, for documentaries on battered children and rat epidemics; Edgar Allan Poe Award nominations, Mystery Writers of America, 1975, for *Jump Cut,* and 1977, for *Freeze Frame.*

WRITINGS:

NOVELS

The Face Out Front, Popular Library (New York City), 1977.
The Devil's Breath, Pinnacle Books (New York City), 1982.
Footsteps, Pinnacle Books, 1982.
Revelation, [Sweden], 1984.
Barking Dogs, St. Martin's, 1994.

"ROBERT CHRISTOPHER" SERIES

Jump Cut, Popular Library, 1974.
Freeze Frame, Popular Library, 1976.
Horizontal Hold, Popular Library, 1978.
Ratings Are Murder, Walker & Co. (New York City), 1985.

"MORONI TRAVELER" SERIES

Baptism for the Dead, Dodd (New York City), 1988.
The Angel's Share, St. Martin's (New York City), 1989.
Gone to Glory, St. Martin's, 1990.
Called Home, St. Martin's, 1992.
The Spoken Word, St. Martin's, 1992.
The Great Reminder, St. Martin's, 1993.
The Hosanna Shout, St. Martin's, 1994.
Pillar of Fire, St. Martin's, 1995.

OTHER

Contributor of short stories to *Ellery Queen's Mystery Magazine.* Stories collected in anthologies, including *Best Detective Stories of the Year 1975,* Dutton, 1976; *The Deadly Arts,* Arbor House, 1985; and *Murder California Style,* St. Martin's, 1987.

WORK IN PROGRESS: Novels.

SIDELIGHTS: Robert Irvine's early novels drew on his extensive experience as a television newsman. In a four-volume mystery series that includes *Jump Cut, Freeze Frame, Horizontal Hold,* and *Ratings are Murder,* he featured a character named Bob Christopher, a reporter for a Los Angeles TV station. Christopher is described by Jon L. Breen in *Twentieth-Century Crime and Mystery Writers* as "an animal lover with a persistent weight problem whose bleeding heart is ill-concealed by a wisecracking front." In *Freeze Frame,* the plot concerns corporate wrongdoing; *Horizontal Hold* turns on the murder of an anchorman; and *Ratings Are Murder* provides a murder mystery overlaid with plenty of satire about competition for television ratings. In *Barking Dogs,* Irvine created a new detective team—a tough, female reporter, Vicki Garcia, and Kevin Manwaring, a rebel television producer. In the story, the pair investigates a fire that killed a cultish offshoot of the Church of Latter-Day Saints, also known as the Mormon Church. *Barking Dogs* prompted a *Publishers Weekly* reviewer to describe Irvine as "a writer who is alternately warm and cynical, but always knowing."

Mormonism is central to Irvine's best-known work, the "Moroni Traveler" detective series, set in Salt Lake City. The author was born in that city, which is the seat of the Mormon faith and where, according to Wes Lukowsky in *Booklist,* "life is touched on all levels by the Mormon church." The protagonist of the series—described by Lukowsky as "Salt Lake City's contemporary version of Philip Marlowe"—is named after an ancient prophet revered by the Mormons. He has fallen away from his ancestral faith, making him an outsider in his home town. According to a *New York Times Book Review* contributor, he is "a true rebel hero in the classic private-eye tradition."

The rigid and powerful church establishment is sometimes the villain in these stories; at other times it is Traveler's client. In *Called Home,* Traveler is hired by a resident of a small Mormon town to investigate a suicide. The detective's work is complicated when the whole town closes ranks against him due to his lack of faith. *Called Home* was praised by *Armchair Detective* critic Allen J. Hobin as "a marvelous achievement: evocative, graphic, intense, and involving," and as "an impressive picture of a slice of Latter-day Saints society." In *The Great Reminder,* Traveler goes up against the church's disapproval of probing into the past when he is hired by a man who wishes to repay a debt to a missing person who may have passed away years ago. A subplot involves a missing child who could be Moroni's son. "Irvine expertly unravels a skein of decades-old mysteries in a satisfying addition to his unusual, solid series," affirmed a *Publishers Weekly* reviewer.

Pillars of Fire is singled out by many commentators as one of the strongest entries in the Traveler series. In this book, the detective is hired by the church to investigate Jason Thurgood, a faith healer and cult leader. In another *Booklist* review, Lukowsky declared: "the eighth Traveler mystery is one of the best. It's carefully plotted, there's a touching romantic tryst . . . and . . . some much-needed, wisecracking humor." "Irvine expertly mines his setting for the narrative riches of myth, superstition and religious history," noted a *Publishers Weekly* writer. "His Traveler stories consistently offer thoughtful entertainment."

Irvine told *CA:* "My writing career began in 'the classical manner,' as a reporter assigned to obituaries on a small daily newspaper. Three years later, I was with a large newspaper on the day John Kennedy was shot. The story bewildered my boss, who turned on his television set to see what was happening. In that instant I decided I was in the wrong business. I wanted to be where the action was—in television. I joined a local television station. At that point, however, the station changed anchormen, opting for a ratings-grabber who was part politician, part actor, but never a journalist. I had to flee, landing at KNX-Radio, where I worked my way to the top job and planned the station's transition to an all-news format.

"But television was still my first love, or so I thought. So when the chance came to make the switch, I jumped, this time landing with KABC-TV. Thus, within the space of seven years, I had risen from the dead (obituaries) to news director of one of [the] country's biggest television stations. But, by then, television news had become big business, too important to be trusted to the journalists. The salesman saw to it that show business was substituted for journalism, money for integrity, and power—corrupting power—for sanity. I took refuge in fiction."

BIOGRAPHICAL/CRITICAL SOURCES:

BOOKS

Twentieth Century Crime and Mystery Writers, St. James Press (Chicago), 1991.

PERIODICALS

Armchair Detective, summer, 1986, pp. 244-45; spring, 1992, p. 152.

Booklist, May 15, 1992, p. 1665; July, 1993, p. 1947; March 1, 1994, p. 1184; November 15, 1995, p. 537.

Library Journal, June 1, 1989, p. 151; March 1, 1994, p. 123; October 1, 1994, p. 119; November 1, 1995, p. 110.

Los Angeles Times Book Review, November 12, 1995, p. 11.

New York Times Book Review, April 29, 1990, p. 18; June 24, 1990, p. 22; July 5, 1992, p. 17.

Publishers Weekly, May 19, 1989, p. 71; May 4, 1990, p. 57; April 12, 1991, p. 46; April 26, 1991, p. 58; April 27, 1992, p. 256; May 10, 1993, p. 53; February 21, 1994, pp. 236-37; August 22, 1994, p. 44; September 25, 1995, p. 46.*

J

JACKSON, Dave
See JACKSON, J. David

* * *

JACKSON, J. David 1944-
(Dave Jackson)

PERSONAL: Born July 16, 1944, in Glendale, CA; son of Louis (an aircraft metalworker) and Helen (a homemaker) Jackson; married Neta Thiessen (a writer), October 15, 1966; children: Julian, Rachel Berg, Samantha Sang (a Cambodian foster daughter). *Education:* Judson College, B.A., 1969. *Politics:* Independent. *Religion:* Christian. *Avocational interests:* Bow hunting, fishing, vegetable gardening, camping, mountain bike riding, watching *Mystery* and *Masterpiece Theater* on PBS.

ADDRESSES: Home and office—917 Ashland Ave., Evanston, IL 60202.

CAREER: David C. Cook Publishing Co., Elgin, IL, editor, 1980-85; freelance writer, 1985—. Member of pastoral staff at Reba Place Church, 1973-82.

MEMBER: Children's Reading Round Table (Chicago, IL).

AWARDS, HONORS: Silver Angel Award, Excellence in Media, 1994, for *Listen for the Whippoorwill,* and 1995, for *Attack in the Rye Grass;* Gold Medallion Award, Evangelical Christian Publishers Association, 1994, for *Breaking Down Walls: A Model for Reconciliation in an Age of Racial Strife;* Best Children's Book of the Year, Christian Booksellers Association, 1995, for the "Trailblazer" series; Best Children's Book, Christian Booksellers New Zealand, 1995, for the "Trailblazer" series; C. S. Lewis Award for Best Series, 1995, for the "Trailblazer" series.

WRITINGS:

FOR CHILDREN

(With wife, Neta Jackson) *Hero Tales: A Family Treasury of True Stories from the Lives of Christian Heroes,* Bethany House (Minneapolis, MN), 1996.

"TRAILBLAZER" SERIES; WITH WIFE NETA JACKSON; ILLUSTRATED BY SON, JULIAN JACKSON

The Queen's Smuggler, Bethany House, 1991.
Kidnapped by River Rats, Bethany House, 1991.
Spy for the Night Raiders, Bethany House, 1992.
The Hidden Jewel, Bethany House, 1992.
Escape from the Slave Traders, Bethany House, 1992.
The Chimney Sweep's Ransom, Bethany House, 1992.
The Bandit of Ashley Downs, Bethany House, 1993.
Imprisoned in the Golden City, Bethany House, 1993.
Shanghaied to China, Bethany House, 1993.
Listen for the Whippoorwill, Bethany House, 1993.

Attack in the Rye Grass, Bethany House, 1994.
Trial by Poison, Bethany House, 1994.
Flight of the Fugitives, Bethany House, 1994.
The Betrayer's Fortune, Bethany House, 1994.
Abandoned on the Wild Frontier, Bethany House, 1995.
Danger on the Flying Trapeze, Bethany House, 1995.
The Thieves of Tyburn Square, Bethany House, 1995.
The Runaway's Revenge, Bethany House, 1995.
Quest for the Lost Prince, Bethany House, 1996.
The Warrior's Challenge, Bethany House, 1996.
Traitor in the Tower, Bethany House, 1996.
The Drummer Boy's Battle, Bethany House, 1996.

Several titles in the "Trailblazer" series have been translated into various languages, including German, Norwegian, Korean, Spanish, and Swedish.

"SECRET ADVENTURE" SERIES; WITH NETA JACKSON; ILLUSTRATED BY JULIAN JACKSON

Spin: Truth, Tubas, and George Washington, Broadman (Nashville, TN), 1994.
Snap: How to Act Like a Responsible Almost Adult, Broadman, 1994.
Smash: How to Survive Junior High by Really Trying, Broadman, 1994.
Snag: I'm Dreaming of a Right Christmas, Broadman, 1994.

"STORYBOOKS FOR CARING PARENTS" SERIES, ILLUSTRATED BY SUSAN LEXA

Scared, But Not Too Scared to Think, Chariot Books (Elgin, IL), 1985.
Bored, But Not Too Bored (to Pretend), Chariot Books, 1985.
Tired, But Not Too Tired (to Finish), Chariot Books, 1985.
Angry, But Not Too Angry (to Talk), Chariot Books, 1985.
Shy, But Not Too Shy, Chariot Books, 1986.
Stubborn, But Not Too Stubborn, Chariot Books, 1986.
Disappointed, But Not Too Disappointed, Chariot Books, 1986.
Unfair, But Not Too Unfair, Chariot Books, 1986.

The "Storybooks for Caring Parents" series has been translated into Chinese.

FOR ADULTS

Coming Together, Bethany House, 1978.
Dial 911: Peaceful Christians and Urban Violence, Herald Press, 1981.
(With Patricia Brandt) *Just Me and the Kids: A Course for Single Parents,* D. C. Cook (Elgin, IL), 1985.
(With Matthew and Lea Dacy) *Teen Pregnancy,* D. C. Cook, 1989.
Lost River Conspiracy, Good Books (Intercourse, PA), 1995.

FOR ADULTS; WITH NETA JACKSON

Living Together in a World Falling Apart, Creation House (Carol Stream, IL), 1974.
(Editor) *Storehouse of Family-Time Ideas: Fall and Winter,* D. C. Cook, 1987.
(Editor) *Storehouse of Family-Time Ideas: Spring and Summer,* D. C. Cook, 1987.
(And with Ed Hurst) *Overcoming Homosexuality,* D. C. Cook, 1987.
Glimpses of Glory: Thirty Years of Community: The Story of Reba Place Fellowship, Brethren Press (Elgin, IL), 1987.
(And with Brother Andrew) *A Time for Heroes,* Vine Books (Ann Arbor, MI), 1988.
(And with Kenneth E. Schemmer) *Between Life and Death: The Life-Support Dilemma,* Victor Books (Wheaton, IL), 1988.
(And with Grace A. Wenger) *Witness: Empowering the Church through Worship, Community, and Mission,* Herald Press (Scottdale, PA), 1989.
On Fire for Christ: Stories of Anabaptist Martyrs, Herald Press, 1989.
(Editors with Beth Landis) *The Gift of Presence: Stories that Celebrate Nurses Serving in the Name of Christ,* Herald Press, 1991.
(And with Gordon R. McLean) *Cities of Lonesome Fear,* Moody Press (Chicago, IL), 1991.
(And with Kenneth E. Schemmer) *Tinkering with People* ("What You Need to Know about the Medical Ethics Crisis" Series), Scripture Press, 1992.
(And with Howard Jones) *Heritage & Hope: The Legacy and Future of the Black Family in America,* Victor Books, 1992.
(And with Steve Wilke) *When We Can't Talk Anymore: Stories about Couples Who Learned to Communicate Again* ("Recovering Hope in Your Marriage" Series), Living Books (Wheaton, IL), 1992.

(And with Wilke) *When Its Hard to Trust,* Tyndale House, 1992.
(And with John D. Bradley) *Switching Tracks: Advancing Through Five Crucial Phases of Your Career,* Fleming H. Revell (Grand Rapids, MI), 1994.
(And with Raleigh Washington and Glen Kehrein) *Breaking Down Walls: A Model for Reconciliation in an Age of Racial Strife,* Moody Press, 1994.
(And with Steve Wilke) *When Alcohol Abuses Our Marriage,* New Leaf Press, 1995.
(And with Wilke) *When the Odds Are Against Us,* New Leaf Press, 1995.
(And with Wilke) *When We Fight All the Time,* New Leaf Press, 1995.

Living Together in a World Falling Apart has been translated into Swedish and Finnish.

WORK IN PROGRESS: Research on circuit-riding preachers in the early 1800s; a second volume of *Hero Tales.*

SIDELIGHTS: An author of juvenile fiction and adult self-help books, Dave Jackson has received widespread commendation for his fictional biographies about young men and women whose lives are influenced by historical Christian figures. Jackson is perhaps best known for the "Trailblazer" series of books he initiated with his wife and coauthor Neta Jackson in 1991. The "Trailblazer" works are fictionalized biographies of men and women whose pioneering efforts left a significant mark on history and Christianity.

In addition to coauthoring the "Trailblazer" series, Jackson and his wife teamed to create a collection of "Secret Adventure" books featuring lively action designed to teach children Christian virtues and underscore positive values. The same thematic emphasis permeates Jackson's *Lost River Conspiracy,* a story about a young Mennonite man who becomes involved in a fierce Indian war. While traveling home to Lost River, Oregon, Abraham Miller meets a young pioneer named Mary and her father. When Miller hears that a war has broken out near Mary's home, he decides to try to help diffuse the situation between the Modoc tribe and the United States Army. Miller, acting as a go-between for the Army's Peace Commission and the Modoc warriors, tries to resolve the conflict. After his peace-keeping efforts fail and war erupts, Miller chooses to remain with the Indian tribe and attempt to right the many injustices they suffered at the hands of the United States government. Writing in *Voice of Youth Advocates,* Lisa Prolman commended Jackson's ability to create a character who "shows how a person can stand for his or her beliefs even when those beliefs run counter to majority opinion." Although admitting the book's opening was "slow-going," Prolman also said that she found the book "compelling" after a few chapters and appreciated the afterword about the history of the Modoc uprising in 1872. In *Booklist,* a critic found Jackson's recreation of Captain Jack and Scarface Charley, two famous Modoc warriors, "very much to life." Furthermore, the critic praised Jackson's "sure sense" of northern Nevada and the lava beds into which the defeated Indians retreat.

BIOGRAPHICAL/CRITICAL SOURCES:

PERIODICALS

Booklist, April 1, 1995, p. 1391; September 1, 1995, p. 56; November 1, 1995, p. 455; January 1, 1996, p. 834; March 15, 1996, p. 1264.
Bookstore Journal, October, 1994, p. 99.
Christianity Today, November 9, 1992, p. 76.
Los Angeles Times Book Review, September 7, 1986.
School Library Journal, December, 1995, p. 104.
Voice of Youth Advocates, April, 1996, p. 26.

* * *

JACKSON, John N(icholas) 1925-

PERSONAL: Born December 15, 1925, in Nottingham, England; son of Alexander (a teacher and clergyperson) and Phyllis E. (Oldfield) Jackson; married Kathleen M. Nussey, May, 1951; children: Andrew, Susan, Paul. *Education:* University of Birmingham, B.A., 1949; University of Manchester, Ph.D., 1960. *Religion:* Anglican.

ADDRESSES: Home—80 Marsdale Dr., St. Catharines, Ontario L2T 353, Canada.

CAREER: Herefordshire County Council, Herefordshire, England, research officer, 1950-53;

Hull County Borough, Hull, England, senior planning assistant, 1954-56; University of Manchester, Manchester, England, lecturer in town and country planning, 1956-65; Brock University, St. Catharines, Ontario, professor of applied geography, 1965-91, professor emeritus, 1991—, head of department, 1965-70. *Military service:* Royal Navy (British).

WRITINGS:

Surveys for Town and Country Planning, Hutchinson University Library, 1963.

Recreational Development and the Lake Erie Shore, Niagara Region Development Council, 1968.

The Industrial Structure of the Niagara Region, Brock University (St. Catharines, Ontario), 1971.

The Canadian City: Space, Form, Quality, McGraw-Ryerson, 1972.

(Editor with J. Forrester) *Practical Geography,* McGraw-Ryerson, 1972.

Welland and the Welland Canal, Mika, 1975.

St. Catharines, Ontario: Its Early Years, Mika, 1976.

A Planning Appraisal of the Welland Urban Community, Department of Public Works (Ottawa), 1976.

Land Use Planning in the Niagara Region, Niagara Region Study Review Commission, 1976.

(With John Burtniak) *Railways in the Niagara Peninsula,* Mika, 1976.

(Contributor) Lorne H. Russwurm and Ken B. Beesley, editors, *The Rural-Urban Fringe: Canadian Perspectives,* Department of Geography, Atkinson College, York University, 1981.

(With Fred A. Addis) *The Welland Canals: A Comprehensive Guide,* Welland Canals Foundation, 1982.

The Four Welland Canals: A Journey of Discovery in St. Catharines and Thorold, Vanwell Publishing, 1988.

Names across Niagara, Vanwell Publishing, 1989.

(With Sheila M. Wilson) *St. Catharines: Canada's Canal City,* St. Catharines Standard (St. Catharines, Ontario), 1992.

The Welland Canals and Their Communities: Engineering, Industrial, and Urban Transformation, University of Toronto Press (Toronto, Ontario), 1997.

JACKSON, Neta J. 1944-

PERSONAL: Born October 26, 1944, in Winchester, KY; daughter of Isaac (a school administrator) and Margaret (a teacher) Thiessen; married Dave Jackson, October 15, 1966; children: Julian, Rachel Berg, Samantha Sang (a Cambodian foster daughter). *Education:* Wheaton College, B.A., 1966. *Politics:* Independent. *Religion:* Christian. *Avocational interests:* Horseback riding, flower gardening, camping, mountain bike riding, watching *Mystery* and *Masterpiece Theater* on PBS, genealogy, creating photo albums.

ADDRESSES: Home and office—917 Ashland Ave., Evanston, IL 60202.

CAREER: David C. Cook Publishing Co., Elgin, IL, editor, 1980-85; freelance writer, 1985—.

MEMBER: Children's Reading Round Table (Chicago, IL).

AWARDS, HONORS: Silver Angel Award, Excellence in Media, 1994, for *Listen for the Whippoorwill,* and 1995, for *Attack in the Rye Grass;* Gold Medallion Award, Evangelical Christian Publishers Association, 1994, for *Breaking Down Walls: A Model for Reconciliation in an Age of Racial Strife;* Christian Booksellers Association, Best Children's Book of the Year, 1995, for the "Trailblazer" series; Best Children's Book, Christian Booksellers New Zealand, 1995, for the "Trailblazer" series; C. S. Lewis Award for Best Series, 1995, for the "Trailblazer" series.

WRITINGS:

FOR CHILDREN

Loving One Another—Beginner's Stories on Being a Good Friend, Questar Publishers (Sisters, OR), 1994.

(With husband, Dave Jackson) *Hero Tales: A Family Treasury of True Stories from the Lives of Christian Heroes,* Bethany House (Minneapolis, MN), 1996.

"TRAILBLAZER" SERIES; WITH HUSBAND, DAVE JACKSON; ILLUSTRATED BY SON, JULIAN JACKSON

The Queen's Smuggler, Bethany House, 1991.

Kidnapped by River Rats, Bethany House, 1991.

Spy for the Night Raiders, Bethany House, 1992.

The Hidden Jewel, Bethany House, 1992.
Escape from the Slave Traders, Bethany House, 1992.
The Chimney Sweep's Ransom, Bethany House, 1992.
The Bandit of Ashley Downs, Bethany House, 1993.
Imprisoned in the Golden City, Bethany House, 1993.
Shanghaied to China, Bethany House, 1993.
Listen for the Whippoorwill, Bethany House, 1993.
Attack in the Rye Grass, Bethany House, 1994.
Trial by Poison, Bethany House, 1994.
Flight of the Fugitives, Bethany House, 1994.
The Betrayer's Fortune, Bethany House, 1994.
Abandoned on the Wild Frontier, Bethany House, 1995.
Danger on the Flying Trapeze, Bethany House, 1995.
The Thieves of Tyburn Square, Bethany House, 1995.
The Runaway's Revenge, Bethany House, 1995.
Quest for the Lost Prince, Bethany House, 1996.
The Warrior's Challenge, Bethany House, 1996.
Traitor in the Tower, Bethany House, 1996.
The Drummer Boy's Battle, Bethany House, 1996.

Several titles in the "Trailblazer" series have been translated into various languages, including German, Norwegian, Korean, Spanish, and Swedish.

"SECRET ADVENTURE" SERIES; WITH DAVE JACKSON; ILLUSTRATED BY JULIAN JACKSON

Spin: Truth, Tubas, and George Washington, Broadman (Nashville), 1994.
Snap: How to Act Like a Responsible Almost Adult, Broadman, 1994.
Smash: How to Survive Junior High by Really Trying, Broadman, 1994.
Snag: I'm Dreaming of a Right Christmas, Broadman, 1994.

"PET PARABLES" SERIES

The Parrot Who Talked Too Much, Multnomah Press (Portland, OR), 1991.
The Hamster Who Got Himself Stuck, Multnomah Press, 1991.
The Cat Who Smelled Like Cabbage, Multnomah Press, 1991.
The Dog Who Loved to Race, Multnomah Press, 1991.

FOR ADULTS

A New Way to Live, Herald Press, 1983.
Building Christian Relationships, Bethany House, 1984.
Who's Afraid of a Virgin, Wolf?, Meriwether Publishers (Colorado Springs, CO), 1991.
From Sod Shanty to State Senate (a biography of C.R. Thiessen), Castle Rock Publishers (Evanston, IL), 1992.

FOR ADULTS; WITH DAVE JACKSON

Living Together in a World Falling Apart, Creation House (Carol Stream, IL), 1974.
(Editor) *Storehouse of Family-Time Ideas: Fall and Winter,* D. C. Cook (Elgin, IL), 1987.
(Editor) *Storehouse of Family-Time Ideas: Spring and Summer,* D. C. Cook, 1987.
(And with Ed Hurst) *Overcoming Homosexuality,* D. C. Cook, 1987.
Glimpses of Glory: Thirty Years of Community: The Story of Reba Place Fellowship, Brethren Press (Elgin, IL), 1987.
(And with Brother Andrew) *A Time for Heroes,* Vine Books (Ann Arbor, MI), 1988.
(And with Kenneth E. Schemmer) *Between Life and Death: The Life-Support Dilemma,* Victor Books (Wheaton, IL), 1988.
(And with Grace A. Wenger) *Witness: Empowering the Church through Worship, Community, and Mission,* Herald Press (Scottdale, PA), 1989.
On Fire for Christ: Stories of Anabaptist Martyrs, Retold from Martyrs Mirror, Herald Press, 1989.
(Editor with Beth Landis) *The Gift of Presence: Stories that Celebrate Nurses Serving in the Name of Christ,* Herald Press, 1991.
(And with Gordon R. McLean) *Cities of Lonesome Fear,* Moody Press (Chicago), 1991.
(And with Kenneth E. Schemmer) *Tinkering with People* ("What You Need to Know about the Medical Ethics Crisis" Series), Scripture Press, 1992.
(And with Howard Jones) *Heritage & Hope: The Legacy and Future of the Black Family in America,* Victor Books, 1992.
(And with Steve Wilke) *When We Can't Talk Anymore: Stories about Couples Who Learned to Communicate Again* ("Recovering Hope in Your Marriage" Series), Living Books (Wheaton, IL), 1992.
(And with Wilke) *When Its Hard to Trust,* Tyndale House, 1992.

(And with John D. Bradley) *Switching Tracks: Advancing Through Five Crucial Phases of Your Career,* Fleming H. Revell (Grand Rapids, MI), 1994.
(And with Raleigh Washington and Glen Kehrein) *Breaking Down Walls: A Model for Reconciliation in an Age of Racial Strife,* Moody Press, 1994.
(And with Steve Wilke) *When Alcohol Abuses Our Marriage,* New Leaf Press, 1995.
(And with Wilke) *When the Odds Are Against Us,* New Leaf Press, 1995.
(And with Wilke) *When We Fight All the Time,* New Leaf Press, 1995.

Living Together in a World Falling Apart has been translated into Swedish and Finnish.

WORK IN PROGRESS: Research on circuit-riding preachers in the early 1800s.

SIDELIGHTS: One-half of a husband-wife writing duo, Neta J. Jackson is the coauthor of several series of children's books, including one focusing on the lives of important Christian figures in history. Interestingly, Jackson told *Bookstore Journal* that while growing up, she never aspired to be a writer, but instead an artist. "I loved to draw and was horse-crazy as a kid. . . . But in junior high, I started writing stories about horses instead of just drawing them. Eventually, my interest in writing stories overtook my interest in art."

Along with her husband Dave, Jackson began the "Trailblazer" series in 1991, a fictionalized biography series about men and women who had a significant impact on history and Christianity, such as Harriet Tubman, Martin Luther, and Menno Simons. In *The Betrayer's Fortune,* for instance, fifteen-year-old Adriaen begins to question his Anabaptist faith when his mother is imprisoned for her beliefs. Set in the early 1500s, the story shows how a young man struggles with his faith in a God who allows suffering among His followers. Writing in *Booklist,* Shelly Townsend-Hudson praises the "compelling" plot which follows the growth of "an initially unsympathetic boy into a courageous young man."

Jackson tries to teach readers about history by creating fictional characters whose lives are influenced by real men and women from the past. *Danger on the Flying Trapeze* features a fourteen-year-old boy who convinces his mother to join a traveling circus after his father dies. While preforming at the Chicago World's Fair, Casey loses his courage on the trapeze bar after a bad fall. However, he happens to meet the evangelist D. L. Moody who encourages him to try the stunt again. Casey succeeds and decides to continue following the teachings of Moody. While in a *Booklist* review Townsend-Hudson complains that the references to Moody are slight, not allowing the reader to "gain a real sense of the man," she does go on to say that Jackson's biographical sketch of Moody "will interest some readers." In *School Library Journal,* Renee Steinberg contends that "the message is heavy-handed and the characters are flat," but she is enthusiastic about the dramatic events in the book, saying "there is a lot of action."

Jackson told *CA* that the "burning issue" she and her husband share is "the need to confront racism in ourselves and our culture, and to work for racial reconciliation in every area of our lives—but especially the church."

BIOGRAPHICAL/CRITICAL SOURCES:

PERIODICALS

Booklist, April, 1, 1995, p. 1391; September 1, 1995, pp. 54, 56; January 1, 1996, p. 834; March 15, 1996, p. 1264.
Bookstore Journal, October, 1994, p. 99.
Christianity Today, November 9, 1992, p. 76.
School Library Journal, December, 1995, p. 104.

* * *

JACOBS, William Jay 1933-

PERSONAL: Born August 23, 1933, in Cincinnati, OH; son of Louis (a merchant) and Fannie (a homemaker; maiden name, Kletter) Jacobs; married Phoebe Lloyd (an art historian), November 27, 1959 (marriage ended); married Susan Meyers (a professor); children: (first marriage) Catherine Elizabeth, Adam Eleazar. *Education:* University of Cincinnati, B.A. (history; with high honors), 1955, M.A., 1956; Columbia University, Ed.D., 1963; graduate study at Rutgers University. *Politics:* Social Democrat. *Religion:* "Ethical Humanist within the Judaeo-Christian tradition." *Avocational interests:* Travel, including past visits to the People's Republic of China, Cuba, India, Northern Africa, and the Soviet Union.

ADDRESSES: Home and office—William Jay Jacobs Associates, Inc., 5 Mayfair Ln., Westport, CT 06880.

CAREER: Hamilton County Public Schools, Hamilton County, OH, teacher of American and European history, 1956-58; Walden School, New York City, history teacher, 1959-60; River Dell Regional Schools, Oradell, NJ, chairman of department of history, 1960-64; Hofstra University, Hempstead, NY, assistant professor of education, 1964-65; Rutgers University, New Brunswick, NJ, assistant professor of social studies education, 1965-68, associate director of NDEA Institute in History, 1966; Harvard University, Cambridge, MA, master teacher in Master of Arts in Teaching Program, 1967; Job Corps Plans and Programs, Washington, DC, special assistant to the chief, 1967-68; Hunter College of the City University of New York, New York City, associate professor of social studies education, 1968-70; Ramapo College of New Jersey, Mahwah, professor of education and director of Division of Teacher Education and Physical Education, 1970-73, distinguished visiting professor of education, 1973-74; Darien Public Schools, Darien, CT, coordinator of history and the social sciences, 1975-93. William Jay Jacobs Associates, Inc. (educational consultants), Stamford, CT, president, 1974—. Adjunct teacher or graduate assistant at University of Cincinnati, Rutgers University, Brooklyn College of the City University of New York, Columbia University, and Harvard University. Member of Joint Committee of National Council for the Social Studies (NCSS) and the Children's Book Council (CBC), 1984-88; member of National Advisory Board for World Federalist Association; member of National Advisory Council for the Social Democrats. Consultant to publishers, including McGraw's Junior Book Division, 1965-75, Holt, Macmillan, Glencoe, and Scholastic.

MEMBER: American Historical Association, Authors Guild, Authors League of America, Phi Beta Kappa.

AWARDS, HONORS: William Howard Taft Fellow in History, 1956; *World Book Encyclopedia* Fellow, 1963; Ford Foundation Fellow, 1967-68; Yale University Visiting Fellow, 1977-78, 1980-91, 1989-90, and 1992-96; Notable Children's Books in Social Studies selection, National Council for the Social Studies and Children's Book Council, and Best Children's Books of 1979 selection, Child Study Association, both 1979, both for *Mother, Aunt Susan and Me: The First Fight for Women's Rights;* Fulbright Fellow in India, 1980; Child Study Association Best Children's Books of 1983 selection, and Books Across the Sea selection, both 1983, both for *Eleanor Roosevelt: A Life of Happiness and Tears;* Urban League Educational Award for Contributions to Intergroup Understanding, 1983; National Endowment for the Humanities Fellow, 1983; Academic Freedom Award, Northeast Regional Council for the Social Studies, 1988; Woodrow Wilson Fellow in History, 1989; Notable Children's Books in Social Studies selection, 1990, for *Ellis Island: New Hope in a New Land.*

WRITINGS:

FOR CHILDREN

Search for Freedom: America and Its People, Glencoe (New York City), 1973, new edition, 1982.
Hannibal: An African Hero, McGraw (New York City), 1973.
Edgar Allan Poe: Genius in Torment, McGraw, 1975.
Women in American History, Glencoe, 1976.
Mother, Aunt Susan and Me: The First Fight for Women's Rights, Coward (New York City), 1979.
Eleanor Roosevelt: A Life of Happiness and Tears, Coward, 1983.
Ellis Island: New Hope in a New Land, Scribner (New York City), 1990.
Washington, Scribner, 1991.
Lincoln, Scribner, 1991.
Mother Teresa: Helping the Poor, Millbrook Press (Brookfield, CT), 1991.
War with Mexico, Millbrook Press, 1993.
Search for Peace: The Story of the United Nations, Scribner, 1994.
They Shaped the Game: Ty Cobb, Babe Ruth, Jackie Robinson, Scribner, 1994.
Dwight D. Eisenhower: Soldier and Statesman, F. Watts (New York City), 1995.

"VISUALIZED BIOGRAPHY" SERIES

Prince Henry the Navigator, F. Watts, 1973.
Hernando Cortes, F. Watts, 1974.

Samuel de Champlain, F. Watts, 1974.
William Bradford of Plymouth Colony, F. Watts, 1974.
Roger Williams, F. Watts, 1975.
Robert Cavelier de La Salle, F. Watts, 1975.

"TWENTIETH CENTURY BIOGRAPHIES" SERIES

Hitler, Glencoe, 1976.
Churchill, Glencoe, 1976.
Stalin, Glencoe, 1976.
Mussolini, Glencoe, 1980.
Truman, Glencoe, 1980.
Roosevelt, Glencoe, 1980.

"FIRST BOOK" SERIES

Cortes: Conqueror of Mexico, F. Watts, 1994.
LaSalle: A Life of Boundless Adventure, F. Watts, 1994.
Pizarro: Conqueror of Peru, F. Watts, 1994.
Champlain: A Life of Courage, F. Watts, 1994.
Magellan: Voyager with a Dream, F. Watts, 1994.
Coronado: Dreamer in Golden Armor, F. Watts, 1994.

"GREAT LIVES" SERIES

Human Rights, Scribner, 1990.
World Government, Scribner, 1992.
World Religions, Scribner, 1996.

OTHER

Mill River Bridge at Main Street and Other Poems, Byzantium Press, 1986.
America's Story (textbook), Houghton (Boston), 1990.
History of the United States: Beginnings to 1877 (textbook), Houghton, 1992.

Contributor to *World Book Encyclopedia* and *The New Book of Knowledge.* Contributor of more than forty articles and reviews to education journals and other magazines, including *Teachers College Record, Ms., People, New York Times Book Review, Urban Review,* and *Horn Book.* Children's book review editor of *Teachers College Record,* 1966-69. Member of National Board of Advisors, 1980-84, and book review editor, 1986-88, for *Social Education;* member of National Advisory Board for *Biography Today* (magazine).

WORK IN PROGRESS: A book on baseball pitchers.

SIDELIGHTS: The many historical accounts and biographies by William Jay Jacobs introduce children and young adults to significant events and figures throughout the course of American history. In such works as *Mother, Aunt Susan and Me: The First Fight for Women's Rights, Eleanor Roosevelt: A Life of Happiness and Tears, Lincoln, Washington,* and *Search for Peace: The Story of the United Nations,* Jacobs provides both historical facts and data as well as descriptions of the personalities and qualities of the people involved; he brings Elizabeth Cady Stanton, Susan B. Anthony, Eleanor Roosevelt, Abraham Lincoln, George Washington, and several others to life for his young readers.

All of the history Jacobs researches and writes about is of special significance to him because of his family background. He told *CA:* "My mother came to America on her own from Austria at the age of twelve, becoming a household maid for the songwriter, Oscar Hammerstein. My father escaped from Hungary just before being taken into that country's army. On arrival in this country he became qualified for citizenship and joined the United States Army. Hence, America to me is more than just a place of residence. It is a passion."

This passion has led Jacobs to excel in his varied career, which includes several different levels of teaching, involvement in numerous groups, organizations, and causes, and extensive traveling throughout the world. Another major part of this career involves the writing of children's books. It was through another author, John R. Tunis, that Jacobs first realized his potential in this field. Having been influenced by Tunis's writing while he was growing up, Jacobs once told *CA:* "Many years later, as a college professor, it was my pleasure to know John Tunis personally. We became friends. As one outgrowth of that friendship I was able to refine my goals as a writer. Tunis helped me understand my potential contribution as a biographer and historian writing especially for children. He impressed me, too, with the importance of sheer hard work—research, revision, rewriting—involved in the production of a book, one ultimately worthy of young readers."

Out of this hard work has come a large library of historical books for young people. In *Mother, Aunt Susan and Me: The First Fight for Women's*

Rights Jacobs describes the women's rights leaders Elizabeth Cady Stanton and Susan B. Anthony through the voice of Stanton's daughter Harriot, who recounts their early efforts to get the vote for women and the beginnings of the struggle to get the Equal Rights Amendment passed. The first-person narrator, asserts a *Bulletin of the Center for Children's Books* contributor, gives *Mother, Aunt Susan and Me* "an intimacy and immediacy that make the details of the fight for equality vivid."

Personal aspects of Eleanor Roosevelt's life and character are also revealed in Jacobs's biography of this former first lady. Starting with Roosevelt's difficult childhood and moving through her transformation into adulthood, Jacobs provides insights into her relationships with her husband and children as well as describing her political and social influences. *Eleanor Roosevelt: A Life of Happiness and Tears,* writes Barbara Bader in *Kirkus Reviews,* is "a coherent, generally honest and affecting life of Eleanor Roosevelt for young people—as an unfavored child, and a deeply hurt wife, 'determined to live her own life.'" Joyce Milton similarly maintains in the *New York Times Book Review:* "Jacobs's biography gives us a woman who was a strong personality in her own right, and who had to face and resolve continuing conflicts between her own goals and the demands of being Mrs. Roosevelt and First Lady."

Portraits of two of America's most famous Presidents are given in Jacobs's 1991 works *Lincoln* and *Washington.* Once again, the author focuses on the personal traits of these great men, not just their historical achievements; descriptions of the qualities that made Lincoln and Washington great leaders make up the bulk of these brief biographies. *Booklist* contributor Kay Weisman states that Jacobs's "emphasis on personality development . . . will help young readers to appreciate the true significance of both great leaders."

Not all of Jacobs's history books are biographies, however. The author writes the history of an organization in *Search for Peace: The Story of the United Nations.* The history of war and conflict are described as part of the background for the United Nations, as well as the actual events that led to the founding of the organization. The group itself, and its complex structure and different agencies, as well as its future, are also discussed. *Search for Peace* "is intelligent, comprehensive, and well written," observes Julie Corsaro in *Booklist.*

One of Jacobs's personal interests—the game of baseball—is covered in his biography *They Shaped the Game: Ty Cobb, Babe Ruth, Jackie Robinson.* Descriptions of both the contributions to baseball and the controversial personal lives of all three of these well-known and influential sports figures make up this account. "Jacobs does a commendable job of presenting accurate, interesting information," points out Tom S. Hurlburt in *School Library Journal.* Susan DeRonne further states in *Booklist* that the "book includes interesting details about these men's lives and marriages as well as some simple philosophical musings about values and 'greatness.'"

It is the greatness of all his subjects that Jacobs tries to get across to his young audience. "Now, by creating textbooks and biographies, I am able to reach a very special audience: young people searching for models, trying to understand themselves," he once explained to *CA.* "My primary task, perhaps, is to introduce them to that great reservoir of recorded history from which our civilization has drawn inspiration. Clearly there are models—Hannibal and Jefferson and Lincoln; Galileo and Shakespeare and Gandhi and Jesus. Because of those past lives, and vicarious contact with them, the lives of young people can become fuller and richer. Presented in imaginative narrative form, people of past ages can provide companionship. They also can help today's readers retain what F. Scott Fitzgerald once described as a 'capacity for wonder.'"

BIOGRAPHICAL/CRITICAL SOURCES:

PERIODICALS

Booklist, September 15, 1979; July, 1990, p. 2091; September 1, 1991, p. 50; July, 1994, p. 1934; September 1, 1994, p. 38; January 15, 1995, p. 910.

Bulletin of the Center for Children's Books, September, 1975, p. 12; January, 1980; May, 1990, p. 215.

Kirkus Reviews, July 1, 1975, p. 720; September 15, 1979, p. 1070; November 1, 1983, p. J213.

New York Times Book Review, November 13, 1983, pp. 44, 53.

School Library Journal, March, 1975, p. 98; November, 1975, p. 91; February, 1984, p. 74; June, 1990, p. 131; July, 1991, p. 81; November, 1992, p. 129; January, 1994, p. 118; August, 1994, p. 163; February, 1995, p. 108.

Voice of Youth Advocates, October, 1990, p. 244; August, 1996, p. 179.

* * *

JACOBUS, Lee A. 1935-

PERSONAL: Born August 20, 1935, in Orange, NJ; son of Ernest W. and Julia R. Jacobus; married Joanna J. Miller (a massage therapist), April 5, 1958; children: Sharon Grania, James Diarmuid. *Education:* Brown University, A.B., 1957, A.M., 1959; Claremont University Center (now Claremont Graduate School), Ph.D., 1968. *Avocational interests:* Music (a lifelong piano student), art, photography, computers, drama.

ADDRESSES: Home—1 Meadow Wood Rd., Branford, CT 06405. *Office*—Department of English, University of Connecticut, U-25, Storrs, CT 06269.

CAREER: Mary C. Wheeler School, Providence, RI, teacher of English, 1959-60; Western Connecticut State College, Danbury, instructor in English, 1960-66; University of Connecticut, Storrs, assistant professor, 1968-71, associate professor, 1971-77, professor of English, 1977—. Summer instructor at Phillips Exeter Academy, 1962, and Columbia University, 1967; visiting professor at Brown University, 1981.

MEMBER: International James Joyce Society, Modern Language Association of America, American Committee for Irish Studies, Milton Society of America.

AWARDS, HONORS: Fellow of William Andrews Clark Memorial Library, University of California, Los Angeles, 1968; University of Connecticut Research Foundation grant, 1968, 1971, 1972; Connecticut Commission on the Arts grant, 1975-76; postdoctoral fellow, Yale University, 1982-83 and 1996-97.

WRITINGS:

Improving College Reading, Harcourt (New York City), 1967, 6th edition, 1992.

(Editor) *Issues and Response,* Harcourt, 1968, revised edition, 1972.

(Editor) *Aesthetics and the Arts,* McGraw (New York City), 1968.

Developing College Reading, Harcourt, 1970, 5th edition, 1995.

(Editor) *17 from Everywhere: Short Stories of the World,* Bantam (New York City), 1971.

(With William T. Moynihan) *Poems in Context,* Harcourt, 1974.

(With F. David Martin) *Humanities through the Arts,* McGraw, 1975, 5th edition, 1997.

John Cleveland, Twayne (Boston, MA), 1975.

(Contributor) Donald B. Gibson, editor, *Black American Poets,* Prentice-Hall (Englewood Cliffs, NJ), 1975.

Sudden Apprehension: Aspects of Knowledge in "Paradise Lost," Mouton (The Hague), 1976.

The Sentence Book, Harcourt, 1977, 3rd edition, 1989.

(Editor) *The Longman Anthology of American Drama,* Longman (New York City), 1982.

(Editor) *A World of Ideas,* St. Martin's (New York City), 1983, 4th edition, 1994.

Humanities: The Evolution of Values, McGraw, 1986.

The Bedford Introduction to Drama, St. Martin's 1989, 3rd edition, 1997.

Writing as Thinking, Macmillan, 1989.

Shakespeare and the Dialectic of Certainty, St. Martin's, 1992.

Literature: An Introduction to Critical Reading, Prentice-Hall, 1996.

The Compact Bedford Introduction to Drama, St. Martin's, 1996.

Teaching Literature: Theory and Practice, Prentice-Hall, 1996.

Advanced Composition, Oxford University Press (Oxford, England), 1998.

PLAYS

Fair Warning, produced in New York City at American Theatre for Actors, 1987.

Long Division, produced in New York City at American Theatre for Actors, 1988.

OTHER

Contributor of articles to scholarly journals and of

poems and short stories to literary magazines. Editor in chief, *LIT: Literature Interpretation Theory;* advisory editor, Oxford University Press, 1994—. Referee, *Rhetoric Review* and *Modern Language Studies.*

WORK IN PROGRESS: A novel, *Emma Now;* a book on Milton's use of Rhetoric and Logic.

SIDELIGHTS: Lee A. Jacobus told *CA:* "Most of my writing has been in the field of college textbooks. They grow naturally out of my teaching, which constantly presents me with opportunities for solving problems in ways that have not been tried before. I am committed to humanistic scholarship and values, and textbooks offer me a chance to touch many people at an age when they are likely to listen and learn. High quality texts are a kind of treasure, and I aim to add to that treasure as much as I can. Besides texts, I naturally write scholarship in the fields of seventeenth-century English literature and modern Irish literature. In addition, I have been writing plays, two of which were performed in New York in an Off-Broadway theater on 54th Street.

"After finishing my scholarly book on Shakespeare, I decided that I would return to fiction at my earliest opportunity. I am currently at work on a novel while working on a book on writing for Oxford University Press."

* * *

JAFFE, Rona 1932-

PERSONAL: Born June 12, 1932, in New York, NY; daughter of Samuel (an elementary school teacher and principal) and Diana (a teacher; maiden name, Ginsberg) Jaffe. *Education:* Radcliffe College, B.A., 1951.

ADDRESSES: Home—201 East 62nd St., New York, NY 10021. *Office*—c/o Ephraim London Buttenweiser, 875 Third Ave., New York, NY 10022. *Agent*—Janklow & Nesbit Associates, 598 Madison Ave., New York, NY 10022.

CAREER: File clerk and secretary, New York City, 1952; Fawcett Publications, New York City, associate editor, 1952-56; writer, 1956—. Associate producer of made-for-television movie *Mazes and Monsters,* CBS-TV, 1982. Founder of the Rona Jaffe Foundation; administrator of the Rona Jaffe Prizes in Creative Writing program at Radcliffe University.

WRITINGS:

NOVELS

The Best of Everything, Simon & Schuster (New York City), 1958.
Away from Home, Simon & Schuster, 1960.
The Cherry in the Martini, Simon & Schuster, 1966.
The Fame Game, Random House (New York City), 1969.
The Other Woman, Morrow (New York City), 1972.
Family Secrets, Simon & Schuster, 1974.
The Last Chance, Simon & Schuster, 1976.
Class Reunion: A Novel, Delacorte (New York City), 1979.
Mazes and Monsters: A Novel, Delacorte, 1981.
After the Reunion: A Novel, Delacorte, 1985.
An American Love Story, Delacorte, 1990.
The Cousins (Literary Guild and Doubleday Book Club selection), D. I. Fine (New York City), 1995.

OTHER

The Last of the Wizards (juvenile), Simon & Schuster, 1961.
Mr. Right Is Dead (novella and five short stories), Simon & Schuster, 1965.

Contributor of stories, essays, and articles to various magazines.

ADAPTATIONS: The Best of Everything was filmed in 1959 by Jerry Wald; *Mazes and Monsters* was adapted as a 1982 CBS-TV movie.

SIDELIGHTS: "In Rona Jaffe," notes Elaine Dundy in the *Times Literary Supplement,* "we have a good storyteller who is a good storywriter as well." Jaffe has written numerous bestsellers, including her first novel, *The Best of Everything.* The book, described by Judy Klemesrud in the *Chicago Tribune* as a "novel about New York career girls trying to sleep and claw their way out of the steno pool," brought the author both fame and fortune while still in her twenties.

In several ways *The Best of Everything* is like many of Jaffe's later novels. The book deals with life in New York City, focuses on conflicts in male/female relationships, and follows the stories of several main characters—three characteristics often found in her work. In one of Jaffe's most ambitious novels, *Family Secrets,* for example, some thirty-two characters appear over the course of the story.

Reviewers commenting on Jaffe's later books almost always compare the work being reviewed to Jaffe's first novel, thereby continuing interest in it. Written in the late fifties, the book has a distinctly pre-women's liberation movement slant which places it firmly in that decade. Although the women in *The Best of Everything* have jobs, they are not career women; men and the possibility of marrying one of them are far more important to these women than their work. At one point in the story one of the women characters thinks to herself: "It's hell to be a woman . . . ; to want so much love, to feel like only half a person, to need so much. What was it Plato had said? A man and a woman are each only half a person until they unite. Why hadn't he made that clearer to the men?"

Some critics, such as Judith Christ, objected to Jaffe's depiction of women in *The Best of Everything,* but the author asserts that the work gives an accurate picture of life in the fifties. According to Jaffe, the characters have much in common with people she knew or interviewed while doing research for the book. Jaffe explained to Klemesrud: In the fifties "girls were brought up to fulfill the image of what boys wanted. They feigned great interest in things they hated because they were only supposed to talk about the boys' interest. . . . They always tried to look their best. . . . It was all part of the fifties rat race toward the altar."

The fifties also play an important role in Jaffe's *Class Reunion,* a novel that has been described as an updated version of Mary McCarthy's story about coming of age in the 1930s, *The Group.* Alluding to McCarthy's title, a *Time* reviewer observes, "Change Vassar to Radcliffe, the '30s to the '50s, take away the wry tone, and you have Rona Jaffe's readable reworking, *Class Reunion.*" In her *Washington Post* review of the book, Lynn Darling notes that in the novel Jaffe "follows the trials and tribulations of eight members of the Class of '57 . . . as they try to crawl out from under the mind-numbing conformity of the '50s." Darling sees Jaffe's novels as a sort of exorcism of unpleasant memories. "Her observations," Darling comments, "are edged in irony, but like any veteran of a vicious war, past skirmishes are with her still, and she is still in the trenches."

In *Class Reunion* and other novels written since *The Best of Everything,* Jaffe deals with married as well as single women and how they cope with more significant dilemmas than how to catch a man. Divorce, cocaine addiction, teenage suicide, and other contemporary problems are dealt with in detail. But, while Jaffe's recent novels are praised for their readability as well as her skill in capturing the essence of life in New York City, reviews are often mixed.

In the *New York Times Book Review* Katha Pollitt, for example, calls *Class Reunion* "a wry and very readable tale," while in Eve Zibert's *Washington Post* review of the same book, the critic finds the novel "like a soap opera, . . . absorbing and embarrassing at the same time." And, while Nora Johnson in her essay on *The Last Chance* in the *New York Times Book Review* comments, "You have to keep reading Jaffe, she's competent and dependable, and she piles on the delicious details," in Nora Peck's review of *After the Reunion* appearing in the same journal, the critic notes, "Though the soul-searching in this novel may be on the level of [the television programs] "Dynasty' or "Dallas,' it proves equally entertaining."

An American Love Story, Jaffe's eleventh novel, took some particularly harsh blows from reviewers. "Rarely has a novel depressed me more, or made me feel older," declares Joyce Slater in the *Atlanta Journal-Constitution.* "One expects more of Ms. Jaffe, a pioneer in the genre we now call 'glitz.'" The novel's central character is Clay Bowen, a charismatic television producer, and the plot relates the unhappy fates of four women in his life: Laura, a ballerina who becomes his wife; Susan, a writer, who becomes his mistress; Bambi, an agent who supplants Susan; and Nina, Clay's daughter. All four "ooze talent and beauty," according to Slater, yet all nearly ruin their lives trying to hold onto Clay—even though, in the reviewer's opinion, "It's hard to understand why any sane woman would cross the street to spit on his shoes." *Boston Globe* reviewer Richard Dyer concurs that Clay's character is not well-realized;

in his words, the producer "seems to be a neutral screen onto which [the female characters] project their fantasies. . . . The effect of this . . . is disastrous," making the women in the story difficult to understand and, therefore, unsympathetic. Still, Dyer notes that *An American Love Story* "springs to momentary life when Jaffe writes about something she has actually experienced," citing "an amusing sequence depicting egos in conflict during the filming of a television miniseries." Ilene Cooper also praises Jaffe's sharp portrait of Hollywood life, and adds that even if the character of Clay is weak, the author "writes her women well."

Jaffe's next novel, *The Cousins,* was more favorably reviewed. In it, the author focused closely on one character, Olivia Okrent. A large cast of relatives provides a backdrop for Olivia's struggle to resolve a life crisis. The crisis is brought on by the infidelity of the man she loves and has lived with for ten years—Roger Hawkwood, her partner in a Manhattan veterinary practice. A *Washington Post Book World* writer claims to have experienced some frustration while reading the book because so many fascinating secondary characters are treated so briefly, but she concludes that "overall, *The Cousins* is very rewarding because the masterful Jaffe does such a good job of portraying Olivia, an honorable woman facing some tough choices." A *Publishers Weekly* contributor claims that many elements of the story may be familiar to Jaffe's fans, but goes on to say: "Fictional familiarity can breed contentment. . . . Jaffe has not lost her wit, her keen eye for human frailties and her ear for the small but telling remark."

While Leslie Garis does not propose a completely positive view of Jaffe's work, her *Ms.* review of *Family Secrets* does offer a brief summary of the qualities in Jaffe's writing that critics and readers alike find most appealing: "Breezy, immediate, conversational, elliptical—Rona Jaffe writes like [French novelist] Francoise Sagan's American cousin. She's more clean-cut, and less arrogant than Sagan, but their detachment, their simple statements that reduce complex emotional development to one measurable moment, their readiness to describe a childhood in a paragraph, are similar in spirit, if not in content. And when their subjects match their style, both writers carry it off brilliantly." In a *New York Times* interview with Alex Witchel, Jaffe commented that her own aim is always to "write more than a good story that in some ways can be helpful to women. If one little girl is sitting alone in a studio apartment thinking she's the only one having a tragic affair and realizes she's not, then it's worth it. And for me, certainly, books are always great company."

BIOGRAPHICAL/CRITICAL SOURCES:

BOOKS

Bestsellers 90, Issue 3, Gale (Detroit), 1990.

PERIODICALS

Atlanta Journal-Constitution, May 6, 1990, p. L9.
Booklist, February 15, 1990, p. 1121; July, 1995, p. 1836.
Book World, November 9, 1969.
Boston Globe, May 9, 1990, p. 92.
Chicago Tribune, May 27, 1968.
Cosmopolitan, September, 1985, p. 34.
Detroit News and Free Press, May 13, 1990.
Entertainment Weekly, September 22, 1995, p. 75.
Ladies Home Journal, December, 1981, p. 81.
Library Journal, August, 1995, p. 117.
Listener, January 25, 1968.
Los Angeles Times Book Review, November 10, 1985; July 27, 1986; April 15, 1990, p. 8.
Ms., November, 1974.
New Leader, November 7, 1966.
New Yorker, August 30, 1976.
New York Times, October 2, 1969; June 16, 1991, p. L18; November 8, 1995, p. C1.
New York Times Book Review, May 2, 1965; October 2, 1966; September 28, 1969; October 29, 1972; October 27, 1974; September 5, 1976; July 31, 1977; July 8, 1979; July 22, 1979; November 8, 1981; September 22, 1985.
Observer, March 8, 1970; June 8, 1975; October 17, 1976.
People, October 19, 1981, p. 117.
Publishers Weekly, March 2, 1990, p. 76; July 31, 1995, pp. 70-71.
Saturday Review, September 6, 1958; May 8, 1965.
Spectator, February 6, 1982.
Time, May 21, 1965; October 7, 1966; July 2, 1979.
Times Literary Supplement, February 1, 1968; August 8, 1975.
Virginia Quarterly Review, winter, 1977.
Wall Street Journal, November 29, 1985.
Washington Post, June 23, 1979.

Washington Post Book World, June 24, 1973; September 13, 1981; August 25, 1985; July 13, 1986; October 22, 1995, p. 8.

* * *

JANSEN, Jared
See CEBULASH, Mel

* * *

JOHNSON, Lois Walfrid 1936-

PERSONAL: Born November 23, 1936, in Starbuck, MN; daughter of Alvar Bernhard (a clergyman) and Lydia (a business manager and bookkeeper; maiden name, Christiansen) Walfrid; married Roy A. Johnson (an elementary school teacher and delinquency prevention counselor), June 26, 1959; children: Gail, Jeffrey, Kevin. *Education:* Gustavus Adolphus College, B. A. (magna cum laude), 1958; University of Oklahoma, graduate study, 1968-71. *Politics:* Independent. *Religion:* Christian. *Avocational interests:* Spending time with family and friends, hiking, biking, swimming, cross-country skiing, reading, listening to music, playing the piano, traveling, photography.

ADDRESSES: Office—c/o Bethany House, 11300 Hampshire Ave. S., Minneapolis, MN 55438.

CAREER: English teacher, Wayzata, MN, 1958-59; author and speaker, 1969—. Writer's Digest School, editorial associate, 1974-77. Teacher of writing for children and adults at schools, libraries, and universities. Presenter at writing workshops and conferences, 1971—.

MEMBER: Society of Children's Book Writers and Illustrators, Children's Reading Round Table of Chicago, Council for Wisconsin Writers.

AWARDS, HONORS: Distinguished Alumni Citation, Gustavus Adolphus College, 1983, for body of work; Gold Medallion, Evangelical Christian Publishers Association, and C. S. Lewis Medal for Best Series Published in 1988, both 1989, both for "Let's-Talk-about-It Stories for Kids" series, including *You're Worth More than You Think!, Secrets of the Best Choice, Thanks for Being My Friend, You Are Wonderfully Made!;* Book Award of Merit for Distinguished Service to History, State Historical Society of Wisconsin, 1991, "Adventures of the Northwoods" series; Silver Angel Award, Excellence in Media, 1991, for *The Disappearing Stranger,* 1992, for *Trouble at Wild River,* 1994, for *The Runaway Clown,* 1995, for *Disaster on Windy Hill,* and 1996, for *Escape into the Night;* Arthur Tofte Juvenile Book Award, Council for Wisconsin Writers, 1992, for *Trouble at Wild River;* Award of Merit, Excellence in Media, 1993, for *Grandpa's Stolen Treasure;* C. S. Lewis Honor Book (Silver Medal), 1995, for *Escape into the Night.*

WRITINGS:

FOR CHILDREN

Just a Minute, Lord, Augsburg (Minneapolis), 1973.
Aaron's Christmas Donkey (picture book), Augsburg, 1974.
Hello, God!: Prayers for Small Children (picture book), Augsburg, 1975.
You're My Best Friend, Lord, Augsburg, 1975.

"LET'S-TALK-ABOUT-IT STORIES FOR KIDS" SERIES

Secrets of the Best Choice, Navpress (Colorado Springs, CO), 1988.
You're Worth More Than You Think!, Navpress, 1988.
Thanks for Being My Friend, Navpress, 1988.
You Are Wonderfully Made!, Navpress, 1988.

"ADVENTURES OF THE NORTHWOODS" SERIES

The Disappearing Stranger, Bethany House (Minneapolis), 1990.
The Hidden Message, Bethany House, 1990.
The Creeping Shadows, Bethany House, 1990.
The Vanishing Footprints, Bethany House, 1991.
Trouble at Wild River, Bethany House, 1991.
The Mysterious Hideaway, Bethany House, 1992.
Grandpa's Stolen Treasure, Bethany House, 1992.
The Runaway Clown, Bethany House, 1993.
Mystery of the Missing Map, Bethany House, 1994.
Disaster on Windy Hill, Bethany House, 1994.

"RIVERBOAT ADVENTURES" SERIES

Escape into the Night, Bethany House, 1995.
Race for Freedom, Bethany House, 1996.
Midnight Rescue, Bethany House, 1996.
The Swindler's Treasure, Bethany House, 1997.

FOR ADULTS

Gift in My Arms: Thoughts for New Mothers, Augsburg, 1977.
Either Way, I Win: A Guide for Growth in the Power of Prayer, Augsburg, 1979.
Songs for Silent Moments: Prayers for Daily Living, Augsburg, 1980.
Falling Apart or Coming Together: How You Can Experience the Faithfulness of God, Augsburg, 1984.

OTHER

Also author of over 225 shorter pieces, including articles, poetry, and song lyrics. Some of Johnson's work has been published in the United Kingdom, Australia, New Zealand, and other English-speaking countries throughout the world, translated into twelve languages for publication in other countries, and printed in braille for the blind.

WORK IN PROGRESS: Additional novels for the "Riverboat Adventures" series; revised edition of *Either Way, I Win.*

SIDELIGHTS: A former high school English teacher, Lois Walfrid Johnson is the creator of several popular pre-teen books, including the "Riverboat Adventures" series. This series revolves around the experiences of twelve-year-old Libby Norstad who, after living with a rich aunt in Chicago, joins her riverboat captain father. In the first book, *Escape into the Night,* Libby meets Caleb, her father's thirteen-year-old cabin boy. A conductor on the Underground Railroad, Caleb is involved in helping slaves escape from the South, which forces Libby to examine her own thoughts about slavery. Soon, Libby finds herself in the midst of a dangerous struggle to help three runaway slaves find freedom. Applauding the "fast-paced plot," *Booklist* reviewer Lois Schultz praised Johnson's ability to weave history "with well-developed characters, believable dialogue, and crisp description." In a *School Library Journal* review, Joyce Adams Burner lauded the depth of Johnson's characters, "especially Libby, whose transformation from a spoiled brat into a self-sacrificing heroine rings true."

Lois Walfrid Johnson told *CA:* "Often people ask me, 'How did the "Adventures of the Northwoods" series begin?' Some time ago, my husband and I moved from Minneapolis to northwest Wisconsin. I began hearing stories from people who had been friends and neighbors for three and four generations. I valued these stories and the way of life they represented. I felt that these memories, and the values, love, and courage they represented, were too good to be lost.

"Then one warm May evening when the air was sweet with lilac and plum blossoms, I took a walk near our home. I came to a field where trees had grown up inside the cellar of an old house. As I looked at the broken foundation of what had once been a log home, I asked myself, *What if a farm family lived here? What if there was a girl named Kate who moved from Minneapolis to northwest Wisconsin? What if she had a step-brother named Anders who teased her all the time? And someone like Erik who could become a special friend?* That was the beginning. I kept thinking about Kate, Anders, Erik, and the Windy Hill folks until I felt as though that family were mine.

"Because I want readers to have fun with my novels, I often include a mystery. I try to write about universal problems true to any time of history. Sometimes the experiences of my characters reflect my own life. Before our marriage, my husband, Roy, was a widower, just like Papa Nordstrom. When Roy and I were married, Roy's daughter, Gail, became our flower girl. In time, two additional children, Jeffrey and Kevin, were born and grew tall like Anders and Erik. While Kate is my viewpoint character, I wanted strong male characters because of my experience in having sons.

"I set the series in 1906-7 for two reasons. Those were transition years in northwest Wisconsin. It was still possible to see the old way of doing things—horse power, hand pumps, clearing of the land. Yet the new was coming in—electricity, rural telephones, even automobiles. Also, Big Gust, a much loved 360-pound, seven-foot, six-inch Swedish immigrant, was the village marshall in Grantsburg, Wisconsin during those years.

"Whenever I could, I used historic characters—people who actually lived in the time and place about which I wrote. I wove the lives of these people into what my fictional characters were doing. A note at the front of each novel tells which characters really lived.

"Kate had Irish and Swedish parents, and soon discovered that she, Harry Blue, and Rev. Pickle were the only non-Swedes in the Trade Lake area. Being Swedish was true to the settlement of that part of northwest Wisconsin, but I also wrote out of what I knew from my own background.

"Within the novels are 'secrets' that reflect both my family and that of my husband, Roy. We are still close to the immigrant heritage that made America strong. As a young woman, Roy's mother came from Norway. In a wave of homesickness she had her picture taken and sent back to her family. The result was the family picture described in *The Disappearing Stranger* and other novels. Roy's father also immigrated from Norway, and the two met in Milwaukee.

"Carl Nordstrom is named after two more immigrants—my Swedish grandfather, Carl Johnson, and my Swedish grandmother, Mathilda Nordstrom. While a young woman, Grandma worked on a farm outside Walnut Grove, Minnesota, and often watched wagon trains pass through to settle in the West.

"When Grandpa and Grandma Johnson were married, they bought a farm on the banks of Plum Creek. My father grew up there, and many of my stories about runaway horses come out of his experience in riding and breaking broncos. Years later, during summer vacations, my sisters and I often played in Plum Creek. From where we waded, the water flowed under a bridge into the land once owned by the family of Laura Ingalls Wilder.

"The Danish side of my family is also represented in the Northwoods novels. When my Grandpa Christiansen came to America, he worked for about a year to save enough money to bring my grandmother and their three-year-old daughter, Lydia, across the Atlantic. While passing through Ellis Island, Grandma and Lydia had pieces of paper pinned on their coats, as described in *Grandpa's Stolen Treasure*.

"Although they are called Swedish, that novel described my Danish grandparents as they looked when I was a child. From that point on, the story was fiction, or so I thought. A few months after the book was published, I learned that when Grandma came to Rochester, Minnesota, as an immigrant, there was a mix-up at the depot. Grandpa 'lost' her and Lydia for an entire day! As you might guess, three-year-old Lydia grew up to be my mother.

"Some of the country school experiences in the Northwoods novels also came out of my own childhood. I attended my first four grades in a two-room country school on the shores of Goose Lake, near Scandia, Minnesota. Miss Sundquist gives spelling words exactly as my teacher, Miss Guslander, did. There were drafts through the knotholes in the floor at Goose Lake, too, as well as box socials, a woodshed, and a large wood stove. Even as a child, I knew it was special to attend a school with woods and water for a playground.

"In addition to being a wonderful encourager, my husband, Roy, helps me in the development of ideas. After writing a number of Northwoods novels, I told him, 'I'm having so much fun doing this. I'll miss my characters when it's time to stop. What could we do next?'

"That morning Roy went out for coffee. Taking a napkin, he wrote down some thoughts. When he told me his idea for the 'Riverboat Adventures' series, I said, 'That's it!'

"We felt that by having my main characters live on the steamboat *Christina,* they could travel as needed to make a story work. For three years, while I was still writing 'Northwoods' novels, Roy and I traveled up and down the Mississippi River, researching for ideas and historical accuracy. Soon the year 1857 became especially interesting to me. I could reflect the golden era of steamboats, for rivers were the highways of that time. I could show the pioneers using those steamboats to reach their new homes along the waterways of the Midwest. But I could also bring to life the social and political upheaval of the times by telling thc story of the Underground Railroad.

"Again I use a girl as my viewpoint character—Libby, who comes from Chicago to join her father, a steamboat captain. Again I use strong boy characters—Caleb, who has worked with the Underground Railroad since the age of nine, and Jordan, a fugitive slave who escapes from his cruel master. With every novel I try to create strong reader interest by having fast moving plots and cliff hangers at the end of each chapter. I also seek to reflect important truths of our American heritage, giving perspective on the freedoms sought in the Declaration of Independence.

"To research these books, my husband and I visited Underground Railroad sites in a number of states. We grew to love and value the runaway slaves about whom we learned. We grieved about their hardship and suffering. We also respected their courage and daring, as well as the integrity and honor of the people who helped them.

"When readers write to say, 'I want to know what happens to Jordan's family,' I feel deeply moved. I, too, want to discover what happens to his family! "By now Libby, Caleb, and Jordan have become part of our lives. When Roy and I talk, we sometimes say, 'Could Libby do that?' Often we think of something that would be perfect for such a leap-before-she-looks person. Other times we decide, 'No, that would fit Caleb or Jordan better.' Like my readers, we often wonder, *What will these characters do next?*"

BIOGRAPHICAL/CRITICAL SOURCES:

PERIODICALS

Booklist, November 15, 1995, p. 559.
Children's Book Watch, September, 1991, p. 3.
Library Journal, October 15, 1974, p. 2721.
School Library Journal, October, 1995, p. 134.
Voice of Youth Advocates, June, 1984, p. 120; February, 1985, p. 51.

K

KALECHOFSKY, Roberta 1931-

PERSONAL: Born May 11, 1931, in Brooklyn, NY; daughter of Julius (a lawyer) and Naomi (maiden name, Jacobs) Kirchik; married Robert Kalechofsky (a mathematician), June 7, 1953; children: Hal, Neal. *Education:* Brooklyn College, B.A., 1952; New York University, M.A., 1956, Ph.D., 1970. *Politics:* Liberal. *Religion:* Jewish. *Avocational interests:* Animal rights, vegetarianism, history.

CAREER: Micah Publications, Inc., Marblehead, MA, publisher, 1975—.

MEMBER: Amnesty International, National Writers Union (charter member), Association of Jewish Book Publishers, Anti-Slavery Society, Jews for Animal Rights (founder).

AWARDS, HONORS: Fellowship in creative writing, National Endowment for the Arts, 1982; fellowship in fiction, Massachusetts Council on Arts, 1987; Kind Writers Make Kind Readers award, Fund for Animals, for *A Boy, a Chicken and the Lion of Judah.*

WRITINGS:

George Orwell, Ungar (New York City), 1973.
Justice My Brother, Writers' Cooperative (Montreal), 1974.
Stephen's Passion, Micah, 1975.
Orestes in Progress, Micah, 1976.
La Hoya, Micah, 1976.
Solomon's Wisdom, Micah, 1978.
(Editor with husband, Robert Kalechofsky) *Echad: An Anthology of Latin American Jewish Writings,* Micah, 1980.
Rejected Essays and Other Matters, Micah, 1980.
(Editor) *Phoenix Rising: Contemporary Jewish Writing,* Micah, 1982.
Bodmin, 1349: An Epic Novel of Christians and Jews in the Plague Years, Micah (Marblehead, MA), 1982.
(Editor with Robert Kalechofsky) *South African Jewish Voices,* Micah, 1982.
(Editor with Robert Kalechofsky) *Jewish Writing from Down Under: Australia and New Zealand,* Micah, 1984.
Haggadah for the Liberated Lamb: Bilingual Edition, Hebrew and English, revised edition, Micah, 1988.
(Editor with Robert Kalechofsky) *The Global Anthology of Jewish Women Writers,* Micah, 1990.
Autobiography of a Revolutionary: Essays on Animal and Human Rights, Micah, 1991.
(Editor) *Judaism and Animal Rights: Classical and Contemporary Responses,* Micah, 1992.
Haggadah for the Vegetarian Family: An Egalitarian Traditional Service, Micah, 1993.
Justice, My Brother, My Sister: Life and Death in a Mexican Family, Micah, 1993.
A Boy, a Chicken, and the Lion of Judah: How Ari Became a Vegetarian (juvenile), illustrated by Anselm Atkins, Micah 1996.
K'tia, A Savior of the Jewish People (short stories), Micah, 1996.
(Editor) *Rabbis and Vegetarianism: An Evolving Tradition,* Micah, 1996.
The Jewish Vegetarian Year Cookbook: Reading and Recipes, Micah, 1997.

Kalechofsky's works have been translated into Italian.

WORK IN PROGRESS: Job Enters a Pain Clinic, short stories; research on social reform movements of the nineteenth century: women's rights, abolition of slavery, liberation of Jews from ghettos and civic disabilities, animal rights.

SIDELIGHTS: Roberta Kalechofsky told *CA:* "As a publisher, independent scholar, and writer, publishing and research feed my writing life as continuous acts of communication. I began Micah Publications as a small, independent press in 1975 to solve a specific publishing problem as a writer, but came to realize that publishing was another form of communication. In 1985, when I became actively involved with the Animal Rights movement, my press became a vehicle for publishing material for this movement, which I regard as the leading edge of a new sensibility. My children's book for vegetarian children, *A Boy, a Chicken, and the Lion of Judah,* was awarded the Kind Writers Make Kind Readers Award from the Fund for Animals.

"Unfortunately, publishing also seriously reduces one's time for writing, and there is a persistent tension between writing and publishing—as there is for me between being a wife and mother. I also like to garden, take dancing and aerobic classes, walk an hour a day, and be physically active. I like to cook and read cookbooks, and I have written one. I even like to clean house sometimes. These activities, or what I call 'living' as opposed to writing, also create tension and the need to search for balance between life and fiction, whose purpose is to create an alternative life.

"My fiction, which often is historical fiction, using original chronicles and documents, has found a particularly appreciative audience in Italy. My novella, *La Hoya,* was translated into Italian and published in Italy as *Veduta Di Toledo* by Palomar. It received excellent reviews in major Italian papers and has been used in several college courses on American writers at the University of Florence. Several other stories of mine have also been translated into Italian and published in Italian-language anthologies.

"My historical fiction deals with the inter-relationship between Jews and Christians, which I regard as a primary theme in European civilization."

KAVAN, Anna 1901-1968
(Helen Ferguson)

PERSONAL: Original name, Helen Emily Woods; name changed by deed poll; born 1901, in Cannes, France; died of a drug overdose, December 5, 1968, in London, England; daughter of C.C.E. and Helen (Bright) Woods; first husband, Donald Ferguson (divorced); second husband, Stuart Edmonds (divorced); children: (first marriage) one son (deceased). *Education:* Attended boarding schools in England, Switzerland, and the United States; privately educated.

CAREER: Writer.

WRITINGS:

NOVELS UNDER NAME ANNA KAVAN

Change the Name, J. Cape (London), 1941.

The House of Sleep, Doubleday (Garden City, NY), 1947, published in England as *Sleep Has His House,* Cassell (London), 1948.

A Scarcity of Love, Angus Downie, 1956, reprinted, McGraw (New York City), 1974.

Eagles' Nest, P. Owen (London), 1957.

Who Are You?, Scorpion Press, 1963.

Ice, P. Owen, 1967, with an introduction by Brian W. Aldiss, Doubleday, 1970.

Mercury, foreword by Doris Lessing, P. Owen, 1994.

The Parson, P. Owen, 1995.

STORY COLLECTIONS UNDER NAME ANNA KAVAN

Asylum Piece and Other Stories, J. Cape, 1940, Doubleday, 1946.

I Am Lazarus, J. Cape, 1945.

A Bright Green Field and Other Stories, P. Owen, 1958.

Julia and the Bazooka and Other Stories, edited and with an introduction by Rhys Davies, P. Owen, 1970, Knopf (New York City), 1975.

My Soul in China: A Novella and Stories, edited and with an introduction by Rhys Davies, P. Owen, 1975.

My Madness: The Selected Writings of Anna Kavan, edited by Brian W. Aldiss, Picador (London), 1990.

NOVELS UNDER NAME HELEN FERGUSON

A Charmed Circle, J. Cape, 1929.

The Dark Sisters, J. Cape, 1930.
Let Me Alone, J. Cape, 1930, reprinted under name Anna Kavan, with an introduction by Rhys Davies, P. Owen, 1974.
A Stranger Still, John Lane (London), 1935.
Goose Cross, John Lane, 1936.
Rich Get Rich, John Lane, 1937.

OTHER

(Under name Anna Kavan, with K. T. Bluth) *The Horse's Tale,* Gaberbocchus (London), 1949.

Contributor to *Harper's Bazaar, New Yorker* and *Horizon.*

SIDELIGHTS: Anna Kavan's writing career had two distinct phases: her early novels, published in the 1930s under her married name of Helen Ferguson, were conventional romance stories; but beginning with *Asylum Piece and Other Stories,* published in 1940 under the name Anna Kavan—one of the fictional characters featured in her novel *Let Me Alone*—Kavan left her old name and life behind. In the *New Statesman,* Stanley Reynolds commented that this renaming was "rather as if Dickens had changed his name by deed poll to David Copperfield." Reynolds pointed out that the decision to adopt this particular name "is even more interesting when you consider that Kavan is not the heroine's original surname but the name of the hated and despised husband of the novel." Under her new name, Kavan wrote stories concerned with the disintegrating psychological states of characters suffering from mental illness. Kavan, according to John Woodburn in the *Saturday Review,* "concerned herself with the unbalanced mind, the pathos and terror of the intellect in the tragic act of slipping its tether to reality."

The new subject matter was based on Kavan's own tragic life. From the 1930s until her death in 1968, Kavan was a heroin addict who suffered from mental breakdowns, compulsions to suicide and desperate attempts at withdrawal from drug addiction. Her stories, filled with mentally fragile characters trying to cope with a world that makes no sense to them, are less concerned with linear plots than with states of mind; they are so autobiographical in nature that they exist on the border between fiction and nonfiction. "With Anna Kavan," wrote Max Egremont in *Books and Bookmen,* "the stories and novels are so subjective in tone that it is as if she wishes, in reality, to write her own spiritual autobiography but, rather than do this, has dressed up her sufferings and longings in fictional terms."

As a child Kavan traveled extensively with her wealthy, emotionally cold mother, with whom she maintained a love-hate relationship all her life. This relationship generated a rage which frequently surfaced in her writings. In the short story, "A World of Heroes," she wrote: "What could have been done to make me afraid to grow up out of such a childhood? Later on, I saw things in proportion, I was always afraid of falling back into that ghastly black isolation of an uncomprehending, solitary, oversensitive child."

After her second marriage ended, like the first, in divorce, Kavan entered a Swiss clinic where she received treatment for mental disorders. She recorded her experiences at the clinic and published them as a series of sketches entitled *Asylum Piece and Other Stories,* her first book to bear the name Anna Kavan. In an article in *Books and Bookmen,* Rhys Davies called *Asylum Piece* "extraordinarily moving and original." Leo Lerman, writing in the *Saturday Review of Literature,* confided that *Asylum Piece* "will probably never be a best seller. It tells no story or even stories: telling a story was not the author's problem. . . . *Asylum Piece* conveys moods, emotions, and mental situations. . . . [It] is definitely experimental writing, but experimental writing of a very high order." In his review of the book for the *New Republic,* John Farrelly observed that "in the best of these stories, Miss Kavan has created with poetic devices those states of mind between reality and illusion in which contradictions hold each other in a terrified embrace. This is the hell of souls lost within themselves, and she has charted the territory of loneliness they inhabit and has registered the persistent single voice that forms their silence."

Kavan's *The House of Sleep* tells of a nameless young woman who is succumbing to mental disintegration. Diana Trilling, reviewing the novel for the *Nation,* called it a "kaleidoscope of the subjective states of an increasingly disordered mind, recorded half as if from within the sick mind itself and half as if through the eye of an outsider much too closely identified with her subject." She concluded that "nothing makes it worth reading." Woodburn, however, described *The House of Sleep* as "a strange, softly terrifying book. It is difficult not to yield helplessly to its beauty, and it is impossible not to be profoundly disturbed by it."

Ice, which is often categorized as science fiction because of its vision of a dystopian world, is the tale of two men (possibly the same man with two personalities) pursuing an elusive and enigmatic woman through a landscape of snow and ice. The time is the next glacial age, the world is threatened with destruction by ice, and the two men fantasize that the woman they pursue is the "snow-queen, the elusive ice-woman," as Adrianne Marcus explained in the *Pacific Sun Literary Quarterly.* "Past, present and future intermingle," Marcus wrote of the novel, "and the deliberate confusion of reality and imagination are chillingly present." Marcus argued that Kavan's language possesses the "intensity of metaphor" and that many passages and descriptions in the book have a surreal quality. "*Ice,*" Janet Byrne wrote in *Extrapolation,* "is a searing interior monologue broken up by unexpected dream segments and other fragments from another time and place." According to Byrne, the larger destruction of the world in the novel is echoed in the characters' mental states. The "rampant confusion and destruction," Byrne explained, "mirror the inner turmoil of the protagonist, providing an appropriate background both for Kavan's concentration on the subjective experience of her characters and for the author's prophetic and highly subjective importunings." Marcus described *Ice* as "one of those rare books that has achieved an underground reputation."

A registered addict for nearly thirty years, Kavan found escape from reality through heroin. She suffered from acute depression and attempted suicide twice. Davies, a personal friend for many years, believed that the heroin acted as a preservative of both sanity and physical energy for Kavan. In addition to being able to write novels and numerous short stories—despite her addiction—she also purchased and renovated old houses on Campden Hill and did editorial work for a literary magazine. Kavan also designed and presided over the building of the modernistic house in which she spent the last twelve years of her life.

The story collection *Julia and the Bazooka* deals with Kavan's life as a drug addict. The "bazooka" of the title story was her nickname for the syringe she used to inject her heroin. Writing in the *Guardian Weekly,* Robert Nye found that what emerges from the stories in *Julia and the Bazooka* "is the boredom and the cold, the inner emptiness and death-wishing deadness of the hardened addict." Nye believed that while some of the stories in the collection "fail to rise above the level of an organised hysteria," the best of them "should not be missed by anyone who cares for contemporary writing." A critic for the *Times Literary Supplement* claimed that *Julia and the Bazooka* gives the impression not only that "Kavan was a very good writer but that it was drugs, and her paranoic state of mind, that made her good. Because of her despair, because of her experience of hallucination and psychedelic vision, because of her willing, even persuasive, acceptance that she was doomed, she seems to have been capable of extraordinary insight and perfect control over the words in which she describes what it is like to be herself."

When British authorities imposed new and tighter regulations on drug addicts, Kavan was forced to attend regularly scheduled sessions which she considered to be disciplinary punishment, but she attended them out of fear that the National Health Service workers would hold back her drug supply. This reinforced her idea of the inimical world she often described in her novels. Davies remarked that in spite of this, Kavan always returned to the "valid discipline" of her stories and that "their clarity of style, their spurning of sensationalism, and their own code of logic were another justification of her vision."

Kavan died with a loaded syringe in her hand. Jill Robinson, in an article in the *New York Times Book Review,* commented: "The facts of one's difficult existence do not guarantee literature. Anna Kavan is not interesting because she was a woman, an addict or had silver blond hair. She is interesting because her work comes through with a powerful androgynous individuality and because the stories are luminous and rich with a fresh kind of peril. She knows how to pull us into her world, her dreams and nightmares—how to have all of it become ours."

BIOGRAPHICAL/CRITICAL SOURCES:

BOOKS

Callard, David A., *The Case of Anna Kavan: A Biography,* P. Owen, 1992.

Contemporary Literary Criticism, Gale (Detroit), Volume 5, 1976, Volume 13, 1980, Volume 82, 1994.
Crosland, Margaret, *Beyond the Lighthouse: English Women Novelists in the Twentieth Century,* Taplinger (New York City), 1981, pp. 186-192.
Kavan, Anna, *Ice,* introduction by Brian W. Aldiss, Doubleday, 1970.
Kavan, *Julia and the Bazooka,* edited and with an introduction by Rhys Davies, P. Owen, 1970, Knopf, 1975.
St. James Guide to Science Fiction Writers, 4th edition, St. James Press (Detroit), 1996.

PERIODICALS

Anais: An International Journal, Number 3, 1985, pp. 55-62, 75-6.
Belles Lettres, spring, 1994, p. 65.
Booklist, February 15, 1996, p. 991.
Books and Bookmen, March, 1971; June, 1978, pp. 43-4.
Bookwatch, March, 1996, p. 8.
Extrapolation, spring, 1982, pp. 5-11.
Guardian Weekly, March 14, 1970, p. 21.
Journal of the Fantastic in the Arts, Volume 3, number 2, 1991, pp. 14-21.
Kirkus Reviews, February 1, 1996, p. 162.
Library Journal, September 15, 1993, p. 104.
Listener, March 12, 1970.
Modern Fiction Studies, summer, 1994, pp. 253-77.
Ms., September, 1975, p. 42.
Nation, September 20, 1947, pp. 291-92.
New Republic, September 23, 1946, pp. 355-56.
New Statesman, January 11, 1974; March 16, 1973; March 28, 1975.
New Statesman & Society, April 20, 1990, p. 37.
New York Times Book Review, May 11, 1975.
Observer Review, January 17, 1971.
Pacific Sun Literary Quarterly, May 15, 1975.
Publishers Weekly, September 27, 1993, p. 46; October 31, 1994, p. 44; March 13, 1995, p. 60; January 15, 1996, p. 457; February 12, 1996, p. 59.
Saturday Review, August 23, 1947, p. 15.
Saturday Review of Literature, August 10, 1946, p. 9.
Spectator, January 31, 1976.
Textus: English Studies in Italy, Number 4, 1991, pp. 119-146.
Times Literary Supplement, September 14, 1967; March 12, 1970, p. 275; February 5, 1971, p. 144; June 14, 1974, p. 644; May 11, 1990, p. 496; June 25, 1993, p. 21; August 19, 1994, p. 22; June 16, 1995, p. 24.
Village Voice, April 7, 1975, p. 33.
World Literature Today, winter, 1977; summer, 1995, pp. 581-582.

OBITUARIES:

PERIODICALS

New York Times, December 7, 1968.
Times (London), December 6, 1968.*

* * *

KELLER, Beverly L(ou)
(B. L. Harwick)

PERSONAL: Born in San Francisco, CA; daughter of Wearne E. and Ruth (Burke) Harwick; married William Jon Keller, June 18, 1949 (died, 1964); children: Lisa, Kristen, Michele. *Education:* University of California, Berkeley, B.A., 1950.

CAREER: Author, newspaper columnist, and feature writer.

MEMBER: Society for the Prevention of Cruelty to Animals (director and officer for Yolo County, 1976-78; 1991-93).

AWARDS, HONORS: Fiona's Bee was selected a Best Book of 1975 by *School Library Journal.*

WRITINGS:

FOR CHILDREN

Fiona's Bee, Coward (New York CIty), 1975.
The Beetle Bush, Coward, 1976.
Don't Throw Another One, Dover!, Coward, 1976.
(Under name B. L. Harwick) *The Frog Prints,* Raintree Editions, 1976.
The Genuine Ingenious Thrift Shop Genie, Clarissa Mae Bean and Me, Coward, 1977.
Pimm's Place, Coward, 1978.
The Sea Watch, Four Winds Press (New York City), 1981.
Fiona's Flea, Coward, 1981.
The Bee Sneeze, Coward, 1982.

My Awful Cousin Norbert, Lothrop (New York City), 1982.
No Beasts! No Children!, Lothrop, 1983.
A Small, Elderly Dragon, Lothrop, 1984.
When Mother Got the Flu, Lothrop, 1984.
A Garden of Love to Share, Parker Brothers (Beverly, MA), 1984.
Rosebud, with Fangs, Lothrop, 1985.
Desdemona: Twelve Going on Desperate, Lothrop, 1986.
Only Fiona, HarperCollins (New York City), 1988.
Fowl Play, Desdemona, Lothrop, 1989.
Desdemona Moves On, Bradbury (Scarsdale, NY), 1992.
Camp Trouble, Scholastic (New York City), 1993.
The Amazon Papers, Browndeer (San Diego), 1996.

OTHER

The Baghdad Defections (adult suspense novel), Bobbs-Merrill (Indianapolis), 1973.
Consumer Skills, Quercus, 1986.
A Car Means Out, Quercus, 1987.
Cliffhanger, Quercus, 1987.
Beam Me Up, He Said, Quercus, 1987.

Also contributor to textbooks, including *Hide and Seek,* Scott Foresman, 1985. Contributor to anthologies, including *The Best from Fantasy and Science Fiction,* edited by Edward Ferman, Doubleday, 1974; and *The Random House Book of Humor for Children,* Random House, 1988. Contributor to periodicals, including *Atlantic, Magazine of Fantasy and Science Fiction, Cosmopolitan,* and *American Voice.* Some of Keller's books have been published in Japanese and Spanish.

ADAPTATIONS: *Fiona's Bee* has been produced as an audio recording by Listening Library in 1976, re-released, 1991.

WORK IN PROGRESS: A series for children.

SIDELIGHTS: Beverly L. Keller is the author of two popular series of children's books, one about a dog-loving girl named Fiona and another starring a pre-teen protagonist named Desdemona. The story of ten-year-old Fiona Foster begins in *Fiona's Bee* when she purchases a dog dish in hopes of befriending a dog and its owner. However, Fiona doesn't expect a bee to land on her hand and interfere with her friend-making plan. Instead of panicking, the brave girl reasons that if she slowly walks to an area packed with flowers, the insect will fly off in search of sweet nectar. The scheme works, but with an unexpected bonus—along the way to the park she meets many new friends impressed by her pet bee. A critic in *Kirkus Reviews* lauded Keller's "sharp, empathic humor," while in *Horn Book,* Ann A. Flowers described the story as "simple and kindly."

In *Only Fiona,* Keller's third book in the series, Fiona and her family have moved to a new town and once again she finds herself in the uncomfortable situation of making new friends. By the end of the story, Fiona does gain new playmates, but not without causing a few problems. Intensely interested in the welfare of animals, she interrupts neighborhood events, including two outdoor weddings, first to save a beetle, and then to help a bumblebee. Although she contended that Fiona's naivety and a "determined cuteness" detract from the story, Zena Sutherland added in *Bulletin of the Center for Children's Books,* "the writing style is brisk and the dialog and characters convincing." Calling Fiona a "real, three-dimensional person," a *Kirkus Reviews* critic stated that children should be entertained by Fiona's antics and applauded "Keller's sharply portrayed characters."

In 1983, Keller introduced young readers to the world of Desdemona Blank in *No Beasts! No Children!* After her parents separate, Desdemona and her five-year-old twin brother and sister go and live with her psychologist father in the only place in the city which allows both kids and pets. When the rich landlord tries to evict the Blank family because of all the commotion they and their animals make, he is surprised to discover that his son Sherman spends much of his free time with Desdemona. In the end, the landlord allows the family to stay and even realizes that he should give more time and attention to his own son. Zena Sutherland of the *Bulletin of the Center for Children's Books* wrote that the "characters are exaggerated but colorful and funny, as is the dialogue," but found the "intensity of the ceaseless action" a bit tiresome. In *School Library Journal,* Elaine E. Knight praised the swift, humorous action, saying "the misadventures of this menagerie are irresistible."

Desdemona's spirited adventures continue in *Desdemona: Twelve Going on Desperate,* Keller's

1986 sequel to *No Beasts! No Children!* In this fast-paced story, Desdemona and her family must fight her landlord's plan to level the family's house and build luxury condos on the site. Making matters worse, the landlord, who hopes to be elected mayor, is also the father of Sherman, Desdemona's best friend. Mixups always seem to happen to Desdemona—she mistakes a bottle of varnish for shampoo and serves dog food instead of truffles at a party she caters for Sherman's father. Yet throughout the book, Desdemona keeps her head up and eventually helps her family keep their home. Ilene Cooper of *Booklist* described Keller's characters as "strong and funny" and Betsy Hearne of the *Bulletin of the Center for Children's Books* praised Keller's "gift to connect absurd characters, themes, and situations with a logical certainty that builds into farce." In a *School Library Journal* review, Linda Wicher called Desdemona's life "zany and appealing," while noting that Keller manages to include some "food for thought about slumlords, image-conscious politicians, and true friends."

Fowl Play and *Desdemona Moves On* continue the series about the Blank family. In *Fowl Play,* Desdemona decides to help her vegetarian friend's crusade against the eating of turkeys for Thanksgiving. Always finding herself in messy situations, Desdemona discovers that the printer confused her "save-a-turkey" flyers with ones advertising adult entertainers after she and Sherman already inserted them in the program for the school play. Although *Booklist* reviewer Ilene Cooper criticized some of Keller's minor persons as "stock characters who are little more than cartoons," she went on to applaud the "funny moments as well as several sobering ones that work well." Ranking Keller's Desdemona with Lois Lowry's Anastasia and Constance Greene's Al, *School Library Journal* contributor Sally T. Margolis lauded Keller's even handed approach to teaching children about animal rights without sounding like a "tract."

Once again, in *Desdemona Moves On,* the Blank family is facing eviction, this time just before Christmas. However, Desdemona's father finally manages to secure a new house which even has a swimming pool. After they move in, they are surprised to find the Chinese Olympic swim team practicing every day in their back yard. While she cautioned in *School Library Journal* that "some situations seem contrived," Mary Lou Budd claimed "the plot flows smoothly" and suggested this book for reluctant readers.

In 1996, Keller ventured into the world of young adult literature with her fast-paced book *The Amazon Papers.* When she's not working on cars or reading a book of philosophy, fifteen-year-old protagonist Iris Hoving—a straight-A student whose disappointed mother would rather her daughter be a popular cheerleader—is desperately seeking the attention of a handsome high school dropout and pizza delivery boy, Foster Prizer. When her mother goes on vacation, Iris arranges to meet Foster at a pool hall, but the evening becomes a disaster when Iris suffers a broken foot and vandals strip her mother's car. "Iris' narrative voice is dryly rueful and oddly suitable for a bright, unconventional young woman exasperatedly trying to figure out how she 'fits,'" noted Janice M. Del Negro of the *Bulletin of the Center for Children's Books.* In a *School Library Journal* review, Susan R. Farber called Iris "a wonderful, fully fleshed-out character," and praised the "true to life" ending in which Iris realizes she needs the help of an adult to get everything back in order.

Keller told *CA:* "As a child, I didn't live anywhere, but travelled with my parents. Wherever we stayed, my father let it slip that he was really Lawrence Tibbett, the great Metropolitan opera star, secretly married to my mother, who was really Gertrude Ederle, the first woman to swim the English Channel. My mother weighed ninety pounds and was terrified of any body of water larger than a bathtub, but fortunately, nobody pressed her to do a few strokes.

"I knew what it was like to be treated like a star. We had flowers and fruit baskets and prime tables. Now and then the band leader would beg my father to honor the guests with an aria. Now and then my father obliged.

"So we changed schools often. By the time I was in high school, I'd attended thirteen schools, and in the process missed learning English grammar entirely. One compensates.

"I married in my junior year at UC Berkeley, and as soon as I was graduated, began writing a newspaper column at forty cents a column inch. As soon as I sold one piece to the *Atlantic* and another to *Women's Home Companion,* I decided that I would never work again for forty cents a column inch.

"By this time we had two daughters, and we lived for the next few years in Baghdad and Beirut. I got caught in a camel migration in Iraq, and we arrived in Beirut in time for the Suez Canal crisis. At its height, we drove through the Middle East and Europe, sleeping in abandoned villas on the Aegean, arriving in Rome at the outbreak of the Hungarian Revolution.

"We lived in a penthouse which had belonged to Count Ciano, Mussolini's son-in-law. It wound around the building—vast terraces, a marble foyer, bar, and sitting room, an enormous den full of assegais, spears, shields, guns . . . and there were rooms I never cared to enter.

"Afterward we traveled third class by rail through Europe with two small children, which explains why I have looked my age for many years.

"I started doing precinct work when I was seven, passing out political flyers, and continued doing political volunteer work for years, serving as county co-chair for several presidential campaigns.

"If you have ever seen the Booth cartoon, 'Write about Dogs,' you may have some inkling of my working conditions. My dogs, which are large and many, doze and shed on bills, correspondence, and work in progress. I also knock myself out for cats in trouble, shelter spiders, and feed ants. I can't say my friends understand, but they're fond of me."

BIOGRAPHICAL/CRITICAL SOURCES:

PERIODICALS

Booklist, December 15, 1975, p. 582; July 15, 1976, p. 1602; October 15, 1982, p. 317; September 1, 1983, p. 87; May 1, 1984, p. 1248; October 1, 1986, p. 273; October 15, 1986, p. 359; April 1, 1989, p. 1385.

Bulletin of the Center for Children's Books, April, 1976, p. 126; October, 1976, p. 26; May, 1977, p. 144; May, 1978, p. 143; June, 1981, p. 196; June, 1982, p. 190; March, 1983, p. 153; June, 1984, p. 188; July, 1984, p. 207; December, 1986, p. 70; January, 1988, p. 93; March, 1989, p. 173; November, 1996, p. 101.

Horn Book, April, 1976, p. 151; August, 1984, p. 466.

Kirkus Reviews, June 15, 1973, p. 659; October 1, 1975, p. 1128; June 1, 1976, p. 633; December 1, 1976, p. 1263; January 1, 1978, p. 3; February 15, 1979, p. 195; March 1, 1981, p. 283; August 1, 1981, p. 939; February 1, 1983, p. 121; April 15, 1988, p. 619; February 15, 1989, p. 294.

Library Journal, August, 1973, p. 2342.

New York Times Book Review, August 19, 1973, p. 13.

Publishers Weekly, June 25, 1973, p. 69; June 4, 1982, p. 67.

School Library Journal, December, 1975, pp. 31, 62; December, 1976, p. 64; March, 1977, p. 133; March, 1978, p. 130; February, 1979, p. 43; May, 1981, p. 82; November, 1981, p. 106; February, 1982, p. 37; August, 1982, p. 98; December, 1982, p. 77; May, 1983, pp. 32, 72; May, 1984, p. 81; October, 1984, p. 148; October, 1985, p. 174; November, 1986, p. 90; April, 1988, p. 101; May, 1989, p. 110; December, 1992, p. 112; October, 1996, pp. 147-148.

Voice of Youth Advocates, August, 1984, p. 147; December, 1996, p. 271.

* * *

KELLY, H(enry) A(nsgar) 1934-

PERSONAL: Born June 6, 1934, in Fort Dodge, IA; son of Harry Francis and Inez Ingeborg (Anderson) Kelly; married Marea Tancred, June 18, 1968; children: Sarah Marea, Dominic Tancred. *Education:* Attended Creighton University, 1952-53; St. Louis University, A.B., 1959, A.M. and Ph.L., 1961; Harvard University, Ph.D., 1965; postgraduate study at Boston College, 1964-66, and American Academy in Rome, 1966-67. *Politics:* "Independent, out of Democratic." *Religion:* Roman Catholic.

ADDRESSES: Home—1123 Kagawa St., Pacific Palisades, CA 90272. *Office*—University of California, Los Angeles, Department of English, 405 Hilgard St., Los Angeles, CA 90095. *E-mail*—kelly@humnet.ucla.edu.

CAREER: Society of Jesus (Jesuits), Wisconsin Province, scholastic seminarian, 1953-66;

Harvard University, Society of Fellows, Cambridge, MA, junior fellow, 1964-67; University of California, Los Angeles, assistant professor, 1967-69, associate professor, 1969-72, professor of English and medieval-renaissance studies, 1972—.

MEMBER: Medieval Academy of America (fellow), Medieval Association of the Pacific (president, 1988-90).

AWARDS, HONORS: Guggenheim fellow, 1971-72; National Endowment for the Humanities fellow, 1980-81, 1996-97.

WRITINGS:

The Devil, Demonology, and Witchcraft, Doubleday (New York City), 1968, revised edition, 1974 (published in England as *Towards the Death of Satan,* Geoffrey Chapman, 1968).
Divine Providence in the England of Shakespeare's Histories, Harvard University Press (Cambridge, MA), 1970.
Love and Marriage in the Age of Chaucer, Cornell University Press (Ithaca, NY), 1975.
The Matrimonial Trials of Henry VIII, Stanford University Press (Stanford, CA), 1976.
Canon Law and the Archpriest of Hita, Medieval and Renaissance Texts and Studies (Binghamton, NY), 1984.
The Devil at Baptism: Ritual, Theology, and Drama, Cornell University Press, 1985.
Chaucer and the Cult of the Saint Valentine, E. J. Brill (Long Island City, NY), 1986.
Tragedy and Comedy from Dante to Pseudo-Dante, University of California Press (Berkeley, CA), 1989.
Ideas and Forms of Tragedy from Aristotle to the Middle Ages, Cambridge University Press (Cambridge, England), 1993.
Chaucerian Tragedy, Boydell and Brewer, 1997.

Contributor to professional journals, including *Church History, Journal of Religion, Modern Philology,* and *Ricardian.* Coeditor, *Viator: Medieval and Renaissance Studies* (annual of the Center for Medieval and Renaissance Studies, University of California, Los Angeles), 1970-90.

WORK IN PROGRESS: Chaucer and Religion; Medieval Antecedents of American Due Process.

KING, Kimball 1934-

PERSONAL: Born February 5, 1934, in Trenton, NJ; son of James and Virginia (Martin) King; married Harriet Richards Lowry, December 27, 1955; children: Scottow, Caleb, Virginia. *Education:* Johns Hopkins University, B.A., 1956; Wesleyan University, Middletown, CT, M.A., 1960; University of Wisconsin—Madison, Ph.D., 1964.

ADDRESSES: Home—610 North St., Chapel Hill, NC 27514. *Office*—Department of English, University of North Carolina, Chapel Hill, NC 27514. *E-mail*—jkking@email.unc.edu; fax: 919-962-3520.

CAREER: University of North Carolina, Chapel Hill, assistant professor, 1964-68, associate professor, 1968-81, professor of English, 1981—.

MEMBER: Modern Language Association of America, South Atlantic Modern Language Association, Bechett Society, Pinter Society, Thomas Wolfe Society.

WRITINGS:

(Editor) Thomas Nelson Page, *In Old Virginia,* University of North Carolina Press, 1972.
Twenty Modern British Dramatists, Garland Publishing (New York City), 1977.
Ten Modern Irish Playwrights: A Comprehensive Annotated Bibliography, Garland Publishing, 1979.
Ten Modern American Playwrights: An Annotated Bibliography, Garland Publishing, 1982.
August Baldwin Longstreet, G. K. Hall, 1984.
Sam Shepard: A Casebook, Garland Publishing, 1989.
Hollywood on Stage, Garland Publishing, 1997.

Contributor to literature journals. Managing editor, *Southern Literary Journal.*

* * *

KINGHORN, Kenneth Cain 1930-

PERSONAL: Born June 23, 1930, in Albany, OK; son of Kenneth (a businessman) and Eloise (Rye) Kinghorn; married Hilda Hartzler, June 4, 1955; children: Kathleen, Kenneth, Kevin, Kent.

Ethnicity: "White-Anglo." *Education:* Ball State University, B.S., 1952; Asbury Theological Seminary, B.D., 1962; Emory University, Ph.D., 1965.

ADDRESSES: Home—1083 The Lane, Lexington, KY 40504. *Office*— Office of the Dean, Asbury Theological Seminary, 204 N. Lexington Ave., Wilmore, KY 40390. *E-mail*—ken_kinghorn@ats.wilmore.ky.us; fax: 606-858-2371.

CAREER: Ordained United Methodist minister, 1965; Asbury Theological Seminary, Wilmore, KY, associate professor, 1965-70, professor of history of theology, 1970-82, dean, 1982—.

WRITINGS:

Contemporary Issues in Historical Perspective, Word Inc. (Waco, TX), 1970, reissued as *Current Issues in Historical Perspective,* Lay Renewal Press.
Dynamic Discipleship, Revell (Old Tappan, NJ), 1973.
Fresh Wind of the Spirit, Abingdon (Nashville, TN), 1975.
Gifts of the Spirit, Abingdon, 1976.
Christ Can Make You Fully Human, Abingdon, 1979.
Discovering Your Spiritual Gifts: A Personal Inventory Method, Francis Asbury (Wilmore, KY), 1981.
A Celebration of Ministry: Essays in Honor of Frank Bateman Stanger, Francis Asbury, 1982.
The Holy Spirit and You, University of the Air, 1987.
Secularism and America: Controversy for the 1990s, Bristol Books, 1990.
The Gospel of Grace: The Way of Salvation in the Wesleyan Tradition, Abingdon, 1992.

Contributor of articles to periodicals.

WORK IN PROGRESS: A fiction trilogy; a book on the early Methodist class meetings; *A History of American Methodism.*

* * *

KINKLEY, Jeffrey C(arroll) 1948-

PERSONAL: Born July 13, 1948, in Urbana, IL; son of Harold Vernon (an educator) and Emily Jane Robinson Kinkley; married Chuchu Kang (an econometrician); children: Matthew Kang. *Education:* University of Chicago, B.A., 1969; Harvard University, M.A., 1971, Ph.D., 1977.

ADDRESSES: Home—8 Laurel Lane, Bernardsville, NJ 07924. *Office*—Department of History, St. John's University, 8000 Utopia Parkway, Jamaica, NY 11439.

CAREER: Harvard University, Cambridge, MA, lecturer in history, 1977-79; St. John's University, Jamaica, NY, assistant professor, 1979-86, associate professor of Asian studies, 1986-87, associate professor, 1987-93, professor of history, 1993—. Chair of Modern China Seminar at Columbia University, 1987-88.

MEMBER: American Historical Association, Association for Asian Studies, Phi Beta Kappa.

AWARDS, HONORS: Fellow, Committee on Scholarly Communication with the People's Republic of China, 1980 and 1989-90, and American Council of Learned Societies, 1982, 1986, and 1987.

WRITINGS:

The Odyssey of Shen Congwen, Stanford University Press (Stanford, NJ), 1987.
(Translator with others) Zhang Xinxin and Sang Ye, *Chinese Lives: An Oral History of Contemporary China,* edited by W. J. F. Jenner and Delia Davin, Pantheon (New York City), 1987.
(Translator) Hsiao Ch'ien, *Traveller without a Map,* Hutchinson (London), 1990, Stanford University Press, 1993.
Shen Congwen bixia de Zhongguo shehui yu wenhug (title means "Shen Congwen's Vision of Chinese Society and Culture"), East China Normal University Press (Shanghai), 1994.

EDITOR

After Mao: Chinese Literature and Society, 1978-1981, Council on East Asian Studies, Harvard University (Cambridge, MA), 1985.
(And author of introduction) Chen Xuezhao, *Surviving the Storm: A Memoir,* M. E. Sharpe (Armonk, NY), 1990.
(With Helmut Martin) *Modern Chinese Writers: Self-Portrayals,* M. E. Sharpe, 1992.

(And translator with others) *Imperfect Paradise: Stories by Shen Congwen,* University of Hawaii Press (Oahu), 1995.

Editor of Chinese section of *Fiction,* 1987; assistant editor, *Journal of Asian Studies,* 1991-94. Member of editorial board, *Republican China.*

WORK IN PROGRESS: Under Surveillance: Modern Chinese Writing about Crime.

SIDELIGHTS: Although a professor of history at St. John's University, Jeffrey C. Kinkley is an expert in modern Chinese literature who has written, edited and translated a number of important works in the field. Kinkley once told *CA:* "My primary interest has been analyzing twentieth-century Chinese literature as a witness to history. I have also introduced contemporary Chinese authors to an American audience through translations."

The essays Kinkley gathered together for his first book, *After Mao: Chinese Literature and Society, 1978-1981,* explore the many forms of literature suddenly allowed in Communist China again following the death of Communist party chairman Mao Tse-Tung. Under Mao's rule, literature was tightly controlled by the Communist Party and such popular genres as romance and science fiction were harnessed to propaganda purposes. With the relaxation of China's censorship after Mao's death, Chinese literature regained some of its traditional vitality. The essays in *After Mao,* according to C. N. Canning in *Choice,* "expand our view of mainland China's broad and complex literary scene." Robert E. Hegel, writing in *World Literature Today,* finds that *After Mao* "should be on the reading list of everyone seriously interested in contemporary world literature."

Kinkley turned his attention to Chinese author Shen Congwen in his study *The Odyssey of Shen Congwen.* Known for his novels, short stories and essays, Shen was born in the West Hunan area of China and featured that region in all of his fictional works. Because of Chinese prejudice against the people from his region, Shen endured decades of indifference from the literary establishment of China. In the 1950s the author was forced to undergo "re-education" by Communist authorities, during which he was forced to confess imaginary crimes and publicly reavow faith in the Maoist revolution. In the Cultural Revolution of the 1960s, Shen was once again persecuted and sent for re-education. Not until 1979 was he officially exonerated. Kinkley based his book on a series of interviews done with the author, his family and others. This information was then thoroughly cross-checked where possible with relevant written records. The resulting book offers "a brilliant literary biography of Shen's life, times, thought, and art," as Jerome Ch'en writes in the *American Historical Review.* Michael S. Duke, writing in *World Literature Today,* claims that *The Odyssey of Shen Congwen* "will be the definitive book on Shen for some time to come." In 1995 Kinkley edited *Imperfect Paradise: Stories by Shen Congwen,* a collection of the author's shorter works set in his native West Hunan. Reviewing the title for the *New York Times Book Review,* Jonathan Spence calls Kinkley "the leading expert in the West on the work of Shen Congwen."

BIOGRAPHICAL/CRITICAL SOURCES:

PERIODICALS

American Historical Review, February, 1989, pp. 196-197.

Choice, October, 1985, p. 304; February, 1988, p. 914; April, 1994, pp. 1249-1251.

Journal of Asian Studies, February, 1986, p. 377.

New York Times Book Review, December 17, 1995, p. 15.

Times Literary Supplement, July 1, 1988, p. 728.

World Literature Today, spring, 1986, p. 360; summer, 1988, p. 507.*

* * *

KNOX, James
See BRITTAIN, William (E.)

* * *

KOCH, Kenneth 1925-

PERSONAL: Surname is pronounced "coke"; born February 27, 1925, in Cincinnati, OH; son of Stuart J. and Lillian Amy (Loth) Koch; married Mary Janice Elwood, June 12, 1954 (died, 1981); married Karen Culler, December 29, 1994; children: Katherine. *Education:* Harvard University, A.B., 1948; Columbia University, M.A., 1953, Ph.D., 1959.

ADDRESSES: Home—25 Claremont Ave. #2B, New York, NY 10027. *Office*—414 Hamilton Hall, Columbia University, New York, NY 10027.

CAREER: Rutgers University, Newark, NJ, lecturer, 1953-58; Brooklyn College (now of the City University of New York), Brooklyn, NY, lecturer, 1957-59; Columbia University, New York City, assistant professor, 1959-66, associate professor, 1966-71, professor of English and comparative literature, 1971—. Director of Poetry Workshop at the New School for Social Research, 1958-66. Exhibitions of Koch's collaborative work were held at the Ipswich Museum, England, 1993, and at the Tibor De Nagy Gallery, New York City, 1994. *Military service:* U.S. Army, 1943-46.

AWARDS, HONORS: Fulbright fellow, 1950-51, 1978, and 1982; Guggenheim fellow, 1960-61; grant from the National Endowment for the Arts, 1966; Ingram Merrill Foundation fellow, 1969; Harbison Award, 1970, for teaching; Frank O'Hara Prize, 1973, for *Poetry;* Christopher Book Award and Ohioana Book Award, both 1974, for *Rose, Where Did You Get That Red?: Teaching Great Poetry to Children;* National Institute of Arts and Letters award, 1976; Award of Merit for Poetry from American Academy and Institute of Arts and Letters, 1986; National Book Critics Circle nomination, 1988, for *One Thousand Avant-Garde Plays;* Bollingen Prize, Yale University, 1995; elected member, American Academy of Arts and Letters, 1995; Rebekah Johnson Bobbitt National Prize for Poetry, Library of Congress, 1996, for *One Train: Poems.*

WRITINGS:

POETRY

Poems, Tibor de Nagy Gallery, 1953.
Ko; or, A Season on Earth (also see below), Grove (New York City), 1959.
Permanently, Tiber Press, 1960.
Thank You and Other Poems, Grove, 1962.
Poems from 1952 and 1953 (limited edition), Black Sparrow Press (Santa Barbara, CA), 1968.
The Pleasures of Peace and Other Poems, Grove, 1969.
When the Sun Tries to Go On, Black Sparrow Press, 1969.
Sleeping with Women (limited edition), Black Sparrow Press, 1969.
The Art of Love, Random House (New York City), 1975.
The Duplications (also see below), Random House, 1977.
The Burning Mystery of Anna in 1951, Random House, 1979.
Days and Nights, Random House, 1982.
Selected Poems, 1950-1982, Random House, 1985.
On the Edge, Viking (New York City), 1986.
Seasons on Earth (includes *Ko; or, A Season on Earth* and *The Duplications*), Penguin (New York City), 1987.
Selected Poems, Carcanet (Manchester, England), 1991.
One Train: Poems, Knopf (New York City), 1994, Carcanet, 1997.
On the Great Atlantic Rainway: Selected Poems, 1950-1988, Knopf, 1994.
(Editor, with others, and author of introduction) Joseph Ceravolo, *The Green Lake Is Awake: Selected Poems,* Coffee House Press (Minneapolis, MN), 1994.

FICTION

(With Alex Katz) *Interlocking Lives,* Kulchur Foundation (New York City), 1970.
The Red Robins (also see below), Random House, 1975.
Hotel Lambosa and Other Stories, Coffee House Press, 1993.

NONFICTION

Wishes, Lies and Dreams: Teaching Children to Write Poetry, Chelsea House (New York City), 1970.
Rose, Where Did You Get That Red?: Teaching Great Poetry to Children, Random House, 1973.
I Never Told Anybody: Teaching Poetry Writing in a Nursing Home, Random House, 1977, revised edition, Teachers and Writers Collaborative (New York City), 1997.
Les Couleurs des voyelles: Pour faire ecrire de la poesie aux enfants, Casterman (Paris), 1978.
Desideri Sogni Bugie, Emme Edizioni (Milan), 1980.

(With Kate Farrell) *Sleeping on the Wing: An Anthology of Modern Poetry, with Essays on Reading and Writing,* Random House, 1981.

(With Farrell) *Talking to the Sun: An Illustrated Anthology of Poems for Young People,* Metropolitan Museum of Art/Holt (New York City), 1985.

The Art of Poetry (literary criticism), University of Michigan Press (Ann Arbor), 1996.

PLAYS

Little Red Riding Hood, produced in New York City at the Theatre de Lys, 1953.

Bertha, first produced in New York City at Living Theatre, 1959, produced as an opera, music by Ned Rorem, c. 1971, published in *Bertha and Other Plays,* 1966.

Pericles, produced Off-Broadway, 1960, published in *Bertha and Other Plays,* 1966.

The Election, produced in New York City at Living Theatre, 1960, published in *A Change of Hearts: Plays, Films, and Other Dramatic Works, 1951-1971,* 1973.

George Washington Crossing the Delaware, produced Off-Broadway, 1962, published in *Bertha and Other Plays,* 1966.

The Construction of Boston, produced Off-Broadway, 1962, produced in Boston as an opera, music by Scott Wheeler, 1990-91, published in *Bertha and Other Plays,* 1966.

Guinevere, or the Death of the Kangaroo, produced in New York City at New York Theatre for Poets, 1964, published in *Bertha and Other Plays,* 1966.

The Tinguely Machine Mystery, or the Love Suicides at Kaluka, produced in New York City at the Jewish Museum, 1965, published in *A Change of Hearts: Plays, Films, and Other Dramatic Works, 1951-1971,* 1973.

Bertha and Other Plays (also see below; includes *The Return of Yellowmay, The Revolt of the Giant Animals, The Building of Florence, Angelica, The Merry Stones, The Academic Murders, Easter, The Lost Feed, Mexico,* and *Coil Supreme*), Grove, 1966.

The Moon Balloon, produced in New York City in Central Park, 1969, published in *A Change of Hearts: Plays, Films, and Other Dramatic Works, 1951-1971,* 1973.

The Artist (opera based on poem of the same title; music by Paul Reif), produced in New York City at Whitney Museum, 1972.

A Little Light, produced in Amagansett, NY, 1972.

A Change of Hearts: Plays, Films, and Other Dramatic Works, 1951-1971 (also see below; contains *Bertha and Other Plays, E. Kology, Without Kinship, Youth, The Enchantment,* and ten filmscripts: *Because, The Color Game, Mountains and Electricity, Sheep Harbor, Oval Gold, Moby Dick, L'Ecole Normale, The Cemetery, The Scotty Dog,* and *The Apple*), Random House, 1973.

The Gold Standard, produced in New York City, 1975, published in *Bertha and Other Plays,* 1966.

Rooster Redivivus, produced in Garnerville, NY, 1975.

The Red Robins (based on novel of the same title; produced in New York City at Theater at St. Clement's, 1978), Theatre Arts, 1979.

The New Diana, produced in New York City at New York Art Theatre Institute, 1984.

A Change of Hearts (opera), produced in New York City at Medicine Show Theatre Ensemble, 1985, published in *A Change of Hearts: Plays, Films, and Other Dramatic Works, 1951-1971,* 1973.

Popeye among the Polar Bears, produced in New York City at Medicine Show Theatre Ensemble, 1986.

One Thousand Avant-Garde Plays, produced by Medicine Show in New York City at the Marymount Theatre, 1987, Knopf, 1988.

The Gold Standard: A Book of Plays, Knopf, 1996.

OTHER

Contributor to *Penguin Modern Poets 24,* Penguin, 1974; contributor of fiction, poetry, and plays to magazines, including *Art and Literature, Locus Solus, Poetry, Raritan, Grand Street,* and *New York Review of Books.* Member of editorial board of *Locus Solus,* 1960-62.

ADAPTATIONS: The Art of Love was adapted for stage by Mike Nussbaum and produced in Chicago, IL, 1976.

WORK IN PROGRESS: A book of poetry and a book about poetry, *The Pleasures of Poetry,* to be published by Simon & Schuster, 1998.

SIDELIGHTS: Kenneth Koch, winner of the 1995 Bollingen Prize, has published numerous collections of poetry, avant-garde plays, and short fiction while also serving as one of the nation's best-known creative writing teachers. Associated with the New York School of poetry for most of his career, Koch has used surrealism, satire, irony, and an element of surprise in many of his poems. However, "his satires are more than mere jokes," explained Roberta Berke in her *Bounds Out of Bounds: A Compass for Recent American and British Poetry:* "they have a serious purpose of literary and social criticism." Koch explores an assortment of emotions in his poetry, but in an era seemingly dedicated to deep seriousness he has refused to relinquish lightness or a sense of humor. According to Phoebe Pettingell in *The New Leader,* Koch's works "convey his perennial freshness in at least two senses of that word: novelty and cheekiness. He has a subtle grasp of the nuances of language as well as a gift for hilarious parody, and behind his casual, friendly manner there is formidable technique and learning."

Koch is "the funniest serious poet we have," according to David Lehman in *Newsweek.* And although Peter Stitt maintained in the *Georgia Review* that the author's "greatest commitment as a poet is to not making very much sense, to not taking things very seriously," other critics have contended that Koch's poetry has an underlying seriousness and praise him for his imagination and originality. "His playfulness, in tone and technique, has often caused him to be underrated," stated *Salmagundi* contributor Paul Zweig. "But it is just his great capacity for humor, based on so much more than mere irony, that makes him important. He has reclaimed the humorous for serious writers of poetry and for that we are in his debt."

Koch is generally considered one of the founders of The New York School of poetry, which came into existence in the 1950s. At the time, the poets who were working within the "school"—including John Ashbery, Frank O'Hara, and Koch, among others—hardly considered themselves trend-setters. The name "New York School" was coined for them by Donald Allen for an anthology he was editing in the late 1950s, and it suggested a spirit of novelty and experimentation that well suited its young practitioners. "The so-called New York School assembled its own outsider identity from some of the same sources as the Beats: an urban male savvy, sometimes inflected with Jewish and gay sensibilities, and an openness to avant-garde work in other media," wrote Christopher Benfey in *The New Republic.* "Kenneth Koch has been a conspicuous member of the New York School, often chronicling its exploits and mourning its losses." *Dictionary of Literary Biography* contributor Michael Adams observed that Koch "has characterized the New York School style as 'anti-traditional, opposed to certain heavy uses of irony and symbolism. . . . I think we may have been more conscious than many poets of the surface of the poem, and what was going on while we were writing and how we were using words.'"

Like other poets of the New York School, Koch uses stream-of-consciousness in his writing and stresses the importance of the present moment and the ordinary. In his essay in *Comic Relief: Humor in Contemporary American Poetry,* John Vernon pointed out that Koch, "like most poets of the New York school, . . . often spices his poems with references to pop culture, deliberate cliches, archaisms, or both academic and romantic phrases and words." Pettingell, for one, concluded that the pop references and personal asides notwithstanding, Koch's work has stood the test of time quite well. "Today, Robert Lowell and Allen Ginsberg are looking pretty hoary to the students of Generation X, and Eliot seems as remote as the late Victorian authors," the critic maintained. "The joke is that those bards of the passing scene, Ashbery and Koch, continue to flourish. Indeed, today they appear to exemplify the tenets of postmodernism."

Koch's first book of poetry, entitled simply *Poems,* began the critical debate over the seriousness of his work. Finding the book "tasteless, futile, noisy and *dull,*" Harry Roskolenko further contended in *Poetry* that "Koch writes lazy verse and is precious and puerile." This negative review prompted a rebuttal from Frank O'Hara, who asserted in *Poetry* that Koch "has the other poetic gift: vivacity and go, originality of perception and intoxication with life. Most important of all, he is not *dull.*" *Washington Post Book World* contributor Michael Lally agreed, claiming that "Koch's work is always entertaining and usually enlightening." The poems in Koch's debut work cover a diversity of subjects; F. W. Dupee claimed in the *New York Review of Books* that "Koch is fond of making poetry out of poetry-resistant stuff. Locks, lipsticks, business letterheads, walnuts, lunch and fudge attract him; so do examples of inept slang, silly sentiment, brutal behavior and stereotyped exotica and erotica." Employing the bizarre humor of surrealism and the techniques of abstract expressionism, Koch crafts poems that emphasize form and sound. And the words that Koch selects to present his subjects surge together "like an express train of exuberant sounds," observed *Poetry* contributor David Lehman, adding that "the poet takes a great deal of delight in the sounds of words and his consciousness of them; he splashes them like paint on a page with enthusiastic puns, internal rhymes, titles of books, names of friends . . . and seems surprised as we are at the often witty outcome."

Koch seems to thrive on the intensity in writing a new poem, and many of his poems deal with the poetic imagination and the actual act of creating poetry. *Poetry* contributor Paul Carroll explained: "Koch celebrates that splendid faculty with which men make poetry. His poems embody the poetic imagination as it rejoices in the ebullience of its health and freedom, its fecundity, its capacity for endless invention, its dear, outlandish ability to transform everyday, pragmatic reality into an Oz or a tea-party at the March Hare's house, its potency in, possibly, achieving a bit of immortality as a result of having brought forth some children of the soul." In "The Pleasures of Peace," the title poem in *The Pleasures of Peace and Other Poems,* Koch presents this theme of the creative mind at work through Giorgio Finogle and another poet. Both poets are writing a poem about the pleasures of peace, and thus find themselves competing against one another. This is but one example of the author's "celebration of the excitement of the imagination as it begins to create," according to Carroll.

In *The Art of Love,* Koch's "voice is unperturbed, offering serene and careless advice on the arts of love and poetry for those who have ears and can hear," said Paul Wilner in *Village Voice.* Writing in *Poetry,* J. D. McClatchy referred to the book as an "erotic romp," and Wilner further described it as "updating Ovid by reinventing the alphabet of emotion." Zweig added that Koch's "humor has an edge of satire; his ebullient absurdity slides into an original form of social and cultural criticism, as in 'The Artist' and 'Fresh Air,' both enormously funny epics about the impossibility of art." In the poem "The Art of Love," Koch parodies several advice-giving documents and tries to "enable both poet and reader to distance feelings, ideas, experiences, so as to perceive them strangely, freshly, as if they were rare or even alien curiosities, *objects d'art,* perhaps, in some great Bloomingdale's of the imagination," asserted Sandra M. Gilbert in *Poetry.* The drawback to this form of presentation is that detachment can filter in. *Shenandoah* contributor Conrad Hilberry observed, for instance, that "[Koch's] poems, like pop art, present great simplicity but maintain so much ironic distance that they make the ordinary reader uneasy." However, Aram Saroyan maintained in the *New York Times Book Review* that the poems in *The Art of Love* embody "the ability to move the reader, plain but beautiful language that should appeal to a wide audience, a general graciousness of spirit that has long been an unremarked-on hallmark of Koch's writing, and last but not least, outright wisdom."

"Every book of poems by . . . Koch seems to be a new beginning, a starting over, a trying-out of new voices, styles and idioms," observed John Boening in his *World Literature Today* review of *Days and Nights.* This anthology contains a wide variety of poems, in which, explained Mark Hillringhouse in the *American Book Review,* "Koch has paid more attention to physical detail and places his emotions directly and concretely into the poem." The poems encompass such subjects as love, aging, loneliness, the past, and the future. One of the pieces, "To Janice," is "moving, intimate, smiling, tender, touching and inventive," according to Boening, who added that it alone "is worth the price of the book." And the title poem, "Days and Nights," is phrased in such a way so as to evoke "a whole spectrum of emotions; from lost time to old friends, to travels and defeats to fears of writing itself," asserted Hillringhouse. "Koch sets out to explore a new landscape that is honest to the act of writing and to the process of the imagination."

On the Edge consists of two lengthy poems, "Impressions of Africa" and "On the Edge," the second being "more ambitious, ranging widely over the facts and fiction of . . . Koch's life," in the words of *New York Times Book Review* correspondent John Ash. The poem moves back and forth between past and present, according to Denis Donoghue in *Commonweal,* "memories and currencies of sentiment jostling one another within the strong propriety of the cadence." *Washington Post Book World* contributor Peter Davison saw the allusions the poem relies on as "calculated to exclude outsiders, to make the non-belonger feel stupid, to make the reader ransack for a footnote."

Ash, however, viewed the book as taking "great risks," and claimed that "we cannot do better than judge it by his [Koch's] own demanding criteria, set out in his 'Art of Poetry.' Does it astonish? Is it sufficiently modern? Is it written in his own voice? Is it devoid of 'literary, "kiss-me-I'm-poetical" junk'? Is it 'serious without being solemn, fresh without being cold'? The answer, in all cases, must be affirmative."

A new poem, "Seasons on Earth," and two of Koch's previously published comic epics, "Ko; or, A Season on Earth" and "The Duplications," comprise *Seasons on Earth.* The book provides "a poetic memoir that glances back at the time during which he wrote the earlier poems, a genre at which Koch's discursive talents have proved particularly masterful," commented Gary Lenhart in the *American Book Review.* Lenhart added that the title poem continues the mastery of the narrative, "but new urgencies threaten to move the poet away from the strict adherence to form characteristic of the earlier poems." Adams described *Ko; or A Season on Earth* as "a comic epic modeled partially after Byron's *Don Juan* and Ariosto's *Orlando Furioso*" that "details the misadventures of a group of outlandish characters who flit about from continent to continent, reality to unreality." Among other things, the poem relates the story of Ko, a Japanese college student who comes to the United States to play baseball. Lenhart says that the poem "is bursting with the exuberance of a sensuous young poet impatient with the literary world." In the *Washington Post Book World,* Terence Winch regarded "The Duplications" as "something of a nonsense epic whose seriousness lies more in the demonstration of Koch's impressive technical skill than in the narrative itself." There are many "duplications" in the poem, maintained Winch, but the most important ones are the rhymes. And although the poem is a narrative, Winch also suggested that the way in which Koch's mind works and the language he uses deserve more attention than the actual story. Koch's "work is important for its singularity as for its exuberant invention, inspired fluency, and histrionic imagination," concluded Lenhart.

Aside from writing poetry, Koch has also experimented with teaching poetry to children and to the elderly. In 1968 he began his experiment with the children at P.S. 61, a New York City elementary school. *New York Times* contributor Lisa Hammel described the reception Koch received from his students: "The fifth grade class stood up and cheered so wildly when the tall man with a mop of wavy hair came into the room, he might have been a baseball player. Or an astronaut. But he wasn't. The man . . . who seemed to invade rather than come into the room was their poetry teacher." *Wishes, Lies, and Dreams: Teaching Children to Write Poetry* describes how writing became exciting for these students and includes some of the poetry they wrote. The title of the book actually came from some of the teaching methods Koch used. *Saturday Review* contributor Herbert Kohl considered the work "perhaps the best book I have read portraying the joy and excitement young people experience when writing in a happy place where people care about their work." Kohl emphasized the environment Koch was able to create, stating that "Koch's classes were obviously fun. There was noise, movement, life. In a deathly quiet and clean environment, the most interesting ideas are immediately sterilized."

Although the students in Koch's class wrote some exceptional poetry, Koch didn't stop there. John Gardner wrote in the *New York Times Book Review* that "the children themselves felt a need for something more. Koch's response was to shift the experiment to 'teaching great poetry to children,' thus broadening the tradition available to them." The record of this experiment and its tremendous results is *Rose, Where Did You Get That Red?: Teaching Great Poetry to Children.* Koch would distribute and read a poem such as William Blake's "The Tyger," and then discuss it with the children until they understood its central idea. Then, he would have his students work on their own writing, some of which Gardner labeled "brilliant" and "terrific." Although not everyone could be as successful a teacher as Koch, concluded Gardner, his methods "will work for everyone at least some of the time. His two books could—*should*—be the beginning of a great revolution."

Koch also worked with another group of seemingly unlikely poets, the residents of Manhattan's American Nursing Home. *I Never Told Anybody: Teaching Poetry Writing in a Nursing Home* "is a collection of the patients' poems and Koch's highly readable account of how he coaxed his students along," commented a *Time* contributor. At first unresponsive, the elderly and infirm students learned "to summon and repeat words joyfully, to exaggerate enthusiastically, to celebrate contrasts, to become immersed in nature, to imagine all sorts of places, to put themselves into many different kinds of shoes," wrote Robert Coles in the *New York Times Book Review.* Koch explained to the *Time* reviewer that he hopes other homes will offer such workshops, but not just as "therapeutic busywork. . . . As therapy it may help someone to be a busy old person, but as art and accomplishment it can help him to be fully alive. It was cheering to find such a lot of life and strength in the nursing home. I hadn't known that there was so much passion and wit." The author also told *CA* that he profited creatively from the experience: "Teaching others to write poetry was a sort of practical use of discoveries I'd made writing poems, an applied science, something like engineering rather than physics. But I'm very glad to have been able to do that teaching."

Koch has also written many short plays, as full of parody, satire, and irony as his poems. Denis Donoghue suggested in a *New York Review of Books* essay that in *Bertha and Other Plays,* "Koch implies in his smiling way that nothing is too silly to be said or sung, provided we know exactly how silly it is." In the *New York Review of Books,* Stephen Spender described the plays in *A Change of Hearts: Plays, Films, and Other Dramatic Works, 1951-1971* as being "written in a variety of styles, parodying other styles." Koch is extremely inventive, concluded Spender, "and has the funniness which comes out of exuberant vitality." The more recent *One Thousand Avant-Garde Plays,* which contains 112 miniature verse plays, was considered to be "a pure act of poetic invention" by David Lehman in the *Washington Post Book World.* The cast of characters in these plays includes Lord Byron, Bozo, Olive Oyl, a Chinese cook, Little Red Riding Hood, Watteau, and hippopotami. "These brief plays are not fragments but full-blown dramas distilled to the action at the heart of each," asserted Lenhart, concluding that "one can only applaud [Koch's] insistence on making plays that are at once intelligent and entertaining."

Although many critics applaud Koch's poems and plays for their frivolity and nonsense, other critics believe that the whimsy in his work prevents it from being taken seriously. Koch told *CA* that he resents the label "comic poet" and does not feel it does justice to his work. "If whoever says comic means by that not serious, I certainly hope it's not accurate," he said. "I think some of my work is funny, but if it's not also serious I've been wasting a lot of time. My intention is never mainly to be satirical but to be lyrical, or to do some sort of lyrical reportage, to try to get at what experience is like—sometimes the comic is a part of it, or may be part of what helps me to find it." Lenhart, for one, has insisted that Koch has had admirable success with humor, satire, and irony. "As poet, dramatist, anthologist, and teacher, he has consistently attempted to reclaim for poetry areas of sensibility considered out of bounds in our stretch of the twentieth century," the critic concluded.

Koch's more recent works demonstrate the poet's willingness to continue experimenting in a variety of forms. In 1994 he released two poetry collections, and the following year he published a volume of short-short stories. All three books earned significant critical response, with the poetry collections cited as factors in awarding Koch the Bollingen Prize. In a *Chicago Tribune* review of both of the poetry collections, Paul Hoover declared: "Koch is an extravagant improviser, natural formalist and borscht-belt comedian. His poems have daring, ease and sprezzatura; they are formally accomplished without pomposity. . . . *On the Great Atlantic Rainway* reveals a poet of intimacy and size, lyricism and intelligence. Because his work is light-hearted, it has been accused of triviality. Yet in poems like his hilarious polemic, 'Fresh Air,' Koch shows the fiercely moral nature of the true satirist. Koch wishes to relieve poetry of false height and forced sentimentality." While Benfey noted that some of Koch's work leaves the poet himself "ripe for parody," he nonetheless observed: "Koch seems to have such a good time writing poetry that any carping feels like party-pooping."

Hotel Lambosa is a collection of short fiction, variously described in reviews as short-short stories, prose poems, and vignettes. The pieces blend biography, fable, and magic realism as they reveal new facets of Koch's imagination. "I don't know if *Hotel Lambosa* is the 'best' work Koch has done, but it's astonishingly mature and wise—also surprising," wrote Peter Johnson in the *American Book Review.* "*Hotel Lambosa* exhibits . . . range in subject and vision. Myths get rewritten, geographical details are recorded, and real and imaginary characters stumble across real and imaginary landscapes, or perhaps they're one and the same. . . . It's [Koch's] maturity as a writer—his general ability to suggest 'big ideas' simply—that makes this collection worth the read." *World Literature Today* contributor Bernard F. Dick noted that, with *Hotel Lambosa,* "one is in the presence of a poet who knows how to distill images into metaphor and structure a story so it culminates in a climax."

A longtime professor of creative writing and comparative literature at Columbia University, Koch makes his home in New York City. "I seem to go on being influenced, and encouraged, by what I read," he told *CA*. Koch, in turn, has become influential upon the generations of young writers who have followed him, as well as upon critics and readers of his works. Bernard F. Dick observed that the author's body of work depicts "a poet's progress, beginning with self-conscious experimentation in the usual way of finding a voice and ending with a voice as distinctive and resonant as the ones that echo through the poetry." Dick added that Koch's poems "attest to a creative power and its gradual refinement, as life and art, the playful and the profound."

BIOGRAPHICAL/CRITICAL SOURCES:

BOOKS

Berke, Roberta, *Bounds Out of Bounds: A Compass for Recent American and British Poetry,* Oxford University Press (Oxford, England), 1981.

Chevalier, Tracy, editor, *Contemporary Poets,* St. James Press (Detroit, MI), 1991.

Cohen, Sarah Blacher, editor, *Comic Relief: Humor in Contemporary American Literature,* University of Illinois Press (Champaign, IL), 1978.

Contemporary Literary Criticism, Gale (Detroit, MI), Volume 5, 1976, Volume 8, 1978, Volume 44, 1987.

Dictionary of Literary Biography, Volume 5: *American Poets since World War II,* Gale, 1980.

Dupee, F. W., *"The King of Cats" and Other Remarks on Writers and Writing,* Farrar, Straus (New York City), 1965.

Howard, Richard, *Alone with America: Essays on the Art of Poetry in the United States,* Atheneum (New York City), 1969.

John Ashbery and Kenneth Koch: A Conversation, Interview Press, 1965.

Koch, Kenneth, *The Art of Love,* Random House, 1975.

PERIODICALS

American Book Review, May, 1984; November-December, 1986; May, 1989; February, 1994, pp. 12, 19.

Booklist, May 15, 1993, p. 1674.

Chicago Tribune Books, July 9, 1995, p. 6.

Commonweal, November 29, 1985.

Comparative Literature Studies, June, 1980.

Georgia Review, fall, 1985.

New Leader, January 30, 1995, pp. 14-15.

New Republic, August 2, 1969; March 13, 1995, pp. 39-42.

Newsweek, September 16, 1985.

New York Review of Books, May, 1963; October 20, 1966; September 20, 1973; August 14, 1980; April 8, 1993, p. 36.

New York Times, November 21, 1970; April 10, 1977; January 19, 1978; January 12, 1979; February 7, 1995.

New York Times Book Review, February 11, 1968; December 23, 1973; September 28, 1975; April 10, 1977; April 20, 1986.

Poetry, March, 1955; June, 1955; September, 1969; November, 1971; August, 1976; August, 1978.

Publisher's Weekly, April 5, 1993, p. 71; May 30, 1994, p. 45.

Review of Contemporary Fiction, fall, 1993, pp. 221-22.

Sagetrieb, spring, 1993, p. 131.

Salmagundi, spring-summer, 1973.

Saturday Review, March 20, 1971.

Shenandoah, spring, 1978.

Studies in Short Fiction, winter, 1995, pp. 102-05.

Time, April 4, 1977.

Times Literary Supplement, February 20, 1987.

Village Voice, May 18, 1972; December 20, 1973; November 24, 1975.

Washington Post Book World, August 3, 1975; April 17, 1977; January 12, 1986; April 13, 1986; August 28, 1988; January 1, 1995, p. 8.

World Literature Today, winter, 1984; winter, 1994, p. 142; autumn, 1995, pp. 800-801.

Yale Review, July 1985.

* * *

KRAMER, Rita 1929-

PERSONAL: Born April 30, 1929, in Detroit, MI; daughter of William R. and Sophie (Joffe)

Blumenthal; married Yale Kramer (a physician), March 18, 1951; children: Deborah, Mimi. *Ethnicity:* "American." *Education:* University of Chicago, B.A., 1948. *Religion:* Jewish.

ADDRESSES: *Agent*—Michael Congdon, Don Congdon Associates Inc., 156 Fifth Ave., New York, NY 10010.

CAREER: Freelance writer, editor, and researcher, 1960—. CBS Learning Center, worked as coordinator of infancy research; U.S. Department of Education, served as member of Elementary Education Study Group and Elementary School Recognition Panel, and as a member of the board of directors of Fund for the Improvement and Reform of Schools and Teaching.

WRITINGS:

(With Lee Salk) *How to Raise a Human Being,* Random House (New York City), 1969.

Maria Montessori: A Biography, Putnam (New York City), 1976, published with a foreword by Anna Freud, Hamish Hamilton, 1989.

Giving Birth: Childbearing in America Today, Contemporary Books (Chicago), 1978.

In Defense of the Family: Raising Children in America Today, Basic Books (New York City), 1983.

At a Tender Age: Violent Youth and Juvenile Justice, Holt (New York City), 1988.

Ed School Follies: The Miseducation of America's Teachers, Free Press (New York City), 1991.

Flames in the Field, Penguin UK, 1996.

Work represented in anthologies. Contributor of articles, stories, and reviews to magazines, including *New York Times Magazine, Commentary, Public Interest, American Heritage, Wilson Quarterly,* and *City Journal,* and newspapers.

SIDELIGHTS: In 1896, Maria Montessori became the first woman graduate of an Italian medical school; later she turned her talents to reforming the fields of early childhood and special education. "Thanks to Rita Kramer, Montessori's latest biographer," notes *Village Voice* contributor Donald M. Kaplan, "we now have a trustworthy and compelling account of the life and career of this most brilliant educator, *Maria Montessori: A Biography.*" While Montessori's teaching methods have endured, many aspects of the professor's life have been overlooked; to rectify this, "Kramer has done some marvelous detective work in uncovering obscure facts about Montessori's life, and fitting them together to shed important light on her activities," remarks Barbara Castle in *Best Sellers.* Donald G. MacRae similarly observes in *New Statesman* that "Kramer has written a continually interesting book about Montessori and has not flagged in her researches into a life led in so many countries and an influence so widely exercised." The critic adds that *Maria Montessori* "is, as the author claims, something more than a life: it is also a contribution to intellectual and social history." "Kramer has captured precisely the circumstances of Montessori's achievement," maintains Kaplan. "For Kramer gives us not only a faithful portrait of a truly marvelous woman; Kramer's biography is also a travelogue, a chronicle of the first half of the century and, not least, a history of a social and intellectual struggle to liberate . . . the mind of the child."

Montessori was a natural subject for Kramer to investigate, for the author has been a longtime child advocate. Her 1983 work *In Defense of the Family: Raising Children in America Today,* for example, proposes "that parents should and must reclaim for themselves the primary responsibility of nurturing, guiding and teaching their children," describes *Commonweal* contributor Janet Scott Barlow. The critic asserts that Kramer's book "does more than leave its mark; it scores a bullseye. . . . That this particular book will doubtless be viewed in some circles as either radical or reactionary says [something about our times]," adds Barlow. *In Defense of the Family*'s suggestion that a parent (preferably the mother) remain at home with the child for at least its first three years has produced controversy among family advocates, researchers, and feminists. *New Republic* contributors Peter and Margaret O'Brien Steinfels, for example, believe that "it is no exaggeration to say that [Kramer's] book is a diatribe against feminism, which is never mentioned except disparagingly." The Steinfels elaborate, noting that "there is not the least acknowledgement that feminists have addressed any real problems"; Judith K. Davison similarly comments in the *New York Times Book Review* that "Kramer simply ignores many realities" about women's motives for remaining in the workplace after giving birth. Jane O'Reilly similarly criticizes Kramer for slighting issues such as the "feminization of poverty." Writing in the *Nation,* she asserts that it is "futile to suggest the solution [to family problems] lies in putting women back in the home—and, by unavoidable implication, keeping men out of it."

Kramer, however, responds in a *People* article that her book is directed toward a specific audience, not all parents. "I'm not prophesying doom for the offspring of every woman who doesn't have a man in the house and has to work to support her kids. . . . I'm addressing myself to the ambivalence of middle-class mothers who have options." *Commentary* contributor Chester E. Finn notes that while Kramer "harbors what many will deem old-fashioned views," *In Defense of the Family* "is not an exercise in finger-wagging or tradition mongering. Rather, Mrs. Kramer's image of the proper ordering of family and society is grounded in her understanding of child development, of human psychology, and of the requisites for the emergence of an autonomous young adult." Finn adds that the author does consider potential objections to her philosophy: "The objective reader will see that Mrs. Kramer has worked her way through these issues and is confident—I think justly so—of her conclusions." In addition, Kramer provides a theoretical basis for her assertions that a home environment with continuous parent involvement is crucial to a child's development; Elizabeth Cleland comments in the *Washington Post* that *In Defense of the Family* "offers 46 pages of detailed notes to reinforce her conclusions." "Rita Kramer suggests that parenthood is not only a noble, but an enobling task," contends Barlow. "She writes that one of the challenges of this task is to be 'tolerant while maintaining your standards.' True to her own advice, she has written a noble book which, like a good parent, provides the confidence of sure expectations and the safety of loving limits."

In another study involving children's issues, *At a Tender Age: Violent Youth and Juvenile Justice,* "Rita Kramer takes you to the edge of the abyss and lets you have a long, terrifying look," describes James Q. Wilson in *Commentary*. "The abyss is Family Court in New York City as it struggles to cope with violent, abused, and disorderly youth. The terror comes not only from seeing the violent ones," elaborates the critic, "but, worse, from seeing the inability of the court to do much except return them to the environment from which they came." Kramer's extensive research into the working of the juvenile justice system led her to encounter such subjects as a twelve-year-old who participated in the gang-rape and beating of an elderly woman and who had previously raped and murdered another; a year later he was released from rehabilitation and was soon spotted near the scene of a similar rape/beating. "Why was so obviously dangerous a boy left at large?," asks *Los Angeles Times Book Review* contributor George Cadwalader. "The answer, says longtime child advocate Rita Kramer in . . . her excellent and thought-provoking study . . . , lies in the 'obsolescent philosophy' behind a system that fails 'either to restrain or retrain the young.'"

This system, writes the author, has been undermined by conflicting court procedures. While the original concept of the juvenile justice system was to act in place of the parents when a child was "at risk," whether from abuse, criminal activity, or delinquency, later directives steered the court into an adversarial relationship where the focus is on the juvenile's "rights" and not his protection or rehabilitation. "[Kramer] has written an angry, unsettling book in which the impressive weight of her nuts-and-bolts reporting is to some extent undermined by an intemperate tone," remarks Susan Jacoby in the *New York Times Book Review.* The critic admits, however, that "anger is an understandable response to a system that fails to protect the community because it gives so much more weight to the age of the criminal than to the nature of the crime." Cadwalader concurs, noting that *At a Tender Age* "provides countless examples to prove that *parens patria,*" the concept of the court acting as parent, "doesn't work. . . . The sobering message implicit in this important book is that we must look instead at all the aspects of our society that contribute to producing [juvenile criminals]." "If a governor or mayor wants to make a lasting difference in New York City," concludes Wilson, "let him go with Mrs. Kramer and peek into the abyss of Family Court, and then set himself the task of reconstituting it along saner lines. If he is not willing to do this he should stop making speeches about crime."

BIOGRAPHICAL/CRITICAL SOURCES:

PERIODICALS

Best Sellers, July, 1976.
Commentary, May, 1983; July, 1988.
Commonweal, August 10, 1984.
Harper's, October, 1969.
Los Angeles Times, March 9, 1983.
Los Angeles Times Book Review, May 15, 1988.

Nation, July 9, 1983.
New Republic, May 16, 1983.
New Statesman, April 14, 1978.
New York Times Book Review, May 8, 1983; April 10, 1988.
People, March 14, 1983.
Times Literary Supplement, May 26, 1978; April 12, 1996.
Village Voice, August 16, 1976.
Washington Post, February 11, 1983.

* * *

KREEFT, Peter 1937-

PERSONAL: Surname is pronounced Krayft; born March 16, 1937, in Paterson, NJ; son of John (an engineer) and Lucy (Comtobad) Kreeft; married Maria Massi, August 18, 1962; children: John, Jennifer, Katherine, Elizabeth. *Ethnicity:* "Dutch." *Education:* Calvin College, A.B., 1959; graduate study at Yale University, 1959-60; Fordham University, M.A., 1961, Ph.D., 1965. *Religion:* Roman Catholic.

ADDRESSES: Home—44 Davis Ave., West Newton, MA 02165. *Office*—Department of Philosophy, Boston College, Chestnut Hill, MA, 02167; fax: 617-332-9173.

CAREER: Villanova University, Villanova, PA, instructor in philosophy, 1961-65; Boston College, Chestnut Hill, MA, assistant professor, 1965-69, associate professor of philosophy, 1969—.

AWARDS, HONORS: Woodrow Wilson fellowship, 1959-60; Danforth fellowship, 1966-67; *Love Is Stronger than Death* was nominated for the American Book Award in the religion/inspirational category, 1980.

WRITINGS:

C. S. Lewis, Eerdmans (Grand Rapids, MI), 1969, published as *C. S. Lewis: A Critical Essay,* Christendom College Press (Front Royal, VA), 1988.
Love Is Stronger than Death, Harper (New York City), 1979.
Heaven, the Heart's Deepest Longing, Harper, 1980.
Everything You Ever Wanted to Know about Heaven . . . but Never Dreamed of Asking, Harper, 1982.
Between Heaven and Hell, Inter-Varsity Press (Downers Grove, IL), 1982.
The Unaborted Socrates, Inter-Varsity Press, 1983.
The Best Things in Life, Inter-Varsity Press, 1984.
Yes or No?: Straight Answers to Tough Questions about Christianity, Servant Publications (Ann Arbor, MI), 1984.
(With Richard Purtill and Michael MacDonald) *Philosophical Questions,* Prentice-Hall (Englewood Cliffs, NJ), 1984.
Prayer: The Great Conversation, Servant Publications, 1985.
The Source, Thomas Nelson (Nashville, TN), 1985.
For Heaven's Sake, Thomas Nelson, 1986.
Making Sense Out of Suffering, Servant Publications, 1986.
Socrates Meets Jesus, Inter-Varsity Press, 1987.
A Turn of the Clock, Ignatius Press (San Francisco, CA), 1987.
Spiritual Journeys, Daughters of St. Paul (Boston), 1987.
The Reality of God's Love, Servant Publications, 1988.
Fundamentals of the Faith, Ignatius Press, 1988.
Letters to Jesus, Ignatius Press, 1989.
Three Philosophies of Life: Job, Ecclesiastes, Song of Songs, Ignatius Press, 1989.
(Author of introduction and conclusion) J. P. Moreland and Kai Nielson, *Does God Exist?: The Great Debate,* Thomas Nelson, 1990.
Making Choices, Servant Publications, 1990.
You Can Understand the Old Testament, Servant Publications, 1990.
(Editor) *Summa of the "Summa,"* Ignatius Press, 1991.
Reading and Praying the New Testament, Servant Publications, 1991.
(Editor and author of notes) *Christianity for Modern Pagans,* Ignatius Press, 1993.
The Snakebite Letters, Ignatius Press, 1993.
A Shorter Summa, Ignatius Press, 1993.
(With R. Tacelli) *Handbook of Christian Apologetics,* Inter-Varsity Press, 1993.
Your Questions, God's Answers, Ignatius Press, 1994.
The Shadowlands of C. S. Lewis, Ignatius Press, 1994.
(With A. von Hildebrand) *Women and the Priesthood,* Franciscan University Press, 1994.

The Angel and the Ant, Servant Publications, 1994.
C. S. Lewis for the Third Millennium, Ignatius Press, 1994.
Angels and Demons, Ignatius Press, 1995.
Ecumenical Jihad, Ignatius Press, 1995.
The Journey, Inter-Varsity Press, 1996.

WORK IN PROGRESS: A catechism based on the new *Catechism of the Catholic Church;* a novel, *Sea of Angels.*

SIDELIGHTS: Peter Kreeft writes that his main interests are philosophy in literature, philosophy of religion, East-West dialogue, mysticism, and existentialism. His books sometimes dramatize both sides of a moral issue. For instance, *The Unaborted Socrates* is an imaginary dialogue between Socrates and a doctor, a lawyer, and a psychiatrist in an abortion clinic. C. S. Lewis, John F. Kennedy, and Aldous Huxley—who in real life all died on the same afternoon in 1963—meet in *Between Heaven and Hell* to discuss three world views (theism, humanism, and pantheism). And in *Socrates Meets Jesus,* Kreeft places the philosopher in Harvard Divinity School to dramatize a conversion through rational argument.

Kreeft told *CA:* "*Sea of Angels* will be an angel's-eye view of the connection between Jesus Christ, dead Vikings, Muslim philosophers, soul-surfers, sassy Black feminists, Dutch Calvinist seminarians, fat Jewish mother substitutes, Alexandr Solzhenitsyn, two-and-a-half dead popes, sea serpents, the dooms of the Boston Red Sox, the Great Blizzard of '78, the seduction of the sea, post-abortion trauma, the Arab-Israeli wars, and the third millennium."

* * *

KREJCI, Jaroslav 1916-

PERSONAL: Surname rhymes with "Strachey"; born February 13, 1916, in Czechoslovakia; son of Jaroslav (a civil servant) and Zdenka (Dudova) Krejci; married Anna Cerna (a principal lecturer at Preston Polytechnic), May 11, 1940 (died July 31, 1995). *Ethnicity:* "Czech." *Education:* Charles University, Prague, D.Jur., 1945.

ADDRESSES: Office—Lonsdale College, Lancaster University, Lancaster LA1 4YT, England; fax 1524-843934 and 2-23-13-882. *E-mail*—a.taylor@lancaster.ac.uk.

CAREER: State Planning Office, Prague, Czechoslovakia, secretary to the chairperson, 1945-48, head of department of national income, 1948-50; State Bank, Prague, research worker, 1950-53; Czechoslovak Academy of Sciences, Prague, research worker, 1968; Lancaster University, Lancaster, England, lecturer in comparative social and cultural analysis, 1970-76, professor in School of European Studies, 1976-83, professor emeritus, 1983—. External associate professor at Graduate School of Political and Social Sciences, Prague, 1948-50, and Technological University, Prague, 1950-52; Academy of Sciences of the Czech Republic, director of Centre for Research into Socio-Cultural Pluralism at Institute of Philosophy, 1994—. Member of advisory body for economic analysis for the deputy prime minister, Prague, 1968; Josef Hlavka Economic Institute, Prague, honorary chairperson, 1994—.

MEMBER: International Society for the Comparative Study of Civilizations, Czechoslovak Society of Arts and Sciences, Czech Learned Society, British Association of Soviet and East European Studies.

AWARDS, HONORS: Award for participation in Czech resistance movement during World War II, 1946; Charles University Memorial Medal, 1991; Josef Hlavka Award, Czechoslovak Academy of Sciences, 1992, for "outstanding scholarship."

WRITINGS:

Duchodove rozvrstveni (title means "Income Distribution"), [Prague], 1947.
Uvod do planovaneho hospodarstvi (title means "Introduction to the Planned Economy"), [Prague], 1949.
Volkseinkommensvergleich: Osterreich CSSR (title means "National Income Comparison: Austria-Czechoslovakia"), Verlag des Osterreichischen Gewerkschaftsbundes (Vienna, Austria), 1969.
Social Change and Stratification in Postwar Czechoslovakia, Columbia University Press (New York City), 1972.
Social Structure in Divided Germany, St. Martin's (New York City), 1976.

(Editor) *Sozialdemokratie und Systemwandel,* Dietz, 1978.
(With V. Velimsky) *Ethnic and Political Nations in Europe,* St. Martin's, 1981.
National Income and Outlay in Czechoslovakia, Poland and Yugoslavia, St. Martin's, 1982.
Great Revolutions Compared, St. Martin's, 1983.
Before the European Challenge: The Great Civilizations of Asia and the Middle East, State University of New York Press (Albany), 1990.
Czechoslovakia at the Crossroads of European History, I. B. Tauris (London), 1990.
The Human Predicament: Its Changing Image, St. Martin's, 1993.
Society in a Global Perspective, SLON (Prague), 1993.
Great Revolutions Compared: The Outline of a Theory, Harvester, 1994.
(With P. Machonin) *Czechoslovakia, 1918-92: A Laboratory for Social Change,* Macmillan (London), 1996.
(Editor) *Human Rights and Responsibilities in a Divided World,* Filosofia (Prague), 1996.

Contributor to books, including *Comparative Economic Performance,* edited by A. Graham and A. Sowden, Methuen, 1990; *Neo-Fascism in Europe,* edited by L. Cheles, R. Ferguson, and M. Vaughan, Longman, 1990; and *The Far Right in Western and Eastern Europe,* Longman, 1995. Contributor to *Review of Income and Wealth, Soviet Studies, Sociological Analysis, Journal of Religious History, History of European Ideas, Journal of Communist Studies, Czech Sociological Review,* and other periodicals.

WORK IN PROGRESS: Memoirs.

SIDELIGHTS: Jaroslav Krejci spent the years from 1954-60 in a labor camp in Czechoslovakia. He told *CA:* "The communist regime in Czechoslovakia found my approach to macroeconomics (my original specialization) subversive. It also taught me a lesson: it is not economic interests and relationships but new great ideas (religions or world views) shared by sufficiently large numbers of dedicated people that decide the turning points in history. As a result I have turned to the study of such ideas. My key work is the book *The Human Predicament: Its Changing Image*. The subtitle of its amended Czech version, published by Charles University Press in 1996, reads 'Spiritual Foundations of Diversity in Civilization.' The study of various ways of coping with death and making sense of life leads to the assumption of particular paradigms of the human predicament. Their developments (cross-breedings, rifts, wanings, revivals, and mutations) are explanatory pointers to the understanding of the meandering course of world history.

"My memoirs refer mainly to my father's role in the Czech-German cohabitation and/or confrontation before and during World War II (for a time, he was prime minister), my involvement in the anti-Nazi and anti-communist resistance movements, my experience of the communist labour camps, of exile in the UK, and of my return and rehabilitation at home. Particular attention is given to the social and political background of the reported events. A German translation is envisaged."

* * *

KUNITZ, Stanley (Jasspon) 1905-

PERSONAL: Born July 29, 1905, in Worcester, MA; son of Solomon Z. (a manufacturer) and Yetta Helen (Jasspon) Kunitz; married Helen Pearce, 1930 (divorced, 1937); married Eleanor Evans, November 21, 1939 (divorced, 1958); married Elise Asher (an artist), June 21, 1958; children: (second marriage) Gretchen. *Education:* Harvard University, A.B. (summa cum laude), 1926, A.M., 1927.

ADDRESSES: Home—37 West 12th St., New York, NY 10011-8502.

CAREER: Poet. *Wilson Library Bulletin,* New York City, editor, 1928-43; Bennington College, Bennington, VT, professor of English, 1946-49; Potsdam State Teachers College (now State University of New York College at Potsdam), Potsdam, NY, professor of English, 1949-50; New School for Social Research, New York City, lecturer in English, 1950-57; Poetry Center, Young Men's Hebrew Association (YMHA), New York City, director of poetry workshop, 1958-62; Columbia University, New York City, lecturer, 1963-66, adjunct professor of writing in School of the Arts, 1967-85. Member of staff of writing division, Fine Arts Work Center, Provincetown,

1968—. Fellow, Yale University, 1969—; visiting senior fellow, Council of the Humanities, and Old Dominion Fellow in creative writing, Princeton University, 1978-79. Director of seminar, Potsdam Summer Workshop in Creative Arts, 1949-53; poet in residence, University of Washington, 1955-56, Queens College (now Queens College of the City University of New York), 1956-57, Brandeis University, 1958-59, and Princeton University, 1979. Danforth Visiting Lecturer at colleges and universities in the United States, 1961-63; visiting professor, Yale University, 1972, and Rutgers University, 1974. Lectured and gave poetry readings under cultural exchange program in USSR and Poland, 1967, in Senegal and Ghana, 1976, and in Israel and Egypt, 1980. Library of Congress, Washington, DC, consultant on poetry, 1974-76, honorary consultant in American letters, 1976-83. *Military service:* U.S. Army, Air Transport Command, 1943-45; became staff sergeant.

MEMBER: American Academy and Institute of Arts and Letters (secretary, 1985-88), Academy of American Poets (chancellor, 1970—), Poets House (founding president, 1985-90), Phi Beta Kappa.

AWARDS, HONORS: Garrison Medal for poetry, Harvard University, 1926; Oscar Blumenthal Prize, 1941; Guggenheim fellowship, 1945-46; Amy Lowell travelling fellowship, 1953-54; Levinson Prize, *Poetry* magazine, 1956; *Saturday Review* award, 1957; Harriet Monroe Poetry Award, University of Chicago, 1958; Ford Foundation grant, 1958-59; National Institute of Arts and Letters award, 1959; Pulitzer Prize, 1959, for *Selected Poems, 1928-1958;* Brandeis University creative arts award medal, 1964; Academy of American Poets fellowship, 1968; New England Poetry Club Golden Rose Trophy, 1970; American Library Association notable book citation, 1979, for *The Poems of Stanley Kunitz, 1928-1978;* Lenore Marshall Award for Poetry, 1980; National Endowment for the Arts senior fellowship, 1984; Bollingen Prize in Poetry, Yale University Library, 1987; Walt Whitman Award citation of merit, with designation as State Poet of New York, 1987; Montgomery Fellow, Dartmouth College, 1991; Centennial medal, Harvard University, 1992; National Medal of Arts, 1993; National Book Award, 1995, for *Passing Through: Later Poems, New and Selected;* Shelly Memorial Award, 1995. Litt.D., Clark University, 1961, Anna Maria College, 1977; L.H.D., Worcester State College, 1980, and SUNY-Brockport, 1987.

WRITINGS:

POETRY

Intellectual Things, Doubleday, Doran (New York City), 1930.

Passport to the War: A Selection of Poems, Holt (New York City), 1944.

Selected Poems, 1928-1958, Little, Brown (Boston), 1958.

The Testing-Tree: Poems, Little, Brown, 1971.

The Terrible Threshold: Selected Poems, 1940-70, Secker & Warburg (London), 1974.

The Coat without a Seam: Sixty Poems, 1930-1972, Gehenna Press (Northampton, MA), 1974.

The Lincoln Relics, Graywolf Press (Townsend, WA), 1978.

The Poems of Stanley Kunitz: 1928-1978, Little, Brown, 1979.

The Wellfleet Whale and Companion Poems, Sheep Meadow Press (Riverdale-on-Hudson, NY), 1983.

Next-to-Last Things: New Poems and Essays, Little, Brown, 1985.

Passing Through: Later Poems, New and Selected, Norton (New York City), 1995.

EDITOR

Living Authors: A Book of Biographies, H. W. Wilson (Bronx, New York), 1931.

(With Howard Haycraft) *Authors Today and Yesterday: A Companion Volume to "Living Authors,"* H. W. Wilson, 1933.

(With Haycraft) *The Junior Book of Authors: An Introduction to the Lives of Writers and Illustrators for Younger Readers,* H. W. Wilson, 1934, second revised edition, 1951.

(With Haycraft) *British Authors of the Nineteenth Century,* H. W. Wilson, 1936.

(With Haycraft) *American Authors, 1600-1900: A Biographical Dictionary of American Literature,* H. W. Wilson, 1938, 8th edition, 1971.

(With Haycraft) *Twentieth Century Authors: A Biographical Dictionary,* H. W. Wilson, 1942, first supplement, 1955.

(With Haycraft) *British Authors before 1800: A Biographical Dictionary,* H. W. Wilson, 1952.

Poems of John Keats, Crowell (New York City), 1964.

(With Vineta Colby) *European Authors, 1000-1900: A Biographical Dictionary of European Literature,* H. W. Wilson, 1967.

(And author of introduction) Ivan Drach, *Orchard Lamps,* Sheep Meadow Press, 1978.

Selections: University and College Poetry Prizes, 1973-78, Academy of American Poets, 1980.

(Author of introduction) *The Essential Blake,* Ecco Press, 1987.

CONTRIBUTOR

John Fischer and Robert B. Silvers, editors, *Writing in America,* Rutgers University Press (Rutgers, NJ), 1960.

Anthony J. Ostroff, editor, *The Contemporary Poet as Artist and Critic,* Little, Brown, 1964.

Vineta Colby, editor, *American Culture in the Sixties,* H. W. Wilson, 1964.

Robert Lowell and others, editors, *Randall Jarrell, 1914-1965,* Farrar, Straus (New York City), 1967.

Contributor to poetry anthologies, including *War Poets: An Anthology of the War Poetry of the 20th Century,* edited by Oscar Williams, John Day, 1945; *The Criterion Book of Modern American Verse,* edited by W. H. Auden, Criterion, 1956; *How Does a Poem Mean?,* edited by John Ciardi, Houghton, 1959; *Modern American Poetry,* edited by Louis Untermeyer, Harcourt, 1962; *American Lyric Poems: From Colonial Times to the Present,* edited by Elder Olson, Appleton, 1964; *The Distinctive Voice,* edited by William J. Martz, Scott, Foresman, 1966; *Where Is Vietnam?: American Poets Respond,* edited by Walter Lowenfels, Doubleday-Anchor, 1967; *Norton Anthology of Modern Poetry,* edited by Richard Ellmann and Robert O'Clair, Norton, 1973; *Fifty Years of American Poetry: Anniversary Volume for the Academy of American Poets,* Abrams, 1984; and *Contemporary American Poetry,* edited by A. Poulin, Jr., Houghton, fourth edition, 1985. Also contributor to periodicals, including *Atlantic, New Republic, New Yorker, Antaeus, New York Review of Books, American Poetry Review,* and *Harper's.*

OTHER

(Translator with Max Hayward) *Poems of Anna Akhmatova,* Little, Brown, 1973.

(Translator) Andrei Voznesensky, *Story under Full Sail,* Doubleday, 1974.

Robert Lowell: Poet of Terribilita, Pierpont Morgan Library (New York City), 1974.

A Kind of Order, a Kind of Folly: Essays and Conversations, Little, Brown, 1975.

Interviews and Encounters with Stanley Kunitz, edited by Stanley Moss, Sheep Meadow Press, 1993.

General editor, "Yale Series of Younger Poets," Yale University Press (New Haven, CT), 1969-77.

Also contributor of translations to: Andrei Voznesensky, *Antiworlds,* Basic Books (New York City), 1966; Voznesensky, *Antiworlds* [and] *The Fifth Ace,* Anchor Books (New York City), 1967; and Yevgeny Yevtushenko, *Stolen Apples,* Doubleday (Garden City, NY), 1971.

SIDELIGHTS: Poet Stanley Kunitz "has always been a fine and quiet singer," according to James Whitehead in *Saturday Review.* A published poet, editor, and translator for the greater part of the twentieth century, Kunitz has exerted a subtle but steady influence on such major poets as Theodore Roethke, W. H. Auden, and Robert Lowell. In addition, he has provided encouragement to hundreds of younger poets as well. His output has been modest but enduring: since 1930 he has published only eleven volumes of poetry. "I think that explains why I am able to continue as a poet into my late years," Kunitz once explained in *Publishers Weekly.* "If I hadn't had an urgent impulse, if the poem didn't seem to me terribly important, I never wanted to write it and didn't. And that's persisted." While the complexity of Kunitz's initial works delayed critical attention, in 1959 he received a Pulitzer Prize for his third poetry collection, *Selected Poems, 1928-1958.*

Many critics suggest that Kunitz's poetry has steadily increased in quality in the intervening years; as *Virginia Quarterly Review* contributor Jay Parini observed: "The restraints of [Kunitz's] art combine with a fierce dedication to clarity and intellectual grace to assure him of a place among the essential poets of his generation, which includes Roethke, Lowell, Auden, and Eberhart." This place was confirmed in 1995, when Kunitz was honored with the National Book Award for *Passing Through: The Later Poems, New and Selected.*

Kunitz's early poetry collections, *Intellectual Things* and *Passport to the War: A Selection of Poems,* earned him a reputation as an intellectual poet. Reflecting their author's admiration for English metaphysical poets like John Donne and William Blake, the intricate metaphorical verses in these collections were recognized more for their craft than their substance. Thus, they were somewhat slow to garner widespread critical attention. "In my youth, as might be expected, I had little knowledge of the world to draw on," Kunitz explained to *CA*. "But I had fallen in love with language and was excited by ideas, including the idea of being a poet. Early poetry is much more likely to be abstract because of the poverty of experience." Also, as *New York Review of Books* contributor Vernon Young observed, Kunitz "is notable for his intelligence, and intelligence tends to wait a longer time for recognition or acquires it within a relatively limited circle."

Kunitz followed his Pulitzer Prize-winning *Selected Poems, 1928-1958,* with *The Testing-Tree: Poems,* a collection in which the author "ruthlessly prods wounds," according to Stanley Moss in the *Nation.* "His primordial curse is the suicide of his father before his birth. The poems take us into the sacred woods and houses of his 66 years, illuminate the images that have haunted him. . . . [Kunitz] searches for secret reality and the meaning of the unknown father. He moves from the known to the unknown to the unknowable—not necessarily in that order." And Robert Lowell commented in the *New York Times Book Review:* "One reads [*The Testing-Tree*] from cover to cover with the ease of reading good prose fiction. . . . I don't know of another in prose or verse that gives in a few pages the impression of a large autobiography." Discussing the self-revelatory nature of his work, Kunitz told *CA:* "By its nature poetry is an intimate medium, . . . Perhaps that's why it is so dangerously seductive to the creative spirit. The transformation of individual experience—the transpersonalization of the persona, if you will—is work that the imagination has to do, its obligatory task. One of the problems with so much of what was called, in the '60s, confessional poetry was that it relied excessively on the exploitation of self, on the shock effect of raw experience. My conviction is that poetry is a legendary, not an anecdotal, art."

Published in 1971, *The Testing-Tree* was perceived by critics as a significant stylistic departure for its author. Lowell, for example, commented in the *New York Times Book Review* that the two volumes "are landmarks of the old and the new style. The smoke has blown off. The old Delphic voice has learned to speak 'words that cats and dogs can understand.'" *Dictionary of Literary Biography* contributor Marie Henault concurred: "*The Testing-Tree* [reveals] a new, freer poetry, looser forms, shorter lines, lowercase line beginnings. . . . Overall the Kunitz of this book is a 'new' Kunitz, one who has grown and changed in the thirteen years since *Selected Poems.*" Gregory Orr offered this view in *American Poetry Review:* "There *is* a stylistic shift, but more deeply than that there is a fundamental shift in Kunitz's relation to the world and to his life."

Asked to comment on this stylistic shift in *Publishers Weekly,* Kunitz noted that "My early poems were very intricate, dense and formal. . . . They were written in conventional metrics and had a very strong beat to the line. . . . In my late poems I've learned to depend on a simplicity that seems almost nonpoetic on the surface, but has reverberations within that keep it intense and alive. . . . I think that as a young poet I looked for what Keats called 'a fine excess,' but as an old poet I look for spareness and rigor and a world of compassion." If Kunitz's earlier poems were often intricately woven, intellectual, lyricized allegories about the transcendence of physical limitations, his later work can be seen as an emotive acceptance of those limitations.

While Kunitz's style has changed, his themes have not. One of Kunitz's most pervasive themes concerns the simultaneity of life and death. "It's the way things are: death and life inextricably bound to each other," he explained to *CA*. "One of my feelings about working the land [as a gardener] is that I am celebrating a ritual of death and resurrection. Every spring I feel that. I am never closer to the miraculous than when I am grubbing in the soil." He once revealed in the *New York Times:* "The deepest thing I know is that I am living and dying at once, and my conviction is to report that dialogue. It is a rather terrifying thought that is at the root of much of my poetry." Other themes concern "rebirth, the quest, and the night journey (or descent into the underworld)," explained the poet in *Poetry.*

Kunitz's willingness to explore such serious themes has prompted critics to applaud his courage, and to describe him as a risk taker. Analyzing one of Kunitz's better-known poems, "King of the River," from *The Testing-Tree, New York Times Book Review* contributor Robert B. Shaw wrote: "Kunitz's willingness to risk bombast, platitude or bathos in his contemplation of what he calls 'mystery' is evident in [this poem]. Mystery—of the self, of time, of change and fate—is not facilely dispelled but approached with imaginative awe in his work; in our rationalistic century this is swimming against the stream. This is a form of artistic heroism; and when Kunitz's scorning of safety meshes firmly with his technical skills, the outcome is poetry of unusual power and depth." Mary Oliver similarly observed in *Kenyon Review* that "what is revealed, then, is courage. Not the courage of words only, but the intellectual courage that insists on the truth, which is never simple."

Kunitz reveals within his works an optimism that is apparent in *Next-to-Last Things: New Poems and Essays,* his celebration of rural life published in 1985. A collection of twelve poems, several prose essays, and an interview from the *Paris Review, Next-to-Last-Things* reflects the poet's love of nature, acts of conscience, and the loneliness that comes from both age and creativity. *New York Times Book Review* contributor R. W. Flint observed: "The sharp and seasoned good humor Stanley Kunitz brings to the poems, essays, interviews and aphorisms in *Next-to-Last Things* is a tonic in our literary life. . . . Paradox and complication entice him, and he now cheerfully discusses a body of poetry, his own, that he rightly finds to have been 'essentially dark and grieving—elegiac.'"

In *Next-to-Last Things* critics found that both Kunitz's perception of the themes of life and death and his style had undergone further transitions. *Chicago Tribune Book World* contributor James Idema noted that Kunitz's poetry had become yet more austere: "The poems that open the book are leaner than those from the early and middle years, narrower on their pages. . . . Some of them are serene and melancholy, as you might expect. Most reflect the sky-and-weather environment of his Provincetown summer home, where he is most comfortable confronting 'the great simplicities.' But the best ones are full of action and vivid imagery."

Passing Through: The Later Poems, New and Selected encapsulates much of Kunitz's later oeuvre and includes nine new works of poetry. "The Wellfleet Whale," a nature poem that speaks to a finback whale run aground, is accompanied by "Touch Me," wherein the artist characteristically contemplates an earthbound immortality. The collection, which earned its ninety-year-old author the National Book Award for poetry, is considered to possess an assured poetic voice and a heightened vision sensitive to subtleties and nuances of life filled with meaning. "In youth, problems come to you out of the blue," Kunitz told Mary B. W. Tabor in the *New York Times*. "They're delivered at your doorstep like the morning news. But at this age," he added, "one has to dig."

Although Kunitz's style has changed over his seven decades as a poet, his methods have not. A notebook and a pen render a sketch; many late nights over a manual typewriter result in a finished poem. What he does not find satisfactory, he destroys. "I don't want my bad poems to be published after I'm not around to check them," he told Tabor.

"I don't try to preordain the form of a poem," Kunitz revealed to *CA,* discussing his personal experience of the poetic craft. "There's a good deal of automatism in the beginning, as I try to give the poem its head. Most of all I am looking for a distinctive rhythm. . . . I want the poem to grow out of its own materials, to develop organically." The organic quality of a poem is of primary importance to Kunitz. "I write my poems for the ear," he explained. "In fact, my method of writing a poem is to say it. The pitch and tempo and tonalities of a poem are elements of its organic life. A poem is as much a voice as it is a system of verbal signs. I realize that ultimately the poet departs from the scene, and the poems that he abandons to the printed page must speak for themselves. But I can't help wondering about the influence on posterity of the technical revolution that will enable them to see and hear, on film and tape, the poets of our century. Suppose we had videotapes of Keats reading his ode 'To Autumn' or Blake declaiming 'The Marriage of Heaven and Hell'!"

BIOGRAPHICAL/CRITICAL SOURCES:

BOOKS

A Celebration for Stanley Kunitz on His 80th Birthday, Sheep Meadow Press, 1986.

Contemporary Literary Criticism, Gale (Detroit), Volume 6, 1976, Volume 11, 1979, Volume 14, 1980.

Dictionary of Literary Biography, Volume 48: *American Poets, 1880-1945,* second series, Gale, 1986.

Henault, Marie, *Stanley Kunitz,* Twayne (New York City), 1980.

Hungerford, Edward, editor, *Poets in Progress,* Northwestern University Press (Chicago), 1962, revised edition, 1967.

Kunitz, Stanley, *Interviews and Encounters with Stanley Kunitz,* Sheep Meadow Press, 1993.

Mills, Ralph J., Jr., *Contemporary American Poetry,* Random House (New York City), 1965.

Orr, Gregory, *Stanley Kunitz: An Introduction to the Poetry,* Columbia University Press (New York City), 1985.

Ostroff, Anthony J., editor, *The Contemporary Poet as a Critic and Artist,* Little, Brown, 1964.

Rodman, Selden, *Tongues of Fallen Angels,* New Directions (Newton, NJ), 1974.

Rosenthal, M. L., *The Modern Poets: A Critical Introduction,* Oxford University Press (New York City), 1960.

PERIODICALS

American Poetry Review, March/April, 1976; July,1980; September/October, 1985.

Chicago Tribune Book World, December 22, 1985.

Contemporary Literature, winter, 1974.

Harper's, February, 1986.

Iowa Review, spring, 1974.

Kenyon Review, summer, 1986, pp. 113-35.

Nation, September 20, 1971.

New Yorker, October 16, 1995, p. 50.

New York Quarterly, fall, 1970.

New York Review of Books, November 22, 1979.

New York Times, July 7, 1979; March 11, 1987; August 29, 1993, sec. 9, p. 3; November 30, 1995, p. B1, C18.

New York Times Book Review, November 11, 1965; March 21, 1971; July 22, 1979; April 6, 1986, p. 11.

Paris Review, spring, 1982.

Poetry, September, 1980.

Prairie Schooner, summer, 1980.

Publishers Weekly, December 20, 1985; November 20, 1995, pp. 17, 20.

Saturday Review, September 27, 1958; December 18, 1971.

Sewanee Review, winter, 1988, pp. 137-49.

Times Literary Supplement, May 30, 1980.

Virginia Quarterly Review, spring, 1980.

Washington Post, May 12, 1987.

Washington Post Book World, September 30, 1979.

Yale Literary Magazine, May, 1968.

Yale Review, autumn, 1971.*

L

LANCASTER, David
See **HEALD, Tim(othy Villiers)**

* * *

LANDON, Michael de L(aval) 1935-

PERSONAL: Born October 8, 1935, in Saint John, New Brunswick, Canada; son of Arthur Henry Whittington (a brigadier general in the Canadian Army) and Elizabeth Worthington (Fair) Landon; married Doris Lee Clay, December 31, 1959 (divorced, 1980); married Carole Marie Prather Casey (a businesswoman), February 28, 1981; children: (first marriage) Clay de Laval, Letitia Elizabeth. *Education:* Worcester College, Oxford, B.A. (with honors), 1958, M.A., 1961; University of Wisconsin—Madison, M.A., 1962, Ph.D., 1966. *Politics:* Independent. *Religion:* Episcopalian. *Avocational interests:* Gardening, cooking.

ADDRESSES: Home—P.O. Box 172, University, MS 38677. *Office*—Department of History, University of Mississippi, University, MS 38677. *E-mail*—hslandon@olemiss.edu.

CAREER: Manor House School, Horsham, Sussex, England, history teacher, 1957; Dalhousie Preparatory School, Ladybank, Fife, Scotland, assistant master of history, 1957-58; Lakefield College School, Lakefield, Ontario, assistant master of French, 1958-60; University of Wisconsin—Madison, teaching assistant, 1961-63, project assistant, 1963-64; University of Mississippi, assistant professor, 1964-67, associate professor, 1967-72, professor of history, 1972—, acting director of libraries, 1986-87, acting chair, Department of Modern Languages, 1996—. Visiting associate professor, University of Wisconsin—Madison, 1971.

MEMBER: American Historical Association, American Society for Legal History (member of board of directors, 1982-84; secretary-treasurer, 1988—), American Association of University Professors, Royal Historical Society (London; fellow), Conference on British Studies, Eta Sigma Phi, Phi Alpha Theta, Phi Kappa Phi, Oxford Society.

AWARDS, HONORS: American Philosophical Society research grant, 1966-67, 1973-74.

WRITINGS:

The Triumph of the Lawyers, University of Alabama Press (University), 1970.

The Honor and Dignity of the Profession: A History of the Mississippi State Bar, 1906-1976, University Press of Mississippi (Jackson), 1979.

Erin and Britannia: The Historical Background to a Modern Tragedy, Nelson-Hall (Chicago), 1981.

The Challenge of Service: A History of the Mississippi Bar's Young Lawyers, University Press of Mississippi, 1995.

The Political Career of Sir John Maynard, Serjeant-at-Law, 1604-1690, 1997.

Contributor to *Per Se, Enlightenment Essays, Proceedings* of the American Philosophical Society, and other journals.

SIDELIGHTS: Michael de L. Landon wrote *CA:* "With my history of the Mississippi State Bar, published in 1979, I feel that I have achieved a mature writing style of my own with which I am reasonably content."

* * *

LANE, Edward
See DICK, Kay

* * *

La PALOMBARA, Joseph 1925-

PERSONAL: Born May 18, 1925, in Chicago, IL; son of Louis (a tailor) and Helen (Teutonico) La Palombara; married Lyda Mae Ecke, June 22, 1947 (divorced); married Constance Ada Bezer, June, 1971; children: (first marriage) Richard Dean, David D., Susan Dee. *Ethnicity:* "Italian-American." *Education:* University of Illinois, A.B., 1947, M.A., 1950; Princeton University, M.A., 1952, Ph.D., 1954; University of Rome, graduate study, 1952-53. *Politics:* Democrat. *Avocational interests:* Book collecting, fishing.

ADDRESSES: *Home*—50 Huntington St., New Haven, CT 06511-1333. *Office*—Department of Political Science, Yale University, New Haven, CT 06520. *E-mail*—lapalom@minerva.cis.yale.edu; fax 203-776-6532.

CAREER: Oregon State College (now University), Corvallis, 1947-50, began as instructor, became assistant professor of political science; Princeton University, Princeton, NJ, instructor in politics, 1952; Michigan State University, East Lansing, assistant professor, 1953-56, associate professor, 1956-58, professor of political science and chairperson of department, 1958-64; Yale University, New Haven, CT, professor of political science, 1964-65, Arnold Wolfers Professor of Political Science, 1965—, chairperson of department, 1974-78, 1982-84, director of Institution for Social and Policy Studies, 1987-92. Visiting professor at University of Florence, 1957-58, University of California, Berkeley, 1962, and Columbia University, 1965-66. Michigan Citizenship Clearing House, director, 1955; Social Science Research Council, staff member, 1966-73; Conference Board of New York, senior research associate, 1975-80; U.S. Embassy, Rome, Italy, cultural attache and first secretary, 1980-81. Inter-University Consortium on Political Research, member of executive committee, 1968-70; Social Science Research Council/American Council of Learned Societies, chairperson of Western European foreign area fellowship program, 1972-76. Transparency International, member of board of directors, 1995—; Italian-American Multi-Media Corp., president; consultant to Brookings Institution, Twentieth-Century Fund, Agency for International Development, Foreign Service Institute, and to several major U.S. and European corporations.

MEMBER: International Political Science Association, American Political Science Association (vice president, 1977-78), American Society for Public Administration, Society for Italian Historical Studies, Italian Social Science Association, Societa Italiana di Studi Elettori, Phi Beta Kappa, Phi Kappa Phi, Phi Eta Sigma.

AWARDS, HONORS: Fellow, Center for Advanced Study in the Behavioral Sciences, 1961-62, and Rockefeller Foundation, 1963-64; Order of Merit, Republic of Italy, 1964; M.A., Yale University, 1964; Ford Foundation faculty fellow, 1969; Guggenheim fellow, 1971-72; named Knight Commander, Order of Merit, Republic of Italy, 1974; Guido Dorso Prize (Italy), 1985; fellow of European University Institute and Wissenschaftszentrum Berlin, both 1996.

WRITINGS:

The Initiative and Referendum in Oregon, Oregon State College Press (Corvallis), 1950.

The Italian Labor Movement: Problems and Prospects, Cornell University Press (Ithaca, NY), 1957.

Guide to Michigan Politics, Michigan State University (East Lansing), 1960.

(Coeditor) *Elezioni e comportamento politico in Italia,* Comunita, 1962.

Bureaucracy and Political Development, Princeton University Press (Princeton, NJ), 1963.

Interest Groups in Italian Politics, Princeton University Press, 1964.

Italy: The Politics of Planning, Syracuse University Press (Syracuse, NY), 1966.

(Editor with Myron Weiner) *Political Parties and Political Development,* Princeton University Press, 1966.
(With others) *Crises and Sequences in Political Development,* Princeton University Press, 1971.
Politics within Nations, Prentice-Hall (Englewood Cliffs, NJ), 1974.
(With Stephen Blank) *Multinational Corporations and National Elites,* Conference Board of New York (New York City), 1976.
(With Blank) *Multinational Corporations in Comparative Perspective,* Conference Board of New York, 1977.
(With Blank) *Multinational Corporations and Developing Countries,* Conference Board of New York, 1979.
(With others) *Assessing the Political Environment,* Conference Board of New York, 1980.
Democracy, Italian Style, Yale University Press (New Haven, CT), 1987.

Contributor to books, including *Imaginari a confronto,* edited by Carlo Chiarenza and William L. Vance, Marsilio (Venice, Italy), 1992; *L'Italia fra crisi e transizione,* edited by Mario Caciagli, Franco Cazzola, and others, Laterza (Bari, Italy), 1994; and *Dove va la societa italiana,* edited by Ivo Colozzi and Michele La Rosa, Franco Angeli (Milan, Italy), 1996. U.S. correspondent, Sviluppo Quotidiani Group, 1991—. Contributor to numerous periodicals, including *Nation, Yale Review, Corriere della sera* (Milan), *La Repubblica* (Rome), *World Politics,* and *Pacific Spectator.* Editor-in-chief, *Italy Italy,* 1988—.

WORK IN PROGRESS: Politics and the Multinational Corporation, completion expected in 1998.

SIDELIGHTS: Joseph La Palombara told *CA:* "I write because I wake in the morning, get up, and begin another day. Like many others who do the same thing, I resent interferences with my writing, sometimes even the ones (like teaching or consulting) that I otherwise enjoy. Beyond this 'anatomical' impulse, I write because, unless I do, my thoughts about so many different things of interest to me would remain somewhat inchoate, jumbled, and perhaps too much ruled by emotion rather than reason.

"My work is primarily influenced by the shape that politics and economics take, both in the United States and abroad. I am passionately interested in the processes whereby political and economic power are exercised. At times, I write about these things as an academic, which means that attention is paid to theory and method, evidence, argument, and the strict rules of inference. I also write as a journalist, in the hope that what I have to say will reach a larger, more general audience. Like most writers, I want to be read!

"As for writing process, for years I refused to use a typewriter, preferring to compose, rewrite, and edit on a lined yellow pad. I now use a personal computer and find it frustrating no longer to be able to identify a first, second, and 'n'th draft. I prefer to write in the morning and, unless I find several hours of relatively uninterrupted time, what emerges will have to be trashed. I find it productive to leave a piece of writing lie for awhile, and then to revisit it. Invariably I am horrified at the quality which I had earlier judged good, or even superior.

"Although I am primarily an academic writer, I have paid a lot of attention to the better writers of fiction and exposition. I also keep close to my heart and hand George Orwell's famous essay on academic writing about politics!"

* * *

LAURENTI, Joseph L(ucian) 1931-

PERSONAL: Born December 10, 1931, in Hesperange, Luxembourg; naturalized U.S. citizen, 1953; son of Ernest (a lawyer) and Angelina (Dal Canton) Laurenti; married Alice Luellen Watson, June 10, 1967. *Ethnicity:* "Italian." *Education:* University of Illinois at Urbana/Champaign, B.A. (cum laude), 1958, M.A., 1959; University of Missouri—Columbia, Ph.D., 1962. *Politics:* Democrat. *Religion:* Roman Catholic.

ADDRESSES: Office—Department of Foreign Languages and Literatures, 206 Stevenson Hall, Illinois State University, Normal, IL 61790-4300; fax 309-438-8038.

CAREER: University of Illinois at Urbana-Champaign, Urbana, instructor in Spanish, 1958-59; University of Missouri—Columbia, instructor in Spanish, 1959-62; Illinois State University, Normal, assistant professor, 1962-63, associate professor, 1963-66, professor of Spanish and Italian, 1966—. Edition Reichenberger (publisher), member of editorial board. *Military service:* U.S. Army, Intelligence, 1952-54; served in Germany, Italy, and France.

MEMBER: International Association of Hispanists, International Association of Philologists, Modern Language Association of America (chairperson for Bibliography Committee, Italo-Hispanic Section), American Association of University Professors, American Association of Professors of Italian, American Association of Teachers of Spanish and Portuguese, Asociacion de Bibliografia Espanola (life member), Asociacion de Cervantistas (life member), Midwest Modern Language Association, Illinois Association of Teachers of Modern Languages, Sigma Delta Pi (president of University of Illinois chapter, 1958-59).

AWARDS, HONORS: Grant from Intercambios Culturales Hispano-Americanos, Barcelona, Spain, 1984; fellow, Newberry Library, 1986; grants from Program for Cultural Cooperation between Spain's Ministry of Culture and the U.S. Government, 1989, 1994, Diputacion Provincial de Sevilla, 1991, 1994, and Gutenberg-Gesellschaft, 1992; Antonio Nicolas Prize, Syracuse University, 1992; Medal of Order of Don Quixote, Sigma Delta Pi.

WRITINGS:

Lazarillo de Tormes: Estudio critico de la segunda parte de Juan de Luna (title means "Lazarillo de Tormes: A Critical Study of the Second Part of Juan de Luna"), Studium, 1965.

Ensayo de una bibliografia de la novela picaresca espanola (title means "A Bibliographic Essay of the Spanish Picaresque Novel"), Consejo Superior de Investigaciones Cientificas, 1968.

Estudios sobre la novela picaresca espanola (title means "Studies in the Spanish Picaresque Novel"), Consejo Superior de Investigaciones Cientificas, 1970.

Los prologos en las novelas picarescas espanolas (title means "Critical Prefaces in the Spanish Picaresque Novel"), Castalia, 1971.

(With Alberto Porqueras Mayo) *Ensayo bibliografico del prologo en la literatura* (title means "A Bibliographic Essay of the Prologue in Literature"), Consejo Superior de Investigaciones Cientificas, 1971.

(With Joseph Siracusa) *Relaciones literarias entre Espana e Italia* (title means "Literary Relations between Spain and Italy"), G. K. Hall (Boston), 1972.

Bibliografia de la literature picaresca: Desde sus origenes hasta el presente, AMS Press (New York City), 1973, translation published as *A Critical Bibliography of Picaresque Literature,* G. K. Hall, 1973, revised edition published as *A Bibliography of Picaresque Literature from Its Origin to the Present,* AMS Press, 1981.

(With Siracusa) *The World of Federico Garcia Lorca,* Scarecrow (Metuchen, NJ), 1974.

(Editor with Mayo) *Antonio de Guevara en la biblioteca de la universidad de Illinois,* S.A. Impresores, 1974.

The Spanish Golden Age (1472-1700), G. K. Hall, 1979.

A Catalog of Rare Books in the Library of the University of Illinois and in Selected North American Libraries, G. K. Hall, 1979.

A Catalog of Spanish Rare Books (1701-1974) in the Library of the University of Illinois and in Selected North American Libraries, Peter Lang (New York City), 1984.

(With A. Porqueras Mayo) *Estudios bibliograficos sobre la Edad de Oro,* Puvill Libros (Barcelona, Spain), 1984.

Hispanic Rare Books of the Golden Age (1470-1699) in the Newberry Library of Chicago and in Selected North American Libraries, Peter Lang, 1989.

(Editor with Vern Williamsen) *Varia hispanica estudios en los siglos de oro y literature moderna: Homenaje a Alberto Porqueras Mayo,* Edition Reichenberger (Kassel, Germany), 1989.

Catalogo bibliografico de la literatura picaresca (Siglos XVI-XX), Edition Reichen-berger, 1991.

(With Mayo) *Nuevos estudios bibliograficos sobre la Edad de Oro: Fondos raros y colecciones en la Biblioteca de la Universidad de Illinois,* Puvill Libros, 1994.

U.S. correspondent for *AZB Revista de Cultura Internacional* and *Quaderni Ibero-Americani.* Contributor of more than 200 articles and reviews to journals in France, Spain, Italy, Japan, Korea, Germany, Mexico, Puerto Rico, Argentina, and the United States, including *Modern Language Journal.* Member of editorial board, *Quaderni Ibero-Americani.*

SIDELIGHTS: Joseph L. Laurenti told *CA:* "I believe that in this world there is something that is worth more than the joys derived from material possessions, better than fortunes, better than health itself, and that is the devotion to the arts and sciences. Everything that we see, feel, touch, and create is an expression of God's intelligence, and while we are here on this planet, we cannot achieve the ecstasy and exultation of our own spirit and talent without first nurturing that intelligence with our daily love, virtues, and work for each other. This has always been my motivation throughout life."

* * *

LEE, Dennis (Beynon) 1939-

PERSONAL: Born August 31, 1939, in Toronto, Ontario, Canada; son of Walter and Louise (Garbutt) Lee; married Donna Youngblut, June 24, 1962 (divorced); married Susan Perly, October 7, 1985; children: (first marriage) two daughters, one son. *Ethnicity:* "Anglo plus Irish." *Education:* University of Toronto, B.A., 1962, M.A., 1964.

ADDRESSES: *Agent*—WCA, 94 Harbord St., Toronto, Ontario, Canada M5S 1G6.

CAREER: Writer. University of Toronto, Victoria College, Toronto, Ontario, lecturer in English, 1964-67; Rochdale College (experimental institution), Toronto, resource person, 1967-69; House of Anansi Press, Toronto, cofounder and editor, 1967-72. Macmillan of Canada, editorial consultant, 1973-78; McClelland & Stewart, poetry editor, 1981-84. Lyricist for television series *Fraggle Rock,* 1982-86.

AWARDS, HONORS: Governor-General's Award for Poetry, 1972, for *Civil Elegies;* award from Independent Order of Daughters of the Empire, 1974; Canadian Association of Children's Librarians, Best Book Medals, 1974 and 1977, and English Medal, 1975, named to Hans Christian Andersen Honour List and recipient of Canadian Library Association award, both 1976, all for *Alligator Pie;* Philips Information Systems Literary Award, 1984; Vicky Metcalf Award, Canadian Authors' Association, 1986, for body of work for children; officer, Order of Canada, 1994; Toronto Arts Award, 1995, for lifetime achievement.

WRITINGS:

POETRY

Kingdom of Absence, House of Anansi (Toronto, Ontario), 1967.

Civil Elegies, House of Anansi, 1968, revised edition published as *Civil Elegies and Other Poems,* 1972.

Wiggle to the Laundromat (juvenile), New Press, 1970.

Alligator Pie (juvenile), Macmillan (Toronto), 1974, Houghton (Boston), 1975.

Nicholas Knock and Other People (juvenile), Macmillan, 1974, Houghton, 1975.

The Death of Harold Ladoo, Kanchenjunga Press, 1976.

Garbage Delight (juvenile), Macmillan, 1977, Houghton, 1978.

The Gods, McClelland & Stewart, 1979.

Jelly Belly (juvenile), Macmillan, 1983.

The Dennis Lee Big Book (anthology), Macmillan, 1985.

The Difficulty of Living on Other Planets (some poems previously published in *Nicholas Knock and Other People* and *The Gods*), Macmillan, 1987.

The Ice Cream Store (juvenile), HarperCollins (New York City), 1991.

Riffs, Brick, 1993.

Ping and Pong (juvenile), HarperCollins, 1993.

Nightwatch: New and Selected Poems, 1968-96, McClelland & Stewart, 1996.

Dinosaur Dinner (With a Slice of Alligator Pie) (juvenile), Knopf (New York City), 1997.

OTHER

(Coeditor) *The University Game* (essays), House of Anansi, 1968.

(Editor) *T.O. Now: The Young Toronto Poets* (poetry anthology), House of Anansi, 1968.

Savage Fields: An Essay in Cosmology and Literature, House of Anansi, 1977.

The Ordinary Bath (juvenile), McClelland & Stewart, 1977.

Lizzy's Lion (juvenile), Stoddart, 1984.

(Editor and author of introduction) *New Canadian Poets, 1970-1985* (poetry anthology), McClelland & Stewart, 1985.

Also coeditor of two high school poetry anthologies.

ADAPTATIONS: Coauthor, with Jim Henson, of story adapted by Terry Jones for the screenplay of the Henson Associates Inc./Lucasfilm Ltd. production, *Labyrinth,* 1985.

WORK IN PROGRESS: Body Music: Literary Essays.

SIDELIGHTS: In a speech delivered at the 1975 Loughborough Conference in Toronto and reprinted in *Canadian Children's Literature,* Canadian author Dennis Lee examines the way his attitude toward children's verse evolved. As an adult and parent, he contemplates Mother Goose and discovers: "The nursery rhymes I love . . . are necessarily exotic. . . . But they were in no way exotic to the people who first devised them and chanted them. . . . The air of far-off charm and simpler pastoral life which now hangs over Mother Goose was in no way a part of those rhymes' initial existence. . . . The people who told nursery rhymes for centuries would be totally boggled if they could suddenly experience them the way children do here and now, as a collection of references to things they never see or do, to places they have never heard of and may never visit, told in words they will sometimes meet only in those verses."

Out of concern that his own children were learning that "the imagination leads always and only to the holy city of elsewhere," Lee decided to build his imaginary "city" from the language of familiar objects—elements of contemporary life made extraordinary by their unique use and sound in verse. Maintaining that "you are poorer if you never find your own time and place speaking words of their own," he believes the "fire hydrants and hockey sticks" of today can be the stuff of nursery rhymes, just as curds and whey were for children of a previous time. Thus, he says, "to look for living nursery rhymes in the hockey-sticks and high-rises that [children know] first-hand [is not] to go on a chauvinistic trip, nor to wallow in a fad of trendy relevance. It [is] nothing but a rediscovery of what Mother Goose [has been] about for centuries."

Lee's poetic narratives, tongue-twisters, and riddles have been compared to the nonsense verse of Lewis Carroll and A. A. Milne. Lee, however, emphasizes the here-and-now objects of daily life in his work—things children may or may not recognize. Canadian places, history, politics, and colloquial diction, as well as purely invented words, all play a part in his pieces. Many critics feel the readability and repeatability of the poems—rather than references to far-away places—are what fascinates young children. As Betsy English writes in *In Review: Canadian Books for Children,* the strong rhythms, rhymes, and other sound devices in Lee's work produce "a sense of gaiety, an appeal that shouts for reading aloud."

BIOGRAPHICAL/CRITICAL SOURCES:

PERIODICALS

Books in Canada, February, 1980, p. 21; December, 1984, p. 12; December, 1993, p. 37.
Canadian Children's Literature, number 4, 1976; number 33, 1984, p. 15; number 42, 1986, p. 103; number 52, 1988, p. 56; number 63, 1991, p. 61-71; number 67, 1992, p. 102.
Canadian Forum, February, 1986, p. 38.
Canadian Literature, autumn, 1989, p. 228.
Canadian Materials, March, 1992, p. 86; March-April, 1994, p. 46.
Christian Science Monitor, October 5, 1984, p. 88.
Essays on Canadian Writing, spring, 1988, p. 110-22; spring, 1994, p. 126-31.
In Review: Canadian Books for Children, spring, 1971; winter, 1975.
New Yorker, December 1, 1975, p. 184.
New York Times Book Review, November, 1977, p. 47.
Poetry, February, 1970, p. 353.
Quill & Quire, November, 1983, p. 25; November, 1984, p. 11; August, 1985, p. 44; fall, 1991, p. 35; October, 1993, p. 28.
Saturday Night, January, 1978, p. 74; November, 1979, p. 61.

* * *

LEE, Warner
See BATTIN, B(rinton) W(arner)

* * *

LENT, John A(nthony) 1936-

PERSONAL: Born September 8, 1936, in East Millsboro, PA; son of John (a railroad worker) and Rose Marie (Marano) Lent; married Martha Meadows, June 17, 1961 (divorced November 15, 1985); married Roseanne Kueny, July 9, 1988; children: (first marriage) Laura, Andrea, John Vincent, Lisa, Shahnon. *Ethnicity:* "Italian-American." *Education:* Ohio University, B.S.J. (with honors), 1958, M.S. (with highest honors), 1960; graduate study at University of Guadalajara, summer, 1961, and Syracuse University, 1962-64; University of Oslo, certificate, 1962; Sophia University, Tokyo, certificate, 1965; University of Iowa, Ph.D. (with highest honors), 1972.

ADDRESSES: Home—669 Ferne Blvd., Drexel Hill, PA 19026. *Office*—Department of Broadcasting, Telecommunication, and Mass Media, Temple University, Philadelphia, PA 19122.

CAREER: West Virginia Institute of Technology, Montgomery, instructor in English and journalism, and director of public relations, 1960-62, assistant professor, 1965-66; Wisconsin State University—Eau Claire (now University of Wisconsin—Eau Claire), assistant professor of journalism, 1966-67; Marshall University, Huntington, WV, assistant professor of journalism, 1967-69; Universiti Sains Malaysia, Penang, Malaysia, coordinator and lecturer in mass communications, 1972-74; Temple University, Philadelphia, PA, associate professor, 1974-76, professor of communications, 1976—. Visiting lecturer, De La Salle College, Manila, Philippines, 1964-65; visiting associate professor, University of Wyoming, 1969-70. Participated in Indian Media Study Tour, New Delhi, summer, 1980. Has chaired and organized panels, lectured, presented papers, and spoken at national and international conferences and symposia in forty-three countries.

MEMBER: International Association for Mass Communication Research (chair of comic art and visual communications working groups), Association for Asian Studies, Asia Mass Communication Research and Information Centre, Latin American Studies Association, Caribbean Studies Association, Popular Culture Association (founding chair, Asian Popular Culture group), Malaysia/Singapore/Brunei Studies Group (founding chair), Philippine Studies Group (executive board), Asian Cinema Studies Society (chair), Sigma Delta Chi, Sigma Tau Delta, Phi Alpha Theta, Kappa Tau Alpha.

AWARDS, HONORS: Fulbright scholar to Philippines, 1964-65; Benedum research award, Marshall University, 1968; vice chancellor research awards, Universiti Sains Malaysia; library collections at Ohio University and Alvina T. Burrows Institute named for Lent; two Broadcast Preceptor Awards, 1979; Bethany College (Bethany, WV), Benedum Research Award, and Benedum Distinguished Visiting Professor Award, 1987; Paul Erdman Outstanding Research Award, Temple University, 1988; Ray and Pat Browne National Book Award, 1994; exceptional award salary adjustment, Temple University, 1995-96.

WRITINGS:

Journalism Study of New York Colleges and High Schools, Newhouse Communications Research Center, Syracuse University (Syracuse, NY), 1963.

(Editor) *Readings on the Foreign Press,* West Virginia Institute of Technology, 1965.

Philippine Mass Communications Bibliography: First Cumulation of Sources on Areas of Advertising, Journalism, Newspaper, Magazine, Public Relations, Radio, Television, Movies, [Fort Worth], 1966.

Newhouse, Newspapers, Nuisances: Highlights in the Growth of a Communications Empire, Exposition Press (Smithtown, NY), 1966.

Three Research Studies, West Virginia Institute of Technology, 1966.

Philippine Mass Communications: Before 1811, after 1966, Philippine Press Institute, 1967.

(Editor) *The Asian Newspapers' Reluctant Revolution,* Iowa State University Press (Ames), 1971.

Asian Mass Communications: A Comprehensive Bibliography, School of Communications and Theater, Temple University (Philadelphia, PA), 1974.

Commonwealth Caribbean Mass Communications, State University of New York Press (Buffalo), 1975.

Guided Press in Southeast Asia, State University of New York at Buffalo, 1976.

Third World Mass Media and Their Search for Modernity: The Case of Commonwealth Caribbean, 1717-1976, Bucknell University Press (Cranbury, NJ), 1977.

(Editor) *Cultural Pluralism in Malaysia: Polity, Military, Mass Media, Education, Religion, and Social Class,* Center for Southeast Asian Studies, Northern Illinois University (DeKalb), 1977.

Asian Mass Communications: A Comprehensive Bibliography, 1977 Supplement, Temple University, 1978.

(Editor) *Broadcasting in Asia and the Pacific: A Continental Survey of Radio and Television,* Temple University Press, 1978.

(Editor) *Malaysian Studies: Present Knowledge and Research Trends,* Center for Southeast Asian Studies, Northern Illinois University, 1979.

Topics in Third World Mass Communications, Asian Research Service, 1979.

The Use of Development News, AMIC, 1979.

Caribbean Mass Communications: A Comprehensive Bibliography, African Studies Association (Waltham, MA), 1981.

(Editor) *Newspapers in Asia: Contemporary Trends and Problems,* Heinemann Educational (Exeter, NH), 1982.

New World and International Information Order: A Resource Guide and Bibliography, AMIC, 1982.

Women and Mass Media in Asia: An Annotated Bibliography, AMIC, 1985.

Malaysian Studies: Archaeology, Historiography, Geography and Bibliography, Northern Illinois University, 1985.

Comic Art: An International Bibliography, privately printed, 1986.

Global Guide to Mass Media, K. G. Saur (Ridgewood, NJ), 1987.

Videocassette Recorders in the Third World, Longman (New York City), 1989.

The Asian Film Industry, University of Texas Press (Austin), 1990.

(Editor) *Caribbean Popular Culture,* Popular Press, 1990.

Mass Communications in the Caribbean, Iowa State University Press, 1990.

Women and Mass Communications: An International Annotated Bibliography, Greenwood Press (Westport, CT), 1991.

(Editor) *Transnational Communications: Wiring the Third World,* Sage (Beverly Hills, CA), 1991.

Bibliography of Cuban Mass Communication, Greenwood Press, 1992.

(Editor) *Social Science models and Their Impact on the Third World,* College of William and Mary (Annandale, VA), 1992.

Cartoonometer: Taking the Pulse of the World's Cartoonists, WittyWorld Books, 1994.

Animation, Caricature, and Gag and Political Cartoons in the United States and Canada: An International Bibliography, Greenwood Press, 1994.

Comic Books and Comic Strips in the United States: An International Bibliography, Greenwood Press, 1994.

Comic Art of Europe: An International Comprehensive Bibliography, Greenwood Press, 1994.

(Editor) *Brunei and Malaysian Studies,* College of William and Mary, 1994.

(Editor) *Asian Popular Culture,* Westview (Boulder, CO), 1995.

A Different Road Taken: Profiles in Critical Communication, Westview, 1995.

Comic Art in Africa, Asia, Australia, and Latin America: A Comprehensive International Bibliography, Greenwood Press, 1996.

Also contributor to numerous books; also coauthor of filmstrip *Pied Type, a Load of Coal and the Laser;* also compiler of slide presentations on Asia and the Caribbean for Vis-Com, Inc., 1972, 1975. Book reviewer, *Choice,* and numerous other periodicals. Contributor to periodicals, including *European Broadcast Review, Television Quarterly, Journal of Communication, Journalism Quarterly, Quill, Gazette* (Amsterdam), *Asian Studies, Silliman Journal* (Philippines), and *Estudios Orientales* (Mexico). Founding editor of *Berita: Newsletter of Malaysia/Singapore/Brunei Studies Group* and *Asian Studies at Temple Newsletter;* editor, *Asian Cinema;* founding managing editor of *WittyWorld;* associate editor and book review editor of *Asian Thought and Society;* book review editor, *Studies in Latin American Popular Culture;* contributing editor, *Comics Journal* and *New Asia Review;* associate editor of *International Communications Bulletin,* 1970-72; assistant editor of *Media History Digest* and *Communication Booknotes;* bibliographer for *Journalism Quarterly,* 1969-92; member of editorial board of periodicals, including *Crossroads, World Media Report, Philippine Research Bulletin, Human Rights Quarterly, Asian Profile, Indian Journal of Communication, Journal of Asian Pacific Communication, Gazette,* and *Komunikasi.*

WORK IN PROGRESS: Books on cartoons and comics, labor and media worldwide; bibliographies on comic art worldwide and women and mass communications; an encyclopedia on the cinema of Asia.

SIDELIGHTS: John A. Lent has traveled in Europe, Asia, Australia, Africa, Latin America, and the Caribbean. He developed and taught the first international communications courses at University of Wisconsin—Eau Claire, Marshall University, University of Wyoming, and Universiti Sains Malaysia. He has also supervised an archaeological excavation in Canada, edited an underground newspaper, and helped organize FREE, a group for racial equality in West Virginia. Lent believes that writing comes from rigid discipline; he has now abandoned his earlier practice of writing all night in favor of a strict daytime schedule of 40-60 hours per week.

* * *

LESTER, David 1942-

PERSONAL: Born June 1, 1942, in London, England; U.S. citizen; son of Harry (a bookie) and Kathleen (Moore) Lester; married Jean Mercer (a psychologist and author under names Gene Lester and Jean Mercer), April 15, 1967 (divorced, 1977); married Mary E. Murrell (a professor of criminal justice), July 20, 1979 (divorced, 1983); married Bijou Yang (an economist), October 22, 1987; children: (first marriage) Simon. *Ethnicity:* "Caucasian." *Education:* Cambridge University, B.A., 1964, M.A., 1968, Ph.D., 1991; Brandeis University, M.A., 1966, Ph.D., 1968. *Politics:* None. *Religion:* None.

ADDRESSES: Home—RR 41, 5 Stonegate Ct., Blackwood, NJ 08012. *Office*—Psychology Program, Richard Stockton State College, Pomona, NJ 08240. *E-mail*—fac137@pollux.stockton.edu; fax: 609-748-5559.

CAREER: Wellesley College, Wellesley, MA, instructor, 1967-68, assistant professor of psychology, 1968-69; Suicide Prevention and Crisis Service, Buffalo, NY, research director, 1969-71; Richard Stockton State College, Pomona, NJ, associate professor, 1971-74, professor of psychology, 1975—, chair of department, 1971-74, coordinator of criminal justice program, 1977-78. Executive director, Center for the Study of Suicide, Blackwood, NJ, 1993—.

MEMBER: International Academy of Suicide Research (cofounder, 1990), International Association of Suicide Prevention (president, 1991-95), American Association of Suicidology (Proceedings editor, 1988-95), Chinese Association for Crisis Intervention.

AWARDS, HONORS: Research grant, National Institute of Mental Health, 1967-68, Radcliffe College research support program, 1993; Medal of Honor from University of Padua, 1990; Outstanding Achievement Award, Asociacion Mexicana de Tanatologicia, 1994; Dublin Award, American Association of Suicidology, 1997.

WRITINGS:

(With Gene Lester) *Suicide: The Gamble with Death,* Prentice-Hall (Englewood Cliffs, NJ), 1971, second edition, Charles, 1997.

Why Men Kill Themselves, C. C. Thomas (Springfield, IL), 1972, third edition published as *Why People Kill Themselves,* 1992.

Comparative Psychology: Phyletic Differences in Behavior, Alfred Publishing (Sherman Oaks, CA), 1973.

A Physiological Basis for Personality Traits, C. C. Thomas, 1974.

(With G. Lester) *Crime of Passion: Murder and the Murderer,* Nelson-Hall (Chicago), 1975.

Unusual Sexual Behavior: The Standard Deviations, C. C. Thomas, 1975.

The Use of Alternative Modes of Communication in Psychotherapy: The Computer, the Book, the Telephone, the Television, the Tape Recorder, C. C. Thomas, 1977.

(With B. H. Sell and K. D. Sell) *Suicide: A Guide to Information Sources,* Gale (Detroit, MI), 1980.

Psychotherapy for Offenders, Pilgrimage Press (Berkeley, CA), 1981.

(With Mary E. Murrell) *Introduction to Juvenile Delinquency,* Macmillan (New York City), 1981.

The Psychological Basis for Handwriting Analysis, Nelson-Hall, 1981.

The Structure of the Mind, University Press of America (Lanham, MD), 1982.

Gun Control: Issues and Answers, C. C. Thomas, 1984.

(With A. Levitt) *Insanity and Incompetence: Case Studies in Forensic Psychology,* Pilgrimage Press, 1984.

The Murderer and His Murder, AMS Press (New York City), 1986.

The Death Penalty, C. C. Thomas, 1987.

Suicide as a Learned Behavior, C. C. Thomas, 1987.

(With M. Braswell) *Correctional Counseling,* Anderson Publishing (Cincinnati, OH), 1987, third edition, 1997.

The Biochemical Basis of Suicide, C. C. Thomas, 1988.

Suicide from a Psychological Perspective, C. C. Thomas, 1988.

Why Women Kill Themselves, C. C. Thomas, 1988.

Can We Prevent Suicide?, AMS Press, 1989.

Questions and Answers about Suicide, Charles, 1989.

Suicide from a Sociological Perspective, C. C. Thomas, 1989.

(With R. Clarke) *Suicide: Closing the Exits,* Springer-Verlag, 1989.

Understanding and Preventing Suicide, C. C. Thomas, 1990.

Psychotherapy for Suicidal Clients, C. C. Thomas, 1991.

Questions and Answers about Murder, Charles, 1991.

(With B. Danto) *Suicide behind Bars,* Charles, 1993.

The Cruelest Death: The Enigma of Adolescent Suicide, Charles, 1993.

Suicide in Creative Women, Nova Science, 1993.

Understanding Suicide, Nova Science, 1993.

Patterns of Suicide and Homicide in America, Nova Science, 1994.

Theories of Personality, Taylor & Francis, 1995.

Serial Killers, Charles, 1995.

Patterns of Suicide and Homicide around the World, Nova Science, 1997.

Encyclopedia of Famous Suicides, Nova Science, 1997.

(With Bijou Yang) *Economic Perspectives on Suicide,* Nova Science, 1997.

Suicide in American Indians, Nova Science, 1997.

EDITOR

Explorations in Exploration, Van Nostrand (New York City), 1969.

(With G. Brockopp) *Crisis Intervention and Counseling by Telephone,* C. C. Thomas, 1973.

Gambling Today, C. C. Thomas, 1979.

The Elderly Victim of Crime, C. C. Thomas, 1981.

Suicide '89, American Association of Suicidology, 1989.

Current Concepts of Suicide, Charles, 1990.

Suicide '90, American Association of Suicidology, 1990.

Suicide '91, American Association of Suicidology, 1991.

Suicide '92, American Association of Suicidology, 1992.

Suicide '93, American Association of Suicidology, 1993.

(With M. Tallmer) *Now I Lay Me Down: Suicide in the Elderly,* Charles, 1994.

Emile Durkheim: "Le Suicide" One Hundred Years Later, Charles, 1994.

Suicide '94, American Association of Suicidology, 1994.

(With S. Canetto) *Women and Suicidal Behavior,* Springer-Verlag, 1995.

Suicide '95, American Association of Suicidology, 1995.

(With A. Leenaars) *Suicide and the Unconscious,* Jason Aronson (New York City), 1996.

Contributor of over 1,500 articles to periodicals, including *Journal of Clinical Psychology, American Anthropologist, Journal of General Psychology, Nature,* and *Clinical Psychologist.* Founder and coeditor, *Crisis Intervention,* 1969-71; member of editorial advisory board, *Current Contents (Social and Behavioral Sciences);* member of editorial board, *Omega,* 1971—, *Suicide and Life-Threatening Behavior,* 1981—, *Crisis,* 1993—, *Death Studies,* 1994—, and *Archives of Suicide Research,* 1995—.

SIDELIGHTS: David Lester told *CA:* "When I first wrote personal notes for *CA,* I was hoping to branch out into journalism and fiction. A lack of success pushed me back into my primary field—death studies and especially suicide. I have published some thirty books since 1988, almost all on aspects of death, and I have received increasing recognition in the field, leading to invitations to lecture in the United States and abroad. One of my goals now is to have a paperback best-seller on death. My recent book on serial killers did not make it, but I have one in progress on life-after-death. However, I have this inability to write for the mass market and to abandon my scholarly habits of having footnotes and references.

"What is my primary motivation for writing? Part of my motivation stems from my adolescent years when I studied physics and wanted to be the successor to Einstein. I love scientific knowledge and the process of acquiring it. I would have liked a Nobel Prize. The same motivates my work on suicide, but I also would like fame—not the kind of fame that one gets from being on a television talk show (I turn down all such invitations) but rather recognition from peers in the field.

"Why am I fascinated by death? Only recently did I consider this question. I was born in London in 1942 and spent the first three years of my life living in an air-raid shelter. My mother said that I was very sensitive to the impending cues to bombings, and so perhaps I developed a fear of death quite early in life. My adult preoccupation with death and suicide may be the psychoanalytic defense of intellectualization. By acquiring knowledge, I gain control over my death anxieties and death wishes. (Oh, wouldn't a course of psychoanalysis have been fun if I could have afforded it?)"

* * *

LEVI-STRAUSS, Claude 1908-

PERSONAL: Born November 28, 1908, in Brussels, Belgium; son of Raymond (a painter) and Emma (Levy) Levi-Strauss; married Dina Dreyfus, 1932 (divorced); married Rosemarie Ullmo, 1946 (divorced); married Monique Roman, April 5, 1954; children: (second marriage) Laurent; (third marriage) Matthieu. *Education:* Universite de Paris, licence, 1929, Agregation, 1931, Doctorat es Lettres, 1948.

ADDRESSES: Home—2 rue des Marronniers, Paris 75016, France. *Office*—Laboratoire d'Anthropologie sociale, 52 rue du Cardinal-Lemoine, Paris 75005, France.

CAREER: Universidade de Sao Paulo, Sao Paulo, Brazil, professor of sociology, 1935-39; New School for Social Research, New York, NY, visiting professor, 1941-45; French Embassy, Washington, DC, cultural counselor, 1946-47; Musee de l'Homme, Paris, France, associate curator, 1948-49; Sorbonne, Ecole Pratique des Hautes Etudes, Paris, director of research, 1950-82, College de France, Paris, professor of social anthropology, 1959-82, honorary professor, 1982—.

MEMBER: Academie francaise, National Academy of Sciences, American Academy and Institute of Arts and Letters, British Academy, Royal Academy of the Netherlands (foreign member), Academy of Norway (foreign member), Royal Anthropological Institute of Great Britain (honorary fellow), American Philosophical Society, London School of African and Oriental Studies.

AWARDS, HONORS: Honorary doctorates from University of Brussels, Oxford University, Yale University, University of Chicago, Columbia University, Stirling University, Universite Nationale du Zaire, University of Uppsala, Laval University, Universidad Nacional Autonoma de Mexico, Johns Hopkins University, Harvard University, and Visva Bharati University, India; Viking Fund Medal, Wenner-Gren Foundation, 1966; Commandeur de l'Ordre Nationale du Merite, 1971; Erasmus Prize, 1975; Grand-Officier de la Legion d'Honneur, 1991; Commandeur de l'Ordre des Palmes Academiques; Commandeur des Arts et des Lettres; Commandeur de la Coronne de Belgique; Cruzeiro do Sul.

WRITINGS:

La Vie familiale et sociale des Indiens Nambikwara, Societe de Americanistes, 1948.

Les Structures elementaires de la parente, Presses Universitaires de France, 1949, translation by J. H. Bell and J. R. von Strumer published as *The Elementary Structures of Kinship,* Beacon (Boston, MA), 1969.

Race et histoire, Gonthier, 1952.

Tristes Tropiques, Plon, 1955, revised edition, Adler, 1968, partial translation by John Russell published as *Tristes Tropiques,* Criterion (Torrance, CA), 1961 (published in England as *A World on the Wane,* Hutchinson, 1961), complete translation by John Weightman and Doreen Weightman, J. Cape (England), 1973, Atheneum (New York City), 1974.

Anthropologie structurale, Volume 1, Plon, 1958, translation by Claire Jacobson and Brooke Grundfest Schoepf published as *Structural Anthropology,* Basic Books (New York City), 1964, Volume 2, Plon, 1973, translation by Monica Layton, Basic Books, 1977.

Entretiens avec Claude Levi-Strauss, edited by Georges Charbonnier, Plon-Julliard, 1961, translation published as Conversations *with Claude Levi-Strauss,* J. Cape, 1969.

La Pensee sauvage, Plon, 1962, translation published as*The Savage Mind,* University of Chicago Press, 1966, revised edition, Adlers Foreign Books, 1985.

Le Totemisme aujourd'hui, Presses Universitaires de France, 1962, translation by Rodney Needham published as *Totemism,* Beacon, 1963, revised edition, Penguin (New York City), 1969.

Mythologiques, Plon, Volume 1: *Le Cru et le cuit,* 1964, Volume 2: *Du Miel aux cendres,* 1967, Volume 3: *L'Origine des manieres de table,* 1968, Volume 4:*L'Homme nu,* 1971, translation by J. Weightman and D. Weightman published as *Introduction to a Science of Mythology,* Volume 1: *The Raw and the Cooked,* Harper (New York City), 1969, Volume 2: *From Honey to Ashes,* J. Cape, 1973, Harper, 1974, Volume 3: *The Origin of Table Manners,* Harper, 1978, Volume 4: *The Naked Man,* Harper, 1981.

The Scope of Anthropology, J. Cape, 1968.

Discours de reception a l'Academie francaise, Institut de France (Paris), 1974.

La Voie des masques, two volumes, Skira, 1975, enlarged edition, Plon, 1979, translation by Sylvia Modelski published as *The Way of the Masks,* University of Washington Press (Seattle, WA), 1982.

(With Jean Marie Benoist) *L'Identitae: Saeminaire interdisciplinaire,* B. Grasset (Paris), 1977.

Myth and Meaning: Five Talks for Radio, University of Toronto Press (Canada), 1978, Schocken, 1979.

Le Regard eloigne, Plon, 1983, translation by J. Neugroschel and P. Hoss published as *The View from Afar,* Basic Books, 1985.

Paroles donnees, Plon, 1984, translation by Roy Willis published as *Anthropology and Myth: Lectures, 1957-1982,* Blackwell, 1987.

La Potiere jalouse, Plon, 1985, translation by Benedicte Chorier published as *The Jealous Potter,* University of Chicago Press, 1988.

Introduction to the Work of Marcel Mauss, Routledge & Kegan Paul (England), 1987.

(With Didier Eribon) *De pres et de loin,* Jacobs, 1988.

Comparative Mythology, Johns Hopkins University Press (Baltimore, MD), 1988.

(With Eribon) *Conversations with Claude Levi-Strauss,* translation by Paula Wissing, University of Chicago Press, 1991.

Saudades do Brasil: A Photographic Memoir, translation by Modelski, University of Washington Press, 1995.

The Story of Lynx, translation by Catherine Tihanyi, University of Chicago Press, 1995.

SIDELIGHTS: Often ranked with Jean-Paul Sartre and Andre Malraux as one of France's greatest modern intellectuals, Claude Levi-Strauss is "the last uncontested giant of French letters," as James M. Markham describes him in the *New York Times.* Acclaimed for his studies of primitive mythology and for his autobiographical book *A World on the Wane* (*Tristes Tropiques*), Levi-Strauss is also credited with founding the movement known as structural anthropology, "the search for underlying patterns of thought in all forms of human activity," as Markham defines it. So pervasive is Levi-Strauss's influence in such diverse fields as language theory, history, and psychology that George Steiner claims in his *Language and Silence: Essays on Language* that "an awareness of Levi-Strauss's thought is a part of current literacy." Marshall D. Sahlins believes the professional attention accorded Levi-Strauss is almost "unparalleled in the history of anthropology."

Tristes Tropiques, Levi-Strauss's study of Brazilian Indians, is "one of the great books of our century," according to Susan Sontag in her *Against Interpretation and Other Essays.* As much a rationale for anthropology as it is a study of a primitive people, the book asks why Western culture is the first to study other cultures and it explores the role of the anthropologist. Sontag finds the book to be "rigorous, subtle, and bold in thought. It is beautifully written. And, like all great books, it bears an absolutely personal stamp; it speaks with a human voice." This personal dimension is noted by Richard A. Shweder in the *New York Times Book Review,* who describes *Tristes Tropiques* as the book in which Levi-Strauss "transformed an expedition to the virgin interiors of the Amazon into a vision quest, and turned anthropology into a spiritual mission to defend mankind against itself."

In his *Introduction to a Science of Mythology,* Levi-Strauss attempts to systematize myths, discover their underlying structures, and expose the process of their creation. James Redfield in *Thinkers of the Twentieth Century* sees the massive four-volume work as "a book about human nature—if we understand that 'nature' here means the mind, which is to say, the sense that things make." "Levi-Strauss was intrigued by the way that languages as well as myths of different cultures resembled each other and appeared to be structured in a similar fashion," Edith Kurzweil explains in *The Age of Structuralism: Levi-Strauss to Foucault.* Steiner credits Levi-Strauss with "seeking a science of mythology, a grammar of symbolic constructs and associations allowing the anthropologist to relate different myths as the structural linguist relates phonemes and language systems. Once the code of myths is deciphered and is seen to have its own logic and translatability, its own grid of values and interchangeable significants, the anthropologist will have a tool of great power with which to attack problems of human ecology, of ethnic and linguistic groupings, of cultural diffusion. Above all, he may gain insight into mental processes and strata of consciousness which preserve indices. . .of the supreme event in man's history—the transition from a primarily instinctual, perhaps pre-linguistic condition to the life of consciousness and individualized self-awareness." Although Kurzweil admits that Levi-Strauss's structuralist approach has not been wholly successful in studying mythology, "his theory of the elusive, unconscious structures did lead to the creation of various new subjects of inquiry such as the relationships between the structures of all signs in language, their function within messages, and their rapport with other sign systems, such as music, gestures, [and] body language."

Several observers find that how Levi-Strauss expresses his ideas is as important as what he says. He often presents an intellectual position only to tear it down, uses irony and digression, and ranges over a number of seemingly unrelated subjects—all while displaying a mastery of such diverse fields as linguistics, psychiatry, genetics, and neuroscience. "Levi-Strauss once described his own rather cultivated, but sometimes savage, mind as the intellectual equivalent of slash-and-burn agriculture," Shweder reports. "The prose of Levi-Strauss," Steiner writes, "is a very special instrument, and one which many are trying to imitate. It has an austere, dry detachment. . . . It uses a careful alternance of long sentences, usually organized in ascending rhythm, and of abrupt Latinate phrases. While seeming to observe the conventions of neutral, learned presentation, it allows for brusque personal interventions and asides." "There is more to understanding Levi-Strauss than knowing what he himself has written," adds Godfrey Lienhardt. "Perhaps beyond any other living anthropologist he has established a dialogue with part of the intellectual public, appearing to speak personally to educated general readers and engaging them in his own processes of analysis and reflection." "The outstanding characteristic of his writing . . . ," Edmund Leach maintains in his study *Claude Levi-Strauss,* "is that it is difficult to understand; his sociological theories combine baffling complexity with overwhelming erudition." Leach goes so far as to say that "Levi-Strauss is admired not so much for the novelty of his ideas as for the bold originality with which he seeks to apply them. He has suggested new ways of looking at familiar facts; it is the method that is interesting rather than the practical consequences of the use to which it has been put." But Lienhardt identifies Levi-Strauss's writing as "an exhortation to wonder at the complex creativity of mankind, to revere it and finally to see through it."

Levi-Strauss cheerfully admits that his books "are hard to understand" and that he "stands outside of the anthropological mainstream," notes a writer for *Newsweek.* "'I think,' he says, 'I'm a school by myself.'" With Sartre and Malraux dead, and their leftist politics increasingly discredited, Levi-Strauss now holds a unique and powerful position in the French intelligentsia. But though he is widely respected, he refuses to accept the role of "prophet," a role long common among French philosophers. Markham quotes Pierre Bourdieu explaining that "one of [Levi-Strauss's] effects has been to change the nature of the French intellectual, to propose something more modest." David Pace, writing in *Claude Levi-Strauss: The Bearer of Ashes,* reports that Levi-Strauss "has made no real effort to disseminate his ideas of cultural progress to a large popular audience or to translate them into any political movement. On the contrary, he has taken every opportunity to deny the importance of his own speculations on these topics and to focus attention upon his technical achievements in structural anthropology."

Speaking to Markham, Levi-Strauss identified his deep concern for "a certain number of values which are those of my society and which I consider to be threatened. They are threatened by the Soviet Union, by Islamic fundamentalism, and by the demographic growth of the Third World." Among these values are the importance of a national culture over a world "monoculture" and the ideal of the traditional peasant who lives close to nature. Yet Pace finds "something fundamentally nihilistic about Levi-Strauss's world-view. . . . There is neither a serious effort to protect the things which he sees as threatened nor an attempt to abandon his attachment to them. He himself has described his own position as a 'serene pessimism.'"

"For 25 years," Shweder notes, "[Levi-Strauss] has been the object of adoration and scorn in the English-speaking world." Redfield reports that "it is possible that . . . later ages will speak of our time as the age of Levi-Strauss. . . . He is a maker of the modern mind, and has influenced many who have never read him, and some who have quite mistaken ideas about what he says." As Joan Bamberger writes: "Whatever the future impact of [Levi-Strauss's] work, certainly the anthropological study of myth will never be the same."

BIOGRAPHICAL/CRITICAL SOURCES:

BOOKS

Contemporary Literary Criticism, Volume 38, Gale (Detroit), 1986.

Girard, Rene, *"To Double Business Bound": Essays on Literature, Mimesis, and Anthropology,* Johns Hopkins University Press (Baltimore), 1978.

Kurzweil, Edith, *The Age of Structuralism: Levi-Strauss to Foucault,* Columbia University Press (New York City), 1980.

LaPointe, Francois Y. and Claire C. LaPointe, *Claude Levi-Strauss and His Critics: An International Bibliography of Criticism (1950-1976), Followed by a Bibliography of the Writings of Claude Levi-Strauss,* Garland Publishing (New York City), 1977.

Leach, Edmund, *Claude Levi-Strauss,* Viking Press (New York City), revised edition, 1974.

Pace, David, *Claude Levi-Strauss: The Bearer of Ashes,* Routledge & Kegan Paul, 1983.

Rossi, Ino, editor, *The Logic of Culture: Advances in Structural Theory and Methods,* J. F. Bergin Publishers, 1982.

Sontag, Susan, *Against Interpretation and Other Essays,* Farrar, Strauss (New York City), 1966.

Steiner, George, *Language and Silence: Essays on Language, Literature, and the Inhuman,* Atheneum (New York City), 1967.

Thinkers of the Twentieth Century, St. James (Chicago), second edition, 1987.

PERIODICALS

Atlantic, July, 1969.

Book Week, February 9, 1964.

Book World, November 9, 1969.

Commentary, May, 1968.

Globe and Mail (Toronto), May 14, 1988.

Hudson Review, winter, 1967.

Kenyon Review, March, 1967.

Listener, May 23, 1968.

Nation, March 16, 1970.

Natural History, June/July, 1973.

New Republic, July 22, 1969; May 18, 1974.

Newsweek, February 23, 1967.

New York Review of Books, November 28, 1963; October 12, 1967.

New York Times, December 31, 1969; December 21, 1987.

New York Times Book Review, June 3, 1973; April 14, 1985.

Reporter, April 6, 1967.

Saturday Review, December 31, 1966; May 17, 1969.

Spectator, May 12, 1961; March 21, 1969.

Time, June 30, 1967.

Times Literary Supplement, May 12, 1961; June 15, 1967; September 12, 1968.

* * *

LIEBER, Robert J(ames) 1941-

PERSONAL: Born September 29, 1941, in Chicago, IL; married Nancy Lee Isaksen, June 20, 1964; children: Benjamin Yves, Keir Alexander. *Education:* University of Wisconsin, B.A. (with high honors), 1963; Harvard University, Ph.D., 1968.

ADDRESSES: Office—Department of Government, Georgetown University, Washington, DC 20057-1034.

CAREER: University of California, Davis, assistant professor, 1968-72, associate professor, 1972-77, professor of political science, 1977-81, chair of department, 1975-76 and 1977-80; Georgetown University, Washington, DC, professor of government, 1982—. chair of department, 1990-96. Visiting fellow, St. Antony's College, Oxford, 1969-70; fellow, Woodrow Wilson International Center for Scholars, 1980-81; guest scholar, Brookings Institution, 1980-81. Research associate, Harvard University Center for International Affairs, 1974-75, and Atlantic Institute, Paris, 1978-79. Coordinator of Middle East issues in Dukakis presidential campaign, 1987-88. Participant in Washington Institute's presidential study group on U.S. policy in the Middle East, 1987-90.

MEMBER: International Institute for Strategic Studies, American Political Science Association, Council on Foreign Relations. Phi Beta Kappa.

AWARDS, HONORS: NDEA Title IV fellowship in political science, University of Chicago, 1963-64; postdoctoral research training fellowship, Social Science Research Council, 1969-70; International Affairs fellowship, Council on Foreign Relations, 1972; Guggenheim fellowship, 1973; Rockefeller International Relations fellowship, 1978-79; Ford Foundation grant, 1981; fellow, Woodrow Wilson International Center for Scholars, 1980-81.

WRITINGS:

British Politics and European Unity: Parties, Elites, and Pressure Groups, University of California Press (Berkeley), 1970.

Theory and World Politics, Winthrop Publishers, 1972.

(Coauthor) *Contemporary Politics: Europe,* Winthrop Publishers, 1976.

Oil and the Middle East War, Harvard University Center for International Affairs (Cambridge, MA), 1976.

The Oil Decade: Conflict and Cooperation in the West, University Press of America (Lanham, MD), 1986.

No Common Power: Understanding International Relations, Scott, Foresman (Glenview, IL)/ Little, Brown (Boston), 1988, third edition, Harper Collins (New York City), 1995.

EDITOR

(Coeditor and contributor) *Eagle Entangled: U.S. Foreign Policy in a Complex World,* Longman (New York City), 1979.

(Contributor) *Will Europe Fight for Oil?,* Praeger (New York City), 1983.

(Coeditor and contributor) *Eagle Defiant: U.S. Foreign Policy in the 1980s,* Little, Brown, 1983.

(Coeditor and contributor) *Eagle Resurgent?: The Reagan Era in American Foreign Policy,* Little, Brown, 1987.

(Coeditor and contributor) *Eagle in a New World: American Grand Strategy in the Post-Cold War Era,* Harper Collins, 1992.

OTHER

Contributor to periodicals, including *International Security, International Affairs* (London), *American Political Science Review, Politique Etrangere, Harper's, New York Times,* and *Washington Post.*

WORK IN PROGRESS: Writing on American foreign policy and U.S. relations with Western Europe and the Middle East.

SIDELIGHTS: Robert J. Lieber told *CA* that his "other credits include faculty and party politics, 'killer tennis,' and a walk-on part in the Alfred Hitchcock film classic 'North by Northwest.'"

* * *

LIPSYTE, Robert (Michael) 1938-

PERSONAL: Born January 16, 1938, in New York, NY; son of Sidney I. (a principal) and Fanny (a teacher; maiden name, Finston) Lipsyte; married Marjorie L. Rubin (deceased); married Katherine L. Sulkes; children: (first marriage) Sam, Susannah. *Education:* Columbia University, B.A., 1957, M.S., 1959.

ADDRESSES: *Home*—New York, NY. *Agent*—Theron Raines, Raines & Raines, 71 Park Ave., Suite 4A, New York, NY 10016.

CAREER: *New York Times,* New York City, copyboy, 1957-59, sports reporter, 1959-67, sports columnist, 1967-71 and 1991—; *New York Post,* New York City, columnist, 1977; Columbia Broadcasting Service, Inc. (CBS-TV), New York City, sports essayist for program *Sunday Morning,* 1982-86; National Broadcasting Company, Inc. (NBC-TV), New York City, correspondent, 1986-88; Public Broadcasting Service (PBS-TV), New York City, host of program *The Eleventh Hour,* 1989-90; writer. Has also worked as a journalism teacher and radio commentator. *Military service:* U.S. Army, 1961.

AWARDS, HONORS: Dutton Best Sports Stories Award, E. P. Dutton, 1964, for "The Long Road to Broken Dreams," 1965, for "The Incredible Cassius," 1967, for "Where the Stars of Tomorrow Shine Tonight," 1971, for "Dempsey in the Window," and 1976, for "Pride of the Tiger";

Mike Berger Award, Columbia University Graduate School of Journalism, 1966 and 1996; Wel-Met Children's Book Award, Child Study Children's Book Committee at Bank Street College of Education, 1967, for *The Contender; New York Times* outstanding children's book of the year citation, and American Library Association best young adult book citation, both 1977, for *One Fat Summer;* New Jersey Author citation, New Jersey Institute of Technology, 1978; Emmy Award for on-camera achievement, Academy of Television Arts and Sciences, 1990, as host of the television program *The Eleventh Hour.*

WRITINGS:

(With Dick Gregory) *Nigger,* Dutton (New York City), 1964.
The Masculine Mystique, New American Library (New York City), 1966.
The Contender, Harper (New York City), 1967.
Assignment: Sports, Harper, 1970, revised edition, 1984.
(With Steve Cady) *Something Going,* Dutton, 1973.
Liberty Two, Simon & Schuster (New York City), 1974.
SportsWorld: An American Dreamland, Quadrangle (Chicago), 1975.
That's the Way of the World (screenplay; also released under title *Shining Star*), United Artists, 1975.
One Fat Summer, Harper, 1977.
Free to Be Muhammad Ali, Harper, 1978.
Summer Rules, Harper, 1981.
Jock and Jill, Harper, 1982.
The Summerboy, Harper, 1982.
The Brave, HarperCollins (New York City), 1991.
The Chemo Kid, HarperCollins, 1992.
The Chief, HarperCollins, 1993.
(With Peter Levine) *Idols of the Game: A Sporting History of the American Century,* Turner (Atlanta), 1995.

"SUPERSTAR LINEUP" SERIES

Jim Thorpe: Twentieth-Century Jock, HarperCollins, 1993.
Arnold Schwarzenegger: Hercules in America, HarperCollins, 1993.
Michael Jordan: A Life above the Rim, HarperCollins, 1994.
Joe Louis: A Champ for All America, HarperCollins, 1994.

OTHER

Author of screenplay *The Act,* 1982; creator and writer of the three-part television documentary *Idols of the Game,* TBS, 1995; also scriptwriter for *Saturday Night with Howard Cosell.* Author of introduction to C. L. James, *Beyond a Boundary,* Pantheon, 1984. Contributor to periodicals, including *TV Guide, Harper's Magazine, Nation, New York Times, New York Times Book Review, New York Times Magazine,* and *American Health.* Advisory editor for *Sports and Society,* edited by Gene Brown, Arno Press (New York City), 1980.

Lipsyte's papers are housed in the De Grummond Collection, University of Southern Mississippi and the Kerlan Collection, University of Minnesota.

SIDELIGHTS: Robert Lipsyte, a journalist who left the medium to write books, spent fourteen years covering sports for the *New York Times,* from the late 1950s to the early 1970s. Lipsyte gained national attention as a result of his sports columns, and Paul D. Zimmerman, in a *Newsweek* review of Lipsyte's book *Sports World: An American Dreamland,* called the author "the most original and elegant writer on the sports staff" of the *New York Times* during his tenure. Lipsyte began writing books while still on staff at the paper. His publications for young adults have been praised as unsentimental books featuring characters who experience a transformation through a combination of hard work and adherence to ethics. Not surprisingly, the majority of the author's books also involve aspects of athletics and, because of his experience as a sportswriter, Lipsyte is considered an authority in the field of children's sports stories. Offering advice in an article for *Children's Literature in Education,* the author commented, "I don't think we have to make any rules for sports books for children beyond asking that they present some sense of truth about the role of sports in our lives."

For Lipsyte, this means providing realistic portraits of athletes who do not lead idyllic lives solely because of their physical abilities, but must contend with ordinary problems in other areas of their lives. The author also believes the importance of physical ability should be downplayed because many people, especially youngsters who haven't had the time to develop skills in other areas, may be humiliated when they are unable to display athletic prowess. In an article for *Children's Literature in Education,* Lipsyte commented, "Sports is, or should be, just one of the things people do—an integral part of life, but only one aspect of it. Sports is a good experience. It's fun. It ought to be inexpensive and accessible to everybody." He added, "In our society, sports is a negative experience for most boys and almost all girls. . . . They're required to define themselves on the basis of competitive physical ability." And, according to Lipsyte, sports programs are elitist because individuals with only average ability are quickly weeded out of the system.

These problems, evident in organized sports, have led Lipsyte to refine his own philosophy regarding athletic involvement and question the appropriateness of the nation's fixation with all levels of athletic competition. The author maintains that a subculture exists in American society based on the myth that such practices as obeying a screaming coach, suppressing individualism for the team's sake, and playing through pain are noble pursuits. He alleges that media coverage of sporting events promotes this myth and invites spectators to triumph vicariously through the exploits of their favorite superstars instead of participating in sports themselves. As a sportswriter, Lipsyte was an integral part of this subculture he has christened "SportsWorld," and his disillusionment with certain athletic conventions has thus been deemed noteworthy. In his work *SportsWorld: An American Dreamland,* Lipsyte recapitulates his career as a sportswriter, using encounters with athletes in baseball, football, basketball, boxing, and tennis to give examples of and validate his philosophy.

Elaborating on his displeasure with "SportsWorld," Lipsyte explained in his book, "Sometime in the last fifty years the sports experience was perverted into a SportsWorld state of mind in which the winner was good because he won; the loser, if not actually bad, was at least reduced, and had to prove himself over again, through competition. . . . SportsWorld is a grotesque distortion of sports. . . . It has made the finish more important than the race." The author is disconcerted that such maxims have been readily accepted by the American public. He argues that "very few people seem to be questioning SportsWorld itself, exploring the possibility that if sports could be separated from SportsWorld we could take a major step toward liberation from the false values, the stereotypes, the idols of the arena that have burdened us all since childhood."

Statements such as these in *SportsWorld* prompted reviewers to categorize Lipsyte as a disenchanted writer harboring an intense dislike of sports. Disappointed with the book's emphasis on the negative aspects of sports, Roger Kahn, writing in the *New York Times Book Review,* admitted "I admired his column and I wanted to like his book. But *SportsWorld* lacks a sense of joy." In a review of *SportsWorld* in the *New York Review of Books,* Garry Wills reasoned, "If you take Lipsyte's advice and cease to care about professional sports, there is nothing much left to care about in his book." Lipsyte, however, foresaw such criticism and proclaimed at the conclusion of the book: "I am no hater of athletes and my book is not antisports, although these will be the reflex charges." Instead, the author claims he questions athletic procedures and policies because of his affinity for sports. Noting the contentious nature of the work, Zimmerman deemed *SportsWorld* "a persuasive volume of dissent," and added, "Read him, and you will never look at a sports event in quite the same way again."

In the opening chapter of *SportsWorld,* Lipsyte exposes his childhood association with athletics. He remarked: "I was never an avid spectator sports fan. Although I grew up in New York while there were still three major league baseball teams in town, I didn't attend my first game until I was 13 years old. I was profoundly disappointed. . . . I went to only one more game as a paying customer. The third one I covered for *The New York Times.* I attended few sports events as a child, but there was no escaping SportsWorld. That's in the air. I grew up in Rego Park, in Queens, then a neighborhood of attached houses, six-story apartment buildings, and many vacant jungly lots. We played guns in the lots, Chinese handball against thc brick sides of buildings, and just enough stickball in the streets and schoolyard to qualify . . . as true natives. There was no great sporting tradition in the neighborhood."

Apparently no precedent of athletic participation existed in Lipsyte's family. Instead, intellectual pursuits were stressed due to the fact that both of his parents were teachers and the family's house contained many books. The young Lipsyte spent hours reading and decided early on to become a writer. He received an undergraduate degree in English from Columbia University in New York and planned to continue his education by attending graduate school. Yet, unpredictably, his career as a sports reporter began. In *SportsWorld* he recalled, "In 1957, a few days after graduation from Columbia, I answered a classified ad for a copy boy at *The Times*. I wanted a summer job to pay my way out to graduate school in California. . . . The job was at night, from 7 to 3, and it was in the sports department, filling paste-pots, sharpening pencils, and fetching coffee for the nights sports copy desk." Despite his decidedly unglamorous entrance into the sports department, Lipsyte opted to stay and eventually graduated from his gopher status. He continued in *SportsWorld:* "I moved from copy boy to statistician to night rewrite reporter. I wrote high school sports and occasional features, often on my own time, and I was sometimes let out to catch a celebrity passing through town or make a fast grab between editions for a quote to freshen up someone else's limp story."

Lipsyte seemed enamored with the newsroom's colorful figures and hectic pace and was eager to test his writing skills. He earned his first major assignment for the paper in 1962, covering the New York Mets in that baseball team's first year of existence. The author also learned to write within space constraints while heeding deadlines. In the 1984 edition of his book *Assignment: Sports* Lipsyte explained, "Writing under deadline is often exhilarating, and if you're lucky and the event has moved you, a rhythm develops and the story just flows out of the typewriter." However, he noted the drawback that "at night in a chilly arena, with the clock moving toward the deadline, that moment comes when even the best story in the world, finished too late, is worthless."

Lipsyte recalled that the 1960s were an excellent time to break into the sportswriting field because of the surge in the appeal of sports as family entertainment and the exposure of athletic contests on television. These developments generated a change in the configuration of articles in the sports page. Previously, stories were essentially game summaries, written for the benefit of those who had not attended the competition. As television gained popularity and more people were able to watch various sporting events, fans looked to newspaper articles to give them unique information about a team or athlete. As Lipsyte acknowledged in *SportsWorld,* this meant that "the sportswriter had to offer his reader fact and opinion unavailable elsewhere, and that meant controversy, bold speculation, and outspoken second-guessing."

In addition to the evolution of reporting, the social conflicts of the 1960s, beginning with the civil rights movement and continuing in the wake of the Vietnam War, profoundly influenced athletes and thus sports stories. Lipsyte chronicled the exploits of many sports figures and tried to demythicize his subjects by reporting about their successes on the field as well as the troubles they faced in their everyday lives. The author was deemed controversial because of his tendency to infuse social and political issues in his sports column. Defending this approach in his book *Assignment: Sports,* an edited collection of his columns, Lipsyte argued, "Politics, race, religion, money, the law—all play roles in sports . . . sports is no sanctuary from reality." Yet, his philosophy had some supporters in the newspaper industry. In *SportsWorld* he admitted, "My age-group counterparts on other papers seemed pleased when I started covering . . . the growing discontent of athletes; racism, sexism, distorted nationalism, the sports-politics interface. By appearing in *The Times,* these stories got instant credibility. It became easier for other writers to get such stories past their own editors. Such is the power-by-default of *The Times.*"

Lipsyte's most controversial columns inevitably involved the boxer Muhammad Ali, previously named Cassius Clay. In the 1960 Rome Olympics, Clay won a gold medal and publicly credited the United States with progress in race relations. As a professional boxer in 1964, however, he converted to the Islamic religious denomination called the Black Muslims, a black separatist sect which adheres to strict rules and seeks to limit contact of its members with whites. As part of his religious conversion, the boxer subsequently changed his name to Muhammad Ali. Some members of the American public viewed his involvement with the Black Muslims as a rebuke against the United States—the country that had afforded Ali the opportunity to become a champion. Many periodicals, including the *New York Times,* initially refused to address the boxer by his newly adopted Islamic name. Ali's religious beliefs came to the forefront again in 1967 when he refused to serve in the Vietnam War, complying with a Black Muslim precedent. This act resulted in the rescindment of his boxing title and a forced three-year hiatus from fighting. In addition, Lipsyte recalled in *SportsWorld* that *The Ring,* a boxing magazine, "refused to designate a Fighter of the Year in 1967 because 'most emphatically is Cassius Clay of Louisville, KY not to be held up as an example to the youngsters of the United States.'"

Lipsyte, who began covering the boxing beat for the *New York Times* in 1964 and followed Ali's career for more than three years, witnessed the controversy firsthand. Yet, in contrast to the negative perception some members of the American public had of Ali, Lipsyte viewed Ali's expressions of individuality with respect. In his biography of the boxer titled *Free to Be Muhammad Ali,* the author categorized Ali as "far and away the most interesting character in that mythical kingdom I call SportsWorld." Ali's outspokenness—manifested in snappy, original sayings—also offered the author plenty of material with which to write stories. In *SportsWorld,* the author recalled, "Every time I wrote about Ali in those days I would get a flood of letters praising me for being courageous or liberal or irreverent, attacking me for being unAmerican or a nigger-lover or a fool. The letters more or less neutralized each other. But sometimes [in reference to the ongoing Vietnam War] I would get a sad, thoughtful letter reminding me of all the young Americans coming home in rubber bags while Ali and I were free to prattle."

The title *Free to Be Muhammad Ali* refers to an incident that occurred after the young Clay had defeated Sonny Liston in 1964 to assume the heavyweight championship. After reporters questioned his lifestyle, values, and religious philosophy, Ali replied, according to Lipsyte in *SportsWorld,* "I don't have to be what you want me to be, I'm free to be who I want." Lipsyte remembered that the remark "was very simple, but at that time, coming from a brand-new heavyweight champion of the world, it was profound and revolutionary. A declaration of independence from *SportsWorld.*" In *Free to Be Muhammad Ali,* Lipsyte recounts episodes of the fighter's life and supplies illustrations of his charismatic nature. Mel Watkins, writing in the *New York Times Book Review,* categorized the work as "a thoughtful, complex portrait of one of America's greatest athletes" and added that the reader derives a sense of Ali's personality and "the affection and respect the author feels for him as an athlete and as a man."

Lipsyte drew upon his experiences as a boxing writer to produce his first novel for young readers, *The Contender.* The protagonist, Alfred Brooks, is an orphaned seventeen-year-old boy living in Harlem. A recent high school dropout, Alfred lives with his aunt and works as a stock boy in a grocery store. The work chronicles the metamorphosis of the aimless Alfred into a disciplined young man with long-term goals. He achieves this change by applying principles he learns while training to be a boxer. Offering universal advice in one of these training sessions, his manager Donatelli insists, "Everybody wants to be a champion. That's not enough. You have to start by wanting to be a contender. . . . It's the climbing that makes the man. Getting to the top is an extra reward." After months of training, Alfred enters the ring and wins several matches as an amateur. Donatelli, sensing that Alfred does not have the killer instinct required to be a top boxer, advises him to quit fighting competitively. Alfred insists on fighting once more against a worthy opponent to see if he has the requisite courage to be a contender. Although ultimately losing the contest, Alfred discovers an inner resolve that will help him in everyday life. At the book's conclusion, Alfred has plans to go back to school and open a recreation center for the children of Harlem.

The novel was commended for its trendsetting treatment of athletic participation. Unlike the common theme of sports as a vehicle out of the ghetto, Lipsyte's *Contender* presents sports involvement as a form of discipline that will help his protagonist survive and be productive in his same environment. Approving of this realistic approach, John S. Simmons, writing in *Elementary English,* remarked that "tribute to the author lies in the fact that in his search for himself, Alfred has scaled no Matterhorn peaks at the novel's conclusion." Instead, Simmons noted, the protagonist's "gains are modest and his successes frequently tainted with fear, reproach, and self-depreciation." Nat Hentoff, writing in the *New York Times Book Review,* remarked that "whenever Lipsyte writes about boxing itself he indicates how intensely evocative he can be," but hastened to add that "when he leaves the gym and the ring . . . Lipsyte is too often content to map the road to salvation" for Alfred. Edward B. Hungerford, writing in

Book World, concluded by calling *The Contender* "a fine book in which interest combines with compassion and enlightenment."

In the fall of 1967, Lipsyte left the boxing beat to begin writing a general sports column for the *New York Times.* In *SportsWorld* he remarked, "It was an exciting time to be writing a column, to be freed from the day-to-day responsibility for a single subject or the whims of the assignment desk. For me, after more than three years with Ali, the newly surfaced turmoil in sports seemed a natural climate." Responsible for three columns a week for the *New York Times,* Lipsyte had the freedom to choose his topics, but was still forced to adhere to stringent space limitations. He continued in *SportsWorld,* "Professionally, there is a challenge, for a while at least, to creating within formalized boundaries. Over an extended period of time, however, it's a poor way to transmit information." The author also confessed, "As that second year slipped into a third year, as the column became progressively easier to write, . . . I found I was less and less sure of what I absolutely knew."

Lipsyte's columns became the source for his 1970 work titled *Assignment: Sports,* in which he edited his writings from the *New York Times* to appeal to a younger audience. In 1984, he revised the first edition to incorporate the changes in sports, specifically the emergence and acceptance of the female athlete. As with *SportsWorld, Assignment: Sports* serves as a historical guide of American athletics. The author provides an account of the Black Power protests in the 1968 summer Olympics and offers portraits of sports figures, including football's Joe Namath, boxing's Ali, and baseball manager Casey Stengel. Sam Elkin, writing in the *New York Times Book Review,* credited Lipsyte "with the skill of a fine fiction writer for nuance" and added the "readers meeting him for the first time, regardless of age-group, have a rare treat in store."

Despite the acclaim his columns received, Lipsyte left the *New York Times* in the fall of 1971. In *Assignment: Sports* he remarked, "I knew I'd miss the quick excitement of deadline journalism. . . . But I wanted more time to think about what I had seen during the past fourteen years, and more space to shape those thoughts into characters and stories." During the next eleven years he wrote books, taught journalism at college, visited schools to talk about his books, wrote jokes for a television show called *Saturday Night with Howard Cosell,* and spent nine months at the *New York Post* writing a column about the people of that city. Although Lipsyte admitted to sometimes missing his old job at the *New York Times* he reasoned, "Mostly I enjoyed a deeper, richer creative challenge. It was a wonderful time. I remember with pleasure the months of traveling slowly through the back roads of my imagination."

In the late 1970s and early 1980s, Lipsyte wrote what he deemed a fifties trilogy consisting of the books *One Fat Summer, Summer Rules,* and *The Summerboy.* The author shares similarities with his protagonist, Bobby Marks, who also comes of age in the fifties and conquers an adolescent weight problem. Each book is set in a resort town in upstate New York called Rumson Lake, where Bobby's family spends each summer. Lipsyte presents the maturation process of his protagonist from the age of fourteen to eighteen. In the trilogy, Bobby faces problems, but overcomes them by relying on determination, hard work, and positive values. Critics have endorsed the novels for tackling adolescent dilemmas in a realistic manner and for offering believable first-person narration.

The first installment, *One Fat Summer,* depicts the protagonist as a fourteen-year-old nicknamed the "Crisco Kid" because he weighs more than two hundred pounds. Wishing to hide his flabby body beneath baggy winter clothes, Bobby dreads the family's annual migration to Rumson Lake. The protagonist must also contend with Willie Rumson, a town bully who dislikes "summer people" such as the Marks family, and takes out his frustrations by subjecting Bobby to public humiliation. During this particular summer Bobby must also endure the snide comments of Dr. Kahn, who employs the youngster as a landscaper. Despite the aching muscles and blisters he is afflicted with during his stint of manual labor, Bobby loses fifty pounds over the summer and, more significantly, gains the self-esteem necessary to stand up to Willie and Dr. Kahn. When describing the protagonist, Stephen Krensky, writing in the *New York Times Book Review,* commented that "refreshingly, he is neither precocious nor off-beat . . . but simply a normal boy in abnormal circumstances."

The second book of the trilogy, *Summer Rules,* chronicles Bobby's adventures as a sixteen-year-old. Although eagerly looking forward to socializing during the summer, Bobby is forced by his father to work as a counselor at the Happy Valley Day Camp. Here the protagonist meets Sheila, his first real girlfriend. Unfortunately, she is also the cousin of Harley, a spoiled nine-year-old who has experienced emotional problems since his mother's death. The book recounts Bobby's budding romance with Sheila and his tribulations as a counselor. A building fire nearly kills some of the campers and, based on his past record, Willie Rumson, Bobby's nemesis from *One Fat Summer,* is falsely arrested on the suspicion of arson. Bobby knows that Harley actually set the fire, but struggles with his conscience to determine if telling the truth will cause the boy more distress and alienate Sheila. Several critics approved of the sophisticated subject and praised Lipsyte's writing style.

Bobby returns as an eighteen-year-old in the novel *The Summerboy*. The protagonist begins his summer job at Lenape Laundry thinking that the town girls will be impressed by his new status as a college student. Instead, his coworkers shun him because he is an affluent "summerboy." The owner of the laundry, Roger Sinclair, allows his workers to toil in unsafe working conditions and will fire anyone who complains. Bobby, who wants to be accepted by the other workers, must decide whether to side with the boss and keep his job, or stand up for the other employees. After a serious accident at the laundry, Bobby leads a protest and is fired, but the demonstration forces Sinclair to improve conditions.

Lipsyte was forced to battle his own problems beginning in the summer of 1978 when he was diagnosed as having testicular cancer. In his book *Assignment: Sports* he recalled, "Like most people, we regarded cancer as one of the most dreaded words in the language; if not a death sentence, we thought, at least it meant the end of a normal, productive life. We knew very little about cancer, but we learned quickly. After surgery, I underwent two years of chemotherapy. I was sick for a day or two after each treatment, and I lost some strength and some hair, but we were amazed at how normally my life continued: I wrote, I traveled, I swam and ran and played tennis. After the treatments were over, my strength and my hair returned. There was no evidence of cancer. I was happy to be alive, to be enjoying my family, to be writing."

Lipsyte's next book, *Jock and Jill,* involves themes of social responsibility and the use of pain-killing drugs in athletics. In the book, Jack Ryder, a high school pitching ace, breaks up with his girlfriend of two years to date Jill, a socially aware girl who has taken therapeutic drugs for emotional problems. He then joins Jill's coalition with Hector, a Hispanic gang leader, to lobby for better conditions in the housing projects of New York City's ghettos. Early in the work it appears that Jack has a perfect life, but it is gradually revealed that his younger brother is mentally retarded and his father cannot afford Jack's college tuition. Consequently, the protagonist, though receiving cortisone shots to relieve the pain in his arm, must rely on his pitching skills for a scholarship. As Jack prepares to pitch for his high school team in the Metro Area Championship in Yankee Stadium, he ponders his varying responsibilities to his father, coach, teammates, and the girl he has fallen in love with. Jack has the chance to be a hero in the game, but instead decides to use his platform to benefit Jill and Hector. The protagonist selflessly interrupts his no-hitter game in the seventh inning to protest the false arrest of Hector. Critics generally considered that Lipsyte skillfully handled the numerous elements in the story. John Leonard, writing in the *New York Times Book Review,* commented that the author "has a number of pitches to make in this engaging and didactic novel" and added, "On the big game, Mr. Lipsyte is superb."

Following the publication of *Jock and Jill,* Lipsyte began another career as a television correspondent. In *Assignment: Sports* he recalled, "One day in the spring of 1982, Shad Northshield and Bud Lamoreaux, the executive producers of the CBS 'Sunday Morning' show, asked me if I'd like to appear on television. It would mean hitting the road again and writing on deadline, learning a new field and meeting new people. . . . [It] would be like starting all over again." Lipsyte took the challenge and, after leaving *Sunday Morning,* worked as a correspondent for NBC-TV and became the host of *The Eleventh Hour* PBS program, a combination talk and interview show.

Despite his detour into broadcasting, Lipsyte continues to observe and comment upon college athletics. Serving as a senior fellow at the Center for the Study of Sport in Society at Northeastern University, the author has studied the alienation of college and professional athletes from the general public as well as the problems this isolation causes when an athlete's career is finished. He wrote in the *New York Times Magazine,* "I have begun to understand the problems of the temporarily rich and famous trying to become ordinary people." Lipsyte believes that once athletes retire, they experience difficulty adjusting to a lifestyle that lacks the structure and discipline of a sports team.

For Lipsyte, these issues serve as another indication of the dangers of mythicizing athletic involvement. The author wishes sports to once again be popular recreation instead of an industry that offers false hopes of stardom to millions of youngsters. As a writer, Lipsyte has attempted to present athletic participation in a proper perspective for young readers. In an article for *Children's Literature in Education,* Lipsyte concluded, "If we write more truthfully about sports, perhaps we can encourage kids to relax and have fun with each other—to challenge themselves for the pleasure of it, without self-doubt and without fear."

Although Lipsyte took an eight-year break from composing books, the urge to write never left him. In 1991, he published *The Brave,* a sequel to *The Contender,* his best-selling book. The author had received numerous letters in the years since *The Contender*'s publication all posing a common question—"what happened next?" to Alfred. Lipsyte once said: "I began to wonder what happened to Alfred too. In the psychosis that is writing, you begin to think that some of your characters really lived." The idea for *The Brave*'s plot was formed while Lipsyte was on a journalism assignment at an American Indian reservation. There he met and talked with a young man who described his fear of being stuck on the reservation where there were high levels of disease, alcoholism, and unemployment. At the same time, he was also afraid of leaving the reservation and facing the "white" world and possible rejection and prejudice. Nonetheless, he ran away to New York City for a few days. Although he was caught and forced to return home, the action was one of personal triumph. Lipsyte admired the boy's bravery and said "The idea of this runaway meeting Alfred Brooks marinated in my mind for a few years."

Lipsyte was able to act on this potential plot after the PBS television program he hosted was suddenly canceled. Ironically this happened in June, which Lipsyte called his "lucky month for starting books." In *The Brave,* Sonny Bear, a seventeen-year-old half-Indian runaway, meets Alfred Brooks in New York City. Alfred is now a forty-year-old police sergeant who seeks to curtail drug trafficking in the city. Sonny unwittingly becomes a pawn in the drug war, yet is rescued by Alfred, who teaches him how to box. Explaining the police officer's urge to help out the youngster, Lipsyte said, "Alfred wanted to pass on what he learned from Donatelli," his old boxing manager who gave advice that changed the course of Alfred's life when he was a teenager. A reviewer for *English Journal* compared Lipsyte's long-awaited sequel favorably with *The Contender.* "It has the same emphasis on personal growth through physical challenge." "In addition," noted the reviewer, "there's a larger political message" about the struggles of Native Americans in the wider national context. In 1993, Lipsyte added a third book to his young adult boxing series, *The Chief.* This novel follows Sonny Bear as he boxes his way from the reservation to Hollywood and back in a quest for a shot at the heavyweight title. The book highlights both the physical challenges and the challenges of the citizens of SportsWorld, all trying to get their piece of the action. "As usual," commented Susan R. Farber in *Voice of Youth Advocates,* "Lipsyte's writing is as hard-hitting as the sport he obviously loves. Heavy on dialogue and definitely not for the squeamish, this fast-paced book will be favorite among his many fans."

During 1991, the same year that *The Brave* was published, Lipsyte returned to the *New York Times* to write one sports column a week. The author said that his comeback as a sportswriter was "all part of the return to writing, the recommitment. I wanted to see how the world had changed—how I had changed. It was a terrific challenge; people might tell me that 'anything you had to say, you said twenty years ago.'" As for the changes in sports and the sportswriting field since his first stint in 1957, Lipsyte added, "The stakes are higher in sports now, but *I'm* more different than sports are. The writers are much better—they are better educated and sharper in perception." The author also pointed out that when he began, most writers were white males. "Now there are more women and blacks. There is beginning to be a representation of America" in the sports department.

After returning to his sports column at the *New York Times,* Lipsyte also returned to chronicling twentieth-century sports stars and the world of sports for both young people and adults. With HarperCollins, he launched the "Superstar Lineup" series of sports biographies with his 1993 *Jim Thorpe: Twentieth-Century Jock.* He followed with books on Arnold Schwarzenegger, Michael Jordan, and Joe Louis. He also cowrote with history professor Peter Levine *Idols of the Game: A Sporting History of the American Century.* In profiling the greats in a wide variety of sports, men and women, whites and minorities, the authors present, in the opinion of *New York Times Book Review* contributor Carolyn T. Hughes, "their subjects [as] literally symbols of different periods in 20th-century America." Hughes is not completely convinced of Lipsyte's and Levine's argument, but she conceded that "one does not have to agree totally with the authors to enjoy their book." Lipsyte helped TBS turn the book into a three-part television documentary, with episodes on the great men of sports, the great women, and the business of sports.

BIOGRAPHICAL/CRITICAL SOURCES:

BOOKS

Cart, Michael, *Presenting Robert Lipsyte,* Twayne (New York City), 1995.

Children's Literature Review, Volume 23, Gale (Detroit), 1991.

Contemporary Literary Criticism, Volume 21, Gale, 1982.

Twentieth-Century Young Adult Writers, St. James Press (Detroit), 1995.

PERIODICALS

Booklist, March 15, 1981, p. 1023; April 1, 1982, p. 1014; September 1, 1982, p. 36; December 1, 1993, p. 682; February 1, 1994, p. 1005; March 1, 1995, p. 1237.

Book World, November 5, 1967, p. 43.

Children's Literature in Education, spring, 1980, pp. 43, 44, 45, 47.

Elementary English, January, 1972, p. 117.

English Journal, December, 1980; April, 1992, p. 85; November, 1992, p. 89.

Entertainment Weekly, December 8, 1995, p. 62.

Harper's Magazine, September, 1985.

Horn Book Magazine, September-October, 1993, p. 634.

Library Journal, October 1, 1995, p. 89.

Los Angeles Times, November 27, 1995, p. F1.

Nation, May 25, 1985.

Newsweek, November 24, 1975, pp. 120-121.

New York Review of Books, October 30, 1975, p. 6.

New York Times, November 7, 1988.

New York Times Book Review, November 12, 1967, p. 42; May 31, 1970, p. 14; November 8, 1975, p. 5; July 10, 1977, p. 20; March 4, 1979, p. 32; April 26, 1981, pp. 68-9; April 25, 1982, p. 34; April 10, 1983, pp. 29-30; November 5, 1995, p. 22.

New York Times Magazine, February 16, 1986; November 30, 1986, p. 59; May 22, 1988.

People Weekly, March 25, 1985.

Publisher's Weekly, September 27, 1993, p. 65; September 25, 1995, p. 40.

School Library Journal, May, 1994, p. 125; October, 1994, p. 135; December, 1994, p. 124.

Voice of Youth Advocates, December, 1993, pp. 294, 322; February, 1994, p. 398; June, 1995, p. 122.

Wilson Library Bulletin, March, 1995, p. 106.

* * *

LORD, Shirley

See ROSENTHAL, Shirley Lord

M-O

MALKIEL, Burton Gordon 1932-

PERSONAL: Born August 28, 1932, in Boston, MA; son of Sol and Celia (Gordon) Malkiel; married former wife Judith Atherton, July 16, 1954; married Nancy Weiss (dean of the College, Princeton University), July 31, 1988; children: (first marriage) Jonathan. *Education:* Harvard University, B.A., 1953, M.B.A., 1955; Princeton University, Ph.D., 1964.

ADDRESSES: *Home*—76 North Rd., Princeton, NJ 08540. *Office*— Department of Economics, Princeton University, Princeton, NJ 08544. *E-mail*—bmalkiel@pucc.edu; fax: 609-258-6419.

CAREER: Smith Barney & Co., New York City, associate, 1958-60; Princeton University, Princeton, NJ, assistant professor, 1964-66, associate professor, 1966-68, professor of economics, 1968-81, Gordon S. Rentschler Memorial Professor of Economics, 1969-81, chair of department, 1974-75, 1977-81; Yale University School of Organization and Management, New Haven, CT, dean, 1981-87; Princeton University, Chemical Bank Chairman's Professor of Economics, 1988—. Member of board of directors of several companies, including Prudential Insurance Company of America, 1973—, and Vanguard Group of Investment Companies, 1977—; member, President's Council of Economic Advisors, 1975-77; governor, American Stock Exchange, 1978—. *Military service:* U.S. Army, 1955-58; became first lieutenant.

MEMBER: American Economic Association, American Finance Association (president, 1979; member of board of directors, 1979-84).

AWARDS, HONORS: D.H.L., University of Hartford, 1971.

WRITINGS:

The Term Structure of Interest Rates: Expectations and Behavior Patterns, Princeton University Press (Princeton, NJ), 1966.

(With Richard E. Quandt) *Strategies and Rational Decisions in the Securities Options Market,* MIT Press (Boston), 1969.

A Random Walk down Wall Street, Norton (New York City), 1973, sixth edition, 1996.

(With George M. von Furstenberg) *The Government and Capital Formation: A Survey of Recent Issues,* American Enterprise Institute (Washington, DC), 1978.

The Inflation Beater's Investment Guide: Winning Strategies for the 1980s, Norton, 1980, new edition published as *Winning Investment Strategies: The Inflation-Beaters Guide,* 1982.

(With John G. Cragg) *Expectations and the Structure of Share Prices,* University of Chicago Press (Chicago), 1982.

Global Bargain Hunting: Investment Opportunities in Emerging Markets, Simon & Schuster, 1997.

WORK IN PROGRESS: Research on securities markets.

* * *

MALLON, Thomas 1951-

PERSONAL: Born November 2, 1951, in Glen Cove, NY; son of Arthur Vincent (a salesperson) and Caroline (Moruzzi) Mallon. *Education:* Brown University, B.A., 1973; Harvard University, M.A., 1974, Ph.D., 1978.

ADDRESSES: *Home*—230 Saugatuck Ave., Westport, CT 06880.

CAREER: Writer. Vassar College, Poughkeepsie, NY, professor of English, 1979-91.

AWARDS, HONORS: Rockefeller Foundation fellow, 1986-87; Ingram Merrill Award, 1994.

WRITINGS:

Edmund Blunden (biography), G. K. Hall (Boston), 1983.
A Book of One's Own: People and Their Diaries, Ticknor & Fields (New York City), 1984.
Arts and Sciences: A Seventies Seduction (novel), Ticknor & Fields, 1988.
Stolen Words: Forays into the Origins and Ravages of Plagiarism, Ticknor & Fields, 1989.
Aurora 7 (novel), Ticknor & Fields, 1991.
Rockets and Rodeos and Other American Spectacles (essays), Ticknor & Fields, 1993.
Henry and Clara (novel), Ticknor & Fields, 1994.
Dewey Defeats Truman, Pantheon (New York City), 1997.

Contributor of articles and reviews to literature journals, newspapers, and national magazines, including *American Spectator, American Scholar, Civilization, Harper's, New York Times, Washington Post,* and *Wall Street Journal.* Literary editor, *Gentleman's Quarterly,* 1991-95.

SIDELIGHTS: Thomas Mallon has won acclaim for his historical novels *Aurora 7* and *Henry and Clara,* which several reviewers see as being informed by the penchant for painstaking research that is evident in the author's nonfiction works. Mallon's nonfiction efforts, which formed the bulk of his early output, have received critical praise as being serious yet highly readable. "For all his aptitude, Mr. Mallon has been slow to sidle up to fiction; there has been a curious retardation to his career," John Updike observes in the *New Yorker.* But with historical fiction, Updike comments, Mallon "has found forms expressive of his modern disquiet and given his furtive, ominous themes grandeur. He has shown himself to be . . . one of the most interesting American novelists at work."

One of Mallon's earliest works was *A Book of One's Own: People and Their Diaries. Los Angeles Times* critic Richard Eder asserts that "Thomas Mallon, who has read hundreds of diaries, has written a marvelous book about them. It is a basket full of good things, and some of the best are his own. . . . [Mallon] has sat in libraries listening to famous and obscure voices. Pepys, Virginia Woolf, Dostoevsky, of course; and also a London spinster who spent her life in a boarding house, and a bed-ridden Boston patrician whose diary runs 30,000 pages. Here we are, they told him. Here they are, he tells us." Eder and other reviewers are pleased by the broad scope of Mallon's book, noting that he gives as much deference to the famous, the rich, and the noble, as to the unknown, the poor, and the lowly. In her *New Yorker* assessment, Naomi Bliven describes *A Book of One's Own* as "inclusive . . . but not a bit long-winded. It is learned but never pedantic. It is also charming, diverting, and exceptionally intelligent. The book is literary criticism, yet it is something more—a knowing, sympathetic, but not soppy commentary on humanity. . . . By bringing together so many diverse people at their most candid. . . . Mallon offers us a glimpse of human possibility we could get no other way." In the opinion of *New York Times Book Review* contributor and poet Brad Leithauser, Mallon "lets the diaries speak for themselves," with each chapter of the work devoted to a specific type of diarist, like chroniclers, travelers, creators, confessors, and so forth. To Leithauser, "the book proves winsome and ingratiating. . . . Some of the book's most affecting passages come from diaries of pioneer women whose lives were 'unremarkable' in the sense of not being surprising, given their surroundings. But what surroundings!"

Mallon's first novel, *Arts and Sciences: A Seventies Seduction,* is, according to *Newsday* reviewer Edward Guereschi, "the type of revenge comedy every disenchanted graduate student vows to write once he has passed from the cave into the sunlight." This is a coming-of-age novel about the awkward youthful Artie as he pursues his graduate degree in literature from Harvard University. Artie's difficult first weeks push him close to a nervous breakdown; indeed, he has the impulse to throw people into oncoming traffic, to destroy rare books from the university library, and the like.

Georgia Jones-Davis remarks in the *Los Angeles Times Book Review:* "Imagine if Keats had somehow re-materialized in the fall of 1973 as a . . . graduate student in English at Harvard. That's partly what Thomas Mallon is up to" in *Art and Sciences.* Jones-Davis adds that Artie, "a Keats worshiper, really is a Keats clone—a 113-pound mass of quivering, nervous energy and sensibility." "Into all of this," notes Roger Davis Friedman for Chicago *Tribune Books,* "comes Angela Downing, the 28-year-old blonde English divorcee who wins Artie's heart through her knowledge of Greek [since Artie fears failing this subject foremost]. . . . Artie and Angela's romance is far-fetched but more often than not entertaining in a smirky way. Angela is all the things Artie is not: spoiled, rich, unbearably witty, and purposefully dumb. One might call her an intellectual coquette." According to Jones-Davis, at the end of the academic year "Artie finds himself standing a little taller," while Angela "is exhibiting signs of emotional wear and tear. This is all *Sturm-und-Drang* in a teacup stuff. . . . 'Arts and Sciences' is a sweet, frothy story that tries to illustrate, as Keats put it, 'how necessary a World of Pains and troubles is to school an Intelligence and make it a Soul.'" Although some reviewers consider the novel slight and merely good for a few laughs, Guereschi believes it "shows it seams with bravado, charm and tenderhearted wit. . . . This is a skillful fictional debut." And *USA Today* contributor David Guy insists that "Mallon is a deft writer with a light touch and the sense to let a small subject remain small. He has produced a novel that seems perfectly suited to its theme, its humor shot through with wisdom."

Mallon followed *Arts and Sciences* with a nonfiction work. In *Stolen Words: Forays into the Origins and Ravages of Plagiarism,* he explores in depth several examples of plagiarism's perpetrators and victims (or those who thought themselves victims). He covers disputes over materials ranging from scholarly books to television series', his focus a period extending from the sixteenth century to the 1980s. In a *New York Times* review, Christopher Lehmann-Haupt writes that *Stolen Words* "remains specific and detailed yet manages to cover so much ground and blow away so much of the fog surrounding plagiarism." *New York Times Book Review* contributor Walter Kendrick criticizes Mallon for sometimes providing excessive and unnecessary information, but praises him for producing "a beguiling portrait of the plagiarist . . . as an oddly plaintive psychopath." Kendrick concludes: "The subject is dismal, but 'Stolen Words' seldom fails to make it lively, engrossing and provocative."

Mallon's second novel, 1991's *Aurora 7,* focuses on events encountered by a variety of people on May 24, 1962, the day astronaut Scott Carpenter performed the dangerous feat of orbiting the earth three times. A young boy, Gregory Noonan, who is fascinated by Carpenter's mission, vanishes from his school. His parents must deal with this and other pressures—his father with business troubles, his mother with the difficulties of living up to the early-1960s ideal of domesticity. The book also provides a look at many other characters against a background loaded with period touches, including numerous references to the popular culture of the time. Then-U.S. President John F. Kennedy even makes a brief appearance.

Washington Post Book World reviewer Marianne Gingher praises *Aurora 7* for historical accuracy: "Mallon got every detail right. You're back there in 1962, practically innocent again. You're part of history." Beyond this, Gingher comments, Mallon also has created a rich universe of characters, and the reader cannot help being interested in their fates. The result, she says, is a novel that "is vast with insight, charming and provocative." A *New Yorker* critic finds that Mallon has utilized his "talent for scrupulous historical research" in the service of an engaging story, making *Aurora 7* "a gift-wrapped time capsule."

Mallon's 1993 book of essays, *Rockets and Rodeos and Other American Spectacles,* covers topics as diverse as former U.S. Vice President Dan Quayle, the Sundance Film Festival, and the vigil before an execution at the San Quentin penitentiary. In a review for *USA Today,* Stephen Goodwin says the book is full of "precise, detailed and vivid reporting." *Rockets and Rodeos,* he writes, has "no grand vision to unveil" but it contains numerous small revelations that "are more revealing than any full-blown, formal portrait."

Mallon went from essays on twentieth-century America to a novel of nineteenth-century America for his third work of fiction. 1994's *Henry and Clara* is the fictional account of Henry Rathbone and Clara Harris, the couple who were in the theater box with President and Mrs. Abraham

Lincoln the night that Lincoln was fatally shot by John Wilkes Booth. Mallon originally intended to write a straight historical treatment of the couple, but, finding the available material inadequate, turned their story into a novel. "Mallon retraced the rough trajectory of Henry and Clara's courtship and marriage, stopping at a point where the facts threatened to corset his narrative and his psychological speculation," explains John Blades in the *Chicago Tribune*. He managed to do this, Blades notes, without trivializing history—in marked contrast to some writers of historical fiction.

In Mallon's account, Henry and Clara's lives certainly are blighted by their presence at the assassination, but they encounter other difficulties as well. Brought up as stepbrother and stepsister in a wealthy family in upstate New York, they encounter parental opposition to their love affair. Henry is moody and temperamental even as a boy; these aspects of his character become more pronounced after his experiences as a soldier in the Civil War and the night at Ford's Theater, where he suffers a near-fatal knife wound at the hands of Booth. He also must endure questions about his conduct that night—about whether he could have saved the president.

Henry and Clara brought Mallon praise for his historical research, his storytelling facility, and the meshing of these two factors. "The period details are generously supplied, but they rarely . . . detract from the central erotic and psychological drama of the loving couple," Updike writes in the *New Yorker*. The novel covers many years and touches upon many historical facts, but remains compelling throughout, Updike adds. "Perhaps one should have attempted a historical novel of one's own" to appreciate this feat, the reviewer says. *Washington Post Book World* contributor George Garrett asserts that "the fabric of the story is magically seamless. . . . Scene by scene the powerful story is superbly told." *Publishers Weekly* named *Henry and Clara* one of the best books of 1994.

BIOGRAPHICAL/CRITICAL SOURCES:

PERIODICALS

Boston Globe, February 1, 1988.
Chicago Tribune, October 10, 1994.
Los Angeles Times, November 18, 1984.
Los Angeles Times Book Review, February 14, 1988.
Newsday, February 14, 1988.
New Yorker, January 21, 1985; March 11, 1991, p. 92; September 5, 1994, pp. 102-05.
New York Times, November 17, 1984; December 7, 1989.
New York Times Book Review, March 31, 1985; March 13, 1988; October 29, 1989, p. 13.
People Weekly, May 20, 1985.
Tribune Books (Chicago), March 20, 1988.
USA Today, March 4, 1988; February 24, 1993, p. 20.
Washington Post, February 3, 1988; February 17, 1991, p. 7.
Washington Post Book Review, February 3, 1985; August 14, 1994, p. 5.

* * *

MALONE, Michael (Christopher) 1942-

PERSONAL: Born November, 1942, in NC; son of Thomas Patrick (a psychiatrist) and Faylene (Jones) Malone; married Maureen Quilligan (a professor of English), May 17, 1975; children: Margaret Elizabeth. *Education:* Attended Syracuse University; University of North Carolina, A.B., M.A., 1963-66; Harvard University, M.A., A.B.D., 1967-73. *Politics:* Democrat. *Religion:* Episcopalian.

ADDRESSES: Home—32 Commerce St., Clinton, CT 06413. *Agent*—Peter Matson, Sterling Lord Literistic, Inc., 1 Madison Ave., New York, NY 10001.

CAREER: Writer. Instructor at various colleges, including Yale University, Connecticut College, University of Pennsylvania, and Swarthmore College, 1967—. Lecturer, reader, and panel member. Board member for several arts organizations, including Connecticut Opera Company.

MEMBER: International Association of Crime Writers, PEN America, Writers Guild of America, Dramatists Guild, Authors Guild, Authors League of America, Dramatists Guild, National Book Critics Circle, Writers and Publishers Alliance.

WRITINGS:

NOVELS

Painting the Roses Red, Random House (New York City), 1975.
The Delectable Mountains, Random House, 1977.
Dingley Falls, Harcourt (San Diego, CA), 1980.
Uncivil Seasons, Delacorte (New York City), 1983.
Handling Sin, Little, Brown (Boston), 1986.
Time's Witness (mystery), Little, Brown, 1989.
Foolscap, Little, Brown, 1991.

PLAYS

Defender of the Faith (play), produced at Yale Divinity School, 1981.
Washington Slept Here (screenplay), Metro-Goldwyn-Mayer, 1986.
Handling Sin (screenplay adapted from his own novel), Twentieth-Century Fox, 1987.
The Rich Brother (television script), VISN Cable Network, 1989.

NONFICTION

Psychetypes: A New Way of Exploring Personality, Dutton (New York City), 1977.
Heroes of Eros: Male Sexuality in the Movies, Dutton, 1979.

OTHER

Stories represented in anthologies, including *Fast Forward, Incarnation,* and *O'Henry Prize Stories.* Contributor of stories to literary journals and magazines. Contributor of articles and reviews to magazines, including *Viva, Nation, Human Behavior, Harper's, Playboy, Mademoiselle,* and *New York Times Book Review.*

ADAPTATIONS: Film rights to *Uncivil Seasons* were bought by Warner Bros.

SIDELIGHTS: Michael Malone's novels are sprawling picaresques featuring large casts of characters, numerous plot complications, and an exuberant humor. The author of mainstream novels as well as mysteries, Malone renders both genres in an expansive manner in the tradition of such earlier novelists as Charles Dickens, Henry Fielding and Miguel de Cervantes. Critics cite his ability to combine rollicking entertainment with literary seriousness.

The setting of Malone's *Dingley Falls* is described by *New York Times Book Review* critic Alan Cheuse as a town "inhabited by more homey, colorful characters than all of Winesburg, Ohio, Raintree County and Batavia, NY, put together." He adds, "There are scores of [characters], all neatly listed in a cast sheet preceding the first chapter—and they stroll, stalk, hitchhike, jog, or drive police cars, motorcycles, bicycles, jalopies, sports cars or fire engines along the town's simple streets and bordering highways. Each is convinced that life in Dingley Falls, U.S.A., is neither comic nor tragic but merely life."

Calling *Dingley Falls* "a wonderful novel, impressive in every way, and constantly absorbing and entertaining," Susan Fromberg Schaeffer notes in the *Chicago Tribune Book World* that the book "takes its structure from a metaphor Malone uses early in the [novel]: that of the spider and his web. Just as each person is at the center of his own web, so each web is entangled in larger webs, and the plot of 'Dingley Falls' is to uncover the two largest webs in which the townspeople are entangled. . . . Everything in this book sparkles and rings true." *Washington Post* reviewer Pat McNees finds *Dingley Falls* to be "schizophrenic in tone and concept," but concludes that this "imperfect novel [is] so full of energy and gems of characterization, so successful at creating a sense of place and people, that you forgive it its excesses and awkwardness, are sorry when it's finished, and look forward to the author's next book. There's talent there, and life. One senses Malone will grow."

Malone took another look at the American south in the comic novel *Handling Sin.* In this story, a minister leaves his church for life on the road with a black woman who is young enough to be his granddaughter, and his son—the novel's hero—combs the American south trying to find him. Along the way, the son is mugged by Satan-worshippers and rescued by nuns. He learns, explains Laszlo J. Buhasz of the Toronto *Globe and Mail,* "that there is more to life than membership in the Chamber of Commerce, a comfortable retirement plan and smug entrenchment in the middle class." Critics recommend the book for its striking a balance between serious moral issues and rollicking humor. A *New York Times Book World* reviewer claims that in this "irreverent, unafraid comedy," the author's "twists and turns and surprises are downright phenomenal, verging on genius." A *Washington Post Book World* reviewer explains: "*Handling Sin* is a larky tale that asks us to take its merry adventures at face value. We do gladly. It's somewhat later . . . that we realize it's something wiser and deeper. . . . It's a parable of love and reconciliation. It's also a celebration of plain old fun as one of God's great pedagogical devices. . . . It's a delightful book." Concludes Buhasz, "Malone has written a winner that deserves to become a humor classic."

Uncivil Seasons—a mystery novel—also "bears Malone's imprint," a *Washington Post Book World* reviewer observes. The Malone hallmarks include "the vividly drawn ambience," "a stylish gift for language," and "a tender and believable romance," as well as lively characters. While detectives Justin Savile and Cuddy Mangum unravel a murky mystery in a small Southern town, Malone raises larger questions about the human condition. Evan Hunter, writing in the *New York Times Book Review,* believes that, with Savile and Mangum, Malone has "created two of the most memorable police detectives ever to appear in mystery fiction." Rising above the mystery genre in the manner of Umberto Eco's *The Name of the Rose* and Italian novelist Leonardo Sciascia, *Uncivil Seasons* with its vivid scenes and wry humor invites rereading.

Reviewers of *Time's Witness* remark that Malone's depiction of life in Piedmont is as fully drawn as the novels of William Faulkner, and more fun to read. In this mystery-thriller, Malone put prejudice and the death penalty on trial. "There's a lot to savor in *Time's Witness*" in addition to "an unusually fine sense of reality in a place and time," claims the critic for the *Chicago Tribune;* the novel's "thoroughly satisfactory ending . . . send[s] the reader to the shelves for Malone's earlier work." A *New York Times Book Review* critic concludes, "Malone peoples his fiction with large, quirky casts, and his readers come to know not only what these characters eat, drink, chew, whistle, sing, listen to, read . . . and dream, but—most important, most especially in 'Time's Witness'—what they believe." Malone also provides "a complex and satisfying plot, a rich panorama," and "a moral vision."

When *Foolscap* was published in 1991, Malone was again complimented for his ability to create a large, spirited novel. Writing in *Bloomsbury Review,* Carla Seaquist calls *Foolscap* "a rollicking take on the conflict of Art vs. Life. Which has priority? What price art? What constitutes living? *Foolscap* bursts with events, vivid characters, literary and theatrical asides, tight dialogue, high humor. . . . The pleasures of Malone's fluid storytelling are many." The elaborate plot centers on Theo Ryan, a young university professor. Tidy and conservative in his ways, Theo is commissioned to write the biography of Ford Rexford, an aging, legendary playwright. Rexford's messy, sprawling, passionate life is nearly the opposite of Theo's, and in time, the large-souled artist transforms the young scholar.

"Malone knows drama from Shakespeare to *South Pacific,* and his worldview seems that of a cockeyed optimist," comments Paul Elie in *Commonweal.* "With *Foolscap,* which is about plays and playwrights, he has contrived a spirited comedy that is as innocently entertaining as a movie musical." Elie praises Malone's carefully constructed plot and his clever writing, but he finds the author's characterizations and thematic development weak. *Los Angeles Times Book Review* contributor Mindi Dickstein also rates *Foolscap* as highly entertaining, but in her view, "Malone's gift for comedy is matched only by his ability to zero in on the darker underside of his characters' lives." She concludes: "The result is that with a few poignant but well-placed serious moments, Malone achieves a depth of character not usually found in such a comic novel."

BIOGRAPHICAL/CRITICAL SOURCES:

BOOKS

Contemporary Literary Criticism, Volume 43, Gale, 1987, pp. 280-85.

PERIODICALS

Armchair Detective, summer, 1995, pp. 320-327.

Bloomsbury Review, January/February, 1993, pp. 14-15.

Chicago Tribune, April 24, 1989.

Chicago Tribune Book World, June 15, 1980; November 28, 1983; April 20, 1986.

Christian Science Monitor, March 26, 1986, p. 21.

Commonweal, February 14, 1992, pp. 27-28.
Globe and Mail (Toronto), June 21, 1986.
Kirkus Reviews, February 15, 1975, p. 196.
Library Journal, January 1, 1977, p. 127.
Los Angeles Times Book Review, August 10, 1980; April 6, 1986, p. 3; March 8, 1992, p. 9.
Nation, August 30, 1980, pp. 195-196; June 21, 1986, pp. 860-862.
Newsweek, June 2, 1986.
New York Times Book Review, May 11, 1980, pp. 14, 29; November 13, 1983, p. 14; April 13, 1986, p. 11; April 5, 1987; April 23, 1989.
Publishers Weekly, March 3, 1975, p. 64.
Times Literary Supplement, January 9, 1987.
Washington Post, May 26, 1980.
Washington Post Book World, November 20, 1983, p. 10; April 13, 1986, pp. 3, 13.
Yale Review, January, 1993, pp. 155-158.*

* * *

MANO, D. Keith 1942-

PERSONAL: Born February 12, 1942, in New York, NY; son of William Franz (a business executive) and Marion Elizabeth (Minor) Mano; married Jo Margaret McArthur, August 3, 1964 (divorced, 1979); married Laurie E. Kennedy (an actress), July 18, 1980; children: (first marriage) Roderick Keith, Christopher Carey. *Education:* Columbia University, B.A. (summa cum laude), 1963. *Politics:* Conservative. *Religion:* Eastern Orthodox.

ADDRESSES: Home—392 Central Park West, Apt. 6P, New York, NY 10025.

CAREER: Writer. X-Pando Corp. (building materials manufacturer), Long Island City, NY, vice president, 1965-86. Actor with Marlowe Society in England, 1963-64, and with National Shakespeare Company, 1964-65.

AWARDS, HONORS: Kellett Fellow, Clare College, Cambridge, 1963-64; Woodrow Wilson fellowship, 1965-66; *Bishop's Progress* was named one of year's ten best novels by *Time* magazine, 1968; Modern Language Association award, 1969, for *Bishop's Progress; Playboy* nonfiction award, 1977; Literary Lion Award from New York Public Library, 1987.

WRITINGS:

NOVELS

Bishop's Progress, Houghton (Boston), 1968.
Horn, Houghton, 1969.
War Is Heaven!, Doubleday (New York City), 1970.
The Death and Life of Harry Goth, Knopf (New York City), 1971.
The Proselytizer, Knopf, 1972.
The Bridge, Doubleday, 1973.
Take Five, Doubleday, 1982.
Topless, Random House (New York City), 1990.

OTHER

Resistance (play), first produced in New York City at the Judith Anderson Theater, June 2, 1988.

Also author of scripts for television series, including *St. Elsewhere, L. A. Law,* and *Homicide.* Contributor to numerous magazines and newspapers, including *Esquire, New York Times Book Review, People, Playboy,* and *Sports Illustrated.* Contributing editor and author of column, "The Gimlet Eye," *National Review,* 1972-89; former film reviewer and contributing editor, *Oui.*

SIDELIGHTS: D. Keith Mano is a novelist whose books are inventive, satirical, and extravagant. "He is," Joan Reardon explains in the *Los Angeles Times,* "a razzle-dazzle kind of writer—a Renaissance man reincarnated as a magical word processor." "Just a little too much is just enough for Mr. Mano," claims Geoffrey Wolff of the *New York Times Book Review.* "Not for him peace and quiet, the ordinary. He cherishes crisis, calamity and farce; he drives at full throttle, straight pipes howling." Underneath the surface turmoil, however, his stories speak of religious salvation in a society lacking moral values. "As a novelist," Mano explains in his article for the *Contemporary Authors Autobiography Series,* "I am a conservative, committed to Western traditions. I consider myself a Christian writer, though some reviewers have called me a Christian pornographer. . . . In my novels I have tried to relate traditional Christianity to the concerns of the modern world."

Between 1968 and 1973, Mano published six novels in quick succession. These books established his reputation as what Peter S. Prescott of

Newsweek calls "one of our most exciting younger writers." His first novel, *Bishop's Progress,* the story of an ailing bishop's spiritual rebirth during a twelve-day stay in a hospital, won two major awards and moved R. V. Cassill, writing in the *New York Times Book Review,* to remark that "the luminous talents of D. Keith Mano have produced a work which is, at the same time, witty, disturbing, entertaining, grave, full of suspense, and a prolonged meditation on the riddle of faith in our epoch." But the novel also contains some humor which several reviewers found distasteful. Gillian Tindall of the *New Statesman* believes that "instead of revealing the true predicament of his central character . . . Mr. Mano obscures it with the purely gruesome [such as] a sadistic doctor [who] botches injections and enemas." But Barry H. Leeds, in an article for *Saturday Review,* finds that *Bishop's Progress* sets the pattern for the serious concerns of Mano's later fiction. The novel, "which recounted the pilgrimage of a spiritually lazy bishop from imminent damnation to salvation through suffering and a new recognition of his own mortality," Leeds writes, "forms the keystone of a carefully structured body of work."

Horn, Mano's second novel, also concerns a clergyman. In this story an Episcopal priest is sent to a church in Harlem, where he encounters and tries to accommodate Horn, the leader of a black power group. The priest's efforts to make peace with Horn lead him to a better understanding of racial tensions. As Arthur Curley writes in *Library Journal,* "black-white (as well as black-black and white-white) differences and relationships emerge as complex and subtle matters which can never be understood in terms of social cliches, either pernicious or well-intentioned in nature." Despite the differences between the two men, they develop an admiration and respect for each other. Shane Stevens of *Book World* complains that "the usual fare of racist rallies, sex orgy and firebombings" can be found in *Horn.* Stephen F. Caldwell of the *New York Times Book Review* finds the novel to be "a fine young writer's tale about two men who might reasonably expect to find the worst in the other but instead find the best."

Mano turned to the subject of war in *War Is Heaven!,* a look at a U.S. military intervention in a Central American conflict. "As were Mano's first two books," remarks Caldwell, "*War Is Heaven!* is about the complexity and ambiguity of good and evil." The story focuses on two soldiers who represent opposing views of religious belief. Sergeant Clarence Hook has a strong faith, while Corpsman Andrew Jones is a sour nonbeliever. Their conversations about their roles in the war reveal the tensions and paradoxes of the situation. L. J. Davis of *Book World* calls *War Is Heaven!* "disturbing, powerful, and often downright irritating. . . . Mano's book, nevertheless, remains a work of considerable imaginative power."

The Death and Life of Harry Goth is a black comedy in which Harry Goth, an industrial sanitation supply salesman, learns that he is dying of leukemia. This discovery paradoxically gives him a renewed energy for life. In the course of the story, most of Harry's eccentric family is killed, he gets bloated and bald from a quack cancer cure, and, following the advice of his hermit brother, he hides away in his house, refusing to confront the world. "Mano," Tom McHale writes in the *New York Times Book Review,* "is a gutsy writer with an extravagant vision of the universe. His real genius . . . is in somehow keeping a funeral ship, heavily laden with pathos and parable, afloat, while it is buffeted by howling gales of laughter." Frank Day, writing in the *Dictionary of Literary Biography,* calls the novel "talented black humor, deft and wicked, reminiscent of Evelyn Waugh."

In *The Proselytizer,* Mano tells the story of television evangelist Kris Lane, an excessive and perverse man whose sexual exploits are fully depicted in the course of the novel. "There is no note of hope, no celebration of indomitable spirit," Leeds maintains. "Instead, there is compassion in this black humor and real wisdom. This is not as enjoyable a book as *Bishop's Progress* or *Harry Goth,* nor is it as well balanced between high seriousness and humor; yet it takes Mano's vision a step farther than those books did. And it may be more difficult to forget." Other critics, however, found fault with *The Proselytizer.* Writing in the *New York Times Book Review,* Geoffrey Wolff admits that Mano "manages some startling scenes. He pushes the vocabulary of sexual congress beyond its previous boundaries. . . . But he has left out whatever it is that translates little losers like Harry Goth into great fictional characters." Prescott, too, was disappointed by the book. "A miss for Mano this time," he comments, "but like most misses by really good authors, it makes better reading than most bland successes."

In 1973, Mano published *The Bridge,* a novel set in the distant future in a world free of all forms of environmental pollution. The cost for such a clean environment, however, has been high. Plant, animal, and insect life flourish everywhere, nearly overrunning human life. Strict governmental prohibitions prevent many kinds of activity. Those who ate meat have been put to death. One character, Dominick Priest, comes to learn of Christianity and converts. But his knowledge of the religion is incomplete, and the manner in which he practices his faith includes the cannibalistic slaughter of primitives. The novel's disturbing subject matter bothered some critics. J. F. Cotter of *America,* for example, maintains: "I cannot remember reading a more repellent novel. . . . I would never read a book like this of my own sweet will." But R. V. Williams of *Best Sellers* claims that "Mano's striking imagery, his slashing irreverence, the savagery of his satire, and the never-ceasing drive of his imagination make the reading of this book a provocative and deeply troubling experience."

It was not until 1982 that Mano published his next novel, *Take Five.* The idea for the book took hold of him shortly after writing *The Bridge,* but writing it took some nine years. "I'm very proud of myself for having hung in all those years," Mano tells C. H. Simonds of *National Review.* He adds, "There were times when I could have just given up, times when I couldn't even remember who the characters were."

Mano did a tremendous volume of work for magazines during the years he spent writing *Take Five,* including articles for *Playboy, Oui,* and other men's magazines. In his article for the *Contemporary Authors Autobiography Series,* Mano notes the many unusual experiences he underwent to produce these stories: "I lived as a transvestite; had my skeleton bent by Rolfers; sank, glub, underwater in a rebirthing tank. I met incestuous fathers and people who knew all about cannibalism. I gave blood; pretended I was a wino; went under hypnosis; had myself put away in a goofy garage." These experiences were relayed in what Mano describes as his "side-of-the-mouth, attention-hooking voice. . . . When your prose is in direct visual competition with soft, nubile young women all set for some antic hay, you better talk *loud,* brother."

Some of the extravagance of Mano's nonfiction reappears in *Take Five,* "a picaresque epic which satirizes contemporary politics, sexuality and religion," according to Jack Sullivan of the *Washington Post.* It is, Sullivan believes, "full of energy, invention and great gusts of hot air." John Leonard of the *New York Times* explains that *Take Five* "is long enough for three ordinary novels." Because the protagonist, Simon Lynxx, is an unappealing, obnoxious character, the novel proved a challenge for some reviewers to evaluate. As Sullivan remarks, "It is difficult to convey in a short review the full unpleasantness and tedium of [Simon's] ugly tantrums."

Take Five traces the story of filmmaker Simon Lynxx as he tries to raise money for his latest project, a film entitled "Jesus 2001". During the course of the novel, which is told in Joycean verbal pyrotechnics and is loaded with wild humor, Simon loses his physical senses one by one, ending up completely cut off from the world around him. It is at this point that Simon attains spiritual salvation. "No man," Hugh Kenner comments in *National Review,* "has ever found a crazier way to write a book about the Christian faith."

Simon Lynxx attracts the most comments from reviewers, primarily because of his outspoken opinions on sexual and racial questions. He is, V. D. Balitas notes in *America,* "a boisterous, obscene (his language wearies as it combines a pseudo-Wildean wit, the raunchiness of the legendary longshoreman and an exaggerated bigotry reminiscent of [Archie] Bunker and [Don] Rickles), egotistical young film maker." Through this character, Mano comments satirically on a number of topics. "More than half of *Take Five* is hilarious, even when it is vile," notes Leonard. "Mr. Mano speaks in many tongues, all of them vipers. What he tells us about Hollywood, the art world, Episcopalianism, homosexuality, Jewish motherhood, black huckstering, Eastern religion, Queens night life, Freud . . . and white dwarves is savage, but it is also very, very funny. You will laugh, and then feel guilty about it." Some critics were harsh on Mano for creating a character like Simon. Writing in *Nation,* Gerald Jay Goldberg finds Simon to be a "sexist, racist, bigot and bully, with an ego the size of Quasimodo's hump."

The novel itself had its share of criticism as well. Sullivan complains that *Take Five* "is clever, even virtuosic, but it is ultimately only an intellectual good-old-boy novel." Robert M. Adams, in an article for the *New York Review of Books,* finds that Simon's conversion at novel's end is unconvincing. "Simon the capering, obnoxious punchinello is the mainspring of the action; at least some of the pieties that he joyfully desecrates deserve the vigorous boot he gives them," Adams writes. "That pious ending seems to leave the door uncomfortably open to cheap edification."

But many critics find much to praise in *Take Five.* Leonard calls it "a novel about 300 years of American history, a low-budget movie singing the song of assimilation. It is a novel about art, especially modernist art; its many parodies, puns and anagrams serve as a thesis on the nature of metaphor and play." Leonard sees Simon's ultimate salvation to be well handled by Mano: "The last 40 pages . . . depict salvation as persuasively as Joyce did damnation in *Portrait of the Artist as a Young Man.*" Reardon concludes that *Take Five* "challenges a reader's better judgement; its hero makes Prometheus look like a pussy cat, and its sheer verbal pushiness cowers an audience into attention. Simon Lynxx said it best: 'Only outrages—howls—get any air time in this society.'"

The central character of *Topless* bears little outward resemblance to Simon Lynxx. He is Father Mike Wilson, a well-meaning Episcopal priest from Nebraska who ends up managing his brother Tony's topless nightclub in New York City after Tony's unexplained disappearance. The priest leaves his affluent parish and his fiancee to take this uncomfortable assignment; he does so because the bar provides a means of support for Tony's wife and four children. Father Mike's life becomes even more complicated after several of the club's dancers are murdered and he is tagged as a suspect. The novel is written as a diary by the priest.

"*Topless* is a neat little . . . cross between *Diary of a Country Priest* and . . . *Silence of the Lambs,*" comments Christopher Buckley in the *National Review.* "It's also a savagely funny send-up of the current state of Episcopalianism while, oddly, reaffirming the ineluctable—to Christians—necessity of Grace, whatever weird, personal highway one travels in order to get it." Buckley applauds Mano as a keen observer of things bizarre and incongruous; this facility, Buckley says, makes *Topless* a novel full of fascinating detail. Kinky Friedman, critiquing for the *New York Times Book Review,* praises Mano as evoking the atmosphere of a topless bar with accuracy, but is not so impressed with the novel's diaristic style. "Father Mike Wilson's interminable self-analysis, within which he charts every spiritual tic of his life, is almost as tedious as Nebraska," Friedman asserts. "Still, the story manages to wiggle and jiggle its way to a cross-cultural conclusion that may, indeed, even be shocking to readers who are *not* Episcopalian." This conclusion, a *Publishers Weekly* reviewer adds, is "somewhat contrived" but ultimately satisfactory.

Writing in his contribution to the *Contemporary Authors Autobiography Series,* Mano explains how he reconciles the sometimes offensive material found in his novels with his basically Christian message. "In a profane age," he states, "the profane must be taken unawares and in their own tongue. . . . You might say that the end, doubtful as it is, cannot justify the means. But the Flood was a means. Saint Paul's blindness. And the crucifixion. God does not go gently into our self-imposed night."

BIOGRAPHICAL/CRITICAL SOURCES:

BOOKS

Contemporary Authors Autobiography Series, Volume 6, Gale (Detroit), 1988.

Contemporary Literary Criticism, Gale, Volume 2, 1974; Volume 10, 1979.

Dictionary of Literary Biography, Volume 6: *American Novelists since World War II,* second series, Gale, 1980.

PERIODICALS

America, October 27, 1973; August 7-14, 1982.

Best Sellers, September 15, 1973.

Book World, March 23, 1969; May 10, 1970.

Christianity and Literature, spring, 1979.

Hudson Review, autumn, 1972.

Library Journal, April 1, 1969.

Los Angeles Times, July 15, 1982.

Nation, June 26, 1982.

National Review, August 11, 1970; June 11, 1982; May 27, 1983; September 23, 1991, pp. 51-54.

New Statesman, February 7, 1969.

Newsweek, April 5, 1971; March 27, 1972.

New Yorker, April 8, 1972.

New York Review of Books, June 10, 1982.

New York Times, April 30, 1982; June 8, 1988.
New York Times Book Review, February 18, 1968; March 9, 1969; June 21, 1970; March 14, 1971; April 23, 1972; May 23, 1982; August 11, 1991, p. 14.
Prairie Schooner, winter, 1968-69.
Publishers Weekly, June 7, 1991, pp. 56, 58.
Saturday Review, July 15, 1972.
Time, April 18, 1969; April 20, 1970; September 10, 1973.
Times Literary Supplement, June 11, 1970.
Washington Post, July 17, 1982.

* * *

MARA, Jeanette
See CEBULASH, Mel

* * *

MARKGRAF, Carl 1928-

PERSONAL: Born July 18, 1928, in Portland, OR; son of Carl Bertschi and Elizabeth (McNutt) Markgraf; married Mary Barbara Irene Fleming, November 13, 1951; children: Cecily B., Elinor M., Karl F., Lise M., Thomas B., Paul E., Anna D. *Ethnicity:* "Caucasian/Cherokee." *Education:* Attended University of California, Berkeley, 1946, and Multnomah College, 1947-48; University of Portland, A.B. (cum laude), 1951, M.A., 1954; University of California, Riverside, Ph.D., 1970. *Politics:* Democrat.

ADDRESSES: Home—2224 Northeast 26th Ave., Portland, OR 97212. *Office*—c/o Department of English, Portland State University, Portland, OR 97207.

CAREER: High school teacher of English in Hood River, OR, 1954-57; Marylhurst College, Marylhurst, OR, instructor, 1957-60, director of drama, 1957-63, assistant professor of English, 1960-63; Portland State University, Portland, OR, assistant professor, 1966-70, associate professor, 1970-75, professor of English, 1975-96, professor emeritus, 1997—, assistant head of department, 1972—, acting head of department, 1973-74, assistant dean of arts and letters, 1980-82. New Theatre, Portland, member of board of directors, 1967-68, executive vice president, 1968-69, president, 1969-70. *Military service:* U.S. Navy, 1948-49. U.S. Army Reserve, 1956-64; became first lieutenant.

MEMBER: American Association of University Professors, Alpha Psi Omega, Delta Phi Alpha.

WRITINGS:

(Editor) *Problems in Usage,* Teaching Research Commission, State of Oregon, 1969.
(Editor) *Oscar Wilde's Anonymous Criticism,* Xerox Corp., 1970.
(With Alex Scharbach) *Making the Point: Challenge and Response,* Crowell, 1975.
Punctuation, Wiley (New York City), 1979.
J. M. Barrie: An Annotated Secondary Bibliography, ELT Press (Greensboro, NC), 1989.

SCREENPLAYS FOR TELEVISION

Marylhurst College (documentary), broadcast on KGW-TV, November, 1957.
A Woman Wrapped in Silence, broadcast on KGW-TV, December, 1957.
The Play of Daniel, broadcast on KGW-TV, December, 1958.

OTHER

Contributor to books, including *The Letters of John Addington Symonds,* edited by Herbert M. Schueller and Robert L. Peters, Wayne State University Press (Detroit), 1967; and *The 1890s: An Encyclopedia of British Literature, Art, and Culture,* edited by G. A. Cevasco, Garland Publishing (New York City), 1993. Adaptor of seven plays into radio scripts, including Aeschylus' *Agamemnon* and William Shakespeare's *Twelfth Night* and *Taming of the Shrew,* all broadcast as part of the *Northwest Artists* series, 1951-52. Contributor to periodicals, including *South Atlantic Quarterly, Victorian Studies,* and *English Literature in Transition.*

WORK IN PROGRESS: Annotated bibliographies of writings about Harley Granville Barker and Gilbert Murray.

SIDELIGHTS: Carl Markgraf once told *CA:* "From a childhood interest in writing plays and radio scripts came an interest in theater that eventually led to an M.A. in theater and ten years of theater and radio production and direction. Pressure to acquire the Ph.D. led me back to graduate school in English, and there a specialization in Victorian literature focused on the later Victorians, especially Oscar Wilde and John Addington Symonds."

* * *

MARKS, Stan(ley)

PERSONAL: Born in London, England; taken to Australia at the age of two; son of Sidney and Sally Marks; married Eve Mass (a crafts lecturer and designer); children: Lee (daughter; deceased), Peter. *Education:* Attended University of Melbourne.

ADDRESSES: *Home*—348 Bambra Rd., South Caulfield, Victoria, Australia 3162.

CAREER: Began working for an Australian country newspaper; later a reporter and theater critic for *Melbourne Herald,* Melbourne, Australia; reporter for newspapers in England, 1951, and in Montreal, Quebec, and Toronto, Ontario, 1952-53; correspondent for Australian newspapers in New York City, 1954-55; Australian Broadcasting Commission, Melbourne, public relations supervisor, 1958-64; public relations officer of Trans Australia Airlines, 1965-67; Australian Tourist Commission, Melbourne, public relations manager, 1968-86. Has given numerous radio talks in Australia, Canada, London, and the United States; has done a workshop with *Thunder on Anzac Grove.*

MEMBER: Australian Journalists Association, Australian Society of Authors, Society of Australian Travel Writers.

AWARDS, HONORS: Neighborhood Watch Award of Distinction, for work with organization.

WRITINGS:

God Gave You One Face (novel), R. Hale, 1964.
(Contributor) *Walkabout's Book of Best Australian Stories,* Landsdowne Press, 1968.
Graham Is an Aboriginal Boy, photographs by Brian McArdle, Methuen (London), 1968, Hastings House (New York City), 1969.
Fifty Years of Achievement, Methuen, 1972.
Animal Olympics, Wren (Australia), 1972.
Rarua Lives in Papua New Guinea, Methuen, 1974.
Ketut Lives in Bali, Methuen, 1976.
(Author of text) William Andrew David Brodie, *St. Kilda Sketchbook,* Rigby, 1980.
Malvern Sketchbook, Rigby, 1981.
Welcome to Australia, Methuen, 1981.
Out and About in Melbourne, Methuen, 1988.
St. Kilda Heritage Sketchbook, Cosmos, 1995.

Author of plays, *Is She Fair Dinkum?,* 1968, *When a Wife Strikes,* 1970, *Everybody Out,* and *Thunder on Anzac Grove.* Also author of stories for two records for children, including *Montague the Mouse Who Sailed with Captain Cook.* Author of book *Melbourne Holocaust Museum and Research Centre,* 1994. Also contributor of short story to *Australia/New Zealand Yearbook,* 1985. Originator of a comic strip, *Ms.,* for Australian newspapers, including *Melbourne Herald, Auckland Star,* and *Christchurch Star,* 1975-80. Contributor of feature stories and articles to Australian and overseas journals.

Several of Marks's books have been published in Danish, Hebrew, and Braille.

ADAPTATIONS: *God Gave You One Face* was optioned for a locally-made movie, 1988.

SIDELIGHTS: Stan Marks has a strong interest in the arts, youth, and in promoting better understanding between nations. As early as 1951 he suggested that an All-British Commonwealth Arts Festival should be held regularly; later he began urging that a Youth Council be established at the United Nations to get the world's young closer to policy-making. A Commonwealth Arts Festival eventually did take place, and the Youth Council idea earned him an invitation to the 1960 White House Conference on Youth. Also in the 1960s, he advocated an "Ideas Bank" for international peace, where people might send suggestions to be sifted through for possible discussion ("just one good idea might save that button being pushed"). His books reflect these concerns as well as his interest in aborigines.

Marks told *CA* that his writings deal with topical themes. *God Gave You One Face* is about a woman in Australia who confronts the camp guard who killed her parents, in front of her, in a World War II camp, and *Thunder on Anzac Grove* explores what happens when an aboriginal family moves onto a diverse Melbourne street of ten homes, and what it means for the different groups with their different backgrounds, prejudices, and emotional reactions.

While researching *Graham Is an Aboriginal Boy,* Marks lived for ten days with the Arunta tribe near Alice Springs in Australia's Northern Territory, learning to hunt with a boomerang and to enjoy a diet of bush bananas and figs. He has also lived in other villages in New Guinea and Bali while researching his books. Marks told *CA* that these experiences have shown him that "all people really require [the] same things, especially [the] ability to survive with some dignity—a sense which over the centuries (I guess, since dawn of time) certain peoples, of all races, creeds, and self-righteousness, have felt they knew the answers and could dictate (or impose) their wills on others."

He adds: "I also worry about the international communications explosion. With all the power of good in our world-wide TV, radio, computer, satellite, and other links, we seem to be not using it effectively. Why this incredible leaning towards violence in our entertainments and leisure activities? Why? Is it really something inborn? Why are so many ready to die for something—is it easier than to TRY and live for it? Isn't it time we came together to give today's people a chance—not future generations? When do we start to think of all peoplekind? I hope, in some small way, my writings have sown some seeds of better understanding of each other, of the importance of each person, that no one has the only answer. With so much to live for, people seem bent on destruction."

In 1997, Marks told *CA* that he has written "a great deal about how we might use all the modern 'miracles' of communication to bring this old world of ours closer and, hopefully, eliminate many of today's problems and ills. [I believe] with computers, the Internet, satellites, television, radio, newspapers and so on, we can come closer and realise, while keeping our differences, we are still all part of one ever-narrowing world. One world or none." He concluded that he has "exchanged letters with many world leaders, including renowned writers, who have encouraged [me] to pursue [my] ideas and plans."

MARSHALL, (Sarah) Catherine (Wood) 1914-1983

PERSONAL: Born September 27, 1914, in Johnson City, TN; died of heart failure, March 18, 1983, in Boynton Beach, FL; daughter of John Ambrose (a minister) and Leonara (Whitaker) Wood; married Peter Marshall (a minister), November 4, 1936 (died January, 1949); married Leonard Earle LeSourd (an editor and publisher), November 14, 1959; children: (first marriage) Peter John. *Education:* Agnes Scott College, B.A., 1936. *Religion:* Presbyterian.

CAREER: Writer. National Cathedral School for Girls, Washington, DC, member of faculty, 1949-50; Chosen Books Publishing Co., Lincoln, VA, treasurer and partner, beginning 1968. Trustee, Agnes Scott College.

MEMBER: National League of American Pen Women, Phi Beta Kappa.

AWARDS, HONORS: Named "Woman of the Year" in the field of literature, Women's National Press Club, 1953; D.Litt., Cedar Crest College, 1954, and Westminster College, 1979; Paperback of the Year Award, *Bestsellers* magazine, 1969, for *Christy;* L.H.D., Taylor University, 1973; American Book Award nomination, 1980, for *The Helper.*

WRITINGS:

A Man Called Peter: The Story of Peter Marshall, McGraw (New York City), 1951.

(With Peter Marshall) *God Loves You,* McGraw, 1953, published as *God Loves You: Our Family's Favorite Stories and Prayers,* 1967.

To Live Again, McGraw, 1957.

Beyond Our Selves, McGraw, 1961.

Christy (novel), McGraw, 1967.

Something More, McGraw, 1974.

Adventures in Prayer, Chosen Books (Lincoln, VA), 1975.

The Helper, Chosen Books, 1978.

(With Leonard E. LeSourd) *My Personal Prayer Diary,* Chosen Books, 1979.

Meeting God at Every Turn: A Personal Family Story, Chosen Books, 1980.

Catherine Marshall's Story Bible, Chosen Books, 1982.

(Author of text) *Thornbird Country,* Warner Books (New York City), 1983.

Julie, McGraw, 1984.
A Closer Walk, edited by LeSourd, Chosen Books, 1986.
Catherine Marshall's Storybook for Children, edited by David Hazard, Chosen Books, 1987.
Light in My Darkest Night, Chosen Books, 1989.
The Inspirational Writings of Catherine Marshall, Inspirational Press (New York City), 1990.
Footprints in the Snow: More Stories about God's Mysterious Ways, Dimensions for Living (Nashville, TN), 1992.
The Best of Catherine Marshall, edited by LeSourd, Chosen Books, 1993.
Unlocked Dreams: A Collection of Poems, Thomas Nelson (Nashville, TN), 1994.
(With LeSourd) *Quiet Times with Catherine Marshall,* Chosen Books, 1996.

EDITOR AND AUTHOR OF INTRODUCTION

Peter Marshall, *Mr. Jones, Meet the Master* (also see below), Revell (Old Tappan, NJ), 1949, revised edition, 1950.
P. Marshall, *Let's Keep Christmas,* McGraw, 1953.
P. Marshall, *Prayers of Peter Marshall,* McGraw, 1954.
P. Marshall, *Heart of Peter Marshall's Faith* (excerpt from *Mr. Jones, Meet the Master*), Revell, 1956.
P. Marshall, *Friends with God: Stories and Prayers of the Marshall Family,* McGraw, 1956.
P. Marshall, *First Easter,* McGraw, 1959.
P. Marshall, *John Doe, Disciple: Sermons for the Young in Spirit,* McGraw, 1963.
The Best of Peter Marshall, Chosen Books, 1983.

OTHER

Contributor to periodicals, including *Reader's Digest.* Woman's editor, *Christian Herald,* 1958-60; roving editor, *Guideposts,* beginning 1960.

ADAPTATIONS: A Man Called Peter was filmed by Twentieth Century-Fox in 1955.

SIDELIGHTS: An enormously popular inspirational writer, Catherine Marshall was known for her many books about the Christian faith, for editing her late husband Peter Marshall's sermons and inspirational writings, and for writing the young adult novel *Christy. Christy* has proven its continuing popularity by inspiring a continuing series of books featuring the young female character.

Following the death of her husband, Peter Marshall, in 1949, Catherine Marshall edited a collection of his sermons. Peter Marshall had served as the chaplain for the U.S. Senate from 1947 until 1949; the collection of his writings attained a place on the bestseller list within a few weeks of publication and remained there for almost a year.

In 1951, Marshall wrote a biography of her husband, *A Man Called Peter: The Story of Peter Marshall.* Another success, the book remained on the bestseller lists for three years and was later adapted as a motion picture. "The best stories are those that really happened," commented Clarence Seidenspinner in the *Chicago Sunday Tribune* about the book. Seidenspinner found that "none of the novels concerning the ministry, written during the last few years, touches the heart and appeals to the mind in the way that Catherine Marshall does in telling the story of her husband." A. P. Davies in the *New York Times* stated: "Catherine Marshall writes extremely well. Those who do not accept her religious viewpoint will nevertheless admit that she presents it with grace and charm."

Recalling the experience of writing her husband's biography, Marshall told *McCall's:* "Literature, if it is accurately to reflect life, must at times reach past the reader's intellect to the emotional level. In order to achieve that, the writer has to *feel* something as he writes. There were times during the writing of *A Man Called Peter* when reliving . . . my life with Peter was almost too much for me. . . . Particularly [when] I wrote the chapter on Peter's death. Not only did I have to re-experience every vivid detail . . . , but there was [also] the necessity of holding that emotion in check. I am convinced that real communication in writing always has to be disciplined."

In 1967 Marshall published *Christy,* a novel about a young girl at the turn of the century who goes to the rugged mountains of Appalachia to work as a teacher. Marshall based the novel on her mother's actual life. "The idea for the novel," she once explained to *CA,* "was born from experiences in the life of my mother who, as a sheltered, nineteen-year-old girl went to live among and teach the inhabitants of the Great Smoky Mountains of eastern Tennessee. [She was] determined to make herself useful in any way possible and [in the manner] acceptable for young women of the early twentieth century. Readers of all ages can identify with Christy because her spirit exists in everyone, whether young or old, male or female."

Christy has proven to be both a critical and popular success. Elizabeth Thalman in *Library Journal* found that Marshall "gives a clear impression of the proud Scotch-Irish mountaineers and their harsh, lonely lives." Adele Silver in the *New York Times Book Review* described *Christy* as "the same mixture of family, faith, and fortitude" to be found in Marshall's nonfiction books. I. N. Pompea in *Best Sellers* called *Christy* a "highly charming novel." At the time of her death in 1983, over 4 million copies of *Christy* were in print.

The story of *Christy* has proven so popular that Word Publishing has launched the Christy Juvenile Fiction Series. Adapted by C. Archer from the original story by Marshall, these books retell many of Christy's adventures for younger readers. By early 1997, eleven books in the series had been published.

BIOGRAPHICAL/CRITICAL SOURCES:

PERIODICALS

Best Sellers, October 15, 1967, p. 27.
BookPage, January, 1996.
Chicago Sunday Tribune, October, 7, 1951.
Christian Century, October 11, 1967, p. 84.
Christian Science Monitor, October 12, 1967, p. 5.
Library Journal, October 1, 1967, p. 92.
Look, March 6, 1956.
McCall's, August, 1953.
New York Herald Tribune Book Review, October 28, 1951.
New York Times, October 7, 1951.
New York Times Book Review, November 22, 1967, p. 70.
Reader's Digest, July, 1953.
Time, October 13, 1967, p. 50.

OBITUARIES:

PERIODICALS

AB Bookman's Weekly, April 11, 1983.
Chicago Tribune, March 20, 1983.
Los Angeles Times, March 19, 1983.
Newsweek, March 28, 1983.
New York Times, March 20, 1983.
Publishers Weekly, April 15, 1983.
School Library Journal, May, 1983.
Washington Post, March 20, 1983.*

* * *

MARWICK, Arthur 1936-

PERSONAL: Born February 29, 1936, in Edinburgh, Scotland; son of William Hutton (a lecturer) and Maeve (Brereton) Marwick. *Ethnicity:* "Scottish." *Education:* University of Edinburgh, M.A. (first class honours), 1957; Balliol College, Oxford, B.Litt., 1960.

ADDRESSES: Home—67 Fitzjohn's Ave., London NW 3, England; fax: (01908) 653750. *Office*—Department of History, Open University, Milton-Keyes, Buckinghamshire, England. *E-mail*—a.j.-marwick@open.ac.uk.

CAREER: University of Aberdeen, Aberdeen, Scotland, assistant lecturer in history, 1959-60; University of Edinburgh, Edinburgh, Scotland, lecturer in history, 1960-69, director of studies, 1964-69; Open University, Bletchley, England, professor of history, 1969—, dean of arts, 1978-84. Visiting professor at State University of New York at Buffalo, 1966-67, Stanford University, 1984-85, Rhodes College, Memphis, TN, 1991, University of Perugia, Italy, 1991; visiting scholar, Hoover Institution, 1984-85; directeur d'etudes invite, L'Ecole des hautes etudes en sciences sociales, Paris, 1985.

MEMBER: Royal Historical Society (fellow).

AWARDS, HONORS: D.Litt., Edinburgh University, 1981.

WRITINGS:

The Explosion of British Society, 1914-1962, Pan Books (England), 1963, revised edition published as *The Explosion of British Society, 1914-1970,* Macmillan (London), 1971.

Clifford Allen: The Open Conspirator, Oliver & Boyd (England), 1964.

The Deluge: British Society and the First World War, Bodley Head (England), 1965, Little, Brown (Boston, MA), 1966, new edition, Macmillan (New York City), 1991.

Britain in the Century of Total War: War, Peace, and Social Change, 1900-1967, Little, Brown, 1968.

The Nature of History, Macmillan, 1970, Knopf (New York City), 1971, revised edition, Macmillan, 1989.

War and Social Change in the Twentieth Century: A Comparative Study of Britain, France, Germany, Russia, and the United States, St. Martin's (New York City), 1974.

The Home Front: The British and the Second World War, Thames & Hudson (England), 1976.

Women at War, 1914-1918, Croom Helm (London), 1977.

Class: Image and Reality in Britain, France, and the USA since 1930, Oxford University Press (New York City), 1980, revised edition, Macmillan, 1990.

British Society since 1945, Penguin (New York City), 1982, revised edition, 1989, revised edition published as *Britain since 1945,* A. Lane, 1991, updated edition, 1996.

Britain in Our Century: Images and Controversies, Thames & Hudson, 1984.

Beauty in History: Society, Politics, and Personal Appearance, Thames & Hudson, 1988.

Culture in Britain since 1945, Blackwell, 1991.

EDITOR

(With Christopher Harvie, Charles Kightly, and Keith Wrightson) *The Illustrated Dictionary of British History,* Thames & Hudson, 1980.

Class in the Twentieth Century, St. Martin's, 1986.

Total War and Social Change, St. Martin's, 1988.

(With Clive Emsley and Wendy Simpson) *War, Peace, and Social Change in Twentieth-Century Europe,* Open University Press, 1989.

(With Wendy Simpson) *War, Peace, and Social Change. Documents: Europe 1900-1955,* Open University Press, 1990.

(With others) *Europe on the Eve of War, 1900-1914,* Open University Press, 1990.

(With others) *War and Change in Twentieth-Century Europe,* Open University Press, 1990.

The Arts, Literature, and Society, Routledge, 1990.

OTHER

Contributor of articles and reviews to learned and popular journals, including *Journal of Contemporary History.* Contributor to books, including *Memoirs of a Modern Scotland,* edited by Karl Miller, Faber, 1970; and *Developments in Modern Historiography,* edited by Henry Kozicki, St. Martin's, 1993. General consultant for *Britain Discovered: A Pictorial Atlas of Our Land and Heritage,* M. Beazley (London), 1982.

WORK IN PROGRESS: The Age of Missed Opportunities: British Politics, 1914 to the Present, for Blackwell; *Culture in Western Europe since 1945,* for Oxford University Press; *The Sixties: Social and Cultural Change in Britain, France, Italy and the U.S.A., c. 1958-c. 1974*; editing and contributing to *The International Cultural Revolution of the 1960s.*

SIDELIGHTS: Class and society in the twentieth century is the subject of much of Arthur Marwick's research, culminating in such works as *Class: Image and Reality in Britain, France, and the USA since 1930* and *British Society since 1945.* The author often uses quotes from members of various social stations to illustrate his theses; in Shirley Robin Letwin's *Spectator* review of *Class,* the critic notes some examples: "A nightwatchman, whose wife was described as a prostitute, looks down on the owner of his lodging house as 'working-class.' But a [driver] regards the owner of [a liquor shop], who takes lodgers, as a privileged 'boss.' A stable boy, in awe of his 'boss,' the greatest man in town, nevertheless invites him home to dinner, only to discover that [the boss] uses the word 'yis,' which establishes that he is really 'working-class.' A housepainter describes himself as 'working-class,' but an engineer's turner, on the other hand, insists that he is an 'artisan.'"

In *British Society since 1945* Marwick contends that "from the point of view of the vast majority of the British people, as little interested as ever in major national concerns, the most significant changes in values were probably those related to sexual mores and social relationships." The author "does not ignore structural questions, like the rediscovery of poverty and the new dimensions of social inequality, but nor does he dwell on them," according to *Times Literary Supplement* critic Peter Clark."[Marwick] prefers to illuminate his themes obliquely with the anecdotal insight and the telling quotation. He has achieved his aim in breaking new ground and now that he has done so it will be easier for others to follow."

Marwick once told *CA* that *Beauty in History: Society, Politics, and Personal Appearance,* "against the vociferous opposition of cultural theorists and some feminists, opens up a new area of historical research, the social and political implications of personal appearance, male and female." He added: "In evaluating beauty we should not, as all previous writers have done, look simply at what painters *painted,* as fashion writers *decreed,* nor even at one or two individual beauties and what was *said* about them; we must look at what people actually *did.*"

Marwick told *CA:* "While I was researching in the United States on my new book on the nineteen sixties, an American remarked to me: 'Say, I never knew you guys had a sixties over there.' In fact, this is a pioneering comparative study covering France and Italy as well as Britain and America. I believe that too much attention has been focused on the minority of pop stars, beautiful people, etc., and on the protests and rioting. These all were important, but I'm concentrating on the transformation in the lives and liberties of ordinary people.

"I am a leading proponent of source-based non-metaphysical history, and a leading critic of such neo-Marxist poststructuralist commentators as Hayden White, as can be seen from my contributions to *Developments in Modern Historiography,* edited by Henry Kozicki, and the *Journal of Contemporary History,* January, 1995."

BIOGRAPHICAL/CRITICAL SOURCES:

PERIODICALS

Listener, July 31, 1980.
New York Review of Books, December 16, 1969.
New York Times, December 27, 1965.
Spectator, June 14, 1980.
Times (London), June 19, 1980.
Times Literary Supplement, July 23, 1982; January 11, 1985.

MATTHEWS, William 1942-

PERSONAL: Born November 11, 1942, in Cincinnati, OH; son of William P., Jr., and Mary E. (Sather) Matthews; married Marie Harris (a teacher), May 4, 1963 (divorced, 1974); married Arlene Modica, September 23, 1985 (one source says 1984) (divorced); children (first marriage): William, Sebastian. *Education:* Yale University, B.A., 1965; University of North Carolina at Chapel Hill, M.A., 1966.

ADDRESSES: Home—523 W. 121st St., New York, NY 10027. *Office*—English Department, City College of City University of New York, Convent and 138th St., New York, NY 10031.

CAREER: Wells College, Aurora, NY, instructor in English, 1968-69; Cornell University, Ithaca, NY, assistant professor of English, 1969-74; University of Colorado, Boulder, associate professor of English, beginning 1974; University of Washington, Seattle, professor of English, 1978-83; City College, New York City, writer in residence, 1985—. Writer in residence, Emerson College, 1973-74; visiting lecturer, University of Iowa, 1976-77; visiting professor, University of Houston, 1981, 1983. Codirector of Lillabulero Press and coeditor of *Lillabulero* (poetry journal), 1966-74; member of editorial board for poetry, Wesleyan University Press, 1969-74; advisory editor, L'Epervier Press, 1976—. Member of literature panel, National Endowment for the Arts, 1976—; member of board of directors, Associated Writing Programs, 1977—.

MEMBER: PEN, Poetry Society of America (president, 1984-88).

AWARDS, HONORS: National Endowment for the Arts fellowship, 1974, 1983-84; Guggenheim fellowship, 1980-81; Ingram Merrill Foundation fellowship, 1983; National Book Critics Circle Award for poetry, 1995, for *Time & Money: New Poems.*

WRITINGS:

POETRY

(With Russell Banks and Newton Smith) *15 Poems,* Lillabulero Press (Northwood Narrows, NH), 1967.

Broken Syllables, Lillabulero Press, 1969.

Ruining the New Road: Poems, Random House (New York City), 1970.

The Cloud, Barn Dream Press (Boston), 1971.

The Moon, Penyeach Press (Baltimore), 1971.

(With Robert Bly and William Stafford) *Poems for Tennessee,* Tennessee Poetry Press (Martin), 1971.

Sleek for the Long Flight, Random House, 1972.

Without a Mouth, Penyeach Press (Norfolk, VA), 1972.

Sticks and Stones, Pentagram Press (Milwaukee), 1975.

(With Mary Feeney, translator from the French) Follain, *A World Rich in Anniversaries,* Grilled Flowers Press (Iowa City), 1979.

Rising and Falling, Atlantic-Little, Brown (Boston), 1979.

Flood, Atlantic-Little, Brown, 1982.

A Happy Childhood, Atlantic-Little, Brown, 1984.

Foreseeable Futures, Houghton (Boston), 1987.

Blues If You Want, Houghton, 1989.

Selected Poems and Translations, 1969-1991, Houghton, 1992.

Time & Money: New Poems, Houghton, 1995.

OTHER

An Oar in the Old Water (pamphlet), Stone Press (San Francisco), 1974.

(With Feeney, translator from the French) Jean Follain, *Removed from Time* (pamphlet), Tideline Press, 1977.

Curiosities, University of Michigan Press (Ann Arbor), 1989.

Contributor to numerous anthologies; also contributor of articles and reviews to periodicals. Advisory editor, *Tennessee Poetry Journal,* 1970-72; poetry editor, *Iowa Review,* 1976-77; contributing editor, *Gumbo,* 1977—.

SIDELIGHTS: William Matthews's poetry has earned him a reputation as a master of well-turned phrases, wise sayings, and rich metaphors. He is sometimes identified as a member of the "deep image" movement, along poets like W. S. Merwin, James Wright, and Robert Bly. Poets in this school often tend to allow one strong image to dominate each poem and to evoke many strong feelings and associations. Much of Matthews's poetry explores the themes of life cycles, the passage of time, and the nature of human consciousness. In another type of poem, he focuses on his particular enthusiasms: jazz music, basketball, and his children. His early writing was free-form and epigrammatic, and considered derivative by some critics. But as his career has progressed, he has adopted a more formal structure and garnered growing praise. Writing in the *Bloomsbury Review,* Christopher Merrill identified Matthews as "one of our most alert and engaging poets."

Matthews's first major collection, *Ruining the New Road: Poems,* was described by Paul West in *Book World* as a group of "terse but ripe little poems. . . . It exposes, it warms, it warns." West identified Matthews's appreciation of nature and his unflinching view of human foibles as outstanding features of the book. "Matthews is ever conscious of the risks we run in life and his meter and his metaphors take the kinds of chances real poetry needs if it is to succeed," declared a *Virginia Quarterly Review* contributor. The reviewer also noted that Matthews, "with a distinctive lyric sense and literal toughness, confronts the almost hidden terrifying aspects of life around us." *Poetry* commentator F. D. Reeve, however, found Matthews's style in *Ruining the New Road* only partly successful. "Images weave back and forth among the poems, picking up associations which, sharp in separate poems, do not easily translate," Reeve observed. For instance, he pointed out, ashes are gloves in one poem, but are pulled over the eyes in another.

The understated nature of Matthews's early verse elicited comment from many reviewers. Jack Hicks reported in a *Carolina Quarterly* essay on *Ruining the New Road:* "His voice is unique, personal, but one not heard immediately or sharply. Because he does not knock you down, he requires reading and rereading—and even then his work does not announce itself. . . . Readers who insist on a poetry of ecstasy, one that frays or strokes nerve endings, will likely rush through and by these poems." Matthews's understatement proved deceptive to Dave Smith, who confessed in an *American Poetry Review* piece on the poet's 1979 collection, *Rising and Falling:* "Perhaps too hastily, I thought his earlier poems had the odd property of losing substance upon rereading. This new collection has singular depth, weight, and clarity. Everything in it is touched with intensity and taken care of with integrity. . . . The poems of *Rising and Falling* do not glitter or dazzle, but shed a steady light." Peter Stitt, writing in the

Georgia Review, was similarly enthusiastic about the collection, declaring that "there is a richness of image and metaphor in this volume that shows itself everywhere—in complete poems, in passages, in single lines. . . . Matthews does indeed have a magical way with words, an agile, graceful style; this is the best book yet produced by one of our most articulate younger poets."

The 1982 collection *Flood,* full of water imagery, reflected further refinement of Matthews's craft, according to some critics. *Georgia Review*'s Stitt commented that the poems showed greater structural discipline than Matthews's previous work, indicating "the operation not just of a free and surprising imagination, but of a powerful and controlling intellect as well." In *Poetry,* Bonnie Costello observed another development in evidence in *Flood:* "Matthews moves from outward observation to inward questioning. But his objectivity . . . never compromises lyricism." In a later summary of Matthews's career, though, *Contemporary Poets* contributor Jay S. Paul called *Flood* "marred by repetitive imagery, trite conceptions, and thematic confusion."

In *A Happy Childhood,* Matthews set out to investigate the psychological aspects of human life, using the theories of Sigmund Freud to inform some of his verses. Freud is in fact "the muse of *A Happy Childhood,*" according to *Washington Post Book World* contributor David Lehman. Matthews "renews Freud's metaphors . . . or propounds new ones. . . . Most of all, Matthews emulates the poet in Freud, fastening on our errors and dreams and accidental patterns as badges of enchantment, clues to a mystery that retains something of its inscrutability even as it fosters new forms of revelation." In the *Georgia Review,* Stitt was less positive in his assessment of the collection, finding it somewhat "solemn and pompous; the poet is preaching at us, repeating the cliches of our age (accurately called by many the Age of Analysis) as though they were spontaneous revelations. Far too much of the book is like this, a heavily worked up burden of wisdom the reader longs not to have to bear." John Lucas, contributor to *New Statesman,* identified Matthews's poems as part of "that very self-conscious American tradition of the child as holy innocent," and found them full of synthetic sentiment. Lucas described some of the poems as "gooey," others "gruesome," and one, "Civilisation and Its Discontents," offensive for its borrowing from Robert Frost. *New York Times Book Review* writer David Kalstone, however, lauded *A Happy Childhood.* "These poems restore some sense of mystery and play to Freud's explanations and challenge the easy fictions people make of them." He praised the poems' "counterpoint of assurance and irrationality," in which "the skillful, elegant analyst becomes as comically self-deluding as the rest of us." He concluded that *A Happy Childhood* is "Mr. Matthews's writing at its strongest, open to the interplay of narrative and song."

In *Foreseeable Futures,* Matthews gave readers thirty-six poems, thirty of them written in the same form, with five tercets each. The swift passage of time and the weight of mortality are dominant themes, but J. D. McClatchy advised in the *New York Times Book Review* that "it would be misleading to call this a gloomy book. . . . Mr. Matthews finds human joys brightening the unlikeliest places—a plate of pasta or Bach's skeleton—and wants to juggle them with dark truths." *Poetry* reviewer Robert B. Shaw commented on a detached quality in the work: "Matthews sounds equally distanced whether he is writing about music, spring, a plane crash, or a vasectomy." This quality is not necessarily desirable, Shaw said, but noted some poems in the collection break out of this pattern, such as "Recovery Room," showing a "real fierceness," and "Photo of the Author with a Favorite Pig," which the reviewer dubbed "charming" and deceptively lighthearted.

In *Blues If You Want,* Matthews focused on jazz, with many poem titles taken from favorite jazz tunes. *Kenyon Review* contributor Fred Chappell thought the collection was occasionally marred by "self-indulgence," but on the whole "warm" and "genial." In the *Bloomsbury Review,* Christopher Merrill pointed out the poet's exploration of the relationship between music and language, and lauded Matthews's "curiosity" and "wit."

"Things that don't last" are the subject of Matthews's 1995 collection, *Time & Money: New Poems,* according to a *Publishers Weekly* writer. The more than forty poems gathered here range from meditations on a visit to New York City by Ronald Reagan, to reflections on the death of Matthews's father, to a eulogy for jazz musician Charles Mingus. Several reviewers noted the ironic voice Matthews expresses in the poems, with notably different shadings from one piece to the next. Donna Seaman in *Booklist,* calling the works "fine, quietly furious poems," also praised Matthews for the linguistic gifts evident in the collection.

BIOGRAPHICAL/CRITICAL SOURCES:

BOOKS

Contemporary Authors Autobiography Series, Volume 18, Gale (Detroit), 1994.
Contemporary Literary Criticism, Volume 40, Gale, 1986.
Contemporary Poets, fifth edition, St. James Press (Detroit), 1995.
Dictionary of Literary Biography, Volume 5: *American Poets since World War II,* Gale, 1980.

PERIODICALS

Aegis, fall, 1975.
American Book Review, March-April, 1984, p. 16.
American Poetry Review, November-December, 1979, pp. 33-37.
Black Warrior Review, spring, 1975.
Bloomsbury Review, May-June, 1990, pp. 27-29.
Booklist, July, 1995, p. 1855.
Book World, May 31, 1970, pp. 6-7.
Carolina Quarterly, spring, 1971, pp. 99-101.
Georgia Review, summer, 1980, pp. 428-40; fall, 1982, pp. 675-85; winter, 1984, pp. 857-68; spring, 1992, pp. 150-66.
Ironwood, Volume 3, 1973.
Journal and Constitution (Atlanta) December 31, 1989, p. N8.
Kenyon Review, summer, 1990, pp. 168-76.
Library Journal, July, 1995, p. 84.
New Statesman, September 20, 1985, p. 29.
New York Times Book Review, October 21, 1979, p. 26; July 1, 1984, p. 14; July 26, 1987, p. 9.
Ohio Review, spring, 1972.
Poetry, July, 1971, pp. 234-38; January, 1974, pp. 241-47; June, 1980, pp. 164-70; May, 1983, pp. 106-13; July, 1987, pp. 234-35.
Publishers Weekly, May 29, 1995, p. 77.
Shenandoah, fall, 1993, pp. 65-74.
Virginia Quarterly Review, autumn, 1970, p. CXXXIV.
Washington Post Book World, August 19, 1979; September 2, 1984, p. 6.
Words, winter, 1974.

MAY, Elaine Tyler 1947-

PERSONAL: Born September 17, 1947, in Los Angeles, CA; daughter of Edward T. (a physician) and Lillian (an art historian and family-planning educator; maiden name, Bass) Tyler; married Larry L. May (a historian and author), March 7, 1970; children: Michael Edward, Daniel David, Sarah Lillian. Ethnicity: "Jewish." *Education:* University of California, Los Angeles, A.B. (cum laude), 1969, M.A., 1970, Ph.D., 1975.

ADDRESSES: Home—88 Arthur Ave. S.E., Minneapolis, MN 55414. *Office*—American Studies Program, 104 Scott Hall, University of Minnesota, Minneapolis, MN 55455; fax: 612-624-3858. *E-mail*—mayxx002@maroon.tc.umn.edu.

CAREER: U.S. Senate, Washington, DC, research intern with Committee on Intergovernmental Relations, 1969; California State University, Fullerton, instructor in history, 1971-72; California State University, Los Angeles, instructor in history, 1972-73; Princeton University, Princeton, NJ, instructor, 1974-76, assistant professor of history, 1976-78; University of Minnesota, Minneapolis, assistant professor, 1978-81, associate professor of American studies, 1981-89, professor of American studies and history, 1989—, associate dean, College of Liberal Arts, 1987-92, chair, American Studies Program, 1992-96, member of women's studies governing council; University College, Dublin, Ireland, Mary Bell Washington professor of American history, 1996-97. Public speaker; humanities commentator for Minnesota Public Radio, 1981; project director, organizer, and moderator.

MEMBER: American Historical Association, Organization of American Historians, American Studies Association (president, 1995-96), American Association for the Advancement of the Humanities, National Organization for Women, Social Science History Association, Women Historians of the Midwest.

AWARDS, HONORS: Research fellow at Princeton University, 1975-77, Princeton Inn fellow, 1976; Mellon fellow at Harvard University, 1981-82; research scholar at Radcliffe College, 1982; fellow of American Council of Learned Societies, 1983-84; grant from National Endowment for the Humanities, 1983, 1985-87; research grant from Rockefeller Foundation, 1995-96.

WRITINGS:

Great Expectations: Marriage and Divorce in Post-Victorian America, University of Chicago Press (Chicago), 1980.

Homeward Bound: American Families in the Cold War Era, Basic Books (New York City), 1988.

Pushing the Limits: American Women, 1940-1961, Oxford University Press (New York City), 1994.

Barren in the Promised Land: Childless Americans and the Pursuit of Happiness, Basic Books, 1995.

Contributor to books, including *The American Family in Social-Historical Perspective,* 3rd edition, edited by Michael Gorden, St. Martin's (New York City), 1983; *Recasting America: Culture and Politics in the Age of Cold War,* edited by Larry May, University of Chicago Press, 1989; and *The War and American Culture,* edited by Lewis Erenberg and Susan Hirsch, University of Chicago Press, 1996. Contributor of more than a dozen articles and reviews to history and women's studies journals and newspapers.

SIDELIGHTS: Elaine Tyler May once told *CA:* "Everywhere we turn we find people bemoaning, or celebrating, the imminent collapse of the American family. And yet, the cry has been heard before. In the midst of every era that has undergone tremendous social change, the family has appeared threatened. The family continues to survive, although it is continually transformed, through each major historical upheaval. My work is prompted in part by an effort to understand these changes and the massive popular concern over the fate of the family.

"As a historian, I find it fascinating to see the same concerns emerge in different historical contexts. Why is the 'emancipation of women,' for example, continually blamed for the erosion of the family? As a feminist as well as a spouse and a mother, I find it imperative that the emancipation of women not be on a collision course with the survival of the family. In my own research and writing, I have found that the problems of family life are more the result of the failure of public institutions to support families than they are a result of women's increasing equality. Although historians are not in the business of making predictions, it is my own feeling that when public life is revitalized in support of men, women, and children, we will find true mutuality and equality in the home. On that day in the hopefully near future, perhaps we will stop blaming families for the nation's problems and begin addressing the problems directly. Families at that point will be intact because they will express the desires of the individuals within them—whether those families are united by marriage, blood, or friendship. We will then find a new meaning of 'family life' altogether."

* * *

MCALLISTER, CASEY
See BATTIN, B(rinton) W(arner)

* * *

McCLELLAND, Doug 1934-

PERSONAL: Born July 16, 1934, in Plainfield, NJ; son of William Vincent and Elna (Whitlock) McClelland. *Ethnicity:* "Scottish-Danish." *Education:* Attended Newark, NJ, public schools.

ADDRESSES: Home—704 Madison Ave., Bradley Beach, NJ 07720.

CAREER: Newark Star-Ledger, Newark, NJ, reporter, late 1940s; *Newark Evening News,* Newark, arts editor, 1952-56; *Record World Magazine,* New York City, editor, 1961-72. Lecturer on motion pictures.

AWARDS, HONORS: Two-time recipient of James R. Quirk Award.

WRITINGS:

The Unkindest Cuts, A. S. Barnes (San Diego, CA), 1972.

(Contributor) *The Real Stars,* Curtis Publishing (Indianapolis, IN), 1973.

Susan Hayward: The Divine Bitch, Pinnacle Books (New York City), 1973.

Down the Yellow Brick Road, Pyramid Publications, 1976.

The Golden Age of "B" Movies, Charterhouse, 1978.

(Contributor) *Hollywood Kids,* Popular Library, 1978.
Hollywood on Ronald Reagan, Faber & Faber (Winchester, MA), 1985.
Hollywood on Hollywood, Faber & Faber, 1985.
StarSpeak, Faber & Faber, 1987.
Blackface to Blacklist, Scarecrow, (Metuchen, NJ), 1987.
Eleanor Parker: Woman of a Thousand Faces, Scarecrow, 1989.
Hollywood Talks Turkey, Faber & Faber, 1989.
Forties Film Talk, McFarland & Co. (Jefferson, NC), 1992.

Contributor of articles to *Hollywood Studio Magazine, Films of the Golden Age, Film Fan Monthly, After Dark, Films and Filming, Films in Review, Filmograph, Screen Facts, Asbury Park Press,* and *The Many Worlds of Music.* Author of liner notes for record albums.

BIOGRAPHICAL/CRITICAL SOURCES:

PERIODICALS

Los Angeles Times Book Review, October 16, 1983.
People Weekly, June 8, 1987.

* * *

McFEE, Michael 1954-

PERSONAL: Born June 4, 1954, in Asheville, NC; son of William Howard (a postal clerk) and Lucy (Farmer) McFee; married Belinda Anne Pickett (a physician's assistant), June 16, 1978; children: Philip Pickett. *Education:* University of North Carolina, B.A. (summa cum laude), 1976, M.A., 1978.

ADDRESSES: Home—2514 Pickett Rd., Durham, NC 27705. *Office*—Department of English, Greenlaw CB 3520, University of North Carolina, Chapel Hill, NC 27599-3520.

CAREER: Duke University, Durham, NC, instructor in continuing education, 1982-83; North Carolina State University at Raleigh, lecturer in English, fall, 1983; University of North Carolina, Chapel Hill, visiting lecturer in poetry, spring, 1984; University of North Carolina, Greensboro, visiting instructor, fall, 1985; Cornell University, Ithaca, NY, visiting assistant professor, summer session, 1986-88; Lawrence University, visiting poet, winter, 1988; University of North Carolina, Chapel Hill, lecturer in creative writing, 1990-95, assistant professor of English, 1995—. Has also taught at Appalachian Writers' Workshop, Duke University Writers' Conference, and the Writers' Center at Chautauqua, NY. Gives poetry readings.

MEMBER: Poets and Writers, Inc., Phi Beta Kappa.

AWARDS, HONORS: Discovery/*The Nation* Award, 1980; scholar at Bread Loaf Writers' Conference and Reynolds Homestead Writers' Conference, both 1980; first prize from *Crucible,* 1980; Pushcart Prize, 1981-82; North Carolina Arts Council fellowship in poetry, 1985-86; Ingram Merrill Foundation fellowship in poetry and fiction, 1986; National Endowment for the Arts fellowship in poetry, 1987-88; Durham Arts Council seasonal grant, 1991-92.

WRITINGS:

(Contributor) Jeffrey Richards, editor, *An Introduction to Film Criticism,* 3rd edition, Department of English, University of North Carolina (Chapel Hill, NC), 1977.
(Contributor) *Pushcart Prize VI: Best of the Small Presses,* Pushcart (Wainscott, NY), 1981.
Plain Air (poems), University Presses of Florida (Gainesville, FL), 1983.
(Editor) *The Spectator Reader,* Spectator Publications, 1985.
Vanishing Acts (poems), Gnomon Press (Frankfort, KY), 1989.
Sad Girl Sitting on a Running Board, Gnomon Press, 1991.
To See (with photographs by Elizabeth Matheson), North Carolina Wesleyan College Press, 1991.
(Editor) *The Language They Speak Is Things to Eat: Poems by Fifteen Contemporary North Carolina Poets,* University of North Carolina Press, 1994.
Colander (poems), Carnegie Mellon University Press (Pittsburgh, PA), 1996.

Work represented in anthologies, including *No Business Poems,* 1981; *New North Carolina Poetry: The Eighties,* edited by Stephen E. Smith, Green River, 1982; *Anthology of Magazine Verse and Yearbook of American Poetry; Light Year,*

1984-89; *The Bedford Introduction to Literature,* 1987; *The Faber Book of Movie Verse,* 1993; *Sweet Nothings: An Anthology of Rock & Roll in American Poetry,* 1994; *For a Living: The Poetry of Work,* 1995. Contributor of several hundred poems, articles, and reviews to magazines, including *New Yorker, Poetry, Hudson Review, Nation, Georgia Review, Parnassus, Ploughshares,* and *Southern Poetry Review.* Poetry editor of *Carolina Quarterly,* 1977-79; book editor of *Spectator,* 1980-93; book critic for National Public Radio, WUNC-FM, Chapel Hill, NC, 1982-94.

WORK IN PROGRESS: Another collection of poems, as yet untitled.

SIDELIGHTS: Michael McFee told *CA:* "Why do I write poetry? Because I have to. Because if I don't, I feel physically ill after a while. Because nothing else gives me more pleasure than to get the best words in the best order. Because I've been doing it for over 20 years, and it's become a way of thinking and seeing and encountering the world, a habit of being. Because I've had some success at it, both on my own terms and others'. Because I love it.

"What influences me, provokes me into poetry? Things. Things noticed, overheard, smelt, felt, touched. Things that become images jotted on napkins while driving, or phrases on the sheets of paper I always carry folded in my pocket so I don't lose a poem-seed when it appears. Things that generate lines in my notebook, stanzas in manuscript, drafts in the typewriter, finished poems on the computer.

"Why do I write on the subjects I have chosen? In a way, it's not that I've chosen them: they've chosen me, and I simply have to be alert to their call and then write about them. Over the years, through five books, those subjects have changed: the landscape of my native North Carolina mountains (*Plain Air*); the people living there—myself, my relatives, my mother (*Vanishing Acts, Sad Girl Sitting on a Running Board*); photographs (the collaborative *To See*); common objects *(Colander).* If I'm lucky, those subjects will continue to change, to challenge me as a writer. Who know where the poems will lead?

"All along, though, whether writing free verse or the occasional form, I've tried to maintain an integrity of line and stanza, a freshness of image, a clarity of voice, and the constant possibility of surprise—in 'plot,' in wit, in metaphor, in whatever way the poem seems to require. I want my poetry to give as much pleasure as possible, in the mouth, in the eye and ear, in the mind."

BIOGRAPHICAL/CRITICAL SOURCES:

PERIODICALS

Durham Morning Herald, February 5, 1984.

* * *

McLEOD, Wallace (Edmond) 1931-

PERSONAL: Born May 30, 1931, in Toronto, Ontario, Canada; son of Angus Edmond (a printing press operator) and Mary A. E. (Shier) McLeod; married Elizabeth M. Staples (a teacher), July 24, 1957; children: Betsy, John, James, Angus. *Ethnicity:* "White." *Education:* University of Toronto, B.A., 1953; Harvard University, A.M., 1954, Ph.D., 1966; American School of Classical Studies, Athens, additional study, 1957-59. *Politics:* Conservative. *Religion:* Presbyterian.

ADDRESSES: *Home*—399 St. Clements Ave., Toronto, Ontario, Canada M5N 1M2. *Office*—Victoria College, University of Toronto, Toronto, Ontario, Canada M5S 1K7; fax: 416-585-4584.

CAREER: Trinity College, Hartford, CT, instructor in classical languages, 1955-56; University of British Columbia, Vancouver, instructor in classics, 1959-61; University of Western Ontario, London, lecturer in classics, 1961-62; University of Toronto, Victoria College, Toronto, Ontario, assistant professor, 1962-66, associate professor, 1966-74, professor of classics, 1974-96, professor emeritus, 1996—, associate chair, 1975-78, acting chair of classics department, 1978-79. Prestonian lecturer, 1986. Member of Society of Blue Friars; fellow of Philalethes Society (president, 1992).

MEMBER: Classical Association of Canada, American Philological Association, Archaeological Institute of America, Society of Archer-Antiquaries, Ancient Free and Accepted Masons.

AWARDS, HONORS: Canada Council fellowship, 1970-71.

WRITINGS:

Composite Bows from the Tomb of Tut'ankhamun, Griffith Institute, 1970.
(Editor and contributor) *Beyond the Pillars: More Light on Freemasonry,* Grand Lodge of Canada, 1973.
(Editor and contributor) *Meeting the Challenge: The Lodge Officer at Work,* Grand Lodge of Canada, 1976.
(Editor and author of introduction) *The Sufferings of John Coustos: A Facsimile Reprint of the First English Edition, Published at London in 1746,* Masonic Book Club, 1979.
(Editor and contributor) *Whence Come We?: Freemasonry in Ontario, 1764-1980,* Grand Lodge of Canada, 1980.
Self Bows and Other Archery Tackle from the Tomb of Tut'ankhamun, Griffith Institute, 1982.
(Editor and author of introduction) *The Old Gothic Constitutions: Facsimile Reprints of Four Early Printed Texts of the Masonic Old Charges,* Masonic Book Club, 1985.
The Old Charges: The Prestonian Lecture for 1986, privately printed, 1986.
(Editor and author of introduction) *Wellins Calcott, a Candid Disquisition: A Facsimile Reprint of the First English Edition, Published at London in 1769,* Masonic Book Club, 1989.
For the Cause of Good: A History of the First Twenty-Five Years of the Masonic Foundation of Ontario (1964-1989), Masonic Foundation of Ontario, 1990, reprinted with a new preface, 1993.
The Grand Design: Selected Masonic Addresses and Papers of Wallace McLeod, Anchor Communications, 1991.

Contributor of about 150 articles and 350 reviews to professional journals. *Phoenix,* associate editor, 1965-70, acting editor, 1973, acting review editor, 1976-77, 1989-90, 1993-94, acting associate editor, 1985-86.

WORK IN PROGRESS: The Quest for Light: Selected Masonic Papers of Wallace McLeod.

SIDELIGHTS: Wallace McLeod participated in archaeological excavations at Lerna, Greece, and Gordion, Turkey, in 1958.

MEYER, Carolyn (Mae) 1935-

PERSONAL: Born June 8, 1935, in Lewistown, PA; daughter of H. Victor (a businessman) and Sara (Knepp) Meyer; married Joseph Smrcka, June 4, 1960 (divorced, 1973); married E. A. Mares (an historian, poet, and playwright), May 30, 1987; children: Alan, John, Christopher. *Education:* Bucknell University, B.A. (cum laude), 1957. *Politics:* Liberal. *Religion:* Episcopalian.

ADDRESSES: Home—202 Edith Boulevard, N. E., Albuquerque, NM 87102. *Agent*—Amy Berkower, Writers House Inc., 21 West 26th St., New York, NY 10010.

CAREER: Freelance writer, 1963—. Institute of Children's Literature, instructor, 1973-79; Bucknell University, Alpha Lambda Delta Lecturer, 1974; guest lecturer at various schools and organizations.

AWARDS, HONORS: Notable book citations, American Library Association (ALA), 1971, for *The Bread Book: All about Bread and How to Make It,* 1976, for *Amish People: Plain Living in a Complex World,* and 1979, for *C. C. Poindexter; New York Times* best book citation, 1977, for *Eskimos: Growing Up in a Changing Culture;* best book for young adults citations, 1980, for *C. C. Poindexter,* 1980, for *The Center: From a Troubled Past to a New Life,* 1986, for *Voices of South Africa: Growing Up in a Troubled Land,* 1992, for *Where the Broken Heart Still Beats: The Story of Cynthia Ann Parker,* 1993, for *White Lilacs,* 1995, for *Drummers for Jericho,* and 1996, for *Gideon's People; Voice of Youth Advocates* YASD best books citations, 1988, for *Denny's Tapes* and *Voices of South Africa: Growing Up in a Troubled Land;* Pennsylvania School Librarians Association author of the year award, 1990.

WRITINGS:

FOR CHILDREN; NONFICTION

Miss Patch's Learn-to-Sew Book, Harcourt (New York City), 1969.
(Self-illustrated) *Stitch by Stitch: Needlework for Beginners,* Harcourt, 1970.
The Bread Book: All about Bread and How to Make It, Harcourt, 1971.

Yarn: The Things It Makes and How to Make Them, Harcourt, 1972.

Saw, Hammer, and Paint: Woodworking and Finishing for Beginners, Morrow (New York City), 1973.

Milk, Butter and Cheese: The Story of Dairy Products, Morrow, 1974.

Christmas Crafts: Things to Make the 24 Days before Christmas, Harper (New York City), 1974.

People Who Make Things: How American Craftsmen Live and Work, Atheneum (New York City), 1975.

Rock Tumbling: From Stones to Gems to Jewelry, Morrow, 1975.

The Needlework Book of Bible Stories, Harcourt, 1975.

Amish People: Plain Living in a Complex World, Atheneum, 1976.

Lots and Lots of Candy, Harcourt, 1976.

Coconut: The Tree of Life, Morrow, 1976.

Eskimos: Growing Up in a Changing Culture, Atheneum, 1977.

Being Beautiful: The Story of Cosmetics from Ancient Art to Modern Science, Morrow, 1977.

Mask Magic, Harcourt, 1978.

The Center: From a Troubled Past to a New Life, Atheneum, 1979.

Rock Band: Big Men in a Great Big Town, Atheneum, 1980.

(With Charles Gallenkamp) *The Mystery of the Ancient Maya,* Atheneum, 1985, revised edition, 1995.

Voices of South Africa: Growing Up in a Troubled Land, Harcourt, 1986.

Voices of Northern Ireland: Growing Up in a Troubled Land, Harcourt, 1987.

A Voice from Japan: An Outsider Looks In, Harcourt, 1988.

Japan: How Do Hands Make Peace?, McGraw (New York City), 1990.

In a Different Light: Growing Up in a Yup'ik Eskimo Village, Simon & Schuster, 1996.

FOR CHILDREN; FICTION

C. C. Poindexter, Atheneum, 1978.

Eulalia's Island, Atheneum, 1982.

The Summer I Learned about Life, Atheneum, 1983.

The Luck of Texas McCoy, Atheneum, 1984.

Elliott & Win, Atheneum, 1986.

Denny's Tapes, Macmillan (New York City), 1987.

Wild Rover, Macmillan, 1989.

Killing the Kudu, Macmillan, 1990.

Where the Broken Heart Still Beats: The Story of Cynthia Ann Parker, Harcourt, 1992.

White Lilacs, Harcourt, 1993.

Rio Grande Stories, Harcourt, 1994.

Drummers of Jericho, Harcourt, 1995.

Gideon's People, Harcourt, 1996.

Jubilee Journey, Harcourt, 1997.

"HOTLINE" SERIES; FOR YOUNG ADULTS

Because of Lissa, Bantam (New York City), 1990.

The Problem with Sidney, Bantam, 1990.

Gillian's Choice, Bantam, 1991.

The Two Faces of Adam, Bantam, 1991.

OTHER

Author of columns "Cheers and Jeers" 1967-68, and "Chiefly for Children," 1968-72, and of multi-part series on crafts and women, consulting editor for "Right Now" section, 1972, all for *McCalls* magazine. Contributor of articles and book reviews to periodicals, including *Accent on Leisure, Americana, Family Circle, Golf Digest, Los Angeles Times, Publishers Weekly, Redbook,* and *Town & Country.*

SIDELIGHTS: Carolyn Meyer has achieved notable success as a writer of both fiction and nonfiction for children and young adults. In addition to her highly praised novels—which include a series featuring high school students who staff a counseling hotline—she has written several works that introduce younger readers to people coming from a variety of cultural backgrounds. The day-to-day lives of Yup'ik Eskimos, the Amish, people from both sides of racially divided South Africa and religion-torn Northern Ireland, and even rock stars have come under Meyer's perceptive scrutiny and been depicted within her books. Several of her works have received accolades from such sources as the American Library Association and the *New York Times.*

A bookworm from an early age, Meyer made her first serious effort at writing as "a way to stay sane and alive after the housework was done," as she explained in the *Junior Literary Guild* magazine. After submitting short stories to several magazines, one was finally published. Interestingly, it was published entirely in shorthand; although this fact did not deter readers of the periodical containing it—a secretarial magazine—no one in her family could read it. This first success led Meyer to undertake the first of many book-length projects—1969's *Miss Patch's Learn-to-Sew Book.*

From these first efforts in juvenile nonfiction, Meyer soon became successful enough to center her life around being a writer. From her interest in how-to books, she began to expand her works to include books inspired by personal experience. A trip to her childhood home in Pennsylvania resulted in *Amish People: Plain Living in a Complex World,* which was praised by *New York Times Book Review* critic Edward Hoagland as "an excellent introduction to Amishism."

Soon after the publication of *Amish People,* Meyer met Bernadine Larsen, a Caucasian ex-nun who had married into an Eskimo family in Alaska; the two women worked together on Meyer's next book, *Eskimos: Growing Up in a Changing Culture.* Meyer "narrates with respect and tenderness the melancholy story of representative villagers in the remote bush, caught between an ancient, now-decaying folk culture and the powerful incursions of the new one in its crassest frontier forms," according to Saul Maloff in the *New York Times Book Review.*

From the northernmost reaches of North America, Meyer moved to the continents of Europe and Africa for her next books, which included *Voices of Northern Ireland: Growing Up in a Troubled Land* and *Voices of South Africa: Growing Up in a Troubled Land.* Meyer spent five weeks in South Africa interviewing young people of both black and white background as part of her research for the latter book, which a *Kirkus* reviewer hailed as a "brilliant study" of a nation torn by race.

In addition to her work in journalistic nonfiction, Meyer also discovered the ability to transform her life and the lives of those she met into the stuff of fiction. Her first published novel was 1978's *C. C. Poindexter,* which features a fifteen-year-old girl who is six-foot-one and still growing. While grappling with both her parents' divorce and the height that makes her feel like a gawky misfit at school, C. C. struggles to discover the direction her own life should take. Meyer based the book on her own feelings of insecurity as a youngster, during which time her lack of coordination made her dread recess. One of Meyer's sons helped inspire her second novel, *Eulalia's Island,* in which thirteen-year-old Sam is dragged along on a family vacation to the Caribbean, where he meets a black St. Lucian girl named Eulalia and gains a new appreciation of both family and self.

After spending over a decade living in suburban Connecticut, Meyer moved to the Southwest, and has since lived in both New Mexico and Texas. She has set many of her young adult novels—including *The Luck of Texas McCoy, Elliott & Win,* and *Wild Rover*—in this region, discovering inspiration in many of the people she has met there. In *The Luck of Texas McCoy,* the title character—a sixteen-year-old girl—inherits her family's ranch in New Mexico and must battle to keep it running. A *Bulletin of the Center for Children's Books* reviewer had high praise for the novel, noting that "the characterization and writing style are far superior to those in most western-setting horse stories."

Despite her relatively recent success as a young adult novelist, Meyer continues to intersperse her novels with nonfiction, sometimes even combining the two, as with 1992's *Where the Broken Hear Still Beats: The Story of Cynthia Ann Parker.* Based on the true story of a nine-year-old white girl who was stolen from her parents by a Comanche raiding party and raised as an Indian before being "rescued" by the U.S. cavalry and returned to her white relatives twenty-five years later, the historical novel received high praise from reviewers. "I enjoy writing fiction, but the lure of nonfiction remains strong," Meyer has noted in an autobiographical essay published in *Something about the Author Autobiography Series.* "Sometimes I think the two kinds of writing come from different parts of the brain—one from the imaginative, childlike side, the other from the intellectual, rational, disciplined adult half." Balancing the two has resulted in a series of successes for Meyer, whose recent works of historical fiction have brought her critical praise, awards, and a growing young adult readership.

BIOGRAPHICAL/CRITICAL SOURCES:

BOOKS

Something about the Author Autobiography Series, Volume 9, Gale (Detroit), 1990.

PERIODICALS

Booklist, December 1, 1992, p. 659; October 1, 1994, p. 328; June 1-15, 1995, p. 1753.
Bulletin of the Center for Children's Books, October, 1976; April, 1978; October, 1984; November, 1986; November, 1987.
Children's Literature in Education, March, 1980, pp. 53-54.
Horn Book, August, 1976; February, 1978; December, 1978, pp. 646-47; October, 1982, pp. 520-21; February, 1988, p. 87.
Junior Literary Guild, March, 1976, p. 47.
Kirkus Reviews, February 1, 1986, p. 215; September 1, 1986, p. 1377; September 1, 1987, p. 1323; August 1, 1989, p. 1163.
New York Times Book Review, May 9, 1976, pp. 14-15; December 18, 1977, p. 23.
Publishers Weekly, June 27, 1986, p. 96; July 27, 1990, p. 236; May 8, 1995, p. 296.
School Library Journal, September, 1982, p. 141; February, 1985, p. 86; November, 1990, pp. 50-51, 140; September, 1992, pp. 278-79; October, 1993, p. 152; June, 1994, p. 133.
Voice of Youth Advocates, October, 1986, pp. 146-47; April, 1988, p. 48; April, 1993, pp. 27-28; December, 1993, p. 296; October, 1994, p. 212.

* * *

MIDDLEBROOK, (Norman) Martin 1932-

PERSONAL: Born January 24, 1932, in Boston, England; married Mary Sylvester, September 7, 1954; children: Jane, Anne, Catherine. *Ethnicity:* "Human race." *Education:* Attended schools in England "and the University of Life." *Politics:* Independent. *Religion:* Agnostic. *Avocational interests:* Golf, bowls ("a la Francis Drake"), travel, giving guided tours of the Western Front battlefields.

ADDRESSES: Home and office—48 Linden Way, Boston, Lincolnshire, England. *Agent*—A. P. Watt & Son, 20 John St., London, England.

CAREER: Poultry farmer in Boston, England, 1956-81. *Military service:* British Army, 1950-52.

WRITINGS:

The First Day on the Somme, Allen Lane (London), 1971, Norton (New York City), 1972.
The Nuremberg Raid, Allen Lane, 1973, Morrow (New York City), 1974.
Convoy, Allen Lane, 1976, Morrow, 1977.
(Contributor) Edward Marshal and Michael Carver, editors, *The War Lords,* Weidenfeld & Nicolson (London), 1976.
(With Patrick Mahoney) *Battleship,* Allen Lane, 1977, Scribner (New York City), 1979.
The Kaiser's Battle, Allen Lane, 1978.
(Editor) *Private Bruckshaw's Diaries,* Scolar Press, 1979.
The Battle of Hamburg, Allen Lane, 1980.
The Peenemunde Raid, Bobbs-Merrill (New York City), 1982.
The Schweinfurt-Regensburg Mission, Scribner, 1983.
Operation Corporate, Viking (New York City), 1984.
The Bomber Command War Diaries, Viking, 1985.
The Berlin Raids, Viking, 1985.
The Fight for the "Malvinas," Viking, 1989.
(With wife, Mary Middlebrook) *The Somme Battlefields,* Viking 1991.
Arnham 1944, Viking, 1994.

SIDELIGHTS: Martin Middlebrook told *CA:* "In my opinion there is no such thing as a 'last word' in history, and anyone who thinks he/she has written a 'definitive' book is a fool."

BIOGRAPHICAL/CRITICAL SOURCES:

PERIODICALS

Times Literary Supplement, December 26, 1980.
Washington Post Book World, May 18, 1986.

* * *

MILLS, Daniel Quinn 1941-

PERSONAL: Born November 24, 1941, in Houston, TX; son of Daniel Monroe (an engineer) and Louise (Quinn) Mills; married Joyce Smith, 1971 (divorced); children: Lisa Ann, Shirley Elizabeth. *Ethnicity:* "English-Irish." *Education:* Ohio Wesleyan University, B.A., 1963; Harvard University, Ph.D., 1968.

ADDRESSES: Office—Harvard Business School, Harvard University, Boston, MA 02163.

CAREER: Massachusetts Institute of Technology, Cambridge, assistant professor, 1968-71, associate professor, 1971-74, professor of management, 1974-76; Harvard University, Harvard School of Business Administration, Cambridge, professor of business administration, 1976—. Chair of construction industry stabilization committee, U.S. Department of Labor, 1973-74; member, National Commission of Employment Policy.

MEMBER: American Economic Association, Industrial Relations Research Association.

WRITINGS:

Industrial Relations and Manpower in Construction, MIT Press (Boston, MA), 1972.
Government, Labor, and Inflation: Wage Stabilization in the United States, University of Chicago Press (Chicago), 1976.
Labor-Management Relations (includes instructor's manual), McGraw (New York City), 1978, 5th edition, 1995.
Employment and Unemployment Statistics in Collective Bargaining, National Commission on Employment and Unemployment Statistics, 1978.
(Editor with Julian E. Lange) *The Construction Industry: Balance-Wheel of the Economy,* Lexington Books (Lexington, MA), 1979.
Industrial Relations in Transition, Wiley (New York City), 1984.
(With Malcolm Lovell, George Lodge, and Bruce Scott) *Competitiveness and the U.S. Economy,* Howard University Press (Washington, DC), 1984.
The New Competitors: A Report on American Managers from the Harvard Business School, Wiley, 1985.
Not Like Our Parents: How the Baby Boom Is Changing, Morrow (New York City), 1987.
The IBM Lesson: The Profitable Art of Full Employment, Times Books (New York City), 1988.
The Radical Executive, Wiley, 1990.
Rebirth of the Corporation, Wiley, 1991.
The Empowerment Imperative, Human Resource Development Press (Amherst, MA), 1994.
The Gem Principle & Six Steps to Creating High Performance Organization, Wiley, 1994.
Staying Afloat in the Construction Industry: Economic & Political Trends for the 1990s, BNI (Los Angeles), 1996.
(With Bruce Friesen) *Broken Promises: An Unconventional View of What Went Wrong at IBM,* Harvard Business School Press (Boston, MA), 1996.

Contributor to business and management journals.

SIDELIGHTS: Daniel Quinn Mills once told *CA:* "I have always been interested in the way individuals in our society relate to large organizations and in how organizations deal with other organizations. My work began with government activities, then focused on unions. Now it is centered on management. Writing is both a way to communicate ideas and to receive feedback."

BIOGRAPHICAL/CRITICAL SOURCES:

PERIODICALS

Los Angeles Times Book Review, February 7, 1988.

* * *

MOCHE, Dinah (Rachel) L(evine) 1936-

PERSONAL: Born October 24, 1936, in New York, NY; daughter of Bertram A. (a lawyer) and Mollie (Last) Levine; married I. Robert Rozen, September 5, 1955 (died November 17, 1966); children: two daughters, two stepsons. *Education:* Harvard University/Radcliffe College, B.A. (magna cum laude), 1958; Columbia University, M.A., 1961, Ph.D., 1976.

ADDRESSES: Home—P.O. Box 98, Rye, NY 10580-0098. *Office*—Department of Physics, Queensborough Community College of the City University of New York, Bayside, NY 11364.

CAREER: Columbia University, Radiation Laboratory, New York City, research assistant in physics, 1961-62; Bronx Community College of the City University of New York, Bronx, NY, instructor of physics, 1963-64; instructor of physics at Fashion Institute of Technology, 1964-65; Queensborough Community College of the City University of New York, Bayside, NY, lecturer,

1965-66, instructor, 1966-69, assistant professor, 1969-77, associate professor, 1977-78, professor of physics, 1979—. Participant in (and sometimes director of) national meetings.

MEMBER: American Physical Society, American Association of Physics Teachers, National Science Teachers Association, New York State Association of Two-Year College Physics Teachers, Phi Beta Kappa, Sigma Xi.

AWARDS, HONORS: National Science Foundation grant, 1974-75, faculty fellowship, 1976, National Science foundation grant, 1978-80.

WRITINGS:

JUVENILE, UNLESS OTHERWISE INDICATED

What's Up There?: Questions and Answers About Stars and Space, Scholastic (New York City), 1975.
Magic Science Tricks, Scholastic, 1977.
Astronomy: A Self-Teaching Guide (adult; updated regularly), Wiley, 1978, completely revised and expanded fourth edition, 1996.
Mars, F. Watts (New York City), 1978.
Search for Life Beyond Earth, F. Watts, 1978.
The Astronauts, Random House (New York City), 1979.
The Star Wars Question and Answer Book About Space, Random House, 1979.
Radiation: Benefits/Dangers, F. Watts, 1979.
Life in Space (adult), A & W Visual (New York City), 1979.
More Magic Science Tricks, Scholastic, 1980.
My First Book about Space: A Question and Answer Book, illustrated by R. Z. Whitlock, Golden Press (New York City), 1982.
We're Taking an Airplane Trip, illustrated by Carolyn Bracken, Golden Press, 1982.
Astronomy Today (updated regularly), illustrated by Harry McNaught, Random House, 1982, completely revised and expanded edition, 1995.
If You Were an Astronaut, Western Publishing (Racine, WI), 1985, second edition, 1992.
Amazing Space Facts, illustrated by R. W. Alley, Western Publishing, 1988, second edition, 1992.
The Big Book of Real Spacecraft, Grosset & Dunlap (New York City), 1989.
The Golden Book of Space Exploration, with paintings by Tom LaPadula, Western Publishing, 1990.
Amazing Rockets, illustrated by John Nez, Western Publishing, 1990.

Author of multimedia presentation, *Women in Science,* American Association of Physics Teachers and National Science Teachers Association, 1975. Contributor of articles and reviews to professional journals and popular magazines. Contributing editor of *Science World,* 1976-77; member of editorial board of *Physics Teacher,* 1974-77, and of review board of *American Journal of Physics,* 1977—.

SIDELIGHTS: Dinah Moche told *CA:* "I aim to make science accessible, interesting, and exciting for people of all ages. I want my books to be accurate and enjoyable. To me, science and writing are fun."

BIOGRAPHICAL/CRITICAL SOURCES:

PERIODICALS

American Journal of Physics, October, 1976.
Booklist, October 1, 1978, p. 296; June, 1, 1979, p. 1493; November 15, 1979, p. 507; April 1, 1983, p. 1036; January 15, 1984, p. 730; December 1, 1984, p. 489.
Physics Teacher, September, 1976; February, 1979.
School Library Journal, January, 1983, p. 72.
Science Books and Films, September, 1979, p. 80; May, 1980, p. 281; January, 1981, p. 132; May, 1982, p. 254; September, 1983, p. 30; January, 1988, p. 159; January, 1991, p. 16.

* * *

MOHAN, Brij 1939-

PERSONAL: Born August 9, 1939, in Mursan, India; came to the United States in 1975, naturalized citizen, 1983; son of Ram Pershad Sharma and Ram Shreedevi Sharma; married Prem Sharma; children: Anupama Sharma, Sanjaya Sharma. *Ethnicity:* "Indo-American." *Education:* Agra University B.A., 1958, M.S.W., 1960; University of Lucknow, Ph.D., 1964.

ADDRESSES: Home—1573 Leycester Dr., Baton Rouge, LA 70808. *Office*—School of Social Work, Louisiana State University, Baton Rouge, LA 70803.

CAREER: University of Lucknow, Lucknow, India, research supervisor and research scholar, 1960-64, lecturer in social work, 1964-75; University of Wisconsin—Oshkosh, academic specialist, 1975-76; Louisiana State University, Baton Rouge, associate professor, 1976-81, professor of social work, 1981—, dean of School of Social Work, 1981-86, director, doctoral program in social work.

MEMBER: International Council on Social Welfare, International Association of Schools of Social Work, International Consortium on Social Development, National Association of Social Workers, American Association of University Professors, Council on Social Work Education.

AWARDS, HONORS: Government of India University Grants Commission research scholar, 1960-63; fellow of UNESCO, 1968.

WRITINGS:

India's Social Problems, Indian International Publications, 1972.

Social Psychiatry in India, Minerva Associates, 1973.

New Horizons of Social Welfare and Policy, Schenkman (Cambridge, MA), 1985.

(Editor) *Toward Comparative Social Welfare,* Schenkman, 1985.

Denial of Existence: Essays on the Human Condition, C. C Thomas (Springfield, IL), 1987.

The Logic of Social Welfare, St. Martin's (New York City), 1988.

Glimpses of International and Comparative Social Welfare, ISFED, Inc., 1989.

Global Development: Post-Material Values and Social Praxis, Praeger (New York City), 1992.

Eclipse of Freedom: The World of Oppression, Praeger, 1993.

Democracies of Unfreedom: United States and India, Praeger, 1996.

Contributor of more than 150 articles and reviews to journals in the social sciences. Founder and editor-in-chief of *New Global Development: Journal of International and Comparative Social Welfare;* member of editorial board of *Psychology: A Journal of Human Behavior* and *Social Development Issues.*

WORK IN PROGRESS: Unification of Social Work; Echoes of Nothingness: A Phenomenological Essay on Social Reality; The Mantras of Mayhem, fiction.

SIDELIGHTS: Brij Mohan told *CA:* "I write because I *exist.* As an act of 'self-purification,' to paraphrase Sartre, writing assumes the significance of both catharsis and praxis. Aside from its therapeutic import, it helps construct the ethics of personal and social development.

"Primarily, my writings reflect the transformation of my consciousness. My first encounter with human tragedy was at my father's clinic in Mursan where I witnessed the cruelty and helplessness of poverty and misery. I grew up thinking of a system where want and deprivation would cease to thwart human aspirations. My search for truth and existence continues. The writings of Ghandi, Sharad Chandra, Nirala, Shakespeare, Firaq, Freud, Marx, Hemingway, Camus, and Sartre helped me understand the beauty and banality of the human condition.

"I don't write unless I must. The drive, however, is perennial. I wanted to unravel the dialectics of freedom in a scientific manner. The outcome is a recently completed trilogy: *Global Development: Post-Material Values and Social Praxis, Eclipse of Freedom,* and *Democracies of Unfreedom.* The work in progress includes Unification of Social Work which seeks to undergird the knowledge-based transformation of social reality. Echoes of Nothingness is a phenomenological essay on human reality. The Mantras of Mayhem is a fictional study of an interpersonal plague that devalues the meaning of the American dream.

"The meanings of truth, reality and existence facilitate the formulation of the subjects I write about. My encounter with reality—the plight of an ordinary person, my sense of freedom, the workplace conditions, alienation, and the corresponding challenges—has helped me grow as an individual in search of substance and dignity."

MOORE, Patrick (Alfred Caldwell) 1923-

PERSONAL: Born March 4, 1923, in Pinner, Middlesex, England; son of Charles (an army officer) and Gertrude (White) Moore. *Education:* Educated at private schools in England. *Politics:* Conservative. *Avocational interests:* Cricket, tennis, chess.

ADDRESSES: Home—39 West St., Selsey, West Sussex, England. *Agent*—Hilary Rubinstein, A. P. Watt, Ltd., 26-28 Bedford Row, London WC1R 4HL, England.

CAREER: Freelance writer. Regular host on British Broadcasting Corporation (BBC) television program, *The Sky at Night,* 1957—; Armagh Planetarium, Armagh, Northern Ireland, director, 1965-68. Lecturer in Europe and the United States on astronomy and related topics. *Military service:* Royal Air Force, Bomber Command, 1940-45; navigator; became first lieutenant.

MEMBER: International Astronomical Union, Royal Astronomical Society (fellow), British Astronomical Association (director of lunar section, 1965—; director of Mercury and Venus section, 1954-63; president, 1982-84), Royal Society of Arts (fellow), Children's Writers Group of London (chair, 1964-65).

AWARDS, HONORS: Lorimer Gold Medal, 1962, for services to astronomy; Goodacre Gold Medal, 1968; Officer, Order of the British Empire, 1968; Guido Horn d'Arturo Medal, Italian Astronomical Society, 1969; Amateur Astronomers' Medal, New York City, 1970; D.Sc., University of Lancaster, 1974, Hatfield Polytechnic, 1988, and University of Birmingham, 1990; Jackson-Gwilt Medal, 1978; Klumpke-Roberts Award, Astronomical Society of the Pacific, 1978; Commander of the British Empire, 1988.

WRITINGS:

SCIENCE FICTION NOVELS

The Master of the Moon, Museum Press (London), 1952.
The Island of Fear, Museum Press, 1954.
The Frozen Planet, Museum Press, 1954.
Destination Luna, Lutterworth Press (London), 1955.
Quest of the Spaceways, Muller (London), 1955.
Mission to Mars, Burke (London), 1955.
World of Mists, Muller, 1956.
The Domes of Mars, Burke, 1956.
Wheel in Space, Lutterworth Press, 1956.
The Voices of Mars, Burke, 1957.
Peril on Mars, Burke, 1958, Putnam (New York City), 1965.
Raiders on Mars, Burke, 1959.
Captives of the Moon, Burke, 1960.
Wanderer in Space, Burke, 1961.
Crater of Fear, Harvey House (New York City), 1962.
Invader from Space, Burke, 1963.
Caverns of the Moon, Burke, 1964.
Planet of Fire, World's Work (Tadsworth, England), 1969.
Spy in Space, Armada (London), 1977.
Planet of Fear, Armada, 1977.
The Moon Raiders, Armada, 1978.
Killer Comet, Armada, 1978.
The Terror Star, Armada, 1979.
The Secret of the Black Hole, Armada, 1980.

NONFICTION

Guide to the Moon, Norton (New York City), 1953, published as *Survey of the Moon,* 1963, published as *New Guide to the Moon,* 1976.
Suns, Myths, and Men, Muller, 1954, revised edition, Norton, 1969, published as *The Story of Man and the Stars,* Norton, 1955.
(With A. L. Helm) *Out into Space,* Museum Press, 1954.
The Boy's Book of Space, Burke, 1954, Roy (New York City), 1956.
The True Book about Worlds around Us, Muller, 1954, published as *The Worlds around Us,* Abelard Schuman (New York City), 1956.
A Guide to the Planets, Norton, 1954, published as *The New Guide to the Planets,* 1972, revised edition, Sidgwick and Jackson (London), 1993.
(With Hugh Percival Wilkins) *The Moon,* Macmillan (New York City), 1955.
Earth Satellite: The New Satellite Projects Explained, Eyre and Spottiswoode, 1955, published as *Earth Satellites,* Norton, 1956, revised edition, Norton, 1958.
The Planet Venus, Faber (London), 1956, Macmillan, 1957, revised edition (with Garry Hunt), Faber, 1982.
Man-Made Moons, Newman Neame (London), 1956.

(With Hugh Percival Wilkins) *How to Make and Use a Telescope,* Norton, 1956, published as *Making and Using a Telescope,* Eyre and Spottiswoode, 1956.

The True Book about the Earth, Muller, 1956.

Guide to Mars, Muller, 1956, Macmillan, 1958, revised edition, Muller, 1965.

The True Book about Earthquakes and Volcanoes, Muller, 1957.

Isaac Newton (for children), Black (London), 1957, Putnam (New York City), 1958.

Science and Fiction, Harrap (London), 1957, Folcroft Editions (Folcroft, PA), 1970.

The Amateur Astronomer, Norton, 1957, revised edition published as *Amateur Astronomy,* 1968, 11th edition published as *The Amateur Astronomer,* 1990.

The Earth, Our Home, Abelard Schuman, 1957.

Your Book of Astronomy, Faber, 1958, revised edition, 1979.

The Solar System, Methuen (London), 1958, Criterion (New York City), 1961.

The Boy's Book of Astronomy, Roy, 1958, revised edition, Burke, 1964.

The True Book about Man, Muller, 1959.

Man on the Moon, Newman Neame, 1959.

Rockets and Earth Satellites, Muller, 1959.

Astronautics, Methuen, 1960.

Star Spotter, Newman Neame, 1960.

Guide to the Stars, Norton, 1960, published as *The New Guide to the Stars,* 1975.

Stars and Space, Black, 1960.

Conquest of the Air: The Story of the Wright Brothers, Lutterworth Press, 1961.

(With Henry Brinton) *Navigation,* Methuen, 1961.

The Picture History of Astronomy, Grosset & Dunlap, 1961, published as *Astronomy,* Oldbourne (London), 1961, revised edition published as *The Story of Astronomy,* Macdonald, 1972, revised edition published as *Patrick Moore's History of Astronomy,* Macdonald, 1983.

The Stars, Weidenfeld and Nicolson (London), 1962.

(With Henry Brinton) *Exploring Maps,* Odhams Press, 1962, Hawthorn (New York City), 1967.

(With Henry Brinton) *Exploring Time,* Odhams Press, 1962.

(With Paul Murdin) *The Astronomer's Telescope,* Brockhampton Press (Leicester), 1962.

(With Francis J. Jackson) *Life in the Universe,* Norton, 1962, revised edition, Routledge & Kegan Paul (London), 1987, Norton, 1989.

The Planets, Norton, 1962.

The Observer's Book of Astronomy, Warne (London), 1962, 6th edition, 1978.

Telescopes and Observatories, Day, 1962.

Space in the Sixties, Penguin (London), 1963.

Exploring the Moon, Odhams Press, 1964.

The True Book about Roman Britain, Muller, 1964.

(With Henry Brinton) *Exploring Weather,* Odhams Press, 1964.

The Sky at Night 1-7, Eyre and Spottiswoode, 2 volumes, and British Broadcasting Corp. (London), 5 volumes, 1964-80, volume 1, Norton, 1965.

(With Francis L. Jackson) *Life on Mars,* Routledge, 1965, Norton, 1966.

(With Henry Brinton) *Exploring Other Planets,* Odhams Press, 1965, Hawthorn, 1967.

Exploring the World, Oxford University Press (London), 1966, F. Watts (New York City), 1968.

The New Look of the Universe, Norton, 1966.

Exploring the Planetarium, Odhams Press, 1966.

Legends of the Stars, Odhams Press, 1966.

Naked-Eye Astronomy, Norton, 1966.

Basic Astronomy, Oliver and Boyd (Edinburgh), 1967.

(With Henry Brinton) *Exploring Earth History,* Odhams Press, 1967.

(With Peter J. Cattermole) *The Craters of the Moon,* Norton, 1967.

The Amateur Astronomer's Glossary, Norton, 1967, published as *The A-Z of Astronomy,* Scribner, 1976, revised edition published as *Patrick Moore's A-Z of Astronomy,* Stephens, 1986, Norton, 1987.

Armagh Observatory: A History 1790-1967, Armagh Observatory (Armagh), 1967.

Exploring Rocks, Odhams Press, 1967.

Exploring the Galaxies, Odhams Press, 1968.

Exploring the Stars, Odhams Press, 1968.

Space, Lutterworth Press, 1968, Natural History Press (New York City), 1969.

The Sun, Norton, 1968.

Moon Flight Atlas, Rand McNally (Chicago), 1969, revised edition, Mitchell Beazley (London), 1970.

Astronomy and Space Research (bibliography), National Book League (London), 1969.

The Development of Astronomical Thought, Oliver and Boyd, 1969.

The Atlas of the Universe, Rand McNally, 1970, revised edition published as *The Mitchell Beazley Concise Atlas of the Universe,*

Mitchell Beazley, 1974, published as *The Concise Atlas of the Universe,* Rand McNally, 1974, published as *The New Atlas of the Universe,* Crown (New York City), 1984.

(With Henry Brinton) *Gunpowder, Treason: November 5, 1605,* Lutterworth Press, 1970.

Astronomy for O Level, Duckworth (London), 1970, published as *Astronomy for GCSE,* 1989.

Seeing Stars, Rand McNally, 1971.

Mars, the Red World, World's Work, 1971.

The Astronomy of Birr Castle, Mitchell Beazley, 1971.

Can You Speak Venusian: A Guide to Independent Thinkers, David & Charles, 1972, Norton, 1973.

(With David A. Hardy) *Challenge of the Stars,* Rand McNally, 1972, published as *The New Challenge of the Stars,* Mitchell Beazley-Sidgwick & Jackson, 1977, Rand McNally, 1978.

(With Desmond Leslie) *How Britain Won the Space Race,* Mitchell Beazley, 1972.

Stories of Science and Invention, Oxford University Press, 1972.

(With Lawrence Clarke) *How to Recognise the Stars,* Corgi (London), 1972.

The Southern Stars, Timmins (Cape Town, South Africa), 1972.

Color Star Atlas, Crown, 1973, published as *Patrick Moore's Colour Star Atlas,* Lutterworth Press, 1973.

The Starlit Sky, Timmins, 1973.

Man, the Astronomer, Priory Press (London), 1973.

(With Charles A. Cross) *Mars,* Crown, 1973.

The Comets: Visitors from Space, Reid, 1973, published as *Comets,* Scribner, 1976, published as *Guide to Comets,* Lutterworth Press, 1977.

Watchers of the Stars: The Scientific Revolution, Putnam, 1974, revised edition published as *The Great Astronomical Revolution: 1543-1687 and the Space Age Epilogue,* Albion, 1994.

(With Iain Nicolson) *Black Holes in Space,* Ocean (London), 1974, Norton, 1976.

The Astronomy Quiz Book, Carousel (London), 1974, published as *Patrick Moore's Astronomy Quiz Book,* G. Philip (London), 1987.

The Young Astronomer and His Telescope, Reid, 1974.

Let's Look at the Sky: The Planets, Volume 1, *Let's Look at the Sky: The Stars,* Volume 2, Carousel, 1975.

Legends of the Planets, Luscombe (London), 1976.

The Next Fifty Years in Space, Taplinger, 1976.

The Stars Above, Jarrold (Norwich), 1976.

(With Pete Collins) *The Astronomy of Southern Africa,* Hale (London), 1977.

(With Charles A. Cross) *The Atlas of Mercury,* Crown, 1977.

Guide to Mars (not the same as 1956 book), Lutterworth Press, 1977, Norton, 1978.

Wonder Why Book of Planets, Volume 1, *Wonder Why Book of the Earth,* Volume 2, *Wonder Why Book of Stars,* Volume 3, Transworld (London), 1977-78 (*Stars* published separately, Grosset & Dunlap, 1979).

Man's Future in Space, Wayland, 1978.

The Guinness Book of Astronomy Facts and Feats, Guinness Superlatives (London), 1979, 3rd edition published as *The Guinness Book of Astronomy,* Guinness, 1988, 4th edition, 1992.

Fun-to-Know-About Mysteries of Space (for children), Armada, 1979.

(With Clyde Tombaugh) *Out of Darkness: The Planet Pluto,* Stackpole (Harrisburg, PA), 1980.

The Pocket Guide to Astronomy, Simon & Schuster (New York City), 1980, revised edition published as *Patrick Moore's Pocket Guide to the Stars and Planets,* Mitchell Beazley, 1982.

(With Magnus Pyke) *Everyman's Scientific Facts and Feats,* Dent, 1981.

The Moon (atlas), Rand McNally, 1981.

(With Garry Hunt) *Jupiter,* Rand McNally, 1981.

William Herschel, Astronomer and Musician, P. M. E. Erwood-Herschel Society, 1981.

The Unfolding Universe, Crown, 1982.

(With Garry Hunt) *Saturn,* foreword by Archie E. Roy, Rand McNally, 1982.

What's New in Space? (for children), Carousel, 1982.

(With Garry Hunt) *The Atlas of the Solar System,* Mitchell Beazley, 1983, published as *Atlas of the Solar System,* Rand McNally, 1983.

Countdown! or, How Nigh Is the End?, Joseph-Rainbird (London), 1983.

Travellers in Space and Time, Park Lane (London), 1983, Doubleday, 1984.

The Space Shuttle Action Book (for children), illustrated by Tom Stimpson, Random House (New York City), 1983.

(With John Mason) *The Return of Halley's Comet,* Norton, 1984.

Patrick Moore's Armchair Astronomy, Norton, 1984.

(With Peter Cattermole) *The Story of the Earth,* Cambridge University Press, 1985.

Stargazing: Astronomy without a Telescope, Barron's, 1985.

(With Heather Couper) *Halley's Comet Pop-Up Book,* Crown, 1985.

How to Make the Most of Your Telescope, Longman, 1985.

The Sky at Night, foreword by Will Wyatt, Norton, 1985.

(With Iain Nicolson) *The Universe,* Macmillan, 1985.

Astronomy for the under Tens, Philip (London), 1986, published as *Astronomy for the Beginner,* Cambridge University Press, 1992.

Patrick Moore's A-Z of Astronomy, Stephens, 1986, Norton, 1987.

Astronomers' Stars, Routledge, 1986, Norton, 1989.

Exploring the Night Sky with Binoculars, Cambridge University Press, 1986, 3rd edition, 1996.

TV Astronomer: Thirty Years of "The Sky at Night," Harrap (Kent, England), 1987.

Stars and Planets, Exeter (New York City), 1988, published as *Philip's Guide to Stars and Planets,* Philip, 1993.

Space Travel for the under Tens, Philip, 1988, published as *Space Travel for the Beginner,* Cambridge University Press, 1992.

The Planet Neptune, Ellis Horwood, 1988, 2nd edition published as *The Planet Neptune: An Historical Survey before Voyager,* Wiley, 1995.

(With Garry Hunt) *Atlas of Uranus,* Cambridge University Press, 1989.

The Amateur Astronomer, Cambridge University Press, 1990.

Universe for the under Tens, Philip, 1990, published as *The Universe for the Beginner,* Cambridge University Press, 1992.

Mission to the Planets: The Illustrated Story of Man's Exploration of the Solar System, Norton, 1990.

Earth for the under Tens, Philip, 1991.

Patrick Moore's Passion for Astronomy, David & Charles, 1991.

Guide to the Night Sky, Philip, 1991.

Sir John Herschel, Explorer of the Southern Sky, William Herschel Society (Bath, England), 1992.

Fireside Astronomy: An Anecdotal Tour through the History and Lore of Astronomy, Wiley, 1992.

(With Garry Hunt) *Atlas of Neptune,* Cambridge University Press, 1994.

Philip's Atlas of the Universe, Philip, 1994, published as *Atlas of the Universe,* Rand McNally, 1994.

The Starry Sky, illustrated by Paul Doherty, Copper Beech Books (Brookfield, CT), 1995.

The Stars, illustrated by Paul Doherty, Copper Beech Books, 1995.

The Sun and Moon, illustrated by Paul Doherty, Copper Beech Books, 1995.

Comets and Shooting Stars, illustrated by Paul Doherty, Copper Beech Books, 1995.

The Planets, illustrated by Paul Doherty, Copper Beech Books, 1995.

Hard Choices: Environmentalists and the Forest, Heartland Institute (Chicago), 1995.

EDITOR

Space Exploration, Cambridge University Press, 1958.

Yearbook of Astronomy (annual), Norton, 1962—.

Practical Amateur Astronomy, Lutterworth Press, 1963, published as *A Handbook of Practical Amateur Astronomy,* Norton, 1964.

Against Hunting, Gollancz, 1965.

William R. Corliss, *Some Mysteries of the Universe,* Black, 1969.

Astronomical Telescopes and Observatories, Norton, 1973.

Modern Astronomy: Selections from The Yearbook of Astronomy, Norton, 1977.

The Beginner's Book of Astronomy, Sidgwick & Jackson, 1978.

The Astronomy Encyclopaedia, Mitchell Beazley, 1987, published in the United States as *The International Encyclopedia of Astronomy,* introduction by Leif Robinson, Orion Books (New York City), 1987.

The Observational Amateur Astronomer, Springer (London), 1995.

The Modern Amateur Astronomer, Springer, 1995.

Small Astronomical Observatories: Amateur and Professional Designs and Constructions, Springer, 1996.

TRANSLATOR

Gerard de Vaucouleurs, *The Planet Mars,* Macmillan, 1950, revised edition, Faber, 1951.

Evry L. Schatzman, *The Structure of the Universe,* Weidenfeld & Nicolson, 1968.

J. Andrade e Silva and G. Lochak, *Quanta,* Weidenfeld & Nicolson, 1969.

Jean Emile Charon, *Cosmology,* Weidenfeld & Nicolson, 1970.

E. M. Antoniadi, *The Planet Mercury,* two volumes, Reid, 1974-75.

OTHER

Perseus and Andromeda (play; music by Moore), produced in Shoreham, Sussex, 1974.

Theseus (play; music by Moore), produced in 1982.

SIDELIGHTS: Patrick Moore is a prolific author of books for young readers on astronomy and space travel. Since 1957 he has also hosted the British Broadcasting Corporation (BBC) television series *The Sky at Night,* a science program about astronomy. Moore's interest in space travel has also led him to write several science fiction novels for children.

Moore's interest in astronomy began early; he joined the British Astronomical Association at the age of eleven, the youngest member in the group's history. At the age of thirteen Moore published his first paper, a study of craters located in the Mare Crisium area of the moon. After serving in the Royal Air Force during the Second World War, Moore was offered the chance to write a nonfiction book about the moon. *Guide to the Moon* was such a success that the publishers asked for further astronomy titles. "I had intended," Moore explains in his essay for *Something About the Author Autobiography Series (SAAS),* "to go to university as soon as I could, and take my degree in the usual way, but I never had time."

Moore's nonfiction books have been critically praised for their clear explanations of scientific principles. Speaking of *Astronomers' Stars*—which tells the stories of certain significant stars and the astronomers who discovered them—a critic for *Publishers Weekly* states that for "those who read this thoroughly engaging book, the night sky will never be the same." *The Starry Sky,* an overview of the primary objects visible in the night sky, "is well-sequenced and entertaining," writes Dennis Ashton in the *Times Educational Supplement.* Ashton concludes that *The Starry Sky* "provides youngsters with a factual, visually memorable introduction to space."

While his nonfiction books range over a variety of scientific subjects, Moore's science fiction novels usually feature young heroes who become associated with a scientific group engaged in space research. Due to circumstances, the protagonist is entrusted with a special mission during which he displays a resourcefulness and courage which gain the respect of the scientists who employ him. "The appeal of this storyline is fairly obvious," argues Gary Coughlan in the *St. James Guide to Science Fiction Writers.* "It displays successful adolescent involvement in an adult world, though a greatly simplified and idealised one. A display of truth, integrity, and courage is sufficient to achieve one's desire, and there are no authority conflicts to establish problems between the adolescent and his elders, since the authority displayed by the scientists stems only from their great knowledge of a given situation, and the motivation for accepting their authority is made obvious: death in space if the mission fails. In this respect, Moore's novels reflect an updating of traditional tales of this type, and in that context, a fairly successful updating."

Moore's prolific writing brought him to the attention of the BBC in 1957 when the network wanted to develop a monthly program on astronomy. *The Sky at Night,* hosted by Moore since its debut on April 26, 1957, has covered such varied topics as eclipses around the world, the appearance of Halley's Comet, fringe believers in such things as flying saucers and a flat Earth, and the manned space programs of England, the United States, and the Soviet Union.

Speaking of his career as a writer and television host, Moore writes in *SAAS:* "I was lucky; I came on the scene when there were not many people writing about astronomy, and my entry into television was another piece of sheer good fortune. I simply happened to be 'available,' and I was presenting programmes at the time when the space age started, in October 1957, with the launch of Russia's first artificial satellite, *Sputnik I.* That is why *The Sky at Night* has lasted for so many years; it is not due to any skill on my part, and I am not conceited enough to think otherwise."

Moore points out that his career has brought him into contact with many of the greats in aviation and space history. "I rather feel that I span the ages," he writes in *SAAS*. "I am proud to know Neil Armstrong, as well as almost all the other moon men. I knew Yuri Gagarin, the Russian who made the very first spaceflight way back in 1961. And when I was myself learning how to fly, in 1940, I actually met Orville Wright, who made the pioneer flight in a heavier-than-air machine at the turn of the century."

In 1984 Moore had Minor Planet No. 2602 named in his honor by Dr. E. Bowell of the Lowell Observatory.

BIOGRAPHICAL/CRITICAL SOURCES:

BOOKS

St. James Guide to Science Fiction Writers, 4th edition, St. James Press (Detroit), 1996.
Something about the Author Autobiography Series, Volume 8, Gale (Detroit), 1989.

PERIODICALS

Astronomy, March, 1990, p. 91; February, 1994, p. 96; August, 1995, p. 84.
Bloomsbury Review, November, 1988, p. 29.
Canadian Geographic, May-June, 1996, p. 87.
Christian Science Monitor, December 8, 1987, p. 20.
Earth Science, fall, 1989, p. 33.
Library Journal, July, 1989, p. 103; June 1, 1992, p. 166.
Los Angeles Times Book Review, November 29, 1987, p. 10.
Nature, November 16, 1995, p. 320.
Publishers Weekly, June 16, 1989, p. 62; June 22, 1990, p. 42.
School Library Journal, January, 1989, p. 108; April, 1990, p. 154; July, 1995, p. 73.
Sky and Telescope, February, 1991, p. 164; June, 1995, p. 55; April, 1996, p. 57.
Times Educational Supplement, March 10, 1995, p. R2.
Tribune Books (Chicago), December 2, 1990, p. 16.
Village Voice Literary Supplement, December, 1985, p. 30.
Washington Post Book World, December 6, 1987, p. 10.
Whole Earth Review, spring, 1991, p. 72.
World and I, April, 1989, p. 259.*

MOORE, Thomas (William) 1940-

PERSONAL: Born October 8, 1940, in Detroit, MI; son of Thomas Benjamin (a plumbing instructor) and Mary (a homemaker; maiden name, Owens) Moore. *Education:* De Paul University, B.A., 1967; University of Michigan, M.A., 1969; University of Windsor, M.A., 1972; Syracuse University, Ph.D., 1975. *Avocational interests:* Woodworking, playing the piano.

ADDRESSES: Home and office—P.O. Box 291, Shutesbury, MA 01072.

CAREER: Glassboro State College, Glassboro, NJ, assistant professor of psychology, 1975-76; Southern Methodist University, Dallas, TX, assistant professor of religious studies, 1976-83; practicing psychotherapist, West Stockbridge and Amherst, MA, 1985-92; writer and lecturer, 1992—. Founder and director of the Institute for the Study of Imagination; fellow of Dallas Institute of Humanities and Culture.

AWARDS, HONORS: Syracuse University fellow, 1972; research grant from Glassboro State College, 1976; grant from Van Waveren Foundation, 1990.

WRITINGS:

The Planets Within, Bucknell University Press (Cranbury, NJ), 1982.
Rituals of the Imagination, Pegasus Foundation, 1983.
(Editor and author of introduction) James Hillman, *A Blue Fire: Selected Writings,* Harper (New York City), 1989.
Dark Eros: The Imagination of Sadism, Spring Publications (Woodstock, CT), 1990, revised edition, 1994.
Care of the Soul: A Guide for Cultivating Depth and Sacredness in Everyday Life, HarperCollins (New York City), 1992.
Soul Mates: Honoring the Mysteries of Love and Relationships, HarperCollins, 1993.
Meditations: On the Monk Who Dwells in Daily Life, HarperCollins, 1994.
The Re-Enchantment of Everyday Life, HarperCollins, 1996.

Also author of *A Permian Symphony,* "for two narrators and a large symphony orchestra," music by John David Earnest. Contributor of numerous articles concerning Jungian and archetypal psychology to books and periodicals.

WORK IN PROGRESS: Philodendron, a novel.

SIDELIGHTS: Thomas Moore is a scholar, theologian, and therapist whose books focus on the lack of spirituality in modern life, and ways to revive it. Michael S. Kimmel, a reviewer for the *Los Angeles Times Book Review,* finds that although Moore's philosophy is rooted in conservative theology, the author also "rides the crest of the New Age's second wave," tapping into a profound desire for meaning in life. Moore's work is much more grounded than most in the genre, according to Kimmel, who observes: "There's nothing glamorous or seductive in his books, no channelers with crystals counting up past lives, no mythopoetic male drummers off bonding in the woods, no Birkenstock-footed purveyors of herbal elixirs as conduits to cosmic consciousness. Moore promises less—much less. His books may tap into that same hunger for meaning, but his table is set with much simpler fare. His recipe for soul food offers contemporary seekers a turn inward, a groping toward something deeper and more authentic, a way to ground experience in ways less tangible and material, and yet deeply fulfilling and satisfying."

Moore's first popular success was *Care of the Soul: A Guide for Cultivating Depth and Sacredness in Everyday Life,* published in 1992. It was on bestseller lists for many months and sold more than a quarter million hardcover copies. William A. Davis of the *Boston Globe* comments that *Care of the Soul* is "about self-discovery and self-acceptance rather than techniques for self-improvement and realization of one's potential, the gist of most pop-psych books." In this volume, Moore urges readers to embrace a "soulful" acceptance of life as it is, rather than pursue a doomed quest for perfection. Davis notes: "Like Zen, Moore says, soulfulness recognizes that life is full of foolishness and absurdities. 'It's not inspiring—it's about not being able to find all the answers'. . . . Caring for the soul usually involves striving less and listening more, Moore says. 'You have to stop trying to understand everything and stop trying to make everything better through heroic efforts.'"

In his next book, *Soul Mates: Honoring the Mysteries of Love and Relationships,* Moore concentrates on a soulful approach to personal relationships. Then, in *Meditations: On the Monk Who Dwells in Daily Life,* he draws on the many years he spent in a Catholic monastery before deciding to embrace secular life instead of the priesthood. According to a *Publishers Weekly* reviewer, *Meditations* "makes a simple point: The monastic life offers lessons that, once learned, will enhance the spiritual dimension of daily life." The text is comprised of brief prose selections, referred to by the author as "seeds," each of which illuminates a valuable aspect of monasticism.

In 1996, Moore brought forth a sequel to his bestseller *Care of the Soul. The Re-Enchantment of Everyday Life* focuses on how to experience spiritual growth amid the mundane details of everyday life. "This important book will dare many to believe that life really is full of enchantment," according to a *Publishers Weekly* reviewer, "if only we can go beyond our habitual literal-mindedness and narcissism to experiment with that broader state of attunement that Moore calls soul."

Commenting on Moore's entire body of work, Kimmel muses that the author "answers a difficult call, to minister to the loss of soul in contemporary life . . . and to do it in a style that is immediately accessible for mass readers, and instantly usable in everyday life. . . . Drawing on Jungian archetypes, ancient mythologies and folksy philosophy, Moore's books are prose-poems of compassion and tenderness. His soothingly graceful prose is a balm for egos battered by hostile takeovers, anguished divorces and do-it-to-them-before-they-do-it-to you public philosophy."

BIOGRAPHICAL/CRITICAL SOURCES:

PERIODICALS

Booklist, December 1, 1993, p. 659; November 15, 1994, p. 559; January 1, 1996, p. 868.

Boston Globe, May 3, 1992, p. B42; July 13, 1992, p. 38.

Boston Globe Magazine, March 6, 1994, p. 9; April 21, 1996, p. 18.

Christian Century, June 1, 1994, p. 584.

Commonweal, August 14, 1992, p. 35; September 9, 1994, p. 20.

Entertainment Weekly, July 8, 1994, p. 49.

Library Journal, October 15, 1993, p. 111; March 1, 1994, p. 138, p. 1; January, 1995, p. 109; June 15, 1995, p. 111.

Los Angeles Times Book Review, January 17, 1993, p. 14; March 27, 1994, p. 1.

New York Times Book Review, March 11, 1990; August 16, 1992, p. 25.

New York Times Magazine, April 23, 1995, p. 44.

Psychology Today, May-June, 1993, p. 28; March-April, 1994, p. 26.

Publishers Weekly, April 6, 1992, p. 42; December 13, 1993, p. 57; November 14, 1994, p. 34; April 8, 1996, p. 60.

U.S. Catholic, August, 1993, p. 48; April, 1994, p. 48.

Utne Reader, January, 1993, p. 120.*

* * *

MORA, Pat(ricia) 1942-

PERSONAL: Born January 19, 1942, in El Paso, TX; daughter of Raul Antonio (an optician) and Estella (a homemaker; maiden name, Delgado) Mora; married William H. Burnside Jr., July 27, 1963 (divorced, 1981); married Vernon Lee Scarborough (an archaeologist), May 25, 1984; children: (first marriage) William, Elizabeth, Cecilia. *Education:* Texas Western College, B.A., 1963; University of Texas at El Paso, M.A., 1967. *Politics:* Democrat.

ADDRESSES: Agent—3423 Oakview Place, Cincinnati, OH 45209.

CAREER: El Paso Independent School District, El Paso, TX, teacher, 1963-66; El Paso Community College, part-time instructor in English and communications, 1971-78; University of Texas at El Paso, part-time lecturer in English, 1979-81, assistant to vice president of academic affairs, 1981-88, director of University Museum and assistant to president, 1988-89; writer and speaker, 1989—; gives presentations and poetry readings nationally and internationally. W. K. Kellogg Foundation, consultant, 1990-91. Member of Ohio Arts Council panel, 1990; member of advisory committee for Kellogg National Fellowship program, 1991-94. Host of radio show, *Voices: The Mexican-American in Perspective,* on National Public Radio-affiliate KTEP, 1983-84.

MEMBER: International Reading Association, Poetry Society of America, Academy of American Poets, Society of Children's Book Writers, National Council of Teachers of English, Texas Institute of Letters, National Association of Bilingual Educators.

AWARDS, HONORS: Creative writing award, National Association for Chicano Studies, 1983; *New America: Women Artists and Writers of the Southwest* poetry award, 1984; Harvey L. Johnson Book Award, Southwest Council of Latin American Studies, 1984; Southwest Book awards, Border Regional Library, 1985, for *Chants,* 1987, for *Borders,* and 1994, for *A Birthday Basket for Tia;* Kellogg National fellowship, 1986-89; Leader in Education Award, El Paso Women's Employment and Education, 1987; Chicano/Hispanic Faculty and Professional Staff Association Award, University of Texas at El Paso, 1987, for outstanding contribution to the advancement of Hispanics; named to *El Paso Herald-Post* Writers Hall of Fame, 1988; National Endowment for the Arts fellowship, 1994.

WRITINGS:

POETRY

Chants, Arte Publico (Houston), 1984.

Borders, Arte Publico, 1986.

Communion, Arte Publico, 1991.

Agua Santa/Holy Water, Beacon Press (Boston), 1995.

Work represented in anthologies, including *New Worlds of Literature,* Norton (New York City), and *Woman of Her Word: Hispanic Women Write.*

FOR CHILDREN

A Birthday Basket for Tia, illustrated by Cecily Lang, Macmillan (New York City), 1992.

Listen to the Desert: Oye al desierto, Clarion (New York City), 1994.

The Desert Is My Mother/El desierto es mi madre, with art by Daniel Lechon, Pinata Books (Houston), 1994.

Agua, Agua, Agua, illustrated by Jose Ortega, GoodYearBooks, 1994.

Pablo's Tree, illustrated by Lang, Macmillan, 1994.

(With Charles Ramirez Berg) *The Gift of the Poinsettia,* Pinata Books, 1995.

Confetti (poems), illustrated by Enrique Sanchez, Lee & Low (New York City), 1995.

The Race of Toad and Deer, illustrated by Maya Itzna Brooks, Orchard Books, 1995.

Uno, dos, tres/One, Two Three, illustrated by Barbara Lavallee, Clarion, 1996.

Tomas and the Library Lady, illustrated by Raul Colon, Knopf (New York City), 1997.

This Big Sky (poetry), Scholastic, in press.

The Rainbow Tulip (picture book), Viking, in press.

OTHER

Nepantla: Essays from the Land in the Middle (nonfiction), University of New Mexico Press (Albuquerque), 1993.

House of Houses (memoir), Beacon Press (Boston), 1997.

Contributor of articles and poems to periodicals, including *The Best American Poetry, 1996, Daughters of the Fifth Sun, Prairie Schooner, Latina: Women's Voices from the Borderland, Calyx,* and *Ms.*

WORK IN PROGRESS: Aunt Carmen's Book of Practical Saints, a poetry collection.

SIDELIGHTS: Pat Mora is acknowledged as a leader in the contemporary movement to recognize and express the many voices of the Hispanic population—and especially those of Latinas—in the United States. Her collections of poems for children and adults reflect her experiences as an American woman of Mexican heritage. By portraying her native traditions as well as the physical surroundings of the Southwest desert, Mora gives voice both to herself and her people. As a poet and an author of children's books, she is essential to the movement to understand and uphold Mexican American culture. The author herself comments in a *Horn Book* essay: "I take pride in being a Hispanic writer. I will continue to write and to struggle to say what no other writer can say in quite the same way."

Born in El Paso, Texas, Mora was raised by her parents—Estella (Delgado) and Raul Antonio Mora, an ophthalmologist—as well as by her grandmother and her mother's half-sister. She received her bachelor's degree in 1963 from Texas Western College and married soon after graduation. Earning a master's degree from the University of Texas—El Paso in 1967, Mora held teaching positions at the secondary, post-secondary, and college levels; however, after her divorce in 1981, she began to devote herself more seriously to writing. Her poetry gained rapid acclaim, winning the Creative Writing Award from the National Association for Chicano Studies in 1983, and both the *New America: Women Artists and Writers of the Southwest* Poetry Award and the Harvey L. Johnson Book Award in 1984. Mora continues to write, lecture and give readings of her work. She is also collaborating with others to have April 30th designated as Dia de los Ninos: Dia de los Libros, a national celebration of children and bilingual literacy.

Mora's first two collection of poems, *Chants* and *Borders,* are steeped in the aura of the Southwest, celebrating that region's desert landscape. Throughout these works she explores the theme of identity, especially that of woman and her connection with the various forms of the "earth mother"—the *curandera,* or healer, and the *abuelita,* the nurturing grandmother. In an essay for *The Desert Is No Lady: Southwestern Landscapes in Women's Writing and Art,* Tey Diana Rebolledo notes that in Mora's poetry collections, "Nature and the land . . . become allies of the woman hero. Keeping her in touch with her self, they are a kind of talisman that enables her to make her way through the alienations of male society, and also of the received female traditions of a limited society, whether represented by the history of Spain or Mexico."

In her third collection, *Communion,* Mora departs her beloved Southwest and relates impressions gained from her subsequent travels. She finds herself experiencing daily life in Cuba ("The Mystery"), overwhelmed by the aura of the big city ("New York: 2 a.m."), and washing at the Yamuna River in central India ("The Taj Mahal"). In these poems women's identities remain the prevalent concern as Mora explores the implicit questions: "Who am I? Who are we?" In doing so, however, she consciously avoids didacticism. "I try not to have a message when I start out," Mora insists in *This Is about Vision: Interviews with Southwestern Writers,* writing on the subject of message poetry. "I really do. If I have a message then I say to myself, 'That's great, but that's not a poem.' I like to begin with an idea, a line, an image and see where it goes. But I am stubborn enough that a lot of my deep feelings are obviously going to come in, because of the way I see the world."

In addition to verse, Mora has written several prose commentaries that have been collected and published in *Nepantla: Essays from the Land in the Middle*. These, too, address themes of what it means to be a woman and a Chicana; they synthesize the experiences of a culture attempting to grasp its identity and make its voice heard. In a *Nation* review of *Nepantla,* Ray Gonzalez observes that the work is important "because it allows a Chicana writer to present strong opinions, dreams and commitments—all of them backed by a tough voice of poetic experience." *Bloomsbury Review* contributor Mary Motian-Meadows likewise praises *Nepantla,* noting of Mora: "Her experiences as an American woman of Mexican descent are integrated into a rich mosaic of insights that include the best of both worlds."

Because the elements of the Southwest are so prevalent in her work, Mora has been labeled a "regional" writer. Although she has expanded her view to encompass women's experience in other parts of the world, the author agrees that her Southwest emphasis is very important. As many scholars point out, the experiences of the Chicana have been virtually ignored in American society; writers such as Mora empower Hispanics—especially Hispanic women—through a celebration of the native traditions which lie at the heart of their cultural identity. "For a variety of complex reasons," Mora once told *CA,* "anthologized American literature does not reflect the ethnic diversity of the United States. I write, in part, because Hispanic perspectives need to be part of our literary heritage; I want to be part of that validation process. I also write because I am fascinated by the pleasure and power of words."

That "validation process" has also been a strong incentive for Mora to produce children's literature and juvenile poetry for and about Hispanic Americans. Through a series of bilingual books and stories that feature Hispanic protagonists, she has sought to establish pride in heritage for young Chicanos. "There is particular pleasure for me in poetry, there's just no doubt about that, but I see children's books as very close to that," the author explains in *This Is about Vision.* "I have very strong feelings that Chicano kids need good children's books, well illustrated, from big publishing houses, and that is something I would really like to work at."

As for the muse that drives her, Mora relates in *This Is about Vision:* "I think one of my big reasons for writing poetry is to help people feel less lonely; that's what poetry did for me. . . . I was able to read women writers and feel less lonely, and so any time my poetry does that for somebody, that is probably my definition of success."

BIOGRAPHICAL/CRITICAL SOURCES:

BOOKS

Balassi, William, John F. Crawford, and Annie O. Eysturoy, editors, *This Is about Vision: Interviews with Southwestern Writers,* University of New Mexico Press, 1990, pp. 129-139.

Hispanic Literature Criticism, Volume 2, Gale (Detroit, MI), 1994, pp. 844-854.

Norwood, Vera and Janice Monk, editors, *The Desert Is No Lady: Southwestern Landscapes in Women's Writing and Art,* Yale University Press (New Haven, CT), 1987, pp. 96-124.

Notable Hispanic American Women, Gale, 1993, pp. 280-282.

PERIODICALS

Bloomsbury Review, September/October, 1993, p. 5.

Horn Book, July/August, 1990, pp. 436-437; November/December, 1994, pp. 723-724.

Nation, June 7, 1993, pp. 772-774.

Publishers Weekly, December 5, 1994, p. 76.

San Jose Studies, spring, 1989, pp. 29-40.

School Library Journal, October, 1994, p. 112.

* * *

MORGAN, Fidelis 1952-
(Morgan Benedict, a joint pseudonym)

PERSONAL: Born August 8, 1952, in Salisbury Plain, England; daughter of Peter Horswill (a dentist) and Fidelis (a painter; maiden name, Morgan) Morgan. *Ethnicity:* "Irish/English." *Education:* University of Birmingham, B.A. (with honors), 1973.

ADDRESSES: Home—London, England; fax: 0181-673-0283. *Agent*—(Scripts and plays) ICM, 76 Oxford St., London WC1, England; (books) Brian Stone, Aitken Stone, 29 Fernshaw Rd., London SW10 0TG, England.

CAREER: Professional actress and writer. Has performed at Citizen's Theatre, Glasgow, Scotland, 1983-88, with the Paines Plough Tour, 1987, at the Royal National Theatre, on television, and elsewhere. Has lectured and given workshops at many universities and drama schools, including University of Birmingham, University of Bristol, University of Leicester, University of Liverpool, University of Glasgow, University of Strathclyde, and University of London.

AWARDS, HONORS: Named Most Promising Playwright by *Financial Times,* 1985, for *Pamela;* commission from Liverpool Institute of Performing Arts, with Jill Benedict, to write a large-cast play.

WRITINGS:

The Female Wits, Virago (New York City), 1981.
Wedlock/Deadlock (play), first produced in London at King's Head Theatre, 1984.
A Woman of No Character, Faber (London), 1986.
Bluff Your Way in Theatre (humor), Ravette, 1986.
(With Giles Havergal) *Pamela* (dramatic adaptation of Samuel Richardson's novel), Amber Lane, 1987.
The Well-Known Troublemaker, Faber, 1988.
A Misogynist's Source Book, J. Cape (London), 1989.
(Editor with Patrick Lyons) *Restoration Women's Comedies,* J. M. Dent (London), 1989.
(Editor) *The Female Tatler,* J. M. Dent, 1992.
The Years Between, Virago, 1994.
My Dark Rosaleen (novel), Heinemann (London), 1994, Mandarin (New York City), 1995.
Wicked, Virago, 1995.

Also author of unpublished plays, including *Lady Audley's Secret, Madonna and Child, Trilby,* and *The Lucky Chance.* Coauthor with Jill Benedict of unpublished film scripts *Scapegoat* (under the joint pseudonym Morgan Benedict) and *The Diamond Necklace Affair.* Contributor of articles and reviews to periodicals, including *Daily Mail* and *The Observer.*

WORK IN PROGRESS: Coauthor with Jill Benedict: *Pettylambkin,* a thriller (under the joint pseudonym Morgan Benedict); *The Queen's Necklace,* a historical novel; and *Fragments from the Life of Marie Antoinette,* a play.

SIDELIGHTS: Fidelis Morgan told *CA:* "Motivation: I love research and sculpting a story. Also when I've finished writing most things I like to reshape them and take them on the road. In the last year I have toured platform shows of *The Female Wits, The Female Tatler,* and *Wicked.*

"Influence: Boredom drives me to work. Can't bear a day off.

"Process: Total immersion and thinking about the project night and day, then sit down and write in a long spurt.

"Inspiration: Patricia Highsmith, Wilkie Collins, and the people in history who have become myths."

BIOGRAPHICAL/CRITICAL SOURCES:

PERIODICALS

Times Literary Supplement, March 20, 1987.

* * *

MOSKOWITZ, Robert (A.) 1946-

PERSONAL: Born October 27, 1946, in Newark, NJ; son of George (a certified public accountant) and Carolyn (Handler) Moskowitz; married Francine Levy (a hospital administrator), June 30, 1968; children: Jake, Alex. *Education:* University of Pennsylvania, B.A., 1968; graduate study at New School for Social Research, 1969-71.

ADDRESSES: Home—4741 Larkwood Avenue, Woodland Hills, CA 91364; fax: 818-224-4343. *Office*—Crown Communications Group, P.O. Box 6375, Woodland Hills, CA 91365. *E-mail*—robertam@ix.netcom.com. *Agent*—Brenda Feigen Associates, 10158 Hollow Glen Circle, Bel Air, CA 90077; fax: 310-271-0606.

CAREER: Prentice-Hall, Inc., Englewood Cliffs, NJ, management editor, 1968-70; consultant in private practice, 1970—. Developer of the Personal Productivity Audit, a computer-scored paper-and-pencil instrument used to evaluate white collar employee productivity, 1978. Has appeared as commentator on CNBC Television and elsewhere, 1992—.

MEMBER: PEN, Authors Guild, Independent Writers of Southern California.

AWARDS, HONORS: Silver medal, New York Television and Film Festival, 1979, for film *Time Management for Supervisors.*

WRITINGS:

Time Management for Supervisors (screenplay), released by Education for Management, 1979.
How to Organize Your Work and Your Life, Doubleday (New York City), 1981, revised edition, 1993.
(With wife Francine Moskowitz) *Parenting Your Aging Parents,* Key Publications (Woodland Hills, CA), 1991.
Out on Your Own—Everything You Need to Know before, during, and after Leaving the Nest, Key Publications, 1993.
The Small Business Computer Book: A Guide in Plain English, Upstart Publishing (Dover, NH), 1993.

AUDIO TAPES

Personal Selling, with workbook, American Management Association (New York City), 1974.
Total Time Management, with workbook, American Management Association, 1975.
Basic Business Psychology, with workbook, American Management Association, 1977.
How to Avoid Personal Obsolescence, with workbook, American Management Association, 1977.
Assertiveness for Career and Personal Success, with workbook, American Management Association, 1977.
Creative Problem Solving, with workbook, American Management Association, 1978.
How to Evaluate Performance and Assess Potential, with workbook, American Management Association, 1979.
Real Estate Investors Toolbox, Hume Financial Publishers (Atlanta, GA), 1985.
Financial Planning When Your Time Is Limited, Hume Financial Publishers, 1988.

OTHER

Contributor of articles to newspapers and national magazines, including *Capitalist Reporter, Computer Decisions, ComputerWorld, Free Enterprise, Internet World, Investor's Business Daily, Journal of Accountancy, Los Angeles Times, PC Times, Popular Computing, Software News, Sylvia Porter's Personal Finance,* and *Your Money.* Contributor to books, including *Marketing Handbook, Volume 2: Marketing Management,* edited by Edwin E. Bobrow, Dow Jones Irwin, 1985. Editor and publisher of newsletters, including *High Profit Investing,* 1983-87; *Tele-News,* 1993—; and *Practical Supervision,* 1994—. Writer, director, and producer of industrial films and videos. Script supervisor and coordinating producer for 10-part television adaptation of his book *Your Aging Parents,* Public Broadcasting System, 1995. Author of other cassettes and workbooks for American Management Association, including *Successful Delegation* and *Using Managerial Authority.*

SIDELIGHTS: Robert Moskowitz once told *CA:* "I write to share what I learn. My titles reflect my personal odyssey. I try to set myself up for experiences that I can translate into published works. For instance, I restored a one-hundred-year-old home and wrote about it in a magazine series. My personal struggle is to write deeper and deeper experiences—to move away from simple behavior and add more sense of feeling, motivation, and meaning to my material."

* * *

MOSLEY, Walter 1952-

PERSONAL: Born 1952 in Los Angeles, CA; married Joy Kellman (a dancer and choreographer). *Education:* Attended Goddard College; received degree from Johnson State College; attended City College of the City University of New York, beginning 1985.

ADDRESSES: *Home*—New York, NY. *Agent*—c/o W. W. Norton, 500 Fifth Ave., New York, NY 10110.

CAREER: Formerly a computer programmer; now a writer.

AWARDS, HONORS: Shamus Award, Private Eye Writers of America, and Edgar Award nomination, best new mystery, Mystery Writers of America, both 1990, both for *Devil in a Blue Dress.*

WRITINGS:

Devil in a Blue Dress, Norton (New York City), 1990.
A Red Death, Norton, 1991.
White Butterfly, Norton, 1992.
Black Betty, Norton, 1994.
R. L.'s Dream, Norton, 1995.
Gone Fishin', Black Classic Press, 1996.
Always Outnumbered, Always Outgunned: The Socrates Fortlow Stories, Norton, 1997.

ADAPTATIONS: Devil in a Blue Dress was released as a feature film starring Denzel Washington in 1995.

WORK IN PROGRESS: More titles in the "Easy Rawlins" series.

SIDELIGHTS: "A good private-eye novel . . . is not really about violence; it's about the fallibility of people, about the grotesqueries of modern life, and not least it is about one man, the detective, who defines the moral order." This statement, from *Washington Post* reviewer Arthur Krystal, captures the essence of Walter Mosley's widely praised detective stories. The author's novels are the start of an ongoing series of hard-boiled detective tales featuring Ezekiel "Easy" Rawlins, who reluctantly gets drawn into investigations that lead him through the tough streets of black Los Angeles. There Easy operates in a kind of gray area, where moral and ethical certainties are hard to decipher. "The Rawlins novels . . . are most remarkable for the ways they transform our expectations of the hard-boiled mystery, taking familiar territory—the gritty urban landscape of post-World War II Los Angeles—and turning it inside out," writes David L. Ulin in the *Los Angeles Times Book Review.* "Mosley's L.A. is not that of Raymond Chandler, where tycoons and hoodlums cross paths on gambling boats anchored off the Santa Monica coast. Rather, it is a sprawl of black neighborhoods largely hidden from the history books, a shadow community within the larger city, where a unique, street-smart justice prevails."

Ironically, Mosley had ambitions other than writing early in his career. Born in Los Angeles, he made his way to the East Coast, where he began his professional life as a computer programmer. Then one day in New York, he told D. J. R. Bruckner of the *New York Times,* "I wrote out a sentence about people on a back porch in Louisiana. I don't know where it came from. I liked it. It spoke to me." From that moment, he defined himself as a writer and fulfilled the dream of many would-be authors bound to an office: he quit to devote his full attention to his craft. He continues to write the way he began: "First there is a sentence. Then characters start coming in."

In 1990, readers first met Mosley's Rawlins—and his short-tempered sidekick, Mouse—in *Devil in a Blue Dress.* The novel is set in 1948, when many black World War II veterans, like Easy, found jobs in the area's booming aircraft industry. When Easy loses his job, he grows concerned about the source of his next mortgage payment—until he is introduced to a wealthy white man who offers him a way to make some quick cash: he will pay Easy one hundred dollars to locate a beautiful blonde woman named Daphne Monet, who is known to frequent jazz clubs in the area. Easy takes the job but soon realizes that the task is far more dangerous than he imagined.

Mosley followed *Devil in a Blue Dress* with *A Red Death,* set five years later. In the sequel, Easy has used stolen money to buy a couple of apartment buildings and is enjoying the life of a property owner. But he gets into a jam with the Internal Revenue Service, and his only way out is to cooperate with the FBI by spying on a union organizer suspected of being a Communist. Again, he gets mired in complications as he tries to make sense out of a dark underworld of extortion and murder.

Mosley's third novel, *White Butterfly,* fast-forwards to 1956. Easy is married and has a new baby, and his businesses are going well. When three young black women—"good-time girls"—are brutally slain, the crimes are barely reported. But when a white student at the University of California, Los Angeles, meets a similar death, the serial killings finally make headlines. In the meantime Easy is hired by the police to help investigate. His inquiries take him through bars, rib joints, and flophouses until he makes the startling discovery that the latest victim, the daughter of a city official, was a stripper, known by her fans as the "White Butterfly." In fact, nothing in the novel is as it appears, but Easy sorts through the corruption and deception to solve the mystery—at a terrible price to his personal life.

Observer correspondent Nicci Gerrard comments: "In Mosley's fictional world, there's no such things as innocence. There's hope (which Mosley calls naivete), and anger (which Mosley calls sense). There's law (white law), cops (the real criminals) and justice (which exists only in a heaven he doesn't believe in). There's love (which he calls heartache), and trying (failure), and then, of course, there's trouble."

By the time Mosley's next Rawlins novel, *Black Betty,* was published in 1994, the author had earned an important endorsement. President Bill Clinton let it be known that Mosley was one of his favorite writers and the Rawlins books among his favorite reading. Not surprisingly, *Black Betty* sold 100,000 copies in hard cover and helped to earn Mosley a multi-book contract for further novels in the series. As the action in *Black Betty* commences, "Easy" Rawlins is well into mid-life and the 1960s are in full swing. Once again in need of extra money—this time to help support two street children he has taken in—Rawlins agrees to search for a woman he knew back in Houston named Black Betty. The story, to quote *Chicago Tribune Books* reviewer Paul Levine "is a tale of mendacity and violence told with style and flair from the perspective of the black experience—or rather Mosley's unique version of it." Levine calls the book "a sizzling addition to the color-coded series" and adds that the author ". . . captures a time and place with dead-on perfect detail and evocative language."

Mosley left his popular detective behind temporarily in 1996 and published his first non-genre novel, *R. L.'s Dream.* Set in New York City in the late 1980s, the novel explores an unconventional friendship struck in hard times and offers meditations on blues music, especially the unparalleled work of Robert "R. L." Johnson. The story unfolds when Atwater "Soupspoon" Wise, dying of cancer and evicted from his skid row apartment for nonpayment of rent, is taken in by a young white neighbor named Kiki Waters, who has troubles of her own. According to Ulin, *R. L.'s Dream* "is less about life in the modern city than about the interplay between past and present, the way memory and reality intersect. Thus, although Soupspoon and Kiki may share living quarters and a certain fundamental bond, both are essentially lost in their own heads, trying to come to terms with personal history in whatever way they can."

Mosley's first mainstream novel has found many fans among the critics. *Entertainment Weekly* contributor Tom De Haven calls the book a "beautiful little masterpiece, and one probably best read while listening, very late at night, to *Robert Johnson: The Complete Recordings.*" In the *San Francisco Review of Books,* Paula L. Woods noted that the novel is "a mesmerizing and redemptive tale of friendship, love, and forgiveness . . . without doubt, the author's finest achievement to date, a rich literary gumbo with blues-tinged rhythms that make it a joy to read and a book to remember." A *Publishers Weekly* correspondent observes that in *R. L.'s Dream* Mosley's work "achieves a constant level of dark poetry" and concludes that the book is "a deeply moving creation of two extraordinary people who achieve a powerful humanity where it would seem almost impossible it should exist."

According to biographical notes appearing in *Devil in a Blue Dress,* Mosley's successful novels incorporate narrative skills that he learned from his father and from "thousands of his 'cousins'" who, like Easy, had moved to Los Angeles in the years after the war and who passed the time by telling stories. As a result of this oral heritage, Mosley presents "a black world of slang and code words that haven't been delivered with such authority since Chester Himes created his Harlem detective stories," assessed Herbert Mitgang in the *New York Times.* Commenting on Mosley's strength as a writer, *Chicago Tribune Books* reviewer Gary Dretzka surmised that the author demonstrates "his ability to tell an interesting period story in an entertaining and suspenseful manner and to create dead-on believable characters whose mouths are filled with snappy dialogue." Clarence Petersen of the *Chicago Tribune* praised "the rhythm of his prose" and the "startling originality of his imagery," presented with an "unselfconscious ease." Beyond capturing both the music and the nuances of his characters' language, Mosley uses his stories to explore issues of race and class. Commented Digby Diehl in the *Los Angeles Times Book Review,* "The insightful scenes of black life . . . provide a sort of social history that doesn't exist in other detective fiction." The critic added, "He re-creates the era convincingly, with all of its racial tensions, evoking the uneasy combination of freedom and disillusion in the post-war black community."

Mosley told *Los Angeles Times* writer Don Snowden that he visualizes about nine books in the Rawlins series and plans to bring the narrative up to the 1980s. His aim is less to create a memorable gumshoe than it is to explore the ethical dilemmas that the character constantly faces. He summed up his achievement for D. J. R. Bruckner of the *New York Times:* "Mysteries, stories about crime, about detectives, are the ones that really ask the existentialist questions such as 'How do I act in an imperfect world when I want to be perfect?' I'm not really into clues and that sort of thing, although I do put them in my stories. I like the moral questions."

BIOGRAPHICAL/CRITICAL SOURCES:

BOOKS

Mosley, Walter, *Devil in a Blue Dress,* Norton, 1990.

PERIODICALS

Armchair Detective, spring, 1991; winter, 1992.
Bloomsbury Review, November, 1990.
Boston Book Review, October 1, 1995.
Chicago Tribune, July 1, 1990; June 19, 1991; July 21, 1991; June 28, 1992; August 24, 1992, p. 1.
Entertainment Weekly, August 18, 1995, pp. 47-48.
Esquire, June, 1994, p. 42.
Essence, January, 1991.
Globe and Mail (Toronto), July 18, 1992.
Hungry Mind Review, October 1, 1995.
Los Angeles Times, May 5, 1992.
Los Angeles Times Book Review, July 29, 1990; July 12, 1992; June 5, 1994, p. 3; August 6, 1995, pp. 3, 8.
Nation, September 18, 1995, pp. 290-91.
Newsweek, July 9, 1990.
New York, September 3, 1990.
New Yorker, September 17, 1990.
New York Times, August 15, 1990; September 4, 1990; August 7, 1991; August 7, 1992.
New York Times Book Review, September 6, 1992; June 5, 1994, p. 13; August 13, 1995, pp. 11-12.
Observer (London), October 23, 1994, p. 20.
People, September 7, 1992, p. 105.
Publishers Weekly, May 29, 1995, p. 65.
Quarterly Black Review, October 1, 1995.
San Francisco Review of Books, February, 1991; September/October, 1995, pp. 12-13.
Times (London), May 2, 1991.
Tribune Books (Chicago), June 16, 1991; June 28, 1992; June 26, 1994, p. 3.
USA Weekend, June 11, 1993.
Vanity Fair, February, 1993, p. 46.
Village Voice, September 18, 1990.
Wall Street Journal, July 24, 1991.
Washington Post, June 22, 1990.
Washington Post Book World, August 16, 1992; August 20, 1995, p. 7.
West Coast Review of Books, May, 1990.

* * *

MUELLER, Virginia 1924-

PERSONAL: Born March 22, 1924, in Sheboygan, WI; daughter of Arno and Cora (Hoogstra) Kernen; married Walter A. Mueller (a teacher), July 20, 1946; children: Linda (Mrs. Jerome Medlin), Christine (Mrs. Reed Simon), Walter David, David John. *Education:* Attended Rhinelander School of Art (University of Wisconsin Extension); additional study through Institute of Children's Literature. *Religion:* Protestant. *Avocational interests:* Collecting antiques, visiting historical sites, reading, classical piano.

ADDRESSES: Home—N4359W CTH A, Plymouth, WI 53073.

CAREER: Freelance writer, 1975—.

WRITINGS:

JUVENILES

Noises and Sounds, Columbia Broadcasting System (New York City), 1968.
The King's Invitation: Matthew 2:1-14 for Children, illustrated by Jim Roberts, Concordia (St. Louis, MO), 1968.
The Secret Journey: Matthew 2:13-23 for Children, illustrated by Betty Wind, Concordia, 1968.
What Is Faith?, edited by Judith Sparks, Standard Publishing (Cincinnati, OH), 1969.
The Silly Skyscraper, Concordia, 1970.

Who Is Your Neighbor?, edited by Judith Sparks, Standard Publishing, 1973.
Clem, the Clumsy Camel, Concordia, 1974.
Monster and the Baby, illustrated by Lynn Munsinger, Whitman, Albert (Niles, IL), 1985, Puffin Books (New York City), 1988.
A Playhouse for Monster, illustrated by Lynn Munsinger, Whitman, Albert, 1985, Puffin Books, 1988.
A Halloween Mask for Monster, illustrated by Lynn Munsinger, Whitman, Albert, 1986, Puffin Books, 1988.
Monster Can't Sleep, illustrated by Lynn Munsinger, Whitman, Albert, 1986, Puffin Books, 1988.
Jacob's Ladder, Concordia, 1990.
Monster Goes to School, illustrated by Lynn Munsinger, Whitman, Albert, 1991.
Monster's Birthday Hiccups, illustrated by Lynn Munsinger, Whitman, Albert, 1991.
Dinosaur Shares a Book, Houghton (Boston, MA), 1991.
In the Morning, illustrated by Diane Jaquith, Houghton, 1991.
A Great Day for Llama, Houghton, 1995.

WITH DONNA LUGG PAPE

Bible Activities for Kids, Bethany Fellowship, Books 1 and 2, illustrated by Carol Karle, 1980, Books 3 and 4, 1981, Books 5 and 6, 1982.
Think Pink Solve and Search Puzzles, Xerox Publishing, 1980.
Texas Puzzle Book, Eakin Publications (Austin, TX), 1981.
Arkansas Puzzle Book, Rose Publishing (Little Rock, AK), 1983.
Louisiana Puzzle Book, Eakin Publications, 1983.
Wisconsin Puzzle Book, Bess Press (Honolulu, HI), 1984.
Tennessee Puzzle Book, Winston-Derek (Nashville, TN), 1984.
Hawaii Puzzle Book, Bess Press, 1984.
California Trivia Puzzle Book, Bess Press, 1985.
Vermont Puzzle Book, Countryman Press (Woodstock, VT), 1987.
(With Carol Karle) *Florida Puzzle Book*, Pineapple Press (Englewood, FL), 1996.

OTHER

Also author, with Donna Lugg Pape, of *Country Music Puzzle Book*. Contributor to *Humpty Dumpty, Turtle*, and juvenile religious magazines. Mueller's works have translated into French, Japanese, Portuguese, Spanish, and Welsh.

WORK IN PROGRESS: Jenny's Bargain, an Americana story that deals with overcoming prejudice.

BIOGRAPHICAL/CRITICAL SOURCES:

PERIODICALS

Booklist, September 1, 1986.
Publishers Weekly, August 22, 1986.
School Library Journal, December, 1985, December, 1986.

* * *

MYERS, J(ohn) William 1919-

PERSONAL: Born December 1, 1919, in Huntington, WV; son of Condon William (an engraver and tool and die maker) and Mary Olive (Fox) Myers; married Nancy Hortense Paxton, July 6, 1942 (divorced); married Helen File Fleming, November 28, 1981; children: (first marriage) Martha Ann, Lenora Ellen, Nancy Louise, John Charles. *Education:* Ohio Wesleyan University, B.A., 1951; Bowling Green State University, M.A., 1952. *Politics:* Liberal Democrat. *Avocational interests:* Cooking, baking, making wines.

ADDRESSES: Home—105 Fulton St., Lyons, OH 43533. *Office*—Humanist Education Press, Inc., 109 North Adrian St., Lyons, OH 43533.

CAREER: Ordained a minister in Methodist Church, 1948; minister, Ohio Annual Conference of the Methodist Church, 1944-54; transferred to the Unitarian Church, 1956; minister, Horton Unitarian Universalist Church, Horton, MI; minister, Jersey Universalist Church, 1974-78; minister, Lyons Unitarian Universality Church, Lyons, OH, 1978-81. Journeyman letterpress and lithographic printer, editor, publisher, book designer, and freelance writer, 1954—. Lecturer on poetry and religion.

MEMBER: American Academy of Poets, Poetry Society of America, Catholic Poetry Society of America, American Translators Association, Ohio Poetry Society, Poetry Society of Virginia.

AWARDS, HONORS: Honorary degree from Kletzing College (now Vennard College), 1952; nomination for Pulitzer Prize in Poetry, 1964, for *Green Are My Words;* London Literary Circle award, 1967, for poem "Prayer for a House I Never Had"; citation for achievement in poetry, Ohio House of Representatives, 1993.

WRITINGS:

POETRY

Evening Exercises, Humanist Education Press, 1956.
These Mown Dandelions, Ohio Poetry Review Press, 1959.
My Mind's Poor Birds, Elgeuera Press, 1963.
Alley to an Island, New Merrymount Press, 1963.
Green Are My Words, New Merrymount Press, 1964.
Sun Bands and Other Poems, Georgetown Press (San Francisco, CA), 1964.
Anatomy of a Feeling, New Merrymount Press, 1966.
Variations on a Nightingale, New Merrymount Press, 1968.
A Greene County Ballad, New Merrymount Press, 1972.
The Sky Is Forever, New Merrymount Press, 1974.
Something Will Be Mine, New Merrymount Press, 1976.
Annotations 1951, New Merrymount Press, 1977.
Stones of Promise, New Merrymount Press, 1977.
(Translator of Friedrich Nietzsche's text to the Frederick Delius choral work) *A Mass of Life,* New Merrymount Press, 1980.
Homage to Dionysius: Selected Poems of Friedrich W. Nietzsche in Translation, New Merrymount Press, 1982.
Juliet and God (poetic play), New Merrymount Press, 1983.
Apprentice to the Muse: First Poems, New Merrymount Press, 1986.
Painful Knowledge: Homage to Schopenhaur, Poems after the Aphorisms, New Merrymount Press, 1987.
Amphion in Appalachia, New Merrymount Press, 1987.
Rediscovered Country, New Merrymount Press, 1988.
Episode Pt. Marion, New Merrymount Press, 1995.
Stones of Realization (collected poems), New Merrymount Press, 1996.

OTHER

Also translator from the German of poetry of Johann W. Von Goethe, Friedrich Hoelderlin, Joseph von Eichendorff, Friedrich Rueckert, Edward Moerike, Reiner Kunze, Gottfried Keller, Richard Dehmel, Stefan Anton George, Hermann Hesse, Franz Werfel, and Karl Krolow. Reviewer for *Chicago Sun-Times.* Contributor of poems and bibliographies to over sixty periodicals, including *Bitterroot, Twentieth-Century Literature, Descant, New York Herald Tribune, Cardinal Poetry Quarterly, South and West,* and *Laurel Review.* Editor, *Mid-Lakes Humanist* (American Humanist Association publication), 1956-59, *Ohio Poetry Review,* 1957-59, *Anthropos, the Quarterly of Humanist Poetry,* 1958-59, Ohio Poetry Society *Bulletin,* 1958-59, and *Poetry Dial,* 1959-61; poetry editor, *Humanist,* 1961-62; advisory and contributing editor, *Dasein: The Quarterly Review,* 1962—.

WORK IN PROGRESS: Opus Guyandotte, a collection of poems; *A Long Time Learning,* an autobiography; *White Rocks: A Poetic Legend.*

SIDELIGHTS: J. William Myers told *CA:* "As I approach what are doubtless the last decades of my life there is a perspective—to chase a metaphor is the enduring thing. So I desire, down deep, to fly above this time of cheap ethics, unbelievable illiteracy and a fear of man's demise, to live in the hope something of mine will sing beyond the ruin. This means I have purposed to make use of the symbol knowing it to be a symbol and never to be mistaken for reality."

BIOGRAPHICAL/CRITICAL SOURCES:

PERIODICALS

Adrian Telegram, February 9, 1980.
Columbus Dispatch, May 22, 1969.
Newark Advocate, May 1, 1978.
Observer-Reporter (Washington, PA), June 23, 1969.
Record-Outlook (McDonald, PA), November 18, 1971.

* * *

NAHA, Ed 1950-
(D. B. Drumm, Michael McGann)

PERSONAL: Born June 10, 1950, in Elizabeth, NJ; son of George Harry and Christina Agnes (McGann) Naha. *Education:* Newark State College, B.A., 1972. *Politics:* "Ranting liberal." *Avocational interests:* "Reading, drinking, rowdy behavior in general."

ADDRESSES: Home—Santa Barbara, CA 93105. *Agent*—Harvey Klinger Agency, 301 W. 53rd St., New York, NY 10019.

CAREER: CBS Records, New York City, manager of East Coast publicity, 1972-75, associate producer of East Coast artists and repertory, 1975-77; *Future Life,* New York City, coeditor, 1977-80; writer.

WRITINGS:

Horrors-From Screen to Scream: An Encyclopedic Guide to the Greatest Horror and Fantasy Films of All Time, Avon (New York City), 1975.
The Rock Encyclopedia, Grosset, 1978.
(Editor) *1941: The Official Movie Magazine,* O'Quinn Studios (New York City), 1979.
(Editor) *The Beatles Forever,* O'Quinn Studios, 1980, published as *John Lennon and the Beatles Forever,* Tower Books (New York City), 1980.
The Science Fictionary: An A-Z Guide to the World of SF Authors, Films, and TV Shows, Seaview (El Cerrito, CA), 1980.
(With Eric Seidman) *Wanted, by the Intergalactic Security Bureau: 20 Full-Color Posters of the Most Wanted Alien Criminals,* Bantam (New York City), 1980.
The Paradise Plot (futuristic mystery), Bantam, 1980.
The Films of Roger Corman: Brilliance on a Budget, Arco (New York City), 1982.
The Suicide Plague (futuristic mystery), Bantam, 1982.
The Making of "Dune," Berkley (New York City), 1984.
The Con Game, Dell (New York City), 1986.
Robocop (novelization of screenplay), Dell, 1987.
Breakdown, Dell, 1988.
Dead-Bang: A Novel (novelization of screenplay by Robert Foster), Berkley, 1989.
Ghostbusters II: A Novel (novelization of screenplay), Dell, 1989.
On the Edge, Pocket Books (New York City), 1989.
Orphans, Dell, 1989.
Razzle-Dazzle, Pocket Books, 1990.
Robocop II (novelization of screenplay), Jove (New York City), 1990.
Cracking Up, Pocket Books, 1991.

NOVELS; UNDER PSEUDONYM D. B. DRUMM

First, You Fight, Dell, 1984.
The Road Ghost, Dell, 1985.
The Stalking Time, Dell, 1986.
Hell on Earth, Dell, 1986.
The Children's Crusade, Dell, 1987.
The Prey, Dell, 1987.
Ghost Dancers, Dell, 1987.

NOVELS; UNDER PSEUDONYM MICHAEL McGANN

The Marauders, Jove, 1989.
Blood Kin, Jove, 1989.
Liar's Dice, Jove, 1990.
Convoy Strike, Jove, 1990.
The Ghost Warriors, Jove, 1990.
Blood and Fire, Jove, 1991.
Fortress of Death, Jove, 1991.

SCREENPLAYS

Camp Bottomout, New World Pictures, 1984.
The Wizard Wars, New World Pictures, 1984.
Troll, Empire Pictures, 1986.
Dolls, Empire Pictures, 1987.
(With Tom Schulman) *Honey, I Shrunk the Kids,* Disney, 1989.
Omega Doom, Filmwerks, 1996.
The Ransom of Red Chief, Hallmark/ABC-TV, 1997.

Also author of screenplay *Thanksgiving.*

OTHER

Author of columns "Screen Scoops," *New York Post,* 1980—, "Nahallywood," *Heavy Metal,* 1983—, and "L.A. Offbeat," *Starlog,* 1983—. Contributor to various magazines and newspapers.

WORK IN PROGRESS: "I'm toiling on a mystery novel taking aim at the current melding of religion and politics as well as a TV series set in medieval Japan."

SIDELIGHTS: Best known for his ability to merge science fiction and mystery in crime stories set in the future, Ed Naha's work covers many genres: science fiction, mystery, horror, detective fiction, film novelizations, and nonfiction. For example, *The Paradise Plot* introduces an unlikely hero named Harry Porter who must solve a string of murders aboard an orbiting space colony. Porter and other Naha characters exhibit the behavior typical of modern detective fiction heroes: they smoke, drink, cast a jaundiced eye on police procedures, and have strong opinions about everything from the villains they pursue to rock and roll. *Armchair Detective* reviewer Bernard A. Drew cites Naha for his "skillful and humorous way with descriptions, characterizations, and interactions."

Naha's work within the film industry includes novelizations of such popular movies as *Robocop* and *Ghostbusters II,* as well as nonfiction titles like *The Films of Roger Corman: Brilliance on a Budget* and *The Making of "Dune."* In a *Library Journal* review of *The Films of Roger Corman,* William H. Lyles described the work as "a balanced, objective view of an artist who ought to be taken seriously." A *S.F. Chronicle* review of *The Making of Dune* likewise noted that Naha "has done considerable writing related to the film industry before, and it is evident that he knows his subject." The author's forays into screenplay include the highly successful *Honey, I Shrunk the Kids.*

Naha told *CA:* "I have always suspected my mother of taking strange drugs prior to my birth. This would explain my wanting to work long hours and spew out many words for very little money. It is a gratifying existence, in a sado-masochistic sense. I would recommend writing full time to all those interested in designer hair shirts.

"On a slightly more serious note—a somber F-sharp—I think I have always tried, in both my fiction and nonfiction, to entertain and enlighten readers in an accessible manner. I've never felt that a 'fun' read necessarily meant a lightweight one. I've also always enjoyed being sneaky and flaunting trends whenever possible without people ever noticing it.

"Since science fiction and mystery tomes often boast determined, two-fisted and goal-oriented heroes, I made my futuristic sleuth an ordinary guy who gets stuck in extraordinary circumstances and who dearly desires to extricate himself from said circumstances with all his limbs intact. So much for goals.

"In terms of film, since the current trend seems to lean towards 'R'-rated sex and/or violence flicks, I decided to try to fashion my scripts in the 'PG' territory. I managed to write and sell three in a year, two comedies and a fantasy-adventure.

"I'm not sure what all of this proves except, perhaps, it serves as an illustration that you don't have to be a convicted murderer-friend of Norman Mailer to pay your rent via writing . . . although, let's face it, it probably helps.

"Basically, I'd like to construct a literary career along the same lines as Quentin Tarantino's cinematic one. You know, convince the public that blood, gore, cliched dialogue and comic-book behavior is intellectual; do some bad acting, roll my eyes on talk shows and then, put my name on a series of rock and roll compact discs that has absolutely nothing to do with my life's work. Either that or make a sandwich."

BIOGRAPHICAL/CRITICAL SOURCES:

BOOKS

St. James Guide to Science Fiction Writers, fourth edition, St. James (Detroit), 1996.

PERIODICALS

Armchair Detective, spring, 1990, pp. 237-38.
Baltimore News American, June 6, 1982.
Booklist, Volume 78, number 15, p. 996.
Creem, May, 1982.
Kirkus Reviews, November 1, 1984, p. 1043.
Library Journal, March 1, 1976, p. 737; October 15, 1981, p. 2047; November/December, 1984, p. 2294.
Los Angeles Herald Examiner, December 5, 1982.
New York Daily News, June 14, 1981; November 21, 1982.
Publishers Weekly, November 16, 1984, p. 63.
Quill & Quire, April, 1981.
S.F. Chronicle, June, 1985, p. 42.
Science Fiction Review, summer, 1985, p. 34.
Seattle Post-Intelligencer, May 18, 1982.
Village Voice, December 15, 1975.

Voice of Youth Advocates, June, 1981, p. 44; June, 1985, p. 147; April, 1988, p. 40; October, 1989, pp. 214-15.

Washington Post Book World, December 28, 1980.

* * *

NASKE, Claus-M(ichael) 1935-

PERSONAL: Born December 18, 1935, in Stettin, Germany; son of Alfred (an army officer) and Kaethe (Salomon) Naske; married Dinah Ariss (a teacher), May 20, 1960; children: Natalia-Michelle Nau-geak, Nathaniel-Michael Noah. *Ethnicity:* "German, of east and west Slavic descent." *Education:* University of Alaska, B.A., 1961; University of Michigan, M.A., 1964; Washington State University, Ph.D., 1970. *Politics:* Independent.

ADDRESSES: Office—Department of History, University of Alaska Fairbanks, Fairbanks, Alaska 99775. *E-mail*—ffcmn@alaska.aurora.edu.

CAREER: Farm laborer in Palmer, Alaska, 1954-56; surveyor in Palmer and Fairbanks, Alaska, 1957-61, and Monterey, CA, 1962; Bureau of Indian Affairs, Barrow, Alaska, teacher, 1964-65; Juneau-Douglas Community College, Juneau, Alaska, instructor in history and political science, 1965-67; University of Alaska Fairbanks, 1969—, began as assistant professor, professor of history, 1981—, head of department of history, 1986-90, executive director of University of Alaska Press. Member of board of directors of Pacific Northwest History Conference, 1970—. Consultant to Bureau of Land Management, Alaska Department of Transportation and Public Facilities, and Alaska Department of Law. *Military service:* U.S. Army Reserve.

MEMBER: Association for Canadian Studies in the United States, Canadian Historical Association, Western History Association, Alaska Historical Society, Tanana-Yukon Historical Society (past president).

WRITINGS:

An Interpretive History of Alaskan Statehood, Alaska Northwest Publishing (Edmonds, WA), 1973, second revised edition published as *A History of Alaskan Statehood,* University Press of America (Lanham, MD), 1985.

(With Herman Slotnick) *Alaska: A History of the Forty-Ninth State,* Eerdmans (Grand Rapids, MI), 1979, second edition, Oklahoma State University Press (Stillwater), 1987.

(With William R. Hunt and Lael Morgan) *Alaska,* Abrams (New York City), 1979.

Edward Lewis "Bob" Bartlett of Alaska: A Life in Politics, University of Alaska Press (Fairbanks), 1980.

(With Ludwig J. Rowinski) *Anchorage: A Pictorial History,* Donning (Norfolk, VA), 1981.

(With Rowinski) *Fairbanks: A Pictorial History,* Donning, 1981, second revised edition, 1995.

(With Rowinski) *Alaska: A Pictorial History,* Donning, 1983.

(With Hans Blohm) *Alaska,* Oxford University Press (New York City), 1984.

Paving Alaska's Trails: The Work of the Alaskan Road Commission, University Press of America, 1986.

Ernest Gruening: Alaska's Territorial Governor, 1939-1953, in press.

Contributor to *Proceedings* of the 27th and 29th Alaska Science Conference, 1976 and 1978. Also contributor to numerous periodicals, including *American Historical Review, Pacific Northwest Quarterly, Alaska Journal, Choice,Journal of the West, Military Affairs, Pacific Historian, Western Historical Quarterly, B.C. Quarterly,* and *Western Legal History.*

SIDELIGHTS: Claus-M. Naske told *CA:* "I am damn glad I made it to America and was able to leave Europe behind. American society is fascinating—I wake up each morning, realizing with great joy that I am doing what I want to do, and getting paid for it on top of it all. What a life!"

Waske more recently told *CA:* "Love to write—how can one be a historian and not write? Still write by hand on legal pads. Use computer for letters, memos. Enjoy life to the fullest."

* * *

NUWER, Hank

See NUWER, Henry

NUWER, Henry 1946-
(Hank Nuwer)

PERSONAL: Born August 19, 1946, in Buffalo, NY; son of Henry Robert (a truckdriver) and Teresa (a maid; maiden name, Lysiak) Nuwer; married Alice M. Cerniglia, December 28, 1968 (divorced, 1980); married N. Jenine Howard (an editor), April 9, 1982; children: (first marriage) Henry Christian; (second marriage) Adam Robert Drew. *Education:* Buffalo State College, B.S., 1968; New Mexico Highlands University, M.A., 1971.

ADDRESSES: Home—1706 Taft Place, #A, Richmond, VA, 23233. *Office*—Journalism Program, University of Richmond, VA 23173.

CAREER: Freelance writer, 1969—. Professor at Clemson University, 1982-83, Ball State University, and University of Richmond, 1995-97; editor-in-chief of *Arts Indiana Magazine,* 1985-89. Consultant, NBC television movie, *Moment of Truth: Broken Pledges,* 1994.

WRITINGS:

UNDER NAME HANK NUWER

(With William Boyles) *The Deadliest Profession* (novel), Playboy Press, 1980.
(With Boyles) *A Killing Trade* (novel), Playboy Press, 1981.
(With Boyles) *The Wild Ride* (novel), Playboy Press, 1981.
(With Boyles) *Blood Mountain* (novel), Playboy Press, 1982.
(With Carole Shaw) *Come Out, Come Out, Wherever You Are* (nonfiction), R & R Press, 1982.
Strategies of the Great Football Coaches, F. Watts (New York City), 1987.
Strategies of the Great Baseball Managers, F. Watts, 1988.
Rendezvousing with Contemporary Authors, Idaho State University Press, 1988.
Recruiting in Sports, F. Watts, 1989.
Steroids, F. Watts, 1990.
Broken Pledges: The Deadly Rite of Hazing, Longstreet Press (Atlanta, GA), 1990.
Sports Scandals, F. Watts, 1994.
How to Write Like an Expert about Anything, Writers Digest (Cincinnati, OH), 1995.

Also editor with Robert G. Waite of *Rendezvous at the Ezra Pound Centennial Conference,* 1986. Contributor to periodicals, including *Saturday Review, Harper's, Inside Sports, Nation, Outside, Success,* and *Sport.*

WORK IN PROGRESS: "I am collecting my essays into one volume and am completing a second book detailing the strained relationship between college students and administrators. The second project is tentatively titled *The Uneasy Alliance,* and it is under contract to Indiana University Press. I am also working on a historical project examining women's education and another examining the lives of American women of Japanese descent who for one reason or another remained as unwelcome aliens in Japan during World War Two."

SIDELIGHTS: Hank Nuwer told *CA:* "My first books and magazine articles were humorous, frivolous, satirical and adventurous pieces that reflected both the times in the seventies and early eighties and my own thrill-seeking tendencies. I wrote about playing minor-league baseball on assignment, accompanying a part-time bounty hunter on his appointed rounds, visiting herders in remote sheep camps out West, and flying the unfriendly skies of Idaho with a rescue pilot. From 1983 to 1990, I began thinking of myself more as a journalist and less and less as an entertainer, writing mainly about health, fitness, and sports. My work after 1990 tends to be serious and spiritual: personal essays, a book examining deaths resulting from fraternity initiations, a history of women's education, and investigative journalism.

"Buffalo State College teacher and author Fraser Drew has been my lifelong mentor. Since 1982 my wife Jenine, an editor, has not only served as a trusted editor but also as a friend and counselor. In the seventies and eighties I heeded advice from authors Jesse Stuart, Gian-Carlo Bertelli, Robert Laxalt, Ron Rash, Mark Steadman, Richard Etulain, Jim Harrison, and David Mamet. An editor at Longstreet Press named Jane Hill, and Poynter Institute for Media Studies writing coaches Roy Clark and Donald Fry, helped me discipline my writing style. In the mid-nineties Indiana author Susan Neville, a regular contributor to *Arts Indiana Magazine* which I then edited, inspired me to write personal essays.

"The major career satisfaction I've had as a journalist is that my *Broken Pledges* has helped illuminate the problem of hazing to help eliminate deaths by hazing. As a teacher I feel fulfilled because some of my own students have become authors and editors."

BIOGRAPHICAL/CRITICAL SOURCES:

PERIODICALS

Boston Globe, October 2, 1990.
Chicago Tribune, March 22, 1994.
Denver Post Contemporary Magazine, November 9, 1980.
Los Angeles Times Book Review, April 16, 1981.
New York Times, January 27, 1993; December 21, 1994.
Wall Street Journal, November 18, 1994.

P-Q

PADGETT, Ron 1942-
(Harlan Dangerfield)

PERSONAL: Born June 17, 1942, in Tulsa, OK; married; children: one son. *Ethnicity:* "Caucasian." *Education:* Columbia University, A.B., 1964.

ADDRESSES: Home—342 East 13th St., New York, NY 10003.

CAREER: St. Mark's-in-the-Bowery, New York City, poetry workshop instructor, 1968-69; poet in various New York City Poets in the Schools programs, 1969-76; writer in the community, South Carolina Arts Commission, 1976-78; St. Mark's Poetry Project, New York City, director, 1978-81; Teachers and Writers Collaborative, New York City, director of publications, 1982—. Cofounder, Full Court Press (publishers), New York City, 1973.

AWARDS, HONORS: Boar's Head Poetry Prize and George E. Woodberry Award, Columbia University, both 1964; Gotham Book Mart Avant-Garde Poetry Prize, 1964; recipient of numerous fellowships and grants, including Fulbright fellowship, 1965-66, and Guggenheim fellowship, 1986.

WRITINGS:

POETRY COLLECTIONS

In Advance of the Broken Arm, "C" Press, 1964.
(With Ted Berrigan and Joe Brainard) *Some Things,* "C" Press, 1964.
2/2 Stories for Andy Warhol, "C" Press, 1965.
Sky, Goliards Press (Bellingham, WA), 1966.
(With Berrigan) *Bean Spasms,* Kulcher Press, 1967.
Tone Arm, Once Press, 1967.
(With Brainard) *100,000 Fleeing Hilda,* Boke, 1967.
(With Tom Clark) *Bun,* Angel Hair Books, 1968.
Great Balls of Fire, Holt (New York City), 1969.
(With Jim Dine) *The Adventures of Mr. and Mrs. Jim and Ron,* Cape Gouliard Press, 1970.
Sweet Pea, Aloes, 1971.
Poetry Collection, Strange Faeces Press, 1971.
(With Brainard) *Sufferin' Succotash* [bound with *Kiss My Ass* by Michael Brownstein], Adventures in Poetry, 1971.
(With Berrigan and Clark) *Back in Boston Again,* Telegraph, 1972.
(With Dine) *Oo La La,* Petersburg Press (New York City), 1973.
Crazy Compositions, Big Sky (Southampton, NY), 1974.
(With others) *The World of Leon,* Big Sky, 1974.
Toujours l'amour, SUN (New York City), 1976.
Arrive by Pullman, Generations (Paris), 1978.
Tulsa Kid, Z Press (Calais, VT), 1979.
Triangles in the Afternoon, SUN, 1980.
How to Be a Woodpecker, Toothpaste Press (West Branch, IA), 1983.
(With Katz) *Light as Air,* Pace Editions, 1988.
New & Selected Poems, David Godine (Boston), 1995.

EDITOR

(With Berrigan) Tom Veitch, *Literary Days,* "C" Press, 1964.

(With David Shapiro) *An Anthology of New York Poets,* Random House (New York City), 1970.
(With Bill Zavatsky) *The Whole Word Catalogue 2,* Teachers and Writers (New York City)/ McGraw (New York City), 1976.
(With Nancy Larson Shapiro) *The Point: Where Teaching and Writing Intersect,* Teachers and Writers, 1983.
The Complete Poems of Edwin Denby, Random House, 1986.
The Teachers and Writers Handbook of Poetic Forms, Teachers and Writers, 1987.

OTHER

(With Berrigan) *Seventeen: Collected Plays,* "C" Press, 1965.
(Translator) Guillaume Apollinaire, *The Poet Assassinated,* Holt, 1968.
(Translator) Pierre Cabanne, *Dialogues with Marcel Duchamp,* Viking (New York City), 1970.
(Adaptor with Johnny Stanton) Henry Caray, *Chrononhotonothologos,* Boke, 1971.
Antlers in the Treetops (novel), Coach House Press (Chicago), 1973.
(Translator with Zavatsky) Valery Larbaud, *The Poems of A. O. Barnabooth,* Mushinsha (Tokyo), 1974.
(Translator) Cendrars, *Kodak,* Adventures in Poetry, 1976.
(Translator) Apollinaire, *The Poet Assassinated and Other Stories,* North Point Press (Berkeley, CA), 1984.
(With Raymond Roussel) *Among the Blacks* (memoir), Avenue B, 1988.
(Translator) Blaise Cendrars, *Complete Poems,* University of California Press (Berkeley), 1992.
Blood Work: Selected Prose, Bamberger Books, 1993.
Ted: A Personal Memoir of Ted Berrigan, The Figures, 1993.

Contributor, sometimes under pseudonym Harlan Dangerfield, to periodicals.

SIDELIGHTS: "Ron Padgett is the grand old *young* man of the New York School of poets," asserts *Village Voice* contributor Aram Saroyan, a school which, as Gilbert Sorrentino describes it in the *New York Times Book Review,* "relies on highly sophisticated, urban statement, seemingly artless when it is most artificial, and ingenuous when it is most shrewd." The critic explains: "The poems defy criticism by proffering the reader a brilliantly polished but false naivete. This is consciously done." Padgett's poems in particular "defy explanation and specification, appearing incoherent on the surface," Caroline G. Bokinsky notes in a *Dictionary of Literary Biography* essay, "but once the surface is penetrated, the private world of the poet emerges. Ron Padgett brilliantly transforms mundane experience into the subject of the poetry," Bokinsky continues, "through subtle humor, wordplay, and a childlike fascination with the world."

In *Triangles in the Afternoon* and *Tulsa Kid,* for example, Padgett's poems deal with such commonplace things as Cheez-Its, chocolate milk, and kitchen matches, as *New York Times Book Review* contributor Donna Brook observes. The critic believes that "for both what he discusses and how he goes about discussing it . . . , Ron Padgett can be called a champion of American language and experience." "Padgett has an ability to play games with his free-flowing imagination," claims Bokinsky, "allowing him to grab an image and take off with it. . . . Padgett seeks in the mundane something that will excite the imagination: banal, trite, everyday words and phrases of language can be exciting," the critic adds. "I feel good about Padgett's work," Brook states, "the way it wakes, shakes, and charms, and I carry it around even when I don't coherently defend it to myself." As Bokinsky summarizes, the poet "never ceases from exploring the mystery of the commonplace while giving pleasure as he illuminates the trivial."

Praising Padgett's 1995 collection of poems, *New & Selected Poems, Voice Literary Supplement* contributor Karen Volkman writes: "This *New & Selected* is a fine sampling of a restless, hilarious, and haunting lyric intelligence, a 'phony' whose variable voices form a rare and raucous orchestration: the real thing."

BIOGRAPHICAL/CRITICAL SOURCES:

BOOKS

Dictionary of Literary Biography, Volume 5: *American Poets since World War II,* Gale (Detroit), 1980.
Kostelanetz, Richard, editor, *The New American Arts,* Horizon, 1966.

PERIODICALS

American Book Review, March/April, 1981.
New York Times Book Review, March 31, 1968; September 19, 1976.
Village Voice, December 7, 1967; January 24, 1977.
Voice Literary Supplement, September, 1996, p. 21.

* * *

PARKER, Barry (Richard) 1935-

PERSONAL: Born April 13, 1935, in Penticton, British Columbia, Canada; immigrated to the United States, 1961, naturalized citizen, 1980; son of Gladstone (a garage owner) and Olive (Young) Parker; married Gloria Haberstock, 1962; children: David. *Education:* University of British Columbia, B.A. (with honors), 1959, M.Sc., 1961; Utah State University, Ph.D., 1967.

ADDRESSES: *Home*—750 Fairway Dr., Pocatello, Idaho 83201. *Office*—Department of Physics, Idaho State University, Pocatello, Idaho 83209. *E-mail*—parker@physics.isu.edu.

CAREER: Weber State College, Ogden, UT, lecturer, 1963-65, assistant professor of physics, 1965-66; Idaho State University, Pocatello, associate professor, 1967-75, professor of physics, 1975—.

MEMBER: American Physical Society, Sigma Xi (president, 1974-75), Sigma Pi Sigma.

AWARDS, HONORS: Science writing prize, McDonald Observatory, 1980, for the article "The Gravitational Lens."

WRITINGS:

Concepts of the Cosmos: An Introduction to Astronomy, Harcourt (New York City), 1983.
Einstein's Dream: The Search for a Unified Theory of the Universe, Plenum (New York City), 1986.
Search for a Supertheory: From Atoms to Superstrings, Plenum, 1987.
Creation: The Story of the Origin and Evolution of the Universe, Plenum, 1988.
Invisible Matter and the Fate of the Universe, Plenum, 1989.
Colliding Galaxies, Plenum, 1990.
Cosmic Time Travel, Plenum, 1991.
The Vindication of the Big Bang, Plenum, 1992.
Stairway to the Stars, Plenum, 1994.
Chaos in the Cosmos, Plenum, 1996.

Contributor to books, including *Astronomy: Selected Readings,* edited by Michael Seeds, Benjamin-Cummings (Redwood City, CA), 1980, and *Encyclopaedia Britannica.* Contributor to scientific journals and popular magazines, including *Astronomy, Star and Sky, Fly Fisherman, Fishing World, High Country,* and *Angler.*

WORK IN PROGRESS: The Quest for Extraterrestrial Life, for Plenum; a novel; a juvenile popular science book.

SIDELIGHTS: Barry Parker once told *CA:* "It's difficult to say why one writes, but in my case I suppose it's because I thoroughly enjoy the challenge of taking a scientific subject—or any difficult subject, for that matter—and making it understandable and enjoyable for a popular audience. The emphasis here should, I firmly believe, be placed on the word 'enjoyable'; it's not enough just to make the material understandable.

"My first book, *Concepts of the Cosmos,* resulted from many years of teaching astronomy and writing popular articles on the subject. I felt that the majority of astronomy books on the market were not enjoyed by most students, and I hoped I could produce a book that would at least partially overcome this. Once I had completed it I found I was hooked—well hooked—and I immediately started a second book. It is also oriented, to some degree, towards astronomy, but it is much narrower in scope than the previous book. Titled *Einstein's Dream,* it is the story of man's search for a unified theory of the universe.

"Although much of my writing has been in the area of popular science, I am also an enthusiastic outdoorsman and have published many articles on fishing, backpacking, and so on. 'Write about the things that you enjoy most,' someone once said to me, and I guess I've taken that advice."

Parker more recently told *CA:* "I enjoy interpreting science for the general public and have several books in mind that I would like to do. I am currently a professor at Idaho State University, where I teach many of the topics I write about, but I will be retiring soon and will have considerably more time to write. With this extra time, I hope to expand my horizons to include fiction and, perhaps, juvenile or children's books."

BIOGRAPHICAL/CRITICAL SOURCES:

PERIODICALS

Los Angeles Times, November 20, 1987; October 11, 1988.
New York Times Book Review, January 10, 1988.

* * *

PARKER, Hershel 1935-

PERSONAL: Born November 26, 1935, in Comanche, OK; son of Lloyd and Martha (Costner) Parker; married Joanne Johnson (an English professor), June 29, 1963 (divorced, 1979); married Heddy Richter (a librarian), 1981; children: (first marriage) Alison, Sabrina. *Education:* Lamar State College (now Lamar University), B.A., 1959; Northwestern University, M.A., 1960, Ph.D., 1963.

ADDRESSES: *Office*—Department of English, University of Delaware, Newark, DE 19716. *E-mail*—hparker@brahms.udel.edu.

CAREER: Telegraph operator for Kansas City Southern Railway, 1952-59; University of Illinois at Urbana-Champaign, assistant professor, 1963-65; Northwestern University, Evanston, IL, assistant professor, 1965-68; University of Southern California, Los Angeles, associate professor, 1968-70, professor of English, 1970-77, Bruce R. McElderry Research Scholar, 1977-79; University of Delaware, Newark, H. Fletcher Brown Professor, 1979—.

MEMBER: Melville Society.

AWARDS, HONORS: Woodrow Wilson fellowships, 1959-60 and 1962-63; Guggenheim fellowship, 1974-75; University of Southern California Creative Scholarship and Research Award, 1977; fellowship from Center for Advanced Study, University of Delaware, 1981-82.

WRITINGS:

EDITOR

The Recognition of Herman Melville: Selected Criticism since 1846, University of Michigan Press (Ann Arbor, MI), 1967.
(With Harrison Hayford) Herman Melville, *Moby-Dick: An Authoritative Text* (includes reviews and letters by Melville, analogues and sources, and criticism), Norton (New York City), 1967.
(And contributor with Hayford and G. Thomas Tanselle) *The Writings of Herman Melville,* Northwestern University Press and Newberry Library, thirteen volumes, 1968-96.
(With Hayford) *Moby-Dick as Doubloon: Essays and Extracts, 1851-1970,* Norton, 1970.
Melville, *The Confidence-Man: His Masquerade; An Authoritative Text* (includes backgrounds and sources, reviews, criticism, and annotated bibliography), Norton, 1971.
Shorter Works of Hawthorne and Melville, C. E. Merrill (Columbus, OH), 1972.
Norton Anthology of American Literature, Volume 1, Norton, 1979, 4th edition, 1994.
(Series editor) *A Reader's Guide to the Short Stories of Nathaniel Hawthorne,* G. K. Hall (Boston, MA), 1979.
(With Brian Higgins) *Critical Essays on Herman Melville's "Pierre; or, The Ambiguities,"* G. K. Hall, 1983.
(With Kevin J. Hayes) *Checklist of Melville Reviews,* revised edition, Northwestern University Press, 1991.
Critical Essays on Herman Melville's "Moby-Dick," G. K. Hall, 1992.
(With Brian Higgins) *Herman Melville: The Contemporary Reviews,* Cambridge University Press (New York City), 1995.
(With Jay Leyda) *The New Melville Log,* five volumes, Gordian Press, forthcoming.

OTHER

Flawed Texts and Verbal Icons: Literary Authority in American Fiction, Northwestern University Press (Evanston, IL), 1984.
Herman Melville: 1819-1851, Johns Hopkins University Press (Baltimore, MD), 1996.

Contributor of articles to *American Literature, Studies in Short Fiction, New York Historical*

Society Quarterly, Modern Language Quarterly, Nineteenth-Century Fiction, Papers of the Bibliographical Society of America, Mississippi Quarterly, Studies in the Novel, and other literary journals. Contributor of the Melville chapter to the annual volume of *American Literary Scholarship,* 1972-80. Guest editor of *Studies in the Novel,* spring, 1978.

WORK IN PROGRESS: Continuing work on the final volume of *The Writings of Herman Melville* for Northwestern University Press and Newberry Library.

SIDELIGHTS: Hershel Parker told *CA:* "My early education was checkered, even for someone whose half Choctaw and Cherokee father jounced about South Texas oil fields in the Depression and Oregon defense plants during World War II before backtrailing to a farm in Oklahoma. After the 11th grade I hired out as a railroad telegrapher in Louisiana, where I finished high school and introductory college English courses by correspondence from the University of California and then attended a California junior college for a year. For two years I held a job as night telegrapher in Port Arthur, Texas, while attending Lamar State College of Technology in Beaumont full time. A Woodrow Wilson fellowship got me off the railroad and into Northwestern in 1959. Thereafter my education was conventional. I completed my master's the next year, 1960, and (aided by a Woodrow Wilson dissertation fellowship) my Ph.D. in 1963.

"In 1962 my archival research on Melville and Politics made me a belated member of the group of 1940s Melville scholars who had set themselves to discover what could be known factually about Herman Melville. That research led to my becoming Associate General Editor of *The Writings of Herman Melville* in 1965. I contributed half the "Supplement" to Jay Leyda's 1969 edition of *The Melville Log* and since 1986 have been working on the third edition, *The New Melville Log,* now several times the length of the earlier editions. Through the decades I have brought news to Melvilleans—from the shocking false newspaper headline 'Herman Melville Crazy' and the tantalizing fact that Melville had completed an unknown lost novel, *The Isle of the Cross,* to the many wholly new episodes in my biography, one of which (Melville's presentation of *Moby-Dick* to Hawthorne in the dining room of the Curtis Hotel in Lenox) ends the first volume.

"In the early 1970s in California (far from the eastern archives) my study of Melville's texts and the relationships between textual-biographical evidence and literary criticism led me into a second career as a textual critic and theorist. In the mid-1970s at USC I created a then-unique course in the aesthetic implications of textual and biographical evidence. Later, my relating textual evidence to the creative process and cognitive psychology led to the controversial *Flawed Texts and Verbal Icons* (1984), in which I brought to bear on literary criticism and theory fresh evidence from the texts of Mark Twain, Stephen Crane, Henry James, F. Scott Fitzgerald, Norman Mailer, and other American writers. This pioneering work int he now-burgeoning field where textual and literary theory merge outraged many because it demonstrated that authors could lose control of meaning; it outraged others because it demonstrated that authors had never been in control of meaning in the first place. For this book I have been identified (or misidentified) as 'textual objectivist,' 'hermeneut,' a 'textual primitivist,' and an 'antiformalist,' and compared to and contrasted with E. D. Hirsch, G. Thomas Tanselle, Jacques Derrida, Jerome McGann, Donale Reiman, Hans Walter Gabler, among others.

"Uniting my work as textual theorist and as Melvillean is my lifelong concern for tangible evidences of the creative process, fascination with the laws of cognitive psychology and human memory, belief that archival research allows a scholar to arrive closer to the truth, and respect for the enlightening and nurturing power of narrative. In 1995, commenting on my contrasting the assumptions of film critics with the assumptions of literary critics, David C. Greetham declared that having 'blazed' a 'rhetorical trail' years before, Hershel Parker as a theorist 'may have come into his own,' may have 'found his time.' That may be true of my work as a theorist, but it is in the Melville biography, it seems to me, that the two sides of my career have fused into one."

BIOGRAPHICAL/CRITICAL SOURCES:

PERIODICALS

New York Times Magazine, December 15, 1996.
Times Literary Supplement, February 15, 1985.

PATRICK, Robert 1937-

PERSONAL: Born September 27, 1937, in Kilgore, TX. *Ethnicity:* "Caucasian." *Education:* Attended Eastern New Mexico University for three years.

ADDRESSES: Home—1837 North Alexandria Ave., No. 211, Los Angeles, CA 90027.

CAREER: Playwright, actor, director, and songwriter. Worked as dishwasher, autopsy typist, accounts receivable correspondent, astrologer, and reporter. Caffe Cino, New York City, waiter, doorman, and stage manager, 1961-63; Old Reliable Theatre Tavern, New York City, playwright-in-residence, 1967-71.

MEMBER: New York Theatre Strategy, Playwrights Cooperative, Actors Studio.

AWARDS, HONORS: Show Business best Off-Off Broadway playwright award, 1968-69, for *Joyce Dynel, Fog,* and *Salvation Army;* nominated for *Village Voice* "Obie" award, 1973; Glasgow Citizens' Theatre International play contest, first prize, 1973, for *Kennedy's Children;* Rockefeller Foundation playwright-in-residence grant, 1973; Creative Artists Public Service grant, 1976; International Thespian Society Founders Award, 1980; Robert Chesley Foundation Lifetime Achievement in Gay Playwrighting Award, 1996.

WRITINGS:

Untold Decades: Seven Comedies of Gay Romance, St. Martin's (New York City), 1988.

Temple Slave (novel), Masquerade Press (New York City), 1994.

PLAYS

The Haunted Host, first produced at Caffe Cino, November 29, 1964.

Mirage, first produced at La Mama, July 8, 1965.

The Sleeping Bag, first produced at Playwrights' Workshop, June, 1966.

Indecent Exposure, first produced at Caffe Cino, September 27, 1966.

Halloween Hermit, first produced at Caffe Cino, October 31, 1966.

Cheesecake, first produced at Caffe Cino, 1966.

Lights, Camera, Action, first produced at Caffe Cino, June 8, 1967.

The Warhol Machine, first produced at Playbox Studio, July 18, 1967.

Still-Love, first produced at Playbox Studio, July 18, 1967.

Cornered, first produced at Theatre Gallery, January 26, 1968.

Un Bel Di, first produced at Theatre Gallery, January 26, 1968.

Help, I Am, first produced at Theatre Gallery, January 26, 1968.

Camera Obscura, first produced at Caffe Cino, produced Off-Broadway at Cafe au Go Go, May 8, 1968.

The Arnold Bliss Show, first produced by New York Theatre Ensemble, April 1, 1969.

A Bad Place to Get Your Head, first produced at St. Peters Church, July 14, 1970.

Bread-Tangle, first produced at St. Peters Church, July 14, 1970.

Picture Wire, first produced at St. Peters Church, August 13, 1970.

I Am Trying to Tell You Something, first produced at The Open Space, August, 1970.

Shelter, first produced at Playbox Studio, November, 1970.

The Richest Girl in the World Finds Happiness, first produced at La Mama, December 24, 1970.

Hymen and Carbuncle, produced by the Dove Company, 1970.

A Christmas Carol, first produced at La Mama, December 22, 1971.

Youth Rebellion, first produced at Sammy's Bowery Follies, February, 1972.

Play by Play (first produced at La Mama, December 20, 1972), Samuel French, 1975.

Something Else, first produced by New York Theatre Ensemble, January, 1973.

Ludwig and Wagner, first produced at La Mama, February, 1973.

Mercy Drop, first produced at W.P.A. Theatre, March, 1973.

Simultaneous Transmissions, first produced at Kranny's Nook, March 1, 1973.

The Track of the Narwhal, first produced in Boston, MA, at Boston Conservatory, April 28, 1973.

Kennedy's Children (first produced at Clark Center, May 30, 1973, produced on the West End at Arts Theatre Club, May, 1975, produced on Broadway at Golden Theatre, November 3, 1975), Samuel French (London), 1975, Random House (New York City), 1976.

Cleaning House, first produced at W.P.A. Theatre, June 27, 1973.

Hippy as a Lark, first produced at Stagelights II, June, 1973.

Blue Is for Boys, produced in Hollywood, CA, at Deja Vu, September, 1973, produced Off-Broadway at Corner Loft Studio, January, 1987.

The Golden Circle, first produced by Spring Street Company, September 26, 1973.

Love Lace, first produced at Pico Playhouse, 1974.

How I Came to Be Here Tonight, first produced at La Mama Hollywood, March 21, 1974.

Orpheus and Amerika, first produced in Los Angeles, CA, at Odyssey Theatre, April, 1974.

Fred and Harold, and One Person, first produced in London, 1976.

My Dear, It Doesn't Mean a Thing, first produced in London, 1976.

My Cup Runneth Over (first produced in Brooklyn, NY, at Everyman Theatre, November 3, 1977), Dramatists Play Service, 1979.

Judas, first produced in Santa Monica, CA, April, 1978.

T-Shirts, first produced in Minneapolis, MN, at Out-and-About Theatre, October 19, 1978.

Mutual Benefit Life (first produced by Production Company, October, 1978), Dramatists Play Service (New York City), 1979.

Bank Street Breakfast, first produced by the Fourth E, February, 1979.

Communication Gap, first produced in Greensboro, NC, 1979.

The Family Bar, first produced at Deja Vu, 1979.

Big Sweet, first produced in Richmond, VA, January, 1984.

No Trojan Women, produced in Wallingford, CT, July, 1985.

Explanation of a Xmas Wedding, produced at Theatre for the New City, December 29, 1987.

Michelangelo's Models, Dialogus Press (Dallas), 1994.

Bread Alone, Dialogus Press, 1994.

The Trial of Socrates, Dialogus Press, 1994.

Also author of *Diaghilev and Nijinsky.*

PLAYS; FIRST PRODUCED OFF-OFF BROADWAY AT OLD RELIABLE THEATRE TAVERN

See Other Side, April 1, 1968.

Absolute Power over Movie Stars, May 13, 1968.

Preggin and Liss, June 17, 1968.

The Overseers, July 1, 1968.

Angels in Agony, July 1, 1968.

Salvation Army, September 23, 1968.

Dynel, December 16, 1968.

Fog, January 20, 1969.

I Came to New York to Write, March 24, 1969.

Joyce Dynel, April 7, 1969.

The Young Aquarius, April 28, 1969.

Oooooooops!, May 12, 1969.

Lily of the Valley of the Dolls, June 30, 1969.

One Person, August 29, 1969.

Angel, Honey, Baby, Darling, Dear, July 20, 1970.

The Golden Animal, July 20, 1970.

COLLECTIONS

Robert Patrick's Cheep Theatricks! (contains *I Came to New York to Write, The Haunted Host, Joyce Dynel, Cornered, Still-Love, Lights, Camera, Action, Help, I Am, The Arnold Bliss Show, One Person, Preggin and Liss,* and *The Richest Girl in the World Finds Happiness*), edited by Michael Feingold, Winter House, 1972.

One Man, One Woman (contains *Mirage, Cleaning House, Cheesecake, Something Else, Love Lace,* and *Bank Street Breakfast*) Samuel French, 1975.

Mercy Drop and Other Plays (contains *Mercy Drop, Ludwig and Wagner, Diaghilev and Nijinsky, Hymen and Carbuncle,* and *The Family Bar*), Calamus (New York City), 1980.

OTHER

Also author of *Sketches,* first produced in 1966, *Silver Skies, Tarquin Truthbeauty,* and *The Actor and the Invader,* all produced in 1969, *La Repetition* and *Sketches and Songs,* both produced in 1970, *Songs,* produced in 1972, *Imp-Prisonment* and *The Twisted Root,* both produced in 1973, and several other plays variously produced 1979-85, including *All in the Mind, The Sane Scientist, Twenty-four Inches, The Spinning Tree, Report to the Mayor,* and *Bread Alone.* Contributor to anthologies, including *Collision Course, New American Plays 3, The Off-Off Broadway Book,* and *West Coast Plays 5.* Contributor to periodicals, including *Saturday Review, Astrology Today, Playbill, Gaysweek,* and *New York.*

Recorded *Pouf Positive* on Harvey Fierstein's *This Is Not Going to Be Pretty,* Plump Records, 1996.

ADAPTATIONS: *My Cup Runneth Over* was produced for public television. *Kennedy's Children,* which has been translated into some forty languages, has been produced on television in several countries.

WORK IN PROGRESS: *All at Sea,* a musical comedy; *Sound,* a screenplay; *The Way We War,* a screenplay.

SIDELIGHTS: Robert Patrick is one of theater's most prolific playwrights. With some seventy Off-Broadway one-act and full-length works to his credit, Patrick is still best known primarily for one work—*Kennedy's Children*—that made it to Broadway. "Patrick is something of a maverick, an urchin in a middle-aged body, a Texas drifter with an obsession for story telling," according to Maggie Hawthorn in a *Seattle Post-Intelligencer* article. "[He] is, by his own admission, voluble. He loves to talk about the theater, about people, about himself, about America." He is also one of the early proponents of gay drama—"many gay theaters in America and abroad have opened with [my] work," as the author once told *CA.*

Kennedy's Children depicts the barroom confessions of five representatives of the sixties, yet, according to Patrick, the play is not primarily concerned with the era. As Patrick notes to Robert Berkvist of the *New York Times,* the play's theme "is the loss of heroes. And it's not about the sixties, it's about now, about why we have become what we are." As Patrick was completing the work, he goes on to say, he found that the characters "were each a different aspect of the lost-hero theme: one had killed his hero, another had seen his hero betrayed, another had tried to be a hero."

"A play is primarily a shared experience which exists only in performance," Patrick once told *CA.* "Its immediacy is its special quality. Unlike films and literature, which record experiences that once happened, a play presents an event. Its *reality* makes it a powerful moral and psychological tool. Theatrical artists who do not communicate consciously, communicate helplessly and unconsciously."

Patrick more recently told *CA:* "My sole reason for writing is to entertain myself. I write what I would like to see on a page, a stage, or screen. I imagine a marquee or book cover with a certain title on it, then, in imagination, enter the theater or open the book and write down what I find there. My influences are every book, play, or film I've ever encountered, and the personal experiences that delight, enlighten, or frighten me. I don't like life very much; I prefer art. I am aware that art strikes deeply into the human consciousness, and release for publication or production only those works I wish to have in the heads of the people around me. Ideas create our world; art instills ideas; artists create our world. I'd like to help create a wiser, kinder, wittier world."

BIOGRAPHICAL/CRITICAL SOURCES:

BOOKS

Authors in the News, Volume 2, Gale (Detroit), 1976.

Feingold, Michael, editor, *Robert Patrick's Cheep Theatricks!,* Winter House, 1972.

Poland, Albert, and Bruce Mailman, editors, *The Off-Off Broadway Book,* Bobbs-Merrill, 1972.

PERIODICALS

Newsweek, November 17, 1975.

New York Times, May 4, 1975; September 3, 1975; November 9, 1975; June 23, 1978; January 29, 1987; December 29, 1987.

Seattle Post-Intelligencer, April 18, 1976.

Time, November 17, 1975.

* * *

PENN, Ruth Bonn
See ROSENBERG, Ethel (Clifford)

* * *

PERLMAN, Mark 1923-

PERSONAL: Born December 23, 1923, in Madison, WI; son of Selig and Eva (Shaber) Perlman; married Naomi Waxman, 1953; children: Abigail Ruth. *Education:* University of Wisconsin, BA, 1947, M.A., 1947; Columbia University, Ph.D., 1950.

ADDRESSES: Home—5622 Bartlett St., Pittsburgh, PA 15217. *Office*—Department of Economics, University of Pittsburgh, Pittsburgh, PA 15260.

CAREER: Princeton University, Princteon, NJ, instructor, 1947-48; assistant professor at University of Hawaii, Honolulu, 1951-52, and Cornell University, Ithaca, NY, 1952-55; Johns Hopkins University, Baltimore, MD, assistant professor, 1955-58, associate professor of political economy, 1958-63; University of Pittsburgh, Pittsburgh, PA, professor of economics, history, and economics of public health, 1963—, university professor of economics, 1968—, chair of department of economics, 1965-70. Harvard University, research associate, 1955-57, lecturer, 1957-58. Senior Fulbright lecturer at Melbourne University, 1968; official faculty visitor and visiting fellow, Clare Hall, Cambridge Unviersity, 1976-77; adjunct scholar of American Enterprise Institute, 1980—; resident scholar at Rockefeller Foundation Center, Villa Serbelloni, Bellagio, Italy, 1983. Visiting lecturer at other universities, including three in Vienna, Austria, 1982; Kiel, Germany, 1987; Augsberg, Germany, 1995; Chemnitz, Germany, 1996. Member of Johns Hopkins survey team evaluating public health in Brazil, 1960, and Johns Hopkins medical team in Taiwan and Turkey, 1962-64; member of Princeton Institute for Advanced Study, 1981-82.

MEMBER: International Union for the Scientific Study of Population, History of Economics Society (vice president, 1977; president-elect, 1983-84; president, 1984-85), American Economic Association (member of executive committee, 1968-80), Economic History Association, Economic History Society, Population Association of America, Royal Economic Society, American Jewish Historical Society, Athenaeum (London).

AWARDS, HONORS: Ford Foundation fellow, 1962-73; Chinese Academy of Social Science Distinguished Scholar Award, National Academy of Science, 1983.

WRITINGS:

Judges in Industry: A Study of Labor Arbitration in Australia, Cambridge University Press (New York City), 1954.

Labor Union Theories in America: Background and Development, Row, 1958, new edition, Greenwood Press (Westport, CT), 1976.

The Machinists: A New Study in American Trade Unionism, Harvard University Press (Cambridge, MA), 1961.

Democracy in the International Association of Machinists, Wiley (New York City), 1962.

(Editor) *Human Resource in the Urban Economy,* Resources for the Future, 1963.

(With Timothy D. Baker) *Health Manpower in a Developing Economy,* Johns Hopkins University Press (Baltimore), 1967.

(Editor with Charles Levin and Benjamin Chinitz, and contributor) *Spatial, Regional, and Population Economics: Essays in Honor of Edgar M. Hoover,* Gordon & Breach (New York City), 1972.

(Editor with Norval Morris, and contributor) *Law and Crime: Essays in Honor of Sir John Barry,* Gordon & Breach, 1972.

(Editor) *Economics of Health and Medical Care,* Halsted (New York City), 1974.

(Editor and contributor) *The Organization and Retrieval of Economic Knowledge,* Halsted, 1977.

(Editor with Gordon K. MacLeod and contributor) *Health Care Capital: Competition and Control,* Ballinger (Cambridge, MA), 1978.

(Editor with J. van der Gaag) *Health, Economics, and Health Economics,* North-Holland (New York City), 1981.

(Editor with K. Weiermair) *Studies in Economic Rationality: X-Efficiency Examined and Extolled,* University of Michigan Press (Ann Arbor), 1990.

(Editor with A. Heertje) *Evolving Technology and Market Structure: Studies in Schumpeterian Economics,* University of Michigan Press, 1990.

(Editor with N. H. Ornstein) *Political Power and Social Change: The United States Faces a United Europe,* AEI Press (Washington, DC), 1991.

(Editor with C. E. Barfield) *Capital Markets and Trade: The United States Faces a United Europe,* AEI Press, 1991.

(Editor with Barfield) *Industry, Services, and Agriculture: The United States Faces a United Europe,* AEI Press, 1991.

(Editor with F. M. Scherer) *Entrepreneurship, Technological Innovation, and Economic Growth: Studies in Schumpeterian Economics,* University of Michigan Press, 1992.

(Editor with Yuichi Shionoya) *Innovation in Technology, Industries, and Institutions: Studies in Schumpeterian Perspectives,* University of Michigan Press, 1994.

(Editor with Shionoya) *Schumpter in the History of Ideas,* University of Michigan Press, 1994.

The Character of Economic Thought, Economic Characters, and Economic Institutions: Selected Essays by Mark Perlman, University of Michigan Press, 1996.

(Editor with Ernst Helmsteadter) *Behavioral Norms, Technological Progress, and Economic Dynamics: Studies in Schumpterian Economics,* University of Michigan Press, 1996.

OTHER

Contributor to numerous books, including J. Braeman, R. H. Bremmer, and D. Brady, editors, *Twentieth-Century America,* Ohio State University Press, 1968; Kevin M. Cahill, editor, *The Untapped Resource,* Orbis, 1971; J. P. Nieuwenhuysen and P. J. Draker, editors, *Australian Economic Policy,* Melbourne University Press, 1977; Jacob S. Dreyer, editor, *Breadth and Depth in Economics,* Lexington Books, 1978; Herbert Giersch, editor, *Capital Shortage and Unemployment in the World Economy: Symposium 1977,* Mohr, 1978; William Fellner, editor, *Contemporary Economic Problems,* American Enterprise Institute, Volume I, 1979, Volume II, 1980, Volume III, 1981, Volume IV, 1982; Helmut Frisch, editor, *Schumpeterian Economics,* Praeger, 1981; Warren J. Samuels, editor, *Research in the History of Economic Thought and Methodology: A Research Annual,* Volume I, JAI Press, 1983; Bela Gold and others, editors, *Technological Progress and Industrial Leadership: The Growth of the U.S. Steel Industry, 1900-1970,* Lexington Books, 1984; Julian L. Simon and Herman Kahn, editors, *The Resourceful Earth,* Basil Blackwell, 1984; Henry W. Spiegel and Samuels, editors, *Contemporary Economists in Perspective,* JAI Press, 1984; Horst Hanusch and others, editors, *Staat und Okonomie heute,* Verlag, 1985; William Alonso and Paul Starr, editors, *The Politics of Numbers,* Russell Sage, 1987; Arthur F. Burns, *The Ongoing Revolution in American Banking,* AEI, 1987; Horst Hanusch, editor, *Evolutionary Economics: Applications of Schumpeter's Ideas,* Cambridge University Press, 1988; Joseph E. Stiglitz, *The Economic Role of the State,* AEI, 1989; James H. Cassing and Steven L. Husted, editors, *Capital, Technology, and Labor in the New Global Economy,* AEI, 1989; contributor and editor with Friederich A. von Hayek and Frederick B. Kaye of *An Interpretation of Bernard de Mandeville: Fable of the Bees,* 1990; Stephen S. F. Frowen, editor, *Unknowledge and Choice in Economics,* 1990; Warren J. Samuels, editor, *Research in the History of Economic Thought and Methodology: A Research Annual,* Volume 8, 1991; Warren Samuels, editor, *New Horizons in Economic Thought,* Edward Elgar, 1992; and Horst Klaus Rechtenwald and Horst and Hanusch, editors, *Economics Science in the Future by Eminent Scholars,* 1992.

Coeditor, "Cambridge University Surveys of Economic Literature," 1977-96, and "Cambridge Surveys in Economic Politics and Institutions," 1991-95. Contributor to journals. Member of editorial board, *Industrial and Labor Relations Review,* 1953-55; founding and managing editor, *Journal of Economic Liteature,* 1969-81; founding editor, *Portfolio on International Econimic Perspectives* (journal of U. S. Department of State), 1973; co-managing editor, *Journal of Evolutionary Economics,* 1991-96.

WORK IN PROGRESS:The Development of Economic Ideas: Philosophical Traditions and Rhetorical Styles, and *The Development of Economic Ideas: Factors of Production and Professionalism,* both with Charles R. McCann, Jr., for University of Michigan Press.

SIDELIGHTS: Mark Perlman told *CA* that his motivation for writing stems from the desire to provide "undergraduates with a broad-based liberal arts approach to the economics discipline. Most of my research stems from what is involved in the teaching process—that is, in building up then explaining databases." Influences on his work, he further explained, "are described in my autobiographical essay, 'What Makes My Mind Tick,' to be found in my collection *The Character of Economic Thought, Economic Characters, and Economic Institutions: Selected Essays by Mark Perlman.* There I note several institutional factors like the coming of World War II and changes about the perception of economics as a body of thought—changes which surfaced as early as 1947 with the publication of Paul Samuelson's *The Foundations of Economic Analysis* and which became dominant during the 1970s." Perlman further recogized the influences of his father, the Australian crinimologist John Barry, and colleagues Simon Kuznets and Fritz Machlup on his thinking. When translating his hypotheses into writing, he told *CA* that "from an empirical standpoint, the actual writing goes through a minimum of three drafts—from getting the story straight to telling it expeditiously."

* * *

PERRIN, Noel 1927-

PERSONAL: Born September 18, 1927, in New York, NY; son of Edwin Oscar (an advertising executive) and Blanche Browning (Chenery) Perrin; married Nancy Hunnicutt, November 26, 1960 (divorced, 1971); married Annemarie Price, June 20, 1975 (divorced, 1980); married Anne Spencer Lindbergh (a children's book writer), December 26, 1988 (died December 10, 1993); children: (first marriage) Elisabeth, Amy. *Education:* Williams College, B.A., 1949; Duke University, M.A., 1950; Trinity Hall, Cambridge, M.Litt., 1958. *Religion:* Episcopalian.

ADDRESSES: Home—R.R. Box 8, Thetford Center, VT 05075. *Office*—Department of Environmental Studies, Dartmouth College, Hanover, NH 03755. *E-mail*—noel_perrin@dartmouth.edu.

CAREER: Daily News, New York City, copy boy, 1950-51; *Medical Economics,* Oradell, NJ, associate editor, 1953-56; University of North Carolina, Woman's College, Chapel Hill, instructor, 1956-59; Dartmouth College, Hanover, NH, assistant professor, 1959-64, professor of English, 1964-93, chairperson of department, 1972-75, adjunct professor of environmental studies, 1993—. *Military service:* U.S. Army, Artillery, 1945-46, 1950-51; became first lieutenant; served in Korea; received Bronze Star.

MEMBER: Phi Beta Kappa.

AWARDS, HONORS: Guggenheim fellowships, 1970, 1985.

WRITINGS:

A Passport Secretly Green (essays), St. Martin's (New York City), 1961.

Dr. Bowdler's Legacy: A History of Expurgated Books in England and America, Atheneum (New York City), 1969, Macmillan (New York City), 1970.

Amateur Sugar Maker, University Press of New England (Hanover, NH), 1972.

Vermont: In All Weathers, Viking (New York City), 1973.

(Editor) *The Adventures of Jonathan Corncob, Legal American Refugee,* David Godine (Lincoln, MA), 1976.

First Person Rural: Essays of a Sometime Farmer, illustrated by Stephen Harvard, David Godine, 1978.

Giving Up the Gun: Japan's Reversion to the Sword, 1543-1879, David Godine, 1979.

Second Person Rural: More Essays of a Sometime Farmer, illustrated by F. Allyn Massey, David Godine, 1980.

Third Person Rural: Further Essays of a Sometime Farmer, woodcuts by Robin Brickman, David Godine, 1983.

A Reader's Delight, University Press of New England, 1988.

(With Kenneth Breisch) *Mills and Factories of New England: Essays,* photographs by Serge Hambourg, Abrams (New York City), 1988.

Last Person Rural, David Godine, 1991.

Solo: Life with an Electric Car, Norton (New York City), 1992.

Columnist for *Vermont Life,* 1976-81, *Boston Magazine,* 1978-79, and *Washington Post Book World,* 1981-88. Contributor to periodicals, including *New Yorker, Country Journal, Vermont Life,* and *Horticulture.*

SIDELIGHTS: Noel Perrin was an English professor at Dartmouth College and is the author of such scholarly works as *Dr. Bowdler's Legacy: A History of Expurgated Books in England and America* and *Giving Up the Gun: Japan's Reversion to the Sword, 1543-1879.* Since his move to the Vermont countryside at the age of thirty, however, Perrin has written several books about his experiences as a part-time farmer there. Four of these books, *First Person Rural: Essays of a Sometime Farmer, Second Person Rural: More Essays of a Sometime Farmer, Third Person Rural: Further Essays of a Sometime Farmer,* and *Last Person Rural,* contain essays previously published in magazines like *Country Journal* and *Vermont Life* and have been highly praised for their unaffected style, wit, and abstention from the pitfalls of idealizing life in a bucolic setting.

In *First Person Rural,* Perrin fills most of the book's pages with practical advice for the novice or part-time farmer on how to tend grounds, buy supplies, and keep pipes from bursting during the bitter-cold Vermont winters. The essays in *Second Person Rural,* notes *Washington Post Book World* contributor Stephen Goodwin,"are more reflective, less concerned with *How-to* than with the meatier question, *Why?*" The answer to this question, at least for Perrin, "is that he likes what he's doing." Extolling the joys of raising animals and crops, making one's own butter, and tapping trees for real maple syrup, the author is nevertheless "no rustic romantic," according to Doris Grumbach's *Saturday Review* article. "When he writes about rural existence he sees all the flies in the idyllic ointment . . . [and the] interesting thing is, Noel Perrin has never become indifferent to the pleasures of the city."

The author does insist, however, on the importance of keeping the rural separate from the urban so that the countryside might be spared the fate of becoming a mere tract of city suburbs; and in *Second Person Rural* he proposes an immigration test in which newcomers to the countryside would be issued one-year visas that would be revoked by a board of native farmers should candidates prove incapable of raising their own livestock. In this way, a large outflow of urbanites might be prevented from settling the farmlands. As for Perrin himself, by the time he wrote *Third Person Rural* he felt confident enough in his assimilation into country life to declare: "I am so deeply into rurality that my own [suburban] childhood conditioning has almost been overcome."

As an expounder of the delights of rural living, Perrin has been favorably compared to another well-known writer on the subject. "No writer since E. B. White," avers Goodwin, "can make puttering around a small farm sound so satisfying. Perrin's prose style is as unaffected as White's, and he is always deft, droll, and thoroughly civilized." Another *Washington Post Book World* critic, Peter Davison, similarly remarks that "like E. B. White, [Perrin] can make amusing what we wood-splitters, hay-makers, pig-sloppers encounter as dreary labor." "He is to farming," Davison also asserts, "what that eloquent physician, Lewis Thomas, is to medicine." After the positive reception of all three of these books, Robert W. Glasgow laments in the *Los Angeles Times Book Review* that "Perrin says that [*Third Person Rural*] is the last volume in his trilogy of published essays. I am among the readers who implore him not to stop."

BIOGRAPHICAL/CRITICAL SOURCES:

BOOKS

Perrin, Noel, *Third Person Rural: Further Essays of a Sometime Farmer,* David Godine, 1983.

PERIODICALS

Los Angeles Times Book Review, December 18, 1983.
New York Review of Books, October 11, 1979.
New York Times Book Review, November 9, 1969; July 23, 1978; July 15, 1979; October 26, 1980; January 8, 1984; April 17, 1988.
Saturday Review, October 14, 1978.
Time, October 3, 1969; July 24, 1978.
Times Literary Supplement, May 7, 1970; December 4, 1981.
Washington Post Book World, August 12, 1979; November 2, 1980; November 27, 1983; February 5, 1995.

* * *

PERRIN, Ursula 1935-

PERSONAL: Born June 15, 1935, in Berlin, Germany; came to the United States in 1938, naturalized citizen, 1944; daughter of Max (a physician) and Gretchen (Kemp) Gutmann; married Mark Perrin (a physician), August 25, 1956; children: Thomas, Christopher, Nicholas. *Education:* Smith College, B.A., 1956. *Politics:* Democrat. *Religion:* Protestant.

CAREER: Writer.

MEMBER: Authors Guild, Authors League of America.

WRITINGS:

NOVELS

Ghosts, Knopf (New York City), 1967.
Heart Failures, Doubleday (Garden City, NY), 1978.
Unheard Music, Dial (New York City), 1981.
Old Devotions, Dial, 1983.
The Looking-Glass Lover, Little, Brown (Boston), 1989.

Cool's Ridge, Permanent Press (Sag Harbor, NY), 1996.

SIDELIGHTS: In her novels, Ursula Perrin often writes on two related themes: young women coming of age and the friendship between two women. Her first novel, *Ghosts,* for example, combines the two themes by dealing "poetically with coming of age in the 1950s and the relationship between two sisters," according to a critic in *Belles Lettres. Old Devotions* focuses on the friendship between two old schoolmates as they reach middle age. Abigail McCarthy in the *New York Times Book Review* finds that at a certain point in the novel, "the reader begins to realize with what intensity this ordinary story is being told, how full of foreshadowing and foreboding it is."

In *The Looking-Glass Lover,* Perrin again structures her story around the relationship between two women. Barbara and Claire are cousins who seem to be complete opposites in temperament and abilities. Barbara is overwhelmed by her life as a single mother raising three teenaged children. Claire, married to a successful but emotionally-distant doctor, has recently lost her son in a skiing accident. She feels alone and neglected. "The relationship between these two neatly contrasting cousins—and the ways they use each other's lives to break through the barriers of helplessness and sterility that are entrapping them—are where the looking glasses come in," writes Gary Krist in the *New York Times Book Review.* Krist believes that the concept of the mirror-like differences between the two women, "while potentially engaging, never evolves into anything more than a perfunctory literary device." But a critic for the *Los Angeles Times Book Review* explains that the "novel is slung between the lives, imaginations, lovers and children of [the] two cousins" and that "the voices of the cousins are the success in the book." A *Publishers Weekly* reviewer finds that Perrin "writes with energy and compassion about the quiet desperation in ordinary lives" and "provokes insight and touches responsive chords."

BIOGRAPHICAL/CRITICAL SOURCES:

PERIODICALS

Atlanta Constitution, April 18, 1996, p. D5.
Belles Lettres, fall, 1988, p. 22.
Bestsellers, April 1, 1967, p. 9.
Booklist, June 1, 1967, p. 1034; February 1, 1979, p. 854.
Chatelaine, May, 1983, p. 4.
Chicago Sunday Times, November 15, 1981; January 23, 1983.
Chicago Tribune, November 22, 1981.
Glamour, February, 1983, p. 168.
Kirkus Reviews, July 15, 1978; May 15, 1989.
Library Journal, June 1, 1989, p. 148.
Los Angeles Times, November 20, 1981; February 20, 1983.
Los Angeles Times Book Review, August 6, 1989, p. 6.
Ms., July, 1983, p. 22.
New York Times Book Review, April 30, 1967, p. 40; February 6, 1983, pp. 10-22; June 26, 1988, p. 46; August 20, 1989, p. 11.
Publishers Weekly, January 9, 1967, p. 58; September 15, 1978; November 19, 1982; June 9, 1989, p. 53; January 15, 1996, p. 43.
Tribune Books (Chicago), March 24, 1996, p. 4.
Voice Literary Supplement, March, 1983, p. 3.
Winston-Salem Journal, February 6, 1983.*

* * *

PINOAK, Justin Willard
See PROSSER, H(arold) L(ee)

* * *

PRICE, (Edward) Reynolds 1933-

PERSONAL: Born February 1, 1933, in Macon, NC; son of William Solomon and Elizabeth (Rodwell) Price. *Education:* Duke University, A.B. (summa cum laude), 1955; Merton College, Oxford, B. Litt., 1958.

ADDRESSES: *Home*—4813 Duke Station, Box 99014, Durham, NC 27708. *Office*—Department of English, Duke University, Durham, NC 27706. *Agent*—Harriet Wasserman Literary Agency, Inc., 137 East 36th St., New York, NY 10016-3528.

CAREER: Duke University, Durham, NC, instructor, 1958-61, assistant professor, 1961-68, associate professor, 1968-72, professor of English, 1972-77, James B. Duke Professor of English, 1977—, acting chair, 1983. Writer-in-residence at

University of North Carolina at Chapel Hill, spring, 1965, University of Kansas, 1967, 1969, 1980, and University of North Carolina at Greensboro, 1971; Glasgow Professor, Washington and Lee University, 1971; faculty member, Salzberg Seminar, Salzberg, Austria, 1977. National Endowment for the Arts, Literature Advisory Panel, member, 1973-77, chair, 1977.

MEMBER: American Academy and Institute of Arts and Letters, Phi Beta Kappa, Phi Delta Theta.

AWARDS, HONORS: Angier Duke Scholar, 1955; Rhodes Scholar, 1955-58; William Faulkner Foundation Award (notable first novel), and Sir Walter Raleigh Award, both 1962, for *A Long and Happy Life;* Guggenheim fellow, 1964-65; National Association of Independent Schools Award, 1964; National Endowment for the Arts fellow, 1967-68; National Institute of Arts and Letters Award, 1971; Bellamann Foundation Award, 1972; Lillian Smith Award, 1976; Sir Walter Raleigh Award, 1976, 1981, 1984, 1986; North Carolina Award, 1977; D. Litt., St. Andrew's Presbyterian College, 1978, Wake Forest University, 1979, Washington and Lee University, 1991, and Davidson College, 1992; National Book Award nomination (translation), 1979, for *A Palpable God: Thirty Stories Translated from the Bible with an Essay on the Origins and Life of Narrative;* Roanoke-Chowan Poetry Award, 1982; National Book Critics Circle Award (best work of fiction), 1986, for *Kate Vaiden;* Elmer H. Bobst Award, 1988; Fund for New American Plays grant, 1989, for *New Music;* R. Hunt Parker Award, North Carolina Literary and Historical Society, 1991; finalist for the Pulitzer Prize in fiction, 1994, for *The Collected Stories.*

WRITINGS:

NOVELS

A Long and Happy Life, Atheneum (New York City), 1962.
A Generous Man, Atheneum, 1966.
Love and Work, Atheneum, 1968.
The Surface of Earth, Atheneum, 1975, reprinted, Scribner (New York City), 1995.
The Source of Light, Atheneum, 1981, reprinted, Scribner, 1995.
Mustian: Two Novels and a Story, Atheneum, 1983.
Kate Vaiden, Atheneum, 1986.
Good Hearts, Atheneum, 1988.
The Tongues of Angels, Atheneum, 1990.
Blue Calhoun, Atheneum, 1992.
Michael Egerton, Creative Education (Mankato, MN), 1993.
The Promise of Rest, Scribner, 1995.

PLAYS

Early Dark: A Play (three-act play; adapted from *A Long and Happy Life;* first produced Off-Broadway at the WPA Theater, April, 1978), Atheneum, 1977.
Private Contentment, Atheneum, 1984.
New Music (trilogy; contains *August Snow, Night Dance,* and *Better Days;* produced in Cleveland, OH, November, 1989), Atheneum, 1990.
Night Dance, Dramatists Play Service (New York City), 1991.
Better Days, Dramatists Play Service, 1991.
August Snow, Dramatists Play Service, 1991.
Full Moon and Other Plays, Theatre Communications Group (New York City), 1993.

POETRY

Late Warnings: Four Poems, Albondocani, 1968.
Lessons Learned: Seven Poems, Albondocani, 1977.
Nine Mysteries: Four Joyful, Four Sorrowful, One Glorious, Palaemon Press, 1979.
Vital Provisions, Atheneum, 1982.
The Laws of Ice, Atheneum, 1985.
House Snake, Lord John (Northridge, CA), 1986.
The Use of Fire, Atheneum, 1990.

OTHER

The Names and Faces of Heroes (stories), Atheneum, 1963.
Permanent Errors (short stories and a novella), Atheneum, 1970.
(Author of introduction) Henry James, *The Wings of the Dove,* C. E. Merrill (Columbus, OH), 1970.
Things Themselves: Essays and Scenes, Atheneum, 1972.
Presence and Absence: Versions from the Bible (limited edition; originally published as a pamphlet by the Friends of Duke University Library), Bruccoli Clark (Bloomfield Hills, MI), 1973.

A Palpable God: Thirty Stories Translated from the Bible with an Essay on the Origins and Life of Narrative, Atheneum, 1978.
A Final Letter, Sylvester and Orphanos, 1980.
The Annual Heron (limited edition), Albondocani, 1980.
Country Mouse, City Mouse, North Carolina Wesleyan College Press (Rocky Mount, NC), 1981.
The Chapel, Duke University, Duke University Press (Durham, NC), 1986.
A Common Room: New and Selected Essays, 1954-1987, Atheneum, 1988.
Real Copies, North Carolina Wesleyan College Press, 1988.
Clear Pictures: First Loves, First Guides (memoir), Atheneum, 1989.
Back before Day, North Carolina Wesleyan College Press, 1989.
The Foreseeable Future: Three Long Stories, Atheneum, 1990.
An Early Christmas (stories), North Carolina Wesleyan College Press, 1992.
The Collected Stories, Atheneum, 1993.
A Whole New Life: An Illness and a Healing, Atheneum, 1994.
The Honest Account of a Memorable Life: An Apocryphal Gospel, North Carolina Wesleyan College Press, 1994.
(Editor and contributor) *The Three Gospels: The Good New According to Mark, the Good News According to John, an Honest Account of a Memorable Life,* Scribner, 1996.

Also author of *Oracles: Six Versions from the Bible* (limited edition), Friends of the Duke University Library. Contributor of poetry, reviews, and articles to numerous magazines and newspapers, including *Time, Harper's, Saturday Review,* and *Washington Post.* Contributor to books, including *The Arts and the Public,* University of Chicago Press, 1967; and *Symbolism and Modern Literature: Studies in Honor of Wallace Fowlie,* Duke University Press, 1978. Editor, *The Archive,* 1954-55; advisory editor, *Shenandoah,* 1964—. Writer, with James Taylor, of the song "Copperline."

Price's books have been translated into over sixteen languages, including French, German, and Italian.

SIDELIGHTS: Reynolds Price wears many hats—novelist, short story writer, poet, playwright, essayist, teacher—but he is perhaps best known for his works that feature the backroads and small towns of his native North Carolina. While Price dislikes the "southern writer" label, he nevertheless acknowledges the influence of venerable southern authors such as Eudora Welty. "One of the things [Welty] showed me as a writer was that the kinds of people I had grown up with were the kind of people one could write marvelous fiction about," he told the *Washington Post.* By concentrating on those aspects of the rural South that he was most familiar with, Price has created a body of work noted for both its unique sense of place and offbeat cast of characters. A bout with cancer of the spinal cord left Price paralyzed from the waist down in 1984; while the experience changed Price's physical world, it also led to one of the most fertile periods of his career (including the publication of his much-acclaimed novel *Kate Vaiden*). Price explained his prolific output to the *Washington Post* by saying: "I don't write with a conscious sense of the hangman at my door, of my own mortality. But I am a tremendously driven person, and I have gotten more so since sitting down. Words just come out of me the way my beard comes out. Who could stop it?"

Price was born in Macon, North Carolina. His father was a traveling salesman who stayed close to home, while his mother was an "eccentric rogue" whose individuality left a large mark on her young son. Early on, Price found he had an aptitude for writing. His skill eventually won him a scholarship to Duke University and, after graduation, a Rhodes Scholarship for study at Oxford University. After his return from England, Price accepted a teaching position at Duke University, where his students have included Anne Tyler and Josephine Humphries. Price still resides in North Carolina, preferring to remain where he feels most comfortable: near his students in a house filled with memorabilia he affectionately refers to as "a *lotta* stuff."

Price received a great deal of praise for his first novel, *A Long and Happy Life.* Primarily the story of country girl Rosacoke Mustain, *A Long and Happy Life* was especially lauded for its sense of style and strong characterizations. Richard Sullivan noted that "there's not a wasted word. The characters . . . all jump with vitality," while Gene Baro termed Price's observations "vivid and acute." Baro added that Price "passes that ultimate test of a novelist: he has the ability to create a character that is memorable." Interestingly, many critics compared the stylistic and thematic concerns of *A Long and Happy Life* to those found in Price's highly praised 1986 novel, *Kate Vaiden.* According to Michael Spector of the *Washington Post,* Price was surprised by the association. Price told Spector: "My God, [*A Long and Happy Life*] is such an old book now in my life I no longer feel like the person who wrote it. I don't happen to feel by any means that it was the best book I ever wrote, or even the best before *Kate Vaiden.*"

Much of the praise given to both *A Long and Happy Life* and *Kate Vaiden* related to Price's strong characterizations of women. According to Elaine Kendall of the *Los Angeles Times Book Review,* "*A Long and Happy Life* belonged almost entirely to the heroine of Rosacoke Mustain, and each of the novels and stories following that stunning debut have been enlightened by unforgettable female protagonists. *Kate Vaiden* is the ultimate extension of Price's thesis, a first-person-singular novel written as the autobiography of a woman coming of age in the South during the Depression and war years." "At once tender and frightening, lyrical and dramatic, this novel is the product of a storyteller working at the height of his artistic powers," Michiko Kakutani commented in the *New York Times.* Price maintained that in focusing on characters like Kate, he was attempting to debunk the idea that "a man cannot 'understand' a woman and vice versa." By giving his female and male characters complex personas and motivations, Price created what he described for Kendall as "a contained look at a human hero," a character who is as much everywoman as everyman.

Carefully drawn characters constitute just one hallmark of Price's work. In novels such as *The Surface of Earth* (1975) and *The Source of Light* (1981)—which tell the stories of Eva Kendal and Forrest Mayfield and their descendants—Price explored the boundaries of narrative, especially those that exist between written and spoken language, and the tension that arises between the individual and the family. "Basically, all my novels and short stories are invented, with little pieces of actual, observed reality and dialogue. The speech of my characters often comes from natives of eastern North Carolina, which is my home country," Price told Herbert Mitgang of the *New York Times.* Price's use of language was heavily influenced by the Southern oral tradition. This tradition of tale-telling, with its heavy emphasis on history and drama, has offered a wealth of thematic concepts for Price. He told Elizabeth Venant of the *Los Angeles Times Book Review* that "as long as there remains anything that's recognizably Southern—this strange society with a tremendously powerful black presence in it, its very strong connections with some sort of Christianity, a major heritage as an agrarian society, a slave-owning past, a tragic war fought and lost on the premises—as long as there's any kind of continuing memory of that, then I think literature will continue to rise from it."

Price concluded the story of the Mayfields in *The Promise of Rest.* Set in the 1990s, this novel centers on Hutchins, the grandson of Eva Kendal and Forrest Mayfield, who has become a poet/professor ensconced in his position in the English department at Duke University. He is divorced and his only son has left the family far behind for a life as an architect in New York City. But, when Hutch discovers that his son is suffering the ravages of AIDS, he travels north to bring the boy home to die. Here, noted John Gregory Brown in the *Los Angeles Times Book Review,* "Price takes on the horror of AIDS, a subject that seems a far departure from the usual bodily tragedies and triumphs of will that run like a swelling stream through the Southern novel." Yet, continued Brown, "this subject is no departure at all, for what is AIDS if not one more of this earth's unspeakable tragedies . . . bringing families together and tearing them apart."

"A book about the death from AIDS of a young man whose only sin was love should be urgent and alarming. It should risk detail," Peter S. Prescott wrote in the *New York Times Book Review.* But, the reviewer added, "Mr. Price musters no such feeling, and this is his novel's principal failure." In the opinion of *Washington Post Book World* contributor Bruce Bawer, however, "There is, to be sure, much that is moving and memorable here. Compared to the earlier Mayfield novels, this one is direct, authentic and at times heartbreaking in its urgency; at best, it has a spare spiritual power." Bawer noted Price's depiction of the tension between the goals of the individual and those of the family, but for Bawer, this characteristic weakened the book. "In the end, this book feels at odds with itself," he wrote, "torn between a respect for individual integrity and the notion that family counts above all." Brown conceded that "this novel is less successful than so much of

Price's earlier work. But," he continued, "the very sincerity of *The Promise of Rest,* its unflinching gaze, its awful candor, can only leave the reader sad and grateful for such a book."

Price drew on his memories of growing up in this "strange society" in order to write *Clear Pictures: First Loves, First Guides.* Begun during a particularly painful period in the author's convalescence from cancer treatments, *Clear Pictures* covers the first twenty-one years of the his life. In this memoir, Price spends a great deal of time discussing the influence of his parents, especially his mother Elizabeth (who, he admits, was in many ways the model for Kate Vaiden). Price also recreates, in great detail, the small towns that formed the backdrop of his youth: Macon, Asheboro, and Warrenton. *Clear Pictures* met with an enthusiastic reception from critics, many of whom were impressed by Price's ability to depict the past in vibrant detail. Jonathan Kirsch of the *Los Angeles Times Book Review* remarked that Price "has returned to the secret world of his own childhood, a place where others have found a threatening and dangerous darkness, but Price discovered only the purest light. To be sure, he found suffering and terror and even death, and he describes them in sometimes heartbreaking detail, but *Clear Pictures* still glows with that bright, healing light." "Remarkable for its Proustian detail," noted Genevieve Stuttaford of *Publishers Weekly.* "This lucid biography portrays a mind learning to trust and reach out to the world."

Since the onslaught of his cancer, Price has drawn much of his own inspiration from a past made clearer by self-hypnosis. First prescribed as an analgesic for the pain of his illness, the self-hypnosis opened a floodgate of memories. "The sensation was so powerful that I felt as if I'd whiffed a potent drug," Price wrote in *Clear Pictures.* "As I began to feel the gathered force of so much past, I turned to write a story I'd planned but never begun." Price also used these memories when writing *The Tongues of Angels,* a novel about a precocious young boy's turbulent stay at summer camp. On one level a very basic look at camp life, *The Tongues of Angels* also contains discussions heavily grounded in philosophic thought. Many of Price's friends were moved by the book, especially those who had attended summer camp themselves. Price expressed his surprise at this development to John Blades of the *Chicago Tribune:* "I hadn't realized what a nerve I was touching. It seems that most of my friends, certainly those who are middle-aged, have strong and pleasant memories of their weeks, sometimes years, at summer camp. And they look back with a lot of fondness on the goofy but loveable institution that summer camp was in those days."

Price was careful not to let his illness and the restrictions it imposed impede either his life or his work. A basically happy man who claimed "I think I am programmed to laugh every five minutes," Price also resisted for many years the urge to reveal the secrets of his recovery. "I don't feel ready yet to say, 'Look at me. Didn't I go through this wonderfully?,'" he told Venant. "I don't want to give the devil ideas. 'Oh you think you have gotten through this wonderfully, do you? Well then try this.'" The author eventually became comfortable enough with the fact of his recovery that he could write about the experience. The memoir *A Whole New Life: An Illness and a Healing* follows Price from the early, unrecognized signs through diagnosis, surgery, and other treatments to recovery and adaptation to his new life in a wheelchair. Of Price's account, *Time* contributor William A. Henry III wrote, "Joltingly frank, the dryly written tale ranges from religious visions . . . to matter-of-fact discussions of the mechanics of paraplegic excretion." Geoffrey Wolff commented in the *Washington Post Book World,* "There is about *A Whole New Life* an atmosphere of ferocious sanity and serenity."

The story of *A Whole New Life* is the story of a man in a battle for his life. And, as Richard Selzer observed in the *Los Angeles Times Book Review,* "The man who emerges from these pages is feisty, gritty, angry, sometimes snobbish and, notwithstanding, most appealing. He makes no effort to portray himself as a saint or a martyr." Yet, because Price is also an author, this memoir of an illness promises new insights into a terrible condition. "Rarely if ever has a patient of Price's writerly gifts taken on the story of physical devastation," Henry maintained. "The weight of the subject has somewhat muted and simplified his normally fizzy prose. But the events emerge with awful clarity." Selzer concluded with gratitude that Price was able with time to look back on his experience. "There can be no sweeter use made of adversity than this act of generosity that comes in the form of a book," Selzer wrote.

In recent years, Price has been encouraged by the return of many aspiring young writers to their Southern roots. While some of these authors find inspiration in the fast pace of urban areas like Atlanta, others are rediscovering the story-telling tradition so closely identified with Southern culture. Price has also derived great pleasure and inspiration from his teaching and his students, many of whom maintain contact with the author long after they leave school. When teaching his writing course, Price completes the same writing tasks that he assigns his students. "I discovered earlier that I couldn't offer only one story for discussion, because the students were afraid of insulting the teacher," Price related to *Publishers Weekly*. "But if I do all the fairly elementary exercises required right from the beginning, that gives the students a truer sense that I'm in the same canoe as they are. They give me a quiet, fresh pair of glasses."

By writing along with his students, Price has also renewed his interest in the short story, a form he had put aside for many years. Together with his older stories, some of the new stories written during his courses provided the material for *The Collected Stories,* which was nominated for a Pulitzer Prize. Reviewing the collection for the *Washington Post Book World,* Sven Brikerts concluded: "Price is a superb storyteller. His idiom, pitched to the rhythms of natural speech and built up of things seen, touched and tasted, is fresh and compelling, and he homes in unfailingly on the details that matter. This compendium, spanning the work of decades, shows off the full range of his talents."

Price's novels, short stories, and memoirs have often manifested a religious sensibility that reflects not only his upbringing but also his experience as a writer. In *The Three Gospels: The Good New According to Mark, the Good News According to John, an Honest Account of a Memorable Life,* Price offers his translation of the Gospels of Mark and John and his own gospel. The result, according to Larry Woiwode in the *Washington Post Book World,* is a valuable book for anyone desiring a better understanding of these cornerstones of the Christian faith. "His prefaces to each are excellent," wrote Woiwode. "In fact, if anyone wanted an introduction to the Gospels, or wondered why they should have one, I would turn them first to Price's book, rather than any contemporary theologian. Price's book is that good, tempering a breadth of scholarly study with his good sense as an intuitive storyteller." The reviewer added that Price's versions make "a wonderfully engrossing book. It moves with a care and lucidity that should offend few . . . and should provide a new perspective for many."

BIOGRAPHICAL/CRITICAL SOURCES:

BOOKS

Contemporary Literary Criticism, Gale (Detroit), Volume 3, 1975, Volume 6, 1976, Volume 13, 1980, Volume 43, 1987, Volume 50, 1988, Volume 63, 1991.

Dictionary of Literary Biography, Volume 2: *American Novelists since World War II,* Gale, 1978.

Humphries, Jefferson, editor, *Conversations with Reynolds Price,* University Press of Mississippi (Jackson, MS), 1991.

Kimball, Sue Leslie, and Lynn Veach Sadler, editors, *Reynolds Price: From "A Long and Happy Life" to "Good Hearts,"* Methodist College Press (Fayetteville, NC), 1989.

Ray, William, *Conversations: Reynolds Price & William Ray,* Memphis State University (Memphis, TN), 1976.

Schiff, James A., *Understanding Reynolds Price,* University of South Carolina Press (Columbia, SC), 1996.

PERIODICALS

America, October 15, 1988, p. 259; July 28, 1990, p. 67; August 31, 1991, p. 121; March 16, 1996, p. 18.

Atlanta Constitution, May 31, 1995, p. C2.

Atlanta Journal and Constitution, May 10, 1992, p. N8; June 14, 1992, p. N10; May 29, 1994, p. N8; August 14, 1994, p. M1; May 28, 1995, p. K10.

Boston Globe, June 2, 1992, p. 55; June 6, 1993, p. B41; May 21, 1995, p. 77.

Chicago Tribune, May 11, 1990; May 26, 1994, sec. 5, p. 2; February 11, 1996, sec. 15, p. 1.

Christian Century, July 10, 1991, p. 678; November 23, 1994, p. 1108; November 22, 1995, p. 1128; June 5, 1996, p. 633.

Christian Science Monitor, June 25, 1986, p. 21; June 8, 1992, p. 14.

Commonweal, August 12, 1988, p. 438; December 1, 1989, p. 678; May 22, 1992, p. 17; December 3, 1993, p. 22; June 17, 1994, p. 24; December 2, 1994, pp. 24, 29.

Detroit News, July 17, 1989.

Globe and Mail (Toronto), July 2, 1988.

London Review of Books, April 23, 1987, p. 18.

Los Angeles Times, July 12, 1993, p. E3.

Los Angeles Times Book Review, July 10, 1986; May 17, 1987, p. 13; January 3, 1988, p. 10; May 22, 1988, p. 3; August 3, 1989; May 27, 1990, p. 3; July 22, 1990, p. 14; June 16, 1991, p. 7; June 21, 1992, p. 12; May 22, 1994, pp. 1, 8; May 7, 1995, p. 1; July 16, 1995, pp. 4, 15.

Nation, July 30, 1990, p. 139; March 13, 1995, p. 58; March 20, 1995, pp. 391-94.

National Review, June 7, 1993, p. 68; October 24, 1994, p. 73.

New England Journal of Medicine, June 23, 1994, p. 1834.

New Republic, September 29, 1986, p. 40; July 4, 1988, p. 34.

Newsweek, June 23, 1986, p. 78; July 17, 1989, p. 54.

New Yorker, September 22, 1986, p. 116; August 14, 1989, p. 91.

New York Review of Books, September 25, 1986, p. 55.

New York Times, June 24, 1986; January 4, 1987; June 26, 1989; August 26, 1989; November 4, 1989; May 8, 1992, p. C28; May 18, 1996, p. 7.

New York Times Book Review, June 29, 1986, p. 1; February 14, 1988, p. 21; May 8, 1988, p. 10; June 4, 1989, p. 10; May 13, 1990, p. 13; July 7, 1991, p. 5; May 24, 1992, p. 10; February 28, 1993, p. 1; July 4, 1993, p. 8; July 10, 1994, p. 9; May 14, 1995, p. 9; May 19, 1996, p. 12.

Observer (London), February 22, 1987, p. 29.

Poetry, August, 1991, pp. 282-84.

Publishers Weekly, March 13, 1987; April 21, 1989; December 15, 1989; January 24, 1991; March 14, 1994, p. 55; May 9, 1994, p. 51; January 8, 1996, p. 25; April 8, 1996, p. 60.

San Francisco Review of Books, July, 1995, pp. 25-27.

Southern Living, September, 1990, p. 126; September, 1992, p. 38; May, 1994, p. 142.

Southern Review, autumn, 1980, p. 853; spring, 1986, p. 329; summer, 1988, p. 686; spring, 1992, pp. 371-89; winter, 1993, p. 16.

Time, July 10, 1989, p. 62; May 14, 1990, p. 89; May 23, 1994, pp. 66-67; May 22, 1995, p. 73.

Times (London), February 5, 1987.

Times Literary Supplement, May 22, 1987, p. 558.

Tribune Books (Chicago), January 25, 1987, p. 6; December 13, 1987, p. 3; April 17, 1988, p. 6; June 26, 1988, p. 1; June 11, 1989, p. 6; May 6, 1990, p. 3; June 2, 1991, p. 6; May 16, 1993, p. 1; September 25, 1994, p. 5; June 11, 1995, p. 3.

USA Today, June 27, 1986, p. D4; May 13, 1992, p. D4; June 18, 1993, p. D4; February 11, 1994, p. D7.

Variety, March 21, 1994, p. 66.

Voice Literary Supplement, June, 1988, p. 13.

Wall Street Journal, June 26, 1992, p. A9.

Washington Post, September 7, 1986; January 13, 1987.

Washington Post Book World, July 6, 1986, p. 1; February 14, 1988, p. 6; April 10, 1988, p. 5; June 18, 1989, p. 3; May 6, 1990, p. 3; June 2, 1991, p. 1; May 10, 1992, p. 5; May 30, 1993, pp. 1, 7; June 12, 1994, pp. 1, 10; July 16, 1995, p. 4; May 5, 1996, pp. 4-5.

World Literature Today, spring, 1994, pp. 370-71.

OTHER

Clear Pictures, Public Broadcasting System (PBS), 1995.*

* * *

PROSSER, H(arold) L(ee) 1944-
(Harold Lee Prosser; Lee Prosser; pseudonym: Justin Willard Pinoak)

PERSONAL: Born December 31, 1944, in Springfield, MO; son of Harold and Marjorie (maiden name, Firestone) Prosser; married Grace Eileen Wright, November 4, 1971 (divorced, March 3, 1988); married Debra Jeanann Phipps, December 6, 1994; children: (first marriage) Rachael Maranda, Rebecca Dawn. *Education:* Santa Monica College, A.A., 1968; attended California State University, Northridge, 1968-69; Southwest Missouri State University, B.S., 1974, M.S.Ed., 1982; New Mexico Theological Seminary, Santa Fe, certificate of ordination, 1994; has studied under writers Paul Bowles, Alan Casty, and Christopher Isherwood. *Religion:* Affiliated with Unity Church, and Vedanta Society. *Avocational interests:* Fishing.

ADDRESSES: Home—P.O. Box 185, Oologah, OK 74053.

CAREER: Sociologist and writer, 1963—. Proprietor of Justin Willard Pinoak Bookshops, 1969—. Ordained minister, 1994; founder and director, Oneness Center for Spiritual Living, Roswell, NM, 1995-96.

MEMBER: Vedanta Society, Foundation for Shamanic Studies, Gerina Dunwich's Pagan Poets Society, Huna Research.

WRITINGS:

UNDER NAME H. L. PROSSER

Dandelion Seeds: Eighteen Stories, Angst (Selma, OR), 1974.
The Capricorn and Other Fantasy Stories, Angst, 1974.
The Cymric and Other Occult Poems, Mafdet Press, 1976.
The Day of the Grunion and Other Stories, Mafdet Press, 1977.
Spanish Tales, Mafdet Press, 1977.
Goodbye, Lon Chaney, Jr., Goodbye (novelette), W. D. Firestone Press, 1977.
Summer Wine (pamphlet), W. D. Firestone Press, 1979.

UNDER NAME HAROLD LEE PROSSER

Robert Bloch, Borgo (San Bernardino, CA), 1984.
Charles Beaumont, Borgo, 1985.
(Contributor) Carl B. Yoke, *Phoenix from the Ashes: The Literature of the Remade World,* Greenwood, 1987.
Frank Herbert: Prophet of Dune, Borgo Press, 1987.
Desert Woman Visions: One Hundred Poems, Cougar Creek, 1987.
Jack Bimbo's Touring Circus Poems, Cougar Creek, 1988.
The Work of J. N. Williamson, Borgo Press, 1988.
(Contributor) Marilyn Fletcher, *Reader's Guide to 20th Century Science Fiction,* American Library Association (Chicago, IL), 1989.

UNDER NAME LEE PROSSER

Shamanic Poems: 100 Poems, Cougar Creek, 1991.
Wiccan Poems: 100 Poems, Cougar Creek, 1992.
Vedanta Poems: 100 Poems, Cougar Creek, 1993.
Running from the Hunter (biography of Charles Beaumont), Borgo, 1996.

OTHER

Author of short fiction under pseudonym Justin Willard Pinoak. Contributor to magazines, including *Doppelganger, Imagine, Antaeus, Dialogue, Moon, Night Magic, Singing Guns Journal,* and *Social Education.*

Manuscripts collected at University of Wyoming, Laramie, and Donnelly Library, New Mexico Highlands University at Las Vegas, NM.

WORK IN PROGRESS: Shamanism: Becoming a Healer; Astral Travel; The Shaman's Herb Guide.

SIDELIGHTS: H. L. Prosser, who has published under his full name Harold Lee Prosser and under the name Lee Prosser, told *CA:* "My heritage is English, Scottish, Welsh, American Cherokee Indian; taken together, they spell American, and that about sums up my genealogy."

He also wrote: "I feel it is the duty of any good writer to create in clear, concise, correct English if he truly wants to communicate and share with the reader. To do otherwise is to be dishonest. Don't write for a select elite, for when they are gone your work dies with them; but do write for the common man and woman—like [Ernest] Hemingway, [Charles] Dickens, [Mark] Twain, and [Edgar Allen] Poe did—for they are the ones who will keep your work alive long after you're gone. It is all right to experiment creatively, but remember you're writing for the reader as well as yourself, and if the reader fails to understand, then you've accomplished nothing of lasting value.

"The two greatest influences on my writing have been writers Paul Bowles and Christopher Isherwood. I learned my skills through hard work and study, and experimentation, but these two individuals taught me the ropes. Without their early influence and encouragement, I wouldn't be writing today.

"Since 1963, I have written over nine-hundred works for publication. I enjoy live classical and jazz concerts; outdoor sports and hiking; collecting postcards; visiting new locales; taking journeys to nature locations and ghost towns; and cats. My interest since 1960 in the vedic literature of Ancient India and writings of early Christianity have had an impact on my philosophical leanings.

"I enjoy all genres of writing. I have a preference for fantasy fiction. My belief on reading is that it is one of the most precious gifts a person can give to a child, and reading should be encouraged at all levels of public and private education. A good writer should encourage peace as an alternative to world holocaust whenever possible, either verbally or in writings. The themes which appear most frequently in my own writings are: individuality; the outcast and the loner; love; the struggle of the individual for both inner and outer peace; cats.

"I try to write honestly about what I know, have seen, and encountered; like all authors, my work does contain autobiographical elements. I think it would be interesting to fall in love with a friendly extraterrestrial woman, and visa versa, and see what happens, and also, to have a friendship with a mermaid family—a touch of whimsy in one's life helps eliminate many rough edges of existence! Life is what you make of it! Among my favorite books are: *Bhagavad-Gita;* John Steinbeck's *The Acts of King Arthur and His Noble Knights; The Upanishads;* The Holy Bible; Swami Chetanananda's *Avadhuta Gita of Dattatreya; The Collected Stories of Ray Bradbury;* and the collected poems of Emily Dickinson, Robert Frost, Theodore Roethke, along with contemporary American Indian poetry."

BIOGRAPHICAL/CRITICAL SOURCES:

PERIODICALS

Angst Review, January, 1977.

* * *

PROSSER, Harold Lee
See PROSSER, H(arold) L(ee)

* * *

PROSSER, Lee
See PROSSER, H(arold) L(ee)

R

RADOSH, Ronald 1937-

PERSONAL: Born November 1, 1937, in New York, NY; son of Reuben (a milliner) and Ida (Kreichman) Radosh; married Alice Schweig, 1959 (divorced, 1970); married Allis Wolfe (a consumer's union consultant), October 15, 1975; children: (first marriage) Laura, Daniel; (second marriage) Anna. *Education:* University of Wisconsin—Madison, B.A., 1959, Ph.D., 1967; University of Iowa, M.A., 1960. *Politics:* "Democratic socialist." *Religion:* Jewish.

ADDRESSES: *Home*—220 W. 93rd St., Apt. 3D, New York, NY 10025. *Office*—Department of History, Queensborough Community College of the City University of New York, Bayside, NY 11364. *Agent*—Betty Anne Clarke, 28 East 95th St., New York, NY.

CAREER: Queensborough Community College of the City University of New York, Bayside, NY, instructor, 1964-68, assistant professor, 1968-71, associate professor, 1971-78, professor of history, 1978—. Member of graduate faculty at City University of New York Graduate Center.

MEMBER: PEN, American Historical Association, Organization of American Historians, Radical Historians Organization, Columbia University Faculty Seminars in U.S. Civilization.

AWARDS, HONORS: Research grants from Institute of Education Affairs, 1987, Smith Richard Federation, 1987, and Bradley Foundation, 1988.

WRITINGS:

(Editor with Louis Menashe) *Teach-Ins U.S.A.,* Praeger (New York City), 1967.

American Labor and United States Foreign Policy, Random House (New York City), 1969.

(Editor) *Eugene V. Debs,* Prentice-Hall (Englewood Cliffs, NJ), 1972.

(Editor with Murray N. Rothbard) *A New History of Leviathan,* Dutton (New York City), 1973.

Prophets on the Right: Profiles of Conservative Critics of American Globalism, Simon & Schuster (New York City), 1975.

(Editor) *The New Cuba: Paradoxes and Potentials,* Morrow (New York City), 1976.

(With Joyce Milton) *The Rosenberg File: A Search for the Truth,* Holt (New York City), 1983.

(With Harvey Klehr) *The Amerasia Spy Case: Prelude to McCarthyism,* University of North Carolina Press (Chapel Hill, NC), 1996.

Also author, with others, of *El Salvador: Central America in Cold War,* 1982. Contributor of articles and reviews to magazines, including *Nation, New Republic, Progressive, In These Times,* and *Dissent,* and newspapers. Member of editorial board of *Marxist Perspectives.*

SIDELIGHTS: Historian Ronald Radosh has studied and written about many aspects of modern history, including labor, politics in Cuba and Central America, and espionage. Two of his best known books are *The Rosenberg File: A Search for the Truth* and *The Amerasia Spy Case: Prelude to McCarthyism.* In the first, Radosh and his coauthor Joyce Milton take a fresh look at the espionage trial of Julius and Ethel Rosenberg, the husband and wife who were convicted as Soviet spies in 1951 and executed in 1953. The Rosenbergs were said to have provided vital information on the atomic bomb to the Soviets. This act was deemed "worse than murder" by the judge in their case, Irving R. Kaufman, who also blamed the couple for "Communist aggression in Korea, with the resultant casualties exceeding 50,000," according to *Newsweek* writer Jim Miller. Much of America accepted that judgement, but many others held that the Rosenbergs were innocent, and were framed in the name of anti-Communist hysteria.

Radosh and Milton reach a conclusion somewhere between the two extremes. They contend that Julius Rosenberg was indeed an important member of a Soviet spy ring, and that he did provide information concerning the atomic bomb to Soviet officials; that Ethel Rosenberg knew of her husband's activities and assisted him minimally, but that she was not deeply involved, and that her prosecution was a government ploy intended to force a confession from her husband; that the sketches and notes passed on by Julius Rosenberg were not highly significant, being only confirmation of atomic secrets the Soviets already possessed; and that some evidence used against the Rosenbergs in their trial was highly questionable—probably even false.

"The authors of 'The Rosenberg File' say they believed the Rosenbergs were innocent until their study of the documents in the case required them to reassess their views," notes Alan M. Dershowitz in a *New York Times Book Review* article. "The evidence that Julius Rosenberg played a central role in a Soviet spy ring emerges from so many independent, indeed mutually antagonistic sources that it is impossible to discount." Dershowitz praises the authors for the thoroughness of their research, and concludes that their book will provide a starting point for all further discussion of the still-controversial case: "Now that Mr. Radosh and Miss Milton have convincingly demonstrated Julius Rosenberg's guilt, we can turn to the important task of insuring that legal injustices, whether directed against the innocent or the guilty, are not tolerated even in times of political hysteria."

Radosh examines another espionage case in a book coauthored with Harvey Klehr, *The Amerasia Spy Case: Prelude to McCarthyism.* The *Amerasia* case predated that of the Rosenbergs, and is less well known. It was highly significant, however, as it was the first major postwar spy case, and was held up by Senator Joseph McCarthy as proof that the State Department had been infiltrated by Communists. The central figures in the case were Philip Jaffe, editor of a pro-Communist periodical entitled *Amerasia,* and John Stewart Service, a member of the State Department and an expert on China. Jaffe and some of his colleagues at the magazine were Communist sympathizers, and were found in possession of hundreds of classified documents; Service had passed information on to them in the hopes of damaging U.S. support for Chiang Kai-shek's Chinese government, which he did not regard as fit for alliance with the United States. After the arrests of Jaffe, Service, and several others, however, the case unraveled in a web of cover-ups, spurious charges, and cheap political moves. In the end, it never even went to trial.

Radosh and Klehr are commended by numerous reviewers for their conscientious investigation of the case. They "sift through an enormous amount of material," notes John Corry in *American Spectator.* "The research is impeccable, and the judgments are judicious." Reviewing *The Amerasia Spy Case* in *New York Times Book Review,* William L. O'Neill declares: "Mr. Klehr and Mr. Radosh carefully point out the many important links between the Amerasia case and the McCarthy era. And although they do not develop the incident's bizarre and comic aspects as much as they might have, their wonderful material enables readers to see many of the participants with their pants down. People who want to believe that all victims of McCarthyism were innocent will not care for this book. But anyone with an open mind and a taste for deception will find it valuable, even gripping."

Radosh told *CA:* "I agree with the views of my mentor, William Appleman Williams, that the study of history does not allow us to reach back to the past and find ready-made answers for today. Rather, it does allow us to learn how we got to where we are, so that individually and collectively we can formulate relevant alternatives for the present and become actors in making our own history. History can then become both a way of learning and looking at the past, as well as a way of breaking the chains of an earlier era. My own work is written in this spirit."

BIOGRAPHICAL/CRITICAL SOURCES:

PERIODICALS

American Spectator, October, 1983, p. 32; June, 1996, pp. 60-62.
Atlanta Journal-Constitution, June 13, 1986, p. A27.
Atlantic, October, 1983, p. 122.
Commentary, October, 1983, p. 66.
Commonweal, March 9, 1984, p. 151.
Nation, April 10, 1982, p. 440.
National Review, November 25, 1983, p. 1486.
New Republic, March 3, 1982, p. 37; October 31, 1983, p. 30; October 22, 1990, pp. 9-10; August 7, 1995, pp. 25-27.
Newsweek, September 12, 1983, pp. 79-80.
New York, August 29, 1983, p. 98.
New Yorker, September 12, 1983, p. 156.
New York Times, September 13, 1987, p. B2.
New York Times Book Review, August 14, 1983, pp. 1, 14, 18; March 31, 1996, p. 24.
Progressive, November, 1983, p. 38.
Publishers Weekly, December 11, 1995, p. 64.
Time, August 22, 1983, p. 69.
Washington Monthly, October, 1983, p. 60.
Whole Earth Review, winter, 1989, p. 118.*

* * *

RAYMOND, E. V.
See GALLUN, Raymond Z.

* * *

REUTHER, David L(ouis) 1946-

PERSONAL: Born November 2, 1946, in Detroit, MI; son of Roy L. (a labor leader) and Fania (Sonkin) Reuther; married Margaret Miller (a photographer), July 21, 1973; children: Katherine Anna, Jacob Alexander Louis. *Education:* University of Michigan, B.A. (with honors), 1968.

ADDRESSES: Home—271 Central Park W., New York, NY 10024. *Office*—William Morrow and Co., Inc., 1350 Avenue of the Americas, New York, NY 10019.

CAREER: Lewis-Wadhams School, Westport, NY, teacher of humanities, 1968-70; Children's Book Council, Inc., New York City, editor, 1972-75; Scholastic Book Services, New York City, senior editor of Four Winds Press, 1975-82; William Morrow and Co., Inc., New York City, began as vice president and editor in chief of Morrow Junior Books, 1982—, became senior vice president.

MEMBER: Authors Guild, Authors League of America, American Library Association.

WRITINGS:

(With Roy Doty) *Fun to Go: A Take-Along Activity Book* (juvenile), Macmillan (New York City), 1982.
Save-the-Animals Activity Book (juvenile), Random House (New York City), 1982.
(Editor with John Thorn) *The Armchair Quarterback,* Scribner (New York City), 1982.
(Editor with Thorn) *The Armchair Aviator,* Scribner, 1983.
(Editor with Thorn) *The Armchair Mountaineer,* Scribner, 1984.
(With Thorn) *The Hidden Game of Baseball: A Revolutionary Approach to Baseball and Its Statistics,* Doubleday (New York City), 1984.
(Editor with Thorn) *The Armchair Book of Baseball,* Scribner, 1985.
(Editor with Terry Brykczynski) *The Armchair Angler,* Scribner, 1985.
(With Thorn) *The Complete Book of the Pitcher,* Prentice-Hall (Englewood Cliffs, NJ), 1988.
(Editor with Thorn) *The Armchair Traveler,* Prentice-Hall, 1988.
(With Thorn) *Total Baseball,* Warner Books (New York City), 1989, second edition, 1991.
(With Thorn) *The Whole Baseball Catalog,* Simon & Schuster (New York City), 1990.

* * *

ROSENBERG, Ethel (Clifford)1915-
(Eth Clifford, Ruth Bonn Penn, David Clifford)

PERSONAL: Born December 23, 1915 in New York, NY; married David Rosenberg (a publisher), October 15, 1941; children: Ruthanne Zipporah Lazar.

ADDRESSES: Home—1075 Miami Gardens Dr. #102W, North Miami Beach, FL 33179-4600. *Agent*—Ted Chichak, 1040 First Ave., Suite 175, New York, NY 10022.

CAREER: Writer. David-Stewart Publishing Co., Indianapolis, IN, editor and writer, 1959-70.

AWARDS, HONORS: Best Children's Books selection, *Saturday Review* and *New York Times,* 1961, for *Red Is Never a Mouse;* Young Hoosier Award, Association for Indiana Media Educators, 1982, for *Help! I'm a Prisoner in the Library;* Sequoyah Award, Oklahoma Library Association, 1986, for *Just Tell Me When We're Dead.* Clifford also received an Artist's Fellowship Award from the state of Florida in 1987 for her body of work.

WRITINGS:

UNDER NAME ETH CLIFFORD, EXCEPT AS INDICATED

FOR CHILDREN; FICTION

The Year of the Second Christmas, illustrated by Stan Learner, Bobbs-Merrill (Indianapolis), 1959.

Red Is Never a Mouse, illustrated by Bill Heckler, Bobbs-Merrill, 1960.

(With husband, David Rosenberg, under pseudonym David Clifford) *No Pigs, No Possums, No Pandas,* Putnam (New York CIty), 1961.

A Bear before Breakfast, illustrated by Kelly Oechsli, Putnam, 1962.

A Bear Can't Bake a Cake for You, illustrated by Jackie Lacy, E. C. Seale (Indianapolis), 1962.

(Under pseudonym Ruth Bonn Penn) *Mommies Are for Loving,* illustrated by Ed Emberley, Putnam, 1962.

Pigeons Don't Growl and Bears Don't Coo, illustrated by Esther Friend, E. C. Seale, 1963.

(With husband, David Rosenberg, under pseudonym David Clifford) *Your Face Is a Picture,* E. C. Seale, 1963.

(Under pseudonym Ruth Bonn Penn) *Simply Silly,* illustrated by Joseph Reisner, E. C. Seale, 1964.

The Witch That Wasn't, illustrated by Jean Dorion Kauper, E. C. Seale, 1964.

(With Leo C. Fay) *Curriculum Motivation Series: A Necessary Dimension in Reading* (contains *Blue Dog, and Other Stories; The Flying Squirrels, and Other Stories; The Almost Ghost, and Other Stories; The Barking Cat; Better Than Gold;* and *Three Green Men*), illustrated by Carol Burger, Lyons and Carnahan, 1965.

Why Is an Elephant Called an Elephant?, illustrated by Jackie Lacy, Bobbs-Merrill, 1966.

The King Who Was Different, illustrated by Francoise Webb, Bobbs-Merrill, 1969.

The Year of the Three-Legged Deer, illustrated by Richard Cuffari, Houghton (Boston), 1972.

Search for the Crescent Moon, illustrated by Bea Holmes, Houghton, 1973.

Burning Star, illustrated by Leo and Diane Dillon, Houghton, 1974.

The Wild One, illustrated by Arvis Stewart, Houghton, 1974.

The Curse of the Moonraker: A Tale of Survival, Houghton, 1977.

The Rocking Chair Rebellion, Houghton, 1978.

The Killer Swan, Houghton, 1980.

The Strange Reincarnations of Hendrik Verloon, Houghton, 1982.

The Remembering Box, illustrated by Donna Diamond, Houghton, 1985.

I Never Wanted to Be Famous, Houghton, 1986.

The Man Who Sang in the Dark, illustrated by Mary B. Owen, Houghton, 1987, published as *Leah's Song,* Scholastic (New York City), 1989.

I Hate Your Guts, Ben Brooster, Houghton, 1989.

The Summer of the Dancing Horse, Houghton, 1991.

Will Somebody Please Marry My Sister?, illustrated by Ellen Eagle, Houghton, 1992.

Family for Sale, Houghton, 1996.

"JO-BETH AND MARY ROSE" SERIES; ILLUSTRATED BY GEORGE HUGHES

Help! I'm a Prisoner in the Library, Houghton, 1979.

The Dastardly Murder of Dirty Pete, Houghton, 1981.

Just Tell Me When We're Dead, Houghton, 1983.

Scared Silly, Houghton, 1988.

Never Hit a Ghost with a Baseball Bat, Houghton, 1993.

"HARVEY" SERIES

Harvey's Horrible Snake Disaster, Houghton, 1984.

Harvey's Marvelous Monkey Mystery, Houghton, 1987.

Harvey's Wacky Parrot Adventure, edited by Patricia MacDonald, Houghton, 1990.
Harvey's Mystifying Raccoon Mix-Up, Houghton, 1994.

"FLATFOOT FOX" SERIES; ILLUSTRATED BY BRIAN LIES

Flatfoot Fox and the Case of the Missing Eye, Houghton, 1990.
Flatfoot Fox and the Case of the Nosy Otter, Houghton, 1992.
Flatfoot Fox and the Case of the Missing Whoooo, Houghton, 1993.
Flatfoot Fox and the Case of the Bashful Beaver, Houghton, 1995.
Flatfoot Fox and the Case of the Missing Schoolhouse, Houghton, 1997.

NONFICTION

(With Willis Peterson) *Wapiti, King of the Woodland,* Follett, 1961.
Ground Afire: The Story of Death Valley, photographs by Ansel Adams, Follett, 1962.
(Under pseudonym Ruth Bonn Penn) *Unusual Animals of the West,* photographs by Willis Peterson, Follett, 1962.
(With Raymond Carlson) *The Wind Has Scratchy Fingers,* Follett, 1962.
(With Richard E. Kirk and James N. Rogers) *Living Indiana History: Heartland of America,* illustrated by George Armstrong and David Kinney, David-Stewart, 1965.
(With Leo C. Fay) *Curriculum Enrichment Series: A New Dimension in Reading* (contains *Look at the Moon* and *Tommy Finds a Seed*), illustrated by Carol Burger, Lyons and Carnahan, 1965.
(With others) *War Paint and Wagon Wheels: Stories of Indians and Pioneers,* illustrated by David Kinney, Bill Harris, and Polly Woodhouse, David-Stewart, 1968.
(Compiler) *The Magnificent Myths of Man,* edited by Leo C. Fay, Globe Book Company, 1972.
(Editor) *The Third Star: The Story of New Jersey* (textbook), Third Star Publishing, 1974.
Show Me Missouri: A History of Missouri and the World Around It, illustrated by George Armstrong, Russell E. Hollenbeck, and Gene Jarvis, Unified College Press, 1975.

Also contributor of four books to "Reading for Concepts" series, McGraw-Hill, 1970. Contributor to *Basic Science Series,* McGraw-Hill, 1968; *Reading Incentive Series,* McGraw-Hill (Webster Division), 1968; *Pacesetters in Personal Reading,* Lyons and Carnahan, 1969; *Health and Safety Series,* Globe Book Company, 1970; *Living City Adventures,* Globe Book Company, 1970; *Pathways to Health,* Globe Book Company, 1970; and *Pre-Primer Stories for Series 360,* Ginn and Company, 1971. Also lexicographer for *Compton's Illustrated Science Dictionary,* Compton's Encyclopedia Company, 1963; *Dictionary of Natural Science* (2 volumes), Compton's Encyclopedia Company, 1966; and *Discovering Natural Science,* Encyclopedia Britannica, 1967.

FOR ADULTS

Go Fight City Hall (fiction), Simon & Schuster (New York CIty), 1949.
Uncle Julius and the Angel with Heartburn (fiction), Simon & Schuster, 1951.
(Under name Eth Clifford Rosenberg; with Molly Picon) *So Laugh a Little* (fiction), Messner (New York City), 1962.

Also contributor to *Best Humor Annual, 1949-50,* 1950, and *Best Humor Annual, 1951,* 1951, both edited by Louis Untermeyer and Ralph E. Shikes, Holt. Contributor to *A Treasury of Jewish Humor,* edited by Nathan Ausubel, Doubleday, 1951, and *Tales of Our People,* edited by Jerry D. Lewis, Bernard Geis Associates, 1969.

Some of Clifford's papers and manuscripts have been collected by the Division of Rare Books and Special Collections of the University of Wyoming, the Bicentennial Library of California State College in California, and the Kerlan Collection at the Walter Library of the University of Minnesota.

ADAPTATIONS: The Rocking Chair Rebellion was adapted for television by NBC-TV.

SIDELIGHTS: The author of more than eighty children's books, Ethel Rosenberg, better known under her pseudonym of Eth Clifford, is especially praised for the well-received *Year of the Three-Legged Deer, The Killer Swans, The Remembering Box,* and mysteries with a humorous twist such as *Help! I'm a Prisoner in the Library* and *Just Tell Me When We're Dead.* Clifford has, however, written a wide range of books, both fiction and nonfiction, for children and adults. Her adult fiction title, *Go Fight City Hall,* was a bestseller when it appeared in 1949.

"I never, ever thought I would be a writer," Clifford confided in an essay for *Something about the Author Autobiography Series* (*SAAS*). "Writers I regarded as a race apart. They were tall, and handsome, and male. They were brilliant, and witty, and flawless. . . . Then I made an extraordinary discovery. All writers were not necessarily male!. . . But of course, I told myself, these women were tall and beautiful. I was tiny, and certainly not beautiful, so I automatically disqualified myself. . . . I wrote, of course, very early on. I accepted the fact that this did not make me an author. Authors were very special people. I was very class-conscious!"

Whether or not she considered herself a writer, Clifford was a reader from an early age. Born in Manhattan, she moved with her family to rural New Jersey for a time, and then to Philadelphia where her father's employment took him. Clifford was eight when her father died, and the family moved to Brooklyn to live among their relatives. Clifford's father's death was a defining moment of her childhood. "I understood that I would never see him again," she wrote in *SAAS*. "Never hear his voice, never see him smile." It was then that Clifford turned to the solace of fiction—both reading and writing. "I think that somehow that was when I became a writer. Making up stories gave me power—power to create people and situations, power to control what they said and did."

At age seventeen, Clifford met the man she would later marry, someone who loved books as much as she. After marriage and the turmoil of the war years in the 1940s, the two started the David-Stewart Publishing Company, which developed a range of books and educational materials from inception to writing to packaging. Clifford had been writing short stories and publishing them in magazines throughout the 1940s, and the success of her first two novels, *Go Fight City Hall* and its sequel, *Uncle Julius and the Angel with Heartburn,* were encouraging. "And then suddenly, my direction changed," Clifford explained in *SAAS*. "My husband listened each evening as I told stories to our daughter at bedtime. She snuggled down in her pillow, thumb in mouth, ready for story time. One evening, when she was fast asleep, David told me, 'You ought to write those stories down.'" Thus was launched a career in children's books that has lasted nearly four decades.

One of her first children's books, *Red Is Never a Mouse,* was about colors. Chosen as one of the 100 best books of the year by *Saturday Review* and the *New York Times,* that book convinced Clifford to devote full time to writing for children "of all ages," as she put it in *SAAS*. Her early efforts were mainly picture books for young children as well as first readers for school curricula. By the 1970s, however, she was writing longer novels for middle-grade and young adult readers. *The Year of the Three-Legged Deer,* inspired by Clifford's visit to a pioneer museum in Indiana where the family had moved, was set on the Indiana frontier in 1819 and based on actual events. In this story, trader Jesse Benton is married to a Lenni Lenape Indian and has a son and daughter by her. His son brings home an injured deer which his daughter, Chilili, raises. Jesse purchases the freedom of a slave who has saved his son's life, but intolerance and bigotry soon rip the family apart, and Chilili is killed by Indian-hunting whites. Jesse's wife and son decide to go back to their people, joining their removal westward to Missouri. Jeanette Swickard of *Booklist* thought that Clifford's novel presented a "thought-provoking dramatization of the evils of prejudice." Clifford commented in *SAAS* that readers still complain about the death of Chilili: "'Why did you let Chilili die? Can you write the book over again and let her live?' one child begged." Another frontier story—based on the life of Frances Slocum—informs *Search for the Crescent Moon,* the tale of a 15-year-old boy who, along with his grandfather, goes on a search for the old man's twin sister, kidnapped by Indians as a child. Virginia Haviland, writing in *Horn Book,* commented that in this work Clifford "is in full command of her historical material and knows how to invent and present dramatic actions."

Clifford expanded on this technique of fictional biography and history with two books somewhat further afield: one set in Spain, the other in the South Pacific, and both in the nineteenth century. *The Wild One* is the embellished partial biography of young Santiago Ramon y Cajal, winner of the Nobel Prize for medicine in 1906, and of his punishing upbringing that nearly squelched his genius. Desiring to be an artist, the young Santiago was sent to strict schools by his stern doctor father, and became interested in medicine only when his father sought his help in the infirmary and allowed him to use his artistic skills to sketch anatomy drawings. "Santiago's escapades as embellished here make lively reading," noted a *Kirkus Reviews* critic, "and Clifford brings the time and place of his teen-age years to dramatic life." Zena Sutherland of the *Bulletin of the Center for Children's Books* concluded in her review that "the book has good period detail, a sensitive treatment of relationships, strong characterization, and a vigorous style." Clifford's South Pacific novel, *The Curse of the Moonraker,* was based on a true incident: the sinking of a passenger ship in the South Pacific in 1866. Just fifteen passengers survived on the Auckland Islands for a year and a half until being rescued. Told from the point of view of a thirteen-year-old cabin boy, Clifford's Robinson Crusoe narrative "is a gripping one," according to *Horn Book* reviewer Mary M. Burns, "because of the ingenuity by which [the shipwrecked people] battled and defeated the emotional and physical obstacles to their survival." *School Library Journal* contributor Robert Unsworth felt that the novel, on balance, was "a good story, well told, and it deserves a reading."

With *The Rocking Chair Rebellion,* Clifford left the realms of history for contemporary fiction. In this story, protagonist Opie is fourteen and a somewhat reluctant volunteer at the Maple Ridge Home for the Aged where a former neighbor, Mr. Pepper, is an unwilling guest. Pepper and some other residents try to buy a house of their own in Pepper's former neighborhood and set up a communal home for the aged. The neighbors, however, dig in their heels and take the seniors to court. Opie's lawyer father successfully handles the case in this novel which has, according to *Bulletin of the Center for Children's Books* reviewer Zena Sutherland, "a crisp style, sharp characterizations, and humor." *The Rocking Chair Rebellion* was adapted for television by NBC-TV, and several months after publication, a "rebellion" mirroring that in Clifford's book actually took place in Chicago. "Fiction turned into fact!" Clifford wrote in *SAAS.* "That was a joyous moment for me."

Lighthearted, often humorous adventures form the core of some of Clifford's most popular books, those centering on the exploits of sisters Jo-Beth and Mary Rose. Their first adventure, *Help! I'm a Prisoner in the Library,* has the two accidentally locked overnight in a children's library after their father has run out of gas in a blizzard. Spooky sounds abound, the pair save the injured librarian who lives upstairs, and by morning all is well when their father shows up to rescue them. Mary I. Purucker in *School Library Journal* called it a "funny, fast-moving, suspenseful, and engaging easy-to-read tale," and a *Kirkus Reviews* critic noted that the book is a "cozy adventure, easy to read in a sitting." A runaway cousin and bank robbers at an amusement park figure in another Mary Rose and Jo-Beth romp, *Just Tell Me When We're Dead.* Craighton Hippenhammer commented in *School Library Journal* that "lots of laughs and fast-paced action follow," and *Bulletin of the Center for Children's Books* reviewer Zena Sutherland noted that there was "plenty of danger and action for thrill-lovers." A deserted mining town in California with a very life-like ghost fuels the engine of *The Dastardly Murder of Dirty Pete,* a novel with "verve and suspense," according to *Publishers Weekly,* and an unscheduled visit to a bizarre shoe museum gets Jo-Beth and Mary Rose in hot water in *Scared Silly.* With the fifth novel in the series, *Never Hit a Ghost with a Baseball Bat,* Clifford has the sisters explore a haunted trolley museum, fashioning a book which *Booklist* dubbed "another great in the series."

Two distinctive books by Clifford from the 1980s deal with loss and remembrance, handling serious problems with poignancy while avoiding sentimentality. *The Killer Swan* presents something of a paradox with a male white swan, a cob, that attacks its young. Lex, the young protagonist, whose father recently committed suicide, saves one of the cygnets from its father's attack, and ultimately is forced to kill the cob after it attacks a friend's dog. Clifford draws the analogy between the behavior of the cob—actually set off because of the pain it is experiencing from an injured eye—and Lex's father who took his own life. *Publishers Weekly* declared that "Clifford is at her impressive best," and Frank Perry, writing in *Voice of Youth Advocates,* while noting Clifford's "keen insight and sensitivity," concluded that *The Killer Swan* was more than just an animal story: "It is a human story for all persons fortunate enough to read it." *The Remembering Box* also deals with loss, when young Joshua's grandmother dies. But she has left Joshua with a legacy of memories out of her trunk full of mementos, a heritage that bridges the generational and cultural gaps between the two. Hanna B. Zeiger of *Horn Book* noted that "Eth Clifford has succeeded in opening a remembering box for her readers, giving them a glimpse into the world of their grandparents." A *Bulletin of the Center for Children's Books* commentator called the book a "moving remembrance within a remembrance," and Micki S. Nevett in *School Library Journal* wrote that "this warm and loving relationship between a boy and his grandmother is beautifully depicted."

Two separate series also employ Clifford's blend of zany humor and action/mystery writing. The "Harvey" series features young Harvey Willson and sometimes his cousin Nora, with whom he has a tenuous relationship. And most of all, the books feature adventures with various animals: a snake, a monkey, a parrot, a raccoon. *Horn Book* reviewer Elizabeth S. Watson commented of *Harvey's Marvelous Monkey Mystery* that "the real focus is on plenty of action. Children who are looking for the next step after easy readers will find new friends in these books. . . ." Ilene Cooper of *Booklist* found the book "warm, realistic, and certainly funny." Reviewing *Harvey's Wacky Parrot Adventure* for *Booklist,* Deborah Abbott noted that this was "another breezy read for Harvey fans," and Christina Dorr in *School Library Journal* concluded that *Harvey's Mystifying Raccoon Mix-Up* is a "lively page-turner that draws readers into the action and won't disappoint them." The second series to employ Clifford's penchant for mysteries with a light touch are the "Flatfoot Fox" books for younger readers, featuring the Fox as a great detective. These easy-to-read chapter books involve cases ranging from recovering the owl's missing "whoooo" to the otter's missing child, and combine the best of mystery and animal stories. Flatfoot Fox and his sidekick, Secretary Bird, team up initially in *Flatfoot Fox and the Case of the Missing Eye* to create a "clever and funny first chapter book," according to Kay Weisman in *Booklist.* They have continued to please through five further installments in their adventures with a mixture of "tongue-twisting alliterations" and "dry comedy," as Stephanie Zvirin noted in a *Booklist* review of *Flatfoot Fox and the Case of the Bashful Beaver.*

Clifford is at her best when she infuses her work with a quirky humor that has become a hallmark of her writing. She can tackle serious themes but, with a dash of humor, turn such books into easy-reads. A strained relationship between cousins once again comes to play with *I Hate Your Guts, Ben Brooster,* in which near-genius Ben arrives to spend a year with his older cousin, Charlie. Rivalry is put on hold while the mystery of a suitcase Ben has mistakenly taken is solved. "Dollops of humor add fun to a book that demonstrates how children can learn to get along without having to be best friends," according to Deborah Abbott in *Booklist.* Pure fun fills the pages of *I Never Wanted to Be Famous,* in which thirteen-year-old Goody is jarred out of his ambition-less state when he saves an infant from choking. A sudden celebrity, Goody now has to deal with the pressures that fame brings as well as the plans his mother has for him. "*I Never Wanted to Be Famous* is a sheer delight to read," commented Civia Tuteur in *Voice of Youth Advocates.* "It is filled with humor."

A *Publishers Weekly* critic, reviewing *I Never Wanted to be Famous,* noted that "Clifford's quick wit and likable characters have won the hearts of fans who revel in such gems as *Help! I'm a Prisoner in the Library, The Dastardly Murder of Dirty Pete,* etc."—which is high praise for someone who thought she could never be one of those "authors". Over the years, Clifford has created a body of work that has pleased, amused, delighted, and encouraged children to read. "Words are the bridges to communication," Clifford wrote in *SAAS.* "Words on the page say: listen, I've been thinking and I want to share my thoughts with you. Perhaps you've had these same thoughts (and feelings) but haven't been able to express them. But when you read these words, you can say to yourself—that's it. She's got it exactly right."

BIOGRAPHICAL/CRITICAL SOURCES:

BOOKS

Sixth Book of Junior Authors and Illustrators, H. W. Wilson (Bronx, NY), 1989.

Something about the Author Autobiography Series, Volume 22, Gale (Detroit), 1996, pp. 23-38.

PERIODICALS

Booklist, November 1, 1972, p. 246; June 1, 1987, p. 1520; September 1, 1989, p. 68; March 15, 1990, p. 1444; December 15, 1990, p. 861; December 15, 1993, p. 753; April 15, 1994, p. 1540; September 15, 1994, p. 135; March 1, 1995, p. 1242; February 1, 1996, p. 932.

Bulletin of the Center for Children's Books, January, 1973, p. 73; March, 1975, p. 107; May, 1978, p. 139; March, 1979, p. 111; April, 1980, p. 148; March, 1981, p. 129; February, 1983, p. 104; February, 1984, p. 104; December, 1985, p. 64; April, 1988, p. 152; July, 1990, p. 261; March, 1992, p. 177; November, 1992, p. 70; November, 1993, p. 77.

Horn Book, October, 1973, p. 464; April, 1978, pp. 162-163; February, 1979, p. 59; April, 1981, p. 189; March-April, 1986, p. 200; July-August, 1987, p. 461.

Kirkus Reviews, October 15, 1974, pp. 1109-1110; December 15, 1979, pp. 1429-1430; November 15, 1994, p. 1524; December 15, 1995, p. 1768.

New York Times Book Review, June 18, 1972, p. 8.

Publishers Weekly, December 12, 1980, pp. 47-48; December 11, 1981, p. 62; April 25, 1986, p. 83.

School Library Journal, March, 1978, p. 125; October, 1978, p. 153; November, 1979, p. 63; November, 1980, p. 84; January, 1982, p. 61; December, 1983, p. 64; December, 1985, p. 87; May, 1986, p. 89; April, 1987, p. 92; October, 1987, p. 124; June, 1988, p. 103; October, 1989, p. 116; March, 1991, p. 170; July, 1991, p. 72; September, 1991, p. 201; June, 1992, p. 112; June, 1993, p. 104; August, 1993, p. 140; October, 1994, p. 120; April, 1995, p. 100; April, 1996, p. 132.

Voice of Youth Advocates, April, 1981, pp. 31-32; August, 1986, p. 140.

* * *

ROSENTHAL, Shirley Lord 1934-
(Shirley Lord)

PERSONAL: Born August 28, 1934, in London, England; came to the United States in 1971; daughter of Francis James (a company director) and Mabel (Williamson) Stringer; married Cyril Lord, January 17, 1960 (divorced December, 1973); married David Jean Anderson (a business consultant), August 3, 1974 (died January, 1985); married A. M. Rosenthal (a *New York Times* columnist), June 10, 1987. *Education:* Attended South West Essex Technical College, Essex, England. *Politics:* Conservative. *Religion:* Roman Catholic.

ADDRESSES: Home—131 East 66th St., New York, NY 10021. *Office— Vogue* Magazine, 140 East 45th St., New York, NY 10017.

CAREER: London Star, London, woman's editor, 1960-61; *Evening Standard,* London, woman's editor, 1961-63; *London Evening News,* woman's editor, 1963-67; *Harper's Bazaar,* London and New York City, beauty and health editor, 1963-73; *Vogue,* New York City, beauty and health editor, 1973-75; Helena Rubinstein, U.S.A., vice president for corporate development and public relations, 1975-80; *Vogue,* beauty director, 1980-94, director of special projects, 1994—. Professional international and domestic tours include "The Shirley Lord Show," "The Shirley Lord Beauty Breakfast," and "A Better Look at Your Life." City commissioner for Craigavon, Northern Ireland.

WRITINGS:

UNDER NAME SHIRLEY LORD

Small Beer at Claridge's (autobiography), M. Joseph (London), 1968.

The Easy Way to Good Looks, illustrated by Martha Voutas, Crowell (New York City), 1976.

You Are Beautiful, and How to Prove It, Sidgwick & Jackson (London), 1978.

Golden Hill: A Novel, Crown (New York City), 1982.

One of My Very Best Friends: A Novel, Crown, 1985.

Faces (novel), Crown, 1989.

My Sister's Keeper, Crown, 1993.

Author of syndicated column, "Be Beautiful," Field Syndicate, 1975—.

WORK IN PROGRESS: A radio series on beauty; *The Crasher,* a novel, for Warner Books, optioned to Miramax Films.

BIOGRAPHICAL/CRITICAL SOURCES:

PERIODICALS

New York Times, October 21, 1982.

New York Times Book Review, October 24, 1982; October 27, 1985; June 11, 1987.

Washington Post Book World, December 5, 1982.

ROSS, Marilyn (Ann) Heimberg 1939-
(Marilyn Markham Heimberg)

PERSONAL: Born November 3, 1939, in San Diego, CA; daughter of Glenn J. (in business) and Dorothy (a real estate broker; maiden name, Scudder) Markham; married T. M. Ross (an advertising executive), May 25, 1977; children: Scott, Steve, Kevin, Laurie. *Ethnicity:* "Caucasian." *Education:* Attended San Diego State University. *Religion:* Church of Religious Science. *Avocational interests:* Dancing, horses, reading.

ADDRESSES: *Home*—P.O. Box 909, Buena Vista, CO 81211; fax: 719-395-8374.

CAREER: Manager of a woman's ready-to-wear business, 1959-69; San Diego-South Bay Trade Schools, San Diego, CA, director of marketing, 1969-74; marketing consultant, advertising copywriter, and writer, 1974-80; About Books, Inc. (nationwide writing and publishing consulting service), cofounder, 1980. Communication Creativity, Buena Vista, CO, president, beginning 1978; Copy Concepts, cofounder, 1978, director, beginning in 1978. San Diego Community College District, instructor, 1975-77. Research Electronics Co., member of board of directors.

MEMBER: Small Publishers Association of North America (SPAN; cofounder, 1996; executive director), Authors League of America, Authors Guild, American Society of Journalists and Authors, National Speakers Association, San Diego Women in Business (founding member of board of directors).

AWARDS, HONORS: First place in nonfiction from Southern Division of California Press Women, 1977, for "Business Bites Back at Internal Crime," 1978, for *Creative Loafing: Shoestring Guide to New Leisure Fun,* and 1979, for *Encyclopedia of Self-Publishing: How to Successfully Write, Publish, Promote and Sell Your Own Work.*

WRITINGS:

(Under name Marilyn Markham Heimberg) *Discover Your Roots: A New, Easy Guide for Tracing Your Family Tree,* Communication Creativity (Buena Vista, CO), 1977.

(Under name Marilyn Markham Heimberg) *Finding Your Roots: How to Trace Your Ancestors and Record Your Family Tree,* Dell (New York City), 1978.

Creative Loafing: A Shoestring Guide to New Leisure Fun, Communication Creativity, 1978.

(With husband, T. M. Ross) *The Encyclopedia of Self-Publishing: How to Successfully Write, Publish, Promote and Sell Your Own Work,* Communication Creativity, 1979, second edition, 1980.

Be Tough or Be Gone, Northern Trails Press, 1984.

The Complete Guide to Self-Publishing, Writer's Digest Books (Cincinnati, OH), 1985, third edition, 1994.

How to Make Big Profits Publishing City and Regional Books, Communication Creativity, 1987.

Big Ideas for Small Service Businesses, Communications Creativity, 1994.

Country Bound!, Dearborn Financial Publishing (Chicago), second edition, 1997.

Ghost writer and editor. Contributor to hundreds of magazines and newsletters, including *Essence, Modern Maturity, Nation's Business, Entrepreneur, Catholic Digest,* and *Westways.* Editor of *People in Motion* (company newsletter), 1971-74, and *SPAN Connection,* 1996—.

SIDELIGHTS: Marilyn Heimberg Ross told *CA:* "Writing serves as my window to the world. It gives me a vehicle to share my knowledge and empower people. I strive to provide books and articles rich in content, yet fun to read.

"My husband Tom and I have been active in the self-publishing movement for two decades. We recently founded the Small Publishers Association of North America (SPAN) to give back to this industry that has been so good to us over the years.

"Through the vehicles of writing, speaking, and consulting, I am blessed with a career that is fulfilling to me and enriching for others."

* * *

ROTHMAN, David J. 1937-

PERSONAL: Born April 30, 1937, in New York City; son of Murray and Anne (Beier) Rothman;

married Sheila Miller, June 26, 1960; children: Matthew, Micol. *Education:* Columbia University, B.A., 1958; Harvard University, M.A., 1959, Ph.D., 1964.

ADDRESSES: Office—Columbia University, College of Physicians and Surgeons, Center for the Study of Society and Medicine, 630 W. 168th St., New York, NY 10032-3702.

CAREER: Columbia University, New York, NY, assistant professor, 1964-67, associate professor, 1967-70, professor of history, 1971—; Bernard Schoenberg professor of social medicine; director of Center for Study of Society and Medicine. Fulbright professor, Hebrew University, Jerusalem, 1968-69; Fulbright professor in India, 1982. Fellow of Center for the Study of History of Liberty in America, Harvard University, 1965-66; member of Committee to Study Incarceration, sponsored by Field Foundation, 1971-72; visiting Pinkerton Professor, School of Criminal Justice, State University at New York, 1973-74; Samuel Paley lecturer, Hebrew University, Jerusalem, 1977; co-director, Project on Community Alternatives, 1978-82; board of directors, Mental Health Law Project, 1973-80, 1982—.

MEMBER: American Historical Association, Organization of American Historians, New York State Academy of Medicine, Phi Beta Kappa.

AWARDS, HONORS: Grants from American Philosophical Society, 1967, and U.S. Department of Health, Education and Welfare, 1968-69; fellowships from Social Science Research Council, 1968, National Endowment for the Humanities, 1971-72, and National Science Foundation, 1972-73; Albert J. Beveridge Prize, American Historical Association, 1971, for *The Discovery of the Asylum: Social Order and Disorder in the New Republic;* fellowships from National Institutes of Mental Health, 1974-75, 1978-81; Law Enforcement Assistance Administration fellow, 1975-76.

WRITINGS:

Politics and Power: The United States Senate, 1869-1901, Harvard University Press (Cambridge, MA), 1966.

(With Neil Harris and Stephan Thernstorm) *The History of the United States: Source Readings,* two volumes, Holt (New York City), 1969.

The Discovery of the Asylum: Social Order and Disorder in the New Republic, Little, Brown (Boston), 1971, revised edition published in 1990.

(With Willard Gaylin, Ira Glasser, and Steven Marcus) *Doing Good: The Limits of Benevolence,* Pantheon (New York City), 1978.

Incarceration and Its Alternatives in 20th Century America, U.S. Department of Justice, Law Enforcement Assistance Administration (Washington, DC), 1979.

Conscience and Convenience: The Asylum and Its Alternatives in Progressive America, Little, Brown, 1980.

(With wife, Sheila M. Rothman) *The Willowbrook Wars,* Harper (New York City), 1984.

Strangers at the Bedside: A History of How Law and Bioethics Transformed Medical Decision Making, Basic Books (New York City), 1991.

(With Aryeh Neier) *Prison Conditions in India,* Human Rights Watch (New York City), 1991.

EDITOR

(With Sheila M. Rothman) *On Their Own: The Poor in Modern America,* Addison-Wesley (Reading, MA), 1972.

(With Stanton Wheeler) *Social History and Social Policy,* Academic Press (New York City), 1981.

(With Steven Marcus and Spephanie A. Kiceluk) *Medicine and Western Civilization,* Rutgers University Press (New Brunswick, NJ), 1995.

(With Norval Morris) *The Oxford History of the Prison: The Practice of Punishment in Western Society,* Oxford University Press (New York City), 1995.

Also editor of *The Sources of American Social Tradition,* 1975, *The World of the Adams Chronicles,* 1976, and *The Sources of American Society.* Advisory editor of Arno's *Poverty in America: The Historical Record,* 1971, *The Family in America,* 1972, and *The Family,* Arno Press (New York City), 1979.

EDITOR WITH SHEILA R. ROTHMAN; "WOMEN AND CHILDREN FIRST" SERIES; PUBLISHED BY GARLAND (NEW YORK CITY)

Children's Hospitals in the Progressive Era: Two Investigations of Substandard Conditions, 1987.

The Consumers' League of New York: Behind the Scenes of Women's Work, 1987.
Dangers of Education: Sexism and the Origins of Women's colleges, 1987.
Divorce: The First Debates, 1987.
Low Wages and Great Sins: Two Antebellum American Views on Prostitution and the Working Girl, 1987.
Maternal Mortality in New York City and Philadelphia, 1931-1933, 1987.
National Congress of Mothers: The First Conventions, 1987.
The Origins of Adoption, 1987.
Risks for the Single Woman in the City, 1987.
Women in Prison, 1834-1928, 1987.

OTHER

Contributor to history journals.

SIDELIGHTS: David J. Rothman makes a significant contribution to the study of public institutions with his book *The Discovery of the Asylum: Social Order and Disorder in The New Republic* (published in a revised edition in 1990). In it, he presents a detailed history of penitentiaries, orphanages, poorhouses, workhouses, and insane asylums in the United States, from the Revolutionary War era until the time of the Civil War. "The boldness and sweep of his arguments and the resonance of his implicitly anti-institutional, antibureaucratic, anti-expert analysis of nineteenth-century prisons, asylums and juvenile reformatories made that book an instant success," remarks Andrew Scull in *Nation.*

Rothman explains that in colonial society, it was widely accepted that poverty, insanity, and criminal behavior were inescapable elements of the human condition, brought on by mankind's inherent sinfulness and God's great plan for the universe. Accordingly, the poor, the infirm, and the lawless were considered an integral part of the larger community. Rothman further notes that by far the strongest force in early American society was that of the household and the family. Therefore, the household was considered the proper place for ill, impoverished, orphaned, or insane citizens. At times, public funds were allocated for the care of such individuals, but they lived within family units—usually their own. Criminals were punished with fines, public humiliation, and—in extreme cases—execution, but they were rarely jailed for long periods.

Society underwent dramatic changes following the Revolution, however. The strength of the household began to crumble. Simultaneously, a belief arose that a utopian world really was possible. The infirm, the indigent, and the criminally inclined came to be seen as deviants from the utopian ideal rather than as integral parts of the imperfect world. The era of social reform dawned, in which it was believed that if only the proper institutions were established, such people could be isolated, reshaped, and then released as model citizens. During the 1820s, 1830s, and 1840s, orphanages, insane asylums, penitentiaries, poorhouses, and other institutions sprang up everywhere, founded on idealistic principles.

By 1850, most of the ideals had faded away. Public institutions still flourished, but their function was acknowledged to be grim and practical, and conditions in them were frequently horrific. Rothman examines the reasons why the institutions were preserved even though they had failed so miserably in their stated aims, and he states that new, experimental alternatives to the continuing tradition of isolating the "problem" members of our society must be explored. An *Antioch Review* contributor praises Rothman's book as "a painstaking effort to place social ills in a social context." *Commonweal* reviewer Peter Steinfels finds the book "fascinating," and a *Library Journal* writer deems it "fundamental to an understanding of our present problems in this institutional sphere." "This is more than a book about 'the discovery of the asylum'; it is also a major study in the development of the American character," declares John Demos in *New York Times Book Review.* "Ever alert to the human dimensions of his subject, Rothman concentrates on the people who founded and supported the first asylums. He explores their stated motives, their unstated premises and their relationship to the larger currents of social change that were building throughout the country. It is, above all, his sure sense of context that gives his study a remarkable vitality. The result is nothing less than a portrait of a whole generation of Americans, caught in a variety of revealing and sometimes contradictory poses," Demos adds.

Rothman focused exclusively on prisons in a book he co-edited with Norval Morris, *The Oxford History of the Prison: The Practice of Punishment in Western Society.* Assessing the volume in *New York Times Book Review,* Yale Kamisar judges it "well-written and intelligently indexed" and "also quite handsome—thanks to the more than 100 paintings, drawings and photographs scattered throughout. Especially poignant are the eight full pages of artwork produced by inmates of the California State Prison System's Art in Corrections program."

BIOGRAPHICAL/CRITICAL SOURCES:

PERIODICALS

Antioch Review, summer, 1971, p. 286.
Booklist, November 1, 1971, pp. 222-23; December 15, 1995, pp. 673, 692.
Commentary, July, 1980, p. 75.
Commonweal, December 3, 1971, p. 238.
Journal of American History, June, 1992, p. 346.
Journal of the American Medical Association, August 14, 1991, p. 851.
Library Journal, April 15, 1971, p. 1381; March 15, 1991, p. 110; November 1, 1995, p. 92; December, 1995, p. 144.
Los Angeles Times Book Review, May 26, 1991, p. 5.
Nation, June 28, 1980, p. 794-6.
New England Journal of Medicine, November 7, 1991, p. 1387.
New Leader, August 12, 1991, pp. 15-17.
New Republic, June 14, 1980, p. 29; February 4, 1985, p. 28; February 26, 1996, pp. 39-41.
New Statesman & Society, March 1, 1996, p. 39.
Newsweek, November 12, 1984, p. 105.
New York Review of Books, June 26, 1980, p. 14; October 22, 1992, p. 21; September 23, 1993, p. 56.
New York Times Book Review, September 26, 1971, p. 41; April 6, 1980, p. 7; May 12, 1991, p. 28; August 6, 1995, p. 22; February 11, 1996, p. 27.
Times Literary Supplement, August 16, 1991, p. 12.
Virginia Quarterly Review, spring, 1972.
Washington Monthly, October, 1984, p. 56.*

* * *

RUARK, Gibbons 1941-

PERSONAL: Born December 10, 1941, in Raleigh, NC; son of Henry Gibbons (a minister) and Sarah (Jenkins) Ruark; married Kay Stinson, October 5, 1963; children: Jennifer Kay, Emily Westbrook. *Ethnicity:* "Caucasian." *Education:* University of North Carolina at Chapel Hill, A.B., 1963; University of Massachusetts, M.A., 1965.

ADDRESSES: Office—Department of English, University of Delaware, Newark, DE 19716. *E-mail*—gruark@udel.edu.

CAREER: University of North Carolina at Greensboro, instructor in English, 1965-68; University of Delaware, Newark, assistant professor, 1968-73, associate professor, 1973-83, professor of English, 1983—.

AWARDS, HONORS: National Arts Council awards for poetry, 1968, and 1971, for *A Program for Survival;* National Endowment for the Arts fellowships, 1979, 1986, and 1993; Saxifrage Prize, 1984, for the poem "Keeping Company."

WRITINGS:

(Editor with Robert Watson) *The Greensboro Reader,* University of North Carolina Press (Chapel Hill), 1968.
A Program for Survival (poems), University Press of Virginia (Charlottesville), 1971.
Reeds (poems), Texas Tech University Press (Lubbock), 1978.
Keeping Company (poems), Johns Hopkins University Press (Baltimore, MD), 1983.
Small Rain (poems), The Center for Edition Works, 1984.
Forms of Retrieval (special edition of *Yarrow*), Kutztown University Press (Kutztown, PA), 1989.
Rescue the Perishing (poems), Louisiana State University Press (Baton Rouge), 1991.

Work represented in numerous anthologies, including *American Literary Anthology #1,* Farrar, Strauss (New York City), 1968; *Best Poems of 1968,* edited by Lionel Stevenson and others, Pacific Books, 1969; *Messages,* edited by X. J. Kennedy, Little, Brown (Boston), 1973; *Best Poems of 1974,* edited by Stevenson and others, Pacific Books, 1975; *Introduction to Poetry,* edited by Kennedy, Little, Brown, 1982; *Introduction to Literature,* edited by Kennedy, Little, Brown, 1983; *1984 Anthology of Modern Poetry,* Monitor Book (Palm Springs, CA), 1984; *The Morrow Anthology of Younger American Poets,* edited by Dave Smith and David Bottoms, Morrow (New York City), 1984; *The Made Thing,* by Leon

Stokesbury, Arkansas, 1987; *The Direction of Poetry,* edited by Robert Richman, Houghton (Boston), 1988; *Vital Signs,* by Robert Wallace, Wisconsin, 1989; *Articles of War,* by Stokesbury, Arkansas, 1990; *Poetry: A HarperCollins Pocket Anthrology,* edited by R. S. Gwynn, HarperCollins (New York City), 1993; and *The Pushcart Prize XV.*

WORK IN PROGRESS: Poems.

SIDELIGHTS: A tape recording of Gibbons Ruark's poems has been placed in the archives of the Library of Congress.

BIOGRAPHICAL/CRITICAL SOURCES:

BOOKS

Chappell, Fred, *Plow Naked,* University of Michigan Press (Ann Arbor), 1993.

Contemporary Literary Criticism, Volume 3, Gale (Detroit, MI), 1975.

PERIODICALS

American Book Review, June/July, 1993.
American Poetry Review, January/February, 1979.
Antioch Review, summer, 1984.
Choice, March, 1979.
Chowder Review, spring/summer, 1979.
Gettysburg Review, spring, 1992.
Kliatt, April, 1992.
Midwest Quarterly, Volume 12, 1971.
Poetry, September, 1984.
Publishers Weekly, July 5, 1991.
Roanoke Times, November 13, 1983.
Saturday Review, December 18, 1971.
Virginia Quarterly Review, autumn, 1971.

S

SAFA, Helen M. Icken 1930-

PERSONAL: Surname is accented on second syllable; born December 4, 1930, in Brooklyn, NY; daughter of Gustav F. (self-employed) and Erna (Keune) Icken; married Manouchehr Safa-Isfahani (with United Nations), December 23, 1962 (died, 1994); children: Mitra; stepchildren: Kaveh, Arya. *Education:* Cornell University, B.A., 1952; Columbia University, M.A., 1958, Ph.D., 1962. *Politics:* Democrat. *Religion:* Protestant.

ADDRESSES: Home—2021 Northwest 15th Ave., Gainesville, FL 32605. *Office*—Center for Latin American Studies, University of Florida, 319 Grinter Hall, Gainesville, FL 32611.

CAREER: New York City Board of Education, New York City, research assistant, 1954; training and evaluation officer, Puerto Rican Department of State, Technical Cooperation Administration, 1954-55; information analyst, Commonwealth of Puerto Rico, Social Programs Administration, 1955-56; consultant in Research Office, New York State Division of Housing, 1956-57; consultant in Research Office, Commonwealth of Puerto Rico, Urban Renewal and Housing Administration, 1959-60; Inter-American Housing and Planning Center, Pan American Union, Bogata, Colombia, temporary consultant, 1961; Syracuse University, Syracuse, NY, assistant professor of anthropology and senior research associate of Youth Development Center, 1962-67; Rutgers University, New Brunswick, NJ, associate professor, 1967-72, professor of anthropology and urban planning, 1972-74, associate director, then director of Latin American Institute, 1970-74, New Brunswick Chairperson of Anthropology, 1974-80, graduate director, 1974-76; University of Florida, Gainesville, director of Center for Latin American Studies and professor of anthropology, 1980-85, professor of anthropology and Latin American studies, 1985—. Has coordinated and participated in numerous conferences throughout the world. Member of review boards, panels, and delegations, 1974—. Fulbright program, member of advisory screening committee, 1974-77, chairperson, 1983-86; member of Inter-American Foundation doctoral fellowship committee, 1987-90.

MEMBER: International Congress of Americanists, American Anthropological Association (fellow), Society for Applied Anthropology (fellow), Latin American Studies Association (member of executive committee, 1974-77; president, 1983-84), American Ethnological Society, National Organization for Women, Phi Beta Kappa.

AWARDS, HONORS: Grant from National Institutes of Mental Health, 1963, 1969-70, 1980-83; grant from U.S. Office of Education, 1966-67; collaborative research grant from Social Science Research Council, 1976-77; grant from Smithsonian Foreign Currency Program, 1978-79; grant from Wenner-Gren Foundation for Anthropological Research conference grant, 1980, 1985, and 1995-96; collaborative grant from National Science Foundation; named distinguished professor, University of Utrecht, Netherlands, 1987, and Northwestern University, 1990; fellow, Kellogg Institute for International Studies, University of Notre Dame, 1989; Rockefeller Foundation grant, 1992-96, for study in Florida and Bellagio, Italy; Rockefeller conference grant, 1996.

WRITINGS:

The Urban Poor of Puerto Rico: A Study in Development and Inequality, Holt (New York City), 1974.

(Editor with Brian DuToit) *Migration and Development,* Mouton (The Hague), 1975.

(Editor with DuToit) *Migration and Ethnicity,* Mouton, 1975.

(Editor with Gloria Levitas) *Social Problems in Corporate America,* Harper (New York City), 1975.

(Editor with June Nash) *Sex and Class in Latin America,* Praeger (New York City), 1976.

(Editor) *Toward a Political Economy of Urbanization in Third World Countries,* Oxford University Press (New Delhi), 1982.

(Editor with Nash) *Women and Change in Latin America: New Directions in the Study of Sex and Class in Latin America,* J. F. Bergin, 1985.

(Editor with Eleanor Leacock) *Women's Work: Development and the Division of Labor by Gender,* Bergin & Garvey (South Hadley, MA), 1986.

(With Carmen D. Deere and others) *In the Shadows of the Sun: Alternative Development Strategies in the Caribbean,* Westview (Boulder, CO), 1995.

The Myth of the Male Breadwinner: Women and Industrialization in the Caribbean, Westview, 1995.

CONTRIBUTOR

Irwin Deutscher and E. Thompson, editors, *Among the People: Encounters with the Urban Poor,* Basic Books (New York City), 1968.

Anuario Indigenista, Volume 39, Inter-American Indian Institute, 1969.

Murray Wax, editor, *Anthropological Perspectives on Education,* Basic Books, 1971.

Peter Orleans and Russell Ellis, editors, *Urban Affairs Annual Review,* Volume 5, Sage Publications (Beverly Hills, CA), 1971.

Charles O. Crawford, editor, *The Family: Structure and Function in Health Crises,* Macmillan (New York City), 1971.

Family and Social Change in the Caribbean, Institute of Caribbean Studies, University of Puerto Rico, 1973.

S. L. Bailey and R. T. Hyman, editors, *Perspectives on Latin America,* Bobbs-Merrill (New York City), 1974.

Boxandall, Gordon, and Reverby, editors, *America's Working Women,* Vintage Book (St. Paul, MN), 1977.

D. Shimkin and others, editors, *Anthropology for the Future,* University of Illinois (Champaign, IL), 1978.

Women and National Development, University of Chicago Press, 1978.

I. Horowitz, J. Leggett, and M. Oppenheimer, editors, *The American Working Class: Perspectives for the 1980s,* Dutton (New York City), 1979.

D. Mortimer and R. S. Bruce-Laporte, editors, *Female Immigrants to the United States: Caribbean, Latin American, and African Experiences,* Smithsonian Institution (Washington, DC), 1981.

J. Nash and M. P. Fernandez Kelly, editors, *Women and the International Division of Labor,* State University of New York Press (Albany, NY), 1983.

N. El-Sanabary, editor, *Women and Work in the Third World,* Center for the Study, Education, and Advancement of Women, University of California, Berkeley, 1983.

Jack Hopkins, editor, *Latin America: Perspectives of a Region,* Holmes & Meier (New York City), 1985.

(Author of preface) Steve Sanderson, editor, *The Americas in the International Division of Labor,* Holmes & Meier, 1985.

H. P. Smith and J. Feagin, editors, *The Capitalist City: Global Restructuring and Communist Affairs,* Basil Blackwell (London), 1987.

Leith Mullings, editor, *Cities in the United States,* Columbia University Press (New York City), 1987.

E. Acosta-Belen and B. Sjostrom, editors, *The Hispanic Experience in the United States,* Praeger, 1988.

S. Stichter and J. Parpart, editors, *Women, Employment and the Family in the International Division of Labor,* Macmillan, 1990.

L. Beneria and S. Feldman, editors, *Unequal Burden: Economic Crisis, Persistent Poverty and Gender Inequality,* Westview Press, 1992.

From Labrador to Samoa: The Theory and Practice of Eleanor Burke Leacock, American Anthropological Association (Washington, DC), 1993.

E. Bonacich and others, editors, *Global Production: The Apparel Industry in the Pacific Rim,* Temple University Press (Philadelphia, PA), 1994.

C. Bose and Acosta-Belen, editors, *Women in the Latin American Development Process,* Temple University Press, 1995.

K. Roy and others, editors, *Economic Development and Women in the World Community,* Praeger, 1996.

V. Moghadam, editor, *Patriarchy and Economic Development,* Clarendon Press (Oxford, England), 1996.

OTHER

Also contributor, June Nash and Juan Corradi, editors, *Ideology and Social Change in Latin America,* 1975. Contributor to numerous periodicals, including *American Anthropologist, Contemporary Sociology, Cultural Survival, Caribbean Studies, Human Organization,* and *Latin American Perspectives.* Guest editor, *American Behavioral Scientist,* March-April 1972, *Signs,* 1981, *New West Indian Guide,* Volume 61, numbers 3 and 4, 1987.

* * *

SCANNELL, Vernon 1922-

PERSONAL: Born January 23, 1922, in Spilsby, Lincolnshire, England; married Josephine Higson, October, 1954; children: Nancy, Tobias, Benjamin (deceased), Jane, John, Jacob. *Education:* Attended University of Leeds, 1946-47. *Politics:* "Romantic Radical."

ADDRESSES: Home—51 North St., Otley, West Yorkshire LS21 1AH, England.

CAREER: Writer. Professional boxer, 1945-46; teacher of English, Hazelwood School, Limpsfield, Surrey, England, 1955-62. Resident poet, village of Berinsfield, Oxfordshire, 1975; visiting poet, Shrewsbury School, Shropshire, 1978-79, and King's School, Canterbury, 1979. Freelance broadcaster. *Military service:* British Army, 1941-46.

MEMBER: Royal Society of Literature (fellow).

AWARDS, HONORS: Heinemann Award for Literature, Royal Society of Literature, 1960, for *The Masks of Love;* Cholmondoley Poetry Prize, 1974, for *The Winter Man;* Society of Authors' Traveling Scholarship, 1984; Poetry Book Society recommendation, for *A Sense of Danger;* Poetry Book Society Choice citation, for *The Loving Game.*

WRITINGS:

POETRY

Graves and Resurrections, Fortune Press (London), 1948.

A Mortal Pitch, Villiers (London), 1957.

The Masks of Love, Putnam (London), 1960.

A Sense of Danger, Putnam, 1962.

Walking Wounded: Poems 1962-1965, Eyre & Spottiswoode (London), 1965.

Epithets of War: Poems 1965-1969, Eyre & Spottiswoode, 1969.

Mastering the Craft (for children), Pergamon (Oxford), 1970.

Selected Poems, Allison & Busby (London), 1971.

Company of Women, Sceptre Press (Frensham, Surrey), 1971.

Incident at West Bay, Keepsake Press, 1972.

The Winter Man, Allison & Busby (Richmond, Surrey), 1973.

Meeting in Manchester, Sceptre Press, 1974.

The Apple-Raid and Other Poems (for children), Chatto & Windus (London), 1974.

The Loving Game, Robson Books (London), 1975.

An Ilkley Quintet, privately printed, c. 1975.

(With Alexis Lykiard) *A Modern Tower Reading 1,* Modern Tower (Newcastle-upon-Tyne), 1976.

New and Collected Poems: 1950-1980, Robson Books, 1980.

Winterlude, Robson Books, 1982.

(With Gregory Harrison and Laurence Smith) *Catch the Light* (for children), Oxford University Press (Oxford), 1983.

Funeral Games and Other Poems, Robson Books, 1987.

The Clever Potato (for children), Century Hutchinson (London), 1988.

Soldiering On: Poems of Military Life, Robson Books, 1989.

Love Shouts and Whispers (for children) illustrated by Tony Ross, Century Hutchinson, 1990.

A Time for Fires, Robson Books, 1991.

Traveling Light (for children), illustrated by Ross, Bodley Head, 1991.

Collected Poems, 1950-1993, Robson Books, 1994.

The Black and White Days, Robson Books, 1996.

Also author of *On Your Cycle Michael,* illustrated by Ross. Contributor to books, including *Maver-*

icks: An Anthology, edited by Howard Sergeant and Dannie Abse, Editions Poetry and Poverty (London), 1957; (with Jon Silkin) *Pergamon Poets 8* (anthology), edited by Dennis Butts, Pergamon, 1970; *Corgi Modern Poets in Focus: 4* (anthology), edited by Jeremy Robson, Corgi Books (London), 1971; and *Poets in Hand,* edited by Anne Harvey, Puffin, 1985.

NOVELS

The Fight, Nevill (London), 1953.
The Wound and the Scar, Nevill, 1954.
The Big Chance, John Long (London), 1960.
The Shadowed Place, John Long, 1961.
The Face of the Enemy, Putnam, 1961.
The Dividing Night, Putnam, 1962.
The Big Time, Longmans, Green (London), 1965.
The Dangerous Ones, (for children), Pergamon, 1970.
A Lonely Game (for children), Wheaton (Exeter), 1979.
Ring of Truth, Robson Books, 1983.

OTHER

(Editor with Patricia Beer and Ted Hughes) *New Poems 1962: A PEN Anthology of Contemporary Poetry,* Hutchinson, 1962.
Edward Thomas (criticism), Longmans, Green, for the British Council, 1963.
The Tiger and the Rose: An Autobiography, Hamish Hamilton (London), 1971.
(With Dannie Abse and Leonard Clark) *Three Poets, Two Children,* edited by Desmond Badham-Thornhill, Thornhill Press (Gloucester), 1975.
Not without Glory: Poets of the Second World War, Woburn (London), 1976.
A Proper Gentleman (autobiography), Robson Books, 1977.
How to Enjoy Poetry, Piatkus (Loughton, Essex), 1983.
How to Enjoy Novels, Piatkus, 1984.
(Editor) *Sporting Literature: An Anthology,* Oxford University Press, 1987.
Argument of Kings (autobiography), Robson Books, 1987.
Drums of Morning: Growing Up in the Thirties, (autobiography), Robson Books, 1992.

Also author of radio scripts *A Man's Game* and *A Door with One Eye,* and of radio opera *The Cancelling Dark,* with music by Christopher Whelan, performed December 5, 1965. Contributor to periodicals, including *Listener, Encounter, London Magazine, Spectator,* and *Times Literary Supplement.*

Some of Scannell's manuscripts are housed at the British Library in London, the Eton College Library, and at the University of Texas in Austin.

SIDELIGHTS: "For more than thirty years [Vernon] Scannell has written poems that meet the challenges of established forms while drawing on his vivid experiences as soldier, boxer, lover, husband and father, tutor and lecturer, broadcaster, drinker, and general survivor," wrote John H. Schwartz in the *Dictionary of Literary Biography: Poets of Great Britain and Ireland, 1945-1960.* A versatile writer who is also recognized for his novels and autobiographies, Scannell is frequently referred to as a "melancholy poet" because of the frequency with which he writes about danger and death, said Schwartz.

Scannell's themes are played out in the field of ordinary everyday living. "Scannell is an observer of life's ordinary cruelties," observed the *Stand*'s David McDuff in a review of Scannell's poetic works, adding that "the theme of war and its 'terrible abstractions', its anti-human rationalisation and normalisation of suffering, goes right through Scannell's oeuvre." "[Scannell's] is a poetry which embraces the immediate, wears and describes the scars of ordinary living, is plain (including plain frightened and plain indignant) about life and death and moral problems, rarely intricate, rarely delicate, always absorbing in its firm yet friendly insistence that the here-and-now of modern urban existence is what almost all of us have to fit into for most of the time," found Alan Brownjohn in a review for *Encounter.* Scannell's poems "inhabit the real world; they concern life as it is lived today," commented Gavin Ewart in the *London Magazine.*

Scannell's style, sometimes compared by critics to Thomas Hardy for its anecdotal elements and O. Henry for its characteristic surprise endings, is frequently noted for "clear and level-headed attitude to life's difficulties" and "consistency of tone, content and purpose" as McDuff related. *London Magazine*'s Roy Fuller cited Scannell's "clear and unpretentious tone" in his review of *Mortal Pitch.* In a review for the *New Statesman,* Alan Brownjohn praised Scannell's "no-nonsense standpoint." In a later *New Statesman* review, Anthony Thwaite cited the "straightforward" appeal of Scannell's work and descriptions that have a "marvelously clean and clear accuracy."

Other early critics of Scannell's work were far less appreciative. Of Scannell's second poetry collection, *A Mortal Pitch,* Roy Fuller wrote in *London Magazine:* "[Vernon Scannell] needs all the help he can muster to make his poems memorable, for his thought is apt to be rather commonplace." Reviewing *The Masks of Love,* Donald Hall went even further in *The New Statesman:* "In most of these poems, the author seems unaware that he is using metaphor. . . . Scannell's meter is sloppy. . . . In short, Scannell lacks art. There are poem-length thoughts but no poems here. . . . I suspect that it is easier to get away with bad writing if you call it poetry."

Scannell has taken his punches and come back stronger over the years, winning respect not only for his endurance, but not infrequently for his skill as well. Commenting on Scannell's next collection, *The Masks of Love,* a reviewer for *The Times Literary Supplement,* commenting specifically on the poem "The Lynching," wrote: "This is the kind of writing that really stops one short. One can only call the quiet underlining of the comparison between the hanged man and the wives ('fastened at the neck / And neat at feet') unemphatic emphasis." The reviewer commended Scannell's "ability to speak through images."

Writing for *New Statesman,* Alan Brownjohn thought Scannell's 1973 collection *The Winter Man,* "arguably his best book yet. He hasn't changed his material or his poetic personality: just found new ways with old subjects, achieved an increasing technical confidence, and written more movingly and interestingly than before." Brownjohn concluded that "all in all, *The Winter Man* represents a most encouraging advance." A reviewer for *The Times Literary Supplement,* shared Brownjohn's sentiments, judging *The Winter Man* Scannell's "best volume to date." The reviewer cited Scannell's "delicate judgment and dramatizing skill."

In 1994, Scannell published the collection *Collected Poems, 1950-1993.* In a 1980 overview of Scannell's poetry, *The Times Literary Supplement* critic Simon Curtis summed things up thus: "[To] those who prefer significant communication to self-expression Vernon Scannell's *Collected Poems* demonstrates much that is right with the plain presentation of mood and reflection, linked to incident and episode; poems that limit themselves to saying something clear." Curtis went on to summarize Scannell's various, recurring themes: "Fatherhood, soldiering, fear death, wry bitterness at aging, love in many aspects, the vulnerability of seemingly-strong characters . . . ; scenes whose backcloth is the railway station, the schoolroom, the bar, the bedroom." All of these themes, Curtis continued, were expressed in "images resolutely ordinary." Reviewing the collection for *New Statesman,* Alan Hollinghurst also seized upon the note of clarity: "the result is a body of work of easy appeal and genuine and likeable personality." Hollinghurst summed up Scannell's work: "He is funny and ironical; but he is not numinous, and his poems are unlikely to haunt the reader. This is partly a consequence of their being well-made, formal and unambiguous, envisaging poetic success in a readily available clarity: this indeed is their achievement and their limitation."

Scannell has used the resources of a rich and varied life to inform his poetry and prose. While never writing in the "confessional" mode of Lowell and other post-war moderns, he has also managed to duck the egoless abstractions favored by the earlier New Critics. Indeed, Scannell is something of a throw-back to the late 19th Century when poets were "approachable." In this sense, his poetry has been compared to Thomas Hardy's in it's anecdotalism, regular metricality and rhyme schemes. A reviewer for *Contemporary Literary Criticism,* took note of the kinds of experiences that forged the personality that is irrepressible in the poetry and prose: "While recuperating from a severe wound he suffered as a soldier in France in 1944, Scannell became demoralized by military life, and following the Allied victory in Europe, he deserted the army. In addition to holding numerous odd jobs, Scannell was a professional boxer. . . . In 1947, Scannell was arrested for desertion and was ordered to spend time in a mental institution before being discharged by the army."

Scannell has treated his life-material gingerly in his poetry, novels and in his autobiographical works. Of *The Tiger and the Rose,* Anthony Thwaite wrote in *The New Statesman:* "Some of its virtues are the virtues of Scannell's poetry: he is straightforward, masculine without being aggressively tough, circumstantial, unphoney." Thwaite demurred about a Scannell proclivity other critics have also noted: "His reflections on the nature of his experiences jar a little, and made me impatient for him to go on again with the experiences themselves, which he describes with a marvelously clean and clear accuracy."

"*The Tiger and the Rose* has the clear, shrill ring of truth," a reviewer in *The Times Literary Supplement* noted. The praise may have inspired the title of Scannell's prize-fighting novel, *Ring of Truth.* D. A. N. Jones in *The London Review* was especially taken with Scannell's treatment of his distaff characters: "As Vernon Scannell grows older he becomes more expert or plausible in his attempts to understand women's ideas and imagine their conversations when no men are present." Roger Lewis in *The New Statesman* gave the work a mixed review. "Though the conversations and bad grammar of dialect pall," Lewis wrote, "the novel is dotted with excellent observations."

Argument of Kings, Scannell's autobiographical novel, was praised by Gerald Mangan in *The Times Literary Supplement:* "[It] is remarkable not only for the disturbing immediacy of its realism, but for acute explorations of complex states of mind." Mangan lauded the "sheer pace and quality" of the book, as well as Scannell's "unusually accurate ear for Scottish speech."

Over the course of his career, Scannell has gained the respect of many critics, a number of whom have cited "The Walking Wounded," as one of the best poems to come out of the Second World War. David McDuff in *Stand* wrote: "There are some poets who work quietly throughout the whole of their lives without either seeking or attracting great attention, but who on reaching later years turn out to have amassed an oeuvre that unquestionably merits it. The poetry of Vernon Scannell is one such body of work."

BIOGRAPHICAL/CRITICAL SOURCES:

BOOKS

Contemporary Literary Criticism, Volume 49, Gale (Detroit), 1988.

Dictionary of Literary Biography, Volume 27: *Poets of Great Britain and Ireland, 1945-1960,* Gale, 1984.

Hay, Phillip, and Angharad Wynn-Jones, *Three Poets, Two Children,* edited by Desmond Badham-Thornhill, Thornhill Press, 1975.

Morrish, Hilary, *The Poet Speaks: Interviews with Contemporary Poets,* edited by Peter Orr, Routledge & Kegan Paul, 1966.

Robson, Jeremy, editor, *Corgi Modern Poets in Focus: 4,* Corgi Books, 1971.

PERIODICALS

London Magazine, Volume 4, number 5, May, 1957.

London Review of Books, February 2-15, 1984.

New Statesman, February 27, 1960; September 17, 1971; December 14, 1973; October 21, 1977; August 22, 1980; December 30, 1983.

The Spectator, August 10, 1962.

Stand, winter, 1992.

Times (London), July 23, 1987.

Times Literary Supplement, February 3, 1961; September 7, 1962; September 17, 1971; January 25, 1974; August 1, 1980; October 15, 1982; July 22, 1983; November 11, 1983; April 10, 1987; October 16-22, 1987.

* * *

SCHNELL, George A(dam) 1931-

PERSONAL: Born July 13, 1931, in Philadelphia, PA; son of Earl Blackwood and Emily (Bernheimer) Schnell; married Mary Lou Williams (in real estate sales), June 21, 1958; *Education:* Pennsylvania State University, M.S., 1960, Ph.D., 1965. *Politics:* Democrat. *Religion:* Reformed Church.

ADDRESSES: Home—29 River Park Dr., New Paltz, NY 12561-2636. *Office*—Department of Geography, Hamner House 1, State University of New York College at New Paltz, 75 S. Manheim Blvd., New Paltz, NY 12561-2499.

CAREER: State University of New York College at New Paltz, assistant professor, 1962-65, associate professor, 1965-68, professor of geography, 1968—, founder and founding chair of department, 1969-94, founder and founding board member of Institute for Development, Planning, and

Land Use Studies. Visiting professor, University of Hawaii, summer, 1966; adjunct professor, Empire State College of the State University of New York, 1974-85. *Military service:* U.S. Army, 1952-54.

MEMBER: Association of American Geographers, National Council on Geographic Education, Pennsylvania Academy of Science, Pennsylvania Geographic Society.

AWARDS, HONORS: National Science Foundation summer fellow, 1965; excellence award, United University Professors of New York State, 1990; distinguished alumnus, West Chester University (PA), 1994; distinguished geographer, Pennsylvania Geographical Society, 1994.

WRITINGS:

(Editor with George J. Demko and Harold M. Rose) *Population Geography: A Reader,* McGraw (New York City), 1970.

(With Kenneth Corey and others) *The Local Community: A Handbook for Teachers,* Macmillan (New York City), 1971.

(With Mark Stephen Monmonier) *The Study of Population: Elements, Patterns, Processes,* C. E. Merrill (Columbus, OH), 1983.

(Coeditor and contributor) *Proceedings of a Conference on Economic Development and the Quality of Life,* Mid-Hudson Regional Development Council, 1986.

(With Monmonier) *Map Appreciation,* Prentice-Hall (Englewood Cliffs, NJ), 1988.

(With Peter Fairweather) *The Shawangunk Mountains: A Critical Environmental Region,* Institute for Development, Planning, and Land Use Studies, 1988.

(With Fairweather) *Bridging the Skills Gap: Identifying Human Resource Priorities for the Mid-Hudson Region,* Mid-Hudson Regional Economic Development Council, 1990.

(With Fairweather and T. Clark) *Locating an Incubator in the Hudson Valley: A Preliminary Marketing Study,* Hudson Valley Technology Development Center, 1991.

(With Fairweather, Ann Davis, Joel Neuman, and Kenneth Toole) *A Regional Economic Development Compact, Actions to Promote Regional Revitalization, An Update of the Mid-Hudson Regional Economic Development Strategy,* Institute for Development, Planning and Land Use Studies, 1994.

Also contributor to numerous publications, including *Guineas and Gunpowder,* by John M. Scherwig, Harvard University (Cambridge, MA), 1969; *Education and Rural Development in Kenya: A Case Study of Primary School Graduates,* by Lewis Brownstein, Praeger (New York City), 1972; *The World's Population: Problems of Growth,* edited by Q. H. Stanford, Oxford University Press (Canada), 1972; *Readings on West Virginia and Appalachia,* edited by H. Adkins and others, Kendall-Hunt (Dubuque, IA), 1976; *Pennsylvania Coal: Resources, Technology, and Utilization,* edited by S. K. Majumdar and E. W. Miller, Pennsylvania Academy of Science (Easton, PA), 1983; *Hazardous and Toxic Wastes: Technology, Management, and Health Effects,* edited by Majumdar and Miller, Pennsylvania Academy of Science, 1984; *Environmental Radon: Occurrence, Control and Health Hazards,* edited by Majumdar, R. Schmalz, and E. W. Miller, Pennsylvania Academy of Science, 1990; *Natural and Technological Disasters: Causes, Effects, and Preventive Measures,* edited by Majumdar and others, Pennsylvania Academy of Science, 1992; *Conservation and Resource Management,* edited by Majumdar and others, Pennsylvania Academy of Science, 1993; *Medicine and Health Care into the 21st Century,* edited by Majumdar and others, Pennsylvania Academy of Science, 1995; and *Forests: A Global Perspective,* edited by Majumdar and others, Pennsylvania Academy of Science, 1996.

Also author of audio units, "Weather, Climate, and Man," Learning Systems, Inc., 1971. Contributor to proceedings; contributor to geography and other professional journals. Member of editorial board, Pennsylvania Academy of Science, 1968-88; member of editorial and advisory board, Pennsylvania Coal Project; *Pennsylvania Geographer,* guest editor, 1973, member of editorial board, 1988—. Associate editor, *Journal of the Pennsylvania Academy of Sciences,* 1988—. Consulting editor, Exams Unlimited, Inc., 1995—.

WORK IN PROGRESS: A research project, "Aged Migration into the Pocono Mountains."

SIDELIGHTS: George A. Schnell told *CA:* "I enjoy teaching very much, especially undergraduates, and am especially gratified to see them go on to succeed in graduate and professional schools and gain positions of responsibility. This success is very much based upon their ability to communicate—to write—and I hope that helping them to learn to write has become an important part of my role in their academic lives."

* * *

SCHULLERY, Paul (David) 1948-

PERSONAL: Surname is pronounced "shul-air-ee"; born July 4, 1948, in Middletown, PA; son of Stephen Emil (a Lutheran minister) and Judith Catherine (a teacher; maiden name, Murphy) Schullery; married Dianne Patricia Russell (an editor), June 11, 1983 (divorced December, 1988); married Marsha Karle, June 22, 1996. *Education:* Wittenberg University, B.A., 1970; Ohio University, M.A., 1977. *Religion:* Lutheran. *Avocational interests:* Hiking, nature photography, playing guitar.

ADDRESSES: *Home*—P.O. Box 184, Yellowstone National Park, WY 82190.

CAREER: National Park Service, Yellowstone National Park, WY, ranger-naturalist, summers, 1972-77, historian-archivist, winters, 1974-77; Museum of American Fly Fishing, Manchester, VT, executive director, 1977-82; freelance writer and research consultant, Livingston, MT, 1982-86; National Park Service, Yellowstone National Park, resource naturalist and technical writer, 1988-93, Yellowstone Center for Resources, acting chief of cultural resources, 1993-94, senior editor, 1993-95, resource naturalist, 1995—. Affiliate professor of history at Montana State University, 1991—; adjunct professor of American studies at University of Wyoming, 1992—. Member of board of trustees, Museum of American Fly Fishing, 1982—. Consulting researcher, Mount Rainier National Park, 1983.

MEMBER: American Association for the Advancement of Science, Greater Yellowstone Coalition, Theodore Roosevelt Association, Trout Unlimited, Federation of Fly Fishers (senior adviser, 1980—; senior vice president, 1982-83), American Institute of Biological Sciences, Yellowstone Association, Yellowstone Grizzly Foundation, Theodore Roosevelt Association, Montana Historical Society, International Association for Bear Research and Management, Cahokia Museum Society, George Wright Society.

AWARDS, HONORS: Phi Alpha Theta, National History Honorary, 1970; Special Achievement Award for supervisory work from National Park Service, Yellowstone National Park, 1977; award for graphic arts excellence from Printing Industries of America, 1980 and 1981, and from Consolidated Papers, Inc., 1981, all for journal *American Fly Fisher;* overall National Park Service award for excellence in interpretive publications and first place award in Competition of the Conference of National Park Cooperating Associations, both 1984, both for *Freshwater Wilderness: Yellowstone Fishes and Their World; The Bears of Yellowstone* was named one of the outstanding books of 1986 by *Montana* magazine; Special Act Service Award, National Park Service and U.S. Forest Service, 1991, for work on Greater Yellowstone Vision document; Special Act Service Award, National Park Service, 1992, for role in National Park Service's 75th Anniversary activities; citation of excellence in the Sigurd F. Olsen Nature Writing Award competition, 1992, for *Pregnant Bears and Crawdad Eyes: Excursions and Encounters in Animal Worlds;* Austin Hogan Award, The American Museum of Fly Fishing, 1992, for outstanding contributions to *American Fly Fisher;* special citation from the International Association for Bear Research and Management, 1995, for role as coeditor of the proceedings of the 9th international conference on bear research and management; Special Achievement Award, National Park Service, 1996, for outstanding performance as editor and writer; *American Fly Fishing: A History* was named one of the most important trout-related books of the last thirty years by *Trout* magazine.

WRITINGS:

(Editor) *Old Yellowstone Days,* Colorado Associated University Press (Boulder), 1979.

The Bears of Yellowstone, Yellowstone Library (Yellowstone Park, WY), 1980, new edition, Roberts Rinehart (Boulder), 1986.

(Editor) *The Grand Canyon: Early Impressions,* Colorado Associated University Press, 1981.

(Editor) *American Bears: Selections from the Writings of Theodore Roosevelt,* Colorado Associated University Press, 1983.

(With John D. Varley) *Freshwater Wilderness: Yellowstone Fishes and Their World,* Yellowstone Library, 1983.

Mountain Time (memoir), Schocken (New York City), 1984.

(With C. Beasley, C. W. Buchholtz, and S. Trimble) *The Sierra Club Guides to the National Parks: The Rocky Mountains and the Great Plains,* Stewart, Tabori (New York City), 1984.

(Editor) *Theodore Roosevelt: Wilderness Writings,* Peregrine Smith (Layton, UT), 1986.

(Editor and author of new material) Freeman Tildon, *The National Parks,* foreword by William Penn Mott, revised edition, Knopf (New York City), 1986.

(Editor) *Island in the Sky: Pioneering Accounts of Mount Rainier,* Mountaineers-Books (Seattle), 1987.

(With D. Despain, D. Houston, and M. Meagher) *Wildlife in Transition: Man and Nature on Yellowstone's Northern Range,* Roberts Rinehart, 1987.

American Fly Fishing: A History, Nick Lyons (New York City), 1987.

(With Bud Lilly) *Bud Lilly's Guide to Western Fly Fishing,* Nick Lyons, 1987.

(With Lilly) *A Trout's Best Friend,* Pruett (Boulder), 1987.

The Bear Hunter's Century, Dodd (New York City), 1988, reprinted, Stackpole (Harrisburg, PA), 1989.

Pregnant Bears and Crawdad Eyes: Excursions and Encounters in Animal Worlds, Mountaineers-Books, 1991.

(Editor) *Yellowstone Bear Tales,* Roberts Rinehart, 1991.

(With W. Sontag and L. Griffin) *The National Park Service: A Seventy-fifth Anniversary Album,* Roberts Rinehart/National Parks Foundation, 1991.

(Editor with J. Claar) *Bears—Their Biology and Management,* International Association for Bear Research and Management/Yellowstone Center for Resources, Yellowstone National Park, 1995.

Yellowstone's Ski Pioneers: Peril and Heroism on the Winter Trail, High Plains Publishing (Worland, WY), 1995.

Waterton/Glacier: Land of Hanging Valleys, HarperCollins West (San Francisco), 1996.

Shupton's Fancy: A Tale of the Fly-Fishing Obsession, Stackpole, 1996.

(Editor) *Echoes from the Summit,* Harcourt (New York City), 1996.

(Editor) *Mark of the Bear,* Sierra Books (San Francisco), 1996.

(Editor) *The Yellowstone Wolf: A Guide and Sourcebook,* High Plains Publishing, 1996.

Searching for Yellowstone: Ecology and Wonder in the Last Wilderness, Houghton (Boston), 1997.

Also contributor to various publications, including *The Greater Yellowstone Ecosystem: Balancing Man and Nature in America's Wildlands,* with Varley, Yale University Press (New Haven, CT), 1991; *The Great Bear, Contemporary Writings on the Grizzly,* edited by J. Murray, Alaska Northwest Publishing (Edmonds), 1992; *Home Waters, a Fly-Fishing Anthology,* Fireside/Simon & Schuster (New York City), 1992; *Out among the Wolves,* edited by Murray, Alaska Northwest Publishing, 1993; and *Our Living Resources,* National Biological Service, 1995.

Nature columnist and associate editor, *Country Journal,* 1986-88. Contributor to periodicals, including *Country Journal, American West, Field and Stream, National Parks, Outdoor Life, Gray's Sporting Journal,* and *New York Times Book Review.* Editor of *American Fly Fisher,* 1978-83, and *Yellowstone Science,* 1992-96. Book reviewer for a wide variety of technical and popular periodicals.

Pregnant Bears and Crawdad Eyes: Excursions and Encounters in Animal Worlds has been translated into Japanese.

WORK IN PROGRESS: An Eye to the Wild: A Modern Wildlife Watcher's Code; Royal Coachmen: The Lore and Legend of Fly Fishing; (with L. Whittlesey) *Yellowstone Wildlife: A History;* (with B. Lilly) *The Western Fly Fisherman.*

SIDELIGHTS: Paul Schullery once told *CA:* "My work has been in several related areas—conservation history, modern conservation, natural history, sporting history, and modern outdoor sports. Fishing and hunting in North America have not been subjected to one percent of the scholarly scrutiny that has been given to organized games, partly because games, such as football and baseball, are more completely recorded both as far as statistics of the games themselves and as far as the numbers of spectators involved. Field sports, or blood sports, have been passed by in modern scholarship, resulting in a lack of public and scholarly understanding of their place in American culture. Drawn to these activities by my own recreational interests as well as by my related enthusiasms for nature and conservation, I have attempted to encourage the study of field sports by scholars, and have located several fellow enthusiasts with whom I share this project. My essay 'Hope for the Hook and Bullet Press' in the *New York Times Book Review* in 1985 was an attempt to bring the field of 'outdoor writing' to the attention of more people as a legitimate type of writing with a long and fascinating history. It was also an attempt to cast a sympathetic yet critical eye on that field, and thus was a source of some controversy among outdoor writers.

"I have also enjoyed writing about my own outdoor activities; my book *Mountain Time* is a memoir of my years as a Yellowstone Park ranger, and mixes personal anecdote with examination of the place of wilderness recreation in American life and history."

* * *

SCHWARTZ, Amy 1954-

PERSONAL: Born April 2, 1954, in San Diego, CA; daughter of I. Henry (a writer and newspaper columnist) and Eva (a professor of chemistry; maiden name, Herzberg) Schwartz. *Education:* Attended Antioch College; California College of Arts and Crafts, B.F.A., 1976.

ADDRESSES: *Agent*—Jane Feder, 305 East 24th St., New York, NY 10010.

CAREER: Author and illustrator of books for children.

AWARDS, HONORS: Has received many awards for books and illustrations from organizations, libraries, and periodicals, including Parents' Choice Award from Parents' Choice Foundation for *The Crack-of-Dawn Walkers,* Award for Best Picture Book from Association of Jewish Libraries for *Mrs. Moskowitz and the Sabbath Candlesticks, Parents* Certificate of Excellence from *Parents* Magazine for *Annabelle Swift, Kindergartner,* Christopher Award for *The Purple Coat,* and New York Times Book Review Ten Best Illustrated Children's Books, for *A Teeny Tiny Baby.*

WRITINGS:

SELF-ILLUSTRATED

Bea and Mr. Jones, Bradbury (Scarsdale, NY), 1982.
Begin at the Beginning, Harper (New York City), 1983.
Mrs. Moskowitz and the Sabbath Candlesticks, Jewish Publication Society, 1983.
Her Majesty, Aunt Essie, Bradbury, 1984.
Yossel Zissel and the Wisdom of Chelm, Jewish Publication Society, 1986.
Oma and Bobo, Bradbury, 1987.
Annabelle Swift, Kindergartner, Orchard Books, 1988.
(Editor with Leonard S. Marcus) *Mother Goose's Little Misfortunes,* Bradbury, 1990.
Camper of the Week, Orchard, 1991.
(With Henry Schwartz) *Make a Face,* Scholastic, 1994.
A Teeny Tiny Baby, Orchard, 1994.

ILLUSTRATOR

Amy Hest, *The Crack-of-Dawn Walkers,* Macmillan (New York City), 1984.
Eve Bunting, *Jane Martin, Dog Detective,* Harcourt (San Diego, CA), 1984.
Joanne Ryder, *The Night Flight,* Four Winds (Bristol, FL), 1985.
Donna Guthrie, *The Witch Who Lives Down the Hall* (Junior Literary Guild selection), Harcourt, 1985.
Hest, *The Purple Coat,* Four Winds, 1986.
Elizabeth Lee O'Donnell, *Maggie Doesn't Want to Move,* Four Winds, 1987.
Mary Stolz, *The Scarecrows and Their Child,* Harper, 1987.
Larry King, *Because of Lozo Brown,* Viking (New York City), 1988.
I. Henry Schwartz, *How I Captured a Dinosaur,* Orchard, 1989.
Lucretia Hale, *The Lady Who Put Salt in Her Coffee,* Harcourt, 1989.
Hest, *Fancy Aunt Jess,* Morrow (New York City), 1990.
Nancy White Carlstrom, *Blow Me A Kiss, Miss Lillie,* Morrow, 1990.
Stephanie Calmenson, *Wanted: Warm Furry Friend,* Macmillan, 1990.
Pat Brisson, *Magic Carpet,* Bradbury, 1991.
Schwartz, *Albert Goes Hollywood,* Orchard, 1992.
(Editor) David Gale, *Funny You Should Ask,* Delacorte (New York City), 1992.

Kathryn Lasky, *My Island Grandma,* Morrow, 1993.

Hest, *Nana's Birthday Party,* Morrow, 1993.

Kathleen Krull, *Wish You Were Here: Emily Emerson's Guide to the 50 States,* Doubleday (New York City), 1997.

ADAPTATIONS: Bea and Mr. Jones was adapted for television and broadcast on "Reading Rainbow," PBS, 1983; *The Purple Coat* was adapted for television and broadcast on "Reading Rainbow," PBS, 1989.

WORK IN PROGRESS: Illustrating a book for Amy Hest, for Simon & Schuster.

SIDELIGHTS: Amy Schwartz has been recognized by many reviewers as a talented writer and gifted illustrator of children's books. Her stories have been praised for their realistic, yet sensitive portrayal of childhood experiences. Maureen J. O'Brien in a *Publishers Weekly* interview with Schwartz notes that "virtually all of Schwartz's books include one overriding theme that anything is achievable if you just put your mind to it." And Schwartz relates to O'Brien during the interview: "When I'm trying to come up with a story. I think I am more inclined to write about internal victories." As she explains further to *CA:* "I often pick these rather stubborn and determined types as main characters—both in little girls and grandmotherly figures. I think it's a part of me, a part of the people in my family."

Schwartz goes on to describe her early love of books to *CA* in this manner: "Looking back on my childhood, I can easily see a progression of interests that led to my writing and illustrating children's books. Some of my strongest memories from my childhood involve books. I always had the most number of stars in the class for 'Books Read' on the elementary school book awards. I remember looking forward each year to the annual ritual of receiving a book from my grandmother on my birthday.

"I wrote stories and plays in elementary school, and adapted my favorite picture books for school theater productions. I was shy and awkward in real life, but I had an active fantasy life. I was also a real ham on stage. I also loved to draw and paint when I was young, as I still do. I would draw after school, either with friends or on my own. I was usually enrolled in an art class on Saturday mornings. This interest in drawing and painting has been continuous throughout my life."

Commenting on whether she thinks of herself more as a writer than an artist, Schwartz told *CA:* "I actually think of myself as an illustrator first, I suppose because I do more illustrating than writing. And I've drawn and painted since I was a child, whereas the writing still feels fairly new to me."

Schwartz also explains how she became successful. "With me it mainly took sticking with it, being persistent. I'm very glad that I did stick with it, that I didn't give up early and drop the whole thing. Also, before I started doing this, I had the idea—especially with writing—that it was something you did all on your own. With practically all my writing I've gotten help from somebody: a teacher, a friend, my agent, an editor. I think that's also good to know, that it's not something you have to do from start to finish all on your own without getting advice from someone else, an outside reader."

BIOGRAPHICAL/CRITICAL SOURCES:

PERIODICALS

New York Times Book Review, May 17, 1987.

Publishers Weekly, February 26, 1988.

* * *

SCHWEIK, Robert C(harles) 1927-

PERSONAL: Born August 5, 1927, in Chicago, IL; son of Charles Anthony (a candy broker) and Eleanor (Waters) Schweik; married Joanne Lovell (a freelance writer), December 27, 1954; children: Susan, Charles. *Ethnicity:* "Caucasian." *Education:* Loyola University, Chicago, IL, A.B., 1951; University of Notre Dame, Ph.D., 1957. *Avocational interests:* Writing detective stories, chess.

ADDRESSES: Home—27 Newton St., Fredonia, NY 14063. *Office*—Department of English, State University of New York College at Fredonia, Fredonia, NY 14063. *E-mail*—schweik@fredonia.edu; fax: 716-673-3446.

CAREER: Marquette University, Milwaukee, WI, instructor, 1953-58, assistant professor, 1958-65, associate professor of English, 1965-69; State University of New York College at Fredonia, professor of English literature, 1969-78, Distinguished Teaching Professor, 1978—. Visiting professor at Wisconsin State University—Superior, 1969, Universitaet Trier-Kaiserslautern, 1972-73, 1982, and University of Stockholm, 1979. State University of New York, faculty exchange scholar, 1982. *Military service:* U.S. Navy, 1944-45; became seaman first class.

MEMBER: International Association of University Professors of English, Modern Language Association of America, Victorian Studies Association, Thomas Hardy Society (vice president, 1988—).

AWARDS, HONORS: Grants from American Philosophical Society, 1966, State University of New York Research Foundation, 1970, and Deutsche Forschungsgemeinschaft, 1972; fellow of National Endowment for the Humanities, 1981; senior Fulbright-Hays fellowship, 1982.

WRITINGS:

(Editor and author of introduction) Emily Bronte, *Wuthering Heights,* Cambridge Book Co. (Englewood Cliffs, NJ), 1968.

(With Joseph Schwartz) *Hart Crane: A Descriptive Bibliography,* University of Pittsburgh Press (Pittsburgh, PA), 1972.

(With Dieter Riesner) *English and American Literature: A Guide to Reference Materials,* Adler's Foreign Books (Skokie, IL), 1976.

(With Riesner) *Reference Sources in English and American Literature: An Annotated Bibliography,* Norton (New York City), 1977.

(Editor) Thomas Hardy, *Far from the Madding Crowd,* Norton, 1986.

Contributor to numerous books, including *Hardy: The Tragic Novels,* edited by Ronald P. Draper, Macmillan (London), 1975; *Budmouth Essays on Thomas Hardy,* edited by F. B. Pinion, Thomas Hardy Society, 1976; *Thomas Hardy: After Fifty Years,* edited by Lance St. J. Butler, Rowman & Littlefield (Lanham, MD), 1977; *Twilight of Dawn: Studies in English Literature in Transition,* edited by Om Brack, Arizona University Press (Tucson), 1987; *Twentieth Century Literary Criticism,* Volume 32, edited by Paula Kepos and Dennis Poupard, Gale (Detroit), 1989; *A Spacious Vision: Essays on Hardy,* edited by Draper and Philip V. Mallett, Patten Press, 1994; *Essays on Thomas Hardy,* edited by Charles Pettit, Macmillan, 1997; and *The Cambridge Companion to Thomas Hardy,* edited by Dale Kramer, Cambridge University Press (Cambridge, England), 1997.

Also contributor to professional journals, including *Browning Institute Studies, Nineteenth Century Fiction, Victorian Newsletter, Philological Quarterly, College English, English Studies, Quarterly Journal of Speech, Modern Language Notes, Notes and Queries, Papers of the Bibliographical Society of America, Texas Studies in Literature and Language, Analytical and Enumerative Bibliography, Metaphor and Symbolic Activity,* and *Nineteenth-Century Prose;* also contributor to *Ellery Queen's Mystery Magazine.* Member of editorial board, *English Literature in Transition,* 1972—, *Literary Research Newsletter,* 1978-93, *Cithara,* 1979—, and *Alphabetum,* 1994—.

WORK IN PROGRESS: Research on persistent rhetorical strategies in art commentary from the nineteenth century to the present.

SIDELIGHTS: Robert C. Schweik told *CA:* "Trained in the literary history of Britain, and initially focusing my research on the novels of Thomas Hardy, I was gradually led by them to expand the scope of my inquiries from the imaginative elements in Hardy's fiction to include both the study of the imaginative elements of Victorian prose (with particular emphasis on the writings of John Stuart Mill) and of the relationships of nineteenth-century and twentieth-century British literature to painting, music, religion, philosophy, and science. The most recent results of this gradual expansion of research interests have been studies of the impact of religion, science, and philosophy on the writings of Thomas Hardy, of the titling of modern works of music, visual art, and literature, and of the uses of metaphor and other rhetorical devices in contemporary art criticism. This broadening of research interests is largely the result of one thing leading to another—of an interest in the writings of Thomas Hardy leading to a concern for his relationship to the larger cultural context of late nineteenth- and early twentieth-century Europe, and that, in turn, leading to an exploration of the roots of 'modernism' in European art, and that, in turn, to an interest in the origins of the rhetoric of contemporary art criticism. In retrospect, that gradual, progressive expansion of research interests seems reasonable—even logical; from the point of view of the researcher, it was altogether unforeseen."

* * *

SHADWELL, Thomas
See COVER, Arthur Byron

* * *

SHAFFER, Karen A. 1947-

PERSONAL: Born October 12, 1947, in Dayton, OH; daughter of John Richard (an engineer) and Helen Maxine (a homemaker; maiden name, Baker) Shaffer. *Education:* American University, B.A., 1969, J.D., 1972.

ADDRESSES: Home and office—5333 North 26th St., Arlington, VA 22207. *E-mail*—kshaffer@erols.com; fax: 703-532-1816.

CAREER: American University, Washington, DC, director of Placement and Alumni Office of Law School, 1972-73; Interstate Commerce Commission, Washington, DC, attorney, 1974; U.S. Department of the Interior, Washington, DC, attorney in Office of the Solicitor, 1974-78; private practice of law in Washington, DC, 1978-81; U.S. House of Representatives, Washington, DC, counsel to Interior Committee, 1981-85; private practice of law in Arlington, VA, 1985—; Jackson & Kelly (law firm), Washington, DC, attorney, 1990-92. Artists' manager, 1985—. Founder and president of Maud Powell Foundation, 1986—; member of board of directors of Gary Karr Doublebass Foundation, 1984—; secretary of Washington Bach Consort, 1986-88; guest speaker at First American Violin Congress, 1987. Member of National Academy of Sciences Committee on the Disposal of Excess Spoil, 1980-81; consultant to National Coal Council. Lecturer.

WRITINGS:

Maud Powell, Pioneer American Violinist, The Maud Powell Foundation/Iowa State University Press (Ames), 1988.

Maud Powell, Legendary American Violinist (for children), The Maud Powell Foundation (Arlington, VA), 1994.

Contributor to music journals, including *The Maud Powell Signature, Journal of the Violin Society of America,* and *The Strad.*

WORK IN PROGRESS: Editing *The Collected Writings of Maud Powell.*

SIDELIGHTS: Karen A. Shaffer once told *CA:* "*Maud Powell, Pioneer American Violinist* is a seminal work, representing as it does the first history of violin playing in America. The book was an outgrowth of my love for the violin as an amateur violinist and my intrigue with American history. My future literary projects will expand my work on that biography and include extensive lecturing as well as writing. The Maud Powell Foundation, which also grew out of my work on that biography, will seek to bolster other American musicological research.

"Maud Powell (1867-1920) was America's first great master of the violin with an international reputation. She ranked with the European masters, including Ysaye and Kreisler. She was one of the first woman violinists accepted as an equal in a previously all-male field. She premiered fourteen violin concertos in the United States, including ones by Tchaikovsky, Dvorak, and Sibelius. She was a champion of American composers as well. She was the first instrumentalist to record for Victor Talking Machine Company's Red Seal label. She pioneered recital circuits in the United States and molded American musical taste. She developed programming principles still valued today as well as programming tactics that taught previously impatient American audiences appreciation for performances of entire symphonies and concertos. She was an eloquent author of instructive program notes and articles on musical performance and conservation of American ethnic music. She encouraged young performers. She was a tireless performer as soloist and in chamber music, with orchestra and in recital, in large and small concert halls, hospitals, schools, and World War I army camps. She was the first woman to head her own string quartet in which the other members were men. She formed and toured with the Maud Powell Trio in 1908 and 1909. She toured throughout Europe and South Africa, traveling as far west as Hawaii and giving some of the first violin recitals ever heard in the Far West. She was a crusader for sexual equality in music, a humanist, and a consummate performer. In her day, she was America's foremost pioneer in music whose abundant legacy still influences the musical world."

* * *

SIDHWA, Bapsy (N.) 1938-

PERSONAL: Given name sometimes transliterated as Bapsi; born August 11, 1938, in Karachi, Pakistan; came to the United States in 1983 (naturalized, 1992); daughter of Peshotan (in business) and Tehmina (an association president; maiden name, Mama) Bhandara; married Gustad Kermani, January 10, 1957 (deceased); married Noshir R. Sidhwa (in business), January 31, 1963; children: Mohur, Koko, Parizad. *Education:* Kinnaird College for Women, B.A., 1956. *Religion:* Zoroastrian (Parsi). *Avocational interests:* Travel (including the United States, Soviet Union, Iran, Turkey, India, Western Europe), cinema, transcendental meditation, reading, social investigation, working for women's rights, promoting religious tolerance.

ADDRESSES: *Home*—4218 Tasslewood Lane, Houston, TX 77014. *Agent*—Elizabeth Grossman, Sterling Lord Literistic Agency Inc., 65 Bleecker St., New York, NY 10012.

CAREER: Writer and teacher. St. Thomas University, Houston, TX, conducted fiction writing workshop, fall, 1983; Rice University, Houston, conducted novel writing workshops, 1984-86; University of Houston, Houston, assistant professor of creative writing, fall, 1985; Columbia University, New York City, taught in MFA graduate program, 1989; currently writer-in-residence and professor of English at Mount Holyoke College. Has given readings at various institutions, including Mount Holyoke, Amherst, and Williams College; has given readings and interviews on radio and television in Pakistan and for British Broadcasting Corporation (BBC). Pakistan's delegate to Asian Women's Congress, 1975; associated with Destitute Women's and Children's Home, Lahore; with Asia Society of Houston, organizes annual readings and discussions with writers and public figures from the Indian subcontinent.

MEMBER: International Women's Club of Lahore (president, 1975-77), PEN American Center.

AWARDS, HONORS: National Award for English literature, Pakistan Academy, 1985, for *The Bride;* Bunting Fellow, Radcliffe/Harvard, Mary Ingraham Institute, 1986-87; National Endowment for the Arts grant, 1987; visiting scholar at Rockefeller Foundation Study Center, Bellagio, Italy, 1991; SITARA-I-IMTIAZ, Pakistan, 1991; Liberaturepreis, 1991, for *Ice-Candy-Man;* Notable Book of the Year Award, *New York Times Book Review,* 1991, and nomination for Notable Book of the Year, American Library Association, both for *Cracking India*; Lila Wallace-Reader's Digest Award, 1993.

WRITINGS:

NOVELS

The Crow Eaters, Imani Press (Lahore), 1978, Jonathan Cape (London), 1980, St. Martin's (New York City), 1981, Milkweed Editions (Minneapolis), 1992.

The Bride, Jonathan Cape, 1982, St. Martin's, 1983.

Ice-Candy-Man, Heinemann (London), 1988, published as *Cracking India,* Milkweed Editions, 1991.

An American Brat, Milkweed Editions, 1993.

Short stories and articles published in numerous anthologies, including *Without a Guide,* edited by Katherine Govier, and *Kunapipi: Post-Colonial Women's Writing,* edited by Anna Rutherford. Contributor to magazines and newspapers, including *Femina, Civil and Military Gazette, Radcliffe Quarterly, Pakistan Times, New York Times Book Review,* and *Houston Chronicle.*

WORK IN PROGRESS: A collection of essays and a collection of short stories.

SIDELIGHTS: Bapsy Sidhwa, described by one critic as Pakistan's finest English-language novelist, writes stories that reflect her experience as a woman, a member of a religious minority in Pakistan, and as an immigrant to the United States. She told *CA:* "Most of my writing is motivated by a desire to give a voice to the marginalized or misrepresented communities of Pakistan and India, and now that I'm in America, about my American experiences and reaction to my new country. I am writer enough to know that unless the readers are in some way entertained—finding their passions engaged by either the humor or tragedy affecting the characters—they won't stay with the book; and I try to maintain enough tension in the story to keep the pages turning."

Sidhwa's first published novel, *The Crow Eaters,* was the second one she had written, after having received numerous rejection slips for her earlier work. The rejections continued to come for *The Crow Eaters,* which finally was published privately in Pakistan, then picked up by British and American publishers. The novel tells the story of a family from a small village in Central India, adherents of the Zoroastrian (Parsi or Parsee) religion, who emigrate to the large city of Lahore, Pakistan, in search of economic betterment. The head of the family, Faredoon "Freddy" Junglewalla, manages to prosper; he is crafty and unprincipled in business and manipulative of the region's British rulers. He frequently comes into conflict, however, with his mother-in-law, Jerbanoo. The novel, which takes its title from a slang term for overly talkative people, has many comic elements. In *Bloomsbury Review,* Leslie Woolf Hedley calls *The Crow Eaters* "a good-humored satirical mirror of one Parsee family." In a *New York Times Book Review* piece, Carolyne Wright pronounces it "a rollicking comic tale," while Edward Hower, in *World & I,* describes the novel as "a critical but very affectionate look at Sidhwa's community."

In regard to the book, Sidhwa told *CA:* "The Parsis, Zoroastrian descendants of the Magi now settled in the subcontinent, are rapidly becoming an endangered species. The community is too small to exert political pressure and affluent enough to attract the attention and envy of other social groups. Subconscious pressures compelled me to record its traditions and culture. *The Crow Eaters* was written not only to inform, but to entertain. The choice of humor as a vehicle has in no way diminished its truth. In Pakistan, the book has aroused strong and mixed emotions. Its publication was marked by a sham bomb threat."

Sidhwa's first novel, *The Bride,* was published after *The Crow Eaters.* Sidhwa was inspired to write the novel after hearing the story of a young woman who tried to run away from the man she was forced to marry; eventually, the woman was found and killed. The main character in *The Bride* is a young woman named Zaitoon; orphaned in the violence surrounding the partition of Pakistan from India, she is adopted by Qasim, a man from a remote, mountainous area (Zaitoon is from the plains). He brings her up in Lahore, but when she is old enough to marry, he promises her hand to one of his tribesmen in the mountains. Her husband, Sakhi, turns out to be abusive; his society permits no disobedience from women. Zaitoon must decide whether to submit to this treatment or to escape. Sidhwa interweaves Zaitoon's story with that of an American woman living on the subcontinent.

Hower notes that *The Bride,* unlike *The Crow Eaters,* was "anything but a comedy; domestic relations form its most powerful scenes." Elizabeth Berridge, writing in the *Daily Telegraph,* asserts that *The Bride* "reveals to the Western reader a way of life that is completely alien," adding, "the events that follow Zaitoon's marriage to Sakhi are truly chilling." *Observer* reviewer Hermoine Lee remarks, "Ms. Sidhwa's polemical intentions are plain, but elegantly controlled in this delicate and lively novel."

Sidhwa commented to *CA:* "*The Bride* is the story of a Muslim girl and the people with whom she interacts. It is dedicated to the mountainous regions of Pakistan—the Himalayas and Karakorams—and to the deprived and courageous women who make their lives in this spectacular but impoverished part of the country." Sidhwa is quoted in *World & I* as saying that the book "is an indictment of what happens to women in a tribal society. At the same time, I tried to have compassion for these people. . . . You can't blame anyone because they live by this code of honor."

Speaking to *CA,* Sidhwa said of her third novel, *Ice-Candy-Man:* "It is about the partition of India and Pakistan in 1947. The story is told through the eyes of a young Parsi girl who records the upheaval as her Hindu and Sikh neighbors leave and the Muslim refugees arrive. The two main characters who evolve the action are Ayah and an ice-candy peddler: the victim and the predator. There are other victims, other predators: Hindu, Muslim, Sikh, Christian and Parsi. Through them the novel deals with religious and social biases—

and the political considerations that tore a people apart."

Ice-Candy-Man, published as *Cracking India* in the United States, has some autobiographical elements. Like Sidhwa, the young girl, Lenny, is a polio survivor who was kept out of school because of her temporary disability. In *World & I* Sidhwa explains that Lenny was, to an extent, her "alter ego," but far more sophisticated than Sidhwa was at a similar age. The character also shares Sidhwa's religion. The Parsis largely avoided the violence that occurred in the era of the partition; however, other characters, such as Lenny's Hindu nanny Ayah, are members of religions directly involved in the strife.

In the *New York Times Book Review,* Shashi Tharoor comments, "The story is not about partition, though partition looms large in its pages . . . Ms. Sidhwa's novel is about a child's loss of innocence . . . about servants and laborers and artisans caught up in events they barely understand, but in which they play a terrible part." *Belles Lettres* contributor Kamala Edwards commends Sidhwa for her depiction of resilient women characters, but notes, "Although Sidhwa's description of the partition experience is intensely emotional, the novel is not without flaws. Lenny is less than convincing when she mouths adult perceptions, especially about British politics." Richard Ryan, however, asserts in *Washington Post Book World,* that Sidhwa "has told a sweet and amusing tale filled with the worst atrocities imaginable; she has concocted a girlishly romantic love story which is driven by the most militant feminism; above all, she has turned her gaze upon the domestic comedy of a Pakistani family in the 1940s and somehow managed to evoke the great political upheavals of the age."

Sidhwa, who moved to the United States in 1983, shifted the locale of her fiction there with *An American Brat.* The novel focuses on a young Pakistani Parsi woman, Feroza Ginwalla, whose liberal parents send her to the United States to get her away from the influence of Pakistan's Islamic fundamentalists. In America, though, Feroza becomes more free-thinking than her family wished. She transfers from the sheltered atmosphere of a small Mormon college to a large, more permissive public university, where she falls in love with a Jewish man. Alarmed at the possibility of Feroza marrying outside her faith (a Parsi woman who does so is forbidden to practice her religion), her mother, Zareen, makes an emergency trip to the United States. There Zareen confronts her headstrong, assertive daughter—her "American brat."

"*An American Brat* is an exceptional novel, one of such interest that the reader's reservations, while significant, are ultimately of little consequence," according to *Los Angeles Times* reviewer Chris Goodrich. The novel, Goodrich maintains, "suffers from a meandering, literal plot and a tone that doesn't distinguish major insights from minor ones." Ultimately the critic finds, however, *An American Brat* to be consistently interesting, with many fresh observations on American culture and immigrants' lives as it explores "the competing loyalties immigrants feel toward family, culture, heritage, self."

Several other reviewers also remark upon this theme. In the *Washington Post Book World,* Edit Villareal declares that "Sidhwa reveals with a humorous yet incisive eye the exhilarating freedom and profound sense of loss that make up the immigrant experience in America." *World & I* commentator Fawzia Afzal-Khan lauds Sidhwa's "evenhandedness of cultural representation" and terms the author "an equal-opportunity critic: She is aware that all cultural and religious groups derive their sense of identity, in part, by excluding others." Afzal-Khan judges the novel to be marred by its sometimes "pedantic, moralizing tone" and a few bizarre and incongruous scenes, but praises Sidhwa's use of humor and deftness of characterization. Goodrich concludes that *An American Brat* is "a funny and memorable novel."

BIOGRAPHICAL/CRITICAL SOURCES:

BOOKS

Dhawan, R. K., and Novy Kapadia, editors, *The Novels of Bapsi Sidhwa,* South Asia Books (Columbia, MO), 1996.

Jussawalla, Feroza, and Reed Way Dasenbrock, editors, *Interviews with Writers of the Post-Colonial World,* University Press of Mississippi (Jackson, MS), 1992.

Montenegro, David, *Points of Departure: International Writers on Writing and Politics,* University of Michigan Press (Ann Arbor, MI), 1991.

Notable Asian Americans, Gale (Detroit), 1995.

Ross, Robert, editor, *International Literature in English,* Garland (New York City), 1991.

PERIODICALS

Belles Lettres, fall, 1991, pp. 47-48.
Bloomsbury Review, October, 1985.
Boston Phoenix, September 3, 1993.
Daily Telegraph, November 9, 1980; February 24, 1983.
Dallas Morning News, March 22, 1992.
Economist, December 11, 1993, p. 100.
Far Eastern Economic Review, December 15, 1983; March 23, 1995, p. 44.
Financial Times, March 26, 1983.
Good Housekeeping, February, 1983.
Guardian, September 11, 1980.
Houston Chronicle, January 7, 1994.
India Abroad, December 1, 1983.
Kirkus Reviews, August 1, 1993.
LA Weekly, March, 1992.
Library Journal, October 15, 1991; May 15, 1992; November 1, 1993, p. 149.
London Magazine, March, 1988.
London Review of Books, September 15, 1988.
Los Angeles Times, August 9, 1992; January 14, 1994, p. E4.
Los Angeles Times Book Review, August 9, 1992, p. 6.
Massachusetts Review, winter, 1990, pp. 513-33.
Ms., November-December, 1991.
Newsday, September 19, 1991; January 17, 1993; November 7, 1993.
New Statesman, September 19, 1980.
New York Times Book Review, October 6, 1991, p. 11; January 10, 1993, p. 20; January 16, 1994, p. 22.
Nightly Minnesota Daily, January 20, 1994.
Observer (London), September 14, 1980; February 2, 1983.
Publishers Weekly, January 15, 1982; August 1, 1983; July 25, 1991, p. 37; August 30, 1993, p. 76; January 10, 1994.
Radcliffe Quarterly, June, 1993.
Spectator, October 18, 1980; March 5, 1983.
Times (London), September 18, 1980; February 24, 1983; November 2, 1988.
Times Literary Supplement, September 26, 1980.
USA Today, February 11, 1992; February 20, 1993, p. D7.
Washington Post, November 24, 1992, p. E2.
Washington Post Book World, November 24, 1991, p. 10; December 12, 1993, p. 7.
World & I, June, 1992, p. 369; March, 1994, pp. 281, 289-301.
World Literature Today, spring, 1994, p. 436.

—Sketch by Trudy Ring

* * *

SKINNER, Ainslie
See GOSLING, Paula

* * *

SORESTAD, Glen (Allan) 1937-

PERSONAL: Surname is pronounced *Sor*-stad; born May 21, 1937, in Vancouver, British Columbia, Canada; son of John (in sales) and Myrtle (Dalshaug) Sorestad; married Sonia Diane Talpash (in business), September 17, 1960; children: Evan, Mark, Donna, Myron. *Education:* University of Saskatchewan, B.Ed. (with distinction), 1963, M.Ed., 1976. *Avocational interests:* "I am a constantly amazed traveller who loves to see new places, to meet new people and find new friends in the unlikeliest places. I always want to know what lies over the next mountain."

ADDRESSES: Home—668 East Place, Saskatoon, Saskatchewan, Canada S7J 2Z5; fax 306-244-1762.

CAREER: Yorkton Public Schools, Yorkton, Saskatchewan, elementary school teacher, 1957-60, vice principal, 1963-67; Saskatoon Board of Education, Saskatoon, Saskatchewan, elementary school teacher, 1967-69, high school teacher of English, 1969-81; writer, 1981—. Instructor in creative writing at Saskatoon Community College, 1976-81, and University of Saskatchewan—Extension, 1984. Thistledown Press, cofounder, 1975, publisher and director, 1975—. Literary Press Group, executive member, 1983-84; Prairie Publishers Group, president, 1984-85. Writer-in-residence at numerous schools, libraries, and writing programs.

MEMBER: League of Canadian Poets (executive member), Saskatchewan Writers Guild, University of Saskatchewan Alumni Association (vice president, 1966), Saskatchewan Teachers Federation (member of council, 1957, 1963, 1965, 1966).

AWARDS, HONORS: Hilroy fellowship from Canadian Teachers Federation, 1976, for innovative teaching project, "Prairie Writers Workshop"; Canada Council grant, 1976, for completion of *Prairie Pub Poems.*

WRITINGS:

POETRY

Wind Songs, Thistledown Press, 1975.
Prairie Pub Poems, Thistledown Press, 1976.
Pear Seeds in My Mouth, Sesame Press, 1977.
Ancestral Dances, Thistledown Press, 1979.
Jan Lake Poems, Harbour Publishing, 1984.
Hold the Rain in Your Hands, Coteau Books, 1985.
(With Jim Harris and Peter Christensen) *Stalking Place: Poems across Borders,* Hawk Press, 1988.
Air Canada Owls, Harbour Publishing, 1990.
West into Night, Thistledown Press, 1991.
(With Jim Harris) *Jan Lake Sharing,* privately published, 1993.
Birchbark Meditations, Writers on the Plains, 1996.

EDITOR

(With James A. MacNeill) *Strawberries and Other Secrets,* Nelson Canada, 1970.
(With MacNeill) *Tigers of the Snow,* Nelson Canada, 1973.
(With MacNeill) *Sunlight and Shadows,* Nelson Canada, 1974.
(With Christine McClymont and Clayton Graves) *Contexts: Anthology Three,* Nelson Canada, 1984.
(With Allan Forrie and Paddy O'Rourke) *The Last Map Is the Heart,* Thistledown Press, 1989.
Fat Moon, Kalamalka Press, 1993.
(With McClymont and others) *Something to Declare,* Oxford University Press, 1994.

OTHER

Work is included in numerous anthologies, including *A Sudden Radiance,* Coteau Books, 1987; *What Is Already Known,* Thistledown Press, 1995; and *Through the Smoky End Boards,* Polestar Press, 1996. Contributor of poetry and short stories to many periodicals; poems and stories have also been broadcast on CBC-Radio.

ADAPTATIONS: One of Sorestad's short stories was adapted as a television film, broadcast in syndication.

WORK IN PROGRESS: Icons of Flesh, poems; a manuscript of long poems; a growing manuscript of short prose pieces which may be both prose-poems and mini-fictions.

SIDELIGHTS: Glen Sorestad told *CA:* "I continue to write because I can't imagine what else I would rather do and because, if I didn't write, I would be a miserable creature, intolerable to live with. As Alden Nowlan once said when asked why he wrote: 'What else would I do?'

"I am more and more fascinated by the phenomenon of human memory, what we remember and why, and by the discoveries memory holds for the writer in that amazing creative act by which memory is unlocked and manifests itself into poems or stories. So often, it seems, the poem or story is for me a voyage of discovery; this is both the challenge and the reward, the pain and the pleasure."

Sorestad more recently told *CA:* "As far back as I can remember, poetry has always been a part of my life—from my early love of reading and being read to, to being surrounded with music and song, to a one-room country schoolhouse where I not only willingly memorized numerous poems, but actually committed to memory poems that weren't even assigned, simply because it was an easy and pleasurable activity. Strangely, though, while memorizing some awfully didactic but rhythmically pleasing poems by mostly nineteenth-century and earlier British poets, it never once occurred to me then, when I was twelve or thirteen, that I might actually want to try my hand at writing a poem. After all, poems were written by British or American men, mostly dead. So that made poetry a remote art practised in the past by people in distant lands. Still, poems made good reading, and there was something about poetry that worked its way into my blood and wouldn't let go of me once it took hold.

"When I was seventeen, in high school, I chanced upon Anne Marriott's 'The Wind Our Enemy' in our literary textbook. I was unprepared for the discovery that, not only could poems be written by contemporary Canadians, and even women wrote poetry, but they could be written about places you knew, places you'd been, not just Kew in lilac time or Tintern Abbey or the sweet Afton. I was completely stunned to think that the vast prairies and ever-present wind could ever be a suitably poetic subject. Of course, I apparently wasn't the only one who thought this because our teacher never once mentioned this particular poem being included in the text. I didn't rush home and write a sequence of poems about the prairies, though-in fact, it took another fourteen or fifteen years before I began my first fumblings with poems. Once I started though, I was hooked for good.

"It was in Saskatoon that I first began to meet and talk with writers and to read with a tremendous excitement contemporary poets like Andy Suknaski and Pat Lane, Anne Szumigalski and John Hicks, Bob Currie and Gary Hyland. I was hooked for good. In 1973 Andy Suknaski published a few poems of mine in a little chapbook that was the forerunner to my later *Prairie Pub Poems*. By 1975 I had become involved in founding Thistledown Press, and my life was never to be the same. Almost 200 Thistledown books later, I am still involved in helping to ensure that poetry books keep appearing. In the process, I manage to keep turning my own lines into occasional volumes."

BIOGRAPHICAL/CRITICAL SOURCES:

BOOKS

Hillis, Doris, editor, *Voices and Visions,* Coteau Books, 1985.

* * *

SORIN, Gerald 1940-

PERSONAL: Born October 23, 1940, in Brooklyn, NY; son of John (a foreman) and Ruth (a secretary; maiden name, Gass) Sorin; married Myra Cohen (a language teacher), June 9, 1962; children: Anna Bess. *Ethnicity:* "Jewish." *Education:* Columbia University, A.B., 1962, Ph.D., 1969; Wayne State University, M.A., 1964. *Politics:* Democratic Socialist. *Religion:* Jewish.

ADDRESSES: Home—28 Woodland Dr., New Paltz, NY 12561. *Office*—Department of History, State University of New York College at New Paltz, New Paltz, NY 12561. *E-mail*—soring@matrix.newpaltz.edu.

CAREER: State University of New York College at New Paltz, assistant professor, 1965-70, associate professor, 1970-77, professor of history, 1977—, Distinguished Teaching Professor, 1994—, department head, 1986-96, director of Jewish studies, 1983—.

MEMBER: Association for Jewish Studies, American Jewish Historical Society, Organization of American Historians, American Historical Association, American Jewish Congress, Yidisher Visnshaftlekher Institute (Yiddish Scientific Institute; YIVO).

AWARDS, HONORS: Danforth associate, 1970; State University of New York Foundation fellowships, 1970, 1971, 1979, 1983; Living History award, Gomez Foundation, 1996.

WRITINGS:

New York Abolitionists: A Case Study of Political Radicalism, Greenwood Press (Westport, CT), 1971.

Abolitionism: A New Perspective, Praeger (New York City), 1972.

The Prophetic Minority: American Jewish Immigrant Radicals, 1880-1920, Indiana University Press (Bloomington), 1985.

The Nurturing Neighborhood: The Brownsville Boys Club and Jewish Community in Urban America, 1940-1990, New York University Press (New York City), 1990.

A Time for Building: The Third Migration, 1880-1920, Johns Hopkins University Press (Baltimore, MD), 1992.

Tradition Transformed: The Jewish Experience in America, Johns Hopkins University Press, 1997.

SIDELIGHTS: David Brion Davis remarks in *Reviews in American History* that Sorin's *Abolitionism* "gives us a clear and admirable account of the 'rise of immediatism.' He correctly points to the evangelical background of the majority of abolitionists, and arrays a good bit of evidence to oppose the well known theses of David Donald and Stanley Elkins. He gives detailed attention to the black abolitionists, who have so often been ignored by white historians. If Sorin's *Abolitionism* is something less than an imaginative synthesis, it is probably the most readable and informative survey now available."

Gerald Sorin once remarked to *CA:* "Writing history gives me a weapon with which to negotiate a tentative peace with a chaotic universe."

BIOGRAPHICAL/CRITICAL SOURCES:

PERIODICALS

American Historical Review, June, 1991.
American Jewish History, June, 1986.
Reviews in American History, March, 1973.

* * *

SORKIN, Alan Lowell 1941-

PERSONAL: Born November 2, 1941, in Baltimore, MD; son of Martin and Sally (Steinberg) Sorkin; married Sylvia Jean Smardo, September 9, 1967; children: David Lowell, Suzanne Elizabeth. *Ethnicity:* "White." *Education:* Johns Hopkins University, B.A. (with honors), 1963, M.A., 1964, Ph.D., 1966. *Politics:* Republican. *Religion:* Lutheran.

ADDRESSES: Home—1694 Campbell Rd., Forest Hill, MD 21050. *Office*—Department of Economics, University of Maryland, 5401 Wilkens Ave., Baltimore, MD 21228; fax 410-455-1054.

CAREER: Bureau of Labor Statistics, Washington, DC, economist, summers, 1963-64; Research Analysis Corp., McLean, VA, economic analyst, 1966-67; Brookings Institution, Washington, DC, research associate in economics, 1967-69; Johns Hopkins University, Baltimore, MD, assistant professor, 1969-72, associate professor of international health and economics, 1972-74; University of Maryland, Baltimore County, Baltimore, professor of economics and chairperson of department, 1974—. Parttime lecturer at Goucher College and George Washington University, 1966-67; University of Maryland Medical School, adjunct professor, 1974—.

MEMBER: American Economic Association, Phi Beta Kappa, Delta Omega.

AWARDS, HONORS: Grants from Agency for International Development, 1972, and World Health Organization, 1995-96.

WRITINGS:

American Indians and Federal Aid, Brookings Institution (Washington, DC), 1971.
(With K. N. Williams, T. D. Baker, J. S. Newman, and others) *Health and Economic Development: An Annotated, Indexed Bibliography,* Department of International Health, Johns Hopkins University (Baltimore, MD), 1972.
Education, Unemployment, and Economic Growth, Heath Lexington (Lexington, MA), 1974.
Health Economics: An Introduction, Heath Lexington, 1975, third revised edition, Free Press (New York City), 1992.
Health Economics for Developing Nations, Heath Lexington, 1976.
Health Manpower: An Economic Perspective, Heath Lexington, 1977.
The Urban American Indian, Heath Lexington, 1978.
The Economics of the Postal Service: Alternatives and Reform, Heath Lexington, 1980.
Economic Aspects of Natural Hazards, Heath Lexington, 1982.
(Editor and contributor) *Research in Human Capital and Development,* JAI Press (Greenwich, CT), Volume 3 (With Ismail Sirageldin and David Salkever): *Health and Economic Development,* 1983, Volume 5 (with Sirageldin): *Public Health and Development,* 1988, Volume 6 (with Sirageldin and Richard Frank): *Female Labor Force Participation and Development,* 1990, Volume 8 (with Sirageldin): *Nutrition, Food, Policy, and Development,* 1994.
Health Care and the Changing Economic Environment, Heath Lexington, 1986.
Monetary and Fiscal Policy and the Postwar Business Cycles, Heath Lexington, 1988.

Contributor to books, including *Health Planning for Effective Management,* edited by William A. Reinke, Oxford University Press, 1988; *Survey of Social Science: Economics,* edited by Frank Magill, Salem Press (Englewood Cliffs, NJ), 1991; and *The Economic and Social Status of American Indians,* edited by C. Matthew Snipp,

JAI Press, 1997. Editor of the series "Research in Human Capital and Development," JAI Press, 1991—. Also contributor of more than fifty articles and reviews to education and social science journals, including *Journal of Negro Education, Growth and Change: A Journal of Regional Development, Social Forces, College and University, Monthly Labor Review, American Journal of Economics and Sociology, Journal of Economic Studies, Journal of Economic Literature,* and *Journal of Health Administration Education.*

WORK IN PROGRESS: An economic analysis of cholera vaccines in refugee settings, supported by World Health Organization; continuing research on the health status of Native Americans living on or near reservations and the adequacy of Indian Health Service programs to serve this population.

* * *

SPOTO, Donald 1941-

PERSONAL: Born June 28, 1941, in New Rochelle, NY; son of Michael G. (an advertising executive) and Anne (a public relations aide; maiden name, Werden) Spoto. *Education:* Iona College, B.A. (summa cum laude), 1963; Fordham University, M.A., 1966, Ph.D., 1970. *Religion:* Roman Catholic.

ADDRESSES: *Agent*—Elaine Markson Literary Agency, 44 Greenwich Ave., New York, NY 10011.

CAREER: Fairfield University, Fairfield, CT, assistant professor of theology and humanities, 1966-68; College of New Rochelle, New Rochelle, NY, assistant professor and chairman of religious studies, 1968-74; City University of New York, New York City, assistant professor of classics, 1974-75; New School for Social Research, New York City, professor of humanities, 1975-86; University of Southern California, Los Angeles, CA, adjunct professor, 1987-90. National lecturer, American Film Institute, Washington, DC, 1979-82; visiting lecturer, British Film Institute, National Film Theatre, London, 1980-86.

MEMBER: Authors Guild, Writers Guild of America.

AWARDS, HONORS: Edgar Award from Mystery Writers of America, 1984, for *The Dark Side of Genius: The Life of Alfred Hitchcock.*

WRITINGS:

Stanley Kramer, Film Maker, Putnam (New York City), 1978.
Camerado: Hollywood and the American Man, New American Library (New York City), 1978.
The Art of Alfred Hitchcock, Doubleday (New York City), 1979, revised edition published as *The Art of Alfred Hitchcock: Fifty Years of His Motion Pictures,* 1992.
The Dark Side of Genius: The Life of Alfred Hitchcock, Little, Brown (Boston, MA), 1983.
The Kindness of Strangers: The Life of Tennessee Williams, Little, Brown, 1985.
Falling in Love Again: Marlene Dietrich, Little, Brown, 1985.
Lenya: A Life, Little, Brown, 1989.
Madcap: The Life of Preston Sturges, Little, Brown, 1990.
Blue Angel: The Life of Marlene Dietrich, Doubleday, 1992.
Laurence Olivier: A Biography, HarperCollins (New York City), 1992.
Marilyn Monroe: The Biography, HarperCollins, 1993.
A Passion for Life: The Biography of Elizabeth Taylor, HarperCollins, 1995.
The Decline and Fall of the House of Windsor, Simon & Schuster (New York City), 1995.
Rebel: The Life and Legend of James Dean, HarperCollins, 1996.
Notorious: The Life of Ingrid Bergman, HarperCollins, 1997.

Also author of numerous reviews and essays; contributor to magazines and newspapers.

WORK IN PROGRESS: A biography of Gustav and Alma Mahler, 1997.

SIDELIGHTS: Donald Spoto, whose books are regularly published in more than twenty languages, is internationally known for his biographies of, among other subjects, larger-than-life personalities of the theater and film worlds. Ranging from playwright Tennessee Williams and actor Laurence Olivier to film legends Alfred Hitchcock, Marlene Dietrich, Marilyn Monroe, and James Dean, Spoto's works are characterized by meticulous research and extensive interviews. In his books he attempts to acquaint the reader with the life stories of some of the twentieth century's most colorful (and sometimes most tormented) public figures. The critical consensus about his work was aptly summarized by the editor of the *San Francisco Chronicle*'s "Book World" in 1995: "Spoto is neither hack biographer nor vicious expose artist. He is instead a good example of the biographer as advocate—a historian who believes in the intrinsic decency of his subject and explains human foibles with respect and sensitivity."

"The biography per se hardly constitutes a new or noteworthy addition to literary tradition," notes John and Carl Bellante in the *Bloomsbury Review*. "In contemporary times, however, perhaps no one has elevated this particular genre to higher or more scrupulous standards than Donald Spoto. . . . Unlike other writers who specialize in celebrity exposes . . . Spoto combines the discriminating eye of a literary sleuth with the finely honed sensibilities of a discerning critic." In a discussion of his work published in the *Bloomsbury Review,* Spoto explained: "I'm deeply intrigued by how creative people interact with a larger society. Clearly everyone has a private life, and that's terribly important in understanding how a person lives." He added: "Most biographies are simply chronicles or almanac entries. Then he went here, then he did this or that. But our real life, of course, is how we react internally. How we grow or don't grow. How we assess and develop values. How we respond, how we love, how we fear."

A former professor of religion and humanities, Spoto has claimed that he began writing biographies "by accident." Having written three books on film culture and history—including the well-received *The Art of Alfred Hitchcock*—he was approached by his agent about doing a Hitchcock biography soon after the famous film director died in 1980. "My agent said to me, 'There's your next book,'" Spoto recalled in the *Bloomsbury Review*. "I'd been two years without a project. 'You're the logical one to do the Hitchcock biography,' she said. 'I don't know anything about how to write biographies!' She looked at me. 'You're a writer. A scholar. You have a Ph.D. You know how to do research. You're doing the biography!' In two weeks we had a contract."

Winner of the prestigious Edgar Award in 1984, *The Dark Side of Genius: The Life of Alfred Hitchcock* combines historical perspective with voluminous research, interviews, film studies, and anecdotes. Hitchcock emerges, in Spoto's estimation, as perhaps the greatest filmmaker in history, and as man of profound fears. For "those who consider Hitchcock a dark genius," writes Richard Grenier in the *New York Times Book Review,* "Mr. Spoto's book is absolutely compulsory reading." *Time* reviewer John Skow suggests that Spoto "is too shrewd to imagine . . . that an artist is the sum of his quirks. Hitchcock's brilliance was entangled with his personal grotesqueries, but it was real brilliance. . . . His final obsession was secretiveness, but he has been well served by a knowledgeable and revealing biography." Actor Gregory Peck (who appeared in two Hitchcock pictures) endorsed the book as "a biography of unassailable integrity."

Spoto's next biography was *The Kindness of Strangers: The Life of Tennessee Williams,* the first comprehensive treatment of the playwright to appear after its subject's death. Like the other Spoto works, *The Kindness of Strangers* is an unauthorized biography, but in this case the author was given access to Williams's private papers and conducted in-depth interviews with family members who felt free to talk in the wake of the playwright's death. In a review for the *Washington Post Book World,* Jonathan Yardley states that "because Williams led a bewilderingly peripatetic life, and because people moved in and out of that life in equally bewildering numbers, Spoto's chronicle occasionally descends into a rather paralysing recital of arrivals and departures; but he only rarely lapses into the indiscriminate accumulation of meaningless detail that characterizes contemporary American literary biography, and he has many calm, judicious things to say about his subject." Michael Church, writing for the *London Review of Books*, calls *The Kindness of Strangers* "a richly detailed study," while Dan Sullivan of the *Los Angeles Times Book Review* hails it as "possibly the best [biography] of an American playwright since Louis Sheaffer's two-volume study of O'Neill."

Spoto turned to stage and screen star Lotte Lenya as the subject of his next biography. The widow of composer Kurt Weill, Lenya made a name for herself in Germany between the World Wars interpreting the songs that Weill wrote for works by playwright Bertoldt Brecht, including *The Threepenny Opera* and *The Rise and Fall of the City of*

Mahagonny. She fled Europe for America in the mid-1930s and was "rediscovered" by Hollywood and Broadway with her roles in the James Bond film *From Russia with Love* and the musical *Cabaret.* Lenya died of cancer in 1981, having spent the bulk of her career promoting and performing Weill's songs. "This sympathetic book pays tribute to [Lenya's] allure, charm, wit, sadness and genius," notes a *Publishers Weekly* reviewer; *The Times* of London adds that "Spoto is an exact and atmospheric biographer who succeeds in recreating the fevered discord of the German Twenties."

A lifelong aficionado of American film, Spoto returned to that genre with *Madcap: The Life of Preston Sturges.* Spoto chronicles the director's unconventional childhood, which took place in an environment that might have inspired some of Sturges's more fanciful films. His mother, for instance, was a dilettante who became a disciple of the magician Aleister Crowley, leaving Sturges in charge of a thriving cosmetics shop at the tender age of sixteen. *Village Voice* reviewer Katherine Dieckmann calls Spoto's descriptions of the director's private life "far more to the point than Sturges's [autobiography], which downplays his extramarital dallying." Patrick Goldstein, writing for the *Los Angeles Times Book Review,* commends Spoto as "an able, informative biographer . . . [who] is at his best describing Sturges' impossibly exotic upbringing."

Spoto's biographies of major film stars include *Blue Angel: The Life of Marlene Dietrich, Laurence Olivier: A Biography, Marilyn Monroe: The Biography, A Passion for Life: The Biography of Elizabeth Taylor,* and *The Life and Legend of James Dean.* In each case Spoto has striven to bring new perspective to the private lives of the stars in question and, in the case of Marilyn Monroe, has offered a reasonable explanation for her untimely death. In a review of *Marilyn Monroe, New Statesman & Society* contributor Douglas Kennedy concludes: "Spoto is somewhat smitten by his subject—and his immensely readable biography is noteworthy for its lack of sensationalism and its willingness to portray the movie star as an intelligent, yet deeply frightened woman." Likewise in a review of *Blue Angel, Washington Post Book World* correspondent Quentin Crisp commends Spoto for the "great care and subtlety" with which he has approached the elusive star. "Spoto's book is not prurient," the reviewer continues. "It is a genuine attempt to understand this mysterious, self-created and, to some extent, self-deceived woman." *Los Angeles Times Book Review* essayist Paul Rosenfield states that Spoto's biography of Olivier is "thorough and illuminating . . . the best of a dozen books about the actor." And the *Boston Globe* considers Spoto's biography of James Dean "a well-written and researched biography" that brings "a new clarity to the fog that has enveloped the Dean mystique."

Spoto's *The Decline and Fall of the House of Windsor* traces the troubled history of Great Britain's royal family from the times of Queen Victoria to the present. Rather than dwelling upon the scandals of the present generation of royals, Spoto ranges through the twentieth century and, according to *People* magazine reviewer Clare McHugh, "persuasively argues that the current crisis is a natural souring of decades of careful image-building." A *Kirkus Reviews* contributor calls *The Decline and Fall of the House of Windsor* "a gracefully fleshed-out timeline . . . packed with just as much information about famous royal nannies as about who was sleeping with whom." A *Publishers Weekly* reviewer observes that Spoto "has skillfully assembled what could be entitled 'Windsors 101,'" and concludes that the book is an "entertaining and informative tour of a dynasty."

Reflecting on his choice of subjects, Spoto stated in a *Bloomsbury Review* interview: "As far as how I choose my topics . . . I don't pick them. They seem to pick me. I don't mean to sound like a bogus mystic, but somehow the subjects emerge. I'm offered exclusive access to papers or someone puts an idea into my head." He added that he would rather write unauthorized biographies because they do not hinder his objectivity. "Writing an authorized biography can in itself be a hindrance," he explained. "You get friendly with people, and you withhold. Hesitate to go into details about family relationships because you're trying to curry favor." Spoto concluded that when writing biography, "I believe in the Chekhovian approach. You have to know more than you tell."

Donald Spoto once told *CA:* "The writer's vocation is extraordinarily simple, and simply extraordinary—and at the same time a positive joy. It is nothing less than the constant attempt to make order out of chaos, first within himself, then with words, for the healing of the world."

BIOGRAPHICAL/CRITICAL SOURCES:

BOOKS

Contemporary Literary Criticism, Volume 39, Gale (Detroit, MI), 1986.

PERIODICALS

Bloomsbury Review, September/October 1993, pp. 20-21, 25-26.
Boston Globe, May 17, 1996, p. 58.
Chicago Tribune Book World, May 21, 1989, p. 5.
Entertainment Weekly, November 3, 1995, pp. 60-61.
Film Quarterly, spring 1977; summer 1979; summer 1986, p. 35; winter 1992, p. 61.
Kirkus Reviews, September 15, 1995, p. 1338.
London Review of Books, September 5, 1985, p. 14.
Los Angeles Times Book Review, May 26, 1985, p. 4; May 14, 1989, p. 6; May 6, 1990, p. 8; September 27, 1992, pp. 1, 8, 11; May 2, 1993, pp. 2, 8.
Nation, January 6, 1978; July 20, 1985, pp. 54-56.
New Republic, May 13, 1985, pp. 33-36.
New Statesman & Society, May 7, 1993, pp. 40-41.
Newsweek, April 11, 1983.
New York Review of Books, April 26, 1984, pp. 22-24, 32; June 13, 1985, pp. 5-6, 8-10; December 20, 1990, pp. 6, 8-10.
New York Times, March 15, 1983.
New York Times Book Review, November 11, 1979; March 6, 1983; April 21, 1985, pp. 3, 48; April 13, 1986, p. 38; April 30, 1989, p. 12; April 22, 1990, p. 20; August 9, 1992, pp. 3, 16-17; June 11, 1995, p. 45.
Observer, May 9, 1993, p. 58.
People, January 8, 1996, p. 34.
Publishers Weekly, March 17, 1989, p. 88; May 20, 1995, p. 51; October 9, 1995, p. 70; March 4, 1996, p. 44.
Spectator, October 21, 1989, pp. 38-39; October 19, 1991, pp. 42-43; May 1, 1993, p. 38.
Time, May 9, 1983; May 13, 1985, pp. 74-75; April 23, 1990, pp. 96-97.
Times (London), May 19, 1983.
Times Literary Supplement, June 21, 1985, pp. 685-86; December 1, 1989, p. 1335; October 11, 1991, p. 20; December 25, 1992, p. 16; May 7, 1993, p. 9; May 5, 1995, p. 27.
Tribune Books (Chicago), June 10, 1990, p. 8; July 19, 1992, p. 9.
Village Voice, October 18, 1983; September 18, 1990, pp. 73-74.
Village Voice Literary Supplement, February, 1984, p. 7.
Washington Post Book World, April 17, 1983; April 14, 1985, pp. 3, 7; March 30, 1986, p. 12; May 13, 1990, p. 10; December 29, 1991, p. 12; February 23, 1992, p. 3; July 19, 1992, p. 1, 10.

T

TATE, James (Vincent) 1943-

PERSONAL: Born December 8, 1943, in Kansas City, MO; son of Samuel Vincent Appleby (a pilot) and Betty Jean Whitsitt. *Education:* Attended University of Missouri, 1963-64; Kansas State College, B.A., 1965; University of Iowa, M.F.A., 1967.

ADDRESSES: Home—16 Jones Rd., Pelham, MA 01002. *Office*—Department of English, University of Massachusetts, Amherst, MA 01003.

CAREER: University of Iowa, Iowa City, instructor in creative writing, 1966-67; University of California, Berkeley, visiting lecturer, 1967-68; Columbia University, New York, NY, assistant professor of English, 1969-71; University of Massachusetts at Amherst, beginning 1971, began as associate professor, currently professor of English. Poet in residence, Emerson College, 1970-71. Consultant to the Coordinating Council of Literary Magazines, 1971-74, and to the Kentucky Arts Commission, 1979. Member of Bollingen Prize Committee, 1974-75; judge for several poetry contests, including the Lucille Medwick Prize, 1978, the Elliston Book Award, 1978, and the Charles and Cecilia Wagner Award, 1980.

MEMBER: PEN.

AWARDS, HONORS: Yale Younger Poets Award, 1966, for *The Lost Pilot;* named Poet of the Year, Phi Beta Kappa, 1972; National Institute of Arts and Letters award for poetry, 1974; Massachusetts Arts and Humanities fellow, 1975; Guggenheim fellow, 1976; National Endowment for the Arts fellow, 1980; Pulitzer Prize for poetry, 1992, for *Selected Poems;* National Book Award for poetry, 1994, for *Worshipful Company of Fletchers;* Tanning Prize, Academy of American Poets, 1995.

WRITINGS:

POETRY

Cages, Shepherd's Press (Iowa City), 1966.

The Destination, Pym-Randall Press (Cambridge, MA), 1967.

The Lost Pilot, Yale University Press (New Haven, CT), 1967.

Notes of Woe: Poems, Stone Wall Press, 1968.

Camping in the Valley, Madison Park (Chicago), 1968.

The Torches, Unicorn Press (Santa Barbara, CA), 1968, revised edition, 1971.

Row with Your Hair, Kayak Press (San Francisco), 1969.

Is There Anything?, Sumac Press (Fremont, MI), 1969.

Shepherds of the Mist, Black Sparrow Press (Los Angeles), 1969.

Amnesia People, Little Balkans Press (Girard, KS), 1970.

(With Bill Knott) *Are You Ready Mary Baker Eddy,* Cloud Marauder Press (Berkeley, CA), 1970.

Deaf Girl Playing, Pym-Randall Press, 1970.

The Oblivion Ha-Ha, Little, Brown (Boston), 1970.

Wrong Songs, Halty Ferguson (Cambridge, MA), 1970.

Hints to Pilgrims, Halty Ferguson, 1971, 2nd edition, University of Massachusetts Press (Amherst), 1982.

Absences, Little, Brown, 1972.

Apology for Eating Geoffrey Movius' Hyacinth, Unicorn Press, 1972.
Hottentot Ossuary, Temple Bar (Cambridge, MA), 1974.
Viper Jazz, Wesleyan University Press (Middletown, CT), 1976.
Riven Doggeries, Ecco Press (New York City), 1979.
Land of Little Sticks, Metacom (Worcester, MA), 1981.
Constant Defender, Ecco Press, 1983.
Reckoner, Wesleyan University Press, 1986.
Distance from Loved Ones, Wesleyan University Press, 1990.
Selected Poems, Wesleyan University Press, 1991.
Worshipful Company of Fletchers, Ecco Press, 1994.

BROADSIDES

Mystics in Chicago, Unicorn Press, 1968.
Nobody Goes to Visit the Insane Anymore, Unicorn Press, 1971.
A Dime Found in the Snow, Little Balkans Press, 1973.
Marfa, University of Connecticut Library (Storrs), 1974.
Suffering Bastards, Hearsay Broadsheets, 1975.
Who Gets the Bitterroot?, Rook Press, 1976.
The Rustling of Foliage, the Memory of Caresses, Massachusetts Review, 1979.
If It Would All Please Hurry, Shanachie Press, 1980.

OTHER

(With Knott) *Lucky Darryl: A Novel,* Release Press (Brooklyn, NY), 1977.

Work represented in numerous anthologies, including *Heartland: Poets of the Midwest,* edited by Lucien Stryk, Northern Illinois University Press, 1967; *The Norton Anthology of Modern Poetry,* edited by Richard Ellman and Robert O'Clair, Norton, 1973; and *English and American Surrealist Poetry,* edited by Edward B. Germain, Penguin, 1978. Contributor to *Paris Review, Transatlantic Review, New Yorker, Nation, Atlantic, Poetry, Quarterly Review of Literature, Shenandoah,* and other publications. Poetry editor, *Dickinson Review,* 1967-76; trustee and associate editor, Pym-Randall Press, 1968-80, and associate editor of Barn Dream Press.

SIDELIGHTS: Described by John Ash in the *New York Times Book Review* as "an elegant and anarchic clown, a lord of poetic misrule with a serious, subversive purpose," James Tate writes poetry concerned with the playful and creative aspects of language, as well as the limits to what language can express. Some critics fault him for slighting his poetic subjects in favor of the language in which the poems are written, but for Tate, the language of the poem is the poem's ultimate subject. As Philip Dacey remarks in the *American Book Review,* Tate's "subject matter is the folly of subject matter."

A typical Tate poem begins with an unlikely or whimsical situation. Writing in the *Dictionary of Literary Biography,* Stephen Gardner maintains that Tate's poems "are rooted in landscapes that are often—if not generally—bizarre and surreal." His language is charged with metaphor and linguistic inventiveness, similar to that of the surrealist or absurdist writers, and is meant to illustrate the inability of language to express human emotion. Because of his willingness to take extreme chances, Tate tends to "err on the side of adventure rather than caution," according to Harold Jaffe in the *Christian Science Monitor.* "Tate," Dacey comments, "writes as if he were translating from a foreign language he did not understand, relying solely on word-association for method. . . . He has his fun at the expense of language rather than vice versa, acting less to employ it than to expose it."

According to a critic for the *Virginia Quarterly Review,* the strengths and weaknesses of Tate's work "are characteristic of the poet's generation. Freshness, attractive eccentricity, winning irreverence, and a laudable independence give these poems a flavor quite their own; but most of them lack something vital: a purpose, a sense of direction, a goal." Pointlessness is a charge raised by some other critics as well. William Logan of *Poetry* characterizes Tate's poems as "invention without control, ingenuity without purpose, they careen like driverless automobiles, ending at times in a crash of irrelevant simile." In like terms, Dick Allen of the *Hudson Review* has "the feeling that these are mainly smarty-pants nonsense poems, going for the easy chuckle and the virtuoso dance of language."

But many commentators value Tate's work for its ingenuity, exhilarating language, and sheer energy. Norman Rosten in *Saturday Review,* for example, calls Tate "a poet of verbal excitement, sometimes opaque, sometimes of dazzling clarity. His is a unique vision of a man tuned in to a private cosmos with its little mysteries." "Tate's power," claims Marianne Boruch in the *American Poetry Review,* "has always been his verbal energy, his expert and dead serious play which resists conventional design and the sentimental reduction it risks." Though Ash admits that sometimes "Tate's jazzy, oddball version of Surrealism threatens to become automatic," he argues that "these reservations are insignificant when set against the poet's consistent originality and inventiveness." Harper Barnes, writing in the *Washington Post Book World,* believes that Tate "must be included in any discussion of major American poets."

In 1966 Tate won the prestigious Yale Younger Poets Award, the youngest poet, at the age of 23, to ever do so in the award's seventy-three year history. The manuscript that earned him the prize was *The Lost Pilot,* which was published by Yale University Press in 1967. The book's title refers to Tate's father, a pilot who was reported missing over Germany during the Second World War. Critical response to the collection was enthusiastic. Gardner notes that "most reviewers" reacted with "simultaneous praise and amazement—praise for the accomplishment and amazement that one so young had done so much so well." Several reviewers believed that Tate had already developed his own poetic voice: Tate's "low-keyed, off-hand style is his own," as Jaffe remarks. Julian Symons, writing in *New Statesman,* found Tate to be "an ironical, original, self-absorbed poet who glances with amusement at love, humanity, himself."

In subsequent collections Tate established himself as one of the leading poets of his generation. According to Barnes, "Tate is that rare American phenomenon, the prodigy fulfilled." Among his most critically praised books is *Absences,* a collection that Julian Moynahan in the *New York Times Book Review* describes as "meditative, introverted, self-reliant, funny, alarming, strange, difficult, intelligent and beautifully crafted." Brian Swann, in his review of the book for *Library Journal,* calls Tate "a real poet: vigorous, effervescent, adventurous." Speaking of the collection in the *American Poetry Review,* Mark Rudman claims that "*Absences* still moves me more than anything else [Tate has] written. In it he retains elements of despair, anger, rage; it is surrealism with a razor-edge and transcends the boundaries of any *ism.*"

Constant Defender was also praised by many reviewers. In his analysis of the book, Logan believes that Tate "tests himself too little and congratulates himself too much." Yet he describes Tate as "a clever and resourceful poet. He can take a bizarre premise and with it mock the grave anthropologists. . . . He can turn a meditation on an old photograph of himself into an Icelandic saga." Mark Irwin, writing in *World Literature Today,* explains that "Tate has succeeded perhaps more than anyone else in defining 'the disinheritedness' of American culture. His new volume confirms in a wry yet terrifying manner the shallow and confusing nature of our orphaned past."

In an article for the *American Poetry Review,* Donald Revell sees *Constant Defender* as a long meditation on the relationship between our treatment of death and our use of language to describe and deal with death. He explains that the poem "If It Would All Please Hurry," included in the collection and also published separately as a broadside, "engages every one of Tate's major themes—love, death, and the career of words among the loving and the dying—in a single, urgent occasion." In this poem, according to Revell, Tate attacks the language typically found in eulogies. "He reserves his most forceful, moving language for the assault on those rituals surrounding death," Revell writes. "Tate distills that language to an awful clarity. . . . The prescribed ritual speech of the man presiding over the funeral is dead because it is irrelevant. It cannot comfort; it cannot speak to the situation of grief at all."

Tate won the Pulitzer Prize for poetry with *Selected Poems,* a collection of work from nine volumes, from *The Lost Pilot* through 1986's *Reckoner.* "Unlike most books of this kind, Tate's wants to be read sequentially," Ralph Angel observes in his *American Poetry Review* commentary on *Selected Poems.* "Or, if it is read that way, the poetic voice develops as would a character in a particularly good play—complicated and soulful enough to care about, laugh and joke around with, feel for and ultimately worry over." In poems written over the course of twenty years, Tate expresses a wide range of thought and feeling and reacts to a constantly changing environment. Out of all this somehow evolves a consistent vision, Angel notes, adding that the poet "does the hard thing by embracing human complexity . . . James Tate is talented and smart and vulnerable enough to reflect our age." *New York Times Book Review* contributor Richard Tillinghast asserts that the collection demonstrates how Tate "has created a voice and a kind of poem that no one else could have written." Tillinghast goes on to praise both Tate's "highly brainy comedy" and his underlying, sometimes surprising seriousness. In *Hudson Review,* Mark Jarman welcomes the collection and writes that Tate "has edited himself well." While Jarman deems the poet's wordplay occasionally irritating, and sometimes imitative of lesser writers, he also lauds Tate's lack of predictability and finds that many of his poems have retained their impact over the years. "*The Lost Pilot* . . . is still a wonderful read," he notes. Both Tillinghast and Jarman conclude that Tate stands out from, and above, the numerous other poets who have attempted a surrealistic style.

Worshipful Company of Fletchers brought Tate another honor, the National Book Award for poetry. "Awards do not make the man, but in this case the recognitions are well-deserved," comments Amy Gerstler in her *Los Angeles Times Book Review* piece on the book. In *Worshipful Company of Fletchers,* as in previous works, Tate's way with language and quirky wit are much in evidence, Gerstler writes, adding that Tate's humor is frequently humor with a purpose. "I know of no American poet . . . who makes better use of humor as an explorer's tool, to probe thought, experience and emotion," she states. For instance, she points out that in "50 Views of Tokyo," Tate comes up with numerous engaging images as he ponders the doubts and mysteries of life. A *Publishers Weekly* reviewer also has much praise for the collection, applauding Tate's "earnest verbal anarchy [which is] difficult to characterize or resist. Jazzlike, he seems to invent experience, not just poetry, and the effect is exhilarating for a reader." Tate received a further honor in 1995, when the Academy of American Poets presented him with the Tanning Prize, at $100,000 the largest annual literary award in the United States. The prize recognizes poets who have demonstrated extraordinary ability in their craft.

According to Gardner, "Tate's importance in contemporary poetry needs no defense. . . .[His] poetry provides a lively and jolting characterization of the universe. His language is fresh and highly suggestive. And unlike many surrealists—including those who are his followers—he is clearly able to control the situations he creates." Rosten calls Tate "a risk-taker, likely to get out on that real or metaphysical limb and keep cutting, not caring much whether the saw is between him and the tree or not. This is the heady spirit that encourages the adventure of poetry."

BIOGRAPHICAL/CRITICAL SOURCES:

BOOKS

Contemporary Literary Criticism, Gale (Detroit), Volume 2, 1974, Volume 6, 1976, Volume 25, 1983.

Dictionary of Literary Biography, Volume 5: *American Poets since World War II,* Gale, 1980.

The Making of Poetry, Yale University Press (New Haven), 1967.

Shaw, Robert B., editor, *American Poetry since 1960: Some Critical Perspectives,* Dufour Editions (Chester Springs, PA), 1974.

PERIODICALS

AB Bookman's Weekly, July 11-18, 1977.

American Book Review, November-December, 1987, pp. 14-15.

American Poetry Review, November-December, 1976; July-August, 1981; January-February, 1987, p. 43; January-February, 1988, p. 17; May, 1992, pp. 45-46.

Booklist, September 15, 1994, p. 107.

Boston Globe, April 8, 1992, p. 27; November 17, 1994, p. 65.

Carleton Miscellany, fall, 1967.

Christian Science Monitor, July 11, 1967; October 28, 1976.

Commonweal, September 11, 1987, p. 506.

Encounter, December, 1967.

Georgia Review, summer, 1991, p. 383.

Hudson Review, summer, 1967; winter, 1972-73; spring, 1980; autumn, 1987, p. 510; spring, 1992, pp. 158-66; summer, 1995, p. 339.

Library Journal, June 15, 1972; January, 1987; November 1, 1990, p. 93; September 15, 1994, p. 74.

Los Angeles Times Book Review, November 27, 1994, pp. 2, 11.

Nation, April 24, 1967.

New Statesman, June 16, 1967.

New York Times, November 17, 1994, p. C24; November 18, 1994, p. C35; September 20, 1995.

New York Times Book Review, November 12, 1972; March 1, 1987, p. 26; August 30, 1992, p. 12.
Poetry, February, 1968; March, 1971; October, 1971; July, 1977; August, 1980; November, 1984, p. 99; June, 1995, p. 168.
Publishers Weekly, October 19, 1990, p. 53; August 29, 1994, p. 68; November 21, 1994, p. 26.
Saturday Review, June 3, 1967; August 12, 1972.
Sewanee Review, summer, 1980.
Small Press, fall, 1991, p. 74.
South Atlantic Review, November, 1990, pp. 78-86.
Southern Review, winter, 1972.
Sulfur, spring, 1995, p. 218.
Times Literary Supplement, May 18, 1967.
Virginia Quarterly Review, summer, 1967; spring, 1969; autumn, 1970; winter, 1980.
Wall Street Journal, January 19, 1995, p. A16.
Washington Post, September 19, 1995, p. D3.
Washington Post Book World, December 31, 1972; March 3, 1991, p. 6; June 16, 1991, p. 12; December 4, 1994, p. 14.
World Literature Today, spring, 1984.
Yale Review, summer, 1967.*

* * *

TERRY, Margaret
See DUNNAHOO, Terry Janson

* * *

TEZLA, Albert 1915-

PERSONAL: Born December 13, 1915, in South Bend, IN; son of Michael and Lucia (Szenasi) Tezla; married Olive Anna Fox (a psychiatric nurse), July 26, 1941; children: Michael William, Kathy Elaine. *Ethnicity:* "Hungarian American." *Education:* University of Chicago, B.A., 1941, M.A., 1947, Ph.D., 1952.

ADDRESSES: Home—5412 London Rd., Duluth, MN 55804. *E-mail*—atezla@umn.edu; fax 218-525-9062.

CAREER: Employed during his early career as night watchman, shipping clerk, dock worker, lathe operator, and secondary teacher; Indiana University, South Bend, instructor in English literature in Extension Division, 1946-48; University of Minnesota—Duluth, instructor, 1949-53, assistant professor, 1953-56, associate professor, 1956-61, professor of English, 1961-83, professor emeritus, 1983—. Columbia University, visiting professor of Hungarian literature, 1966, visiting scholar, 1975. *Military service:* U.S. Navy, 1942-46; became lieutenant; received Purple Heart and Commendation medal.

MEMBER: International Association of Hungarian Studies (member of executive committee), Hungarian PEN (honorary member).

AWARDS, HONORS: Faculty-staff award from University of Minnesota Student Association, 1958, for contributions to student life outside the classroom; Fulbright research fellow in Vienna, 1959-60; American Council of Learned Societies grants, 1961, 1968; Inter-University Committee research fellow in Budapest, 1963-64; Outstanding Teacher Award, University of Minnesota Student Association, Duluth, 1965; commemorative medal from Institute of Cultural Relations (Budapest), 1970, for contributions to the knowledge of Hungarian culture in the United States; International Research and Exchanges Board research fellowship, 1978; National Endowment for the Humanities research grant, 1978-81; award from ARTISJUS, Agence Litterraire, Theatrale et de Musique (Budapest), 1982, for translations of Hungarian literature; Hungarian Publishers Annual Award, 1985, for translating *Fifth Seal, A Novel,* and *God in the Wagon (Ten Short Stories),* and 1988, for translating *On the Balcony, Selected Short Stories;* award from Presidium of the Hungarian PEN Center, 1986, for his lifework and contributions to Hungarian studies; John Lotz Memorial Award, International Association of Hungarian Studies, 1986, for contributions to Hungarian literary scholarship; Chancellor's Award for Meritorious Service, University of Minnesota—Duluth, 1993; Pro Cultura Hungarica Medallion, Hungarian Ministry of Culture, 1996, for outstanding contribution to worldwide prestige and the reputation of Hungarian culture.

WRITINGS:

An Introductory Bibliography to the Study of Hungarian Literature, Harvard University Press (Cambridge, MA), 1964.
Hungarian Authors: A Bibliographical Handbook, Belknap Press (Cambridge), 1970.
(Editor and contributor) *Ocean at the Window: Hungarian Prose and Poetry since 1945,* University of Minnesota Press (Minneapolis), 1981.

(With daughter, Kathy Elaine Tezla) *Valahol tul, meseorszagban; Az amerikas magyarok, 1895-1920: Somewhere in a Distant Fabled Land,* two volumes, Europa (Budapest, Hungary), 1987.

(Editor) *Three Contemporary Hungarian Plays,* Forest Books (Boston), 1992.

The Hazardous Quest: Hungarian Immigrants in the United States, 1895-1920, Corvina Publishing House, 1993.

TRANSLATOR

Ferenc Santa, *God in the Wagon (Ten Short Stories),* Corvina Publishing House, 1985.

Santa, *The Fifth Seal, A Novel,* Corvina Publishing House, 1986.

Ivan Mandy, *On the Balcony, Selected Short Stories,* Corvina Publishing House, 1988.

Istvan Lazar, *Hungary: A Brief History,* Corvina Publishing House, 1990.

Lazar, *An Illustrated History of Hungary,* Corvina Publishing House, 1992.

Sandor Marai, *Memoir of Hungary, 1944-1948,* Corvina Publishing House, 1996.

Miklos Meszoly, *Once There Was a Central Europe: Selected Short Stories and Other Writings,* Corvina Publishing House, 1997.

Alaine Polcz, *A Woman at the Front,* Corvina Publishing House, 1997.

OTHER

Contributor to books, including *East Central Europe: A Guide to Basic Publications,* University of Chicago Press (Chicago), 1969; *Hungarian Short Stories,* edited by Paul Varnai, Exile Editions (Toronto, Ontario), 1983; *William Rose Benet: The Reader's Encyclopedia,* Crowell, 1984, third edition, Harper (New York City), 1987; and *The Kiss: Twentieth-Century Hungarian Short Stories,* edited by Istvan Bart, Corvina Publishing House, 1993; also contributor to *Academic American Encyclopedia,* Arete Publications, 1980, *World Authors, 1975-1980,* H. W. Wilson (Bronx, NY), 1985, *World Authors, 1980-1985,* H. W. Wilson, 1991, and *Austrian History Yearbook.* Contributor to *New Hungarian Quarterly, Valosag, Hungarian PEN, Hungarian Studies,* and other periodicals.

SIDELIGHTS: The University of Minnesota—Duluth has established the Albert Tezla Scholar/Teacher Award in honor of the author. The award recognizes "faculty members who excel in bringing to the classroom a teaching style that emphasizes the worth of research," Albert Tezla once told *CA.*

Tezla more recently told *CA:* "I look upon my work in Hungarian studies to be mostly that of a utility player meeting the emerging needs of the field that fall within the scope of my competence. Frustrated in my attempt in the late fifties to lay a sound research basis for a projected study of Hungarian romanticism, I chose to create bibliographic tools for Hungarian literature that would enable researchers outside Hungary to review thoroughly the basic materials of the discipline for their projects. So, at age forty-four, I devoted twelve years to the preparation of two basic, annotated bibliographies with locations of cited primary and secondary titles to meet that requirement.

"As that time passed, other large projects I had planned for myself—an ambitious history of contemporary Hungarian literature, for example—necessarily became, instead, the writing of articles, mostly author profiles, for major reference works. With the mounting interest in matters Hungarian, this provided an effective way of informing English-speaking individuals about significant features of Hungarian literature.

"From the very beginning, I was acutely aware of the need to create a larger foreign readership for Hungary's imaginative literature. So, from the early 1960s onward, I gave ever more attention—and now in the years of my retirement continue to give—to translation, mostly from the writings of authors I have come to know personally through the large amounts of time I have frequently spent in Hungary since 1959. It is a rare privilege, indeed, to enjoy their splendid company and to receive their help in solving problems of translation that I encountered in their texts. What priceless memories of our times together! Santa, Mandy, Meszoly—how great my debt to you!

"Two factors led me into the field of immigration studies: my experiences as a second-generation Hungarian and the sharp rise of interest in immigrant history that began in the 1960s. My desire to throw much-needed light on the life of Hungarians through the testimony of those who, like my parents, came to America between 1895 and 1920, resulted in two published documentaries: one in Hungarian, the other in English. Products of more than twenty years of archival research in Hungary, Austria, and the United States, they are a labor of love in memory of my beloved parents, who came to the United States in 1907, and of their generation of immigrants from Hungary. The books represent an effort on my part to make sure, at least to some measure, that what an ethnic Hungarian miners' newspaper of the time reported can never again be said about these people: 'The poor have no history, nobody takes note of the life of the poor. The Janos Wereshes simply live, struggle, and die, and then everybody forgets them.'"

* * *

THIHER, Allen 1941-

PERSONAL: Surname rhymes with "fire"; born April 4, 1941, in Fort Worth, TX; son of Ottah A. (in sales) and Helen (Massy) Thiher. *Education:* University of Texas at Austin, B.A., 1963; University of Wisconsin—Madison, M.A., 1964, Ph.D., 1968.

ADDRESSES: Home—105 Meadow Lane, Columbia, MO 65203. *Office*— Department of Romance Languages, 143 Arts and Science Building, University of Missouri—Columbia, Columbia, MO 65211. *E-mail*—langalln@showme.missouri.edu.

CAREER: Duke University, Durham, NC, assistant professor of French, 1967-69; Middlebury College, Middlebury, VT, assistant professor of French, 1969-76; University of Missouri—Columbia, associate professor, 1976-81, professor of French, 1982—, Middlebush Professor of Romance Languages, 1985-89, Curators' Professor of French, 1990. Universitaet des Saarlandes, exchange professor, 1992.

MEMBER: Modern Language Association of America, American Association of Teachers of French, American Association of University Professors, Society for Literature and Science, Phi Beta Kappa.

AWARDS, HONORS: Fulbright scholarship, 1966-67; Shell Foundation grant, 1973; Guggenheim fellowship, 1976-77; University of Missouri summer research fellowship, 1978, travel grants, 1979 and 1981, and Chancellor's Award for outstanding research in the humanities and the arts, 1981.

WRITINGS:

Celine: The Novel as Delirium, Rutgers University Press (New Brunswick, NJ), 1972.

The Cinematic Muse: Critical Studies in the History of French Cinema, University of Missouri Press (Columbia), 1979.

Words in Reflection: Modern Language Theory and Postmodern Fiction, University of Chicago Press (Chicago), 1984, second edition, 1987.

Raymond Queneau, Twayne (New York City), 1985.

Franz Kafka: A Study of the Short Fiction, Twayne, 1989.

The Power of Tautalogy: The Roots of Literary Theory, Associated University Presses (Cranbury, NJ), 1997.

Contributor to books, including *Actes du Colloque international d'Oxford,* Societe des etudes celiniennes, 1981; *Samuel Beckett: Humanistic Perspectives,* edited by Morris Beja, S. E. Gontarski, and Pierre Astier, Ohio State University Press (Columbus), 1983; and a volume on Franz Kafka, published by Indiana University Press (Bloomington). Contributor of book reviews and essays to journals, including *Modern Fiction, Modern Drama, PMLA, Philological Quarterly, Literature/Film Quarterly, Romance Notes,* and *Kentucky Quarterly of Romance Studies.*

SIDELIGHTS: Allen Thiher once told *CA:* "Like one of Beckett's heroes, I keep trying to make sense of the senseless, which is, I suppose, the central task of literary studies today."

* * *

THOMAS, J(ames) D(avid) 1910-

PERSONAL: Born July 20, 1910, in Holliday, TX; son of William Albert (a clerical worker) and Angie Belle (Wisdom) Thomas; married Mary Katherine Payne, February 22, 1931; children: Deborah Gayle Thomas Fish (deceased), Hannah Belle (Mrs. Dwayne Kissick), John Paul. *Ethnicity:* "Caucasian." *Education:* Attended University of Texas at Austin, 1926-28; Abilene Christian College (now University), A.B., 1943; Southern Methodist University, M.A., 1944; University of Chicago, Ph.D., 1957.

ADDRESSES: Home—1334 Ruswood, Abilene, TX 79601-4647.

CAREER: Minister, Church of Christ, 1937—; City of Lubbock, TX, assistant city manager, 1939-42; Northwest Church of Christ, Chicago, minister, 1945-49; Abilene Christian University, Abilene, TX, associate professor, 1949-57, professor of Bible, 1957-82, professor emeritus, 1982—, head of department, 1970-79, lectureship director, 1952-70. Biblical Research Press (now Abilene Christian University Press), owner, publisher, manager, and editor, 1958-84. Lecturer in Japan, Korea, Taiwan, Hong Kong, and the Philippines, 1958, and in thirty countries during world tour in 1969. *Restoration Quarterly,* president of corporation board, 1974-79. Eastern Little League, founding president, 1939.

MEMBER: Society of Biblical Literature (former president of Southwestern section), American Bible Society (member of advisory board), American Academy of Religion, American Scientific Affiliation, Evangelical Theological Society, Southwestern Philosophical Society.

AWARDS, HONORS: Century Book Award, Family Book Club, 1966, for *Facts and Faith,* Volume 1; *Twentieth Century Christian,* Christian journalism award, 1966, named outstanding educator, 1981; named Kiwanian of the Year, Abilene Kiwanis Club, 1988; Distinguished Christian Service Awards from Pepperdine University and Oklahoma Christian University of Science and Arts, both 1991.

WRITINGS:

We Be Brethren, Biblical Research Press (Abilene, TX), 1958.
Evolution and Antiquity, Biblical Research Press, 1961.
Facts and Faith, Biblical Research Press, Volume 1, 1966, Volume 2: *The Bible and Faith,* 1980.
The Spirit and Spirituality, Biblical Research Press, 1967, second edition, 1982.
(Editor) Frank Pack and Prentice A. Meador, Jr., *Preaching to Modern Man,* Biblical Research Press, 1969.
Self-Study Guide to Galatians and Romans, Biblical Research Press, 1971.
Self-Study Guide to the Corinthian Letters, Biblical Research Press, 1972.
(Editor) *Spiritual Power: Great Single Sermons,* Biblical Research Press, 1972.
Heaven's Window, Biblical Research Press, 1975.
(Editor) *What Lack We Yet?,* Biblical Research Press, 1977.
The Biblical Doctrine of Grace, Biblical Research Press, 1977.
Divorce and Remarriage, Biblical Research Press, 1977.
The Message of the New Testament: Romans, Biblical Research Press, 1982.
The Message of the New Testament: First Corinthians, Abilene Christian University Press (Abilene), 1984.
Second Corinthians: The Message of the New Testament, Abilene Christian University Press, 1986.
The Well-Spring of Morality, Abilene Christian University Press, 1987.
Hebrews-James: The Message of the New Testament, Abilene Christian University Press, 1988.
(Editor) *Evolution and Faith,* Abilene Christian University Press, 1988.
Harmonizing Hermeneutics, Gospel Advocate Press (Nashville, TN), 1991.

EDITOR; "GREAT PREACHERS OF TODAY" SERIES

Sermons of Batsell Barrett Baxter, Biblical Research Press, 1960.
Sermons of George W. Bailey, Biblical Research Press, 1961.
Sermons of Frank Pack, Biblical Research Press, 1963.
Sermons of John H. Banister, Biblical Research Press, 1965.
Sermons of Gus Nichols, Biblical Research Press, 1966.
Sermons of William S. Banowsky, Biblical Research Press, 1967.

Also editor of six other volumes in the series.

EDITOR; "TWENTIETH-CENTURY SERMONS" SERIES

Reuel Lemmons, *The King and His Kingdom,* Biblical Research Press, 1968.
John A. Chalk, *Jesus' Church,* Biblical Research Press, 1969.
Robert C. Douglas, *Freedom in Christ,* Biblical Research Press, 1970.
C. E. McGaughey, *The Hope of the World,* Biblical Research Press, 1971.
Akio Limb, *Because of Jesus,* Biblical Research Press, 1972.
Anthony L. Ash, *The Word of Faith,* Biblical Research Press, 1973.

Joe R. Barnett, *Live, with Peace, Power and Purpose,* Biblical Research Press, 1978.

Also editor of six other volumes in the series.

OTHER

Editor, "Sermons for Today" series, three volumes, 1981—. Contributor to *Journal of Biblical Literature.* Member of board, *Restoration Quarterly,* 1957-89; former staff writer, *Gospel Advocate* and *Twentieth Century Christian.*

SIDELIGHTS: J. D. Thomas once told *CA* that his motivation "is to teach Christians, primarily, so that they in turn may teach others. The time is short and the need is great. The masses do not have the intellectual grasp they should have on the basic issues and the meanings in life. Writing should be done as a contribution to the education of humanity in matters spiritual, for these are the important matters."

Thomas more recently told *CA:* "My primary goal in research and writing has been to 'seek the truth.' The world is generally run on the basis of spiritual ignorance. Admittedly, the Bible is the world's greatest book, yet the average person doesn't grapple with it in any serious way."

His first book, *We Be Brethren,* was written to help solve a problem of interpretation that had developed among his colleagues, and since he had business experience, Thomas decided to publish it himself. This launched his publishing career, which now includes many titles. Several of his books have been translated into other languages.

* * *

TROJANOWICZ, John M.
See TROYANOVICH, John M(ichael)

* * *

TROYANOVICH, John M(ichael) 1936-
(John M. Trojanowicz)

PERSONAL: Surname is pronounced Troy-a-*no*-vich; original surname, Trojanowicz, legally changed, 1966; born August 22, 1936, in Bay City, MI; son of Chester R. (a detective) and Loretta (Duffy) Trojanowicz; married Kathleen Gallagher (a bookkeeper), September 1, 1956 (divorced); children: John L., Stephan J., Mark M., Rita M., Josef G. *Ethnicity:* "Polish-American." *Education:* University of Michigan, B.A. (with distinction), 1960; University of Illinois, M.A., 1961; Michigan State University, Ph.D., 1964; postdoctoral study at University of Tuebingin, 1964.

ADDRESSES: Home—2212 Somerset Blvd., No. 104, Troy, MI 48084. *Office*—Corporate Diversified Services, Inc., 575 East Big Beaver Rd., Suite 270, Troy, MI 48083; fax 810-680-2152.

CAREER: Michigan State University, East Lansing, instructor, 1962-64, assistant professor of German, 1964-68; University of Kansas, Lawrence, associate professor of German and education, 1968-71; Illinois Wesleyan University, Bloomington, professor of modern languages and education, 1971-77, chairperson of department of foreign languages, 1971-74; Volkswagen of America, New Stanton, PA, training and communications administrator, 1977-79, coordinator of engineering liaison in Troy, MI, 1979-81, purchasing agent, 1981-84; Chrysler Corp., Detroit, MI, quality specialist and manufacturing liaison in Mexico, 1984-86, training manager, 1986-91; Skoda Automobilova, Mlada Boleslav, Czech Republic, manager of project coordination, 1992-94; Corporate Diversified Services, Inc., Troy, president, 1994—. Oakland Community College, professor of business, 1983—. President of board of directors, McLean County Mental Health Center, Center for Human Resources. *Military service:* U.S. Army, Security Agency, interpreter and translator in German and Romanian, 1955-58.

MEMBER: American Management Association.

AWARDS, HONORS: Woodrow Wilson fellow, 1960; study grant for Germany, Germanistic Society of America, 1964; travel grant from Republics of West Germany and Austria.

WRITINGS:

(With Kurt W. Schild) *German Conversational Reader,* with instructor's manual and tape program, American Book Co. (New York City), 1969.

German: From Language to Literature, with instructor's manual, Van Nostrand (New York City), 1972.

(Author of instructor's manual for brother's book) Robert C. Trojanowicz, *Juvenile Delinquency: Concepts and Control,* Prentice-Hall (Englewood Cliffs, NJ), 1973, fourth edition, with Merry Morash, 1987.
(Author of instructor's manual) R. C. Trojanowicz and Samuel L. Dixon, *Criminal Justice and the Community,* Prentice-Hall, 1974.
(Under name John M. Trojanowicz; with R. C. Trojanowicz, and Forrest M. Moss) *Community Based Crime Prevention,* Goodyear Publishing (Pacific Palisades, CA), 1975.
(With R. C. Trojanowicz) *Police Supervision,* Prentice-Hall, 1980.
(With Richard E. Dauch) *Passion for Manufacturing,* Society of Manufacturing Engineers (Dearborn, MI), 1993.

Work represented in anthologies, including *Where Dawn Lingers,* National Library of Poetry (Owings Mills, MD), 1996; and *The Best Poems of the Nineties,* National Library of Poetry, 1996. Contributor to periodicals, including *American Foreign Language Teacher, Foreign Language Annals, Die Unterrichtspraxis, Public Personnel Review, Classical Outlook, Bereavement,* and *Texas Foreign Language Bulletin.*

* * *

TUROW, Joseph G(regory) 1950-

PERSONAL: Born April 5, 1950, in New York, NY; son of Abraham (a chemist) and Danuta (Chaikin) Turow; married Judith Forrest (a pediatrician), June 17, 1979. *Education:* University of Pennsylvania, B.A. (with distinction), 1971, M.A., 1973, Ph.D., 1976.

ADDRESSES: Home—321 Bala Ave., Bala Cynwyd, PA 19004. *Office*—Annenberg School of Communications, University of Pennsylvania, 3620 Walnut St., Philadelphia, PA 19104-6220.

CAREER: Drexel University, Philadelphia, PA, lecturer in communications, summer, 1974, 1975; Purdue University, West Lafayette, IN, assistant professor, 1976-81, associate professor of communications, 1981-86, faculty fellow at Fowler House, 1976-77; University of Pennsylvania, Annenberg School of Communications, Philadelphia, associate professor, 1986-90, professor of communications, 1990—. University of California, Los Angeles, visiting assistant professor, summer, 1980, visiting associate professor, summer, 1985. Member of advisory panel of Indiana Arts Commission, 1980-83; Commonwealth Speaker for Pennsylvania Humanities Council, 1989, 1991; advisory board member, Telecourse Project on Mass Communication, WGBH-TV, Boston, 1989-91; advisory board member, WPBT-TV, Miami, 1991—. Member, communication advisory panel, Please Touch Children's Museum, Philadelphia, 1992-93; member, National Endowment for Children's Educational Television (U.S. Department of Commerce), 1995-97; seminar leader; public speaker; guest on television and radio programs.

MEMBER: International Communication Association (Mass Communication Division chair, 1993-97), Speech Communication Association of America, Phi Beta Kappa.

AWARDS, HONORS: Award from Speech Communication Association of America, 1977, for article "Another View of Citizen Feedback to the Mass Media"; David Ross fellowship from Purdue University, 1979, 1980-81; awards from International Communication Association, 1981, for article "Unconventional Programs on Commercial Television: An Organizational Perspective," and 1983, for paper "Corporate Planning Toward the Coming Information Age: How It Will Affect Mass Media Culture"; Russell B. Nye Award for best article from *Journal of Popular Culture,* 1982; National Endowment for the Humanities grants, 1986 and 1994; University of Pennsylvania Research Foundation grant, 1988-89; Ford Foundation grant, 1996.

WRITINGS:

Program Trends in Network Children's Television, 1948-1978 (monograph), Federal Communications Commission (Washington, DC), 1979.
Getting Books to Children: An Exploration of Publisher-Market Relations, American Library Association (Chicago, IL), 1979.
Entertainment, Education, and the Hard Sell: Three Decades of Network Children's Television, Praeger (New York City), 1981.
(Editor) *Careers in Mass Media,* Science Research Associates (Chicago, IL), 1984.
Media Industries: The Production of News and Entertainment, Longman (New York City), 1984.
Playing Doctor: Television, Storytelling, and Medical Power, Oxford University Press (New York City), 1989.

Media Systems in Society: Understanding Industries, Strategies, and Power, Longman, 1992.

Breaking Up America: Advertising and the New Media World, University of Chicago Press (Chicago, IL), 1997.

CONTRIBUTOR

Paul Hirsch, Peter Miller, and F. Gerald Kline, editors, *Strategies for Communication Research,* Sage Publications (Beverly Hills, CA), 1978.

C. Whitney and James Ettema, editors, *Individuals in Mass Media Organizations,* Sage Publications, 1981.

Robert Bostrom, editor, *Communication Yearbook 7,* Sage Publications, 1983.

W. Rowland and B. Watkins, editors, *Interpreting Television,* Sage Publications, 1985.

Phillip Tompkins and Robert McPhee, editors, *Organizational Communication: Traditional Themes and New Directions,* Sage Publications, 1985.

Clifford Johnson, editor, *The Book of Days,* Pierian (Ann Arbor, MI), 1987.

Erik Barnouw, editor, *The International Encyclopedia of Communication,* Oxford University Press, 1989.

B. Dervin, L. Grossberg, and E. Wartella, editors, *Paradigm Dialogues,* Sage Publications, 1989.

The Academic American Encyclopedia, Grollier, 1989.

B. Ruben and L. Lievrow, editors, *Information and Behavior,* Transaction Books (New Brunswick, NJ), 1990.

J. Anderson, editor, *Communication Yearbook,* Sage Publications, 1990.

C. Stratos, editor, *The World of News,* Gnosis Publishing (Athens, Greece), 1991.

J. Curran and M. Gurevitch, editors, *Culture, Society, and the Media,* 2nd edition, Routledge (New York City), 1992.

Lynn Spigel and Michael Curtin, editors, *The Revolution Wasn't Televised,* Routledge, 1996.

OTHER

Author of "Outtakes," a column in *EMMY: The Magazine of the Academy of Television Arts and Sciences,* 1980-82. Contributor of articles and reviews to communications and education journals, including *Communication Research Reports, Journal of Broadcasting, Journal of Popular Culture, The Lancet,* and *Journal of Communication.* Member of editorial board, *Communication Education,* 1978-82, and *Journal of Broadcasting and Electronic Media,* 1985-94, 1996—; advising and contributing editor, *Journal of Communication,* 1981-91, 1996—; assistant editor, *Central States Speech Communication Journal,* 1983-85; member of founding editorial board, *Critical Studies in Mass Communications,* 1984-89; editorial board member, Sage Annual Reviews of Communication Research, 1986—; advising editor, Ablex Communication Book Series, 1988-91.

WORK IN PROGRESS: Research on "new media" and the public relations industry.

SIDELIGHTS: Joseph G. Turow told *CA:* "My primary research and writing revolves around two questions: (1) What forces cause continuity and change in mass media material? and (2) To what extent can publics use those forces to bring about the changes in mass media that they want? The more I learn, the more I realize how complex the answers to these questions are. They are intertwined tightly with the issue of power and control in society. They relate to the broad spectrum of societal resources that define the holders of power and how they use it. And they relate to industrial and organizational processes through which power and control are exercised. Studying this subject is fascinating. Trying to implement changes in the media is more difficult and necessarily frustrating than most people would imagine."

BIOGRAPHICAL/CRITICAL SOURCES:

BOOKS

Benet, James, Arlene Daniels, and Gaye Tuchman, editors, *Hearth and Home,* Oxford University Press, 1978.

Boylan, Robert, Phillip Davison, and T. C. Yu, *Mass Media: Systems and Effects,* Praeger, 1977.

Greenberg, Bradley, *Life on Television,* Ablex Publishing (Norwood, NJ), 1980.

PERIODICALS

AFI Education Newsletter, September-October, 1981.

College and Research Libraries, July, 1979.

Dallas Morning News, October 4, 1981.

Detroit Free Press, January 18, 1981.

HSSE Newsletter, autumn, 1980.

Journal of Communication, spring, 1982.

Journalism Quarterly, August, 1979; spring, 1982.

New York Times, March 25, 1989.

Southern Speech Communication Journal, spring, 1983.
Top of the News, autumn, 1979.
Wilson Library Bulletin, October, 1980.

W-Z

WATERMAN, Andrew (John) 1940-

PERSONAL: Born May 28, 1940, in London, England; son of Leonard and Olive (Smith) Waterman; married Angela Marilyn Hannah Eagle, May 21, 1982 (divorced, 1985); children: Rory John Nolan. *Ethnicity:* "Anglo-Irish." *Education:* University of Leicester, B.A. (with first class honors), 1966; graduate study at Oxford University, 1966-68. *Avocational interests:* Hill-walking, chess, good conversation.

ADDRESSES: *Home*—15 Hazelbank Rd., Coleraine, Londonderry, Northern Ireland. *Office*—University of Ulster, Coleraine, Londonderry, Northern Ireland.

CAREER: University of Ulster, Coleraine, Northern Ireland, lecturer, 1968-78, senior lecturer in English literature, 1978—.

MEMBER: Poetry Society, Association of University Teachers.

AWARDS, HONORS: Cholmondeley Award for Poets, 1977; second prize in Arvon Foundation Poetry Competition, 1981, for *Out for the Elements.*

WRITINGS:

POETRY

Living Room: Poems, (Poetry Book Society choice in England), Marvell Press, 1974.
Last Fruit, Mandeville Press, 1974.
From the Other Country, Carcanet Press, 1977.
Over the Wall, Carcanet Press, 1980.
Out for the Elements (Poetry Book Society recommendation in England), Carcanet Press, 1981.
(Editor) *The Poetry of Chess,* Anvil Press Poetry, 1981.
Selected Poems, Carcanet Press, 1986.
In the Planetarium, Carcanet Press, 1990.
The End of the Pier Show, Carcanet Press, 1995.

OTHER

Contributor to books, including *British Poetry since 1970,* edited by Michael Schmidt and Peter Jones, Carcanet Press, 1980. Contributor of articles and reviews to journals and newspapers, including *London Magazine, Poetry Wales, P.N. Review,* and *Times Literary Supplement.*

WORK IN PROGRESS: Further poems.

SIDELIGHTS: In a *Times Literary Supplement* article, Grevel Lindop characterized Waterman's *Out for the Elements* as "an autobiography framed in a diary: the past recaptured through the preoccupations of the present." The book begins with an introductory set of twenty lyrics titled "Given Worlds," which are memories and insights into Waterman's personal experience; the book continues with another group of "Shorter Poems," and closes with the major works. These include "Anglo-Irish," a discussion of the situation in Northern Ireland from the author's perspective, and "Out for the Elements," a wide-ranging account of the author's travels in England and Ireland during 1979 and 1980.

Reflecting on the poetic achievement in *Out for the Elements* and some of Waterman's earlier efforts, Lindop declared, "One has the impression of a poet who has found his proper direction, and has begun to produce important work." He continued, "*Out for the Elements* is a rare thing: a long poem which is highly readable, as well as thoroughly contemporary in its techniques and its mode of intelligence. It also goes with sensitivity to the heart of several problems that beset modern Britain."

Waterman told *CA,* "Life provides sufficient motivation for writing poetry; that is, one is nagged to articulate response, to use language to explore and try to clarify various areas of experience. Obviously one could enlarge enormously on this."

BIOGRAPHICAL/CRITICAL SOURCES:

BOOKS

Dictionary of Literary Biography, Volume 40: *Poets of Great Britain and Ireland since 1960,* Gale (Detroit), 1985.

Schmidt, Michael, and Peter Jones, editors, *British Poetry since 1970,* Carcanet Press, 1980.

PERIODICALS

Encounter, January, 1982.

Listener, April 15, 1976.

London Review of Books, February 18, 1982.

Times Literary Supplement, April 16, 1982.

* * *

WATKINS, T(homas) H(enry) 1936-

PERSONAL: Born March 29, 1936, in Loma Linda, CA; son of Thomas F. (a newspaper worker) and Orel (Roller) Watkins; married Elaine Otakie, January 26, 1957 (divorced); married Ellen J. Parker, June 12, 1976; children: (first marriage) Lisa Lynn, Kevin Blair. *Education:* Attended San Bernardino Valley College, 1954-56; University of Redlands, B.A., 1958; San Francisco State College (now University), graduate study, 1963-64. *Politics:* Democrat. *Religion:* "Former Catholic, now militantly ecumenical Christian."

ADDRESSES: Home—2226 Decatur Pl. N.W., Washington, DC 20008. *Office*—c/o The Wilderness Society, 900 17th St. N.W., Washington, DC 20006.

CAREER: American West Publishing Co., Palo Alto, CA, *American West* (magazine), managing editor, 1966-69, editor, 1969-70, associate editor, 1970-76; *American Heritage* (magazine), New York City, member of board of editors, 1976-79, senior editor, 1979-82; *Wilderness* (magazine), Washington, DC, editor, 1982-96; The Wilderness Society, Washington, DC, editorial consultant, 1996—. Advisor to Public Broadcasting Series (PBS) seven-part documentary, *The West,* 1996. Chair of nonfiction panel, National Book Award, 1996.

AWARDS, HONORS: Captain Donald T. Wright Award in Maritime Transportation Journalism, 1975, for *Mark Twain's Mississippi;* Robert Marshall Award, 1989, for conservation writing; National Book Award and National Book Critics Circle Award nominations, 1990, and *Los Angeles Times* Book Award, 1991, all for *Righteous Pilgrim: The Life and Times of Harold L. Ickes, 1874-1952.*

WRITINGS:

San Francisco in Color, Hastings House (New York City), 1968.

(With Roger R. Olmsted) *Here Today: San Francisco's Architectural Heritage,* San Francisco Chronicle (San Francisco, CA), 1968.

(With others) *The Grand Colorado: The Story of a River and Its Canyons,* American West, 1969.

California in Color: An Essay on the Paradox of Plenty, Hastings House, 1970.

(With others) *The Water Hustlers,* Sierra Club (SanFrancisco, CA), 1971.

Gold and Silver in the West: The Illustrated History of an American Dream, American West, 1971.

California: An Illustrated History, American West, 1973.

On the Shore of the Sundown Sea, Sierra Club, 1973.

Mark Twain's Mississippi: The Pictorial History of America's Greatest River, American West, 1974.

(With Charles S. Watson, Jr.) *The Lands No One Knows: America and the Public Domain,* Sierra Club, 1975.

John Muir's America, illustrated with photographs by DeWitt Jones, American West, 1976.

(With Olmsted) *Mirror of the Dream: An Illustrated History of San Francisco,* Scrimshaw Press, 1976.

Taken by the Wind: Vanishing Architecture of the West, illustrated with photographs by Ronald Woodall, New York Graphic Society (Boston, MA), 1977.

Gold Country, illustrated with photographs by Stanly Truman, California Historical Society (San Diego, CA), 1982.

(Author of introduction) John Wesley Powell, *Lands of the Arid Region of the United States,* new edition, Harvard Common, (Boston, MA), 1983.

American Landscape, illustrated with photographs by David Muench, Graphic Arts Center (Portland, OR), 1987.

Vanishing Arctic: Alaska's National Wildlife Refuge, Aperture and Wilderness Society (Washington, DC), 1988.

Time's Island: The California Desert, Peregrine Smith and Wilderness Society, 1989.

Righteous Pilgrim: The Life and Times of Harold L. Ickes, 1874-1952, Henry Holt (New York City), 1990.

The Great Depression: America in the 1930's, Little, Brown (Boston, MA), 1993.

(With Dyan Zaslowsky) *These American Lands: Wilderness, Parks, and the Public Lands,* Island Press (Fort Myers Beach, FL), 1994.

(Editor, with Joan Parker Watkins) *The West: A Treasury of Art and Literature,* Hugh Lauter Levin, 1994.

(Editor, with patricia Byrnes) *The World of Wilderness: Essays on the Power and Purpose of Wild Country,* Roberts Rinehart (Boulder, CO), 1995.

Stone Time: Southern Utah, a Portrait and a Meditation, Clear Light (New York City), 1995.

(With Joan Parker Watkins) *Western Art Masterpieces,* Hugh Lauter Levin, 1996.

Southern Utah Wilderness: A Portrait, a History, and a Battle, illustrated with photographs by Muench, BrownTrout, 1997.

Our National Lands, National Geographic Society (Washington, DC), in press.

Contributor of more than 250 articles to numerous periodicals.

WORK IN PROGRESS: By Chaos out of Dream: A History of the United States in the Age of the Great Depression, for Holt.

SIDELIGHTS: T. H. Watkins told *CA:* "Some people call me an historian, some a journalist, some an environmentalist—they're all wrong. I'd prefer to think of myself *first* as a writer—a writer who happens to work in all these areas, as well as anything else which presents itself. I'm in love with words, with the sound and muscularity of phrases. . . . At the same time, I cannot deny a profound dependence upon the historical view, for it seems to me that it provides the essential key to understanding—and understanding is the only shield we have against fate and all its consequences. I learned this essential fact, among other things, from the one writer who has influenced my work, such as it is, more than any other: Wallace Stegner, the novelist and historian who needs no encomiums from me to place him at or very near the head of the small list of this century's major American writers."

BIOGRAPHICAL/CRITICAL SOURCES:

PERIODICALS

Los Angeles Times Book Review, October 15, 1989.

New York Review of Books, April 25, 1991.

New York Times Book Review, December 14, 1969; December 18, 1977.

Publishers Weekly, October 25, 1993.

* * *

WHEELER, Cindy 1955-

PERSONAL: Born May 17, 1955, in Montgomery, AL; daughter of Kenneth Bradford (a school supervisor) and Joanne (a teacher; maiden name Dingus) Wheeler; married Robert Patrick Lee (in publishing), July 26, 1980; children: Sally Virginia, William Patrick. *Ethnicity:* "Caucasian." *Education:* Auburn University, B.F.A., 1977; graduate study at School of Visual Arts, New York City, 1980. *Religion:* Episcopalian.

ADDRESSES: Home—125 Pinedale Rd., Asheville, NC28805. *Office*—The Bookstore on Wall Street, 34 Wall St., Suite 805-C, Asheville, NC 28801. *E-mail*—cwlart@aol.com; fax: 704-258-8501.

CAREER: Zibart's Bookstore, Nashville, TN, children's book buyer and sales clerk, 1977-78; Alfred A. Knopf (publishers), New York City, editorial secretary in juvenile department, 1977-80; freelance illustrator, designer, and writer, 1980—. Lothrop, Lee & Shepherd, assistant to the art director, 1984-85. The Bookstore on Wall Street, coowner.

AWARDS, HONORS: Rose was included in Bologna International Children's Book Fair, 1985; Alabama Author's Award, Alabama Library Association, 1985, for *Marmalade's Christmas Present.*

WRITINGS:

SELF ILLUSTRATED

A Good Day, a Good Night (Junior Literary Guild selection), Lippincott (Philadelphia), 1980.
Rose, Knopf (New York City), 1985.
Spring Is Here! (coloring book), Happy House, 1986.
A Day on the Farm (coloring book), Happy House, 1987.
Sally Wants to Help, Random House (New York City), 1988.
What's in Your Basket?, Scholastic (New York City), 1997.
Early Easter Morning, Scholastic, 1997.

"MARMALADE" SERIES

Marmalade's Snowy Day, Knopf, 1982.
Marmalade's Yellow Leaf, Knopf, 1982.
Marmalade's Nap, Knopf, 1983.
Marmalade's Picnic, Knopf, 1983.
Marmalade's Christmas Present (Junior Literary Guild selection), Knopf, 1984.
The Bookstore Cat, Random House, 1994.
Simple Signs, Viking (New York City), 1995.

ILLUSTRATOR

Charlotte Zolotow, *One Step, Two,* Lothrop (New York City), revised edition (Wheeler not associated with first edition), 1981.
The Scaredy Cats and the Haunted House, Random House, 1982.
Alice Schertle, *That Olive!,* Lothrop, 1984.
Laurel Richardson, *Red House, Blue House,* Peel Productions (Columbus, NC), 1997.

OTHER

Merry Christmas, Little Mouse (coloring book), illustrated by Jan Brett, Happy House, 1986.
A New House for Little Mouse (picture book), illustrated by Stella Ormai, Happy House, 1987.
The Emperor's Birthday Suit, illustrated by R. W. Alley, Random House, 1996.

WORK IN PROGRESS: Writing and illustrating *More Simple Signs,* publication by Viking expected in 1998; writing *Cats,* Random House, 1998; illustrating *Fred Fish,* by Richardson, Peel Productions, 1998.

SIDELIGHTS: Cindy Wheeler once told *CA:* "Writing and illustrating books for children gives me a chance to stay in touch with some of the first emotions I experienced as a child. With each of my books I try to share, simply and clearly, those feelings the way I remember them—uncomplicated, unsuspicious happiness in its purest and most all-encompassing form."

Wheeler more recently told *CA:* "Writing and illustrating books for children is more than something I enjoy doing, however. It is something I *need* to do. For various reasons during my career, I have earned my keep doing other things from time to time. But, like the prodigal son (or daughter), I have always come back to children's books.

"I enjoy working on everything from mass-market board-books to educational software. Whether writing, illustrating, doing computer animation for CD-ROM, or even designing a business card, my goal is always the same: How can I make this project my own? How do I leave *my* signature? It's the desire to meet this challenge that keeps bringing me back, time and time again. The technology has changed so much since I began in this business some twenty years ago, but it seems that the more things change, the more they stay the same. I think that is what I love about children's books. The packaging gets glitzier, but the heart and soul remain the same."

WILBUR, C. Keith 1923-

PERSONAL: Born June 21, 1923, in Providence, RI; son of Clifford Keith (a chemist) and Ruth (Williams) Wilbur; married Ruth Elizabeth Asker, June 29, 1946; children: David Williams, Carol Ann, Bruce Alan, Jody Elizabeth. *Education:* Bates College, B.S., 1948; University of Vermont, M.D., 1952. *Religion:* Congregational (Church of Christ).

ADDRESSES: Home and office—397 Prospect St., Northampton, MA 01060.

CAREER: Salem Hospital, Salem, MA, intern and resident, 1952-53; family practice of medicine in Northampton, MA, 1953-85. Past staff member at Cooley Dickinson Hospital and Smith College infirmary. Chair, Northampton Historical Fair, 1969, and Northampton Historical Commission. Member, Northampton Bicentennial Committee. *Military service:* U.S. Navy, 1942-46; commanded submarine chaser; became lieutenant junior grade.

MEMBER: American Academy of Family Practice (fellow), National Tree Farmers Association, National Wood Carvers Association, Company of Military Historians (fellow), Massachusetts Medical Society, Massachusetts Archaeological Society, Sixth Massachusetts Continentals, Hampshire County Medical Society, Northampton Historical Society, Old DeerfieldPocumtuck Society, College Club (Bates College).

AWARDS, HONORS: Heritage Foundation Award, 1963, for pageant "Rebels and Redcoats."

WRITINGS:

Picture Book of the Continental Soldier, Stackpole (Harrisburg, PA), 1969, also published as *The Revolutionary Soldier, 1775-1783: An Illustrated Sourcebook of Authentic Details about Everyday Life for Revolutionary War Soldiers,* Globe Pequot, 1993.

Picture Book of the Revolution's Privateers, Stackpole, 1973, also published as *Pirates and Patriots of the Revolution: An Illustrated Encyclopedia of Colonial Seamanship,* Globe Pequot, 1984.

Medical Crisis in Washington's Army, Bristol Pharmaceutical Co., 1976.

The New England Indians, Globe Pequot (Chester, CT), 1978.

Revolutionary Medicine, 1700-1800, Globe Pequot, 1980.

(With wife, Ruth E. Wilbur) *Bid Us God Speed: The History of the Edwards Church of Northampton, Massachusetts, 1833-1983,* Phoenix Publishing, 1983.

Tall Ships of the World: An Illustrated Encyclopedia, Globe Pequot, 1986, revised edition, 1996.

Antique Medical Instruments: Price Guide Included, Schiffer, 1987.

Land of the Nonotucks, Northampton Historical Society (Northampton, MA), 1987.

Early Explorers of North America, Globe Pequot, 1989.

Indian Handcrafts, Globe Pequot, 1990.

(Illustrator) Elizabeth Janos, *Country Folk Medicine,* Globe Pequot, 1990.

Home Building and Woodworking in Colonial America, Globe Pequot, 1992.

The Woodland Indians, Globe Pequot, 1995.

Also author of historical pageant "Rebels and Redcoats."

SIDELIGHTS: C. Keith Wilbur once told *CA:* "My boyhood introduction to early American history was unforgettable. It was by the shore of Narragansett Bay that I'd picked up another flat stone to scale across the water. It came as something of a shock to realize that I was holding an arrowhead in my hand chipped to perfection—and I'd very nearly sent it skipping! Untouched for centuries, I had a find that was worth ponderingover and treasuring.

"Once into Indian lore, I made my own headdress, then a wigwam, and a full-sized dugout canoe. Yet the surface of history was only scratched, for the books in the library were filled with exciting narratives of exploration and colonization of these Indian lands. It seems even possible that Old World prehistoric peoples had visited America well before the Viking exploits! The story of America is heady stuff—Jamestown and Plymouth, the French and Indian wars, our independence from King George's heavy hand, the clipper ships probing the seven seas, and so on. No fiction here, just the real adventures by real people who shaped America's destiny.

"Indeed I am fascinated by our early American heritage. It belongs to and is part of all of us. My writings and pen and ink sketches are a way of sharing what I have experienced and learned with our readers."

* * *

WILLANS, Jean Stone 1924-

PERSONAL: Born October 3, 1924, in Hillsboro, OH; daughter of Homer (a teacher) and Ella (Keys) Hammond; married Donald Stone (a lieutenant commander in the military; deceased); married second husband, Richard Willans (a writer and management consultant); children: Suzanne Jeanne. *Ethnicity:* "Caucasian." *Education:* Attended San Diego Junior College.

ADDRESSES: *Home*—368 East Mendocino St., Altadena, CA 91001; fax 818-797-4900.

CAREER: Family Loan Co., Miami, FL, assistant to vice president, 1946-49; U.S. Air Force, General Officers Branch, Washington, DC, civilian supervisor, 1953-55; Blessed Trinity Society, Van Nuys, CA, founder and executive director, 1960-66; *Trinity* (magazine), Los Angeles, CA, editor, 1961-66; Society of Stephen, Altadena, CA, cofounder and executive director, 1967—, vice president and director of Asian Office in Hong Kong, 1968-81. Has lectured and conducted missions throughout the United States and in Canada, Mexico, Great Britain, Indonesia, Taiwan, Hong Kong, and the Philippines.

AWARDS, HONORS: An award from the National Assocation of Pentecostal Women, 1964; received honorary degree of Doctor of Divinity from the American branch of the Church of the East.

WRITINGS:

(Editor with husband, Richard Willans) *Charisma in Hong Kong,* Society of Stephen (Altadena, CA), 1970.

(Editor with R. Willans) *Spiritual Songs,* Society of Stephen, 1970.

The Acts of the Green Apples (autobiography), Society of Stephen, 1973, revised edition, Whitaker House (Springdale, PA), 1974, revised and updated edition, Society of Stephen, 1995.

Author of pamphlets and booklets for the Blessed Trinity Society, 1960-63. Also author and editor, with R. Willans, of *Once There Was a Church, Spiritual Songs,* and *Fire and Wind,* two volumes, for Society of Stephen, 1969-92. Contributor to periodicals, including *Voice, Christian Life,* and *Eternity.*

WORK IN PROGRESS: "(With R. Willans) a sequel to *The Acts of the Green Apples,* an update of the Willanses' ministry, particularly their experiences with the drug addicts and triad gangsters in Hong Kong's underworld; a third volume of *Fire and Wind,* anthologies of testimonies and teaching articles relating to the Pentecostal-charismatic experience and movement."

SIDELIGHTS: Jean Willans' husband, Richard, writes: "Jean is one of the genuine pioneers of the charismatic renewal. In this movement, tens of millions of Christians worldwide—Roman Catholic, Orthodox and Protestant of every hue, clergy as well as laity—have received an experience described biblically as 'baptism in the Holy Spirit' with the manifestation of speaking in unlearned languages (sometimes called glossolalia). This is the same experience which distinguishes the Pentecostal movement. Indeed, most if not all first-generation charismatic renewal leaders received it through contact with Pentecostals; there has always been close fellowship and cooperation between adherents of both movements; and today most knowledgeable observers recognize these two 'waves' as part of the same major current, generally referring to them as the Pentecostal-charismatic movement. However, the groundbreaking accomplishment of Jean and other early charismatics was to demonstrate that the emotionalism which characterized Pentecostalism (resulting in such descriptives as 'holy rollers') is not essential to either speaking in tongues or the other 'charismata' such as healing and prophetic utterance.

"Jean received this Holy Spirit baptism in 1959, while a member of St. Mark's Episcopal Church in Van Nuys, California; and Passion Sunday 1960, when the rector, Fr. Dennis Bennett, preached the experience from the pulpit, isgenerally regarded as the point at which the movement 'went public.' For, although Bennett resigned under pressure that same day, Jean was convinced that nothing less than the key to the dynamism of the early church was at stake, and she put both *Time* and *Newsweek* onto the story (on condition of anonymity). More importantly, she and a few like-minded St. Mark's refugees (they had left rather than comply with a parish-imposed 'gag order') formed the Blessed Trinity Society to continue to spread the word, in the face of strong initial ecclesiastical opposition. The rest, as they say, is history.

"Although it was the phenomenon of highly educated, sedate 'mainline church' folk speaking in tongues that grabbed the headlines initially, more far-reaching effects of the movement have long since become evident. Among the most important are a general resurgence of the charismatic gifts of the Holy Spirit throughout Christendom; and an ecumenicity unprecedented in history—ranging from thousands of grassroots interdenominational prayer groups to high level conclaves where representatives lay aside centuries of institutional division and sacramentally break bread together, not on the basis of compromise, but rather the concrete unity of a shared experience. This ecumenicity is also breaking down racial dividing lines, and from the beginning Jean was one of those leaders who encouraged this development; in recognition of this she was given an award in 1964 by the National Association of Pentecostal Women, an African American group.

"Our work has included introducing many heroin addicts in Hong Kong to the same religious experience described above, which enabled them to withdraw with no pain or sickness, without the use of medication. This drew considerable local and international media attention, including *Time* and *People* articles; and the Hong Kong government has honored our ministry by means of a stone memorial and plaque in the Kowloon Walled City Park, constructed on the site of the notorious area where drug dens once flourished. In addition to our travels, we have undertaken several 'quiet evangelism' tours to the People's Republic of China. In 1996, the American branch of the Church of the East (the ancient communion which evangelized China, including a series of emperors, in the 7th and 8th centuries) conferred upon Mrs. Willans the honorary degree of Doctor of Divinity."

BIOGRAPHICAL/CRITICAL SOURCES:

BOOKS

Hocken, Peter, *Streams of Renewal,* Paternoster, 1986.

Hocken, *One Lord One Spirit One Body,* Word Among Us Press, 1987.

Kelsey, Morton T., *Tongue Speaking,* Doubleday, 1964.

Nichol, John T., *Pentecostalism,* Harper, 1966, revised edition published as *The Pentecostals,* Logos International, 1971.

Quebedeaux, Richard, *The New Charismatics,* Doubleday, 1976, revised edition, Harper, 1983.

Sherrill, John L., *They Speak Other Tongues,* McGraw, 1964, updated edition, Chosen Books, 1985.

PERIODICALS

Los Angeles Times, March 10, 1963; March 17, 1963; November 17, 1963; May 23, 1964; April 20, 1992.

New York Times, November 6, 1977.

People, September 8, 1975.

San Francisco Chronicle, May 9, 1963; May 12, 1963.

Time, March 20, 1978.

* * *

WILLIAMS, C(harles) K(enneth) 1936-

PERSONAL: Born November 4, 1936, in Newark, NJ; son of Paul Bernard and Dossie (Kasdin) Williams; married Sarah Dean Jones, June, 1966 (divorced, 1975); married Catherine Mauger (an editor), April 13, 1975; children: (first marriage) Jessica Anne; (second marriage) Jed Mauger. *Education:* University of Pennsylvania, B.A., 1959. *Avocational interests:* Piano, guitar, drawing.

ADDRESSES: *Home*—82 Rue d'Hauteville, 75010 Paris, France.

CAREER: Poet. Columbia University, New York City, professor of writing, 1981-85; George Mason University, Fairfax, VA, professor of literature, 1982—95. Visiting professor of literature, Beaver College, Jenkintown, PA, 1975, Drexel University, Philadelphia, PA, 1976, University of California, Irvine, 1978, Boston University, 1979-80, Brooklyn College, 1982-83; Franklin and

Marshall College, Lancaster, PA, Mellon visiting professor of literature, 1977; Halloway lecturer at University California, Berkeley, 1986; lecturer at Princeton University, Princeton, NJ, 1996—.

MEMBER: PEN, Poetry Society of America.

AWARDS, HONORS: Guggenheim Fellowship, 1974; Pushcart Press Prize, 1982, 1983, and 1987; National Endowment for Arts Fellowship, 1985 and 1993; National Book Critics Circle Award, 1987, for *Flesh and Blood;* Morton Dauwen Zabel Prize, American Academy of Arts and Letters, 1989; Harriet Monroe Prize, 1993; Lila Wallace-Reader's Digest Grantee, 1993.

WRITINGS:

POEMS

A Day for Anne Frank, Falcon Press (Philadelphia, PA), 1968.
Lies, Houghton Mifflin (Boston), 1969.
I Am the Bitter Name, Houghton Mifflin, 1972.
With Ignorance, Houghton Mifflin, 1977.
The Lark, The Thrush, The Starling, Burning Deck (Providence, RI), 1983.
Tar, Random House, (New York City), 1983.
Flesh and Blood, Farrar, Straus (New York City), 1987.
Poems 1963-1983, Farrar, Straus, 1988.
Helen, Orchises Press (Washington, DC), 1991.
A Dream of Mind, Farrar, Straus, 1992.
Selected Poems, Farrar, Straus, 1994.
The Vigil, Farrar, Straus, 1996.

TRANSLATOR

(With Gregory Dickerson) Sophocles, *Women of Trachis,* Oxford University Press, 1978.
Euripides, *Bacchae,* Farrar, Straus, 1990.
(With Renata Gorczynski and Benjamin Ivry) Adam Zagajewski, *Canvas,* Farrar, Straus, 1991.
(With John Montague and Margaret Grissom) *Selected Poems of Francis Ponge,* Wake Forest University Press (Winston-Salem, NC), 1994.

EDITOR

(And author of introduction) Paul Zweig, *Selected and Last Poems,* Wesleyan University Press (Middletown, CT), 1989.
(And author of introduction) Gerard Manly Hopkins, *The Essential Hopkins,* Ecco (Hopewell, NJ), 1993.

Also contributing editor of *American Poetry Review,* 1972—.

SIDELIGHTS: C. K. Williams is viewed by readers and critics alike as an original stylist. He writes poems in long, prose-like lines that emphasize characterization and dramatic development. His subject matter has developed from political and social protest in his earlier books into bleak descriptions that often show the states of alienation, deception, and occasional enlightenment that exist between public and private lives in modern urban America. Unlike many of his contemporaries who write lyrically self-centered poems or who write poems that witness political events, Williams writes poems of personal and cultural focus, world events and human frailties, rants and reminiscences, realistic portraits and songs of self-awareness. Edward Hirsch called Williams in the *New York Times Review of Books* "simultaneously one of the most documentary and one of the most thoughtful poets working today."

Williams's first book *Lies* was published upon the recommendation of confessional poet Anne Sexton who, according to Allan M. Jallon in the *Los Angeles Times,* called Williams "the Fellini of the written word," and the book received strong initial critical acclaim. M. L. Rosenthal, reviewing the book in *Poetry,* described it as a collection of poems that portrays "psychic paralysis despite the need to make contact with someone." Fred Moramarco in *Western Humanities Review* noted that the poems "sound the grim notes of [William Blake's] *Songs of Experience,*" where "paradox is a quality central to almost each poem in the volume." The final poem in the book, "A Day for Anne Frank," which had been published separately a year earlier, was praised by Alan Williamson in *Shenandoah* as "asurprisingly moving poem, one of the best in the book."

Willaims's next three books all met with continued critical success. *I Am the Bitter Name,* the title of which, as Jascha Kessler pointed out in *Poetry,* "is meant . . . to stand for Death," is largely a collection of protest poems about the fear and hatred nurtured by America's involvement in the Vietnam War, culminating in the long, final poem

"In the Heart of the Beast," about the shooting of students at Kent State University by the Ohio National Guard. In this poem, John Vernon stated in *Western Humanities Review,* "the language is like a whip that lashes out."

Williams's next book, *With Ignorance,* however, shows the first development of the poet's trademark style, where, as James Atlas explained in *Nation,* "the lines are so long that the book had to be published in a wide-page format, like an art catalogue," giving the "poetry . . . an eerie incantatory power." Atlas called the fourteen poems in this collection "parables, plain tales about men and women in extreme situations" which, as Stanley Plumly observed in *American Poetry Review,* alternate "between a sort of street talk storytelling and incandescent lyricism."

Flesh and Blood is a collection of eight-line poems,each of twenty or twenty-five syllables and printed two poems to a page, making them comparable, as Michael Hofmann suggested in the *Times Literary Supplement,* to "[Robert] Lowell's sonnets, or [John] Berryman's Dreamsongs." The poems' subjects, the critic pointed out, are "the by-now familiar gallery of hobos and winos, children and old people, lovers and invalids; the settings, typically, public places, on holidays, in parks, on pavements and metro-stations." Hirsch commented that while these poems "lack the narrative scope and sheer relentless force of Mr. Williams's longer poems, . . . together they have a strong cumulative energy and effectiveness." Hirsch described Williams's poetry as having a "notational, ethnographic quality" that presents "single extended moments intently observed." Even though these poems sometimes read "like miniature short stories, sudden fictions," Hirsch continued, they always present people in situations where they are "vulnerable, exposed, on the edge."

Poems 1963-1983 collects selections from *Lies* and *I Am the Bitter Name,* and reproduces both *With Ignorance* and *Tar* in their entirety. Paul Muldoon, writing in the *Times Literary Supplement,* called it "the book of poems I most enjoyed this year," finding Williams to have "an enviable range of tone" and to be "by turns tender and troubling." Hofmann claimed that the book "has as much scope and truthfulness as any American poetsince Lowell and Berryman."

A Dream of Mind received mixed reviews. William Logan criticized the book in the *New York Times Book Review* as one in which Williams's long-line style has "decayed" from his earlier works into "continual repetition, pointless variation and the automatic cloning of phrases," making the poems "little Xerox machines of technique" in which Williams is "most successful when purely voyeuristic, less when confessional, and least when meditative." Lawrence Norfolk, however, writing in the *Times Literary Supplement,* lauded Williams for his "stubbornness or refusal to turn away" from "uncomfortable or harrowing realities," such as those presented in "Helen," a husband's account of his wife's decline and death. Michael Dirda, writing in the *Washington Post Book World,* favorably judged Williams's "often plain language" that "keeps the reader fascinated as much by his storytelling power as by his telling phrases."

Selected Poems replaces the early poems with work from *Flesh and Blood* and *A Dream of Mind* and contains thirteen new poems. Ashley Brown, in *World Literature Today,* suggested that "Williams has learned from [French novelist Marcel] Proust how to make the power of memory operate to maximum effect," and a reviewer for the *Times Literary Supplement* appreciated Williams's later work, which "strikes a more refined balance between social and individual responsibilities." Williams, in a *Los Angeles Times* interview with Jallon, stated that he believes "the drama of American poetry is based very much on experience. It's coming out of all the different cultures. We're an enormous nation and we have an enormous poetry." Stephen Dobyns, writing in *Washington Post Book World,* described a characteristic Williams poem as one in which there are "variations of meaning pushing toward the increasingly precise." The depth, complexity, and stylistic originality, maintained consistently over a period of twenty-five years, has led Dobyns to name Williams, in his mid-fifties, "one of our major poets."

BIOGRAPHICAL/CRITICAL SOURCES:

BOOKS

Clark, LaVerne Harrell, editor, *Focus 101,* Heidelberg Graphics (Chico, CA), 1979.

Contemporary Literary Criticism, Gale (Detroit), Volume 33, 1985; Volume 56, 1989.

Contemporary Poets, fifth edition, St. James Press (Detroit), 1991.

Dictionary of Literary Biography, Volume 5: *American Poetssince World War II,* Gale, 1980.

Hamilton, Ian, editor. *Oxford Companion to Twentieth-Century Poetry in English,* Oxford University Press, 1994.

PERIODICALS

America, October 30, 1993.

American Poetry Review, fall, 1972, p. 45; winter, 1977; January-February, 1978, pp. 21-32; July-August, 1979, pp. 12-
13; May, 1988, p. 9.

Antioch Review, summer, 1984, pp. 363-374.

Booklist, July 15, 1969, p. 1254; September 1, 1983, p. 23; June 15, 1992, p. 1803; October 1, 1994, p. 232.

Chicago Tribune, December 16, 1987, p. 3; January 16, 1995, p. 10.

Choice, April, 1973, p. 293; September, 1977, p. 867.

Georgia Review, winter, 1983, p. 894; fall, 1993, p. 578.

Hudson Review, spring, 1970, p. 130; spring, 1984, p. 122; winter, 1988, pp. 680-681; summer, 1995, p. 339.

Kliatt Young Adult Paperback Book Guide, summer, 1988, p. 30.

Library Journal, June 1, 1969, p. 2239; February 1, 1972, p. 504; June 15, 1977, p. 1386; October 1, 1983, p. 1880; May 1,1987, p. 72; June 1, 1990, p. 130; May 1, 1992, p. 86.

Los Angeles Times, March 7, 1993, p. 30.

Los Angeles Times Book Review, January 22, 1984, p. 3.

Nation, June 18, 1977, pp. 763-766; December 24, 1983, p. 673; May 30, 1987, pp. 734-736.

National Book Critics Circle Journal, May 15, 1988, pp. 3-4.

New England Review and Bread Loaf Quarterly, spring, 1984, pp. 489-492.

New Republic, August 17, 1992; December 21, 1992; January 25, 1993.

New Statesman and Society, December 23, 1988, p. 36; December 4, 1992, p. 40.

New Yorker, April 29, 1991, p. 42; October 21, 1991, p. 84; April 20, 1992, p. 38; January 11, 1993, p. 111.

New York Times Book Review, July 10, 1977, p. 14; November 27, 1983, p. 13; August 23, 1987, p. 20; March 13, 1988, p. 34; November 15, 1992, p. 15.

Observer, January 8, 1989, p. 46.

Parnassus, fall-winter, 1972, pp. 125-129; January, 1990, p. 115; January, 1995, p. 11.

Partisan Review, summer, 1985, p. 302; March, 1991, p. 565.

Poetry, November, 1971, pp. 99-104; February, 1973, pp. 292-303; September, 1984, pp. 353-355; February, 1988, pp. 431-433; April, 1989, p. 29; December, 1993, p. 164.

Publishers Weekly, April 14, 1969, p. 96; July 22, 1983, p. 126; May 11, 1992, p. 58; August 29, 1994, p. 66; November 7, 1994, p. 41; November 25, 1996, p. 71, November 25, 1996, p. 71.

Reference and Research Book News, December, 1992, p. 34.

San Francisco Review of Books, February, 1987, p. 34.

Shenandoah, summer, 1970, pp. 89-93.

Stand, autumn, 1990, p. 18; winter, 1993, p. 77.

Threepenny Review, summer, 1984, p. 11; fall, 1989, p. 21.

Times Literary Supplement, December 2, 1988, p. 1342; January 20, 1989, p. 59; February 12, 1993, p. 11; December 8, 1995, p. 28.

TriQuarterly, winter, 1988, pp. 224-225.

Village Voice, January 10, 1984, p. 44.

Virginia Quarterly Review, winter, 1992, p. 27.

Washington Post Book World, October 9, 1983, p. 8; January 3, 1993, p. 10; July 30, 1995, p. 8.

Western Humanities Review, spring, 1970, pp. 201-207; winter, 1973, pp. 101-10; summer, 1978, p. 269.

World Literature Today, autumn, 1989, p. 685; winter, 1989, p. 104; spring, 1993, p. 387; summer, 1995, p. 589.

Writer's Digest, February, 1984, p. 55.

Yale Review, October, 1977, p. 72.*

—Sketch by Robert Miltner

* * *

WILLOUGHBY, Hugh
See HARVEY, Nigel

* * *

YOUNG, Rose
See HARRIS, Marion Rose (Young)

ZAPPA, Francis Vincent, Jr. 1940-1993 (Frank Zappa)

PERSONAL: Professionally known as Frank Zappa; born December 21, 1940, in Baltimore, MD; son of Francis Vincent (ascientist) and Rose Marie Zappa; died of prostate cancer, December 4, 1993, in Los Angeles, CA; married first wife, Kay, in 1959 (divorced); married Gail Sloatman in 1969; children: Dweezil, Moon Unit, Ahmet Rodin, Diva. *Education:* Attended Antelope Valley Junior College and Chaffee Junior College.

ADDRESSES: E-mail—www.zappa.com.

CAREER: Composer, performer, producer, screenwriter, and filmmaker. Appeared in motion pictures, including *Head, 200 Motels, Baby Snakes, The Dub Room Special, Video from Hell, Does Humor Belong in Music?, Uncle Meat, The True Story of Frank Zappa's 200 Motels,* and *Funny.* Appeared in television shows, including *The Steve Allen Show, Miami Vice, The Monkees, Saturday Night Live,* and *Class of the 20th Century;* was the voice of the pope in an episode of *Ren and Stimpy;* contributed to the score for the television series *Duckman.*

AWARDS, HONORS: Named pop musician of the year, *Downbeat* (magazine), 1970, 1971, and 1972; Grammy Award for best rock instrumental album, 1987, for *Jazz from Hell;* inducted into the Rock and Roll Hall of Fame, 1995.

WRITINGS:

Plastic People: Songbuch (songbook; in German and English), Frankfurt am Main (Germany), 1977.

Them or Us (The Book), Barfko-Swill (Los Angeles, CA), 1984.

(With Peter Occhiogrosso) *The Real Frank Zappa Book,* Poseidon Press (New York City), 1989.

RECORDINGS

Freak Out!, Verve, 1966.

Absolutely Free, Verve, 1967.

Lumpy Gravy, Verve, 1967.

We're Only in It for the Money, Verve, 1968.

Cruising with Ruben and the Jets, Verve, 1968.

Hot Rats, Bizarre, 1969.

Mothermania—The Best of the Mothers, Verve, 1969.

Uncle Meat (soundtrack; see also below), Bizarre, 1969.

Burnt Weenie Sandwich, Bizarre, 1969.

Chunga's Revenge, Bizarre, 1970.

Weasels Ripped My Flesh, Bizarre, 1970.

Fillmore East, June, 1971, Bizarre, 1971.

200 Motels (soundtrack; see also below), Bizarre, 1971.

Just Another Band from L.A., Bizarre, 1972.

The Grand Wazoo, Bizarre, 1972.

Waka/Jawaka, Bizarre, 1972.

Over-Nite Sensation, DiscReet, 1973.

Apostrophe ('), DiscReet, 1974.

Roxy & Elsewhere, DiscReet, 1974.

One Size Fits All, DiscReet, 1975.

(With Captain Beefheart) *Bongo Fury,* DiscReet, 1975.

Safe muffinz, Amazing Kornyfone (Germany), c. 1975.

Poot face booogie, Amazing Kornyfone, c. 1975.

Zoot Allures, DiscReet, 1976.

Zappa in New York, DiscReet, 1978.

Studio Tan, DiscReet, 1978.

Orchestral Favorites, DiscReet, 1979.

Joe's Garage, Act I (see also below), Zappa, 1979.

Joe's Garage, Acts II and III (see also below), Zappa, 1979.

Sleep Dirt, DiscReet, 1979.

Sheik Yerbouti, Zappa, 1979.

Shut Up 'n' Play Yer Guitar, Barking Pumpkin, 1981.

You Are What You Is, Barking Pumpkin, 1981.

Tinseltown Rebellion, Barking Pumpkin, 1981.

Ship Arriving Too Late to Save a Drowning Witch, BarkingPumpkin, 1982.

London Symphony Orchestra, Barking Pumpkin, Volume 1, 1983, Volume 2, 1987.

The Man from Utopia, Barking Pumpkin, 1983.

Baby Snakes (soundtrack; see also below), Barking Pumpkin, 1983.

Rare Meat, Del Fi, 1983.

Boulez Conducts Zappa: The Perfect Stranger, Angel, 1984.

Francesco Zappa, EMI, 1984.

Them or Us, Rykodisc, 1984.

Thing-Fish, Barking Pumpkin, 1984.

FZ Meets the Mothers of Prevention, Rykodisc, 1985.

Does Humor Belong in Music? (soundtrack; see also below), Rykodisc, 1986.

Jazz from Hell, Rykodisc, 1986.

Joe's Garage (contains *Joe's Garage, Act I,* and *Joe's Garage, Acts II and III*), Rykodisc, 1987.

Broadway the Hard Way, Rykodisc, 1988.
Guitar, Rykodisc, 1988.
You Can't Do That on Stage Anymore (compilation), six volumes, Rykodisc, 1988-92.
Beat the Boots (collection of bootleg recordings), Foo-eee Records, Volume 1 (contains *'Tis the Season to Be Jelly, TheArk, Freaks and Motherfu*#@!, Piquantique, Unmitigated Audacity, Saarbrucken 1979, Anyway the Wind Blows,* and *As an Am, 1981*), 1991, Volume 2 (contains *Electric Aunt Jemima, Our Man in Nirvana, Tengo na minchia tanta, Disconnected Synapses, Swiss Cheese/Fire, Conceptual Continuity, Anyway the Wind Blows,* and *At the Circus*), 1992.
The Best Band You Never Heard in Your Life, Barking Pumpkin, 1991.
Make a Jazz Noise Here, Barking Pumpkin, 1991.
Playground Psychotics, Barking Pumpkin, 1992.
Ahead of Their Time, Barking Pumpkin, 1993.
The Yellow Shark, Barking Pumpkin, 1993.
Civilization, Phaze III, UMRK, 1994.
Frank Zappa (interview picture disc), Baktabak, c. 1994.
Strictly Commercial, Rykodisc, 1995.
Lather, Rykodisc, 1996.
The Lost Episodes, Rykodisc, 1996.
Frank Zappa Plays the Music of Frank Zappa: A Memorial Tribute, Barking Pumpkin, 1996.
Have I Offended Someone?, Rykodisc, 1997.

Also composer and performer on *The Ramblers,* MagpieRecords & Ozz-Good Productions, c. 1984. Composer and/or producer of numerous recordings released as singles.

FILMS; UNLESS OTHERWISE NOTED

(And director, with Tony Palmer) *200 Motels* (screenplay), United Artists, 1971.
(And director) *Baby Snakes,* Barfko-Swill,· 1979.
(And director) *The Dub Room Special,* Barfko-Swill, 1984.
Dupree's Paradise (music score), Barfko-Swill, 1984.
(And director) *Video from Hell,* Barfko-Swill, 1985.
(And director) *Does Humor Belong in Music?,* Barfko-Swill, 1985.
(And director) *Uncle Meat,* Barfko-Swill, 1987.
(And director) *The True Story of Frank Zappa's 200 Motels,* Barfko-Swill, 1988.

Composer of film score for *The World's Greatest Sinner,* 1962; *Run Home Slow,* 1965; *The Dub Room Special,* 1984; and *Video from Hell,* 1985. Author of column in *Guitar Player,* 1982-93.

SIDELIGHTS: Iconoclast Frank Zappa was an enormously prolific recording artist who is remembered today as much forhis outspoken defense of free speech as for his eclectic recordings. During his lifetime Zappa was described as bizarre, disgusting, avant-garde, grotesque, obscene, Dadaistic, and cheesy. The lyrics of his songs, which largely critique contemporary cultural phenomena and middle-class values, were in many cases deemed unfit for public broadcasting. Nevertheless, Zappa was considered by many to be a musical genius, and he never lacked fans. *Chicago Tribune* correspondent Greg Kot called Zappa "one of the most important, and misunderstood, musical figures of the last half-century . . . a serious composer who indulged in juvenile humor, a virtuoso guitarist who on many albums played little or no guitar, . . . an imposing, impenetrable composer who either pandered to or bamboozled his audience with low-brow humor and complex music." *Rolling Stone's* Lester Bangs once wrote: "Frank Zappa probably knows more about music than you and I and 3/4 of the other professional musicians in this country put together. . . . [He] has made an incredible contribution towards broadening the scope of the average American kid's listening habits" (Bang's italics).

Zappa and his band, the Mothers of Invention, which he formed in 1964, made their recording debut with a double album entitled *Freak Out!*. Typical of his subsequent works, the cuts on this first album combine rock, classical, jazz, and rhythm and blues music, and satirically comment on bourgeois status symbols, social practices, and values. Songs such as "Wowie Zowie" and "Go Cry on Somebody Else's Shoulder" mock teenybopper love, while more serious statements are made with tunes like "Trouble Coming Everyday," which Zappa wrote to protest the exploitation of blacks in the 1960s. Zappa sings: "You know something people, I ain't black, but there's a whole lot of times I wish I could say I'm not white." Robert A. Rosenstone in the *Annals of the American Academy of Political and Social Science* declared: "No song writer showed more empathy with the black struggle for liberation than that."

Freak Out!'s title implies that its contents not only put down the "establishment" and its mores, but promote deviant actions, such as "freaking out" on drugs. Zappa, however, was ardently opposed to the use of drugs. According to David Walley in *No Commercial Potential,* Zappa wrote in a letter to the *Los Angeles Free Press* in 1966: "WE, AS A GROUP, DO NOT RECOMMEND . . . VERILY, WE REPUDIATE ANY ANIMAL/MINERAL/VEGETABLE/SYNTHETIC SUBSTANCE, VEHICLE and/or PROCEDURE WHICH MIGHT TEND TO REDUCE THE BODY, MIND, OR SPIRIT OF AN INDIVIDUAL (any true individual) TO A STATE OF SUBAWARENESS OR INSENSITIVITY. . . . THE SORT OF HIGH YOU REALLY WANT IS A *SPIRITUAL HIGH* AND YOU ARE BULLSHITTING YOURSELF IF YOU TRUST *ANY* CHEMICAL and/or AGRICULTURAL SHORT-CUT TO DO IT *FOR* YOU." And Zappa offered a definition of freaking out, without reference to drugs, inside the cover of his first album. Freaking out, according to Zappa, is "a process whereby an individual casts off outmoded and restricting standards of thinking, dress, and social etiquette in order to express creatively his relationship to his immediate environment and the social structure as a whole."

Absolutely Free followed *Freak Out!* in 1967 and again presented Zappa's audience with more songs attacking the bourgeoisie. "Brown Shoes Don't Make It," for example, slams the Protestant ethic: "Be a jerk, and go to work / be a jerk and go to work, / do your job and do it right, / life's a ball—TV tonight . . . / do you love it? / do you hate it? / there it is the way you made it. . . ." "Plastic People" also offers Zappa's opinion of the middle-class, going so far as to include, and subtly insult, some members of his audience: "Plastic People . . . baby you're such a drag . . . go home and check yourself, you think we're singing about someone else, but you're plastic people." "[*Absolutely Free*] adds up to a pretty cogent picture of the hippy's view of American society," wrote Bertram Stanleigh in *Audio.* "And if it's a distorted view, it's still a pithy and clever commentary that makes some pretty telling digs."

Among Zappa's most applauded works is *We're Only inIt for the Money,* a satire on the love, peace, and drug scene of the 1960s flower children, whom Zappa considered as "plastic" as the people against whom the hippies were rebelling. Mocking the lovechild lifestyle, Zappa said in a narrative on the album: "First I'll buy some beads, and then perhaps a leather band to go around my head, some feathers and bells and a book of Indian lore. I will ask the Chamber of Commerce how to get to Haight Street and smoke an awful lot of dope. I will wander arcund barefoot. I will have a psychedelic gleam in my eye at all times. I will love everyone . . . I will love the cops as they kick the shit out of me on the streets." *Rolling Stone* commentator Barret Hansen observed: "Though the Establishment gets well roasted, Zappa saves his sharpest jabs for 'hippies,' brutally exposing the irrelevance of much of their world." Commenting on the album as a whole, Hansen opined: "Zappa's ingenuity in conception of form, in innovation of recording techniques, and in the integration of vastly differing types of music, beggars all competitors. His rhythms and harmonies are truly sublime, and his lyrics contain the most brilliant satire in the whole pop world. . . . Zappa's sounds are put together as painstakingly as a symphony." *Popular Music and Society* contributor Peter Kountz called *We're Only in It for the Money* Zappa's "finest melodic statement. . . . This album illustrates the composer's dependence on the melodic developments of serious contemporary music. The melodies . . . are wide-ranging, asymmetrical, economic and deliberately structured, angular and set within unusual rhythms, harmonies and textures. . . . They are demanding melodies, as demanding as the lyrics they support. And these melodies are suggestive of the direction of melody in serious contemporary music: expansion, innovation and, to some degree, revolution."

By 1967 Zappa and the Mothers of Invention found their success waning; though the group enjoyed well-attended concerts, its record sales were down, due in part to the censoring of their recordings by MGM/Verve records. Fed up with that company, Zappa decided to start his own, calling it Bizarre Productions and Straight Records. Zappa also ventured into filmmaking at this time, laboring on *Uncle Meat,* a promotional film that was only released in 1987. Basically an instrumental album, the soundtrack recording of *Uncle Meat* contains fewer social comments, moving, according to Walley, "away from message-oriented songs toward purer, more 'serious' music." Alec Dubro concurred in *Rolling Stone.* "*Uncle Meat,* more than any of their previous albums, is a serious piece of music. . . . The longer pieces of overdubbings done with such incredible care and painstaking artistry, so exact as to be much closer in structure and in spirit to modern classical music."

Zappa disbanded the Mothers of Invention in 1969, saying he was tired of performing for audiences who applauded for all the wrong reasons. The Mothers went separate ways, and Frank recorded a solo album, *Hot Rats*. The album indicated a change in Zappa's style, from rock to a more eclectic instrumental form. In *Rolling Stone,* Lester Bangs predicted: "If *Hot Rats* is any indication of where Zappa is headed on his own, we are in for some fiendish rides indeed." Zappa also delved into a film project at this time, writing the script and music for *200 Motels*. Although the motion picture was not released until 1971, the score was performed in 1970 by a newly-formed Mothers of Invention and the Los Angeles Philharmonic under the direction of Zubin Mehta at Pauley Pavilion of the University of California, Los Angeles. The ensemble played Zappa's score, in addition to "Intergrales" by Zappa's mentor Edgar Varese. The evening was peppered with Zappa's comments on various lewd subjects and ad libbed activity from the orchestra. At one point all of the orchestra members left the stage and marched into the audience, each musician playing his own composition. In his *Rolling Stone* review of the event, David Felton wrote: "Before 12,000 attentive fans [Zappa] did it marvelously. It was his show almost from the start. Mehta and the Philharmonic were simply new lab toys for his mad genius and they became better people for it."

The movie *200 Motels* was released in 1971 to mixed reviews, many critics comparing it to the Beatles's *A Hard Day's Night*. Vincent Canby of the *New York Times* wrote: "At its heart, '200 Motels' is a subjective 'A Hard Day's Night' in desperate need of the early Beatles. It is Zappa's somewhat put-on, but mostly put-down, vision of what it's like to be Frank Zappa . . . and the Mothers of Invention while touring through a universe that is one big Centerville, U.S.A." *Newsday* correspondent Joseph Gelmis, who thought *200 Motels* perhaps "the most innovative movie of 1971," felt it took "the movie musical 'documentary' its first giant step since *A Hard Day's Night*.. . . Zappa and the Mothers have a reality and dimension that increases the more we learn about them. . . . Few rock musicians are interesting enough to withstand close scrutiny. That was one of the appeals of the Beatles. . . . [*200 Motels*] isn't for Aunt Prudence or little Abby, but it's a new way to look at movies if you're ready."

Although his music never reached the mainstream, popular audience, Zappa consistently enjoyed a loyal following of fans. Despite his steady popularity, however, Zappa often felt he was underrated as a musician, and suggested that marketing, more than talent, is responsible for today's artists' successes. He told John Swenson in a *Guitar World* interview: "If what I'm doing does stay around for a long time, then perhaps it's not really that valuable because the value is determined by how many people want to consume it, and the audience for what I do is unfortunately small because not that many people have been *told* that it's cool to like this. As long as you are told over and over again that the apex of perfection is REO Speedwagon and Pat Benatar, then as long as you believe that that's what's cool, then that's all you will every buy and that's all you will ever listen to and all you will ever admire."

Zappa also expressed frustration concerning the rumors about his antics in concert, particularly the one about his defecating on stage and devouring the matter. He shared his feelings with Swenson: "[People are] still all tied up with questions like 'Well, is he a genius or isn't he?' 'Well, did he shit on the stage and eat it or didn't he?' All dumb stuff like that from sixteen years ago and it doesn't even relate to the present day. You can't beat it. I'm not gonna spend my life going around trying to correct everybody's statistical inaccuracies because I've got other things to do. But by the same token this stuff is hanging over my career like a cloud. . . . I don't eat doo doo. I don't step on baby chickens, I don't do any of that stuff. I'm a real good guitar player. I sing some funny songs sometimes. I'm not that crazy."

There was nothing "crazy" about Zappa's impassioned defense of rock lyrics when members of the federal government sought to impose new censorship laws. In his testimony before Congress—and his highly publicized debates with Tipper Gore and other advocates of censorship—Zappa became a sort of folk hero for free speech and the right of artists to create works as they saw fit. Many of Zappa's views on the subject of censorship can be found in his 1989 memoir *The Real Frank Zappa Book*. Narrated with rich infusions of italic and boldface type, the book also includes Zappa's reminiscences about the early days with the Mothers of Invention and his multitudinous gripes with the music industry. Calling the work "refreshingly unlike the typical rock star autobiography," a *Publishers Weekly* reviewer concluded: "Few popular musicians equal Zappa's audacity or intelligence."

In his *Los Angeles Times Book Review* assessment of *The Real Frank Zappa Book,* Kenneth Turan observed that Zappa had become "the unlikeliest rock star this country—or any other one, for that matter—has produced," adding that the artist was "an opinionated autodidact of the first water . . . [who] loves to mock convention in the best, most deliberately chaotic Dada style." Turan praised the book for the way it "regales us with a series of ad hominem anecdotes about [Zappa's] life and times, showing how he made the transition from youthful goof-off to mature guru."

Zappa was stricken with prostate cancer in his late forties and, unlike many performers, did not dodge the press as his health failed. He died late in 1993 at the age of fifty-two. At the time of his death his entire catalog was being remastered for reissue by Rykodisc, which planned to market them all by the turn of the century. According to Kot, "a couple of these discs are cornerstones of the rock era." The Zappa Family Trust continues to release Zappa's works, many of which he planned before his death.

BIOGRAPHICAL/CRITICAL SOURCES:

BOOKS

Alla Zappa: Festschrift anleasslich der Zark-Expo & Mothers-Konzerte in Zeurich im Mearz, 1976, Painting Box Press (Zurich, Germany), 1976.

Colbeck, Julian, *Zappa: A Biography,* Virgin Books (London), 1987.

Contemporary Literary Criticism, Volume 17, Gale (Detroit), 1981.

Kostelanetz, Richard, editor, *The Frank Zappa Companion: Four Decades of Commentary,* Schirmer Books, 1997.

Lennon, Nigey, *Being Frank: My Time with Frank Zappa,* California Classics Books, 1995.

Miles, *Zappa: Frank Zappa—A Visual Documentary,* Omnibus Press, 1993.

Poroila, Heikki, and Heikki Karjalainen, *Recorded Zappa: Annotated Discography, 1961-1995,* Finnish Music Library (Helsinki), 1995.

Slaven, Neil, *Zappa: Electric Don Quixote,* Omnibus Press, 1996.

Walley, David, *No Commercial Potential: The Saga of Frank Zappa and the Mothers of Invention,* Dutton (New York City), 1972, revised edition published as *No Commercial Potential: The Saga of Frank Zappa, Then and Now,* 1980, second revised edition published as *No Commercial Potential: The Saga of Frank Zappa,* Da Capo Press, 1996.

Watson, Ben, *Frank Zappa: The Negative Dialectics of Poodle Play,* St. Martin's Press, 1995.

Zappa, Frank, with Peter Occhiogrosso, *The Real Frank Zappa Book,* Poseidon Press, 1989.

PERIODICALS

Booklist, April 15, 1989, p. 1411.

Chicago Sun-Times, November 29, 1971.

Chicago Tribune, June 30, 1995, p. R.

Entertainment Weekly, June 9, 1995, p. 63.

Guitar World, March, 1982.

Library Journal, June 1, 1989, p. 108.

Los Angeles Times Book Review, July 2, 1989, p. 1.

Newsday, November 11, 1971.

New York Times, November 11, 1971.

Playboy, January 1974.

Popular Music and Society, Volume IV, 1975.

Publishers Weekly, April 7, 1989, p. 121.

Rolling Stone, April 6, 1968; April 27, 1968; May 31, 1968; December 21, 1968; March 7, 1969; October 1, 1970; November 1, 1970; December 24, 1970; September 30, 1971; December 7, 1971; June 8, 1972; January 2, 1975; December 30, 1976; May 3, 1979; July 26, 1979; February 21, 1980; March 20, 1980.

Stereo Review, March, 1975, pp. 85, 87.

OBITUARIES:

PERIODICALS

Chicago Tribune, December 7, 1993, p. 13.

Gramaphone, March, 1994, p. 13.

Keyboard Magazine, April, 1994, pp. 52-68.

Los Angeles Times, December 6, 1993, p. A1.

New York Times, December 7, 1993, p. B12.

Times (London), December 7, 1993, p. 21.*

ZAPPA, Frank
See ZAPPA, Francis Vincent, Jr.

* * *

ZIOMEK, Henryk 1922-

PERSONAL: Surname is pronounced "*Zyoh*-mek"; born January 8, 1922, in Druzbin, Poland; son of Walenty (a manufacturer) and Jozefa (Fijalkowski) Ziomek; married Patricia Ann De Moor (a piano teacher and organist), August 16, 1956; children: Stanley, John Josef, Paul Henry. *Education:* Attended University of Warsaw, 1939-41; Indiana State University, B.A.,1955; Indiana University, M.A., 1956; University of Minnesota, Ph.D., 1960.

ADDRESSES: *Home*—370 Rivermont Rd., Athens, GA 30606. *Office*—Department of Romance Languages, University of Georgia, Athens, GA 30601.

CAREER: Wisconsin State University—Oshkosh (now University of Wisconsin—Oshkosh), 1956-60, began as instructor, became assistant professor of Latin, Spanish, and French; Butler University, Indianapolis, IN, assistant professor of Spanish and French, 1960-62; Colorado State University, Fort Collins, associate professor of Spanish and French, 1962-64; Ohio University, Athens, professor of Spanish and French, 1964-66; University of Georgia, Athens, professor of Spanish and literature of the Spanish Golden Age, 1966-82, professor emeritus of Romance languages, 1992—. Visiting professor of Spanish, University of Warsaw, 1978. Has worked as a commercial artist and as an anthropologist. *Military service:* Polish Underground Army, 1942-44; became second lieutenant. U.S. Army, 1945; served in France.

MEMBER: Associacion Internacional de Hispanistas, Modern Language Association of America, American Association of Teachers of Spanish and Portuguese, Latin American StudiesAssociation, Polish Institute of Arts and Sciences in America, Comediantes, South Atlantic Modern Language Association, Sigma Delta Pi.

WRITINGS:

Reflexiones del Quijote, Editorial M. Molina, 1971.

(Annotator) Vern G. Williamson, editor, *An Annotated, Analytical Bibliography of Tirso de Molina Studies,* University of Missouri Press (Columbia, MO), 1979.

Lo grotesco en la literatura espanola del Siglo de Oro, Editorial Alcala, 1983.

A History of Spanish Golden Age Drama, University Press of Kentucky (Lexington, KY), 1984.

Compendia de la literatura espanola, Panstwowe Wydawnictwo Naukowe (Warsaw), 1986.

(With Edmund S. Urbanski) *Polish Silhouettes in Nineteenth-*
and Twentieth-Century Latin America, two volumes, Artex Press, 1991.

EDITOR

(And author of introduction) Lope de Vega, *La nueua victoria de D. Gonzalo de Cordoua* (play; paleographic edition), Hispanic Institute, Columbia University (New York City), 1962.

Papers of French-Spanish-Spanish American-Luso-Brazilian Relations, University of Georgia Press (Athens, GA), 1966.

(And author of introduction and notes) de Vega, *El poder en el discreto* (play; critical edition), Editorial M. Molina, 1971.

(And author of introduction and notes) de Vega, *La batalla del honor* (play), University of Georgia Press, 1972.

(And author of introduction and notes) de Vega, *La prueba de los amigos* (play), University of Georgia Press, 1973.

(With Robert W. Linker, and author of introduction and notes) Luis Velez de Guevara, *La creacion del mundo* (play; critical edition), University of Georgia Press, 1974.

(And author of introduction and notes) Velez de Guevara, *El principe vinador* [and] *El amor en vizcaino* (plays), Editorial Ebro, 1975.

(And author of introduction and notes) Velez de Guevara, *Mas pesa el rey que la sangre, y Blason de los Guzmanes* (two plays; critical edition), Editorial Ebro, 1976.

(With Ann N. Hughes, and author of introduction and notes) Velez de Guevara, *Cerco de Roma por el Rey Desiderio* (play; critical edition), Edition Reichenberger, 1992.

Also author of more than fifty articles on Spanish, Spanish-American, and Brazilian literary subjects. Contributor as an abstractor to *Abstracts of English Studies,* 1966-91.

* * *

ZUCKER, Martin 1937-

PERSONAL: Born December 12, 1937, in New York, NY; son of Harry and Rose (a sign language teacher; maiden name, Weidman) Zucker; married Rosita Gottlieb (an artist), August 6, 1978. *Education:* Occidental College, B.A., 1959. *Religion:* Jewish.

ADDRESSES: Home—12405 Aneta St., Apt. 6, Los Angeles, CA 90066. *Agent*—Bob Silverstein, 50 Wilson St., Hartsdale, NY 10530. *E-mail*—mzucker@sprynet.com.

CAREER: Correspondent in Europe and the Middle East for Associated Press (AP), 1965-72; free-lance journalist and founder of *Mideast Media,* 1972-75; freelance writer, 1975—, specializing in health, nutrition, and preventive medicine. *Military service:* U.S. Army, 1959-61.

WRITINGS:

How to Have a Healthier Dog, Doubleday (New York City), 1981.
The Very Healthy Cat Book, McGraw (New York City), 1983.
Pet Allergies: Remedies for an Epidemic, Very Healthy Enterprises, 1987.
(Ghostwriter) *Lindsay Wagner's New Beauty,* Prentice-Hall (Englewood Cliffs, NJ), 1987.
(Ghostwriter) *The Potency Miracle,* Wilshire Books (North Hollywood, CA), 1996.

Contributing editor, *Let's Live.*

SIDELIGHTS: Martin Zucker told *CA:* "The greatest fulfillment I gain from my work is the satisfaction of having written something that hopefully may touch and improve the life of a fellow being."